Sound of Hunger

Sound of Hunger

*One German family's chronicle of the chivalry,
politics, lies, murder and aftermath of war*

Chris Heal

UNIFORM

UNIFORM

Published by Uniform
An imprint of Unicorn Publishing Group
5 Newburgh Street
London W1F 7RG

www.unicornpublishing.org

A catalogue record for this book is available from
the British Library

5 4 3 2 1

ISBN 978-1-911604-41-9

Cover design Unicorn Publishing Group
Typeset by Vivian@Bookscribe

Printed and bound in Great Britain by
TJ International Ltd, Padstow, Cornwall

MIX
Paper from
responsible sources
FSC® C013056

Contents

In Memoriam

Ahlefeldt	Karl-Christian	Verdun	Killed in action	1916
Atkins	Arthur	*Copenhagen*, North Sea	Killed by torpedo	1917
Barney	Harry	*Copenhagen*, North Sea	Killed by torpedo	1917
Brundle	Charles	*Copenhagen*, North Sea	Killed by torpedo	1917
Canaris	Wilhelm	Flossenbürg	Executed	1945
Chaplin	William	*Copenhagen*, North Sea	Killed by torpedo	1917
Dresky	Hans-Wilhelm	*U 33*, Clyde Estuary	Drowned	1940
Fryatt	Charles	Bruges	Executed	1917
Fürbringer	Werner	Brunswick	Illness	1982
Gerth	Eva	California	Illness	1999
Gerth	Erich	Rome	Murdered	1943
Gerth	Ernst	Berlin	Illness	1893
Gerth	Georg	Würzburg	Illness	1970
Gerth	Hedwig	Berlin	Gas poisoning	1923
Gerth	Maria	Würzburg	Illness	1970
Gudgeon	Athol	Gosport Naval Hospital	Died of wounds	1917
Guilcher	Jean	*Victorine Helène*, Atlantic	Killed by shell	1917
Guillou	Jean	*Victorine Helène*, Atlantic	Killed by shell	1917
Hasse	Hugo	Berlin	Murdered	1919
Hammond	Arthur	*Copenhagen*, North Sea	Killed by torpedo	1917
Heal	Tom	Toronto	Illness	1922
Jones	Robert	*Broomhill*, Channel	Killed by shell	1917
Jones	James	*Broomhill*, Channel	Drowned	1917
Liebknecht	Karl	Berlin	Murdered	1918
Luxemburg	Rosa	Berlin	Murdered	1918
Maggs	Ivor	HMS *Kale*, North Sea	Killed by mine	1918
Malcoste	Pierre	*Le Gard*, Atlantic	Killed by shell	1917
Marx	Otto	Theresienstadt camp	Unknown	Unknown
Marx	Solomon	Berlin	Illness	1936
Milliner	Jean	*Victorine Helène*, Atlantic	Killed by shell	1917
Neumann	Willy	POW Camp, France	Unknown	1917
Raabe	Karl	POW Camp, France	Unknown	1920
Rand	Leonard	*Copenhagen*, North Sea	Killed by torpedo	1917
Rathenau	Walther	Berlin	Murdered	1922
Schindler	Paul	POW, Davos-Wiesen	Illness	1918
Tesseraud	–	*Nelly*, Atlantic	Killed by shell	1917
105 civilians		Scarborough, Hartlepool	Killed by shell	1914
3 civilians		Lowestoft	Killed by shell	1915
42 sailors		*Kléber*, Atlantic	Killed by mine	1917
10 sailors		HMT *Arfon*, Channel	Killed by mine	1917
3 sailors		*Indutiomare*, Channel	Killed by torpedo	1917
49 sailors		HMS *Ettrick*, Channel	Killed by torpedo	1917
476 soldiers and crew		*Chaouia*, Straits of Messina	Killed by torpedo	1919

and the many hundreds of thousands of civilians who died because of the British blockade

Abbreviations and Common German Words

Abitur	A set of examinations taken in the final year of secondary school
ASDIC	Allied Submarine Detection Investigation Committee
BA-MA	Bundesarchiv-Militärarchiv, Federal Military Archives, Freiburg, Germany
BIR	Board of Investigation and Research, Royal Navy
BRT	Gross registered tonnage
CID	Committee for Imperial Defence
DNVP	Deutschnationale Volkspartei, German National People's Party
DRASSM	Le Département des Recherches Archéologiques Subaquatiques et Sous-Marines, The Department of Underwater Archaeological Research
ecpad	Etablissement de Communication et de Production Audiovisuelle de la Défense
Fähnrich	Midshipman
Freikorps	Post-World War 1 German para-military unit
Führer	Leader
Great War	World War 1, 1914-1918
GPS	Global positioning system
HVB	Handelsverkehrsbuch code
HMS	His Majesty's Ship
ICRC	International Committee of the Red Cross
Kaiser	Kaiser Wilhelm II, 1890-1919
Kaiserliche Marine	The Imperial German Navy, 1871-1919
Kriegsmarine	Navy of Nazi Germany, 1935-1945
KPD	German Communist Party
KTB	Kriegstagebuch, War Diary
KRA	German War Materials Department
NARA	National Archives and Records Administration, Washington, DC
NID	Naval Intelligence Division, Royal Navy
NMM	National Maritime Museum, Greenwich, London
NSDAP	National Socialist German Workers' Party
OHL	Oberste Heeresleitung, Supreme Army Command, Germany
PGL	Pan-German League
Reichsmark	German currency before the Deutschmark
RN	Royal Navy
Seeoffizier	Naval executive officer
SHD	*Service historique de la Défense,* Historical Defence Service, headquarters Vincennes, France
SHOM	*Service d'Hydrologie et d'Océanographie de la Marine* – the French Navy Hydrology and Oceanography Service
SKM	Signalbuch der Kaiserlichen Marine, German navy signal book
SMS	Seiner Majestät Schiff, His Majesty's Ship
SPD	Sozialdemokratische Partei Deutschlands, Social Democratic Party
TNA	The National Archives, Kew, London
Ufa	Universum Film AG
USPD	Independent Social Democratic Party
VB	Verkehrsbuch code
Weimar	German Republic, 1919-1933
Weltpolitik	German expansionist overseas foreign policy, 1890-1919
ZAN	Zone des Armées du Nord
Zur See	(Naval executive officer) at sea

List of Maps

Principal locations in Europe in *Sound of Hunger*

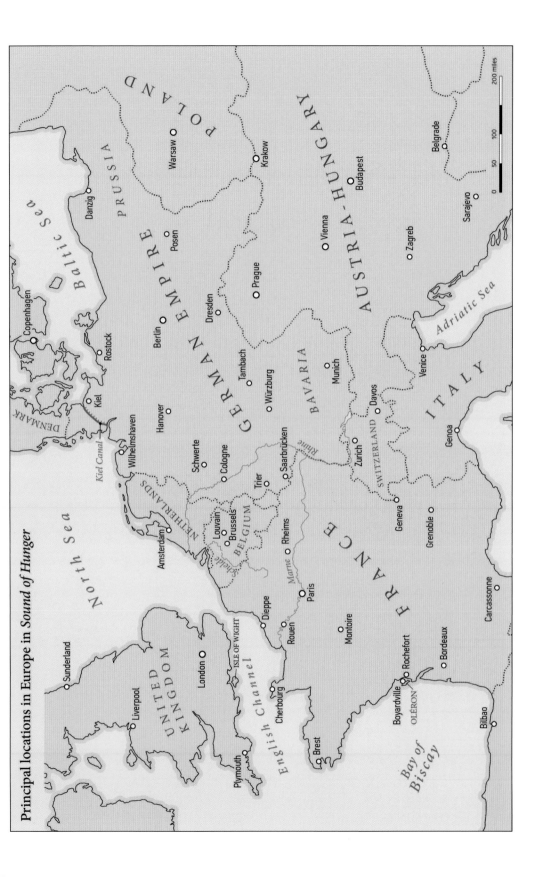

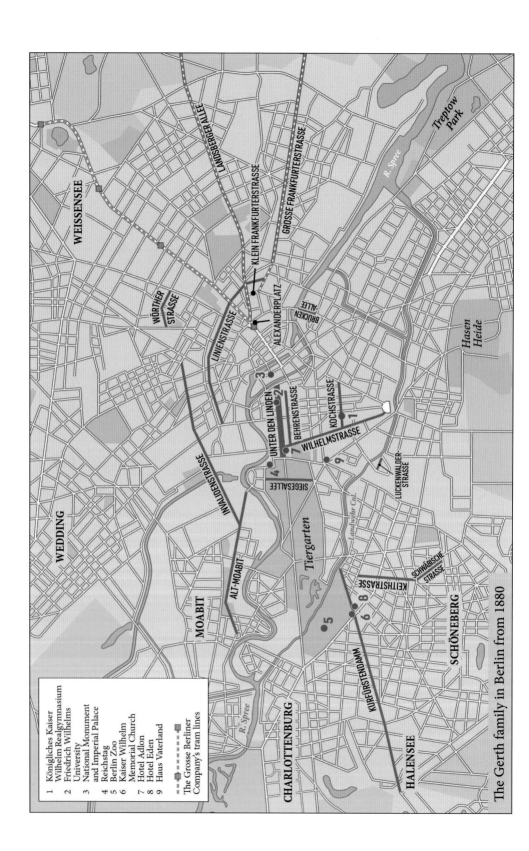

The Gerth family in Berlin from 1880

1 Königliches Kaiser
   Wilhelm Realgymnasium
2 Friedrich Wilhelms
   University
3 National Monument
   and Imperial Palace
4 Reichstag
5 Berlin Zoo
6 Kaiser Wilhelm
   Memorial Church
7 Hotel Adlon
8 Hotel Eden
9 Haus Vaterland

■ ▪ ▪ ▪ The Grosse Berliner
         Company's tram lines

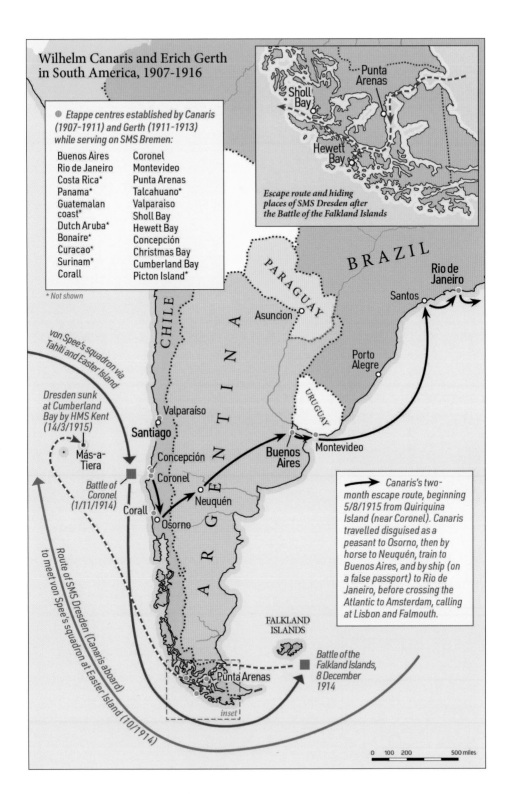

Wilhelm Canaris and Erich Gerth in South America, 1907–1916

● *Etappe centres established by Canaris (1907-1911) and Gerth (1911-1913) while serving on SMS Bremen:*

Buenos Aires	Coronel
Rio de Janeiro	Montevideo
Costa Rica*	Punta Arenas
Panama*	Talcahuano*
Guatemalan coast*	Valparaíso
Dutch Aruba*	Sholl Bay
Bonaire*	Hewett Bay
Curacao*	Concepción
Surinam*	Christmas Bay
Corall	Cumberland Bay
	Picton Island*

* Not shown

Punta Arenas

Sholl Bay

Hewett Bay

Escape route and hiding places of SMS Dresden after the Battle of the Falkland Islands

PARAGUAY

BRAZIL

Rio de Janeiro

Santos

Asuncion

Porto Alegre

CHILE

URUGUAY

von Spee's squadron via Tahiti and Easter Island

Dresden sunk at Cumberland Bay by HMS Kent (14/3/1915)

Más-a-Tiera

Valparaíso

Santiago

Concepción

Battle of Coronel (1/11/1914)

Coronel

Neuquén

Corall

Osorno

Montevideo

Buenos Aires

A R G E N T I N A

Route of SMS Dresden (Canaris aboard) to meet von Spee's squadron at Easter Island (10/1914)

FALKLAND ISLANDS

Punta Arenas

inset

Battle of the Falkland Islands, 8 December 1914

⟶ *Canaris's two-month escape route, beginning 5/8/1915 from Quiriquina Island (near Coronel). Canaris travelled disguised as a peasant to Osorno, then by horse to Neuquén, train to Buenos Aires, and by ship (on a false passport) to Rio de Janeiro, before crossing the Atlantic to Amsterdam, calling at Lisbon and Falmouth.*

0   100   200   500 miles

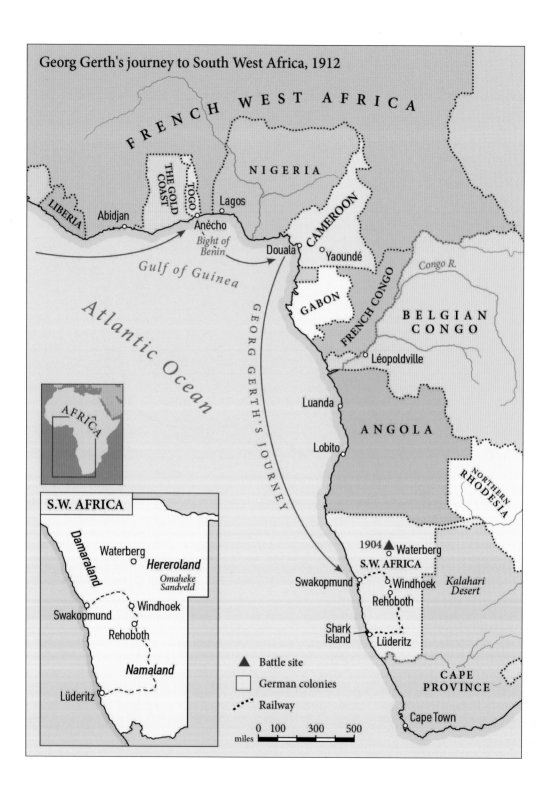

Georg Gerth's journey to South West Africa, 1912

FRENCH WEST AFRICA

NIGERIA

LIBERIA

Abidjan

THE GOLD COAST

TOGO

Lagos

Anécho

Bight of Benin

Douala

Gulf of Guinea

CAMEROON

Yaoundé

GABON

FRENCH CONGO

Congo R.

BELGIAN CONGO

Léopoldville

Atlantic Ocean

AFRICA

Luanda

Lobito

ANGOLA

GEORG GERTH'S JOURNEY

NORTHERN RHODESIA

1904 ▲ Waterberg

S.W. AFRICA

Swakopmund

Windhoek

Rehoboth

Kalahari Desert

Shark Island

Lüderitz

CAPE PROVINCE

Cape Town

S.W. AFRICA

Damaraland

Waterberg

Hereroland

Omaheke Sandveld

Swakopmund

Windhoek

Rehoboth

Namaland

Lüderitz

▲ Battle site

☐ German colonies

⋯ Railway

0   100   300   500

miles

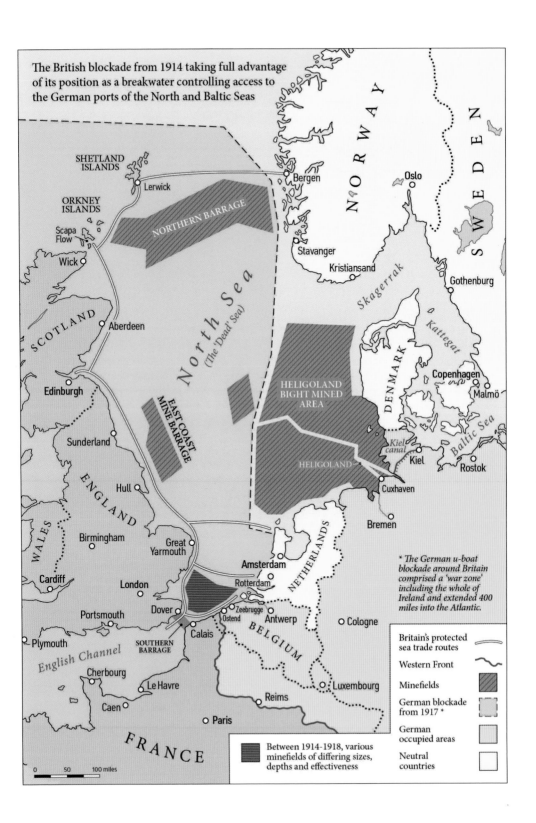

The British blockade from 1914 taking full advantage of its position as a breakwater controlling access to the German ports of the North and Baltic Seas

NORWAY

SWEDEN

SHETLAND ISLANDS

Bergen

Oslo

Lerwick

ORKNEY ISLANDS

NORTHERN BARRAGE

Scapa Flow

Stavanger

Wick

Kristiansand

Gothenburg

SCOTLAND

Aberdeen

North Sea
(The 'Dead' Sea)

Skagerrak

Kattegat

DENMARK

Copenhagen

HELIGOLAND BIGHT MINED AREA

Edinburgh

EAST COAST MINE BARRAGE

Malmö

Baltic Sea

Sunderland

Kiel canal

Kiel

Rostok

HELIGOLAND

Cuxhaven

Hull

ENGLAND

WALES

Birmingham

Bremen

Great Yarmouth

NETHERLANDS

Cardiff

Amsterdam

London

Rotterdam

* The German u-boat blockade around Britain comprised a 'war zone' including the whole of Ireland and extended 400 miles into the Atlantic.

Portsmouth

Dover

Zeebrugge
Ostend

Antwerp

Cologne

Plymouth

SOUTHERN BARRAGE

Calais

BELGIUM

English Channel

Cherbourg

Luxembourg

Le Havre

Reims

Britain's protected sea trade routes

Caen

Western Front

Paris

Minefields

FRANCE

German blockade from 1917 *

0   50   100 miles

German occupied areas

Between 1914-1918, various minefields of differing sizes, depths and effectiveness

Neutral countries

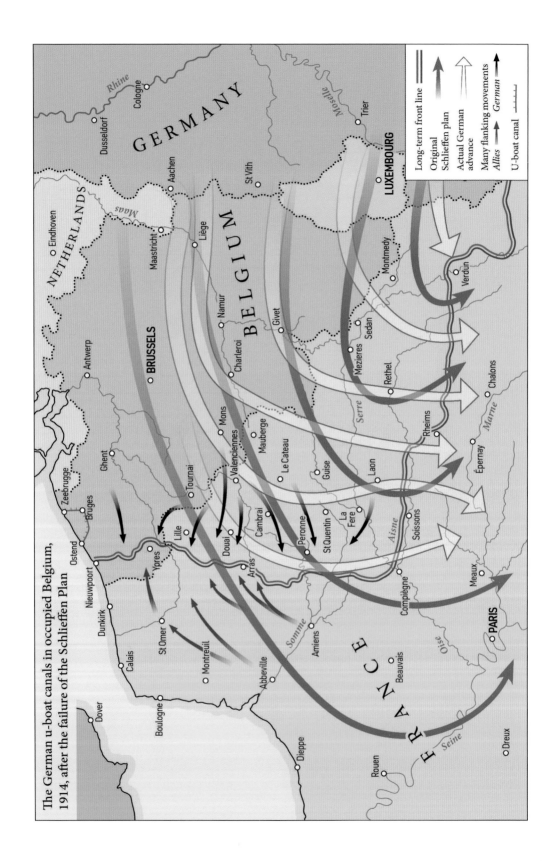

The German u-boat canals in occupied Belgium, 1914, after the failure of the Schlieffen Plan

Legend:
- Long-term front line
- Original Schlieffen plan
- Actual German advance
- Many flanking movements — German
- Allies
- U-boat canal

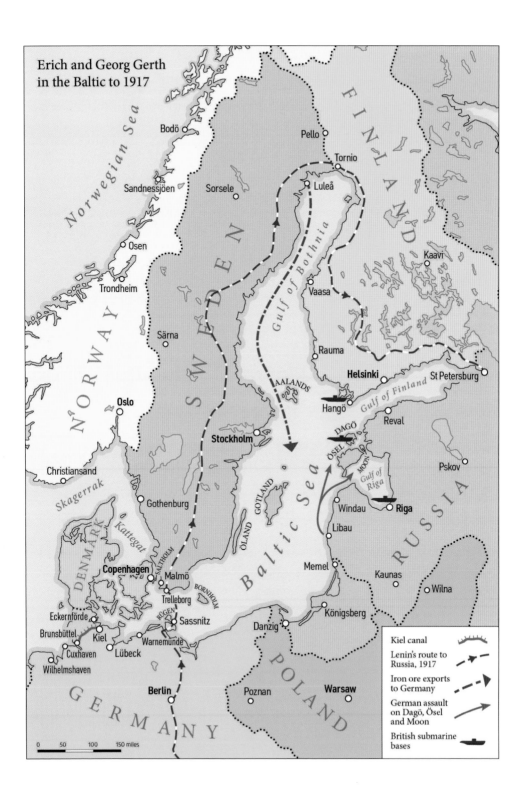

Erich and Georg Gerth
in the Baltic to 1917

Norwegian Sea

Bodö

Pello

Tornio

FINLAND

Sandnessjöen

Sorsele

Luleå

Gulf of Bothnia

Osen

Kaavi

Trondheim

Vaasa

NORWAY

Särna

Rauma

Oslo

SWEDEN

Helsinki

St Petersburg

AALANDS

Hangö

Gulf of Finland

Reval

Christiansand

Stockholm

DAGÖ

Skagerrak

ÖSEL

Pskov

Gothenburg

Kattegat

ÖLAND GOTLAND

MOON

Gulf of Riga

DENMARK

Baltic Sea

Windau

Riga

SALTHOLM

Libau

RUSSIA

Copenhagen

Malmö

Memel

Kaunas

Trelleborg

BORNHOLM

Wilna

Eckernförde

RÜGEN

Sassnitz

Danzig

Königsberg

Brunsbüttel

Kiel

Warnemünde

Cuxhaven

Lübeck

Wilhelmshaven

Berlin

Poznan

Warsaw

GERMANY

POLAND

0   50   100   150 miles

Kiel canal

Lenin's route to
Russia, 1917

Iron ore exports
to Germany

German assault
on Dagö, Ösel
and Moon

British submarine
bases

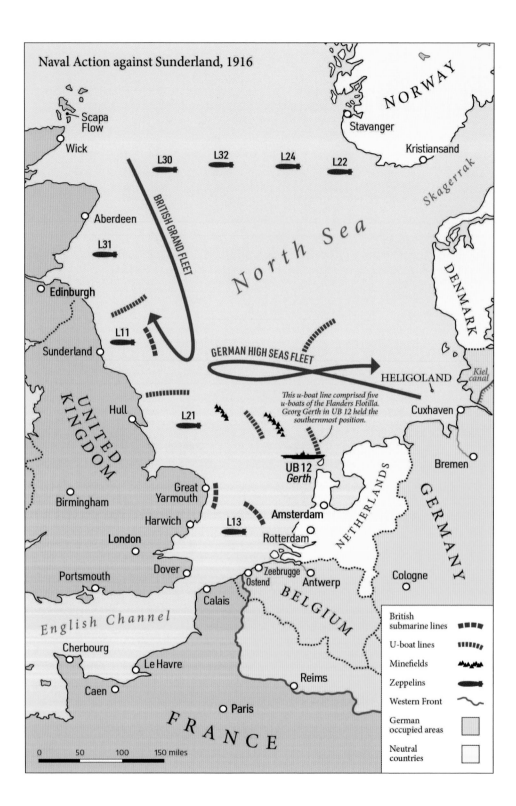

Naval Action against Sunderland, 1916

NORWAY

Scapa Flow
Wick
Stavanger
Kristiansand

L30   L32   L24   L22

North Sea

Skagerrak

Aberdeen

BRITISH GRAND FLEET

L31

DENMARK

Edinburgh

L11

GERMAN HIGH SEAS FLEET

HELIGOLAND

Kiel canal

Sunderland

Hull

L21

This u-boat line comprised five u-boats of the Flanders Flotilla. Georg Gerth in UB 12 held the southernmost position.

Cuxhaven

UB 12
Gerth

Bremen

UNITED KINGDOM

Birmingham

Great Yarmouth

Amsterdam

NETHERLANDS

GERMANY

Harwich

London

L13

Rotterdam

Dover

Portsmouth

Zeebrugge
Ostend
Antwerp

Cologne

Calais

BELGIUM

English Channel

Cherbourg

Le Havre

Reims

Caen

Paris

FRANCE

0   50   100   150 miles

British submarine lines
U-boat lines
Minefields
Zeppelins
Western Front
German occupied areas
Neutral countries

Erich Gerth and the Mediterranean War

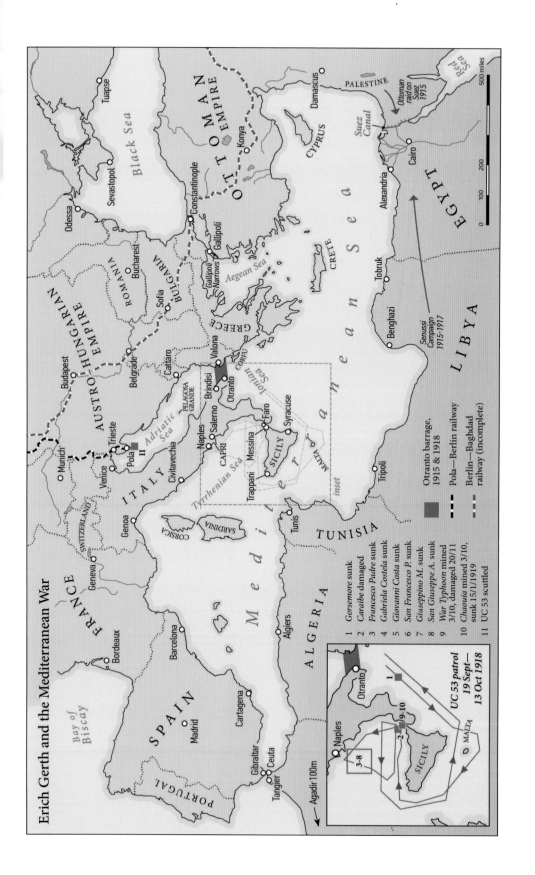

Ottoman raid on Suez 1915

Senussi Campaign 1915–1917

Otranto barrage, 1915 & 1918

Pola—Berlin railway

Berlin—Baghdad railway (incomplete)

1 *Gorsemore* sunk
2 *Caraibe* damaged
3 *Francesco Padre* sunk
4 *Gabriela Costela* sunk
5 *Giovanni Costa* sunk
6 *San Francesco P.* sunk
7 *Giuseppino M.* sunk
8 *San Giuseppe A.* sunk
9 *War Typhoon* mined 3/10, damaged 20/11
10 *Chaouia* mined 3/10, sunk 15/1/1919
11 UC 53 scuttled

UC 53 patrol
19 Sept—
13 Oct 1918

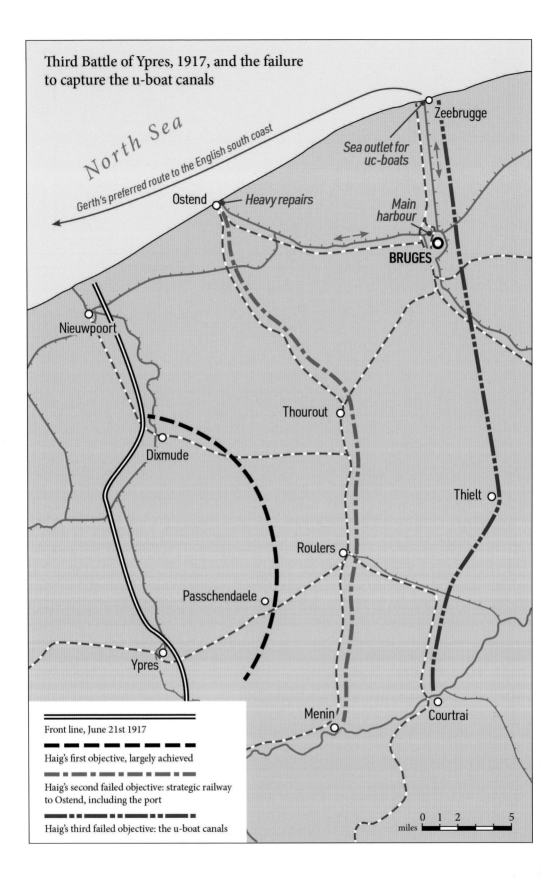

Third Battle of Ypres, 1917, and the failure
to capture the u-boat canals

North Sea

Gerth's preferred route to the English south coast

Zeebrugge

Sea outlet for
uc-boats

Ostend — *Heavy repairs*

Main
harbour

BRUGES

Nieuwpoort

Dixmude

Thourout

Thielt

Roulers

Passchendaele

Ypres

Menin

Courtrai

Front line, June 21st 1917

Haig's first objective, largely achieved

Haig's second failed objective: strategic railway
to Ostend, including the port

Haig's third failed objective: the u-boat canals

0 1 2   5
miles

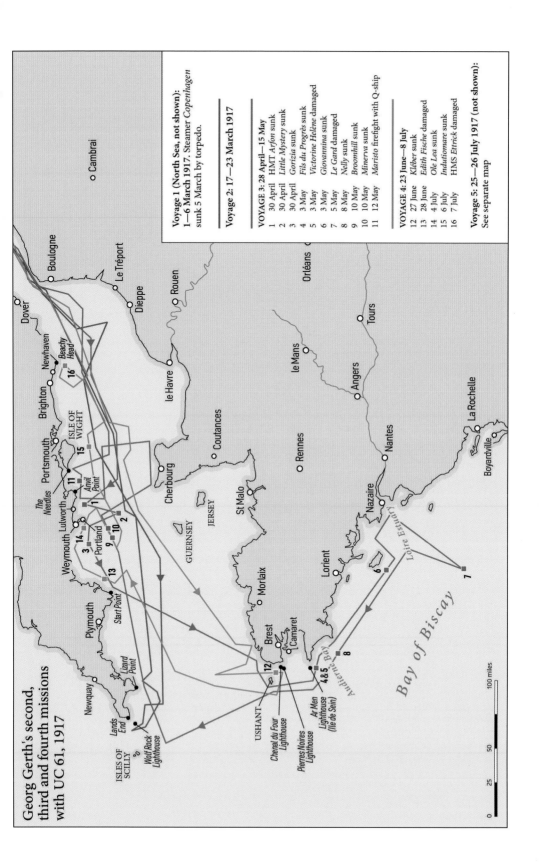

Georg Gerth's second, third and fourth missions with UC 61, 1917

Voyage 1 (North Sea, not shown):
1–6 March 1917. Steamer *Copenhagen* sunk 5 March by torpedo.

Voyage 2: 17–23 March 1917

VOYAGE 3: 28 April—15 May

1	30 April	HMT *Arfon* sunk
2	30 April	*Little Mystery* sunk
3	30 April	*Gorizia* sunk
4	3 May	*Fils du Progrès* sunk
5	3 May	*Victorine Hélène* damaged
6	3 May	*Giovannina* sunk
7	5 May	*Le Gard* damaged
8	8 May	*Nelly* sunk
9	10 May	*Broomhill* sunk
10	10 May	*Minerva* sunk
11	12 May	*Maristo* firefight with Q-ship

VOYAGE 4: 23 June—8 July

12	27 June	*Kléber* sunk
13	28 June	*Edith Fische* damaged
14	4 July	*Ole Lea* sunk
15	6 July	*Indutiomare* sunk
16	7 July	HMS *Ettrick* damaged

Voyage 5: 25—26 July 1917 (not shown):
See separate map

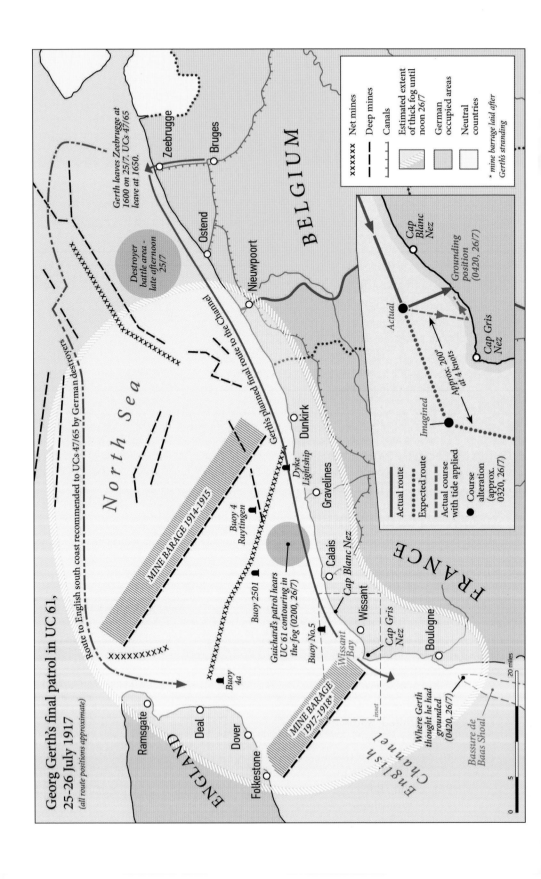

Georg Gerth's final patrol in UC 61,
25-26 July 1917
(all route positions approximate)

ENGLAND

Ramsgate
Deal
Dover
Folkestone

North Sea

MINE BARAGE 1914-1915

Buoy 4a

Buoy 2501

Buoy 4
Ruytingen

Route to English south coast recommended to UCs 47/65 by German destroyers

Destroyer battle area - late afternoon 25/7

Gerth leaves Zeebrugge at 1600 on 25/7. UCs 47/65 leave at 1650.

Zeebrugge
Bruges

Ostend

Nieuwpoort

BELGIUM

Gerth's planned final route to the Channel

Dyke Lightship

Dunkirk

Gravelines

Guichard's patrol hears UC 61 contouring in the fog (0200, 26/7)

Buoy No.5

Calais

Cap Blanc Nez

Wissant Bay

Wissant

Cap Gris Nez

MINE BARAGE 1917-1918*

inset

FRANCE

Boulogne

Where Gerth thought he had grounded (0420, 26/7)

Bassure de Baas Shoal

English Channel

0   5   20 miles

Inset:

Cap Blanc Nez

Actual

Grounding position (0420, 26/7)

Cap Gris Nez

Imagined

Approx. 200° at 4 knots

Course alteration (approx. 0320, 26/7) Gerth's stranding.

Actual route
Expected route
Actual course with tide applied
Course alteration (approx. 0320, 26/7) Gerth's stranding.

Net mines
Deep mines
Canals
Estimated extent of thick fog until noon 26/7
German occupied areas
Neutral countries

* mine barrage laid after Gerth's stranding

Introduction

Among the thousands who march into battle and humbly obey the will of the whole, each one knows how beggarly little his life counts beside the glory of the State, he feel himself surrounded by the workings of inscrutable powers ... Men kill each other who have great respect for each other as chivalrous foes. They sacrifice to duty not only for their life, they sacrifice what matters more, their natural feelings, their instinctive love of mankind, their horror of blood. Their little ego with all its noble and evil impulses must disappear in the will of the whole.[1]

There never was a master plan to write an historical story that centred on World War I. I have always evaded the subject, knew just broad details by osmosis, stayed away from it because it was an awful thing.

I fell across by chance two ordinary German participants – as much as two brothers from Berlin who were u-boat commanders can be described as ordinary. The more that I learned about Erich and Georg Gerth, the more interesting they became. I decided to explore their early lives. Why did they make the choices they did? What influenced them? How did their decisions fit the evolving politics of the time? What was their level of commitment when they went to war? I tarried in the places, with the people and the attitudes that mattered to them: their nineteenth-century family and school, the elitist German naval college, their devotion to the monarchy and the Prussian military system, the German drive for world-wide trade dominance, Admiral Tirpitz's naval adventure, the Kaiser's attempt to unsettle the Middle East and to inflame the Muslim diaspora and the development of the African colonies.[2] From there it was a short step to the Gerths' day-to-day war experiences, the economic blockade of Germany, the boredom of the Baltic, the founding of the Flanders u-boat bases, unrestricted submarine warfare, the virulent propaganda war, French prisoner of war camps and watching families deal with desperate food shortages. The brothers both survived by luck and judgement and faced immediate choices in the post-war fight to the death between a new socialist republic, Bolshevism, and the die-hard right wing they never admitted defeat or blame.

But I'm getting ahead of myself. All of that was a later truth, the product of work on an unplanned book that crept up on me. The first truth was a personal journey that began when I was still in short trousers. That was a simpler time when summer holidays meant the family making its way to Paddington Station in London and catching the steam train for the West Country. Our clothes and last year's bucket and spade were packed in a few suitcases and, when a baby brother arrived, the large perambulator went into the guard's van. As we approached the end of the journey, there was tension. My father had 'made good', left his Somerset roots, and now worked in the capital. Proudly waiting for our arrival on the country platform was his father, Sid, luggage trolley at the ready, for he was the station porter. Other passengers were ignored as my grandfather loaded our suitcases on his barrow. We made the short walk, past the Boer War cannon, to a nearby terraced house where a special and expensive tea of tinned salmon sandwiches, sponge cake and chocolate finger biscuits waited, the makings bought that morning from Uncle Bert's small shop on the corner. We never stayed beyond tea with 'Big Grandma and Grandad'. Their house was too small for a two-week holiday home and conversation was always stilted and embarrassing for a ten-year-old for my father had truly 'moved on'. We made our way over the town bridge, suitcases loaded on the pram, through the river docks, to my mother's parents, 'Little Grandma and Grandad', and our holiday home.

There was a good eight inches of height between the grandfathers. Sid, at over six-feet tall, volunteered for the Coldstream Guards just before being forced into uniform by the Derby Act in 1915.

It took more than two years to overcome political resistance to conscription. But the delay was only possible because of the surge of volunteers. Instead of rioting, the masses were eager to don uniform. No one had foreseen this, so the uniforms had not been prepared.[3]

In 1916, after a freezing winter near Passchendaele, Sid was invalided home with trench fever to long-term unemployment and begging cider for songs in the town's pubs. My mother's father, Alf, served in the Dragoon Guards, a cavalry regiment that was reduced to mounted infantry as the long-sought opportunity to break through the German lines never came.[4] Alf was a deserter before the war, but at the stricture of his bride-to-be, gave himself up in a general amnesty in August 1914, out of duty, but more because of the promise of marriage when the war was won 'by Christmas'.

Sid, always ready with a joke, never talked about his experiences. It was from Alf, with his gruff voice and bristly face, that I received my lasting impression of the Great War: running up the gradual slope, rifle with long bayonet in hand, to the German-held French hill-top town of Monchy-le-Preux. After a couple of hundred yards, Alf was blown up by a shell and received a piece of shrapnel in his neck. It was the only story of that time that he ever told me. He came to, paralysed, as he landed in a pit of ruined bodies and lime with part of his best friend lying next to him. Alf managed a grunt of horror which prompted his sergeant, standing on the grave edge, to discuss with another trooper whether it was worth the effort to climb down and to see if Alf could be saved. Alf got married during his convalescence and returned to the front in the Royal Engineers stoking coal into engines on the railway supply lines behind the trenches.

The story of the mass grave, part charnel pit, formed the nightmare that stayed with me into my twenties; it still visits me occasionally. The dream was one of a pair. Alf had few books; in retirement, he was a gardener and enjoyed a glass of beer and painting watercolour ships. However, in the little bookcase in the corner there was a multi-volume pictorial history of the Great War. I never saw anyone take a book off the shelves, but I did, secretly and guiltily, when I thought myself unwatched. I can still see at night a dozen of those photographs and they brought alive my grandfather's tearful memory.

The war was never discussed again, but the memories lingered so much that I felt I could smell it: musty, acidic and futile. I can now. The smell is triggered by the word 'million'. Every time I hear or read 'million', the taint comes back.

The irony is that I have a life-long interest in history – Byzantium, Carthage, the Mediterranean, Garibaldi and Napoleon – but I never concentrated on, nor touched unless I had to, the Great War. I am a Johnny-come-lately academic. I finished my doctorate at Bristol University when I was sixty-five years old. I cleared the many sub-projects and obligations and had some time free. Early in 2016, I contacted the Maritime Archaeology Trust (MAT), based in Southampton. The Trust had developed a five-year Heritage Lottery-funded project as part of the Centenary of World War I. Called *Forgotten Wrecks*, the continuing intention is to chart and record some 700 south coast sites that resulted from the conflict. The project includes merchant, naval, passenger, troop and hospital ships, and extends to ports, wharfs, buildings and foreshore hulks – anything with a maritime connection.[5] Many of these sites are uncelebrated and unprotected and have been deteriorating above and below water for up to one hundred years.

To begin my probation, I was given two shipwrecks to investigate, the *Minerva* and the *Broomhill*, both merchant steamers and, as was obvious, sunk a few miles apart on the same day in 1917 and, therefore, most likely, by u-boat. The culprit was *UC 61*, a coastal mine-layer, which, after detaching her mines, had forced 'my' two boats to stop with gunfire, encouraged their crews into lifeboats, and then boarded and set bombs on their waterlines, sending them to the bottom. Research at *The National Archives* in Kew established seven other vessels attacked by the same u-boat off the south coast that should be part of the *Forgotten Wrecks* project.[6] I was intrigued and asked for these extra wrecks to be added to my research list.

Part of the project's requirement was to develop limited information about the attacking vessel. *UC 61* was easy to find on the internet; in a small way, the submarine had become a celebrity. Its renown was not because of any heroic deeds. It had run aground in fog in July 1917 on the beach at Wissant a few miles south west of Calais near Cap Gris Nez.[7] All the websites based their tales either on each other or on a few pages in a book written in 1927 by Albert Chatelle, an author who made a good living for many years by writing and producing war memories of the French seaside towns. In the case of *UC 61*, the story ran most prominently in *Calais pendant la guerre 1914-1918*.[8] What was less known was that Chatelle based his elaborated version of *UC 61*'s demise on a forgotten war memoire of a French ensign, Louis Guichard, and on a single contemporary newspaper report. Chatelle's approach to *UC 61* centred on the robust language used by its commander, Kapitänleutnant Georg Gerth on being approached in a small boat by brave but querulous French Coast Guard 2nd Class Stanislas Serin. The stranding was portrayed as an embarrassing navigational error for Gerth. The twenty-six-man crew surrendered willingly to Serin's shaking rifle and were soon marched to Calais for interrogation and to begin their captivity. They were accompanied by a troop of lancers called to the scene and thus *UC 61* was lauded as the only u-boat captured by the Belgian cavalry. The intelligence gain from the wreck and crew was described officially as minimal, particularly as the crew blew up and set fire to their boat. This claim was untrue; the intelligence gained, I found, was substantial.[9]

I soon took serious notice of Georg's older brother, Erich. Erich joined the *Kaiserliche Marine* two years before Georg, but followed him into submarine command two years later in 1918. Georg fought off the south coast of England and the west coast of France; Erich spent his short u-boat career in the Mediterranean. Georg became a philosopher and businessman who relished his privacy. Erich's wider life was fascinating: spying with Wilhelm Canaris in South America; connections to the Battle of Verdun and Baron von Richthofen; to the Spartakist revolution and the murder of communist leaders Karl Liebknecht and Rosa Luxemburg in 1919; covertly preparing the second u-boat fleet for the next war; developing close contacts from Paris with Europe's Catholic hierarchy, even to the Pope-to-be, Eugenio Pacelli, in an attempt to stop a second world war; and dealing with the consequences of the introduction by the National Socialists in 1933 of a law to cleanse German public life of all those with Jewish connections.

Together Erich and Georg's stories allowed the inclusion of many of the awful events that helped the war to develop: famine in the British concentration camps of 1900-02 during the Boer War; the genocide of the Herero and Nama people in German South West Africa between 1904 and 1907; the slaughter of, perhaps, 6,000 Belgian civilians in 1914 and the deportation for slave labour of many more, and the cultural destruction of the Louvain library and Rheims Cathedral, in the German rush to encircle Paris; claimed atrocities by all sides in the u-boat war; and, over twenty years later, the Nazi concentration camps and the carpet bombing of little-militarised German cities in 1944 and 1945.[10]

There are many detailed and considered books that set out to tell the whole story of the Great War and its aftermath, or concentrate on important aspects. This book is not intended as a competitive history, although there is much history within it, and some of that history is new. What I decided to write was not a conventional history, but a personal view of the events that were integral to the Gerth brothers, to see how they were changed by what they heard, were taught and experienced. It is a true story about real people. *Sound of Hunger* is unashamedly intimate in selection, perhaps eccentric in places; a personal journey that explains what was newly found, how it was investigated and understood and became important to laying my demons. The closer my text is to the story of the Gerths, the more original the research; the nearer to the Kaiser, the more I have relied on a host of other authors, selecting those which seemed to have grasped a nub or raised a controversy. There are opinions everywhere; however, these are better seen as signposts for readers who wish to explore further. If I have over-stepped the mark in my free quoting from any source, please forgive my enthusiasm.

In summary, there is no deliberate reason to choose the Gerth brothers for this book. Other crews, another family, might have done just as well. Perhaps that is the point. When politics and profit come to play in war, as they must, it is ordinary families that are caught in the chaos. And Erich and Georg Gerth do provide an exciting and interesting story as well as a helpful literary device. Historian James Joll in 1968 asked why the origins of the war were still studied 'even though every incident in the critical days of July 1914 has been scrutinised, analysed and interpreted again and again'.[11] Since Joll's question, the flood has continued with more books on the subject than on any other topic in history.

> *The crisis of 1914 owes its continuing interest to the fact that it provides an opportunity of trying many different approaches and offering many different types of historical explanation. It is the example of the extent to which what we call International History must in fact embrace all kinds of history, and it suggests that any attempt to insist on a too rigid departmental division of historical studies into economic history, diplomatic history, art history, and so on, must lead to an impoverishment of our historical understanding.[12]*

Choosing what to read on or about the Great War is an alarming task, especially for someone new to the field. Historian Jay Winter described a 'veritable tide of publications ... dizzying in its magnitude'.[13] He felt it would take several working lives just to read the existing literature: in 2004, more than 500,000 titles were listed in the library of the *Bibliothèque de documentation internationale contemporaine* in Paris. Winter's fellow academic, Christopher Clark, wrote that the war had 'spawned an historical literature of unparalleled size, sophistication and moral intensity'.[14] I have read, or in just a few cases skimmed, almost 500 of them.[15] In some cases, choice was determined by careful subject definition, sometimes availability or cost, and it was easy to discard many general histories and other works that concerned the detail of great land battles and their equipment, war in the air, and also spheres of war away from the western approaches. One book often led to others as ideas came together or new avenues of thought opened. Among the surprises was the lack of confidence among present-day historians for contemporary commentators, those who had met the people involved or who were themselves the person who helped make the decisions or carried them out. Amid the propaganda and, sometimes, hatred, I found there was no substitute for proximity described with clarity, a sense of holding hands with historical events.

> *In our own deconstructive times, new historians contrive to shrivel old historians until their information ... is practically discounted, if not discarded. All that is held interesting about their work is its discourse, the subconscious patterning of its information to establish certain contrasts and 'oppositions' required by the society in which the historian operated.*[16]

Selectivity was rife in what I read. For example, three major recent books on the same subject contained almost no overlap in their choice of secondary source material. With the volume of literature available, it is possible to choose which authors to quote and thereby to assemble an impressive battery of 'evidence' to complement any reasonable hypothesis.[17] 'There was always enough complexity to keep the argument going.' This point is made with due regard and gratitude to the many authors quoted in this book.

The twentieth century saw a gradual and deliberate embrace of total war: the willingness of Western civilisation to use food, as well as weapons of increasingly destructive power, in an indiscriminate way against the whole population of an enemy country. I was converted to an awful point of view, that the Great War was not won or lost in the trenches. Indeed, after the Battle of the Marne, much of the slaughter had been in vain – a divisive opinion, I understand, but not frivolously offered. The war in the west had been won at sea off Western Europe. Even there it was not, at heart, a war of munitions and death, but of economic deprivation, of food, or rather famine, and a cold-blooded attempt by each side to starve the enemy civilian populations into submission. The Germans only just failed with their high risk, all-or-nothing response, the unrestricted sinking of the

Atlantic supply ships. The British, with more practice at famine, blockade and war on civilians, had planned for this eventuality over some twenty years. They were, finally, successful after being bolstered by the entry of the USA into the war in 1917 and the greater ability that gave to stem the flow of food and supplies into Germany through the remaining principal neutral countries – Denmark, the Netherlands, Norway and Sweden.

It also became apparent that many of the momentous decisions on both sides were taken by men of limited intellectual breadth and rigour, flawed through pomposity and, in some cases, a lack of morality and proportionality. Joll softly calls this assessment their 'ordinariness'. Luigi Albertini wrote a seminal three-volume work on the origins of the war, predating that of Fritz Fischer which in the 1960s shattered the cosy post-war German consensus on war guilt.[18] Albertini wrote a little kindly of the 'disproportion between [the leaders'] intellectual and moral endowments and the gravity of the problems which faced them, between their acts and the results thereof.'[19] So, from time to time, I have taken advantage of hindsight to be direct.

Byzantine research tentacles spread in many unexpected directions and exposed a complex network of documents, important and famous people, surprises, and coincidences. So, interwoven and interspersed with chapters about the Gerths are stories offering wider explanations, the planning of the economic destruction of Germany and the consequences of its famine, the progress of the u-boat war and the response from London, the British attempt through propaganda to demonise the German nation and to bring America into the war, the terrible treatment of prisoners of war.[20]

It was the realisation that the Great War was a war of deliberate attempted starvation that led to the title of this book, *Sound of Hunger*. For a change from a heavy diet of war books, I had dabbled in the foothills of chaos theory – the butterfly effect – the accumulative influence of unnoticed small margins that tip the balance into something altogether unexpected and, often, more serious. In a simple form, this effect can be found in a Ray Bradbury short story, *The Sound of Thunder*.[21] The title of this book is a homage, a play of words, to his contribution to understanding chaos. All war is chaotic and it is often a matter of luck which action prevails and who lives or dies.

> *The objective nature of war makes it a calculation of probabilities; now there is only one single element still wanting to make it a game, and that element it certainly is not without: it is chance. There is no human affair which stands so constantly and so generally in close connection with chance as war. But together with chance, the accidental, and along with it good luck, occupy a great place in war.*[22]

The Gerths and their u-boats played a small part in the famine war, but at what stage would their sinking of a sail ship of fish bound for a local market prove the tipping point between a suffering, but ordered, society and a population in revolt. This was so feared in 1914 in England that front-line troops were held back from Flanders. In France, there were many smaller-scale food riots as prices climbed and scarcity became common. By January 1917, food prices in Paris had risen 40 per cent since July 1914 and, six months later, by 92 per cent; real wages had fallen by 10 per cent in the same period.[23] In Germany, food riots were sometimes dealt with by machine guns shooting down protesting housewives and, later, were part and parcel of the people's post-war Bolshevik revolution and the armed response.

Sound of Hunger is the sound of the Great War. The book, therefore, is in part about the politics and deliberate application of hunger in war and its use as a bargaining chip in the post-war negotiations. 'Sound' also refers to the Channel, the large passage of water connecting the North Sea to the Bay of Biscay where most of the action in this book was fought.

> *The British policy looked to the use of every possible weapon, legal and illegal, by which the Central Powers could be starved out. It sought, according to Winston Churchill, to treat 'the whole of Germany as if it were a beleaguered fortress, and avowedly sought to starve the whole population – men, women, and children, old and young, wounded and sound – into submission'.*[24]

Soldiers flooded back to Germany and home, mostly in good and proud order, but hungry and jobless. The Allies applied every conceivable pressure on the German negotiation team to force them to sign a dictated peace treaty. The military were quickly stripped of their Grand Fleet and their u-boats so that their ability to fight and to protect themselves from invasion by sea was lost. The French moved gunboats up the Main river and positioned them to fire on Frankfurt should the treaty not be signed.[25] The British demanded that the entire German merchant fleet be handed over. The extent of confiscated railway rolling stock and motor lorries severely reduced the ability both to kick-start the economy and to distribute food and fertiliser. But, crucially, the Allies applied ruthless emotional pressure on ordinary German families and through them on the politicians. The French refused to release prisoners of war even though their own soldiers, and those of the British, had been released on demand in the first months after armistice. In the west, no sizeable German POW group got home until after March 1920.[26] Despite all this, and the signing of what was believed to be an 'unjust peace', the German negotiators used unrelenting propaganda to unite most of the German people in a time of revolution, to gain the upper moral hand over the Allies and to rewrite the history books, especially in the neutral countries and in the United States.[27]

In the views of a small, but significant, number of historians 'the fact that war was waged on women and children, on the elderly – after the Armistice – [was] a war crime'.[28] Having looked at the effects of the continued blockade into 1919, I agree. Historians may argue the actual number of deaths, possibly reaching towards one million, but it is the cumulative effects of stunted growth, retarded mental powers, social collapse and residual hate that matters. One might also argue that the holding back of German prisoners after 1918 was a war crime, especially as so many were housed in inhumane conditions and forced to clear the battlefields of live ordnance and long-dead bodies. Then, of course, the unleashing of the u-boats to fire indiscriminately on unarmed merchant ships and sail-powered fishing fleets was always portrayed in a relentless propaganda war as a differentiator between the moral, God-fearing Allies and the militaristic and vicious Prussians.

Press and public ratcheted up the hatred altogether. The most poisonous racist weekly, John Bull, saw its circulation climb by 300,000 in early 1915, proving there was a good audience for exterminatory rhetoric. The implication and conclusion were clear: no more distinctions between good and bad Germans ... The correct response was retaliation ... In short, kill them all and let God sort them out.[29]

It is customary, even necessary, for an author to declare their personal involvement in the subject under review. Mine is limited. Almost fifty years ago, I dived in thirty feet of water on one of the Falmouth u-boats. At the end of the Great War, 105 u-boats were allocated to Britain as war reparations, eight made it to Falmouth, and two were sunk in gunnery practice. While waiting their fate, the remaining six were caught in a severe winter storm in 1921; one was thrown ashore on Gyllyngvasse beach and the other five on rocks near Pendennis Point.[30] During the dive, I caught the best-tasting turbot ever, halved with my landlady and shared with my companions for breakfast.

I was far advanced with my research before I realised, in addition to the admissions in the opening paragraphs, the appropriateness of the stories of some of my own relatives. Little Grandma, Harriet, had two sea-going brothers:

One, Austin Milner Maggs was a merchant navy chief engineer. On 27 July 1917, his steamer, *Belle of England*, 3,877 tons, built in 1905, was carrying iron ore from Algiers to Barrow. She was an unusual vessel with a hull that was rounded and stepped inward above her waterline.[31] *Belle of England* was torpedoed 155 miles off the Fastnet Rock by *U 95*, commanded by Kapitänleutnant Athalwin Prinz. There were no fatalities, but a destroyer accompanying the small convoy told the men that they could not pick them up for fear of also being hit. Austin spent three days in an open lifeboat before being found and taken to Ireland. His privations damaged his eyesight to the extent that it declined through the rest of his life, eventually costing him his sea-going job.

> [The case of the Alnwick Castle] was typical of hundreds, with the sudden explosion, the disappearance of the great ship, the miserable struggle for life in open boats on a stormy sea by men who had no comforts and no warmth, and who were exposed to the waves and the bitter cold, with every prospect of perishing of starvation and thirst. Many boats were never heard of again; many ships vanished leaving no trace.[32]

The second brother was Engineer Lieutenant Ivor Alphonso Maggs of the River Class torpedo-boat destroyer HMS Kale, 7th Destroyer Flotilla, based at the River Humber. Kale was used in counter-mining operations and anti-submarine patrols and may even have chased UC 61 at some time. Kale hit a British mine in the North Sea on 27 March 1918 while leading a flotilla of four vessels that were transferring from Immingham to Portsmouth; fourteen officers and men were lost, including Ivor Maggs. Commander Harold Denison of the Kale was criticised in a court martial for hazarding his vessel, but lightly dealt with. The wreck was still unfound in 2016; the Admiralty claiming till then that its position was unknown. This was untrue. The Admiralty always knew the precise position of sinking. The court martial and the story behind the sinking were kept secret until 1994; the knowledge was never shared in 1918 with the families of the lost crew members. A close reading of the official papers suggests a cover up to protect a senior officer responsible for failing to issue an up-to-date mine map to Denison.[33] But, that is another story.

Private Tom Heal was the youngest brother of Big Grandad Sid. He was a member of 4th Battalion, Royal Marines Light Infantry, a unit raised for a raid on Zeebrugge with the intention of blocking u-boat access by canal to the sea from their inland base at Bruges; the very path travelled many times by UC 61. These marines landed on Zeebrugge mole from an ageing HMS Vindictive on 23 April 1918 and in a vicious fire-fight lost a third of their men. The operation was instantly, more accurately 'previously', declared a great success; senior Admiralty officers waited for the returning men on the quayside at Dover to hand out gallantry medals. In fact, the raid was an heroic failure as smaller u-boats could pass through the canal the next day at high tide. Larger u-boats diverted to the sea through Ostend. Tom died in Toronto, Canada, in 1926, of tuberculosis and is buried in a pauper's grave.[34]

These personal cases confirmed three lessons which proved invaluable when reviewing either primary or secondary sources for this book: first,

casualty numbers do not tell the whole story of suffering; second, never
blindly trust what is written whatever the source; and, third, even the most
surprising people tell lies and not always for the most evident reasons.

> *If you take the truth from History what is left is an idle unprofitable tale.*
> *Therefore, one must not shrink from blaming one's friends or praising*
> *one's enemies; nor be afraid of finding fault with and commending the*
> *same person at different times. For it is impossible that men engaged*
> *in public affairs should always be right, and unlikely that they should*
> *always be wrong.*[35]

I needed help with my language skills and I am indebted to two translators
who have become friends and surprising Gerth enthusiasts.

Dr Cathrin Brockhaus-Clark, scion of the family behind the *Brockhaus
Lexikon*, helped with contacts with Peter Schultz at the Deutsches U-Boot
Museum at Cuxhaven-Altenbruch where, amongst much other material,
copies of the commanders' *Kriegstagebuch* (KTB – war diaries) of most
of the World War 1 u-boats can be obtained, and with Sebastian Remus
who researched for me in the Department of Military Archives in the
Bundesarchiv in Freiburg.[36] Both institutions provided copious material,
which we sifted through and Dr Brockhaus translated.

The majority of these German naval records have the rubber stamp of
the NID, the Royal Navy Intelligence Department, each with an individual
'PG' number. The suffix 'PG', reportedly standing for 'Pinched from the
Germans', gives the clue to a remarkable story. During the last days of
World War II, Team 55 of the Royal Navy 30 Assault Unit joined US Navy
counterparts of the Forward Intelligence Units in dangerous searches to
capture German intelligence records, taken late in the war from Berlin to
be hidden in out-of-the-way places and destroyed if need be. On 25 April
1945, acting on a discovered letter, the Allied team arrived at Tambach
Castle near Coburg in Southern Bavaria. Here, they found German forces,
including three junior admirals, with the entire German Admiralty record
stretching from 1850 to 1945. The files had been moved at the command
of Grand Admiral Erich Raeder who intended to write the history of the
pre-1914 Imperial German Navy in defence of the Tirpitz strategy.[37] The
military guards ignored the order to burn the files should capture be
imminent and instead used their wood and petrol to keep warm. Included,
among much else, were the war diaries from almost all of the World War
I u-boats.[38] All the files were classified 'Top Secret' and mostly taken to
London, split between the British Admiralty and the American military
headquarters at 20 Grosvenor Square where, after much personal initiative
and hard work, it was decided to microfilm the whole record. This began
in August 1945 and was completed by July 1947 and comprised 3,905 reels
of film, of which 40 per cent contained records from before 1930. In 1962,

the British Admiralty began the snail-like process of returning the original documents to the Federal Republic of Germany.[39] The entire microfilm collection of the years before 1930 was transferred from the Naval History Division of the US Navy to the American National Archives in 1967.

One obvious difficulty with u-boat diaries is that they cannot cover the last voyage of each boat unless other official or Press documents were added later. Another is that many of the accounts, especially those of the Flanders Flotilla, are handwritten in *Sütterlinschrift*, old-style German cursive letters, impenetrable to many living Germans. As some 202 boats were lost by accident and by enemy action in the Great War, there is a large amount of information missing from the diaries including final encounters and a resting place. One of the leaders of the modern-day u-boat hunters is Dr Innes McCartney of Bournemouth University, England, and he has produced a thorough review of the archaeological evidence of those graves.[40] Often joining the teams in the water, McCartney found that of the sixty-three u-boats in the English Channel, 41 per cent were incorrectly identified or unknown. The original source for u-boat wrecks recorded by the British Admiralty in 1919 was 52 per cent wrong.[41] McCartney also gives a useful review, accurate to 2015, of sources for u-boat information.[42] The official German five-volume history of u-boat operations in the Great War was written by Rear Admiral Arno Spindler, based on the German naval archive and never published in English.[43] Indeed, Spindler was one of those captured at Tambach Castle. While there is much to be grateful for in these volumes they do have serious limitations. Those volumes that were written during the Nazi period do not dwell on failures during the first u-boat campaign, as this honesty would not mesh with the success necessary for the philosophy of a master race.

> *Spindler takes pains to present the crews and their war patrols in the best possible light. Chivalry still counted for something in World War I and Spindler wanted it documented … This is not the most glowing official history ever produced but considering the context … we should be grateful that any scholarship was attempted.*[44]

For his last volume, completed after the loss at Tambach Castle, Spindler was denied access by the British to his own records. Modern u-boat histories in German have improved matters.[45] One recent detailed student of the archive goes so far as to say that after the war was lost the 'Imperial Navy studiously sabotaged the creation of an objective history'; Spindler's work being 'full of omissions and misrepresentations'.[46]

Nor were early English efforts any more reliable. British Admiralty files were also treated to almost wanton disregard for future usefulness. Historian Matthew Seligmann notes with some sadness:

> *Seemingly arbitrary decisions taken by British Admiralty records clerks to cull first 93% of the total which was then re-examined twenty-five years later in 1958–61 when it was whittled down to a mere 2% of the original total. The theory was that anything with a long-term political, financial, administrative, legal or historical significance would be retained permanently. The reality, of course, did not live up to the promise.*[47]

The British Government decided on a twenty-eight-volume set of the *History of the Great War Based on Official Documents*. A chapter on the blockade was discarded and rewritten due to continuing legal scruples.[48] With the first volume almost ready in 1923, the Admiralty announced that the role of the u-boat should not be over-emphasised, especially through to April 1917.

> *These chapters provide gloomy reading from the British point of view and there is much in them to encourage potential enemies who may consider that it is in their competence to subjugate the Empire by a large submarine building programme. The encouragement of these ideas by means of an official publication is very much to be deprecated, particularly at a time when we are advocating the abolition of the submarine.*[49]

It was through the endeavours of Cathrin Brockhaus' family in Germany, particularly sister-in-law Doris Brockhaus, that a remarkable discovery was made. Christa-Maria, the youngest daughter of Georg Gerth, was alive and living in rural Germany, her two sons nearby, and she was willing, indeed enthusiastic, to meet and to reminisce about her father. Christa-Maria, who was born in 1939, was Georg's favourite among his four children and spent most time with him, apart from during World War II, and at the end looked after him until he died in 1970. Two days of intensive interviews followed at the family home, including convivial meals. Luckily, each family member spoke more than adequate English.

Jacqui Squire corrected my French emails to potential information sources, but quickly took charge of translating many documents, including deciphering handwritten reports, conducted Internet searches and smoothed the research passage through the French administration at many archives. She became so involved that she volunteered to join several European research trips. The first, in the summer of 2016, included a visit to Calais Citadel where the crew of *UC 61* were first imprisoned; the beach at Wissant where *UC 61* was stranded and where, with the help of local historian and diver Alain Richard and GPS, the remnants of the u-boat were found at low-tide among the holidaymakers; the Pas-de-Calais archives, which includes a separately housed extensive newspaper collection at Arras; and, finally, the war museum at Adinkirke, Belgium, where a remnant of *UC 61* is on display and which was introduced by the curator and now good friend, Guido Mathieu. Alain Richard was extremely free with his extensive knowledge of the coast and other wrecks which play a part in this story, and also to the email introduction of fellow diver and wreck enthusiast Jef Coulon. The second trip, in October 2016, started with a visit in the rain and heavy traffic to the Zeebrugge/Bruges canal, route to the sea for the World War I u-boats of the Flanders Flotilla; a day at the Royal Museum of the Armed Forces and of Military History in Brussels under the thoughtful guidance of World War I expert Rob Troubleyn; a moment's silence at the site of General Cambronne's verbal defiance at the field of Waterloo (and repeated reportedly by Georg Gerth on the beach at Wissant in 1917); time at the Service historique de la Défense in Vincennes, east of Paris, where exciting finds were made; and, finally, an evening visit to an unusual tribute, the cocktail bar *UC 61* in the Paris seventeenth arrondissement.[50] A third trip, a return to Wissant, was largely organised by Jacqui. This time we commemorated the centenary of the stranding of *UC 61* with Georg Gerth's daughter and her sons and with many friends and colleagues.[51] Particular thanks for arrangements, support and associated conference are due to Lieutenant Colonel Henri Lesoin; M Jean-Marie Ball, president of the *Art and History Society of Wissant*; local historian, M Philippe Gallois; and the staff of the Hotel de la baie de Wissant and of the restaurant, La Chaloupe.

Fulsome thanks are due to staff and personal intermediaries who gave freely of their time at various archives: Quoc-Thanh Nguyen, author and expert on Maritime Indochina, for further work at Vincennes and elsewhere in France, especially among German prisoners of war held in that country; Dr Nelson Timothy of the Dokumentationsbibliothek in Davos for information about the care of German prisoners of war transferred to Switzerland; Amélie Lelandais for her efforts among the archives at the Service historique de la Défense at Cherbourg; Guillaume Ange for his unfailingly helpful and meticulous organisation among the photographic and film archives at ecpad in Ivry-sur-Seine, the agency for the French military's *images de la défense*; personal friend, Emanuele Ojetti, in Rome, for his search for the tomb of Erich Gerth, Georg's brother, and for an introduction to Martina Nibbeling-Wriessnig whose detailed delving in the files at the German Foreign Ministry in Berlin was invaluable.

A copy of the original French language report of the interrogation of the German crew of *UC 61* was found in the US National Archives (NARA) in Washington, DC.

In the UK, there were many visits to The National Archives in Kew, and to the Royal Navy Submarine Museum at Gosport under the guidance of George Malcolmson, the Archives Collections Officer of the National Museum of the Royal Navy. Willing help from The Submariners Association provided two contacts: first, on technical matters concerning *UC 61*, Chief Petty Officer David Townsend, a former Royal Navy shipwright and submarine seaman officer and leader of the team that refurbished the RN submarine *Ocelot* for display at Chatham Harbour; and, second, access to a considerable private u-boat library belonging to Peter Holmes, the son of a World War II u-boat commander. Jacqui Squire introduced Captain Chris Phillips, master of the sail training ships *Lord Nelson* and *Tenacious*, Lieutenant RN retired, formerly of HM Submarines, who provided expert and friendly help with navigational issues. And a special thanks to Stephen Fisher of the *Maritime Archaeology Trust* for his considerable early work on the charts of the voyages of *UC 61*.

Of course, the Internet offered several relevant, and not-so-relevant, websites, some maintained by experts and some of these have been particularly useful, especially the forums. I offer a special thanks to Michael Lowrey and the team at uboat.net; to wrecksite.eu; the Great War Forum;[52] the forum at The Aerodrome, which deals with matters aerial;[53] the World War I Royal Navy monographs placed online by the Australian Navy;[54] the comprehensive French newspaper and publication collections at the Bibliothèque nationale de France;[55] Wikipedia; Pages 14–18 Forum;[56] and paid access to Ancestry.co.uk; shipindex.org and many others, individually cited.

I also thank many individuals, some met only by email: Eric Bulteau (*UC-61* bar), Hans-Georg Donner (Glashuette pocket watches);[57] Ann-Marie Fitzsimmons (UK Hydrographic Office), Charlie Fletcher (Liverpool University), Simon Hodgson (Simon Hodgson Photography), Rachel Hunt (National Trust), Anne Inquimbert (SHD, Vincennes), Scott Karabowicz and team (PD Studios), Dr Jarl Kremeier (Würzburg Residence), Matthias Löhr (German Foreign Ministry), Innes McCartney (Bournemouth University), Jim McMaster (UK Submariners Association), Mark Mollan (NARA), Jasmine Noble-Shelley (MAT), Klaus-Peter Pohland (uboatwar.com), Geoff Pringle (oldnautibits.com), Renate Rüb (Berlin archives), Ester Schneider (Villeroy & Boch), Freddy Spuikom (u-boat enthusiast), Simon Stephens (National Maritime Museum), Richard Stone (Bristol University), Rodney Strong (Kingsbridge Local History Group), Deryck Swetnam (Portsmouth University), Tomas Termote (author and nautical archaeologist), Julee Ware (Lighthouse Investigations, Austin, Texas) and François Zoonekyndt (SHD, Cherbourg).

Thanks also to the Unicorn Publishing Group team for their help and assistance in bringing this to fruition. Special thanks to Viv and Douglas for their tireless concentration over the text formatting and indexing.

Just as a final copy was transferred to my publishers, and after a year of enquiry, contact was made with Erich Gerth's family, all now living in the United States. Remarkably all Erich's four children, now in their eighties, were still living in January 2018. Descendants freely shared their startling reminiscences and their few photographs. Thank you to Madeleine, Marc and Roger.

Finally, there are a few explanations. The text includes emphases on racial, religious and sexual differences, sometimes crudely spoken or written, as in the day. These are an essential part of the story. Modern sensibilities may not sit well with this, but the book is not intended to be sanitised history. It is customary to acknowledge that any mistakes in the following pages are entirely my own responsibility. This I happily do, except, of course, that it is not always true. There are just two stylistic points. All footnote references to publications are abbreviations; for the reader to investigate further, as encouraged, it will be necessary to find the full source in the bibliography. Archival and Internet sources are given only in the footnotes.

Please enjoy. It's not all grim.

Chris Heal
Hampshire, UK
February 2018

ENDNOTES

1 Dorpalen, *Heinrich von Treitschke*, p. 149, cited in Padfield, *Dönitz*, p. 14.
2 Chapters 1, 'Brave new world', and 2, particular loyalty to the monarch – *Kaisertreu*.
3 Offer, *Working Classes*, p. 225.
4 Howard, 'Men against Fire, Expectations of War in 1914', pp. 47–48, citing Altham, *The Principles of War*, p. 92.
5 forgottenwrecks.maritimearchaeologytrust.org/home/about-the-project, accessed 5/12/2016.
6 Minesweeper trawler HMT *Arfon*, Norwegian, Uruguayan and Belgian steamers *Ole Lea*, *Edith Fische*, *Gorizia*, *Indutiomare*, the destroyer HMS *Ettrick*, and British merchant schooner *Little Mystery*. Other ships were sunk and damaged by *UC 61* away from the *Forgotten Wrecks* project area. Chapter 6, 'War of the raven'.
7 Chapter 8, 'Final patrol'.
8 Chatelle & Tison, *Calais pendant la guerre*, pp. 161–65. Also referenced in Chatelle & Le Bon, *Boulogne et sa marine pendant la guerre* (1921), pp. 113, 120–21 and in *Base Navale du Havre* (1949), pp. 235–36.
9 Chapter 10, 'Intelligence gift'.
10 Chapter 2.
11 Joll, *Unspoken Assumptions*, p. 5.
12 Joll, *Unspoken Assumptions*, p. 24.
13 Winter and Prost, *The Great War in History*, p. 1. Fischer, *War Aims*, p. xxi.
14 Clark, *Sleepwalkers*, p. xxi. Clark gives a useful summary of the official archival collections, and some of the major memoirs, with their many faults. Schwertfeger: 'A world war of documents'.
15 One of the great unsung successes of the British way of life is the *Inter-Library Loan Service*. Their assistance, through Alton library in Hampshire, was a friendly and almost-always successful service.
16 Ascherson, *Black Sea*, p. 78.
17 Clark, *Sleepwalkers*, pp. xxiv–xxv, makes the same point.
18 Fischer, *War Aims*.
19 Albertini, *Origins of the War*, Vol III, p. 178.
20 Chapter 12, 'Prisoners of war'.
21 Bradbury, *The Sound of Thunder & Other Stories* (1990), particularly p. 207. See also Gleick, *Chaos, Making A New Science*; and Hilton, 'Sea gulls, butterflies, and grasshoppers: A brief history of the butterfly effect in nonlinear dynamics'.
22 Clausewitz, *On War*, Book I, clause 20, p. 19.
23 Strachan, *World War 1*, p. 243.
24 Peterson, *Propaganda for War: The Campaign Against American Neutrality*, p. 83.
25 Boemeke, *Versailles*, Klein, in 'Misunderstood Defeat', p. 207.
26 Chapter 13, 'Guilt and blame'.
27 Chapter 9, 'Your truth, our truth'.
28 Winter, *Versailles Treaty – A Grand Bazaar*.
29 Gregory, 'A Clash of Cultures: The British Press and the Opening of the Great War' in Paddock, *Call to Arms*, pp. 38–39.
30 McCartney, *Lost Patrols*, pp. 51–55. The Falmouth u-boats: *UC 92*, *UB 86*, *UB 97*, *UB 106*, *UB 112* and *UB 128*, the boat of later Admiral Wilhelm Canaris, chief of the *Abwehr* from 1935.
31 wikipedia, accessed 10/12/2016.
32 Wilson, *Great War*, p. 255.
33 TNA, ADM 1/8520/10, 'Loss of Kale by mining'; ADM 156/40, 'Loss of Kale by mining'; ADM 156/42, 'Hazarding vessel'.
34 The records of the preparation for the Zeebrugge raid are held at *The Royal Marines Museum*, Southsea, where there is also a good scale model of the battle site. See also, amongst many: Carpenter, *Blocking of Zeebrugge*; Holloway, *From Trench to Turret*; Howard, *Zeebrugge Affair*; Terry, ed., *Ostend and Zeebrugge*; Warner, *Zeebrugge Raid*; Westerman,

Thick of the Fray at Zeebrugge and the autobiographies of Admirals Bacon and Keyes.

35   Hankey, *Supreme Command*, Vol. I, p. 94, the first British Cabinet Secretary, was fond of quoting Polybius, *The Histories*, trans. Shuckburgh, Vol. I, c. 14, 'He should know the truth of his remark.'

36   Dr Brockhaus's direct forebears were the founders of the famous 'Brockhaus Encyclopaedia' (the German equivalent of the *Encyclopaedia Britannica*) and of the F.A. Brockhaus publishing house in Leipzig in the early nineteenth century (*brockhaus.de*).

37   Seligmann, *Naval Route*, 'Introduction', p. xxi.

38   The complete headquarters war diaries were also later found hidden beneath the doorstep of what became the Royal Navy headquarters at Plön (Paterson, *Black Flag*), p. 93.

39   Farago, *The Game of Foxes*, pp. xi–xv. Kahn, National Archives History Office, 'The German Naval Archives: Tambach' (prologue.blogs.archives.gov/2016/08/31/the-german-naval-archives-tambach/). Kohnen, 'Seizing German Naval Intelligence from the Archives of 1870–1945', *Global War Studies*, Vol. 12, No. 1, 2015, pp. 133–179. *Guides to the Microfilmed Records of the German Navy, 1850–1945*: No. 1, 'Records Relating to U-Boats and T-Boats, 1914–1918', Microfilm Publication M1743 (one roll). McCartney, *Lost Patrols: Submarine Wrecks of the English Channel*, p. 11.

40   McCartney, *Lost Patrols*.

41   *TNA*, ADM 239/26.

42   McCartney, *Maritime Archaeology*, pp. 6–11.

43   Spindler, *Der Krieg zur See 1914–1918: Der Handelskrieg mit U-Booten*, Band 3, Oktober 1915 bis Januar 1917 (1934); Band 4, Februar bis Dezember 1917 (1941).

44   Koerver, *German Submarine Warfare*, pp. x–xi.

45   Bendert, *Die UB-Boote der Kaiserlichen Marine 1914 – 1918. Einsätze, Erfolge, Schicksale* (E S Mittler, Hamburg 2000) and *Die UC-Boote … Minenkrieg mit U-Booten* (2001); Herzog, *Deutsche U-Boote 1906–1966* (Pawlak, Koblenz 1990) and Schröder, *Die U-Boote des Kaisers: Die Geschichte des deutschen U-Boot-Krieges Gegen Großbritannien im Ersten Weltkrieg* (Bernard & Graefe Verlag, Bonn 2003).

46   Koerver, *War of Numbers*, p. 3.

47   Seligmann, *Naval Route*, 'Introduction', pp. xvii–xviii.

48   *TNA*, ADM 116/3424, p. 214.

49   *TNA*, ADM 116/3421, p. 11.

50   'UC-61 Bar', 4 rue de L'Arc de Triomphe (www.uc-61.com). Special thanks are given to Tom and Anne Chattaway for their kindness and hospitality in Waterloo during this expedition.

51   Chapter 18, 'The Long arm of the war'.

52   1914–1918.invisionzone.com.

53   theaerodrome.com/index.php.

54   navy.gov.au/media-room/publications/world-war-i-naval-staff-monographs.

55   bnf.fr/fr/acc/x.accueil.html.

56   pages14-18.mesdiscussions.net.

57   glashuetteuhren.de.

Preface
Behind the Mask

War has generated a distinctive culture. Processes of preparing for, waging, and commemorating war are seen as 'essential elements of history, rooted in psychology', admired and joined in as a martial cultural tradition that with the intensity of its emotions remains central to the lives of those who participate in it. The motivation to fight and die in war is perpetuated by a Culture of War that manifests itself through uniforms, war games, parades, military decorations and war memorials; the creation of war art, martial music, and war museums; and the popular fascination with weapons, war toys, violent computer games, battle re-enactments, collectibles, and military history and literature. The Culture of War makes men and women face death willingly, even enthusiastically.[1]

Two men deep in conversation, interspersed with gaps for thoughtful consideration, strolled through the London park on a warm mid-morning.[2] There was more sorrow than anger in the occasional and evident disagreements. The older man, a major in the Royal Marines, waved his pipe for emphasis; his companion in ill-fitting civilian clothes drew hands from trouser pockets to gesticulate before slumping them home again. Kensington Gardens was a busy thoroughfare of dawdling nannies and perambulators skirted by earnest individuals, head-down going about their wartime business. It was August 1917.

The man in uniform passed unrecognised and yet, for a few days seven years before, was one of the most talked-about men in Britain.[3] Bernard Trench received a much-publicised trial in Germany after being caught red-handed spying on military installations around the Frisian Islands in the North Sea. He spent almost three years in a fortress prison at Glatz in Lower Silesia. Trench, now just turned thirty-seven, was back at his old game, an expert on the u-boat arm of the *Kaiserliche Marine*, which many feared was about to starve England to her knees. His little red books on the personnel and activities of the u-boats were the pride of British Naval Intelligence. At the time of his stroll, Trench was the senior interrogator of u-boat prisoners, particularly their commanders.[4] He spoke fluent German and French with a good grasp of Danish. Trench's adversary was Kapitänleutnant Kurt Tebbenjohanns, aged thirty-one, known as 'Tebben' to all and sundry, recent commander of the coastal mine-laying submarine *UC 44*, and lucky to be alive.

The substance of the morning talk was written up by Trench, checked with Tebben, and then shared with Trench's boss, Reginald Hall, the Director of Naval Intelligence, who had been given the credit for persuading America to join the war; First Lord Sir Eric Geddes, the political head of the Navy; Admiral Sir John Jellicoe, the First Sea Lord and Chief of the Navy Staff. The text of Trench's précis is repeated below in full, first, because it exemplifies so many of the dilemmas investigated in this book and, second, because it is a true clash of cultures. Tebben met Trench's specific enquiries into u-boat operations, especially mine-laying, with a 'polite request that he might be excused from replying'.[5] The official papers support this: they are quite empty of useful military material. What Tebben was happy to do in an 'unusually candid' manner was to discuss aspects of German naval behaviour and his own feelings on these matters and it is this that made Trench's summary of importance to his superiors. If one wants to try to understand the background, the depth of knowledge and level of thinking of the average u-boat commander in World War I, as *Sound of Hunger* sets out to do in its first half, then this 1,800-word document is a good place to start. The subjects debated over two and a half hours ranged from the German theory of war, how the war started, the nature of war crimes, the morality of unrestricted submarine warfare, blockade, the arming of merchant ships and the use and effect of propaganda; all of these are investigated in chapters with particular relevance to the book's two main protagonists and u-boat captains, brothers Erich and, two years younger, Georg Gerth. Tebben ventured that his opinions were typical of his fellow officers. He was a member of the Crew of '05, his cadet year class, when for twelve months among almost four years of training he shared the close confines of a steam-powered sail training ship, the *Stein*, with Erich Gerth and his close friend, Wilhelm Canaris, who was to lead Germany's military intelligence into World War II.

Tebben recalled his two meetings with Trench on 10 and 14 August as a walk in the park with a recognised pre-war spy in which no information was exchanged. 'I was able to cut short all attempts he made to pump me.'[6] Tebben was in the middle of two weeks' solitary confinement with 'totally inadequate rations' on the fourth floor of a military building in South Kensington when Trench visited unexpectedly. Trench announced that he had obtained permission for a walk 'solely out of sympathy for [Tebben's] situation'. Trench, naturally enough, declared himself the winner in the conversation and described his adversary's intelligence as 'not of a high order' and that his 'thinking had evidently never travelled beyond the limits of his professional duties'.[7] The summary, other documents in the Admiralty files, and Tebben's *Abitur*, his pre-university educational qualification, suggest that Trench was a little over-pleased with his conduct of the interview. Letters written at the same time by Tebben to his parents in Braunschweig; his commanding officer at Brunsbüttel, Kapitänleutnant Pasqual; and a colleague in the Pola u-boat flotilla in the Adriatic, Kapitänleutnant Kurt Hartwig, are well written and sensitive.[8] Tebben is careful with his words, meticulous with his instructions, and distraught at the loss of his crew.

> *Please find out about the circumstances of [a leading seaman's widow] and the other poor widows of my brave men, and make such provision for them as is necessary, out of the sum of which I allotted for this purpose in my will.*[9]

The story of the sinking of Tebben's boat is described well enough in the Admiralty files and in Tebben's letters; there are a few reasonable discrepancies, but also some evasions around the exact circumstances of the loss, both parties having something to hide. There is also Tebben's personal recollection many years later when he is prevailed upon to tell the story openly for the first time by his great friend and u-boat ace Ernst Hashagen and which Hashagen recounts in his best-seller, *The Log of a U-Boat Commander*.

> *A happy chance had thrown me in again with Tebben. The fire burned brightly on the hearth and flickered on the faces of the few friends sitting before it ... It is curious that those who have taken part in the war are always unwilling to speak of any dreadful experience. It remains shut up in them, like a dark secret, and but rarely does it fight its way to the light.*[10]

On 31 July 1917, *UC 44* collected her eighteen mines at Heligoland and, after passing through the Dover Straits, arrived off Waterford on the south-east coast of Ireland on the evening of 4 August. At low tide, she laid four mines at the western side of the harbour and then moved to the east to lay five more. Immediately after the ninth mine dropped, there was a violent explosion and the submarine sank to the bottom in about ninety feet of water. It is possible that *UC 44* was lured to a live minefield as part of a well-laid subterfuge by Reginald Hall and British Naval Intelligence. The circumstances of *UC 44*'s sinking are disputed and are discussed in Chapter 10 as part of the intelligence gain from the wreck of *UC 61*, Georg Gerth's boat, stranded four days earlier on the beach at Wissant, south of Calais.[11]

Tebben and two men were trapped, squeezed together above the control room in a pocket of air in the conning tower. The inside of the bottom half of the tower was an integral part of the vessel with no safety hatch to separate the three survivors from the bodies of the twenty-six crew in the flooded boat. Tebben considered giving up and waiting to die of suffocation, but one of the men, recently married and who had just become a father, urged an escape attempt.

> *Tebben had spoken the last words more slowly and with hesitation. His recollection of the details of that dreadful experience now reduced him to silence. We others did not dare to ask him a question. A strange and fearful form had joined us round the fire and peered, greedily questioning, into the eyes of the spokesman. It was the Horror, which had been there to make a fourth that night with those three men in the tower.*

The men waited for the water to rise and compress their pocket of air until it equalled the outside pressure. The hatch opened easily and they popped out. Tebben actually kicked downwards to slow his ascent and to allow the expanding air to escape from his lungs. On the surface, he lost touch with his two comrades. It was a long way to shore and they both succumbed to the cold and the waterlogged weight of their heavy clothing. Tebben swam around for two and half hours fighting the tides. Just when his strength began to fail and he prepared to die, he was picked up by a rowing boat sent from the village of Dunmore. Tebben was well cared for, even when it was realised who he was. He was fed, clothed and packed off to London.

Trench's own history is also full of derring-do. In 1910, Trench and a friend, Lieutenant Vivian Brandon, were part of the crew of the training ship *HMS Cornwall*, which was used for spying operations during its overseas visits by its captain, Reginald Hall. It was not their first escapade: two years before Trench was commended for an investigation into the options for a sea assault on the port at Kiel in the Baltic.[12] Trench and Brandon pleaded guilty at trial in Leipzig and were sentenced to four years' imprisonment. The men were pardoned by Kaiser Wilhelm in 1913 as a personal gesture during the private visit of his first cousin King George and Queen Mary to Berlin. Hall re-employed the men when he headed Naval Intelligence and compensated them after their financial abandonment by the British Admiralty. Trench wrote an excellent 134-page personal diary of their spying, capture and his imprisonment.[13] The novel, *The Riddle of the Sands*, by Erskine Childers, which details German duplicity in the Frisians, was a favourite and read several times by both men before they set out on their adventure and contains startling coincidences.

Précis of two interviews with Kapitänleutnant Kurt Tebbenjohanns, 10 and 14/8/1917[14]

The second interview was largely recapitulatory, to enable the writer [Trench] *to satisfy himself that the notes that he made of the first interview directly represented the substance of the various points discussed, and this was in fact found to be the case, the German submarine commander* [Tebbenjohanns] *assenting to or occasionally modifying the* seriatim *account submitted to him.*[15]

The keynote of the conversation was supplied by the German officer's quotation of the Latin saying audiatur et altera pars, *and the discussion represented a genuine attempt to ascertain as far as possible the 'other fellow's point of view'.*[16]

The first point discussed was the effect of unrestricted u-boat warfare in its practical and moral aspects, and the German officer was compelled to admit as a result of a step-by-step discussion that, in spite of the most careful instructions and utmost precautions, the methods of unrestricted u-boat warfare:[17]

1. *Had resulted in a large number of innocent persons being done to death.*
2. *It followed from 1. that, notwithstanding the fact that a u-boat commander could plead that he was absolved from all responsibility in his capacity of a naval officer fighting for his country, yet the results were such that they did violence to his feelings as a human being, and that such a method of warfare could only be held to be justified by 'iron necessity'. The 'iron necessity' was conceived, not indeed:*

   a. As an attempt to starve out England, an idea which was energetically repudiated, but as representing the policy which it was hoped would largely interfere with the import of all raw materials necessary to the prosecution of the war, so as to bring England to the point of considering the advantage of a 'peace by negotiation'.[18]

   b. And that further it had been determined as the result of the Allies arming their merchant ships.

It was suggested that this view put the cart before the horse, and that the necessity of arming merchant vessels, which it was conceded were entitled to defend themselves, was inter alia *partly a measure of protection for the skipper who, if he relied on ramming as his sole method of defence, was in the event of capture shot as a* franc tireur.[19] *And the accuracy and justice of this analysis was grudgingly admitted.*

As a further explanation of submarine 'atrocities', such as the case of the Belgian Prince, *the German officer suggested that there were of necessity some submarine commanders who were unfavourable examples of the German naval officers, and that there were parallel cases in our service, as was proved by the case of the* Baralong *and* U 27 *and that it was undesirable to pass judgement on such cases until the other side had been heard. It was thereupon pointed* out that a suspense of judgement in the case of the Belgian Prince involved an equal suspense of judgement in the case of the Baralong and U 27, and that the phrase 'proved' was then equally inapplicable to all these incidences, and it was further pointed out that even a layman could construct a case of the other side which a professional could not but admit to be plausible, and this was conceded. Incidentally it appeared that Leutnantkapitän Tebbenjohanns was unaware that the Admiralty had published an official refutation of the charges made in the German account of the incidents connected with U 27.[20]

From the consideration of particular atrocities the conversation then turned to atrocities in general, and the German officer attempted to account for and excuse the progressive growth of atrocities in the course of this war on the ground that they should be judged rather than by their intentions than by their results, and that air raids, e.g. on London and Karlsruhe, had doubtless been aimed at some definite military area in those cities, and that failure to attain purely military objects had incidentally resulted in unexpected and unintentional regrettable results.[21] The German officer was then invited to consider the German theory of war, and in a sequence of logical steps was compelled to admit that bombs on undefended places were merely the logical result of warfare when it ceases to be confined to the combatant forces of a nation and becomes the expression of a struggle between nations. The logical conclusion of the argument appeared so startling to the German that he energetically protested that the conclusion was too horrible to be accepted, though he was compelled to assent to the accuracy of the argument. It was suggested that precisely because these conclusions were latent in the German conceptions, other nations felt compelled to fight them to the bitter end.

From this, the conversation turned to the origins of the war, and the German officer stated that no-one in Germany could understand at the outbreak of war that the infringement of Belgian neutrality really constituted a casus belli, and that the real cause must, therefore, be sought elsewhere.[22] He developed this by stating that it was ridiculous to suppose that England was pledged to maintain the neutrality of Belgium as the Belgische Aktenstücke, 'official file', proved that there was a pre-war understanding by which Belgium had agreed to allow England and France to move troops across her territory in the event of a war with Germany.[23] In the light of these disclosures it was held in Germany that the true causes of the war were to be sought, as far as England was concerned, in the direction of trade rivalry and jealousy of German's growing commercial power, and this compelled Germany to fight for her place in the sun. On being asked to give specific instances in which Germany had before the war suffered any disability either as regard her nationals or her ships in British colonies or in countries under British rule, he confessed that he had never studied the question sufficiently closely to be able to cite chapter and verse and that as a 'simple naval officer' political considerations of this kind were rather outside his beat. He next referred to the 'freedom of the sea', but was constrained to admit that this idea was a purely war conception and became meaningless in times of *peace, and readily assented to the suggestion that if a power that was fighting Germany on land were to ask for a safe conduct for its traders across territory controlled by Germany such a suggestion was 'highly ridiculous'.*[24]

Being asked to particularise the contents of Belgische Aktenstücke, *which had never been published in England, he stated that he had not himself studied them, but had merely represented the views that had been expressed in the German Press.*

He was then invited to consider whether the infringement of Belgian neutrality on a closer analysis did not constitute a sufficient explanation of England's action, in that the conception of a state that felt bound to stand by its treaty obligation and one that recognised no such obligation, involved such a fundamental and irreconcilable antithesis in state ethics as to supply ample grounds for a casus belli.[25] *The German officer, while admitting the immense moral difference involved in the two conceptions considered that ethical considerations had no place in world politics. And on this subject he stated* inter alia, *that a considerable advance towards political freedom had been achieved by the recent changes in the franchise in Prussia, though he did not believe that they would bear fruit rapidly nor did he consider it desirable, as it was his view that any rapid progress must involve a revolution injurious to his country, while gradual and slow change spread over a period from ten to fifty years would be far more beneficial in its results.*[26] *He strongly and bitterly censured the distortions and lies current in the Press of both countries, and he considered that the expressions of hatred such as Lissauer's* Song of Hate, *the* Lusitania *commemorative medal, the trinkets with* Gott strafe England, *etc., were only a passing phase and in no way characteristic of the German people as a whole.*[27]

At the conclusion of the interview he was asked whether the views to which he had given expression were representative of his class, and after some reflection, he replied that, judging by his own intimate friends, they were typical of a considerable section of German naval officers.

By way of comment it may be stated that an unprejudiced estimate of this officer, as gleaned from two talks together, lasting about two and a half hours, would justify the view that he was perhaps unusually candid and genuinely anxious to apply the principle of audiatur et altera pars, *but that his intelligence was not of a high order and that his thinking had evidently never travelled beyond the limits of his professional duties.*[28] *And it was obvious that most of the views that he enunciated had been accepted without any attempt to examine their nature or the basis on which they rested, so that whenever he was driven, in the course of a dialectical discussion, into a corner, he endeavoured to explain his inability to extricate himself from an impasse by the statement that he was only a 'simple naval officer' who had never deeply reflected on matters which he described as belonging to the domain of politics.*

ENDNOTES

1   Wodiczko, *Abolition of War*, p. 9.
2   Bittner, *Royal Marines Spies*, pp. 47–49.
3   *The Times*, London, 'Alleged Espionage In Germany', 12/11/1910.
4   James, *Code Breakers*, pp. 8–10. Beesly, *Room 40*, p. 266.
5   *TNA*, ADM 137/3876, p. 102 and following.
6   Hashagen, *Commander*, pp. 150–162. See also, Grant, *U-Boat Hunters*, p. 55, fn. 214.
7   *TNA*, ADM 137/3897, p. 291.
8   See several references to Hartwig in Chapter 4, 'Erich's war'.
9   ADM 137/3876, pp. 113–18.
10 Hashagen, *Commander,* pp. 150–162.
11 Chapter 10, ' Intelligence gift'.
12 Bittner, *Royal Marines Spies*, pp. 13, 18, 36–37.
13 *Royal Navy Library*, Portsmouth, *Diary of Lieutenant Commander Bernard Frederic Trench during captivity at Glatz 1910-1913*, 28/5/2017. Also *New York Times*, 'Britons Admit Spying', 22/10/1910; W Reader, *At Duty's Call*, pp. 69–71; Seligmann, *Spies in Uniform*.
14 *TNA*, ADM 137/3897, pp. 286–91. For Captain Trench, see Chapter 10.
15 *Seriatim*, 'Taking one subject after another point by point'.
16 *Audiatur et altera pars*, 'Let the other side be heard as well'.
17 Chapter 5, 'The 'very nearly' battle'.
18 Chapter 3, 'Planning a famine'.
19 *Inter alia*, 'Among other things'. Chapter 2, 'Kaisertreu', which discusses *franc-tireurs*. Chapter 6, 'The war of the raven' which includes the execution of Charles Fryatt as a *franc-tireur*.
20 For war crimes by u-boats see Chapter 14, 'Welcome home Erich' including *Belgian Prince* which was sunk by Wilhelm Werner, *U 55*, most of the crew drowning when the u-boat submerged underneath them while they were on deck. In the same chapter is the murder by the British *Baralong* of the German crew of the sunken *U 27* while some were in the water and after others had gained safety aboard a ship.
21 See Chapter 2.
22 *Casus belli*, 'Provokes or justifies a war'. Chapter 2.
23 *Belgische Aktenstücke*, 'Belgian File 1905-1914', produced in Berlin in 1915. Chapter 1, 'Brave new world'.
24 Chapters 1 and 13, 'Guilt and blame', for freedom of the seas.
25 Chapter 2.
26 Chapters 1, 13, 14, 'Welcome home, Erich', and 15, 'Salomon and the film business', for the German franchise and revolution.
27 Chapter 9, 'Your truth, our truth' for both of these 'expressions of hatred'. Tebbenjohanns claimed that he knew the name of the commander of the u-boat that sank the *Lusitania*, but declined to give it. He affirmed it was not Max Valentiner or Otto Steinbrinck. [It was Walther Schwieger, *U 20*]. 'The officer concerned had received positive orders to sink the ship, as definite information had reached Germany that she was carrying munitions of war. The officer was placed in a 'difficult position, and I myself would have acted in the same way under the circumstances, but I should have been very sorry indeed to do it.'
28 Chapter 2 for the debate in Germany on the need for *Abitur* or *Charakter* and the political and social isolation of the naval officer corps.

CHAPTER 1

Brave New World

And the devil, taking Him up into a high mountain, showed unto Him all the Kingdoms of the world in a moment of time, and said unto Him, 'All this power will I give thee, and the glory of them; for that is delivered unto me; and to whomsoever I will, I give it. If thou therefore wilt worship me, all shall be mine.'[1]

Erich and Georg Gerth were proud Prussians, born two years apart in Berlin in the 1880s. They lost their father, Ernst, a successful small businessman, early in life. After passing their final examinations, the *Abitur*, in 1904 and 1906, which qualified them for university study, they were the only two boys from their school years to be taken in as officer cadets in Kaiser Wilhelm II's shiny new navy.[2] By all accounts, they were lucky to be accepted.

Initially, the Kaiser wished to encourage officers in his dramatic creation, the Imperial Navy, to come from a broad church that was more reflective of the newly increased level of education across German society. Selection was to be less aristocratic or socially elite, especially when compared to its main military competitor, the Prussian Army. To support this, the Kaiser, in a cabinet order of 1890, added those of 'noble mind' to those of 'noble birth' as eligible to be 'officer aspirants'.[3] Sons of these 'honourable bourgeois houses in which love of King and Fatherland, a warm heart for the soldierly profession and a Christian upbringing and education' prevailed were now to be admitted.[4] Within ten years, the good intent faltered. One can have too much egalitarianism. At the turn of the century, new imperial guidelines favoured the 'loyal, monarchist lineage and families whose names were registered in the annals of Prussian history'.[5] Erich and Georg, whether they and their wider family realised it or not, were near the bottom of an acceptable social class. To join Germany's naval first estate, the boys' applications would be scrutinised by the president of their administrative district, the local military commander, police agencies and municipal magistrates.[6] After these political, social and financial checks were completed, suitability was assessed by a naval board more interested in the continuity of aristocratic values than in military competence.[7] The final decision on each cadet remained in the hands of the Kaiser. After Erich's acceptance in 1905, and his delivery of two years' satisfactory progress as a cadet, the obstacle of class would be less troublesome for his brother, Georg, in 1907.

The boys lacked the long-term guiding hand and influence of their father. Ernst Gerth owned a felt hat and millinery factory. In 1885, aged fifty-one, he chose his second wife, Hedwig, from among his workers. Ernst made an opportunistic and successful career switch to become general manager of one of Berlin's earliest horse tram companies.[8] A newly-elected city councillor, he died suddenly on New Year's Eve in 1893. Putting the pre-teen boys through secondary school until aged eighteen was the first step. Three and a half years of naval schooling, and afterwards their first year as a lowly-paid junior *leutnant*, would need a familial and formal commitment of more than 8,000 Reichsmarks for each young man.[9]

The Berlin of the Gerths' childhood was not a much loved town, except perhaps by the thousands of hopeful immigrants and the large number of Jews that flocked every year from Brandenburg, East Prussia and Silesia. 'Every other person seemed to have climbed off a train.'[10] The Jews came to Berlin to practise commerce, their expertise developed after long discrimination in the provinces which prevented them from owning land, practising many traditional crafts, or serving in the bureaucracy or the military. Berliners themselves were 'distrustful' of their city, a fledging, upstart capital scrabbling to catch up with the regional centres of Munich, Hamburg, Mainz, Cologne, Dresden, Leipzig and Frankfurt that had for years 'dominated the political and cultural scene'.[11] Industrialist Walther Rathenau called Berlin 'the parvenu of cities and the city of parvenus'.[12]

> From being a capital strictly orientated toward the Prussian monarchy's military needs, a garrison city only recently adorned with a few royal structures in grand classical style, the Berlin of the 1860s was quickly changing to fit its new role as an imperial seat. The Prussian army won three consecutive victories during that decade. Soon after the first victory, over Denmark in 1864, the town began to experience an unprecedented growth. It attracted new inhabitants by projecting the image of a youthful, energetic metropolis, destined for greatness, politically and economically alike.[13]

However, the imperial leadership preferred to be elsewhere. When Otto von Bismarck, the grand old man of German unification, died in 1898 he outwitted his Kaiser's plans for a lavish state funeral in Berlin by leaving instructions that he was to be buried at his country estate at Friedrichsruh.

'Apparently, he did not want to be caught dead in Berlin.'[14] Kaiser Wilhelm II admitted that he never felt really happy in the city, preferring the flattering environment and 'aesthetic surroundings of a small circle of friends' of Potsdam where there was 'always the suspicion of repressed homosexuality ... The bizarre tastes of the emperor and his friends form a chapter in juvenile vulgarity.'[15]

> *Wilhelm lived his life in an elaborate masquerade. He paraded as the consummate soldier-warlord, always in uniform, always fierce, hard, decisive, steady, an amalgam of the 'masculine virtues'. Wilhelm was actually none of these. Slightly feminine in appearance, with delicate health, hypersensitive, squeamish, nervous as a caged animal, and steady as an aspen leaf.*[16]

Wilhelm's father, Friedrich III reigned for only ninety-nine days, diagnosed with throat cancer. His son's greatest fear was that Friedrich would 'team up with the progressive elements in the capital to democratise Germany before he could take control' and threaten his own autocratic ambitions. Wilhelm acted as if his father was already dead, brazenly usurping royal prerogatives. The period of mourning was shortened to only two days and he ordered soldiers to cordon off the cortege route so that Berliners would have difficulty paying respects. 'Wilhelm's objective was to banish his father's memory as soon as possible so that no one could dwell on the possibility that a more liberal Germany might have emerged.'[17]

Despite pretensions to be the 'people's ruler', Wilhelm held many of his subjects in contempt and saw as little of them as possible. He found local citizens harboured 'far too much irreverence toward royal authority'.[18] For this, Wilhelm punished them by his frequent absence. 'Once the Berliners have gone for some time without seeing the imperial carriage, they will come crawling back on all fours.' He could barely bring himself to speak to local dignitaries, perhaps including city councillor Ernst Gerth. He refused to shake hands with the civic delegation who came to present him with a fountain to mark his new status. The statuary depicted Neptune to reflect the imperial love of the seas. For years afterwards, Berliners responded to acts of ingratitude with the phrase, 'But I didn't offer you a fountain'. In 1900 and 1903, he ordered the police to gun down striking workers.[19] However, Kaiser-worship did exist and was especially pronounced among the city's younger middle-class males, many of whom aped the royal moustache by curling their own upward at the tips. The city's bureaucrats and professionals often tried to look and act like mini-Kaisers in their dealings with the lower orders.

What did separate Berlin from its countryside, which was mostly time-wrapped in feudal farming, from every other town in Germany, and from almost every other town in the world, was growth: growth in people, in industries, in employment and in buildings, both monumental and sordid. Paris and London were much larger, but since 1891 the new capital of the new Germany was a permanent building site.

> *An ambitious building programme sought to cope with Berlin's phenomenal growth; entire blocks were razed in the centre of the city to make room for new government buildings, for offices and department stores, while unending rows of apartment houses went up in the suburbs. New plants and factories, railroads and canals, stations and harbour facilities reflected the city's economic advance: schools, theatres, and lecture halls sprang up in response to its educational and cultural needs. Berlin ... presented a picture of breathless activity and confident growth, symbolic of the rising prestige and prosperity of that country.[20]*

The twenty-six-year period from Wilhelm's ascension to the throne in 1888 to the outbreak of the world war in 1914 brought 'tremendous change and plenty of cause to boast about urban progress and technological innovation'.[21] Art critic Karl Scheffler said the city was condemned 'always to be becoming, never to being'.[22] City planner Sir Peter Hall wrote that Berlin in the late nineteenth century 'could fairly claim the title of high-tech industrial centre of the world: the Silicon Valley of its day'. Mark Twain called Berlin 'the German Chicago' because of the two cities' breathtaking mutability, but Twain decided Chicago was the 'more venerable'. The Baedeker guide in 1903 declared that since 'three-quarters of [Berlin's] buildings are quite new it suffers from a certain lack of historical interest'.

At the time of German unification in 1871, the city had 865,000 inhabitants. It grew to more than a million by 1877 and reached two million by 1905. By the eve of the war, the population had doubled again to nearly four million making its sixty square kilometres the most densely populated in the world.[23] Worker migrants settled in the suburbs to the south and east and in 'islands' in the more central Charlottenburg and Schöneberg generating a remarkable growth in large high buildings. It was an exciting time for Germans everywhere, and Berlin was at the centre of it all. 'The city's dynamism was contagious; its achievements, glorious.'[24] Berlin came to house an enormous industrial infrastructure as it competed with the Ruhr as the armaments and munitions centre of the country.[25] Berlin was also the financial capital. Behrenstraße, site of several major banks as well as the Imperial Bank, intersected Wilhelmstraße, a 'symbol of the active negotiations between the sectors of government, industry and commerce'.

One of the engines of growth was Berlin's pioneer development of urban transport.[26] Here, Ernst, the Gerth boys' father, was a leading light. Berlin had a steam railway by 1870; the world's first electric streetcar was introduced in Lichterfelde in 1881. The new Stadtbahn, inaugurated in 1882, was Europe's first viaduct railway, a kind of city-within-a-city, containing under its brick archways a wealth of shops, storerooms, warehouses and pubs. Berlin registered its first automobile in 1892 to Rudolf Herzog, a department store owner. When Wilhelm bought his Daimler in 1898, he insisted that the first distinctive registration, 1A-1, should be his and took Herzog to court in a failed attempt to force a transfer. 'While this may have been taken as a setback for absolutism, the fact that this case was raised at all showed once again that in modern Berlin the remnants of feudalism remained much in evidence.'[27] The Kaiser's car horn was tuned to the thunder-motif from Wagner's *Das Rheingold*. The constructions of a subway system started in 1896 with the first line opening a decade later. By the turn of the century Berlin was served by twelve railway lines and ten long-distance train stations. The most impressive of these, Friedrichstraße, was a 'far cry from the pitiful hovels that [once] passed for stations [not long before].'

The core of the city's transport system before 1900 was the horse drawn tram which the Prussian military promoted to transport workers when the enlarged artillery workshops moved from the Kupfergraben to Spandau.[28] Passenger numbers increased from two and a half million in 1872 to three million in 1873 and to six million in 1874. Ernst Gerth was initially general manger then president of the *Neue Berliner Pferdebahn-Gesellschaft*, the 'New Berlin Horse Railway Company', which gained permission in 1875 to build a line from Alexanderplatz to Weißensee.[29] A trial took place on 29 December 1876 with the official opening on New Year's Day.

Ernst was the third and preferred name of Wilhelm August Ernst Ludwig Gerth, born in 1834, who married Wilhelmine Knoll, daughter of a Brandenburg barber and bonesetter, in 1862. Ernst's father, Carl August Gerth, was a local apothecary in Linienstraße. Ernst trained as a mechanical engineer and, by 1867, owned a milliner's shop and quickly moved into a felt and straw-hat factory in Invalidenstraße. His reversion to his engineering skills began with the birth of the New Berlin Tram business when Ernst Gäbler bought thirty-eight hectares of the Weißensee Castle estate and turned a large portion to speculative housing.[30] The streets were named partly after battles of the Franco-Prussian War of 1871–1872 and the district became known as the French Quarter.[31] Gäbler needed to provide easy access to the centre of the city in order to sell his dwellings and thus set up a tram company in 1876. The line ran to central Alexanderplatz with stops at Greifswalderstraße and Antonplatz. Weißensee Castle was also home from 1874 to a popular amusement park with lake terrace, bandstand, carousels, two dance halls and various beer houses. In 1879, this line carried 625,979 passengers although there were only 20,000 residents in Neu-Weißensee. Profitability came second to the sale and rising value of the housing plots.[32]

As well as an entrepreneur, Gäbler was also a state official with posts in the Ministry of Justice, the Berlin police department, and in the

administrative offices of the Prussian Navy. It is, therefore, possible that
Gäbler first met Ernst Gerth through city business or, perhaps, he bought
his hats from him. Another possibility is that Ernst's elder brother, Heinrich
Gerth, provided the contact as he was a Royal Counsellor of Justice with
offices in Wilhelmstraße.[33] It would also be simple if Gäbler was the contact
that provided entry for the aspirant navy officers, Erich and Georg Gerth,
but Gäbler died of typhoid in 1876 well before the boys were born.

Gäbler thus missed the opening of his tram service on New Year's
Day 1877, the first service of its kind in the city. An additional licence to
Friedrichsberg was acquired from the city authorities. Ernst Gerth oversaw
its rapid development. The Friedrichsberg extension opened in 1878 and
the line was extended the following year to Friedrichsberg Station, then
in 1881 through Landsbergerstraße and Landsbergerallee to the new
municipal stockyards and slaughterhouse near Lichtenburg, and, in 1883,
connections were made with the other Berlin tramway, *Große Berliner
Pferde-Eisenbahn*, and into the city centre. Berlin was a 'city of vending
machines and newspaper kiosks, telephones and trams'.[34] In 1895, the city
had eight times as many telephones per head of population as London.

Ernst Gerth married his first wife, Wilhelmine, in 1862. Their only child,
Marie, died in 1865 within a year of her birth. At Wilhelmine's death from
dropsy in 1884 she was a bedridden invalid with a spinal cord injury. Ernst,
aged fifty-one, married again fourteen months later to Hedwig Boch, aged
twenty-four, clearly known for some time as what ... his wife's nurse, an
employee, a long-time affair? In 1883, two sisters, 'Bock' milliners, were
living at Große Frankfurterstraße 4, just around the corner from Ernst
and Wilhemine's home at Kleine Frankfurterstraße 1. In 1886, almost nine
months to the day after marriage, Hedwig Gerth presented Ernst with a
son, Erich Gerth and, two years later, Georg Gerth.[35] A third son, Carl,
drowned about age three in a courtyard fountain or decorative pool. A
nanny had left the three brothers playing, momentarily unsupervised.[36]
This must have been a scarring incident with the truth difficult to establish.
Carl died just a short time before his father's own death in 1893.[37]

When Ernst died, the board of directors 'deeply mourned the painful
loss of this worthy man who with tireless diligence and total commitment
dedicated his powers to the [tram] company for many years'.[38] With
the driving force gone and the company not in sufficient profit to pay
a dividend, the directors looked to protect their investment. Hedwig
left the apartment that came with the job above the forty-passenger-car
depot in Landsbergerallee and had to find herself some suitable new
accommodation.[39] She first returned to Kleine Frankfurterstraße where,
perhaps, her sister still lived.[40] Next year, 1895, with some of the money
from her inheritance, she bought a house at Dessauerstraße 19, near to
the boys' school; in 1900 she bought and moved to Luckenwalderstraße
7, with eleven other people renting apartments from her; and, finally, in

1908, with the boys safely at naval college, she was able to free capital by downsizing to an apartment at Keithstraße 22, where she lived for the rest of her life. She never remarried.

Management of *Neue Berliner* was taken over by the firm's partner and competitor, *Große Berliner*. Motor transport quickly made headway against traditional horse drawn vehicles. The first motor taxi was introduced in 1899 and the tram companies responded with their first electric service. As both companies intended a full electrification of their trams, the city authorities demanded a merger which took place on New Year's Day 1900 under a new company, *Große Berliner Straßenbahn*.[41] The Landsbergerallee depot was closed in 1901 and demolished the following year. The last horse-drawn car, which ran to the municipal insane asylum, was taken out of service in 1902. However, six years later, Berlin still had 52,000 workhorses in the city.

The boys were eight and six years old when they lost their father and, about the same time, their baby brother Carl. There was just a short time to share Ernst's company. There would surely have been many visits to the depot beneath their home with men at work repairing trams and caring for the 167 horses. There must have been many opportunities for tram rides. Although they were young, they may have sat on their parents' shoulders to witness major events of the day. In 1889, Bismarck left Berlin to begin his rural retirement and the local citizenry 'displayed an outpouring of warm sentiment for the old man'.[42] People crowded shoulder to shoulder along his route to the Lehrter railway station. 'Like a flood, the crowd surged toward the carriage, surrounding, accompanying, stopping it momentarily, hats and handkerchiefs waving, calling, crying, throwing flowers.' The same year, one memory would have stuck with a three-year-old Erich when Buffalo Bill Cody's Wild West Show came to the Kurfürstendamm, a street modelled on the Champs-Elysées in Paris. Over 60,000 Berliners watched performances. The Kaiser was a man, Berliners said, who could not attend a funeral without wanting to be the corpse. Few were surprised when the star of the show, Annie Oakley, asked for a volunteer from the audience to smoke a cigar whose ash she would shoot off from a distance of thirty paces. Her husband was supposed to step forward, but the young Kaiser leapt from the royal box, 'strutted into the arena, extracted a Havana cigar from a gold case and lit it with a flourish'.[43] Annie walked off the distance, raised her Colt 45, took aim, and blew away the Kaiser's ashes.

Had she blown away the Kaiser instead, the subsequent history of Berlin, Germany, and indeed the entire world might have been different. Annie realised this herself later on. After America entered World War I, she wrote to the Kaiser asking if she could have a second shot.

In 1896, Berlin wanted to ape the Paris of 1889 and host a world exhibition to show off its national prowess. The Kaiser thought better of it and the city fathers were reduced to a National Industrial Exposition in brand new Treptow Park to the far east of the city. It was still larger than any previous exposition anywhere in the world. The exhibits at Treptow Park would have stunned any small boy: hissing steam engines from Borsig, giant cranes from Pintsch, the world's first electric railway from Siemens & Halske, electrical lighting innovations from AEG, and chemicals and dyes from IG Farben. In most cases, the private sector developed and controlled the advanced naval technologies essential to the fabrication of ships and weapons systems.[44] Important innovations such as nickel-steel armour plate could determine the alternatives available to the navy and open new directions in research and development. The owners of most of these businesses in time would become Erich's personal acquaintances. Perhaps Wilhelm was right for, despite five million visitors, the exposition was a financial disaster, but his dismissal was typically churlish.

> *Paris is the great whorehouse of the world; therein lies its attraction independent of any exhibition. There is nothing in Berlin than can captivate the foreigner, except a few museums castles and soldiers. After six days the [Baedeker guide] book in hand he has seen everything and he departs relieved, feeling he has done his duty. The Berliner does not see these things clearly and would be very upset if told about them. However, this is the real obstacle to the exhibition.*[45]

In 1902, the Kaiser presided over the dedication of a new space for display of one of the wonders of the uncovered world, the Pergamum Altar and parts of the newly found Market Gate of Miletus from the Turkish archaeological sites of Priene and Baalbek. 'Germany thereby gained a great advantage over Britain, France, Russia and Austria in the exploitation of the cultural riches of the eastern Mediterranean.'[46] Two years later, the Berlin Secessionist movement was set up by artists frustrated by the Kaiser's 'ridiculous campaign' to control the local art scene and rid it of modern art and impressionism.[47] The final straw was the refusal of the Kaiser to agree to a gold medal for an etching by Käthe Kollwitz.[48] 'Please, gentlemen, a medal for a woman, that's really going too far. That would amount to a debasement of every high distinction. Orders and honours belong on the chests of deserving men.'[49] Secessionists complained and were banned from exhibiting at Germany's exhibition at the 1904 St Louis World Fair in America. They responded with a wildly successful exhibition of their own in Berlin. The result was the opposite of the Kaiser's intention: the works of Karl Hauptmann and Max Liebermann became widely popular. This defiance of the Kaiser resulted in all military officers being forbidden to attend the event in uniform.

Wilhelm's architectural contribution to Berlin turned out to be variable, but in the building site of their youth Erich and Georg would have seen the rise of many governmental buildings, churches, prisons, barracks and hospitals. The particular imperial love was for monuments of which so many were built that it was 'practically impossible to turn a corner in central Berlin without encountering some outsize statue in bronze or marble'.[50] 'Virtually all of the architectural additions betrayed their sponsor's conviction that a structure could only be impressive if it were weighted down with heavy historical baggage.' During the 1890s, Wilhelm cleared away the houses on the west front of his palace to build a massive *National Monument* featuring a large statue of his grandfather, Wilhelm I, to whom he was much closer than he was to his father. 'The monument is long gone and unlamented', remembered by few.[51] The Gedächtniskirche, the 'Kaiser Wilhelm Memorial Church', was also built to honour his grandfather. The church was dedicated in 1891 and designed to be a focal point of Berlin's 'New West', beyond the Tiergarten, the newly fashionable district. It was also where the Gerths' mother, Hedwig, was to be buried. In 1894, the new Reichstag parliament building was completed after ten years' work, 'something like a cross between the Paris Opéra and a Palladian palazzo'. Its architect, Paul Wallot had been charged with capturing the German spirit in stone and he 'perhaps unwittingly achieved this through the eclectic confusion of his design'. Bismarck called it the 'ape house'. The architectural addition of which the Emperor was most proud was the Siegesallee, 'Victory Avenue', an avenue in the Tiergarten lined with marble busts of Hohenzollern heroes and built in 1901. Wilhelm provided the drawings for the figures himself, many looking like his close friends. 'The project merely added to Berlin's reputation for portentous posturing.'

> *Everything, literally everything, was American new – and newer – German new! And the cabbies were the largest, fattest, most broad-backed, most thick-through and* Deutschiest *looking creatures I have ever beheld.*[52]

Both boys attended a day pre-school and then for nine years the *Königliches-Kaiser-Wilhelm-Realgymnasium*. This was a prestigious secondary school, founded in 1747. The school split in 1797, the second part became the *Friedrich-Wilhelm-Gymnasium*, one of the leading classical grammar schools in Prussia, teaching Latin and Greek with many famous students, including Otto von Bismarck, Walther Rathenau, to become head of AEG, and Adolf von Trotha, later admiral, the last two destined to have far-reaching influence on Erich Gerth's life. The original secondary school became the Gerths' Realgymnasium in 1882. Both schools, together with the girls' school, *Elisabeth-Schule*, were situated close together at the western end of Kochstraße.

The Realgymnasium that Erich and Georg attended focused on modern foreign languages, natural sciences and practical skills. Some of the school records exist, including annual reports.[53] Erich started at the Realgymnasium in October 1895, almost ten years old, and left, aged eighteen, in October 1904 after passing his final exams, one of nine successful students; Georg Gerth was a student from the autumn of 1894 to the autumn of 1906, one of seventeen who passed. The curriculum listed in 1905 for students in their last two years consisted of thirty-one lessons, plus two optional, each week: mathematics five, four each for Latin and French, three each for German, English, history, physics; and two for religious education, chemistry and drawing; the optional two to be taken from singing, physical education, physics/chemistry laboratory work and technical drawing. For the previous two years, geography and biology were also compulsory. Georg was clearly not short of a Reichsmark for he donates twice, three and five Reichsmarks, in his last years to the student stipend fund for 'worthy students in need'.

Perhaps the most heartfelt description of turn-of-the-century school days comes from writer Stefan Zweig, albeit his experiences were in Vienna.[54] In those days of 'enlightened' liberalism, only an education regarded as academic and leading to a university really counted. He found the path to university was a long one.

> You had to spend five or six hours a day sitting on a wooden bench for five years of elementary school and eight of grammar school. In your free time, you did your homework. It was more than too much, leaving almost no time for physical exercise, sporting activities, walking, and above all none for light-hearted amusements ... It still strikes me as incredible that today children will talk to their teachers naturally, almost on a par with them, and that they hurry to school free of fear, instead of with a constant sense of inadequacy ... As soon as we entered the hated school building we had to keep our heads down, so to speak, to avoid coming up against the invisible yoke of servitude. School, to us, meant compulsion, dreary boredom, a place where you had to absorb knowledge of subjects that did not seem worth knowing, sliced into neat portions ... The old style of teaching meant a dull, dreary kind of learning for the mere sake of learning, not for the sake of life.

Zweig was brought up to respect the status quo as 'perfect, our teachers' opinions as infallible, a father's word as final, brooking no contradiction, and state institutions as absolute and valid for all eternity'. Young people should not be allowed too easy a time. Before they were allowed rights they were supposed to learn that they had duties, 'above all the duty of total obedience'.

> From the first, it was to be impressed that we had not done anything in life, we had no experience, we must be grateful for anything that

we were allowed, and that we had no right to ask questions or make demands ... The distrust of any young person as 'not quite reliable' was rife in all circles of society.

The two modern preoccupations of teenage boys got short shrift in Zweig's writings.[55] 'Going out with girls seemed to us a waste of time, since in our intellectual arrogance we regarded the opposite sex as intellectually inferior by their very nature, and we didn't want to spend our valuable time in idle chatter.' The lack of serious physical education in the syllabus also seems at odds with today's expectations. Enthusiasm for sport had not yet spread from Britain to the continent of Europe. It was considered a 'rather violent occupation' and a grammar school boy felt he ought to be ashamed to indulge. 'It would be quite hard to get a modern young person to understand the extent to which we ignored, even despised all sporting activities.'

The Realgymnasium did have a school rowing club and 'Kaiser Wilhelm' regularly won the 'Kaiser cup' in the annual regatta. There were also many expeditions on Berlin's River Spree, but there is no mention of the Gerth boys in the crews, which in itself is not proof of their lack of participation.

The origins of Berlin were as a garrison town and in Prussian militarised society, which 'permitted easy interaction between front-line soldiers and the civilian population, a grave security issue for the authorities'.[56] 'There was an air of officiousness in the city, attempting to tame Berlin's restlessness and to contain it within the straightjacket of Prussian order.'[57] In the parks of Paris and London, visitors could lie down on the grass; in Berlin's Tiergarten they found the sign *'Verboten'.* Contemporary visitors used descriptors like *severe, ordered, serious, obedient, disciplined.* Military monuments were never far away, nor the endless parades, brass bands in the parks, soldiers in 'fantastic uniforms on the grand central avenues and smart cafés'. Berliners joked that their air stank of gunpowder.[58] Wilhelm almost doubled the number of officers and men by 1913. Uniformed officers seen in Piccadilly or the Champs Élysées usually meant a state occasion, but it was everyday in Berlin. 'Not only did the soldiers move along the street with rigid measured steps like machines, but they were copied by the street-seller, the coachman, the porter, even the beggar.'[59] The new Wilhelmine officers were 'insufferable, unbearable prigs'. 'Prussian soldiers and Berlin infantry regiments marched and trained in the Halensee beyond the Zoo and in the Kurfürstendamm, where the Kaiser and Kaiserin sometimes strolled by themselves.'[60] All of these were regular parts of the Gerths' experiences. The military cloak extended even to the boys' home on Luckenwalderstraße. Apartment buildings, occupying large blocks of land, were referred to as *Mietkasernen*, literally 'rented barracks', a reference to their 'anonymous, uniform and quasi-military character'. Perhaps, Erich and Georg joined other young men on a *Vogelwanderung*, 'bird hike', as part of an imperial scout troop one early morning in Grunewald, the forested areas to the west of the city.

The Kaiser was also the patron of the Realgymnasium and the school regularly received book donations on nautical issues. One of Wilhelm's favourite books, which he kept on the bed-table of his yacht, was probably not one of the presents. In historian Tuchman's view, if Wilhelm had 'confined his reading to *The Golden Age*, Kenneth Grahame's dreamlike story of English boyhood in the world of cold adults, it is possible there might have been no world war'.[61]

> *The excitement of the thing was becoming thrilling. A Black Flag must surely be fluttering close by. Here was evidently a malignant contrivance of the Pirates, designed to baffle our gun-boats when we dashed up-stream to shell them from their lair. A gun-boat, indeed, might well have hesitated, so stout was the netting, so close the hedge: but I spied where a rabbit was wont to pass, close down by the water's edge; where a rabbit could go a boy could follow, albeit stomach-wise and with one leg in the stream ... No-one would have suspected Edward of being in love, but that after breakfast, with an over-acted carelessness, 'Anybody who likes,' he said, 'can feed my rabbits,' and he disappeared with a jauntiness that deceived nobody in the direction of the orchard. Now, kingdoms might totter and reel, and convulsions change the map of Europe; but the iron unwritten law prevailed, that each boy severely fed his own rabbits. There was ground then for suspicion and alarm.*[62]

If *The Golden Age* might have saved millions of lives, there were two of Wilhelm's favoured books which promoted the opposite and both found their way onto the shelves of the Realgymnasium: the first, American Admiral Alfred Mahan's *The Influence of Sea Power on History*, appeared in 1890 and revolutionised German naval thinking; the second, Georg Wislicenus's *Deutschlands Seemacht*, of 1895, enflamed national passions and cemented the German view of Mahan's teachings into the popular consciousness. The Kaiser saw to it that copies of Mahan were placed aboard every ship in the imperial fleet, and in colleges and schools like the Realgymnasium. If two books ever set up the thinking for a war, it was these two.

> *In his day, Mahan has even been blamed for starting the First World War, while his defenders claim that he was some sort of Delphic oracle whose writings claim all the clues to the future.*[63]

Wilhelm always had an active interest in naval affairs. There were youthful memories of visits to Kiel and Plymouth, his readings in naval history, recollections of British naval reviews, visits to the regattas at Cowes.[64] In 1895, he proudly exhibited his painting, *Sea Battle*, depicting the attack of a torpedo flotilla upon a squadron of ironclads. But it was Mahan's view, that of an American, not an Englishman for all their supposed naval superiority in history and strategy, which most helped shape the young emperor's outlook.[65] 'Instantly an immense vision opened before the impressionable Wilhelm: Germany must be a major power upon the oceans as upon land.' Concerned by lack of suitable and extensive colonies and by the unstable international situation, specifically the Spanish-American and Boer wars, the Kaiser complained bitterly, 'We have dire need of a fleet.'[66] Possessing a navy at this time was a sign of national greatness and power, and a strong naval force was thought necessary for a nation to 'compete for economic and political influence around the world'.[67] Having joined the industrial revolution about a century too late, the German leadership was embarrassed by a relative lack of empire and the subsequent limited opportunities for global growth. All of the western European seaboard nations from Denmark to Portugal, even, humiliatingly, Belgium, had substantial and profitable colonial possessions. Germany did have smaller protectorates of limited integral value in West, South West and East Africa as well as Samoa and parts of New Guinea; Austria-Hungary had nothing.[68] This was 'particularly galling to the ambitious and chauvinistic German emperor' who was determined to have a world voice commensurate with his self-esteem.'[69]

Navalism became the 'overriding strategic concept of the day'. In *Sea Power*, Mahan demonstrated that he who 'controls communications by sea controls his fate'; the master of the seas is master of the situation. Large battle-fleets and a concentration of force would decide control of the oceans. Possession of select bases on island or continental peripheries were more valuable than the control of large land masses.[70] Mahan staked his concept by describing in individual chapters a series of major sea battles, drawn from his talks at the US Naval War College, and drawing sometimes oblique conclusions. Ultimately, 'navalism was the belief that national prestige without seapower was impossible'. The Naval Office ordered Mahan's book to be translated into German. It was to serve as a 'naval bible', designed to justify the need for large naval expenditures. The work was a bestseller throughout Europe.

Wislicenus, author of the illustrated book on German seapower, *Deutschlands Seemacht*, was a 'passionately committed naval officer'. The first edition sold out within six weeks, and publisher Brockhaus quickly put out a second printing in Christmas 1895. *Deutschlands Seemacht* turned out to be a blockbuster. The prized editions quickly made Wislicenus and his ideas into 'household familiars'.[71] With ammunition like Wislicenus and Mahan, it is surprising that more of the Gerths' schoolfellows did not apply for naval college.

Its overwhelming success took everyone by surprise: the author, the foreign office, the admiralty, and even the prestigious firm of Brockhaus which had published it. As Admiral Hugo Pohl of the Imperial Navy later observed, Wislicenus had written what was in the hearts of many Germans, and bookdealers' profits seemed to indicate that the philosophy of navalism had already permeated all geographical regions and all social levels of Germany.

Bismarck's constitution made the Kaiser, who was also King of Prussia, the most powerful ruler in the world. 'Standing giant-like over the *Bundesrat*, the moribund executive body of the empire, and the Reichstag, which could not initiate new legislation, was the federal executive, composed of the Kaiser and his Chancellor.'[72] By privilege of *Kommandogewalt*, the royal command, the Kaiser could appoint and dismiss his chancellor, all federal officials, and all officers in the Prussian Army – a state within a state – and those in the navy.[73] He held complete control of foreign policy, could declare war and make peace, and was the supreme commander of all imperial armies. 'He was answerable to no-one.'

The Prussian Navy dated from the 1848 Revolution when it was founded by German liberals by means of public subscription to demonstrate their country's newly found national unity and freedom. By the time of Wilhelm's accession, the monarch's role was defined in Article 53 of the Constitution of 1871. 'The navy of the empire is united under the supreme command of the Kaiser. The organisation and structure of the same is within the jurisdiction of the Kaiser, who appoints the officers and civil servants of the navy and receives a direct oath of allegiance, an oath also to be sworn by other ranks.' For officers, the oath was sworn on the flag or a drawn sword. The oath clearly defined the young officer's allegiance to Kaiser rather than to the nation, Reichstag, or constitution.[74]

I swear a personal oath to God the Almighty and All-knowing that I will faithfully and honourably serve His Majesty the German Kaiser, Wilhelm II, my Supreme War Lord, in all and any cases, on land and at sea, in peacetime and in wartime, regardless where this may be; [that I] will promote all that benefits and serves His Highness, but defend him from injury and prejudice; [that I] will completely obey the Articles of War that have been read to me, and will act in a manner proper and suitable for a righteous, intrepid, honourable and duty-loving soldier. So help me God through Jesus Christ to salvation. Amen.[75]

If Wilhelm was the petulant Kaiser who wanted a real navy to replace the paltry affair that he had inherited, it was Rear Admiral Adolf Tirpitz who gave it to him. In 1897, the Kaiser, recognising the need for a man who would deliver naval strength whatever the counter-arguments, recalled Tirpitz from the Far East Cruiser Squadron to take command of the *Reichsmarineamt* (RMA), the imperial naval office.[76] Tirpitz was an acknowledged and ardent believer in Mahan's advocacy of an aggressive naval policy. With his 'All-Highest Cabinet Order' of 1898, the Kaiser gave Tirpitz a free hand in construction and the selection of the types of ships that would join the fleet. Tirpitz enjoyed 'absolute control over the development of the German navy'.[77] Unsurprisingly, 'German industry joined the Kaiser in hailing Tirpitz's energy and determined leadership'.[78]

> *The Germans showed the worst tendency, out of all the naval powers, to misinterpret and misunderstand Mahan. Tirpitz was obsessed with Mahan's dictum that commercial dominance had to be backed by military superiority, and believed that Great Britain would use her navy to crush German trade rivalry ... and felt that a huge fleet would be necessary to do so. This resulted in the hideous dilemma of having to out-build the world's biggest shipbuilding nation and to outstrip the most successful navy, which happened to sit astride Germany's overseas communications ... Germany's leaders sought to ward off a danger which was largely imaginary by using a challenge to the British which they could never hope to substantiate.[79]*

Tirpitz was a man of strong personality and unusual talents, most not suited to a great thinker. Despite his squeaky, high-pitched voice, he was a charismatic, fierce, manipulative leader. He exhibited ruthless and unlimited ambition; his wish to be imperial chancellor was an open secret in the political circles of Berlin.[80] Devlin describes him as a 'gigantic Neptune of a man with a forked beard and an almost pathological hatred of the British; the bogeyman for all good English children'.[81] A few facts belie an absolute hatred. Tirpitz sent his two daughters to study at Cheltenham Ladies College in England which his wife had also attended.[82] He knew his future opponents, the British royals and dignitaries such as Winston Churchill and Admiral John Jellicoe, because he met them every year at the Cowes Regatta at the Isle of Wight off the English south coast and in June at Kiel Week, a gala international regatta with yacht races, balls and other festivities. Kiel was the Kaiser's answer to Cowes, which was hosted by his grandmother, Queen Victoria. Tirpitz also had reason later to be grateful to Churchill. His son, Wolfgang, was aboard the light cruiser *Mainz* in 1914 when it was sunk in a confused action in the fog off Heligoland. 'Despair gripped the family' until a message arrived from Churchill via the US Embassy in Berlin. 'Tell Admiral Tirpitz that his son is safe and unwounded.'[83]

The 'polar opposite of the Emperor', Tirpitz, with Wilhelm, demonstrated a single vision, the expansion of the Imperial Navy to become at least the second largest in the world after the British, which although still an imposing force in 1900, was 'in certain respects a drowsy, inefficient, moth-eaten organisation'.[84] Tirpitz pursued his objective against any objections or facts.[85] 'There had been no humiliation or provocation by another power, no logical need, other than the combined will of these so radically different Siamese twins.' From 1900 to 1914, Tirpitz quadrupled the German fleet from 256,000 to almost one million tons. To achieve this he had direct access to the Kaiser at all times. He was the 'spider in the web, holding all the threads', and the unofficial Supreme Commander of the Fleet. History has been damning of his decisions and of his intellectual capabilities. His reading of Clausewitz and 'total war' fallaciously turned the concept to 'victory in the first and only great naval battle'.[86] Admiral Woodward studied Tirpitz closely:[87]

> *Neither a profound political philosopher nor a profound student of history, [Tirpitz] never attempted to analyse the political terms which he borrowed from current literature; his historical illustrations give one the impression of facts learned, carefully but uncritically, from lectures and text-books at military colleges. The importance of his views is to be found not in their scientific value, but in the fact that they were shared by the Emperor William II. [The Kaiser], though he was most anxious to strengthen the German navy, had not thought out a naval policy. The Emperor liked tall ships as an earlier Hohenzollern had liked tall soldiers. He was impressed by the power of the England; jealous of the impregnable position held by the British fleet. There was more than an undercurrent of rivalry in his desire to see Germany strong at sea as on land; yet the Emperor had not considered the measure of strength which would be sufficient, and refused to think of England as an enemy. The Emperor's imagination was turbulent, overcharged with emotions of a second-rate order, over-filled with military sentimentality, overawed by the traditions of his military ancestors and the influence of his military entourage.*

Wilhelm was 'suffered, not enjoyed, by many Germans', who nonetheless remained intensely loyal to the royal ethos.[88] His chancellors were weak, not the men to direct an all-powerful general staff, an arrogant navy, a confused and divided foreign office, and an increasingly divided Reichstag. Particularism reigned at all levels of command: generals, admirals, and diplomats 'had no sense of mutual trust, and seldom worked together in a common cause'. Historians Asprey and Herwig piled on the character deprecation.

> *Wilhelm's refusal to face reality, his unwillingness to be alone, his extreme Cäsarenwahnsinn, [Caesar's madness], with its delusions of either prosecution or grandeur, his nervousness and instability, inability to concentrate, constant talking, incessant travelling, charm on the one hand, rudeness, vulgarity and even cruelty on the other, his military*

*posturing exemplified by upturned moustaches waxed into place each
morning by a barber who always travelled with him, his utter conceit:
a postcard picture of the Kaiser, signed by his own hand, was, in his
own estimation, one of the most priceless gifts he could bestow.*[89]

*The Kaiser's vanities must appear to the modern reader both amusing
and pathetic. His participation in gaudy fleet reviews and his love
for naval garb evoked sarcastic jibes from his contemporaries ...
He apparently never realised his limitations, nor the dignity and
responsibility necessitated by his august position. He eventually diluted
his authority not least by issuing countless trivial orders like, in 1913,
requesting gentlemen of the Army and the Navy to 'dance neither the
Tango nor One-step nor Two-step in uniform and to avoid families in
which these dances are performed.'*[90]

Britain's Prime Minister, Lord Salisbury, thought Wilhelm not in complete
possession of his senses. Bismarck thought him like a balloon. 'If one did
not hold him fast on a string, he would go no-one knows whither.' Many
thought him insane.[91] To Max Weber it seemed as if 'we were ruled by a
bunch of maniacs'.[92]

Tirpitz believed fervently that a powerful battle fleet would deter Britain
from eliminating Germany's growing commercial and colonial access to
the North Sea. Without such a 'risk fleet', Germany's further economic
growth would 'lie at the mercy of rapacious rivals, and it would decline
to the status of a poor agricultural state'.[93] With a large fleet, 'Greater
Germany' could control and protect the colonies and markets, which
were the preconditions for becoming one of the four world powers of the
twentieth century. 'The fleet programme was one of the salient aspects
of Wilhelmine Germany's unpredictable and unruly foreign policy and
contributed towards the tensions that led to the First World War.' Tirpitz
explained his case in a memorandum attached to a funding request to
the Reichstag.[94] The German empire, for the security of its economic
development and world trade, needed peace, on land and sea, not indeed
'peace at any price, but peace with honour, satisfying the just requirements
of Germany'.

*A naval war for economic interests, particularly for commercial
interests, would cost Germany's opponents little if the German coasts
could be blockaded. The enemy would cover his war expenditure by
the improvement of his own trade. Hence the only effective means of
protecting German overseas trade and colonies lay in the construction
of a battle-fleet. The fleet must be of sufficient strength that even the
strongest naval power would not attack it without endangering its own
position in the world. For this purpose it was not absolutely necessary*

for the German battle-fleet be as strong as that of the greatest naval Power. This latter Power would not, as a rule, be able to concentrate all its forces against Germany. In any case, the defeat of the German fleet would so weaken the enemy that, in spite of his victory, his own naval position in the world would be insecure; that is to say, the German navy would have damaged the victorious fleet to such an extent that it could no longer meet a coalition of other Powers.

This 'risk theory' had already been outlined by Tirpitz in 1896, but, in truth, the theory kept Tirpitz's true objectives from everyone, including the Reichstag and the naval officer corps. It was a subterfuge, not designed for defence, but to force Germany's entire foreign policy to encompass colonial expansion. Germany either gained concessions to enable its 'place in the sun' or would come to one great Armageddon of the sea against the British.[95] Crucial documents released after the war, and others found at Tambach Castle at the end of World War II, 'leave no doubt that the Imperial German Navy deliberately challenged the Royal Navy'.[96] Tirpitz planned for his navy to be ready for war with sixty capital ships by the early 1920s, and had planned both the need for gradual 'brick on brick' law change back in 1898 and the excuses and reasons to deliver them. He assured the Kaiser that he would 'remove the disturbing influence of the Reichstag on your Majesty's intentions concerning the development of the Navy'.

Tirpitz assembled a complex series of alliances and pressure groups to gather approval for the considerable amount of money needed for his Kaiser's ambitious play fleet. The alliances constituted a veritable house of cards and Tirpitz's success in constructing the individual layers with so little glue was remarkable.[97] Within six years, his ideas were so taken up by colonialists, vested industrial interests, extreme nationalists and the public at large that naval expansion took on a life of its own. It was all the more remarkable because the fleet, which Tirpitz never led operationally, became a significant contributor to the eventual war and because its purpose was never accepted by many of its commanders. It did not achieve Tirpitz's stated aims, failed to relieve the British blockade, declined a great North Sea battle, and was largely scuttled at Scapa Flow.[98] Its idle and managerially incompetent officers brought about a mutiny of the battleship crews in the Baltic that provided the spark that ended the career of its co-founder, Kaiser Wilhelm. Tirpitz's 'luxury fleet', as Churchill dubbed it, can be seen today as a catastrophic error and an overwhelming national embarrassment.[99] It was a wasteful diversion of national treasure which should have been used to produce far-reaching and beneficial improvements to trade and social well-being. The icing on the mess was Tirpitz's continuing resistance to research and investment in a nascent submarine force despite cogent internal opposition and which, towards the end of the war, provided Germany's only real chance of victory.[100]

> *Between 1890 and 1905 the deplorable naval policy of the Kaiser and the pressures exerted by the Pan-German League, the Navy League, and other nationalists did grave harm to Germany's reputation, but did not place her in direct peril.* [101]

Tirpitz immediately launched the modern era of military propaganda to mould public opinion. The popularisation of the navy with the press, learned societies, universities and related institutions pressurised the Reichstag and enabled Tirpitz to claim that he was following the will of the masses. His highly efficient machine made the Naval Office the forerunner of the twentieth-century propaganda ministries. [102]

> *We organised meetings and lectures, and made special efforts to get in touch with the Press on a large scale. We instituted tours to the waterside and exhibited the ships and the wharves; we turned our attention to the schools and we called upon authors to write for us; stacks of novels and pamphlets were the result. Prizes were to be given by the Ministry of Education to the schools.* [103]

The Press and Information Branch, *Abteilung für Nachrichtenwesen und allgemeine Parlamentsangelegenheiten* formed the nucleus of the later Naval Intelligence Service, known as 'N' for *Nachrichtenbüro*. It co-ordinated the preparation of parliamentary papers, promoted naval bills, and published popular works on sea power. 'N' developed in 1899 the periodical *Nauticus: Jahrbuch für Deutschlands Seeinteressen*, which 'argued the economic and political cause for the non-military reader' through a broad spectrum of officers, writers and academics. The preface to its 1908 edition explained, 'The first issues appeared at the time of the first naval bills and were designed as aggressive promotional material in support of the great task of the time, namely convincing the German people of the truth that a defence capability at sea is a condition of life for any state that wants to thrive and not fritter away its paltry existence.' The issue also included a major survey of the concepts and technology of the submarine. The *Marine-Rundschau*, 'Naval Observations', was turned from a technical journal into a popular magazine, with an increased circulation and enlarged budget. By 1901, eleven Berlin and thirty-one provincial newspapers subscribed to ready-made stories produced by the anonymous 'N'. Mahan's *Sea Power* was translated and distributed. 'Political and industrial leaders were invited to attend naval reviews, officers courted the favour of the Reichstag deputies, popular journals and books glorified naval history, and naval uniforms became the vogue, especially for children.' Capital ships were named after monarchs and princes from all over Germany, especially drawing in Bavarian royalty, while twenty new battleships took the names of regional states and provinces and twenty-five light cruisers were named for mainly inland German cities.[104] Ritualistic launches and on-going contact and new programmes all encouraged local civic and scholastic commitment to 'their ship', the navy and its growth.

Annual fleet manoeuvres formed the basis for stirring reports; most of them totally fictionalised versions of what actually had taken place. The navy's own information officers contrived the stories with a modicum of truth in order to feed the curiosity of civilian reporters which could not otherwise be controlled. In this way press censorship influenced, shaped and in some cases even stage-managed public opinion in order to 'increasingly interest the public in the institutions and needs of the Kriegsmarine.' The navy, in modern terms, had become a media event.[105]

The chief instrument of propaganda was the *Deutscher Flottenverein*, the 'German Navy League', which spread the 'gospel of navalism and naval prestige'. The League was founded in 1898 mostly with money from Alfried Krupp of the armaments firm and covertly from Tirpitz's naval office. Its objective was to 'emancipate large sections of the community from the spell of the political parties by arousing their enthusiasm for this one great national issue'. Led by Krupp, heavy industry supported the Naval League generously. The 'Central Union of German Industrialists' was particularly active. Within three years of its foundation, the League had 240,000 private members and 600,000 by 1900 when Britain's Navy League, had only 25,000 subscribers. The members of the League came mainly from a bourgeois background. Many were employed in the upper civil service, the clergy, the teaching professions, commerce and industry. 'These groups also later provided the majority of naval officers for the fleet.'[106] In May and September 1906, the League took twenty-five final year students of the Realgymnasium sixth form, one assumes including Georg Gerth, on visits to the trade port in Hamburg and to the naval base in Kiel. Could this have been the final career spark which encouraged Georg to join his brother in the naval cadet corps?

The League was conceived originally as a non-political organisation in which membership should be available to all who supported the monarchy. 'No self-respecting monarchist could safely question the League's existence without placing himself beyond the pale of legitimate dissent ... alongside the Social Democrats, Frenchman and Poles.'[107] The League became central to political debate about the direction of the navy and, at its climax in 1908, the League split into adherents of Tirpitz's approved direction supplied by the naval office and others who saw this as insufficient and sought to criticise the government for growing the fleet too slowly and in too timid a manner.[108] The propaganda had taken a life of its own separate from its master. Because the League separatists did not have to 'pay for these policies or realise them in fact, they were free to demand immediate, grandiose successes'.[109] Agitation grew 'recklessly and embraced the revolutionary potential of German foreign policy'. 'Mere nationalism developed into dynamic, high-stakes, imperialist, and populist ultra-nationalism.'

Other groups, the Colonial League and the Pan-German League (PGL), strongly supported Tirpitz's objectives. The Colonial League with 20,000 members, in 1897, distributed 250,000 brochures and seven million pamphlets in one year on the navy's behalf. The PGL was a different and worrying organisation.

> *Demands which the PGL proclaimed years before Hitler surfaced in German politics were a chilling anticipation of the programmes which the National Socialists attempted to put into practice.*[110]

Pan-Germans demanded first the consolidation of German-occupied territories throughout the world. Those in Europe would be housed in a giant central-European state which would include large swathes of territory cut out of western Europe and eastern France and emptied of their native inhabitants. This new state would provide raw materials, commercial outlets, strategic security and living space for a burgeoning German population. 'That this venture would require general war was self-evident.' The PGL executive was at the forefront of anti-Semitism in Imperial Germany. Leading Pan-Germans publicly advocated not only the exclusion of Jews from public life but also the suppression of socialists, ethnic minorities and assorted other groups of people whom the League identified as enemies of the race. The organisation was formally founded in 1891 and because of its open programme foreign journalists quickly sounded the alarm. The London *Times* called the PGL the *enfant terrible* of German chauvinism. Enjoying the backing of German heavy industry, the PGL had ready access to the men who ruled in Berlin and 'used its influence to help prepare a war of aggression'. The League stood 'undeniably at the ideological forefront of naval agitation; it provided Tirpitz and his supporters with ideas that were propagated to serve industrial interests'. The organisation championed an extravagant and aggressive programme calling for unrestrained building of warships to challenge the British, the demise of the Hapsburg monarchy, and constructing an empire to include an ethnic community so far-flung that it embraced the Boers in South Africa.

> *The German people had to be aroused to their destiny and Bernhard von Bülow, new Foreign Minister [from 1897], and Rear Admiral Alfred von Tirpitz [who was] responsible for naval building and manoeuvring the necessary budget through the Reichstag set about their task with such skill and energy and achieved such success that it was not long before they were trying to restrain the effusions of Pan-Germans.*[111]

The PGL was a foremost advocate of the variety of nationalism known as *völkish*. Pan-Germans insisted that human life was founded on groups that were ethnically defined – by language, culture, tradition and race. 'Ethnicity was an existential fact, the most natural and genuine characteristic of any human being.' The *völkish* philosophy was a direct challenge to the Marxist proposition that human existence was governed by economic forces, and that the fundamental unit of human organisation was social class.

Because of its ties to Catholic-baiters and anti-Catholic themes, there were only two chapters of the PGL in Catholic Bavaria that are worth mentioning and one of these was in Würzburg. Würzburg was to play a major role in Georg Gerth's life after the war through his marriage into the Catholic Leinecker family. It would seem Georg was not an instinctive pan-German.

It was impossible to introduce such a sudden, intensive and all-embracing propaganda campaign without a worsening of the long-term ambivalent relationship with the British nation and its navy. One should always remember that the Kaiser's mother was Queen Victoria's eldest child, Vicky, the princess royal of England, and that on Victoria's deathbed in 1901, it was Wilhelm who held her hand and stroked her hair.[112] However, looking west from Germany, the first object seen by the navalists was Great Britain positioned like a 'giant breakwater across all Germany's routes to the overseas world'. The Imperial Navy was consciously and strenuously preparing for the day of reckoning when the 'younger, more virile, harder-working, more efficient German navy, riding the tide of history, would wrest the trident from the aging mistress of the seas in a great battle in the North Sea'.[113] Anti-English feeling was 'deliberately fostered' by those who directed propaganda in favour of a larger navy'.[114] This anti-British passion resulted in vehement verbal aggressiveness and popular doggerel rhymes calling on German men and women to give the British a 'good hiding'. A report in the *Contemporary Review*, alarming as it was, still failed to convey to British readers the extent of the hatred the Boer War had created in Germany.[115] 'Political agitators of the Right at once sensed the popularity of Anglophobia and were quick to seize the opportunity for making political capital of what had become Germany's most beloved hatred.'[116] Pan-Germanic meetings, societies of so-called German and Christian Socialism, and the Navy League, demonstrated against the British. Bülow wrote from Windsor in November 1899 that 'German feeling was far more anti-English than English feeling was anti-German'.

German chauvinism was joined to racism and imperialism, and these in turn were made to reaffirm Germany's superiority, stress its unique culture of 'inwardness' and celebrate its artistic, primarily musical, soul.[117]

The next addition to Tirpitz's house of cards order was intended to stem the mounting tide of socialism. The SPD, the social democratic party, emerged from an amalgam in 1875 of the *Allgemeiner Deutscher Arbeiterverein*, the 'General German Workers' Association', founded in 1863, and the *Sozialdemokratische Arbeiterpartei Deutschlands*, the 'Social Democratic Workers' Party', founded in 1869. In 1879, aristocracy and bourgeois united under the slogan 'rye and iron' to create an alliance of Rhenish big business interests and East Elbian agricultural interest. This *Sammlungspolitik*, 'Coalition Policy', was strongly supported by Tirpitz. 'The domestic success of the naval programme stemmed largely from this pact and, in 1898, the landowners voted in favour of naval expenditures that were bound to benefit primarily the industrialists while the latter promised to support increased tariffs on agricultural products.'[118] Tirpitz also saw that the *Sammlungspolitik* was a strong palliative against social democratic ideas. He intended that 'Germany's immense economic power, coupled with the anticipated prestige inherent in an ambitious programme of overseas expansion, would arrest further demands for a more representative parliament by the SPD and the liberals and at the same time would turn the energies and ambitions of Germany's middle classes towards colonial expansion.'

> *Instead of trying to accommodate the political system to the needs of the emerging industrial society, naval expansion was resorted to in order to preserve the political power of the pre-industrial agrarian, bureaucratic and military elites.*[119]

The final card layer, a coalition with the major industrialists, was always going to be the easiest to secure following *Sammlungspolitik* and given their naked self-interest. However, the relationship between buyer and seller was often tense. For the most part, German shipbuilders learnt their trade abroad, in England or at the naval construction school at Copenhagen.[120] After the unification of Germany, Great Britain still built most of Germany's ships. The large private investment needed in Germany to gear up facilities would be expensive especially as the industrialists rarely knew what the navy wanted. While the burgeoning navy was unimaginable without the backing of Germany's largest firms, the discussion always came down to profit and control. Early in his term, Tirpitz 'correctly surmised that the Krupp firm would just as soon profit from selling to Germany's enemies as supply the German navy'. The initial flow of orders to the naval armaments industry lacked a strategic plan and, therefore, uniformity; the existing fleet was a hodgepodge of different types of ships. By 1905, many of the most important shipyards were not ready to build the projected dreadnought types because their slips were not wide enough. All six of the major private yards began a crash programme to alter their facilities. The naval office planned in the following year to locate a new research institute at Berlin

Marienfelde and another for materials testing at Stuttgart. The latter would complement those at Charlottenburg, the Berlin Technische Hochschule, and the purchasing department offices in Düsseldorf, Essen and Berlin.

> *Many industrialists wanted to co-operate with the navy for reasons of patriotism and profit, but not to the extent of endangering their hold on the market or depriving themselves of the initiative in setting policy, prices and research and development priorities. Leading naval officers held sharply contrasting points of view. Building warships was not business as usual, the [Naval Office] refused to be treated as an ordinary customer. Instead Tirpitz demanded long-range commitments from industry and a degree of control over quality and price that went far beyond the traditional relationship between buyer and seller. Tirpitz also felt that the navy had to assume the dominant role in its relationship with the arms merchants.*[121]

While the leaders of Germany's large businesses would benefit from a dramatic increase in naval building, and the worldwide expansion which was expected would follow, they also suspected that the Reichstag would not vote sufficient appropriations. They needed to help Tirpitz as much as they could, but they also needed to keep their options open. Industry quickly put money and muscle behind the 'public' agitators, the Pan-German League and the Navy League.

Wilhelm cultivated close friendships with prominent wealthy Jews, the so-called *Kaiserjuden*, who included the shipbuilder Albert Ballin; the bankers Max Warburg, Carl Fürstenberg and Ludwig Max Goldberger; the 'Cotton-King' James Simon; and the coal magnate Eduard Arnhold.[122] These relationships provided useful opportunities to support the naval programmes, but they sometimes involved 'soliciting funds in support of various pet causes', as each of these powerful Jews sought acceptance as 'true Germans'.[123] The contacts also 'respected Wilhelm's genuine interest in men who had acquired wealth by their own efforts'. While government ministers complained how difficult it was to gain access to the Kaiser, Wilhelm found the time for long meetings with, for instance, Walther Rathenau, the head of AEG, in at least twenty meetings during the last years before the outbreak of war.

With the public in full supportive voice and the votes of the conservatives, landowners and industrialists secured, success in the Reichstag needed one more alliance and this was provided by Tirpitz's relationship with the Catholic Centre Party and its leader Ernst Lieber. Lieber 'looked beyond the religious and regional character of his party and fancied that support for the naval issue could make it the premier national party in Germany'.[124] He hoped that aiding Tirpitz would help broaden the freedom and influence of the Catholic Church and establish his party as the arbiter in Reichstag disputes. In 1903, Germany's Catholic illustrated magazine, *Stadt Gottes: Illustrirte Zeitschrift für das katholische Volk,* devoted a section to the submarine, the new naval craft. 'At first glance this seems an unlikely vehicle for disseminating naval ideas.'[125] However, Catholic conservatives had long since been persuaded by Tirpitz's publicity onslaught that naval expansion was the surest means for securing influence in both national and world affairs. The Catholic Centre party vociferously supported Tirpitz's naval bills.

The Reichstag passed the First Navy Law in 1898 and the Second in 1900.[126] The first called for the construction of nineteen battleships, eight armoured cruisers, twelve large and thirty smaller cruisers; the capital ships were to be automatically replaced after twenty-five years. The second law doubled the size of the fleet to thirty-eight battleships, twenty armoured cruisers and thirty-eight small cruisers. Whereas in 1898, the parliamentary deputies had set an upper limit of just over four billion Reichsmarks, the second law set no limit.

Tirpitz went to the Reichstag in 1906, 1908 and 1912 with three *Novellen,* supplementary laws, with further detailed projections of naval needs. The first and the last passed in the wake of two foreign-policy crises, those over Morocco in 1905 and 1911, and these alarms gave Tirpitz added grist. He was able to sidestep the financial pressures bearing down on the politicians.[127] He rode a wave of self-inspired Navy League and Pan-German propaganda, inflamed public sentiment and the base self-interest of the industrialists. He had the vociferous backing of the Kaiser. 'Opposition to his dream fleet was tantamount in Wilhelm's eyes to treason.'[128] Tirpitz was ruthless at eliminating rivals in the navy, but could relate to people according to the demands of the moment. He 'handled contacts in the Reichstag with seasoned grace', sending its leaders thorough memoranda to keep them well informed on naval affairs and 'frequently engaging them in personal conversations or encouraging his subordinates to do so'.[129] The naval office responded to all questions from the Reichstag, arranging as necessary tours of the Imperial Navy yards for Reichstag deputies. Tirpitz had the necessary votes in his pocket. It was an unholy alliance of Catholics and Pan-Germans, of cold money and naked nationalism. All of these triumphal contracts, stories and emotions, closely reported in the country's newspapers, provided the backdrop for the decisions of many young men to join the excitement and opportunity provided by the German Navy.

Six large cruisers were added to the fleet in 1906 and additional funds were granted to widen existing canals and expand dock facilities in order to accommodate the huge dreadnoughts. The second *Novelle* in 1908 stipulated that the battleships would be replaced at twenty years, five years earlier than previously agreed. Maintenance costs, training centres, personnel increases were to be made automatically depending on the number of ships in service. Finally, in 1912, the third *Novelle* increased the fleet to forty-one battleships, and twenty large and forty small cruisers.

The coming to power of Admiral von Tirpitz held back any further submarine design in Germany, except for one or two private ventures, for a period of over ten years. The reason given by Tirpitz was that he did not wish to supply anything to the German navy that was not fully developed and proved, and the submarine was certainly not in this category. At the same time he emphasised that the geography of the German coast with its shallow water meant that submarines were not suitable for its defence. The real reason was however probably more profound. Tirpitz was trying at this time to build up a German fleet into an ocean-going navy with a powerful battle fleet, and he clearly wanted no rivals to this policy. A submarine force would be much cheaper and, if it could be shown to be capable of defending the homeland, might well have been preferred by the Reichstag. In these circumstances, it is understandable that Tirpitz played down submarine development in Germany.[130]

Thanks to the success of the 1906 and 1908 Supplementary Naval Laws, some additional funds were squeezed out and the pace of the u-boat programme quickened. Eleven boats were laid down and research and development increased, one and a half million Reichsmarks each year in 1905 and 1906. For each of the next two years, the figure rose by one million, finally leaping to five million Reichsmarks in 1909. Tirpitz still showed a consistently negative attitude. 'I refused to throw away money on submarines as long as they could only cruise in home waters and therefore would be of no use to us.'

The German Navy objected properly to the use of steam and petrol for underwater propulsion.[131] Nevertheless, many saw that if submarines could be developed for use offensively they would be of considerable value especially against Great Britain. With the development of the Körting heavy-oil engine in Hanover in 1905, the Imperial Navy's technical objections fell away. The Germans built their first unsuccessful boat during 1906. Their second submarine was not completed until 1908, but from 1907 onwards they embarked on a programme of large 'overseas' submarines. In 1912, secret trials in the North Sea confirmed worthwhile patrols off the English coasts. Altogether, forty-two 'overseas' type submarines were ordered between 1908 and 1914, of which twenty-nine had been completed before war broke out. The Germans then had twice as many 'overseas' submarines built or building as the British. Tirpitz later claimed that he had waited until he was sure that submarines were an effective offensive weapon and had then built them in quantity for the express purpose of using them against Great Britain.[132] Many on his staff disagreed with his retroactive interpretation. In fact, in 1912, Tirpitz still refused to allow u-boats to participate in winter manoeuvres, but during Tirpitz's summer holidays in South Germany, Admiral Eduard von Capelle, his chief aide, managed to include them.[133]

Here was the time, in the year or so immediately before 1905 that Erich and Georg Gerths' career plans were formed. They both chose to become naval officers in the Imperial Navy, one of the best-loved institutions in Wilhelmine Germany. The populace 'showered their affection and adulation' upon the *Blauen Jungen*, the 'bluejackets'.[134] Applications were made in writing towards the end of 1904 and 1906 and the young men had until May of their cadet entry year to make their case for acceptance, pass boards and examinations, submit written proofs and, not least, to find the money.

Their success as applicants was the more unusual as none of their co-students in their academic years chose the same path. Whatever had determined Erich and Georg on their course, did not appeal to their fellows or their parents. All had grown up in Berlin's world of discipline and respect, surrounded by Wilhelm's military statues, marching soldiers and arrogant Prussian officers. The excitement of immigrants, rapid urban growth and the fruits of international respect, from Wild West shows and cultural events to industrial exhibitions abounded. Young men were caught in the thrill of expansion, a coming empire, and a rightful place in the sun. They heard the vehement criticism of the arrogant British who stood literally in the way, and dismissed the traitorous counter-arguments of the social democrats. Behind Tirpitz's incessant bravado and rhetoric, there was, for the sea-goers, the promise of travel to foreign lands as successful traders and colonial masters and, perhaps, glorious battle. The nation was caught up in probably the 'most totemic of all modern armaments competitions prior to the Cold War'.[135] Throughout school, the Gerths experienced the steady drip of visits to naval installations, the pull of emotion-tugging books and carefully placed newspaper articles, and the clarion calls of family and the pervasive outpourings of the Pan-German and Navy Leagues. With this weight of excitement, much of it coldly manufactured, the question might more properly be why the two Gerths were not accompanied by a group of fellow thrusters. Yet Berlin was renowned for its thorough disrespect for the Kaiser and his expensive pretensions and perhaps these dislikes of an undemocratic establishment held greater sway. However, the lure of the navy won through and the Gerths left the company of their childhood friends and, given the nature of the officer corps they were to join, they probably left them forever.

Ironically, at much the same time as the bravado and promise of Tirpitz's propaganda caught the Gerths' imagination in the first years of the twentieth century, this was also the moment when the integral and naïve flaws in the Tirpitz plan slowly became clearer; his great dream started to unravel and his powers began to wane.

Outwardly, Germany was 'on the climb to major-power status', an industrial juggernaut steadily producing more steel than Britain, exporting more goods, her population expanding as rapidly as the 'expansionist dreams so fervently preached by the Pan-Germans and Navy Leaguers in their frantic pursuit of the Kaiser's and their own *Weltpolitik*, 'expansionist' ambitions'.[136] German per-capita purchasing power rose more than 70 per cent from 1871 to 1913 and the population in cities with more than 50,000 inhabitants increased from twelve to 36 per cent. The on-going industrialisation required a rethink of farming methods. 'More and more fodder, fertiliser and other intermediate products as well as human foodstuffs were imported to ensure that agriculture grew at a sufficient pace.'[137] Germany's major food trades were for Russian barley, American grains and Norwegian fishmeal. Between 1887 and 1912, imports rose by almost 250 per cent to ten million Reichsmarks and exports to nine million Reichsmarks. 'The balance of trade had thus become unfavourable and the restoration of a favourable balance had become one of the essential tasks of German economic policy. No other country could show a comparable increase in imports.'[138] By 1913, Germany was still leading in exchanges with European states, although the balance was down by 30 per cent and overall trade was now in deficit. The industrialists, banks and oil companies spread the risk by gaining facilities outside of Germany's small share of international influence. Joint planning with government was encouraged and led to ownership of foreign mines, or at least concessions or shares.[139] Iron and steel was exported to Australia, South America, China and, even, Britain. The need for extra steel refining capacity took heavy industry to the iron deposits of Krivoi Rog and Tchiaturi in the Ukraine and the Caucasus. Partnerships were made over the Anatolian and Baghdad railways. Overseas countries, the tropics and, above all, South America, were supplying an increasing proportion of vital raw materials like fertilisers. These widening trade routes were increasingly vulnerable to malicious interference.

The Germans worked to undercut and squeeze rivals out of markets.[140] British industrialists knew but rarely acknowledged that there was also a marked superiority in new German manufactures like organic chemicals and electrical goods. The British press carried bitter stories of the 'unfair' tactics of German salesmen spying on British trade practices, pandering to foreign countries and seducing them to the extent of, heaven forbid, translating brochures into their own language.[141] George Schreiner, an American news correspondent operating in Germany for most of the war, noted:

Germany's industrials do not seem to have been content with merely entering a foreign market and then supplying it with that good tact which makes the article and its manufacturer respected. Instead of that they began to dump their wares in the new field in such masses that soon there was attached to really good merchandise the stigma of cheapness in price and quality. A proper sense of proportion would have prevented this. There is no doubt that German manufacturers and exporters had to undersell foreign competitors but for the sake of 'hogging' the markets that they should turn to cheap peddling was nothing short of criminally stupid – a national calamity.[142]

Chancellor Bethmann-Hollweg stated that the British 'looked upon a Germany that kept on growing as an unwanted and troublesome intruder on the sanctity of British supremacy over the commerce and oceans of the world'.[143] Modern machinery, highly trained technicians, rapid application of scientific discoveries to production techniques, and a will to adapt to the purchaser's wishes 'all helped Germany forge ahead'.[144] Britain's earlier industrial revolution meant that by the 1910s much of its manufacturing suffered from comparative technological backwardness and a lack of new investment. 'A considerable portion of the profit from British industry was being invested in high-interest yielding portfolios and securities abroad, rather than being re-invested in industrial modernisation at home.' British supremacy was being challenged, but it was due as much to British complacency that leads were lost, opportunities missed and markets overtaken. Better quality, cheaper goods were also coming from America and Japan, but mostly from Germany.[145]

This prosperous picture was marred by increasing internal dissention, growing insistence on electoral and financial reforms, and increasingly powerful trade union demands for industrial and agricultural legislation. Liberal Reichstag members wanted to bring imperial Germany into the modern political world. A ruling aristocracy wanted imperial Germany to remain in the Junker tradition of government by the few for the few. Liberals wanted to cut arms spending. Conservatives demanded a bigger navy and a stronger army.[146]

Tirpitz wanted to confront Britain with the ultimate risk, forcing a reticence to do battle for fear of significant loss. Tirpitz and many of his supporters 'chose to believe that Britain could not or would not act to prevent the inevitable change in the naval balance of power' as the German High Seas Fleet grew.[147] What was not thought through was that the British would interpret the construction of the German fleet as the ultimate challenge to their national welfare. The change in the British political climate between 1902 and 1904 'destroyed the international foundation of the risk theory and propelled Germany into a full-scale arms race before Tirpitz expected or realised it.'

All sorts of sober-minded people in England began to be profoundly disquieted. What did Germany want this great navy for? Against whom, except ours, could she measure it, match it, or use it? For a war against France or Russia in the North Sea and in the Baltic, a German fleet with less than half of this strength would have been more than sufficient.[148]

The Boer War confirmed a suspicion held by many in Britain in the latter part of the nineteenth century that the country's powers were in decline. Other, more vigorous, states were pressing forward, eager to assume Britain's role as the world's leading industrial and maritime nation. No longer confident that it could depend for its safety solely on the strength of its far-flung economic and naval resources, British sought to repair its defences early in the twentieth century with a system of international alliances. The long-held policy of 'splendid isolation' was jettisoned and diplomatic links forced with France, Russia and Japan.[149]

The British reached an agreement with France in 1904 which further reduced the German North Sea threat: the British would safeguard the North Sea and French channel coasts while the French took charge of the Mediterranean releasing British capital ships from Gibraltar to glower at the Germans at Wilhelmshaven and Kiel.[150]

The British never appreciated that the French entente was for Germany a potential threat to their safety, but no more did the Germans realise that in a world of armament races, Realpolitik and imperialistic rivalries, naval supremacy was vital to Britain's interests.[151]

From 1905, the German fleet replaced the French and Russian navies as the benchmark for British naval strength. It was now the greatest challenge to the maritime supremacy upon which Britain depended and consequently endangered the use of Britain's chief weapon, blockade.[152] Britain's trade routes in the Atlantic were not threated by German battleships and cruisers in the North Sea.[153] The battleships, in particular, were hamstrung for they did not have the range to twice run the gauntlet around the British fleet based in Scotland and could not be used in lengthy coal-consuming battle or commercial war in the Atlantic. For instance, the *Deutschland* class battleships that came into service from 1903 could travel far less than 5,000 nautical miles when cruising comfortably.[154] In battle conditions, or in a chase, the distance dropped critically.

Another British response to the perceived German threat was the 'Dreadnought' revolution that made all other battle fleets around the world instantly obsolete. The naval armaments clock was set back to zero. HMS *Dreadnought* launched in 1906 had a top-speed of twenty-one knots, twice the firepower of previous ships and incorporated many revolutionary technical innovations. Every older battleship was now marginalised as a 'pre-dreadnought'. 'The aura of peace and prosperity which had graced

Wilhelm's reign was suddenly dashed.'[155] Tirpitz was quick to react; the first German Dreadnoughts put to sea in 1907. By 1909, twelve British and ten German dreadnoughts were either under construction or already in service. 'For one brief moment in history, it looked as though the Imperial Navy would be able to manage the establishment of a fleet equal to the Royal Navy.'[156] The situation was not tenable. The Royal Navy doubled its construction programme in 1909. Britain laid eight new keels in a clear signal that a one-third superiority over the Imperial Navy would be maintained at any price. By rule of thumb, therefore, the enemy could be annihilated. Britain sought to end the arms race in 1912, but the Kaiser, under pressure from Tirpitz, rejected the proposal.

For all of these reasons, Tirpitz came under increasing attack from senior German naval staff and free thinkers. From 1905 to 1908, Tirpitz began an 'uphill battle against criticism from energetic opponents who took him to task for his relentless devotion to the risk theory and the battleship'.[157]

In spite of scathing attacks by newly retired Vizeadmiral Karl Galster, Rear Admiral Curt von *Maltzahn*, Kapitän Lothar Persius and Kapitänleutnant Wolfgang Wegener, the admiral kept to his course and struck back at his detractors. Tirpitz's 'most trenchant critic' was Galster, who 'caused quite a stir when he went public with his condemnation of the battle fleet programme' in 1907.[158] Galster condemned the military futility of the 'risk fleet', dismissing out of hand the 'wishful thinking' that it was possible to compensate for inferiority by gaining a technological edge over the world's largest and most experienced navy. He confirmed that Germany's few battleships could do nothing to protect colonial and trade communications. 'This was the most damning strategic criticism ever levelled at the construction policy in Tirpitz's time.'[159] Galster also advocated quicker development of the u-boat. *Maltzahn* thought that the navy should first build a fleet of overseas cruisers to foster Germany's commercial interests. Persius championed the u-boat and, after his retirement, became a formidable foe. His series of books and articles praising the possibilities of the u-boat in a commercial war persistently took Tirpitz to task. When Tirpitz's theories fell from favour during the war and he reluctantly retired, Persius administered the *coup de grace*. In a book entitled *Die Tirpitz Legende*, Persius 'indicted the admiral's strategic dogma and blamed him for Germany's lack of preparedness to fight a u-boat war in 1914'. In three position papers written in the summer of 1915 for circulation within the navy, Wegener's challenge caught the imagination of the younger members of the officer corps, possibly including the newly commissioned Gerth brothers. Wegener dissected the risk theory and questioned the value of the decisive battle which formed the core of Tirpitz's theories. While he did not repudiate the battle fleet, he also, shockingly, 'accused Tirpitz of being ignorant of how to use it'.[160]

Tirpitz was ruthless with his critics.[161] He classified officers such as

Galster, Maltzahn and Persius as 'enemies of the navy' and had their writings banned while they remained in the service. Galster and Maltzahn, in particular, were ostracised by the Reichsmarineamt in a campaign organised by the Information Bureau because Tirpitz felt their ideas challenged the primacy of the battleship.

The first concrete sign of Tirpitz's waning influence came in 1912. The Kaiser and his cabinet endorsed decisions to rebalance the budget towards the army, an improved social budget and a broader fiscal foundation.[162] The navy had grown twice as fast as the army since 1909 and Tirpitz, tactics exposed, now faced arguments over high prices, inefficiency, too high profits, monopolies and evidence that ships were cheaper abroad, particularly in Britain. 'After intense debates, it became obvious that the days of rapid growth and rich appropriations had come to an end.' The vote signalled the end of fourteen years of political success for Tirpitz.

Meanwhile, the gathering success of the socialists appalled Wilhelm and his advisers. From 1878 to 1890, any grouping or meeting that aimed at spreading socialist principles was banned under the Anti-Socialist Laws, but the party still gained support in elections. In 1890, when the ban was lifted and the SPD could again present electoral lists, the party adopted its current name. The first May Day celebrations of the workers' movement took place in Berlin on that 1 May. Although now legal, the SPD 'remained an outlaw in establishment eyes'.[163] The Kaiser warned that in the unlikely event of securing a Reichstag majority, the party would 'at once proceed to plunder the citizens'. No party meeting could take place without a police officer keeping watch and taking notes of speeches. The government banned its employees from joining the party and forbade the sale of SPD newspapers at railway station newsstands. The Kaiser's advisers told him to be 'determined to treat the Social Democrats not as a party, but to fight them with means of coercion as revolutionaries against state and order'.[164] The Kaiser did not quite want to go that far, but did want to ban all SPD meetings and to hand out jail sentences for those 'who defame the memory of dead German princes'.

By the late 1890s, Bismarck had concluded that his efforts to reconcile Germany's working classes to the authoritarian state through a mixture of *Butterbrot und Peitsche*, 'buttered bread and whip', had failed.[165] Miners in the national coalfields were waging devastating strikes for higher wages; the SPD was growing apace and making effective alliances with other opposition parties in the Reichstag. Berlin, with its huge working class population and 'obstreperous Reichstag delegation', seemed to Bismarck like a 'growing cancer, likely to infect and destroy the political system he had created'. In 1890, Bismarck decided that the only way to deal with the fractious workers was to throw away the buttered bread and to lay on the whip. More specifically, he proposed extending the Anti-Socialist laws indefinitely and, if labour protested, bringing in troops to discipline them.

He also wanted the Reichstag to be abolished and replaced by a chamber beholden to the large landowners and industrialists. 'He planned, in other words, a state coup against the existing political system and he was willing to risk civil war to carry it out.' The Kaiser thought initially that he could win over the workers with limited additional reforms and, of course, his charisma. It was a clash of ideas and personality and, therefore, Bismarck had to go. Conversely, by 1894, Wilhelm realised that the rift was causing damage to his personal prestige and he arranged that when he summoned Bismarck to Berlin the encounter was presented as a 'moment of great reconciliation'. Even a return visit later in the year to Bismarck's country estate did not help. 'Bismarck's contemptuous estimate of the young Kaiser had not changed in the slightest, and for Wilhelm the overpowering shadow of the 'old man in the Saxon Forest' remained a constant irritation.'[166]

Allegations of subversive and dangerous activities were not helped by the SPD's anthems.[167] A good example is the *Workers' Marseillaise* which was usually sung at the end of party meetings with a revolutionary rephrasing of the famous Lutheran song, *Ein' feste Burg ist unser Gott*, 'A Stronghold is Our God':

> *A call resounds from land to land*
> *The poor should clasp each other's hand*
> *And call a halt to tyranny*
> *And stop the slave's agony.*
> *The drums are beaten dully,*
> *The red flags flutter briskly:*
> > *Let us live working or die fighting.*

August Bebel, the SPD leader, rejected the accusations and claimed his party was not revolutionary, but was rather for reform; neither was it unpatriotic because it 'wanted a freer and more beautiful Fatherland'.[168] The unpatriotic groups were the ruling classes 'because they imposed the burden of military expenditure mainly on the workers whose patriotism they distrusted and to whom they would not grant equal rights and social recognition'. The real revolutionaries were the big industrialists.

The government did not have many options: the Bismarck solution, complete repression of the Social Democrats, if necessary by coup d'état and the abolition of the Reichstag; democratisation by first giving the middle classes a greater share in government and by subsequently integrating the Social Democrats into the national community; or a continued isolation of the Social Democrats. The first had been rejected decisively by the Kaiser when he fired Bismarck. Democratisation was 'beyond the vision' of Wilhelm and of his officials. The emperor and his government elected the third, easiest course; they continued to isolate the labour movement while not blocking its membership among the working class.[169] This last was preferred, especially because of the electoral strength of the German left between 1893 and 1906. 'In the short run this policy of isolation was convenient; in the long run, it was bound to be dangerous in times of external crisis.' By 1912, the party claimed the most votes of any German party. An absolute majority of Berliners voted for the SPD in the Reichstag elections. The party polled 34 per cent of the votes of the Reichstag and had a million members by 1914; it held 110 of the 396 seats in the Reichstag, more than 220 in the state diets, more than 2,800 in the city parliaments and councils and more than 9,000 in rural communities.[170] Despite their increasing wealth, the merchants in the great cities, especially Berlin, joined the SPD, not at all for their socialist policies, but for their prominent opposition to Wilhelm. 'Their hatred of the Junker power in the civil administration and army alike was united in their derision of and annoyance with the want of culture displayed by the governing classes.'[171] Despite all of these pending upheavals, with their hints of revolution, Imperial Germany approached World War I with an impressive record of internal stability.

> *No constitutional change had occurred in the Reich and Prussia; there had been crises of personnel and prestige, but none of them had seriously shaken the constitutional defences of the Emperor, his government, his army and navy, and his conservatives who affirmed their monarchist loyalty at the same time that they put their own political and economic interests over national interests. Democratisation had made some advance primarily in southern Germany, but on the federal level it was not more than a tendency and in Prussia not more than a possibility for the future.*[172]

While the Gerths were safely tucked up at cadet school, or out of harm's way in the naval fleet after graduation, they were protected from all of these dilemmas. Tirpitz's large ships were sliding out of the dockyards ready to provide future glory and career opportunity. Initially, u-boats did not seem like an officially approved or pleasant option. Junior leutnants were prohibited from intercourse with their more worldly-wise technical officers and, especially with their crews, their nearest contact with the socialist workers in the ports. The Gerths knew little of the political arguments between government, industry and the social democratic movement and, what they did know, came from right-thinking newspapers, from instruction by their blinkered and arrogant superiors, or by consensus debate in their equally insular officers' mess.[173] The anti-war machinations of the Reichstag and the fervent singing of the *Workers' Marseilles* on board the fleet were light years away. During and immediately after the war years, as Erich and Georg emerged from their chrysalises and became more mature, it was not into the enjoyable butterfly world of uniform and prestige that they anticipated. The old stabilities disappeared. As the world order changed and challenged their beliefs, perhaps they suddenly realised they had not been provided with the skills to cope.

As the Kaiser and Chancellor Bethmann much later realised, risk strategy worked both ways. In August 1914, Germany was quite unready to challenge Britain.[174] As a result, they decided throughout most of the war to keep their fleet bottled up because it was of more value, they hoped, in favourable peace negotiations than in risky naval battles. The Kaiser also feared for his little 'darlings' and could not bear to think of them 'shattered by gunfire, smeared with blood ... or sinking beneath the waves'.[175]

ENDNOTES

1   Richter, *Family life in Germany under the Blockade*, p. 2, adapted from the *Bible*, Matthew, 4:8–10.
2   Padfield, *Dönitz*, p. 19.
3   29/3/1890.
4   Herwig, 'Soziale Herkunft und wissenschaftliche Vorbildung des Seeoffiziers der Kaiserlichen Marine vor 1914', *Militärgeschichtliche Mitteilungen, 10, 1971*, p. 86, cited in Mueller, Canaris, p. 4.
5   *Marine-Rundschau*, 1900, Vol. 63, p. 193.
6   Herwig, *Naval Officer Corps*, pp. 38–39, 50.
7   Horn, *Mutiny*, p. 7.
8   Annual Business Report, 1893, *Neue Berliner Pferdebahn-Gesellschaft*, 20/3/1894, courtesy Michael Grunwald, Berlin Verkehrsbetriebe (BVG).
9   The costs suggested for each year of cadetship covered clothes and uniform, 'parental support', social obligations, status, and books and amounted to 7,235 Reichsmarks, plus additional expenses for riding, fencing, dancing and 'miscellaneous costs' (Herwig, *Naval Officer Corps*), p. 55.
10 Large, *Berlin*, pp. 9, 50.
11 Large, *Berlin*, p. xxi.
12 Rathenau, 'Die Schönste Stadt der Welt', *Die Zukunft 26*, 1899.
13 Volkov, *Rathenau*, p. 1.
14 Large, *Berlin*, p. 57.
15 Asprey, *German High Command*, pp. 144–45.
16 Hull, *Entourage*, p. 27. Rosenberg, *Imperial Germany*, pp. 35–36.
17 Large, *Berlin*, pp. 51–52.
18 Large, *Berlin*, pp. 53, 61.
19 Asprey, *German High Command*, pp. 144–45.
20 Dorpalen, *Treitschke*, p. 194.
21 Large, *Berlin*, pp. 47–49.
22 Scheffler, 'Berlin: Ein Stadtschicksal', cited in Emmerson, *1913*, p. 69.
23 berlin.de/the-royal-capital, accessed 12/2017.
24 Volkov, *Rathenau*, p. 2.
25 Davis, *Everyday Life*, pp. 18–19.
26 Large, *Berlin*, pp. 82–85.
27 Large, *Berlin*, p. 84.
28 Zimmermann, *Die Bahn, die Berlin bewegt*, pp. 19–22.
29 Pohl, 'Neue Berliner', p. 91.
30 Ernst Gäbler bought the land from Gustav Adolf Schön who speculated on Berlin's expansion by parcelling and selling parts of the Weißensee Castle estate, which he

bought for 700,000 thalers from Friedrich Wilhelm Lüdersdorff. Schön set up a building company with Gäbler, the builder Hermann Roelcke, and the bankers Busse & Co to further profit from one parcel. Among the street names were many of Schön's family, friends and business associates: GustavAdolfstraße, Schönstraße, Albertinenstraße, Amalienstraße, Antonplatz, Gäblerstraße, Magnusstraße and Roelckestraße (wikipedia).

31   From 1951, most of the streets were rebuilt after war damage and named after composers.

32   Zimmermann, *Die Bahn, die Berlin bewegt*, pp. 19–22.

33   Carl August Heinrich Gerth, born 1862, married Caroline Wilhelmine Louise Thiede. There were seven children of which three sons were Heinrich Carl Wilhelm Emil Georg Ernst Gerth, born 1830, died 26/11/1870, married 18/7/1861, Brandenburg, Friederike Wilhelmine Emilie(a) Leben; Wilhelm August Ernst Ludwig Gerth, born 12/7/1834, Berlin, died 31/12/1893, married, first, Wilhelmine Ida Knoll 5/4/1862; and Carl August Gerth, born 7/1/1837, reservist, 2nd Field Regiment, 1st Dragoon Guards, Artillery Brigade, Prussian Army, married 8/2/1863, Wilhelmine Dorothea Schultze (ancestry.com).

34   Emmerson, *1913*, p. 61.

35   Erich Ernst Heinrich Gerth, born 25/4/1886; Georg Carl Gerth, born 3/3/1888; Carl August Gerth, born 17/7/1889 (ancestry.com).

36   Email, Madeleine Prendergast, 15/1/2018.

37   Family picture of Ernst with his three sons dated 5/1890.

38   *Geschäftsbericht der Neuen Berliner Pferdebahn-Gesellschaft für 1893*, 'Annual company report of the New Berlin Horse Tram Company for the year 1893', 20/3/1894 for the general meeting on 5/4/1894.

39   Jung, 'New Berlin Horse Railway Company', pp. 4/17–18; Pohl, 'New Berlin Horse Railway Company', pp. 1/2–11 and pp. 2/32–38.

40   Two widows, A and M Boch (possibly the same person), are recorded at different times living with Hedwig in Luckenwalderstraße.

41   Grunwald, private email, 5/4/2017.

42   Baroness von Spitzemberg, *Tagebuch*, cited in Large, *Berlin*, p. 55. Ullrich, *Bismarck*, p. 107.

43   Large, *Berlin*, p. 62.

44   Weir, *Kaiser's Navy*, p. 2.

45   Large, *Berlin*, pp. 81–82.

46   Large, *Berlin*, p. 76.

47   Rosenberg, *Imperial Germany*, p. 40.

48   One of Kollwitz's best-known etchings which shows children reaching upwards with begging bowls, is used as the cover of Vincent's *Politics of Hunger*.

49   Large, *Berlin*, pp. 71–73.

50   Large, *Berlin*, pp. 57–59.

51   Ladd, *Ghosts of Berlin*, p. 54.

52   Dreiser, cited in Emmerson, *1913*, pp. 59–60.

53   Jahresbericht : über das Schuljahr Ostern, Königliches, Kaiser-Wilhelm-Realgymnasium zu Berlin (digital.ub.uni-duesseldorf.de/ulbdsp/periodical, pageviews/4162345, 4162580, 4162690), accessed 3/2017.

54   Zweig, *World of Yesterday*, pp. 51–57.

55   Zweig, *World of Yesterday*, pp. 60, 78.

56   Davis, *Everyday Life*, p. 20.

57   Emmerson, *1913*, pp. 62–64.

58   Richie, *Faust's Metropolis*, pp. 203–4.

59   Richie, *Faust's Metropolis*, p. 206.

60   Padfield, *Dönitz*, pp. 10–13.

61   Tuchman, *August 1914*, p. 367.

62   Grahame, *Golden Age*, pp. 11, 16.

63   Preston, 'Introduction', in Mahan, *Influence of Sea Power*, p. 6.

64   Herwig, *Naval Officer Corps*, p. 11.

65   Vincent, *Politics of Hunger*, p. 27.

66   Herwig, *Naval Officer Corps*, p. 11.

67   Weir, *Kaiser's Navy*, p. 1.

68 Wolfgang Mommsen, 'Debate of German War Aims', pp. 47–72. West Africa for the Germans was Cameroon and the River Volta region of modern Ghana; South West Africa, Namibia; and German East Africa which combined Burundi, Rwanda, and Tanganyika (now mainland Tanzania).
69 Asprey, *German High Command*, p. 27.
70 Hadley, *Count Not the Dead, p. 6.*
71 Hadley, *Count Not the Dead, pp. 7–8.*
72 Asprey, *German High Command*, pp. 146–48.
73 Rosenberg, *Imperial Germany*, p. 34.
74 Herwig, *Naval Officer Corps*, pp. 23–24.
75 *Marine-Taschenbuch*, 1905, pp. 278–79. Herwig, *Naval Officer Corps*, p. 67, fn. 4: Catholics were to end the oath with, 'So help me God and his holy gospel. Amen'; Jews with, 'So help me God. Amen', but only if they had already been baptised.
76 Herwig, *Naval Officer Corps*, pp. 12–13.
77 Weir, *Kaiser's Navy*, pp. 13, 19.
78 Weir, *Kaiser's Navy*, p. 11.
79 Preston, 'Introduction', in Mahan, *Influence of Sea Power*, p. 10.
80 Koerver, *War of Numbers*, p. 36. Tuchman, *August 1914*, p. 368.
81 Devlin, *Too Proud*, p. 190.
82 Kelly, *Tirpitz*, pp. 71–72.
83 Wolfgang Tirpitz was one of 348 survivors whom the British had pulled from the North Sea after the action. He spent the rest of the war in a prison camp.
84 Marder, *Dreadnought*, Vol. 1, p. 6.
85 Koerver, *War of Numbers*, pp. 14–15, 36.
86 Clausewitz, *On War*, Book 8, Chapter 2. Herwig, 'Total Rhetoric'.
87 Woodward, *Great Britain and the German Navy*, pp. 19–20.
88 Asprey, *German High Command*, p. 31.
89 Asprey, *German High Command*, pp. 148–49.
90 Herwig, *Naval Officer Corps*, pp. 31–33, 73. Clark, *Iron Kingdom*, p. 564.
91 Hull, *Entourage*, p. 16.
92 Röhl, *Kaiser, Hof and Staat*, p. 10. Hull, *Entourage*, p. 7.
93 Hobson, *Imperialism at Sea*, p. 1.
94 Reichstag, Navy Law, 1898.
95 Herwig, *Naval Officer Corps*, p. 11.
96 Seligmann, *Naval Route*, 'Introduction', p. xxi. For the story of Tambach Castle, see 'Introduction' to this book.
97 Herwig and Trask, *Naval Operations Plans*, p. 40. 'The Tirpitz bandwagon provided a scaffold of cultural, economic, political, military and vulgar Darwinistic timber for the new structure.'
98 Weir, *Kaiser's Navy*, pp. 6–7.
99 Churchill, *World Crisis*, p. 61.
100 Weir, *Kaiser's Navy*, p. 33.
101 Turner, *Origins*, pp. 113–15.
102 Hadley, *Count Not the Dead, pp. 6–13.* Herwig, *Naval Officer Corps*, pp. 6–7. Meyer, *Die Propaganda der deutschen Flottenbewegung 1897–1900*, p. 26.
103 Tirpitz, *Memoirs*, Vol. 1, pp. 112–13.
104 Rüger, *Great Naval Game*, pp. 146–47.
105 Hadley, *Count Not the Dead, pp. 6–9.*
106 Herwig, *Naval Officer Corps*, pp. 7–8.
107 Eley, 'Radical Nationalism and the German Navy League', p. 332.
108 Chickering, *Most German*, pp. 253–56.
109 Hull, *Absolute Destruction*, pp. 105–6.
110 Chickering, *Most German*, pp. 1, 2, 9, 12, 74, 76–79, 234.
111 Padfield, *Dönitz*, p. 15.
112 Asprey, *German High Command*, p. 141.
113 Padfield, *Dönitz*, pp. 10–13, 24.

114   Woodward, *Great Britain and the German Navy*, pp. 26–27.
115   *Contemporary Review*, Vol. LXXVII, 6/1900, pp. 881–82.
116   Koebner, *Imperialism*, pp. 245–46.
117   Volkov, *Rathenau*, p. 44.
118   Herwig, *Naval Officer Corps*, pp. 4–6.
119   Seligmann, *Naval Route*, 'Introduction', p. xliii.
120   Weir, *Kaiser's Navy*, pp. 10–13.
121   Weir, *Kaiser's Navy*, pp. 2–3, 81–83.
122   Clarke, *Kaiser Wilhelm*, pp. 351–52.
123   Volkov, *Rathenau*, p. 3.
124   Weir, *Kaiser's Navy*, p. 23.
125   Hadley, *Count Not the Dead, p. 11.*
126   First Navy Law, 10/4/1898; Second Navy Law, 14/6/1900. Herwig, *Naval Officer Corps*,
       pp. 8–12.
127   Weir, *Kaiser's Navy*, p. 79.
128   Hull, *Entourage*, p. 115.
129   Weir, *Kaiser's Navy*, pp. 22–23.
130   Hezlet, *Submarine and Sea Power*, pp. 12–13.
131   Hezlet, *Submarine and Sea Power*, pp. 17–20.
132   Hezlet, *Submarine and Sea Power*, pp. 12–13.
133   Herwig, *Naval Officer Corps*, p. 27, fn. 3.
134   Horn, *Mutiny*, p. 3.
135   Seligmann, *Naval Route*, 'Introduction', p. xv.
136   Asprey, *German High Command*, p. 148.
137   Blum, 'Living Standards in Germany', p. 557.
138   Fischer, *War Aims*, p. 12.
139   Grebler, *Cost of the War*, p. 23. Helfferich, *Deutschlands Wohlstand*, pp. 79–80.
140   Fischer, *War Aims*, pp. 17–19.
141   Docherty & Macgregor, *Hidden History*, p. 59.
142   Schreiner, *Iron Ration*, pp. 21–22.
143   Ewart, *Roots and Causes of the Wars*, Vol. II, pp. 680–81.
144   Docherty & Macgregor, *Hidden History*, p. 58.
145   Landes, *Unbound Prometheus*, p. 327.
146   Asprey, *German High Command*, p. 148.
147   Weir, *Kaiser's Navy*, pp. 101–2.
148   Churchill, *World Crisis*, p. 23; Koerver, *War of Numbers*, pp. 15–16. Seligmann, *Naval
       Route*, 'Introduction', p. xxiii.
149   Barnett, *British Food Policy*, p. 5.
150   Woodward, *Great Britain and the German Navy*, pp. 38–42.
151   Marder, *Dreadnought to Scapa Flow*, Vol. 1, p. 177.
152   Weir, *Kaiser's Navy*, pp. 77–78.
153   Wegener, *Strategy*, pp. 154–55.
154   Gröner, *Warships*, Vol. 1, p. 21.
155   Hull, *Entourage*, p. 236.
156   Koerver, *War of Numbers*, pp. 16–17.
157   Weir, *Kaiser's Navy*, p. 76.
158   Hobson, *Imperialism at Sea*, pp. 261, 265. Glaster, *Welche Seekriegs-Rüstung braucht
       Deutschland?*
159   Weir, *Kaiser's Navy*, pp. 77–78. Hobson, *Imperialism at Sea*, p. 271.
160   Weir, *Kaiser's Navy*, p. 142.
161   Weir, *Kaiser's Navy*, pp. 83–84.
162   Weir, *Kaiser's Navy*, pp. 118–21.
163   Harmer, *Luxemburg*, p. 27.
164   Roth, *Social Democrats*, p. 115.
165   Large, *Berlin*, p. 54; Ullrich, *Bismarck*, pp. 103–5.

166 Ullrich, *Bismarck*, pp. 111–12.
167 Roth, *Social Democrats*, p. 91, citing Schuster, *Die Social-Demokratie*, p. 162. The anthem was based on *Psalm 46*.
168 Roth, *Social Democrats*, p. 124.
169 Roth, *Social Democrats*, pp. 83–84.
170 Roth, *Social Democrats*, p. 287. For more background, see Berlau, *German Social Democratic Party, 1914–1921*; Lidtke, *Outlawed Party: Social Democracy in Germany, 1878–1890*; Orlow, *Common Destiny: Comparative History of the Dutch, French, and German Social Democratic Parties, 1945–1969*; Schorske, *German Social Democracy, 1905–1917*.
171 Rosenberg, *Imperial Germany*, p. 40.
172 Roth, *Social Democrats*, p. 285.
173 Preface, 'Behind the mask'. Also Chapter 2, 'Kaisertreu'.
174 Hull, *Scrap of Paper*, p. 212.
175 Tuchman, *August 1914*, p. 368.

Kaisertreu

The vast majority of executive officers joined the navy not because it was a German federal rather than particular entity, nor because through it they hoped to achieve German Weltpolitik, nor because it was a bourgeois rather than an aristocratic creation, nor for any other sophisticated reason. The truth of the matter is that many joined out of a sense of youthful adventurism … in short, the romance of the sea inspired by various writers, better opportunities for advancement, a longing for travel abroad, and a hankering for practical rather than academic occupations.[1]

To its officer recruits, the navy was the status symbol of the modern German Empire, the 'melting pot' of Germany.[2] Its ships flew the Imperial black, white and red banner, but were funded by the Reichstag. The navy had its own state secretary in the cabinet appointed by the Kaiser, but it chose its cadets from all German cities and states. At least, that was the forward-looking picture presented to the general public. Internally, at the turn of the century, command officers grappled with the acute problem of whether *Charakter* or *Bildung*, 'noble lineage' or 'formal education', was the leading desired attribute for new entrants.[3] At stake was the soul of the *Kaiserliche Marine*.

The military ethos, embodied in the officer's honour code, was more rigid, more exclusive, than civilian standards of behaviour. *Charakter* was the Prussian code word for a 'constellation of qualities' which included good birth, correct upbringing, propriety, and, something harder to evaluate today, adherence to noble values and judgements and particular loyalty to the monarch – *Kaisertreu*.[4] Cadets with *Charakter* could be relied upon to provide a consistent flow of bureaucratic virtues, like efficiency, duty and service. They would loyally and successfully expedite business as long as they were not challenged by more intellectual demands like creating policy or managing complex technical problems. This dramatic contrast was exemplified within the Germany military. From 1872, the Bavarian Army recognised the changing face of warfare and required its officer recruits to have graduated from high school with their *Abitur*. In contrast, in the Prussian Army of 1897, the diminution of the 'better class' had become so serious that 'noble' targets were set. At least 60 per cent of all new officers were to be of aristocratic family. As a counterbalance, 60 per cent of all non-commissioned officers were to come from rural areas so as to exclude the unsuitable democratic elements more likely among city recruits.[5] This Prussian military exclusiveness continued throughout the war. It was not until 1919 that the army accepted that the *Abitur* should be a necessary admission criteria for its officers.[6]

> [Charakter] *was also stereotypically masculine. The virtues it touted were hardness, decisiveness, strength, obedience and control. Under this scheme of things the merits of diplomacy and politics were suspect as manifestations of indecision or weakness. The overvaluation of military manliness predisposed a contingent within the entourage to vigorous or bellicose policies. This was equally if not more true for men who feared that they did not measure up to the masculine ideal. Wilhelm himself is the most perfect single example of this paradox.*[7]

Dash and daring was no longer enough among the *Seeoffiziere, the* executive sea officers. As the modern ships built under the First Navy Law of 1898 neared completion, the navy, even more than the army, required great numbers of skilled technicians to manage rapid mechanisation and technical advances, especially in range-finding, gun-sighting and gun-firing. Officers needed to be better educated and trained and, sad to say, education was not a high priority among the junior sons of the Prussian nobility.

Bildung gradually won the day, but *Charakter* was the long-term victor. In 1894, some 40 per cent of naval cadets possessed the *Abitur*. Between 1898 and 1905, the percentage of *Abituriente* of each annual intake more than doubled until, by 1909, it reached 75 per cent.[8] By the start of the war, this had increased to about 90 per cent. If a young man with military leanings did not have his 'high school certificate', then the navy was a declining option. Admiral Prince Henry of Prussia, younger brother to the Kaiser and later to be Georg Gerth's commanding officer in the Baltic, acknowledged the problem, but not the reason that lay behind it. As so often with the nobility, birthright was the factor which trumped competence. Henry led the resistance to a better-educated officer corps. He feared 'creating two classes' of officer: the number of less well-educated recruits from 'good old families' would reduce if preference was given to those better trained to handle the complexities of an up-to-date fleet 'but who do not bring with them the upbringing or the [necessary] ethical and social attitudes'. Behind it all was the fear that the more recruits that were accepted from the less desirable elements of society, the greater would be the reluctance of desirable families to send their sons to the navy. The fleet would be in social decline and down that long road lay potentially undesirable political consequences like egalitarianism and democracy.

Once entered and embraced by young cadets, the autocratic prejudice of the officer corps made it difficult to escape the intellectual consequences. The tentacles of monarchical dedication were far-reaching, especially when, in the case of Wilhelm II, the subject of the sworn obligation was so evidently blemished. Finding human flaws, which then must be ignored or covered up, required paradoxically an increased level of commitment in order to turn a blind eye and to carry on. It was a recipe for future trouble. In the view of a British observer, the 'whole navy without exception [was] absolutely devoted to [the Kaiser], not only as their emperor but also particularly in a personal sense.'[9] The excellent historian of the Imperial cadet corps, Herwig, made the telling observation that 'lingering emotional attachment to the corps on the part of former officers of both Wilhelm II's *Kaiserliche Marine* and Adolf Hitler's *Kriegsmarine* have made the study of naval personnel policies a sensitive undertaking for German historians'.[10]

The Kaiser's personal influence was, for better of worse, of paramount importance. He saw himself and tried to act as the embodiment of naval service by nurturing a paternalistic relationship with his fleet.[11] On 1 January 1900, as Tirpitz's great expansion was getting underway, the Kaiser made a famous, emotional, if disjointed, declaration of mission in an address to the naval officers of the Berlin garrison:

> And as my grandfather did for the Army, so I will, for my Navy, carry on unerringly and in similar manner the work of reorganisation so that it may also stand on an equality with my armed forces on land and so that through it the German empire may also be in a position abroad to attain that place which it has not yet reached.[12]

In fact, what Wilhelm did was in almost every important way less useful than the work of his grandfather, Friedrich III. Habitually wearing the uniform of an admiral of one navy or another, Wilhelm involved himself in many aspects of his navy, from policy to everyday routines which, in other navies, were dealt with at much lower levels of command. 'In the early days this was excused as innovative and caused some stir.' Every new entrant was personally mulled over before final acceptance. Regular case reviews of the Honour Courts, summary trials of officers charged with offences against the Code of Service Discipline, reveal just how closely Wilhelm monitored the comportment of even his most junior officers. The Kaiser's judgement on minor cases of immorality and offence to the officer class invariably meant dismissal from the navy. 'The message was clear: naval service meant personal and prestigious service.'

This need to meddle in most things, but to direct nothing, came to a head in 1909 when Tirpitz gained the Kaiser's approval to dissolve the navy's supreme command. The result was that a dozen naval institutions reported directly to a new structure that Tirpitz was able to control because the Kaiser was unable to lead.[13] This fundamental point is supported by many historians. Wilhelm's 'significance lay less in the imposition of an autocratic will than in a chronic failure of leadership'.[14]

> *Wilhelm's daily routine vacillated around the navy, world power politics, domestic policy, travel, historical paintings and card games. Whoever was able to gain the Emperor's ear usually got what he wanted. One day he commanded the navy to build more u-boats, the next day to construct new battleships. He intervened sporadically down to the lowest level in every naval affair. Weak nerves and hysteria, an inability to perform serious and disciplined work, and a notorious reluctance to make difficult decisions, hindered the monarchy from effective leadership of the navy. During a war this could only have catastrophic results.*[15]

The advance of the *Abituriente* gradually altered the language of those serving officers outside the high command. Their war interests reflected social origins; their fathers were, in the main, senior civil servants, merchants, academicians, bankers, pastors and ex-officers. The concerns of the new breed lay less in traditional territorial gains to the east of Prussia; they talked instead of naval bases, oil concessions, commercial agreements and overseas trading posts.[16] These were the aims of an industrious class of merchants and entrepreneurs. The strong bourgeois element in the *Seeoffizierekorps* also placed the young officers at the forefront of the anti-England wing because they thought of the fleet as an instrument of economic expansion. Like their Supreme War Lord, they developed an 'ambivalent relationship with perfidious Albion' as competitor, target and model.[17]

However, while the background of the new intakes may have provided some commercial differentiation, there was a disturbing social downside. 'The non-noble officers reacted to the aristocrats in their ranks by trying to ape the airs of the feudal Junker class, by looking down upon their social inferiors, and by cultivating an excessively gruff and somewhat ludicrous military tone.'[18] Horn found in his study of the 1918 mutiny of the high seas fleet that the 'less desirable' officers abandoned their former liberalism and their approval of social mobility and anxiously closed ranks with the aristocracy to protect themselves against infiltration by the 'lower classes'. The naval officer corps, although the 'special representative of the bourgeoisie in the armed service', quickly took on the 'characteristics of aristocratic privilege'.[19] It was a trait recognised by Padfield, the biographer of the future *Führer*, Karl Dönitz, of the 'Crew of 1910'.[20] He found that over time there was a drive to ...

> ... *foster social exclusiveness by stamping the cadets with the style of the Prussian Army officer; this meant adopting harsh, high rather nasal barking, a deliberately crude, often ungrammatical mode of speech, a prickly concern for personal and caste honour – the duel, the Kaiser's consent to marry, the Court of Honour to try breaches of the code of chivalry, particularly with regard to the duel and relationships with unsuitable women, and on board ship the insistence on exaggerated marks of deference from specialist officers, petty officers and ratings to the person of the élite executive officer.*

Erich was in the 'Crew of '05', as each year's intake class was called. There were 319 applications for 160 places; 159 were accepted and of these 55 per cent had the *Abitur*.[21] In other words, *Charakter* and *Bildung* were almost in balance. In 1907, Georg's Crew year, there were 372 applications for 190 places with 189 chosen. As with Erich's crew, the same proportion, 55 per cent, had passed their *Abitur* suggesting the educational tide was about to turn. Eleven per cent were from noble families, mainly from the lower, relatively impoverished Prussian aristocracy, 66 per cent were from Prussia, and, among the fathers of the rest, ninety were academicians, fifty-two officers of the rank of Colonel or higher, thirty-four merchants or manufacturers, ten estate owners, and ten professionals. Potential Jewish officers were not tolerated other than in the rare cases when they had been baptised. Less than 3 per cent of Georg's crew were from lower social circles like the Gerths. The applicants for 1907 even drew a comment from the interview board who found that they 'left much to be desired with respect to social origins'; eighteen were rejected out-of-hand and a further nineteen still to be processed were 'doubtful'.[22] Undesirable applicants were told that the year's quota had already been filled.

The Gerths were more than just fortunate in climbing this most difficult social hill. Admission by middle-class families could be bolstered through letters of recommendation from high government officials or noble friends. Somewhere in the background, there had to be a guiding hand to encourage the Gerth boys in their choice and determination, someone with sufficient status to make acceptance even thinkable. There are a number of possibilities. There is the chance of an unknown 'outside-the-family' benefactor. Perhaps the school played a role? Despite the concern by the selection authorities at the low social class of many applicants, it still needed to fulfil a notional quota from the 'new' Germany. Two fatherless young men, evidently keen and educationally qualified, were appropriate porthole dressing. From within the family, there were three possibilities. Erich and Georg had two suitable uncles. One, Heinrich, was a senior royal judicial counsellor In Berlin, but who died in 1897 before their cadetship. The other, Carl, was a dragoon officer in a Prussian artillery brigade whose longevity and fate are not known. Either could have left appropriate connections. The third option was Richard Leinecker of Würzburg who in 1869 married Heinrich's daughter, Anna, first cousin to the Gerth boys. This was a close cross-family relationship as shown by Georg Gerth's own marriage to Anna's daughter after the war. Richard was a career soldier, an *Oberstleutnant*, a lieutenant colonel, in the Royal Bavarian Army, a respecter of *Abitur*, and of sufficient rank to be accepted by the naval selection process. If, additionally, the Gerths' widowed mother was able to fund the required financial commitment through her inheritance and property sales then the social hill had been climbed. Family leaders were obliged to pledge in writing per young man approximately 8,000 Reichsmarks over four years, almost £40,000 or 44,000 Euro at a current approximate value.[23] All that remained was to pass the formal entrance criteria.

In a remarkable parallel, the background and qualifications of Karl Dönitz, future leader of the u-boats in World War II and final Führer of the Third Reich, were similar to the Gerths. They were all Berlin-born with grandfathers who ran an apothecary corner shop, and with uncles in law and in the military.[24] Dönitz's education and school qualified him for entry, but his social status only just made the grade.[25] The decision to admit Dönitz and the Gerths rested initially with the Sea Cadet Entrance Commission, which deliberated in private without minutes or the necessity to reveal its reasons.

Much of the information on the cadet selection process and training comes from two surviving contemporary manuals: *Instructions for the replenishment of the naval officer corps with regulatory statutes*, 1909, and *Instructions for the training of naval cadets on the school ships*, 1910. Both training booklets were published by the Imperial Navy Office in Berlin through the firm of Mittler & Sohn, purveyor of books to the royal court. Today, Mittler are a giant of German publishing. Their Berlin publishing house in 1910 was at Kochstraße 68–72 next door to the Gerth boys' Kaiser Wilhelm Realgymnasium at Kochstraße 66.

Cadet admissions were once a year, generally in May, by written application submitted in the last three months of the year before. Candidates were recommended to spend at least six months at Oxford, Cambridge or Grenoble to prepare for language tests; there is no evidence of the Gerths following this advice although Georg was noted in later life for speaking 'Oxford English'. Potential cadets were invited for personal interview and medical examination at the Navy School in Kiel.[26] The general knowledge anticipated in the entry exam included English and French, writing, translation, reading comprehension, and 'fluent free speaking'; maths; natural sciences, mainly physics; and technical drawing and sketching. Documentary evidence was required: a birth certificate;

a personal details form, with name, nationality and *curriculum vitae* and whether both parents were still alive; father's name, status, place of residence; mother's name and maiden name; a statement of religion with certificates of baptism and confirmation; a list of any relatives in the army or navy; details of education including annual school and *Abitur* reports; a certificate proving the ability to swim continuously for thirty minutes; medical and dental certificates; and a commitment to provide the finances for training, equipment, uniform and day-to-day expenses.

General Albrecht von Stosch, who held the portfolio of Ministry of Marine in 1872, and his successor, Count Leo von Caprivi, also an army general, instilled the junior service with the military *esprit de corps* and transferred to it the drill and regulations of the Prussian Army.[27] The next three leaders until 1897 were, at least, admirals. Admiral Ludwig von Schröder, the hard man of the later Flanders coastal command, Georg's future commanding officer, announced to cadets, 'The military leader does not need intelligence but *Charakter*'. *Charakter* was built by courses on horseback riding, one hour per week; dancing, two hours; and visits to local theatres and concerts. The cadets' commander organised the curriculum and supervised the training while his first officer supervised practical training, checked progress and dealt with deficiencies. The junior naval cadet officer was the personal tutor who also controlled the individual's 'economic situation and clothing matters' and looked after 'personal interests and provided advice and care'. Physical agility and practical skills, especially when handling weapons, were important. 'A simple way of life should be seen as a virtue.'

> *The officers* [charged with training] *sought to inculcate the ethos and standards of the service. Personal decency, appearance and bearing were the highest priority; the Imperial Navy was very much the junior service, a parvenu, and exhibited all the characteristics of the parvenu. The compulsions of its officers were to be in attitude and conduct more noble than the nobility of the sword. Duty fulfilment was the highest moral value – the Kantian principle of the Categorical Imperative, an 'unconditional moral obligation which is binding in all circumstances and is not dependent on a person's inclination or purpose'. Do nothing that offends against the moral basis of good behaviour.*[28]

After six weeks' basic infantry training, the cadets were sent to school ships for the rest of the first year.

> *Dönitz and fifty-four others went to the training cruiser* Hertha. *Here, during a cruise in the Mediterranean, they learned the basic sailors' skills practically about the ship and in the boats, also acquiring a grounding in navigation, gunnery and engine room practice – and spending three debilitating weeks stoking the boilers. It was a strenuous*

regime deliberately made in the nature of an ordeal. They had to learn
in just over ten months what officers in the Royal Navy, who entered at
thirteen, picked up over five years.[29]

The most famous of Erich's fellow cadets in the Crew of '05 was Wilhelm
Canaris, future head of the *Abwehr*, the Nazi military intelligence. Both
were the only ones in their years of their prominent schools to join the
navy.[30] The influence of Canaris extended considerably over Erich Gerth's
war and beyond and, through his family, into the 1930s. As training lasted
three-and-a-half years, there was plenty of time for the 159 chosen trainees
to get to know each other. However, Wilhelm and Erich were thrown
together even more closely. After a few weeks of infantry training, Canaris
and Gerth were part of the sixty-strong group assigned to the fully rigged
training ship *SMS Stein* where they lived cheek by jowl for almost a year.
Georg Gerth's assignment two years later was aboard the school ship *SMS
Freya*, a converted cruiser. As with Dönitz, it was a harsh regime.

Brutal punishments were still in vogue and practised on the cabin boys,
the nucleus of the future petty officer corps, who were also trained in
these school ships. Flogging was still common and for minor breaches
of the regulations cabin boys were still tied to the mast.[31]

The cadets had to climb each of *Stein*'s three top masts before breakfast.
'They were required to scrub the decks with sand and stone like common
mariners, learned to ward off sleep in standing night watches, were
instructed in reefing and furling and generally handling the ship's rig in
all states of wind and weather.' Training voyages, concentrating on sail,
not steam, took them regularly into the North Sea, and there were trips to
Skagen, Iceland, and to the Mediterranean and into the Atlantic.[32] Training
to become a *Fähnrich zur See*, 'midshipman', an automatic promotion after
one year, focused on tidiness, punctuality, prudence and decisiveness. 'As
future representatives of the military and social elite, the midshipmen were
introduced to the rigorous code of honour of the naval officer corps and
the strict caste system below the *Seeoffiziere*: deck officers at the bottom,
above them torpedo and ordnance officers, then the engineers and finally
at the top were the navigators.'

Daily working hours started at 0545 in harbour, 0620 at sea, with
physical exercises each morning before washing. Shopping, waiters, room
cleaning were provided and when there were no facilities for washing on
land sailors would 'launder the hammocks, bed linen and work clothes of
the cadets for an additional fee'. There were tailors and cobblers on board
the ships who repaired clothing and shoes for a fixed charge. Additional
courses included fencing, gymnastics and swimming. Some unexpected
books were included. As well as an 'emergency' German/English

dictionary, there were English course books, Kron's *The Little Londoner* and *The Little Seaman*, and an English letter writer.[33] Readers included Cradock's *Whispers from the Fleet*; Picard and Freemantle's *Nautical Terms*; and Plunkett's *The Modern Officer of the Watch*, plus international books on war, history, law and dictionaries, and, of course, any authors, like Mahan, chosen personally by the Kaiser.[34]

The midshipmen moved to the naval school for professional sciences for twelve months where the emphasis was on engineering; then a year's preparation for the main examination for executive officer. If successful, and most were, there followed six months of individual courses in gunnery, torpedo warfare and infantry-field practice.[35]

> *Four-berth rooms in the Navy School at Flensburg-Mürwik* [from 1910] *on the coast of Schleswig-Holstein were home for the next year. Here the training was almost entirely theoretical, the main subjects were navigation and seamanship, which included naval regulations; they also learned engineering, gunnery, mining, hydraulics, mathematics, shipbuilding, ship recognition and had an hour a week of French and English.*[36]

At Kiel, the cadets were expected to behave as officers and gentlemen. The Navy School was run with Spartan strictness. Drinking, smoking, gambling, and music-making were forbidden while in quarters. The cadets were only allowed to enter public houses frequented by executive officers.[37] Candidates were advised that emphasis would be on practical training and education of *Charakter* encouraging leadership, promoting a noble mind, polite manners, confidence and respect. When abroad, proficiency in foreign languages was essential and an interest in and understanding of other countries and people was encouraged. Trips also provided a chance for the officers to 'observe the social manners of the cadets and to improve these, if necessary'. 'Every opportunity to visit foreign war ships and interesting technical sites should be taken.'

In the autumn of the fourth year at the passing-out ceremony, cadets swore the oath of allegiance to the Kaiser in the courtyard of the Naval College, were confirmed as a *Leutnant zur See*, and were sent to their naval stations.

Among a long list of nautical instruments, models, fencing and gymnastics equipment, there was a requirement for a *Beobachtungsuhr*, an observation watch. Georg Gerth managed to keep only one possession from his time in the *Kaiserliche Marine*, his *Beobachtungsuhr*, which he wore after World War II on a watch chain. His daughter remembered how he 'wound it every day, three forward turns, two backwards; it was never serviced.'[38] The watch remains a treasured article with the family in 2017. It was made by the *Glashütte* company and is recently dated to the war years when it would have cost about 350 Reichsmarks. *Glashütte* made high precision pocket watches with a particularly easy to read clock face incorporating an oversized second indicator. The double lid is embossed with the Imperial crown; identification codes signify a navy service watch. Those observation watches used in u-boats had radium illuminated faces, which Gerth's does not, and this suggests that it was likely bought for training, to celebrate passing-out in 1910 or, a little later, for use aboard *Amazone*, Georg's first major posting. In 2017, good examples of these watches could cost up to 4,000 Euros.[39]

Many senior officers later claimed that Germany's naval officer service from the time of Tirpitz's dramatic expansion was more open, more liberal, more cosmopolitan and less Prussian.[40] This was barely the case; it acted more as a model of old-German feudal military discipline and snobbish hierarchy that had been extended to cater for some aspiring grammar school boys. For Hans-Ulrich Wehler, the Empire's salient structural face remained the continued social and political predominance of Prussia's landed nobility in a time of rapid industrialisation and social change.[41] The newly unified Germany was a thinly veiled autocracy, a 'military despotism designed to preserve Prussia, its monarchy, and its Junkers supporters'.[42] The Crew of 1912, for example, showed how little had really changed. Among the fathers of those sons enrolled were at least twenty-five noblemen, forty-nine naval and military officers, twelve estate owners, eleven clergymen, sixteen professors or academicians, thirty-five industrialists or merchants and only two farmers.[43]

As soon as the navy's new officer entrants found their bearings, they looked to climb the social ladder, picking up the absurdities of their aristocratic comrades, desperately seeking acceptance, and becoming fanatically loyal to a monarch who was shown at every juncture to have clay feet. Converts to an established way of life can become the more committed adherents. 'The policies of the officer corps consisted on the one side of servility and conspiracy to win influence over the Kaiser, and on the other side of curtailing as much as possible the politics of parliament.'

The treatment by the executive levels of fellow officers, if inferior, was appalling by any measure of modern management. Despite their age, skill and experience, the engineer officers, the deck officers and the medical staff, all of whom actually ran the ships, were 'treated with contempt by regular officers'.[44] The youngest and most inexperienced ensign outranked any engineer officer aboard the ship, even if the engineer was a lieutenant commander. These technically-skilled men, who generally needed twelve to twenty years to achieve their rank, were forbidden any upward social intercourse. The opportunity to enjoy their own meeting rooms or clubs was denied. During the war, when there was a critical shortage of experienced sea officers throughout the navy, not a single deck officer among the hundreds capable of handling such a job was promoted into the officer corps. 'Even the army was more liberal than this.' The isolation of the executive corps was all but complete. If this was the treatment of those officers in the lower classes, then the handling of the ordinary seamen truly was dismissive and feudal.

The outlook of the executive ranks became increasingly constrained. First, Tirpitz suspended the fleet's remit to cruise outside of the North Sea. The cadets were therefore 'deprived of their only chance to come into contact with different peoples, other forms of government and other views of life'. The few remaining cruises took place in the Mediterranean Sea where, as Prince Henry observed, they merely provided the cadets with 'opportunity for corruption and confusion in sexual matters'. In 1910, the navy dropped the requirement for a working knowledge of foreign languages for most sea officers as there was 'no longer a need'. Then, Tirpitz confined his ships to unattractive bases like Kiel and Wilhelmshaven, neither of which provided a 'rich and varied social life or cultural diversions'. At the eve of World War I, the executive officers were 'socially stagnating'. 'The more commands in foreign waters were restricted in the last decade proceeding the outbreak of war, the deeper the executive officer sank with regard to ethics [and] the quicker he dropped to the intellectual level of the army officer.'[45]

As opportunities to mix with outsiders slowly disappeared, these narrow minded young men turned, naturally enough, to drink, gambling and debt. Mess conversations must have been naïve, repetitive and arrogantly self-affirming. Perceived, perhaps sought-after, slights were dealt with by a duelling code that was encouraged. Even the officers' manhood, their bravery, on which so much self-pride would rest, was left to wither by an executive order to remain inactive for most of the war.

The Kaiser further deepened the isolation of his naval officer corps by declaring in 1907 that 'during military education, questions of a social political nature were not to be raised'.[46] 'While this was in keeping with the general principle of keeping politics out of the armed forces, it was to prove a tremendous disadvantage a decade later.' When the fleet faced the problems of the strike in 1917 and the revolt in 1918, officers were pitifully ill-equipped. They 'lacked all of the skills for normal interaction and when faced with a dilemma had only recourse to class superiority and rank'. Continuing attempts were made by the admirals to arrest the spread of socialist ideas among the crews and to stop them attending political meetings in their spare time.[47] These attempts, communicated by their disconnected officers, must have appeared farcical to the men. The navy even forbade its musical concerts from being advertising in socialist party newspapers. Among the wider corps, desperate conversations took place on the possible abolition of universal suffrage and the banning of the Social Democratic Party.

[The officers] *acquired rigid and often narrow-minded views, notably on matters on which they knew next to nothing. One of these was*

> politics. They tended to equate the SPD with 'subversion', Jews with
> either 'social democracy' or 'international finance', and subjects such
> as universal suffrage in Prussia, democracy, or capitalism with
> 'conspiracy'. This reflected their conscious adaptation of the Prussian
> Army officers' prejudiced outlook, a trait composed of snobbism,
> arrogance and ignorance.[48]

When the war was eventually lost and the humiliation of the High Seas
Fleet officers complete, it was no surprise that so many of them turned
to the paramilitary *Freikorps* to continue the fight against, particularly,
the communists. It was the naval *Freikorps* from Kiel and Wilhelmshaven
that took the leadership over their army comrades-in-arms in political
assassinations and brutal suppression, and at the centre of events in
Berlin.[49] It was to be expected that many of these men were leaders in the
practice of denial and deception about the real causes of failure. They also
began and led, even before the first war ended, the covert operations to
prepare a u-boat fleet for the second war to come.

How did Erich and Georg Gerth develop in this maelstrom? Were their
personalities forever warped by their claustrophobic and damaging training?

As the Gerths left the naval college in 1908 and 1910, they entered a
dangerous world in which the burgeoning German fleet played an increasing
role. In the sixteen years preceding the Great War, there were only three
– 1903, 1907 and 1910 – in which there was no crisis that could have
developed into European war.[50] Many of these episodes are long forgotten,
but every year, and all around Erich and Georg, was the sound of martial
drums in exotic places.[51] The American and German fleets clashed in the
Philippines in 1898 during the American war against Spain over Cuban
independence. The United States gained all of Spain's colonies outside of
Africa in the treaty, including the Philippines, Guam and Puerto Rico with
the exception of Cuba, which became a US protectorate. The Kaiser gave
an inflammatory speech in Damascus that same year seeking a foothold
in Persia and threatening British India through an uprising in Turkey.[52]
Britain retreated from the West Indies in 1901 'thanks to which America
was able to make Columbia her satellite and to undertake construction of
the Panama Canal singlehandedly'. At the turn of the twentieth century,
German merchants dominated overseas trade and banking in Venezuela,
Brazil and Argentina. Following a civil war in Venezuela, Krupp's local
railway became central to a debt dispute. Britain, Germany and Italy
implemented a joint blockade in defence of their South American
interests in 1902. Anglo-Franco-Russo alliances hardened through fear
of German designs on the Baltic coast. In 1908, as the Ottoman Empire
began to crumble, Austria-Hungary announced the annexation of Bosnia
and Herzegovina in an action timed to coincide with Bulgaria's declaration
of independence. This resulted in severe regional tensions, particularly

between Russia and Serbia. The annexation, however, provided greater security for the Austro-Hungarian fleet at the ports of Pula and Cattaro, future home for the German Adriatic u-boat fleet of which Dönitz, Canaris and Erich Gerth were submarine commanders in 1918.[53]

The land appropriations which attracted the attention of the German public, and the putative naval cadets, in the pre-war years, and which nudge into the story of the Gerths' development, came from European colonisations following the scramble for Africa. In 1880, the continent was ruled mostly by Africans and was largely unexplored by Europeans. Within twenty-two years, most of the continent had been appropriated by five European nations and by one man, Leopold II, King of the Belgians. Many of these acquisitions quickly descended into atrocities against the local populations: the Belgian use of slave of labour to export valuable cargoes of rubber and ivory from the Congo from 1885 to 1908, the British pursuit of Transvaal gold and a land highway from Cape Town to Cairo in the war against the Dutch Boers between 1899 and 1902, and the German genocide against the Herero and Nama people of modern-day Namibia from 1903 to 1908.[54] Contiguous with these disasters were two other events in North Africa which each almost brought about war. The Germans, possibly seeking a Mediterranean naval base, squared up to French dominance in Morocco, first in 1905 and 1906 and, second, against the deployment of substantial French troops in 1911, known as the Agadir Crisis. In 1905, the Kaiser visited Tangier and reprised his inflammatory visit to Damascus seven years earlier when he toured the city on a white horse and provoked the French by declaring support for the Sultan. There were many other similar African episodes in the period that are not of direct concern, for instance, the machine-gun suppression of the Maji-Maji uprising in 1905 in German East Africa, the Zulu revolt in Natal against the British in 1906, and slavery and wanton wholesale murder in the French Congo in the same year.

A characteristic of all of these demonstrations of European power and greed was the level of disregard for the welfare of the local people, indeed often of their indiscriminate slaughter. They were tribes, black and white, who valued their independence and were bemused and angered by the duplicity and ferocity they faced and, in which, they were often partially complicit. In the wider scheme of money and politics, they were simply in the way.

The second Boer War had a particular effect in the Netherlands and Germany. The maltreatment of their kin helped persuade the Dutch to stay neutral throughout the Great War and allowed, initially at least, a relaxed attitude to trading food and war supplies with the German nation in defiance of the British blockade. The Boer War produced a 'tidal wave of anti-British sentiment in the Reich'. 'The attitude of public opinion in Germany and the language of the German press were violently anti-English, and went far beyond mere unfriendliness.'[55] The Press denounced the British 'buccaneering' adventure, insulted the British Army as a pack of mercenaries, slandered Queen Victoria in gross caricatures, and hailed British reverses with gusto.[56] One cartoon showed the Queen, accompanied by the royal family, presenting the Victoria Cross to a thirteen-year-old soldier because he had 'outraged' eight Boer women.[57] These 'outbursts of feeling' had more effect and caused more disquiet in Great Britain than, for instance, Tirpitz's concurrent plans for the rapid expansion of the Germany Navy.

The South African Boers fought a force three times larger to maintain their independence against the gold grab of the mining magnates. In a clear warning about what would happen if any European power later declared war against Britain, the Royal Navy announced food as contraband and seized cargoes from the United States bound for the Boers before they could enter the neutral port of Lourenço Marquès in Portuguese East Africa. Supplies were reduced to a trickle.[58] Following American protests, the British placed agents in the port buying up all supplies as soon as they were landed. This was a foretaste of British actions in neutral Norway fifteen years later. The British annexation of the internationally recognised republics of Transvaal and Orange Free State was poorly organised and badly provisioned. Death by disease was three times greater than death in battle; the Boers were 'frustratingly brilliant' at reading and using the landscape. Lord Kitchener took command of the embarrassed British forces in November 1900 and 'determined to end the war no matter what it took'.[59]

What it took he thought, were three extreme tactics that he resolutely applied: the removal of the entire civilian population to internment camps; the systematic sweeping of the republics with flying columns, whose job was maximum destruction of property and food; and the erection of a grid of cement blockhouses linked by barbed wire, which was to expand to cover the entire area of the republics.

Selective burning of farms, begun in March 1900 as reprisal, 'swiftly expanded into the wholesale destruction of farms and villages' in a new policy of laying waste. Isolated concentration camps, euphemistically called 'camps of refuge', were built to house Boer women and children. Tens of thousands starved through a mixture of callousness and incompetence, which eventually shocked the western world. Emily Hobhouse became the untiring voice of humanity. 'I call this camp system a wholesale cruelty ... To keep these camps going is to murder the children.'[60] When her report of 1901 with its many recommendations was debated in the House of Commons, Hobhouse, who attended, wrote, 'No barbarism in South Africa could equal the cold cruelty of that indifferent House'.[61]

Every one of those children who died as a result of their halving of their rations, thereby exerting pressure onto their family still on the battlefield, was purposefully murdered. The system of half rations stands exposed, stark and unashamedly as a cold-blooded deed of state policy employed with the purpose of ensuring the surrender of men whom we were not able to defeat on the field.[62]

'Kitchener is not remembered in South Africa for his military victories. His monument is the camps [which] have left a gigantic scar across the minds of the Afrikaners: a symbol of deliberate genocide.'[63] Statistics placed before the British parliament estimated the camp death rate at approaching 12 per cent, which Lloyd George called a 'policy of extermination'.[64] A modern study places the rate at 24 per cent, which reduced to 7 per cent when the camps were removed from military administration and soon thereafter fell to 2 per cent.[65] The war cost 20,000 British lives and £200 million, the Boers lost more than 7,000 men and 28,000 women and children, the indigenous blacks more than 14,000.[66] Joseph Conrad's *Heart of Darkness*, while started in 1897, had imperialism, the Boer War and the Belgian Congo massacres in its sights. Also published in 1902, John Hobson's polemic, *Imperialism: A Study*, was another famous and influential by-product.

In 1901 there was as yet no elaborate general theory of imperialism in existence. Imperialism and anti-imperialism were still sentiments and beliefs of vague and varying content within the British Isles ... The Boer War was more than a local clash of two nations and opposing political and economic interests. It was more than a chapter in history of the industrialisation of Africa. In the career of imperialism, it was an essential turning point. It made the word an international slogan in Europe ... It originated in England.[67]

Among the German-leaning Belgian Foreign Office, and in the country's senior conservative and Catholic circles, there was open resentment of Britain for leading the international campaign at the turn of the century against the 'hideous abuses of their avaricious king, Leopold II, in the Congo'.[68] Leopold was attacked and chased over many years for the slaughter and mutilation knowingly carried out in his name and the charge was led initially by British liberals.

The Congo was a personal state, the property of one capitalist of genius. Leopold had ridden the world's rubber boom like a man on a trapeze ... By 1902, rubber sales had risen fifteen times in eight years and constituted over 80% of exports, worth over £1.64 million. The rubber grew wild and the method of harvesting was cheap ... Leopold did not reinvest his profit in the Congo according to the unwritten code practised in colonies elsewhere to benefit both the natives and the

European investors. Leopold saw no reason why he should ... His own
patrimony, fifteen million francs, £600,000, had been lavished on the
Congo in those grim years when everyone except Leopold thought that
it would go bankrupt. He had put his fortune into the Congo. Now he
intended to reap the benefit.[69]

At the end of the day, there was no proof of malpractice until Edmund
Morel, a clerk by day in the West African office of the Liverpool shipping
line Elder Dempster, and a writer of growing repute by night for prestigious
journals like the *Pall Mall Gazette* and *The Speaker*, fell upon the evidence in
his company's ledgers. Vast quantities of rubber were reaching the Antwerp
market, but there was no corresponding export to the Congo to pay for it,
except guns, chains, ordnance and explosives for the Belgian traders and
military. The natives were not paid to bring the rubber out of the jungle.
'The officials must be using forced labour, beating and shooting the rubber
out of them.' Morel discovered that the King's well-regarded philanthropy in
Belgium was founded on systemic 'legalised robbery enforced by violence'.
Morel said that he was 'giddy and appalled' ... 'It must be bad enough to
stumble upon a murder. I had stumbled upon a secret society of murderers
with a King for a croniman.'[70] Morel produced a privately-funded, heavily
detailed and argued exposé in 1903, *The Congo Slave State*, in a determined
effort to keep the pressure on the British Government to take action using
international treaties.

Almost never has one man, possessed of no wealth, title, or official post,
caused so much trouble for the governments of several major countries.
Morel knew that officials like foreign secretary Sir Edward Grey would
act only 'when kicked, and if the process of kicking is stopped, he will do
nothing'. To this kicking, Morel devoted more than a decade of his life.[71]

The result on one bout of 'kicking' was that the British Consul for the Congo,
Roger Casement, was to travel to the interior, 160 miles by fever-ridden
river above Leopoldville to where the rubber zone began, and to make a
full report. Casement became known as the 'father of twentieth-century
human rights investigations' and was honoured in 1905 for his report on
Leopold's atrocities.[72] He was knighted in 1911 for his investigations into
human rights abuses in Peru and was hanged by the British in 1917 for his
war-time support, with German backing, of Irish independence.[73]

While the killing in the Congo was of 'genocidal proportions, it was not
strictly speaking, a genocide'.[74] Leopold's men were looking for labour
and in the course of that search, deaths were by-products. Few officials
kept statistics of something 'considered so negligible as African lives':
babies thrown into the long grass to die so that their mothers could carry
commercial loads, rape without end, villages erased for failing to provide

rubber quotas and men lined up so that they could all be shot with a single bullet. The all-pervasive image was the bounty paid for tens of thousands of hacked-off hands of all sizes to show punishment had been duly done.[75] Chronicler of the events, Adam Hochschild, estimated in 1999 that the death tally was about ten million; a Congolese scholar, Isidore Ndaywel è Nziem, who published in the same year, thought perhaps half of the population, about thirteen million died.[76] One Belgium military gentleman whose involvement was closely criticised was General Jules Jacques, 1st Baron Jacques de Dixmuide, who was so insulted when his cavalry were mocked about the 'capture' of Georg Gerth's u-boat in 1917.[77]

The protest became international involving, particularly, the United States. Leopold twisted and turned as he sought to safeguard his plunder. Eventually he dodged his pursuers by giving his private Congo to the Belgian state for a substantial pay off. The affair became embroiled in preparations for the likely European conflict. One of the biggest secrets of World War I was claimed to be a military pact that Britain made with Belgium in 1906 as the price for Britain acknowledging the Belgian state's 'annexation' of Leopold's Congo.[78] Belgium declared that she was ready to fight anyone who invaded – German, French or British.[79] All three considered it even though the five-power Treaty of London of 1839 'guaranteed' a concerted reaction to threats to Belgian's independence. But, what was one of them, Russia or Austria, many hundreds of miles away, to do if another signatory, say Prussia, made the attack to defeat a third, France.[80] France had violated or laid plans to 'violate Belgium's sovereignty twenty times throughout her history'.[81] Soon after the end of the war, King Albert I, Leopold's son, accused the French premier of admitting that he 'deeply regretted' not invading Belgium in 1914. The invaded Belgian territory quickly housed the German u-boat base at Bruges which was Georg Gerth's base from 1916 to 1917.

> *The start of the war was all predicated on a myth: the myth of Belgian neutrality. From 1906 onwards, Britain's military link with Belgium was one of the most tightly guarded secrets*[82] *... Britain's director of military operations, Sir Henry Wilson, spent the summer months of 1906 reconnoitring the Belgian countryside on his bicycle, taking careful notes of the lie of the land, canals, railway crossings and church towers that would one day serve as observation posts. A gigantic map of Belgium, indicating the routes armies might follow, covered the entire wall of his London office.*[83]

Ewart, the contemporary Canadian lawyer, in his impressive though often disregarded forensic investigation of the causes of the war, thought Britain's indignation about 'plucky little Belgium' was most likely a convenient political smokescreen for a long-term intention to join a war when it came. In the days before the war declaration, Britain first accepted only the necessity of using the Royal Navy to protect the northern coasts of France.[84] Within twenty-four hours, the cabinet agreed to intervene only if there was a 'substantial' violation of Belgian neutrality. Parliamentary indignation all but disappeared within a year as the British government sought to justify its military actions. However, moral concern did provide the legal nicety for war.[85] 'The first German footfall in Belgium salvaged the situation.'[86] Bertrand Russell, Avner Offer and Isabel Hull summarised:

> *National law is designed to suppress violence, but the main purpose of international law is in actual fact to afford the sort of pretext which is considered respectable for engaging in war with another Power. A Great Power is considered unscrupulous when it goes to war without previously providing itself with such a pretext.*[87]

> *The record of international war in the first world war, and of maritime law in particular, suggests its primary function, which was to provide a casus belli. No infringement of the law could actually force a nation into war against its better judgement. But if statesmen wanted to fight, then international law provided the justification. It allowed belligerents to don the garments of legality. No-one compelled Britain to intervene when Belgium was invaded. Britain did so on a point of law.*[88]

> *Military necessity and the laws of war are on opposite ends of a seesaw – the more power you grant to military necessity, the less the law applies or is obligatory, so the stakes are very high.*[89]

Erich Gerth had a standard introduction to life as a junior navy officer undertaken while reports from the Congo filled the newspapers. His final training months were spent on the ageing battleship *Kaiser Karl der Grosse* until May 1908 when the ship was decommissioned in Kiel and sent to the Baltic reserve, made obsolete by the new dreadnoughts.[90] During his time with *Kaiser Karl der Grosse*, Erich participated in the normal peacetime routine of training cruises and fleet manoeuvres. There was a summer cruise in 1907 in the North Sea, returning to the Baltic via the Kattegat. This was followed by the regular cruise to Norway in July. During the autumn manoeuvres, which lasted from August to early September, landing exercises were conducted in northern Schleswig. The winter training cruise went into the Kattegat in November. In May 1908, the fleet went on an exercise into the Atlantic instead of its normal restricted voyage in the North Sea. Erich's first fully-fledged posting was to the light cruiser *Königsberg* where he stayed as one of fourteen officers until at least May 1910. The *Königsberg* served with the High Seas Fleet's reconnaissance force and frequently escorted the Kaiser's yacht, *Hohenzollern*, on formal visits including Heligoland in March 1910 and the funeral of King Edward VII in May that year. This was the celebrated Parade of Kings, when over fifty royal horsemen, a 'swaggering cavalcade of emperors, kings, crown princes, archdukes, grand dukes and princes', followed the slowly trundling coffin through the streets of London. The commander of *Königsberg* from December 1909 to September 1910 was Fregattenkäpitan Adolf von Trotha, who had a significant influence on Eric's career in Berlin after the war.[91] Trotha and Gerth successfully escaped censure when the *Königsberg* collided with another light cruiser, the brand new *Dresden*, in February 1910 in Kiel Harbour, even though significant damage was caused to both ships. The *Dresden*, with Erich's fellow cadet Canaris as adjutant, was the ship sunk by the British at the Chilean island of Más-a-Tierra in 1915 after the Battle of the Falklands.[92] Gerth followed this appointment with a few months in a land-based artillery detachment, a customary pattern of alternating ship and shore commands.[93] In 1911, he left for South America to become a spy.[94]

Georg Gerth's first seagoing appointment was for just over two years, until the end of 1911, on the *Preußen*, a pre-dreadnought battleship and 'good sea boat'. *Preußen* was a result of Tirpitz's 1898 Naval Law and was commissioned into the fleet in 1905. During Gerth's service she was stationed in Wilhelmshaven and Kiel as part of the II Battle Squadron.[95] Gerth then spent the whole of 1912 in a coveted posting aboard the *Panther* on the West African station. *Panther* was one of six Iltis-class gunboats built for service in Germany's colonies with a range of just under 4,000 miles and a complement of nine officers and 121 crew. *Panther* had an interesting early career in a number of trouble spots. The year of her commissioning, 1902, she sank a Haitian rebel ship which had hijacked a German steamer carrying weapons to the Haitian government. A few months later, she took part in the naval blockade of Venezuela where later she bombarded Fort San Carlos near Maracaibo. *Panther* received considerable damage in return fire from, ironically, the Krupp gun within the fort and was forced to retire. In 1905, *Panther* sent men ashore to search for a German deserter at the Brazilian port of Itajahy, where, somewhat farcically, they kidnapped the wrong man. The incident became known as the 'Panther Affair'. In 1911, *Panther* became notorious when she was sent to Agadir during the Second Moroccan Crisis. The ship's mission was to apply pressure on the French as they attempted to colonise Morocco, and also to extract compensation in French Equatorial Africa for Germany's loss of influence in North Africa. By the time of Gerth's service in 1912, the boat's duties took her to Togo, the Cameroons and to South-West Africa, all seized by the Germans in 1884, where she paraded as a statement of naval might. In one of the few memories of this time, Christa-Maria, Georg's daughter, remembers her father describing African huts and the general living conditions of the natives.

Georg Gerth travelled to join *Panther* at the beginning of 1912, probably aboard a steamer of the Woermann Line, one of the largest German shipping companies trading into Africa. Woermann made their early money by supplying cheap potato spirit to African natives and the company used its knowledge of West African ports to advise and assist the German government on the colonial acquisitions of 1884. The firm was also complicit in the South-West African death camps during the Herero and Nama wars.[96] This was Georg's first trip outside Europe and might have been a tug on his emotions and political ideas had he known what he was looking at as he steamed by. The Republic of Liberia began in 1822 as a settlement of the American Colonization Society which believed black people would face better chances for freedom in Africa than in America. Almost 20,000 freed and free-born black people returned to Africa. Liberia declared its independence in 1847, but was not recognised by the USA until 1862 during the American Civil War. Gerth then passed the recently acquired German colonies of Togo and Cameroon and traversed the Bight of Benin and the Guinea coast from where Europeans had bought upwards of ten million slaves. Next came the Belgian Congo, Leopold's previous fiefdom, with atrocities still underway in its interior and, finally, to German South-West Africa which was in the dying days of its own particular genocide.

One might expect a large detachment of the crew of the *Panther*, the symbol of German naval power in the region, to be at Windhoek on 27 January 1912, having travelled by the new slave-built railway from the coast at Swakopmund. It was the Kaiser's birthday, an event 'always celebrated with a degree of patriotic fervour in South-West Africa'. However, this was a special occasion centred on the unveiling of the 'Rider Statue', a *Schutztruppe*, a colonial trooper, in uniform. Around seven o'clock in the morning, before the summer heat, citizens passed along Kaiser-Wilhelmstraße with window displays of imported luxuries, Gartenstraße where hot water springs fed the new swimming pool, and through the Memorial Gardens with its manicured lawns and duck ponds. The main speaker was the new governor, Theodore Seitz, who explained that the statue was to honour the dead and to encourage the living to build on what had been a hard war, 'fought selflessly for the love of the Fatherland' against the native population. The venerated soldier announced to the world that 'we are masters of this place, now and for ever'.[97]

> *What had once been the home of the Herero was now a European city in miniature ... The Germans were masters not only of South-West Africa's future, but of its past. Their version of the war had been set in stone and was now cast in bronze. The inauguration of the Rider Statue was the culmination of the process of historical denial and distortion. The brutality of the settlers in the years leading up to the war, General von Trotha's Extermination Order and the concentration camp system were expunged from official history.[98]*

The Herero were cattle herders in the area known as Damaraland; their southern neighbours and traditional enemies were the pastoral Nama, related to the Hottentot. In 1883, Franz Lüderitz fraudulently bought a stretch of coast from the local chieftain. Twenty years of inter-tribal fighting, skirmishes with German settlers, and various broken treaties resulted in some of the Nama under Henrik Witbooi rising against the Germans in 1903, mainly over land rights. By this time, the Herero were seen by many Germans as cattle thieves and a source of slave labour while others called for their extermination.[99] The Herero rebellion, under paramount chief Samuel Maharero, began in January 1904 along the railway line from the coast to Windhoek.[100] There is good evidence that the bitter fighting that followed was sparked by a Lieutenant Ralph Zürn, the local station commander, who was renowned for his 'utter contempt for the Herero'. Herero fighters pursued unpunished German rapists, killed settlers in their beds, burned farms and the German garrisons were 'desperately assailed'. *Panther*'s predecessor, the gunboat *Habicht*, landed eighty-five marines; 500 marine volunteers followed in February and twenty-seven of these were killed in the fighting.

Kaiser Wilhelm sent General Lothar von Trotha, 'man enough not to let moral or political qualms cloud his judgement', to crush the revolt 'by fair means or foul'. When the civilian governor Hermann von Wissmann learned that Trotha was being considered as commander, he tried to prevent the appointment. He called Trotha 'a bad leader, a bad African, and a bad comrade'.[101] After murderous service in East Africa, Trotha was in China as part of the international force to quell the Boxer Uprising. He was present at the public execution of the assassins of German ambassador Baron Wilhelm von Ketteler in Peking and led the punitive expedition to the Ming graves to punish Boxers for murdering Chinese Christians.

By August, most of the Herero had concentrated in a strategic dead end, the Waterberg plateau, a stony upland on the western edge of the Omaheke sandveld, leading to the great Kalahari desert. The Battle of Waterberg was deliberately indecisive and the Herero escaped through a gap carefully left in Trotha's net. When the Herero had been hustled into the desert, Trotha sealed off the last waterhole to ensure they died of thirst.

> *A great number, especially the old, ill and women and children, died of starvation and thirst as they ran for their lives through the desert. But a great many were also shot to death, for the conduct of the war changed with the Battle of Waterberg. The brutal potential of colonial war, sporadically evident now burgeoned into methodical regularity ... Trotha issued orders that no quarter was to be given to the enemy. No prisoners were to be taken, but all, regardless of age or sex, were to be killed. Trotha said, 'We must exterminate them, so that we won't be bothered with rebellions in the future' ... 'The Germans killed thousands*

and thousands of women and children along the roadsides … I saw this
every day.' After the battle, Trotha assembled the few prisoners and
hanged the men.[102]

In October, Trotha issued his infamous Extermination Order 'of which
there are few parallels in modern European history outside of the Third
Reich':

I, the Great General of the Mighty Kaiser, von Trotha, address this letter
to the Herero people. The Herero are no longer considered German
subjects. They have murdered, stolen, cut off ears and other parts from
wounded soldiers, and now refuse to fight on, out of cowardice. I have
this to say to them … the Herero people will have to leave the country.
Otherwise I shall force them to do so by means of guns … Every Herero
whether found armed or unarmed, with or without cattle will be shot. I
shall not accept any more women or children. I shall drive them back.

The Germans then turned their attention to a short war with the Nama.
Late in 1906, after three days in the fetid hold of a Woermann Line
steamer, 2,000 Nama prisoners were offloaded at Lüderitz and marched
in single file along the narrow causeway to Shark Island to join the
thousand existing Herero inmates. It was a concentration camp, rather an
extermination camp, one of six across the country, of the utmost brutality,
without facilities, a place where the captive local population was taken to
be worked and starved to death and which they did at a daily body count
of over twenty. The camp was plainly visible to the white inhabitants of
Lüderitz. An industry developed around the supply of body parts. 'In the
Swakopmund concentration camp in 1905, female prisoners were forced
to boil the severed heads of their own people and scrape the flesh off the
skulls with shards of broken glass'.[103] The camp physician at Shark Island,
Dr Hugo Bofinger, used the inmates for his studies into scurvy, a condition
that was endemic in the camp.[104] He injected his living subjects with a
range of substances, including arsenic and opium, and then performed
autopsies to gauge the results. Bofinger also sealed skulls preserved in
alcohol in tins for export to the Institute of Pathology at the University
of Berlin where they were used by racial scientist Christian Fetzer in
experiments designed to demonstrate the anatomical similarities between
the Nama and the anthropoid ape. Shark Island can certainly be placed in
the same sentence as Auschwitz and Buchenwald.

Georg Gerth would have known some of the horror of his South-West
African destination from spirited public debate in Germany. In 1906, Georg
Lebedour, a deputy of the Social Democratic party, raised the issue of the
Shark Island death camp in the Reichstag.[105] Debates in 1906 and 1907
'about the annihilation of some of the natives and the total slavery of others'

led to a bitter impasse and the defeat of the colonial budget. There was genuine horror at the activities of the government and the army in South-West Africa. The Reichstag elections of 1907 were fought on a single issue, South-West Africa.[106] It became known as the 'Hottentot election', so called because of the nationalist atmosphere whipped up by the Pan-Germans during the campaign. The Social Democrats gained half a million votes and yet lost half of their seats. The remainder of the Herero population was reduced by 1907 to about 20 per cent of its size and was living out of sight in desert camps when Gerth arrived in 1912; they were 'discovered' in 1915 by 'shocked' South African troops when they invaded the colony.[107]

From Zurich, Christian philosopher and pacifist, F. W. Förster, warned that the world was entering a new era of wars; the new conflicts were radically different from the old type of war. 'They arose in the midst of industrial power and science. Their political doctrine was imperialism, the doctrine of the military conquest and economic exploitation of weaker races. The American war against Spain and the British war against the Boers were mere preludes of the new imperialist era and its devastating conflicts.'[108]

After a year on the West Africa Station, Gerth left at the beginning of 1913 for the Baltic and a tour aboard the torpedo training ship, *Württemberg*. His return, presumably, included some time on leave in Berlin to see his mother and to give her some African gifts.

Visitors to Berlin, over a million of them in 1913, found a city full of nervous, unchannelled energy; a city wrapped in itself in the mantle of the German Reich but which was, inside, still the provincial capital of Prussia; a city which was reckoned the most modern in Europe, an industrial powerhouse and a capital of science; a city on parade.[109]

In late July, Chancellor Theobald von Bethmann Hollweg lost control of policy to the experts on the German General Staff. 'Their calculations were not political but military, and their decisions and requirements precipitated the world war.'[110] Germany began battle without war aims. Historian Fischer in his thoroughly documented study of German objectives thought the war represented a 'deep-rooted drive to turn Germany into a world power'.[111] The outbreak of war in 1914 was essentially a tragedy of miscalculation. Unbothered by political complexities, the military's single goal was complete military victory, but the country was not in a good position for a long conflict. 'Her industrial combines demanded massive quantities of diverse imported raw materials to continue production, just as her peoples demanded massive amounts of imported food.'[112] The navy that would have to protect the sea-lanes was untried in warfare and was inferior in strength to the Entente navies should Britain choose to join the war. There had been no joint planning with the army: the Admiralty was a closed corporation, its war plan nebulous in the extreme, its command ranks split almost beyond repair. On 31 July, the Imperial War Department placed the navy on alert. More than 250 units readied themselves: thirty-eight battleships, forty cruisers, and more than 170 destroyers, torpedo boats and others. The twenty-four submarines were a small fraction of the fleet.[113] The Imperial Navy's main combat strength lay in its capital ships of the High Seas Fleet in Wilhelmshaven. But, by Imperial order, the fleet was to remain passive. There would be no sorties in search of battle. Submarines, minelayers and torpedo boats were to generate enemy losses until reaching Tirpitz's goal, a balance of power with the Royal Navy.[114] In his capacity as Secretary, Tirpitz was not concerned with naval operations, but because of his renown a special decree on 30 July 1914 granted him the right to give his opinion to the Kaiser.

The declarations of war against Serbia and Russia and then France and Britain early next month was followed by an upsurge of popular nationalism later affectionately known as the 'August Days'.

> [This was a period in which] *differences of class, confession, and religion seemed erased and the people, the Volk, appeared to be all of one mind ... Both Left and Right looked back beyond the Weimar and remembered the exemplary national unity achieved at the beginning of the war. In ordinary conversations, neighbourhood festivals and war memorial services, Germans reportedly turned over the memory of August 1914 and vividly remembered this uplifting side to war, the unforgettable experience of the crowds, the heartfelt departures at train stations, the intimate community of the front lines.*[115]

Hitler reported that the declaration of war produced a sense of Germanness that filled him in Munich with ecstasy. Hitler amazingly picked himself out in 1930 'in the moment' of crowd enthusiasm in a photograph by Heinrich Hoffmann. For the rest of his life, Hitler 'struggled to retrieve the unshakable union based on ethnic-based nationalism and public self-sacrifice'. In his eyes, the summer of 1914 was memorable because it had created a new and crucial subject, the German *Volk*, unencumbered by past history or inequities and finally unified to claim its Imperial destiny.

> *Kaiser Wilhelm greeted the war in an enthusiastic speech in Berlin on the first day of August. 'The streets of Berlin were thronged with crowds, singing and cheering for war,' the American ambassador, James Gerard, reported. 'An order was given that all communications including letters, telegrams and telephonic conversations must be in German, and that only German should be spoken on the street. After explaining how war had been forced on Germany, the Kaiser told his audience 'to go to church and pray'.*[116] *In Berlin, open-air services were held, thousands and thousands attending.*[117] *The Kaiser ended his*

speech with a peroration that swept the empire. 'For my part there are no more political parties, for me there are only Germans.' Three days later in the Reichstag, he continued, 'We are not driven by the pleasure of conquest; an inflexible will inspires us to reserve what God has given us for ourselves and for all future generations ... With a clear conscience and with clean hands we take up arms in self-defence that has been forced upon us. Aggressive neighbours must be defeated.' The army held centre stage. 'Soldiers marching to their trains were buried beneath garlands of flowers and flowers dangled from the cavalry lances as the dragoons marched down Unter den Linden in the rain.'

However, as many, if not more, Berliners demonstrated against the war as for it. On Tuesday 28 July, perhaps 100,000 working-class people attended Social Democrat meetings, held mostly in the outlying proletarian neighbourhoods of the metropolis.

As these ended, around nine in the evening, smaller parades pressed into the city centre in an attempt to 'desacralize' the national sites at which the patriots had gathered three days earlier. For the most part the marchers were blocked by the police under the strict usual orders to keep what the government considered to be subversive Social Democrats away from Unter den Linden and the Schloss. Nonetheless, several thousand anti-war demonstrators managed to slip through police lines. Their parades provoked mostly bourgeois merrymakers sitting in cafés in the well-remembered Sängerkreig, 'singing competition', in which choruses of the workers' anthem The Marseillaise *interrupted patriotic renditions of* The Watch of the Rhine.[118]*

Some citizens were anxious to draw cash before there was a serious run on the banks. It was a week before creditors were reassured. Already food was seen as a problem and Berliners began what was to be a four-year necessity to hoard. 'Grocery stores were mobbed, the prices of flour, potatoes and salt soared.'

The sense of inevitability and the sense of relief, as the crisis mounted and as war came, were partly due to the technical sequence of mobilisation plans and to the fact that politicians, even if they wanted to, could not stop the military machine once it was in motion, and partly to the fact that many of Europe's leaders saw in the international crisis a distraction from internal problems. But it is also due, I suggest, to the fact that by 1914 the ideas of both Darwin and of Nietzsche had become widely assimilated, so that there were many people in Europe, both among rulers and ruled, who thought of life in terms of the struggle for survival, or who were looking for an opportunity to transcend the limitations of their ordinary lives and to find a new set of values in which they believed would be a new and enriching experience.[119]

On 2 August, the Belgian government refused to allow the Germans passage through their country. The German invasion began two days later.

On the fourth of August, several German uhlans, black and white pennants fluttering at the tips of their lances, crossed into Belgian territory. Their passage did not go unnoticed. In a nearby thicket, a Belgian lookout hastily scrawled a few words on a leaf from his notebook and then fastened a message to the leg of a carrier pigeon. The bird took wing, circled the thicket once, and then made for Liège. The First World War was under way.[120]

Four days later, on 8 August, the American ambassador in Brussels, Brent Whitlock, was sent a note by the Germans which repeated a 'solemn assurance that it is not her intention to appropriate Belgium to herself and that such an intention is far from her thoughts. Germany is still ready to evacuate Belgium as soon as the state of war will allow her to do so.'[121] At the discussions at the Treaty of Versailles in 1920, this unprovoked invasion became the great admission of responsibility and guilt accepted by the Germans.

The original great idea, the old Schlieffen Plan, a war on two fronts against both France and Russia, was inherited only in concept from Helmuth von Moltke, the Elder, revered victor of the wars of 1870, and uncle to Moltke the Younger, leader of the coming invasion.[122] As developed by the dysfunctional German general staff, the plan required about sixteen divisions more than the Prussian war ministry in charge of troop strength had provided. 'German army organisation was radically segregated.'[123] Schlieffen understood that Germany could 'only hope to win by relentless attack' and that a complete victory was necessary before the Allies could regroup and 'ultimately make its superior weight felt'.[124] In the west, Schlieffen planned first to swing massive armies through Belgium and the Netherlands, bypassing the main French strength and taking Paris from behind, all within six weeks. Troops would then be transferred by railway to reinforce the eastern front and the slower-moving Russian forces. It would all be over in a few months if focus and momentum were maintained.[125] France would be permanently reduced, suffer seizures and reparations, and by default Germany would control the Channel and Atlantic coastline.

However, in his strategic memorandum, Schlieffen 'never mentions barbed wire, pays little attention to the deadly effect of machine guns, and ignores the French quick-firing 75mm artillery'.[126] 'Farcical over-planning' was provided by his later military followers but no attention to chance and chaos.[127] And, if the French had gone on the defensive and used their machineguns and artillery, instead of walking line abreast Napoleonic-like with bright uniforms into battle, 'the Schlieffen Plan was bound to fail'.[128]

> *The extension of the battlefield, and its apparent emptiness, was a direct consequence of Europe's industrialisation. The principles of breech-loading and rifling in firearms and artillery were finally allied to mass production in the last third of the nineteenth century. In 1815, at Waterloo, the infantry soldier's musket had a minimum effective range of 150 yards and a rate of fire of two rounds a minute; a century later, the infantry rifle could range almost a mile, and, fed by a magazine, could discharge ten or more rounds a minute. A machine-gun, firing on a fixed trajectory, could sweep an area with 400 rounds a minute.*[129]

The Schlieffen Plan was altered late on for fear of Dutch resistance and the likely immediate involvement of the British in support. Schlieffen's successor as chief of the General Staff from 1906, Moltke the Younger, with his aide Erich Ludendorff, gradually rethought. It was not that the Dutch Army was any match for the Germans, but it was of a sufficient size to delay matters critically, allowing the French more time to recover.[130] At the beginning of 1905, Moltke the Elder told the Kaiser, in contrast to Schlieffen, that a future war 'will be a national war which will not be settled by a decisive battle but by a long wearisome struggle with a country that will not be overcome until its whole national force is broken, and a war which will utterly exhaust our own people, even if it were victorious'.[131] If Moltke the Elder was right and the war did become drawn out, and if Britain sought to impose a blockade, then a neutral Netherlands, emboldened by its Boer War memory, would give Germany an unimpeded and protected outlet to the sea. In 1910, Rotterdam provided Germany with her second most-used port. The coastal defences on the River Scheldt were strengthened at the behest of the Prussian general staff in case of a British landing. Moltke declared, 'For us, it will be of the utmost importance to have in Holland a country whose neutrality will assure imports and exports. It will have to be the windpipe that enables us to breathe.'[132]

> *Risk was at the heart of the plan, as once its most astonishing feature and its most consequential. The most daring military plan of its age, the Schlieffen Plan required feats of marching, provisioning, re-supply, and co-ordinated communications that were unparalleled at the time and that the German Army was in fact unable to accomplish in 1914. More than this, the plan proposed not merely to defeat the two major powers that surrounded and outnumbered Germany, but to defeat one of them in merely six weeks ... It risked Germany's entire future on the outcome of a single battle.*[133]

The decision to send the British Expeditionary Force, commanded by Field Marshall Sir John French, took a further two days.[134] Four members of the British cabinet announced their resignation in protest.[135] There was open talk of letting the far larger French Army take the brunt of the German attacks until the expected British forces were ready. Lord Kitchener, Secretary of State for War, thought that Britain should delay its major effort until 1917, by which time the 'Continental armies would have fought each other to a standstill and the British could take the credit for ending the war'.[136] After the last minute, five divisions, almost the total of the standing army, were sent to Flanders only because economic pressure would work too slowly to save France; one division was kept in England for a mistaken fear of anti-war riots and food shortages.[137] 'Poverty had become a key issue of strategy and of national survival. In the minds of those who feared it, the menace combined the traditional violence of the bread riot with the modern one of political revolution.'[138]

> The Staff studies of recent years had all pointed to the probability that our most formidable danger in going to war was an internal danger. Since the Navy could not guarantee the flow of food and raw materials to this country during the first weeks of the war, it was apprehended that our preparations might be paralysed by popular disturbances aroused by the menace of starvation and widespread cessation of employment. Labour, in fact, might be forced by hunger into an attitude of dangerous antagonism.[139]

During the week of the passage of the transports, 'not so much as a torpedo boat was sighted. Nothing stirred.'[140] The troop ships made 137 separate crossings of the Channel from 14–18 August while, 'all the time, the whole of the British Grand Fleet, with its attendant squadrons and flotillas, patrolled in taut expectancy, watching for the white wake of a torpedo, listening for the wireless signal that would say the German fleet had come out upon the high seas'. The navy, whose existence had been a chief factor in bringing on the war, had no effective role designed for it when war came.'

There had been a complete lack of co-ordination between the German military and either Chancellor Bethmann or their naval counterparts as they worked on their separate war plans.[141] Bethmann knew of the Schlieffen Plan, but conducted foreign policy in 1914 without regard to it and without consulting military or naval leaders. Even Tirpitz was not allowed to know the war plan for the great weapon he had forged until 30 July when the operational orders were shown to him. 'He discovered the secret; there was no plan.'

> The General Staff had apparently not informed Admiral von Tirpitz of the planned invasion of Belgium in the event of a two-front war. The

younger Moltke had decided in 1909 that army and navy should operate independently of each other at the start of hostilities, each following its individual plan. The navy was not to interfere with the landing of any British Expeditionary Force in France since Moltke believed that the army could handle the situation by itself. The navy, in turn, did not include the army in its plans. In 1911, Admiral von Holtzendorff, then Chief of the High Seas Fleet, did not envisage joint army-navy talks in the event of war because the element of surprise and superior German materiel and training would guarantee victory at sea.

Moltke the Younger had to squeeze his armies into a much smaller gap than if the Netherlands had also been used. Just as Moltke the Elder had worried about Dutch Army resistance, Belgium's stand slowed the pace of the German advance. The main Belgian citadel at Liège fell, but twelve more fortresses needed to be reduced and troops had to be left behind as a result.[142]

The process of forgetting the killings of Leopold's Congo received an unexpected boost when Belgium itself became victim instead of conqueror … During the next four years, first the British and then the American governments used the sufferings of 'brave little Belgium' to whip up war fever in countries that had not themselves been attacked. Newspaper stories, cartoons, posters, and patriotic speeches not only denounced the actual brutalities that had taken place; they went further. The Germans, it was said, crucified Belgian babies on the doors of houses. And, in a striking but unconscious echo of the imagery of the Congo, the press in Allied countries reported that German soldiers were cutting off the hands and feet of Belgian children … These shocking reports of severed hands and feet were so widespread that a rich American tried to adopt maimed Belgian children; but, even with offers of a reward, none could be found.[143]

French and Belgian resistance, and the German fear of *franc-tireurs*, the 'free shooter' or civilian gunman, led the Germans to a policy of *Schrecklichkeit*, 'frightfulness', which was summarised by the French nation as the 'most infamous atrocity' at Rheims and by Allies generally as the 'Rape of Belgium'. Hull identified seven forms of violence: executions, arson, burning of whole villages, hostage taking, use of human shields, killing unarmed prisoners of war and pillage.[144]

The Germans displayed a shocking disregard for the rights of other nations, especially of the smaller states. Even the contemptuous treatment that German's major ally, Austria-Hungary, received was completely motivated by the sentiment that Germany as the strongest power on

*the continent could claim immunity from the laws which would prevent
her from establishing herself as a world power like Britain, Russia or
the United States. Social Darwinism served as the justification for this
untrammelled pursuit of power politics. The superiority of the German
race over the Slav and Latin races was generally declared to be a proven
fact of history.*[145]

The Germans bombarded Rheims Cathedral on 20 September 1914
because they claimed that the French were using the spire for artillery
observation.[146] The cathedral was the site of the coronation of France's
kings, and its 'ruins quickly came to represent the scar that war inflicted
on the national psyche'. This was soon followed by heavy destruction in
Belgian Louvain, which entailed severe damage to the fifteenth-century St
Peter's Church, the burning down of the Old Market and the fourteenth-
century Cloth Hall, and, most important of all, the destruction of the
eighteenth-century University Library. The loss included a quarter of a
million books, 800 incunabula (books printed in Europe before 1501) and
950 manuscripts. 'It was the worst act of cultural desecration in more than
a century, involving a university town the equal of Oxford or Heidelburg.'
Hugh Gibson, the newly-arrived secretary of the United States legation
inspected Louvain as it was being destroyed. A 'fat German Landsturmer'
told him that he was acting under 'definite orders':

> *We shall make this place a desert. We shall wipe it out so that it will be
> hard to find where Louvain used to stand. For generations people will
> come here to see what we have done and it will teach them to respect
> Germany and to think twice before they resist her. Not one stone on
> another I tell you* – kein Stein auf einander![147]

Some Belgian civilians reportedly did fight back and many more paid for
it summarily with their lives. 'People as far up as the Chancellor's office in
Berlin knew about the atrocities, but accepted them tacitly.'[148] 'Executions in
small towns, all men from sixteen to sixty, thousands shot on the meadows
... No-one dares say anything against military necessity.' Over the next few
weeks, 5,521 civilians in Belgium and 896 in France were shot, mostly, it
was alleged, out-of-hand.[149] There were major massacres in Andenne (262
dead), Dinant (674), Aarschot (156), Ethe (218) and Tamines (383). The
German military no doubt felt genuine horror and disgust of the *franc-
tireur*, borne of the Franco-Prussian war in 1870–71 and the Herero war.[150]
The Hague Conventions recognised the right of an invaded people to rise in
resistance, provided they formed themselves in organised bodies and were
identifiable as belligerents. 'Is it not the first duty of the citizen to defend
his fatherland?' The Germans opposed this interpretation. They explicitly
did not recognise the right of civilians to resist invasion and thought

international recognition of mass forced enlistment and of guerrilla war would remove limits on war and lead to barbarism.[151] The local population was not permitted in the German code to fire on soldiers; to do so was a despicable act. The fighting was to be an affair between professional land armies: relatively fluid; officered by landowning noblemen; stolid, semi-professional infantrymen marching directly into a concentrated line of fire; glorious cavalry-led pitch battles; limited artillery; and conducted in local battlefields that were chosen by chance or experience.[152] In previous wars, peasants were unlucky to get directly involved. Villagers often continued working their fields as brightly-coloured soldiery marched to and fro. 'The peasants of the north and east had become hardened to it; it was almost a matter of routine. Besides, there were often rich pickings when the mayhem was over. The German principles continued to the negation of the rights of merchant and passenger ships to resist u-boat sinkings and was to have fatal and far-reaching consequences.

The 'imagined reality' of an escalation of warfare to encompass mass, government-orchestrated civilian insurrection against conventional forces was 'so powerful that it helped produce widespread violence against civilians, along with a full, official self-defence that the German government maintained throughout the war and the Weimar Republic'.[153]

> The treachery of the franc-tireurs became an obsession almost as acute as the torments of aching feet. The incidents reported were always based on hearsay, rarely confirmed by personal experience; but they produced the same effect. There was no doubt as to the existence of a Belgian Resistance movement. Numerous acts of sabotage were committed (especially of telephone lines) and some (at least) of the shots fired at troops came from civilian weapons. But this resistance was sporadic, unorganised, although the German High Command claimed it was an authentic, secret army, encouraged and supplied by the Belgian government and by Paris. What is more, the German troops had been indoctrinated – 'conditioned' was the word used – even before they entered Belgium. Through the mobilisation centres German propaganda had spread rumours of atrocities committed by civilians (which always took the same form, particularly the putting out of soldiers' eyes). Historians and eye-witnesses all agree that these measures were far more severely applied in Belgium than in France. In any case, the franc-tireur complex acted as a useful stimulant to discipline on the line of march.[154]

Some historians argue that there was a 'strong vein of anti-Catholicism among German Protestant regiments and social Darwinist dismissal by some officers of the right of small nations to exist'.[155] Tuchman's view was that to the world Louvain 'remained the gesture of a barbarian'. 'Belgium clarified issues, became to many the "supreme issue" of the war ... Belgium was a precipitant of opinion and Louvain was the climax of Belgium'. Matthias Erzberger, soon to be appointed head of Germany's propaganda, found that Belgium 'aroused almost the entire world against Germany'.[156]

German deportations are a much under-discussed aspect of the years of Belgian and French occupation. Some 23,000 Belgian and French civilian deportees disappeared into German camps in the first weeks of the war.[157] At first, the unfortunates were restricted to men of military age and stopped them slipping away to fight by using them for forced labour close behind the lines. By March 1916, the German war minister demanded 400,000 forced deportees to replace German factory workers called into the army. Deportations began in earnest in October and they arrived at ill-equipped former POW camps where they waited many weeks to be placed in factories. The experiment was a disaster. The deportations were halted in February 1917 after 60,000 men had been transferred and repatriations started. A further 60,000 men, women and children were also moved to do military work behind the lines and were never released during the war. The official Belgian report says that among deportees to Germany over 3 per cent died, over 5 per cent were maimed or permanently invalided, 6.5 per cent had scars from ill-treatment, 4.4 per cent had frostbite and 35.8 per cent were ill when returned. In addition to compensating for important lost labour, the Kaiser quickly authorised arbitrary contributions from the Belgian authorities and requisitioned factories 'reducing Belgium's population to extreme poverty'. By war's end, of 260,000 businesses in Belgium, only 3,013 survived. Bethmann regarded the whole affair as an 'unimportant sideshow' using the English blockade as an excuse 'through which our people have been relegated to an existence of misery for generations'.

When the Belgian field army retired into Antwerp, two German reserve corps 'which had been under orders to push forward towards the coast towards Calais', were diverted to form part of the force masking the Belgians' last-ditch stronghold.[158] The Siege of Antwerp lasted until mid-October.

The British were specially concerned in preventing the fall of Antwerp, and were vitally interested in barring the way to the Channel ports from which the Germans could threaten transport of troops from England to France and block the avenues of water-borne traffic converging on London.[159]

The Belgian troops finally retreated south from Antwerp and they stood their ground on the last open area stretching from Dixmuide to the North Sea. It was here in a joint Allied action that Admiral Pierre-Alexis Ronarc'h (of later great importance to Georg Gerth) achieved immortality as the 'Lion of Flanders' while commanding his mostly fellow Bretons in the *Brigade de fusiliers marins*. In one of the Bavarian regiments, originally

3,600 men, facing Ronarc'h during the four days at Dixmude, nearly 3,000 were killed or wounded. One of the survivors was a twenty-four-year-old private, an Austrian volunteer named Hitler. He was later awarded the Iron Class First Class and was wounded three times through to 1918.[160]

> *Admiral Ronarc'h is a Breton; his guttural, sonorous name is almost a birth-certificate. His short, sturdy, broad-shouldered figure is crowned by a rugged, resolute head, the planes strongly marked, but refined, and even slightly ironical; he has the true Celtic eyes, slightly veiled, which seem always to be looking at things afar off or within.[161]*

In the north, the front was unstable. If the Germans bypassed the left of the Allied lines, they would 'cut England from France'.

> *It is necessary to stop them at all costs. It was then that the Ronarc'h Brigade intervened, formed for the most part by sailors not riflemen. Reservists of commerce and fisheries, a robust troop, disciplined, accustomed to the marine climate. The brigade was sent too late to rescue Antwerp. Ronarc'h's 6,000 men stood at Ghent and stopped the Germans in front of the town of Melle long enough to allow the Belgian army to escape. Then disengagement, a hopeless march across Belgium without light, without supplies. On 15 October, Ronarc'h was ordered to stop and hold Dixmuide for a week. He stood for a month alongside the French, Belgian and English troops. The 'Race for the Sea' was won;. Dunkirk and a slice of Belgian territory were saved from invasion.[162]*

The French made their great recovery on the River Marne in the most important land battle on the Western Front. For the next few weeks, first the French or the British, then the Germans, attempted reciprocal attacks to outflank each other on the seaward side of the Marne. Moves gained and lost ground, failed through slowness of manoeuvre, met quickly entrenched troops and, eventually, reached impasse. Each impasse triggered a further outflanking movement and so, bit by bit, stalemate after stalemate, the front finally reached the sea at Nieuwpoort around 19 October and there was nowhere else to go.[163] The town was not a chosen destination; it was just the place by chance at the end of the line. To the great surprise of the advancing Germans, they captured the ports of Ostend and Bruges largely intact and against only light resistance. This gift was at the behest of the British Army 'which expected to turn the German flank and drive the Germans out of Belgium' and then use the ports as supply points.[164]

The ill-named 'Race to the Sea' now became the 'Battle of Flanders'. Both sides tried to break through in two, particularly costly and indecisive battles on the Yser in late October and for a month the first encounter at Ypres until 22 November. At the Yser, the Channel ports became the main objective. Erich von Falkenhayn, the new chief of the German general staff, sought to inflict an 'annihilating blow' by capturing Calais and Dunkerque, but was stopped by fierce resistance and deliberate flooding behind Nieuwpoort.[165] The resistance included British naval support, the monitors *Humber, Severn* and *Mersey* sent from the Dover Patrol.[166]

> *The assailants came on in close order and deep masses. They were new formations, fresh from Germany, with a stiffening of veterans. They were boys of sixteen and corpulent men nearing forty years of age. They marched into fire with admirable courage, several ranks deep, singing patriotic songs ... Rifle and machine guns poured torrents of lead into these moving masses. Entire ranks were mown down.[167]*

By Christmas, despite desperate manoeuvres by both sides, including German attempts to right their failure to capture the Channel ports, the beginnings of a line of trenches, a 'narrow belt of congealed horror', ran from Nieuwpoort to Switzerland.[168]

> *The concentrated destruction, the staggering numbers of young men expended to reclaim a few acres of blood-drenched mud, the eerie, lunar landscape of the combat zone were images etched on the minds of generations ... who faced each other across a narrow killing ground, and who were driven to nervous exhaustion by the constant danger, filth, wetness, noise, death of comrades, and anticipation of one's own demise that, for many years, the First World War was dismissed as an aberration, an alpine failure of human intelligence and imagination.*

The British poured more and more men into an unplanned slugfest. Despite, or maybe because of, developments in the science of land war – machine guns, artillery, mines, barbed wire, poisonous gas, aircraft, tanks – it looked unwinnable and, therefore, interminable. This at least was the view of von Falkenhayn and he moved the German Army to strongly fortified defensive positions able to be held with significantly fewer troops. This enabled him to transfer much-needed divisions to the Eastern Front. British generals did not agree, finding a war of defensive attrition inimitable to their natural instincts:

> *The idea that a war can be won by standing on the defensive and waiting for the enemy to attack is a dangerous fallacy, which owes its inception to the desire to evade the price of victory.[169]*

By the end of 1914, about one-tenth of France was held by the Germans. 'Materially it was of enormous importance.'[170] Losses included almost 80 per cent of French coal, almost the whole of the iron resources which, together with the great steel and textile factories of the north, had been lost for the whole of the war. 'Without this aid it is improbable that the Germans would have endured' the next four years. Replacing the lost coal meant imports from Britain and America, bought with borrowed money that meant a serious loss of wealth and credit, which by 1917 was exhausted.[171] Direct borrowing, mostly from the United States, brought a foreign debt in France of over thirty billion gold francs.[172] Over a quarter of a million French soldiers were dead: 90,000 British, many of them from the original British Expeditionary Force.[173] The German Army had lost 80,000 men in October around Ypres alone. Defeat at Ypres in 1914 had destroyed the Schlieffen dream of encirclement. '*Vernichtungsstrategie*, the strategy of annihilation, had given way to *Ermattungsstrategie*, the strategy of attrition.'[174] Three years of futility followed. The lines scarcely moved one mile one way or the other until the final failed gamble of the major German spring offensive of 1918. Von Falkenhayn concluded that a decisive victory could not be won on the western front. In the Kaiser's view, 'We stand completely alone and must suffer defeat with dignity'.[175]

> *No greater mistake was made by the German generals throughout the war when, in the first rapid advance towards Paris, they failed to occupy the Channel ports.[176] Dazzled by the brilliant prospect of seizing the enemy capital, they were blind to the value of the prize which lay ready to their hand, and that golden opportunity was lost forever. It is difficult to over-estimate the crippling effect which the loss of these ports would have had on the whole activity of the British forces in France, and the intensity of the six weeks' conflict which raged round Ypres [in 1914] is a measure of Germany's bitter desire to retrieve this initial error.[177]*

However, the navy through Tirpitz and the Deputy Chief of the Admiralty Staff, Rear Admiral Paul Behncke, though impotent in affecting the army's conduct, both shared a clear objective on the annexation of Flanders. The latter insisted on 2 September 1914, that,

> *All of Belgium must become German in order to weaken France permanently and to break England's power and influence on the continent. If Germany maintained control of all business, introduced German teachings in schools and churches, and suppressed ... Belgian nationalist agitation, then the land would in time become German. Behncke also wanted to annexe the French coast as far as Boulogne and, in return for compensation to the Netherlands, the Scheldt River.[178]*

As a result, late in 1914, while they waited for the day when Dunkerque and Calais would fall into their hands, the Germans looked to make the best use of the just over thirty miles of coast now available to them between the front line at Nieuwpoort and the border with neutral Netherlands at the River Schelde.[179] Admiral Ludwig von Schröder was brought back from retirement in Berlin by Tirpitz to command the *MarineDivision, Flandern*, and later the entire Flanders coastline. The Division, an unusual hybrid of naval and military units, became the *MarineKorps* in November 1914 and, as its head, Schröder now reported directly to the Kaiser.[180]

Until this time, the larger, more heavily armed, 'overseas' submarines constituted the entire u-boat force as part of the High Sea Fleet, headquartered in Wilhelmshaven.[181] Schröder set up a group to choose the best sites for Germany's naval station in newly-captured Flanders, to include the coastal ub- and uc-boats, and he asked Kapitänleutnant Karl Bartenbach to lead it.[182] Bartenbach was already hugely experienced having joined the navy as a cadet in 1899 and, after a career mostly in torpedo-boats, commanded the submarine *U 1* for two years until 1910. Before the outbreak of war, he held increasingly senior positions in u-boat management. The new base was to focus on submarines and torpedo boats and therefore had to be relatively safe from sea bombardment. Antwerp, although badly damaged in the fighting and with its quays deliberately destroyed in the Allied withdrawal, still had considerable ship-building facilities and potential for repair work, but was not suitable as a forward base as its ships would have to pass through Dutch waters to reach the sea. Bartenbach chose inland Bruges with its extensive canal network to the sea as the centre of operations.[183]

> *Trade through the Straits of Dover into the Thames could only be threatened by submarine warfare – only the large u-boats could have been used while the smaller u-boats could hardly have been of value owing to their minimal cruising radius. Possession of Flanders freed us from this situation, revolutionising our impact.[184]*

In January 1915, some 4,000 labourers arrived from Kiel to begin the construction of the Imperial dockyards at Bruges and Ostend. By March, the work was so far advanced that the Flanders Submarine Flotilla was formed and its leadership fell naturally to Bartenbach.[185] He was promoted Korvettenkapitän in July 1915. At Bruges, he quickly became a respected u-boat leader with, in some cases, a fanatical following.

> *Bartenbach recognized [the need] to maintain our inner strengths for the greatest performance. It was Bartenbach who installed in us the highest clarity of purpose, a wild hatred, an iron will and a readiness for self-sacrifice bound up with love for the soil of the homeland. This holy ardour, this spirit of the Flanders U-Flotilla, was to be the foundation stone for our success and the terrorisation of the enemy.[186]*

The four men who were to lead the struggle for most of the war of the North Sea and the Straits of Dover were now in place. For the Germans, Admiral Ludwig von Schröder commanded all naval and military forces in invaded Flanders with Korvettenkapitän Karl Bartenbach in charge of his u-boats, based in Bruges. For the Allies, Admiral Pierre Ronarc'h, the hero of Dixmuide, from 1915 led the French naval forces between Nieuwpoort and Antifer, about twenty kilometres north of Le Havre, in what was called the *Zone des Armées du Nord* (ZAN). Based in Dunkerque, Ronarc'h's mission was to keep German ships and submarines out of the Dover Channel. Ronarc'h worked in close collaboration with his counterpart and personal friend, Reginald Bacon, from April 1915 Admiral of the British Dover Patrol, and acknowledged to be the 'cleverest officer in the Royal Navy'. From 1916, Georg Gerth was to fight for Bartenbach and Schröder in Flanders and was face-to-face with Ronarc'h and Bacon. In the last year of the u-boat war, Erich Gerth travelled to the Adriatic to join Dönitz, Canaris and other future leaders to further the Kaiser's dream to close the Suez Canal and to threaten Britain's connections to India.

Of Erich Gerth's Crew of '05, thirty-seven cadets served as commanders of u-boats in World War I, fifteen of whom died. In Georg Gerth's Crew of '07, forty-one died in World War I, thirty-seven on u-boats, and a further fourteen lost their lives in World War II.[187]

ENDNOTES

1   Herwig, *Naval Officer Corps*, pp. 60–61.
2   Herwig, *Admirals*, p. 208.
3   Herwig, *Naval Officer Corps*, pp. 46, 47, 51. Mueller, *Canaris*, p. 4.
4   Hull, *Entourage*, pp. 293–96.
5   Ferguson, *Pity*, p. 89.
6   Herwig, *Dynamics*, p. 83.
7   Hull, *Entourage*, pp. 293–96.
8   Mueller, *Canaris*, p. 4.
9   Captain H L Heath, British naval attaché, Berlin 6/10/1910 (*TNA*, ADM 116/940B), cited in Padfield, *Dönitz*, p. 25.
10 Herwig, *Naval Officer Corps*, p. vii.
11 Hadley, *Count Not the Dead*, pp. 6–7.
12 *Marine-Rundschau*, Vol. 11, No. 1, 1900, pp. 132–34. Mueller, *Canaris*, p. 1.
13 Koerver, *War of Numbers*, pp. 34–35.
14 Clark, *Kaiser Wilhelm*, p. 363.
15 Kelly, *Tirpitz and the Imperial German Navy*, p. 378. Granier, *Die deutsche Seekriegsleitung im Ersten Weltkrieg*, Vol. 1, p. 22.
16 Herwig, *Admirals*, p. 209
17 Herwig, *Naval Officer Corps*, p. 92.
18 Horn, *Mutiny*, p. 7.
19 Drascher, 'Zur Soziologie des deutschen Seeoffizierskorps', p. 568.
20 Padfield, *Dönitz*, p. 23.
21 Herwig, *Naval Officer Corps*, p. 62.
22 Herwig, *Naval Officer Corps*, p. 57.

23 history.ucsb.edu/; usinflationcalculator.com (both accessed 3/2017).

24 Padfield, *Dönitz*, pp. 10–13.

25 Padfield, *Dönitz*, pp. 20–21.

26 The Naval School at Kiel was replaced by a new, purpose-built academy at Flensburg-Mürwik, the 'Red Castle', during 1910 to accommodate the increased numbers of officers to be trained under the Tirpitz Naval Laws. Erich Gerth was probably trained only at Kiel while Georg's term may have spanned both establishments.

27 Herwig, *Naval Officer Corps*, pp. 1–4.

28 Padfield, *Dönitz*, pp. 22–23. Immanuel Kant, *Groundwork of the Metaphysics of Morals*, 1785.

29 Padfield, *Dönitz*, pp. 21–22.

30 *BA-MA*, Freiburg, MSG 2/18635, 'Chronik Crew 1905'.

31 Padfield, *Dönitz*, p. 23.

32 Mueller, *Canaris*, p. 5.

33 Richard Kron, *A Concise Account of the New Life and Ways of the English with Special Reference to London, Supplying the Means of Acquiring an Adequate Command of the Spoken Language in All Departments of Daily Life; The Little Seaman: A Concise Account of Naval Organisation ... with Special Reference to the British Royal Navy.*

34 Christopher Cradock was the admiral who led the British Fleet to defeat at the Battle of Coronel in 1914. His book was published in 1908 (Chapter 4, 'Erich's War'). Ernest Picard and Sydney Robert Fremantle, *Nautical Terms and Phrases in French and English* (1890). Reginald Aylmer Ranfurly Plunkett-Ernle-Erle-Drax, *The Modern Officer of the Watch*, 1910.

35 Herwig, *Naval Officer Corps*, p. 63.

36 Padfield, *Dönitz*, p. 27.

37 Herwig, *Naval Officer Corps*, p. 63.

38 Handwritten letter, Christa-Maria Gerth, Georg Gerth's daughter, to the author, 18/12/2016.

39 With thanks to Herr Hans-Georg Donner (*Glashuette* pocket watches), www.glashuetteuhren.de/about/, private emails, 2016.

40 Herwig, *Naval Officer Corps*, p. ix.

41 Wehler, *Das Deutsche Kaiserreich*, p. 249.

42 Hull, *Entourage*, pp. 2–6, 253.

43 Horn, *Mutiny*, p. 6.

44 Horn, *Mutiny*, pp. 8–9.

45 Persius, *Menschen und Schiffe*, p. 35.

46 Herwig, *Naval Officer Corps*, pp. 64–65.

47 Martel and Joll, *Origins*, p. 88.

48 Herwig, *Naval Officer Corps*, p. 94.

49 Chapter 13, 'Welcome home, Erich'.

50 Ewart, *Roots and Causes*, Vol. 1, p. 5.

51 Fischer, *War Aims*, pp. 22–32.

52 Chapter 4.

53 Chapter 4.

54 Pakenham, *Scramble*, p. xvii.

55 Woodward, *Great Britain and the German Navy*, p. 2.

56 Herwig, *Luxury Fleet*, p. 50. The Kaiser sent a telegram in 1895 pledging German support to the insurgent Boers.

57 Woodward, *Great Britain and the German Navy*, p. 56.

58 De Souza, *Question of Treason*, pp. 82, 89.

59 Hull, *Absolute Destruction*, p. 183. Pakenham, *Scramble*, p. 577.

60 Hobhouse, 'Report of a Visit to the Camps', p. 6.

61 Hobhouse, *The Brunt of the War*, p. 128.

62 Stead, cited in Barnard, *Concentration Camps 1899–1902* was the campaigning editor of the *Pall Mall Gazette*. Drowned with the sinking of *Titanic*, Stead was reputed to be about to receive the Nobel Peace Prize (attackingthedevil.co.uk, accessed 1/2017).

63   Pakenham, *Boer War*, p. 495.
64   Pakenham, *Boer War*, p. 508.
65   Spies, *Methods of Barbarism?*, p. 256.
66   Pakenham, *Scramble*, p. 581.
67   Koebner, *Imperialism*, pp. 248–49.
68   MacMillan, *War That Ended Peace*, p. 586.
69   Pakenham, *Scramble*, pp. 585–611.
70   *Croniman*: old word for 'partner in crime'.
71   Hochschild, *King Leopold's Ghost*, p. 209.
72   Ascherson, *King Incorporated*, Chapter XXVIII, 'The Casement Report'.
73   Hochschild, *King Leopold's Ghost*, pp. 284–87.
74   Hochschild, *King Leopold's Ghost*, pp. 225–26; Chapter 11, 'A Secret Society of Murderers';
     Chapter 15, 'A Reckoning'; p. 314.
75   Pakenham, *Scramble*, Chapter 32, 'The Severed Hands'.
76   Other historians see these figures as exaggerated and put much weight on a pandemic
     of sleeping sickness which decimated central Africa at the time. See Ascherson, *King
     Incorporated*, pp. 251–52.
77   Chapter 18, 'The long arm of the war'.
78   Fuehr, *Neutrality of Belgium*, p. 72; Ritter, *Schlieffen*, pp. 87–89; Strachan, *First World War*,
     p. 50; Docherty & Macgregor, *Hidden History*, p. 108.
79   Hull, *Scrap of Paper*, pp. 30–31.
80   Martel and Joll, *Origins*, p. 31.
81   Degrelle, *Born at Versailles*, p. 97.
82   Docherty & Macgregor, *Hidden History*, pp. 348–49.
83   Docherty & Macgregor, *Hidden History*, p. 134. Ferguson, *Pity of War*, p. 63.
84   Martel and Joll, *Origins*, pp. 36–37.
85   Ewart, *Roots and Causes*, Vol. I, pp. 131–41. Also, *The Times*, 8/3/1915.
86   Tooley, *Western Front*, p. 39.
87   Russell, *Justice in War-time*, p. 22.
88   Offer, *Morality*, p. 111.
89   Hull, *Scrap of Paper*, p. ix. For an excellent review, Chapters 5–6, pp. 141–210.
90   Gröner, *German Warships*, Vol. I, pp. 18–21, 143.
91   Chapter 13.
92   Chapter 4.
93   Wegener, *Naval Strategy*, pp. xviii–xix.
94   Chapter 4.
95   Gröner, *German Warships*, Vol. I, pp. 14–16, 104–5, 105–6.
96   Olusoga & Erichsen, *Kaiser's Holocaust*, pp. 40, 167.
97   *Kolonial-Post*, 1937, p. 6.
98   Olusoga & Erichsen, *Kaiser's Holocaust*, pp. 231–32.
99   Bridgman, *Revolt of the Hereros*, p. 130.
100 Pakenham, *Scramble*, Chapter 33, 'Kaiser's First War'; Olusoga & Erichsen, *Kaiser's
     Holocaust*, Chapters 8–9, 'Rivers of Blood and Money', 'Death Through Exhaustion'.
101 Hull, *Absolute Destruction*, pp. 26–27.
102 Hull, *Absolute Destruction*, pp. 46–49, 56–57.
103 Olusoga & Erichsen, *Kaiser's Holocaust*, Chapter 12, 'The Island of Death'.
104 In 1914, Bofinger was the garrison physician in Stuttgart (Frowde, *History of Medicine*).
     See also, from 1913, the work of Eugen Fischer, *Die Rehoboth Bastards*, the first successful
     application of modern Mendelian genetics to human anthropology. Rehoboth was a
     town fifty miles south of Windhoek which contained a mixed-race tribe, the Bastars,
     pushed out of the Cape by the Boers. Fischer was a German professor of medicine,
     anthropology and eugenics and, later, a member of the Nazi Party. He was director of
     the Kaiser Wilhelm Institute of Anthropology, Human Heredity, and Eugenics, and
     was appointed rector of the Frederick William University of Berlin, now Humboldt
     University, by Adolf Hitler. Fischer's ideas informed the Nuremberg Laws of 1935
     which served to justify the Nazi Party's belief in German racial superiority. Hitler read

Fischer's work while he was imprisoned in 1923 and used it to support the ideal of a pure Aryan society (wikipedia).

105 Olusoga & Erichsen, *Kaiser's Holocaust*, pp. 221–22.

106 Hobson, *Imperialism at Sea*, p. 316.

107 *Whitaker Report*, United Nations Economic and Social Council Commission on Human Rights, 2/7/1985. Nuhn, *Sturm über Südwest: Der Hereroaufstand von 1904*, stated that because in 1904 there were 40,000 Herero living in German South-West Africa and therefore, 'only 24,000' could have been killed. Sarkin-Hughes, *Colonial Genocide and Reparations Claims in the 21st Century*, puts the number at 100,000.

108 Koebner, *Imperialism*, p. 247.

109 Emmerson, *1913*, p. 59.

110 Hull, *Absolute Destruction*, p. 200.

111 Turner, *Origins*, pp. 113–15.

112 Asprey, *German High Command*, p. 31.

113 Koerver, *War of Numbers*, pp. 32–33. Gröner, *Kriegsschiffe*.

114 BA-MA, RM 2/1957, pp. 52–53.

115 Fritzsche, *Germans into Nazis*, pp. 3–7, 18–26.

116 Asprey, *German High Command*, pp. 48–51.

117 Fritzsche, *Germans into Nazis*, p. 13.

118 Fritzsche, *Germans into Nazis*, pp. 3–7, 18–26.

119 Joll, *Unspoken Assumptions*, p. 22.

120 Degrelle, *Born at Versailles*, p. 103.

121 Clark, Sleepwalkers, p. 551.

122 Ritter, *Schlieffen Plan*. Turner, 'Significance of Schlieffen', in Kennedy, *War Plans of Great Powers*, p. 199. Hull, *Absolute Destruction*, pp. 163–171.

123 Hull, *Absolute Destruction*, pp. 107–8.

124 Hull, *Entourage*, p. 256.

125 Offer, *Agrarian Interpretation*, p. 5. Raico, 'Turning Point', *Great Wars and Great Leaders*, p. 14.

126 Turner, 'Significance of Schlieffen', p. 202.

127 Hull, *Entourage*, p. 256.

128 Turner, 'Significance of Schlieffen', p. 218, fn. 19.

129 Strachan, *First World War*, pp. 44–45.

130 Frey, 'Bullying the Neutrals, The Case of the Netherlands', pp. 227–29.

131 Strachan, *First Word War*, pp. 43–45.

132 Ritter, *Schlieffen Plan*, p. 166. Strachan, *First Word War*, p. 46.

133 Hull, *Absolute Destruction*, p. 166.

134 Ewart, *Roots and Causes*, Vol. 1, pp. 513–516. Herwig, *Marne*, pp. 64–67.

135 Martel and Joll, *Origins*, p. 35. Those who resigned were: John Morley, who also stood against the Boer War; John Elliot Burns, who never returned to politics; John Allsebrook Simon, who, later, was one of only three men to serve as Home Secretary, Foreign Secretary and Chancellor of the Exchequer; and Lord Beauchamp. Simon and Beauchamp subsequently reversed their decision.

136 Strachan, *First World War*, p. 173.

137 TNA, CAB 16/5. Offer, *Working Classes*, p. 217. Tuchman, *August 1914*, p. 402.

138 Offer, *Working Classes*, pp. 208–9.

139 Corbett, 'Historical Report on the Opening of the War'; see Offer, *Working Classes*, p. 224.

140 Tuchman, *August 1914*, pp. 366–67.

141 Herwig, *Naval Officer Corps*, pp. 175–76. Hull, *Absolute Destruction*, pp. 200, 204.

142 MacMillan, *War That Ended Peace*, p. 595.

143 Hochschild, *King Leopold's Ghost*, pp. 295–96.

144 Hull, *Scrap of Paper*, pp. 52–53.

145 Holborn, 'Introduction', in Fischer, *War Aims*, p. xiii.

146 Nolan, 'Eagle Soars', in Paddock, *Arms*, p. 59.

147 Gibson, *Journal from Our Legation*, pp. 154–72.

148 Koerver, *War of Numbers*, p. 39.

149   Horne and Kramer, 'War Between Soldiers', pp. 154–56. Strachan, *First World War*, pp. 51–52. Read, *Atrocity Propaganda*, pp. 78–103.

150   Hobson, *Jingoism*, pp. 38–39. Hull, *Absolute Destruction*, p. 118.

151   Hull, *Absolute Destruction*, p. 117.

152   In fact, 70 per cent of all casualties on the western front were attributed to artillery (Strachan, *First World War*), p. 309.

153   Horne and Kramer, 'War Between Soldiers', p. 167.

154   Blond, *Marne*, p. 39. Also Horne and Kramer, 'War Between Soldiers', p. 165.

155   Horne and Kramer, 'War Between Soldiers', p. 165.

156   Tuchman, *August 1914*, pp. 357–60.

157   Hull, *Absolute Destruction*, pp. 212, 232–42.

158   Hankey, *Supreme Command*, Vol. I, p. 193.

159   Edmonds, *Military Operations: France and Belgium, 1914*, Vol. 1, p. 463.

160   Asprey, *German High Command*, p. 49.

161   Goffic, *Epic of the French Marines*, p. 7.

162   *The Berthaudière*, 'The Brigade Ronarc'h', *The Telegram of Brest and the West*, No. 6114, 6/11/1964. Also, Essen, *Invasion & War in Belgium*, pp. 279–319; Goffic, *The Epic of Dixmude*.

163   The date of the end of the 'Race to the Sea' is disputed by several days by several historians.

164   Hankey, *Supreme Command*, Vol. I, pp. 205–7. Karau, *Naval Flank*, p. 11.

165   Foley, *German Strategy*, p. 102.

166   Essen, *Invasion & War in Belgium*, pp. 303–4.

167   Essen, *Invasion & War in Belgium*, p. 316.

168   Porch, *French Army*, p. 190.

169   *Field Marshal Sir Douglas Haig, Commander in Chief of the British Armies in France and Flanders, Seventh Despatch 'Features of the war', Fourth Supplement, London Gazette, 8/4/1919*. See also Howard, 'Men against Fire, Expectations of War in 1914, *International Security*, 1984, which summarises the contemporary debate.

170   Cruttwell, *History Great War*, p. 37.

171   Vincent, *Politics of Hunger*, pp. 13–15.

172   Landes, *Unbound Prometheus*, p. 363.

173   Strachan, *First World War*, pp. 278–79.

174   Asprey, *German High Command*, p. 129.

175   28/10/1914.

176   See Ritter, *Schlieffen Plan*; Blond, *Marne*.

177   Koerver, *German Submarine Warfare*, p. 189.

178   Herwig, *Admirals*, p. 212.

179   Information about the Flanders Flotilla and its operations in Bruges, Ostend and Zeebrugge is taken principally from original files at Freiburg and from Karau, *Naval Flank of the Western Front*; Ryheul, *Marinekorps Flandern*; Swetnam, 'The Flanders U-Boat Flotilla', MA dissertation; and Termote, *Krieg Unter Wasser*.

180   Wilhelm II sought to screen his military from the scrutiny of the Reichstag; appointing all officer personally outside of parliamentary control. Forty army and eight naval officers had the right of direct audience (*Immediastellung*) (Herwig, *Dynamics of Uncertainty*), p. 82.

181   Terraine, *Business in Great Waters*, p. 17.

182   Hezlet, *Submarine and Sea Power*, p. 52.

183   Thomas, *Raiders*, pp. 224–25.

184   Wegener, *Strategy*, pp. 174–75.

185   Koerver, *German Submarine Warfare*, p. 190.

186   Fürbringer, *FIPS: Legendary U-Boat Commander*, p. 68.

187   *BA-MA*, Freiburg, MSG2/18641, p.10.

CHAPTER 3
Planning a Famine

Germany was beaten because she was dependent for her very existence on trade with her enemies. But trade means exchange of goods. If Germany lived by selling her products to [Britain], we lived equally by selling our products to Germany. Our blockade cut Germany off from all alternative sources, and so starved her out; but there were moments during the war when Germany, by her submarine campaign, came so near to cutting us off that for some months we read the lists of sunken ships with our hearts in our mouths. It was a frightful starving match, and for nearly a year we were racing neck to neck, or at least seemed to be; for we did not know how impossible it was for Germany to keep up her submarine fleet.[1]

Starving local populations to death was no new idea. Eric Osborne claims that the first recorded instance of a blockade was during the Peloponnesian War in the fifth century BC. As long as men fought, armies would surround unrepentant or fearful cities, cut off food and water supplies, and wait. Citizens held out because of uncertainty as to their fate after a forced surrender. Britain was the first naval power to implement a systematic blockade during the Seven Years' War when from 1756 the Royal Navy sealed off major ports, such as Brest and Toulon, with the goal of forcing the French fleet to fight the blockading force.[2] In 1793 and 1795, 1812–1814, and in the Crimean War, Britain stopped food shipments to its enemies.[3] The United States Government used blockade successfully against their secessionist brothers in the American Civil War of the 1860s.[4] In 1899, the Polish military strategist Ivan Bloch argued that the future of war 'is not fighting, but famine, not the slaying of men, but the bankruptcy of nations and the break up of the whole social organisation'.[5] Bloch's warning was timely and appropriate. In the year it was made, the British declared food destined for the Boers as contraband at the neutral port of Lourenço Marquès.

At the beginning of the Great War, much emotive language was used to support the British blockade of Germany and its allies. Increasingly during the war, and during the blockade's continuance as a vital part of pressure brought to bear in subsequent peace negotiations, the voices in opposition became strident. Its consequences in human terms were long-lasting and devastating. The blockade was not a 'starvation policy' for a town or localised area, but a preparedness to embrace 'untargeted mayhem'.[6] According to Winston Churchill, the intent was to treat 'the whole of Germany as if it were a beleaguered fortress', and avowedly sought to 'starve the whole population – men, women and children, old and young, wounded and sound – into submission'.[7] Sir Charles Ottley, secretary to the Director of Naval Intelligence, prophesised that British sea power would slowly grind the German people 'exceedingly small' and that 'grass would sooner grow in the streets of Hamburg'. He confidently predicted that 'wide-spread dearth and ruin would be inflicted' upon Germany.[8] In the beginnings of a response, in November 1914, Admiral Tirpitz told an American journalist that Germany had the means in the form of u-boats to intercept the bulk of Britain's food imports. The German Press began to agitate for 'employing the new weapon'.[9] The call became a *mêlée* of prominent financiers, shipping and industrial magnates, politicians and scientists.[10] Two distinguished German professors from the University of Berlin added that Britain 'with brutal frankness has established the starvation of our population as a war aim'.[11] If German proposals were going to violate international law, Britain had set the precedent. The scholars explained how much Britain depended on imports and recommended a 'combined air and undersea attack, with u-boats to destroy shipping and Zeppelins to attack food warehouses in the ports'.

One can understand if the British blockade was viewed retrospectively for many years as nationally awkward and not greatly discussed. 'The very existence of the struggle is probably unsuspected by the majority of Englishmen'.[12] What began in 1914 was of a different scale and scope from anything before attempted using the economy of, initially, one nation to beggar another. At the time, the strategy of stopping the flow of food and raw materials, of communication and finance, into an enemy state was presented not as an innovation, but as an 'age-old' weapon of war.[13]

> The [parallel between siege and blockade] *was deliberately misleading – the trade relations and shipping technologies that made modern food blockades possible were recent innovations that had little in common with medieval sieges. Sieges had generally relied on physically surrounding a select area and entirely cutting it off from the outside word, with the aim of literally starving the enemy into surrender, a strategy that was inapplicable to an entire nation. In contrast, naval blockades relied on disrupting transnational trade relations, aiming not*

for the literal starvation of the population but for the collapse or total
restructuring of the national economy.

The British later admitted looking 'to the use of every possible weapon, legal and illegal, by which the Central Powers could be starved out'.[14] In 1937, the First Lord of the Admiralty, Mr Alfred Duff Cooper, stated '... we did everything in our power to starve the women and children in Germany'.[15] Much of the blockade's detail and its effects were kept secret until after World War II. However, there is now considerable material available at British, American and German archives and the blockade has been slowly but increasingly subject to serious academic review. However, even today, it is more the property of historians than the man-in-the-street.

British policy was never limited to one of starvation; it had the wider objective of a war of economic annihilation and, as a result, became a complex structure.[16] In a review in 2007, Greg Kennedy argued that, by 1916, the decisive blockade was 'perhaps the only potential war winning strategy' with money markets, shipping, strategic raw materials and industrial power being the arenas.[17] 'The intelligence provided by the entire machinery of the blockade was first and foremost directed at the political, not the military, effects.'[18] The strategy was a 'conglomerate of various uses of British power' and designed to 'strengthen and co-ordinate the machinery for exerting economic pressure'.[19] Because of this, the overall lead on the blockade strategy was given in February 1916 to a politician in the Foreign Office and not to an admiral. The politician was Lord Robert Cecil, an interesting choice because of his deep religious convictions and commitment to pacifism.[20]

The British plans followed considerable experience in blockade implementation during the Napoleonic wars when its application forced Russia to withdraw from the French trade embargo against Britain – the Continental System. As a result, Napoleon invaded Russia with disastrous consequences for his republic. Strategic plans in 1902 centred on possible conflict with Russia, which was seen as a great threat, particularly to India.[21] In 1894, British relations with France and Russia deteriorated when they had formed an alliance. Precautionary proposals called for a blockade against the French colonies rather than France itself 'because most of France's colonies were dependent on the motherland for food, blockading them would compel their surrender'.[22]

The possibility of a blockade of German ports arose as early as 1903.[23] In August 1906, Captain Henry Campbell took charge of the Navy's Intelligence Department's (NID) trade division. He collected statistics on German and British trade in the principal overseas markets and saw that they showed an increase in German market penetration all over the world. 'But for Campbell this was evidence of German weakness, not strength. He was taking the measure of Germany's overseas trade as a target for

British sea power' and saw that serious 'distress would be severely felt throughout [Germany's] whole commercial and industrial structure, and all the elements of the population depending thereon'.[24] He began to study economic blockade as an offensive weapon.[25] In July 1908, Campbell submitted a long study which suggested that, 'if sea carriage of food and raw materials to Germany was prevented, then land transport by rail over land frontiers would be of no avail. A sea blockade of Germany would reduce the German workman to a state which he feels to be intolerable; want of employment, high costs of living are the first steps towards this financial embarrassment, once this latter is achieved it is believed that no nation can continue to struggle for long.'[26]

That same year, Rear Admiral Edmond Slade, NID's Director, presented the navy's considered strategy:

> *The case of Great Britain and Germany are not dissimilar as regards their wealth-producing sources. This country is practically dependent on industrial production, and so to a very great extent is Germany. This condition implies a necessity for raw material, consequently a dependence on the sea. Our need for overseas supplies may be the greater, but our power to obtain those supplies is also greater, largely due to our superior geographical position … A stoppage of imports or even a mere rise in the prices of raw materials and foodstuffs, in both countries, must tend to produce a position which might become intolerable. The destructive mechanism was ultimately financial: unable to export, Germany would suffer distress, unemployment and finally bankruptcy.*[27]

On Christmas Eve 1908 with the London Naval Conference on international maritime law in session, the Foreign Office delegate, Eyre Crowe, reported to Foreign Secretary Grey that First Sea Lord Admiral Jackie Fisher regarded the whole exercise as a farce.[28] 'Fisher told me personally three days ago that in the next big war, our commanders would sink every ship they came across, hostile or neutral, if it happened to suit them. He added, with characteristic vehemence, that we should most certainly violate the Declaration of Paris and every other treaty that might prove inconvenient.[29] Three years later, Fisher wrote:

> *Perhaps I went a little too far when I said I would boil the prisoners in oil and murder the innocent in cold blood, etc, etc. But it's quite silly not to make war damnable to the whole mass of your enemy's population, which of course is the secret of maintaining the right of capture of private property at sea.*

This was supported three years later in 1911 when a staff officer reported that Fisher evidently allowed the Declaration of London with the deliberate and 'characteristic' intention of tearing it up in the event of war.[30] 'The Germans are sure to infringe it in the early days of the war, then with great regret we tear it up. If they don't infringe it we must invent an infringement.' [31]

By comparison with her all-round industrial capacity, Germany was poor in raw materials and these resources were scattered virtually all over the world.[32] Only coal, zinc, salt products and ceramic materials were sufficiently available. The shortage of raw materials was bound to be a decisive factor in a war that was at least as much an economic struggle as a military fight. 'It was a lack of raw materials, together with the labour shortage, that imposed upon German industry the heavy reduction of activity.'

In other important groups, as for example in iron ores, asphalt, hides and skins, timber tanning substances, resins, fats, phosphates, large imports of raw materials were necessary. The fundamental weakness was the domestic lack in precious materials, copper, nickel, tin, mercury, manganese, graphite, asbestos, nitrates and textile fibres. A similar almost absolute scarcity existed in oil, sulphur, and many other basic materials of the chemical industry. There was, moreover, an increasing need for indispensable tropical raw products such as rubber ... Even the heavy industries had surpassed the capacity of Germany's raw material resources to supply their tremendous growth. In 1912–1913 Germany had to import of the average about 25% of her iron ore and lead consumption and as much as 78% of her copper consumption ... It would appear that of about ten million workers, some four million men depended directly on raw materials from abroad.[33]

The lack of raw materials brought about the 'semi-militaristic organisation of the whole economy'. About 200 *Kriegsgesellschaften*, 'war companies', were run nominally by general staff officers with an entrepreneur as the individual quasi-commanding officer. There was even a Sauerkraut War Company, taken over in 1917 by the Imperial Vegetables and Fruit Office. German industry, previously driven by expansion, was confronted with the tremendous task of devising substitutes.[34] *Umstellung*, 'adaptation', was the catchword of the war years. An ever-growing sector of German industry produced arms and ammunition. There was also a large change over to indirect war production. Grebler cites a few extreme examples: a mortar and stone factory produced artificial honey and substitute fibres; a silk mill made bedsteads for hospitals; manufacturers of lace turned to the making of bandaging materials. Over the whole range of industry, machinery was adapted to the use of substitute materials.

German agricultural imports nearly doubled between 1900 and 1912.[35] In 1913, Germany's food imports exceeded exports by £100 million;

£172 million for raw materials; finished goods by £248 million.[36] A rapid population increase in the last third of the nineteenth century saw a corresponding growth in demand for food imports and, with the general rise in prosperity, a shift from vegetable to animal products. Grain and animal feed accounted for 25 per cent of all German imports in the last decade before World War I. Germany could not exist without maritime trade if she was to be supplied with foodstuffs and raw materials. Her agriculture was notoriously dependent upon fertilisers, three of which, potash, phosphates and nitrogen were essential. The soil in inland Prussia was so quickly exhausted that it could be sown only every twelve years.[37] Germany's deposits at Saxony supplied unlimited quantities of potash, but she imported 50 per cent of her phosphatic fertilisers from the United States and Northern Africa, and Chile sent her more than half her nitrogenous fertilisers in the form of nitrates.

The soil across much of Brandenburg was of poor quality. In some areas, especially around Berlin, the ground was so sandy and light that trees would not grow on it. In this respect, little had changed by the mid-nineteenth century, when an English traveller approaching Berlin from the south at the height of summer described 'vast regions of bare and burning sand; villages, few and far between, and woods of stunted firs, the ground under which is hoar with a thick carpeting of reindeer moss'.[38]

Germany imported one and a half million tons of wheat from the United States because of her own emphasis on the better-suited rye of which she exported two million tons. She consumed six million tons of barley and only produced half, the balance coming from Russia which also supplied 20 per cent of her fodder. The United States supplied nearly all Germany's cotton, three-fifths of her copper, and three-quarters of her mineral oils; the Argentine, much wool and many hides; British India, textile plants and oleaginous grain.

Late in 1914, the German minister of war Erich von Falkenhayn set up an agency to take stock of the raw materials within both the Reich and the occupied territories, particularly Belgium.[39] 'Each commodity was the subject of its own raw materials company', and managed by a board drawn from the firms to which the materials were allocated. The creation of a Nitrate Commission in Germany had an immediate importance as Germany's munition manufacture was at once badly hit by the loss of peacetime Chilean supplies for which it was grossly unprepared. 'Finding a new source of nitrogen for weaponry was a far more pressing initial concern than food shortages.'[40] German chemist Fritz Haber's new nitrogen-fixation technique using synthetic ammonia, first used on an industrial scale in 1913, was expected to produce nitrogen for both fertilisers and explosives and, because it essentially extracted nitrogen from the air, was near limitless.[41] Without Haber and Bosch, Germany would have run out of munitions, probably by the spring of 1916. The Haber-Bosch process was so valued that Article 172 of the Treaty of Versailles specified that it should be made available to the Allies.[42] Munitions also demanded great amounts of glycerine produced from fats and the German population was urged to reduce its intake at the dinner table in order to provide propellant for shells and lubricant in factories and transport. Fat, for Germany, became a key resource as 40 per cent of its dietary requirement at the beginning of the war was imported. Its lack from 1917 was a primary cause of the famine which impoverished the civilian population, especially the poor and vulnerable.[43] Cotton was another vital ingredient for production of explosives and resulted in tension as Great Britain sought to restrict its supply from the United States and thereby cut deeply into American farmers' profits.

In 1914, the initial blockade against Germany was a largely British affair, but, despite all the pre-war discussion, was strategically and tactically muddled. In the first years of the twentieth century, the world seemed ready for an agreement on international regulation of the rules of sea war.[44] Britain was in a cleft stick, unable to agree internally what regulation it favoured. Did Britain view itself as primarily a neutral when it came to future conflicts or should she plan for a belligerent role? The stances were legally contradictory and inimical. 'Undiminished belligerent rights and the widest possible freedom for neutrals are opposite principals. They cannot co-exist. Enlarge the one and you impair the other.'[45] 'Britain's interests as a neutral, a besieged island and an aggressive belligerent were simply not compatible with each other.'[46]

On the eve of the Great War, the British had pulled their warships back to safer northern waters.[47] Foreign Secretary Grey proposed a formal blockade of the German North Sea coast on 12 August 1914. Despite reluctance on the part of the Admiralty and some Cabinet members, torn between the unattractive options of a close or distant blockade, Churchill, Grey and Prime Minister Herbert Asquith persuaded the Cabinet to invoke the principle of continuous voyage, where a final, not initial, destination was all important, and apply it to food as conditional contraband. 'Here was the doctrine of continuous voyage, alive, spitting, and sharp of claw.'[48] Sir Cecil Spring-Rice, Britain's ambassador in Washington, admitted that the practical effect was to make everything absolute contraband.

Britain feared the 'observational blockade': positioning its ships close to German ports and, therefore, making easy targets for coastal batteries, gunboats and submarines. Britain used its 'belligerent rights', the power assumed by fighting a war, to interrupt any maritime trade with Germany to develop a safer long-range blockade and introduced an ever-lengthening list of proscribed cargoes.[49] The 'highly dubious legality of the Cabinet's August decision was ignored.'[50] The decision 'violated agreements reached in Paris and London, and even the Prize Court Proceedings under British law'. At war, supposedly to save neutral Belgium, the British on 25 August, threatened the neutral Dutch with starvation unless they limited food imports to peacetime levels. As casualty lists grew, British ruthlessness became popular at home. British sea power allowed a 'cavalier treatment' of maritime law and Britain soon announced that it would blockade foodstuffs bound for Germany. Food was 'as essential to the forces as bullets and therefore equally seizable; there is really no difference with regard to the consideration of food as contraband of war'.[51] The stage was set for food to become one of the main instruments of the warfare for both sides.[52]

Despite the regular use of the word, a legal 'blockade' of Germany, many believe, was never declared. However, the British Foreign Office felt that they had said enough to make the blockade official in a statement issued in January 1916.[53] A word here on the last source: Archibald Bell was selected by the Foreign Office to write the official history of the blockade, based mainly on Foreign Office papers, partly on those from the Admiralty, and not at all on those from the Board of Trade. It was separated from the often questionable official history of *Naval Operations* on which Bell had assisted Sir Henry Newbolt because it was found to be 'unsuitable for publication'. With over half a million words on almost 900 pages, the book remained confidential until 1961 when almost everyone involved was dead and there was no-one to question about its errors and evasions.[54]

With no competing explanation of events, subsequent generations of historians have tended to treat it as the definitive study on the subject – despite the fact that an absence of footnotes and restriction of access to original documents made it impossible to verify Bell's narrative of events or retrace the steps that led him to his conclusions.

Despite all these caveats, the results of blockade, or use of belligerent rights, were effectively the same. Bonar Law, Chancellor of the Exchequer, the day after the Armistice in 1918, claimed in the House of Commons,

Even at the end this sudden downfall of that military Colossus, whose feet of clay had been hidden, was not caused entirely – I doubt if it was caused mainly – by the military position. It was caused by the result of the blockade, which has sapped the whole foundations of Germany, both military and civil alike.[55]

The distant blockade was only possible because of Britain's fortunate geography and because it had built a naval fleet of a size to be able to exploit it. The British islands formed a 'great breakwater across German waters thereby limiting the passage of vessels to the outer seas to two exits, the one on the South at Dover, narrow, easily blocked and contained, and the other on the North'.[56] 'All shipping that tried to go through the Dover Straits was endangered. Soon the upper tracts of the North Sea swarmed with ships bearing neutral traffic.'[57]

The distant northern blockade is a story of gradual evolution, first with ageing merchant cruisers, then with more appropriate ships, more nets and American mines.[58] Practical experience meant the navy could be specific in their requirements: vessels which could stay on station in the worst possible weather with a large radius of action, and could carry enough stores and coal to do so for long periods; had good accommodation and space spare for a prize crew; were ready to carry prisoners; speed not paramount; eight 4.7-inch guns, but 6-inch quick-firing preferred.[59] It is a classic tale of naval derring-do interspersed with the occasional muddle and much dispute. The British War Plan was for the Tenth Cruiser Squadron to patrol the forty miles between the Orkneys and the Shetlands, and the one hundred miles from the Shetlands to the nearest point of Norway.[60] Its mission was to deny island anchorages to the Germans, to intercept German vessels of war and merchant vessels and to sink or capture them, and to stop all neutral vessels proceeding to German ports. The ship's commanders on the other hand were 'obliged to be careful' how they behaved to the European neutral states: Great Britain was accustomed to Dutch butter and Danish hams; France kept her powder factories in production with nitrates from Norway. The Allies, and Great Britain in particular, were 'reluctant to lose the custom of these European neutrals whom they were trying at the same time to ration. Anxiety as to their balance of trade, by which the rate of exchange of the pound and, consequently, of the franc was maintained, caused them at times to tolerate consignments of merchandise sent by their own traders to neutrals, in spite of some uncertainty as to its ultimate destination'.[61]

At the beginning 'only a tenth [of traffic] could be inspected by the British and so ship after ship passed by bearing, no doubt, goods destined for ports leading to their enemies.'[62] Before operations fully commenced, the *Kaiser Wilhelm der Grosse* slipped into the Atlantic to conduct a German trade war.[63] Still not explained satisfactorily today, ships carrying German reservists who were answering their country's call were given free passage through the blockade by the British Admiralty. Among them was Sub-Leutnant Karl Dancker, Georg Gerth's second-in-command on *UC 61* who, at the beginning of 1915, returned from New York on a Norwegian ship. One possible suggestion for the laxity concerning neutral ships with German cargoes was offered by Maurice Parmelee, an American and close participant in the blockade management from 1918, 'The British government followed the policy at first of permitting Germany to import some of the less important commodities, in order to encourage it to accumulate a large debt in neutral countries which might lead to a financial crisis'.[64]

German merchantmen, almost overnight, were bottled up at home or abroad wherever they happened to be; over 1,000 ships, 3.9 million tons, were laid up in neutral ports because they 'dared not put to sea'.[65] Of these, the Allies captured 900,000 tons; about 1.4 million tons fled to safety in North and South American ports; 1.3 million tons in Asia; and 1.6 million tons in a home fleet in the Baltic and North Sea. Within weeks 'the world's second largest merchant fleet disappeared from the oceans'.[66] Throughout the war no foreign merchant ship reached a German harbour from the westward.[67] German ports were closed to foreign merchant vessels and that part of the Tenth Cruiser Squadron's work became a non-event. Surprisingly, no serious attempt was made by the Germans to undermine the distant North Sea blockade.

Early in 1915, Churchill was publicly satisfied with the way the blockade was going and content to vilify German u-boats and to gloss over any British responsibility. In his statement to the House of Commons on the naval estimates, he said:

> Germany cannot be allowed to adopt a system of open piracy and murder, or what has hitherto always been called open piracy and murder, on the high seas, while remaining herself protected by the bulwark of international instruments which she has utterly repudiated and defied, and which we, much to our detriment, have respected. There are good reasons for believing that the economic pressure which the Navy exerts is beginning to be felt in Germany. We have, to some extent, restricted their imports of useful commodities like copper, petrol, rubber, nickel, manganese, antimony, which are needed for the efficient production of war materials and for carrying on modern war on a great scale. The tone of the German Chancellor's remarks, and the evidences of hatred and anger against this country which are so apparent in the German Press, encourage us to believe that this restriction is proving inconvenient. We shall, of course, redouble our efforts to make it so. So far, however, we have not attempted to stop imports of food. We have not prevented neutral ships from trading direct with German ports. We have allowed German exports in neutral ships to pass unchallenged. The time has come when the enjoyment of these immunities by a State which has, as a matter of deliberate policy, placed herself outside all international obligations, must be reconsidered. A further declaration on the part of the Allied Governments will promptly be made which will have the effect for the first time of applying the full force of naval pressure to the enemy.[68]

The situation became quickly serious, but the Germans found relief in two directions: her European conquests and her bordering neutral states. The goods of the captured territories were immediately available, particularly, for instance, coal from Belgium and north-eastern France, and, over time, wider booty from more distant parts like north-eastern Italy, Romania,

Serbia and Poland.[69] What did occupy the full attention of the Tenth Cruiser Squadron was intercepting trade by everyone, including the United States, and, notoriously, Great Britain herself, with the neutral states to Germany's west and north that enjoyed access to the Atlantic: Holland, Denmark, Norway and Sweden. Together with the other neutrals, Switzerland, Italy, Greece, Romania and Bulgaria, they were all prepared, to some degree or another, and for considerable profit, to pass goods through to Germany and her allies. The preoccupying matter for the British was to monitor, restrict or redirect trades to Norway, Sweden, Denmark and Holland, and to try to compel these neutrals to work for the Allies.[70] This activity centred on Scandinavia, but Holland was the true heart of Britain's economic warfare and its constituent blockade.[71]

The French agreed wholeheartedly with the imposition of the naval blockade, indeed they demanded quicker and more rigorous results. Traditionally, the navy had never loomed large in French strategic thinking and they lacked suitable maritime resources; their fleet's major role was in supporting colonial conquests in Africa and Indochina.[72] French attention was, understandably, on the vulnerable north-western frontier with Germany. Louis Guichard, the most important French writer on the blockade, consistently portrays the French role as one of trying to stiffen policy, and with negotiations with their Swiss neighbours, and it was for this reason the French eventually included a Minister for Blockade in their War Cabinet in November 1917.[73] The position had wider priorities as it was also responsible for the eventual reintegration into France of the German-occupied Alsace-Loraine. One of the minister's regular duties was to complain about the way the 'high-handed' British failed to consult the French on important matters about the blockade except in the 'most perfunctory way'.[74]

Incidentally, continuing the glut of coincidences that fill this story, this Guichard was the same ensign who later almost achieved glory with his 'toy boat' at Wissant beach shortly after Georg Gerth's last u-boat, *UC 61*, stranded in 1917.[75]

The continuation of British trade with Germany after the declaration of war takes a little understanding. It was also difficult to accept for many at the time. 'It went on briskly and was winked at by the Board of Trade.'[76] The Trade and Agriculture Ministries tried to promote as many exports as possible 'so as to pay for imports with income even at the risk of indirect trade with the enemy through re-export by neutrals'.[77] The fear, whatever the morality when compared to the deaths on the Western Front, was of a rapid and uncontrolled trade deficit with an accompanying destabilised foreign exchange rate.[78] In November 1914, Maurice Hankey, secretary to the Committee of Imperial Defence, told the British government that 'drastic means must be taken to prevent British subjects succumbing to the temptation of continuing their trade with [the enemy].[79] In July 1915, the financial secretary to the Treasury confided to Prime Minister Asquith that 'trade with Germany was occurring on a large scale in London'. Even as late as July 1916, the Board of Trade charged that 'this country had been supplying the enemy through neutral countries'. The subject is well covered by John McDermott in 'Trading with the Enemy' who points out that in 1914 the Liberal government and the business community exhibited a strong *laissez-faire* attitude consistent with a country that depended for survival on exports. Business arrangements were considered private and confidential. However, as the losses on the Western Front mounted, sentiment moved naturally for more control and criminalisation in the face of about 1,600 applications for trading permits each day. Convictions with inconsistent penalties followed through the *Trading with the Enemy Act* of 1914. For instance, one firm was fined £2,000 for arranging the exportation of iron ore into Germany from Sweden. Mr W. D. Dick tried to sell coal to Germany and was sent to prison for five years. However, as McDermott points out, fines were more severe for trade in bicycle handlebars, women's handbags and pickled eggs.[80] Tougher regulation led to 'enemy' businesses being wound up, a total of 591 by war end, including Continental Tyre, Bayer, AEG, Bosch and Zeiss. Some British companies were 'virtually created from the forced sale of German assets', including English Electric and General Electric.

> By 1916, emotion coupled with economic opportunism produced an all-out assault on German businesses in the United Kingdom which law and custom had hitherto protected. Under the cover of national interest, the British government and its bureaucracy pursued a policy … reminiscent of the privateers of Elizabethan England.

By December 1914, Cabinet Secretary Hankey declared in a widely circulated memo in government circles that 'our main military effort against German territory is unattainable for the present.[81] The principal weapon remaining is economic pressure and this is the greatest asset we have in the war. Economic pressure, however, appears to be breaking down to a certain extent owing to the enormous trade with Holland and Denmark, and at the best is a weapon slow in operation'. The duplicity did not stop there, as Lambert noted, 'One might well argue that the greatest untold scandal in World War I – though admittedly the case is largely circumstantial – was the degree to which contraband trade was financed by the City of London and carried across the Atlantic in British ships.'[82] During the whole war, it was impossible for the British government to 'mend these holes in the British financial system; the resistance of the banks was 'simply too strong'.[83] Alwyn Parker, the deputy of the Foreign Office Contraband Committee, wrote in 1915 to his head Sir Eyre Crowe, 'It is perfectly sickening to think that these banks are making profits at the expense of our soldiers' lives'.[84] Parker was 'shunted' to become Foreign Office librarian in 1919.[85]

Britain's man on the spot in the northern neutral countries was its naval attaché in Scandinavia from 1912 to 1919, Rear Admiral Montagu Consett, also local head of the Secret Intelligent Service. No other British officer enjoyed his freedom of travel or level of access to businessmen, trade associations and governments across Sweden, Norway and Denmark.[86] His reminiscences were published in 1923 when his frustration with what he had observed foamed over. Here is one example, an extract from a letter he wrote early in the war to a superior:

> It seems to me that when we are so hard-pressed these valuable by-products [ammoniacal liquor from British gas coal] *should, in return for our coal, be placed at our disposal in order to help us kill Germans, instead of being used by neutrals as a fertiliser for producing, amongst other things, grease for our enemies from which they obtain glycerine for their explosives in order that they may kill Englishmen.*[87]

If the British, as a belligerent nation, were guilty of some double standards when it came to trade with 'neutrals', then the position of the United States as a distant neutral showed no immediate constraint because of its fierce commitment to its own rights to free movement of goods. 'The truism that the world is economically interdependent became grimly apparent in 1914.'[88] No country was capable alone of feeding and clothing its population. Every belligerent needed the neutral merchant. However, for the Allies, while respecting neutrality and remaining friendly with a necessary supplier, there was also at the same time the dilemma of denying that supplier access to an enemy. For the British, shipping from Australia and India was in short supply and, when available, took considerably longer to deliver goods. The United States was therefore the most important source of supply for both Britain and France and there were 'weighty reasons for not offending'. Naturally, the Americans continued to insist on their neutral rights to supply Scandinavia, even at levels far exceeding pre-war deliveries, and knowing full well that the final destination was Germany.[89] This concept of 'continuous voyage' – the real final destination as opposed to what was claimed on the manifest – became a cornerstone of the legal debate.[90] America's protests against the blockade gradually weakened as industrial profits taken from the Allies made a stronger claim. 'When British orders for arms and ammunition began to pour in, protest waned and died.'[91] Magnificent profits were made as the war turned America from a 'debtor nation into the world's greatest creditor'.[92] The American economy had 'surged ahead' as their farmers and factories 'poured out wheat, pork, iron and steel'.[93] The United States became the 'banker to the Europeans' as its share of world production soared. At the end of the war, the accumulated debt of the Allied powers amounted to $16.3 billion of which $7.1 billion was owed to the United States.[94]

By the end of October 1914, President Wilson had 'persuaded himself and the American people' that the United States was a committed neutral.[95] 'By international law, however, American behaviour was in no way neutral. Instead, the United States had become 'a partner, and not always a silent partner in the allied campaign to strangle Germany'. Their protests against the British concentrated upon the individual case, but did not challenge policy even as it became more stringent'.[96] Even though a 'majority was in sympathy with the Allied cause, at least 90 per cent of its population eagerly desired to keep out of the war'. There were also many business people, recent descendants of European immigrants many of whom were anti-English, or at least, pro-German.[97] The United States Census of 1910 counted a total population of the United States of almost 92 million. Defined only by place of birth of individuals or of both of their parents, not grandparents or earlier settlers, this number included over eight million people who were first or second-generation Germans, almost three million Austro-Hungarians, over four million Irish, almost three million Finno-Russians and over two million Italians amounting to a potentially hostile 22 per cent or twenty million people. Arthur Zimmermann of the German foreign office had told US sources that 'perhaps it was as well to have the whole world against Germany, and that in case of trouble there were 500,000 [military] trained Germans in America who would join the Irish [-Americans] and start a revolution'.[98] The threat was taken as seriously meant.

In 1914, exports from New York to Denmark and Sweden both increased by over 85 per cent. Antagonising the United States was not in Britain's best interests. However, with her fleet blockading entry to the European neutral states, and serious doubts about the final destination, Britain had the means to intervene in the American traffic with the European neutrals and she did. Complaints, angry words, threats and subversion were daily bedfellows. The American Government 'deplored American trade being excluded from the markets of neutral nations adjacent to Germany'.[99] 'To attain her end, England was willing to risk a serious quarrel with the United States, "or even a war with us rather than yield"'.[100] In 1915, the United States declared the British blockade illegal:

> ... it has been conclusively shown that the methods employed by Great Britain to obtain evidence of enemy destination of cargoes bound for neutral ports and to impose a contraband character upon such cargoes are without justification; that the blockade upon which such methods are partly founded, is ineffective, illegal, indefensible; that the judicial procedure offered as a means of reparation for an international injury is inherently defective for purpose; and that in many cases jurisdiction is asserted in violation of the law of nations ...[101]

The American cross-Atlantic flow was slowly stemmed by gradually increasing, by negotiation or by *force majeure*, the number of declared contraband items. More and more American goods, on top of easily agreed war munitions, were restricted: textiles, rubber, copper, wheat and, eventually, all foodstuffs. 'Foodstuffs, with a hostile destination, can be considered contraband of war only if they are supplies for the enemy's forces. It is not sufficient that they are capable of being so used.'[102] The Americans sought and received formal assurance from the German government that any foodstuffs imported into Germany directly or indirectly from the United States would not be used by the German armed forces. The Germans even offered to have food distributed by American organisations. 'Naturally, the British gave no serious consideration to this suggestion.'

'In an effort to force the United States to assist in these restrictive measures, Great Britain next delicately threatened to forbid the shipment of essential raw materials from the British colonies to the United States.'[103] The situation was always complicated by a legal contrast between absolute contraband, that which was always deemed to be helpful to an enemy, and conditional contraband, that which might or might not be for military use, based on destination.[104]

However, Avner Offer suggests the American posture was, in part, diplomatic huffing and puffing:

> A few weeks into the war, the [British] government ignored the Declaration [of London] and applied a policy of interdicting goods intended for Germany with no exception. American protest was insincere and ineffectual. But when the Germans began their submarine campaign, America responded with great indignation. President Wilson turned a blind eye, for example to the mining of international waters by Britain, but invoked international law to enter the war against Germany, first as an active supplier of the Allied war economy, and later as a belligerent.[105]

In 1920, Consett was appointed the naval adviser to the Supreme Council in Paris. His book on the effects of the blockade on neutral nations was raised twice in the House of Lords as peers tried to get answers to some of the questions that he raised.[106] Now an admiral, it was Consett's view that from the start of the war 'goods poured into Germany from Scandinavia, and for over two years Scandinavia received from the British Empire and the Allied countries stocks which, together with those from neutral countries, exceeded all previous quantities and literally saved Germany from starvation'.[107] His views, trenchantly reported, were at complete variance to information summaries prepared for the British war cabinet. Sir Edward Carson, First Lord of the Admiralty, wrote early in 1917:

All the evidence available tends to show that, with some minor exceptions, practically no goods coming from overseas are getting through to Germany ... The chief minor exceptions are certain colonial goods, such as tobacco, coffee, cinchona from the Dutch colonies, and wines and spirits, as to which we have had a good deal of difficulty with the French. It is possible that, in addition to these, there might be some slight leakage by way of Sweden ... With regard to [Norway, Denmark and the Netherlands] practically none of the export trade to Germany consists of overseas goods. [108]

An enquiry on the central themes of Consett's book was called for in 1923, but the idea was quickly quashed by the government as it was 'not considered that any good purpose would be served by reopening this intricate and difficult subject'. Consett was criticised for an 'improper proceeding for an ex-servant of the Crown to make use of knowledge which he acquired in his official capacity'.[109] By 1925, in another debate, it was noted that none of Consett's charges had been refuted.

The first half of the war was a period of unparalleled prosperity for Scandinavia. As cargoes came crowding onto the wharves of Copenhagen, Gothenberg, Christiana (Oslo) and others, they were transferred in German vehicles to ships plying to and from Germany using British coal as fuel 'which was greatly appreciated'.[110] Consett wrote again in 1918 to the British Minister at Stockholm:

It may not be generally known in official circles, but it is nevertheless a fact that among a large section of American businessmen very bitter feeling exists against England because they believe that during 1915 to 1917 while interfering with American exports to Scandinavia and Holland we were ourselves exporting to these countries similar goods which either reached the enemy directly or indirectly. For instance, they say that, while we refused to allow the International Harvester Company to supply Denmark with agricultural machinery, British agricultural machinery was reaching Denmark and in some cases was being discharged from ships straight into German railway trucks for transit to Germany. They also considered that we had no right to interfere with their export of oil-seeds and the products of these seeds, seeing that during a period of two years our imports of copra to Denmark from British colonies were three times greater than the pre-war average. Again, in view of the fact that British coal was being used in Danish dairies working for Germany, the Americans do not consider that we were justified in any way in interfering with the imports of oil for internal combustion engines required for Danish fishing craft, especially as the export of fish from Denmark to Germany was a pre-war trade, whilst the export of Danish butter to Germany was entirely a war venture. [111]

Britain's Atlantic blockade did not extend to the internal workings of the Baltic. As long as the Russians were kept at bay in the north and west, the Germans were able to continue to use with impunity their many coastal u-boat and ship-buildings works; the sea for naval training and for the delivery of u-boats to other theatres of war, often directly through the Kiel Canal; and to continue uninterrupted fishing. As well as land communications by train directly into Germany from Denmark, there was an unimpeded flow of goods by ship from Sweden.[112] There are three channels into the Baltic, the Great and Little Belts, and the Sound. Denmark's first act in 1914, under pressure from Germany, was to mine the Great Belt, the only easy passage for the large ships of the British fleet. The southern end of the narrow Little Belt was controlled by Germany; it became a valuable alternative route for the German fleet and for its u-boats. The Sound was blocked by an elaborate arrangement of mines, nets and under-water obstructions and was guarded by German destroyers and gunboats, based in Denmark and maintained by supplies which came, directly or indirectly, from the British.

The general Scandinavian sympathies, thought Consett, were that Sweden was pro-German, Norway pro-British, and Denmark pro-Danish.[113] Norway only became an independent state in 1905 when it had deeply offended Swedish sensibilities by throwing off her control. Paradoxically, it was Norway that received most attention from the architects of Britain's economic warfare; it was, claimed Consett, the 'worst treatment' handed out in Scandinavia.[114] Speaking at the outbreak of war, the Norwegian Prime Minister explained the complexity of his country's position:

Since war has broken out among a number of foreign powers the Norwegian and Swedish governments each declares it to be its avowed purpose under the war conditions which have arisen, to maintain to the uttermost its neutrality toward all the belligerent powers – and a promise not be hostile to each other ... Commerce has been continuous between England and Norway for centuries. Many of the Norwegian 80,000 sailors have served on British ships. Nearly all Norwegians speak English. The Norwegian democratic government is modelled on the British parliament. There were over 1½ million Norwegians in American in 1914. Its Queen Maud was the daughter of the late Edward VII. German influence is also profound in Norway. The Teutonic influence is intermingled with British influence. Schoolbooks came from Germany. Many of Norway's men of science, jurists, doctors, philologers, theologians, mathematicians, engineers, artists have been residents of Germany or completed their training there. They have a Lutheran church and great affiliation with German music ... So while Norway's dynastic, political and commercial associations are largely English, Norwegian culture, education, literature, art, science and religion have their roots in German soil.[115]

In 2016, Paul Vigness wrote an excellent and detailed explanation of Norway's invidious position trapped as it was between the two leading belligerents.[116] 'Norway was buffeted about alternatively and often simultaneously by them, as one Power scored a diplomatic triumph and the prestige of its enemy thereby seemed to be threatened.' The British Foreign Office managed a Contraband Committee with agencies in every neutral country neighbouring Germany. These agencies were charged with finding ultimate destinations for suspected goods on a 'continuous voyage' to Germany.[117] By the end of 1916, there were over 200 British trade spies in Norway; Christiana alone housed more than one hundred. The British had a huge library of information about every aspect of neutral trading, which 'enabled them to detect the enemy interest behind the innocent façade'.[118] Suspected ships were required by agreement or force to call at designated British ports for inspection and, if the owner was less than co-operative, inspection could take a considerable time.[119] Delivery deadlines would be missed, profits 'eaten up', and perishable goods spoiled. Where contraband cargo was suspected, shippers were forced to appear before British prize courts suffering further costs and delays. The British arbitrated upon their own actions. Pressure mounted across the board. In May 1915, the British Government 'informed Norwegian coal importers that any dealer trading directly or indirectly in coal with Germany would be refused further supplies'.[120] Each firm was required to report its consumers and also to submit a list of firms ineligible to receive coal. Failure to comply meant Norwegians firms would be placed on an all-powerful 'Black List' with limited opportunity for appeal. Although coal could be obtained from Germany at that time, 'no Norwegian importer dared to trade in it, as such activity automatically would forbid him any connection with British trade'.

Coal used for fuel in ships is termed bunker coal; its principal supply anywhere in the world except America and the Far East was under British control.[121] Britain 'supplied bunker coal only where she saw fit to do so', especially to neutral vessels which may trade with one of her enemies. Terms were devised whereby neutral vessels, particularly Norway's large merchant fleet, were 'persuaded to enter actively into the service of the Allies'. As a condition for receiving coal, vessels suitable for North Sea and Channel shipping were required to complete two voyages of advantage to the Allies before a third voyage could be chosen at the will of the neutral owner.

These mechanisms of economic warfare, applied by the British to a neutral but friendly power, bolstered the Atlantic blockade:

> *Application of the doctrine of 'continuous voyage' permitted practically unlimited authority and control of the belligerent Allies over neutral trade; all ships travelling to neutral countries were required to be inspected in British ports voluntarily or otherwise; organisation of a Contraband Committee with its network of agents increased the*

effectiveness of search and investigation; numerous trade agreements with neighbouring neutrals placing them on a rationing basis and thereby reduced to a minimum the supplies available for enemy trade; utilisation of the scheme of bunker control; and hovering above all, as an effective weapon against violations, the blacklist – all contributing toward the purposeful objective of the economic subjugation of the Central Powers.[122]

One further economic weapon was brought to bear on Norway. During the first two years of the war, fish was the principal diet in German trains and restaurants.[123] Germans stood waiting, cash in hand, as Norwegian fishing boats reached port; four times the normal fish export reached Germany from Norway in 1915. 'Norwegian fishermen realised large profits.' However, as 85 per cent of the fishing equipment, including coal, salt, petroleum and wool, was obtained from the British, fish buyers soon had to sign a declaration that nothing would reach Germany. Then, the British decided to purchase all fish 'surreptitiously in the open market through a go-between' and made £10 million pounds available. Another door was closed.

It was not until the Americans entered the war in 1917 that the British blockade became a true 'Allied' blockade. Lambert notes that the British government in the summer of 1915 were worried that the blockade might even be counter-productive and seriously considered its abandonment'. He places the blame largely, if true, on an 'incapacity to coordinate and integrate departmental action'.[124] In fact, the British quickly developed an efficient bureaucratic system, mainly because until American intervention they were largely acting alone.[125] Government committees studied statistics compiled by thousands of clerks and analysts and indexed materials that were to be 'targeted by the navy so that Germany could be denied what it needed most'. Spies and other ground assets were another essential piece of the puzzle; the blockade 'lived and died with good intelligence flowing into the UK'.[126] Wilson committed wholeheartedly to the blockade and ensued that every loophole left open by the Allies for the potential reprovisioning of Germany was closed'.[127] Effectiveness immediately increased considerably as the Allies now controlled nearly all the markets of the world. Economic encirclement of the central powers was brought about almost automatically. Supplies to the neutral states themselves all but dried up as well and their main anxiety was no longer reprovisioning Germany, but themselves.[128]

Putting in place a sea blockade, and its accompanying economic actions, when added to the cost of an unexpectedly drawn-out war, cost Britain a great deal of money. Other countries had, at least, set up or planned for large standing armies; Britain did not because of her strategy of 'limited liability'. The small British Expeditionary Force 'needed to be multiplied and equipped as soon as possible'.[129] British industry was found incapable of supplying the increased demands of the armed services – heavy guns, high explosives, fuses, trucks, gun sights, aero-engines and light machine guns and, in the case of the Royal Navy's unanticipated anti-submarine war, mines, nets, torpedoes, depth charges, fast patrol craft, minesweepers, patrol aircraft, destroyers, let alone inventions and development work.

Much of this money came from British exports to the Americas, selling overseas assets and by borrowing, mostly from War Bonds or from the New York and Chicago markets. This led to an 'unnerving degree of dependence'. In October 1916, the British chancellor warned his cabinet that 'by next June or earlier, the President of the American Republic will be in a position, if he wishes, to dictate its own terms to us'. During the war, Britain earned £2.4 billion from invisibles, mainly shipping; sold altogether £236 million of foreign investments and borrowed £1,365 million from foreign countries, of which over £1 billion was from the United States.[130] Ironically, Britain re-lent about half their borrowings to Russia which was never recovered. The resulting National Debt arising from the Great War was not paid off until 2015.[131] The nominal value of the UK's public debt rose from £650 million in 1913 to £7,829 million in 1920; the interest bill increased from £24 million to £332 million over the same years.[132] Economic historian Niall Ferguson claimed that the 'German inferiority' was partly due to the British naval blockade, but that it was also, and perhaps even more, because Germany lacked the invisible earnings; the reserves of overseas assets, which were anyway largely in enemy hands; or the assets abroad to finance a large trade deficit.[133] Germany's debt rose to thirty times its pre-war level.

Historiographical writing on the British blockade occupies only a small pocket of the outpouring on the wider Great War; some important general histories manage to dismiss it in a paragraph or two, all of which, thought Eric Osborne, was a 'glaring omission because of the enormous role that it played in the defeat of the Central Powers in the war'.[134] Emotion and human scale has taken narrative to the trenches; the sea war, especially the Falkland Islands, Jutland and the Dardanelles; and to the great political questions of how and why did the war start and what and at what cost did the peace conference at Versailles achieve? 'Allied' historians also claim that the blockade is under-researched; this mostly is a perceived lack of available German resources and insufficient raw numbers.[135]

Some recent theories suggest that the u-boat commanders were wrong to place so much blame on the blockade for their families' hunger. In fact, many of their preconceptions, and those of today, are misplaced, 'the illogicality of the hunger blockade thesis'.[136] Rather they should have looked at the foolishness of the Kaiser and his military chiefs in declaring war on their biggest customers, specifically Britain, Russia and France, thereby depriving Germany of vital foreign exchange.[137] Making enemies of these customers also stopped Germany's access to key commodities that they controlled. All of these were 'more decisive in shifting the military balance than shortages of food'.

Georg Gerth and his last u-boat, *UC 61*, were military beneficiaries of the neutral trade. When war broke out, Germany lost her supplies of French and high-quality Spanish iron ore. This serious loss was made good: Germany took 4–5 million tons of iron ore a year from Sweden and its haulage to the coast by the Swedish railways used British coal.[138] The resulting high-grade steel was essential for submarine building and was used on *UC 61*. Its delivery across the Baltic to *UC 61*'s Weser construction yard at Bremen was made by Swedish steamers also powered by British coal. So pressing had Sweden's demand for shipping become because of this and similar Baltic trades, that 450,000 tons of Scandinavian shipping was leased to bring urgent supplies from America and elsewhere, notably free from German u-boat attack.[139]

Nickel ore was hauled by lorries from Norwegian mines to local factories which were also powered by British coal.[140] Norway was Germany's only outside source of nickel during the war; her own stocks being meagre. Practically all of Norway's nickel exports went to Germany where, because of the metal's ability to impart strength to steel, it was used for the coating of torpedoes and for the outer skin of u-boats like *UC 61* to where it was hauled by Norwegian steamers powered, again, by British coal. Consett tabled the extent of the annual shipments. The British signed over £1 million to the largest Norwegian nickel factory in an agreement to limit nickel exports. However, the amounts set were higher than the firm's capacity and, claimed Consett, the British were bound not to interfere with the supply of nickel to Germany. The agreement, and the identity of the advisors to the British, was kept secret at the time. It was not until May 1917 that the nickel shipments were stopped, not by Britain's intermediaries, but by the Norwegians themselves because of the horrific sinkings of unarmed Norwegian steamers by u-boats.[141]

Consett made a direct connection between a Canadian businessman, James Dunn, later knight of the realm, and the various nickel interests and challenged Dunn by letter. Canada, because of its own interest in nickel, had refused to allow the metal to be placed on the Allies contraband list – as had England, tin; and France, aluminium.[142] The sketchy story is a good example of borderline deals involving 'British' businessmen and neutrals at that time. Dunn arranged for the Norwegian company to ship all its nickel to Canada for which it was paid £100,000 a month in compensation. Consett claimed that immediately after Dunn received his letter, Dunn went directly to the nickel factory in Christiana and found the factory was 'practically destroyed by fire'.[143] The nickel company was 'handsomely compensated by the British government'. Alternative views were provided by biographers. Dunn's fellow Canadian and friend, newspaper tycoon Lord Beaverbrook, wrote a panegyric on Dunn ... 'though his name was known to fame'. Other British political friends included Prime Minister Herbert Asquith, and two future Prime Ministers, Winston Churchill and Andrew Bonar Law, another Canadian. Beaverbook explained that Dunn was employed as a 'man of determination, vision and personal courage' to save the nickel from the Germans.[144] When warning was received that Germany was contemplating the invasion of Norway, Dunn was sent to put the mines out of action, all of this, supposedly, unknown to Consett, then head of the regional secret service.

Duncan McDowell explains more of the workings of the British American Nickel Company (BANCo), established in Ontario in 1913.[145] Dunn was its leading light in Europe, where he was already delivering 3–4,000 horses a month from the American mid-west to the French Army. Dunn also offered the British, French and Russian governments large quantities of blankets, ammunition, steel rails, Argentine beef and military clothing. 'War', for Dunn, 'was chiefly a case of business as usual.' Whatever the truth of the nickel project, Dunn offered his services for nothing to help the British government to buy the Norwegian nickel company on condition only that Dunn could buy it 'equitably' from the British at war end. In return, the British government provided a $6 million guarantee of BANCo's securities. 'As with so many of Dunn's business promotions, somebody else accepted the immediate risk and he stood to reap the ultimate reward.'

> *The effectiveness of the blockade was a subject of major controversy in Britain during the war. Proponents of hitting Germany harder and who therefore objected to solicitude for law or neutral rights claimed in Parliament and in the Press that the Foreign Office's leadership had made the blockade nugatory. Echoes of that charge are visible in the defensiveness of the blockade's official historian, Bell, and perhaps also in the hyperbole of writers like Basil Liddell Hart, who claimed that the blockade 'ranks first' in the causes of German defeat. Too few modern historians of the war devote much attention to the blockade or venture a view about its efficacy. But the best summary, by McKercher, is unequivocal. He calls its success 'undeniable': 'The Allied blockade policies pursued from August 1914 to April 1917 [when the United States entered the war and made the blockade airtight] had disrupted the German economy, increased food shortages and created domestic unrest.*[146]

In Lloyd George's view, Germany was 'broken almost as much by the blockade as by military methods.'[147] It was a view shared by most German economists. Throughout the war, Germany carried on military operations almost entirely outside her own territory. The Russian invasion of East Prussia 'affected no vital part of her economy' and was a brief, if bloody, confrontation. Economic losses caused directly by military operations were of subordinate importance.' The blockade was the outstanding economic fact in Germany's war history.'[148] While the Allies could reach out to the whole world, except for Central Europe, for resources, Germany was forced with her limited associates into isolation. The process of adaptation caused severe difficulties. Had substantial supplies been available from abroad, there would have been far less a burden of human and domestic resources. Total imports from neutral countries over the period of the war amounted to about one quarter of what might be expected in peace time with the 'bulk of imports occurring in the first two years. Supplies from Germany's allies were important, but did not make up shortfalls. Bulgaria and Turkey furnished cotton, wool, silk, oil, tobacco and metals. The relationship with Austria was a drain on the German economy. 'On the whole, Germany's allies were a costly asset to her in terms of foreign trade and war finance'; by the end of the war they owed Germany 12 billion gold Reichsmarks.

The occupied territories were a 'doubtful asset' to Germany's war economy. In the east, Romania was an exception because of her large grain, timber and oil resources; the oil wells had been destroyed early in the war, but were restored after occupation in 1916. The granary of the Ukraine failed to fulfil the expectation of the Brest-Litovsk Treaty in 1918. Poland provided substantial coal and timber only. In the west, vast supplies of raw materials were secured in 1914 and 1915 after the invasion of Belgium; large stocks of copper, cotton, wool, oils and fats were seized in the port of Antwerp and in Belgian factories. 'Substantial booty' was obtained in the industrial regions of Northern France, particularly in the textile area of Roubaix-Tourcoing. All of these brought temporary relief, but the vast territories required heavy investment in materials and labour, laying roads and communications, opening new coal mines, especially in Belgian Campine, and new industrial establishments. 'In one respect only were these territories a profitable field of exploitation.' From 1917, whole industrial plants were requisitioned on a large scale and taken to Germany. Swathes of France and Belgium, particularly, were impoverished as their plants were reduced to 'bare skeletons'.

ENDNOTES

1 Shaw, 'Preface', in Richter, *Family Life*, pp. 7-8.
2 Osborne, *Blockade*, p. 6. Mahan, *Influence of Sea Power upon the French Revolution*.
3 Hull, *Scrap of Paper*, p. 164.
4 Four years of civil war left up to 750,000 soldiers dead, a higher number than the American military deaths in the two world wars combined.
5 Lambert, *Armageddon*, p. 2.
6 Devlin, *Too Proud to Fight*, pp. 158–67, 191–200.
7 Churchill, *World Crisis, 1915*, p. 215.
8 Offer, *Agrarian Interpretation*, p. 232.
9 Offer, *Agrarian Interpretation*, p. 354.
10 Tarrant, *U-Boat Offensive*, p. 14.
11 Offer, 'Bounded Rationality', p. 183.
12 Consett, *Triumph of Unarmed Forces*, p. ix.
13 Weinreb, *Modern Hungers*, p. 16.
14 Peterson, *Propaganda*, p. 83.
15 *Time*, 2/8/1937, p. 17.
16 Vincent, *Politics of Hunger*, p. vi. For brevity, the word 'blockade' was used originally to cover the gamut of economic warfare employed against the Central Powers and the author continues that practice.
17 Kennedy, 'Intelligence and the Blockade', *Intelligence and National Security*, pp. 699–700.
18 Kennedy, 'Intelligence and the Blockade', p. 717.
19 Hankey, *Supreme Command*, pp. 547–48.
20 At the outbreak of the war, Cecil worked for the Red Cross and then became Vicar-General to the Archbishop of York. In September 1916, he wrote and circulated to the Cabinet a 'Memorandum on Proposals for Diminishing the Occasion of Future Wars'.
21 Clark, *Sleepwalkers*, p. 138.
22 Osborne, *Blockade*, pp. 14–15.
23 Robertson, 'The Military Resources of Germany, and Probable Method of their Employment in a War between Germany and England', 7/2/1903 (*TNA*, CAB 38/4/9), published 23/2/1904, Intelligence Department, War Office. Grimes, *Strategy and War Planning*, Chapter 2, 'Early Planning against Germany, 1902-6'.
24 Vincent, *Politics of Hunger*, p. 35.
25 Offer, *Working Classes*, pp. 213–16. Lambert *Armageddon*, pp. 109–120.
26 Captain H Campbell, 'German Trade in Time of War – Effect on the Industrial Output of the Country Due to a Call to Colours, and Due to a Scarcity of Raw Materials' (July 1908), (*TNA*, ADM 137/2872). Neilson, *Makers of War*, p. 21; Docherty & Macgregor, *Hidden History*, p. 119; Strachan, *First World War*, p. 35; Ferguson, *Pity of War*, p. 86. Offer, *Agrarian Interpretation*, pp. 231–32.
27 'The Economic Effect of War on German Trade' (Admiralty memorandum, Committee of Imperial Defence Paper E-4, 12/12/1908), p. 25, printed as Appendix V, 'Report of the Sub-Committee of the CID to Consider the Military Needs of the Empire', 7/1909, with additional tables in Appendix V1 (*TNA* CAB 16/5). Offer, *Working Classes*, p. 216.
28 Offer, *Morality*, p. 106.
29 The Paris Declaration Respecting Maritime Law, 16/4/1856, was signed after the Treaty of Paris which ended the Crimean War. Signatories agreed to abolish privateering; that a neutral flag covered an enemy's goods, with the exception of contraband of war, and were not liable to capture; and that blockades, in order to be binding, must be maintained by a force sufficient to prevent access to the coast of the enemy.
30 Offer, *Morality*, pp. 108–9.
31 Grant Duff, diary 22, 24/2/1911, folios. 50–51; *Churchill Collage Archives Centre*, Grant Duff papers 2/1.
32 Grebler, *Cost of the War*, pp. 13, 34.
33 Goebel, *Deutsche Rohstoffwirtschaft im Weltkrieg*, 1930, quoted in Grebler, *Cost of the War*, p. 12.

34   Grebler, *Cost of the War*, pp. 37, 51–52.

35   Teuteberg, 'Food Provisioning', Zweiniger-Bargielowska, *Food and War*, p. 59.

36   Guichard, *Blockade*, pp. 10–11. Strachan, First World War, pp. 45–46. Molodowsky, 'Germany's Foreign Trade', *Quarterly Journal of Economics*, 1927.

37   Clark, *Iron Kingdom*, p. 3.

38   Clark, *Iron Kingdom*, p. 1, from Howitt, *Rural and Domestic Life of Germany* (1842), p. 429.

39   Strachan, *First World War*, p. 165.

40   Weinreb, *Modern Hungers*, pp. 17–18.

41   Bown, *Damnable Invention*, pp. 218–231. Haber received the 1918 Nobel Prize for ammonia production, not for 'prolonging the war', but for 'for agricultural innovation' which was believed at the time to be the solution to the world's hunger. Haber spent much of the war developing chlorine gas for military purposes and personally supervised its first use at the second Battle of Ypres in the spring of 1915.

42   'In 1913, Chile was supplying two-thirds of the global nitrate demand, yet by the 1930s this was reduced to a mere 7 per cent. The effect was to cause catastrophic devastation of the Chilean economy and throw tens of thousands out of work,' Bown, *Damnable Invention*, pp. 231–32.

43   Chapter 11, 'Immense cemetery'.

44   For those wishing to immerse themselves in the pre-war machinations: both in 2012, Grimes, *Strategy and War Planning*, particularly Chapter 6, 'The Solidification of Dual Strategies, 1911–14', and Lambert, *Armageddon*, almost 700 pages. Osborne's *Blockade of Germany*, 2004, is a helpful start. All these histories, and many more in adjacent footnotes, discuss the political and legislative niceties and disputes in *The Declaration of Paris*, 1856; The second Peace Conference which met at The Hague, 1907; *The Declaration of London*, 1908; *The Naval Prize Bill*, 1911, unratified by the British government, but signed by its conference representatives – maritime rights being 'slippery and elusive affairs' (Consett, *Triumph*), p. xi.

45   Thomas Gibson Bowles, 'The Declaration of London', *The Nineteenth Century*, 5/1909.

46   Offer, *Morality*, p. 105.

47   Wegener, *Strategy*, p. 37, fn. 2. Marder, *Dreadnought*, Vol. 1, p. 372.

48   Tuchman, *August 1914*, p. 373.

49   Bell, *Blockade of Germany*, preface, p. iv. Siney, *The Allied Blockade*, pp. v–vi. Hankey, *Supreme Command*, Vol. I, pp. 95–96.

50   Kelly, *Tirpitz*, pp. 391–92.

51   Weinreb, *Modern Hungers*, p. 15.

52   Hull, *Scrap of Paper*, p. 176.

53   *British Foreign Office*, 'Statement of the Measures adopted to Intercept the Seaborne Commerce of Germany', Miscellaneous No. 2, 1916 (Parmelee, *History of the Blockade*), pp. 39–40, Appendix 3.

54   Lambert, *Armageddon*, pp. 12–13.

55   *Hansard*, House of Commons, 12/11/1918, Vol. 110, cc2568–639.

56   Ranft, ed, *Beatty Papers*, Vol. 1, pp. 145–46. Marder, *Dreadnought*, Vol. II, p. 3.

57   Vigness, *Neutrality*, p. 33.

58   Lambert, foreword, in Cobb, *Preparing Blockade*, pp. xv, xviii, xxi. Also, Poolman, *Armed Merchant Cruisers*.

59   Cobb, *Preparing Blockade*, preface, p. xviii, p. 13.

60   Admiral Dudley de Chair, *Sea is Strong*, pp. 166–216, particularly pp. 166–9. Also, Chatteron, *Big Blockade* (1932), Dunn, *Blockade* (2016); Hampshire, *Blockaders* (1980) and Grainger, *Maritime Blockade* (2003), which includes contemporary reports.

61   Guichard, *Naval Blockade*, pp. 2–3.

62   Vigness, *Neutrality*, p. 33.

63   Poolman, *Armed Merchant Cruisers*, p. 33. The *Kaiser Wilhelm der Grosse* was a luxury passenger liner which gained the *Blue Riband* for Germany on the Atlantic route. She was modified to an all-third-class ship to take advantage of the lucrative immigrant market to the United States and, then, as an auxiliary cruiser during World War I. She destroyed three ships before being defeated in the Battle of Río de Oro off West Africa by the British cruiser

HMS Highflyer in August 1914. The wreck was rediscovered in 1952 and dismantled.

64   Parmelee, *Blockade and Sea Power*, p. 243.
65   Guichard, *Naval Blockade*, pp. 9–10, suggests 724 German and Austrian steamers. Lambert, *Armageddon*, p. 212. Vigness, *Neutrality*, p. 40. Marreo, 'Logistics for Commerce War', *The Mariner's Mirror*, pp. 455–64. Hankey, *Supreme Command*, pp. 545–46.
66   Koerver, *War of Numbers*, p. 38.
67   Hashagen, *Commander*, p. 31.
68   15/2/1915 (Churchill, *World Crisis*), p. 285.
69   Kramer, 'Blockade', Winter, *World War One*, Vol. 2, p. 488.
70   Vigness, *Neutrality of Norway*, pp. 5–6. 'The later entrance of Italy, Greece and Romania into the war on the side of the Allies, and of Bulgaria on the side of the Central Powers, reduced the line of contact with the neutral world.'
71   Lambert, foreword, in Stephen Cobb 'Preparing for Blockade', p. xv; quotes Corbett, *Some Principles of Maritime Strategy* (London, 1911).
72   Porch, 'French Army in the First World War' in Millett, *Military Effectiveness*, Vol. 1, p. 204.
73   Kramer, *Blockade*, p. 472, seems to disagree. See also Laurens, *Le blocus et la guerre sous-marin* (A Colin, Paris 1924).
74   Lambert, *Armageddon*, p. 452.
75   Chapter 8, 'Final patrol'.
76   Cruttwell, *History of the Great War*, p. 192, fn. 1.
77   Koerver, *War of Numbers*, p. 49.
78   Lambert, *Armageddon*, Chapter 3.
79   McDermott, 'Trading with the Enemy', p. 202, quoting from *TNA*, CAB 17/102B, 1/11/1914, 'Report on the Opening of the War'; Montagu to Asquith, 3/7/1915, *Bodleian Library*, Asquith Papers, I/14; memorandum, Kennedy, 12/7/1916, *TNA*, FO 899/11.
80   McDermott, 'Trading with the Enemy', pp. 210–19.
81   Hankey, *Supreme Command*, Vol. I, p. 248.
82   Lambert, *Armageddon*, p. 355.
83   Koerver, *War of Numbers*, p. 51.
84   Lambert, *Armageddon*, p. 358.
85   Lambert, *Armageddon*, p. 601. Letter 14/1/1915.
86   Consett, *Triumph of Unarmed Forces*, p. 133.
87   Consett, *Triumph of Unarmed Forces*, p. 130.
88   Phillips, *American Participation in Belligerent Commercial Controls* (1933), p. 675. See also, Coogan, *End of Neutrality*, which leads to considerable further reading.
89   Guichard, *Blockade*, pp. 2–3.
90   Vigness, *Neutrality*, p. 43. Osborne, *Blockade*, p. 30.
91   Koerver, *German Submarine War*, p. xvi.
92   Cruttwell, *History of the Great War*, p. 199.
93   MacMillan, *Paris 1919*, p. 10.
94   O'Brien, 'Economic Effects', *History Today*, p. 24.
95   Kelly, *Tirpitz*, p. 392.
96   Coogan, *Neutrality*, p. 193.
97   Ferguson, *Pity*, p. 223.
98   Asprey, *German High Command*, p. 171.
99   Guichard, *Blockade*, p. 27. For a useful article on the role of Canada in ameliorating the effect of the blockade on American shipping, see Kennedy, 'The North Atlantic Triangle', *Journal of Transatlantic Studies*.
100 British Ambassador Page to the US Secretary of State, 15/10/1914, US Foreign Relations, Supplement, 1914, p. 248, in Phillips, *Participation*, pp. 675–76.
101 US Secretary of State Lansing to British Ambassador Page, London, 21/10/1915 (Parmelee, *Blockade and Sea Power*), pp. 67–68.
102 Peterson, *Propaganda*, p. 73.
103 Peterson, *Propaganda*, p. 75.
104 Osborne, *Blockade*, p. 34.
105 Offer, *Morality*, p. 111.

106 House of Lords debates: 27/6/1923, Vol. 54, c. 647–54; 1/4/1925, Vol. 60, c860–76.

107 Consett, *Triumph of Unarmed Forces*, p. x.

108 Carson, 'Memorandum to War Cabinet on trade blockade' 1/1/1917 (*TNA*, CAB 1/22), folios 1–2. Cinchona, plant source of quinine. See also, 'Memorandum to War Cabinet on trade blockade' 1/1916 (*TNA*, CAB 1/15); and 'Summary of Blockade Information, 26/1/1917–24/1/1918, Nos 1–52 (*TNA*, FO 902/40).

109 Lambert, *Armageddon*, p. 11.

110 Consett, *Triumph*, p. 71.

111 Consett, *Triumph*, p. 287.

112 Consett, *Triumph*, pp. 89–90.

113 Consett, *Triumph*, p. 92.

114 Consett, *Triumph*, p. 106.

115 Vigness, *Neutrality*, pp. 22–23, 8/8/1914.

116 Vigness, *Neutrality*, p. 85. What follows concentrates on the Norwegian dilemma. For a Dutch view, Marc Frey, 'Bullying the Neutrals, The Case of the Netherlands', in Chickering and Förster, eds., *Great War, Total War*, which offers considerable further reading.

117 Vigness, *Neutrality*, p. 47.

118 Devlin, *Too Proud*, p. 183.

119 Peterson, *Propaganda for War*, pp. 73–75.

120 Vigness, *Neutrality*, p. 54.

121 Vigness, *Neutrality*, p. 56.

122 Vigness, *Neutrality*, pp. 56–57.

123 Vigness, *Neutrality*, pp. 71–84.

124 Lambert, *Armageddon*, p. 499.

125 Vincent, *Politics of Hunger*, pp. 35–36.

126 Janicki, 'British Blockade', *Student Pulse*.

127 Vincent, *Politics of Hunger*, p. 48.

128 Guichard, *Blockade*, pp. 3–4.

129 Kennedy, *First World War*, pp. 33–34.

130 Vincent, *Politics of Hunger*, p. 15.

131 George Osborne, then British chancellor, repaid some £1.9 billion owed to just over 100,000 'people' who held war bonds issued in 1917, the last of the Great War debt. The Debt Management Office estimated that Britain had paid some £5.5 billion in total interest on the loans.

132 O'Brien, 'Economic Effects', *History Today*, p. 23.

133 Ferguson, *Pity*, p. 253.

134 Osborne, *Blockade*, p. 1.

135 Sadly unread, through lack of an English translation: Wilhelm Groener, *Lebenserinnerungen, Jugend, Generalstab, Weltkrieg* (Vandenhoeck & Ruprecht, Göttingen 1959) and Anna Roerkohl, *Hungerblockade und Heimatfront. Die kommunale Lebensmittelversorgung in Westfalen während des Ersten Weltkrieges* (Steiner, Stuttgart 1991).

136 Kramer, 'Blockade and economic warfare', in Winter, ed, *Cambridge History of First World War*, Vol. II, pp. 460–489.

137 Kramer, *Blockade*, pp. 477–79.

138 Consett, *Triumph*, p. 80.

139 Consett, *Triumph*, p. 83.

140 Consett, *Triumph*, pp. 196–203.

141 Chapter 5, 'The 'very nearly' battle'.

142 Koerver, *War of Numbers*, p. 50.

143 Kristiansands Nikkelrafferingsverk (KNR).

144 Beaverbrook, *Courage*, p. 94.

145 McDowell, *Steel at the Sault*, pp. 113–17.

146 Hull, *Scrap of Paper*, pp. 199–200. McKercher, 'Economic Warfare', *Oxford Illustrated History*, pp. 125, 132.

147 House, *Intimate Papers*, pp. 163–64.

148 Grebler, *Cost of the War*, pp. 73–75.

CHAPTER 4

Erich's War

One of the things that has served to convince us that the Prussian autocracy was not and could never be our friend is that from the very outset of the present war it has filled our unsuspecting communities and even our offices of government with spies and set criminal intrigues everywhere afoot against our national unity of counsel, our peace within and without our industries and our commerce. Indeed it is now evident that its spies were here even before the war began; and it is unhappily not a matter of conjecture but a fact proved in our courts of justice that the intrigues which have more than once come perilously near to disturbing the peace and dislocating the industries of the country have been carried on at the instigation, with the support, and even under the personal direction of official agents of the Imperial Government accredited to the Government of the United States. Even in checking these things and trying to extirpate them we have sought to put the most generous interpretation possible upon them because we knew that their source lay, not in any hostile feeling or purpose of the German people towards us (who were, no doubt, as ignorant of them as we ourselves were), but only in the selfish designs of a Government that did what it pleased and told its people nothing. But they have played their part in serving to convince us at last that their Government entertains no real friendship for us and means to act against our peace and security at its convenience. It means to stir up enemies against us at our very doors.[1]

Erich Gerth's war began long before the shooting started. In the spring of 1911 he took the port railway from Bremen to Bremerhaven to claim one of the fifty cabins on the Norddeutscher Lloyd steamer *Chemnitz*.[2] Gerth was a member of small party of new officers travelling to join the light cruiser *Bremen* on its East American Station. *Chemnitz* arrived at Galveston in Texas on 25 May; *Bremen* was waiting in port to collect her replacements, who reported the next day. Gerth's own posting was unusual: he was to become an agent for German naval intelligence.

Bremen was seven years into a ten-year posting charged with promoting and protecting German commercial endeavours in Central and South America, and with flying the flag in visits to the United States.[3] At almost 4,000 tons, she carried a main battery of ten 4.1-inch guns and two 18-inch torpedo tubes. *Bremen* was accounted a good sea boat, although when reaching her top speed of around twenty-three knots, she took on a lot of water while rolling up to 20 per cent.[4] The ship was built in 1902 at the AG Weser yard in Bremen, which provided her name, and also built both of the u-boats commanded during the coming war by Erich's brother, Georg.

Erich Gerth's career before joining the *Bremen* had been conventional for a new officer. After concluding his sea cadet training and receiving his commission as Leutnant zur See in 1908, he joined the High Seas Fleet for a year and a half aboard the light cruiser *Königsberg*. Then followed a year with the Naval Artillery Department during which time he gained his automatic promotion to Oberleutnant.

Something had marked Gerth out as suitable for his new role. Apart from the intellect evident during training, and his natural urbane and sociable manner, it may have been his association with the man who preceded him as a spy in South America, Wilhelm Canaris.

Towards the end of their time together as sea cadets, in November 1907, both Gerth and Canaris were awarded the *Kronenorden*, the Prussian Order of the Crown, in the gift of the Kaiser, which came in six levels of importance. Their junior medal was given to commissioned officers for services to the crown of a general nature, more of a thank you or a pat on the back than a reward of great honour. The Kaiser doled out at least three to British worthies in 1899 for making the arrangements for his official visit to Great Britain which, of course, included time to see his grandmother, Queen Victoria. A further two British officials received awards for similar duties when the Prince of Wales visited the Kaiser in Berlin in 1902 for birthday celebrations. At least forty-two sea cadets who went on to become u-boat commanders received the *Kronenorden* before the war began. As these officers' dates of entry are spread over time, it is probable that the top cadets in each year were recognised in this way.

Officers got promoted in the German naval officer corps because of time served, not because of competence. By an imperial decree in 1899, all officers were listed in order of length of service and promotion from one rank to the other followed strictly according to whoever headed these lists. The final decision always rested with the Kaiser. The system concentrated on the 'expulsion of the undesirable rather than on the promotion of the most highly desirable.[5] 'Only in the case of submarine commanders in World War I were exceptions made, as the road from Leutnant to Kapitänleutnant was [later] somewhat shortened by the exigencies of war.' Normally it took three years from leutnant to oberleutnant and a further four years to Kapitänleutnant. Canaris and Gerth received their early promotions within days of each other: Fähnrich (midshipman), April 1906; Leutnant, September 1908; but then it seems Gerth slipped a little behind: Oberleutnant, August 1910 (Canaris), January 1911 (Gerth); and Kapitänleutnant, November 1915 (Canaris), December 1915 (Gerth), although some records suggest Gerth's last promotion was delayed until August 1916. This is the rank at which Gerth's career rested, while Canaris went on in 1938 to become a Vizeadmiral and the head of the *Abwehr*, the Nazi military intelligence. Canaris led a complex life with many secrets; there is much evidence that he traded information with the British whom he certainly met during World War II. He was tortured and garrotted in 1945 at the Flossenbürg concentration camp after he finally admitted playing a leading part in the plot to assassinate Adolf Hitler on 20 July the year before.

Canaris preceded Gerth by just over a year in the *Bremen*; his tour of South American duty lasted two years from November 1907 to November 1909, including a visit to Haiti during the revolution of 1908. Canaris became the adjutant of *Bremen*'s commander, Kapitän Albert Hopman, and accompanied him on visits to friends in the South American interior.[6] *Bremen* travelled widely: her duties took her round Cape Horn to Chilean ports like Punta Arenas, but most of her time was spent near the principal German interests on the east coast. In 1908, *Bremen* began a five-month tour of South America with stops at Buenos Aires, Rio de Janeiro, Costa Rica, Panama, Guatemala and the Dutch Antilles. In the autumn of 1909, she joined other cruisers including the *Dresden* in celebrations in the United States and, early in 1912, was there again, this time with the battlecruiser *Moltke*, on a goodwill cruise recognising US President William Taft. Wherever she went great parties were thrown for the *Bremen*'s crew as she received the 'typical fanatical welcome accorded to German warships by the patriotic and nationalistic expatriate community' of those times.[7] There were 10,000 Germans in Buenos Aires and 30,000 across Argentina; the breadwinners were mostly business people, engineers, technicians and farmers, but the number also included many military instructors who trained the Argentine Army.

All in all, there was plenty of time and opportunity for Canaris and Gerth to be about their covert tasks. These duties involved the setting up and development of what the Germans called Etappe Centres; an etappe was historically a staging post or a place where troops on the march stayed overnight. From 1898, naval officers overseas began establishing secret intelligence posts.[8] These *Etappendienst* could be run by several men, or a single person, depending on the ports and countries in which they operated. The centres gathered and transmitted by radio, intelligence on the shipping movements of Germany's future enemies. They also negotiated berthing contracts within neutral states; sought information on secluded anchorages on the mainland and on coastal islands; and investigated options for coal and wood for refuelling in emergency. The

British had a parallel and equally concealed worldwide network that used brokerage firms, ships' captains and consulates.

Canaris was given contact addresses in Brazil, Chile and Argentina to set up networks of informers. He expanded the circle of agents and set up an offshore message re-transmission system using ships fitted with wireless telegraphy owned by Norddeutsche Lloyd, HAPAG, and the Kosmos Line. Their task was to make night-time calls at Corall, Coronel, Talcahuano and Valparaiso to collect telegrams from ashore and to signal their contents to German warships at sea. It was at these meetings with land agents that Canaris began to acquire the Spanish language as he became familiar with the countries of Central and South America. The system worked and 'later the entire cruiser squadron operating in South American waters relied on the network of Canaris's spies and report ships'.

When Gerth arrived in South America, he took over Canaris's work. This is recognised by Gerth's obituary written many years later by Matthias Löhr, an official at the German Foreign Office in Berlin with access to ministry files.[9] Löhr's information about Gerth's intelligence career is based in part on Gerth's handwritten, sanitised application to join the German foreign office in 1922. Gerth wrote:

> *I spent many years abroad, in particular, Spain, Italy and the remaining Mediterranean countries, in North and South America and in Africa. During a permanent stay abroad which lasted several years as a member of the admiralty staff I was involved in a special military political mission and had the opportunity to study political and economic conditions, write military-political reports, extend my knowledge in foreign languages, adapt to foreign ways of thinking and gain confidence in official communication with foreign personalities and offices.*[10]

The document contains subtle gilding, immediately recognisable today to anyone whose duties include reading job applications. There is, also, the first hint of a little more, the beginnings of untestable exaggerations, the borrowing of the overheard experiences of others. As Gerth's story unfolds, especially after the war, it is evident that Gerth had a much-welcomed personality, instantly popular with many, a partygoer, and a good teller of stories. The international extravaganzas with their swirling dances and enthusiastic ladies that Gerth enjoyed aboard the *Bremen* were a long way from his fatherless teenage years in Berlin. As a young adult, life initially came easily. Perhaps inventing some small and harmless excitements in his past so as to move nearer to the centre of the 'in-crowd' was a natural thing to do.

> *We were inundated with invitations, ate at tables covered with the most glorious mantles, adorned with the rarest orchids, the finest porcelain,*

*silver plate and golden dessert spoons, were seated next to stylish ladies
who wore expensive perfume and metre-long necklaces of pearls: we
made trips in automobiles and dog-carts, danced the two-step and
generally 'had a good time'.*[11]

Ten years later in 1932, Gerth was pleading special circumstances because
of his past military service while employed in the foreign office. He wrote
that he was used on 'various different' missions at home and abroad.
'For example', he explained, 'I was entrusted for three years with the
organisation of the intelligence service in North and South America and
the cruiser war in the Atlantic Ocean in case of war, a task that I fulfilled
to the full satisfaction of the admiralty staff.'[12]

Note the multiplicity of 'missions' of which he was the 'organiser'.
Twenty-eight months away became rounded to thirty-six. Now, we have
included 'North America', something his predecessor, Canaris, never
discussed. North America did not offer the opportunities for refuelling or
hiding armed cruisers that were provided in the south. As a neutral country,
ship movements were readily discussed in the American newspapers and
needed no cloak and dagger discovery. Work in North America would
entail something darker, perhaps the establishment of sleeper cells for
later, possible, terrorist attacks.

The Germans were particularly upset that the United States, despite
being neutral, was sending munitions to the Allies. Indeed, before the
British blockade, many Americans, driven by profit, defended their neutral
right to supply whomever they wished. One arch culprit from Germany's
perspective was the giant Bethlehem Steel Company. The Germans,
somewhat naively, did nothing to hide their intentions in circulars from
their military representative, Dr E. Fischer, which were reprinted in the
Swiss press in 1914. These called for volunteers to look for employment in
munitions companies like Bethlehem Steel and, when settled, to undertake
sabotage – unless, of course, the notice was engineered by the British or the
French as an elaborate defamatory ruse to arouse American indignation.

*In all branch establishments of German banking houses in Sweden,
Norway, Switzerland, China and the United States, special military
accounts have been opened for special war necessities. Main
headquarters authorizes you to use these credits to an unlimited extent
for the purpose of destroying factories, workshops, camps, and the most
important centres of military and civil supply belonging to the enemy.
In addition to the incitement of labour troubles, measures must be taken
for the damaging of engines and machinery plants, the destruction
of vessels carrying war material to enemy countries, the burning of
stocks of raw materials and finished goods, and the depriving of large
industrial centres of electric power, fuel and food. Special agents, who*

will be placed at your disposal, will supply you with the necessary means for effecting explosions and fires, as well as with a list of people in the country under your supervision who are willing to undertake the task of destruction.[13]

Widespread sabotage certainly occurred before and after the United States entered the war in 1917. Fifty acts of terrorism are on record and thirty of these took place in the New York City and New Jersey area. These acts were managed through the German embassies in New York and Washington, headed by the diplomat Count Johann von Bernstorff, and all vigorously denied at the time. They included $10 million in damages to thirty-six cargo ships as they crossed the Atlantic and caused by the placement in cargo holds of pencil bombs with delayed timers. This team was led by master spy Franz von Rintelen. Elsewhere, munitions factories were hit by explosions and a large ammunition store near the Statue of Liberty, its contents destined for the Allies in Europe, was blown up in 1916. It is possible, of course, that Gerth was involved in some of the advanced planning for this mayhem, but it does seem unlikely that, after the conclusion of his tour on the *Bremen*, he was shipped back to a deck position in the Baltic with all his North American contacts and skills left behind. When President Wilson urged Congress on 22 April 1917 to confirm a declaration of war on Germany, he gave the German spy system in America as the fourth of his reasons alongside the use of unrestricted submarine warfare, the sinking of neutral merchant ships, and the Zimmermann telegram which encouraged Mexico to attack the United States.[14]

In his foreign office application of 1922, Gerth claimed that during his naval years he took language examinations in English, French and Spanish and that he achieved fluency in all three. He also claimed to be able to communicate in Italian. However, when asked if he was prepared to take a preliminary language examination in English and French, he requested a delay. This seems a little odd for an applicant for a scarce and prestigious position in the tough times just a few years after the end of the Great War. But there may have been good reasons. In fairness, Gerth's secondary school in Berlin, the Königliches Kaiser Wilhelm Realgymnasium, provided its pupils in their last two years with thirty-one compulsory lessons a week, including four in Latin and three each in English and French.[15] His mother was reported to speak French well and his brother, Georg, was competent in English and French. As well as the Spanish, which would have greatly benefitted from South American travels, there was an extensive Italian community in Montevideo which may well have been on Gerth's itinerary and provided important fodder for his intelligence network.[16]

Gerth, foreign adventure over, travelled home in September 1913 on the *Hans Woermann*, a 4,000-ton passenger, freight and mail ship of the Woermann Line of Hamburg. For the next two years until the end of 1915,

Gerth served as watch officer on fleet duties in the Baltic on SMS *Hessen*, sister ship to the SMS *Preußen* on which brother Georg spent eighteen months around 1909.

No doubt both Canaris and Gerth wrote detailed notes of their intelligence network; presumably Gerth's work in South America was an updating and an improvement of that already done by Canaris. Contact details and emergency bases and their facilities would then be issued to warships sent to fight in the South Atlantic and to the auxiliaries ordered to supply them. Ironically, it was Canaris who came to make use of their combined knowledge and, therefore, in a way, be grateful to Gerth for his efforts.

In 1914, Canaris was again appointed an adjutant, this time on the cruiser SMS *Dresden,* which was sent to replace *Bremen* on the East American Station. *Dresden* arrived off the Mexican naval base of Veracruz in January to be greeted by two Mexican gunboats. Civil war had broken out. The newly installed President Victoriano Huerta faced a revolt led by the 'bandit' Pancho Villa. American oil workers and their families came under threat and US troops were landed. Because of his language skills, Canaris was in the thick of negotiations and often conducted dangerous trips ashore. With the European war declared in 1914, *Dresden* was ordered to stay on station and to carry out a 'trade war', common code for sinking enemy merchant shipping. After much naval activity, the expansion of Canaris's spy network, and the regular use of the *etappe* facilities on the mainland, *Dresden* met and joined at Easter Island with Admiral Count Maximilian von Spee's squadron of heavy cruisers crossing the Pacific from China.[17] The fleet ran into three British cruisers at Coronel off the coast of Chile on 1 November 1914, two of which were sunk with all hands.[18] This was the first British naval defeat since 1812.

A month later and seeking rapid revenge, 'two hastily despatched British battle cruisers' with workmen still board – *Invincible* and *Inflexible* – caught up with Spee near the Falkland Islands as he attempted to raid the British supply base at Port Stanley. Spee believed rumours, against the advice of his senior commanders, that the islands were undefended because their ships had left to put down a new Boer uprising in South Africa. The British fleet, commanded by Vice Admiral Doveton Sturdee, caught Spee at his most vulnerable. Sturdee rapidly sank six of Spee's ships, including the sister heavy cruisers *Scharnhorst* and *Gneisenau*, killing 2,200 men, including Spee and his two sons.[19] The one German escapee was the *Dresden* whose cat and mouse flight from the British involved use of several scouted havens and *etappes* including Sholl and Hewett Bays, near Punta Arenas; Christmas Island; and eventually Cumberland Bay on Robinson Crusoe's island of Más-a-Tierra. Here she was eventually found and sunk illegally in neutral waters by the British cruiser *Kent*. Canaris conducted negotiations with the British under the roar of *Kent*'s guns. Canaris escaped from Chilean internment in August 1915 and after a 'boy's own' two-month trip home involving horseback, train and ships on a false passport, and which included a stopover in Falmouth, England, reached Germany.[20] While Canaris received the hero's welcome, another of his and Erich Gerth's classmates, Oberleutnant Kurt Hartwig, the *Dresden*'s torpedo officer, also escaped internment and got back to Germany in July before Canaris made his attempt.[21]

At the beginning of 1914, Gerth's new ship, *Hessen* was a powerful if vulnerable ship with four eleven-inch guns in twin turrets fore and aft of the central superstructure, fourteen 6.7-inch guns and eighteen 3.45-inch quick-firing guns. She also had six 18-inch torpedo tubes submerged in her hull.[22] *Hessen* was a typical Tirpitz battleship, quickly made obsolete by Admiral Jackie Fisher's dreadnoughts, and coming to the end of its days.[23] Gerth, in different roles, was to stay in the Baltic area for almost the entire war; he left for his Mediterranean posting in April 1918. His brother Georg overlapped in the period until June 1916 and one assumes they found some time to meet.

Gerth and the *Hessen* saw action if only from a distance. The ship provided background support for the bombardment of Scarborough, Hartlepool and Whitby on 16 December 1914. While Hartlepool was a legitimate target as a naval town, the attacks on the undefended watering holes of Scarborough and Whitby as the unsuspecting population sat down to breakfast was declared a war crime.[24] Winston Churchill, in full hyperbolic flight, proclaimed that the 'stigma of the baby-killers of Scarborough will brand its officers and men while sailors sail the seas'. The British Navy's lack of defensive preparedness or offensive reaction reflected badly. It was the first time for 247 years that foreign naval guns had 'spilled blood on English soil'.[25] In total, 105 men, women and children were killed and 525 wounded. There was no fleet engagement, although it almost happened: Admiral Friedrich von Ingenohl thought skirmishes between destroyer screens meant that the British Grand Fleet would shortly arrive and he ran for home.

In April the next year, German battlecruisers, with Gerth in the *Hessen* in attendance, bombarded Yarmouth and Lowestoft in a tip-and-run raid timed to coincide with the Irish Republican Army's (IRA) Easter Rising in Dublin.[26] Before the raid started, the German flagship, the battlecruiser *Seydlitz*, was damaged by a mine and had to return. At Lowestoft, the German fleet destroyed two shore batteries, 200 houses and killed three civilians and wounded twelve. Poor visibility constrained the operation and this was made worse when the attacking fleet commanded by Rear Admiral Friedrich Bödicker failed to press home a real advantage when engaged with weaker British forces and turned for home.

Gerth's principal ships did not fare well. After participating in the Battle of the Gulf of Riga in August 1915, *Bremen* returned there for a second attack and struck a pair of Russian mines off Windau, now Ventspils in

Latvia, losing 250 men. The *Hans Woermann*, the ship that brought Gerth home from South America, was captured in 1914 by HMS *Cumberland*, renamed the *Gold Coast*, and transferred to the Elder Line of Liverpool. She was torpedoed in 1917 off the Irish Coast by *UC 47*, commander Paul Hundius, a close acquaintance of Erich's brother Georg. *Hessen* was withdrawn from active service in 1917, disarmed and her four large guns were sent to the Western Front and mounted on rail trucks. *Hessen* was used as a depot ship, allowed to stay in Germany after the war under the Treaty of Versailles, and became an ice-breaker and a remote-controlled target ship. After World War II, she was ceded to Russia where she acted as a target ship until scrapped in 1960.

The commander of *Hessen*, Kapitän Rudolph Bartels, felt Gerth was 'suited for employment in staff offices and also suitable for the position of submarine commander'.[27] Early in February 1916, Erich Gerth moved to Libau in Courland as director of the 'E-Stelle' where he stayed until the end of June the following year. Gerth explained that the admiralty staff 'made use of the experience which I gained in the aforesaid activities in America and deployed me until the Russian collapse for a special mission'.

Here we have Gerth again with another 'special mission'. If the mission followed experience in the Americas, as claimed, it would have involved setting up *etappe* stations in enemy territory of Russia or Finland, which, given the relative compactness of the Baltic, and the lack of Russian vessels travelling to Scandinavia, seems unlikely. There is no evidence of Gerth visiting Denmark, Finland, Norway or Sweden and he spoke no Baltic languages. Nothing has been found of the 'E-Stelle' despite investigation except a suggestion that it stood for *Erprobungsstelle*, a trial centre, possibly for marine aircraft. Nothing is known of Gerth's time at the centre either. In 1917, the German Marine Air Forces in the Baltic area were commanded by Kapitänleutnant Hermann Berthold, with three flying stations at Libau, Windau and Angernsee.

What could be the truth of all of this? Gerth's timing seems a little out. He left his post in June 1917, but claimed that he stayed until the Russian 'collapse'. Could Gerth have been involved in some way? There are some intriguing possibilities, particularly in March at Sassnitz on Rügen Island on the German Baltic coast. Originally, the Germans sought unsuccessfully to encourage non-Russian nationalities to rebel against the Tsar. When the Germans switched their support to internal social revolution, the effect was 'world-shaking'.[28] Certainly, in February 1917, female workers in the Russian capital of St Petersburg marched through the streets calling for food, the ousting of the Tsar and an end to the war. The next day, a multitude of men and women joined them on the streets. Troops refused orders to fire on the protestors and mutinied. On 2 March, Tsar Nicholas II abdicated and a provisional government was formed. Next month, the Germans aided thirty-two members of two opposing factions, Vladimir Lenin with his exiled Bolshevist supporters and a group of Julius Martov's Mensheviks, to journey from Zurich to St Petersburg. A sealed German train took the group to Sassnitz, where there would have been German military oversight, and from there by ferry and train to Trelleborg in Sweden, then Helsinki, and finally across the Finnish border into Russia. In Russia, the Germans backed the Bolsheviks with substantial finances.[29] War minister Alexander Kerensky took over the short-lived provisional government in June. It was not until October, four months after Gerth had left, that Vladimir Lenin, after a period in hiding in Helsinki from early August, called for the successful Bolshevik *coup d'état* against the Kerensky government. Lenin returned from self-exile in October to demand action from the Bolshevik Central Committee. The *coup* in St Petersburg was led by Leon Trotsky and Josef Stalin and ended when the Winter Palace was occupied easily by a small group while the Kerensky cabinet was in session.[30]

However, from a German military perspective, the Russian 'collapse', when Gerth said he left his post, did not happen until the next year in March 1918. The German Army was then just eighty-five miles from St Petersburg. The Russians were beaten, the imperialist treaty of Brest-Litovsk was forced on 3 March and the fighting stopped.[31] A great swathe of land from the Baltic to the Crimea and the northern shores of the Black Sea was transferred to German control; the captured lands included Estonia and Latvia which were intended as fiefdoms for the Kaiser's close family. It had always been part of Chancellor Bethmann's plan to 'thrust back the Russian border as far as possible from Germany's eastern frontier' and to break her domination over the non-Russian vassal peoples.[32] Freed by the collapse, the Germans moved substantial forces quickly to the Western Front to support Operation Michael, Hindenburg and Ludendorff's last-ditch spring offensive in 1918.[33] The German Supreme Command also hoped against all logic to extract a million tons of grain from the 'unwilling population of the Ukraine'.[34] They were sadly disappointed. Conditions were 'utterly chaotic' and the puppet regime was incompetent. The truth had to be covered with propaganda.[35] Ukrainian peasants forcibly resisted German Army requisitions by destroying their half-ripened crops.[36] Even when added to the 'ruthless draining' of supplies from Romania, Poland and the Baltic States, and the rape of the captured territories in the west, Germany still found herself far from self-sufficient.[37]

Apart from the possibility of acting as a 'guard' for Lenin at Sassnitz, there are two other options for Gerth's 'secret mission' at Libau. The first may have involved preparations for the German invasion of the Baltic islands of Dago, Moon and Ösel at the head of the Gulf of Riga, now Hiiumaa, Muhu and Saaremaa off the north-west coast of Estonia, in October 1917. This action finally ended the High Seas Fleet's inactivity since the Battle of Jutland over a year before.[38] Some 25,000 German soldiers, accompanied by ten dreadnoughts, 350 other vessels, a half-dozen Zeppelins, and eighty aircraft (possibly with Gerth's involvement), took the islands in the most successful amphibious operation of the war. The Gulf of Riga was opened to German warships and threatened Russian naval bases in the Gulf of Finland. An estimated 20,000 Russians were captured.

The second option is probably far-fetched and comes back to Canaris. After his promotion to Kapitänleutnant, he spent a few days with the Navy Inspectorate at Kiel in November, but transferred at the end of the month to the Intelligence Section of the Admiralty Staff. On 4 January 1916, under the cover name of 'Carl', Canaris arrived in Spain with a covert mission to set up an *etappe* system for the supply of German u-boats in the Atlantic and *en route* to the Mediterranean, and to create a network of informers to report the movement of enemy shipping.[39] By the end of January, 'information centres' were installed in Santander, Seville, Cadiz, and Melilla while those at Algeciras, La Linea, Tripoli, Huelva, Tangier, Barcelona, Vigo and Corunna were in preparation. Canaris was not acting alone, but his assistants are not named in the military record. For a while, Canaris went back to Germany suffering from a bout of malaria caught in South America. On his return, British naval intelligence in 'Room 40' in London was on the case. It was clear to the Germans that there was also a source in their Spanish embassy leaking information to the French. In addition, the German codes were broken and the British and the French were reading radio traffic between Berlin and its three main espionage centres in Madrid, Barcelona and San Sebastian.

Late in February, Canaris left for Genoa using a Chilean passport in an attempt to get to Switzerland. He was held by the Italians and it took a month for him to get back to Spain. Canaris complained of a 'very harsh time under arrest', which included 'long interrogations and foul treatment'.[40]

By June, it was decided to get Canaris out of Spain as his life was thought to be in danger. Kapitänleutnant Lothar von Arnauld de la Perière, commander of *U 35*, missed Canaris during a twenty-four hour stopover at Cartagena on 21 June as Canaris was forbidden to 'sneak aboard'. On 14 September, Canaris tried again to board the u-boat, but the attempt failed due to bad weather. Then, on 29 September, at a rendezvous point off the Spanish coast at Salitrona Bay, Canaris was finally collected by Arnauld in *U 35* and taken to the Cattaro u-boat base in the Adriatic, arriving on 9 October 1916. The number of Allied trawlers and a submarine near the pick-up strongly suggested the leaks from the embassy continued. Canaris returned to Germany and on 24 October, with the Kaiser's personal approval, received the Iron Cross 1st Class. He was then assigned to the Navy Staff Inspectorate of Submarines. On 11 September 1917, probably desperate for a return to action, he took up training as a u-boat commander.

Is there a possibility that Gerth could again have followed in Canaris's wake? Could the time as director of the Baltic marine aircraft centre have been a cover? If it was a post in command of marine aircraft, it was one

for which he had no credentials. Might he have been assisting Canaris in
Spain as the obvious choice of assistant following their similar experiences
in South America? Gerth claimed in 1922, as noted, to have served in
Spain, Italy and Africa. There is no record of Gerth doing this, but Canaris
served in all three during his Spanish mission, the last two in Genoa and in
Tangier and Tripoli, and so might a close accomplice. It is always possible
that one of Gerth's early large ships made stopovers in Africa: he spent
seven months on SMS *Kaiser Karl der Grosse* at the end of his sea cadetship
in 1907 and 1908, but the pre-dreadnought battleship was a part of the High
Seas Fleet and remained in the North and Baltic Seas; and followed that
with a year aboard the light cruiser *Königsberg* which was not sent to Africa
until 1914. However, just as Canaris was in Spain, Italy and the north of
Africa in 1914, so Gerth's brother Georg was stationed off West Africa in
the gunboat *Panther* in 1912 and early in 1913. If there was any imaginary
credit claimed by Gerth by association, there were plenty of close sources.

There is one other element that gives pause. Canaris made royal contact
during his time in Spain. A British agent jealously reported that Canaris
was often seen in deep conversation with the king. When seeking to escape
Spain, Canaris was threatened with kidnap by the French and British secret
services. Discussions took place as to whether the Spanish king should be
alerted to the need to keep a confidential watch on Canaris's safety. In 1922,
in his foreign office application, Gerth gave several surprising referees
all of which would be contacted by the conscientious German ministry.
In other words, a false referee would severely hinder the employment
application. On Gerth's list of Prussian and Bavarian residents were Their
Royal Highnesses Prince und Princess Ludwig Ferdinand von Bayern and
Maria de la Paz de Bourbon, the Spanish infanta and daughter of Queen
Isabella II; His Excellency Pablo Soler, ambassador to his Majesty the King
of Spain; His Excellency Diego von Bergen, the Italian ambassador; and
Monsignor Eugenio Maria Giuseppe Giovanni Pacelli, the papal envoy,
later in 1939 to become Pope Pius XII. Clearly these contacts need later
discussion, but for now they show an extraordinarily high level of political
and religious intimacy with the upper echelons of Spanish and Italian
Catholic society.[41]

Gerth began his u-boat training in June 1917, a few months before
Canaris. The physical criteria were higher than other branches of the
service: no history of heart or vascular diseases, a muscular body with
healthy skin, good teeth, and perfect ears, nose and throat, good hearing
and no colour blindness.[42] Speech had to be perfect with no stuttering
and Gerth had to present a family history showing no hereditary disease,
particularly tuberculosis. The age limits were between eighteen and
thirty years, but this was raised in 1917 to thirty-five; Gerth was thirty-
one and possibly the rule change was timely. Applicants needed to weigh
between sixty and eighty kilograms and be no taller than 180 cm to move

easily through a cramped submarine. Applicants also needed to pass a psychological profile and to have no criminal record; any crime committed during u-boat service meant an immediate transfer.

> *The best and most intelligent of our officers have been transferred to cruisers, torpedo boats and submarines ... With few exceptions those who have remained behind don't have much on the ball ... The fact that it was possible to select the supply of the needed personnel for our submarines ... was largely due to the fact that the German fleet served as a means of training a reserve of personnel from which officers, petty officers and special enlisted ratings could be carefully selected.*[43]

The emphasis laid on preparing the submarine crews can be seen in the increase of the training establishment in the Kiel – Eckernförde Bay areas on the Baltic coast. The number of men rose from 175 at the start of the war to nearly 900 by July 1916: their facilities included the mother ship *Vulcan*; three permanent target ships, including *Amazone* in which Erich's brother Georg recently served; a residential ship; nine submarines; seven torpedo boats; and a considerable number of training staff. Emphasis was on u-boat familiarisation, engines, navigation, diving, secret documents, signals, radio and decoding, seamanship, gunnery, torpedo maintenance and firing ... and many more. One of the, perhaps, unexpected subjects was training in role playing with captains and crew of investigated and destroyed ships, and the recommended behaviour in the event of capture, which seems to have been of little use to Georg Gerth in 1917.[44] One u-boat directive instructed commanders to capture, when possible, captains and engineering officers of sunken ships to stop them returning to the Allied skill pool.[45]

Commanders were expected to have the 'ability to take quick decisions, stay calm and keep a clear head in critical situations where duty must be done in difficult circumstances'.[46] Training an officer for command could take up to seven months. Erich Gerth took ten months, but this may be because, by 23 September, he was commander of a Kiel training boat, *UB 76*, an appointment which lasted for five weeks and suggests that Gerth was accounted a success. On 1 December 1917, the long-term head of the Submarine Training School, Korvettenkapitän Theodor Eschenburg, wrote that on the course for submarine commanders Gerth showed 'keen interest, diligence and deep thoroughness. Also, his practical achievements were good; he navigated with good vision and great confidence below and above the water, calmly carried out the attack and remained mostly unseen even at close distance. His hit results including the night shooting can be described as very good.'[47]

During May 1918, Kapitänleutnant Gerth travelled overland by train through Vienna to the Mediterranean u-boat bases in the Adriatic and reported to the Führer der U-boots, Kapitän zur See Theodor Püllen.[48] The Germans decided to start submarine warfare in the Mediterranean in 1915 to assist the Turkish forces being heavily shelled by Allied ships in the Dardanelles.[49] It was an offensive military operation. Several u-boats were sent to disrupt warships and the supplies to the Gallipoli front. Later, the German u-boats in the Adriatic fleet 'only received orders from the Austrian command for military missions which were rare as the Austrians never ventured further than the Ionian Sea'.[50] The German Admiralty directed all instructions for commercial warfare either through Püllen or directly to boats at sea.

Behind the immediate support for Turkey lay a much more extensive strategy that had its roots well before the start of the war. Germany's rise to become a world power, thwarted by the colonial land grabs outside of Europe of the previous centuries, was thought to be dependent on the disintegration of the British Empire.[51] The promotion of independence of large parts of the British Empire was itself a long-term German war aim. In a famous speech in Damascus in November 1898, made the day after a speech in Jerusalem full of strong support for Christianity, the Kaiser declared himself the protector over all Muslims:

> *Deeply moved by this imposing spectacle* [the Damascus reception] *and likewise by the consciousness of standing on the spot where held sway one of the most chivalrous rulers of all times, the great Sultan Saladin, a knight* sans peur et sans reproche, *who often taught his adversaries the right conception of knighthood, I seize with joy the opportunity to render thanks, above all to the Sultan Abdul Hamid for his hospitality. May the Sultan rest assured, and also the three hundred million Mohammedans scattered over the globe and revering him as their caliph, that the German Emperor will be and remain at all times their friend.*[52]

'The British', the Kaiser wrote in 1906, 'had better understand that war with Germany means the loss of India and therefore a world war'.[53] It was a theme to which he returned regularly. In 1914, before the start of the war, the Kaiser wrote to the German ambassador in St Petersburg, 'England ... must have the mask of Christian peaceableness torn publicly off her face ... Our consuls in Turkey and India, agents, etc, must inflame the whole Mohammedan world to wild revolt against this hateful, lying, conscienceless people of hagglers; for if we are to be bled to death, at least England shall lose India.' Setting the Islamic world afire was an integral part of Germany's official policy. As part of a continuation 'by other means' of this policy, the German-Turkish alliance of 2 August 1914 was concluded with an 'eye to unleashing a pan-Islamic movement, which was to lead off with a Holy War'. On the same day, the retired Freiherr

Max von Oppenheim, the man who had inspired the Kaiser's Damascus speech, was recalled to the foreign ministry. 'Taking up his ideas of 1898, he recommended Holy War and pan-Islamic propaganda as the most effective weapons for revolutionising the Islamic world and, as a first step, he proposed that expeditionary forces should be sent to Persia and Egypt.'

> *While the German armies were trying to overrun France in their first onset, the German government, in collaboration with the general staff, was working out a far-reaching programme of revolution, which was directed equally against the British Empire and imperial Russia. These activities began immediately on the outbreak of war. They were at first a means of strategic warfare; they were intended on the other hand, to delay the Russian deployment on Germany's eastern frontier and keep part of the Russian armies tied down by internal unrest, and on the other hand, to draw off part of the British fleet to overseas stations and make it difficult for France to raise recruits in her colonies. The most vulnerable points of Britain and France seemed to be among their colonial subjects while Russia offered fields for subversion among her non-Russian peoples.*[54]

The u-boat bases in the Adriatic added support to the strategic goals. They aided Turkey, first, by guarding the Gallipoli narrows and the Bosphorus so as to sever communications between the European allies in the Mediterranean and the Black Sea with its Russian ports and, second, as an advanced force by which Germany could attack Britain's empire at her two most vulnerable points, India and Egypt. For both these countries, the Suez Canal and its shipping was of supreme importance. The delivery of Sir Roger Casement, with guns and ammunition for the IRA, was just another example of marrying national aspirations, in this case those of the Irish, with a weakening of the British Empire. Casement was landed by German submarine to facilitate a rebellion against British rule across the country during the Easter Rising of 1916.[55]

The Mediterranean flotilla was headquartered in an old Austro-Hungarian cruiser *Maria Theresia* anchored in the main base at Pola, where they shared a shipyard with a large Austrian fleet. The town name was spelled 'Pola' in Italian but 'Pula' in Croatian. The town had a rich Illyrian and Roman history and from 1813 had been part of the Hapsburg Empire. Its commercial and military language was German. Gerth was to be in the Adriatic for less than six months and his immediate discussions would be with Austrian and German colleagues. This was not the time to achieve his claimed fluency in Italian through mixing with a minority Italian community.

Cattaro, now Kotor, Montenegro, was the advance base with a repair ship from where all missions started and finished because of its proximity to the entrance to the main sea and the security of the one hundred fathom line.[56] The Austrians had taken the port from the Italians with little fight. Later, Fiume, now Rijeka, Croatia, and Trieste at the head of the gulf were added to the fleet anchorages to provide u-boats with more extensive facilities for three-monthly overhauls. All these ports on the eastern shore of the Adriatic are deep-water harbours, 'resembling Norwegian fiords' and are protected for almost the 'whole length of the coast by a fringe of islands'. This is in sharp contrast to the Italian Adriatic coast where the limited ports are much exposed. In three of those recurring connections in the small world of the German navy officer corps, the senior administration staff officer at Cattaro was Kapitänleutnant Hubert Aust, the second administrative staff officer at Pola was Kapitänleutnant Hermann von Fischel, and Oberleutnant Kurt Hartwig, commanding *U 32* and *U 63*, who had been on the *Dresden* with Canaris in Chile, were all class mates of Erich Gerth at the naval academy crew of 1905.[57]

> *We merely added German personnel and material to these two plants in order to increase their efficiency, but unfortunately did not undertake to enlarge or extend them such as was done by the very energetic commander, Bartenbach, at Bruges and Ostend in Flanders.*[58] *The result was that at the climax of the submarine activities in the Mediterranean, it took longer and longer to repair the boats. In 1918, this became really serious. The chief of the submarine division took energetic steps and ordered extensive improvements and enlargements to Pola and Cattaro as submarine bases. The repair shops, etc, at Trieste and Fiume were also enlarged and increased in efficiency through proper measures. As a result of the Austrian collapse, these measures unfortunately were never entirely carried out. It was tragic that we never succeeded in getting hold of Valona; the passage through the Otranto narrows would have then been considerably easier.*[59]

A new fixed barrage of mine nets was laid to 150 feet by the British in the Otranto Straits to block access by the u-boats to the Mediterranean. This was to enhance an inefficient first attempt at a barrier made in 1915, which had accounted for only one submarine.[60] The new work began in April 1918 and was not completed until September. It was an out-and-out failure. Between April and August, Adriatic u-boats made 121 passages by simply diving underneath or, occasionally, around the obstacle. The nets had the 'adverse effect of increasing the u-boats' offensive potential once they were out in the Mediterranean because the convoy escorts were denuded in order to increase the strength of the barrage patrol'. This resulted in the overall loss rate of Mediterranean convoys being twice as high as those in the Atlantic, even though there the ships travelled out of convoy for much of the war.[61]

Another May arrival at Pola with Gerth was Oberleutnant Martin

Niemöller, an old Adriatic hand, who noticed that the 'intimacy of 1916 had disappeared, but the spirit survived, as did the good custom that all German submarine officers should address one another as *Henry*, irrespective of rank and real name'.[62] There were two other 'Henrys' who would become particularly famous in World War II: Oberleutnant Karl Dönitz, the future leader of the u-boats; and, as one could expect, Canaris. The history of the German Mediterranean Flotilla is 'largely the history of three or four conspicuously able commanders, who stand out among a number of quite mediocre performers'.[63] Most striking overall was the disproportionate success rates for a small number of u-boat aces: twenty-two of some 400 u-boat commanders in the Great War realised more than 60 per cent of all Allied merchant sinkings; only 4 per cent of all u-boats sank 30 per cent of all merchant shipping lost.[64]

Pola was at one end of, perhaps, the most humorous tale of the u-boats in the Mediterranean. It involved *UC 20* which was often employed in 1916 to transport rifles, machine guns and hand grenades to the Senussi, a religious sect resident in Libya and Egypt. The Germans and the Ottomans persuaded the Grand Senussi, Ahmed Sharif es Senussi, to declare jihad and to attack British-occupied Egypt from the west. This would divert British forces from a proposed Ottoman raid on the Suez Canal from Palestine. On one of *UC 20*'s voyages the crew was presented with a camel by the grateful Grand Senussi. Pride challenged, the captain decided to ship the beast home. The submarine went as close inshore as possible while the camel was driven into the sea but, when released from its tether, it paddled off at full speed. 'The commanding officer carried out a faultless attack with a 90 degree track angle and blew as the bows were just under the camel's belly. The boat rose and the camel lay on the bows, forelegs to port and hindlegs to starboard.'[65] The beast was hauled onto the deck and made fast. The next morning the captain told his watch officer that, if the boat had to dive on the way back to Pola, 'it's all up for the camel'. The watch officer had an answer. 'We can dive quite well with the camel ... With the boat at 4½ fathoms, the camel's head will just be sticking out above the surface. I have already marked it on the depth gauge.' Twice during the crossing, *UC 20* dived to evade enemy ships and each time came the order, 'Go to camel depth'. Close to the entrance to Pola, *UC 20* passed through a fishing fleet and the captain could not resist diving once more. 'A frightful horror seized the fishermen, who only saw the head and hump approaching and consequently believed it to be some fearful sea-monster. Setting all sail, they fled hastily.' There is, today, a herd of wild camel on the Pola peninsular where tales are told in the waterfront bars of a fearful creature of the deep.[66]

Chief among the able commanders in the Mediterranean was the leading u-boat ace, Arnauld de la Perière, who had rescued Canaris from Spain, and who sank 193 merchant ships with a total of 453,369 tons; two warships,

2,500 tons; and damaged eight ships, 34,312 tons.[67] A close second was the entirely ruthless Kapitänleutnant Max Valentiner who sank over 140 ships and was the third ranking ace of the war. In November 1915, Valentiner torpedoed the Italian passenger liner *Ancona* without allowing time for the passengers to abandon ship with the loss of 200 lives. Valentiner flew the Austro-Hungarian flag during the attack as, at that time, Germany was not at war with Italy. Rather than admit the truth and risk an Italian war, the Germans forced Austria-Hungary to admit falsely that it was one of their own submarines. Further, Austria-Hungary pretended to discipline a non-existent u-boat commander, and to pay reparations to Italy. A month later, Valentiner was branded a war criminal after sinking the passenger liner *Persia* without warning, contrary to international law at that time, and killing 343 of the 519 people aboard.[68] Both men survived the war. Arnauld was killed in 1941 in an aircraft accident at Le Bourget airport near Paris, France, while Valentiner died in 1949 in Sønderborg, Denmark.[69]

Gerth found Canaris had beaten him to the Adriatic by six months where he was appointed the admiralty staff officer at Pola and he had also been acting Führer for two months. These quick promotions were unusual as Canaris had no u-boat leadership experience although his training record praised him highly. Perhaps, as the Mediterranean flotilla was under the direct command of naval staff in Berlin, they wished to have their own man in place.[70] Canaris was not in the Adriatic to greet Gerth as he had returned to Kiel in March to pick up a new boat, *UB 128*, and was much delayed in a traumatic return journey.[71]

Canaris had a poor start to his tour in the Adriatic. His first u-boat, *U 38*, was in constant repair for two months. In the replacement, *UC 27*, Canaris was sent in November to mine the entrances to the Algerian harbours used by the Allies.[72] There were technical problems: the gyrocompass failed and engine sealing rings leaked. The sea was too rough for torpedo attacks.

> *The watch on the deck wore oilskins and were lashed to the rails in lifebelts, as every other sea broke over us with full force, sweeping us right off our feet.*[73]

A December voyage nearly ended in disaster as two mines exploded prematurely; torpedo attacks in January off Sardinia were unsuccessful; there were more technical faults. That month, only five u-boats were operational in the Adriatic, the other twenty-eight were in the dockyard or undergoing maintenance. Extensive refits had to be taken 4,000 miles to Germany. 'Mechanical breakdowns and the inability to put them right quickly were probably as much responsible as convoying for eventually bringing down the number of Allied ships lost to u-boats in the Mediterranean.'[74] This view was endorsed by the later Vizeadmiral Andreas Michelsen, commander of the High Seas Fleet's submarines from

June 1917 until the end of the war, who explained that not much was done at Pola and even less at Cattaro. '[This was] negligence for which they paid dearly. The German submarines had need of big repair works and [not having them] reduced the gains in the theatre of operations that the Mediterranean offered and which could have been so profitable.'[75]

Canaris was moved to command *U 47*, which was another dockyard case. Then, at the start of 1918, he was concurrently given *U 34*, a hugely successful boat with almost one hundred sinkings to her name. On his first trip with *U 34*, the engine malfunctioned and Canaris had to return.[76] 'Finally, off the Algerian coast on 28 January he sighted a heavily laden French steamer escorted by a cruiser and a trawler.'[77] His first torpedo struck the *Djibouti* amidships and she sank with her cargo of phosphate and case oil.[78]

By the time Gerth got to sea in July, Canaris was already well ahead. It was a depressing time to start active patrols as May was the 'most disastrous' month for the flotilla which lost five submarines, three to armed patrols, *U 39* interned at Cartagena, and *UB 52* torpedoed by the British submarine *H 4*.[79]

Gerth's first operational u-boat was *U 47*, Canaris's cast off.[80] Gerth took it over on 18 June when it was under repair at Pola and he spent a frustrating three months dealing with a series of technical problems that mirrored Canaris's introduction. He had his first outing on 13 July with a trimming trial in the harbour and then moored alongside *Maria Theresia* to prepare for a test voyage. Two days later, he sailed out with the torpedo boat *A 82* and fired eleven practice torpedoes near Cap Porer. After an engine test the next morning, and heavy leakage from a hatch, two torpedoes were fired at him by one or two enemy submarines; two periscopes were spotted nearby. More days of testing followed while the hatch still leaked. On one of the trips when he was trialling a new wire cutter, Gerth accidently cut some unexpected Austrian telegraph cables.

Early in August, Gerth took the flotilla chief, Püllen, out for a final trial off Cap Porer and getting the all clear, started that afternoon taking on provisions and equipment. The hatch started leaking again and the mission was postponed for twenty-four hours. Gerth took an Austrian pilot as he wound his way south through the channels inshore of the Adriatic islands. He met *UB 105*, Kapitänleutnant Wilhelm Marschall, and swopped stories, handed the pilot over to an Austrian torpedo boat, and continued above and below water to patrol off the Italian coast near Pelagosa Grande.[81]

> *The cook stretched up his arms to us in the conning tower with tin cups and a steaming plate of pea soup and pork in his hands. I put the plate on my knees and dipped out its contents. The moisture which forms in large drops on the ceiling during long trips underwater fell down on my head and into my plate and left small splotches of oil in the pea soup as a sign they were real drops of u-boat sweat.*[82]

erwig Gerth with her sons, Erich
d Georg, taken in Berlin, possibly in
ourning clothes at the death of her
isband, Ernst Gerth, in 1893. *Family
chive.*

Ernst Gerth and his three sons, Carl,
Erich and Georg. Carl drowned, about
age three, in a courtyard fountain while
playing with his two brothers, briefly
unsupervised. *Family archive.*

A delightful twentieth-century tram
ticket of the *Berliner Pferde Eisenbahn.*
Landesarchiv, Berlin (02405M).

iblicity picture of a horse-drawn tram from Ernst Gerth's company in Berlin in 1890.
ftung Deutsches Technikmuseum (VI.1.003 Foto-SLG, DTMB01574).

Crowds hear the declaration of mobilisation in Berlin, July 1914. *Alamy*.

Annie Oakley shot a cigar from the mouth of Kaiser Wilhelm II during Buffalo Bill Cody's Wild West Show in Berlin in 1889. After America entered the war in 1917, Oakley wrote to the Kaiser asking if she could have a second shot.

MISS ANNIE OAKLEY
(LITTLE SURE SHOT)
CABINET PORTRAIT

ABOVE AND BELOW: Naval officer cadet Erich, about 1905, with his mother, Hedwig, and George, a new officer perhaps five years later, with Hedwig beginning to show her years. *Family archive.*

Ernst Gerth in junior naval officer's uniform, left, and Georg, a cadet, about 1910. *Family archive.*

The two manuals which governed the Gerth boys' lives while cadets: Instructions for the replenishment of the naval officer corps with regulatory statutes, 1909, and Instructions for the training of naval cadets on the school ships, 1910. *Author's archive.*

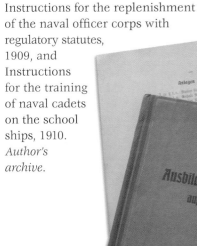

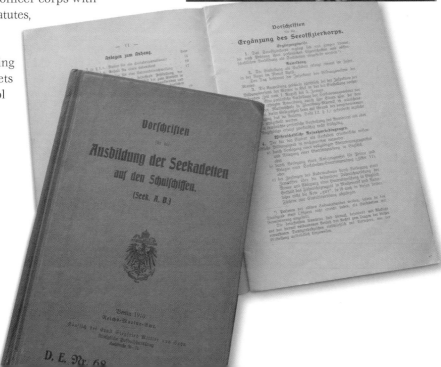

The German Imperial Naval Academy (*Marineakademie*) at Kiel.

Georg Gerth's school ship, SMS *Freya*, a converted cruiser.

Wilhelm Canaris and Erich Gerth were among sixty cadets assigned in 1905 to the fully-rigged training ship SMS *Stein* where they lived cheek by jowl for almost a year.

The only picture of one of the boys in cadet training: Georg, centre, staring at camera. *Family archive*.

The *Beobachtungsuhr*, an observation watch, Georg Gerth's sole remaining possession from his time in the *Kaiserliche Marine*. *Frédéric Gerth*.

Georg Gerth's posting in 1912 on the West African station, the gunboat SMS *Panther*.

The light cruiser, SMS *Amazone*, Georg's first major posting in the Baltic in 1914.

South American spy-ship for Wilhelm Canaris and Erich Gerth before the war, the light cruiser SMS *Bremen*.

Pre-dreadnought battleship, SMS *Preussen*, Georg Gerth's first sea-going appointment until 1911.

The light cruiser, SMS *Dresden*, in the Kaiser Wilhelm (Kiel) Canal; sunk by the British with Wilhelm Canaris aboard in 1915 off the Chilean coast.

ABOVE: The 'Black Tom' sabotage in New Jersey city, USA, in 1916 by German agents, perhaps a postscript to the pre-war work of Canaris and Erich Gerth?

RIGHT: A missionary points to the severed hand of a villager in Leopold's Congo.

Leopold II of Belgium, responsible for the brutal exploitation of his personal fiefdom, the Congo Free State.

Edmund Morel, uncovered the horror of the Congo and devoted much of his life to ending it.

Roger Casement, honoured in 1905 for his report on Leopold's atrocities in the Congo.

Herero prisoners. *Getty Images.*

If two books caused the inflamed passions in Germany that led to the war, it was these two. *Author's archive.*

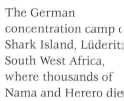

The German concentration camp (Shark Island, Lüderit: South West Africa, where thousands of Nama and Herero die

The brutal command(of the German forces in South West Africa, Lothar von Trotha, wl led the genocide of th Herero people.

The British concentration camp at Bloemfontein, Orange Free State, during the Second War of Independence, where many Boer woman and children died through disease and malnutrition.

The opening ceremor for the 'Rider Statue', a *Schutztruppe*, in Windhoek, South Wes Africa, on 27 January 1912, the Kaiser's birthday. Is Georg Gei in the crowd?

On 6 August, a water-cooling pipe broke in *U 47* which caused serious damage. With the starboard engine not working, Gerth headed back to Cattaro for repairs. He tried to get on patrol again on 10 August, sailing out with an Austro-Hungarian torpedo boat and *U 35*.[83] *U 35* was Arnauld de la Perière's worn-out boat which he commanded from November 1915 to March 1918. It was also the most successful u-boat of the war, active since 1914, with 236 ships sunk or damaged. In the Straits of Otranto Gerth sighted two ships, possibly older Italian cruisers, one of which steered towards the u-boat. Gerth dived to sixty metres, the port engine had to be switched off because of overheating and water began coming in through the long-faulty hatch. It was back to base again avoiding an enemy submarine which could not fire a torpedo because of the heavy swell. Gerth called in at Spalato, modern day Split, to fix a small engine fault, but workers at Cattaro could not handle the larger repairs so it needed a further retreat to Pola, where Gerth handed in his torpedoes and planned an optimistic fourteen days in docks. In September, an additional two weeks of tests and repairs were needed.

With *U 47* seemingly beyond repair, Gerth was given command in September of another suspect boat, *UC 53*, of the same basic type as *UC 61*, his brother Georg's final command, and had just a week to prepare himself and his crew.[84] The boat had undergone extensive maintenance in Trieste throughout July and August. After laying mines north of Messina strait, he was ordered to sail to the Tyrrhenian Sea and to look for merchant ships. It was a ferocious start to his operational u-boat career. He sailed from Cattaro on 19 September and the next day at South Adria was seen by three destroyers and survived twenty-two depth charges.

> *A pallid corpse-like countenance peered out at me from one of the bunks, and retched and retched. At this sight, my own stomach began to turn again, and I could barely contain myself. The atmosphere below was really beyond description. The damp, warm, almost stifling air, saturated as it was with oil, made me feel sicker than ever … I fled from this oil-reeking domain and tried to get some sleep on my bunk. Though hitherto it had been the cold that made me curse my fate, it was now the foul air that made breathing a torture and would not let me sleep. Sweat broke from all my pores; I tossed about and tried to wedge myself in every conceivable position so as not to be flung out by a sudden heave of the boat. Those five hours of rest, that were mere restlessness and torment, seemed eternal, and the summons to turn out came almost as a relief. Exhausted and shattered, without a wink of sleep, I hoisted myself out of my bunk and went to my post in the control-room.*[85]

When Gerth surfaced, a hot air balloon signalled with lanterns to some armed trawlers who presented him with another eighteen depth charges.

The following evening in bright moonlight he passed the chain barricade at Otranto at periscope depth because of six armed trawlers ahead. He found his boat was down by the stern with a strong starboard list. The regulator flooded.

At dawn on 22 September, Gerth saw a laden steamer guarded by two armed trawlers travelling on the route from Malta to Corfu. He fired a torpedo at 380 metres and hit the steamer's bow. Down at fifty metres, he endured ten depth charges from the escorts which left splinters on the deck of his boat. The steamer sank and armed trawlers closed on the site of the sinking while a French four-funnel destroyer dashed about at great speed. After the escorts had picked up the full crew and left the area, Gerth found on papers among the lifeboats that he had sunk the English steamer *Gorsemore*, 3,079 tons, carrying coal from Barry in South Wales to the Italian port of Taranto. The lifeboats were in 'very good condition and well equipped' with emergency ration packs labelled 'For Army and Navy Use'. UC 53 replenished its fresh provisions from a floating cooling cabinet.

> [The ship] screamed and groaned like a fatally wounded beast, till the sea closed over her masts and funnel. Gurgling and bubbling, white eddies, boats and wreckage. Even some minutes afterwards great wooden beams, tearing themselves loose deep below, shot violently up and through the surface ... The ship's death agony stood long in my memory. The seaman, in his heart of hearts, is a good-humoured, generous fellow. For him each ship has a soul. But war turns hearts to steel. Had we not been attacked? Then draw swords! And forward with our u-boats, ruthless, against British trade, the life-nerve of the United Kingdom.[86]

For the next few days Gerth cruised the Malta Channel and Medina Bank in a strong sea, heavy rain and bad visibility. The boat was too heavy and low-lying. There were problems with the ventilation and leaks caused flooding. On 26 September, he ran into a small cargo steamer and an armed trawler which opened fire forcing an emergency dive.

> 'Diving stations!' The order suddenly rang out from the conning-tower. In an instant the deck was empty. Everyone jumped, climbed, or swung himself on to the conning-tower; and thence down the open hatchway. The tall periscope is soon in place. Quickly down the smooth iron greasy ladder; and don't let the great seaman's boots above you crash on to your fingers! And mind your head and your bones in this iron tube, plastered with iron plates, levers, screws, and wheels, and now crammed with scrambling men. In less time than it takes to describe, everyone from on deck has dashed to his appointed place, inside the conning-tower, in the control-room, or in one of the other compartments of the vessel. Last of all the commander climbs into the conning-tower

and the heavy hatch is fastened above his head. The oil-engines are switched off and the electric motors started. Just as the commander stands at the periscope in the conning-tower, the eye of the u-boat, so in the control-room, the brain of the vessel, the chief engineer stands at the centre periscope.[87]

Thunderstorms after dark meant the radio had to be switched off; no radio messages were received the next day because of atmospheric disturbance. On 28 September, at the northern entrance of Messina Strait, Gerth entered the 'perilous currents and whirlpools of Scylla and Charybdis' and logged praise for his navigation officer, Oberleutnant S Peters, for his careful navigation. Near Faro, Gerth fired a second torpedo at a half-laden steamer. There was a loud detonation and Gerth speculated he had ignited a cargo of ammunition. It was the French steamer *Caraibe*, 2,976 tons. Six depth charges followed. Gerth went north, submerged, but found the boat too heavy, sagging by the stern, so he surfaced and spent the day sorting out his torpedoes, reloading and recharging his batteries.

At this time, Gerth's torpedoes, and those of all the Mediterranean German and Austrian boats, were made by British armaments firms Vickers and Armstrong which each held a large proportion of the shares of Whitehead & Co, the torpedo manufacturer with works at Fiume. An ex-secretary to the Committee of Imperial Defence was also a director of Armstrong, Whitworth, and a director of Armstrong's Italian firm, Armstrong Pozzuoli, on the Italian coast.[88] Labour MP Philip Snowden was like a dog with a bone with the story and was unsparing with his criticism of the directors of these companies. His pursuit lasted well into the 1930s but, eventually, to no avail.[89]

'Numerous individuals sitting in the warm comfort of Westminster or their exclusive London clubs of grand gothic cathedrals profited from the torpedoes that sent thousands of brave British seamen to cold graves. These men made untold fortunes on the products of death and misery.[90]

A piston on *UC 53*'s portside engine disintegrated and put that engine out of order for several days reducing maximum speed to six knots. Gerth then caused mayhem with a series of small Italian sailing vessels. On the morning of 30 September in the Gulf of Salerno, he used his machine gun to stop *Francesco Padre*, 101 tons, based in Palermo, travelling in ballast from Naples to Messina. Gerth then sank her with explosive cartridges and released the crew in their tender.[91] Next in a group came *Francesco P*, seventy tons, travelling from Castellamare to Messina with a cargo of wood, sunk by cartridges following some gun practice after the crew were also released in their tender; then *Isanna I*, a mere five tons, with empty barrels for Salerno. The crew 'had no tender and the boat no value so released sailing boat after cutting its sails'. Close to Capri, Gerth spotted three more sailing boats which he approached at dusk and stopped two of them with his machine gun, *Gabriele Costa*, 105 tons, and *Giovanni Costa*, 102 tons, and then sank them with cartridges. Both were sailing in ballast from Genoa to Messina. Gerth then chased the third sailing boat while towing the tender of *Gabriele Costa* and carrying her crew on the deck of *UC 53* when a destroyer moved swiftly towards them. The crew of *Gabriele Costa* were put into their tender and Gerth made an emergency dive to twenty-five metres.

> *It was a touching scene which, in spite of our inner joy, was hard on our nerves, as every true sailor regards the sailing-ship as a remnant of romance, dying out faster and faster in these days. This was truly the reason why now and at other times our hearts ached for each sailing ship which we had to sink.*[92]

Early the next morning, 1 October, Gerth stopped and repeated his routine with the sailing boat *San Giuseppi A*, fifty-six tons, travelling from Civitavechia to Trappani in ballast and, later that afternoon, the sailing boat *Giuseppino M*, thirty-nine tons, Trappani to Castellamare with a cargo of wood.

> *At 0900, I came across a bunch of large two-master schooners of the French deep-sea fleet. Once in their midst, I used their dories to ferry my prize crews from one schooner to the next, sinking them as they went. Within ninety minutes we had finished. Twelve large schooners, each with holds brimming with fish, lay wrecked on the seabed. The loss of the fish, and more to the fishing boats, would make an impression on French food supplies.*[93]

The next day it rained and the radio was switched off because of storms. On 3 October, Gerth finally discharged his two rows of nine mines in the Strait of Messina unnoticed by Allied patrols.[94] Here was an inherently brave or foolhardy act as Gerth had previously fired torpedoes while eighteen potentially unstable mines were still aboard, each capable of being activated by shock waves.

> *We turned and began laying our mines. The after-compartment, which contained our main mine tubes, was the scene of hard and perspiring work … The engineer officer had charge in the control room and maintained the boat at a uniform depth by admitting the correct volume of water to compensate for the weight of each mine as it was dropped, while standing by to dive at any moment.*[95]

From there on Gerth was dogged by more engine problems. On 4 October, he saw a hospital ship in a convoy of four steamers protected by six armed trawlers, but could not get into position because only one main engine was working and his maximum speed was only six knots. Oil consumption was high and his range of operation was subsequently reduced. In the Messina Strait, *UC 53*'s periscope was seen by three armed trawlers as Gerth manoeuvred for a torpedo shot at a 4,000-ton tanker. On 6 October, men worked to repair the starboard engine and its exhaust valve, the boat vulnerable and unable to dive. Lubrication oil consumption remained so high that Gerth decide to return while looking for opportunities to attack between Marritimo and Skerkibank, and off Syracuse. While both engines were running, that on the portside was restricted to four cylinders. Oil consumption was now excessive restricting him to one engine at a time and leaks were causing oil to burn in the cylinders.

> *The only thing that we could not grow accustomed to was the fact that half the ship's company were seasick and the remainder had to clean up all day long.*[96]

It was now an emergency run home by the shortest route before the oil ran out. By 10 October, after passing Gozo and Malta, *UC 53* was limping through rain, hail storms and zero visibility. On 12 October, in the Strait of Otranto, heading northward on a zig-zag course, Gerth finally established radio contact with headquarters and reported his successes and forced return to 'Cleopatra'. The next day, *UC 53* sailed into the Bay of Cattaro and moored at the stone barracks.

> *Who can understand the joy of a commander's heart when, sitting by his narrow writing table, he is carefully working out his report to his superiors? 'Have sunk X steamers, X sailing ships.' All around me were the happy faces of the crew. All were satisfied, every danger past and forgotten, thanks to the strength of youth and their stout hearts.*[97]

This was Gerth's sole operational patrol of the war. He reported that he was out for twenty-four days, travelled 2,803 sea miles above water, 337 submerged. His eighteen mines had been laid and he had sunk one steamer and damaged another by torpedo, and six small sailing vessels sent to the bottom by thirty-eight cartridges, 6,509 tons altogether. Perhaps sinking the clutch of Italian vessels was a trifle wanton at this very late stage of the war, but he had behaved meticulously to their crews? There were no injuries or deaths. Canaris's total by war end was four largish steamers totalling 23,592 tons. Gerth had been plagued by mechanical problems. His flotilla commander was underwhelmed:

*First operation of new commander. Minelaying task completed
successfully. A different route should have been selected for the journey
both ways* (via Adventure Bank) *as there would probably have been
opportunities to drop mines there. While navigating at periscope depth
the boat accidentally brushed against the top link of a net of the buoy line
Otranto-Fano. Criticism of reporting sailing-in via radio transmission
message. Flooding of the starboard regulator was the result of an
operating error. The list of the boat during surface travel should have
been identified as an indicator of an irregularity. The oil engine fault
was caused by an error during the last maintenance works which now
means further delays as all pistons will have to be replaced for checks.
The cause for the boat's excessive lubricating oil consumption will have
to be determined during repair works.*[98]

Eighteen days later, *UC 53* was blown up and sunk by the Germans as one of
ten unseaworthy boats in the Adriatic.[99] Kapitän Püllen and his first officer
Kapitänleutnant Otto Schultze witnessed the start of the collapse of their
Austrian allies.[100] In January in Pola, Austrian naval shipyard workers with
'revolutionary sentiments' began a general strike demanding better living
conditions and an end to the war. The Austrians were joined in the strike
by some 1,500 German workers from Kiel who were helping to maintain
the u-boats in the Adriatic. The strike was suppressed by the Austro-
Hungarian Navy leadership backed by German land forces. However, on
1 February, sailors on the larger ships of the Austro-Hungarian fleet in
Cattaro mutinied. Their commanders decided it would be better to sink
the fleet before there was any chance that the sailors could take the ships
to Italy. They asked Püllen and his u-boats to stand by. The situation was
resolved temporarily, but remained tense throughout the summer with
sporadic acts of severe indiscipline.[101] Mutinies broke out again in October
on the Austrian warships. Püllen realised that if the Austrians sued for
a separate peace then his u-boats could become bargaining chips.[102] On
24 October, the Kaiser and Chancellor Price Max von Baden officially
terminated unrestricted submarine warfare and four days later Rear-
Admiral Adolf von Trotha announced to the government that the u-boats
were being recalled following the army's announcement that it was unable
to continue the fight in France.[103]

*Püllen sought permission to withdraw from the Adriatic and, sworn
to secrecy, he received permission the next day* [25 October]. *Püllen
felt bound to warn Admiral Miklos Horthy, the last commander-in-
chief of the Austro-Hungarian Fleet, and later Regent of Hungary
from 1920–1924, and also the senior Austrian officer at Cattaro,
Linienschiffskapitän Seitz. Evacuation of the flotilla offices at Pola
began on the 28th and at Cattaro on the 30th. Between the 29th and
31st thirteen [actually fourteen] u-boats all left for Germany while*

two more which were on patrol, U 34, Johannes Klasing, and UC 73,
Franz Hagen, received orders to follow them immediately.[104] Püllen was
concerned that a third, UC 74, Adelbert von der Luhe, [probably Hans
Schüler] *which was then off Asia Minor had insufficient fuel and her*
commander opted for internment in Spain.

At a day's notice, all seaworthy u-boats were to return forthwith to Germany
to be available for a 'last stand'. No passengers were to be accommodated.
Boats not ready to sail within twenty-four hours were to be scuttled.[105] At
Pola, on 27 October, torpedo boat *A 51* and a dockyard tug towed out seven
u-boats, including Gerth's *UC 53*, and they were sunk with explosives. The
bases at Cattaro and Pola were destroyed. The flotilla staff and the crews
of the scuttled boats, several hundred men including Gerth, left for home
overland by railway via Vienna on 28 October. There were followed by the
1,500 German dockworkers. This was not a good time to travel. The Austro-
Hungarian front lines were disintegrating, especially towards Italy. The
Bulgarian front had collapsed completely. Nationalist movements seized
their chance to break away from the Hapsburg Empire and to try to set up
their own governments in Albania, Bohemia, Bosnia, Croatia, the Czech
and Hungarian lands, Moravia and Silesia. At the same time, 'a wave of
Spanish influenza hit railroad personnel in Vienna, making idle 8,000 cars
of rolling stock'.[106] In a volatile situation, it was a dangerous trip home for
Gerth and his colleagues.

Niemöller was uncertain to the last minute whether his boat, *UC 67*,
would be seaworthy enough to make the return journey:

> *While the overland convoy, which included many ship's boats, crossed*
> *the inner harbour of Pola on its way to the railway station, we carried*
> *out our first diving trial after the refit and it proved quite successful.*
> *The only outstanding defect was the conning-tower hatch-cover joint,*
> *which was badly worn. The dockyard was empty and deserted, so that*
> *a new jointing ring was unobtainable. A new ring was cut out of a piece*
> *of asbestos sheet. We spent a night over the job and I cannot forget how,*
> *on that last evening in Pola, four young Austrian naval officers came*
> *aboard asking for a passage to Germany. 'What for?' 'We should like to*
> *fight for Germany to the end.' It was enough to make one weep, but I*
> *could not accede to their request. The boat was already heavy enough*
> *and it was impossible to compensate for the additional weight of four*
> *men with their provisions, water and baggage. We went to sea on 29*
> *October in company with UC 22.[107]*

The mass return of the serviceable u-boats was one of the most poignant and
heroic stories of the dying days of the war. Gibson, an early UK submarine
historian, noted forcefully that the u-boat commanders remained steadfast

to the last.[108] 'The nervous tension and physical discomforts; the terrible experiences of crews which had escaped death by a hair's breath; the ever-increasing losses; the uncertainty as to the fate of those who never returned – all such were factors which might be expected to sap endurance and self-confidence in the bravest. Companionship in danger, active service, adventure – all these things preserved and upheld discipline.'

These poorly maintained Adriatic boats needed to travel across the Mediterranean, through the Bay of Biscay, and all the way round Ireland and Scotland to Norway and then to the German coast. The Royal Navy had been forewarned of the flotilla's departure and was patrolling in considerable numbers. Special patrols were organised around Gibraltar from 29 October. At least five u-boats were spotted and at least three were engaged, but only one, possibly, did not make it because of enemy action.[109] *U 34*, Leutnant Johannes Klasing, was claimed sunk by the Q-ship HMS *Privet*. Waiting to approach the narrows, Canaris was forced to watch from a distance off Gibraltar while *U 34* was depth-charged to destruction.[110] Another observer was Dönitz who was on Gibraltar on his way to a prison camp in Britain. The month before, his *UB 68* had been forced to the surface by mechanical difficulties and the boat was sunk by shellfire.[111] However, the loss of *U 34* at this date is disputed.[112] The Gibraltar Straits were passed at night by the scattered fleet at periscope depth with great difficulty. Here are the views of Canaris and Niemöller:

> From the Spanish side strong beams illuminated the waters to the North Africa coast throughout the night, creating a lit area patrolled by numerous small warships and a submarine lurking in the shadows. Canaris wrote that 'under the Moroccan coast are many patrol boats. They present the greatest danger. Basically, they are large American motorboats and small torpedo boats that are very difficult to make out in the darkness.' The situation was not promising ... Canaris bet everything on a single card: he attempted to run submerged below the light barrier. A steamer followed him and seven depth charges tumbled down; both electric rudders failed. It was the most dangerous moment of his u-boat career. Now he got lucky; when the screws of the enemy ships became inaudible he surfaced; a destroyer was so close that it screened him from the patrol boats searching the waters. He remained unseen and in the early hours slipped unnoticed through the last light barrier.[113]

> As we come up that night close to Ceuta and try to enter the straits, we observe that things are pretty sticky here. We come up against a line of patrolling drifters so close together that there is nothing for it but to turn east again and to attempt a passage on the north side, close under the Rock of Gibraltar. Here at 2200, we meet two torpedo boats carrying lights, so that we begin to wonder whether the war is over.

They are, however, followed by darkened patrol vessels and we are quite glad when the wind increases to gale force, as it affords us concealment. A French destroyer even slides past within one hundred yards of us. By daybreak we are in the Atlantic and steering for the open sea.[114]

On the way out of the Straits, on 9 November, two days before an unanticipated armistice, *UB 50*, Oberleutnant Heinrich Kukat, twice torpedoed the 16,350-ton British battleship *Britannia* on convoy duty at the western entrance to the Straits killing fifty-one – 'the last British warship to be sunk in the war'.[115]

The u-boats met on 15 November off Finisterre and held a commanding officers' meeting. Niemöller spent much of the next few days with Kukat on *UB 50*. They had to decide whether to seek internment in a Spanish port or to continue to Germany.

We had heard a good deal about the conditions prevailing in Germany through the German wireless press reports and enemy reports and, as this information reached us en clair, *it was, of course, known to the ships' companies. No trouble was experienced with any of them. The crews were absolutely unaffected ... The attitude of the ships' companies decided us to make for home as we did not want to miss the coming upheavals in the reformation of Germany ... We simply could not believe that the press accounts which kept coming to us gave us a true picture of the state of Germany and of the spirit of its people and we had vague hopes that, perhaps, very shortly, another political upheaval would efface the shame of the incidents of 9 November.*[116]

When the remaining u-boats reached Norway, they were given permission by radio to pass through the fjords. Niemöller was met at Bergan Fjord on 24 November by a Norwegian torpedo boat which escorted him to Lervik for a Mediterranean reunion. From there, a flotilla of eleven submarines made a short stop at Haugesund, then travelled through the Skagerrak and entered Kiel Harbour where they arrived on 29 November. There was no hero's welcome; the ports of Wilhelmshaven and Kiel were 'in the grip of mutiny'.[117] Perhaps Gerth, or at least some of his fellow commanders of the scuttled Adriatic u-boats, safely back in Berlin after their difficult train journey, travelled quickly to the Baltic to congratulate their comrades on their return? Nine days before, the first of 172 u-boats to be surrendered under the terms of the Armistice had already been handed over to the British at Harwich.[118] The Pola boats followed over the next few weeks.

Gerth started the war earlier than most with his activities in South America in 1911. While his direct involvement in the war ended in its last weeks with his train journey from Pola through Austria to Germany, he left some bitter memories. U-boat commanders in all waters were under orders to record carefully the position of mines that they laid in accordance with an international agreement against the day after the end of the conflict when unfound mines could be raised and the seas made safe. Clause 24 of the 11 November armistice gave the Allies the right to 'sweep up all mine fields and obstructions laid by Germany outside German territorial waters, and the positions of these are to be indicated'.[119] Gerth had delivered his mine maps in Pola, but there was clearly not enough time for much, if any, work to be done before 20 November when the 3,116-ton British steamer *War Typhoon* hit one of his mines nine miles off the Cape of Rasolcolmo, north of Messina. There were no casualties and the ship made it safely to harbour.

More might have been expected in mine clearance by next year when, on 15 January, another of Gerth's mines sank the French passenger and general cargo ship *Chaouia*, 4,334 tons.[120] The ship disappeared at night in just a few minutes with the loss of 476 troops, mainly Greek. There were 184 survivors, most saved by the British steamer *Daghestan*.[121] *Chaouia* was hit in the Straits of Messina on her way from Marseille to Batoum, or Batumi, today one of the major port cities in Georgia. At that time, it was held by the British, whom the Greeks were to reinforce. The previous occupiers, the Turks under Kemal Atatürk, had ceded the town under the Treaty of Brest-Litovsk.

There were only two recorded losses to u-boats in 1919. The other was the torpedo boat *Torpilleur 325* sunk seven days after the *Chaouia* with eighteen casualties, also French and also mined in the Mediterranean. *Torpilleur 325*'s mine was laid by Otto Gerke from *UC 27*, Canaris's second boat.

The *Chaouia* was therefore the penultimate boat of the war to be lost to a u-boat. It accounted for the twenty-second largest loss of life. Naturally enough all thirty-four ships on this list of sinkings with over 250 casualties were warships, troopships and passenger ships. Gerth knew about the men killed on the *Chaouia* after the war had ended, but denied it was his mine. He later told his wife, Eva, that the German admiralty 'had to hang the sinking on somebody and they decided to assign it to him'.[122] One can understand why Erich or Eva Gerth might say that, but the facts do not agree. *Chaouia*'s approximate reported sinking was at 38°18'N, 15°41'E.[123] When compared with Erich's handwritten mine charts, this position is too close to his first tranche of nine mines to suggest that any other u-boat might have been involved.

ENDNOTES

1 Wilson, *War Messages*, 65th Congress, 1st Session, Senate Document No. 5, Serial No. 7264, Washington, DC, pp. 3–8, 22/4/1917.
2 *Deutsches U-Boot Museum*, Cuxhaven, Löhr, 'Obituary and naval record: Erich Gerth'. norwayheritage.com.
3 Mueller, *Canaris*, p. 6.

4 Gröner, *German Warships*, Vol. 1, pp. 102–4.

5 Herwig, *Naval Officer Corps*, pp. 31–33, 73.

6 *BA-MA*, Freiburg, N 326/5, Albert Hopman: 'Diary'.

7 Mueller, *Canaris*, p. 6.

8 Mueller, *Canaris*, pp. 7–12.

9 Herr Löhr's interest in u-boats stems from his twice great uncle Alfred Gerke who died when *U 102* was sunk by a mine on the Northern Barrage while homeward bound in September 1918. All forty-two crew were lost. Löhr was instrumental in the identification of *U 102* when it was found by sonar in 2006 and investigated by divers in 2007.

10 *Auswärtige Amt*, Das Politische Archiv, Berlin, 004389, Vol. 2.

11 Hopman, 'Assessments', Canaris-IfZ, quoted in Mueller, *Canaris*, p. 7.

12 *Auswärtige Amt*, Das Politische Archiv, Berlin, 004386, Vol. 1.

13 *Freie Zeitung*, Berne, 2/11/1914, placed by German General Headquarters.

14 Chapter 5, 'The 'very nearly' battle'.

15 'School records' (digital.ub.uni-dusseldorf.de), accessed 3/2017.

16 Trevelyan, *Garibaldi's Defence of the Roman Republic*, Vol. 1, pp. 26–41.

17 Mueller, *Canaris*, Chapter 2, 'The Last Epic Voyage of the Dresden'.

18 Asprey, *German High Command*, p. 133. Marder, *Dreadnought*, Vol. II, pp. 104–18.

19 Marder, *Dreadnought*, Vol. II, pp. 118–29. Mueller, *Canaris*, pp. 14–15.

20 Mueller, *Canaris*, pp. 19–20.

21 wikipedia.

22 Gröner, *German Warships*, Vol. 1, pp. 18–20.

23 Massie, *Dreadnought*. Marder, *Dreadnought*, Vols. 1 & 2. Lambert, *Naval Revolution*.

24 Massie, *Castles of Steel*, pp. 319–27.

25 On 8/6/1667, a Dutch fleet attacked Sheerness Naval Fort in the Thames Estuary, and landed troops. Four days later the Dutch sailed up the River Medway and towed back to Holland the eighty-gun *Royal Charles*, the Navy's largest ship.

26 Massie, *Castles of Steel*, pp. 555–59. Marder, *Dreadnought*, pp. 424–27.

27 Löhr, 'Obituary'.

28 Holborn, 'Introduction', in Fischer, *War Aims*, p. xiii.

29 Fischer, *War Aims*, pp. 365–75.

30 Lenin died in Russia of a stroke 1923; Trotsky was murdered in Mexico on Stalin's orders in 1940; Stalin died of a cerebral haemorrhage in his dacha in Russia in 1953, but his chief of the NKVD, the secret police, Lavrentiy Beria claimed to have poisoned him; Kerensky died of heart disease in New York City in 1970 and, because the Russian Orthodox church would not bury him there, he was interred in Putney Vale Cemetery in London.

31 Kitchen, *Silent Dictatorship*, pp. 157–184. Hull, *Absolute Destruction*, p. 199.

32 Fischer, *War Aims*, pp. 103–6.

33 Chapter 13, 'Guilt and blame'.

34 Arnold-Forster, *Blockade*, p. 27.

35 Feldman, *Army, Industry and Labour*, p. 461.

36 Howard, 'Social and Political Consequences', p. 165.

37 Chapter 11, 'Immense cemetery'.

38 Barrett, *Operation Albion*.

39 Mueller, *Canaris*, pp. 20–25.

40 Mueller, *Canaris*, p. 22.

41 Chapter 16, 'Erich's Jewish problem'.

42 Termote, *Krieg unter Wasser*, pp. 115–17.

43 Mulligan, *Neither Sharks*, p. 34.

44 Chapter 12, 'Prisoners of war'.

45 Mulligan, *Neither Sharks*, p. 40. This instruction was repeated in 1942.

46 *BA-MA*, Freiburg, RM 27-XIII/214, Vol. 8.

47 Löhr, 'Obituary'.

48 The initial leader, Commander Kophamel, returned to Germany to take over the converted mercantile submarine *U 151* (Koerver, *Submarine Warfare*), p. 218.

49 Gayer, *Submarine Warfare*, pp. 5–6.

50   Laurens, *Histoire de la Guerre Sous-Marine Allemande*, p. 367.
51   Fischer, *War Aims*, pp. 120–22.
52   Schierbrand, *Kaiser's Speeches*, p. 321.
53   Fischer, *War Aims*, pp. 120–24.
54   Fischer, *War Aims*, pp. 120–154.
55   Chapter 2, 'Kaisertreu'.
56   Koerver, *Submarine Warfare*, pp. 218–20.
57   Fischel became at admiral. He died in a prison camp near Moscow five years after the end of World War II. His son, Unno, died commanding *U 374* in 1942 (uboat.net).
58   Chapter 2.
59   Gayer, *Submarine Warfare*, pp. 7, 29.
60   Tarrant, *U-boat Offensive*, p. 63.
61   Mulligan, *Neither Sharks*, p. 38. Chapter 5.
62   Niemöller, *From u-boat*, pp. 116–17.
63   Koerver, *Submarine Warfare*, pp. 218–19.
64   Mulligan, *Neither Sharks*, p. 40.
65   Hashagen, *Commander*, pp. 127–29. There are variations on the story elsewhere.
66   Other sources suggest three camels were eventually transferred, two by *UC 20* and one by *UC 73*; on one trip *UC 20*'s camel was accompanied by a sheep (1914–1918.invisionzone.com/forums/topic/96831-disposal-of-a-camel, accessed 10/2017). The author's preferred version is as it was recorded by Hashagen.
67   uboat.net.
68   At the time of sinking, *Persia* was carrying a large quantity of gold and jewels belonging to the Maharaja Jagatjit Singh. The wreck was located off Crete in 2003 at a depth of 3,000 metres and an attempt was made to salvage the treasure located in the bullion room. The salvage attempt met with limited success, retrieving artefacts and portions of the ship, and some jewels.
69   Bridgland, *Outrage*, Chapter 8, 'Max Valentiner Strikes Twice', pp. 121–135.
70   Robert Derencin, uboat.net.
71   Mueller, *Canaris*, pp. 29–30. *UB 128* was the boat that the author dived on at Falmouth in 1972, 'Introduction'.
72   *BA-MA*, Freiburg, RM 97/1785, KTB, *UC 27*.
73   Niemöller, *From u-boat*, p. 24.
74   Compton-Hall, *Submarines*, pp. 221–22.
75   Laurens, *Histoire de la Guerre Sous-Marine Allemande*, p. 367.
76   *BA-MA*, Freiburg, RM 97/753, KTB, *U 34*.
77   Mueller, *Canaris*, pp. 26–28.
78   uboat.net.
79   Gayer, *Submarine Warfare*, p. 7. Koerver, *Submarine Warfare*, p. 224.
80   *Deutsches U-Boot Museum*, Cuxhaven, KTB, *U 47*.
81   Wilhelm Marschall was a World War I u-boat ace with over forty ships sunk. From 1934, he captained the pocket battleship *Admiral Scheer*. During the Spanish Civil War, he commanded the German naval forces off the Spanish coast. Promoted admiral in 1939, he flew his flag in the battleship *Gneisenau* and led the German naval force which intercepted and sank the British auxiliary cruiser *Rawalpindi* off the Faroe Islands. In 1940, Marschall with *Gneisenau*, and her sister-ship *Scharnhorst*, sank in a two-hour action the British aircraft carrier *Glorious* and her accompanying destroyers, *Acasta* and *Ardent*, while *Scharnhorst* was badly hit by one of *Acasta's* torpedoes.
82   Spiegel, *U-202*, p. 48.
83   *Deutsches U-Boot Museum*, Cuxhaven, KTB, *UC 47*.
84   *Deutsches U-Boot Museum*, Cuxhaven, KTB, *UC 53*.
85   Leading Seaman Schlichting, 'Hurricane', Neureuther, *U-Boat Stories*, p. 99.
86   Hashagen, *Commander*, p. 66.
87   War artist Claus Bergen, 'My U-Boat Voyage', Neureuther, *U-Boat Stories*, p. 11.
88   Murray, *Krupp's International Armaments Ring*, p. 179.
89   Docherty & Macgregor, *Hidden History*, p. 142.

90 Interpreted from Labour MP Philip Snowden, *Hansard, House of Commons*, Debate, 5/5/1915, Vol. 71, c1091; 8/11/1934, Vol. 293, ccl1293–1416. Murray, *Krupp's International Armaments Ring*, pp. xiii–xiv, 176–84.

91 Spindler's annotations on *UC 53*'s KTB, dated 11/2/1941, see 'Introduction'.

92 Spiegel, *U-202*, p. 30.

93 Fürbringer, *Legendary*, p. 46.

94 Nine mines north-east of Capo Peloro, from 38°17'6N – 15°40'6E, course 58°; nine mines north of Capo Rasolcolmo, from 38°19'75N – 15°33'1E, course 1°; 3/10/1918 (Zu Minenkarte Nr. 22, KTB), p. 19.

95 Niemöller, *From u-boat*, p. 34. The mine tubes of *UC 53* were at the front of the boat.

96 Niemöller, *From u-boat*, p. 23.

97 Spiegel, *U 202*, p. 73.

98 Gibson, *Submarine War*, p. 183.

99 Destroyed: Cattaro: *U 72*, Hermann Bohm. Fiume: *UB 129*, Karl Neumann. Pola: *U 47*, Karl Bunte; *U 65*, Clemens Wickel; *U 73*, Fritz Saupe; *UB 48*, Wolfgang Steinbauer; *UC 25*, Karl Dönitz (Dönitz switched command to *UB 68* 2/7/1918); *UC 34*, Hans Schuler; *UC 53*, Erich Gerth. Trieste: *UC 54*, Otto Loycke. Two torpedo boats, *A 51* and *A 82*, were also destroyed.

100 Schultz became a grossadmiral in 1936 and was a career-long mentor to Dönitz (Padfield, *Dönitz*), pp. 96–97. His son, Heinz-Otto, died in command of *U 849* in the South Atlantic in 1943.

101 Niemöller, *From u-boat*, pp. 147–56.

102 Wilson & Kemp, *Mediterranean Submarines*, pp. 185–86.

103 Herwig, *Naval Officer Corps*, pp. 240–41.

104 *U 33*, Gustav Siess; *U 35*, Heino von Heimburg; *U 38*, Clemens Wickel; *U 63*, Kurt Hartwig; *UB 49*, Adolf Ehrensberger; *UB 50*, Heinrich Kukat; *UB 51*, Ernst Krafft; *UB 105*, Rudolph Peterson; *UB 128*, Wilhelm Canaris; *UC 20*, Hermann Rohne; *UC 22*, Eberhard Weichold; *UC 27*, Otto Gerke; *UC 52*, Carl Heinrich Sass; and *UC 67*, Martin Niemöller.

105 Mueller, *Canaris*, pp. 30–31.

106 Hollweg, *First World War*, p. 435.

107 Niemöller, *From u-boat*, pp. 149–50.

108 Gibson, *Submarine War*, p. 182.

109 Laurens, Histoire de la Guerre Sous-Marine Allemande, p. 386. Wilson & Kemp, *Mediterranean Submarines*, p. 186. Koerver, *Submarine Warfare*, p. 210. uboat.net.

110 Mueller, *Canaris*, p. 31.

111 Padfield, *Dönitz*, p. 90. uboat.net.

112 uboat.net: 'Likely lost well before that date', implying that this was an unsuccessful attack on another u-boat.

113 Mueller, *Canaris*, p. 31.

114 Niemöller, *From u-boat*, p. 153.

115 Gayer, *Submarine Warfare*, p. 8. Niemöller, *From u-boat*, pp. 147–156. Kukat's brother Hans, also a World War I u-boat commander, *UC 78*, was rammed by the steamer *Queen Alexandra*, west of Cherbourg, on 9 May 1918, all twenty-nine crew were lost (uboat.net).

116 Niemöller, *From u-boat*, pp. 154–56.

117 Mueller, *Canaris*, p. 33.

118 uboat.net.

119 This responsibility was reinforced in the armistice agreement, 11/11/1918 (Appendix 6, 'Military Clauses on the Western Front').

120 uboat.net.

121 *Daghestan* was sold on many times. In 1938, she was bombed and sunk at Alicante in a Spanish Nationalist air attack. She was raised and eventually sank at sea in 1951 (mariners-list.com).

122 Private email, 3/3/2018.

123 uboat.net.

CHAPTER 5

The 'Very Nearly' Battle

We found our efforts dogged by the issue that had inspired [our conferences] in the first place for we failed to produce a definition of 'total war' that could command general assent ... About one thing we could agree. The great industrial wars of the twentieth century witnessed the systematic erasure of distinctions between the military and civilian spheres, combatants and non-combatants. Civilians were as critical to the outcome of both conflicts, and as likely to become victims, as were soldiers. Home fronts were essential to the material and moral support of armies, navies and air forces. As a consequence, civilians also became a legitimate, if not the preferred, target of military violence, whether in the form of genocide, strategic bombing, or starvation by naval blockade. At the least, we concluded, the term 'total' described the fact that the two world wars encompassed the lives of every man, woman and child in the belligerent states.[1]

In January 1917, Georg Gerth was in Kiel at the UAK, the u-boat acceptance commission, busy preparing his new u-boat for war at sea.[2] After serving a five-month apprenticeship aboard one of the early 'sewing machines', *UB 12*, Gerth was allotted in December a greatly improved UC Series II mine-laying boat, built at the Weser Yard in Bremen, one of the ninety-six u-boats launched there during the Great War. Gerth's fitting out party, led by Petty Officer Peter Kleinsorg, worked for almost a month to master the new diesel and electric power units and the increasingly complex control systems.[3] It is doubtful whether Gerth, twenty-nine years old, could have been prouder or more determined to serve his country. Dönitz described himself as 'mighty as a king' when he assumed his first command, *UC 25*, a year later.[4]

Yet, the summons received by Gerth and the other captains to conferences on Wednesday 17 January changed everything. The gloves were to come off in a high-risk gamble. Gerth and his fellow commanders were to hear that the future of the German nation was in their hands. Ludendorff and

Hindenburg had recently replaced Falkenhayn in the army's supreme command, but all three pressured the Kaiser to order the indiscriminate sinking of Allied merchantmen without warning. Unrestricted submarine warfare was intended to destroy the enemy's food supply. The intention was to 'force England to make peace and thereby decide the whole war'. On 9 January 1917, after much indecision, Wilhelm agreed, and the onslaught was set to begin on 1 February. The episode 'closely repeated the formal patterns of the Schlieffen Plan', a high stakes single throw of the dice using maximum force over a short period without a back-up plan. 'Among officers, widespread happiness at the decision was probably the most common response.' At the onset, Germany had 111 submarines of which only thirty-two could be on station at any one time and not all of these in British waters. 'This was a staggering shortfall. The twinning of wishful thinking and risk, the hallmarks of the Schlieffen Plan, had now moved firmly into the realm of the unreal'.[5] In an outbreak of rose-tinted history and hopeful exaggeration, the Kaiser declared:

> *In the impending decisive battle, the task falls upon my navy of turning the English war method of starvation, with which our most hated and most obstinate enemy intends to overthrow the German people, against him and his allies by combating their sea traffic with all the means in our power. In this work, the submarine will stand in the first rank. I expect that this weapon, technically developed with wise forethought at our admirable yards, in co-operation with all our other naval fighting weapons and supported by the spirit which, during the whole course of the war, has enabled us to perform brilliant deeds, will break our enemy's war will.[6]*

There is no list of the number of meetings held that day to announce the same 'most secret' message sent from the admiralty staff, nor which one Gerth attended. The u-boat force had a dysfunctional command structure.[7] Submarines at Wilhelmshaven came under a Führer der Unterseeboote, Hermann Bauer, who was accountable to the Chief of the High Seas Fleet. U-boats at Bremen came directly under the auspices of the Commander of the Baltic Fleet, headquartered at this time at Libau.[8] Other long-distance submarine cruisers came under the Naval Office. Karl Bartenbach, Gerth's immediate superior, was head of the Flanders flotilla, one step away from the Kaiser, while command of the u-boats in the Mediterranean were 'even more confusing' and were commanded notionally by the Chief of the Admiralty Staff.[9] In Fregattenkäpitan Bauer's view, the whole u-boat force should have been 'organised and united under one command', preferably his.[10] He was at a loss why this had not been done. The answer was the Kaiser's inability to manage his private navy. The navy was in peace and war a federal German institution directly under his jealous guardianship.

'It requires no great imagination to gauge whether this system of direct access to an impressionable and volatile monarch by nearly fifty senior officers, not counting department heads, enhanced military effectiveness.'

Bauer led the Wilhelmshaven conference. He regretted that preparation of a large number of u-boats for the coming campaign was hindered by the icy conditions of the current severe winter.[11] An almost full transcript of the conference survives, taken by British divers from the wreck of Tebbenjohanns' *UC 44* off Waterford later that year.[12] Bauer was a torpedo man with great experience of large ships; he commanded the light cruiser SMS *Hamburg* before taking over I Unterseebootsflotille in March 1914 and, in April 1915, the original and entire German submarine force at Wilhelmshaven. Bauer came straight to the point.

> *Energetic action is required, but above all rapidity of action. The submarine war is therefore to be prosecuted with the utmost vigour. No vessel must remain afloat, the sinking of which is authorised. Orders must be carried out with exactitude, doubts must be cleared up before going to sea. Such consideration has hitherto been shown to submarine crews, that now the greatest efforts are to be expected from them. Leave is only possible when repairs to the boat are not affected by it. For this reason, food allowances of submarines are increased. The sole aim is that each boat shall fire her entire supply of ammunition as often as possible. The standard of achievement is not each separate enterprise, but the total result over any given period. Therefore, short cruises, short visits to the dockyard, considerable curtailment of practices. If a submarine is at sea for fourteen days in each month and fires her full supply of torpedoes and a corresponding amount of gun ammunition, that constitutes the best form of practice. During periods of overhaul, only what is absolutely necessary is to be done. The crew and reserve personnel are to be made the utmost use of.*

Bauer then diverted into a curious order of important matters. First, he attacked the prevalence of venereal disease 'which must be eliminated in future'. Next, he insisted on more care when manoeuvring submarines, 'damage in harbour must be absolutely avoided'. He told his men that their object was to 'cut England off from traffic by sea and not to achieve occasional results at far-distant points'. U-boats were to take up stations close to the English coast where merchant shipping had to converge. If the weather turned bad, captains were to submerge their boats and wait it out and not waste time by seeking better conditions elsewhere, not an order reflected by Georg Gerth's practice.

All u-boats were to travel through the English Channel so as to shorten cruises, going first to the North Hinder light vessel, then the deepest channel past *Buoy 2501*, and taking advantage of the light buoys in the

Straits of Dover.[13] Habitation lights ashore in France were still burning as in peace time, but frequently with diminished power.

Bauer listed the principal advantages of 'ruthless submarine warfare'. These included the ability to attack while submerged all armed or suspect ships; the extra option of night attacks because no identity checking of targets was needed in the war zone; no need for warning shots when attacking by gun; and, as no inter-boat communication was needed with an attacked vessel, the only criteria for positioning the u-boat was a military one. Bauer called for a 'sharp look-out' especially for enemy ships hidden under the lee of attacked vessels. He also listed areas that needed special care. Top of the list was the danger from 'submarine traps', or Q-ships, whose 'broadside offensive capability' was kept hidden until the submarine was lured in close. Boats about to be sunk by u-boat gunfire should be approached from aft with no men on deck beyond those actually required. This would reduce the danger of being rammed and provide cover from the guns of submarine traps. Bauer recommended always keeping 'way' on the u-boat so as to give immediate responsive control and thus make a retaliatory attack, especially by enemy submarines, more difficult. Normally, only one torpedo was to be fired against a stopped ship which should then be finished by gunfire. One torpedo tube was to be kept loaded and flooded for emergencies. Bauer made one error in his instructions. He claimed that 'if a ship allows herself to be torpedoed, she will either be no trap or she will have ceased to be dangerous'; decidedly not the case with Commander Gordon Campbell and his fellow Q-ship skippers who often loaded their holds with timber in order to stay afloat after the first 'invited' torpedo.[14]

Within the navy command's prediction to 'bring England to its knees' in six months there were 'two backhanded acknowledgements that the whole house of cards was extremely fragile'.[15] First was the caveat that the programme had to be launched by 1 February 1917 otherwise the American harvest would save England. Second was the admission that 'bringing England to its knees' did not mean 'materially forcing it to quit, but making the cost so great that England, unwilling to make the same heroic sacrifices as Germany, would negotiate on Germany's terms. That is, it was at base, a psychological argument.'

Gerth would undertake another month of sea trials before he left Kiel on 19 February. His route from the Baltic would take him along the sixty-one miles of the Kaiser Wilhelm Canal from Kiel to the North Sea exit at Brunsbüttel and, from there, via Heligoland to Bartenbach's base at Bruges. Gerth's first full-blown assault patrol with UC 61 was not for another six weeks. However, his fellow commanders with their shackles released made immediate and serious inroads into the merchant shipping supplying Britain. These unleashed commanders believed in their new orders; for them it was not a gamble, but a cast-iron plan to win the war. U-boat captives brought to London in 1917 laughed at the 'merest suggestion of German defeat; their attitude was not that of prisoners, but of conquerors'.[16] They regarded themselves as heroes due to be sent home in a few months when the war was won. The possible entry of the United States into the war 'affected them about as much as would a declaration of war from Mars'.

> *So now, in February 1917, Germany had declared unrestricted u-boat warfare. We would have six months, so they said, to pull it off. In these six months, we would have to give everything we had to force the Allies to the negotiating table. Germany's hopes had been placed into the hands of the u-boat arm. We had been entrusted with an endeavour imbued with the highest level of responsibility, to commit ourselves to the uttermost for Germany.*[17]

> *As we are blockading Germany with surface ships, so the Germans are attempting to blockade us with submarines. They have raised an entirely new naval problem ... The Germans are buoyed up with the hope that they can starve us. We must disappoint them and in so doing we shall win the war. They are going to turn loose an increased number of submarines; they intend to use them with the utmost ruthlessness.*[18]

A flurry of supporting 'most secret' orders was issued from Berlin by the chief of the admiralty staff in Berlin, Admiral Henning von Holtzendorff, a strong proponent of unrestricted submarine warfare and, at whose door, lay the principal responsibility for the decision.[19] The orders show that, despite the many months of argument and scheming between various factions in the navy, the army high command and the Kaiser and his family, many important details had not been thought through. The additions and corrections continued over several weeks.[20] The Kaiser's vacillation and sudden final agreement had left much not yet done.

On 12 January, von Holtzendorff insisted in a memorandum that the initial effect of the new submarine attack should be 'as striking as possible' in order to intimidate neutral shipping.[21] A 'barred' area around the British coast should be occupied continuously.[22] The document also dealt with concerns about enemy and neutral ships caught at sea on 1 February, which had not known of the new situation when they sailed. Hospital ships found outside the area were exempted. With provisos, neutral steamers, Belgian relief ships, unarmed enemy passenger steamers and neutral sailing vessels were given up to a few weeks' grace before being treated as targets. By the day after the conference, similar early leniency was to apply to American passenger steamers and to Dutch passenger paddle steamers.[23] Afterwards, one American steamer a week would be permitted to run to and fro between the USA and Falmouth and one Dutch paddle steamer on a weekday between Flushing and Southwold. These ships were given prescribed routes and instructed on their markings, their hulls and superstructures painted with alternative red and white stripes and flying their ensign and a large red and white check flag at each masthead. On 26 January, with just days to go and several u-boats already at sea, complexity began.[24] Commanders were asked to bear in mind that, under the Prussian-American Treaty, American ships could only be sunk when more than half of their cargo comprised finished war material; the timber agreement with Sweden was continued; the promise that ships would be safe if carrying foodstuffs of Danish origin to England was rescinded; no more safe passes would be issued by the consuls in Spain for fruit ships. Shooting on sight, it seems, was to be more difficult than initially announced and not so automatic.

Admiral Reinhard Scheer's view was typically expressed, clinging to a Tirpitz doctrine that was publicly maintained by many political and military leaders throughout and after the war: 'England forbore to risk her superior fleet in battle, and her naval policy in the war was confined to this: to cut Germany off from all supplies by sea, and to starve her out by withholding food and raw materials.'[25] There is no mention here of Germany's political directive not to risk its own High Seas Fleet in battle. Tirpitz did 'not trust that the British would obey the rules; he also wanted to be free to wage commercial war against Britain'.[26] It was a perfect case of adjusted hindsight as Tirpitz sought to evade his years of low investment in u-boat development. Interestingly, Tirpitz first vacillated and then urged caution: a full submarine blockade was unprecedented and new questions would emerge about international law still based on rules from the days of sail; there were not yet enough u-boats for a proper enforcement. Tirpitz's alternative suggestion, not taken up, was that Schröder in Flanders should declare a blockade of the mouth of the Thames. This would bring an added benefit of not upsetting the Americans as their passenger liners all docked at Liverpool.[27]

The issue of food was paramount in German military and political thinking, but, paradoxically, the Germans had done little to prepare for food shortages. The few academics and businessmen who raised the matter were ignored. Many believed that the British would never declare food as contraband, which they promptly did in 1914. Tirpitz had already noted the importance of neutral ports, especially in Belgium and the Netherlands, and pointed out that if food and raw materials were classified as contraband, even access to neutral ports could not circumvent a British blockade. He felt the pinch would not come for eighteen months, but even if grain was available from the east, the railroads would not have sufficient capacity to replace maritime imports. Stockpiling grain, let alone raw materials, would be an admission that a long war was possible. As with the Schlieffen Plan, to suggest a possible failure would be 'tantamount to defeatism'. Also, the Imperial Treasury would not countenance the immense cost of amassing and storing the 'necessarily huge quantity of grain'. 'For a short war, stockpiling was unnecessary. For a long war, it was impossible.'[28]

German naval propagandist, Admiral Carl Hollweg, declared that 'the submarine will guarantee the future freedom of the seas and will forever wrest the hunger whip from the cruel hands of the English naval despotism'.[29] As the campaign got underway, Dr Karl Helfferich, Imperial Secretary of the German Interior, declared:

> In this life and death struggle by hunger, England believed herself to be far beyond the reach of any anxiety about food. A year ago, it was supposed that England would be able to use the acres of the whole world, bidding with them against the German acres. Today, England sees herself in a situation unparalleled in her history. Her acres across the sea disappear as a result of the blockade, which our submarines are daily making more effective around England. We have considered; we have dared. Certain of the result, we shall not allow it to be taken from us by anybody or anything.[30]

This was like old times for those in the German u-boat fleet who had managed to stay alive until 1917. Two previous unrestricted submarine offensives against Allied shipping, one each in 1915 and 1916, had both foundered for the same reason: angry responses from the United States when its neutral ships were threatened or its citizens killed.

In November 1914, the leaders of the German fleet laid their concerns before Admiral von Pohl, chief of the naval staff. Little was to change in the rationale over the war years.

> As England is trying to destroy our trade it is only fair if we retaliate by carrying on the campaign against her trade by all possible means. Further, as England completely disregards International Law in her actions, there is not the least reason why we should exercise any restraint in our conduct of the war. We can wound England most seriously by injuring her trade. By means of the u-boat we should be able to inflict the greatest injury. We must therefore make use of this weapon, and do so, moreover, in the way most suited to its peculiarities. The more vigorously the war is prosecuted the sooner will it come to an end, and countless human beings and treasure will be saved if the duration of the war is curtailed. Consequently, a u-boat cannot spare the crews of steamers, but must send them to the bottom with their ships. The shipping world can be warned of these consequences, and it can be pointed out that ships which attempt to make British ports run the risk of being destroyed with their crews. This warning that the lives of steamers' crews will be endangered will be one good reason why all shipping trade with England should cease within a short space of

time. The whole British coast, or anyway a part of it, must be declared to be blockaded, and at the same time the aforesaid warning must be published. The declaration of the blockade is desirable in order to warn neutrals of the consequences. The gravity of the situation demands that we should free ourselves from all scruples which certainly no longer have justification. It is of importance too, with a view to the future, that we should make the enemy realise at once what a powerful weapon we possess in the u-boat, with which to injure their trade, and that the most unsparing use is to be made of it.[31]

Economic life in Germany had only been slightly affected by January 1915. The admiralty staff knew, however, that as the months went by the actions of the British in stopping ships and seizing cargoes would be intensified and they could form a good idea of the pressure the Allies could bring to bear upon the neutrals. 'She was still breathing normally, but was haunted by fears of suffocation; she beheld herself as it were a fortress, already beset, a state of mind which was itself becoming an obsession. This obsession was one of the reasons which impelled Germany to embark systematically upon the adventure of submarine war.'[32] In retaliation, the Germans declared a war zone around the whole British and Irish coasts. This first offensive was announced in a German proclamation on 4 February 1915. The arguments were consistent; the offensive was 'not conceived initially as a war-winning measure, but as a form of retaliation for the British blockade'.[33]

Since the beginning of the present war, Great Britain has carried on a mercantile warfare against Germany in a way that defies all the principles of international law ... The British Government has put a number of articles in the list of contraband which are not or at most only indirectly useful for military purposes and, therefore, according to the London Declaration as well as according to the universally recognised rules of international law, may not be designated contraband. She has further actually abolished the distinction between actual and relative contraband ... She does not even hesitate to violate the Paris Declaration ... The neutral powers have generally acquiesced in the steps taken by the English Government ... For her violations of international law Great Britain pleads the vital interests which the British Empire has at stake, and the neutral powers seem to satisfy themselves with theoretical protests ... Germany must now appeal to these same vital interests to its regret ... Just as England has designated the area between Scotland and Norway as an area of war, so Germany now declares all waters surrounding Great Britain and Ireland including the entire English Channel as an area of war, and thus will proceed against the shipping of the enemy.[34]

The first attack officially began on 18 February 1915, but was pre-empted by submarine commanders in the days before when they sank eleven Allied ships, five by torpedo without warning.[35] Seven other vessels were attacked, but managed to escape. On 24 February, Bauer, in Emden, gave his commanders their orders for the new commercial warfare according to prize rules to be carried, presaging his similar talk almost two years later.[36] U-boat historian Tarrant concluded the 'aggressive tactics of the u-boat commanders was evidence that the naval command was unleashing a force over which they could not exercise proper control'. Archibald Bell concurred, 'A handful of naval officers, most of them under thirty years of age, without political training, and isolated from the rest of the world by the nature of their duties, were thus given a vague and indefinite instruction to give a thought to politics before they fired their torpedoes'.[37] The Germans said they would try to 'destroy every enemy ship that is found in this area of war without its always being possible to avert the peril that thus threatens persons and cargoes. Neutrals are therefore warned against further entrusting crews, passengers, and wares, to such ships. Their attention [is] also called to the fact that it is advisable for their ships to avoid entering this area, for even though the German naval forces have instructions to avoid violence to neutral ships insofar as they are recognisable, in view of the misuse of neutral flags ordered by the British Government and the contingencies of naval warfare their becoming victims of torpedoes directed against enemy ships cannot always be avoided'.[38]

> *The first event of the Great War was the isolation of Germany by the British blockade. No paragraph of the laws of maritime warfare, as recognised by all Sea Powers, permitted Britain to hold up neutral ships by force on their way to Germany with foodstuffs or other non-warlike cargoes. Britain was the first to wage war, not against the German armies and fleets, but against the German nation and its non-combatants, its women and children. The next step was the German answer. We declared a prohibited area around Britain and dispatched our submarines to break the enemy blockade and damage enemy commerce. An eye for an eye, a tooth for a tooth.*[39]

In the first few months of the campaign, the Germans managed an average of about half a dozen u-boats at sea each day and they acted mainly in the area between the southern Irish coast and the coast of France. Only twenty-one boats were available, eight of them obsolete; all of them required long periods of maintenance in port. 'This was not sufficiently appreciated by the naval command.'[40] The campaign provided the British with exactly the excuse they sought. In counter-retaliation, on 1 March, the British and French Governments declared themselves 'free to detain and take into port ships carrying goods of presumed enemy destination, ownership or origin'.

By month end, the British put into operation a distant 'blockade' which was beyond their international legal rights.[41]

The first u-boat campaign's limited success turned, in part, on indecision about the choice of passage, either north around Scotland, thereby losing time, or directly south through the English Channel. To protect the Channel, the British laid 7,154 mines in twenty-two fields by February 1915. 'This mine barrage proved no obstacle to the u-boats because the British mines were defective. Apart from being visible on the surface at low water they commonly failed to explode when struck. Moreover, about 4,000 mines either sank uselessly to the bottom or drifted away owing to the sinkers being too light.'[42] Another measure was a twenty-mile boom of heavy steel nets from Folkestone to Cap Gris Nez. Heavy seas and corrosion rendered the boom 'impracticable' and it was abandoned in May and mostly removed. These nets, and the action of British drifters towing nets, caused Führer Bauer to instruct his u-boats to travel north because of the 'grave danger'.[43] Meanwhile, the u-boats of the Flanders Flotilla went south with no great hardship.

> Under the 'unrestricted' campaign, the u-boat commanders all affirm that they gave ships warning whenever they could. They were, their own people insist, ordinary men carrying out orders, and did so as humanely as normal for ordinary men who were living the abnormal lives of under-sea raiders. Also, it was economic wisdom to torpedo ships only when they could be sunk in no other way. A u-boat could carry only a limited supply of torpedoes, and these big missiles were mighty expensive.[44]

The American government warned the Germans about attacks on its ships and citizens in strong terms in what it called 'strict accountability' in February 1915:

> If the commanders of German vessels of war … should destroy on the high seas an American vessel or the lives of American citizens, it would be difficult for the Government of the United States to view the act in any other light than as an indefensible violation of neutral rights which it would be very hard indeed to reconcile with the friendly relations now so happily subsisting between the two governments … If such a deplorable situation should arise, the Imperial German Government can readily appreciate that the Government of the United States would be constrained to hold the Imperial German Government to a strict accountability for such acts of their naval authorities and to take any steps it might be necessary to take to safeguard American lives and property and to secure to American citizens the full enjoyment of their acknowledged rights on the high seas.[45]

Peterson noted that this American protest was founded on the false premise that the United States was privileged to speak not only for American vessels, but also on behalf of American citizens on Allied and other vessels. 'No other neutral appears to have fallen into this error.'[46] The decks of British ships were British 'soil'. 'If this position were carried to its logical extreme, President Wilson could have pressured Germany not to carry out aerial bombardment of London because American citizens might inadvertently be killed.'[47] The Americans also tried mediation. Wilson proposed that Germany discontinue the u-boat war if Britain abandoned the blockade of food to be delivered to German ports. On 28 February, the Germans accepted, but 'in desultory fashion' the British rejected the proposal on 15 March and Wilson let the British off with a 'flaccid protest'.[48]

In March 1915, the British passenger ship *Falaba* sailing out of Liverpool carrying munitions and passengers, was torpedoed *by U 28*, commander Georg-Günther von Forstner. There were 104 casualties, one of which was an American. According to historian Raico, the ensuing note to Berlin 'entrenched Wilson's preposterous doctrine, that the United States had the right and duty to protect Americans sailing on ships flying a *belligerent* flag'. Later, John Bassett Moore, with over thirty years' senior experience of international law, agreed.

> *What most decisively contributed to the involvement of the United States in the war was the assertion of a right to protect belligerent ships on which Americans saw fit to travel and the treatment of armed belligerent merchantmen as peaceful vessels. Both assumptions were contrary to reason and to settled law, and no other professed neutral advanced them.*[49]

On 1 May, the American tanker *Gulflight* was torpedoed by *U 30* off the Scilly Isles.[50] The ship did not sink, but three men died, the master from a heart attack and two crew from drowning 'after jumping overboard in panic'.[51] The sinking of the British passenger liners *Lusitania*, *Arabic* and *Hesperian* in May, August and September 1915 off the Irish coast were human and public relations disasters. There were a total of 1,270 casualties. *Lusitania*, in particular, was listed as a British auxiliary cruiser and was built to be able to act as a hunter-killer of German ocean raiders.[52] It also had munitions in its cargo although it was not armed as the Germans first claimed. The German ambassador, Count Johann von Bernstorff in Washington warned the American public against travelling before its sailing.[53] 'These issues are irrelevant; the law demanded visit, search, and safety of those aboard regardless.'[54] The outcry was enormous and, after an extensive exchange of diplomatic notes between the United States and Germany, the Kaiser folded to America pressure and ordered that no more large passenger ships were to be sunk.

Following the *Lusitania* affair, the Americans offered a surprising compromise. If Germany accepted cruiser rules for submarines, by stopping ships to inspect cargoes and, if sinking was justified, first allowing crews into lifeboats, disavowed the attack on the *Lusitania* and paid reparation, the United States would work to get Britain to give up the 'most objectionable aspects of its blockade'. However, if Germany continued with illegal sinkings, then the United States would see that as 'deliberately unfriendly'. Disagreements within the German command followed and they made no response to the offer.

> *The US offer was the greatest diplomatic opportunity that Germany received in the war, for it promised to end Germany's continental isolation, move the United States away from Britain, and open further benefits from American co-operation. It was an important and genuine offer.*[55]

There was another point of view on the effect on public consciousness of the sinking of the liner. Schreiner, the American news correspondent operating in Germany, observed:

> *Nothing weaned the German public so much away from the old order of government as did the Lusitania affair. The act seemed useless, wanton, ill-considered. The doctrine of governmental infallibility came near to being wrecked. The Germans began to lose confidence in the wisdom of the men who had been credited in the past with being the very quintessence of all knowledge, mundane and celestial. Admiral Tirpitz had to go.*[56]

When news of the sinking of the *Arabic* was received in Berlin, Chancellor Bethmann sent a telegram to the imperial headquarters asking whether the Kaiser's order to spare large liners had been rescinded and was told it had not. 'Suddenly, Bethmann understood that the navy had simply refused to obey the imperial order'.[57] Bethmann found that, with the next case of the *Hesperian*, the navy had gone 'rogue' and openly opposed the Kaiser's order again. In September, u-boat commanders were re-ordered to sink no more merchantmen without a warning which would allow crews to seek safety in the lifeboats.[58] He also discovered that Tirpitz had inflated the number of submarines at Germany's disposal by counting those under construction.[59] Otto Steinbrinck, who was to travel behind Georg Gerth on his last voyage down the Zeebrugge canal in July 1917, said that he had 'let forty ships in the channel go by which, under unrestricted warfare, he could have sunk'. Some exaggeration, perhaps, as 'in the short term, the quantity of tonnage sunk actually rose rather than fell, as surfacing enabled the u-boats to use their guns and so economise on torpedoes'.[60]

Wilson's Secretary of State, William Jennings Bryan, tried to reason with the President: 'Germany has the right to prevent contraband going to the Allies and a ship carrying contraband should not rely on passengers to protect her from attack – it would be like putting women and children in front of an army. He reminded Wilson that a proposed American compromise whereby Britain would allow food into Germany and the Germans would abandon submarine attacks on merchant ships had been welcomed by Germany but rejected by England. Finally, Bryan blurted out: 'Why be shocked by the drowning of a few people, if there is to be no objection to starving a nation?' In June, convinced that the Administration was heading for war, Bryan resigned.[61]

The Kaiser's government 'quickly and unequivocally adopted a moderate position that subordinated military considerations to political ones, primarily with a view to avoid American belligerence.'[62] Bauer felt the campaign should have been continued because the United States was not ready, nor willing, to join the war at that time.[63] The English blockade, which 'contravened the law of nations', gave Britain a two-and-a-half year lead, causing 'severe hardship in Germany with the first hunger strikes in Berlin and Braunschweig in the summer of 1916 followed by the turnip winter – *Kohlrübenwinter*. The Kaiser fired Admiral Gustav von Bachmann, and his deputy, Admiral Paul Behncke, because of disagreement over the conduct of the u-boat war. Admiral Henning von Holtzendorff was appointed chief of staff in September 1915 to implement the Kaiser's new policy, but Holtzendorff was quickly persuaded by Tirpitz to the cause of u-boat warfare. This was the same Tirpitz who, before 1905, had scorned submarines and had relentlessly worked to implement a naval strategy wholly dependent on a single great battleship encounter, probably in the North Sea.[64] 'Holtzendorff became an ardent fighter for Tirpitz's cause once he was fully committed to it.'[65]

On 12 November 1915, the Germany navy high command, the Admiralstab ordered the ub-boats of the Flanders Flotilla to operate against troop transports entering or leaving the French Channel ports.

This order was a dead letter for three months for it was not until March 1916 that the Flanders Flotilla was reinforced by boats of the UBII class which alone were sufficiently powerful to operate effectively in the central parts of the English Channel ... The order had been drafted in such a way as to intimate, quite erroneously as it turned out, that passenger ships were only plying on the Folkestone Boulogne route, and that vessels on all other cross-Channel routes could be sunk without warning and without fear of disregarding the pledges made to the United States that passenger ships of every nationality were to be spared molestation.[66]

The second unrestricted campaign began on 4 February 1916 with just one u-boat at sea. Its origin was a desperate plan by General Erich von Falkenhayn, chief of the general staff, which he presented to army and navy leaders at a conference on 30 December.[67] The campaign was short-lived and ended in April and died for the same reason as the first. Falkenhayn's plan recognised that Germany's future food supply was giving serious cause for concern. There were many local and temporary shortages of some kinds of food, but the real problem lay with declining imports of fodder and fertilisers caused by the British blockade. Without the free use of nitrates, the poor and sandy German soil would not yield anything approaching normal harvests, especially the production of cereals. The longer the war went on, the worse matters would become. 'Germany faced the possibility of being starved into suing for peace even though her armies were undefeated in the field.' Falkenhayn offered a two-part approach. The first was a major new land offensive against the French fortified town of Verdun, 'which the French would have to fight to the last man to hold' as it was the gateway to Paris. The essence was to 'turn the approaches into an abattoir into which the French forces would be drawn and bled to death; the actual capture of the town was secondary'. France would be out of the war by the end of 1916. The second was to revive the u-boat campaign in home waters with the object of discouraging Britain, so that with France beaten, she would be inclined to make peace. German shipping experts had, wrongly, worked out a formula that seventy u-boats, would produce Allied losses that would be unsupportable. Falkenhayn felt that unrestricted submarine warfare would cause 'eight to ten times more sinkings' and that he was 'absolutely sure England would finally be ready for peace within three months'.[68] Offer points out that Germany's frame for Britain's capitulation varied over the next year between three and eight months suggesting that the 'time constraint was not entirely derived from economic calculations, but was a prior constraint on the plan'.[69]

Time was working against Germany. In the summer of 1916, the view was that neither side could survive another winter of war. By December, the Germans thought that the prospect of another year of war 'could no longer be faced. In a war of attrition, an already exhausted Germany was bound to lose because it had fewer resources.' However, casualty rates for all armies on the Western Front were unacceptably high. In France, 'where concern with the plunging birth rate had reached almost hysterical proportions by 1914, critics were especially harsh in condemning the cavalier disregard for human life sometimes exhibited by the high command'.[70]

Not long after the German 'victory' at the Battle of Skagerrak/Jutland, Admiral Scheer told the Kaiser in a seemingly complete break with Tirpitz's strategic plan that 'not even the most successful result from a high seas battle will compel England to make peace'.[71] He pointed out Germany's geographic disadvantages and the British superiority that made it impossible to break the blockade. The only remedy was 'the crushing of English economic life through u-boat action against English commerce'.[72] He supported Falkenhayn in the resumption of unrestricted submarine warfare.

More wrangling between the military and the politicians followed until, in March, the u-boats were given permission to sink without warning all ships except passenger vessels.[73] The incident, which caused uproar during this campaign, was on 24 March. Oberleutnant Herbert Pustkuchen, *UB 29*, twenty-six years old, saw through his periscope a steamer about to enter Dieppe with, he thought, its upper decks crowded with troops. Pustkuchen torpedoed her without warning. It was not a troop ship, but the French cross-channel steamer *Sussex* with 325 passengers on her usual trip from Folkestone. *Sussex* had to be beached with her bows blown off.[74] There were twenty-five Americans among the fifty casualties, four of whom were injured.[75] The American response, delivered a month later on 20 April was to the point:

> *If it is still the purpose of the Imperial Government to prosecute relentless and indiscriminate warfare against vessels of commerce by the use of u-boats without regard to what the government of the United States must consider the sacred and indisputable rules of international law and universally recognised dictates of humanity, the government of the United States is at last forced to the conclusion that there is but one course it can pursue. Unless the Imperial Government should now immediately declare and effect an abandonment of its present methods of u-boat warfare against passenger and freight-carrying vessels, the government of the United States can have no other choice but to sever diplomatic relations with the German Reich altogether. This action the government of the United States contemplates with the greatest reluctance but feels constrained to take on behalf of humanity and the rights of neutral nations.[76]*

The Germans noted that during this summer they had stopped, searched unsuccessfully for contraband, and let continue some 300 ships of 700,000 tons.[77] 'It was no rare thing for the mate, or some other trusted assistant of the commander, to have to bring up numerous documents to the conning tower before the attack.' These documents were then gone over to ascertain whether a vessel could be sunk or not – 'a painful and almost impossible task'. The Germans gave the Americans their justification for attacks like that on the *Sussex* and summarised their case:

> *In self-defence against the illegal conduct of British warfare, while fighting in a bitter struggle for national existence, Germany had to resort to the hard but effective weapon of submarine warfare. As matters stand, the German Government cannot but reiterate its regret*

that sentiments of humanity, which the Government of the United States extends with such fervour to the unhappy victims of submarine warfare, have not been extended with the same feeling to the many millions of women and children, who, according to the avowed intention of the British Government, are to be starved, and who by suffering are to force the victorious armies of the Central Powers into an ignominious capitulation.

There was no question that British actions were illegal, as the Germans never tired of pointing out. Their protests became strident at times and showed evident frustration because no one was listening. The British advanced their stranglehold in firm and steady steps in order to test reactions from the neutral powers, especially the United States.[78] The blockade plans to apply the concept of continuous voyage to conditional contraband was in violation of the Declaration of London, signed by the British, but formally unratified. 'Guilty until proven innocent became the new law' of the British-controlled seas. The Royal Navy had even incorporated the provisions of the Declaration into its manuals. Britain also circumvented the valid Declaration of Paris which stated that a blockade against a whole nation had to be effective against all ports to be obligatory and that could not be the case with Germany because the Baltic was completely unblockaded.[79] Because the British for the first part of the war were an absent force in the Baltic they began a continuous expansion of the contraband list in order to stop a widening range of goods reaching Scandinavia and therefore nullifying those countries' Baltic trades with Germany.

German civilian statesmen paid attention to their diplomats' warnings about the strength of American opinion and were soon able to prevail over the generals and the admirals: on 4 May the scope of the submarine campaign was again severely restricted. On 25 April, all u-boats in the High Seas Fleet and the Flanders Flotilla ub-boats were ordered to return to base. The German naval staff decided again to attack the troop transports across the channel. Bartenbach authorised numerous mine-laying expeditions near Calais, but reported that 'results could be expected if they were permitted to torpedo transports without warning' which was, at the time, prohibited.[80] In July, Bartenbach ordered Leutnant Otto Steinbrinck in *UB 18* to Le Havre and the mouth of the Seine where he attempted forty-one attacks. All were broken off because his rules of engagement were impossible to fulfil. He managed to sink only seven small steamers and ten sailing vessels. One might have expected a more determined effort on the part of the naval staff to interfere with direct cross-Channel traffic which supplied the armies in France with men and material, but except for mine-laying in the approaches to Calais, Boulogne and Le Havre, they steered clear of these well-protected channel convoys and confined their activities chiefly to the western end of the Channel and the west coast of France.[81]

> *In March 1916, there was a new exchange of notes with the United States of America. Germany promised to conduct the submarine war strictly in accordance with International Prize Law, which was as good as to renounce it altogether ... We only had permission to fire at ships of war, and they did not show themselves in the open sea.*[82]

America's angry response to Germany's two previous attempts at unrestricted submarine warfare had succeeded because of Germany's politicians' fear that America might enter the war. By May, Chancellor Bethmann saw that the economic position was so serious, the longing of the people for peace so widespread, that she must 'grasp at every possibility of achieving peace'.[83] Yet there remained an overriding concern that interference from American president Woodrow Wilson would not help Germany: it would undermine their western war aims and Wilson himself was thought to be unfavourable at heart to the German cause. This fear that Wilson would make a positive offer of mediation was tangible. If it happened it would need to be in such terms that it would be refused by the British. To keep America onside, Germany could not be seen to be unhelpful. In the summer of 1916, the United States held more political levers than it was inclined to use. Would the United States, even if acting only in support of its own perceived neutral commercial rights, force the Allies to ease up on the attempt to starve Germany into submission? Would Wilson attempt to inaugurate peace negotiations that stood any chance of success? 'The economic situation of the Allies had become so difficult that Wilson, by means of an embargo, could have compelled them to eliminate the most glaring of their illegalities from their blockade procedure. Their financial dependence upon the United States would also have forced the British and the French to enter into peace negotiations if Wilson applied pressure.'[84] Fathoming these knots led to surreal and emotional discussions among the German army and naval commanders.

> *At the time of the visit of the Chief of Naval staff to Bruges on 7 August 1916, Bartenbach attempted to get the rules changed allowing him to attack cross-Channel troop transports, but the reply on the 15th said that conditions on the Somme 'were not such as to warrant bringing America into the war'.*[85]

On patrol in *UB 21* in October 1916, Ernst Hashagen noted that of the seventeen days in which his boat was at sea, the weather was so bad on eleven that no aggressive action was possible. On five days, twenty Scandinavian neutral ships were stopped and searched and seven were sunk. 'All but two of the remainder, which all had to be let go, were carrying food to or coal from Britain.'[86] Hashagen was a year classmate of Erich Gerth in 1905.[87]

For the period of the thirty months from the start of the war, the u-boats' campaigns against commerce were a constant mêlée of changing regulation and constraint. At one time, they had to comply with the strictest international law, applying the rule of stop and search; at the other end the u-boats could sink any enemy merchant shops found in the war zone, whether armed or not. 'In general, the Germans went as far towards a totally unrestricted campaign as their relations with neutral states allowed. The term "restricted campaign" has not therefore a very precise connotation'.[88]

Despite the setbacks, Holtzendorff remained committed to unrestricted submarine warfare and worked hard for its return. During 1916, he produced half a dozen drafts, and one official paper on 27 August, which received minimal support, of an argument to re-persuade the Kaiser on the need for aggressive u-boat action. In this, he was supported by Karl Bartenbach of the Flanders Flotilla and by the High Seas Fleet commanders.[89] Chancellor Bethmann began to 'swim in Müller's waters'.[90] Müller, as head of the Kaiser's navy cabinet, saw his pre-conditions for turning loose the submarines fulfilled in the late summer: certainty about Rumania, which joined the Allies on 27 August, and a good German harvest. On 22 December, a final memorandum was submitted to Hindenburg, who had replaced Falkenhayn after the failures at Verdun. It became the 'pivotal document for Germany's declaration of unrestricted u-boat warfare in 1917'.[91] After the order to begin the invasion of France and Belgium, it was also the most important German document of the war.

The situation by December provided a more favourable hearing for Holtzendorff's views. The German armies had sustained serious losses during the battles of 1916 and the promise of a quick victory, no longer attainable on land, was most attractive. Hindenburg and Erich Ludendorff, credited victor of both battles of Liège and Tannenberg and now army quartermaster general, assumed control of the German land forces in August 1916. Early in the next month, they visited army commanders on the Western Front and received a 'frightening picture' which persuaded them that the German Army must move to the defensive.[92] The slaughter could not be allowed to continue. The construction work on the famous defensive Hindenburg line gave the generals options: 'forming a basis for an eventual land offensive, a strong foundation from which peace discussions could begin, or as a background to the adoption of unrestricted submarine warfare'.[93] In October, Hindenburg and Ludendorff agreed with Holtzendorff's plan. Concerns about Holland and Denmark entering the war on the side of the Allies had receded.[94] Despite losses, there was better news in December: two offensives had been stopped, the British on the Somme and the Russians in Ukraine; Romanian intervention proved to be a 'thing of straw'. 'The public and the press were blasting the Kaiser for his weak-kneed stance on u-boat warfare.' 'The public were made aware of the possession of an infallible weapon. From this point on, it was impossible to tear submarine warfare from the heart of the nation'.[95] At the same time, the Kaiser and Chancellor Bethmann, remained firmly committed to a policy of moderation. The balance was finally tipped by the Allied rejection of a German peace initiative in December 1916. On 30 December 1916, the French handed the American Ambassador in Paris the replies of the Entente countries:

> *A suggestion without any condition for initiating negotiations is not an offer of peace. The so-called proposal, devoid of substance and of precision ... appears less as an offer of peace than a manoeuvre of war ... In reality, the overture made by the Central Powers is but an attempt calculated to work upon the evolution of war and of finally imposing a German peace ... It is with full realisation of the gravity, but also of the necessities of this hour, that the Allied Governments, closely united and in perfect communion with their peoples, refuse to entertain a proposal without sincerity and without import. They affirm once again that no peace is possible as long as the reparation of violated rights and liberties, the acknowledgement of the principle of nationalities and of the free existence of small states shall not be assured; as long as there is no assurance of a settlement to suppress definitely the causes which for so long a time have menaced nations and to give them the only efficacious guarantees for the security of the world.*[96]

Meanwhile, during the latter part of 1916, the u-boat commanders chafed:

> *Out there on the open sea, and especially in the English Channel, when one saw the amount of shipping converging on Britain in an incessant stream, when one saw how busily the enemy was engaged in importing from all quarters of the globe the materials that reinforced his strength for the fight against us, one saw the writing on the wall in a way that was not apparent to people in the homeland, or to the army, or those in high politics. How bitter is the knowledge that we actually had it in our hands to reduce this stream to a trickle so that one day the stream would have dried up completely. On that day the enemy would have been compelled to sue for peace. Though undefeated, the Royal Navy would have had to admit defeat. Meanwhile we pursued the shipping war according to Prize Regulations, laid our mines, sank as much tonnage as we could with our hands tied behind our backs and constantly sought to improve our handling skills.*[97]

> *What use were principles and rules? It was War. For what purpose was the right of capture on the seas? It was only necessary to extend the principle a little, and apply it correctly: then Germany would soon be*

starved out. In a word, Blockade! The situation became desperate. How long could a population hold out in such a hunger war? No one knew of any effective counter-measure. And then the War itself supplied the answer. A new weapon entered the lists, the u-boat.[98]

Holtzendorff's arguments in favour of reintroducing the unrestricted campaign revolved around two issues. First, progressive arming of merchantmen would offset any increase in efficiency and numbers of u-boat assets if they continued to adhere to cruiser rules. Second, the 'failed' American wheat crop of 1916 would offer a unique opportunity to starve Great Britain into submission quickly.[99] The latter, persuasive, argument was inspired by a study of Dr Richard Fuss, the director of a renowned Magdeburg-based banking institute. In February 1916, Fuss postulated that if the u-boats sank enemy merchant tonnage at a rate of 630,000 tons per month, Britain would be compelled to sue for peace within five to six months simply because there would not be sufficient merchant tonnage available both to carry the necessary grain imports and to sustain the war economy at the same time.[100] A colleague, Professor Hermann Levy, concurred, pointing out that wheat imports were the 'Achilles heel of the British economy'.[101] 'The findings of these two alleged experts were passed on to Bethmann, who asked that they be kept top secret. However, Admiral Georg von Müller distributed them to no less than 228 military posts; in all, almost 500 copies of these reports were circulated among military and naval leaders.[102]

The attraction of a swift and decisive victory at sea was irresistible and became an obsession with many senior German naval officers who secretly deplored their admiralty's strategic passivity. There was limited opposition in the Reichstag and from business. In July, Matthias Erzberger, the leader of the Catholic Centre Party, said that 'all our calculations as regard the submarine war are false'. He argued for a return to a defensive war and that 'we must do everything possible to find a way which favours the conclusion of a peace this year'.[103] Influential businessmen Max Warburg thought that, however great the impact on British food supplies, the risk of alienating the United States was too grave. 'If America is cut off from Germany,' he argued, in February 1916, 'that means a 50 per cent reduction in Germany's financial strength for the war, and an increase of 100 per cent for England's and France's ... Everything should ... be done to avoid a breach with America.'[104] 'The war is lost if [unrestricted submarine warfare] goes ahead: financially, because our loans will no longer be bought; economically, because the masses of raw materials which we continue to get from abroad and which we cannot do without will be cut off.'[105] Germany's policy towards the United States came down to a 'race between peace and unrestricted submarine warfare: on the one hand diplomatic efforts to bring the war to a close; on the other mounting pressure by the naval and military leaders, as well as powerful factors of public opinion, for the indiscriminate use of the u-boat arm'.[106]

The Fuss study was endorsed by a host of German financial and economic experts. While American entry into the war would become more likely, although something to be avoided if at all possible, there would be insufficient time or ships for their troops to make a significant difference. Ludendorff expected American belligerency, but declared that without unrestricted submarine warfare Germany would be defeated.[107] He was prepared 'to accept the risk [of a break with the United States]'.[108] Admirals Tirpitz, Hipper and Souchon enthusiastically endorsed the latest naval action, believing that a massive undersea offensive against commerce would end the war before an important United States' intervention. Admiral von Capelle, Tirpitz's successor, told the Reichstag on 1 February, 'From a military point of view, I rate the effect of America coming on the side of our enemies as nil'.[109] Not to be outdone, Holtzendorff swore that no American soldier would ever set foot on the European continent. The Kaiser havered and then cracked at two contrived conferences at his headquarters in Pless, present day Pszczyna in Poland, on 22 December 1916 and, finally, on 9 January, adding that he 'fully expected America's entry into the war' but that this was 'irrelevant' to the outcome of the struggle. Hindenburg placed immense pressure on Bethmann to withdraw his opposition. Dirk Steffen notes that Crown Prince Wilhelm and Empress Auguste Viktoria, as well as numerous other courtiers, 'railed publicly against defeatist elements that opposed a measure that was bound to bring victory and implored the Kaiser to give in to Holtzendorff's request for unrestricted u-boat warfare'.[110] The 'hapless' Bethmann made a half-hearted attempt to stave off the inevitable but eventually yielded to the collective bullying: 'if the military authorities consider the unrestricted u-boat war a vital instrument then I am not in a position to contradict them'.[111]

Bethmann was also accused of undermining the Kaiser by supporting the spread of radicalism in Germany.[112] Hindenburg delivered the *coup de grace* by refusing to work with him any longer. Bethmann left on 13 July 1917. This was the 'final victory of the u-boat faction among the German leaders'.[113] It was now 'to the death' and an end to Bethmann's dream of salvaging a middle ground where a public peace move might create conditions where the new u-boat war might be achieved without a break with the United States.[114]

Economic warfare now carried on by both sides aimed for the complete destruction of the enemy's home front.[115]

> *Spring 1917 … was a crucial time when u-boats were working most feverishly. At all costs we knew we had to maintain against Allied merchant shipping the high success rates which were a prerequisite for an early conclusion to hostilities in Germany's favour. For what*

would become of Germany if we should fail? The spectre of this grim question overshadowed each of us. We discussed it often with the men, reassuring them repeatedly that we would eventually overcome the enemy Entente, and they were convinced.[116]

Terraine saw the decision as a 'moment for history to take note of; from the very foundation of the empire, the army had provided the power base of German policy; from 1 August 1914, it had been the motor of the war. Now Germany's thrust was transferred from her great and revered Army to the young and relatively untried Navy – a revolutionary change indeed, and a measure of the defeats that she had sustained, chiefly on the Western Front'.[117]

In spite of the late date at which this decision for energetic warfare was arrived at, it was generally greeted with joy at the front as a relief from the continual vacillating policy which had existed up until then, and, in spite of the fact that there existed certain fears as to whether the material was sufficient to carry through the operation.[118]

Doubts existed as to whether six months was a long enough time to starve Britain to her knees. There was a 'certain tension' in the u-boat bases. The first assumption was that recreational periods in port would be shortened or abolished entirely as 'unnecessary as the assumption of a long war ended. Secondly, a target of six months would 'justify greater risks with the submarines'.

If, more likely when, the German u-boats antagonised the Americans yet again, and the Americans entered the war as a result, few could claim surprise. Perhaps the Americans would blink again, but it seemed unlikely. Tirpitz felt that Germany must be 'willing to risk active American participation, since the United States was already supplying Britain to such a degree that formal belligerence would make little difference'.[119] The Germans were resigned to fighting the Americans and, if so, the u-boats would sink their troop transports as they crossed the Atlantic. From the beginning of the war in 1914 with the Schlieffen Plan, Tirpitz's great North Sea battle, then successive u-boat campaigns which needed a quick and decisive victory before American involvement, the horror of Verdun in 1916, Ludendorff's *Michael* spring offensive of 1918, Admiral Hipper's proposed naval Armageddon in the North Sea at war end, the scuppering of the fleet at Scapa Flow, German strategy seemed characterised by an 'exceptionally high willingness to gamble' with annihilation.[120] They were 'irresistibly attracted by risky strategies designed to bring victory in the short run'.[121] In all four cases, Germany 'embarked on an offensive ... almost, it seems, for the sake of the struggle itself. It attempted to break a political impasse with a military gamble, with little regard for the odds. It pitched professional zeal and the intensity of desperation against superior material forces.'[122] Offer suggests that one of the 'primary features of intuitive reasoning is the excessive confidence people have in their own prospects and judgement. Military men are prone to this kind of delusion. With egos already inflated by deference and flattery, where bluster is the norm, it is easy for soldiers to lose their sense of reality.'[123] 'Insanity in individuals is something rare but in groups, parties, nations and epochs it is the rule.'[124] Now, came the biggest gamble of all.

The massacre of merchant shipping in the waters around the British Isles began in earnest and Admiral Holtzendorff's promise that Britain would be 'starved into surrender seemed on its way to realisation'.[125] An Australian woman, Caroline Cooper, living in Leipzig, noted on 18 February 1917 that the u-boat war had been going on since the first of the month.[126] 'It amuses me to mention that we still get the London *Times* daily to the people who believe the lies in the daily papers here, '56,000 tons sunk daily', 'Nothing that enters the prohibited waters left afloat', and so on. But I notice that those who were prophesying that England would be on her knees in three weeks are getting somewhat silent on the matter already.' Lord Maurice Hankey, British Cabinet Secretary, recalled every morning reading a list of the sinkings for the previous twenty-four hours and, on the days in April 1917 when they rose above 50,000 tons, it 'preyed upon my mind, the more so because I was convinced that the Admiralty's arrangements were not what they should be. For the first and only time in the war I suffered from sleepless nights'.[127] Holtzendorff estimated that sinking 600,000 tons a month would finish Britain.[128] In February, it was 520,000 tons, by March 564,000 tons (when *UC 61* became operational) and, in April, the 'figure soared above the German admiral's most extravagant hope: 860,000 tons of shipping were destroyed' all achieved with about 150 u-boats of which fewer than half were at sea at any given moment. However, 21 per cent of April's number came down to one spectacular cruise in the Mediterranean by u-boat ace Kapitänleutnant Lothar von Arnauld de la Perière.[129] On 12 March, the Russian Empire collapsed and many more German troops were released for the Western Front. The situation in Britain was desperate, but, of course, the public did not know that in April they had only enough food in their country to last at the most six weeks.[130] US Admiral William Sims claimed: 'Could Germany have kept fifty submarines constantly at work on the great shipping routes in the winter of 1917, nothing could have prevented her from winning the war'.[131] Fifty u-boats were less than the cost of a single German dreadnought.

Our submarine warfare against British trade had been for Great Britain the most serious problem of the whole war. Only once was England at the end of her resources. That was in April 1917, just as the Unrestricted Submarine Warfare had achieved its first surprisingly great results ... It was then that [Admiral of the Fleet] John Jellicoe [told the Americans]: 'The Germans will win unless we stop these [ship] losses, and stop them soon.'[132]

It was also on 6 April that the inevitable happened: America declared war on Germany after a trio of shocks, bringing with her in short order twenty formerly neutral states.[133] First, anticipating the United States entering the war because of the unrestricted u-boat campaign, the German Foreign Minister Arthur Zimmermann proposed a military alliance with Mexico. His infamous and admitted telegram, sent in January, which called on Mexico to invade the United States with German financial backing, was exposed through a slight of hand by Reginald Hall at the British Naval Intelligence Department. Mexico was offered the reconquest of her lost territories in Texas, New Mexico and Arizona. Unsurprisingly, this revelation 'excited great anger' in the United States.[134] Second, Woodrow Wilson's much anticipated peace negotiations conducted independently with Austria-Hungary were rejected in early February. Third, later that month, two American vessels, *Housatonic*, *en route* from Galveston with a cargo of wheat was sunk by *U 53*, commanded by Kapitänleutnant Hans Rose, off the Isles of Scilly, and *Lyman M Law*, a four-masted schooner with a cargo of wood, by *U 35* under Arnauld de la Perière in the Mediterranean.[135] As Wilson clung to his neutrality by 'offering an elaborate excuse', he did not have time to consider what should be said about the sinking of the Cunarder *Laconia* 'for the news only came in as he was making his speech'. *Laconia* was an 18,000-ton passenger liner *en route* from New York to Liverpool; she was torpedoed off Fastnet on 25 February by *U 50*, Kapitänleutnant Gerhard Berger, twelve people died. During the next few days a Belgian relief ship, *Storstad* was sunk and 'as soon as this unpalatable news was digested', the American steamer *Algonquin* travelling from New York to London with a general cargo was also lost, sunk by *UC 62*, commander Ernst Hashagen, much quoted in these pages. In March, the American tanker *Illinois*, and the steamers *City of Memphis* and *Vigilancia* were sunk, albeit with no casualties. There was a roar of indignation from the American Press. 'White-hot' mobs called for the Kaiser to be hanged and sacked German newspaper offices in the 'worst outbreak of ethnic bigotry'.[136] Still Wilson held on. It was not until 2 April that he appeared before Congress and 'in the most stirring, eloquent language' announced that the United States were at war with Germany and called for a vote. The nation has 'no option but to accept the challenge' and to wage war with all the resources at its disposal.

These seemingly unending losses, which included many neutral ships, so intimidated many Norwegian, Danish, Dutch and Swedish captains that, in February alone, sixty neutral merchantmen in British ports refused to sail. German naval leaders 'purposely opted for a tactic certain to antagonize the world's major neutrals in the slender hope of victory over Britain within six months. Such was the German blueprint for victory in early 1917.[137]

Norway was used in Chapter 3, 'Planning a Famine', as an example of a neutral at war under the blockade and a similar use can be made of her position in the submarine war. In merchant shipping, 'Norway was the principal neutral nation' with a 2,530,000 gross tonnage, contesting with France for fourth position in the world.[138] Norway was dependent on imports to a far greater degree than any other neutral. She needed only slightly more than 10 per cent of her merchant fleet for this, but the goods must all come through waters controlled by the Royal Navy. Her large fleet for hire, 90 per cent of her capacity, was available in principle for profitable trade with any belligerent, but because of the blockade, Germany was not able to use Norway's excess tonnage; that was 'not Norway's fault, but Britain's good fortune'. Norway's situation was not comparable to that of any other nation as the 'prospect of economic gain and for political complications was greater than for other neutrals, because Norway had 'by far the greater trading fleet and at the same time the least ability to fall back on its own production'.

In addition, German u-boats used the three-mile strip of water along the Norwegian shore to reach the Atlantic. 'Viewed internationally, Germany could not fail to see that with Norway in the war British control of the Norwegian coast would complete the blockade.'[139] On 13 October 1916, the Norwegians issued a proclamation saying that u-boats travelling into Norwegian waters, except those needing to shelter, would be seized. Germany was on the brink of declaring war, but the u-boats continued to sink Norwegian merchant ships just as though they were already at war'.[140] It was a peculiar bluff. If the u-boat attacks were a cover for forcing an advantageous trade agreement then, by declaring war, Germany would frustrate her own design.

Freight rates mounted rapidly. For example, the normal rate for coal from Cardiff to Genoa before the war was seven shillings a ton. In January 1916, the charge was seventy-five shillings; in February 1916 it became one hundred shillings. Norway paid severely for the English use of her ships.[141] In August 1916, thirteen ships were lost to u-boats, in October forty-eight, November twenty-eight, then thirty-five, forty-four, forty-one, until in March 1917 sixty-six. In the twelve days from 20 October to 1 November 1916, thirty-three Norwegian ships were lost, nearly three a day. 'The struggle on the sea', said Johan Mowinckel, president of the Norwegian parliament, the *Storting*, 'is becoming more fierce, more desperate, day by day, week by week ... In the submarine, Germany has a weapon which she uses with pitiless harshness also against the neutral'.[142] Even then, the Norwegians were scarcely prepared for the assault which began in February 1917. Thirty-nine Norwegian ships were sunk with the loss of thirty-nine lives; in March sixty-six ships were sunk with the loss of 152 men, the highest figure of the war; next month sixty-one ships with ninety-five lives.[143] Not all submarine attacks on Norwegian ships resulted in the loss of lives. In many instances, the commanders of submarines provided for the safety or rescue of the crews. Of 829 ships sunk by submarines and mines, loss of 1,162 lives occurred on 189. This list does not include a large number of smaller, unregistered boats, and hundreds of men for whose disappearance there has been no accounting.[144]

By war end, Norway had lost half of her tonnage. 'In this grim game the punishment meted out to Norway by Germany was by far the more severe. Her toll of nearly 2,000 Norwegian lives lost established a record for brutality in the treatment of neutrals which is unique in history.'[145] A number of years after the close of the war, compensation negotiations were initiated between Norway and Germany.[146] Germany paid the Norwegian government 6,600,000 gold Reichsmarks to settle for the hardships of the surviving families of the Norwegian seamen killed on unarmed Norwegian ships sunk without warning by German submarines.

The seriousness of the situation was summed up by Ernest Fayle, the seaborne war's official British historian in the 1920s.[147]

The full menace of the unrestricted u-boat campaign could now be seen. It had raged for three months, and in those three months the world's tonnage had been reduced by over two million tons, of which nearly a million and a quarter were British ... compared with such losses, the acquisitions of shipping by new construction or transfer from foreign flags sank into insignificance. New ships of 1,600 gross tons or over, brought into service under the British flag, amounted for the three months to under 200,000 tons. About 60,000 tons had been obtained from other sources, but the net reduction in ocean-going tonnage, after allowing on the one hand for all gains and on the other for war and marine losses, was some 940,000 tons or about 5.66% of the total tonnage available on 1 February. In other words the wastage of ocean-going tonnage was at the rate of nearly 23% per annum. It was, however, the acceleration in the rate of loss during the second half of April which was the most alarming feature in the situation. While the ratio of war losses for the three months (without regard to replacements) was about 7%, or 23% per annum, the losses suffered during the fortnight 17–30 April inclusive were at the appalling rate of over 50% per annum on the available tonnage. On the basis of the same period, it was estimated that the risk to an individual steamer homeward bound from a port more distant than Gibraltar was about 2:11; to an outward-bound steamer, which could be more easily stayed or diverted about 1:14. Her chances of leaving the United Kingdom on such a voyage and returning safely were only about 1:4 ... it was evident that the continuance of losses, even at the average for three months which had elapsed since the opening of the unrestricted campaign, would soon bring the Germans within measurable distance of the decision on which they had staked so much.

Winston Churchill, as he often did, wrote his histories with hubris, partial hindsight, or an excision of inconvenient facts.[148] 'It is commonly said that the German drive to Paris and the unlimited u-boat warfare both "nearly succeeded" ... [For the u-boat warfare] there was never any chance of it. Whereas any one of a score of alternative accidents would have given the German Army Paris in 1914, the sea-faring resources of Great Britain were in fact and in the circumstances always superior to the u-boat attack.'[149]

May 1917 denoted the 'first ebb in the tide of destruction'. British losses, 106 vessels of 320,572 tons torpedoed and fourteen others of 28,114 tons mined, showed a reduction of 193,000 tons, and the world total dropped by a further 284,000 tons, 600,000 tons in total; in June the figure rose to 700,000 tons, and fell by July to 550,000 tons (when *UC 61* left the war). From this point on, monthly results levelled around the 350,000 mark. During the last half of 1917, British shipping was destroyed at the reduced rate of seventy hulls a month. 'In view of the tonnage famine, it was still a very serious rate of wastage.'[150] The undersea war also took its toll of the u-boats. Whereas only twenty boats were destroyed in the first half of 1917, forty-three went to the bottom in the second half of that year.[151]

However, the point was fast approaching when the calculations of the German Admiralty Staff would have had to demonstrate beyond doubt a drastic reduction in the enemy's lines of supply from overseas.[152] The naval staff in Berlin published each month a record of u-boat successes by tonnage. In fact, these numbers were 50 per cent higher than the British figures for the same period. 'Chalking up successes and failures in wartime should always be read with tongue firmly planted in cheek.'[153] This discrepancy increased with the war; by 1918 German figures for Allied tonnage sank was double the number admitted by the British. As far as the German public, the Government and the army was concerned, the navy was happily sinking Allied ships *en masse*. 'Little wonder then at Ludendorff's consternation in the summer of 1918 when he saw that France had become a virtual American military camp. About 200,000 American soldiers a month were being safely transported to Europe in spite of the u-boats.'

Berlin was confident that the people of Britain and France were being forced to make the same sacrifices as those enforced upon Germany by the maritime blockade and that the Entente Cordial would collapse before America became effective ... We u-boat men saw it as ominous that five months of unrestricted submarine warfare were already behind

*us and Berlin now thought that the end was near ... At the beginning of
the six months, officers at the Front believed that the period given was
sufficient. Only at the end of five months did it begin to dawn on us that,
despite the huge inroads into enemy tonnage, the first half-year would
not bring the desired conclusion to our affairs. Why not? We had the
sinking statistics. By how much did the Admiral Staff's declaration of
tonnage sunk exceed the true figure? We discussed this question endlessly
in the mess. We knew the name of more than 50% of all ships sunk by the
u-boat arm. Knowing the names, we knew the registered tonnage. The
error in the estimates lay in the remaining 40% or so, but on the whole
it was likely to be a diminishing error as u-boat commanders obtained
more practice in estimating ship size. If the expected victory had not
been achieved, the fault was not attributable to exaggerated estimates
of tonnage sunk. So where? U-boat commanders knew the answer by
what they observed. We sank ship after ship, a fantastic number, and
yet it always seemed to us that we were failing to make any impression
on the numbers of merchant vessels putting into enemy ports. Where
were they all coming from? Was enemy shipping being better organised
or had the Entente succeeded in chartering a much larger proportion
of the world capacity than was considered possible by German naval
planners? Probably both. It was therefore in the high summer of 1917
that some of us began to suspect that we were not only faced with the task
of destroying the merchant tonnage of the Entente nations, but that we
were pitted in a gigantic battle against practically all the tonnage of the
world. Actually, we were not as clear on the matter as I have expressed
it here, but certainly there was an awareness in the mind of the veteran
underwater seafarers who could compare what we found to be the case
today with how it had been previously. It was of course our duty to
maintain the level of buoyant optimism which had been characteristic of
unrestricted submarine warfare at its outset. In this we were assisted by
the continuing descriptions made by our foreign agents as to the degree
to which our sinkings were having their effect on the comforts of English
life. But what we saw we saw, and in discussions between intimates the
first doubts had begun to emerge about the possibility of victory. I must
emphasise that only in the most intimate circles did these conversations
take place, but they cast a long shadow.*[154]

Optimism was no longer the dominant mood in German circles by the
summer of 1917.[155] Hindenburg's staff were beginning to show concern.
The army's head now regretted that the Admiralty Staff had announced
a specific deadline of October for the submarine victory over Britain.
Bethmann was also becoming apprehensive over the deteriorating
course of the 'last card', afraid that Austria-Hungary would not last out
the year, and that the British would not yield. In June, Bauer became

one of the political casualties and 'ended his three-year battle to deploy the submarine forces fully and most effectively'.[156] The German High Command now understood that the unrestricted campaign was not going to bring Britain to her knees within six months. Rather than give up, the Naval Staff extended its time limit. In July, ninety-five new submarines were ordered for delivery beginning in the summer of 1918.[157] In the midst of the re-jigged planning, u-boat aces travelled around the German empire attending conferences with 'appropriate forecasts and pictures, dramatised their stories, emphasised the liveliness and good spirits of the crews, and showed how the submarine force could never be beaten'.[158]

Many of the u-boat veterans of 1914 were dead by the end of 1917 and most of the remainder were under training for the improved, larger u-boat fleet of 1918. However, this training was often rushed even though there were too many inexperienced newcomers. 'Many of the commanders of 1917–18, by their foolish or imprudent conduct, exhibited their inefficiency.'[159] During the last eighteen months of the war submarines under attack often 'surrendered after a feeble resistance'. The Germans lost 202 u-boats and 5,249 sailors during the war, twenty scuttled, and nineteen by accident, but still surrendered 172 vessels at the armistice and there were a further 149 in various stages of construction.[160] 'Germany was obviously still capable of prosecuting the u-boat campaign with great vigour.'[161] However, the unmanaged nature – 'without sense or purpose' – of u-boat ordering during the war 'despite the heated public and internal debates over unrestricted submarine warfare' is surprising.[162] Just twenty-nine craft were ordered in 1914, seventy-two in 1915, eighty-six in 1916, and sixty-seven in 1917. 'Not a single u-boat building contract was placed in the critical eight months between September 1915 and May 1916. None of the boats ordered in or after May 1916 were completed in time to see service.' Gayer explained that u-boat orders had been held back because of the constantly changing political requirements placed on their use 'prevented a definite decision as to the best type'.[163] Also Admiral von Capelle, now secretary of the navy, was convinced that 'too great a number of submarines existing at the close of the war would have a detrimental effect upon the further development of the fleet insofar as the naval budget was concerned'.

Submarine historian Richard Compton-Hall thought that the 'Great Underwater War was won by the German u-boats, very nearly'. The u-boat men were not to blame for Germany's eventual collapse.[164]

Hermann Bauer, writing at the start of World War II, said,

> *England's crime was the interruption of sea routes to starve people to win her wars, but being at the same time dependent on maritime traffic. The war with submarines remains as the only effective resistance against 'inhumane warfare' the cruelty of which 'exceeds all limits' and a protection against naval tyranny. The legacy of the German*

submarine crews of both world wars will be to end centuries of [British]
tyranny and restore to all mankind the free sea. [165]

Vice Admiral Wolfgang Wegener was an officer in the Imperial German
Navy who later wrote a series of influential works criticising the naval
strategy adopted by Germany in World War I and proposed an alternative
based on threatening the sea lanes of the United Kingdom with both
surface and submarine forces. [166] The *Wegener Thesis* is often regarded
as a significant contribution to German naval strategy in World War II.
Wegener found that as 'valuable as the submarine campaign may have
been, it gained only partial command of the sea'. [167] It was a mirror image
of the British Admiralty's failure. 'The submarine can destroy sea lanes
but cannot protect them. Submarines can dive under a blockade, but
cannot break it. Only a fleet operating from a strategic position can break
a blockade. What success might have crowned the submarine war had the
battle for the gateway [to the Atlantic] been conducted simultaneously?
'We starved in jail and almost succeeded in making our jailor starve with
us, without once reaching for the bread that all the while lay on the table.'

Writing in 1944, an unattributed German naval historian took the
opposite view from the 'u-boat school':

> *The unquestioned hopes placed on the decisive effects of the u-boat war*
> *were grounded in the Great War conception that we would have won*
> *if only we'd had enough u-boats and used them in an all-out effort*
> *without regard for political restrictions. The historical research of the*
> *past twenty years does not support this contention. Nevertheless, it was*
> *disseminated throughout the post-war navy, supported by an extensive*
> *naval literature, and could not be shaken by the doubts raised by the*
> *findings of the Naval Research and Historical Division. Doubtless this*
> *view dominated the thinking of leading naval figures at the beginning*
> *of the current war.* [168]

ENDNOTES

1   Chickering, 'Introduction: Total war and total history', *Great War and Urban Life*, p. 1.
2   *UC 61* KTB, Cuxhaven.
3   Original notes, *SHD*, Cherbourg, SSTe35.
4   Padfield, *Dönitz*, p. 78.
5   Hull, *Absolute Destruction*, pp. 296–98.
6   2/1917, quoted in Sims, *Victory at Sea*, pp. 13–14.
7   Herwig, *Luxury Fleet*, pp. 182, 221.
8   Libau, currently Liepecca in Latvia, took over as headquarters in the Baltic, from Kiel
    and Dantzig, after it was captured from the Russians in May 1915 (Gayer, *Die Deutschen
    U-Boote in ihrer Kriegführung*), p. 1.
9   Herwig, 'Dynamics', pp. 80–82.
10 Bauer, *Als* Führer der U-*Boote*, p. 457.
11 Bauer, *Als* Führer der U-*Boote*, p. 456.
12 *TNA*, ADM 137/3886. Chapter 10, 'Intelligence Gift'. Also, Tarrant, *U-boat Offensive*, p. 46.
13 The Germans placed Buoy 2501 at about 51° 21' N, 2° 6' E.
14 Chapter 6, 'War of the raven'.
15 Hull, *Absolute Destruction*, p. 297
16 Sims, *Victory at Sea*, p. 13.
17 Fürbringer, *Legendary*, pp. 67–68.
18 *Daily Telegraph*, 'Submarine Menace', 25/1/1917, p. 1.
19 *TNA*, ADM 137/3886.
20 Koerver, *German Submarine Warfare*, p. 201.
21 *BA-MA*, Freiburg, German Admiralty Staff order A 1119 O 1, 12/1/1917.
22 *Naval Staff Monographs*, p. 174.
23 Admiralty Staff order A 1580 O 1, 18/1/1917.
24 Admiralty Staff order A 1993 O 1, 26/1/1917.
25 Scheer, *High Sea Fleet*, pp. 265–66.
26 Kelly, *Tirpitz*, pp, 390–91.
27 Kelly, *Tirpitz*, p. 395.
28 Burchardt, *Friedenswirtschaft und Kriegsvorsorge*, pp. 242–44. Offer, *Agrarian Interpretation*,
    pp. 344–45.
29 Hollweg, *Unser Recht Auf Den U-Bootskrieg*, p. 223.
30 2/1917, quoted in Sims, *Victory at Sea*, p. 14.
31 Scheer, *High Sea Fleet*, pp. 273–74.
32 Guichard, *Blockade*, pp. 44–45.
33 Hezlet, *Submarine and Sea Power*, p. 45.
34 Peterson, *Propaganda*, pp. 110–11. Fürbringer, *Legendary*, p. 8. Offer, 'Bounded Rationality',
    p. 183.
35 Tarrant, *U-boat Offensive*, p. 15.
36 Gayer, *Submarine Warfare*, p. 15.
37 Bell, *Blockade*, p. 156.
38 Peterson, *Propaganda*, pp. 110–11.
39 Hashagen, *Commander*, p. 35.
40 Offer, *Agrarian Interpretation*, p. 355, quoting from Spindler, *Wie es zum Entschluss*,
    pp. 5–7.
41 Peterson, *Propaganda*, pp. 73–75.
42 Tarrant, *U-boat Offensive*, pp. 16–18.
43 Bauer, *Als* Führer der U-*Boote*, p. 446. Gayer, *Submarine Warfare*, pp. 26, 28.
44 Lowell, *Raiders*, pp. 79–80.
45 Peterson, *Propaganda*, pp. 111–12.
46 Peterson, *Propaganda*, p. 112.
47 Vincent, *Politics of Hunger*, p. 42.
48 Kelly, *Tirpitz*, p. 399.

49 Raico, 'Turning Point', *Great Wars and Great Leaders*, pp. 25–26. Peterson, *Propaganda*, p. 112.
50 *U 30*, commander, Kapitänleutnant Erich von Rosenberg-Grusczyski.
51 Tarrant, *U-boat Offensive*, p. 20.
52 Seligmann, *Navy Route*, 'Introduction', p. xxxiii.
53 Kelly, *Tirpitz*, p. 399. Gayer, *Submarine Warfare*, p. 9. Also, Simpson, *Lusitania*; Jasper, *Lusitania*.
54 Hull, *Scrap of Paper*, p. 259.
55 Hull, *Scrap of Paper*, p. 261.
56 Schreiner, *Iron Ration*, p. 292.
57 Koerver, *War of Numbers*, p. 119.
58 Lowell, *Raiders*, p. 113. Admiral Franz von Hipper, *Die Schweren Kreuzer der Admiral Hipper-Klasse*: 'under any circumstances'.
59 Hull, *Absolute Destruction*, p. 223.
60 Strachan, *First World War*, pp. 217–19.
61 Raico, 'Turning Point', *Great Wars and Great Leaders*, pp. 26–27.
62 Steffen, 'The Holtzendorff Memorandum', Appendix 2. Winton, *Convoy*, p. 8.
63 Bauer, *Als Führer der U-Boote*, p. 446.
64 Herwig, 'Dynamics', pp. 90–91.
65 Schröder, *U-Boote des Kaisers*, for a blow-by-blow account of the debate in German. Massie, *Castles*, p. 126.
66 Tarrant, *U-boat Offensive*, p. 28.
67 Tarrant, *U-boat Offensive*, p. 25. Hull, *Absolute Destruction*, p. 223.
68 Afflerbach, *Falkenhayn*, p. 392, discussion reported by Karl von Treutler, diplomat and confidant of the Kaiser, to Chancellor Bethmann, c. 14/4/1916.
69 Offer, *Agrarian Interpretation*, p. 358.
70 Porch, *French Army*, p. 191.
71 Halpern, *Naval History*, pp. 328–29.
72 Kelly, *Tirpitz*, p. 414.
73 Kitchen, *Silent Dictatorship*, pp. 111–124.
74 Winton, *Convoy*, pp. 36–37.
75 Koerver, War of Numbers, p. 171, claims eighty casualties.
76 Spindler, *Der Krieg zur See*, Band 3, pp. 119–20. Bell, *Blockade*, pp. 594–95.
77 Gayer, *Submarine Warfare*, pp. 11–12.
78 Vincent, *Politics of Hunger*, pp. 34–38.
79 Bowles, *Declaration of Paris*, p. 140.
80 Gayer, *Submarine Warfare*, pp. 21–22.
81 Koerver, *German Submarine Warfare*, p, 193.
82 Hashagen, *Commander*, p. 88.
83 Fischer, *War Aims*, pp. 287–93.
84 Peterson, *Propaganda*, p. 291.
85 Gayer, *Submarine Warfare*, p. 22.
86 Hashagen, *Commander*, p. 92.
87 Another Hashagen, Hinrich Hermann, deserves special mention as he was, perhaps, the only junior officer to be promoted to command his own u-boat, *U 22*. Hashagen showed 'conspicuous ability' in bringing a boat, *U 48*, the whole way home from the western exit of the Channel around Scotland to Wilhelmshaven, on the surface. His two senior officers had been killed and the submarine rendered unfit to dive as the result of a collision with the sinking British merchant ship *East Point* (Koerver, *German Submarine Warfare*), p. 213. uboat.net. On the way home, Hashagen sank by gunfire the 2,596-ton steel-hulled French sailing bark, *Guerveur*.
88 Hezlet, *Submarine and Sea Power*, p. 65.
89 Birnbaum, *Peace Moves*, pp. 201–2.
90 Hull, *Entourage*, p. 283.
91 Appendix 2. NARA T-1022, roll 847, KdA, folder U.M. 5/II, Copy of memorandum by Admiral von Holtzendorff to Field Marshal von Hindenburg, Berlin, 22/12/1916.

92   Parkinson, *Tormented Warrior*, p. 116.
93   Terraine, *Business in Great Waters*, p. 14.
94   Gayer, *Submarine Warfare*, p. 24.
95   Hollweg, *Betrachtungen zum Weltkriege*, p. 121.
96   Birnbaum, *Peace Moves*, pp. 287–88.
97   Fürbringer, *Legendary*, pp. 59–60.
98   Hashagen, *Commander*, p. 31.
99   Offer, 'Bounded Rationality', pp. 184–88.
100   See also Offer, *Agrarian Interpretation*, pp. 359–61 for an economic view of the rationale.
101   Herwig, *Luxury Fleet*, pp. 196–98.
102   'Die Schiffsraumfrage und die Versorgung im Jahre 1916' (The tonnage issue and the
      British supply situation in 1916), enclosure, memorandum by Admiral von Holtzendorff
      to Chancellor Bethmann, Berlin 27/8/1919 (*NARA*, Washington, T-1022, roll 847, KdA,
      UM 5/II).
103   Lutz, ed., *Documents of the German Revolution*, Vol. 2, pp. 262–66, 6/7/1917. Strachan,
      World War One, p. 266.
104   Ferguson, *Paper and Iron*, p. 138.
105   Ferguson, *Pity*, p. 284.
106   Birnbaum, *Peace Moves*, p. viii. Offer, 'Bounded Rationality', pp. 189–90.
107   Birnbaum, *Peace Moves*, pp. 277–78.
108   Herwig, *Luxury Fleet*, pp. 196–98.
109   Schröder, *U-boote des Kaisers*, p. 208.
110   Steffen, 'Holtzendorff Memorandum'. Birnbaum, *Peace Moves*, p. viii.
111   Notes of a conference between the Chancellor, Hindenburg and Ludendorff in Pless,
      9/1/1917 (Ludendorff, ed., *Urkunden der Obersten Heeresleitung über ihre Tätigkeit*), p. 323.
112   Hull, *Entourage*, p. 287.
113   Birnbaum, *Peace Moves*, p. ix.
114   Birnbaum, *Peace Moves*, p. 259. Offer, *Agrarian Interpretation*, p. 5.
115   Peterson, *Propaganda*, p. 109.
116   Fürbringer, *Legendary*, pp. 88–90.
117   Terraine, *Business in Great Waters*, pp. 15–16.
118   Gayer, *Submarine Warfare*, p. 26.
119   Kelly, *Tirpitz*, p. 407.
120   Chapter 13, 'Guilt and blame'.
121   Ferguson, *Pity*, pp. 282–83. Peterson, *Propaganda*, pp. 109, 305. Seymour, *American
      Neutrality*, p. 58. Hull, *Entourage*, p. 255.
122   Offer, 'Bounded Rationality', p. 193.
123   Offer, *Agrarian Interpretation*, p. 363.
124   Friedrich Nietzsche, *Beyond Good and Evil*, Chapter 4, 'Maxims and Interludes', 156.
125   Massie, *Castles*, p. 715.
126   Cooper, *Behind the Lines*, Letters 1914–1918.
127   Hankey, *Supreme Command*, Vol. 2, p. 640.
128   Ludendorff, *War Memories*, Vol. 2, p. 603.
129   Compton-Hall, *Submarines*, p. 264. Chapter 4, 'Erich's war'.
130   Lowell, *Raiders*, pp. 216–17.
131   Sims, *Victory at Sea*, p. 48. Massie, *Castles*, pp. 726–27.
132   Hashagen, *Commander*, p. 20.
133   Bauer, *Als Führer der U-Boote*, p. 447.
134   Bell, *Blockade*, pp. 614–15. Compton-Hall, *Submarines*, p. 263.
135   uboat.net.
136   O'Keefe, Theodore, 'Introduction', Degrelle, *Born at Versailles*, p. v.
137   Herwig, *Luxury Fleet*, pp. 196–98.
138   Vigness, *Neutrality*, pp. 16, 56.
139   Vigness, *Neutrality*, p. 101.
140   *Daily Chronicle*, 26/10/1916.
141   Vigness, *Neutrality*, pp. 90–96.

142 Vigness, *Neutrality*, p. 105.
143 Gibson, *Submarine War*, p. 204.
144 Vigness, *Neutrality*, p. 122, fn. 74, p. 123.
145 Vigness, *Neutrality*, p. 85.
146 Vigness, *Neutrality*, p. 170.
147 Fayle, *Seaborne Trade*, Vol. 3, pp. 92–93.
148 There are now many useful reviews of Churchill's standing. 'Churchill never had a principle that he did not in the end betray' (Raico, 'Turning Point', *Great Wars and Great Leaders*), p. 54. Ben-Mosche, *Churchill: Strategy and History*, pp. 329–33. Aigner, *Winston Churchill*. Ponting, *Churchill*.
149 Churchill, *World Crisis*, p. 736.
150 Gibson, *Submarine War*, pp. 183, 191.
151 Herwig, *Luxury Fleet*, p. 227.
152 Fürbringer, *Legendary*, pp. 88–90.
153 Koerver, *German Submarine Warfare*, p. xxxvi–xxxvii.
154 Fürbringer, *Legendary*, pp. 88–90.
155 Herwig, *Luxury Fleet*, p. 227.
156 Bauer, *Als Führer der U-Boote*, p. 463.
157 Massie, *Castles*, p. 738.
158 Laurens, *Le Blocus et la Guerre sous-marine*, p. 193.
159 Gibson & Prendergast, *German Submarine War*, p. 183.
160 Herwig, 'Total Rhetoric'. The positions of seventy-five u-boats have been discovered since the end of the war (uboat.net).
161 Tarrant, *U-boat Offensive*, p. 74.
162 Herwig, 'Total Rhetoric'.
163 Gayer, *Submarine Warfare*, p. 24.
164 Compton-Hall, *Submarines*, p. 300.
165 Bauer, *Als Führer der U-Boote*, pp. 464–69.
166 Chapter 1, 'Brave new world'.
167 Wegener, *Strategy*, pp. 62–63.
168 Mulligan, *Neither Sharks*, p. 41.

CHAPTER 6

The War of the Raven

We junior sub-lieutenants dreamed of flying and submarines, of destroyers and airships, as it seemed such hard lines to waste one's life as a watch keeper in a sword belt, on the quarter-deck of a moored ship of 23,000 tons, whilst one's comrades-in-arms and friends waged the war which drained the life blood of all young Germany.[1]

On Saturday, 1 August 1914, the German ambassador at St Petersburg delivered his country's declaration of war to Russia in its first formal act of 'defensive aggression'. The day before, Georg Gerth, an oberleutnant with less than one year's seniority, reported as watch officer to his latest ship, SMS *Amazone*. This was a ship in decline and surely not the prestige posting of Georg's dreams. *Amazone* was launched in 1900 in Kiel at a cost of just under five million German Reichsmarks, one of ten members of the *Gazelle* class, the first modern light cruisers for Tirpitz's Imperial Navy.[2] Her days in the overseas reconnaissance force of the High Seas Fleet with a full complement of thirteen other officers and 243 enlisted men, had just ended; *Amazone* was to start the war as a coastal defence ship; too worn out, too slow at a reducing twenty-one knots, too lightly armed with ten 10.5 cm guns and two torpedo tubes, and too thinly-armoured to withstand dreadnought weaponry with a deck less than an inch thick.[3] In another two years, even this limited coastal assignment was too onerous for *Amazone*; she was stripped of her guns and designated a u-boat training ship. The following year, in 1917, she no longer went to sea and sat out the war as a barracks for navy regiments.[4]

Gerth's previous ship, SMS *Württemberg*, another old lady, a twenty-three-year-old armoured frigate, was based in Kiel.[5] His new posting meant a move about 500 miles along the Baltic coast to Danzig, modern day Gdańsk in Poland. *Württemberg*, in use as a torpedo and test ship since 1906, was the last of the four Sachsen class boats, the others all taken out of active service in 1910 and used as target hulks for the fleet. Here, on the south-eastern shore of the Baltic Sea, Gerth had spent the last eight months honing and passing on his newly-gained torpedo skills to naval ratings and sea cadets. Altogether, Gerth was to spend over two-and-a-half years based in the Baltic, with four mostly uneventful months on the *Amazone*.

The Baltic, despite its surface area being equivalent to almost 75 per cent of the North Sea, is one of the lesser-known seas of Europe to those who do not live nearby. It connects to the North Sea through the Kattegat, controlled by Denmark, and the Belt Seas, with their dangerous rocks and narrow and shallow channels. Because there is little tidal flow into the Atlantic, Baltic water is brackish and, as a result, almost half of its surface can ice over in winter. Its major cities include Copenhagen, Stockholm, Helsinki and St Petersburg.

The significance of the Baltic area in 1914 was both military and commercial. It was a maritime and land front between Germany, which, since reunification in 1871, occupied much of the southern coast including modern-day Poland, Lithuania, Latvia and Estonia, and with Russia, which controlled Finland. There were many German ports, Danzig, Eckernförde, Kiel, Königsberg, Memel (modern day Klaipėda), Libau (from 7 May 1915, modern day Liepāja), Lübeck, Riga (from 3 September 1917) and Stettin, connected to Berlin by canal. All of these were of strategic significance for safe military shipbuilding, including the u-boat fleet, for relatively secure open water for naval training and for protected commerce. Being nearest to the exit allowed Germany to bottle up Russia's capital ships in the Gulf of Finland. In effect, Russia was blockaded in the Baltic by Germany forcing alternative supply routes either by railway through Sweden and Finland, or in ice-free months around the top of Norway to Archangel, or lengthy journeys from the Crimea if the Bosphorus could be passed, or from Russia's eastern seaboard on the Pacific Ocean. The Germans used their Baltic navy to bombard Russian-controlled cities, like Riga and Reval, modern day Tallinn, to support military advances. The Kaiser Wilhelm Canal, sixty-one miles long, from Kiel to Brunsbüttel was opened by the Emperor in 1895 and provided Germany with a direct route within its own territory from the Baltic to the North Sea. By 1914, the canal had been widened to take dreadnought battleships.[6] Neutral Sweden and, for different political reasons, Russian-occupied Finland, had significant pro-German elements in their populations.[7] The Baltic provided Germany with the easiest route to trade with Scandinavia. Through neutral Norway and Denmark, Germany received vital food and war supplies which often originated in Allied countries or the United States.[8] Pro-German Sweden underpinned the German war effort by, particularly, swopping iron ore from Lulea for coal. The main danger to these sea transfers came from Russian and British submarines.

It was in this Baltic maelstrom of politics and weather that Gerth and the *Amazone* were to guard the Baltic against Allied submarine attacks.

The British declined to send surface ships through the Skagerrak and the heavily-mined Kattegat and instead decided in October 1914 to send three submarines to operate alongside the Russians at their base at Lapvik.[9] Only two, *E 1* and *E 9*, made it; the third *E 11* found the defences of the Belt too alert and aborted. On 18 October, the first day of entering the Baltic, *E 1* fired two torpedoes at the armoured-deck cruiser, *Victoria Louise*, like *Amazone* reduced through age to coastal defence; both missed, one narrowly astern and the second ran down the side of the vessel after it was spotted and the vessel swung to starboard under full helm.[10] German coastal defences therefore knew immediately of the British submarine intrusion. News reached the Baltic Sea commander-in-chief, Grand Admiral Prince Heinrich of Prussia, the Kaiser's younger brother, later that morning. Increased patrols were ordered. On 20 October, *E 1* entered Danzig Bay and its captain saw through his periscope three cruisers lying in the inner basin. They were Gerth's ship, the *Amazone*, and the *Lübeck* and *Augsburg*. All three had recently returned from a raid towards the Gulf of Finland in company with *U 26*, commander Kapitänleutnant Egewolf Freiherr von Berckheim, who successfully torpedoed the Russian cruiser *Pallada*.[11] All 597 men on the *Pallada* died.[12] *E 1* was unable to attack *Amazone* and her two sister ships and turned for the Russian base at Libau. *Lübeck* and *Augsburg* were two more ageing light cruisers, both survived the war and were handed over in 1920 as part of the Versailles peace treaty, *Lübeck* to the British and *Augsburg* to the Japanese.[13]

In 1916, in a covert interview in Copenhagen, ambassador Sir Henry Lowther at the British Legation reported his informant explaining that 'nothing would hasten the end of the war more quickly' than the sinking of ships trading between Sweden and Germany in the Baltic.[14] 'A bold game in these waters during the next two months is the one thing dreaded by both Germany and Sweden.' When the German naval attaché visited a few weeks before, he 'showed great uneasiness' because he had to deal with eleven English and Russian submarines.

Early in December, Gerth was transferred from *Amazone* to a shore position as third Admiral staff officer in the Baltic Sea's Coastal Defence Cruiser Division, the *Küstenschultz-Division der Ostsee*, where he stayed until October 1915.[15] Nothing is known of his duties. The division was commanded at that time by Vizeadmiral Robert Mischke who reported to Prince Heinrich. The Prince's main family residence was at Kiel Castle, burned to the ground during World War II, from where the Prince conducted his command's business with his admiral's flag flying from one of the towers.

It may be here that one of the few comments ever made by Georg Gerth to his family about his time in the Imperial Navy has its roots. His work as a flag officer might well have taken him into respectful contact with Prince Heinrich. Gerth's family, in the 1960s, were expressing surprise when they learned that the Kaiser had a wizened arm. Gerth, sitting in the corner with a book and his customary glass of red wine, rarely spoke, but at the mention of the Kaiser's arm he said, 'I knew that. I played tennis with him once while he was on an inspection tour'.[16] Tirpitz, meeting the prince aboard *Blitz* in 1872, commented that William's 'crippled arm is somewhat noticeable, especially because of his various manoeuvres to try to make the bodily characteristic not noticeable'.[17]

[The Kaiser's] *breech delivery by forceps required over ten hours and resulted in nerve damage that irretrievably affected his left arm.*[18] *A breach baby, he had been pulled from the womb with such force that his left arm was wrenched from his socket, severing some ligaments ... Doctors wrapped his arm in the carcases of freshly slaughtered rabbits, administered electric shock treatments, and made him wear a kind of straightjacket designed to prevent him turning his head to the left.*[19]

A further four British E-class submarines were sent out in August 1915: *E 8*, *E 18* and *E 19* got through to the Baltic while *E 13* ran aground in Danish waters between Malmö and Copenhagen. *E 13* was scuttled after two German torpedo boats under direct orders from Vizeadmiral Mischke, Gerth's superior, opened fire on her with torpedoes, machine-guns and shell fire from a range of 300 yards. Firing continued after the men abandoned ship and took to the shallow water. The engagement ended when the Danish torpedo boat *Søulven* placed herself between the submarine and the two German ships. Fifteen *E 13* crew members were killed.[20]

Such a monstrous outrage on international law and neutral rights is in keeping with the methods Germany has consistently pursued. She has transformed war into wholesale murder, regardless of the dictates of humanity and of the restrictions imposed by civilisation. The unjustifiable slaughter of the men of E 13 is one more notch on the long score we have to settle with the homicidal brood of Prussia.[21]

Four older British C-class submarines were then stripped down and towed to Archangel in the summer of 1915 from where they were barged by canal and river to St Petersburg, reassembled and, in the spring of 1916, joined the flotilla. There were now two attempted blockades in place, that of the Germans on the Russian fleet, and that of the British and Russian submarine flotillas on the Swedish iron ore trade. A great deal of merchant shipping was sunk including, in one day, 22,000 tons by *E 19*. The Germans were quickly forced to employ a convoy system, a regime rejected in the Atlantic by the British Admiralty for several years at great cost in merchant shipping to Great Britain and the Allies.[22]

In July 1915, the Germans began a land offensive which included an amphibious operation on the Baltic flank. To support the landing, they brought in battle cruisers from the High Seas Fleet.[23] This must have been a major preoccupation for the Baltic naval staff while Gerth was in post at the Coastal Defence Division. The armoured cruiser *Prinz Adalbert* was seriously damaged by an *E 9* torpedo, *E 19* sank the light cruiser *Udine* and, the next month, August 1915, *E 1* torpedoed and damaged *Moltke,* one of four battle cruisers travelling in line abreast with a close escort of destroyers.[24] *Moltke* was able to continue under her own power, but the attack so disconcerted flotilla commander Admiral Franz von Hipper that he signalled a return to harbour. The action, much lauded by the Russians, 'in no small part contributed to the cancellation of the German landings at Riga'.[25] The repaired *Prinz Adalbert* was torpedoed and sunk by *E 8* in October. Gerth's ship, *Amazone*, had two near misses by torpedo, the first failure was off Cape Arkona in May when *E 1* missed from a thousand yards, the second was at the Battle of the Gulf of Riga when *E 18* was unsuccessful.

Somewhere in the middle of all this British submarine activity, Gerth made the decision for a serious career change. He applied to become a u-boat captain and was accepted to undergo training. It is likely that, with the u-boat school based in the Baltic, Gerth mixed with other potential officer applicants. The stream of requests for volunteers would have crossed his desk and the opportunity regularly discussed in the officers' mess where he may also have met von Berckheim, the Baltic u-boat ace, and his fellow commanders. It was apparently the 'most experienced and venturesome executive officers and non-commissioned officers' who volunteered for submarine service to overcome the boredom of fleet life.[26] In contrast to Britain's Navy, where officers specialised in torpedoes, gunnery, navigation or signalling, their German counterparts received intensive training in all these fields, but did not commit to a particular branch. This facilitated, say, the ability to move a gunnery officer from a cruiser to command a u-boat.[27] Perhaps also it was the lure of command at a junior rank; dissatisfaction, even, with an outlook of more big ship life; but, certainly, a desire in Georg to swap his shore job for another involving action and an ability to hit back. The discontent of executive officers was reflected by the popular slogan scrawled up on the walls on Wilhelmshaven, *'Lieb' Vaterland, magst ruhig sein, die Flotte schläft im Hafen ein*, 'Dear Fatherland, Rest assured. The fleet lies in harbour – moored'.[28]

Historian Bouton takes a different view about the crews that manned the u-boats. No continuous extensive use of submarines had been made up to the middle of the winter of 1915, but by March 1916 many u-boats were being sent out. At first, they were manned by volunteers, and there had been a surplus of volunteers, for the men of the submarine crews received special food, more pay, liberal furloughs and the Iron Cross after the third trip.[29] 'Within a year, however, conditions changed decidedly.' The men of the fleet reckoned that a submarine rarely survived its tenth trip. The view of Seaman Richard Stumpf aboard the battleship *Helgoland* was that the 'best and most intelligent of our officers have been transferred to cruisers, torpedo boats and submarines ... With a few exceptions those who have remained behind don't have much on the ball'.[30] By 1918, official 'qualification reports' declared submarine lieutenants as 'proven, enthusiastic, and energetic officers of whom we can be proud' while the reports on lieutenants in the fleet were 'very unfavourable'.

> *The Admiralty naturally published no accounts of boats that failed to come back, and this added a new terror to this branch of the service. Volunteers were no longer to be had. The result was that drafts were resorted to, at first from men of the High Seas fleet, and later from the land forces. Such a draft came to be considered as equivalent to a death sentence.* [31]

The submarine offensive 'greatly strained the internal cohesion of the naval officer corps'. The two arms of the navy grew apart: battleships and cruisers fretted in harbour to the frustration of their battle-hungry junior officers.[32] With the German fleet bottled up in Wilhelmshaven and Kiel, the answer was *Kleinkrieg*, 'small operations to erode the Royal Navy's superiority through the use of mines, coastal batteries and submarines'.[33] When the British had 'lost a few battleships, the strengths of the two sides would be more equal and the High Seas Fleet would be able to risk a [Tirpitzian] battle'. Small ship commands meant prospects were only available to younger people and not in sufficient numbers to 'persons in higher stations in life'.[34] Many of the best junior officers transferred to the u-boats, often replaced on the capital ships by cadets or reservists. For returning u-boat skippers, mostly lowly lieutenants and junior captains, the fleet's problems were a world away: dog-tired after two or three weeks at sea cramped in a noisy, smelly, uncomfortable and tense tin their immediate needs were a lengthy wash, fitful sleep and relentless alcohol.[35] The pressure never lifted; their boat had to be repaired, re-provisioned, and got back to sea.

Gerth's u-boat training lasted for nine months from October 1915.[36] It was sometime in this period that he gathered the nickname *Die Rabe*, 'The Raven', which was used openly by officers and crew and stuck with him for the rest of his naval career and was even recorded by the British Admiralty.[37] Gerth arrived in Bruges in June 1916 to take command of *UB 12*. Commanders were cloistered from the general run of military strategy, seldom mixed with the traditional officers of the Grand Fleet, and serviced their boats in remote parts of Bruges and Ostend.

> *Since the u-boats operating from the Flanders base slipped in and out on short forays, an especial kind of under-sea craft was developed.*

This craft was dubbed the ub-boat. These ub-boats were small and stumpy and had a far shorter radius of action than the u-boat. Some were so tiny that they were nicknamed sewing machines. Their crews numbered only about twenty, and even then were frightfully crowded in the narrow space.[38]

UB 12 was 'a Type 1' submarine, the smallest of Germany's u-boats, which, while variously useful, were not going to win the war for Germany. Designed in most part before the start of war and built until 1915 at the Germania and Weser yards in Hamburg and Bremen, they cost about 700,000 Reichsmarks.[39] *UB 12* left Bremen in sections carried by railway for final assembly at the Imperial Dockyard at Hoboken, Antwerp. Between Antwerp and its Flanders base there was a careful practice of 'breaking-in' when deficiencies in material and construction were discovered. 'The responsible flotilla commander worked continually to stop leaks so as to remove treacherous oil and petroleum tracks.'[40]

Less than twenty-eight metres overall and weighing 141 tons submerged, *UB 12* had a single diesel engine driving a three-bladed propeller, supported for submerged running by two sixty-one cell batteries. Accounted poor sea-boats with limited manoeuvrability, Type 1 ub-boats could travel a maximum of 1,650 nautical miles at a leisurely five knots on the surface, perhaps forty-five miles at four knots underwater before recharging, and were, therefore, constrained to the North Sea. Only a few hardy commanders ventured as far south as Dover. Their single skin hulls were increasingly vulnerable to improving Allied mines, depth charges and bombs.

UB-1 boats received much criticism as being too slow, too small and not powerful enough with their single propulsion. On the surface, they could not catch up with fleeing merchantmen and they did not have enough endurance to remain submerged for long periods. After an hour under water the batteries usually ended up depleted ... Heavy swell and stormy circumstances made it impossible to keep at periscope depth. The constant vibrations, pitching and rolling made the compass deviate and put delicate instruments out of action.[41]

Fighting power was limited, 'almost laughable – feeble instruments of war', consisting of two 45 cm torpedo tubes below the waterline at the bow and only one torpedo for each.[42] If a ub-boat on the surface tried to stop a ship, it had only personal weapons and one Maxim machine gun with 1,600 rounds to enforce its will. To prevent seawater damage, the machine gun had to be hauled up with every surfacing and fixed to the conning tower on a detachable pedestal.[43] The gun was little use against aircraft because it could not be angled high enough. If there was any aggressive response from a target ship, *UB 12* carried no deck gun and had to beat a hasty retreat. It took thirty-three seconds to dive from a standing start, twenty seconds if trimmed ready and underway, and the normal depth limit was fifty metres.

> *The longitudinal stability of these ub-boats was delicate; when diving at more than four to six degrees inclination the deck area tended to act as a sheer plane forcing the boats to a deeper angle and unless vigorous action was taken they eventually stood on their heads.* [44]

When a torpedo was fired, compensation tanks, we were designed to flood and therefore compensate for the sudden loss of the 770-kilogram weight. With too little water, the bow shot to the surface; with too much water, the u-boat would almost immediately sink to the bottom. One commander, Oberleutnant Otto von Heimburg, *UB 14* and *UB 15*, was one of the first to disparage the early 'sewing machine' motion of his u-boat after an 'iron tadpole' had been fired. [45]

> *I was knocked sprawling as the boat made a wild leap. It took me bewildered moments to figure what had happened. I had never fired a torpedo from a sewing machine before, and had not anticipated what would happen. The boat was so small that when relieved of the weight of the torpedo at the bow she popped up like a jack-in-the-box. 'To the bow,' I yelled, 'to the bow'. And every man who could leave his station scrambled to the bow, the combined weight bringing it down level.* [46]

UB 12 had nine commanders over its life of three-and-a-half years and accounted for only twenty-four enemy and neutral vessels which carried contraband. Thirteen of these were small fishing boats of the Lowestoft fleet, most much less than half the size of *UB 12*, which were all threatened by machine gun, stopped, boarded, and scuttled with explosives. After the end of Gerth's captaincy in November 1916, *UB 12* was the first of its class to be rebuilt at the bow end when the torpedo tubes were removed and the forward of its four watertight compartments was adapted to take four external mine chutes, each containing two mines. [47] As a consequence, *UB 12*'s last eight victims were all indiscriminate minings.

> *'Mystery' Q-ships went on bravely tackling the enemy. The Lowestoft armed smacks, for instance, during 1916 had some pretty stiff tussles, and we know now that they thoroughly infuriated the Germans, who threatened to have their revenge. Looked at from the enemy's aspect, it certainly was annoying to see a number of sailing smacks spread off the coast, each obviously trawling, but not to know which of them in a moment could cut her gear and sink the submarine with a gun. It was just that element of suspense which made a cautious German officer*

very chary of going near these craft, whereas he might have sunk the
whole fishing fleet if he dared.[48]

Primary evidence on individual u-boat activity comes from flotilla records
held at the military archives in Freiburg; from Gerth's own daily war diary
– Kriegstagebuch – handwritten in old German and, for this book, acquired
from the u-boat museum at Cuxhaven; and admiralty records held mostly
at Kew near London, particularly reports of sightings, actions and sinkings
which include official interviews with the captains of lost ships.[49] An
excellent and quick overview of a u-boat's and a commander's activities
can be found at the voluntary website *uboat.net*.

Georg Gerth was in charge of *UB 12* for just over four months of routine,
short-range voyages and little obvious success. Gerth took over the u-boat
from Oberleutnant zur See Wilhelm Kiel on 26 June 1916 while it was
undergoing repairs and maintenance in the Bruges shipyard. Kiel's
most recent victim, a 4,777-ton British steamer in ballast from Hull for
Philadelphia, was *UB 12*'s single torpedo success.[50] Gerth was now the sole
officer commanding a thirteen-man crew.

Events moved even more quickly than I anticipated. Before we had fully
mastered the rudiments of the innumerable novelties and intricacies of
a submarine and with heads still buzzing from things as yet unknown
to us, eg automatic vents, crash dives, blowers and trimming pumps,
ballast and diving tanks were at sea.[51]

In many respects, *UB 12* was a lucky boat, making ninety-eight patrols.
Gerth's flotilla leader, Karl Bartenbach, used his ub-boats for training his
new leaders. Within a few months, usually only three or four, the slightly
experienced and briefly blooded commanders were transferred as quickly
as possible to the new more powerful and more dangerous uc-boats
coming off the production lines in 1917 and 1918. Of these new uc-boats
for *UB 12* commanders, Kiel's *UC 18* was sunk by gunfire from a stricken
British Q-ship *Lady Olive* off St Malo; two were rammed; depth charges and
mines claimed two more.[52] Only three of *UB 12*'s nine captains survived
the war. *UB 12*'s last commander Oberleutnant Ernst Schöller was lost with
all hands without trace, probably mined, in August 1918 in the North Sea,
one the few unfound u-boat wrecks of the Great War.[53]

Gerth was out in UB 12, his new command, the day after the hand over
so it can be assumed he took on most if not all of the existing crew. Smaller
German submarines were usually stationed as 'outposts' at the entrances to
the German Bight, as it was believed, especially after the Battle of Jutland,
that England would 'endeavour to recover lost prestige by attempting
an advance. But this did not occur.'[54] German submarine officers bridled
under their restricted role as 'mobile sentry boxes'.[55] So, Gerth was to

take up standard three-day sentry duty – the 'outpost' – off the Flanders coast and to have care of big torpedo boats and larger submarines as they sailed into and back from the North Sea. Radio messages would be sent from 1100 to 1110 and from 1200 to 1210. He was to take carrier pigeons for emergency messages back to Bruges. It was a training exercise.

> *The coast was in a constant state of alert for surprise landings by the British. Belgian Flanders was protected by countless artillery emplacements, but it was still considered a worthwhile precaution always to have a couple of small u-boats on station just off the coast. This sentry duty was much deprecated as there was rarely, if ever, any contact with the enemy, yet we were obliged to remain in the state of the highest alertness at all times ... Our Flotilla Chief began to edge us farther and farther offshore until finally his bagful of u-boats went across the North Sea to the enemy: finally, we were operating off the English coast itself. Now at last we felt we were real u-boatmen: now we could get busy in the murderous manner we had dreamed of all these weeks and months![56]*

Throughout the 131 days of his *UB 12* career, Gerth seized chances in slack times while on patrol or on sentinel duty to practise his diving, navigation and torpedo attack procedures. He was trained to keep his records simple and direct with no emotional language. The records include the hand-annotated charts of his voyages with a key: one line with arrow – journey above water, two lines with arrow – journey under water, dotted line with arrow – drifted above water, circle with a cross in middle – sea bed.

When the expected attack by the British fleet did not materialise, the Flanders Flotilla was allowed a more offensive role. There is no doubt that *UB 12* and its crew was driven hard. If the boat was available, it went to sea. The names and locations of the North Sea shoals, Bligh, Terschelling, Schaar, Schouwen, Spon, Thornton and Rabe Banks, with additional light vessels at Maas and North Hinder, and the many friendly buoys, all became daily companions. Gerth made fifteen voyages down the Bruges Canal to Zeebrugge with *UB 12*. He was in command for 3,107 hours and, of that, spent 1,384 hours at sea, 45 per cent of his available time. Perhaps, most importantly, an almost equivalent time, 41 per cent was spent in maintenance or repairs; several times the boat was forced to return early. Gerth had regular problems with injection valves, and, also on the engine, the fuel pump and valve, the oil pump, noisy cylinders and the manometer, which measured gas pressure. A new radio aerial had to be fitted, the hydroplane became restricted, and the main hatch would not open necessitating a crewman squeezing out through the torpedo-loading hatch. The few free hours were spent waiting in Bruges for loadings or sitting out bad weather.

UB 12 saw limited fighting, but lived with daily Allied anti-submarine patrol vessels and destroyers in a seemingly crowded sea. Gerth was in his first action on his second day when he was fired at by destroyers. Once, Gerth took on a British destroyer with a torpedo shot which missed; an eventuality he blamed on his torpedo crewman. On another occasion, four destroyers with a small cruiser at their centre headed zigzagging 'at great speed' towards the partly-submerged u-boat. The cruiser passed fifty metres away without seeing the periscope. In all, Gerth was forced to dive twenty-six times and was under attack twice by a depth charge, once from aircraft machine guns, and once from the hidden cannon of a Q-ship, which had been disguised as a fishing vessel, and left him with five big holes in his decking. *UB 12* was taken to the seabed nine times to sit out persistent searches which included being swept by wire and hydrophones.

> *All ears are laid against the boat's sides to pick up any sound. Everything remains quiet. We repeat the procedure at fifty feet and still hear nothing.*[57]

Gerth took two small food steamers after threatening them with his machine gun. One was sunk and the other seized as a prize; one fishing smack was also sunk by explosives. *Rilda* was a British steamer, built by R. Smith of Preston in 1883, and operated by E. Ellingsen of Christiana. She carried 'general cargo', but Gerth claimed it was food. His men rowed to the boat, set explosive charges and handed her crew over to a passing Dutch steamer. There were no casualties. A prize court confirmed the sinking of the ship and the greater part of the cargo as unlawful. However, part of the cargo was replaced.[58] *Niobe* was travelling from Amsterdam when Gerth captured her, took her captain aboard as a hostage, and ushered the ship to Zeebrugge where she was retained with part of her cargo. This was the second time *Niobe* had been taken as a prize. The first was by *U 36*, Kapitänleutnant Ernst Graeff, on 10 May 1915. The owners, NV Koninkl of Amsterdam, appealed to a German Prize Court sitting in Hamburg on 10 July that year which ruled there was no case because the vessel was 'merely brought into Cuxhaven for examination and was then released forthwith'. Vizeadmiral Spindler described the seizure as a 'remarkable achievement' as Gerth had to rely on machine guns and carbines to stop the ship.[59] Gerth's last success was *Margorie*, a 55-ton British fishing vessel owned by C. H. Crews of Lowestoft, which was stopped and sunk with explosives. The wreck has never been found although it is estimated to be one mile east of Smiths Knoll.[60] Nobody was hurt aboard *UB 12* during Gerth's tenure, nor were there any casualties from his actions.

Apart from a lack of any great success against enemy ships, Gerth was closely involved in two of the main naval events of 1916, and one minor action. The two major events were of different characters and neither brought any credit to Germany's naval forces.

In the first, *UB 12*, with fellow ub-boats from Flanders, spent an abortive couple of days in August as a part of a second elaborate attempt by Admiral Reinhard Scheer to entice the British Grand Fleet into a u-boat trap.[61] A first attempt earlier in the year ended in a 'complete and disappointing failure'. However, it did lead inadvertently, but directly, to the Battle of Jutland.

A few months after that battle, Scheer laid his second trap. He took elements of the High Seas fleet across the North Sea during the night of 18 August 1916 to bombard supposedly military targets around the town of Sunderland the next morning. The British Grand Fleet would then sail to seek combat, but would be forced to approach the town through a broad channel between the coast and the inner edge of three minefields. These large well-charted minefields had been laid by the Germans earlier in the war off the Tyne, Humber and western part of the Dogger Bank. Five 'U-lines', u-boats holding linear formations, with a total of twenty-four u-boats were to be ready and waiting for the Grand Fleet. Two of these lines comprised nine Flanders ub-boats. Separate from the anticipated main action, their task was to guard the southern flank of the High Seas Fleet's advance and to attack light British naval forces from Harwich if they became involved. Gerth and *UB 12* were at the end of U-line II, twelve miles off Texel, the largest and most populous island in the Dutch Frisians.

The operation was mostly a tactical failure. The British intercepted signals announcing the High Seas Fleet's departure and put to sea at 1600 on the 18th, before the Germans had actually sailed. Scheer was 'dissuaded from bombarding Sunderland by a false report made by a scouting Zeppelin which mistook the light craft of the Harwich force for a detached squadron of enemy battleships'. He turned away from Sunderland to chase the 'phantom' battleships. That afternoon, with the Grand Fleet closing from the north and the south barred by the Humber minefield, Scheer headed home.

> *The German navy's reliance upon dirigibles left the fleet constantly at the mercy of fog, wind, sleet and snow, with regard to reconnaissance. Shore command never appreciated that the British not only routinely intercepted their signals to the fleet, but that they expeditiously deciphered them in Room 40 at the Admiralty, with the result that the Grand Fleet was often out to sea before the High Sea Fleet had hoisted anchors.*[62]

German successes came early the next day, the 19th, when u-boats in the first line of attack were on their way to their ambush positions. Two light cruisers in the screen covering the British battleships as they moved south were sunk. At 0445, *U 66*, commander Kapitänleutnant Thorwald von Bothmer, hit the 5,250-ton *Falmouth* with two torpedoes. 'Despite being repeatedly attacked by escorting destroyers and an armed trawler' and suffering depth charge attacks and partial flooding, Bothmer dogged *Falmouth*, firing further torpedoes which missed. At noon, when *Falmouth* which was crawling along under tow, *U 66*, Kapitänleutnant Otto Schultze, fired two torpedoes which finished the ship, killing eleven crew. Schultze survived the war and was appointed Konteradmiral in 1931. Just before six that same morning, *U 52*, Oberleutnant Hans Walther, fired two successful torpedoes at the modern 5,400-ton *Nottingham* and, half an hour later, a third, which sank her. Thirty-eight men died. Walther died the following year with all hands when *UB 75* was mined off Scarborough.

UB 12 took no direct part in the action, saw nothing of consequence, and, after suffering engine problems, went home to Bruges.

However, strategically, the Scarborough operation was much more successful although Scheer did not realise it at the time. Admiral Jellicoe understood that the whole point of the German operation was a submarine trap. For fear of the u-boats and with two cruisers lost, he saw 'great peril' that could not be risked again.

> *Mines had already made it too dangerous for the Grand Fleet to enter the area south of Horns Reef and east of 5°E. Admiral Jellicoe now reckoned that he ought not to go south of 55° 30'N or east of 4°E at any time and 'only west of the same longitude if a really good chance of action with the High Seas Fleet presented itself. Furthermore, he did not believe that he should go south of the Dogger Bank at all unless all classes of ship, including light cruisers, had destroyer screens. As he knew he had not enough destroyers for the purpose, it was tantamount to saying that the Grand Fleet would in future have to stay north of the Dogger Bank.*[63]

In the minor naval action, Gerth formed another U-line with three Flanders ub-boats around 18 October and was told that German and enemy naval forces were to be anticipated. German Navy Zeppelins participated in a High Seas Fleet sortie, escorted by torpedo boats, but German and British ships failed to make contact. Admiral Scheer barely mentions this expedition other than stating that he left the most vulnerable part of his fleet in reserve and that he remembered that his torpedo boats could not go as far as planned due to adverse weather conditions.[64] Five Zeppelins suffered serious mechanical breakdowns during the operation.

Mention of Zeppelin raids provides an opportunity to recognise the variety of naval occupations taken by Gerth's colleagues among the sea cadets in the 'Crew of 1907'. Among his forty-eight fellow cadets aboard SMS *Freya* in the arduous first ten months of training was Kapitänleutnant Kurt Frankenberg, later commander of the Zeppelin *L 21*. Frankenberg had already flown his airship three times to England in 1916. In November, ten Zeppelins took off on a bombing mission from Nordholz, the Imperial Navy's principal airship base near Cuxhaven.[65] Little damage was done at various haphazard targets as the Zeppelins turned for home or were shot down. Only *L 21* remained. She was rebuffed by guns or baffled by blackouts at Barmston, Leeds, Barnsley and Macclesfield, but dropped bombs on Sharton and Dodworth and a series of impromptu targets in the Potteries. *L 21* was tracked to Yarmouth and had lucky escapes from pursuing British aircraft and anti-aircraft guns. Then, Frankenburg was found by three Royal Navy Air Service pilots flying BE 2C aircraft. The first was Flight-Lieutenant Egbert Cadbury, heir to the chocolate empire, who emptied four Lewis drum canisters into the gasbag with no immediate effect. The second plane's gun jammed in the cold air. The third pilot, Flight Sub-Lieutenant Edward Pulling fired only two shots before his gun also jammed. As he pulled away, *L 21* burst into flames and, said Pulling, 'within a few seconds became a fiery furnace'. The crew of the airship kept firing until *L 21* fell into the sea about eight miles east of Lowestoft. There were no survivors. Pulling received the Distinguished Service Order; Cadbury and his colleague, Flight Sub-Lieutenant Gerard Fane, the Distinguished Service Cross.

The second main naval event of 1916 involving Georg Gerth was the infamous 'Captain Fryatt' affair which, in the eyes of the British, summed up everything that was rotten about Prussian Germany and the u-boats in particular. The saga had its roots in the genuine German horror and disgust, borne of the Franco-Prussian war in 1870–71, of the *franc tireur*, the 'free shooter' or civilian gunman.[66] This aversion was extended somewhat tenuously by the Germans to the negation of the rights of merchant and passengers ships to resist u-boat sinkings. The treachery of the *franc-tireurs* became a German 'obsession'.[67]

In 1913, Winston Churchill, then First Lord of the Admiralty, stirred the pot when he proposed that in wartime British merchant ships should be armed in self-defence. He saw no paradox in claiming that if the guns and gunners were provided by the Royal Navy, then the ships could retain their civilian status.[68] The Germans strongly disagreed, but were isolated and reluctantly gave way on the principle of self-defence at a conference held that year in Oxford by the Institute of International Law.[69] Early in the war, Churchill's rhetoric raised the temperature again. Many remarks have been attributed to him, several unsatisfactorily sourced, and, if true, probably off-the-cuff.[70] They included orders to 'immediately engage the enemy, either with armament if they possess it, or by ramming if they do not', that British vessels should treat the crews of captured u-boats as 'felons' and not to accord them the status of prisoners of war.[71] 'Survivors should be taken prisoner or shot whichever was the 'most convenient'. White flags were to be fired on 'with promptitude'. Any master who surrendered his ship 'will be prosecuted'. The Germans reportedly became aware of Churchill's orders when *U 21*, Oberleutnant Otto Hersing, stopped and sank the British freighter *Ben Cruachan* early in 1915 and found a copy aboard.[72]

More diplomatically, the Admiralty certainly issued a secret order on 10 February 1915, repeated in June 1916, which said that no British merchant vessel 'should ever tamely surrender to a submarine, but should do her utmost to escape', including steering away at full speed if a u-boat was seen on the surface.[73] If the u-boat appeared suddenly close ahead, the merchant ship was to 'steer straight for her at your utmost speed' and the submarine 'will probably then dive'.

This order soon became known as the 'ramming order', but the Admiralty had been careful to avoid the use of the word 'ram' in the order because of its connotations of attack rather than defence.[74]

One of the merchant shipmasters to receive the Admiralty order was Captain Charles Fryatt of the Great Central Railway Company. In March, as captain of the unarmed steamer *Wrexham*, on the Tilbury to Hook of Holland route, Fryatt turned away from a surfaced u-boat, *U 12*, ordered full speed and, over forty miles, outpaced it. The deckhands assisted the stokers to make sixteen knots; *Wrexham* arrived at Rotterdam with scorched funnels. Fryatt's employers gave him a gold watch in gratitude. Later that month, off the Maas Lightship, bound for Rotterdam, Fryatt in the *Brussels* of the Great Eastern Railway Company, attempted to ram *U 33*, after its commander Kapitänleutnant Konrad Gansser had ordered him to stop. The u-boat crash dived and only narrowly avoided being hit. By the time Gansser surfaced, *Brussels* was gone.[75] This time, Fryatt's gold watch came from the British Admiralty. In June, *Brussels* twice escaped u-boat attacks and, in July, was missed by a torpedo. *Brussels* was not allowed to mount a gun because she would be forbidden the use of Dutch ports had she done so.[76]

Here the accounts differ. One report notes that Fryatt's 'charmed life and its publicity in Holland angered the Germans and a naval operation was mounted to catch him'.[77] On 22 June, five days before Gerth's first patrol in *UB 12*, Fryatt left Rotterdam for Tilbury, calling at the Hook of Holland. There were sinister tales of lights showing from the coast, a flare, a passenger on deck signalling to shore.[78] The next day, *Brussels* was captured by five German torpedo boats from the Flanders Flotilla and taken into Zeebrugge, later to Bruges, and Fryatt and his crew were sent to a civilian internment camp at Ruhleben near Berlin.[79] British Foreign Office papers state that Fryatt was only forty-eight hours in Ruhleben after which he was taken back alone to Bruges.[80] During his time at Ruhleben, Fryatt was quartered in Barrack No. 1 under a man called Turnbull, 'a notoriously pro-German civilian', who claimed Fryatt had boasted to him of his u-boat exploits. Turnbull was given a six-week holiday by his German captors and was then freed. U-boat historian Termote has a different story. *Brussels* was boarded at sea by crewmen from Torpedo boat *G-102*. An unfound British Admiralty report of 1920 stated that Fryatt had been invited to dine with u-boat officers in the cellar restaurant of their casino in a large manor house in Fort Lapin in the Saint-Peters area of Bruges.

> *Bruges, naturally, was not only the rendezvous, but it was also the playground for the Flanders' u-boat men when off duty between raids. The under-sea flotilla chiefs had their headquarters in one of the oldest buildings in the ancient Belgian city [built by the Jesuits] ... When meal-time came they adjourned to another place, a sumptuous private mansion, a place of spacious rooms, lofty ceilings, carved woodwork, and crystal chandeliers ... an old rathskellar, a cellar which you entered by arched doorways two feet thick ... the nightly congregating place ... walls decorated with frescoes by a submarine commander. For living quarters they scattered about in private houses deserted by their owners.*[81]

> *[The commanders] told [Fryatt] that he was a gentleman and they were on friendly terms up to the moment he saw fit to show off his watch [with his citation for attempting to ram U 33 the previous year]. The atmosphere took a 180° degree turn and he was immediately apprehended and imprisoned.*[82]

Importantly, it was not until 16 July that the Dutch reported that Fryatt had been charged with sinking a German submarine. Termote's version, and the chain of events, does suggest that the plot to capture Fryatt, rather than just the *Brussels*, is an invention. If the Germans knew who they had captured, they presumably would not have sent him to Berlin at all. *U 33*, of course, had not been sunk and, equally, the Germans knew this. The four-hour trial was held eleven days later, 27 July, at Bruges Town Hall. Before a court convened by Admiral Ludwig von Schröder, the head of the Flanders *MarineKorps*, Fryatt was found guilty of being a *franc tireur* and sentenced to death, which was immediately confirmed.[83] One basis for the charge was his watch inscription. Fryatt claimed throughout that he was attempting to evade an anticipated torpedo and had not tried to ram *U 33*. Gansser was in the Mediterranean and did not appear, but sent his second-in-command. Fryatt was not properly represented and was not informed of his rights of appeal. He was executed by firing squad that evening at 1900. He had a wife and seven children. An execution notice was published in Dutch, French and German, signed by Schröder:

> *The English captain of a merchant ship, Charles Fryatt, of Southampton, though he did not belong to the armed forces of the enemy, attempted on 28 March 1915 to destroy a German submarine by running it down. For this he has been condemned to death by judgement this day of the Field Court Martial of the Navy Corps, and has been executed. A ruthless deed has thus been avenged, belatedly but just.*

The British response was, seemingly, one of surprise and genuine horror. British Prime Minister Herbert Asquith spoke of 'utmost indignation', 'atrocious crime', and being 'impossible to conjecture to what atrocities [the Germans] may proceed'.[84] Lord Claud Hamilton, MP, chairman of the Great Eastern Railway, and aide-de-camp to Queen Victoria for ten years, called the execution 'sheer, brutal murder'. Propagandists 'presented Fryatt as a civilian martyr to be ranked with Edith Cavell', the nurse executed for helping over 250 Allied soldiers in occupied Belgium to get back to England through neutral Netherlands.[85] A war crime was declared and retaliation threatened. The Germans investigated and decided correct procedure had been followed.[86] After the war, public funerals were held for both returned bodies of Cavell and Fryatt in St Paul's Cathedral, London. A memorial still stands in London's Liverpool Street Station. In the Canadian Rockies, there are two mountains named for Fryatt and Cavell.

Fryatt's story is worth telling both for its own sake and to demonstrate the different values and strength of feeling on both sides of the submarine war, not least among the u-boat captains. What of Gerth's involvement? The connections are circumstantial, but repay consideration. First, Gerth arrived in Bruges on or about 22 June, the day of Fryatt's capture. He was a new commander who had not yet taken a u-boat to sea in anger when *Brussels* was taken by her prize crew to Zeebrugge and up the canal to Bruges.[87] As a loyal and committed twenty-eight-year-old naval officer in a new post, Gerth would have offered his full support to his commanders and been anxious to soak up the style and opinions of his free-booting comrades. If Fryatt was immediately entertained to dinner in Bruges by the u-boat commanders, then it is likely that Gerth was in attendance. He would have heard Fryatt's stories, seen his watch, and felt the icy change in atmosphere in the cellar. If this part of the story is apocryphal, and Fryatt's connection with *U 33* was not realised until later, then, by July, the whole Flanders Flotilla would have been ablaze with the story of Fryatt's impending court martial. Schröder was Bartenbach's immediate superior and both would have been closely involved in all decisions and, in all probability, instigated them. The military court was held at Bruges Town Hall with five adjudicating officers, one of whom was a serving u-boat commander. The ranks of these men are given, but their names have been omitted from the German report.[88] Might Gerth have attended the court in solidarity that morning along with the few 'unoccupied' commanders in Bruges? He took *UB 12* to sea at 1750 that evening, just two hours before Fryatt was shot.

Did the episode make any impression upon Gerth's Prussian fervour? His involvement in the story is not yet over. On 4 November, Gerth left Bruges and *UB 12* for a short leave and afterwards went up to the Baltic where his new charge, *UC 61*, was being finished at Bremen. Gerth moved the boat to Kiel and brought it to combat readiness with its first crew.

*In November 1916, I was entrusted with the command of UC 70 ...
The policy of unrestricted submarine warfare ... led to the design and
construction of a new type of u-boat which, [with its] much improved
mine-laying capacity, did at least boast an engine plant which brought
the whole British coastline within its range. [The boat] displaced 450
tons instead of 160 tons, carried eighteen mines instead of twelve, was
fitted with one underwater and two surface torpedo tubes, and an
88-mm deck gun. The powerful diesels provided a top speed of twelve
knots. The boat was capable of remaining below much longer ... and
was considerably more habitable.*[89]

*[This was] the busy time of the first diving and steaming trials. No u-boat
was allowed to leave for active service till she was in every respect in
perfect trim. Finally came the firing exercises at the Submarine School
in Eckernförde. To save time, we were towed to the firing position by
torpedo-boats. These exercises were chiefly intended to test the ability
of the commanding officer. Here he must show whether, under warlike
conditions, he not only had his boat absolutely in hand, but also how
to attack and how to hit.*[90]

Gerth travelled through the Kiel Canal and stopped near the entrance at
Brunsbüttel. On one trip, *U 62*, commanded by Ernst Hashagen, was forced
to stop over there because of fog. The officers were asked to join the port
pilots for a drink, 'mostly old sailing ship skippers, many with white beards
and all deep-sea men'.[91] The u-boat men listened to the tall stories of long
ago and then responded with their own modern tales:

*When we are on the bottom we can see everything that goes on around
us under the sea. A big, curved steel plate is slid noiselessly to one
side. A curtain is raised by means of two levers, revealing a dark glass
window. Then we press a button, and at a bound the deep-sea night is
turned into day in the rays of a powerful searchlight. The thick glass
is quite clear and transparent, so that we can distinguish every detail.
We see the great curious fishes shooting up, and the crabs, lobsters, and
starfish moving among the corals and submarine flowers.*

One of the engineers explained that when it got tedious on the bottom,
the men often climbed out through the diving lock. It was quite simple,
he said, to allow the water in and to bite on the rubber mouthpiece on the
diving helmet. It was difficult climbing down the boat's side, which was as
'slippery as an eel'. 'Then we go for our stroll. We all carry lamps and sharp
axes in case of danger. A stroll on the sea bottom is a fine affair.'

UC 61 moved down the coast, passed the Netherlands, to be met by an
escort:

German u-boat UB 4 *hove in sight directly ahead, sent by the Chief of the Flanders Flotilla, Korvettenkapitän Bartenbach, to escort us through the German minefields on the Belgian coast. We made Zeebrugge that afternoon, berthing an hour later at Bruges, to be received by the Flotilla chief and the representative of the Naval Corps. That evening Bartenbach made a speech of welcome in the officers' club.*[92]

Back in Bruges, on 1 March, Gerth made the customary first short operational cruise for a new uc-boat and crew, five days without mines in the Hoofden off the Dutch coast.[93] *UC 61* was a much more offensive boat than *UB 12*: five torpedoes and a serious deck gun. Bartenbach ordered the boat to a designated patrol square to look out for convoys and to disturb the traffic between England and Holland.[94] Gerth sailed in the evening, took up his position and, for the next three days in a reasonable sea with good visibility, saw nothing. He was reduced to making practice runs under water. On his last full day, at 0938, ten miles off the North Hinder light vessel, in a quickly freshening sea and rising wind, with visibility cut by snowdrifts, he saw a steamer with escorts. Gerth takes up the story in the laconic style of his Kriegstagebuch:

Sighted steamer with two destroyers, dived, ran attack, both engines full speed straight ahead. Realised afterwards it was the English steamer Copenhagen *on route to Holland. Bow shot at steamer, distance about 1,500 metres, steamer speed 16 knots. Hit in the engine room. Steamer stops, lies abeam of the sea, both destroyers circle it. Crew leaves the steamer in ship's boats; destroyers cannot go alongside in the heavy sea. Steamer lies without list; stern significantly lower. Released second torpedo 400m from stationary steamer. Failed shot, can only be explained by faulty course of torpedo, probably as a result of the heavy sea. Although going almost constantly full speed,* UC 61 *cannot be held at depth, several times whole conning tower comes above water and is apparently being seen. Destroyer approaches* UC 61 *at great speed. Went to depth, departed. Afterwards headed again towards site of the attack. Sighted nothing else in the very limited field of vision due to high sea [now reported as a gale]. Surfaced very near destroyer, dived. Surfaced. Hatches and thick spars/booms are floating around. Sighted nothing of the steamer. Immediately afterwards sighted two destroyers quite close. Dived. Surfaced. Steamer is briefly visible through fog. Tried to run it down, however steamer is not sighted again.*

What made the *Copenhagen* special for Gerth, Bartenbach and the Flanders Flotilla was that she was a sister ship of Charles Fryatt's *Brussels* in the Great Eastern Railway passenger fleet. That probably was cause enough to enjoy sinking the *Copenhagen*, but there was another reason to dislike and distrust vessels in this fleet: a further sister ship, the Great Eastern's SS *Antwerp*, originally called *Vienna*, was the second Q-ship commissioned in 1915 by the Royal Navy and she was a well-known nuisance to the Flanders u-boats.[95]

Copenhagen left Harwich for the Hook of Holland at 0400, escorted by the destroyers *Sylph* and *Minos* and was near the end of her passage when hit.[96] The Admiralty received a report of the torpedoing at 0959 from the destroyer *Nimrod*.[97] The crew, passengers and despatches were taken off by *Sylph*, which brought them to Harwich with the destroyers *Matchless* and *Lookout*, arriving at 1400. *Nimrod* was ordered not to sink *Copenhagen*, but to let her drift.[98] Arrangements the next day to send out a search and towing party were abandoned because of continuing thick fog and a rough sea. *Copenhagen* did drift about two miles before she sank. The wreck is lying upright in a trough between two sand waves in about twenty-six metres and with little superstructure remaining.[99]

> *For a moment ... I reflected on the morality of the impending situation. On the one hand, the honourable seamen on that ship, true to the highest traditions of their calling, had willingly placed their lives in the greatest danger to save [others]. And all the thanks they were going to get for it was a German torpedo.*[100]

The 2,570-ton *Copenhagen*, built by John Brown at Clydebank, was by far and away the biggest haul to date of Gerth's short career.[101] The German command placed the boat at about 5,000 tons; figures at this time were being routinely inflated as reports passed up the chain of command. Passenger accommodation was spread over three decks amidships, with room for 320 in first class. There was a full-width sixty-two-seat dining room on the lower deck. The Germans noted the success on Monday, 5 March. It was not observed by Gerth because of the counterattack by the two British destroyers; but the loss was confirmed by newspaper reports.[102] The sinking was notified by telegram to the Kaiser by the Chief of the Admiralty Staff who explained that 'it was well known that the vessel was permanently cruising in convoy between Holland and England, so it is even more pleasing that the ship was successfully sunk while escorted by destroyers'. Six British crewmen were reported dead, four were married, and all were working in the engine room where Gerth's torpedo hit. Whether they died in the explosion or from subsequent drowning is moot. These were the first people killed by Gerth.[103]

What a difference in attitude nine months made in the submarine war. In July 1916, Fryatt was executed because he tried to save his ship and possibly tried to ram *U 33*. Nobody died. The following February, the Germans declared unrestricted submarine warfare. The next month, *U 61* sank the *Brussels'* sister ship *Copenhagen* by torpedo without warning in the same area of sea as the attempted ramming, six died, and hardly a murmur was heard. Actually, there was a little murmur based on some confused information. *Copenhagen* had been a hospital ship and, in some reports, had only reverted to passenger traffic on the day of her sinking, and others suggested she was still carrying wounded. But, this would not be true from neutral Holland, and the story quickly disappeared.

Flushed with the success from the sinking of *Copenhagen*, *UC 61* spent a customary couple of days in maintenance and then moved through the canal to the dry dock in Ostend for repairs to her oil tanks. Back in Bruges, Gerth took his eighteen mines aboard for the first time when he was ordered by Bartenbach to lay them in sets off Beachy Head and Newhaven. Afterwards, he was to cruise the Scillies looking for merchant targets. The u-boat sailed for Zeebrugge on 17 March in the company of *UC 17* and *UC 65*. *UC 61*'s second patrol was the nightmare voyage, perhaps saved from farce only by an heroic and lucky cruise home to Bruges where all of the torpedoes, and possibly the mines, were unloaded and handed back. There is a small mystery as Gerth does not mention laying mines during his voyage, something he normally noted meticulously both in his war diary and in a separate mine chart. *UC 61* did make the Lizard in its approach to the Scillies so was well past the area where the mines were to be laid.

> *Because a mine cannot distinguish the nationality of a ship that runs into it, The Hague Convention of 1907 had agreed to keep the open seas free of these lethal weapons floating beneath the ocean's surface. Belligerents were permitted to lay offensive minefields only in hostile territorial waters; that is, within three miles of an enemy's coast. Nevertheless, because the North Sea is generally shallow and therefore particularly suitable for moored contact mines, the German navy, preparing for war, began accumulating a large stock with the intention of using them aggressively … from the first day of war German ships and submarines placed over 25,000 mines in the North Sea, most of them in defiance of The Hague Convention … Britain was wholly unprepared for large-scale mining.*[104]

Half way down the English Channel, overcast with a choppy sea, *UC 61* was briefly caught in crossfire between opposing destroyers with shells landing dangerously close. Gerth went to the seabed at twenty-six metres, surfaced an hour later, and was quickly caught in a destroyer's searchlight.

> *The one great risk a submarine runs when lying on the bottom is that her tanks may not be absolutely tight. If they are not, a leakage of air or oil may occur through vent valves or seams, and the bubbles rising to the surface may betray her.*[105]

More shells landed nearby and Gerth went to the bottom again. The next morning, he dived twice before destroyers and in the early afternoon spotted a sailing ship and opened fire, which immediately brought the attention of five armed trawlers, two of which guarded the ship while the others conducted a search. Trawler *Sapper* flashed an alert to the Admiralty.[106] Two more patrol vessels passed close by while *UC 61* moved under water. Early that evening, Gerth passed *UC 21*, returning to Zeebrugge, whose jubilant commander, Oberleutnant Reinhold Saltzwedel, would surely have passed on the news of fifteen ships sunk during his patrol, including that morning the 5,225-ton American tanker *Illinois*, scuttled off Alderney. Neither Saltzwedel nor *UC 21* would survive the year. Next day, Gerth reached the Lizard after brief brushes with a u-boat hunter and several destroyers.

The morning of 20 March was overcast and blowing a gale. Before first light, Gerth's gyro-compass failed and he was obliged to take magnetic bearings to the Wolf Rock lighthouse, a lonely rock some eight miles from the Scillies towards Lizard Point. Wolf Rock gets its name from the howling sound made when strong winds blow through its fissures. *UC 61* spotted some steamers, but failed in the swell to get into position for torpedo firing. Funnel smoke signalled the arrival of two armed trawlers that spotted Gerth's periscope; the swell had adversely affected his depth control. The u-boat dived to forty metres to escape the depth charges that followed. The sea was now so bad that any torpedo attack was impossible. The trawlers followed, one either side, tracking *UC 61* with sound detectors.

One u-boat, located by hydrophones and then heavily depth-charged, fell silent beneath the waves. Then a propeller was heard faintly turning or attempting to turn ... a slight grating or squeaking such as might have been made by damaged machinery. This noise lasted a few seconds and stopped. Presently it started up again and then once more it stopped. The submarine made a little progress, but fitfully; she would go a few yards then pause. The surface vessels dropped more depth charges and listened again. Then there was a lumbering noise such as might be made by a heavy object trying to drag its hulk along the muddy bottom; this was followed by silence, showing that the wounded vessels could move only a few yards. By now, the surface vessels had used all of their depth charges and could only wait. All night long, the listeners reported scraping and straining noises from below but these grew fainter and fainter. They listened for hours and then, the following afternoon, heard a sharp piercing noise ... Only one thing in the world could make a sound like that ... the crack of a revolver. More of these pistol cracks followed, counted by the listeners above. In all, twenty-five shots came from the bottom of the sea. Then silence.[107]

Gerth tried a course change and dropped to fifty metres. Then, catastrophe

as both electric motors, which gave him underwater power, began to
malfunction. Gerth recorded what happened next in unusual length in his
Kriegstagebuch and also repeated the story for his interrogators in Calais
in July.[108] Between the two tales, which are combined here, the trawlers
grew into destroyers and, one suspects, other details changed dependent
upon the audience.

> *The stuffing boxes of the two crankshafts of the submarine were not
> tight and were leaking considerably. The torpedo and engine bilge
> pumps filled with water owing to the negligence of the sailor in charge
> of the engines who did not report the initial problem. To avoid being
> rammed, and still more to avoid the depth charges, the submarine dived
> to a great depth, about sixty metres.*

Sixty metres was the tested maximum depth for a uc-boat, 'but they will
dive to greater depths in case of serious emergency'.[109] The emergency
kit was minimal. 'Every submarine must carry in the second forward and
second aft compartment a bag containing appliances for stopping leaks,
including at least the following articles: about twenty wooden plugs, ten
mallets of various sizes, one hammer, two chisels, two punches of different
sizes, one pair of pliers, one box of matches, two candles and tow.'[110]

> *The deep dive made matters worse; a serious amount of water was
> flooding into the boat. Gerth tried desperately to reach the surface.
> Because of all the water collecting in the stern, the boat broke through
> at a sharp angle with, perhaps, a third of the boat pointing out of
> the water. A sloop opened fire which obliged Gerth to dive again with
> all speed. The boat's bow now being down, the water, which had
> accumulated aft, rushed forward. The boat sank at a twenty-five
> degree angle to forty metres. The electric motors were completely fused.
> Gerth stabilised the boat and came to the surface using compressed
> air. He found himself in a very rough sea with snow and hail gusts
> and very limited visibility. The trawlers were nowhere to be seen. The
> oil engines were switched on and UC 61 headed out to sea. The gyro-
> compass, which had stabilised, failed again. Chief Engineer Johannes
> Giese worked a small miracle to get some electric power through and
> began to charge the batteries. Some patrol vessels were evaded and UC
> 61 was forced to dive again at about midnight. The starboard engine
> began to malfunction and both electric motors were unstable with no
> chance of repair.*

At three o'clock the next morning, Gerth abandoned his mission. He could
not make a controlled dive and would be stationary and vulnerable under
water so he began a remarkable voyage from Lands End back to Zeebrugge.

After a slow day and night's travel, he decided as he approached the pinch at Dover to spend the following daylight hours on the seabed and he settled to forty-two metres off Beachy Head. However, the boat shifted so badly in the swell that, after an hour, he decided to continue taking the middle channel between Beachy Head and Le Tréport. In one piece of good news, the gyro-compass righted itself. No one noticed *UC 61* as it crawled up the French coast. Thankfully, one of the net buoys was unlit, but all other shore lights and other buoys were burning as usual. Just after midday on 23 March, *UC 61* moored at Bruges. Gerth had been at sea for a lifetime of just over eighty hours.

UC 61 spent a month in dry dock at Ostend and by 28 April was provisioned and ready for sea again.[111] Much of his spare time during the month would have been spent in the officers' mess at Bruges; it was here that he was remembered by fellow commander Werner Fürbringer,

> *Among his fellow sailors in the mess, always the burning cigar between his fingers and the red wine in the background, he spread a special atmosphere of comfort, combined with utmost openness for any humour. Reliability of character, high intellectual abilities, unshakable calm and not least his personal courage distinguished him as a first-class human being and an outstanding officer. He enjoyed a maximum of respect and popularity among his peers.*[112]

Bartenbach gave his commanders hand-written orders, usually instructing three uc-boats to sea at the same time, but with different destinations. Gerth left Bruges in the early hours that Saturday accompanied by *UC 65*, which was ordered to the inner Firth of Clyde, and *UC 69*, bound for the steamer passage at Belle Île and Quiberon Bay off the south coast of Brittany.[113] The British intercepted Gerth's radio messages from the Straits of Dover for both his inward and outward voyages.[114] Because his call sign was known, they knew that *UC 61* was on patrol. Gerth took his boat to the bottom in order to wait for the right tide to drop his mines. Shortly after midnight, he laid two mines at four metres below mean sea level (as with all of his mines) at the Needles off the Isle of Wight; after twenty minutes four more were laid one and a half miles away; just over an hour later there were three more at Anvil Point; and then three more at St Alban's Head. It was customary for each of these uc-boats to be assigned a particular mine-laying area, which formed the primary objective in subsequent cruises.

The losses among the uc-boats of the Flanders Flotilla were proportionately high. 'This has been said to be due to indifferent diving qualities and to the absence of a watertight hatch between conning tower and hull'.[115] However, the core work performed in the vicinity of the coast and of harbour entrances was inherently dangerous. Mines slid weighted out of the tubes to the sea floor as the u-boat passed overhead; if the mines stuck in the shaft or rose prematurely the u-boat was at fatal risk. At least nine of the seventy-nine uc-boats launched before 1918 were thought to have been casualties of their own mines. Altogether, by information gathered by 2013, some 40 per cent of all u-boats destroyed in World War I were the known victims of friendly or enemy mines and a further 14 per cent had an unknown fate.[116]

> *The customary six obliquely mounted bow shafts or tubes discharged a normal load of eighteen mines through the boat's bottom. The German mines operated as follows. Both mine and sinker went to the bottom, where the dissolution of a soluble plug allowed the partially air-filled mine to float up toward the surface until a hydrostatic device was activated at the desired depth. The line connecting the mine to the sinker was then snubbed. The sinker had arms that swung out when it reached the bottom in order to stabilise it. The drawback of this system was that the two ropes connecting mine to sinker allowed substantial swaying and variance at depth, while the soluble release mechanism at times dissolved as soon as the mine was released, with the result that it came up and struck the submarine. The so-called German 'egg' mine was fitted with the Hertz horn, a lead tube containing sulphuric acid in a glass container. Impact with a ship broke the glass, allowed the acid to flow onto carbon / zinc elements and thus produced an electric current that fired the detonator attached to the explosives.[117]*

At about half past three in the morning, Gerth surfaced in a near-calm sea and started his diesel engines to recharge his electric batteries and his compressed air containers. The schooner *Little Mystery* was sighted at six thirty. Her captain, John Greet, greatly experienced with his ship, was on a south by east course, twenty-five miles south-south-east from Portland Bill on the Dorset coast. Greet was *Little Mystery*'s best-known master. Born in 1867 in St Blazey, Cornwall, he passed his master's certificate at Fowey in 1894, aged twenty-nine.[118] Greet's own father was blind and lived by teaching the blind. In 1917, Greet's second wife, Rhoda, waited at home in Plymouth with their twelve-year-old daughter, also Rhoda. *Little Mystery* was alone in a smooth sea and, through the slight haze, she was visible from six miles away. Despite all sails set, she was making only a vulnerable three knots in the light breeze from the north. *Little Mystery*'s cargo was 168 tons of coal, shipped by Hansa Brothers, loaded at Cardiff and bound for Cherbourg where it was consigned to Messrs I. Cavroy of Paris.[119]

The area around Portland harbour was busy in 1917 patching up merchant ships, unloading trains with munitions and loading them into transports for the Western front.[120] The Portland naval authorities were also responsible for controlled sailings in the French coal trade, a lifeline to the French economy since the Germans had captured their north-eastern industrial heartlands in 1914, including 74 per cent of its coal production.[121]

Two months before, matters became so serious that the French prime minister sent a three-man delegation at a day's notice from Paris to London asking for them 'to be received without delay by Mr Lloyd George and the competent British authorities on questions relating to coal'.[122]

> The French Government are faced by an extremely grave crisis caused by the coal shortage in France. This shortage has already necessitated the closing down of a number of factories engaged in work of national defence. M. Briand fears that if the present state of affairs is prolonged there will be an interruption in the production of the most important requirements. The French Government consider that it is essential to address to the British Government an urgent appeal begging them to make a serious effort capable of remedying this state of affairs.[123]

Little Mystery's 168 tons of coal may have been a pinprick but, for all her small size, her voyage was a part of the British response to the French plea. The coal was undisputed war contraband at any stage of the conflict. Colliers bound for Cherbourg and ports west, and colliers with speeds less than eight knots bound for Brest and the Bay of Biscay ports, assembled at Portland under a French-run scheme.[124] This arrangement precluded small schooners like *Little Mystery* who were at the mercy of the wind and, on this day, was moving at walking pace. At seven in the morning, John Greet sighted a submarine on the surface two miles away to the north east and closing quickly.[125] He immediately threw all of his weighted confidential papers overboard. There was no escort or Allied patrol boat in sight and no radio to call for help. Greet kept to his course for thirty minutes.[126] Gerth stopped his diesels in order to approach his prey under water, but kept watch through the periscope. *UC 61* surfaced about two hundred yards away on the port side close to the schooner's stern; this manoeuvre was designed to lessen the damage if the u-boat found their prey was actually a trap. *Little Mystery*'s capture was slightly farcical – no torpedo was fired as these were too expensive to expend on a small schooner and, besides, there were still six mines aboard which may have been set off accidentally by the release of compressed air; no warning shell either from the 88mm cannon, no machine gun fire. Twenty-nine-year-old Gerth stood in his conning tower when close alongside and fired six or seven shots from his pistol and that was enough. At the first shot, *Little Mystery* hove to, its crew decided sensibly not to return fire with their own hand weapons. A Russian able seaman, Carl Eglit, was hit in the muscle in his left arm. Was Gerth's aim random? There was no jostling in the flat sea. A pistol shot to an arm could as easily be a pistol shot to the head. Greet, Eglit and the three other crew, two British and a Portuguese, immediately got into their 'almost new' rowing boat to cross to *UC 61* taking with them as directed their ship's papers.

What the crew saw at close quarters was a u-boat with a black hull and large grey conning tower, all in old paint, a canvas bridge screen, one gun and a periscope. An arrangement was noticed in the bows, circular with teeth, like a saw. Three officers and six men were on deck. Two of the officers were in 'duffle clothing', one in a blue uniform. The men were in 'civilian clothes and appeared dirty and unkempt'. One of the men had a cap ribbon of the Flanders Flotilla, another wore a ribbon of SMS *Derfflinger*, a famous battlecruiser of the Kaiserliche Marine.[127]

> *After supper we were allowed, in turns, to go out on to the upper deck and smoke a cigarette. When I went up, the Commander ... told me to paint out the large white figures on the side of the hull, so that the enemy might not discover the boat's number.*[128]

Greet was told by a junior officer who spoke good English that he should have got his boat in the water more quickly. He was kept on *UC 61* while a boarding party laid a single explosive device on *Little Mystery*'s waterline. The party also scoured the schooner for food, described in one official report as 'looting'.[129] Greet made no such claim except that the German commander 'seized my ensign' and volunteered that he was allowed to return to the ship to get his compass and was told he could take some of his photographs as well. 'We saved a few things.'

> *On the deck a medley of boxes and chests of cocoa, coffee and expensive tea, sacks of wonderful American meal, fresh butter and globes of margarine, cordage, unused nets, oilskins, rubber boots that did not fit the crew, fine white English bread, English marmalade, ham and bully-beef, bacon and beans, two bars of good soap, tobacco and various oddments. All these things, which were now completely strange to us, we had removed from a few paltry enemy fishing-boats, while in Germany the women and children were starving and dying of inanition, or supporting life on vile, injurious, almost uneatable food-substitutes. The poor in Germany thought of old days as they sat over their watery turnips; while in the cabins of these trawlers, which we happened to have sunk just at dinner time, were plates filled with, what seemed to us, lavish helpings of good fresh roast meat and potatoes, such as we only saw in dreams.*[130]

The bomb exploded shortly before eight o'clock and *Little Mystery* sank in five minutes going down by the stern, apparently in one piece. In the thirteen months fourteen days beginning with Boxing Day 1916, Stephens, *Little Mystery*'s owners, lost ten vessels, of which nine were by enemy action, mostly by u-boats. What seems certain is that these sinkings 'represented a heavy loss for which they received no compensation'.[131]

Greet and his crew pulled towards Portland and, at just before ten o'clock, sighted *Royalo*, an armed trawler, which 'from a very far distance' [four miles] opened fire on the u-boat with eight rounds.[132] *UC 61* moved out of sight of *Royalo* above water and after a time submerged showing her periscope. *Royalo* picked up Greet and his crew and took them to Weymouth. It was not yet midday.

What makes for a favoured victim among the over 7,000 vessels hit by u-boats in World War I? A personal reaction to a curt mention in a list of misery? Something of beauty destroyed for small gain? A name that promised allure? An unknown grave?

> *In the hazy distance, the mountains of the Emerald Isle rose some 2,000 feet above the sea. Against this lovely background moved a full-rigged ship under sail. Our first sailing-ship! .... One shell after another tore great holes in the hull below the water-line. At every hit the whole rigging quivered, and great clouds of dust and powder floated up through the sails and spars high above the masts. A quarter of an hour later the proud sailing-ship, now full of water, began to move, turned uncertainly, and once more ran before the wind. Her stern was noticeably down in the water. Her sails flapped: still struggling against her end, she turned once more, and, swaying several times to port and starboard, quivered and sank by the stern, almost majestically, with all sails set.*[133]

Little Mystery, a 114-ton wooden two-masted schooner, was built in 1887 by shipwright William Date at his yard on the Dart River near Kingsbridge, Devon.[134] She was bought that July by John Stephens, a Cornish small ship owner and entrepreneur, trading from his home port of Fowey and its sub-ports of Charlestown, Mevagissey and Par.[135] While Stephens and his son Edward with his wife Mary Ann shared ownership of half the boat, the rest was split among another twenty people – 'the butcher, the baker, the master, the manager and by widows and orphans and by local land-owning families'.[136] One of Stephens' schooners, *Little Beauty*, made a profit of £450 in her first year's trading and the money was distributed to the shareholders by one of the owner's sons 'walking through the Fowey streets and the lanes of the surrounding countryside carrying a jingling wash-leather bag of golden sovereigns'.[137]

> *By national standards [Stephens] was not an enterprise of importance or particular significance, merely one of the many that were planted, grew and blossomed ... in Victorian England only to fade ... after the Great War. However, the Stephens' fleet did last for more than seventy years, managing over fifty vessels during that time. At its largest in 1902, the fleet comprised seventeen ships, averaging just 130 tons gross apiece. Early on, the fleet became known as the Company of Little*

> *Ships because some of them had names beginning with Little – 'a fleet within a fleet'. 'The distinction had a certain ambiguity since all of the vessels were little, but only ten – but never more than five at once – were Little.' All were sailing ships with light crews which included some of the fastest passage-makers of their kind, trading as far as the Indian Ocean and the South Atlantic, though concentrating on the western ocean and, in poor economic times, the coasting business.* [138]

The first *Little* in the Stephens' fleet was *Little Beauty*, built at Polruan, Cornwall, in 1875, 'so called because her timber was too small to be used in another ship, the *Ocean Swell*, being built at the same time'.[139] *Little Mystery* was the sister ship of the *Little Wonder*, launched a year before her in 1886 from the same yard.[140] In 1893, *Little Gem* was added to the fleet, another sister ship of *Little Mystery* 'from whose model she was built, the measurements of the two vessels hardly differing'.[141] They were singled-decked, carvel-built boats, eighty-four feet long and noted for their clean lines, square stern and full female figureheads. In 1894, *Little Mystery* was reduced to 95 tons following the addition of a lower forecastle, sail room, bosun's store, master's room and a chart room.[142]

Little Mystery and her sisters epitomised their half-namesakes, the 'small fry of the ocean', and mostly traded to Newfoundland with salt, returning with dried cod.[143] 'Until the beginning of the first world war there were nearly always six or seven of these vessels on the Atlantic.' The Boon brothers of Bideford recalled that maintenance was done at a yard local to them.[144] John Stephens would come from Fowey, sitting in his own small folding chair, watching work in progress on a *Little* or other fleet ship:

> *Of all the schooners we saw, those ships were the most perfect. They were all coloured green under the waterline and painted black above, their decks were scrubbed, their masts scraped and varnished – for they could afford to do those things in those days. The apprentices used to work overtime scraping off the surplus pitch after the caulking and thereby seeking to supplement their five shillings per week. Even then, Mr Stephens would be sitting there ... to make sure that we did a perfectly good job.* [145]

Captain R. A. Fletcher wrote a love-book to the world of tall ships, but amongst its pages he made space to laud the small schooners which he saw, year in year out, 'thrash their way back and forth' across the Atlantic, chiefly carrying fish from Newfoundland, St Pierre, and Miquelon to Gibraltar or to Spanish or French ports.[146] The Stephens' ships performed winter and summer with a 'regularity which spoke volumes for the seamanship of those who commanded them and was a glowing testimony to the strength of their construction, their suitability for their work, and the excellence of their equipment'. Fletcher named particularly *Little Secret* and *Little Mystery* as well known – 'the romance of the sea can never die out while such vessels and such crews as manned them are afloat'.

> *Once I saw one of these ocean-going schooners showing what she could do in a howling North Atlantic gale, with the sea running mountains high ... The sailing ship I was in was under reduced canvas. As the schooner crossed our bows less than half a mile distant we could see her leaning over until her lee gunwale was under water. Her three little scraps of sail, looking not much bigger than handkerchiefs, tore her along at a great pace amid a smother of foam, and clouds of heavy spray and sometimes green water swept her from end to end. We could see two oilskin-clad figures at the wheel; they must have been firmly lashed or they would have been washed away. She seemed a living, a mad thing as she rushed down the slope of one wave and up the next, bounding ahead in a fashion that even the famous Dreadnought, the 'wild boat of the Atlantic' ... could not have surpassed.*

Basil Greenhill, life-long champion of ships like *Little Mystery*, continued the paean: 'These schooners did not often heave-to, indeed they ran often until it was too late to heave-to.[147] Their particular danger, of course, was that of being pooped and swept clean by a fast, following sea.' The common method of combating this danger was to tow a hawser behind the vessel in order to slow her down and smooth her wake. 'With a heavy sea, a small mistake would mean lost spars, perhaps a smashed wheel, cleared decks and a broach-to.'

There had been no sign of *Little Mystery* breaking up on the surface; Greet reported her 'sinking stern first'. The charted position is 50° 10′ N; 2° 13′ 9″ W, but as wreck detective Jan Lettens says this could be one kilometre in any direction.[148] It is possible that some of the coal cargo, which was all carried in the hold, spilled out of the hole in her side on the way down. The bottom here is about sixty metres with varieties of sand, shell, gravel, pebble and mud. The good timber from Date's Dart River yard is likely wearing well, but the decks will be swept clean, the hull will have settled and, at a hold depth of less than eleven feet, her seafloor silhouette will be slight, swept by currents, but possibly covered in snagged nets, sea urchins, peacock worms, anemones, pouting and pollock.[149] *Little Mystery* has no value, is unlikely to show on a sonar, and will probably only be found, if even noticed, by accident.

John Henry Greet, master of *Little Mystery*, was awarded two war honours in 1919 – the First World War *Mercantile Marine War Medal* and the *British War Medal*.[150] After the war he moved from Plymouth to Middlesex, England, where he lived with his daughter Rhoda and her two children. He died in 1934, aged sixty-eight.

It may come as a surprise that *Little Mystery* lives on. Apart from articles and book references, there is a full hull model on a frame on display at the *National Maritime Museum* at Greenwich, London.[151] The model is decked, with a number of crew in sight, fully equipped and rigged with sails set. So popular is *Little Mystery* that a print and a drinking mug with her image are also available.

The loss of *Little Mystery* may be seen as a part of the hastening of the demise of the cargo sailing ship. Losses to World War I u-boats identified to 2016 total 7,241 in sunken and damaged ships. While it is impossible to clearly categorise all of these, or even to be certain about their propulsion in each case, what is sure to just a few percentage error points is that for every ten ships sunk, three were sailing ships, perhaps some 2,171.[152] However, for Basil Greenhill and the Stephens' fleet it was not so simple:

> *During the war, there were a sufficient number for convoys to be made up of schooners alone, and such convoys were escorted by armed vessels of their own class. Many were sunk, others fought successful operations with submarines, and some were borrowed for conversion into Q ships. The wartime losses among the sailing coasters were actually considerable ... but nevertheless many survived and these, together with the vessels taken over from the enemy, schooners bought from Holland during the shipping boom, and a few newly constructed ships, must have made quite a considerable fleet ready to resume normal work after the cessation of hostilities.*[153]

For the Admiralty and for Gerth it was a hectic afternoon and evening. *UC 61*'s morning mines had already been spotted while Gerth moved on, recharging finished, to lay his remaining six mines. Even before *Little Mystery* was sunk, the Admiralty moved to clear the mines at St Alban's Head; that speed brought Gerth's second success of the day, although unknown to him until later. HMT *Arfon*, a coal-burning, ketch-rigged Milford trawler, was requisitioned for war service as part of the general naval mobilisation a few days before war was declared and was converted for minesweeping duties.[154] At 0945, *Arfon*, with the armed trawler *Vera Grace*, was sweeping for an unknown number of the mines laid a few hours earlier. One mine was spotted and exploded by rifle fire, a second hit the fore part of *Arfon* and she sank within two minutes; of the crew of thirteen the ten who worked under cover died.[155]

There was clearly at least one other u-boat operating in the same general area as several reports came in of minor u-boat skirmishes and these are not reflected in *UC 61*'s war diary. All within a few miles of Portland that Saturday: at 1100, SS *Vestalia*, 5,528 tons, exchanged fire with a u-boat until it was driven down by patrols; motor launches 307 and 311 dropped depth charges off Portland Bill at 1130 having seen a wake and claimed a 'kill' which the Admiralty decided was 'improbable'; SS *Oilfield*, 4,005 tons, managed to outrun a u-boat at 1715 ; just before midnight a conning tower was sighted near Lulworth; the collier *Querida* sighted a submarine on her starboard beam in the early hours and opened fire as the u-boat disappeared into the darkness.[156]

On his way that afternoon to the Shambles Bank at Portland, Gerth stayed above water while evading a destroyer. At about 1700, he spotted a steamer and headed for it, then dived to let it pass, approached under water and surfaced to fire about ten shots from his canon. This was the Uruguayan SS *Gorizia* of Montevideo, 1,246 tons, from New York via Falmouth for Le Havre carrying 'general cargo', including oranges.[157] The main steam pipe in the boiler room was the only hit causing an immediate loss of power. *Gorizia* hove to and the mixed-nationality crew of twenty-two took to their lifeboats and pulled clear. *Gorizia* was boarded and, in the same manner as *Little Mystery*, its American master George Rex was kept on *UC 61* while two bombs were attached. Rex noted the u-boat crew's 'greenish-colour duffle suits'. *Gorizia* sank by the stern within five minutes.

> The [steamer] *sank bow foremost in the usual way ... The pressure of air and water flung a little cloud of soot from the funnels of both, the so-called 'black soul', the final farewell of a steamer on its way to the bottom of the sea.*[158]

Finding an American master on *Gorizia* was not the best of luck for Gerth as the Germans remained desperate to keep the United States neutral and out of the war. Gerth, speaking excellent English, listened while Rex protested his American nationality and replied with an unemotional, 'I am very sorry, but war is war'.[159] He then told Rex to get back to his ship's boat as an armed yacht had been spotted. The *Lorna* having heard the gunfire quickly approached the confrontation and let off five shells which fell short of *UC 61* by fifty yards. The u-boat crash-dived and all that remained was for *Lorna* to pick up *Gorizia*'s crew and take them to Weymouth.

Gerth finished his twenty-four hours by recharging his batteries before continuing to the Shambles to drop his last mines. On the way, shortly before midnight, he saw a large, unidentified, steamer running with dimmed lights. Gerth was about to shoot when his u-boat was spotted in the moonlight and the steamer turned and made off. A little later, Gerth was forced to dive before a destroyer. At the Shambles, the moonlight was still strong so Gerth dived *UC 61* to avoid being silhouetted in the bright night at the time of his greatest vulnerability; he laid his six mines at irregular distances.

After a fruitless following day failing to engage two steamers and three sailing ships and being fired at by armed trawlers and destroyers escorting a steamer convoy, and during it all at different hours evading four patrol boats, two trawlers, four destroyers, an airship, and a plane, Gerth prudently headed towards Ouessant [Ushant] off the coast of Brittany.

What had *UC 61* achieved during 30 April? Eighteen mines had been dropped in prime Allied shipping lanes. As some of the mines were quickly spotted, dozens of naval craft were diverted to search for them and others.[160] Naval reports suggest that eleven mines had been found by the end of the day and the cost had been high with the loss of *Arfon* and ten men dead. The confusion did not end there as the next day, Tuesday, 1 May, at 0730, the Commodore-in-Charge of Portland, was forced to close Portland and Weymouth Bay to all traffic 'on account of mines'; at that time only four had been neutralised.[161] The warning was reiterated at 1330, 'no entry, closed until further notice'. The all clear came the next day at 2150, but immediately St Alban's Bay was closed. The disruption to traffic and convoy management was considerable. Gerth had also sunk the ten-year-old steamer *Gorizia* with its cargo of brass and other metals, probably ordered by the French Government and, equally probably, euphemistically placed on the manifest as 'general cargo'.[162] And then there was the loss of *Little Mystery*, with her wounded man and her coal.

And the cost to the Flanders Flotilla of the *Kaiserliche Marine*? The balance sheet shows a day's u-boat running costs, eighteen mines, no torpedoes, ten 88m shells, three bombs, and a magazine of pistol ammunition.

> One source carefully calculated that Britain's fight against the u-boats absorbed the efforts of 770,000 men (including naval and merchant crews, shipbuilders, dockyard workers, and naval ordnance manufacturers) and diverted from other use some 13,000 naval guns, 3,700 searchlights, nearly 46,000 tons of munitions, and 16,327 kilometre's worth of wire for submarine nets.[163]

Within hours of arriving at the French coast the next morning, 3 May, Gerth tersely states that he used his cannon to sink two small French fishing boats, an hour apart. French reports initially stated that both named boats had been sunk, but this was later corrected to just one.[164] This was an inglorious episode and left British naval officers wondering whether two submarines were involved because in the first attack 'the Germans showed an appalling ferocity, killing three men and seriously wounding two others'. One wonders whether Gerth was below and had delegated the sinking of this unimportant boat to a junior officer?

> The necessity for a short, concise, strictly matter-of-fact statement of events dictated our style. Nothing of our sentiments, our inward selves, found expression.[165]

Victorine Helène from Audierne was near the *Ar Men* lighthouse, with an excellent catch of skate when *UC 61* was spotted while it was a mile and a half away.[166] The submarine passed 200 metres astern and opened fire without warning, perhaps a dozen shots, and destroyed the vessel's interior. The dead were Jean Guillou, the owner with three children; Jean Guilcher, nine children; and Jean Noel Milliner.[167] The two injured survivors and an uninjured man stayed hidden in the bottom of the boat for a quarter of an hour while the u-boat left. They tacked east with an oar and used a largely undamaged sail to join a nearby group of fishermen who took them to the Ile de Sein where their wounds were dressed. Apart from the unnecessary violence, there is one discrepancy: the fishermen claimed the u-boat used two guns. This claim is not unusual from inexperienced witnesses under fire for the first time.

Fils du Progres was another tiny craft, this time from Camaret with a crew of seven.[168] The boat was also fishing for skate using a dinghy for the nets. *UC 61* was spotted a mile away, the nets cut, and the dinghy recalled. Another boat nearby did the same and fled. At 100 metres, Gerth shouted something to the fishermen that they did not understand. He then made signs for them to gather in the stern; three shots then landed in the bow. *Fils du Progress* sank within five minutes and the men were left in their dinghy.

That evening, Gerth attacked an armed 3,030-ton Italian steamer *Giovannina* carrying oranges from Catania to Liverpool.[169] After several shots hit the boat, its crew took to their boats without casualties. Gerth dived to close with the vessel, surfaced and sent a party aboard to attach two bombs. The *Giovannina* did not sink immediately so, now in darkness, Gerth put *UC 61* alongside and attached two more. While the boat sank, *UC 61*'s stern came hard against the ship's side. The muzzle door of the underwater aft torpedo tube was buckled and jammed. Gerth spent the next day cruising off the Loire while the muzzle door was freed so that it could be kept shut by water pressure while diving.

Back on patrol shortly after midnight on 5 May, Gerth sighted a steamer in the Loire estuary and gave chase for over five hours. At dawn, now within gun range, he opened fire, hitting twice before the cannon's height adjuster failed, making further shots difficult in a rolling sea. It was the 1,658-ton *Le Gard,* which was ready and replied immediately and accurately. Gerth now took his only casualty of the war when one of his seamen was slightly wounded in the foot by shrapnel. He dived *UC 61* for ten minutes and when he resurfaced found the horizon obscured by smoke shells. The height adjuster was fixed and, as the smoke cleared, the steamer was sighted again. Shooting from the height of *Le Gard*'s deck continued superior and landed too close to *UC 61*. Gerth took the pragmatic option and aborted the combat.

The report from the French master of *Le Gard*, Etienne Robert, survives and is a slightly more excited telling.[170] Particularly, Robert claimed that there were two submarines and that he sank one, a claim dismissed by the Admiralty as 'improbable'.[171] Here are some extracts:

As soon as the first submarine was sighted I ordered the crew to battle stations and three minutes after came the first shell from the submarine's cannon. I ordered 'Open fire'. At the same time, I noticed a second submarine of a lighter colour coming towards us roughly on the first quarter on the port side of the first one and further behind. I then launched seven Berger smoke screens to try and keep the second submarine surrounded by smoke ... At the second shell from the first submarine the main mast was cut and the radio sliced into five pieces; with the seventh shell numerous pieces of shrapnel holed our lifeboats and killed Stoker Pierre Malcoste, grievously wounded the first Stoker Emmanuel Herledan, and lightly wounded Henri Le Guay, Chief Engineer, and Jean Izagard, Second Engineer .... An uninterrupted burst of firing, about thirty rounds, and another shell cut the cables on the aft starboard side peppering the deck and main mast with shrapnel ... I manoeuvred the ship to keep the second submarine within the smoke and to keep the first one astern ... Several shots punctured the gangway and wounded Helmsman Honore Grenier but he did not move from his post ... At the fourteenth firing of Le Gard's cannon we hit the submarine full on at 4,200 metres. Immediately we clearly noticed a vertical flame rising to about twenty metres, and black smoke, quite different from that of the smokescreen, rising in a plume. The submarine went down quickly by the stern, its nose in the air ... The second submarine came out of the smoke and chased us at top speed whilst firing to which we replied straight away ... I gave the orders to the engines to do the impossible ... The battle started again. We replied shot for shot with eight well aimed rounds which forced the submarine to cease firing and to abandon the fight ... During the fight, all the men acted with admirable composure and discipline ... I would like to bring your particular attention to the good conduct of several members of the crew who did their duty courageously without flinching [twenty-one names attached with details of their deeds].

Gerth then took *UC 61* into Audierne Bay for two days to make repairs. The muzzle door caused ongoing problems and the final solution was to completely shut it and to accept that it would take twenty seconds on the surface for it to be opened and to fire a torpedo. A pressure pump which supplied air to the port engine had been running hot and needed a one-and-a-half-day overhaul, but to no avail. When re-assembled it ran hot again. Without the necessary tools it was impossible to fix so the starboard engine was adjusted to double up for air supply. Work was regularly interrupted by the need to dive before French patrols.

In the morning of the second day, the French steamer *Nelly*, 1,868 tons, was seen close by and a gun attack made that was 'tenaciously reciprocated'. Here was another case where two, perhaps three, submarines were seen.

Nelly's master, Francois Seres, estimated that about a hundred shells were fired at his boat over half an hour, which, if true, would be an extraordinary rate of fire by *UC 61*. *UC 61* scored a lucky hit on an ammunition pile at the rear of the vessel causing it to go up 'in great flames and continuing detonations'. One crew member, gunner Tesseraud, was killed, five seriously wounded and seven slightly. The master was found slumped in the watch room, weakened by loss of blood, and was helped off the vessel by his mate. The white flag was raised and the crew hastily disembarked in two lifeboats. *Nelly*, from Oran with wine for Rouen, was sunk with blasting cartridges. The master and six men were held hostage aboard the u-boat while Carstensen, an officer and two other sailors searched the ship and then placed six mines. 'The German officer brutally refused permission to go on board to find medication and bandages for the wounded.' It was from this ship that the money coupons from Oran were found later in the wallet of Stoker Christian Carstensen, a member of the boarding party. After two-and-a-half hours the crew was picked up by the Norwegian steamship *Gustav Vigeland* which showed 'generous sympathy'.

The boarding party was away for three-quarters of an hour and brought back sextants, alidades, a compass, chronometer, arms and three bundles of foodstuffs. The German sailors also asked by sign language for a small barrel of some wine. The u-boat men often searched victims for food or showed ingenuity to relieve their diet. Kapitänleutnant Johannes Spieß tells the story of landing on the remote uninhabited Scottish island of North Rona and using its high ground to look for signs of enemy shipping:

> *I looked for a suitable landing place amidst the sheer cliffs and ordered the little rowing boat to be put into the sea and sent the officer of the watch with three crewmen (one of whom was the cook) ashore, armed with guns and orders to do their best. The crew rowed with enthusiasm. They were spotted a little later climbing to the summit. They then looked for birds' eggs, without success, so went off to shoot sheep. Four were shot and hauled down to the launch; only two would fit in so they floated the other two behind. A number of seals and walruses appeared, attracted by the possibility of seizing some of the booty and they weren't frightened off by pistol shots.*[172]

Could North Rona be the only part of the British Isles held by Germany, albeit only for an hour or so, during the Great War?

For the first time, there were some detailed personal descriptions of Gerth and his men provided by the crew of the *Nelly*. Everyone was dirty. The commander was tall, thin, clean-shaven, blond hair, between thirty-five and forty years, and wore a grey-brown suit without insignia and a 'traditional soft hat as German tourists wear, without the feather'. The Mate was smaller, agile despite being rather fat, with a moustache and chestnut hair. He was dressed in a dark blue jacket with gold buttons and wore a badged naval cap. The sailors wore dirty blue canvas clothes and fatigues. One sailor was wearing a well-worn leather jacket. Another had a jacket in brown material and wore long rubber gloves. They had sailor's hats with ribbons with writing on them. On one you could read SMS *Flotille Standerberg* and on another SMS *Hannover*. The sailors were armed with long revolvers whose holster was fixed to a board, itself fastened to a hook attached to their clothing.

Gerth returned to the English coast and immediately made contacts. Just after midnight on 9 May off Start Point he saw two dimly-lit steamers and gave chase for three hours only to be seen and evaded. At six o'clock he fired a torpedo at another steamer, *Broomhill*, and missed.

> *When there were two of us in the conning tower, there was no room to move, yet when making a torpedo attack the presence of the coxswain was required there. It wasn't easy. I had to work at the periscope, climb up and down, circle round and round and always squashed up against the other person.*[173]

Gerth blamed the failure on the torpedo 'lying too long in an armed condition'. However, he let the ship pass by until he was able to fire twelve shots without warning, about half hitting home, and one carrying away the wheel and compass.[174] Two men died, and one crewman was wounded about the left arm and head. During the shooting another steamer, the French *Daphne* or the British *Treverbyn*, fired shots at *UC 61* 'from a great distance without a chance', but the shots may have been intended for *UC 17* which was nearby. The survivors of the eighteen-man crew of the Admiralty charter, *Broomhill*, a 1,700-ton collier bound from Penarth to Sheerness, took to their lifeboat which was then used by the Germans, as usual, to place bombs aboard fore and aft. *UC 61* submerged at the approach of the trawler *Caliph*, which recovered one body and took the men to Weymouth.

The two men who died on the *Broomhill* were brothers: Robert Jones, aged thirty-seven, and James Jones, forty-four. Both were 'sett makers', following their father in Caernarvonshire as cutters of small stones for road making, acknowledged as one of the hardest and poorest jobs in the country. Both were married with children. James was injured and drowned getting to the lifeboat; Robert died of his wounds and was buried at Melcombe Regis near Weymouth; his widow and parents were unable to attend the funeral. Both men are commemorated at the Merchant Marine Tower Hill Memorial in London. The 'third' wounded Jones may be duplication and the result of confused reporting.[175] Today *Broomhill* is lying on a firm seabed of sand and chalk. The wreck is intact, lying on the starboard side, mostly collapsed, with the stern pointing south. It is a regular dive haunt. There is a large hole in the hull consistent with being scuttled: no decking, hull apparently empty, propeller blades missing.[176] Wreck identifier, diver Nick Chipchase, reported being 'absolutely horrified' by an enormous conger eel that 'reared up above them – like a huge sea serpent – with half its body still hidden within the dark confines of the wreck'.

Just before nine o'clock, *UC 61* surfaced about one and a half miles astern of *Minerva*, a 518-ton Norwegian collier in ballast, and opened fire without warning with some twelve shots one to two minutes apart.[177] In the distance, *UC 17* was shooting at another steamer. *Minerva* continued at nine knots towards two loaded, oncoming steamers thinking they might provide cover or diversion. Four shots hit *Minerva*; one struck her boiler with shrapnel causing steam to escape and the ship to stop. Thormod Forland, the Master, was wounded in the left eye with splinters; the whole crew abandoned ship in one of three lifeboats. One officer and two sailors from *UC 61* boarded to suspend three blasting cartridges from the starboard deck to the water's edge; three or four crew were held on the u-boat while this occurred. Five minutes after the Germans regained the u-boat, an explosion occurred. The ship stood up, stern down, and sank after two minutes in the sight of another Norwegian steamship, the *Freikoll*, 1,169 tons, which escaped. *Minerva*'s account book was seized, but all other papers went down with the ship. The crew rowed for four hours to Burton Bradstock. *UC 61* went alongside *UC 17* to 'borrow' thirty grenades and then left above water going south, not following the other steamers.

After a frustrating and fruitless day, *UC 61* was off St Catherine's Point on the early morning of 12 May charging batteries when Gerth sighted several steamers. He dived and moved to attack a trawler. It was the *Maristo*, a Q-ship trap, commander Lieutenant Peter Nicholson.[178] Gerth could not identify the ship, but he quickly recognised the tell-tale radio masts and then saw a cover near the funnel fall away revealing two guns and, at the stern, a slipway for depth charges. Nicholson had seen the conning tower and watched the submarine dive. When Gerth surfaced, his boat was just twenty-five yards from *Maristo* which then moved at full speed to ram and passed over the conning town with inches to spare. Three depth charges followed; Gerth was forced to break water by the first; the second brought a 'considerable amount of oil' to the surface; the third was set to twenty-five metres to finish the job. At thirty metres, *UC 61*'s fuses were partly blown, the bilge pumps were failing and the boat sank to the seabed at thirty-five metres. Fuses were reinserted and *UC 61* crept away. Gerth surfaced almost an hour later in hazy weather. He found that the ventilation valve for the stern oil bunker had opened despite a lock and oil was gushing out. Problem fixed, he moved on to Portland before having to dive before some destroyers.

Nicholson, a 'cool and reliable officer not given to exaggeration', claimed a sinking; the Admiralty thought he was probably right, but only allowed a damaged u-boat.[179] However, Nicholson was awarded the Distinguished

Service Cross and was asked to recommend two of his crew for Distinguished Service Medals: Second Hand Alexander Robertson and Leading Seaman George Bremner. The Commodore at Portland also awarded a £200 bounty to be distributed among the eighteen-man crew. Nicholson got £40:12:6, well over £3,000 a century later, and the two lowliest telegraphists Atholie Atkinson and Eric Hartman £4:18:9 (almost £400 today, nearly a month's wages) each.[180]

> A u-boat captain drew upon his individual character, skills, training, and experience to master the challenges of seamanship, battle tactics, and above all leadership of his men. Every combat patrol tested a commander's abilities daily, whether in the intricacies of manoeuvring to obtain the best firing position, the split-second decisions in eluding a depth-charge attack, or the constant effort to maintain his crew's morale and efficiency. His severest test required him to set the proper example while under attack, cracking a joke or ostentatiously reading a novel as depth charges detonated around them. As one commander recalled, 'If you had the confidence of your crew, you were almost a god.'[181]

The following day was dense fog until the evening when it suddenly cleared. Gerth tried but failed in a torpedo attack on a convoy and received a depth charge for his effort. There were patrols, destroyers and planes all around.

> The lighthouses at Cap Gris Nez and Dungeness, greatly dimmed, shine across at us ... Off Cape d'Alprecht we are forced to dive, confronted by a host of vessels ... at periscope depth we worm our way through various small steamships, tugs, and patrol-vessels. Soon after midnight we can see the surface again: all hands remain at diving stations. At high speed we approach the barrage ... When ten minutes have passed I observe ... a submarine chaser. In less than half a minute, the sea has closed smoothly above us: and yet, too late ... the thunder is tearing the silence to pieces. All around us roar the bombs. In spite of the still considerable range, we experience a most violent concussion in the boat ... We must take our last remaining chance: remain submerged and dive under the whole area of nets and barrage ... which was still ten miles off ... The giant hull of the boat is humming along close above the bottom. Every now and then it hits the bottom with a jerk that throws us from our feet ... Surely it must get deeper soon ... We steer down again, always with the feeling that we must 'duck our heads' as low as possible to get under the nets. This time our impact with the bottom is unpleasantly severe ... At that moment, the starboard side scrapes heavily against some object on the bottom. There is a thunderous hammering as if great blocks of rock were rolling over us. The boat lists over heavily, rights herself,

strikes bottom heavily again ... Either we find deep water within a few
minutes, or else we run into the deadly arms of the nets and mines ...
Again, the boat strikes bottom: 95 feet. The boat is taken back to her old
course. At the last minute, it seems, we have found the gap. Now we are
under the barrage. A loud explosion behind us: the stern gives a heave,
and the starboard propeller starts to turn irregularly. But otherwise all
is still. We stop engines and drift on. We are alone, and through.[182]

Two days later, 15 May, Garth moored *UC 61* at Bruges after brushes with
more aircraft in the Channel. The boat then spent over a month in dry
dock at Ostend.[183] The repairs included the water pump, which had run
hot at sea as the cooling chambers had been half filled with fine sand.
Pistons pins on each engine were examined; the metal shells had broken
and when all mountings were checked all displayed the same condition.

Gerth's penultimate patrol, the one before the stranding of *UC 61* at
Wissant, was disdainfully dismissed by his subsequent interrogator at Calais.

The results of [UC 61's] war on commerce, though not absolutely verified
by us, seem to have been but mediocre; they were approximately as
follows: a couple of sailing vessels, one British two-masted barque and
one or two steamers sunk by gunfire. Two torpedoes were fired, but
missed. There was again damage to the machinery, which, though not
serious, involved a day and night of repairs. One of the compressors,
by the negligence of the engine-room crew, heated for want of water-
cooling. The packing rings and segments of the piston had to be changed
immediately, and the compressor was entirely overhauled on the return
to Bruges.[184]

Of course, that was all true, but Gerth was less forthcoming about a French
armoured cruiser and a British destroyer. The voyage did not start well.
Gerth was scheduled to sail from Bruges on 3 June with *UC 47* and *UC 48*.
The plan was for *UC 61* to lay mines off Brest and then to attack shipping
in the western exit of the English Channel.[185] Gerth left Ostend on 11
June and set off from Bruges the next day. Late evening, he tested the
u-boat's trimming and the hydroplanes jammed so it was back to Bruges
then down the canal to Ostend for repairs. That took another week. On
21 June, he was back in Bruges to load his torpedoes and mines. The next
day, he found the gauge cock of the front starboard bunker had become
detached due to a poor fastening. Gerth finally sailed on 23 June, twenty
days behind schedule and after a total of thirty-eight days' inactivity. After
he had checked his trimming, passed the Channel net barrier and reached
the Colbart light vessel, he was undertaking regular evasion tactics with
three separate destroyers and an airship.

We naturally have to frequent places where patrols are particularly active in guarding steamer routes, and these prowling trawlers, yachts and destroyers make it difficult to get within torpedo range of any steamers. We abandon many a promising target because the patrols make it impossible for us to break surface and our underwater speed is too low to enable us to take position to attack ... They hunt us with hydrophones, which pick up the beat of our engines, and when they think themselves close enough, they drop their depth charges, which have to be taken far more seriously than the 'crackers' we knew in the summer of 1916. We lose an enormous amount of time in consequence before we can think of another attack. The zigzagging of ships has also become compulsory, while the intelligence service and convoy discipline have been perfected to an astounding extent.[186]

The next day, 25 June, was overcast with intermittent rain as Gerth made his way towards Brest. At half past one the next morning he laid his first set of six mines at Chenal du Four off Ouessant and about the same time the following morning two more sets of six off the Pierres Noires Lighthouse on the approaches to Brest. Within an hour, Gerth picked up an uncoded radio message: the French armoured cruiser *Kléber* had run into his mines.[187]

Kléber after service in the Dardanelles had made an uneventful voyage from Dakar to Brest where she was to be placed in a reserve squadron. One of Gerth's mines was seen drifting on the port side. Captain Lagorio ordered battle stations and reduced speed, but at once struck a second mine below the waterline on the starboard side by the rear boiler room. Sub-lieutenant Thoreux, aboard since the start of the war, described events: 'The resulting fire spread to the coal bunker and soon the cruiser was shrouded in smoke whilst water rushed into sections of the cruiser causing her to take on a list.' The vessel plunged at the bow immediately; the forward boiler room flooded together with the coal bunker which separated it from the ammunition bunkers; water rose quickly onto the deck and filled the second boiler room; electric light, pumps, speaking tubes, electrical control of the helm and telephone network were all lost.

As soon as the explosion took place, the captain gave the order to stop and to put out a distress call on the radio. The engines were put into reverse to move the vessel, but there was limited room for manoeuvre because of the first mine. As *Kléber* gradually settled, arriving ships were unable to attach two lines because of the raised stern. The situation rapidly worsened; the vessel suddenly shuddered when all the forward bulkheads gave way. Despite good order, abandoning ship proved difficult as lifeboats were damaged. Life rafts were launched and men slipped into the water; ten men were killed when the wireless antenna fell onto the lifeboats. Fifteen men died in the boiler room and several others in the explosion. In total forty-two men lost their lives.

No State, not even America, thought it against the dictates of humanity to build submarines for war purposes, whose task it should be unexpectedly to attack warships and sink them with all on board. Does it really make any difference, purely from the humane point of view, whether those thousands of men who drown wear naval uniforms or belong to a merchant ship bringing food and munitions to the enemy, thus prolonging the war and augmenting the number of women and children who suffer during the war?[188]

UC 61 had slipped away into the dawn where Gerth met an unnamed u-boat at a pre-arranged meeting point, dodged some destroyers and, because the weather was worsening in the Bay of Biscay, made for the English coast.

... lockers broke away from the bulkheads and lay all over the cramped compartments; the galley gave up all cooking and if anybody was hungry or even had any appetite – most people refrained from eating, as being devoid of purpose – he just ate odd bits of bread, spread with anything that came to hand.[189]

At Start Point, Gerth lined up the Norwegian schooner-rigged steamer *Edith Fische*, but cancelled the torpedo because at 1,132 tons the ship was too small for the expense. Instead he opened fire with six rounds. One shell hit the bow and another the after deckhouse.[190]

We held up the vessel from a distance by means of a warning shot, gave the crew time to leave their ship, and then destroyed her by means of explosive charges, by shell-fire on the water-line; or if we were in a hurry, with a torpedo. But every torpedo fired cost a thousand pounds. And, above all, we only had a limited number of torpedoes on board. So we used them sparingly.[191]

Two men were slightly wounded. Eighteen crew rushed to the boats and two jumped overboard. Gerth failed to see approaching trawlers, which he blamed on a misty periscope and came under fire forcing a dive. Two distant depth charges followed. The men in the water were picked up by the trawler HMT *Lois* and returned to their ship. *Edith Fische*, in ballast, made it safely to Newport after salvage by the tugs *HS 31* and *Herculaneum*.

The weather worsened again with thick fog and Gerth went to the seabed at thirty-eight metres. The next day he saw a big, empty tanker with some trawlers and, from his stern tube, fired a torpedo that malfunctioned. A destroyer and some patrol vessels were evaded and Gerth went to the seabed again at Beachy Head to sit out the fog, surfacing every two hours to check conditions. In the evening of 30 June, he met *UB 40*. The next three days were full of destroyers, patrol vessels and armed trawlers and two further failed torpedo shots and an interrupted gun attack against steamers. On 4 July, Gerth stopped an unescorted Norwegian steamer which he named as *Ran*. It was the *Ole Lea*, 534 tons, christened *Peritia* in 1880, *Ran* in 1907, *Tosca* in 1914, and *Ole Lea* in 1915, having six owners during its life. Her last owners bought the ship about two months before the sinking, intending to rename her *Ull*, but had not done so by the time of her sinking.[192] The master at sea was clear that he was sailing the *Ole Lea*.[193] In any event, *UC 61* approached on the starboard side from the west, steering in the same direction, but faster, while *Ole Lea* continued on course. *Gerth* fired three rounds at 3,000 yards, hitting twice. *Ole Lea* stopped engines and the crew left the ship in two lifeboats and rowed towards land. Some sources say *Ole Lea* was sunk by torpedo, but only Gerth was present and he is specific that he scuttled the vessel with 'blasting cartridges'. The crew were picked up at five in the morning by a British patrol boat on hearing the firing and were taken to Weymouth.

The well-broken-down wreck of *Ole Lea* is lying in a sandy gravel bed; there is no apparent cargo, but an amount of debris particularly on the port side; a four-bladed propeller. The mid-ships engine and boiler, with remains of a funnel on top, plus forward and stern winches, are easily seen.[194] In 1995, a steam whistle was recovered from the wreck so it became known as the 'whistle wreck' among the South Coast diving fraternity.[195]

Later that day, Gerth missed with another torpedo shot against a steamer, the third failed attempt of this patrol.

> *How incredibly difficult it was, after calculations and manoeuvres that might last hours, to carry out a successful attack and get in a position to fire a torpedo at a ship protected by fast, well-handled, heavily armed escorts. And even at that point came the art of accurately firing the costly instrument after only a second's aim, with one eye, through a periscope constantly dipping up and down with the movement of the water and thus cutting off the field of vision. If the periscope, that was used so cautiously and rarely appeared above the surface, or its inevitable trail of foam or the course of a moving torpedo were discovered too soon by the enemy, the chance of success was gone. The enemy, too, was experienced in the arts of defence, in attack, in deceptive manoeuvres, and in steering zigzag courses that were hard to calculate. On all the enemy's surface vessels there were many practised eyes on the look-out for u-boats; they were set upon our destruction, and there were tempting honours and rewards for every success. What with their u-boat chasers, destroyers, aeroplanes, nets, depth-charges, u-boat traps of all kinds, u-boats, and many other devices, they pressed us very hard. There were mishaps on both sides that for many meant the end.*[196]

The next day was spent charging batteries, waiting for targets and diving frequently before patrols. On 6 July, there was at last, for Gerth at least, a change for the better. In the midst of frequent traffic, one of his torpedoes finally hit and sank a steamer. It was the unescorted 2,900-ton armed collier, *Indutiomare*, flying Belgian colours. *UC 61* was not seen and fired from her second bow tube while underwater. The torpedo's wake was spotted by *Indutiomare*'s master and second mate coming from the south on the starboard side about 200 yards off. The ship's helm was put hard-a-starboard. The torpedo hit, three men were killed and the remaining twenty-two crew took to two lifeboats. *Indutiomare* sank within two minutes. *Indutiomare*'s gunners did not have time to fire, nor did they have a target. The survivors were picked up by the French steamer *Thisbe* and were landed at Portsmouth that afternoon by HMS *Seahorse*. *UC 61* stayed submerged for the next five hours and did not find another target that day.

The final victim of *UC 61*'s career came in the morning of 7 July with another torpedo hit, but it was not as Gerth described the action:

> *Beachy Head: Dived before destroyer. Stayed under water in order to wait for steamer. Sighted convoy consisting of a middle-sized passenger steamer and a deeply loaded steamer with four masts, numerous cargo booms/derricks, size at least 6,000 tons, shepherded by four destroyers, two u-boat hunters and some trawlers. Shot out of first tube at steamer. Hit. Boat is rammed by escort. Went to periscope depth. The attacked steamer has sunk. Slightly astern lies a destroyer bow heavy up to the front funnel under water. Mast and bridge are missing. The whole escort goes at high speed around the damaged destroyer. A hit against the destroyer instead of the attacked steamer is out of the question. It had probably been damaged by ramming.*

Gerth got it wrong. Four destroyers, *Landrail, Beaver, Forester* and *Ettrick*, and four patrol boats, *22, 25, 32, 54,* were escorting a convoy (HH4) of five steamers from Hampton Roads in Virginia, USA, at nine knots.[197] The convoy commander on *Landrail* ordered *Ettrick*, which was astern the convoy, to swop places for *Landrail* to chase up a convoy straggler. *Ettrick* increased speed to seventeen knots to effect this. *Landrail* turned to meet her and spotted a torpedo track crossing half a mile in front, breaking surface three seconds later. Just before eight o'clock, the torpedo struck *Ettrick* by the galley behind the fore bridge, cutting the vessel in two. The fore part turned turtle, remained afloat about five minutes, and then sank after an explosion in the magazine killed all forty-nine men in that part of the ship; the ship's company were at breakfast there at that time. HMT *Sheldon* took off the survivors. *P 25* took *Ettrick* in tow by the stern as the six men who remained on board fought to keep the ship afloat, the three ratings who remained on Ettrick until docked were commended for their conduct: Henry Bell, Bertie Sadler and William Beard. HMS *Seahorse* took over the tow while tugs *Sturdy* and *Alert* used salvage pumps. The remains of *Ettrick* were brought safely to the North Railway Harbour at Newhaven at half past seven.

The convoy commander thought *UC 61* fired at the British oiler *Madrono*. *Ettrick*'s lieutenant thought *Ettrick* was 'evidently' the target. The court of enquiry found that Lieutenant Athol Gudgeon, captain of *Ettrick*, who gave evidence at the naval hospital at Gosport because of his injuries, was 'partially to blame' having only two lookouts instead of the required four, but that 'in view of the state of the surface of the sea ... it was unlikely that the torpedo would have been seen in time to avoid it'. No disciplinary action was taken. Gudgeon died of his wounds one month later, aged thirty-two.

Ettrick was not repaired and was hulked until the end of the war when she was sold for scrap.[198] When is a wreck a wreck? *Ettrick* does not appear on any wreck list as the bulk of the ship was towed to dry dock. However, her bows can be dived on – if they are ever found. The Chief of the German Admiralty Staff sent a report of Gerth's sinkings to his Commander-in-Chief. In the margin of the telegram, the Kaiser wrote 'Good'.[199] Gerth moored at Bruges just before midday on 8 July. His next patrol, his last, ended on 26 July on the beach at Wissant.

After 148 days in command, Gerth had spent 48 days, some 32 per cent, operational, the great majority of the remaining two-thirds under repair and much of that in dry dock. Adding the 108 days for training and delivery from Kiel to Bruges since putting formally into service, *UC 61* was operational for 19 per cent of its life. At a build price of around two million Reichsmarks, the boat cost the German people nearly 42,000 Reichsmarks a 'patrol day' to which must be added the expense of a twenty-six-man crew for training, wages and food (with one man injured); u-boat running and repair costs; and munitions and management overheads. It was an expensive war. The return from Gerth from both *UB 12* and *UC 61* was 26,764 tons of shipping with total crews of 862 men, twelve ships sunk including an ageing armoured cruiser, four ships damaged including a ruined destroyer. Amongst the total were three sailing ships, including *Little Mystery*. Disruption was caused by mine alerts and hunting on, perhaps, twelve days, with some ports closed in the south of England for six of these. There was also the considerable overall cost to the British of combating the u-boats, including mines and net barriers, a dedicated and extensive anti-submarine fleet, as well as aircraft and airships, the raids on the Flanders ports, and the human and munitions burden of the Third Battle of Ypres. Gerth and his two u-boats killed 118 men and wounded twenty-one others. Interestingly, in Gerth's u-boat career, he may never have seen a dead body.

ENDNOTES

1   Niemöller, *From u-boat*, p. 18.
2   Herwig, *'Luxury' Fleet*, p. 28.
3   Gröner, *German Warships*, Vol. 1, pp. 91–102.
4   *SMS Amazone* may have been old, but she was long-lived. One of six cruisers permitted to the Reichsmarine after Versailles, she went back to active duty during the 1920s and served again as a barracks ship in the 1950s and was finally broken for scrap in 1954.
5   Gröner, *German Warships*, Vol. 1, pp. 7–8.
6   Chapter 1, 'Brave new world'.
7   One of Georg Gerth's sea cadet classmates in the Crew of 1907 Horst von Pflugk-Harttung was evicted one after the other from Sweden, Norway and Denmark for organising and arming pro-Nazi factions in the early 1930s. Chapter 14, 'Welcome home, Erich'.
8   Chapter 3, 'Planning a famine'.
9   Submarines *E 1*, *E 9* and *E 11* (McCartney, *British Submarines*), pp. 20–28.
10 Wilson, *Baltic Assignment*, pp. 30–31.
11 Wilson, *Baltic Assignment*, p. 38. Von Berckheim was killed with all of his crew when *U 26* hit a mine off Hanko in the Gulf of Finland the following August. Its wreck has been found by Finnish divers (uboat.net; press release 2/6/2014, Helsinki: hbadewanne.fi).
12 uboat.net.
13 Gröner, *German Warships*, Vol. 1, pp. 102–4, 106–7.
14 *TNA*, FO/371/2679, p. 20.
15 Curriculum vitae, Dissertation, University of Würzburg, 5/1923. For background on the British submarine fleet in the Baltic, a main preoccupation of German Coastal Command (Wilson, *Baltic Assignment*), Chapters 4, '1914: The First Campaign' and 5, '1915: The Opening Moves', pp. 40–77.
16 Interview by the author with Georg Gerth's daughter, Christa-Maria Gerth, at her home in Germany, 16/11/2016.
17 Kelly, *Tirpitz*, p. 38. *Blitz* was one of two steel-hulled ships, the first of any kind in the German Navy, built in the 1880s, and which led to the later *Gazelle* light cruisers.
18 Asprey, *German High Command*, p. 141.
19 Large, *Berlin*, pp. 52–53.
20 'Stricken E13 Shelled', *The Times*, 23/8/1915, p. 6.
21 'The Situation in Russia', *The Times*, 23/8/1915, p. 7.
22 Chapter 5, 'The 'very nearly' battle'.
23 Hezlet, *Submarine and Sea Power*, p. 35.
24 Gray, *British Submarines*, p. 84.
25 McCartney, *British Submarines*, p. 23.
26 Herwig, *Naval Officer Corps*, p. 194.
27 Mulligan, *Sharks Not Wolves*, pp. 33–34.
28 Herwig, *Naval Officer Corps*, p. 180.
29 Bouton, *Abdicates*, pp. 89–90. Gibson, *Submarine War*, pp. 182–83.
30 Horn, *War, Munity and Revolution*, p. 75, cited in Mulligan, *Sharks Not Wolves*, p. 34.
31 Herwig, *Naval Officer Corps*, p. 251. The heavy losses among army aviators had brought about a similar state of affairs at the same time in the army. Volunteers for the fighting planes ceased offering themselves and forced service became necessary.
32 Herwig, *Dynamics*, p. 99. 'This "war of lieutenants" troubled senior officers as submarines required few flag-rank officers. [In February 1917,] when Germany decided to risk all on the u-boat gamble, Admiral Eduard von Capelle, Tirpitz's successor at the navy office, warned that emphasis on submarine building would endanger the long-term capital-ship program and called for the creation of a special "submarine cemetery" after the war.'
33 Strachan, *First World War*, p. 197.
34 Herwig, *Luxury Fleet*, p. 224. 'Personnel considerations weighed heavily in the controversy between the competing schools of thought … u-boats and cruisers do not require admirals. Rear-Admiral Karl Hollweg: 'You must take into consideration how organisation and promotion will function in a navy which has replaced its capital ships

with dirigibles and submarines. This is a problem which has not been solved yet.'

35   Bouton, *Abdicates*, pp. 89–90.
36   For details of commander u-boat training, Chapter 4, 'Erich's war'.
37   *TNA*, ADM 137/4161, 'German Submarine Officers'.
38   Thomas, *Raiders*, pp. 226–27.
39   Gröner, *German Warships*, pp. 22–23.
40   Gayer, *Submarine Warfare*, p. 5.
41   Termote, *Krieg unter Wasser*, p. 36.
42   Terraine, *Business in Great Waters*, p. 20.
43   Termote, *Krieg unter Wasser*, p. 88.
44   Padfield, *Dönitz*, p. 83.
45   Gibson and Prendergast, *German Submarine War*, p. 38. Heimburg was awarded the 'Pour le Mérite' in 1917 having sunk 62,000 tons of enemy shipping, including the British submarine *E 20* and the British troop transport HMS *Royal Edward* in the Mediterranean. At the end of World War II, Soviet forces abducted him, then a fifty-five-year-old retired naval officer, and transported him to a POW camp near Stalingrad where he died in late 1945 (uboat.net).
46   Thomas, *Raiders*, pp. 133–34.
47   *BA-MA*, RM 120/40 U-Boote, Vol. 2: Marinekorps report 12/1916, dated 18/1/1917, to the chief of the admiralty staff. Suggestions made by the Siemens company for this conversion of the oldest ub-boats (UB 1–17) were twice turned down the previous summer ('Inspection of u-boat fleet', 24711, Kiel, 5/8/1916). *TNA*, ADM 137/3899, p. 22. Gröner, *German Warships*, p. 23. Compton-Hall, *Submarines at War*, p. 85.
48   Chatterton, *Q-ships*, p. 52.
49   www.uboot-recherche.de from where scans of the KTBs of individual u-boats for given periods may be bought as cds. See also for *UB 12*, Spindler, *Krieg zur See*, pp. 6, 82, 121, 232.
50   uboat.net.
51   Niemöller, *From u-boat*, p. 19.
52   After receiving cannon fire which wrecked her engine room, *Lady Olive* was ordered 'abandon ship' by *UC 18*. Seaman William Dumaresq sighted the u-boat directly in line with his gun and chanced eight shots which hit the hull. *UC 18* sank with all hands. *Lady Olive* sank later, but its crew in three boats and two rafts were stalked by a second u-boat. The French destroyer *Dunois* rescued her crew the following afternoon after a cat and mouse game and ramming of the second u-boat 'the port propeller guard crashing against the boat so that it ripped out the latter's starboard side'. Dumaresq was awarded the DSM (Chatterton, *Q-Ships*), pp. 104–8. This last claim is rejected by the log of the *Dunois* which mentions only sighting a conning tower and firing at it while continuing to pick up crew (www.memoiredeshommes.sga.defense.gouv.fr), p. 746.
53   U-boat diver Jan Lettens assumes a mining and reports several probable contacts from 1976, most recently on 15/12/2009 at 51°20, 099'N, 01°29, 978'E, using a Trisponder Positioning System: a small object has been located protruding from the edge of a sandbank at a depth between 5.5 and 9.5 metres (wrecksite.eu, accessed 11/3/2017). *Royal Navy Submarines Museum (National Museum of the Royal Navy), Gosport*, 'u-boat Activities and Losses', Vol. 1, p. 153.
54   Gayer, *Submarine Warfare*, p. 21.
55   Hezlet, *Submarine and Sea Power*, p. 25.
56   Fürbringer, *Legendary*, p. 14.
57   Niemöller, *From u-boat*, p. 126.
58   uboat.net. wrecksite.eu. skipet.no. Spindler, *Krieg sur Zee*, Band 3, p. 231.
59   *TNA*, CO 323/801/4. uboat.net. Spindler, *Krieg sur Zee*, Band 3, p. 232.
60   Lettens, www.wrecksite.eu, accessed 12/3/2017.
61   Scheer, *High Seas Fleet*, pp. 224–31. Tarrant, *U-Boat Offensive*, pp. 32–33. Gayer, *Submarine Warfare*, pp. 19–23.
62   Herwig, *Dynamics*, p. 98.
63   Hezlet, *Submarine and Sea Power*, pp. 72–73.

64 Scheer, *High Sea Fleet*, p. 232.
65 *London Gazette*, 5/12/1916.
66 Chapter 2, 'Kaisertreu'.
67 Blond, *Marne*, p. 39.
68 *Hansard*, House of Commons, Vol. L, 1913, c1776–7.
69 Hall, *Law of Naval Warfare*, 1921, p. 55.
70 Among the claimed sources: Churchill, *World Crisis*, pp. 283, 724–5; Coles, *Slaughter at Sea*, p. 114; Griffiths, *World without Cancer*, p. 249; *Richmond Diaries*, 27/2/1915; Simpson, *Lusitania*, p. 36.
71 Simpson, *Lusitania*, p. 36. Richmond Diaries, 27/2/1915.
72 Hersing was known amongst his colleagues as the 'Zerstörer der Schlachtschiffe' – destroyer of battleships: HMS *Pathfinder*, light cruiser, torpedoed off the east coast of Scotland, 1914; HMS *Triumph* and HMS *Majestic*, both battleships, Gallipoli, 1915; *Carthage*, French auxiliary cruiser, Turkey, 1915; *Amiral Charner*, French cruiser, Syria.
73 Hurd, *Merchant Navy*, Appendix A, pp. 436–40. TNA, 'War Instructions for British Merchant Ships', *Admiralty War Staff*, 1/6/1916, ADM 137/2832. TNA, FO 383/494, p. 613.
74 Jamieson, 'Martyr or Pirate?', *The Mariner's Mirror*, p. 198.
75 TNA, FO 383/195, Captain Fryatt's report, 28/3/1915. Hurd, *Merchant Navy*, pp. 308–10.
76 Hurd, *Merchant Navy*, pp. 334–35.
77 Haws, *Merchant Fleets*, pp. 29, 49–50.
78 *New York Times*, 29/7/1916, pp. 1–2.
79 Winton, Convoy, p. 38. Coles, *Slaughter at Sea*, p. 149. Cawley and Woodward, 'Charles Fryatt', BBC, 16/7/2016.
80 TNA, FO 383/521, pp. 78–80.
81 Thomas, *Raiders*, pp. 226–27.
82 Termote, *Krieg unter Wasser*, pp. 173–74.
83 Chapter 2.
84 *Hansard*, House of Commons, Vol. LXXXIV (1916), Col. 2080–1.
85 Jamieson, 'Martyr or Pirate?', *The Mariner's Mirror*, p. 200.
86 TNA, FO 383/497, pp. 554–615. A German commission, the Schüking Commission, confirmed Fryatt's sentence on 2/4/1919 as not in violation of International law, but apologised 'most vividly for the hurry in which the judgement was enforced'. Two panel members dissented as they saw Fryatt's sentence as a 'severe infringement' ('Regulation of the Council of People's Deputies on the composition and proceedings of the Commission investigating the charges of violation of international law in the treatment of prisoners of war in Germany', 30/11/1918, *Reichsgesetzblatt*), p. 1388. *Deutsche Allgemeine Zeitung*, 3/5/1919.
87 *Brussels* was used as a depot ship at Zeebrugge by the torpedo arm of the Flanders Marine. On 23/4/1918, she was damaged in the Zeebrugge raid and on 5/10/1918 sunk by the Germans as a blockship at the head of the mole. In 1919, she was raised and taken back to the River Tyne in England. She ended her days running a twice-weekly service for 600 live cattle between Preston and Dublin (Haws, *Merchant Fleets*), p. 50.
88 TNA, FO 383/497, p. 592.
89 Fürbringer, *Legendary*, pp. 69–70.
90 Hashagen, *Commander*, p. 86.
91 Hashagen, *Commander*, pp. 125–27.
92 Fürbringer, *Legendary*, p. 14.
93 TNA, ADM 137/3898, p. 93; ADM 137/3884, p. 55.
94 Gayer, *Submarine Warfare*, p. 5.
95 Fürbringer, *Legendary*, p. 18.
96 *Shipping*, No. 144, 2/2002, p. 17. The Great Easter Railway ran train services to from London to Harwich from 1854 and obtained powers in 1862 to connect to their own steamships to Rotterdam and Antwerp.
97 TNA, ADM 137/247.
98 Manning, *British Destroyer*, pp. 66, 69, 70, 74, 127–28.

99   Listed as 'probable': *Diver*, 8/2010. wrecksite.eu/wreck.aspx?75582.

100 Fürbringer, *Legendary*, pp. 94–95.

101 Spindler, *Der Krieg zur See*, Band 4, p. 142. Bendler, *Der UC-Boote*, p. 159. *TNA*, BT 110/279, Ship's Register.

102 *BA-MA*, RM 2/1994, p. 252: Telegram from Admiralty Staff to the Kaiser, 7/3/1917. The Kaiser did read the reports for that of the following month which had 'Bravo' noted in the royal hand in the margin.

103 Five names are recorded on the Merchant Navy memorial at Tower Hill in London: Arthur J Atkins, fireman, drowned; Harry Barney, engine donkeyman, drowned; Charles Brundle, fireman, drowned; William Chaplin, fireman, drowned; and Arthur Hammond, fireman, killed. Leonard Rand, fireman, is commemorated at Harwich Cemetery, likely being the only body recovered by one of the destroyers and taken back to their home base (benjidog.co.uk, ancestry.co.uk, accessed 11/2016).

104 Massie, *Castles*, p. 140. Vincent, *Politics of Hunger*, pp. 39–40.

105 Koerver, *German Submarine Warfare*, p. 134.

106 *TNA*, ADM 137/390, sighting 1400, repeat alert to Admiralty 1922.

107 Sims, *Victory at Sea*, pp. 153–54. Massie, *Castles*, p. 737.

108 *TNA*, ADM 137/3898, p. 93. *Gosport*, Admiralty report, 'U-Boats: Activities and Losses', Vol. 1, p. 247.

109 Friedman, *German Warships*, p. 79.

110 *TNA* ADM 137/3886, 'Appliances for stopping leaks'.

111 Bendert, *Die UC-Boote*, p. 159. Spindler, *Der Krieg zur See*, p. 142.

112 Cuxhaven, Georg Gerth, Obituary, MOV 11/1970.

113 All three of these u-boats were wrecked before the year end. *UC 65* was torpedoed by British submarine *C 15* fifteen miles south of Beachy Head on 3/11/1917. The first torpedo hit amidships, but did not explode; the second blew off the stern, sinking her instantly; twenty-two dead, four survivors; career sinkings: 105 ships. *UC 69* was rammed accidently by *U 96* off Cape Barfleur, sinking immediately by the stern; 'its net cutter fouled *U 96*'s bow, for a short time the two boats were locked together. That turned out to be a blessing, because most of *UC 69*'s crew made their way aboard *U 96* by going over the bows. Finally, the bows separated. When *UC 69*'s stern hit the seabed, the after torpedo exploded, killing ten men who were in the water' (Messimer, *Verschollen*), pp. 304, 307.

114 *TNA* ADM 137/3886, 'Report from *UC 61*', 15/5/1917, E.I. No. 146.

115 Koerver, *German Submarine Warfare*, p. 116.

116 McCartney, *Maritime Archaeology*, p. 308.

117 Herwig, *Luxury Fleet*, p. 219.

118 Certificates of Competency, 023292, Fowey: Mate, 18/12/1890, Master 12/4/1894 (*National Maritime Museum*, Master's Certificates). Ancestry.

119 *TNA*, ADM 137/1295, 4/1917.

120 Carter, *Royal Navy at Portland*, p. 39.

121 Strachan, *First World War*, p. 59.

122 Translated letter from the French Embassy, London, 20/2/1917 (*TNA*, ADM 137/1392, French Coal Trade, Jan-Apr 1972), p. 249. The importance of the French coal trade to the Allied war effort is shown by two volumes of letters and orders, each containing some 600 pages. David Lloyd George was the Liberal prime minister of the British wartime coalition government.

123 Aristide Briand, French prime minister over eleven terms. He resigned within a month following the letter over disagreements on his conduct of the war. He received the Nobel Peace Prize in 1926 for his work on territorial peace treaties between the Allies and Germany. This 'coal delegation' was led by René Viviani, French prime minister for the first year of the war.

124 Carter, *Portland*, p. 39.

125 Correlating times from British ships' logs, foreign ships in British waters, u-boat logs, and times ashore is problematic during World War I. Three British naval ships meeting a u-boat mid-Channel, and researched for contact with *UC 61*, recorded times in GMT,

BST and German summer time, but they were not consistent. See discussion 'U-boat time in 1917', *WW1 Forum*, uboat.net.

126   The story of the sinking is taken from *TNA*, ADM 137/1295, /2961 & /4120; uboat. net and pastscape.org.uk, both accessed 17/5/2016; and Larn, *Shipwreck Index*, Vol. 1, Section 6.

127   At Jutland on 28/5/1917, *Derfflinger* was partially responsible for the sinking of two British battlecruisers: with *Seydlitz* she destroyed *Queen Mary* and, with the *Lützow*, sank *Invincible* (Massie, *Castles*), pp. 588–92.

128   Engine-room Artificer Karl Wiedemann, 'My First U-Boat Voyage', Neureuther, *U-Boat Stories*, p. 59.

129   *TNA*, ADM 137/1295, p. 114.

130   War artist Claus Bergen, 'My U-Boat Voyage', Neureuther, *U-Boat Stories*, p. 51.

131   Ward-Jackson, *Stephens of Fowey*, p. 53.

132   *TNA*, ADM 137/675, Weekly Report of Portland Auxiliary Vessels. *Monographs*, Vol. XVIII, fn. p. 448. *Royalo* was mined and sunk off Penzance 1/9/1940 (uboat.net).

133   Bergen, 'My U-Boat Voyage', Neureuther, *U-Boat Stories*, pp. 41–44.

134   'William Date, Shipwrights Yard and the Fruit Schooners', *Knightsbridge Estuary U3A Local History Group*, 16/10/2103.

135   Ward-Jackson, *Stephens of Fowey*, p. 5.

136   *TNA*, BT 110/349/50, *Little Mystery*, Ship's Register (official number 85828). Greenhill, *Merchant Schooners*, Vol. 2, p. 109, and see pp. 111–15, 120–29.

137   Greenhill, 'The Rise and Fall of the British Coastal Steamer', *Mariner's Mirror*, Vol. 27, Issue 3, 1941, p. 250.

138   Ward-Jackson, *Stephens of Fowey*, p. 5, offers the comparison of the *Cutty Sark* (1869) at 863 gross tons – over six times the size of a *Little*; the full-rigged *Preußen* (1902) at 5,548 tons; and the largest sailing vessel, *France II* (1911), at 5,806 tons (a multiple of almost forty-five).

139   Ward-Jackson, *Stephens of Fowey*, particularly pp. 21, 34, 37–38, 76, 84.

140   *Little Wonder* was lost in mid-Atlantic on 24/9/1891. She was on her way from Newfoundland with codfish when in a gale the cargo shifted. The masts had to be cut away and the mate was drowned, though the rest of the crew, lashed to the stumps of the masts, were saved by a passing steamer. Twenty-six people from around Fowey had shares in her (Ward-Jackson, *Stephens of Fowey*), p. 37.

141   84.5 feet x 21.1 x 10.8 (*TNA*, BT 110/349/50).

142   *TNA*, BT 110/349/50.

143   The phrase about 'small fry' is from Lubbock, *Last of the Windjammers*, Vol. 1, pp. 455, 460. In John Stephens' day, 100,000 fishermen were employed in the Newfoundland trade. 'Making fish, involved hand-cleaning, extracting the liver to rot down into cod liver oil, washing, salting and placing in kegs to pickle in a shore-side shed, then spreading out on racks to dry in the sun, and finally weighing in quintals or 112-pound lots (Ward-Jackson, *Stephens of Fowey*), p. 36.

144   The two maintenance yards were Benjamin Tregaskis at Par and at Cleave Houses, on the north bank of the Torridge between Bideford and Appledore.

145   Greenhill, *Merchant Schooners*, pp. 110–11.

146   Fletcher, *In the Days of the Tall Ships*, pp. 32–33.

147   Greenhill, *Merchant Schooners*, pp. 113–14.

148   wrecksite.eu.

149   'The destruction of wooden wreck sites is especially worrying because after the effects of currents and trawling they typically display little relief above the sea bottom' (Bennett, wrecksite.eu forum_15/06/2016). See also Kingsley, 'Deep-Sea Fishing Impacts on the Shipwrecks of the English Channel & Western Approaches'.

150   *TNA*, BT 351/1/54397, both issued 29/4/1921.The *Mercantile Marine War Medal* was instituted by the Board of Trade to reward the war service of the officers and men of the Mercantile Marine who, while only trained as peacetime mariners, continued to serve while running the risk of being attacked at sea during the war. The *British War Medal* was a campaign medal of the United Kingdom which was awarded to officers and men

of British and Imperial forces for service in the First World War (en.wikipedia.org), accessed 27/5/2016.

151   *National Maritime Museum*, SLR1179 (accessed 27/5/2016). The model, dimensions: 860 x 1,174 x 432 mm, was presented to the museum by the builder Max T Davey of Hove, Sussex, in 1969. Other Davey models and prints at *NMM*: two different versions of the mackerel driver *Ebenezer*, 1867, and the sailing brig *Marie Sophie*, 1879 (prints. rmg.co.uk/artist/28383/Max-T-Davey), accessed 27/5/2016; and in the *National Trust Collection*, on loan from *Cotehele Museum*, Cornwall, the *Rhoda Mary* (NT 812819). Davey was a prolific craftsman producing work to a high standard and was known for his style of finishing a model in a more realistic fashion as opposed to the more clinical exhibition style for museum displays. Davey 'also produced accurate and detailed models that could be sailed using radio controlled equipment which was quite rare' (Stephens, Curator of the Ship Model and Boat Collections, NMM, email, 17/6/2016).

152   Database: Lowrey, WW1 forum, uboat.net, 18/5/2016; calculations, the author, 20/5/2016.

153   Greenhill, 'Rise and Fall', p. 256.

154   *Milford Trawlers*, 'Arfon M223', llangibby.eclipse.co.uk, accessed 18/5/2016.

155   *TNA*, ADM 137/3255, 'Court of Enquiry'.

156   Monographs, p. 448; *TNA* ADM 137/1295; ADM 137/442; ADM 137/1296.

157   'Le Havre' was consistently called 'Havre' in Admiralty documents (*TNA*, ADM 137/1295). *Gorizia* was built in 1907 by A Macmillan & Son of Dumbarton, Scotland, as *Glenmount* for the Montreal Transportation Company, Canada, perhaps later SS *Great Lakes*, passing to her last name at the Oriental Navigation Corporation, New York, and, later, Montevideo, shortly before sinking. Sonar contact was established in 1945. In 1988, divers reported the bows blown off (Davies, 24/8/1988, 19/7/1989). Examined by Differential Global Positioning System (DPGS) on 8/5/2003, upright, but partly buried at a depth of forty-two metres at 50° 36'N, 2° 55'W, seventeen miles from Portland Bill (Lettens 27/8/2008; Allen 7/9/2011, wrecksite.eu, accessed 27/5/2016.

158   Bergen, 'U-Boat Voyage', Neureuther, *U-Boat Stories*, p. 50.

159   The Uruguayan *Chargé d'Affaires* quickly took up the sinking of one of its registered ships, looking 'urgently' for further information, but they met the Admiralty 'playing a straight bat' (*TNA*, ADM 137/1295).

160   The Commodore-in-Charge at Portland had forty larger vessels at his disposal for convoy escort, minesweeping and anti-submarine activity, as well as over a dozen motor launches (*TNA*, ADM 137/675).

161   *TNA*, ADM 137/442.

162   One unconfirmed diver report says that *Gorizia* was on charter to the French Government, making her a legitimate target. In 1989, divers reported that most of her cargo of brass had been recovered (wrecksite.eu).

163   Mulligan, *Neither Sharks*, p. 40.

164   *TNA*, ADM 137/4120.

165   Hashagen, *Commander*, p. 242.

166   *TNA*, ADM 137/3988.

167   The two wounded men were Maurice Thymrut and Jean Pierre Salaun. A second Jean Guilcher, possibly a son, was unhurt.

168   *TNA*, ADM 137/3988.

169   uboat.net.

170   *TNA*, ADM 137/3988.

171   *TNA* ADM 239/26.

172   Spieß, *Six Ans de Croisières*, pp. 220–3, *U 19*, 13/4/1918. Wikipedia repeats the story, but for Kapitänleutnant Walter Remy, *U 90*, who claimed to stop at the island during each of his patrols.

173   Chatterton, *Q-ships*, p. 8.

174   *TNA*: ADM 137/1296; ADM 137/2692; ADM 137/4114.

175   *CWGC*, Tower Hill Merchant Navy cemetery. *North Wales Chronicle*, 1/6/1917, courtesy of Wendy Williams.

176 wrecksite.eu.
177 *TNA*: ADM 137/1296; ADM 137/4114.
178 *TNA*: ADM 53/48473; ADM 239/26; ADM 137/1296.
179 *TNA*, ADM 137/1296.
180 McCartney, 'Paying the Prize', *Mariner's Mirror*, 2/2018, pp. 42–43, explains that to keep details of the anti-u-boat war secret the Admiralty suspended all prize payments until after the war.
181 Mulligan, *Sharks Not Wolves*, p. 2.
182 Hashagen, *Commander*, pp. 193–95. Hashagen's account is much abbreviated and occurred after *UC 61*'s stranding. The barrage Hashagen ran from Cap Griz Nez across to Folkestone was not installed until late in 1917. However, the strain and the terror brings to life the few casual lines in Gerth's log.
183 *BA-MA*, RM 3/11186, pp. 21–23.
184 *TNA*, ADM 137/3898, p. 94.
185 Spindler, *Krieg zur See*, Band 4, p. 320. Bendert, *Die UC-Boote*, p. 159.
186 Niemöller, *From u-boat*, pp. 66–67.
187 *Le Petit Journal*, 30/6/1918. uboat.net. forum-auto.com. Un *Livre d'or de la Marine Française, Guerre 1914–1918*; 14-18-marine-livredor.wifeo.com/kleber-croiseur-cuirasse. ph, accessed 1/2/2017.
188 Scheer, *High Sea Fleet*, p. 268.
189 Niemöller, *From u-boat*, p. 25.
190 *TNA*, ADM 137/1341. uboat.net.
191 Hashagen, *Commander*, p. 65.
192 skipet.no/skip/skipsforlis; miramarshipindex.org.nz.
193 *TNA*, ADM 137/1341. uboat.net.
194 wrecksite.eu.
195 Hinchcliffe, *Dive Dorset*, p. 54.
196 Bergen, 'U-Boat Voyage', Neureuther, *U-Boat Stories*, pp. 18–19.
197 *TNA*: ADM 137/3283; ADM 340/60.
198 27/5/1919 to James Dredging Company.
199 *BA-MA*, RM 2/1996, p. 27. 'As late as 1918, Wilhelm still read the war diaries of his submarine commanders and marked each one with his famous marginal notes' (Herwig, *Naval Officer Corps*), p. 28.

CHAPTER 7

Keeping Britain Fed

During the centuries of almost incessant warfare, which came to an end with the defeat of Napoleon, the application of these principles to the defence of merchant shipping had resulted in the unquestioned adoption in time of war of the convoy system. The gathering together of the season's shipping engaged in any particular trade and sailing it in an organised fleet with a naval escort enabled the maximum protection to be afforded. At the same time, it enabled the available naval force to be concentrated where the enemy was bound to come if he wished to do you hurt. So obvious was this to the seamen of Nelson's day that any other system would have been unthinkable to them.[1]

There were many reasons why the great German u-boat gamble was failing. The unsung policy hero was the introduction of controlled 'rationing in the UK by the spring of 1917 driven from the top by Prime Minister Lloyd George. The number of sinkings by u-boats in a time of sustained drought finally forced government to action after the *laissez-faire* approach of the first years of the war. Lord Rhondda led Britain's second attempt at food control with the establishment of a Ministry of Food providing the most important barrier to possible starvation. That year almost a million extra acres of land were worked. 'The vast and demanding system of rationing that Rhondda had established for the British Isles was accepted by the ordinary independent populace because it succeeded in providing fair shares for everyone.'[2] The enterprise was more close run than was admitted except in the most private governmental discussions. For example, that April, British sugar supplies were down to four days. Even as late as February 1918, police in London counted up to 550,000 people standing in food queues.

The prosecution of the war became more arduous for the u-boats. British anti-submarine measures improved by leaps and bounds. However, there were historic divides in British Admiralty thinking which largely mirrored the strategic problems of their German counterparts.[3] Some admirals, followers of Tirpitz, were fixated on the great battle with the German High Seas Fleet which, apart from Coronel and Falklands in the South Atlantic in the early days of the war, and the much-discussed British tactical loss but strategic victory at Jutland, never happened. Captain Herbert Richmond, later Admiral, described as 'perhaps the most brilliant naval officer of this generation', was marginalised in 1913 by Churchill and Jellicoe for his ready criticisms about the navy's lack of strategic rigour.[4] Richmond reminded those around him 'to look at the war as a whole; to avoid keeping our eyes only on the German fleet. What we have to do is to starve and cripple Germany'.[5]

There was a long-term antipathy to the submarine as a defensive or offensive weapon. This led directly to a failure to anticipate or to prepare for the u-boat threat against British food supplies. In some quarters, the championing of protection of the merchant ships was not pursued with vigour. As well as being poorly anticipated, strategic change to protect the primacy of food supply was also slow in coming.[6] Historian Paul Kennedy found little evidence that the quality of the Royal Navy's personnel was 'other than good' with the regularly identified weakness of the 'unimaginative and sometimes simple-minded nature of a disturbingly large array of the senior naval officers in the first two years of the war'. It was not until the 1890s, when the admirals of the Great War 'saw reefing sails in a gale as the ultimate test of manhood, [that] a consensus had at last emerged that warships would shed their sails'.[7] A generation had passed since the last great naval battle with the Austrian wooden ships' victory over the Italian's ironclads at Lissa, off present-day Croatia, in 1866. There was a shocking resistance to trial by the British admirals, let alone introduce a convoy system. This single failure, portrayed as a great success when it finally occurred, almost cost Britain the war. It was the more awful because historic lessons were lost, warnings in, for instance, Mahan's *Influence of Sea Power* ignored, and the same mistake was repeated in World War II. 'What mattered was that merchant ships survive and deliver their cargoes. If they could do that – because the u-boats had been avoided or forced to keep out of the way – it did not matter how many u-boats were sent to the bottom.'[8] This position was reinforced by post-war studies that showed that even though the number of submarines increased later in the conflict the rate of sinking per u-boat declined rapidly after convoy was introduced.[9]

There were many warnings about Britain's vulnerability to economic pressure.[10] The most prescient came in a six-volume work by Jean de Bloch, published in Paris in 1898: *La Guerre Future; aux points du vie technique, economique et politique.*[11] Bloch was an entrepreneur 'almost on the scale of the Rothschilds' and by dint of a varied career had an 'unusual grasp of military logistics'.[12] Historian Avner Offer described the foresight of his work as astonishing.[13] Bloch asked what would be the eventual result of the machine gun and artillery:

At first there will be increased slaughter – increased slaughter on so terrible a scale as to render it impossible to push the battle to a decisive issue ... Then, instead of a war fought out to the bitter end in a series of decisive battles, we shall have to substitute a long period of continually increasing strain upon the resources of the combatants [involving] entire dislocation of all industry and severing of all the sources of supply by which alone the community is enabled to beat the crushing burden ... That is the future of war – not fighting, but famine, not the slaying of men but the bankruptcy of nations and the break-up of the whole social organisation ... The civil population will be, more than anything else, the deciding factor in modern war ... Your soldiers may fight as you please; the ultimate decision is in the hands of famine [which] would strike first at those proletarian elements which, in advanced societies, were most prone to revolution.[14]

In 1900, soldier and politician, Stewart Lygon Murray, began a 'self-imposed mission to alert the country to the dangers of famine in wartime'.[15] In that year, three-quarters of the British population lived in urban districts and were dependent for supplies on retail shops.[16] There was a continuing decline in the number of acres under crops, from twenty-four million in 1872 to under twenty million by 1913. This was worsened by a shift away from grain, especially wheat, and a move to pasture. Much of the resulting imported grain travelled long distances and 'placed a tremendous burden on the nation's shipping'. Murray insisted that a Ministry of Food was needed to prepare a system of rationing for the coming war and, in 1902, he retired from the army in order to run the campaign full-time. After careful preparation, it began in February 1903 with a burst of orchestrated activity that produced a positive result in the space of five weeks. Prime Minister Balfour reluctantly granted a royal commission:

For, if our Empire fall through neglect of proper defence, with it will fall our trade (because, if our rivals are victorious, they will certainly close all the great markets against us) and with our trade will go our wages and our food. And what would then be left to the British working man?[17]

The Royal Commission on Food Supply began its hearings in May; a minority remained unconvinced, but the majority accepted that warships used to protect the food supply could provide a defence from economic disaster and class warfare. By 1914, almost 60 per cent of the food consumed in Britain was imported from overseas, about two-thirds by crude weight and more than half by value.[18] British merchant ships carried 90 per cent of the country's imported food; only 10 per cent sailed in neutral vessels. Therefore, 90 per cent of Britain's food was subject to capture regardless of its status.[19] The upper and middle classes had the choice of home-produced meat and dairy goods and consumed much more animal-derived food than their relative share of the population. The working classes depended more on cereals. They purchased inferior grades of meat, cheese and butter, and took a lot of sugar in their tea and jam, so working-class reliance on sea-borne food was higher even than indicated by the high market share of imports. It was realised that prices would rise sharply at the outset of war 'causing hardships to the poorer sector of the community, particularly unskilled labourers'.[20]

Labour representatives told of 'possible distress and misery, and semi-starvation amongst the working classes'. The Commission was warned of city riots if bread prices rose substantially. Admiral Jackie Fisher warned early on that during May England had three days' food in the country; in September, just enough for three weeks. 'Stop the incoming food for a week or two: what can the Army do?'[21]

Author Arthur Conan Doyle tried another tack. He was frustrated that the government ignored his warnings about the vulnerability of Britain's food supplies to a sustained attack by a small fleet of submarines. He called for work to go ahead on a Channel tunnel. In a short story, *Danger!*, written about eighteen months before the outbreak of war and remarkable for its accurate and detailed predictions, Captain John Sirius, a u-boat commander with eight submarines in the navy of 'one of the smallest powers in Europe' brings England to its knees within weeks.[22] Doyle relayed in his preface how he adopted every possible method to put his views forward to politicians and to the Committee for National Defence, all to no avail. The British may have ignored Doyle, but his views gave some succour to the Germans. Kapitänleutnant Albert Gayer, commander of 3rd Submarine Flotilla, and the Wilhelmshaven captains, saw that in spite of all the u-boats' efforts, 'in spite of all the miles covered, despite the progress achieved in equipment, the success of our submarines since the start of the war up until October 1914 had been very little and that a better result would be achieved by combined actions against the enemy merchant fleet rather than isolated pursuits of warships'.

This idea is not new because Conan Doyle had shown in his war stories how a small enemy state could bring England to its knees by attacking merchant shipping with several submarines. Without doubt Conan Doyle had his reasons for having shown how easy this action would be; for many people in Germany the optimism to which it had given birth however left several submarine officers dreaming.[23]

There had been a real knucklehead tussle in the British admiralty over the development of submarines. If the British admirals could not get their heads around the importance of submarines to themselves, there was little chance of a successful defence being prepared against submarine fleets owned by other nations. Apart from the dominance of its fleet, the Royal Navy was well endowed with industrial assets required to produce naval armaments, and 'could draw upon all the resources of the largest and wealthiest maritime empire in the world'. The Royal Navy either owned or had access to an unrivalled network of naval bases at strategic locations around the globe. British companies dominated the world's mercantile marine, controlled most of the wireless and cable communication networks, and, perhaps most importantly, possessed an effective monopoly on the supply of steam coal outside European waters and the east coast of the United States. Without access to coal and colliers, fleets simply could not move.[24]

In 1900, the French parliament voted £4,750,000 for new flotilla craft – nearly 150 torpedo-boats and submarines. The submarine enthusiasts were 'anxious that [the UK] should start building submarine boats as a reply to the French'. The Royal Navy purchased a single Holland submarine in 1900 and, impressed by its potential, then built five undersea craft under licence. The French Navy began with experiments of its own but later came round to Holland's design. By the summer of 1914, 400 submarines, most of them evolutionary progressions from Holland's original design, existed in sixteen navies.[25] However, Admiral Jellicoe felt that the Germans 'could not possibly build enough submarines to saturate the North Sea for another eight to ten years'. Admiral of the Fleet, George Wilson, was ambivalent:

> The development of submarine warfare must be detrimental to a nation depending on navigation at the surface for its supplies of food and the necessities of life. We cannot stop invention in this direction [and] we cannot delay its introduction longer, but we should still avoid doing anything to assist in its improvement in order that our means of trapping and destroying it may develop at a greater rate that the submarine boats themselves. [To this end] politicians should take all favourable opportunities of enlisting the moral sense of nations against this method of warfare, and above all saying anything to prevent the sternest measures being adopted against the crews of submarine boats when caught in the act of using them.[26]

John Winton found the Navy was 'not nearly so obtuse about the dangers of submarines to surface warships as has often been supposed'.[27] Concerns were raised in 1903 and, from 1910, there were a series of tests at sea with Holland submarines as targets using liquid tar, six-inch guns, towed hydroplanes, rifle grenades, airplanes and sweep nets with explosive charges.

The real submarine champion was Jackie Fisher. In 1904, he wrote a number of letters: 'My beloved submarines are going to magnify the naval power of England seven times more than present.'[28] 'It's astounding to me, perfectly astounding, how the very best amongst us absolutely fail to realise the vast impending revolution in naval warfare and naval strategy that the submarine will accomplish.' 'In all seriousness, I don't think it is even faintly realised – the immense impending revolution which the submarines will effect on us as offensive weapons of war ... it makes one's hair stand on end.'[29] Four years later, he declared that it was 'inevitable when the Germans fully realise the capability of this type of [overseas] submarine – they probably do not do so yet on account of having small experience with them at sea (they have but three to our sixty) – the North Sea and all its ports will be rendered uninhabitable by our big ships – until we have cleaned out their submarines'.[30] The submarine, he repeated constantly, was 'the battleship of the future' and the torpedo the naval weapon of the future. The problem was how to deliver the torpedo to the target.[31]

Considering the achievements of the submarine as a commerce destroyer in the first German war it is astonishing to find that, with one exception, no naval brain on either side had an inkling of what the submarine was going to mean. The exception was Fisher, the erratic genius who was first Sea Lord from 1904 to 1910 (the year in which he predicted that war with Germany would break out in August 1914).[32]

In 1913, Fisher wrote a famous memorandum on 'The Submarine and Commerce', which argued that there was nothing else but for the submarine to sink her capture. 'It must be admitted that, however inhuman and barbarous it may appear, this submarine menace is a truly terrible one for British commerce and Great Britain alike, for no means can be suggested at present of meeting it except by reprisals.' First Lord Winston Churchill disagreed: 'I do not believe [using submarines to sink merchant vessels] would ever be done by a civilised Power.'[33]

Both the Germans and the British abruptly changed their views within a few weeks of the start of the war. The start was inauspicious: a German expedition of ten of their twenty-eight submarines in commission on 6 August sank nothing, but lost one of their number by ramming.[34] 'No one thought of operations against merchant ships.'[35] On 5 September, *U 21*, commander Otto Hersing, sank a British light cruiser, *Pathfinder*, off the Firth of Forth, the first ship sunk to a u-boat; 250 sailors died. Hersing was unusual in that he survived while commanding the same boat for the whole war.[36] Then, on 22 September, *U 9*, Otto Weddigen, torpedoed three aged British armoured cruisers, *Aboukir, Cressy* and *Hogue*, the 'Live Bait Squadron', 'rashly sent on patrol off the Dutch coast without destroyer protection', with the loss of almost 1,500 men.[37] *Aboukir* went down first and the others, thinking that a mine had been struck, were all but stationary while picking up survivors. It was all over in a little over an hour. Weddigen became an immediate national hero, but died with all hands in the Pentland Firth six months later when rammed in *U 27* by HMS *Dreadnought*. If, with a single u-boat, Germany could almost casually sink three cruisers bristling with guns, how vulnerable were unarmed merchantmen?

> *The idea that merchantmen could be dealt with in the same way and even more easily and that their destruction on a large scale could be far more useful than that of three aged cruisers, once it arose, spread rapidly. The feeling that Germany had for her enemies had by now reached a degree of indignation, if not hatred, hot enough to consume scruples; and between the belligerents reprisal and counter-reprisal were succeeding each other swiftly.*[38]

In the first month of the war, both sides had committed serious breaches of international law by mine-laying, restricting international waters to neutral traffic, and by introducing a policy of attempted starvation. Germany entered the war believing in the importance of the sea mine and on the first day laid mines thirty miles off the coast of Suffolk. The cruiser *Amphion* struck one of these on 6 August and 151 lives were lost. Further mines were laid indiscriminately in the North Sea and two merchantmen were sunk.

> *The control of mine-laying by international law was derived from the principle that belligerents had no right to pitch their battles on any land or water that they chose or to make all civilian activity subordinate to the measures. Perhaps this idea now seems ridiculous. In 1945, when the belligerents abandoned the battlefield they had made of Egypt and Libya, they left behind them minefields in which thereafter a huge number of Egyptians were killed or maimed without marking the conscience of mankind.*[39]

The starvation policy was initiated in the British cabinet on 14 August. At a conference at the Foreign Office chaired by Grey, with Churchill and the First Sea Lord to speak for the navy, members heard that the German government had taken over the whole of their country's foodstuffs.[40] This information, laid without evidence, enabled the British to declare as contraband all food imports into Germany in neutral vessels, especially through Dutch ports. The endorsement of this policy by the British cabinet the next day was the decisive move in winning the war, but condemned to misery and death many hundreds of thousands of German civilians, particularly the women, the weak and the children of the poor. 'The fiction helped [the British] to evade an admission of illegality and gave them room for manoeuvre' ... in open blackmail of Holland.[41] The starvation policy was not legally recognised in Britain till a decision of the Privy Council in October 1917.

On 2 October 1914, in response to the German mines, the British Admiralty warned that it would lay a 1,365-square sea mile minefield at the entrance of the Channel into the North Sea. It left free a narrow channel near the English coast, which was only passable within British territorial waters. In early November, the British declared the whole of the North Sea to be a War Zone. Any ships which crossed the area other than by prescribed routes would do so 'at their own peril', and would be exposed to great danger from mines and from warships which would search for suspicious craft with the greatest vigilance. Foreign fishermen were banned from British coastal waters and navigational buoys were to be changed. Fisher predicted that he would now be 'able to control effectively the neutral traffic now so remunerative to Dutch and Scandinavian pockets in feeding Germany'.

> All import trade into Germany both by land and sea was strangled, and in particular the importation of food was made impossible, because the distinction between absolute and relative contraband was done away with. Even the importation of goods that were not contraband was prevented, by taking them off the ships on the plea that contraband might be hidden in them; then when they were landed, either they were requisitioned or detained on the strength of some prohibition of export so that they had to be sold.[42]

On 16 December, the Germans bombarded Scarborough and Hartlepool, scandalising the British Press with this 'war crime'. Grand Fleet commander, Lord Jellicoe, 'expressed surprise that the submarines were not also employed in order to lay a trap', which they did do in 1916.[43]

Meanwhile the u-boats were not only 'eating away the imported food stocks needed by Britain's civilian population, they were also sapping the lifeblood of the Royal Navy itself'. The fleet's newest and most powerful dreadnoughts, its new light cruisers and its destroyers, burned fuel oil. The tankers bringing oil from America were large and slow, presenting fat, easy targets for submarines. So many tankers had been sunk that Britain's reserve of fuel oil had dropped alarmingly; a six-month reserve had shrunk to a supply for only eight weeks. In consequence, the Admiralty ordered Grand Fleet battle squadrons to cruise at no more than three-fifths speed except in emergency.

Although not organised for total war in 1914, there was a reservoir in Britain of scientists, engineers, entrepreneurs and manufacturers who could be mobilized.[44] 'All this took time and was not well organised by a traditionalist Admiralty staff.' Against the u-boats, naval officers and scientists combined to produce far more efficient depth-charges, horned mines, mine nets and barriers, hydrophones laid on the sea bottom, paravanes, and finally detection equipment. Hydrophone units worked as far apart as visibility permitted during daylight, and at night trawlers would shut off their engines and drift while listening for any u-boat on the surface charging its batteries under cover of darkness. By means of hydrophones, listeners could hear a u-boat laying mines; and several groups were thus located.[45] The vigilance of the patrols was unceasing. In March, *UC 55* laid eighteen mines off the Orkneys and reported 'the astounding promptness of the counter-measures; within an hour and a half to two hours after sighting her, twelve destroyers, a submarine chaser, and two sweepers were on the spot'. Another innovation was the depth charge. Johannes Spiess tells of Kapitänleutnant Richard Hartmann in *U 49* returning to Emden in May 1917 and reporting that he had 'passed through a new ordeal'. He had been attacked by 'marine bombs'.[46] 'The tidings created a sensation' because *UC 7*, *UB 44* and *UC 19* had all been destroyed without survivors in the previous ten months.[47]

Much of the improvement in British anti-submarine warfare came in tactics. U-boat commander Hashagen noticed that because of the German's 'self-imposed and periodical pauses' in the submarine war, 'we assisted the British to commission and fit out decoy ships without haste'. After the pause during the winter before unrestricted submarine warfare began again in April 1917, the Germans could see easily that the British had been 'rehearsing'.[48] The British brought in the 'dazzle' scheme of ship painting. Dazzled models of all types of ship were prepared with the intention of falsifying perspective.[49] Other measures included the provision of smoke boxes to put up a screen between the raider and victim; defensive armaments; the reduction of funnel smoke; zigzagging courses; the inconspicuous rig of the standard cargo vessels; and instructional classes for mercantile-marine masters in outwitting the u-boats.

Trawlers were taken in large numbers from Britain's huge fleet of fishing boats and were an important adjunct to British sea power.[50] They did all sorts of 'invaluable drudgery': they laid mines, swept mines, laid nets, acted as anti-submarine craft, often heavily armed with guns and depth bombs, sometimes they acted as Q-ships, relying on their innocent looks. Q-ships came into being at a time when no other method seemed likely to deal with submarines adequately. After early successes, they 'rose in popularity to its logical peak, and then began to wane in usefulness as the submarine adapted herself to these new conditions'.[51] Seaplanes were increasingly used and proved their value as spotters, but were considerably less effective when dropping bombs.[52] In 1915, the British had found that a five- or six-inch gun could easily sink a submarine.[53] Consequently many merchant ships were adapted to take guns, but the work outpaced the supply of weapons and thus was not achieved until the end of 1917.[54] One of the counter-effects was that armed merchantmen were not allowed into American harbours and this became another argument against 'convoy'. Captains were ordered to destroy any u-boat that came within range. Under such circumstances, these commercial vessels should have been classified as men-of-war.[55] The use of neutral flags by British merchant ships added to the difficulties of the submarine commanders. The English liner *Lusitania* raised the American flag to hide its identity on a trip early in 1915. Walther Schwieger, *U 20*, who sank *Lusitania*, commented that 'several British captains were decorated or otherwise rewarded for ramming or attempting to ram submarines'. Schwieger would have been within his rights to ruthlessly destroy the *Lusitania* if her captain was able to and decided to act on his orders.

Despite these efforts it was the reluctant decision of the Royal Navy to introduce the convoy system which actually turned the tide of losses. In May 1917, shipping losses dropped to 616,000 tons, a dramatic decline from the slaughter of April due to the inability of the u-boat fleet to 'maintain the tremendous effort it had made in April.'[56] It was in this period that one of the most dismaying episodes of the British war effort was conducted within the admiralty. Senior naval officers had resolutely set their faces against introducing a convoy system across the Atlantic and in the Mediterranean. This was a tactic that could have been trialled and implemented, to some degree, from the early days of the war when the u-boat threat first became apparent. The Admiralty declined; they wished to control the trade routes, not the shipping which used them. 'Much was talked in the navy of the need, the overriding naval duty, to guard the sea-lanes on which the nation depended. The Royal Navy of 1914 had lost sight of the vital truth.'[57] The navy's approach was 'wasteful in the extreme'.[58]

The Admiralty's continuing principal objections to convoy was that there were not enough escort ships available. By the time the Germans unleashed their third episode of unrestricted submarine warfare in February 1917, the British Navy felt that they did not possess enough destroyers to screen the Grand Fleet, maintain the Harwich force [for the North Sea and the Dutch coast], secure the Channel crossings, and simultaneously protect merchant shipping from submarines.[59] In April 1917, Britain had a commission of about 260 destroyers, many old and badly worn after three years of service. The best one hundred were assigned to the Grand Fleet, and no one wished to send the dreadnoughts into battle without their protective screen.[60] Even so, in February 1917, Beatty reluctantly permitted eight destroyers to be borrowed from the Grand Fleet for anti-submarine work in southern waters ... [among which] the Dover Patrol confronted thirty German u-boats and thirty destroyers based in Flanders. John Winton gives one of many examples of the misuse of resources and it has to be assessed in the context of a total of 3,101 u-boat patrols during the war.[61]

In one week of September 1916, three u-boats operated in the Channel between Beachy Head and Eddystone Light, an area patrolled by forty-nine destroyers, forty-eight torpedo boats, seven Q-ships, and 468 armed auxiliaries – some 572 anti-submarine vessels in all, not

counting aircraft. Shipping in the Channel was held up or diverted.
The u-boats were hunted, but sank thirty ships, and were virtually
unscathed themselves.[62]

The obstinacy was the more distressing because, after all, the navy had
used convoys in differing circumstances since Napoleonic times and from
the beginning of this war for important troop movements.[63]

The British Expeditionary Force was taken across the Channel in convoy;
troops came back from India, were sent to Egypt, to the Dardanelles, the
first Canadian troops aboard fourteen ships in October 1914, and troops
from Australia, New Zealand and South Africa which called at Sierra Leone,
all in convoy. In a jolting statistic, the British Navy successfully convoyed
millions of troops and their supplies across the Channel to France every
day 'without ever losing a man, a gun, or a horse'.[64]

And, yet, convoys were considered, if anything, to be dangerous for
merchantmen. 'Merchantmen were safer, it was confidently believed,
if they were dispersed over a wide area. To assemble them in a convoy
would make the enemy's task easier, as herding a flock of sheep together
made it easier for the wolf to attack them.' The preference was to allow the
sheep to proceed independently down four sparsely guarded lanes into the
embrace of u-boats.[65] 'This view of convoy went in defiance of all of the
navy's history. It was also contrary to normal sheep-rearing practice, as
any shepherd would have confirmed.'[66]

In October 1916, Jellicoe, commander-in-chief of the Grand Fleet, wrote
to the Admiralty a thirteen-point summary of his views on the 'very serious
and ever-increasing menace of the enemy's submarine attack on trade'.
There is no mention of the need to trial convoys of merchantmen; the word
'convoy' is not mentioned at all. His whole argument is about the need to
improve offensive action against the u-boats. Here the record does not help
Jellicoe as the sum of the offensive measures against the u-boats until the
beginning of 1917, almost two and a half years of war, was just forty-six
submarines and this figure includes other causes, like sinking on their own
mines.[67] Jellicoe makes no 'concrete proposals'. His principal suggestion is
the usefulness of forming a committee of young officers with experience in
innovative weapon development to look at methods to solve the problem.
Jellicoe is clearly proud of this summary as he uses it to open one of his
memoirs. It is, in fact, a sad and dangerous example of woolly thinking.

There appears to be a serious danger that our losses in merchant ships,
combined with the losses in neutral merchant ships, may by the early
summer of 1917, have such a serious effect upon the import of food and
other necessities into the allied countries, as to force us into accepting
peace terms which the military position on the Continent would not
justify and would fall far short of our desires.[68]

Following the letter, Jellicoe visited London to discuss it with the Admiralty. He was asked to relinquish the Grand Fleet and to head the anti-submarine work at the Admiralty.[69] After thought, Jellicoe declined because he would be in a 'difficult position'. A few weeks later, Jellicoe was asked by Prime Minister Balfour to become First Sea Lord, which he did on 4 December. Two days later, Lloyd George was appointed Prime Minister; Sir Edward Carson became First Lord of the Admiralty; and Sir Joseph Maclay headed a new Ministry of Shipping to take over the whole business of maritime supply. Almost Jellicoe's first act was to form the Anti-Submarine Division and he called in Rear Admiral Alexander Duff, another convoy rejectionist, to head it.[70] Perhaps the Admiralty was finally to move into a more professional era?

> *Jellicoe had come to the Admiralty to deal with the submarine menace, but once in office and seeing its dimension, he was shaken. 'The shipping situation is by far the most serious question of the day,' he wrote to Beatty at the end of December 1916. 'I fear it is almost too late to retrieve it. Drastic measures should have been taken months ago to stop unnecessary imports, ration the country and build ships. All is being started now, but it is nearly, if not quite, too late.'[71]*

At the beginning of 1917, the official Admiralty staff view was put forward in a pamphlet which stated, quite definitely and emphatically, that convoy was not a sound method of defending trade. Jellicoe worked hard in a memoir to distance himself from the document, 'in the course of preparation for some time prior to my arrival at the Admiralty'; 'I do not think the paper came before me personally'; 'written before unrestricted submarine warfare was in operation' (but not before it was announced).[72] Winton exclaimed that it would be 'difficult to find, even in the long record of Admiralty bureaucracy, a more stupid document and one which more pigheadedly ignored all the lessons of past naval history. It was the more dangerous because it was not the work of a lunatic. It sounded a reasonable measured judgement, taken after all the circumstances had been brought to account.'[73]

> *Whenever possible, vessels should sail singly, escorted as considered necessary. The system of several ships sailing together in a convoy is not recommended in any area where submarine attack is a possibility. It is evident that the larger the number of ships forming the convoy, the greater is the chance of a submarine being enabled to attack successfully, the greater the difficulty of the escort in preventing such an attack. In the case of defensively armed merchant vessels, it is preferable that they should sail singly rather than that they should be formed into a convoy with several other vessels. A submarine could remain at a distance*

and fire her torpedo into the middle of a convoy with every chance
of success. A defensively armed merchant vessel of good speed should
rarely, if ever, be captured. If the submarine comes to the surface to
overtake and attack with her gun the merchant vessel's gun will nearly
always make the submarine dive, in which case the preponderance of
speed will allow of the merchant ship escaping.

The list of objections to convoy were 'like hydra's heads', with fresh ones
growing as soon as one was removed: merchant ship masters, especially
tramp-steamer masters could not keep a proper station one of another;
quartermasters could not steer a straight enough course; convoys could
not be assembled in neutral ports; there were not enough escorts; time
would be wasted assembling convoys; convoys arriving in ports would
overload a dock's capacity; merchant ships had no arrangement to darken
at night; convoys would need to travel at the speed of the slowest ship;
convoys would concentrate a u-boat's targets.[74] Even a number of masters
agreed. At a conference in February 1917, several masters stated that 'it
would be impossible to keep their ships in station when in company with
twelve to twenty other vessels'.[75]

Winton asks how did 'so many able, intelligent and thoughtful men,
who had spent their working lives in the naval service, or who had made a
special professional study of naval history, how did they all come to make
such a colossal collective blunder'.[76] The only answer lay in an obsession
with the sea-lane, which had to be protected by a 'sort of nautical foot
patrol'. Lloyd George described the admirals as like doctors who 'whilst
they are unable to arrest the ravages of disease which is gradually
weakening the resistance of a patient despite all their efforts, are suddenly
confronted with a new, unexpected and grave complication. They go about
with gloomy mien and despondent hearts. Their reports are full of despair.
It is clear that they think the case is now hopeless. All the same, their
only advice is to persist in the application of the same treatment'.[77] The
strongest argument against convoy, and it was strong, was that there were
insufficient ocean-going escorts available before the United States entered
the war and the American supply of destroyers began. Jellicoe repeatedly
offered impassioned justifications of this position and continued with them
long after the war had ended.[78] It came down to the greater evil: the steady
and immediately national-threatening loss of merchantmen and their
supplies or the protection of a Grand Fleet paralysed for fear of mines and
torpedoes and kept idle in harbour against the chance of another Jutland.

Historian Terraine has a more sympathetic view feeling that, despite all the
history of experience for convoys, there was also history with a considerable
force, against convoy. Why did the Admiralty hesitate for so long?

The answer that will always spring readily to the minds of some, and give them full satisfaction, is stupidity; others, taking into account too the characters and qualities of the men concerned – they would not be human if they did not include some degree of prejudice and error – will be less pleased with that answer. As may be supposed, it is too simple ... Those who believe that the Admiralty should have acted earlier are unlikely to change their minds.[79]

One observer remarked at about this time:

... whether we get the better of [the u-boats] or not depends, in my opinion, on whether the Admiralty succeeds in scaling off its semi-opaque upper layer of senior respectabilities who behave with perfect propriety, but have neither knowledge of modern conditions, nor initiative, nor imagination. The beating of the submarines – indeed, naval work as a whole of every description – is a young man's job. Despite its virtues I think there is more obstruction and 'old chappery' in the navy than in any other branch of administration.[80]

With the United States about to enter in the war, Rear-Admiral Sims was sent *post haste* to Europe under an assumed name and in civilian clothes to assess how best the Americans could make a naval contribution.[81] On 10 April, his first day in London and with America now in the war, Sims met with his friend Jellicoe. There is some dispute over what was said, but the import is clear; the conversation has passed into naval history.[82] Here is Sims' version:

A few days spent in London clearly showed that all [our] confidence in the defeat of the Germans rested upon a misapprehension. The Germans, it now appeared, were not losing the war, they were wining it ... [The documents I was shown] disclosed the astounding fact that, unless the appalling destruction of merchant tonnage ... could be materially checked, the unconditional surrender of the British Empire would take place within a few months ...

[Jellicoe said,] as quietly as though he were discussing the weather and not the future of the British Empire. 'It is impossible for us to go on with the war if losses like this continue.'

'What are you doing about it?'

'Everything that we can. We are increasing our anti-submarine forces in every possible way. We are using every possible craft we can find with which to fight submarines.' ...

'It looks as though the Germans are winning the war.'

'They will win, unless we can stop these losses – and stop them soon.'

'Is there no solution to the problem?'

'Absolutely none that we can see now.'[83]

The Prime Minister, Lloyd George, was fast losing patience with his senior admirals who he felt 'lacked resource and drive'.[84] 'Moreover, some very able young officers in the War Staff did not conceal their conviction that the method of routing merchant ships was involving unnecessary losses which could be avoided by the adoption of the convoy system.' There was worse to come for the Admiralty's pride when it transpired, in the same month, that their assessments on convoys had been based on the assumption that 5,000 ocean-going ships called and sailed from the United Kingdom each week. The figure was ludicrously high, but had never been challenged. The awful suspicion dawned on detailed investigation that the figure had no basis in fact whatsoever. 'The suspicion became certainty that the Admiralty collectively had made a supreme ass of itself.'[85] The real daily number was twenty in and twenty out. Winton explains that it was now possible to see 'how dangerously complacent the Admiralty had been'. As long as it was believed that 2,500 ships arrived and another 2,500 ships left British ports every week, the loss of, say, fifty in a week 'did seem unimportant' ... Against the true figures of only 120 to 140 sailings a week, those sinkings 'suddenly leaped into their true and deadly focus'. One in four ocean-going ships was failing to return. This awfulness was hammered home after the war when the merchant and fishing fleet dead could be counted at 15,313 men, 5½ per cent of the total involved, with an 'unknown number permanently disabled or weakened through exposure and wounds'.[86]

Significant and long-lasting changes took place in the British way of life as the government sought ways of cutting imports.[87] Brewing materials were already severely curtailed, but were now limited to one-third of their pre-war bulk. Under the Defence of the Realm Act in 1914, opening hours were reduced for licensed premises to luncheon (1200 to 1440) and supper (1830 to 2130). These restricted public house licencing hours were retained in principle till the late 1980s. Wine imports were heavily reduced and, for the middle classes, wine became a far less common drink. British Summer Time was first established by the Summer Time Act of 1916, beginning on 21 May and ended on 1 October, and was designed to save fuel in response to u-boat sinkings of tankers and to ensure maximum farming time in daylight in Scotland. Just before Christmas in 1916, almost all imports of timber were stopped and the great denuding of British woodlands to supply the coalfields and the army in France began.[88] Domestic house building was delayed because of the loss of wood for construction and this, in turn, led to a lowering of the quality of the national housing stock which plagued Britain's lower classes until the 1960s. The wood seizure resulted later in replacement forests of dreary serried rows of non-native fir trees. The Government tried many ways to increase home food growth. Sir Arthur Lee, Director-General of Food Production, began a number of initiatives in 1917. Interestingly quoting Zoroaster, he called on the churches to encourage Sunday labour in the fields, including drivers to volunteer for six-weeks' night tractor work at sowing time.[89] Lee also tried to put a positive spin on the u-boat's destruction:

> As a nation we owe much to the submarine for it has created an agricultural policy in this country, and will make us more supporting, and therefore safer in the matter of the food supply in the future ... We are paying special attention to small cultivation. If we can get every man to grow something for himself that will help the situation. We are making special efforts to develop that side to meet the requirements of 1917. We want the assistance of private gardeners to advise the small grower. We want the employer to send his gardener to the plots where unskilled people are working to instruct them in their labours. I hope that every vegetable possible will be grown on these plots.[90]

Recent investigation suggests that Britain turned almost four million of common and grasslands into grain and vegetable fields over the last two years of the war.[91] Meat stocks reduced by as much as 24 per cent, but net food output was enhanced by 2.3 million tons. This was further increased by one million tons from town garden allotments. Many of these 'lost' acres never returned to gardens after the war. Allotments became a British way of life and, when under-utilised after World War II, became sites for urban housing.

In an 'almost obscene fashion' the submarine campaign translated into a healthier British nation, even given the absence of 3,000 doctors called to the colours.

> The female death rate in 1917 due to cardiovascular disease, diarrhoeal disease, and complication of pregnancy was well below that of the years 1912 to 1914. The mortality rate due to scarlet fever and rheumatic fever likewise fell in 1916 ... By 1918, per capita calorie intake among civilians was probably higher than it had been in 1914.[92]

In the midst of the opposition to Atlantic convoys, there was independent recognition of the problem and some action. The heavy sinkings by the boats of the Flanders Flotilla in the English Channel during the last quarter of 1916 caused a 39 per cent reduction of deliveries of coal to France. Since the Germans had captured the French north-eastern industrial heartlands in 1914, including seventy-four per cent of its coal production, they needed to import a minimum of one and a half million tons of coal a month to keep vital armament factories in full production.[93] After representations made by the French naval authorities, it was decided to introduce a system of 'controlled sailings' – not convoys because the navy did not support convoys – to ensure the safe and speedy passage of the 800 colliers that crossed the Channel each month.[94] The system that evolved was in fact convoys of up to forty-five colliers, assembled off St Helens, Isle of Wight, escorted by three or four armed trawlers of the Auxiliary Patrol, and taken by night to arrive eight miles off Caen by daybreak.[95] The first convoy of colliers sailed on 10 January 1917. In early February, four coal 'controlled sailings', went every day under escort by armed trawlers; this eventually grew to 800 round trips a month.[96] By the end of April, 2,600 colliers had been conveyed and, although they crossed one of the most consistently lucrative areas of u-boat operations, only five were sunk by u-boat action: a loss rate of a mere 0.19 per cent.

Despite Rear Admiral Duff's earlier objections to the idea of convoy, the variation in speed of merchant ships, their inability to zigzag and tendency to straggle making it impracticable, none of which proved to be valid, he now changed his mind. At the end of April, he minuted Jellicoe on the advisability of introducing a 'comprehensive scheme of convoy'. Tarrant felt that, 'Practical experience had been the catalyst in changing Duff's views.' The 'unexpected immunity for successful u-boat attack on the French coal trade' (together with the success of similar experiments carried out with ships employed in the Dutch trade between the Downs and the Hook of Holland, and trade between Scandinavia and the North Sea ports) afforded Duff 'sufficient reason for believing that we can accept the many disadvantages of large convoys with the certainty of a great reduction in our present losses'.[97] His minute went to Jellicoe on 27 April and made the startling suggestion that 'it would appear that the larger the convoy passing through any given danger zone, provided it is moderately protected, the less the loss to the Merchant Service.' Duff recommended a trial of sixteen merchant ships in convoy from Gibraltar. 'Jellicoe approved although his heart was not in it.'[98] Hankey had a different view as Duff's memorandum to Jellicoe was sent the day after the War Cabinet on 25 April had decided that the Prime Minister should investigate the submarine question.[99] By the time Lloyd George visited the Admiralty on 30 April their 'utmost misgiving' on convoy was now called 'caution' and the seal was set on the decision and 'they carried it out with the utmost energy and competence'.

In the same month, the debate became even more public and critical. The *Daily Telegraph* was emboldened to run a story written by Archibald Hurd asking, 'Will this country ever realise the peril which the enemy's submarine campaign offers to its existence?'[100]

> *From Berlin, it has been announced that these underwater craft offer 'the best and the only means of a speedy victorious ending to the war.' In spite of the losses being sustained by our merchant fleet, there is a tendency on this side of the North Sea to dismiss the matter as of secondary importance, in no way comparable to the offensive on the Western front or the British advance in Mesopotamia. It is forgotten*

*that every warlike activity in which we are engaged is supported from
the sea, and if the Germans succeed in sinking not all, but a certain
proportion of our merchant ships, the war might come to an end, even
though our armies remain undefeated ... Communications from all
parts of the country – particularly with reference to food consumption –
indicate that there is today no full appreciation of the danger in which
we stand.*

There is some evidence that elements of the navy made their own
decisions in the light of local circumstances and that the blockage of
convoy was gradually reduced to distant or intercontinental traffic. A
convoy system was instituted between Lerwick and the Norwegian ports
under the protection of a flotilla leader and six destroyers of the Grand
Fleet.[101] The approved coal convoys were limited to steamers, but there
were a considerable number of small sailing vessels pressed into service
and carrying their small contributions from Welsh ports to France. A small
number of British ships still trading with Holland had been organised in a
loose convoy system on a roughly weekly basis from July 1916, protected
by light forces under Commodore Tyrwhitt at Harwich.[102] Proudly, the
schooner *Little Mystery* sunk by Georg Gerth, provided her own epitaph
as the spur that saved many other schooners on the coal run to France,
including some from her home port in Fowey.[103] Less than a month after
her sinking, the shipping intelligence officer at Portland wrote to the
Admiral's office in Devonport telling him that he had started 'collecting
small ketches and schooners and sending them to France as convoys'
protected by armed vessels:

*One lot of eleven left here about three weeks ago and arrived safely,
and five left Fowey on 17 May. These latter were French and had
one thousand tons of coal between them. They were attacked by a
submarine en route, but the attack was beaten off by the escort. It
is extremely difficult to obtain escorts, but it would appear worthy of
consideration.[104]*

Eight days later, the Admiral concurred. Soon, schooners were made up
into regular convoys in their own right and were escorted by armed sailing
ships.[105] Not only were convoys now allowed, but the possibility of a small
sailing fleet maintaining station had been proved.

On 10 May 1917, a new turn of events 'confounded u-boat commanders':
the trial British merchant convoy reached Plymouth from Gibraltar with
no losses.[106] It was escorted by three armed yachts and two Q-ships and
was met after eight days 200 miles from Devonport by eight destroyers.
This success led to an experimental cross-Atlantic convoy of twelve ships
from Hampton Roads escorted by the cruiser *Roxburgh* and, on arrival,

by eight destroyers. Two slow steamers straggled and one was sunk by a u-boat. 'Despite fog and heavy weather, station keeping had been excellent.' By the end of July, twenty-one Atlantic convoys with 354 ships had been run of which only two had been sunk by u-boats. Convoys 'placed British strengths, both operationally and tactically, against the weakness of the attacking submarines'.[107] The tactics of convoy protection had to be worked out from scratch and training was required so that the frigates and sloops would be 'advantageously positioned around the merchantmen, knew how to react to a u-boat attack, and also how to integrate the new technology of wireless, aircraft, depth-charges, and ultimately ASDIC'. Some of this training was done out of Portsmouth and Queenstown, but the greater part had to be acquired during combat. 'Since the operational concept was a sound one, and the correct technology was becoming available, tactical effectiveness was acquired.' The prime aim was to keep safe the merchant ships; sinking u-boats was a secondary consideration.

The obstructive tide slowly turned. Gainsayers became prophets. Jellicoe described in great detail that when it was decided that convoys were to be introduced, how it could be done.[108] Ports of assembly were organised at Dakar; Gibraltar; Halifax, Nova Scotia; Hampton Roads, Virginia and North Carolina; New York; Sierra Leone; and Sydney.[109] From these ports in 1917, sailings every eight days were inaugurated, with the exception of Gibraltar and Hampton Roads from which sailings took place every four days. Through to August, 8,900 ships were convoyed; sixteen were sunk, a rate of 0.18 per cent. By July, the convoy was a regular occurrence and, whether on the surface or under it, life for the German submarines became more dangerous.[110] While only twenty u-boats were destroyed during the first half of 1917, the toll by the end of the year had risen to sixty-three. Planners in Berlin reacted by enlarging the blockade zones around the British Isles, stepping up production and training crews in the latest tactics at the u-boat school in Eckernförde and, at sea, with a 'target training convoy' at Kiel. At sea, these look-alike merchant ships copied British formations and zigzagging while submarine officers made practice attacks.[111]

Sims' view of the convoy system was that it ...

> ... *should compel any submarine which was planning to torpedo a convoyed ship to do so only in waters that were infested with destroyers. In order to get into position to discharge its missiles the submarine would have to creep up close to the rim that marked the circle of destroyers. Just as soon as the torpedo started on its course, and the tell-tale wake appeared on the surface, the protecting ships would immediately begin sowing the waters with depth-charges. Thus, in the future, the Germans would be compelled to fight for every ship which they should attempt to sink, instead of sinking them conveniently in waters that were free of destroyers, as had hitherto been their privilege.*[112]

By war end, this long affair of 'convoy denial' was seen somewhat differently in the official war histories. Sir Henry Newbolt, poet of 'Drake's Drum' and 'Play up, play the game', took over the story of the war at sea and described the 1917 u-boat fight as 'work undertaken and carried through with anxious resolution, with concentration and great resourcefulness at the Admiralty, and among the officers and men on active service with a combination of carefulness and courage, professional seriousness and cheerful love of sport'.[113]

Hashagen described what it was like when the u-boats came up against the 'well arranged and well worked up' convoys. Again, he credited, this time wrongly, the pause in the submarine war over the winter of 1916 for allowing Allied preparation.[114]

> *Though the submarine had several weapons – torpedoes, guns, scuttling charges, capture, for example – yet against a convoy she was restricted to one weapon, her torpedoes. The modern convoy constructed of three to five columns of vessels of the most varied sizes. At the head steamed, as a rule, an auxiliary cruiser or an old cruiser ... The speed of advance was eight knots. By day they zig-zagged ... by night they held on their course. Ahead, and on either wing, were large covering forces of destroyers. Last came fast patrol-vessels which, if a ship was actually torpedoed, rushed to the spot where the white eddy of the torpedo-shot betrayed the submarine's position, to destroy it by means of salvoes of depth-charges. Right at the tail, far, far astern of the convoy, might sometimes be seen trundling along an untidy, wretched looking tramp – [the Q-ship].*

This was in a time before the Germans could use wireless intercepts or aerial reconnaissance.[115] Dönitz described the tactical problems that he faced:

> *The oceans at once became bare and empty. For long periods at a time, the u-boats operating individually, would see nothing at all, and then suddenly up would loom a huge concourse of ships, thirty or fifty or more of them, surrounded by a strong escort of warships of all types. The solitary u-boat, which most probably had sighted the convoy purely by chance, would then attack, thrusting again and again ... for perhaps several days and nights until the physical exhaustion of the commander and crew called a halt. The lone u-boat might well sink one or two ships, or even several, but that was a poor percentage of the whole. The convoy would steam on. In most cases, no other German u-boat would catch sight of it and it would reach Britain, bringing a rich cargo of foodstuffs and raw materials safely to port.[116]*

This view was supported by interviews with captured u-boat captains. Kapitänleutnant Otto Launburg, *UB 52*, admitted in 1918 that the 'present system of convoy does not favour submarines; the old order of patrols allowed greater freedom of action as we could easily avoid the patrol craft by diving ... Now, every target has an attendant defender'.

Inward convoys were largely in place and working, but convoys continued generally too small and with 'over-abundant escorts'.[117] However, cargoes were not being lost at the same rate as the beginning of the year. The ratio on inward voyages between convoy losses to independent sailing losses reached 18:1. The Germans switched tactics. Monthly sinkings remained high for the rest of the year because, first, the u-boats began operating far further out into the Atlantic and, second, it was now outward ships in ballast that were attacked with the 'lion's share of the slaughter accounted for by the u-boats of Bauer's High Seas Flotilla'.[118] Outwards convoys were slowly arranged and the lack of sufficient escorts was covered by naval ships first escorting departing ships to the edge of the danger zone and, then, waiting there for the next incoming convoy. The logistical arrangements were complex, but the system worked. The Germans were discouraged and doubts began to be voiced about meeting the time target for the capitulation of England. U-boat building plans were reinstated and speeded up; u-boat global sinkings still outpaced the ability to replace the ships.

U-boat losses grew, but only in proportion to the new submarines coming into operation. As a percentage of vessels at sea, these losses were no higher than in previous years. Losses suffered during the summer of 1917 were not a result of any greater efficiency of the British anti-submarine patrols.[119] For example, for nine days in June, the 'most elaborate special hunting operation' involved thirty-five destroyers and fifteen submarines concentrated of known u-boat routes around the north of Scotland.[120] u-boats were sighted sixty-one times and attacked twelve times without causing any loss or damage. Particularly, the 'English did not have the mines up to the job'. The poor quality of the two types of mine which they possessed had been shown through experiment. A submarine was sent into a minefield and hardly one third of the mines which had been touched had exploded. Of the 20,000 mines in stock by April 1917, Jellicoe estimated that 15,000 were hardly able to be used in the barrages against submarines. Two anti-submarine symbiotic tactics did make a noticeable difference. The first was that the British resolved their antipathy to the sea mine and introduced a 'new and vastly more deadly 'H2' horned mine that, secondly, finally closed the Dover Straits to outward u-boats in August 1918 with a deep-mine barrage'.[121] 'At this point a new model, type H, built like a German mine, was put into test. It took a long time to refine it and make it perfect and it was not until October 1917 that a stock of them could be built up and used in the Dover Straits.' The Germans, depending on who managed which u-boat flotilla, insisted on using, then banning, the Dover passage after at least eleven Flanders' boats had been sunk on it.

The Germans had, again, to switch their point of attack. The u-boats now all but abandoned raids far out to sea and chose targets within ten miles of the shore in waters in the Irish Sea, and the English and Bristol Channels. Here, shipping still sailed independently as it travelled to and from convoy assembly or dispersal points. Sinking numbers remained high, but, the losses involved a much higher percentage of smaller vessels. And, again, it was the convoy system that won the day as, by May 1918, coastal convoys became the norm. Coastal convoy had the benefit of aircraft and airship cover and, eventually, this forced the u-boats to change once more, back to deeper waters away from aircraft range and to resort increasingly in the last months of the war to night attacks. In the last months of the war, merchant sinkings fell rapidly until, finally, new construction crossed the 'downward curve of sinkings'.[122]

One little mentioned aspect of the sinkings was the work done to raise lost ships through a special salvage service. In 1916, 190,000 tons were raised; next year with a more efficient service, 518,000 tons; and, in 1918, 884,000 tons. Total salvage over three years amounted to over a million and half tons worth £50 million in ships, bullion and stores.[123]

The German's gambling mindset, previously discussed, can be seen again when the naval campaign had failed. Sinkings continued in 1918, although it was no longer clear what they could achieve.[124] The success rate declined rapidly. More than six million tons were sunk in 1917 and only two million in 1918. 'But the Naval Staff was prepared to jeopardise the peace negotiations in October and November 1918 in order to continue the anti-shipping campaign. Naval fatalism was expressed in the intention of the High Seas fleet to sail out for battle on the very point of Germany's collapse, in late October 1918.' One result was the Germany naval mutiny and the hastening of the German collapse.[125]

It should be asked, rhetorically, what might the Germans have done if the unrestricted campaign of February 1917 quickly came to nothing because of an effective and comprehensive convoy system, perhaps in place, and therefore well-prepared, since the end of 1915? Might the Germans have been driven earlier to a final fatal land assault in France, perhaps in the summer of 1917, rather than as happened in 1918? Might the armistice have been sought up to a year earlier? How many soldiers' lives of all nationalities did the intransigent British admirals cost?

After the blunders of convoy, there remains the question of the Admiralstab miscalculation in the Holtzendorff memorandum.[126] Britain was not brought to her knees within six months. During the decisive six months, British grain reserves more than doubled.[127] Giving grain cargoes a higher priority saw wheat stocks increased from a five-and-a-half-week supply at the end of March to a fourteen-week supply at the end of June. America did come quickly into the war at the rate of 10,000 troops a day and quickly made a large economic difference. The speed of their arrival surprised the Germans who also suffered from a lack of intelligence as to their arrival points.[128] Two million Americans dodged the u-boats by using the Biscay ports and, in doing so, lost only fifty-seven lives when the British troop transport *Moldavia* was torpedoed by *UB 57* off Beachy Head on 23 May 1918.[129] Ironically for the Germans, almost half the American troops escorted to Europe by the US Navy sailed on board eighteen large German ships that had been interned in American ports.[130] America's troops were sufficiently in place in 1918 to provide the support that worn-down French and British armies desperately needed. However, it remained 'close run'. By the end, the British shipping numbers were teetering on the edge of what was required.[131] Sir Leo Chiozza Money, parliamentary secretary for shipping, had calculated that the 'irreducible minimum necessary for the importation of food' was just under five million tons from which the British had only just over 600,000 tons leeway at the end of 1917.[132] 'It is clear, therefore, that although the British had weathered the worst of the storm, the situation remained precarious, and the u-boats, despite the setbacks, still had it in their power to achieve victory in 1918.' The Germans would have succeeded if they had found a tactical answer to convoy. The answer, as World War II showed, was the 'wolf pack', meeting concentrations of merchantmen with co-ordinated concentrations of u-boats, but the German planners failed to recognise this, despite Bauer at Wilhelmshaven raising the matter in 1918, and clinging to the need for an increase in u-boat numbers.[133]

To put it the other way around, the German decision to introduce unrestricted submarine warfare in February 1917 was 'strategically sound'.[134] If the sinkings of the spring of 1917 had been maintained, 'Britain would undoubtedly have been forced into submission by the end of 1917 or the spring of 1918 at the latest'. In that case, France could not have held on alone and the American intervention would have been too late.

The British invented the myth that their anti-submarine measures had beaten the u-boats.[135] Even well into 1918, they downplayed convoy protection as defensive rather than as a combination of defensive and offensive.[136] The navy employed their slowest, oldest vessels in convoy work which amounted to 257 vessels, just 5.1 per cent of their fleet. In March 1918, the navy's anti-submarine faction, with almost no analysis, even suggested reducing the number of convoy escorts by 30 per cent to strengthen their own units. In fact, in the last year of the war, 85 per cent of all shipping losses in the Atlantic and home waters were independent sailings. In the last eighteen months of the war, the u-boats achieved eighty-four successful attacks on convoys and, in sixty-nine of these, only one ship was sunk. The u-boats were forced into underwater attacks and these were limited by the number of torpedoes they carried. Convoys also greatly reduced the number of sinking by mines because the escorts had the latest information on newly-laid minefields.[137]

The first effect of the convoy system was that the ocean suddenly seemed to be devoid of shipping. This was because, strange as it may seem, a convoy of ships was not more likely to be sighted than a single vessel. A single ship will probably be seen by a u-boat lurking within ten miles of its track. A convoy of twenty ships is only two miles wide and so would be seen by a u-boat lying within eleven miles of the centre of the track of one convoy. Five convoys of twenty ships each were not, therefore, very much more likely to be seen than five single ships, and were obviously much harder to find that a hundred independents. The result was that the vast majority of ships when in convoy were never seen, and the greatest advantage of the system was the difficulty the u-boats had in finding the convoys at all.[138]

German-Canadian historian Holger Herwig saw the German calculations to starve Britain as badly wrong, both politically and economically.[139] German naval leaders failed to appreciate the enormous shipbuilding potential of the United States. They ignored the total shipping tonnage available to Great Britain. They had no clear notion of precisely how many ships per month England required to sustain her industry and to feed her subjects. They over-emphasised the importance of wheat, failing to note that other grains could be substituted. London introduced mild forms of rationing, and by adding other types of flour to wheat created a so-called 'war bread' that in 1917–18 saved about thirteen weeks' consumption of wheat flour.[140] They never imagined that rationing would be instituted owing to their conception of the British 'national character'. They did not foresee that Britain could increase her output of foodstuffs by bringing into production resources not yet fully tapped. They did not realise that the London government would rigidly regulate prices, believing that international food prices would skyrocket until Britain could no longer afford to pay them. They also felt certain that shipping and insurance rates would become unaffordable, especially to neutral nations. Finally, they did not take into consideration the available grain reserves – the United States, for example, possessed reserve supplies to cover much of the Allied deficiencies even despite its own poor harvest of 1916. The shortfall was more than made up by Canada, which exported over 70 per cent of its harvest and its wheat exports to Britain in 1917, almost 50 per cent more than the United States.[141]

Scottish historian Niall Ferguson was equally damming. He saw the German's calculations as wrong in every possible respect.[142] They underestimated Britain's ability to expand her own wheat production; the normal size of the American wheat crop (1916 and 1917 were exceptionally bad years); Britain's ability to switch scarce wood from house construction into mine-pit props; the tonnage available to Britain; the British state's ability to ration food in short supply; the effectiveness of convoys; and the ability of the Royal Navy to develop anti-submarine technology. 'Incredibly, they also over-estimated the number of submarines they themselves possessed or could possess: between January 1917 and January 1918 eighty-seven new u-boats were built, but seventy-eight were lost. By 1918, the loss rate among the convoys was down to 1 per cent; for u-boats the figure was over 7 per cent.'[143] By this time, also, America's shipbuilding production had grown so quickly that, by the second quarter, the world was building more ships than it lost; by the third quarter there was a net gain of nearly half a million tons.[144]

For the British establishment, with the official war history written by the orchestrators of the propaganda offensive, the u-boat blockade was all a matter of uncivilised Germans.

> We could only regard it as a hideous crime committed wilfully and by a whole people against law and humanity. Our anger was justified; but it was mainly instinctive. Our perception was clear enough; but it was mainly perception on two practical points, that the attack was dangerous, and that it was characteristic – it marked a true cleavage between the German theory of war and the code hitherto followed by the civilised nations. Looking back, we could trace the dogmatic origins of the German theory among professors and philosophers; and we could find historical records which would go some way to account for a brutality of practice very unusual in war.[145]

There was no mention here of the British economic blockade of Germany and its effects. German indecision combined with astonishing bureaucratic and insular thinking may or may not have cost the war, but it probably cost the peace. The British Admiralty's continuing denial about convoy's effectiveness 'was to cost them dearly in the future' when the u-boats came again.[146]

ENDNOTES

1   Macintyre, *Battle of the Atlantic*, p. 13.
2   Vincent, *Politics of Hunger*, p. 11.
3   Herwig, *Dynamics*, pp. 85, 91. Massie, *Castles*, p. 126.
4   www.navyrecords.org.uk/about-us/leading-figures, accessed 4/2/2017. Marder, *Portrait of an Admiral*.
5   Bennett, *Naval Battles of the First Word War*, p. 258. Strachan, *First World War*, p. 207.
6   Kennedy, *First World War*, pp. 37, 43.
7   Kelly, *Tirpitz*, p. 81.
8   Massie, *Castles*, p. 738. Terraine, *Business in Great Waters*, p. 87. Marder, *Dreadnought*, Vol. V, pp. 102–3. Gayer, *Submarine Warfare*, p. 28.
9   Koerver, *German Submarine Warfare*, p. xxi.
10 Strachan, *First World War*, p. 207.
11 The sixth volume, which summarises the arguments, is available today in English as *Is War Now Impossible?*, and has an introduction using an interview with the British journalist W T Stead.
12 Howard, *Men against Fire*, p. 41.
13 Offer, *Agrarian Interpretation*, p. 11.
14 Bloch, *Is War Now Impossible?*, 'Preface', interview with W T Stead, p. xvi.
15 Offer, *Working Classes*, pp. 211–12. Also, Stewart Lygon Murray, *The Reality of War*.
16 Barnett, *British Food Policy*, pp. 3–4.
17 Murray, *Future Peace and the Anglo Saxons*, pp. 7–8, 108–9.
18 Offer, *Working Classes*, pp. 204–05.
19 Osborne, *Blockade*, p. 36.
20 Barnett, *British Food Policy*, p. 7.
21 Lambert, *Fisher's Revolution*, p. 361.
22 Arthur Doyle, 'Danger! Being the Log of Captain John Sirius', pp. 7–31, also 'Preface', pp. 5–6, in *Danger! and Other Stories*.
23 Laurens, *Histoire de la Guerre Sous-Marine Allemande*, pp. 1–2. Also, Gayer, *Submarine Warfare*, p. 4.
24 Lambert, *Naval Revolution*, pp. 2–3, 47.
25 Massie, *Castles*, p. 123.
26 *TNA*, ADM 1/7515, Minute (21/1/01) by Wilson on 'Submarine Boats'. Lambert, *Revolution*, p. 48.
27 Winton, *Convoy*, pp. 32–33.
28 Fisher to White, 12/3/04, Marder, *Fear God and Dread Nought*, Vol. I, p. 305. Lambert, *Revolution*, p. 83.
29 Fisher to May, 20/4/04, and Fisher to Esher, 23/4/04, Marder, *Fear God and Dread Nought*, Vol. I, p. 308.
30 Fisher, 'The Submarine Question', undated [November 1908], FP4238, Fisher Papers 5/13. Lambert, *Revolution*, p. 183.
31 Massie, *Castles*, p. 123.
32 Devlin, *Too Proud*, p. 190.
33 Winton, *Convoy*, pp. 4–5.
34 Devlin, *Too Proud*, p. 191.
35 Gayer, *Submarine Warfare*, p. 2. Gayer thought eighteen u-boats, not ten, set out for the North Sea ready to intercept British warships.
36 Hersing's second-in-command was Johannes Spieß, *Six Ans de Croisières*, pp. 45–61.
37 Gibson and Prendergast, *Submarine War*, pp. 6–10.
38 Devlin, *Too Proud*, p. 191.
39 Devlin, *Too Proud*, pp. 191–203.
40 *TNA*, FO 372/500/600.
41 Devlin, *Too Proud*, p. 195.
42 Hull, *Scrap of Paper*, p. 184.
43 Gayer, *Submarine Warfare*, p. 3.

44   Kennedy, *First World War*, p. 44.

45   Gibson & Prendergast, *German Submarine War*, p. 188.

46   Gibson & Prendergast, *German Submarine War*, pp. 177–78. Spieß, *Six Ans de Croisières en Sous-marin*.

47   Depth charges were responsible for only one of these u-boats: *UC 19* sunk by British destroyer *HMS Ariel*, 6/12/1916. *UC 7* is presumed to have blown up on a mine north of Zeebrugge while homebound, 5/7/1916; *UB 44* disappeared in the Aegean Sea, 4/8/1916 (uboat.net).

48   Hashagen, *Commander*, p. 107. Massie, *Castles*, p. 720.

49   Gibson, *Submarine War*, p. 177.

50   Lowell, *Raiders*, p. 114.

51   Chatterton, *Q-ships*, p. 270.

52   Gibson, *Submarine War*, p. 180.

53   Peterson, *Propaganda*, p. 198.

54   Jellicoe, *Submarine Peril*, p. 15.

55   Peterson, *Propaganda*, p. 112.

56   Massie, *Castles*, p. 737.

57   Winton, *Convoy*, p. 10.

58   Kennedy, *First World War*, p. 58.

59   Massie, *Castles*, pp. 716–17. Gibson & Prendergast, *German Submarine War*, p. 173.

60   Terraine, *Business in Great Waters*, p. 24.

61   Koerver, *German Submarine Warfare*, p. xii. 'Caveat: many cruises by small UB 1 and UC 1 boats could not be identified.' During the war, u-boats sank 5,408 British, Allied and neutral merchant ships; 10,874,287 BRT.

62   Winton, *Convoy*, p. 40.

63   Jellicoe, *Submarine Peril*, Chapter 8, pp. 96–120. Compton-Hall, *Submarines*, p. 265. John Terraine, *Business in Great Waters*, p. 50.

64   Massie, *Castles*, pp. 728–29.

65   Jellicoe, *Submarine Peril*, p. 16. Terraine, *Business in Great Waters*, p. 42.

66   Winton, *Convoy*, pp. 12–14. Gibson & Prendergast, *German Submarine War*, pp. 173–78.

67   Terraine, *Business in Great Waters*, p. 33.

68   Jellicoe, *Submarine Peril*, p. 2. Churchill, *World Crisis*, p. 719.

69   Jellicoe, *Submarine Peril*, pp. 8–9.

70   Tarrant, *U-Boat Offensive*, p. 39. Terraine, *Business in Great Waters*, p. 24.

71   Massie, *Castles*, p. 717.

72   Jellicoe, *Submarine Peril*, pp. 103–4.

73   Winton, *Convoy*, p. 47.

74   Jellicoe, *Submarine Peril*, pp. 97–103, lists the 'mercantile disadvantages' of convoy. Also, Hankey, *Supreme Command*, pp. 645–48.

75   Gibson, *Submarine War*, pp. 173–74.

76   Winton, *Convoy*, p. 17.

77   Winton, *Convoy*, p. 49.

78   Jellicoe, *Submarine Peril*, pp. 112–18.

79   Terraine, *Business in Great Waters*, pp. 50–51, 59.

80   Oliver, *Anvil of War*, p. 198.

81   Sims, *Victory at Sea*, pp. 1–5.

82   Jellicoe's 'corrections' to Sims' account: *Submarine Peril*, pp. 70–71.

83   Also, Tarrant, *U-Boat Offensive*, p. 50.

84   Hankey, *Supreme Command*, Vol. 2, p. 645.

85   Winton, *Convoy*, pp. 55–56.

86   Winton, *Convoy*, p. 115.

87   Hankey, *Supreme Command*, Vol. 2, pp. 642–43.

88   Herwig, 'Total Rhetoric'.

89   Zoroaster: 'He who sows the ground with care and diligence acquires a greater stock of religious merit than he could gain by the repetition of 10,000 prayers.'

90   *Daily Telegraph*, 'Food Shortage – Not a Moment to be Lost for Sowing Seed', 28/2/1917, p. 1.

91   Herwig, 'Total Rhetoric'.
92   Herwig, 'Total Rhetoric'.
93   Strachan, *First World War*, p. 59.
94   Tarrant, *U-Boat Offensive*, p. 51.
95   *Naval Staff Monographs*, p. 216.
96   Massie, *Castles*, pp. 728–29; see also p. 732.
97   Quoted in Admiralty MS, 'Notes of the Convoy System of Naval Warfare', Part 2. Tarrant, *U-Boat Offensive*, p. 51.
98   Tarrant, *U-Boat Offensive*, p. 52.
99   Hankey, *Supreme Command*, p. 650.
100 *Daily Telegraph*, 26/4/1917, p. 1. Sir Archibald Hurd in the 1920s wrote the three-volume history, *The Merchant Navy* at the request of 'The Historical Section of the Committee of Imperial Defence'.
101 Terraine, *Business in Great Waters*, p. 58.
102 Terraine, *Business in Great Waters*, p. 680.
103 Chapter 6, 'The war of the raven'.
104 *TNA*, ADM 137/1393, French Coal Trade, p. 27, letter dated 21/5/1917. An annotation says the admiral agreed on 29/5/1917. Terraine, *Business in Great Waters*, p. 99.
105 Greenhill, 'Rise and Fall', p. 256.
106 Herwig, *Luxury Fleet*, p. 224.
107 Kennedy, *First World War*, pp. 60–61.
108 Jellicoe, *Submarine Peril*, Ch. 10–11, pp. 142–74.
109 Gibson, *Submarine War*, p. 175.
110 Herwig, *Luxury Fleet*, p. 220.
111 Gibson & Prendergast, *German Submarine War*, p. 186, fn. 1.
112 Sims, *Victory*, p. 92.
113 Newbolt, *Naval History*, p. 115.
114 *Hashagen, Commander*, pp. 217–18.
115 Kennedy, *First World War*, pp. 60–61.
116 Dönitz, *Memoirs: Ten Years and Twenty Days*, p. 4.
117 Terraine, *Business in Great Waters*, p. 64.
118 Tarrant, *U-Boat Offensive*, p. 59.
119 Spindler, *Der Krieg zur See*, Band 4, pp. 2–3.
120 Newbolt, *Naval Operations*, Vol. 5, p. 55.
121 Tarrant, *U-Boat Offensive*, pp. 52–56. Laurens, *Histoire de la Guerre Sous-Marine Allemande*, p. 293. Terraine, *Business in Great Waters*, pp. 27–28. Chapter 10, 'Intelligence gift'.
122 Tarrant, *U-Boat Offensive*, pp. 68–69.
123 Newbolt, *Naval History*, pp. 120–21.
124 Offer, 'Bounded Rationality', pp. 193–94.
125 Chapter 13, 'Guilt and blame'.
126 Offer, *Agrarian Interpretation*, pp. 361–62, 366, gives an economic view of the German failure of argument. Herwig, 'Dynamics', p. 99.
127 Offer, 'Bounded Rationality', p. 194.
128 Ludendorff, *War Memoirs*, Vol. 2, p. 610.
129 uboat.net. Two empty, returning transports were also sunk: *President Lincoln, U 90*, 31/5/1918; *Covington, U 86*, 1/7/1918.
130 Herwig, 'Total Rhetoric'.
131 Hankey, *Supreme Command*, Vol. 2, p. 643.
132 Tarrant, *U-Boat Offensive*, p. 59.
133 Bauer, *Führer der U-Boote*.
134 Tarrant, *U-Boat Offensive*, p. 74.
135 Grant, *U-boats Destroyed*, p. 146.
136 Tarrant, *U-Boat Offensive*, pp. 67–68.
137 Marder, *Dreadnought*, Vol. 5, p. 79.
138 Hazlet, *Submarine and Sea Power*, pp. 94–95.
139 Herwig, *Luxury Fleet*, pp. 196–98.

140   Herwig, 'Total Rhetoric'.
141   Offer, *Agrarian Interpretation*, p. 369.
142   Ferguson, *Pity*, pp. 282–83.
143   Herwig, *Dynamics of Necessity*, p. 104.
144   Arnold-Forster, *Blockade*, p. 28.
145   Newbolt, *Naval Operations*, p. 183, and much more of the same in Ch. VI, 'German Submarine War, The Problem of the U-Boat Blockade'.
146   Tarrant, *U-Boat Offensive*, p. 74.

Erich Gerth, centre, with fellow officers in the Adriatic in 1918. *Family archive.*

Chaouia, sunk by one of Erich Gerth's mines from *UC 53* in 1919, well after war end, with a loss of 476 men.

Graf Karl-Christian von Ahlefeldt-Eschelsmark, Eva Marx's first husband, killed on air patrol over Verdun in 1916.

HMS *Ettrick* in dry dock after her front was blown off by accident by a Georg Gerth torpedo.

Sergeant Lucien Jailler of Escadrille N 15 who claimed Ahlefeldt's aircraft's destruction.

N° 29

Bekanntmachung	Bekendmaking	AVIS
Der englische Handelsschiffs-kapitän	De Engelsche handelsscheeps-kapitein	Le capitaine anglais de la marine marchande
Charles Fryatt	**Charles Fryatt**	**Charles Fryatt**
aus Southampton	van Southampton	de Southampton
hat, trotzdem er nicht der feindlichen Wehrmacht angehörte, am 28. März 1915 versucht, ein deutsches Unterseeboot durch Rammen zu vernichten. Er ist deshalb durch Urteil des Feldgerichts des Marinekorps vom heutigen Tage	heeft, niettegenstaande hij niet tot de vijandelijke krijgsmacht behoorde, op 28 Maart 1915 gepoogd een duitsche onderzeeboot door rammen te vernielen. Hij is daarom door vonnis van het Krijgsgerecht van het Marinekorps, in date van heden,	quoique ne faisant pas partie de la force armée ennemie, a essayé, le 28 Mars 1915, de détruire un sous-marin allemand en le heurtant. C'est pourquoi il a été
zum Tode verurteilt	**ter dood veroordeeld**	**condamné à mort**
und erschossen worden.	en doodgeschoten geworden.	par jugement de ce jour du Conseil de guerre du Corps de Marine et a été exécuté.
Eine ruchlose Tat hat damit späte, aber gerechte Sühne gefunden.	Eene roekelooze daad heeft daarmede hare laattijdige maar gerechtige straf ontvangen.	Un acte pervers a reçu ainsi son châtiment tardif mais juste.
gez. **von Schröder**	(get.) **von Schröder**	(signé) **von Schröder**
Admiral,	Admiraal,	Amiral,
Kommandierender Admiral des Marinekorps.	Bevelvoerende Admiraal van het Marinekorps.	Amiral Commandant du Corps de Marine.
Brügge, den 27. Juli 1916.	Brugge, den 27 Juli 1916.	Bruges, le 27 Juillet 1916.

Execution notice in three languages for Charles Fryatt issued in 1916 by Georg Gerth's commander, Admiral Ludwig von Schröder. *Imperial War Museums (1900-07).*

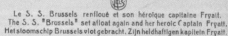

Le S. S. Brussels renfloué et son héroïque capitaine Fryatt.
The S. S. "Brussels" set afloat again and her heroic Captain Fryatt.
Het stoomschip Brussels vlot gebracht. Zijn heldhaftigen kapitein Fryatt.

Charles Fryatt and his ship, *Brussels*, captured by five German torpedo boats in 1916.

UC 58, a sister ship of Georg Gerth's *UC 61*. SHD, Vincennes (MV SS Z 18).

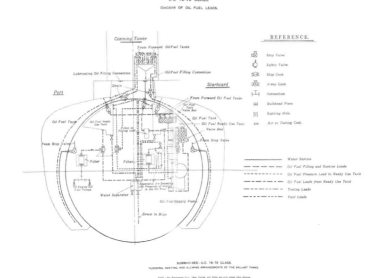

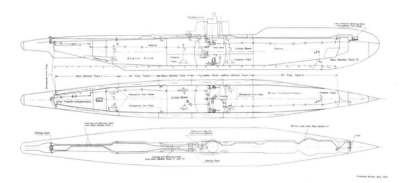

Remastered line drawings of Georg Gerth's *UC 61*. BA-MA, Freiburg.

The French armoured cruiser, *Kléber*, which hit one of Georg Gerth's u-boat mines in 1917; forty-two men died.

Survivors of the sinking of the *Kléber*.

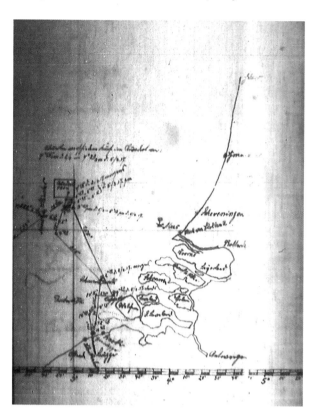

ABOVE: Georg Gerth's hand-drawn chart of his first voyage as commander of *UC 61* in 1917 showing the sinking of the Copenhagen.

RIGHT: One of *UC 61*'s mines taken from the wreck in 1917 to Calais Citadel.

UC 61 on Wissant beach, photographed on 4 August by Edmond Famechon, about a week after stranding. The bows, blown off by the crew's sabotage, have drifted some distance away following high tides and stormy weather. The derrick was built to detach the boat's cannon which was then taken for examination. The unexploded shell hole can be seen in the centre of the picture. ©*Edmond FAMECHON/ECPAD/Defense*

Coastguard 2nd class Stanislas Pierre Louis Serin (probably), hero of the stranding of *UC 61*, inspecting the shell hole in the fairing that streamlines the u-boat's conning tower. ©*Edmond FAMECHON/ECPAD/Defense*

Georg Gerth's copy of the *Signalverkehr*, dated 1911, with the complete hand flag signalling system between the military and merchant ships of the German Navy. The charred book was found in the bottom of *UC 61* in 1917 and re-found in the French military archive in 2017. *SHD, Vincennes (MV SS Gr 43).*

Documents confiscated from the crew of *UC 61* at Wissant Mairie in 1917, also re-found in 2017. *SHD, Vincennes (MV SS Gr 43).*

The live torpedo found in the blown-up wreck of *UC 61* on the beach at Wissant in 1928. *SHD, Cherbourg (MV SS Gr 43).*

The remains of *UC 61* at low tide on Wissant beach in 2016. *Alain Richard.*

Georg Gerth in his officer's cell in the fortress prison at Carcassonne, probably 1918. *Family archive*.

George Gerth and his crew escorted by Belgian lancers from Wissant beach to Calais Citadel in 1917. Gerth is centre, mid-stride. *Royal Museum of the Armed Forces and of Military History, Brussels (Est I/2322)*.

Erich Gerth, left, in an officers' mess, with his 'best friend' Rudi Seuffer, who went down with his u-boat crew in 1918, probably on his way to rescue Georg Gerth from his French island prison. *Family archive*.

The u-boats are out! – reflecting a popular
German verse of WWI and which was found on
Georg Gerth when he was captured.

Allied poster propaganda driven by the u-boat campaign: left, from the British
Ministry of Food in 1916/17 and, right, recruitment for the US Navy, 1917.

CHAPTER 8

Final Patrol

The sand around the wreck of UC 61 *is studded with pieces of black peat from a submerged forest which crumble in the hand. The forest is fifty to sixty feet below the seabed and, at this point, does not expose fossilised tree stumps. It extends across the Channel to England and therefore dates from when England was joined to the Continent as one land mass. This was about 8,000 years ago, between 6225–6170 BC. It is thought that three underwater landslides off Norway, the Storegga Slides, triggered one of Earth's biggest tsunamis. A landlocked sea in the Norwegian trench had burst its banks. The water struck the north-east of Britain with such force that it travelled twenty-five miles inland, turning low-lying plains into what is now the North Sea and, also, marshlands to the south into the Channel.*[1]

The canal from Bruges, Belgium's inland port to the sea at Zeebrugge is seven miles long. It is over 200 feet wide, comfortable enough for two large motor craft to pass at ease, and relatively straight.[2] In 1917, as today, it was lined with many regularly-spaced trees and ran through flat, uninspiring Flemish farmland. Most of the trees were and are Canadian black poplars planted by a proud country for the official opening in 1907.[3] Because of its scenic route, the area bordering the canal was generally quiet. Housing was sparse. There was no large village or heavy industry and the main road and railway to the sea was a mile or so to the west. Local people about their errands occasionally paced the footpath. The adjoining fields were intensively worked, but manually or with horse-powered machinery and transport. There was little activity on a hot afternoon in late July.

However, twenty-five miles away to the west, one of the major bombardments of the war had been underway for four days.[4] General Douglas Haig's British 2nd Army was preparing the German trenches in front of Ypres for a major attack to begin on the last day of the month. The first objective was to push a salient as far as the village of Passchendaele;

the second the main railway line to Ostend when, if the army could advance to Roulers, it would command the key German railway junction in the northern half of the Western Front; the third was the two canals from Bruges to Ostend and to Zeebrugge, including those three towns, and an end to u-boat activity in Flanders. Four months later, the British offensive petered out around Passchendaele in shell-cratered ground churned into mud by heavy rain and became for the British the 'embodiment of the First World War's waste and futility'.[5] There were over half a million British and German casualties and it was here that the Germans used mustard gas for the first time. As a result of the stalemate, six long-planned, daring, amphibious landings of over 13,000 British troops and nine tanks on the Belgian coast and aimed at the u-boat bases were cancelled.[6]

Shortly after lunch, the local quiet around the canal was shattered. There were few things noisier than the twin diesel engines of a u-boat. On a quiet night at sea, the clatter could be heard several miles off as if in invitation to patrolling Allied anti-submarine craft.

The racket was appalling. The noise was so loud in the dangerous quiet that the longer it went on the less comfortable I felt about it.[7]

The passing of today's submarines could be anticipated: for over two years u-boats usually went out to sea on war patrols on a Wednesday or Thursday, but seldom setting out on a Friday or the 13th of the month which were both well-known to bring bad luck.[8] This Wednesday, 25 July, there were two modern mine-laying uc-boats, *UCs 47* and *61*, travelling on the same afternoon from Bruges North Port.[9] Georg Gerth assumed command of the newly commissioned *UC 61* in December 1916 following five months with the much smaller coastal torpedo boat *UB 12*. After its fourth successful, if particularly hard-fought voyage, *UC 61* spent eleven days in repair docks at Bruges and Ostend while Gerth took leave to celebrate his promotion to Kapitänleutnant. This was Gerth's twentieth trip down the canal in two days short of a year of u-boat captaincy. Gerth's previous visit to Ostend the month before had been eventful. In 1917, there were regular, if often ineffective, attacks on all the u-boat dock areas by Allied aircraft and by naval bombardment. During February, in three separate air raids on Bruges, thirteen houses were destroyed, fourteen civilians killed and many more injured; more than 1,200 bombs were dropped on the city that year.[10] On 5 June, *UC 61* was one of four u-boats in Ostend for repairs.[11] At 0320, the British opened a forty-minute bombardment from two monitors, *Erebus* and *Terror*, causing considerable damage to the dockyards, but no casualties.[12] *UC 61* was in a u-boat shelter for work to her engines, rear torpedo tube and front hydroplane and escaped damage; however, *UC 16* was hit and *UC 70* sunk because it was moored alongside a lighter carrying petrol which was struck by a heavy shell.[13]

> *A whistle blew from the deck of* [our u-boat]. *It had been good to feel the solid earth beneath our feet again, but now the time was up; and not a man of our crew was missing. The seamen were on deck, and the mechanics at their engines and dynamos. All the lights on deck were extinguished; only an occasional flash of a torch betrayed where the cables were being cast off. The boat slid down the Bruges Canal to Zeebrugge.*[14]

Among the pigeons that rose and settled on the canal at the din from the two u-boats, one bird might set off at a steadier pace and fly determinedly to the north-west. Many homing pigeons were parachuted into the occupied territories in baskets strapped to Allied agents. Their target was one of a line of Admiralty stationary pigeon lofts spread on the east coast of England from Newcastle-on-Tyne to Hastings. Up to sixty miles, pigeons were practically infallible; more than 95 per cent of the messages sent by pigeon post during the war were safely delivered. As a result, Admiralty Intelligence knew the timing and number of u-boats making for the sea before the day was out and, often, because of identifying marks and other long-gathered data, and radio intercepts, which boats they were and who were their captains. The unknown source of this information was a continuing worry to the u-boat high command.

> *A great disadvantage of* [the German] *situation is how easily enemy agents can observe us. There are probably agents and spies everywhere, but never is gathering information about an adversary as easy as when, for all intents and purposes, he possesses only one harbour and at all times must return to this one port ... While all the intelligence reports that we receive out of England are unreliable – though when reliable, always days late – English intelligence in all cases reaches England within a few hours.*[15]

There was a small irony here as all u-boats carried a few pigeons.[16] These flew in the opposite direction and alerted the u-boat command of Flanders Flotilla in Bruges of significant success or failure. The Flanders u-boats also carried radio, but it was used sparsely and the greatest restrictions on giving movements and positions while at sea were enforced for fear of the British direction-finding radio masts; security on the Flanders boats was by far the strictest of the u-boat flotillas.[17] 'The effect of this secrecy is to reduce the amount of first-hand evidence as regards details of cruises.' The Germans were greatly shocked when they discovered after the war that the British not only had direction finding equipment, but also the codes used for u-boat transmissions; every message that was sent was read by their enemies. *UC 61*'s telegraphist, Otto Bock was aged twenty-two and from Hoisbüttel. He completed seven months' radio training at Wilhelmshaven, joined *UB 12* as his first sea posting and with Seaman Willy Neumann were the only two men who transferred with Gerth to *UC 61*.

Orders to the two uc-boat commanders were handwritten, dated on Tuesday, the day before, and delivered in person by their leader, Korvettenkapitän Karl Bartenbach.[18] The orders were brief and left matters greatly to individual discretion; Bartenbach was well known for allowing unusual flexibility to his men both on and off duty.[19] First, the commanders were given their day of departure and warned that British submarines were currently operating off the coast of Flanders. Second, they were each told to lay their eighteen mines at a spacing and depth setting as they wished, if possible at the turn of the tide, in designated general areas. Third, they were then to conduct 'trade war', sinking any vessel within another broadly named area. Finally, the boat was to return 'according to capability', but at the latest after twelve days. In adopting this managerial approach, Bartenbach followed the tactical doctrine of *Auftragstaktik*: at every level of military command, operational orders took the general form of defining the objectives and leaving the details to be worked out by the subordinate commanders.[20] 'Control was decentralised – essential for opportunistic u-boat warfare – and both the local knowledge and the initiative of subordinate commanders was given full play.'

Bartenbach's orders instructed a third uc-boat, *UC 21*, to join *UC 61* on the trip to Zeebrugge and from there to lay mines at Exmouth, Berry Head and Dartmouth, but by the time *UC 21* arrived from Ostend at Bruges to take on armaments, it needed repairs to its cooling water pump and was delayed for four days. *UC 47*'s mines were destined for the Channel Islands, and those of *UC 61* for the shipping lanes near the *Royal Sovereign* lightship off Eastbourne, and for Newhaven and Brighton.[21]

The course Gerth always laid to pass through the Channel, and shown by his contemporary hand-drawn maps, hugged the French coast whereas many of his fellow captains chose to sail close to the English side where the water was deeper.[22] There is a continuing misconception that travelling by the French coast meant a French Atlantic destination.

> *Reports had been received that the enemy had sealed the Straits of Dover by means of anti-submarine nets which stretched from Dover to Calais. The investigation of the matter had fallen to Oberleutnant Haecker [UB 6], and on completion of this dangerous mission he had been able to report that, whereas the Straits were almost totally netted off, there was a definite gap close under the French coast between Calais and Cap Gris-Nez.*[23]

There has been much confusion about *UC 61*'s destination and it is often claimed that it was heading for the sea lanes around Boulogne or Le Havre.[24] This misinformation was largely caused by commander Gerth who lied several times in interrogation about his route, where he intended to drop his mines and his operational area. These lies were intended as diversions and were disproved quickly by the British and French interrogators, but have proved long lasting in subsequent histories. In fact, after mine laying on the English south coast, Gerth was ordered to the area between the Isle of Wight and Portland Bill, his regular sinking ground. These destinations are supported by Gerth's written orders which are held in Germany and by papers and maps later found aboard his boat.

It was *UC 47* that was headed for Le Havre after mine laying at the Channel Islands; *UC 21*'s later target area was between Land's End and in front of the Bristol Channel. Neither vessel nor their crews would survive the year.[25] In its career, *UC 47* sank fifty-seven ships and damaged eight others. In turn, the submarine was rammed just forward of its conning tower by patrol boat *P57* off Flamborough Head on 18 November; it was then depth-charged twice. British divers recovered its log and charts. *UC 21* was one of the most successful u-boats of the Great War, ninth on the list of ships sunk with ninety-nine vessels; fourteenth on the list of tonnage sunk at 134,063 tons. Less than two months later on 13 September, *UC 21* again left Zeebrugge, this time for the Bay of Biscay and was lost by unknown cause a few days later.

There is one lock on the Bruges Zeebrugge canal, a sea lock, which the u-boat crews had to operate and which often gave departing u-boats a reason to travel together. In early afternoon, *UC 61* arrived in Zeebrugge harbour where up to two dozen ships could shelter in stormy weather. The boat was already fully fuelled, armed and provisioned, but there was a power supply to allow the u-boat's electric motors to be recharged. *UC-61*'s crew of twenty-six probably remained on board as the 'seaside village did not offer many facilities'.[26] Included was one supernumerary, Max Pucknus, aged twenty-eight from Tilsit, who served as a boatswain with the rank of petty officer first class. Pucknus was on a month's loan from the battleship SMS *Schleswig Holstein* in the second squadron of Germany's High Seas Fleet. It was his first cruise in a submarine. These visits by officers of the Fleet were latterly introduced by the German Admiralty to 'vary the monotony of the existence of personnel in large ships and to interest the whole of the navy in the life of submarine crews'.[27] With increasing and high casualty numbers, volunteers for u-boat service had begun to dry up. Eleven obsolete pre-dreadnought battleships were demobilised in the summer of 1916 to release seamen for submarine duty.[28] By the end of 1916, the voluntary system of recruiting for the submarine service was 'entirely abandoned owing not so much to the danger as to the hardship and discomfort of the life, for which the high pay and good food failed to compensate'.[29] From this time onwards the authorities seem to have had considerable difficulty in selecting suitable officers to man the increased number of u-boats. In addition, it became regular practice to 'transfer up to

15 per cent of each crew after every two patrols to assure a continuous flow of experienced men for future u-boats'.[30] In March 1917, an urgent demand for submarine officers was circulated among the ships in the Baltic and, subsequently, the records show many ships being sent insistent calls for the transfer of young officers.

> *The instance of this man [Pucknus] ... is typical and shows the immobility of the personnel on board the [large ships]. This man shipped on board the iron-clad as [a seaman] in 1908, and gained his stripes one by one. He has not been moved since that date, and made no complaint of having been kept nine years on the same iron-clad, every nail of which he knew. The case of this PO does not seem to be exceptional.*[31]

Despite all of the upheaval, Gerth had a relatively stable and experienced, if young, crew. The average age of twenty-three was kept up by Gerth and his helmsman, Andreas Nagel, both twenty-nine, and the oldest man aboard, navigator Hubert Lengs at thirty. On average, the crew had joined up in the first few months of the war. Eighteen of the men had been with Gerth since around the time of the commissioning of *UC 61*; on average each had fourteen months' u-boat experience and half had also served in another boat.[32]

Gerth paused at Zeebrugge to complete formalities and then made his way at 1525 towards the end of the curving thirty-five-metre-high mole, a solid stone breakwater more than a mile long which contained a railway terminus, a seaplane station and large sheds for personnel and material.[33] One of its cannons was mounted on a platform which could be rocked to imitate waves. Flanders Flotilla gunners used it to practice firing at towed targets at sea.[34]

> *At the seaward extremity of the mole was installed a coastal battery equipped with 88 mm rapid fire cannons under the command of Oberleutnant Schutte. His post was in fact the outermost artillery emplacement of the entire Western Front and by reason of his isolated existence at the end of the two-thousand-metre-long breakwater he was known universally as 'The Pope of the Mole'. He was also the most decent fellow in the world. Crewmen aboard u-boats putting to sea or returning were able to obtain from him all their requirements, including drink. Virtually every u-boat passing the mole would pull alongside the molehead to greet the Pope.*[35]

This mole and the sea lock Gerth had just passed through, were the targets in the famed Zeebrugge raid of 1918. This access of the u-boats of Flanders Flotilla to the North Sea remained a preoccupation of the Allies throughout the war. After the failure to break through to the Belgian canals during the last battle around Ypres, the British sought to land a specially raised force of Royal Marines on the mole from an ageing HMS *Vindictive* on 23 April 1918. In a vicious fire-fight a third of their men were lost.[36] The marines were to provide support and cover while three blockships entered the canal. The crews succeeded in sinking the ships at angles to the canal by blowing out their bottoms, releasing tons of cement to the canal floor. The operation was instantly declared a great success; senior Admiralty officers waited for the returning men on the quayside at Dover in order to hand out gallantry medals. In fact, the raid was largely a failure as a smaller u-boat, *UB 16*, was able to pass through the canal two days later at high tide.[37] Larger u-boats temporarily diverted to the sea through Ostend but, by month's end, the average sailings were back to normal.[38] The Germans removed two wooden piers on the western bank of the entrance to the canal near to the sunken ships.[39] Using dredgers, they scooped a fifteen metre-wide passage and the obstructions, bought with so much blood, were nullified. Vice Admiral Sir Reginald Bacon, fired the previous December as head of the Dover Patrol, described the blocking as 'gallantly carried out, but useless'. The Government was forced to admit after the war that the attack had failed and that the 'incorrect information issued to the Nation by the Admiralty was responsible for the elation of the population and the halo which has surrounded this unfortunate operation'.[40]

In the later afternoon when Gerth left the relative safety of Zeebrugge harbour, he first faced the danger of what the Germans called the 'exclusion area', a double row of 1,500 mines, reinforced by nets full of explosives, which had been laid in April 1916.

> The British laid a line of defence directly in front of the Flanders base. It was a line of mine-studded nets and patrol boats placed eighteen miles out from Zeebrugge and extending for thirty-five miles along the coast from the shallow water outside Dunkerque to the shallows of the Scheldt. There was not enough water at the ends for the u-boat to dodge around the barrier. Nor was it possible to dive under the nets. The water along the line was not deep enough. So it had to be a case of slipping through on the surface at night and trying to give the patrol boats the slip.[41]

Gerth always ran the same course from Zeebrugge, travelling at night, and following where he could the route prescribed for merchantmen. He aimed first for British Buoy 4 on the Outer Ruytingen Sandbank (almost halfway from Dunkerque to Nieuwpoort) then picked up the last buoy of the barrage and the Snouw shoal (26 D), guided by the Dyck Lightship off Gravelines. 'This allowed *UC 61* to round the barrage without passing below or above it.'[42] Gerth then passed south of the Dyck lightship, and intended to go north of Buoy 5, between Calais and Cap Gris Nez, well to sea, but near to Wissant. All these buoys, especially another Buoy numbered 2501 twelve miles off Calais, were familiar to the u-boats.[43] 'In the course of time these beacons became the most trusted friends of the submarine flotilla; they were all numbered, and were of the greatest navigation aid in the passage of the Straights of Dover.'[44]

Gerth then planned to hug the French coast, go through the Dover Straits and then to turn south at Cap Gris Nez, passing the Le Colbart Light Vessel. However, there was another major task; he had also to slip round the end of another net barrier filled with mines, laid between September and November 1916, and which stretched from the Goodwins, passed the Outer Ruytingen Bank to Snouw.[45] The nets were reinforced by 2,010 deep mines laid in three rows to the south. Despite having heavy moorings, the tide sometimes dragged the mines into the nets. Also, as the net sagged in many places, it allowed u-boats to pass over. Submarines could easily distinguish the floats of indicator nets and could avoid them in daylight.[46] It is important to understand that these early submarines were essentially surface vessels that could dive rather than modern boats designed to stay underwater for weeks on end. U-boat historian John Terraine was 'surprised how tightly the u-boats were locked to the surface' which in many cases was their downfall as enforced diving used limited battery power and soon required vulnerable time on the surface recharging.[47] On the surface at a maximum speed of almost ten knots, UC 61 had a range of 3,000 nautical miles, or when cruising at six knots, 5,290 miles. Under water, UC 61 relied on the 1,124 cells of its battery-powered electric motors, which were limited to a range of thirty to forty nautical miles at six knots. There had to be a reason to submerge: stealth, safety from attack, positioning for a torpedo strike, and for rest for the crew, probably stopped and settled on the bottom. Even then, the electric motors were needed to replenish the oxygen supply.

> To break through the barrage on a dark night, on the surface, gives the best prospects. The positions of the net and mines are not exactly known and are constantly altered. Should one be forced to pass through under water, the net must be dived under, in the deep-water channel ... For the Flanders boats it was their daily bread, so to speak. On every cruise from Zeebrugge to the western approaches of the Channel they had to pass through, outward and inward bound. Consequently, they knew the position of the barrage, the individual buoys, the tactics of the patrols, and the alterations in the whole barrage-system. They had experience. They were smaller and handier; and from their base close to the Straits they constantly got up-to-date information, and slipped through on the surface, at a favourable moment in darkness and fog. In spite of all this, the Straits of Dover remained, even for them, a permanent source of the greatest danger.[48]

In between the mines and the nets, the u-boat lanes were constantly patrolled by a steady stream of deadly searchers: fast destroyers able to ram, armed trawlers with depth charges, spotter airships, aircraft with bombs, submarines with torpedoes, and many smaller craft with effective guns:

> *The motorboats in pairs with a steel net between them searched through the Channel where they suspected that u-boats were lurking. Every time we stuck up our periscope cautiously in order to look around a bit, it never failed that we had one of those searching parties right in front of us, so that we must submerge in a hurry to a greater depth in order not to be caught by the dangerous nets.* [49]

After Gerth's return to Germany in 1920, he faced a court of enquiry in Bremen; this court was 'invariably held to enquire into the loss of any war vessel from which there were survivors'.[50] The investigation into Gerth's behaviour seems none too serious as he did not attend and was allowed to supply a handwritten report. Gerth described the weather as 'initially hazy'. Even before he reached the buoys of the barrier net, dense fog set in. Fog was prevalent at this time of year, especially in the early hours of the morning. That same day, the British consular general in neutral Rotterdam asked the Admiralty whether to delay the sailing of British ships.[51]

> *I learnt the value of the comparative invisibility of the submarine. The silhouettes of the Englishmen slid by like wraiths, only a few hundred yards away; often indeed so close that we were afraid they would hear the dull hum of the diesel engines, or have their suspicions aroused by the spray as it flung itself from our bows, dashed over the conning-tower and faded into the darkness astern.* [52]

By the time Gerth was within the mine area, he decided that continuing 'did not carry a greater risk than lying on the bottom or returning'. Before crossing the barrage on the surface, commanders watched for the surveillance measures and the lights marking the line of buoys and then moved at a favourable moment.[53] UC 61 carried at the bow great wire scissors for cutting the nets if the boat became trapped. Gerth's story was backed in an interview with the court by Engineer Sub-Lieutenant Johannes Giese who, like Gerth, had just returned from French captivity. Giese, aged twenty-six, and like his commander from Berlin, was an experienced u-boat man with some twenty-one months aboard U 6, which he left, ironically, just before it stranded on the Maas River and the crew were interned, and on U 74, before joining UC 61 from its commissioning.

Gerth wrote that he was 'at complete invisibility' and had to assess his positioning by dead reckoning shaping a course along the coast between Gravelines and Blanc Nez.[54] By one of those strange coincidences, Gerth's men were heard at this task, but not seen. The story was told by twenty-three-year-old Ensign Louis Guichard who wrote several books after the war romanticising his experiences.[55] Guichard was leading a patrol of four small wooden motorboats each with six men. He was trying to catch some sleep below on a small seat when he was called to the deck by a Breton called Bourhis who had heard something strange. They were about two miles from Buoy 4 at two o'clock in the morning.

> *Very gently, we move forward in the dense fog; the night is perfectly calm; the slightest sound of a voice must carry more than a mile. Leaning over the gunwale we strain our ears; the characteristic hum of a combustion engine crosses the night, then stops, very close. We listen intently with beating hearts. A hoarse voice cries out a command in which I distinguish clearly the words 'rechts [right]' and 'auf [left]'. The Germans are very near ... The voice dies away. The submarine is probably trying to grope its way. The hum of the engine resumes, decreases, distancing itself, and we vainly try to follow. After a quarter of an hour the trail is lost.*

Gerth was below and had delegated the navigation of *UC 61* to Warrant Officer Hubert Lengs, from Dortmund, 'feeling quite confident of his course'. It was Lengs' watch and he was 'on duty near the conning tower'. Although Lengs had been through comprehensive training since the winter of 1915, it was his first voyage on a submarine on active service. Perhaps it is a little strange to understand, but it was normal practice for u-boat commanders to leave all navigation matters to those like Lengs with the skills – even in thick fog.

> *The navigation of submarines is entrusted to a warrant officer, who is a specialist in the subject, and is known as a Steuermann. These navigating warrant officers are well up to their work and reliable in taking star and sun sights. In addition, many boats carry a second Steuermann, or a war pilot, whose special qualification is knowledge of the locality in which the submarine is to operate. These war pilots are usually ex-mercantile officers, who obtained an intimate knowledge of Allied ports by years of trading to them in times of peace. The commanding officer does not as a rule interfere in the navigation or concern himself greatly with it. He gives the navigating warrant officer direction to follow a certain route or to work out the course and speed to reach a certain point at a given time. These warrant officers are the right hands of the submarine commanders.*[56]

Close at hand was Gerth's number two, Leutnant Karl Dancker, an experienced ship's officer who, when the war started, was in New York serving on the *Hamburg Amerika Linie*. After a period as adjutant on the obsolete pre-dreadnought battleship SMS *Kaiser Freidrick*, Dancker volunteered for submarine duty in February 1916, served on *UC 24* from October for two months, and then joined Gerth on *UC 61* at its commissioning.[57] The practice of taking along officers of merchant vessels as military pilots proved successful over time, especially with their knowledge of neutral and enemy shipping. 'After these pilots had gained war experience with tried submarine commanders, they were admirably suited to act as advisers to commanders newly assigned to duty at the front.'[58]

> *With an agility to which I am now accustomed, I swing myself on to the floor. There are only sea-boots to put on, for the rest of one's clothing is worn, day and night, during a voyage that may last weeks. Thus, one's toilet is extremely simple, if not particularly thorough. Indeed, washing and shaving are seldom practised of a morning. It becomes easy to study the luxuriance or otherwise of our respective hair and beards ... Water and soap are very precious on board a u-boat. Morning cocoa and bread and marmalade taste delicious under such conditions.*[59]

Lengs was contouring, carrying out soundings with a weight on a line, knowing that if he kept the boat's depth constant he knew his distance from the shore on the portside and would avoid grounding. The shape of the sand banks off Dunkerque on the way to Cap Gris Nez support this as *UC 61* would have to follow a narrow channel with shallow water either side. This was a similar practice to that used by u-boat commanders 'lost' in the Channel who would ground their boat on the bottom to measure their depth and then assess their position against their detailed charts.

Writing in 1920, Gerth thought he had by dead reckoning travelled one hour passed Cap Griz Nez and changed course a little further southwards – 'I do not recall the exact course' – in the middle between Colbart light vessel and the French coast. Immediately afterwards, he said, he stranded at five in the morning (French reports say at 0420, with which Gerth later agreed) near the village of Wissant at high tide. High tide that morning was scheduled at 0457; by low water at 1209 the sea had fallen five and a quarter metres. Gerth's excuse to his superiors was that 'the fault in my ship's position by dead-reckoning can be attributed in my view to the fact that during the previous days there had been an easterly wind which on the evening of my sailing out had turned into a strong westerly wind. The back-flow of the impounded water must have caused an unusual counter current flow'. Gerth attempted to release the boat by using his engines at full power. When this failed he reduced weight by blowing the buoyancy tanks; firing three torpedoes, one from each tube; throwing artillery ammunition over board; and pumping out some bunker fuel. He was hampered by the boat's construction from doing more: compressed air could not be blown in the oil bunkers.

There are significant, but not vital, differences between the information that Gerth gave his interrogators in Calais on the day of grounding, and that given to his superiors three years later. These differences may not be surprising, but everything that Gerth said has to be weighed. He clearly lied several times. First, he ordered his crew to say that UC 61 had left Zeebrugge on 15 July and 'passed round Scotland to Wissant without laying any mines or committing any hostile act'. All of the prisoners, bar one, obeyed this order, but, afterwards 'acknowledged their obvious lie'. Even Gerth was 'easily convinced' that his story was 'too implausible to pass muster'. He had invented it to hide his passage of the Channel barrage. He then claimed that his destination for mine laying was Boulogne and Le Havre, another lie which was taken at face value by his interviewers, newspaper reporters and, later, historians.

Gerth said that around 0420, UC 61 'jerked several times and stranded in the open sea' which was high on a beach. The surface motors failed to move the boat, first full speed ahead, then astern. Then the electric motors were coupled to the diesels without effect. The two loaded torpedoes were fired from the bow tubes, not three as Gerth later claimed. A firing from the third submerged aft tube risked an early explosion on the sand. Two self-propelled torpedoes were found drifting before midday in the sea off Wissant and Admiral Bacon was alerted by telegram.[60] The two spare torpedoes could be loaded from inside of the boat into the after tube but, as that had not been emptied, time and special equipment would be necessary to raise them through the conning tower for external entry into the empty bow tubes. This became important many years later.

While the crew worked, the water was falling. The bay at Wissant Bay is an eight kilometre long picturesque sweep of slowly sloping sand popular as a bathing resort since the nineteenth century.[61] Its tidal speed is considerable; several hundred metres of flat beach are uncovered in not many minutes. It is also the most rapidly eroding shoreline on the French mainland with up to half a kilometre lost since 1917. For Gerth it was a hopeless task not helped by him still not knowing where he was as the fog was hours from clearing. He told his interrogators later that, at first, he thought he had stranded on the Bassure de Baas, a lengthy shoal around the corner of Cap Gris Nez almost seven and a half nautical miles away.[62] There are many contemporary photographs of UC 61 aground. She lay almost parallel with the dunes, which line the shore in front of an uninhabited area about 800 metres east of the village, near to the tiny hamlet of Strouanne, with her bow pointing to Gris Nez. She was travelling from the east, from the direction of Calais, and from Zeebrugge beyond. Wissant's small fishing fleet was tucked up close to the high tide mark near the village. The u-boat's arrival had not been heard. Today's maritime chart suggests that UC 61 had bad luck for there is a depression in the sand leading from the north-east up the beach, only just worth the recording, but large enough to accommodate a u-boat heading in *UC 61*'s precise direction.[63] This took *UC 61* much further towards the shore than would otherwise have been possible. As the sea receded she was left isolated in a little pond. No amount of weight loss would have got her off.

Gerth gave orders to blow up *UC 61* and instructed telegraphist Otto Boch to send a wireless message to Bruges: 'Have run aground apparently Boulogne. Hopeless. *UC 61*.' German monitoring at E-Stelle West of French radio traffic showed that the boat had stranded at Wissant at high tide and 'there was little chance that it would come free again, especially as it has already been noticed by the enemy'. About three hours later, the Calais radio station reported that the boat had come free, '*s'est fait courir*'. Shortly afterwards, the Eiffel Tower station set the record straight reporting that the crew were captured and the interior of the boat aflame.[64] Gerth said he prepared for the explosion with two torpedoes and thirty blasting cartridges (which were intended for use on captured Allied merchantmen). Some of the bombs, 'in particular, were placed near the reserve torpedo under the locker in the engine-room between the motor bearings and close to the shell room'. At around 0600, Gerth noticed four supposed English destroyers, which anchored as close as possible; Belgian cavalry; and 'one or two companies' of Belgian infantry. Much of this information was exaggerated, but, together, did support his 'hopeless' radio signal. The report of the destroyers' arrival was repeated in the classic u-boat history by Harald Bendert.[65]

> *About 0700, the cartridges were attached* [effected under the direction of Karl Dancker] ... *Secret books and notes were destroyed* ... *I instructed my men on what they should say* [under questioning] *and, with the water level still around 1.20 metres and the Belgians about to come aboard, then went with my crew ashore. The detonations ripped the boat completely apart. Accumulator and oil bunker fires completed the destruction.*

On a perhaps slightly lighter note, it may be that *UC 61*'s pigeons were set free in good time. One of the crew was charged with their welfare and would hopefully have been aware of a recent German Admiralty staff instruction that carrier pigeons were not to be shot 'unless there is absolute proof that they are not ours'. This, of course, was not the case. The problem was that the German Naval Air Service had 'not enough good carrier pigeons at present returning to its pigeon houses'. Captured or dead pigeons were to be 'searched for news and handed in to the 2nd Naval Air Division'.[66]

The senior French interrogator noted that when the crew jumped overboard they 'swam ashore easily' [some reports say 'waded'] and gave themselves up. The first bombs were fired just as the Belgians arrived. Later reports suggest that the cavalry captain wanted to go aboard, but

Gerth cautioned him. 'I beg you do nothing. We are all here and my boat will blow up in a moment or two.'[67] Eight to ten minutes later the bombs exploded and, claimed the interrogator, entirely destroyed the central part of the vessel and starting a fire which burnt out the 'whole interior of the hull'. This was not correct: the complete front of the u-boat, which contained her mines, was untouched and there was only limited damage to the central control section under the conning tower. The fire was extinguished by the sea at 1400 at the next high water.

The response to Ensign Guichard's radio alert to the French Admiralty on his encounter with a German submarine arrived at daybreak: 'Go to Wissant where an enemy submarine has run aground'. The telegram wires from Dunkerque to Admiral Bacon in Dover were humming.[68] The first alert was despatched at 0650: 'Hostile submarine ashore at Wissant at 0600'.[69] French light craft are being sent at once. At 0745, news that the crew of three officers and twenty-three men were prisoners, 'but ship damaged by explosions'.

After half an hour at full speed, Guichard's flotilla arrived in front of the dunes shrouded in mist, and they 'contemplated the hull of an abandoned submarine which smoked sadly under a lowering sky'. Sadly, for Gerth, these four small boats were Gerth's exaggerated four English destroyers, a type Gerth knew well from numerous encounters over the last six months. No English vessels were recorded at the scene. The 'one or two companies' of Belgian infantry never did arrive; some of the Belgian cavalry arrived on bicycles. Guichard registered his disappointment:

> We had hoped that we would need to attack the submarine in order to capture it, but we cannot, alas, do anything: the whale lies dry, surrounded by land on all sides. To its right, the small beach town appears vague between two banks of mist: between them and the submarine ... And in front of this surreal landscape we float on the swell, while from invisible Gris Nez the semaphore station siren solemnly bellows its two blasts each minute.

Guichard's enthusiasm for a fight was misplaced. His 'flock' of four new motorboats, recently arrived from America, were viewed by all as like new toys with doll's house living quarters. They would have stood little chance against UC 61's highly-trained crew with their 88mm canon had Gerth decided to stand his ground.

> You remember our old toy motorboats which cost 29 sous? In the bow a little lead cannon, then a mast with its tin flag, and then in the stern, above the two portholes which had been painted in, the hole for the key to start the engine? At this moment I commanded boats which seemed just like them.[70]

The motor launches were part of an order for 580 vessels to *Elco* (Electric Launch Company Inc.) of Bayonne, New Jersey, and, because America was still neutral, were ordered by the Royal Navy through the Canadian Vickers company and assembled by them in Montreal and shipped across the Atlantic as freight.[71] Forty of the boats were passed to France and Guichard was the proud 'owner' of the first four, ML 114–117, renamed with élan by the French as V1–V4.

Guichard signalled to the beach that his flotilla was returning to their sector. As they did a u-turn, an explosion occurred on the coast 'throwing a puff of yellow smoke out of the submarine'.[72] Throughout, the lookouts at the lighthouse and radio station at Cap Gris Nez sent regular telegrams to Dunkerque.[73] At 0720 they heard a 'really big explosion without being able to distinguish in which direction'; at 0830 another explosion to the east in the direction of Wissant. First sight of the u-boat from which thick smoke was pouring came when the weather started to clear at 1200. Two torpedoes floating at sea were reported at 1215. And, at 1610, lookouts noted that the u-boat's bow was resting 'very high in the water which was up to the rear of the conning tower'. The stern was 'completely submerged' and the fire 'seemed extinguished'.

After the pragmatic, if inconsistent, German view of *UC 61*'s stranding, the French story telling of the happenings on the beach was both more romantic and more dramatic. For the Belgians, a little later, perhaps, it was an attempt to move centre stage. This was a surreal event because it was hampered at least until late morning by the mists slowly burning off in the July sun. Serious work was needed to glean secrets from the wreck and its crew, and both needed guarding. Considerable armaments, jettisoned and lying all about, had to be made safe. The inhabitants of Wissant decamped to the sands and milled around excitedly requiring protection for both themselves and for the remains of *UC 61*. Regardless, fisherman dragged boats to the sea for a morning's work. Local dignitaries arrived and made the town hall available for official matters. There was talk of a musical band. Customs officers and coastguards, and Belgian and French military, all armed, strutted to and fro. The squad of forty Belgian cavalry brought their horses and their bicycles. Alerted in Calais by telephone, the most senior officers of the coastal forces were on their way in motor vehicles to take charge and with them brought their official news teams and photographers – and a film cameraman. British allies, who led the local fight at sea against the u-boats, had to be informed and allowed their proper role. Luncheon would be a serious logistical matter for the few local inns; opportunities for a quick profit abounded among those with provisions to sell. Over the next days, journalists arrived in numbers, many instructed to attend from head offices in Paris, and all requiring accommodation, insight and exclusivity. Above it all, heroes were to be found and recognised in this sorely needed national triumph.

It is not surprising that, amongst the hyperbole and daily clamour for new information, and the writing and rewriting, especially many years later in semi-official histories and on the internet, the truth became somewhat opaque.

Picture this: It is shortly before five in the morning. Apart from the steady ripple of the waves on the flat beach, it is fog quiet. This is the time to take the shrimps that have come up with the tide and are trapped in sand pools as the sea falls back. A young shrimp girl, 'une pêcheuse de crevettes', bare-footed, skirt tucked in her bloomers away from the cold water, the pole of a wide-headed net held in both hands, gently scoops her prizes and tips them into the fish bag across her shoulders, her thoughts, as every other morning, elsewhere. Several hundred metres along the coast, as she crosses the bottom of a little bay formed by the lowering tide, a fifty-metre submarine slowly appears.[74]

Thinking she had found a French ship, the unnamed and unsung heroine ran straight to the nearest semaphore and customs post, where M. Charlemagne Honvault was on duty – the same M. Honvault who was eleven years later to play the leading part in the fate of UC 61's carcass. On her way to the semaphore, the shrimp girl met a coastguard who she told of her find. This was Coastguard 2nd Class, Stanislas Pierre Louis Serin, shortly to become a national hero. The coastguard was tasked with cracking down on contraband and collecting everything the tide brought ashore on the sand or on the rocks.[75] By good fortune, Serin's handwritten statement on an official form and made two days after the stranding survives in the French military archives at Vincennes Castle, east of Paris.[76] In it, Serin describes being alerted by Honvault at 0445. There is no mention of the shrimp girl.

> I went to the beach straight away and was joined by the brigadier of customs [Lambert], head of the post, he was accompanied by [two] customs officers [Under Brigadier Delcroix and Officer Tedellec] armed with their guns and I had my revolver. We were taken along the beach up to the submarine (port side) by M. Jean Ternisien, owner of the lugger No. 461.[77] There was a thick fog and we could only vaguely distinguish what had happened [...]. The crew were busy throwing ammunition into the sea, but were doing this on the starboard side – the side facing the open sea – we were unable to see properly what they were doing ... The commander was at his post on the bridge, a large number of the men had their life belts on – one held in his hand a life buoy with the writing 'Unterseeboot'. _The engines were still running_.[78] At the first inquiry by the brigadier of customs, 'Do you speak French?', the commander said, 'Yes'. [It was noted in many reports that Gerth spoke excellent French.] Second question: 'What nationality are you?' No reply. 'English?' Same. Me: 'German?' ... As I know from

*long experience the manoeuvres necessary to refloat a steam ship,
[everything] confirmed to me we had an enemy in front of us and with
the agreement of the brigadier I made ... the owner of the boat put us
ashore at the closest point to go and telegraph Calais. It was then about
... hours when an order came by telephone from the Place de Calais
[ZAN headquarters] to get the crew to disembark immediately. I gave
the order to the boat owner Ternisien to put to sea again. When we
arrived, the crew were getting into the water and after around fifteen
minutes the vessel exploded. It was 0730.*

Over the next few days, various official letters from higher and higher
up the chain of command, even to Vice Admiral Pierre-Alexis Ronarc'h,
supreme commander of the Northern Army Zone (ZAN) at Dunkerque,
and to the Ministry of the Marine in Paris, particularly praised the actions
of Serin and Ternisien.[79] It was pointed out that neither of the men
hesitated to approach the enemy submarine 'even though its situation was
still unclear, and a refloating could have been envisaged'. The two men
had 'bravely done their duty without any fear for what could happen to
them and it was not certain in the first instance whether they would be
exposed to gunfire'. Things turned out peacefully, but 'this was not certain
until after the event'. The Commander of the Marine at Calais, de Bon, put
forward both men for 'official recognition of satisfaction'.

At the extreme, it was the Belgian cavalry which claimed the day.
The lancers of the 5th Regiment spent the summer 'resting' on the coast
near Wissant and, after Serin had effected his capture, were called on to
guard the prisoners who were taken to Wissant Town Hall, and then to
escort them as the crew was walked the same day to Calais Citadel for
interrogation and incarceration.[80] The exaggerations reached their peak in
a newspaper article which turned Coast Guard Serin into a Belgian lancer
who challenged the submarine. 'The response was hubbub. A shot was
fired.' The article continued, 'Cavalrymen first of all, charge at the attack.
In a wave, the squadron resolutely entered the water. They had not gone
more than twenty metres when the crew, as one man, threw themselves in,
too, but with their hands up. We approached them furiously, cries, scuffles,
jostling, splashing around, the victorious and the prisoners reached the
sand and stopped there dripping wet'.[81] The Lancer regiment was quickly
given the life-time soubriquet, 'Submarines'. It wasn't long before this
reporting transmogrified and, later, typically, appeared on the internet in
an otherwise largely correct web report as '*Quand la Cavalerie belge captura
un sous-marin allemande*'.[82]

The coastal commander from Calais, Captain J Rigal, was alerted at
0620 by Calais town hall, which also alerted the Intelligence Service.[83] The
commander made arrangements for every eventuality: mobile artillery to
destroy the submarine from the land; two loads of gun cotton explosives;

men armed with guns; trucks and cars to take them quickly to Wissant. He travelled by car with the marine commander of Calais. On arrival at 0740, Rigal instructed the locking up of the three officers and twenty-three men of the crew with a twenty-man armed guard. He assessed the fuel fire as 'unwise' to approach and unstoppable as it moved forward up the boat and reached the conning tower at 0745; there were explosions every fifteen minutes. 'When the tide put out the fire ... I reckoned that the submarine had been completely disembowelled by the numerous explosions inside it and ravaged by the fire with the exception of the compartments with the mines.' The commander eventually saw to the taking off of the machine gun and small arms and their ammunition, and the collection of the many shells and bombs which lay about after being thrown overboard.

Rigal made some other decisions, one with surprising consequences many years later. While he set the marine commander to carry out a preliminary interrogation of the three officers, he organised the customs officers to search all of the crew. The officers gathered eleven wallets, some money, photographs and several cards and personal papers.[84] The prisoners were allowed to keep their clothes, their food (bread and sausage) and tobacco and cigarettes. Almost one hundred years later at Chateau de Vincennes in Paris, as part of the searches for this story, a brown envelope was opened and out tumbled many of these confiscations. The money was in two parts. First, three notes from the Chamber of Commerce in Oran were found in the wallet of Stoker Christian Carstensen, age twenty-three from Flensburg. Carstensen had been aboard *UC 61* when a boarding party scuttled the French steamer *Nelly* which was carrying wine from Oran to Rouen the previous May.[85] Second, one franc banknotes issued by the Chamber of Commerce at Boulogne were found in the wallet of navigator Hubert Lengs, who, it was noted, spoke French well. Also inside the envelope at Vincennes, taken from Gerth's wallet, was a poem about the u-boat war, *U-Boote heraus!*

u-boats are out![86]

You stormy weather sound,
Now you flow through the lands
It is as if your brazen urge
Now breaks all chaining bonds:
u-boats are out!

As if through snow and winter rage
A spring storm burst –
Now will the rolling, icy flood
A wildest dance spray through:
u-boats are out!

Now will after strangling fear and pain
After heavy, wavering thoughts
To spread the iron seed
The sowing day begin:
u-boats are out!

Now will the wall wrought from ore
Bind even more unbreakable
When the glorious password flies above
As with mighty rattling winds:
u-boats are out!

Now forwards you heroes too big for words
Drive out and bring it to an end
Now we lay Germany's future fate
Into your hero hands:
u-boats are out!

There is no reason to believe that French instructions for interrogating naval prisoners were much different from those issued by the Germans to its own officers.[87] In any event, as a potential taker of prisoners, Gerth would have known these orders and therefore what might happen. He expected his officers and men to be separated immediately and for this reason had given unrecorded instructions to his assembled men before they left the u-boat. This immediate separation by the French was so that the crew had 'no opportunity of talking over their evidence or of influencing each other's statements' because 'the mere presence of officers is liable to make the men more silent and reticent'. Letters, notebooks and any other documents were to be taken from the prisoners at the earliest opportunity and nothing must be thrown overboard or destroyed. There should be a search for secret books. The first interrogation was to take place immediately after capture as 'experience has shown that gratitude for rescue makes [the prisoners] more communicative and trustful than at any other time'. The second interrogation would depend primarily on the capability with which it is conducted and it was therefore 'important to select suitable men for the purpose'. For officers, this also meant equivalence of rank, language skills and familiarity with the enemy's naval organisation.

Général Ditte, military governor general of Calais, hero commander of the Moroccan division at the Battle of the Marne, arrived at 0815; Vice Admiral Ronarc'h at 0900 to take control of the wreck site. There were now three putative authors present. Guichard was shortly to depart in his patrol vessel. Ronarc'h wrote several books, but, sadly, only the first part of his memoirs, which concluded at the end of 1916. He had a stellar naval career and had commanded the legendary soldier fusiliers – 'the girls with red pompoms' – which fought at Dixmude and the Yser in the first months of the war, before taking command of the navy in the North, the ZAN.[88] Général Ditte's history of Calais during the war dealt sparsely with *UC 61* confirming the general events and adding that only Gerth was given a summary interview at Wissant before the crew was marched off to Calais Citadel by the lancers.[89] After looking to the safety of the many onlookers, Ronarc'h's first task was to make *UC 61* safe; wreck it may have been, but the u-boat still carried much of its considerable arsenal.

The uc-series boats had four ways to sink enemy ships and these set Admiral Ronarc'h's priorities.[90] *UC 61* was firstly a mine-layer. The whole area forward of the conning tower was taken up by six slanted 100cm mine shafts, open to the sea, that each carried three mines, one on top of the other, and all eighteen were in place.[91] Two forward torpedo tubes high on the deck each carried a 50cm torpedo ready loaded, but these should not be fired until all of the mines were laid for fear of premature explosion; and yet, they had been fired on stranding and found. Were the mines unstable as a result? There was also a rear tube below the waterline, also possibly with a ready-loaded torpedo. Room within the boat was at a premium and it was assumed in intelligence reports that no spares were carried; and yet two were carried ready to be loaded in the after tube: one was lashed to the roof of the petty officers' quarters; the other was stowed under the locker in the engine room between the bearings of the two diesel motors.[92] All torpedoes had to be lowered into the boat using special cranes; it was no easy matter to take them out again back at Bruges if unused, and especially not on a beach and potentially under fire. On the deck, forward of the conning tower, was an 88mm cannon which could be used for fighting armed steamers, stopping unarmed ships or sinking smaller ones. Standard issue was about 120 rounds 'but this was often considerably exceeded'.[93] If the cannon was deemed 'overkill', *UC 61* had a detachable 13mm machine gun and numerous small arms. Gerth had, earlier in the year, stopped a sailing schooner with only several shots from his pistol. Once aboard a stopped vessel, and with the enemy crew moved to lifeboats, *UC 61* carried a large number of explosive devices with timers, hand bombs, which could be attached to a vessel at the water line and set to explode when the boarding party had safely left.

Ronarc'h firstly ordered the giant net scissors to be detached from the bow and thrown onto the sand so that a wooden crane and pulley system could be installed to remove the cannon and send it with its ammunition to Sevran-Livry, north of Paris, for testing.[94] At the same time, he asked for the mines to be taken off. On 2 August, the u-boat was 'shaken up by bad weather' and had, supposedly, said the lighthouse watchers, turned right around and was facing south. Only one mine had been removed by 13 August, but it had to be sunk at sea, where it possibly remains, because it was impossible to remove the detonator. The work also had to be halted because of the placing of the crane to remove the cannon. The tilt of the wreck made matters worse and the men were nervous of pulling the mines out half-sideways because little was known of the model and its sensitivity. By 1 September, *UC 61* was sinking further into the sand halting the extraction of the mines and their removal to Calais; ten remained on board.

An enemy submarine on the beach of a tourist village, even in wartime, cannot be hidden. It is not going anywhere and can be seen from any number of vantage points. Quickly, local people, Belgian cavalry officers, and tourists from Calais and beyond were out with their cameras.[95] In a few days, postcards were on sale. *UC 61* was to remain a tourist attraction for many years to come. Following the initial story of the wreck and the capture of the crew, the main excitement was the march of the German sailors to Calais Citadel. For this event, a local man, Marius Alix, scooped his competitors and sold his stories as a 'Special Envoy' to the Paris edition of *Le Petit Journal*, one of the four major French daily newspapers.[96] The French authorities were obliged to issue press statements within twenty-four hours and then keep making almost daily statements for the next two weeks.[97] Alix had his first stubs printed the day after the wreck, Friday. On Saturday, he provided additional information, mostly of good accuracy. He knew, for instance, that the wreck was caused by navigational error, how it was fired, that the crew had reached shore without difficulty and that no mines had been sewn. His main coup reached the paper's Sunday edition and described his visit to the submarine at the same time as Ronarc'h and Ditte, the arrival of the crew in Calais, and a personal interview with Gerth, perhaps just a passing shouted exchange in the street.[98] A number of his descriptive passages are worth recalling:

> *The normally calm streets of Calais filled about two o'clock in the afternoon with swarms of people. This is the hour when the throng of these little lace-making fairies return to their workshops.*

> *Framed by Belgian lancers, twenty-two German sailors and two officers paraded past them. Monocle riveted in place, with a surly air, one of the officers seemed satisfied with the curiosity they were creating.*[99] [The monocle represented, beyond all other badges of rank, the affectation and assumed superiority of the Prussian officer class.][100]

> *I wanted to see where this enemy boat was stuck, or what remained of it. Leaving Calais, we took the road, which follows the twisting coastline, past Sangatte, Escalles, and there we were at Wissant, a small town of 900 inhabitants. Everyone, naturally, was on the beach and I could see very clearly, about 600 metres away, the huge wreckage. From afar it looks like some marine monster vomited up by the sea which lay, disembowelled, on its side.*

A cordon of troops keeps the curious at a distance because there is continuing concern about a possible explosion from a forgotten explosive device inside it.

The brave customs officer, a little nervous – who wouldn't be when twenty-four Germans come out of the water towards you and there is only you to receive them – aimed his weapon and warned the officer that if he or his men tried to escape, he would shoot without hesitation.

[Gerth] responded to the ultimatum from the customs official with the word immortalised by Cambronne [merde].[101] The customs official had the good taste not to respond and the German, happy with that and after having confirmed that he was giving himself up, turned back to his crew. The men bustled about the boat a bit then with the water up to their middles reached dry land.

This prize, although pretty much unusable, was pleasing for ... it rid us of a dangerous pirate; a crew trained in submarine warfare since they say – are they bragging – we have sunk **seventeen** *ships.[102]*

The German commander, who speaks our language very well, explained that when he had stopped on the bottom of the seabed to allow his crew to rest they were far from the coast but he had not taken account of the low tide which he believed was not that strong at this location and, furthermore, the falling tide had moved a sandbar against which his boat had rested. Moreover, that morning, thick fog had prevented an accurate assessment of distances.

It is with visible frustration the German officer recounted to those who questioned him the superhuman efforts he made not to fall into our hands. He was no doubt dreaming, seeing himself captured, of the many attacks which were now impossible to commit.

But did his frustration not, above all, give such pleasure to the little lace-makers of Calais who saw him and his crew as evildoers paraded between the Belgian police?

The crew passed through the hamlets of Hervelinghem and Saint-Inglevert. They made a sensational entry into Calais, dressed in black oilcloth suits and the men wearing berets of the same fabric. They took the boulevards Gambetta and Jacquard which led to the Citadel, a multi-walled fortress begun in the late sixteenth century, and moved through the main gate with its portcullis housing and arrow slots.[103] There remains sufficient barred windows and steep steps on the inside of the internal wall to give a good impression of the cells awaiting the men. The major interrogations, each lasting about one hour, took place here. In a few days, the crew was moved to a number of prison holding camps for dispersal.

No self-respecting senior military officer travelled to an opportunity like Wissant beach without their personal official photographers nearby. One photographer made it to the beach on the day of the stranding. A picture, not dramatic, but first, was taken at about midday at some distance along the beach, and shows smoke still rising from the wreck. The four official military reporters arrived at the wreck early in August and produced glass plate pictures in black and white, now held by the French military's audio-visual archive.[104] The first three, Jacques Agié, Edmond Famechon and Charles Winckelsen, were present on the 4th and the fourth, Albert Moreau, on the 6th. While the captions on the photographs are modern, the original '*Légende*' still exists detailing the reporters' own notes and dates of travel. They show, for instance, that Agié was already in Flanders, Famechon and Moreau came from Picardy, and Winckelsen from the Aube and went on to the Oise. Agié's pictures are dramatic and cover the whole wreck under guard at low tide. Famechon concentrated on the firepower of *UC 61*: the mineshafts and the removal apparatus for the canon, and also the damage caused by the explosion. Moreau called in at Calais Citadel first to take a picture of one of the removed mines and then captured an inspection by French and British senior officers who clambered, some with difficulty, up to the deck using flexible rope and metal ladders. Winckelsen covered the same visit, but with close-ups of the officers, who moved among casual French sailors on the deck.

Despite the excellence of these pictures, many of which have been copied and appropriated without reference on the internet, pride of place goes to a film of the wreck taken by Cameraman Daret, also on the 6th.[105] The film lasts one minute thirty-two seconds and shows, in remarkably good quality, *UC 61* under guard at low tide.

How much should all of this considerable information about the sixteen hours or so of *UC 61*'s last voyage be believed? Was it possible for a u-boat to be so hopelessly wrong in its position after so short a journey? The answer, according to Captain Chris Phillips, formerly of HM Submarines, using contemporary charts and tidal information, is 'Yes'.[106] 'I have not made a definitive reconstruction of the boat's movements, but taken a good educated guess based on my understanding of the conditions, likely performance of the submarine, contemporary charts and tables, and my knowledge of the area. In answer to your question: I am pretty sure this would have been an accidental grounding. This is not just because the conditions all point in that direction, but also because I can't see what he would have gained from grounding deliberately.' Should Gerth have been on the bridge at the time of grounding? The answer, given the then practice in the Imperial Navy, and given where he thought he was and his reasonable confidence in his navigating warrant officer, is 'No'.

Even in good visibility, as Gerth is going out on patrol, he would need to conserve his fuel for the patrol as well as keeping some reserve of speed for any emergencies. I reckon on five to six knots passage speed in the better visibility at the start of the voyage, dropping to three to four knots when he entered the fog. Even if he had revolutions set for more speed than this, it is quite possible in the strong westerlies which he mentions that his speed would have been reduced further by the effect of the wind on the submarine and the short choppy waves which would have been thrown up by the wind. At the time of grounding, it was high water, but by no means slack. In fact, in the vicinity of Griz Nez at this state of tide, the tidal stream is at its maximum strength, and Gerth would have been pushing into it since around midnight. So, for most of the period during which he had been in restricted visibility, he would have navigated by dead reckoning. I expect in the circumstances it would be quite easy for him to overestimate his ground speed. I doubt that he would have been going backwards at any stage, but had just been slowed and set more than expected. I deduce that he reached the offing of Dunkerque, and the east end of the mined netting barrage, in better visibility between 2200 and 2359, and then reduced speed marginally due to the restricted visibility at that point. Making about four knots through the water, the combined effect of the two and a half knots' tide and the strong westerly wind have reduced the speed over the ground by more than what he allowed. His dead reckoning position is out. Where he thinks he is altering course out in open water (as he says, an hour beyond Gris-Nez and halfway between Colbart light and the French coast) to continue his transit of the strait, he is actually still well to the east of Gris Nez, halfway between today's Abbeville and CA3 buoys. Had he been where he thought he was the tidal stream, albeit adverse, would have been in a reciprocal direction and would not have affected his course over the ground significantly. However, as he was further east, there was more of an east-going element to the tidal stream, which would have pushed him to the east and hence he grounded off Wissant.

Captain Phillips added a proper and important caveat. He was confident in his deduction 'unless there is another context of which I am not aware'.

Gerth said in his interrogation that on stranding he thought he was on Bassure de Baas over seven miles away. If true, Captain Phillips' work shows that Gerth's mistake was entirely possible. Remember, also, that on stranding Gerth signalled to his headquarters in Bruges that he thought he was near Boulogne which is consistent with stranding on the Bassure de Baas. This information, for background, explains why so many histories, written after war, show the wreck of *UC 61* near Boulogne, well around the corner of Cap Gris Nez.[107] This error is repeated to current times.

If a lie, and Gerth lied often and usually understandably, mostly to deceive his enemies, then Gerth thought he was somewhere else. The reasonable assumption in this case is that Gerth knew exactly where he was and he was there for either an undisclosed or a hidden purpose. Gerth later claimed to Marius Alix that he had 'stopped on the bottom of the seabed to allow his crew to rest'. He had then stranded because of a series of errors and because the retreating tide had 'moved a sandbar against which his boat had rested'. The idea of a tired crew after leaving port just twelve hours before is not credible. Even if true, and *UC 61* were on the bottom near its final resting place, the sea was so shallow that it could never have submerged more than a few feet and this would have been immediately evident inside the boat.

There are a number of other possibilities which can be reasonably rejected. A first thought is that Gerth was, in fact, surrendering, having had enough of the danger of the submarine war. The rate of u-boat losses was increasing after the easier days of 1916. The German Navy lost fifteen u-boats between May and July 1917, but the ratio remained favourable: fifty-three merchant ships were sunk for each u-boat sunk. Moreover, twenty-four u-boats replaced the fifteen lost.[108] Even the brashest of commanders based in Bruges knew that they were unlikely to survive the war and that their death, while glorious, would probably be slow and unpleasant. This inevitability was regularly discussed under drink in the officers' mess. And, yet, despite the probability of death, morale amongst the officers of the Flanders Flotilla remained remarkably high to the end of the war; it remained in many ways the most popular posting. Few officers survived to tell of their experiences.[109]

> From the force of 1,400 that began the war, approximately 18,000 men passed through the submarine combat and support services by war's end, of whom perhaps 11,400 actually served in u-boats. During the war 5,132 u-boat officers and men were killed or died of wounds, and an additional 729 captured – a loss rate of over 51 per cent ... Of 457 u-boat commanders, 152 were killed and thirty-three captured, for a total loss of over 40 per cent.[110]

Across the submarine service, numbers of officers suffered from nervous breakdown or were incapacitated by heart trouble or eye-strain, and the case of *UC 39*, which surrendered on her first cruise after the explosion of a depth charge near her which caused only slight damage, is 'eloquent of both lack of training and shaken nerves'.[111] Certainly, the French interrogators recognised that almost to a man the crew of *UC 61* 'felt little grief for her loss. On the contrary, [the crew] were plainly well pleased to see the end of a life which had assuredly proved rough, uncomfortable and full of danger.' The interrogators agreed that, with the exception of a few hardened 'East Prussians', 'no side or bravado was shown'. There was a 'want of enthusiasm and ardour' which was a great contrast to the 'fine military spirit' shown by the crew of *UB 26* the previous year.[112] If Gerth was planning to give himself up, it was unlikely to be something that he would have shared with his crew for fear of disclosure, disgrace and arrest. If true, Gerth would have ensured he was conning the vessel and not settled below at the crucial moment unless, of course, he already knew before he went below that *UC 61* was committed in Wissant Bay and would never round Cap Gris Nez. It would, at the end, have been spontaneous for he could not plan for the dense fog and, if the fog had not been there, his deck crew would have seen the shore lights. There is nothing in the general papers, interrogations, Gerth's subsequent behaviour or actions or at the court of enquiry in 1920 that adds any support to this theory. Finally, anyone reading the chapters on Gerth's war career or his attempts to escape imprisonment must be impressed by his courage and tenacity. This was not a man tempted to give his boat and crew to the enemy.

For an opposite point of view, there is one press article written two weeks after the wrecking, when exciting news was fast becoming difficulty to find. Eugene Tardieu said in the *Echo de Paris* that he was told that Gerth 'wanted to blow up the boat with himself and the crew rather than be taken prisoner'. Tardieu also claimed that the crew included deserters who had been recaptured and put forcibly aboard and that they had threatened to kill Gerth.[113] This suggestion is unsupported by any British, French or Germany testimony. The crew records show that most of them were volunteers and none of them were deserters. The whole article smacks of over-excited reporting.

For Albert Chatelle, writing in 1949 in his long, lucrative series about seaside towns in war, the finding of one franc banknote on Navigator Lengs may be crucial. 'We don't really know whether the grounding was purely accidental or if the submarine had to come dangerously close to shore to land an officer who was in excess of the normal complement and on whom was found currency notes issued during the war by the Chambers of Commerce of Boulogne and Calais'.[114] Was this just a journalistic fishing trip? There are three immediate errors in Chatelle's interpretation: the money was found on the u-boat's navigator, Lengs, not on supernumerary Pucknus; there was only one note; and the note was issued solely on Boulogne, not jointly with Calais. If Lengs had truly been, even momentarily, considered a spy, his interrogation would have gone differently from that of the rest of the crew and there is no indication of this in any record. The only evidence of different treatment for Lengs is that he was the one crew member moved to the prison camp at Serres-Carpentras where he remained until 1920. At this time, the records are full of summary executions by the French of individuals accused on flimsy evidence of spying. Feelings at large were running high. The case against Lengs is dismissed for want of further evidence. But where did he get his solitary note? This was his first trip aboard *UC 61*; his time beforehand was concentrated in North Germany. If Lengs was not a spy, the case for Gerth moving too close to a beach to either pick up or drop off a spy also falls. There is no mention in Bartenbach's orders of a 'black op', but then there never were hints of this sort of work while there were surely many clandestine operations for the Flanders Flotilla.

In fairness to Gerth, he was not the only commander to hazard his boat in the North Sea in 1917 in difficult weather. In May, *U 59*, Kapitänleutnant Freiherr Wilhelm von Fircks, searching for navigational signals in the fog, ran onto a German mine net south of Horns Reef off the Danish coast and lost thirty-three men.[115] In November, *U 48*, Kapitänleutnant Karl Edeling, drifting while waiting for a full moon, and *U 94*, in heavy seas, both ran aground on the Goodwin Sands.[116] *U 48* was discovered at dawn the next morning by British patrol craft. After a brief exchange of gunfire, scuttling charges were set and the crew abandoned the boat leaving nineteen dead. *U 94*, Kapitänleutnant Alfred Saalwächter, managed to free himself by following Gerth's example and considerably lightening the vessel.[117]

For *UC 61*, there remains one possibility, publicly evident at the time and yet barely mentioned officially by the Allies. It is so relevant, that its omission and lack of subsequent investigation or comment is challenging. *UC 61* had been hit in the conning tower by a shell which did not explode, but could have caused real damage. And, supposedly, Commander Gerth was never asked about it by his interrogators or never mentioned it even to his own superiors. Could this be possible?

On the evidence, the first person to mention the shell hole was Royal Navy Commander Henry Spencer of HMS *Arrogant*, accompanied by Engineer Lieutenant Commander Edwards, quickly sent from Dover for an inspection of the wreck. Spencer's observations were typed up on 29 July, possibly on return to Dover, for Sir Reginald Bacon, Vice Admiral of the Dover Patrol, who received the document the next day.[118] Overall, the report comes a little short and is not hopeful of much that might be of use to the Allies. To be fair, this was an early inspection and Spencer found the interior of the submarine 'a complete wreck'. It might be possible to get more details of remaining intact gear 'when the debris is cleared away'. There is one almost throwaway paragraph deep within the report:

> *The conning tower appears to have been struck by a projectile, as there is a small hole such as a projectile would make on the starboard side of it. Although there is no trace of any further damage inside. This may have been the reason for the grounding of the submarine.*[119]

The next mention was by military reporter Edmond Famechon during his visit on 4 August. In the general caption to his eleven photographs, he typed for his legend, '*UC 61* wrecked at Wissant after having been hit by an English shell and scuttled by her crew'. He added in his own handwriting, 'From information that I could gather, it is assumed that the submarine was hit by a shell to the conning tower (as shown in photo number nine) and came inshore to perform the necessary repairs.'[120]

Photo number nine is a posed close-up of a Frenchman in uniform (hopefully, it is the famed Serin; the gentleman appears in many of the pictures by several photographers) leaning forward and staring intently at a clear round breach of the conning tower, the metal bent inward through impact. The impact is forward and on the right-hand side. There is no evidence of an explosion.

The press got to the story when one of the writers for the Paris edition of *Le Journal* visited the wreck on 13 August: 'It was as a result of a fight that the submarine grounded. It carried, on the left side of the conning tower, a shell hole through which in high seas, waves entered the submarine. To make a repair at night, the pirate came to hide from the waves behind the headland [Cap Gris Nez]. Here it touched a sandbank and grounded.'[121] Here there are a number of errors: the hole is on the starboard side; the sea was calm and not choppy enough to throw 'waves into the submarine' through a three-to-four inch hole four feet above the deck; it was no sandbank, but the beach. But, however, the general point is made.

Finally, *Le Miroir* on 19 August carried a full-page picture and caption, headlined 'The *UC 61* Had Been Hit by a Shell'.[122] This picture, not one recorded by the official photographers, was clearly taken in the first few days as the u-boat's canon was not yet removed. The caption was headed: 'A cross on the conning tower indicates the hole made by a projectile'.

> *In our last edition, we published two photographs of the German submarine, which had just been grounded in the Pas-de-Calais and whose crew were captured. Interest in this catch has doubled by the fact that the U-61 [sic] did not ground following a steering error but because it had been seriously damaged by allied patrols. You can see here a hole in the conning tower of the vessel made by an English or French shell.*

A later report by the Royal Navy added that the conning tower was built of steel plating about half an inch thick and had been penetrated by a small projectile making a jagged hole about three inches in diameter. This UC II class of submarine was developed in 1915 when construction speed was of the essence. They suffered a 'decisive construction error: there was no hatch between the conning tower and pressure hull so that the exposed conning tower became the weakest part of the hull'.[123] As there was no lower conning tower hatch, the pressure hull plating had been covered with a layer of cement up to within one and a half inches of the top of the conning.[124] In other words, the conning tower pressure hull could have been penetrated and, if so, *UC 61* would not be able to dive without substantial repair.

David Townsend qualified as a Royal Navy Shipwright Artificer involved with ship construction and design and then served on both conventional and nuclear submarines as a Seaman Officer.[125] His practical experience is fundamental to his informed view as to the likely source and effect of the shell hole.

> *It is likely that UC 61 sustained a hit from a coastal vessel's 3.5–4 inch gun through the starboard for'd fairing of the fin that streamlines the conning tower.[126] The shell was probably an impact-fused version that failed to explode because of the very thin mild steel superstructure. However, there are a number of essential service pipes and the hatch of the conning tower that could have been damaged by the shell. If the inner hull was breached, the importance of the damage would have forced the commanding officer to seek shelter to attempt repairs. Because of fog, dead reckoning navigation and a high tide, the vessel grounded at the top of the tide and was left stranded.*

> *The casing superstructure is made from light metal (possibly five to ten pound) and the pressure hull is twenty-pound plating. A Royal Navy engineer officer would have worked on the basis that a one-inch thick plate is forty pounds, and therefore the pressure hull would be half an inch thick and the superstructure casing could be as little as one-eighth of an inch thick. The discrepancy in the thickness of the plate is because the casing is 'free-flood' and so not under pressure when dived and merely provides streamlining and protection to external fittings and the conning tower. However, as noted by the RN inspectors, efforts were being made to save metal at this stage of the war.*

A failed explosion from a shell fired by any warship would have caused no surprise at the time. The rapid increase among the Allies in their requirement for artillery shells had 'overtaken the procedures for quality control'.[127] In January 1915, one German observer reckoned that half the shells fired by the French were duds, some because of incompetence and haste, but others because of profiteering and fraud. At the Battle of the Somme in July 1916, 30 per cent of shells failed to explode. Townsend feels that regardless of the lack of explosion the submarine could have been prevented from diving for three reasons. First, the shell severed a compressed air pipe that passed through the fin on the starboard side between the external compressed air tanks. These pipes were used for surfacing by blowing water from the ballast tanks II and III and used to dive and surface the boat.[128] Second, the shell severed the venting lead air cocks situated in the fin which led from the forward oil fuel tanks to the external oil fuel tanks. This could potentially lead to contaminated diesel oil wrecking one of the two diesel engines, or allow diesel to leak to the surface giving the position of the submarine away.[129] Third, the shell may have disrupted the watertight integrity of the upper hatch of the conning tower leading into the submarine. As no lower hatch was fitted for safety as in modern submarines, the boat would have filled quickly with water had the submarine dived with the leak undiscovered. 'Should the submarine be in a collision with a ship passing over the top and damaging the conning tower as it is proud of the pressure hull, there would be no way to isolate the rest of the boat.'

The restriction to one hatch in the UC-series boats was at best a major design compromise, at worst a serious safety fault.[130] If Gerth had come ashore to effect a vital repair to a compromised conning tower, he would have found on inspection, says Townsend, that it was impossible. The fairing gave only an inch or two of space to allow access to the rounded surface behind it and, in this space, would need to be fitted a patch capable of withstanding rapid emergency diving to a depth of, perhaps, four of more atmospheres.

Townsend contends that *UC 61* was hit by a vessel while at sea. The shell would have arrived from the seaward side of the u-boat as it travelled south-west. This makes immediate sense. The possibility that the shot was fired after *UC 61* was beached needs brief consideration, but this option can be swiftly discounted. Nobody knew that the submarine was on the beach until it was spotted when close by the prawn fisher girl. The fog remained dense during the contacts between Gerth and his crew, and a shrimp girl, the coastguard, customs officials and, eventually, the Belgian lancers. Before the fog lifted, the beach was crowded with military and townspeople and remained so. The only Allied vessels ordered to the scene were Ensign Guichard's patrol boats and they did not fire.[131] If a shot was fired from the distance necessary, and to hit *UC 61* at the angle at which it did while lying stationary on the beach, the gun would need to have been in the vicinity of Cap Gris Nez, facing inland and not out to sea, and be fired blind into a crowd of people. Remember, the Gris Nez lookouts could not see *UC 61* until midday.

There was one other mention of the shell hole over ten years later. In 1928, as a side remark to another story, the newspaper *Le Miroir*, described how *UC 61* arrived in Wissant Bay to 'undertake a small repair to its conning tower'.[132]

Townsend only speculates when he suggests possible serious damage. There remains the question of who fired the shot? The vessel could have been French or British. However, most patrols, especially away from the immediate coast, were carried out by the Royal Navy. Contacts with enemy submarines were carefully recorded by the navy for tracking and intelligence purposes. No contact, not even a nearby contact, has been recorded for the necessary hours. Why would any warship keep quiet about a contact or be told to keep quiet about a contact? Why was Gerth not questioned on the matter by the French, or later by the British? Why is there nothing of consequence in the records to reflect the declarations in the Press?

The best answer is that the Allies did not know what happened, but they had been responsible. Something unusual was afoot the night that UC 61 struggled through the fog and the activity was planned to have a major impact on the u-boat war. Admiral Bacon decided to reinstate the coastal net-barrage fronting Zeebrugge, which had been allowed to lapse during the winter months of 1916–17.[133] Bacon was accompanied by Admiral Ronarc'h aboard HMS Broke, a Faulknor class destroyer leader, to witness the laying. Admiral Ronarc'h was therefore unwittingly present off Zeebrugge at the beginning of UC 61's last patrol and then witnessed its aftermath at Wissant. Bacon wrote proudly that twelve miles of nets were laid in one and a half hours.[134]

> It was painfully apparent that the Goodwin-Snouw nets were failing to debar the use of the Straits to u-boats. Admiral Bacon believed that the only way of so doing was to lay a mine barrage across the Channel; but no mines were available. He therefore laid a barrage similar to the coastal mine barrage of 1916. Early on the morning of 25 July [1917], a minelayer laid 120 deep mines along a line about eighteen miles off the coast, and then the drifters laid fifteen miles of mine-nets in position. On 27 July, the line of nets was prolonged still further. This barrage had to be patrolled day and night. Although it acted as a deterrent, the barrage did not prevent submarines from emerging from their base. Actually, on the very day it was laid, UC-61 (Gerth) left Zeebrugge and passed both this obstruction and the Goodwins-Snouw barrier at night.[135]

The nets were laid by Admiralty drifters that were fired on by German destroyers, but HMS Broke and two others, HMS Terror, an Erebus class monitor, and another destroyer leader, HMS Nimrod, drove them off.[136] The remainder of the nets were laid on 27 July and a daily patrol started. The Admiralty did not try to keep the new minefield secret. On 28 July, UB 20 hit a mine and sank with the loss of all hands while on a diving trial off Zeebrugge.[137] On 29 July, Le Petit Calaisien reported from The Hague that the Dutch marine ministry had been told by the British Government that minefield limits had recently been extended and, as a result, the 'safe channel is so narrow that passage cannot be entirely guaranteed'. 'All possible measures' would be taken to ensure safe passage for vessels returning to the Netherlands.[138]

There are two other pieces of evidence. Gerth was inside Zeebrugge mole on the same day as *UC 47*, commanded by Paul Hundius, just appointed Kapitänleutnant. Hundius left Zeebrugge in the haze at 1650 perhaps an hour later than Gerth and was soon signalled by a German destroyer.[139] Two sea areas were being blocked by newly laid barrier nets; 'ahead there are destroyers in combat with English armed forces'. Hundius therefore turned north of Thornton Bank away from the danger in company with *UC 65*. At 1930, Hundius dived *UC 47* to check trim, but it wasn't until 0100 the next morning that he turned south by the Goodwin Sands. When he passed the channel net in deep water by Buoy 2 (2501), the fog was so bad that he decided to stay in the deep channel, taking regular soundings. The fog began to clear around 0700 and, an hour later, Hundius was forced to dive before two monitors and, at 0900, an aircraft. *UC 65* also managed to get through the fog. It was commanded by one of the u-boat aces, Otto Steinbrinck, who, by war end, had sunk just over 200 ships, a surprising number of them small fishing boats. Steinbrinck had returned early to Zeebrugge as he had run out of torpedoes after a successful trip to the English south coast. Pausing only for light repairs and to restock, he was told in Bruges of a 'coastal alarm' with British monitors and destroyers standing south-west of Thornton Bank (and that, on his return, he would be switching command to *UB 57*). After passing the Zeebrugge mole, meeting *UC 47* and being warned by the same German destroyer, Steinbrinck also travelled to the north. By 0100 on 26 July, the sea became calm and smooth and, in a dense fog, *UC 65* 'lightly rammed a fastening buoy of the net barrier'. Undamaged, Steinbrinck turned south where 'other sea signs are neither heard nor seen'. Towards morning, a breeze developed and it became clearer.

As Gerth was surrendering at Wissant, *UC 65* torpedoed HMS *Ariadne*, a cruiser minelayer, off Beachy Head, killing thirty-eight crew.[140] Including *Ariadne*, the Allies had thirteen ships hit on 26 July; the Germans lost two u-boats, *UC 61* and *UB 23*.[141]

So, this would seem to be the simple answer to the hole in *UC 61*'s conning tower? While the u-boat was creeping out of Zeebrugge harbour to start its patrol, it missed the warning from a destroyer and turned left as planned, rather than right as did *UCs 47* and *65*, and sailed through the edge of a major British mine-laying operation. From behind, German destroyers rushed out from Zeebrugge and engaged British warships protecting the mine-laying drifters. *UC 61* received a probable stray hit, possibly friendly fire.[142] If the perpetrator was a British destroyer this is also a ready explanation as to why this engagement with a submarine was not reported. The scrap between destroyers is recorded, but no u-boat is mentioned. It was because no ship saw or aimed at *UC 61*.

Why was the successful hit on *UC 61* not investigated or publicised by the Allies when they later found a hole on the beached wreck? What damage did the shell do? When the first British officer, Henry Spencer, briefly examined *UC 61* and its projectile hole on 29 July, he reported there was 'no trace of further damage inside'. *L'Illustration* may have been first with the story on 18 August when a journalist wrote that there were several holes in the 'light sheet metal of the conning tower', none of which, apart from the main projectile hole, are visible in over thirty photographs. The holes were caused by the bomb explosions. This may be true for small holes to the rear of the structure where the bombs were set, but not for the projectile hole facing forwards. 'If the submarine had really been hit by shells from one of our patrols,' said the journalist, 'the Ministry would have not missed an opportunity of announcing that our sailors had contributed to the loss of the enemy.'[143] *Le Miroir* published the story with a definitive picture the next day. In other words, most observers had missed the projectile hole among the wider post-explosion damage.

But why did Gerth never mention it? The hole appears nowhere in his interrogation. In 1920, when the loss of *UC 61* was investigated perfunctorily by the German Admiralty staff, Gerth does not recall it. Gerth does give a detail conjecture on how he was misled by tides and shifting sands. He was looking naturally for excuses so that the matter of the stranding would be dropped. As a part of his explanation, he turned Guichard's four 'toy' boats into English destroyers. He would surely have grasped the opportunity of a damaged boat that could not dive, especially one that could no longer be inspected.

There is one answer that deals satisfactorily with all the seemingly conflicting information, improbable as it at first seems. Gerth didn't know his u-boat had been hit. On his way south, for whatever reason, probably the sound of the destroyer fight, he may even have sighted a British destroyer, Gerth dived *UC 61*. This would have been an almost unremarkable event. On previous voyages through the channel he had dived *UC 61* over a dozen times to avoid enemy encounters. It would not be something he would remember three years later. There was no log as it burned in the ship. As the ship dived, hatch closed, everyone below deck, the stray shell hit. It pierced the outer fairing on the conning tower, hit the inner structure, failed to explode and rolled harmlessly through the open gap at the bottom and into the sea. At the time of diving, the noise in the u-boat was extreme: air tanks, water tanks, diesel engines, electric motors, loud commands, men rushing to stations. Someone may have heard a dull thump, but there was no damage to the u-boat's water integrity. Everyone got on with their job. When *UC 61* later surfaced, there was no evidence of damage inside the conning tower and the ship was in fog. The hole was out-of-sight on the outside of the conning tower. The imperative was navigation by dead reckoning and checking the boat's depth. The lack of knowledge of the hit also explains why Gerth did not turn back. From his and the crew's perspective, nothing had happened and there was no reason to cancel the mission. When he arrived at Wissant, still in dense fog, the hole was still not seen in the excitement of the moment.

The cannon hole in *UC 61*'s conning tower becomes a tantalising, but real, red herring. The shell was fired unknowingly by a warship, either British or German. It was a dud that caused no damage that impaired the boat or could readily be seen by those aboard. Nobody knew that it had happened. *UC 61* pushed on down the channel and, once free of the Goodwin Snouw barrage, and, as was thought, safely past Cap Griz Nez, was turned south for the open sea. Because of faulty navigation in thick fog and slow speed against a racing high tide, Steuermann Lengs blindly ran the boat ashore. Gerth thought he was stuck on the Bassure de Baas near Boulogne. Instead, he was trapped on the beach at Wissant.

ENDNOTES

1   Bondevik, et al, 'Storegga Slide Tsunami'.
2   11.5km x 70m (110m maximum) x 7m. Currently named *Canal Baudouin*, it is classified 'Class VI' and open to ships of more than 2,000 tons with a draft of 5.5m or less.
3   Populus x Canadensis is a hybrid *Black Poplar* frequently seen along riversides, roadsides and in parks and grown for ornamental planting and timber production. It originated in France in the eighteenth century.
4   The front-line trenches began on the coast near Nieuwpoort and snaked inland to Ypres. Ostend, also connected by canal to Bruges, is about eleven miles north-east of Nieuwpoort, and Zeebrugge about seventeen miles further.
5   Strachan, *First World War*, p. 245.
6   Bacon, *Dover Patrol*, pp. 184–205.
7   Fürbringer, *Legendary*, p. 35.
8   Koerver, *German Submarine Warfare*, p. 196.
9   Osman, *Pigeons in the Great War*, pp. 7–8, 17–27, 45, 50. 'At the outbreak of the war the Belgians had no doubt the finest pigeon service in the world, with headquarters in Antwerp, but before the city's capture on 8 October 1914, Commandant Denuit, chief of the Belgian service, had the lofts and birds all destroyed, thus preventing the Germans using a service that had taken years to become efficient.'
10 Termote, *Krieg Unter Wasser*, pp. 172, 187.
11 *TNA*, London, ADM 137/3818, p. 20. The other boats were *UC 16*, *UC 65* and *UC 70*.
12 *BA-MA*, Freiburg, RM 88/1 FdU Flandern KTB, p. 23. See also Newbolt, *Naval Operations*, Vol. V, Chapter 9; Bacon, *Dover Patrol*, pp. 108–11. A monitor was a relatively small warship, which was neither fast nor strongly armoured, but carried a disproportionately large gun.
13 *UC 61* Kriegstagebuch (KTB), Cuxhaven; interrogation of Lead Stoker Friedrich Becker (SHD, Cherbourg, SSTe35). Many of the pen pictures of the crew which appear in this book are compiled from the same source – the original handwritten notes in French and German made at the crew's formal interrogation.
14 Neureuther, *U-Boat Stories*, p. 134.
15 Wegener, *Naval Strategy of the World War*, pp. 172–73. See also Führer der Unterseeboote Hermann Bauer, briefing, 1/2/1917 (*TNA*, ADM 137/3886): 'Intelligence received from England proves that the British are kept continuously and most accurately informed regarding our submarines and their movements. The greatest reticence is therefore

demanded, particularly in public places, in trains, etc ... Crews are to be instructed repeatedly and explicitly on this matter.'

16 In his later years, Georg Gerth kept a caged canary (Interviews with Georg Gerth's daughter, Christa Gerth, 15–16/11/2016).
17 Koerver, *German Submarine Warfare*, p. 190.
18 *BA-MA*, RM 120–95, Flotilla Order No. 264, 24/7/1917.
19 Koerver, *German Submarine Warfare*, p. 197.
20 Offer, 'Bounded Rationality', p. 196.
21 *UCs 21, 47* and *61* Kriegstagebuch (KTB), Cuxhaven.
22 Termote, *Krieg Unter Wasser*, p. 112.
23 Fürbringer, *Legendary*, p. 15.
24 Grant, *U-Boat Intelligence*, pp. 113–14.
25 uboat.net, accessed 14/12/2016. Messimer, *Verschollen*, p. 286.
26 Termote, *Krieg Unter Wasser*, pp. 156–63.
27 *TNA*, ADM 137/3818, p. 109.
28 Koerver, *German Submarine Warfare*, p. xliv.
29 Koerver, *German Submarine Warfare*, p. 213.
30 Mulligan, *Sharks Nor Wolves*, p. 39.
31 Koerver, *German Submarine Warfare*, p. 23.
32 These figures are compiled from information given by the crew during the initial interrogations after capture at Wissant (SHD, Cherbourg, SSTe35).
33 Newbolt, *Naval History*, p. 127.
34 Termote, *Krieg Unter Wasser*, p. 91.
35 Fürbringer, *U-Boat Commander*, p. 50.
36 British casualties were 214 killed, 383 wounded, nineteen taken prisoner. German losses were ten killed, sixteen wounded (Bacon, *Dover Patrol*), p. 223. Eleven Victoria Crosses were awarded, some later by ballot of the participants.
37 Jellicoe, *Submarine Peril*, pp. 92–93.
38 Jellicoe, 'Foreword' to Bacon, *Dover Patrol*, p. 11. Tarrant, *U-Boat Offensive*, p. 62.
39 Termote, *Krieg Unter Wasser*, p. 161.
40 Newbolt, *Official History of the War, Naval Operations*, Vol. V, pp. 274–77; and, Newbolt, again, *Naval History*, pp. 127–31.
41 Thomas, *Raiders*, p. 230. Also, 'two lines of moored deep contact mines forty miles long and fifteen miles of mined nets had been positioned thirteen miles off the Belgian coast' (Grant, *U-Boat Intelligence*), pp. 61–62.
42 Washington, DC, *National Archives (NARA)*, U Boat Campaign (Enemy): U-Boats, 'Interrogatoire de L'Équipage de *UC 61*' [Interrogation of the Crew of *UC 61*] (45/520/JU/Box 572).
43 Buoys 4 & 5: UK Hydrographic Office, Chart 1872, archive series B24, 'Calais to the River Schelde' at 51° 5' 37"N, 2° 28' 15"E. For Buoy 4, see also Fleet Notices 93, 19/2/1917; 141, 19/9/1917; and 698, withdrawn, 1/12/1917. With thanks for the search by UKHO staff.
44 Gayer, *Submarine Warfare*, p. 13, 'the 'German post-war authority on the submarines'. Also quoted in Bacon, *Memoirs*, p. 155.
45 Gibson & Prendergast, *German Submarine War,* p. 117.
46 *TNA*, ADM 137/3876.
47 Terraine, *Business in Great Waters*, p. xv. Terraine's book, with *U-Boat Offensive*, by Tarrant, lead the field. Both also cover the u-boats in World War II.
48 Hashagen, *Commander*, pp. 179–82.
49 Spiegal, *Adventures of the U 202*, p. 48.
50 KTB, *UC 61*, V4, addendum, pp. 35–39, Cuxhaven. *TNA*, ADM 137/3897, 'Interview with Sub-Lieutenant Peterson, *UC 26*', p. 51. Peterson was one of two survivors from *UC 26* when it was rammed and depth charged by HMS *Milne* off Calais on 8/5/1917.
51 ADM 137/485.
52 Hashagen, *Commander*, p. 44.
53 *SHD*, Vincennes, *Nautical Bulletins*, 'Observations by submarine commanders on crossing the submarine nets of the Pas-de-Calais' (MV SSZ 18, Sous-marins ennemis), pp. 4–25.

54   There is a point at each end of Wissant Bay before leaving the Channel: Cap Blanc Nez
     (White Nose) and the larger Gris Nez (Grey Nose) towards the open sea.
55   Guichard, *Au Large*, pp. 135–38. Guichard was born in Saint Nazaire; he moved to a
     destroyer after a mandatory eighteen months on patrol boats; by the end of the war he
     was ashore as a marine fusilier. He left the navy as a frigate captain (*SHD*, Vincennes,
     MV CC7 4e moderne 3257–9).
56   TNA, ADM 186/407. Also, Koerver, *German Submarine Warfare*, p. 134.
57   It is likely that Dancker left the *Kaiser Freidrick* when she was withdrawn from service
     in February 1915. She was eventually decommissioned in November, thereafter being
     employed as a prison ship and later as a floating barracks. She was scrapped in 1920. *UC
     24* was based in Bruges and moved in February 1917 to the Mediterranean Sea. In May,
     it was torpedoed by the French submarine *Circé* off the entrance to Cattaro harbour with
     twenty-four dead and two survivors.
58   Gayer, *Submarine Warfare*, p. 5.
59   Bergen, 'My U-Boat Voyage', Neureuther, *U-Boat Stories*, p. 17.
60   *TNA*, ADM 137/2096, 26/7/1917; *SHD*, Cherbourg, SSTe35.
61   Sedrati, 'Emblematic case of Wissant Bay', pp. 483–494.
62   The northern end of Bassure de Baas is three miles south from Cap Gris Nez, less than
     one mile from the French coast, nearly opposite Ambleteuse. It is 'shallowest at its
     northern end, perhaps three to four fathoms; its east and west sides of the bank are steep,
     rising from about twelve fathoms'. It is here that there is a knoll of twelve feet of water,
     half a mile in extent in the vicinity of Cap d'Alprech lighthouse 'upon which the sea
     breaks with violence' (Ogden, *Sailing Directions of the North Coast of France*, 1908), p. 3.
63   SHOM chart 7323.
64   RM 88/1, pp. 39–41. There were several other intercepted and conflicting telegrams over
     the next few days. The Kaiser was not told about the loss until 5/8/1917 when a personal
     telegram was sent to him in Berlin by the chief of the admiralty staff of the navy (RM
     2/1996).
65   Bendert, *Die UC-Boote*, p. 159. See also ADM 239/26; ADM 3918; *Naval Staff Monographs*,
     Volume XIX, (C.B. 917R; O.U. 5528[H]), August 1939, p. 207.
66   *TNA*, ADM 137/3886.
67   Chatelle, *Calais Pendant La Guerre*, p. 164.
68   *TNA*, ADM 137/2096.
69   There was an hour difference between French and English times.
70   Guichard, *Au Large*, pp. 82–83.
71   Over twenty of these motor launches received battle honours, the majority of them in
     the blockading of Zeebrugge in 1918. ML 135 played a part in the sinking of *UC 49*, sister
     ship to *UC 61* on 8/8/1918. The launches cost £8,600 each without armament and 200
     were sold after the war for about £275 a boat; those used in the Mediterranean went for
     £50. Reportedly, many were used for smuggling (Colledge and Dittmar, *Index to British
     Warships*, naval-history.net, accessed 23/12/2016).
72   Guichard, *Au Large*, pp. 82–83.
73   *SHD*, Cherbourg, Bundle 4, folder of telegrams.
74   Taken, a little freely, from 'L'échouement du sous-marin boche', *Le Petit Calaisien*,
     28/7/1917.
75   *Le Petit Journal*, 29/7/1917, p. 1.
76   *SHD*, Vincennes, Box MV SS Gr 43, 28/7/1917.
77   Elsewhere in the telegrams: No. 841 HS, a small masted fishing boat.
78   Underlined in original text.
79   Chapter 2, 'Kaisertreu'.
80   *Royal Museum of the Armed Forces and of Military History*, Brussels, AU 9089/2, p. 108. See
     also 4th Regiment HQ correspondence (Box 308, 26/7/1917).
81   Museum Cabour WOII & 2/4 Lancers, Adinkerke, Belgium, framed cutting, 'Le Sous
     Marin', *Le courier de l'Armée*, 30/11/1919.
82   www.1914–1918.be/insolite_sous_marin.php, accessed 8/12/2016. 'When the Belgian
     cavalry captured a German submarine.'

83   Rigal became the French naval attaché in Washington in 1912 and where he wrecked his car in a road accident. He and his car are recorded at the *Library of Congress*, LC-USZ62-108182.

84   *SHD*, Vincennes, MV SS GR 43, p. 6.

85   Chapter 6, 'War of the raven'.

86   Gustav Schüler, *U-Boote heraus!*, translation Cathrin Brockhaus-Clark. In 1914, Schüler (1868–1938) published a patriotic volume of poems and songs 'Wider die Welt ins Feld'; some of these were set to music and became popular with German soldiers during World War I. Early In 1917, a German propaganda film 'U-Boote heraus!' was released.

87   *TNA* ADM 137/3886.

88   Boniface, *Histoire navale Histoire maritime, SHD Library*, Vincennes, GR 16N 2466. Chapter 2.

89   Ronarc'h, *Souvenirs De La Guerre*; Ditte, *Calais*, pp. 111–12 (a rare copy is held at the *Archives départementales du Pas-de-Calais* in Dainville, Arras).

90   *BA-MA*, RM 3872, technical data, 25/5/1916.

91   Gröner, *German Warships, Vol. 2: U-Boats and Mine Warfare Vessels*, pp. 51–52.

92   *TNA*, ADM 137/3818, p. 7.

93   *TNA*, ADM 186/383, 'German Navy, Part 3, Submarines', 3/1917.

94   *SHD*, Vincennes, MV SS Gr 43, letter 1/8/1917 confirming telephone agreement 30/7/1917.

95   The photographs, taken by an unnamed Belgian cavalryman, were included in a personal photograph album which covered family and military service before 1917 and, later, in the Congo (*Royal Museum of the Armed Forces and of Military History*, Brussels, Est I/2322), p. 5.

96   The others were *Le Matin, Le Petit Parisien* and *Le Journal* and all carried good coverage. From being France's largest selling newspaper in the 1860s, *Le Petit Journal* was in relative decline by World War I. However, it still produced almost one million copies helped by a large colour rotary press that could print 200,000 sheets an hour and subsequently had a cover price of five centimes, a third the cost of its competitors (wikipedia, accessed 27/12/2016).

97   The bulk of the remaining press coverage can be found at *The Departmental Archives of Pas-de-Calais* in Arras: *L'Avenir de Marquise*, 2/8/1917 (PG 190/6); *Le Boulonnaise*, 28/7/1917 (PG 49/27); *Croix de Pas-de-Calais* (PG 76/12); *Journal de Berck* (PG 197/9); *La France du Nord*, 30–31/7/1917 (PG 16/96); *L'Independent du Pas-de-Calais*, 29, 31/7, 4/8/1917 (PG 229/34); *Notre Belgique* (PG 106/1); *Patriote de l'Artois* (PG 65/5); *Le Petit Calaisien* (PG 60/16); *Phare de Calais* (PG 8/38); *Reveille de Boulogne* (PG 188/2); and *Le Telegramme*, 27, 29/7/1917 (PG 9/28).

98   *La Bibliothèque nationale de France*, gallica.bnf.fr/ark:/12148/cb32895690j/date. The coverage in *Le Matin* and *Le Petit Parisien* is at the same source.

99   Three officers and twenty-three men were captured.

100 'New Society' cartoon in Feldman, *Army, Industry and Labour*, p. 479.

101 Pierre Cambronne was one of Napoleon's most experienced generals and accompanied him to exile on the island of Elba and then played a leading role in the 'Hundred Days' – the return of Napoleon. He was immortalised in French language for his supposed response, 'Merde', to a demand to surrender the remnants of the Old Guard at the Battle of Waterloo. The response, which Cambronne always denied using, was among the many myths celebrated by Victor Hugo. Gerth's reply was described by Serin (although nowhere is this recorded officially) as 'in the language of Cambronne'.

102 Original emphasis. Twelve ships recorded sunk and four damaged in *UC 61*'s KTB.

103 The Citadel still stands with a narrow walk on top of its inner walls. It is now a large sports complex, 'La Stade du Souvenir', and picnic area with a picturesque second sea gate, 'La Porte de Neptune'. The main gate holds two plaques which commemorate the over 500 French and British soldiers who died in the defence of Calais in 1940.

104 *ecpad: The Etablissement de Communication et de Production Audiovisuelle de la Défense*, Ivry-sur-Seine: Agié SPA 52 X 1995–2000; Famechon SPA 97 R 3524–3534; Moreau SPA 212 M 4196, 4202–4205; Winckelsen SPA 6 OS 81–87.

105 *ecpad*, 14.18 A 708.
106 Phillips, Lieutenant RN retired, master of the sail training ships *Lord Nelson* and *Tenacious*. Assessment delivered by email, 6/8/2016, with addenda 8/8, 12/8, 4/9, 4/12/2016.
107 For instance, Gibson & Prendergast, *German Submarine War* (1931); p. 222, facing; Banks, *Military Atlas* (1975), p. 263; Humphreys, *Dover Patrol* (1998), p. 109.
108 Massie, *Castles*, p. 738.
109 Fürbringer, *Legendary*, p. ix.
110 Mulligan, *Sharks Nor Wolves*, pp. 39–40. The numbers vary with sources, but they are sufficiently accurate to make the general point. Compare with Chapter 14, 'Welcome home, Erich'.
111 Koerver, *German Submarine Warfare*, p. 197.
112 *UB 26* achieved no sinkings. The boat was on only its second patrol when on 5/4/1916 it became entangled in nets from the French destroyer *Trombe* in Le Havre roads. *UB 26*, commander Oberleutnant Wilhelm Smiths, surfaced and scuttled with twenty-one survivors who were imprisoned in France. The wreck was raised, repaired and commissioned by the French on 3/8/1916 as the *Roland Morillot* (uboat.net, accessed 29/12/2016).
113 *SHD*, Cherbourg, 'Echo de Paris', 8/1917 (SSTe35).
114 Chatelle, *La Base Navale du Havre*, pp. 235–36.
115 Gayer, *Submarine Warfare*, p. 27.
116 Gayer, *Submarine Warfare*, p. 28. uboat.net.
117 Several u-boats were stranded during the war, including one commanded by future u-boat Führer Karl Dönitz who ran *U 25* aground and stuck fast on rocks on the Dalmatian Islands. An Austrian destroyer was summoned and pulled the boat off the next day (Padfield, *Dönitz*), p. 82.
118 *TNA*, ADM 137/3898, pp. 132–37. *HMS Arrogant* was used from 1915 as the base flagship for the Dover Patrol at Dover. She also served as a submarine depot ship.
119 ADM 137/3898, p. 133.
120 *ecpad*, 97/3532.
121 *SHD*, Cherbourg, *Le Journal*, Paris edition, 0500, 16/8/1917, article datelined 13/8/1917 (SSTe35).
122 *Le Miroir*, 19/8/1917, p. 14.
123 Koerver, *German Submarine Warfare*, p. xxxviii.
124 *TNA*, ADM 137/3898, p. 122.
125 Townsend passed a full four-year shipwright artificer apprenticeship in HMS *Fisgard* and HMS *Caledonia*, before serving as one of the two shipwrights onboard HMS *Plymouth* for two years on an extended global deployment. Following promotion, David trained at the BRNC Dartmouth and HMS *Dolphin* before taking up various appointments in HMS *Otter*, HMS *Resolution*, HMS *Repulse* and HMS *Revenge* as the torpedo / anti-submarine officer and then as the temporary executive officer of HMS *Revenge* in refit, the temporary first lieutenant in HMS *Walrus*, and finally as the analysis officer (RN) at the Joint Acoustic Analysis Centre. Following retirement from the Royal Navy, David spent some time as the volunteer project leader at the Chatham Historic Dockyard restoring the submarine HMS *Ocelot* using past contacts and foraging in shipyards to obtain missing equipment needed to complete the restoration.
126 The fairing is called a 'fin' in the Royal Navy and the 'sail' in the US Navy and is 'faired' for hydrodynamic effect.
127 Strachan, *First World War*, p. 167.
128 Friedman, edited, *German Warships of World War 1*, description of the compressed air services, p. 315, technical drawings, pp. 356–57.
129 Friedman, *German warships*, technical drawings, pp. 358–59.
130 The reason for the lack of a bottom hatch was a combination of the method used for lowering torpedoes into the boat and of the hoist used for raising and lowering the periscopes which themselves had to pass through the conning tower pressure hull (*TNA*, ADM 137/3898), p. 120.

131 *TNA*, ADM 137/2096.

132 *Le Miroir*, 'On découvre une torpille dans l'épave du sous-marin allemand échoué à Wissant', 'A torpedo discovered in the wreck of the German submarine beached at Wissant', 30/6/1928 (*SHD*, Cherbourg, Box MV SS Gr 43).

133 Jellicoe, *Submarine Peril*, p. 13.

134 Bacon, *Memoirs*, p. 143.

135 Gibson and Prendergast, *German Submarine War*, pp. 193–94.

136 Bacon, *Memoirs*, pp. 143–44.

137 Terraine, *Business in Great Waters*, p. 76. uboat.net.

138 *Le Petit Calaisien*, 30/7/1917.

139 *UCs 21, 47* and *65* Kriegstagebuch (Cuxhaven).

140 *HMS Ariadne*, 11,000 tons, one of seventy-four ships over 10,000 tons sunk by u-boats during the Great War (uboat.net). 'The wreck is blown over a huge area of seabed, nothing sticks up more than one or two meters at the most. We occasionally do it as a second dive with a bit of tide running to cover more of the area' (www.wrecksite. eu/wreck.aspx?10756, accessed 11/1/2017). The next day, Steinbrinck torpedoed the 6,482 British passenger steamer *Candia*, one dead, and the 3,919-ton British steamer *Bellagio*, one dead. In January 1918, Steinbrinck broke down through exhaustion and, on recovery, became first staff officer to Karl Bartenbach.

141 Schooner *Bertha*, Portugal, cargo ship *Locksley*, Norway, barquentine *Venturoso*, Portugal, all scuttled off Villa do Conde, near Oporto (all *UC 69*); schooner *Blanchette*, Italy, and sailing vessel *Gesu E Maria*, Italy, both scuttled off Cape Corse, Corsica (both *U 33*); passenger cargo ship *Carmarthen*, British, near The Lizard, Cornwall, torpedoed, but sank under tow, and Portuguese naval trawler *Roberto Ivens*, mined off Cape Espichel, fourteen dead (both *UC 54*, mining presumed); steamer *Ethelwynne*, British, mined, but towed to port, and French steamer *Flore*, probably mined, both off the Shetlands (both *U 71*); cargo ship *Ludgate*, British, mined off County Cork, twenty-four dead (*UC 51*); passenger steamer *Mooltan*, British, torpedoed off Tunisia with two dead (*UC 27*); refrigerated cargo liner *Somerset*, British, torpedoed off Finistère, France (*U 54*). *UB 23* (fifty-three ships) was depth charged off the Lizard by HMS *PC 60* and put in at Coruña, Spain, three days later where it was interned (uboat.net).

142 On 17 March 1917, Gerth was caught in a similar situation and, with shells landing too close to *UC 61* for comfort, had to dive to escape fire from two opposing destroyers in the North Sea (Chapter 6).

143 Dufossé, *Wissant, 1914–1918*, unpaged, f. 9, quoting *L'Illustration*, 18/8/1917.

CHAPTER 9

Your Truth, Our Truth

That inverted patriotism whereby the love of one's own nation is transformed into the hatred of another nation, and the fierce craving to destroy the individual members of that other nation, is no new thing. Wars have not always, or perhaps commonly, demanded for their origin and support the pervasion of such a frenzy among the body of the people. The will of a king, of a statesman, or of a small caste of nobles, soldiers, priests, has often sufficed to maintain bloody conflicts between nations, without any full or fierce participation in the war-spirit by the lay multitude ... In the long-continued war, the passion of a whole people has, even in old times, been gradually inflamed against another people's, with whom, for reasons usually known to a few, a state of war existed; and such martial animus, once roused, has lasted far beyond the limits of this strife, sometimes smouldering for decades or for centuries.[1]

In the oldest military treatise in the world, *The Art of War*, written in the fifth century BC, Sun Tzu wrote, 'The supreme act of war is to subdue the enemy without fighting'.[2] There is no chapter devoted to propaganda, rather the work is studded with the importance of disinformation, subterfuge and sowing the seeds of doubt. Other early adherents of propaganda, 'word bullets', as a powerful weapon of war included Thucydides in *The Peloponnesian War* and Virgil in *The Aeneid*. Sir Thomas Moore told how the Utopians 'won bloodless victories by undermining their foes with propaganda'.[3] 'They rejoice and vaunt themselves if they vanquish and oppress their enemies by craft and deceit ... Then they glory, then they boast and crack that they have played the men in deed, when they have so overcome, as no other living creature but only man could: that is to say by the might and pursuance of wit.'[4]

In most cases we assign the term 'propaganda' a sinister definition as the presentation of information in an emotionally appealing manner for a purpose that is not candidly announced, and in support of a point of view we would probably debate if we were presented with all the available facts that might bear upon the opinion and were invited to scrutinise the evidence prudently.[5]

U-boat commanders hated the 'lies' told about them by the British, particularly as they experienced directly, and heard about first hand, many examples of duplicity and murder committed by the Royal Navy. There were enough double standards on the other side to excuse one of their own number who was occasionally unstable or murderous. 'Had not England herself, even after the war, spread calumny about the German submarines and their methods? ... Our late enemies should be told that we conducted the war, 'not in kid gloves it is true, but with clean hands'.[6] The u-boat commanders, mostly volunteers, believed in their cause and that they had right on their side.

The confident spirit, the iron sense of duty that knew no rest, remained unchanged. Here were no pirates, nor Huns, whose sole emotions were brutality or joy in murder. They were defending our just cause and our beleaguered land, fighting for their hard-pressed comrades on shore. Like sharp, cleaving knives these small grey boats persistently cut through the enemy's stronghold in just and justified retaliation. What the enemy did, it must also be our right to do.[7]

The German captains recognised the conflicting propaganda. Johannes Spieß, commander of five u-boats throughout the war, knew that whatever was done would tomorrow be lauded in all the German newspapers saying 'that once more we had retaliated on our most hated enemy, thus his inhuman attempt to starve our people had been parried by a horrid and strong blow'.[8] Ernst Hashagen, *UB 21*, was well aware in 1916 of the opposite.[9] He gave the crew of a Swedish schooner *Harald* time to pack gear and 'as I did not wish to leave the fairly large crew in the small and unreliable boat with the weather growing hourly worse, I took the whole of them aboard. The men, frightened and half-frozen, got a plate of thick-pea soup apiece'. In a few hours, the crew were turned over to a Norwegian steamship, which delivered them safely to Sweden. A few weeks later, a cutting from a Swedish newspaper was sent to Hashagen from Berlin. It contained an account of the sinking of the *Harald*, with full descriptions of the accompanying 'bestialities of the Huns'. 'Once more the British agent in Sweden had done his work quickly and well. The British realised what they were fighting for right from the start, and worked from the first day with all their might, with propaganda and calumny as well as everything else.' Daily interactions in the street enforced 'ethnic cleansing': the Germans dropped '*Adieu*' from their goodbyes and dozens of foreign words were deleted from workday vocabularies. At Bad Kissingen, spa guests fined one another for using 'enemy' words – French, five pfennigs; Russian, ten pfennigs; English, fifteen; Italian; twenty.

The Germans used the epithet 'Huns' against the Russians, even before the British took it up against the Germans.[10] The word *Hun* came to the fore when Kaiser Wilhelm in July 1900 addressed the first reinforcements heading to quell the Boxer Uprising in China.[11] Wilhelm told his soldiers, 'You will avenge the death of many Germans and Europeans. When you meet the enemy, you will beat him; you will give no mercy and take no prisoners. As the Huns a thousand years ago made a name for themselves that has lasted mightily in memory, so may the name 'Germany' be known to China, such that no Chinese will ever again even dare to look askance at a German.'[12] The Kaiser's speech was widely reported. Rudyard Kipling's poem *For All We Have and Are*, written early in the war, had used the line, 'The Hun is at the gate', the 'Hun' being a 'crazed and driven foe'. 'Hun' was seized on by the *Daily Mail* immediately after the news of Louvain reached London.[13] 'But the usage of the term took on a very specific resonance.'[14] This can be seen in the headline for a story on 18 November 1914 entitled 'The Heavy Hand of the Hun', which states, 'The horror of Louvain is indescribable, one might think one was in Pompeii.' The use of Hun began to stand for an assault on civilisation itself. The idea of *hunnish* behaviour stemmed from this point. But also, for Kipling, the idea was that England was the epitome of civilisation and 'good'.[15] The idea of *Kultur*, an 'expression of honest conscience, spirituality, and high morality opposed to the artificial forms of mere civilisation', was a major element in German self-propaganda, but it backfired badly.[16] The *Daily Mail* frequently repeated *Kultur* in a negative context and turned it into an expression of derision.

The British blockade, combined with the inefficiency of German government departments and regional military governors, gradually deprived the middle class and the most vulnerable of their daily food. These effects were keenly felt by the u-boat men and this was reflected in their memoirs and in their letters to their families. From February 1917, particularly, the commanders saw their indiscriminate destruction of all vessels in the war zone as a justified retaliation. Sinking of Allied vessels stemmed the flow of war materials, but also, officially and more personally, it was a deliberate attempt to starve in turn their island enemies. It became a literal race to the death with little room for sentiment. As the number and nationality of the boats sank increased, American, British Empire, French, Greek, Italian, Norwegian, Portuguese, South American and Swedish, the u-boat men felt like they fought the whole world.

I remembered the misery of the German Home Front, with our people reduced to starvation level by a merciless naval blockade, and I thought too of the enormous struggle in which Germany was engaged for her very existence. All the Allied freighters we saw out here, every single one of them, were ostensibly proceeding as if on their lawful peacetime occasions, but in reality they stood shoulder to shoulder committed to the defeat of Germany, and they all carried materials for use in the war against Germany. This latter was the argument which had to carry weight with me: these ships had to be sunk inevitably, relentlessly, unsparingly. That much we owed to the German people, even if as seamen we did it with a heavy heart.[17]

Admiral Sir Arthur Wilson, Commander-in-Chief of the Channel Fleet, so despised the submarine's 'underhanded method of attack' that he wanted the Admiralty to announce publicly that all u-boat crews captured in wartime would be hanged as pirates.[18] There was no lower form of life than a u-boat crew and, as news of the Allies' propaganda arrived in Germany, there could be no surprise that the u-boat commanders were incensed. When the Germans captured SS *Ben Cruachan* in October 1915, they found a copy of Winston Churchill's orders to fire on u-boat white flags and giving the choice of capturing or shooting crews.[19] The u-boat captains were appalled that the British Admiralty paid bounties to naval crews who sank submarines, something that would never be countenanced in Germany. 'It is incredible, according to German standards, but it is a fact that [the British] were paid £1,000 per u-boat, which, by the way, they considered far too little.'[20]

What manner of men were these chaps who in wartime won the hatred and bitter execration of half the world? Pirates, they were called, and hanging was the destiny considered just for them. At the same time, it was perfectly clear that they were true stalwarts of the race of adventurers.[21]

The 'pirate' accusation was used to telling effect to rally the u-boat crews and to gather the support of the German population. A typical denunciation came from Admiral Carl Hollweg who led the *Reichsmarineamt* news agency for three years to 1912. Hollweg joined the Navy Cadet School in 1895 and was a devout acolyte of Tirpitz for whom he wrote a publication describing the coming naval war between Britain and Germany. He followed this in 1917 with an emotional defence of Germany's right to use the u-boat.

Ignore the swear words of the enemies calling you 'pirates, barbarians, Huns and child murderers'. The English always cursed their enemies whenever they damaged their trade and, only one hundred years ago, the anger of the French was directed against their current allies, the

English. You should know that the German people back you and respect your dutiful actions and bravery. You should be aware that your deeds will save hundreds of thousands of women and children at home from the English hunger whip and that you will fight to justify the use of a new weapon in this war for the benefit of the whole world. You and your actions help us and will continue to help us to remain a free, upright, unfettered people, to stay German forever. You contribute successfully to this enormous battle for the existence of our people.[22]

In June 1914, Kaiser Wilhelm told President Woodrow Wilson's confidant, Edward House, that Germany did not want war as it was against her best interests, but that she was menaced from every side. 'The primary argument of men around the Kaiser – army generals and naval admirals, the Junker agrarian nobility, Pan-German industrialists, the Navy Leaguers, bankers and conservative politicians – was to prevent an invasion of Germany.

Ample evidence exists to show that neither Russia nor France intended such an invasion, which would not have been supported by either Great Britain or the United States, not in 1914, not even in 1917.' In historian Asprey's view, this was a specious and highly inflammatory argument intended to win over the German people to an aggressive military-industry policy in which greed for new territories and markets and for vast new powers overrode common sense, 'and it succeeded beyond any doubt.'[23]

The Germans introduced, therefore, the first great lie of the war: that Germany had been invaded and was fighting a defensive war. The legend of Allied attack was in part the work of three bright and ambitious general-staff majors at Moltke's headquarters: Walther Nicolai, Hans von Haeften and Max Bauer.[24] Propaganda was their trade. The enemy had attacked defenceless Germany, the French were in Belgium, French planes had bombed Nürnberg and enemy spies were everywhere. Russians dressed as Prussian officers were carrying bottles of typhoid germs to poison the lakes and reservoirs; disguised French officers were racing across Germany in cars packed full of gold for Russia. Strange lights were the work of spies charged with guiding aircraft to German targets.

The infamous 'Aircraft of Nürnberg' was a typical misreported alarm: several French planes had bombed railway lines between the city and Würzburg on 2 August, the day before war was declared. Citing military sources, several German newspapers printed special editions about the shocking violation of international law. The story was traced from Nürnberg railway headquarters through the Bavarian Army Command to the German General Staff. Although quickly corrected, the attack was referenced by Chancellor Bethmann two days later.

The German chancellor and military leaders were dismayed that the Allies had failed to admit that Russia had mobilised first thereby forcing German's hand.[25] The complex logistics of mobilisation and the weeks required for an opposing army to respond were such that any full-scale mobilisation had to be viewed as a pre-declaration of war. The Russians refused to halt their build-up of troops and equipment, aimed initially at Austria-Hungary, but also by default at Germany, despite several frantic appeals by the German diplomatic corps. The Russians were encouraged in their 'dangerous' mobilisation by strong support from French diplomatic channels which included a commitment to fulfil their treaty obligations in the event of a German attack.[26]

Early in August 1914, Prince Bernhard von Bülow called on Bethmann in the Chancellor's Palace in Berlin and described his reception:

> *Bethmann stood in the centre of the room. Shall I ever forget his face …*
> *There is a picture of some celebrated English painter, which shows the*
> *wretched scapegoat with a look of ineffable anguish in its eyes – such*
> *pain as I now saw in Bethmann's. For an instant we neither of us spoke.*
> *At last I said to him, 'Well, tell me, at least, how it all happened.' He*
> *raised his long, thin arms to heaven and answered in a dull, exhausted*
> *voice: 'Oh – if I only knew!' In many later polemics on 'war guilt' I have*
> *often wished it had been possible to produce a snapshot of Bethmann*
> *… at the moment he said those words. Such a photograph would have*
> *been the best proof that this wretched man had never 'wanted war'.[27]*

Bülow is guilty of some obfuscation. Bethmann was determined to use the Austro-Serbian conflict to disrupt the Triple Entente and thereby to break the military and economic encirclement of Germany.[28] But, despite being Chancellor, he did not hold the reins of power. The power lay with a Kaiser who alternated between indecision and hubris, and with his vociferous, sabre-rattling military and naval advisers. In sharp contrast to his interview with Bülow, Bethmann at the first formal session of the Reichstag after the Serbian assassination formalised the 'invasion' lie by a deliberate extension of the truth:

> *Forty-four years we have lived in peace. We are drawing the sword only*
> *in defence of a righteous cause. Russia has set the torch to the house.*
> *It would be a crime to wait until these powers, between which we are*
> *squeezed, break loose. France has already violated the peace. French*
> *flyers have crossed the frontier and have dropped bombs. French*
> *cavalry patrols and infantry companies have broken into Alsace. We are*
> *therefore acting in self-defence. Our troops have occupied Luxembourg*
> *and perhaps are already in Belgium. Our invasion of Belgium violated*
> *international law, but we will atone for the injustice which we have thus*

committed. Whoever is as badly threatened as we are can think only of cutting his way through. We are standing shoulder to shoulder with Austria-Hungary. We have told England that we will attack neither Belgium's sovereignty nor her independence. Germany's great hour of trial has come. Our army is in the field. Our navy is ready for battle. At their back stands a united people.[29]

Britain soon recognised that, with the advent of trench warfare, this was to be a drawn-out war of attrition. In the long term, through emphasising maritime blockade and economic warfare, Britain set out, first, to ruin the financial and industrial systems of Germany and, thereby, bring her militarily to her knees and, second, to bring widespread deprivation to the civilian population to such an extent that its will to support the war was exhausted. The German authorities emphasised that the British blockade was intended to cause starvation, well-backed by jingoistic pronouncements from senior British politicians, but that by scrimping and avoiding waste, hunger could be prevented. Increasing limits on consumption provided an opportunity to improve pubic health by moving to more appropriate diets – less meat, less fat, more vegetables.[30] Several hundred public speakers were enrolled to enlighten the *Volk*.

Civilians, particularly those in the blockaded Central Powers, were forced to deal with rigid competition for goods and services and an increasing dehumanising struggle for survival – an especially hideous struggle because it took place among fellow countrymen. The situation was made worse on the home front because of the distorted view of the war that necessarily developed under a system of strict censorship. Although it was the German civilian who probably suffered the most under a censorship that forced a reliance on underground information provided by soldiers on leave, correspondents, nurses, and others travelling between the fighting line and the home front, all belligerents had to make do to a greater or lesser degree with the half-truths that are so much a part of propaganda. As a tool of war, propaganda produced twisted animosities, profound disillusionment, and an unnecessarily wide gulf between the soldier and his civilian counterpart.[31]

Much of the early success of Germany's ability to accommodate the food blockade was due to its government's 'rapid embrace of propaganda'. In language that would cause instant offence a century later, the government challenged its home front, and especially German women, to accept increasingly draconian limits on individual diets. Women were called upon to disprove a reputation for uncontrolled consumption, for coveting luxury items and for unreasonable hoarding. Taken together and unrestrained, these actions, German women were told, might sabotage the war effort. By acting collectively as a 'voluntary home-front army', women should support the soldiers by fighting the 'battle of the economy'.[32] The government averred that 'every German, above all every German woman, is a soldier in the economic war. Just as our soldiers are dead tired but courageous before the enemy, so at home you must be thrifty and do without.' Only in this fashion would women overcome their 'lack of consciousness' and attention only to their immediate world and would thereby demonstrate their 'willingness to sacrifice' and to fulfil their patriotic obligation.

In Germany in 1917, the British *Aushungerungspolitik*, the 'policy of starvation', was the centre of every day life. It had always been discussed in the Central European Press, but now, however, its actual achievements were openly discussed. 'Shocking conditions were revealed.'[33] During three years of warfare, the public had come to understand that the newspapers were woefully mistaken in downplaying the food blockade and now knew that some of them were in the 'habit of purposefully misleading their readers, as natural results of drastic censorship'. Propaganda extended into the management of the weary army and in the idle High Seas fleet. German troops were bombarded by news from the air of the riots and food shortages at home. One leaflet dropped into the trenches and supply depots contained an *Apostle's Creed* which ended with, 'I believe in the Holy War, a great universal usury, the community of hamsters, the increase of taxes, the shortening of meat rations, and an everlasting shortage of bread. Amen'.[34] Another newspaper report from Munich told of a ministerial decree that, because of a scarcity of clothing, the dead should be buried in paper so that their clothing could be given to the living.

The 'invasion' lie – that Germany had not attacked Belgium, France, Luxembourg and Russia – but was itself first invaded was expanded by a carefully orchestrated campaign led, in part, by German playwrights and authors.[35] England more than France or Russia became the focus of the nation's rage which was built on the 'inhuman' blockade of food intended for women and children. 'Now the conjecture was such that a discussion in the newspapers of the hardship suffered and the damage done by Great Britain's starvation blockade could not but fan the Central States population into a veritable frenzy.'[36] As a result, Britain quickly became Germany's enemy number one, replacing the Russian Slavic menace which had so preoccupied them in the early days of the fighting.[37] A minor Jewish poet, Ernst Lissauer, enshrined Albion's treachery in *Hassgesang gegen England*, the 'Hymn of Hate' which was reprinted in all newspapers, and was read aloud by teachers in class and by officers at the front to their soldiers:

> *We will never forget our hate,*
> *We have all, but a single hate,*
> *We love one, we hate one.*
> *We have one foe, and one alone – England!*

Lissauer was also the author of the slogan *Gott strafe England*, 'May God Punish England' which was popularised by the German Army and widely taken up by intellectuals and the impoverished. The motto became ubiquitous, daubed on the side of buildings, on cufflinks and imprinted on brown coal bricks.[38]

> *What Abraham Lincoln said about public sentiment is particularly true in time of war: 'Public opinion is everything. With public sentiment nothing can fail, without it nothing can succeed.'*[39]

The Germans quickly saw atrocities on the side of the British, but despite having counter messages to promote, they had no sure way of reaching the British or the American publics. There was never a time in Berlin, and generally throughout Germany, from the first declaration of war to the armistice, when the leading American, French, English, Italian and Russian papers could not be bought openly at newsstands.[40] The reverse was not true. Messinger, an historian of British propaganda, argued that the Germans were handicapped by 'organisational confusion' typical of a dysfunctional Imperial government. Many propaganda departments were set up which co-ordinated through regular press conferences, but 'otherwise went their own ways, seldom sharing information or experience, contradicting one another's messages and competing for budget'.[41] German official propaganda also failed to understand foreign audiences. Messinger picked out 'bluntness' and 'extreme nationalism' which led to proclamations of superiority, and 'blustering mannerisms' which, he thought, were 'the consequences of growing up in an autocratic culture where debate was not always permitted and practice in listening to opposing points of view was limited'.

The British propaganda war started long before the shooting began, almost in concert with the Pan-German League's, Tirpitz-inspired, commitment to a large Weltpolitik fleet.[42] From 1905, spy stories and anti-German articles 'bordered on lunacy'.[43] On both sides, before the war, socialists had threatened to oppose war and disrupt mobilisation. However, the war they vilified was a 'tool of imperialism and conquest'. 'In 1914, every belligerent on the continent of Europe portrayed itself as the subject of direct attack.'[44] 'The myth that European men leapt at the opportunity to defeat a hated enemy has been comprehensively dispelled.'[45] The working-class populations of all the powers may not have welcomed the war, but they 'did not reject the duties and obligations it imposed'.[46]

Historians and, some would say, conspiracy theorists, Gerry Docherty & Jim Macgregor, in *Hidden History*, have attacked one of the basic arguments for the British going to war: that militarism had run amok in Germany and the 'fact' that it was seeking world domination through naval and military superiority.[47]

Militarism in the United Kingdom was of God, but in Germany of the Devil and had to be crushed ... Rarely have statistics been so thoroughly abused. An almighty alliance of armaments manufacturers, political rhetoric and newspaper propaganda conjured up the illusion of an enormous and threatening battle fleet. The illusion became accepted, and historians have written that as 'fact' into contemporary history ... In the decade prior to the war, British naval expenditure was £351,916,576 compared to Germany's £185,205,164.[48] The Triple Entente spent £657,884,476 on warships in that same decade, while Germany and Austria-Hungary spent £235,897,978.[49] The peacetime strength of the German army was 761,000, while France stood at 794,000 and Russia 1,845,000,[50] yet the claim that militarism had 'run amok' in Germany was presented as the given truth ... The entire scare was a scam ... the statistics and so-called 'margins' between the British and German navies were grossly misrepresented. Winston Churchill later admitted that 'there were no secret German dreadnoughts, nor had Admiral von Tirpitz made an untrue statement in respects of major construction'.[51]

Opinion in Britain could largely be taken for granted because of the belief in German militarism. However, the war was not brought about by 'popular opinion' as many statesmen claimed.[52] 'The war was justified because it was interpreted as a war of national self-defence. A tenuous and aged treaty obligation, described as a 'matter of honour', bound Britain to defend Belgium if attacked.[53] There was an obligation to come to France's aid, but it was an obligation made by the British foreign secretary in private conversation and without the knowledge of parliament.[54] Gradually, mention was made of Britain's commercial interests: the rivalry of superior German manufactures; fear of Germany's militarisation; and the threat of that militarisation to the Bosphorus and to British India. Little mention was made of the speed with which German colonies in Africa were swallowed by Allied forces, and the capture by the Australians of German interests in the Pacific.

John Ewart declared that the 'chief reason for all this confusion is the practical impossibility (from a war point of view) of permitting investigation and discussion during hostilities'. The French view was that if war was inevitable, it was *notre devoir est de la rendre populaire*, 'a duty to make it popular'.[55]

For that purpose, debate must be silenced; dislike must be whipped into hatred; suggestion as to possible legitimacy in the attitude of the enemy must be suppressed; argument raising suspicion as to the correctness of your own action must be stifled; escaped facts must be distorted or denied; favouring facts must be invented; millions must be spent in an effort to make people believe not that which is true, but that which will

*inflame their passions. Assertion during the war of the righteousness
of your country's action, and condemnation of the villainy of your
enemy's, being essential, and the truth being unknown or, if known,
incommunicable, 'patriotism' was left free to fulminate as it pleased.
And methods of expression of feeling being infinite [varieties of truth will
appear], some honest, and others framed in the pursuance of 'duty'.*[56]

From the first day of war, the French military gained control of the press
from the civil government. At a meeting in Paris on 5 August 1914 it was
announced that 'no news concerning mobilisation and movements of the
army or even diplomatic operations that would react unfavourably upon
the spirit of the army was to be published in the French press'.[57] Only news
from the War Department was to be published. The French had a closer
and more personal view of German stereotypes and joined the British in
attacking their 'warlike and militaristic' nature, which was responsible
for both the war and its atrocities.[58] France fought for its traditional
revolutionary values of democracy and political rights, incorporating the
Catholic Church, while Germany stood for impatient progress and a forced
change in the world order. Much French propaganda emphasised that the
war was a religious war, a 'war by Prussia against Catholicism' and appeals
were made not only to Catholics generally, but 'specifically to Catholics in
Southern Germany'.[59] The French press, at the start of the war, tended to
raise such rhetoric to a fever pitch. The *boche*, as he became widely known,
quickly became the personification of evil, cowardice, and perfidy.[60]
Atrocity stories became part of a larger trend in the representation of the
conflict between France and Germany, which now took on hues of a war to
the death between two 'races', one civilised and the other barbaric.[61] Here,
too, French journalists could draw on pre-war images of a German *Kultur*
'firmly rooted in the desire for conquest and domination, an obsession
with materialism, a methodical and inhuman scientific worldview, and the
cult of Nietzsche and Wagner'.

It is best to see British propaganda in two parts, one fomented by a
virulent Press, egged on in part by the authorities, and the other sometimes
more measured product of the official organisations. The British were
unequivocal in their simple proposition: 'England was good, Germany
was evil.' The primary and overwhelming objective was to win the war
by drawing in the Americans. This strategy, successful in less than three
years, was abetted by the coincidental and helpful loss of American lives
from u-boat attacks. Of great importance in England, but always secondary,
was to keep alive hatred of all things German and thereby smooth the path
for relentless enlistment, a reluctant acceptance of the mounting losses
of husbands and sons, and to bolster the resilience of its citizens against
hardship.[62] From early in 1915, the parliamentary recruiting service issued
regular reports of German atrocities:

It is the duty of every single Englishman who reads these records, and who is fit, to take his place in the King's army, to fight with all the resolution and courage he may, that the stain, of which the following pages are only a slight record, may be wiped out and the blood of innocent women and children be avenged.[63]

Britain was guilty of violations of international law, arguably much more than Germany. Through her international blockade she manipulated the actual economies of neutral countries. Her own atrocities in the field were covered up, repudiated or ignored. Her propaganda was led by simple and clear objectives and, certainly later in the war, was prepared to lie consistently and relentlessly to achieve them. The British were capable of brilliant and rapid responses knowing that a timely truth could build credibility. Immediately following the Battle of Jutland, it seemed likely that the Royal Navy had suffered a disaster as damaged ships limped back to harbour. The navy press bureau, led by Rear-Admiral Sir Douglas Brownrigg, put out an essentially truthful briefing that shocked the nation.[64] However, after Admiral Jellicoe had toured the ports, a second, 'more accurate estimate was released which showed the losses were not major'. Brownrigg felt that the first communiqué, whatever its rights or wrongs, had the effect the world over of re-establishing the navy's reputation for telling the truth. By contrast, the Germans 'suffered irretrievably by their original lying and vainglorious communiqué which they were compelled to alter'.

An early and important propaganda success of the war was that of Germany's war guilt in invading 'plucky' Belgium. From the first, this act placed Germany on the defensive and it governed much that followed, particularly the Allies' conduct at the Versailles peace discussions.[65] In the descent from traditional army-led European wars into the total war that followed in Spain in 1936 and across the whole continent in 1939, an essential element of the degradation was the regularity and variety of war crimes. What was unthinkable in Europe in 1900 became commonplace by the end of 1914. The systematic violence against civilians in the first two months of the war, dubbed by the Allies as the 'Belgian atrocities', became the first staple of propaganda labelling the Germans brutal breakers of international law.'[66] Then came the seemingly wanton destruction by the Germans of heritage sites in France and Belgium.[67] It is difficult in the twenty-first century to recreate the horror that these 'uncivilised' events engendered. They did much, and were propagated as such, to enforce the stereotype of the vicious militaristic and unworthy Prussian. The shootings claimed mostly either innocents dealt with out-of-hand or *franc tireurs*, and was another genuine propaganda gift. Historian Raico thought British propaganda in capitalising on these events was, 'as always, top notch'. Its high point was the Bryce 'Committee on the Alleged Belgian Atrocities'.[68] In the spring of 1915, the British released the 'mendacious' report which was 'a work of raw Entente propaganda, through profiting from the name of a distinguished British writer, the report underscored the true nature of the unspeakable Hun.'[69] Anglophiles everywhere were enraged.

Within a month of invasion, the Belgian government had printed three reports on German war crimes, and the Bryce Committee was the response to calls from the British parliament and press for a local enquiry. Viscount James Bryce was 'an inspired choice' to chair the committee.[70] An opponent of the Boer War, he had studied in Germany, in Heidelberg, Jena and Leipzig. Some 1,200 witnesses were interviewed by British barristers, part of the two million Belgians who had fled the country with over 120,000 arriving in the UK. Bryce asked whether, as chairman, he could interview some of the witnesses, but was told that it was not necessary and none of their stories were directly challenged. Bryce's committee was only to review the findings. His committee found that excesses were ordered or allowed to strike terror into the civil population and to dishearten Belgian troops. Specifically, there were deliberate and systematically organised massacres, civilians were murdered in large numbers, looting and house burning was committed where no military necessity could be alleged, and that women and children were used as shields for the German forces. There was much damning detail in a report that spread around the world and was translated into thirty languages. The witness depositions could not be found after the war. Many writers attacked the report in the inter-war years and it has been vilified for the last one hundred years. 'When the wave of appeasement settled over Europe in the 1920s, the "Belgian atrocities" were interred as propaganda lies until historians in the 1980s and 1990s unearthed them and found they were true.'[71] In contrast to Raico and the other revisionists, the report, thoroughly researched by Jeff Lipkes in 2007, is currently thought to have been substantially vindicated and is no longer a 'prime example of untruthful war propaganda'.[72] Neither the wartime German government nor the Weimar parliament denied the accusations.

From the middle of December 1914, atrocity stories gained massive attention, both in quantity of reporting and in prominence.[73] The German Navy's bombardment of Scarborough and Hartlepool, attended by Erich Gerth, was 'by a considerable margin the most important atrocity story' of 1914 for the British press and its readership. Then came Zeppelin bombings of unprotected British cities. After the use of poison gas at Ypres in April 1915, Valentine Williams unleashed his own interpretation of 'Germanism' in the *Daily Mail* under the title 'The Mind of the Hun':

> *His methods of warfare do not bear comparison with those of even a savage but high-minded people such as the Zulus ... His savagery is not of the assegai and shield variety. It is the cold-blooded employment of every device of modern science, asphyxiating bombs, incendiary*

discs and the like, irrespective of the laws of civilised warfare ... The
bewildering blend of primitive barbarity, low cunning and highly
trained intellect which comprises the word 'Kultur'.[74]

The *Daily Mail*, after the *John Bull* magazine, was always accounted the
most hate-filled national newspaper:

In Belgium, the Germans have treated the villages where any resistance
has been offered to their attack with something like savagery. Peasants
have been shot; houses have been wantonly burnt; hostages have
been seized and maltreated ... Such are the methods of the people who
claim the privileges of culture and civilisation. The wanton attack on
little Belgium has already covered the reputation of Germany with the
broadest discredit.[75]

A few days later, Hamilton Fyfe, in the same newspaper, wrote under the
headline 'The Barbarity of German Troops – Sins against Civilisation', that
there was 'unfortunately no doubt any longer that the Germans have been
making war in a way that is far from being civilised. To call it "savage" or
"barbarous" would be doing a monstrous injustice to uncivilised races ...
Do not think I mean to apply it to all German soldiers or even most of
them ... But that a large number of them have acted not like men but like
devils is now beyond dispute.'[76] To these were quickly added the executions
of nurse Edith Cavell for assisting Allied soldiers to escape from Belgium
and of Captain Charles Fryatt of the passenger ship *Brussels* for, perhaps,
attempting to ram a u-boat.[77] Shortly afterwards, the French executed two
German nurses in similar circumstances, but the Germans said nothing
publicly. Pressed on this is Berlin, the Prussian director of propaganda for
the general staff declared that the French 'had a perfect right to shoot them'.[78]

Quickly, the essential German character was thought to be the root cause
of their atrocious behaviour and early caution was replaced by a 'certainty
of German bestiality'.[79] The British press set about a highly-organised
campaign to depict German nationals as animals capable of any despicable
act. One example which appeared in 1915 in a *Daily Mail* cartoon showed
technologically advanced but under-evolved 'sub-humans' and opened the
possibility of an explanation even worse than cultural differences – that
the Germans as a people were 'intrinsically flawed, probably depraved,
and possibly evil'.[80] The scale of the machinery for disinformation put into
place by the British to enable this conversion, or entrapment, was beyond
anything the world had ever before experienced. It even dwarfed the 1900
propaganda campaigns of Tirpitz and his Naval Office, the forerunner of
the twentieth-century propaganda ministries.[81]

The *Daily Mail* and The Harmsworth Press, pioneer of tabloid journalism
and owned by Alfred Harmsworth, Lord Northcliffe, were later 'demonised

for their hate propaganda' and gained a deserved reputation for an 'unscrupulous readiness to libel the enemy' with sensational stories that excited the gullible. If the popular dailies spread the gospel of anti-German hatred to the working classes, it was *The Times* that was the 'intellectual base and manipulated the elite opinion in Britain, moulding policy and poisoning the climate'.[82] To aid Northcliffe and *The Times*, the British issued accounts of terrible events attributed to the Germans which were purely fictitious. 'By judicious editing and emphasis, they were turned into veritable acts of frightfulness.' It was called officially 'the atrocity drive'. Of course, the 'censor eliminated all reference to actions by soldiers of the Allied countries which might be considered uncivilised'.[83]

There was no end to reports of u-boat war crimes. 'In the North Sea, the Germans have proceeded to show their system of maritime warfare is as cruel and callous as their system of war on land. By scattering mines in the highway of international traffic they have imperilled the shipping of neutral powers and brought the most terrible risks upon innocent non-combatants – women and children.'[84] In the aftermath of the Scarborough bombardment in December 1914, Winston Churchill described the German Navy as 'baby killers'. This was 'easily the strongest invective from a senior politician that had so far been expressed'.[85] Four days later, in an editorial entitled 'The Mark of the Hun', the *Daily Mail* declared that the 'debating habit of flinging articles of The Hague Convention at the enemy' should cease.[86]

Soon, it was a weekly occurrence for the British Press to fulminate against wanton u-boats sending food to the bottom of the seas and even began to portray the British blockade as a justifiable response to this inhumane action instead of being its source. The u-boats sank hospital ships, killed women and children indiscriminately and machined-gunned survivors of merchant ships in lifeboats. Most of the stories were not true and when they were, in a large number of cases, there were extenuating circumstances. By war end, eighteen u-boat captains were listed and sought as war criminals, but none ever stood trial at Leipzig.[87]

These clashes of perception led directly to the greatest single atrocity of the war in British and American eyes, the sinking of the *Lusitania*. However important the *Lusitania* was in shaping American attitudes, the majority of those who died on the ship were British. For many, the *Lusitania* was a real case of 'baby killing'; ninety-four of the victims were children, and thirty-five of the thirty-nine babies on board were drowned. In vain, the Germans pointed out that the ship was an armoured cruiser, carried ammunition, and that proper warning had been given. The sinking was a propaganda disaster. The line of Louvain-Scarborough-Zeppelin-poison-gas-*Lusitania* was now drawn.

Vilification was not limited to the sea war. The Germans constantly did things which 'angered the entire world and these the propagandists exploited to the full'.

> *Such conduct was a natural result of conditions accompanying the*
> *rise of the Reich, a latecomer to the scene of European power ... Every*
> *country on the way up puts a premium on effectiveness and as a result*
> *give position and power to many crass, aggressive, and disagreeable*
> *people. The peculiar situation which faced Germany accentuated this*
> *natural phenomenon. Her youthful impatience caused her to substitute*
> *direct action for the more involved methods which characterise good*
> *politics. Her statesmen, unaccustomed to great power, played their new*
> *part badly.*[88]

There was a well thought through battle plan within the British establishment, first to excite and then to involve the Americans. British propagandists needed to take an ordinary political power struggle and to present it as a fight between the forces of good and evil. If Britain was 'good' and Germany 'evil', it would be a simple step to help the people of the United States to associate with 'good' against 'evil'. If Britain's interests were shown to be America's interests the battle was won: 'the Allies' cause was America's cause' and, when successful, and the tenets of the 'holy war' taken up, the convert becomes the prophet. Those propagandised become propagandists.[89]

Peterson thought that the British were very fortunate: 'The struggle between weary old England and boisterous new Germany readily adapted itself to the stereotype of virtue versus iniquity.' Strachan found the same message. Britain did not present itself as pursuing its own strategic and imperial interests, but as the chivalric knight, first rushing to the aid of brutalised Belgium and second helping to defend France from aggression. 'Britain was fighting to uphold international law and the rights of small nations; its enemy was Prussian militarism.'[90] The mood of the Americans while they remained neutral would make them wish to help the Allies in fighting Germany and, eventually, the tide of commitment would lead America into joining the war.

In cutting the undersea telegraph cables between the United States and Germany, the British began their censorship of what America could and would hear.[91] The next stage was to censor the press in England through the Defence of the Realm Act, 'the famous DORA', which gave control over 'all statements intended or likely to prejudice His Majesty's relations with foreign powers'. Regulation 18 looked to prevent the leakage of militarily-useful information to the enemy, particularly troop and shipping movements. Regulation 27 made it an offence to 'spread false reports', distribute reports likely to cause 'disaffection to His Majesty' or 'prejudice relations with foreign powers', 'prejudice recruiting' or 'undermine public confidence in banks or the currency'. Used carefully, Regulation 27 could be immensely restrictive.[92] By these actions, significant power was already in Britain's hands. Some 90 per cent of the American public received its day-to-day picture of Europe through a distinctly British perspective. 'Few

American newspapers at that time maintained European staffs of their own; while those which did found few trained American foreign correspondents to man them.'[93] As both the American newspapers and press associations covered European politics mainly from London they used, as background, material derived from British newspapers and magazines which were themselves censored by the British government. The censorship of mail, similar to the censorship of press and cable, not only 'served to control information passing between Europe and America' but also allowed the propagandists to input their own information. In 1914, fourteen people worked on British censorship and information production; by Easter 1916 they had grown to about 2,000; early in 1917 there were 3,700 persons in London and 1,500 in Liverpool.[94]

Ferguson saw that wartime Britain 'became by stages a kind of police state'.[95] Through the new profession of advertising, the government had 'become increasingly involved in what amounted to a major psychological offensive against its own citizens' in military recruitment then in activities like the mass marketing of war bonds.[96] In 1916 alone, the Press Bureau, assisted by the secret service department MI7(a) scrutinised over 38,000 articles, 25,000 photographs and 300,000 private telegrams. As *The Nation* justly lamented in May 1916, it was a 'domestic tragedy of the war that the country which went out to defend liberty restricted its own liberties one by one, and that the government that began by relying on public opinion came to fear and curtail it'.

The Press Censorship Committee was replaced in August 1916, by the Press Bureau which was 'the imagination department, the body which dresses up the facts for presentment to the public'.[97] Peterson studied their output and identified their techniques.[98] Arguments were kept simple and all qualifying statements eliminated: the Germans, and only the Germans, broke the law and were brutal. It was vital to tell only that part of the truth which benefitted the central argument and, where there was no evidence to support the proposition, background material was used to imply it. Propaganda was given 'authority' by using big names, by developing quotes for the enemy, and by appealing to legality. Emotional language was constantly used. Above all, there was endless repetition of the core messages.

If there was a 'father' of the British official propaganda service, it was Charles Masterman, a Cambridge man and journalist, well acquainted with many of the great writers of the day. Masterman was asked in August 1914 by Prime Minister Asquith to examine the sudden appearance of German propaganda materials in many countries, including the handing of pamphlets to arriving steamer passengers in New York.[99] German internal propaganda was extensive. 'The domestic press was mobilised for war, receiving weekly lists of topics that should not be covered plus advice on the attitudes that were to be adopted regarding sensitive subjects.'[100] With government support, German papers were circulated to the neutral countries of Switzerland, Holland, Scandinavia and the United States. Both Germany and Britain had 'good reasons for attempting to win the United States to their side. War meant that the two belligerents had each lost their best trading partner – each other.' There is evidence that Asquith's invitation was set up by Lloyd George who had already asked Masterman, 'Will you look into it, Charlie, and see what can be done.' Masterman quickly set up a series of conferences in September. At the first, the invitees, almost all of whom attended, were a breathtaking literary roll call: William Archer, Sir J. M. Barrie, Arnold Bennett, A. C. Benson, Monsignor Hugh Benson, Robert Bridges, Hall Caine, G. K. Chesterton, Sir Arthur Conan Doyle, John Galsworthy, Thomas Hardy, Anthony Hope Hawkins, Maurice Hewlett, W. J. Locke, E. V. Lucas, J. W. Mackail, John Masefield, A. E. W. Mason, Professor Gilbert Murray, Henry Newbolt, Sir Owen Seaman, George Macauley Trevelyan, H. G. Wells and Israel Zangwill. Sir Arthur Quiller-Couch and Rudyard Kipling, both sent messages saying they were willing to assist.

> The group did not include younger authors like Robert Graves and Siegfried Sassoon, who were at the front or about to be called up ... Writers from the Bloomsbury Circle, like E. M. Forster and Virginia Woolf, were not present. The maverick, antagonistic D. H. Lawrence, soon to be harassed by neighbours and the police for his anti-war views, was not invited. And pacifists such as Bertrand Russell were not present and would not have consented to be even if asked.

The result of the first conference was a letter to *The Times* by fifty authors, now swelled by Laurence Binyon, Hubert Henry Davies, Arthur Pinero, H. Rider Haggard and Jerome J. Jerome, declaring 'A Righteous War'.[101] After a preliminary skirmish to point out that the signatories crossed the political spectrum and included 'champions of goodwill towards Germany', the authors majored on the violation of Belgian neutrality:

> Without even the pretence of a grievance against Belgium, [Germany] made war on the weak and unoffending country, and has since carried out her invasion with a calculated and ingenious ferocity which has raised questions other and not less grave than the wilful disregard of treaties. When Belgium in her dire need appealed to Great Britain to carry out her pledge this country's course was clear ... To permit the ruin of France would be a crime against liberty and civilisation ... They excuse all these proceedings by a strange and novel plea. German culture and civilisation are so superior to those of other nations that all steps taken to assert them are more than justified; and the destiny of Germany to be the dominating force in Europe and the world is so manifest that ordinary rules of morality do not hold in her

*case, but actions are good or bad simply as they help or hinder the
accomplishment of that destiny.*[102]

The second conference, held on 7 September, was 'as awesome in its own
way as the first'.[103] It included figures from the cream of the British press
known to readers throughout the world, but pointedly did not include
representatives from pacifist and socialist journals or 'even writers from
journals subsidised by more moderate sectors of Britain's growing labour
movement'. After this meeting, four resolutions regarding the conduct of
propaganda were adopted unanimously: censorship should be minimal,
a co-ordinator should manage the government news, government should
help journalists in their reporting in the Dominions and neutral countries,
and that British diplomats should enlist the help of journalists to correct
errors in foreign [German] news reporting.

With cabinet backing, Masterman set up the War Propaganda Bureau,
which was to concentrate on 'making the British case in Allied and neutral
nations', but not to make propaganda against the enemy or at home.
The organisation was divided on linguistic lines with units dealing with
Scandinavia, the Netherlands, Spain and Portugal and the appropriate
nations of Latin America, Italy and Switzerland, and, most importantly,
the United States. Secrecy, pervasive through all government departments,
and truthfulness, at least in this arm of propaganda work, were the initial
watchwords. Secrecy was helped by setting up the bureau in Wellington
House, Buckingham Gate, in London, a building already housing the
National Health Insurance Commission and 'where the coming and going
of a few more people would be unlikely to attract notice'. 'Wellington House'
became the pseudonym for the operation. The 'inside' staff had impressive
credentials and included Claud Schuster as chief executive officer; Anthony
Hope Hawkins, author of *The Prisoner of Zenda*, was the bureau's literary
adviser. The literary agent was A. S. Watt who recommended to Wellington
House the employment of Muirhead Bone, the prolific war artist, employed
at a salary of £500 a year to make drawings of 'appropriate war scenes' for
propaganda and for historical record.[104] Edwyn Bevan, a prominent classicist
from Oxford University, liaised with military and naval intelligence. Three
historians, Arnold Toynbee, Lewis Namier and J. W. Headlam-Morley were
general advisers. Schuster spent a week in Paris advising the French on
improving their own propaganda departments. Significantly, Wellington
House worked with the Belgian legation and 'functioned as virtually their
entire ministry of propaganda in the early months of the war', which
included the whole period of the 'Belgian Atrocities'.

By June 1915, Wellington House had printed and circulated two and half
million books, official publications, pamphlets and speeches in seventeen
different languages. Among these works were contributions by Anthony
Hope Hawkins who wrote the satirical *The German (New) Testament*,

Germany and the Next War, and *Militarism: German and British*; by G. K. Chesterton, *The Barbarism of Berlin*; and by Sir Arthur Conan Doyle, *The British Campaigns in France and Flanders*. Masterman emphasised to the cabinet that this material was 'not circulated promiscuously, but ... either ... sold or sent with a personal letter' or placed in a library or on a circulation list.

The organisation had a mailing list of 260,000 names of influential people throughout the United States, who were provided with a steady stream of whatever they might need to report on or to discuss about the war, its origin, its history and all the 'varied and difficult questions which arose during its development'. The stream almost knew no bounds. Peterson identified the production and distribution of special pictorial papers; assisting in the placing of articles and interviews designed to influence opinion in the world's newspapers and magazines, especially in America; the wide distribution of pictorial matter, cartoons, pictures and drawings, photographs for insertion in newspapers and periodicals and for exhibition; the production and distribution of cinematograph films; personal correspondence with influential people abroad, especially in America; arrangements for the interchange of visits, of personal tours to neutral and Allied countries and of visits of distinguished neutrals and of representatives of the Allies to this country; the production and distribution of maps, diagrams, posters, lantern slides and lectures, pictures, postcards, and all other possible means of miscellaneous propaganda.[105]

> *Editors, novelists, political experts, essayists, statesmen, university presidents, and men of importance in all walks of life, especially Americans, were given tours of the front. A visitor's chateau was provided for them and there the cuisine was excellent, while food rationing in England tightened under the growing submarine menace. They were chaperoned by most attentive and diplomatic reserve officers who had notes in hand from the Foreign Office about the standing and character of each visitor ... In England, Americans were courted assiduously. Clubs were open to them, teas and dinners were given for them ...[106] The British campaign to induce the United States to come to their assistance affected every phase of American life; it was propaganda in its broadest sense. News, money, and political pressure each played its part and the battle was fought not only in London, New York, and Washington, but also in American classrooms and pulpits, factories, and offices. It was a campaign to create a pro-British attitude-of-mind among Americans, to get American sympathies and interests so deeply involved in the European war that it would be impossible for* [America] *to remain neutral.*[107]

Perhaps the biggest publishing success of the war was *J'accuse!*, written by the German lawyer Richard Grelling. Grelling was born in Berlin, became a dramatist, and was a founding member of the *Deutsche Friedensgesellschaft*, the German Peace Society.[108] The book, which condemned the actions of the Central Powers, enjoyed huge sales in many languages, including English.[109]

> The 'neurosis of war' has indeed become epidemic, like St Vitus's Dance or flagellantism in the Middle Ages. As the Dervishes in the East for hours at a time utter the same formulae of prayer and go through the same contortions with their arms and legs and their bodies until at last they fall down foaming at the mouth and overpowered, so now we have seen the learned men of Germany repeating for months past the same patriotic litanies, the same unproved assertions (assertions indeed of which the contrary is proved); at all times reaching upwards with their arms and legs and indeed their whole body, until in their opinion they and their people surpass all other nations of the earth, and if they do not become like to God, they at least become the chosen people of God ... The workmen and the idle classes however perish and decay. The longer the war lasts, the more surely will German trade, the German system of finance and German manufactures, be deprived of their connections with foreign countries. The seas of the world are open to our enemies, England and France, as well as to the neutral States, and it would be a surprising fact if they did not gradually usurp our place in markets abroad.[110]

The book came into the hands of Jean Jacques Waitz who worked as an interpreter in France with German prisoners of war. Waitz, also known as Hansi, became convinced that 'something should be done to shatter the belief among the Germans that the Fatherland was on the defensive'.[111] Waitz thought to distribute the 400-page book over the German lines. His solution was to invent a letter, supposedly found in the diary of a prisoner of war who marvels at his treatment by the French and describes Grelling's book in which the war guilt of the Germans is clearly shown. This letter was distributed by aircraft over the entire Western Front.

Among the various British bodies in the War and Foreign Offices, was the War Aims Committee, chaired by Captain Guest. Guest set out to reply to pacifist propaganda by means of 'machinery of an educative character' in order that there might be a 'more highly instructed and intelligent determination to prosecute the war to its conclusion than would have been possible if the campaign had never been undertaken'.[112] Being mercilessly obstructionist also helped. Bertrand Russell was quickly renowned for posing difficult questions. He asked whether Germany and England will 'continue to fight and hate each other until one of them is utterly broken?' For the moment, he opined, 'both countries are wholly blind to their own faults, and utterly fantastic in the cries which they attribute to the enemy. A vast but shadowy economic conflict has been invented to rationalise their hostility, which is in fact as irrational and instructive as that of dogs who snarl and fly at each other in the street'.[113] For questions like these, Russell was barred from visiting the towns of Cambridge and Harvard where as a professor of mathematical logic he was based in the universities. Driven to earn a living through a lecture tour, he was told to supply in advance his spoken and responsive lectures on the 'Philosophical Principles of Politics' and then, when protesting that this was nor possible, was banned from several of the towns, as 'prohibited areas', where he had engagements.[114]

In 1918, Northcliffe, who controlled 40 per cent of the morning and 45 per cent of the evening newspaper circulation in Britain, became head of the British propaganda divisions aimed at enemy countries. It was an appointment that greatly alarmed the German high command. *The Star* declared that Northcliffe, next to the Kaiser, had done more than any living man to bring about the war. His virulent attacks on the Germans, especially through the *Daily Mail*, persuaded the Germans to send a warship to shell his house in Broadstairs in an attempt to assassinate him.[115] Northcliffe's residence, Elmwood in Reading Street, still bears a shell hole out of respect for the gardener's wife, who was killed in the attack.[116] After the war, Lloyd George made an excoriating attack on Northcliffe, calling his arrogance 'diseased vanity', possibly in reference to the tertiary syphilis which was to kill him.[117]

One of Northcliffe's first tasks was to establish greater co-operations between the French and British organisations, which had till then been working independently. At a conference in London in March, the French propaganda services were reorganised into two groups: the *Maison de la presse*, concerned particularly with atrocity propaganda, reaching neutral countries, and with work among Catholics, Jews and Protestants in all of Europe; and the *Centre d'action de propaganda contre l'ennemie*, which concentrated on 'tearing down the morals of the enemy, inducing German soldiers to desert, and weakening the power of resistance at the front and among the German people'.[118] It was in the latter that Waitz, the distributor of *J'accuse!*, played a prominent role. Northcliffe immediately directed a programme, managed by H. Wickham Steed, against Austria-Hungary aiming to 'convince the different races of the Hapsburg monarchy that the Allies were determined to secure democratic freedom for them'.[119] The Austrian armies contained large numbers of men who were already nationalists and potentially disloyal. The German troops, however, were far prouder of their supposed single heritage. Northcliffe decided that his division's biggest argument likely to undermine the German soldier was the arrival of the Americans. 'You are almost at the end of your resources in manpower. The Allies have only just begun to pump men out of an enormous new reservoir of inexhaustible depth.' Here, H. G. Wells set out to show that a league of nations stood against the German Army and that the only thing 'between the enemy peoples and lasting peace [was] the predatory designs of their ruling dynasties and military and economic castes; that the design of the Allies [was] not to crush any people but to assure them the freedom of all on the basis of self-determination'.[120] These words were a little less ringing to German ears when they negotiated with the unforgiving Allies between the armistice and the signing of the peace treaty.

Through the avalanche of information, the Germans did little to help themselves. The start of German economic warfare was of 'immense importance to the British in their campaign to create an anti-German climate of opinion within the United States'.[121] The sinking of ships by u-boats was highly advertised, bringing home the distressing submarine warfare to Americans. The Allies claimed that this was proof of German barbarity. The British emphasised that the United States was under threat and the reported atrocities supported this. U-boats killed American crew and passengers and brought a torrent of threats from President Woodrow Wilson. The sinking of the *Lusitania*, with some 130 neutral Americans among 1,201 drowned, was the final straw. At dinner in the American Embassy in London, Ambassador Page remembered:

> *The news seemed to have numbed everyone. There was little or no denunciation, there was no discussion of any consequences of the sinking, except that it was universally accepted that America would enter the war within the month.*[122]

The American press almost unanimously condemned Zeppelin raids on defenceless British towns and the killing of women and children, but 'in the last year of the war British air raids over Germany were five times greater than the total number of air raids on Great Britain during the four years of the war'.[123] When the Americans did enter the war, their own restrictions on the liberty of their citizens were seen as draconian. Even criticising the war in a lodging house became illegal. More than 25,000 Americans were indicted under this legislation of whom nearly one hundred received prison sentences of between ten and twenty years.[124]

Siegfried Heckscher, Reichstag member and chief of the publicity department of the Hamburg-America line, said in September 1918, 'We try to protect our country from enemy espionage and from the work of agents and scoundrels, but with open eyes we leave it defenceless while a stream of poisonous speeches is poured over its people.'[125] One frustrated summariser declared, 'Britain rules the waves and waives the rules'.[126] Another stated, 'One of the greatest qualities which has made the English a great people is their eminently sane, reasonable, fair-minded inability to conceive that any viewpoint save their own can possibly have the slightest merit.'[127]

The first displays of mutinous spirit among the men of the fleet were 'not so much due to revolutionary and radical Socialist propaganda' as to a spontaneous internal dissatisfaction with the conditions of the service itself, particularly the arrogance of the officers and the poor food.[128]

> From birth, the men had been brought up to think along class lines and to wage the proletariat's battle against employers and industrialists. In typical worker fashion, they knew how to strike for their rights and the protection of their interests. When their dreadful living conditions failed to improve during the spring of 1917 and their diet continued to hover near the starvation level, a great tide of war-weariness swept over them. Their officers' one-sided propaganda campaign against reform and in favour of territorial annexations, their refusal to grant food complaint committees, and their prohibition of socialist newspapers and meetings prompted the men to think of organising.[129]

'The Independent Socialists were prompt to discover and take advantage of these conditions. The sailors were plied with propaganda, oral and written.' The character of this propaganda was not generally known until 9 October 1917, when the Minister of the Marine, Admiral von Capelle, speaking in the Reichstag, 'informed the astonished nation that a serious mutiny had occurred in the fleet two months earlier, and that it had been necessary to execute some of the ringleaders and imprison a number of others'.[130] The admirals, in denial, branded the uprising as 'political' and inadvertently gave birth to the myth of 'the stab-in-the-back' to explain the loss of the war. The myth was later embraced by Ludendorff.[131]

Ludendorff wrote extensively in his post-war apologia about the effects of British propaganda which 'literally swamped' the German Army.[132] General headquarters gave rewards for the surrender of propaganda pamphlets, but 'this could not prevent them from poisoning the minds of our soldiers before they were delivered up'. Ludendorff said he 'lifted his hat' to Lloyd George and Clemenceau because they understood what his own 'mean-spirited ministers' did not:

> That in war the morale of the non-combatant is almost as important as that of the combatant. You cannot in modern warfare separate the one from the other. Just as you must discourage your enemy and the whole population of your enemy, you must encourage your own men, and uplift the population behind you. The Statesmen at the back must be the supporting morale reserve of the General at the front.[133]

> Before the enemy propaganda we were like a rabbit and a snake. It was exceptionally clever and worked on a very large scale. Its suggestions had a strong effect on the masses; it worked well together with the actual campaigning, and was unscrupulous as to the means used.

The German people, who had not yet learned the art or the value of silence, had, in their blameworthy frankness, shown by their speech, their writings, and their actions the best line of attack for the enemy propaganda.[134]

Adolf Hitler, later a close student of the propaganda war, went even further: the superiority of British propaganda, or the failure of German propaganda, was the main cause in his view for Germany's demise.[135] The British outpourings were 'vastly superior to German efforts ... Had we any propaganda at all? Alas, I can only reply in the negative. Everything was so inadequate and wrong from the very start that it certainly did no good and sometimes did actual harm ... the effectiveness of [their horror, outrage and atrocity] propaganda was after four and a half years undermining the stamina of our people at home.'[136] Hitler deduced that the 'right use of propaganda was an art in itself and that this art was practically unknown to our bourgeois parties'. It led him as early as 1933 to establish his own ministry of propaganda. In a direct sense, the power of Joseph Goebbels was a tribute to and a mimicry of British success in World War I.

It is a mistake to organise and direct propaganda as if it were a manifold system of scientific instruction. The receptive powers of the masses are very restricted and their understanding is feeble. On the other hand, they quickly forget. Such being the case, all effective propaganda must be confined to a few bare essentials and those must be expressed as far as possible in stereotyped formulas. These slogans should be persistently repeated until the very last individual has come to grasp the idea.

Zweig in his great memoir of the period felt that by war end 'there was no city, no group that had not fallen prey to the dreadful hysteria or hatred' brought about in Germany by the relentless domestic propaganda. The voices of German apologists like Degrelle were lost in the wind:

British propaganda mills had devised horror stories to suit each country's population. They were to be the cannon fodder, and they had to be convinced.[137] *For four years, the concoctions of the London propagandists would ceaselessly fill the ears of millions of gullible people. In big headlines, the press kept pouring out enormous lies about Belgian Red Cross nurses being shot by Hun firing squads; it depicted little girls praying to the Virgin Mary to replace hands that had been savagely chopped off by barbaric Teutons. Then there were the Hun submarines constantly seeking to send American women and children to the bottom of the sea. If these lies are laughable today, they certainly swayed people into a permanent anti-German hysteria in 1919. The cynical British establishment had used the stories to justify sacrificing*

the lives of Englishmen and Scotsmen, and after the war the same
stories justified the subjection and dismemberment of Germany.

Zweig saw the war as of an 'unsuspicious generation'. 'The greatest peril
was the inexhaustible faith of the nations in the single-sided justice of
their cause.'[138] And whereas the excitement of national unity abated, the
'hatred of the enemy remained, continuing as an unfortunate wart on the
peace process. For victor and vanquished alike, the 'consequence of such
hatred could only be tragedy'. A secret report provided by a traveller to
Germany in 1916 was sent from Rotterdam to London and showed how
far and how quickly matters had gone. The traveller was 'first amused and
afterwards disgusted at the insane hatred of the English by every soul of
every class in Germany. Relatives and friends of his who had lived a great
deal in England, had English relatives, and had always been regarded as
Anglo-maniacs, said they believed the most childish things respecting the
English. It was laughable how those who could speak English better than
German adopted this frame of mind.'[139]

As with any successful campaign, its effects are long-lived and enter the
national psyche. Poet and author Henry Newbolt, called with the other
leading British writers into the War Propaganda Bureau at the start of the
war, subsequently became Controller of Telecommunication at the Foreign
Office. Newbolt was asked to finish Sir Julian Corbett's five-volume *History*
of the Great War, published in 1931, and felt able to write these two passages
where he could not have been more specific or more vitriolic.

The struggle, though it seemed to have its origin in smaller causes,
was quickly seen, even by the Germans, to be 'a conflict between two
conceptions of world-politics': that is to say, between two conceptions of
human life. After seeing the two conceptions illustrated on a giant scale,
the judgement of mankind appears to have reaffirmed the old code of
humanity and chivalry, and condemned the new philosophy of Might
and the new methods of Frightfulness. But whether this mood lasts or
not, whether the issue is already decided or must still be fought out in
some more terrible war of liberation, there can be no doubt of the nature
of the fight. [140]

We may achieve something if we consider the German action as the
resultant of a number of interacting forces: first, a particular strain of
the national character, inherited and distinctly traceable for centuries;
second, a tendency to revert to a primitive type of religious feeling; third,
a docility and an emotional instability which made it easy for those in
authority to rouse strong feeling by suggestion; fourth, the propagation
of a Machiavellian theory of the State by professional and military
virtues; fifth, the urgency of the situation created by the policy of the

Naval Chiefs; and sixth, the super-added urgency of the general military position after the breakdown of the German war plan.[141]

And in the same year from respected naval historians Gibson and Prendergast:

The u-boat's campaign was akin to a war-time mafia; like a powerful and virulent secret society, murder and mutilation accompanied by mystery were the marks of its activity. Here one moment and gone the next; wherever they appeared for one fleeting second, the stain of some vile crime as often as not sullied the purity of the sea. To hunt such malignant phantoms was to the pursuers and agents of justice almost as futile and disheartening a task as the chase of a thousand Vanderdeckens.[142]

The following year, 1932, saw one of the first attempts by the British government to censor the BBC in peacetime in what became known as the 'Hashagen Affair'. Ernst Hashagen, a u-boat commander frequently quoted in this book, was one of two German officers from World War I invited to appear on *Hazard*, a series of radio programmes about risky exploits.[143] Zeppelin commander Joachim Briehaupt went first and the talk was 'greeted with a furious letter' from the British Empire Union declaring that the BBC was guilty of a 'callous disregard' for listeners' feelings. The matter was discussed at the top of government where ministers agreed that the Hashagen broadcast should not go ahead and the director-general Sir John Reith was informed. 'Reith stood his ground', but his chairman, J. H. Whitley 'was less resolute and agreed to stop the broadcast'. Whitley protested at the 'bullying'. 'The corporation feels than an incident so contrary to the spirit and intention of the royal charter should not pass without protest. The governors venture to assume that it will not form a precedent.'

Schreiner, the American journalist, had no doubt about his epitaph for the struggle.

There is no greater liar than a censor – nor a more dangerous one. By systematically suppressing one side of an issue or thing, the unpleasant one, he fosters a deception in the public mind that is as pitiful to behold as it is stupendous.[144]

Atrocity historian Read, summarised:

Both sides had unclean hands. Just as both sides invented atrocities to ascribe to the enemy, so did both sides commit atrocities. The Allies, according to reliable witnesses, also 'mopped up' wounded soldiers, bombed civilians, and starved little children. In fact, the Germans as victors, would probably have exhibited quite as much vindictiveness as did the Allies; they had a suspiciously large collection of documents concerning atrocities ready at the end of 1918, on which they had been working for some time. Four years of war and propaganda had left people and politicians with open wounds that would not heal.[145]

ENDNOTES

1   Hobson, *Jingoism*, pp. 1–2.
2   Sun, *Art of War*, p. 1.
3   Read, *Atrocity Propaganda*, p. 1.
4   More, *Utopia*, p. 93.
5   Messinger, *British Propaganda*, p. 9, with an extensive footnote.
6   Hashagen, *Commander*, pp. 19–20.
7   Neureuther, *U-Boat Stories:* Bergen, 'My U-Boat Voyage', p. 2; Wiedemann, 'My First U-Boat Voyage', p. 59.
8   Spiegel, *202*, p. 9.
9   Hashagen, *Commander*, p. 89.
10 Moyer, *Victory Must Be Ours*, p. 99. Fritzsche, *Germans into Nazis*, pp. 40–41.
11 Moyer, *Victory Must Be Ours*, p. 99. Fritzsche, *Germans into Nazis*, pp. 40–41.
12 Hull, *Absolute Destruction*, p. 153, quoting Sösemann, *Die sogenannte 'Hunnenrede'*, pp. 349–50. Compare with the exploits of Lothar von Trotha in China and, later, in South West Africa (Chapter 2, 'Kaisertreu').
13 First published in *The Times*, 2/9/1914.
14 Gregory, 'Clash of Cultures' in Paddock, *Arms*, p. 31.
15 'What stands if Freedom fall? Who dies if England live?'.
16 Gregory, 'Clash of Cultures' in Paddock, *Arms*, pp. 37–38.
17 Fürbringer, *Legendary*, pp. 94–95.
18 Massie, *Castles*, p. 123.
19 Chapter 6, 'War of the raven'.
20 Hashagen, *Commander*, pp. 19–20, 120.
21 Lowell, *Raiders*, p. 4.
22 Hollweg, *Unser Recht Auf Den U-Bootskrieg*, 'Our Right to the Submarine War'. The quote is taken from pp. 235–38, but the theme is repeated throughout.
23 Asprey, *German High Command*, pp. 30–31.
24 Asprey, *German High Command*, p. 50.
25 Hanssen, *Diary of a Dying Empire*, p. 29.
26 Turner, *Origins*, p. 94.
27 Bülow, *Memoirs*, p. 145, quoted in Turner, *Origins*, p. 112. The reference is to Holman Hunt's, *The Scapegoat*.
28 Holborn, 'Introduction', in Fischer, *War Aims*, p. x.
29 Asprey, *German High Command*, pp. 48–49. Hanssen, *Dying Empire*, p. 29.
30 Weinreb, *Modern Hungers*, pp. 32–33.
31 Vincent, *Politics of Hunger*, pp. 8–9, 21–22.
32 Davis, *Everyday Life*, p. 34.

33 Schreiner, *Iron Ration*, pp. 225–26.
34 Bruntz, *Allied Propaganda*, p. 162.
35 Asprey, *German High Command*, p. 135.
36 Schreiner, *Iron Ration*, pp. 225–26.
37 Dunn, *Blockade*, p. 130.
38 The expression and the word 'strafe' gave rise in a 'humorous' and retaliatory adaptation to the term 'strafing', the attacking of ground targets with automatic weapons by low-flying aircraft.
39 Bruntz, *Allied Propaganda*, p. 3.
40 Bouton, *Abdicates*, p. 103.
41 Messinger, *British Propaganda*, pp. 17–18.
42 Chapter 1, 'Brave new world'.
43 Docherty & Macgregor, *Hidden History*, p. 147.
44 Strachan, *First World War*, p. 35.
45 Clark, *Sleepwalkers*, p. 553.
46 Strachan, *First World War*, p. 35.
47 Docherty & Macgregor, *Hidden History*, pp. 135–36.
48 Ewart, *Roots and Causes*, Vol. 1, p. 512.
49 Morel, *Truth and the War*, p. 157.
50 Ewart, *Roots and Causes*, Vol. 1, pp. 510–13.
51 Churchill, *World Crisis*, pp. 23–24.
52 Clark, *Sleepwalkers*, p. 553.
53 Ewart, *Roots and Causes*, Vol. 1, pp. 131–141.
54 Ewart, *Roots and Causes*, Vol. 1, pp. 115–131.
55 Ollivier, *L'Empire Liberal*, Vol. XIV, p. 382.
56 Ewart, *Roots and Causes*, Vol. I, p. 19.
57 *Le Petit Journal*, 6/8/1914. Bruntz, *Allied Propaganda*, p. 9.
58 Peterson, *Propaganda*, pp. 46–47.
59 Bruntz, *Allied Propaganda*, p. 12.
60 Nolan, 'Eagle Soars', in Paddock, *Arms*, p. 58. The origins of the term 'boche' are disputed, but the most convincing etymology is that, in 1870, the popular nickname for the Germans was 'square-heads'. The term *boche* probably derives from *caboche*, a square-headed hobnail used in the making of heavy boots. It thus combines the stereotyped physical appearance of the German soldier with a certain onomatopoetic inelegance. See Lerner, *Das Deutschlandbild in der französischen Literatur*, pp. 183–84.
61 Nolan, 'Eagle Soars', in Paddock, *Arms*, p. 58.
62 Read, *Atrocity Propaganda*, p. 9.
63 *Official Book of German Atrocities*, p. 7.
64 Messinger, *British Propaganda*, pp. 116–17.
65 Peterson, *Propaganda*, p. 50.
66 Hull, *Absolute Destruction*, p. 210.
67 Chapter 2.
68 Raico, 'Great War Retold', *Great Wars and Great Leaders*, pp. 233–34.
69 Raico, 'Turning Point', *Great Wars and Great Leaders*, p. 26. Read, *Atrocity Propaganda*, pp. 201–8. Peterson, *Propaganda*, pp. 51–70.
70 wikipedia.
71 Hull, *Absolute Destruction*, p. 210. For another, opposite view, Messinger, *British Propaganda*, Chapter 5.
72 Lipkes, *Rehearsals*, p. 696.
73 Gregory, 'Clash of Cultures' in Paddock, *Arms*, p. 34.
74 Gregory, 'Clash of Cultures' in Paddock, *Arms*, p. 37.
75 *Daily Mail*, 'German Brutality', 12/8/14, p. 6, quoted in Gregory, 'Clash of Cultures', p. 27.
76 *Daily Mail*, 21/8/14, p. 6.
77 Chapter 6.
78 Messinger, *British Propaganda*, pp. 18–19.
79 Gregory, 'Clash of Cultures', pp. 26–30.

80 *Daily Mail*, 'The Wonders of Science', Kultur cartoons by William Dyson, 1/1/1915, back page, showed two Pickelhaube (spiked German military helmet)-wearing apes in an airplane dropping bombs on civilians.

81 Chapter 1.

82 Docherty & Macgregor, *Hidden History*, p. 147.

83 Peterson, *Propaganda*, pp. 51–52.

84 *Daily Mail*, 'German Brutality', 12/8/14, p. 6.

85 Anthony Gregory, 'Clash of Cultures' in Troy Paddock, *Call to Arms*, p. 35.

86 *Daily Mail*, 'Mark of the Hun', 18/12/14.

87 Chapter 14, 'Welcome home, Erich'.

88 Peterson, *Propaganda*, p. 34.

89 Peterson, *Propaganda*, p. 33.

90 Strachan, *First World War*, p. 61.

91 Chapter 10, 'Intelligence gift'.

92 Gregory, 'A Clash of Cultures: The British Press and the Opening of the Great War' in Paddock, *Arms*, p. 22.

93 Millis, *Road to War*, p. 43, fn.

94 Peterson, *Propaganda*, p. 14.

95 Ferguson, *Pity*, p. 221.

96 Messinger, *British Propaganda*, p. 6.

97 Peterson, *Propaganda*, p. 9.

98 Peterson, *Propaganda*, p. 37.

99 Messinger, *British Propaganda*, pp. 31–35, 54.

100 Messinger, *British Propaganda*, p. 16.

101 'Britain's Destiny and Duty', *The Times*, 18/9/1914, p. 3.

102 Also, Holborn, 'Introduction', in Fischer, *War Aims*, p. xiii.

103 Messinger, *British Propaganda*, pp. 36–40.

104 Bone's drawings for Wellington House were reproduced in a collection called *The Western Front* and were widely circulated: 12,000 copies were sold, 12,000 were used for propaganda and 6,000 were sent to America. The publication was also translated into French as *Agence et Messageries du Figaro*.

105 Peterson, *Propaganda*, pp. 16–17.

106 Peterson, *Propaganda*, pp. 26–27.

107 Peterson, *Propaganda*, p. 4.

108 'The peace movement in Imperial Germany consisted of a small group of well-meaning men and women, who hoped for patriotic reasons to eliminate war by means of an effective international organisation ... These German pacifists found virtually no support ... and were viewed as harmless eccentrics' (Chickering, *We Men*), p. ix.

109 Grelling, now living in Switzerland, was vilified in Germany where his book was banned. He followed *J'accuse!* with *The Crime* in which he attacked his critics, including, sadly, his own son, the philosopher Kurt Grelling. During the Weimar Republic, Grelling's writings were boycotted.

110 Grelling, *J'Accuse*, pp. 7, 9.

111 Bruntz, *Allied Propaganda*, pp. 16–17.

112 *The Times*, 14/12/1917.

113 Russell, *Justice in War Time*, p. 67.

114 Russell, *Justice in War Time*, pp. v–xvii.

115 blueplaquesguy.byethost24.com. Also, *Kent Live News*, 6/8/2017. All versions of this story use the same words and are unattributed; it may be apocryphal.

116 *Kent Today and Yesterday*, 1/1/2010.

117 MacMillan, *Paris 1919*, p. 38.

118 Bruntz, *Allied Propaganda*, p. 18, 198.

119 Bruntz, *Allied Propaganda*, pp. 24–28.

120 Stuart, *Secrets of Crewe House*, pp. 65–86.

121 Peterson, *Propaganda*, p. 109.

122 Simpson, *Lusitania*, pp. 170–71.

123   Peterson, *Propaganda*, p. 64.
124   Ferguson, *Pity*, p. 223.
125   Bouton, *Abdicates*, p. 105.
126   Peterson, *Propaganda*, p. 77.
127   Millis, *Road to War*, p. 64.
128   Bouton, *Abdicates*, pp. 89–90.
129   Horn, *Mutiny*, pp. 98–99.
130   Bouton, *Abdicates*, pp. 89–90.
131   Chapter 13, 'Guilt and blame'.
132   Ludendorff, *War Memories*, Vol. 2, p. 642.
133   Ewart, *Roots and Causes*, pp. 20–21.
134   Ludendorff, *Own Story*, Vol. 1, p. 428.
135   Paddock, 'German Propaganda: The Limits of Gerechtigkeit' in Paddock, *Arms*, pp. 115–16.
136   Hitler, *Mein Kampf*, Chapter VI: 'War Propaganda', pp. 167–75.
137   Degrelle, *Born at Versailles*, p. 523.
138   Zweig, *World of Yesterday*, p. 235.
139   TNA FO 371/2679, received London 20/5/1916, pp. 44–45.
140   Newbolt, *Naval History*, p. viii.
141   Newbolt, *Naval History*, pp. 183–85.
142   Gibson & Prendergast, *German Submarine War*, pp. 186–87. Van der Decken was the captain of the *Flying Dutchman*, whose rash oath meant his ghost ship was doomed to cross the seas for all time, spelling death for all who saw it.
143   bbc.co.uk/historyofthebbc, accessed 7/7/2017.
144   Schreiner, *Iron Ration*, pp. 225–26.
145   Read, *Atrocity Propaganda*, p. 286.

CHAPTER 10

Intelligence Gift

The [British] *cloak of tight secrecy remained until the early 1990s when the Admiralty finally returned captured documents to Germany. By that time, American authorities had made a good number of German* [u-boat] *logbooks available on 35mm microfilm. The absurdity of the Admiralty's dogged tightness can be further illustrated with the fact that copies of a number of the logs in their possession could be viewed in the United States and in German libraries while those in London were still closed to the public.*[1]

Newly-promoted Kapitänleutnant Georg Gerth, commander of *UC 61*, had a cursory chat with his captors at Wissant Town Hall. Serious interviews did not take place until later that day when all the crew were safely marched to Calais Citadel and placed in cells. At least two bilingual French officers, likely more, interrogated the men for about an hour each.[2] It is probable they had experience of interviewing German submariners for their final report reflected first-hand on the lesser enthusiasm for the war of the men of *UC 61* compared to that of the twenty-one crew of *UB 26*, entangled in nets and scuttled off Le Havre in the March of the previous year. Handwritten notes were taken in French and German, depending on the interrogator and the language skills of the crew member. These notes were correlated into a formal report, typed up on 8 August, translated into English, and sent on 11 August to the British liaison officer in Paris. The liaison officer then distributed copies widely to the senior echelons of the Royal Navy. Reginald Hall, the Director of the Navy Intelligence Department (NID) received his copy on the day it was sent and asked that the thanks of the British Admiralty be conveyed to the French for the 'very valuable information obtained from these prisoners'. The original handwritten interview notes survive, given no security classification, as well as early copies of the initial 'Confidential' French '*interrogatoire*', and of the English translation, immediately classified 'Secret' by the British.[3]

These documents, and further copies, are widely dispersed today in Cherbourg, London, Paris and Washington, DC, the latter sent via the American Embassy in Paris to the Force Commander, US Naval Forces, European Waters.

By 11 August, eighteen days after the stranding, the report was mostly too late. Urgent intelligence action had already long been taken: traps set, mines laid, ships sunk, convoys re-routed, codes changed, secret files and assessments of u-boats and officers updated, the wreck three times assessed, armaments, equipment and, even, oil distributed for inspection, and the crew dispersed to prison camps across France.[4] On the day of the stranding, Admiral Bacon in Dover sent a telegram with no time stamp through the commodore in Dunkirk to his opposite number, Admiral Ronarc'h.[5] Bacon said that the Admiralty 'think the French interrogation so good that they could not improve on it'. Ronarc'h was asked to send a copy of the results 'in due course'. Even then, there were fifteen mistakes, several important, in translation from French into English in the formal report sent on 11 August; it is likely from the style that there was more than one translator at work at the same time.

Contrary to a seemingly overall leisurely process, this was an impressively quick set of interrogations and, from what followed within a few days, the telegram sounds more diplomatic, even deliberately misleading, than a true statement. It also shows that there were many early reports long before the more measured document was sent almost three weeks later.

So far, so simple: a u-boat crew captured on a French beach and taken to a French fortress for close examination by French officers who freely share their information with their allies in Britain and America; the French are cordially thanked for the efficiency. The crew was sent on its way, the three officers to a depot at Montoire-sur-le-Loir where they arrived on 5 August and the twenty-three 'other ranks' to holding camp *Gefangenen-Kompagnie 84* in the French military zone, probably in the Department of Oise about fifty kilometres from the front line.[6] However, there is another aspect that only gradually becomes clear and, even when recognised, remains partly opaque. This aspect is the hand of the British NID. Three deficiencies are immediately apparent: the lack of details of the interview with Georg Gerth, compared with his two junior officers, especially as he was reported to have been the 'most talkative'; the absence from the reports of any mention of actions stemming from the most important findings; and the lack of any indication of a serious attempt to collate and to monitor the intelligence gained from aspects of the boat and its fittings.

In today's Admiralty files that are released for public inspection, there are a large number of crew interrogations and also inspection reports of other u-boats, mostly either captured by the British or dived on within a short period of sinking. After reading them all, it is possible to make comparisons about the way u-boat intelligence material was gathered and reported. *UC*

61 was treated in a strikingly different way. Most importantly, its material was gathered mostly in its own files separately from all of the other boats. It is as if the information was held back and intended for release at a much later date. Over eighty pages are missing. Obvious subjects are not covered or are covered casually. As an example, the Admiralty collected in typed books carefully annotated lists of the information discovered from survivors of each class of u-boat. The book for the uc-class has almost one hundred headings listed, from aircraft attacks through to zigzagging, for fifteen uc-boats from March 1916 to June 1918.[7] It is an impressive piece of work. *UC 61* is not mentioned.

The large amount of important information that was collected is scattered around dozens of files in a way that is not common to other reports and interrogations. One possibility is that the lack of administrative rigour may just be a result of much of the work not originating in Britain and, therefore, entering the filing systems in an inconvenient way. This doesn't sit well with the efficient organisation within the NID. The British quickly took control of the many intelligence activities emanating from *UC 61* after stranding. Another possibility is that there is a further file not found, perhaps destroyed or not yet released. The period following 2017, one hundred years after the event, may see some movement in the naval archives at Kew near London and a document will appear quietly in the listing.

Immediately on stranding, Commander Henry Spencer accompanied by a senior technical expert, was despatched from Dover for an inspection additional to the work by the French. Within a few days, almost certainly while *UC 61*'s crew was still at Calais, Bernard Trench interviewed Otto Bock, the u-boat's telegraphist. Working under Reginald Hall, Captain Trench, with Commander Brandon, headed the German section of naval intelligence in Room 40 at the old Admiralty Building in London.[8] After leading a team to interrogate survivors and to recover codebooks from shot-down Zeppelins, Trench was primarily concerned with the u-boat war and put together a team of divers to examine wrecks.[9] He was also the top interrogator of u-boat prisoners.[10] Under interrogation by this most senior of Britain's naval intelligence experts swiftly despatched to Calais, Bock revealed his 'procedures and details of the German Admiralty's system for communication with the u-boats'.[11] Commanders were instructed to listen to the 'Great Bruges Station', one of the captured Belgian broadcasting facilities, at set times each day when they were on the surface and were able; each u-boat sent at least three messages: on arrival and on leaving its operational area and when approaching home so that the torpedo boats and coastal gun crews could be alerted to their return and, in addition, of course, in dire emergency as Gerth had done from Wissant beach.[12] Bock was ordered to listen to the Bruges station at 0100, 0500, 1000, 1500 and 1800 GMT. He also had to listen for special communiqués to submarines which were sent at 1100 through the German Admiralty Station at Nauen in Brandenburg, and for the instructions for all submarines at sea which were sent at 1700 each day from the cruiser *Arcona*, a u-boat support vessel moored in the Ems estuary.[13] The *Arcona* was a sister-ship of the *Amazone*, Georg Gerth's brief posting in the Baltic in 1914.

There was a greater reason why German military radio traffic received close attention. In 1912, the British Committee for Imperial Defence (CID) decided that all German-owned transatlantic cables were to be cut immediately following a declaration of war.[14] Early on the morning of 5 August 1914, the cable ship *Telconia* raised and cut each of the five German cable systems connecting the port of Emden with Spain, Africa and North and South America and, shortly afterwards, a Royal Navy cruiser dragged up two German-owned cables near the Azores. In addition, nine German wireless stations around the world were destroyed by September leaving only two, isolated in Windhoek in German West Africa and Tsingtao in China, with no one to talk to. Only one German cable system, a joint venture with an American company operating between Monrovia in Liberia and Pernambuco in Brazil survived the determined and successful assault, but this was cut early in 1915.

The CID's decision paid Britain a dividend far greater than could have been envisioned and its results were to shape the course and the eventual outcome of the conflict. With the loss of its cable systems at the very outset of the war, Germany was forced to communicate by wireless with its embassies and overseas stations, particularly those in Spain and the Americas.

The 1914 British Naval Annual asserted that there was no threat of interception of radio traffic. However, at that time wireless telegraphy was 'new' technology and its vulnerability to interception seriously underrated. The listening times supplied by Bock of *UC 61* were quickly married to three German naval codes which were assembled by luck by the British in the first few months of the war. The capture of the codes was the stuff of legend, so much so that the navy code breakers in Room 40 dubbed the findings as 'the miraculous draught of fishes' and others, later, wondered whether the stories describing the captures had been made up to cover 'skulduggery'.[15] The first code, the *Handelsverkehrsbuch* (HVB), was used between the German Admiralty and their merchant ships, and was discovered by a Royal Australian Navy captain who tricked the German skipper of the steamer *Hobart*, off Melbourne, who did not yet know that war had begun, into revealing the document's location behind a secret panel by his bed. The second, the *Signalbuch der Kaiserlichen Marine* (SKM), was, supposedly, taken from the clutching arms of a dead German sailor after the light cruiser *Magdeburg* was sunk by two Russian cruisers off the coast of what is now Estonia. The SKM codes were used for major

naval operations and by German flag officers to communicate with the
army and other units.[16] The third, and most unlikely event, involved the
sinking of four old German destroyers during which the books for the VB
code, *Verkehrsbuch*, were thrown over the side in a weighted trunk, only
to be dredged up by accident six weeks later by a British fishing trawler.
Through 'monumental good fortune', all main German codebooks were
collected 'without the Kriegsmarine realising what had happened ... the
German admiralty complacently concluded that no serious consequences
are feared here from the possible loss of [one of the] codebooks'.[17] It was,
principally, the HVB code that was used by the u-boats.

> *As soon as a u-boat began to operate in our waters, her presence and
> her position was known, as a rule, first vaguely by wireless or other
> information, and then in some detail a day of two later when attacks
> were reported or when survivors from sunk ships had been landed and
> questioned.*[18]

UC 61 was lost at the end of July 1917 and, although the tide of u-boat
dominance was just turning, few realised it. Many politicians and admirals
were close to despair. Having, for the first time through Bock's information,
the precise listening times for u-boats at sea, and their transmission
stations, proved a time-saving and mind-concentrating assistance to the
British u-boat hunters. Early in 1915, Room 40's efficiency had been further
improved by the development of a network of direction finding stations.[19]
Positioning was imprecise, accurate only within a five to fifty mile radius,
but that was enough to give the navy a tactical advantage.

> *Direction finding had originally been developed by Marconi from 1911
> onwards ... During January 1915, the first weekly maps based on DF
> information were produced for Military Intelligence, originally detailing
> German wireless positions and later indicating movements not only of
> troops but of Zeppelins and aircraft ... Hall reasoned that giving the
> existing wireless stations DF capability would enable them to track the
> course of German warships.*

Marconi set up a direction finding station on the coast at Lowestoft, the
first of a chain of six stations covering the entire North Sea. By May 1915,
Room 40 had successfully followed the track of a u-boat across the North
Sea from the time it had sailed from its base at Emden. Vice-Admiral Sir
Arthur Hezlet later claimed that radio intelligence was assessed as the 'most
important single factor in the defeat of the u-boats', giving the Admiralty a
fairly complete picture of where the u-boats were, what they were doing,
and where they were going 'and the routing of traffic clear of them'.[20]

The arrival of Trench in Calais for the interview with Bock deserves further attention. All of the *UC 61* crew had already been interviewed by the French, reportedly satisfactorily. It would still be worthwhile for Trench to hop over to Calais, but would he stop at just one interview with Bock? One of Trench's many strengths was his ability to draw information from the u-boat officers that fell into the Allies' hands. Trench's red-covered files on u-boats and commanders, assembled with detailed care, were one of the treasures of the NID.[21] Many a u-boat commander was 'amazed at the amount of information about their Service and its personalities possessed by their interrogators'.

> I was warned to say nothing whatever [in interrogation] whether secret or not ... As officers, we had not allowed our thoughts to contemplate the possibility of capture and our crewmen had not been instructed on the pitfalls to avoid while under interrogation ... When I heard this [British] officer speak freely ... it dawned on me suddenly that the British espionage system in Bruges must be far more efficient than any of us had suspected. The man spoke as though he had been among us in the mess, listening to our chatter. If only I could get a message to Bruges from here![22]

Trench must have taken the opportunity to interview Gerth while he was in Calais and, perhaps, *UC 61*'s other two officers, Karl Dancker and Johannes Giese. This might explain the lack of a serious interview report on Gerth in the main French files. This conjectured dossier was perhaps lost or kept elsewhere because of its important content.

The French interrogation team found the prisoners from *UC 61* 'quite willing to answer questions' and compiled a full list of their names, ranks ages and job descriptions.[23] Only one, Stoker Franz Goosman, the youngest crew member at nineteen years, and a volunteer, refused to give further information. Not surprisingly, there were several spelling errors, particularly with the surnames, and one crewman, Stoker Michael Weidner, was left out of the crew list although this was corrected later. This omission explains the inconsistency in the total crew numbers: there were three officers, Gerth, Dancker and Giese; junior and eight petty officers and non-commissioned officers, Barthold, Bodrich, Gerigk, Kleinsorg, Lengs, Nagel, Naumann and Zäbisch; one supernumerary, Pucknus, who ranked as a sergeant in the French prison system; and fourteen crew members.[24] Most of them spoke easily about their previous ships and their submarine training, but were 'entirely silent' on confidential military matters. Commander Gerth was one of the most talkative of the prisoners and 'answered the most indiscreet questions quite willingly' almost apologising for not knowing more about subjects like new u-boat construction. The crew were not well acquainted with the state of affairs in Germany or even the general results of their submarine campaign.

'The Flanders submarine crews led an isolated existence and their only means of knowing what is going on at home is through carefully censored correspondence and newspapers.' However, the crew was quite open with information about the commissioning of *UC 61*, the training of officers and men, how crews were made up and replaced, and about some of the boat's war voyages. The overall impression from the report is that the French interrogators were somewhat easy-going and sometimes misled. They failed to uncover *UC 61*'s most successful cruise and were left with the impression that the cruise 'though not absolutely verified by us, seems to have been but mediocre'.

Gerth gave freely of his consistent route through the Goodwin Snouw mine and net barrage on each of his four cruises through the Dover Straits. This information had serious consequences for the Flanders Flotilla, as will be discussed shortly. He also described the effectiveness of the Allied bombardments of Ostend and Zeebrugge the previous June, and particularly mentioned the number of dud shells; explained the orders and procedures for laying mines; and gave his opinion on the Allied actions against u-boats which had become far more difficult to deal with since the end of 1916. Boats were now obliged to 'stay constantly on the alert' with the destroyer as the most dangerous enemy. The seaplane and dirigible were the least feared and were 'like tiresome mosquitoes which force the vessel to dive, but whose stings are only superficial'.

> *Our u-boats were safe from sky attack. Small craft, it was possible to build shelters for them. We had regular u-boat stables, quite roomy structures where as many as twenty-five craft could be run in side by side. The shelters were covered with a roof of cement, iron, and gravel more than six feet thick. Bombs which, exploding in soil, would dig a crater nine feet deep would scarcely make a dent in these well-constructed roofs.* [25]

Bacon jumped on Gerth's comments.[26] In a secret letter to the Secretary of the Admiralty, dated 16 August, he said that he was delighted that Gerth's interview showed that not only was his assessment of the limited damage caused by the Ostend and Zeebrugge bombardments correct, but that also a submarine and a trawler were sunk. However:

> *The remark re high explosive shell having many blinds is very painful. After enormous labour to bring off a bombardment on one of the very few days it is possible – faulty fuses appear to have largely reduced the damage done. There should have been no excuse at Zeebrugge as the majority of the ground is firm. I suggest that perhaps our direct action fuses are a mistake in that it is conceivable that the fuse may be deformed on impact before the striker has time to act.*

The response and style of the Admiralty can be seen in the initial response to this Bacon broadside. On 5 September, twenty days after Bacon wrote, a gentleman called Henley, for 'DINO', asked 'CINO' to remark on the paragraph. Duncan, 'CINO', replied two days later suggesting a reply asking Bacon to supply the calibre of shell and number of fuze [sic] and whether they were fitted with false caps 'before any useful remarks can be given'. The next day Henley wrote back concurring that Bacon be asked for details.[27]

Bacon then moved to the attack on Gerth's preferred method of passing the channel barrage as 'of great interest'. He saw the fact that Gerth had passed to the east of Buoy 26D as 'rather a criticism of the French patrols', including, one assumes, Ensign Guichard and his toy boats. He criticised the French interrogators for their lack of confidence, 'Nous gardons l'impression ...'

> The captain of UC 61 having free choice chose the Snouw end five times in succession. I believe the Goodwin end used to be used, but was stopped by the thousand-yard length of net thrown up to the north ... I have laid a similar length on the Snouw bank with white bottles and painted buffs so as to be nearly invisible. Of course, it is next to impossible to stop the end of a barrage short of running the ends ashore and having gates.[28] Gates in tideways are objectionable and lead to accidents. Flanking nets are the only alternative.

Here Bacon was at loggerheads with Winston Churchill, First Lord of the Admiralty, who issued the minutes, and gave detailed guidance to his admirals, from a conference held in 1915.

> The first step should be the closing of the Straits of Dover by lines of nets drifting to and fro with the tide, and each section watched by its respective trawlers and with a proper proportion of armed trawlers and destroyers to attack any submarine entangled. In this moving barrier there should be a gate through which traffic can be passed and it appears necessary that this gate should be so arranged as to force a submarine to come to the surface to pass through it. Destroyers and other armed craft should continually watch the approaches and passages through this gate, and be ready to attack any submarine showing on the surface.[29]

Possibly pausing for breath, Bacon then agreed entirely with Gerth about the relative effectiveness of destroyers and aircraft. 'Destroyers are all important, and aircraft only of use to make the submarine dive, but not to destroy it.' This time, Churchill claimed the strategic credit, 'The first British countermove made on my responsibility was to deter the Germans from surface attack. The submerged u-boat had to rely increasingly on underwater attack and thus ran the greater risk of mistaking neutral for British ships and of drowning neutral crews and thus embroiling Germany with other Great Powers'.[30]

Using the collection of personal notes, official forms and photographs, and the rest, confiscated from the crew at Wissant, UC 61's interrogators then produced a comprehensive and valuable breakdown of the current twenty-five boats of the Flanders Flotilla and their operational status; their commanders, including their experience and assessments on their competence; and a list of the presumed dates and method of loss of twenty-seven u-boats. Time and again in later Admiralty records dealing with individual submarines and their commanders, there is an asterisk followed by a legend similar to, 'Confirmed by prisoners of UC 61'.[31] To this breakdown was added detailed discussion by the prisoners of a further six u-boats which the French considered unlikely to still exist, although some did. These lists were assembled from the comments of the whole crew. All of these deductions were backed by information from a well-placed German spy, the 'disgruntled and avaricious' Dr Karl Krüger.[32] From the earliest days of the war, Krüger delivered a monthly trove, over fifty reports of accurate intelligence information detailing the prevailing situation in all German shipbuilding yards.[33] 'In March 1917, he delivered his masterpiece: the exact numbers of the submarine construction programme.'

Most of the crew's photographs and receipts are annotated on the reverse by the interrogators in French and German with family names, home and military locations, ranks, dates, training and previous war boats. These documents were clearly used to prompt the crew to discuss their personal histories and, in turn, to plot the movement of German vessels and their commanders, and also the experience of their crew members. Taken together, it is, even today, remarkable how many of UC 61's crew's careers can be understood. It is a master class in patient reconstruction. It is also a salutary lesson of what not to take on a military mission where capture is a possibility. None of the items, most illegally withheld, were returned to the crew.

The reduced crew examination report covers thirty-two pages; there are copious details on a wide variety of military subjects including the cross-Atlantic submarine merchant cruiser Deutschland, German naval forces in Flanders, battle cruisers, light cruisers, minelayer cruisers, armaments, specialist training for torpedo and wireless personnel, and general pay and living conditions.

When the mess on the floor beneath the conning tower of UC 61 was cleared, it was soon evident that the interior of the u-boat forward of the engine room, the whole [living space], was not the burned out wreck that was at first supposed or, perhaps, pretended.[34] Several documents, charred around the edges, but still completely readable, came to light including the latest Channel charts and up-to-date codebooks.[35] Gerth's radio assertion to

Bruges that secret papers and notebooks were destroyed was incorrect. One document was Gerth's own copy of the *Signalverkehr*, dated 1911, with the complete hand flag signalling system between the military and merchant ships of the German Navy. This was not vital information, but still a most useful acquisition. As with the personal belongings of the crew found in Vincennes, the signal book slid from another brown envelope in 2016, this time with separated pieces of burnt edging falling to the desk.[36] All of the documents found were handed at Wissant on 28 July to a representative of French naval intelligence sent especially for the collection.[37]

However, the most useful item was a small black bound notebook, full of handwritten notes in pencil, mostly messy and, today, partly illegible. This was Gerth's own notebook. Its contents read like a check list for readying a u-boat for war: postage tariffs, a 1917 calendar, crew details, engine ignition rings, uniform checks, sea boots not handed in, meeting the dockyard accountant, acquisition of carbon dioxide and carbonic acid bottles, dockyard entrance arrangements, visiting the instrument department, washing basins, oil and torpedo receipts, and many more. Interspersed are notes on other u-boats of the Flanders Flotilla: *UC 16*, lost on mines off Zeebrugge; *UC 17*, then commanded by Werner Fürbringer, friend and u-boat ace who wrote Gerth's obituary; and *UC 26*, sunk by the British destroyer HMS *Milne*.[38] A copy of the original German with a French translation was sent on 4 August by d'Andrey, the chief of Military Intelligence, ZAN, with a covering letter, and from there, with two hastily scratched and frequently altered pencil translations into English, to the British authorities at Dunkirk, and thence immediately to Dover.[39] The notebook clearly held vital information. Gerth stated that steamers left Newhaven between 2000 and 2100; this statement was then crossed out. 'Course for entering Newhaven 225°.' Gerth then described, amongst other notes, for instance, Admiralty instructions for vessels 'passing through the channel [they] should shape course from a point eight miles southward of Newhaven and the parallel of 50° 39' N until the *Royal Sovereign* light bears true north'. Four areas where German mines had been reported by the British were listed: a circular area east of Beachy Head on 23 July, northwest of Cherbourg on 21 July, south of Brighton on 16 July, and northwest of Fécamp on 10 July.[40] Evidently, the Germans had read encoded Admiralty warnings of u-boat mined areas. There was also a sketch that showed the mines laid by *UC 62* near the Royal Sovereign Light Vessel on 23 June; this last was one of the areas that Gerth was ordered to mine on his current, but last, patrol. Three days later, Vice-Admiral Bacon sent an encrypted telegram to the Admiralty about the implications:

> From papers found in UC 61 it is evident that she had information of the danger areas declared on the 23 July when she left on the 24 July [25 July]. This shows that the auxiliary code or vocabulary signal book is

useless as a code. She also had good information regarding the routes of vessels in the vicinity of Newhaven.[41]

That same afternoon, Bacon following his telegrams with an explanatory letter in which he said that the route information could have been obtained from a neutral or by intercepted Allied wireless transmission; the danger area information probably by intercepts. He advised that warships passing through the Dover area should in future not use wireless, but should get the latest information by visual signalling with different arrangements for east and for west bound traffic. He added:

> *It is necessary to continue to signal the area as soon as they are known to be dangerous, but I have given orders that the fact of any danger area being declared <u>clear</u> is not to be passed by wireless transmission. It will be sufficient if vessels are informed in ordinary cases when they return to harbour.*[42]

So, within a week, the German's important advantage from code breaking was nullified and an alternative signalling system put in place. Reginald Hall evidently relied on Bacon's discovery when he telegraphed Paris that evening:

> *Vice-Admiral Dover reports that documents from UC 61 show that Germans have information about our minefields, etc, which they probably got from one of our codes being compromised. Please procure me either original or true copies – not translations – of documents – matter is urgent.*[43]

Hall's memorandum of 9 August was also based on Bacon's work. 'It would appear that the Germans have decoded our signals ... The codes concerned can be ascertained from Vice Admiral Dover. Five days later, the Signal Section reported having taken 'necessary steps', a possible euphemism because of what followed.[44] Robert Grant, doyen of u-boat historians, noted that the Admiralty 'had moved faster than that, for by 10 August, the German Admiralty Staff concluded that the British knew that their cipher for the Auxiliary C-14 Code was compromised, since the British had undertaken a wholesale change of ciphers. The German Admiralty Staff asked Bartenbach at Bruges if *UC 61* was carrying decryption materials which might have fallen into British hands. The reply was that the Commander Gerth was a former radio officer and officer on the Admiralty staff and must surely have destroyed secret documents of this sort.[45]

In fact, in 1931, u-boat historians Gibson and Prendergast suggested that the British moved even faster again, and more clandestinely. It was evident that as soon as a minefield was cleared by the British minesweepers and the clearance was announced by code to shipping controllers, the Germans often moved back to the cleared area and re-laid the field hoping to catch now freely-moving shipping unawares. Gibson and Prendergast's version was that a field laid off Waterford in Ireland was carefully chosen and left intact, but it was announced through the broken code that it had been swept. Kurt Tebbenjohanns, commander of *UC 44*, received his written orders to lay mines at Waterford on 30 July, just four days after *UC 61* stranded. In that time, the team at Room 40, had to have found Gerth's notebook, got it to London, realised its significance, devised a plan, put in place safeguards to shipping close to Waterford, and then announced that the harbour entrance area was cleared. Clearly, if this was the case, the notebook was found quickly and all inside *UC 61* was not the hopeless mess that it was supposed to be. If true, it was fast work. The most likely explanation is that plans for the Waterford subterfuge had been in place for some time before *UC 61*'s stranding, but that the discovery of Gerth's notebook added piquancy and certainty. Further poignancy was provided by a strong link between Tebbenjohanns and the Gerth family. Erich Gerth, Georg's brother, was a member of the same sea cadet intake as Tebbenjohanns – the 'Crew of 1905'.[46] Both were assigned as part of a group of fifty-two trainees to the fully-rigged, coal powered training corvette *Stein* in May 1905 and spent the next ten months living cheek by jowl in port and in arduous cruises in the Baltic, the Mediterranean and into the Atlantic.

The idea of a subterfuge sinking gained traction. Secrets often eventually will out and closing a harbour is not a private matter. Grant added in 1969 that the previous minefield had been laid on 14 June by *UC 42*.[47] David Ramsay, official biographer of Sir Reginald 'Blinker' Hall, wrote in 2008 that 'Hall dearly loved a ruse and never more so than when he could wreak havoc on the detested huns'; and confirmed the devious story as an example.[48] William James, who had privileged access to Hall's partly-finished autobiography, said that Hall arranged with Sir Lewis Bayly, the commander-in-chief at Queenstown, Ireland, to 'close the port secretly for a fortnight after the last mines had been laid'. If Grant's mine-laying date of 14 June was right then, that not only rules out *UC 61*, but also suggests the fortnight closure was well over by 4 August. Patrick Beesly suggested the subterfuge did happen, but was connected with interpretations of intercepted broadcasts rather than *UC 61*'s disclosure. Richard Compton-Hall described the affair as 'something like a practical joke'. Gibson and Prendergast were not to be outdone:

> *Patrols rushed to the scene, and picked out of the water the commander ... and a very angry man was he ... his boat blew upon other German mines, laid previously to his arrival. Bitterly did he complain about British carelessness in not clearing the area properly and rendering it safe for his operation. The mine-sweepers had actually made a 'dummy*

counter-mining sweep': they had not cleared away the last-laid patch of German mines.[49]

From Tebbenjohanns' quieter personal account, this narrative may be somewhat excited.[50] Historian Grant changed his mind about *UC 61*'s inadvertent involvement. He decided on fresh research that *UC 44* had blown itself up on its ninth mine which had exploded under the stern; the other eight mines were all collected by British minesweepers.[51]

Her stern is blown up. Bulkhead at after end engine room crumpled and practically the whole of stern abaft the bulkhead wrecked. Damage to bottom extends well forward under engine room.[52]

Unfortunately, Grant told no one publicly of his change of heart. It was not until 2003 that his new research came to light when his publisher finally persuaded him to allow a third book he had written in 1971 to go to print.[53] However, Professor A. Low, writing in 1940, was able to explain Grant's new concern and confirm Gibson and Prendergast's interpretation. Low said that Tebbenjohanns was puzzled as to the reason for the explosion which had blown off the stern of his ship. His first thought was of a premature mine, but enquiry showed he had 'fallen into the trap set for him, for the ninth mine had struck a mine laid on a previous occasion'.[54] Low was clear that Tebbenjohanns was watching outside Waterford, as usual by the Flanders flotilla, as the minesweepers cleared the port, trailing their sweeps and dropping their buoys. The British knew this because of occasional skirmishes between u-boat and minesweepers and also because of the alacrity with which new mines were laid. This time, however, the mine sweeps were dummies and 'the last thing the flotilla wanted to do that day was to bring up a live mine'. Dusk came and *UC 44* crept forward, nosing her way down the 'swept' channel. *UC 44* hit a mine laid previously by *UC 42* just as she laid her ninth 'new' mine, the two mines exploding together.

The story will not quite go away. Despite all the due respect owed to Grant for his copious original research, in this case the weight of evidence, and Low's explanation, suggests he came to the wrong conclusion.

UC 44 was searched by divers with the 'principal object of recovering all books and documents' and copies and originals of those found are in the archives.[55] After weather delays, *UC 44* was eventually salvaged in September as damage was now viewed differently and considered 'slight'. The British Admiralty deemed that it was 'also most important that no information should get out as to how or where she was destroyed'. Why would that be secret if she had blown up on her own mine?

The importance of *UC 61* to NID was again sidestepped. *UC 61* stranded on 26 July and was immediately available for inspection. The explosions and fire, despite statements to the contrary, were largely confined to the engine room. *UC 44* was sunk five days later and not raised until September. Yet:

> It was the recovery whole of UC 44 *(using two divers who worked on UC 5) which proved for the Salvage Section* [of the NID] *to be the intelligence coup of 1917. Undoubtedly this was a key milestone in the understanding of what intelligence treasure troves sunken u-boats could yield.*[56]

Far more likely, it was the slow appreciation of the full treasures of *UC 61*, which drove the Admiralty to return with some urgency to the *UC 44* wreck and to raise it before winter set in. Among the many recovered papers on *UC 44*, there was a record of the conference in January 1917 when u-boat commanders were told of the re-imposition of unrestricted submarine warfare, and also the u-boat's *machinery history* book, published quickly in January 1918.[57] Among the attendant orders found were the instructions that all u-boats were to pass through the English Channel, navigating by Buoy 2501 and the other light buoys, 'without being observed and without stopping' and that u-boats going around Scotland were to 'let themselves be seen as freely as possible in order to mislead the British'.[58] It seems, therefore, that Gerth's implausible claim that he had travelled around Scotland to reach Wissant was a matter of ordered disinformation and, while easily disproved, was not as naive as his interrogators thought.[59] As a result of Gerth's hapless information, on 21 August, Captain W. Fisher, Director of the Anti-Submarine Division, reported to the Chief of Naval Staff that the stranding of *UC 61* and its previous five passages showed it was a 'delusion that submarines operating in the Channel proceed thither north about'.[60] Fisher's evidence included a table showing that from January to August, twenty-seven u-boats were certain to have passed through the Straits, thirty-nine were probable, and thirteen possible.

Grant reported that despite the evidence of *UC 61* and *UC 44*, Bacon paid no attention and insisted that the old barrage east of Dover had been a success.[61] Bacon was fired as head of the Dover Patrol at year end, in part because submarines were getting through the Channel, and was replaced by Acting Vice-Admiral Roger Keyes.[62] In an extraordinary passage in his *Memoirs*, Keyes recounts that on taking up his new appointment he was greeted initially with hostility by Bacon's staff as they denied to a man that 'enemy submarines were passing through the Straights in any numbers ... and to support this view they pointed out that there had been no sinking nor minelaying by submarines in the Dover Patrol area for some time'.[63] Keyes had opened Bacon's safe and passed over to his new staff the information from Fisher's division, and that taken from *UC 44*: 'It is no exaggeration to say that they were astounded when confronted with this very definite evidence.' If Keyes is to be taken at face value, it was over five months since *UC 61* proved the point that the 'terrible losses on shipping south of the Channel and in the western approaches were caused by submarines streaming passed Dover' and it was five months lost. The failure to sink a u-boat on the old Dover barrage seemingly proved to Bacon and his team that there were no submarines there in the first place.

However, this is far from the whole story and Keyes account must be questioned. The antipathy between Bacon and Keyes became legendary. As Bacon's friend, Admiral of the Fleet, Earl Jellicoe, wrote the foreword to Bacon's *Memoirs*. Jellicoe was quite precise:

> *It was recognised by Admiral Bacon in 1917 that the net barrage was not effective in denying the passage to submarines, although it had its uses and caused the enemy considerable loss. Therefore in February 1917 he placed before me plans of a ladder mine-field barrage to be laid between Folkestone and Gris Nez ... A statement to the contrary in Volume V of 'Naval Operations' is incorrect ... It was, of course, the existence of Admiral Bacon's ladder mine-field with its patrol which led to the destruction of twelve German submarines during December 1917 and the year 1918, and to the partial closing of the Straits of Dover to vessels of this type. As so often happens, the credit for this success was given to the Admiral's successor [Keyes] instead of to him.*[64]

In contrast, Jellicoe wrote in one of his own memoirs that it was not until early 1917 that it was realised that 'practically all outward-bound submarines' were adopting the English Channel route.[65] 'Until a short time before this, it was quite the exception for this route to be taken, but it now appeared to be the rule.'

Hew Strachan described Jellicoe as 'a worrier, a centraliser and a hypochondriac'. For him, the German u-boat was always a 'potent threat'; he would never have kept Bacon in post if u-boats rampaged past Dover ignored and unchallenged.[66] By contrast, American Rear-Admiral William Sims, who had been a friend since service together in China in 1901, described Jellicoe as an indefatigable worker, unostentatiously dignified ... all courtesy, all brain, none more approachable, more frank, or open-minded'.[67] This was a palace coup; Jellicoe, well-liked, but deemed 'old school', was fired by letter on Christmas Eve, 1917. For his part, Bacon fought back:

> *The fact that submarines were passing through the Channel was the lever used by certain influences at the Admiralty to oust me ... My differences of opinion with the Barrage Committee, due to my accumulated experience, were used to further the idea that I was obstructive and impossible to work with; yet, in every case, results proved that my contentions were correct and the Committee wrong,*

*which was not to be wondered at as I had had nearly three years' local
experience and they had none.*[68]

The Barrage Committee was a device set up by railways chief Sir Eric
Geddes, recently appointed First Lord of the Admiralty, supposedly to
light a fire under Bacon. Geddes was one of Prime Minister Lloyd George's
'men of push and go', revolutionising in turn small arms production, shell
production, and the military ports and railways, before being sent to the
Admiralty which he found in disarray.

Gerth's description of his five voyages through the barrage had further
consequences. From 30 July to the end of the year, four days after *UC
61*'s stranding, Grant suggests that minelayers began working close to
Zeebrugge, 'precisely on the u-boat route' described by Gerth. During
August, three fields of forty mines were laid, roughly eleven miles to
the north and north-west of Zeebrugge, and on 22–24 September, the
effort was intensified with a further eighty-five mines.[69] The admiralty's
private compilation of mining activity notes that there were twelve days
of new mining in the appropriate area in July, eight in August and ten in
September.[70] Collectively, these new mines may have accounted for three
u-boats: *UC 21*, due back in early October, never returned from a relatively
unsuccessful voyage, its only reported sinking was the scuttling of a sailing
vessel off Ushant on 16 September; *UC 14* did hit the mines just north of
Zeebrugge with the detonation logged at 2215 on 3 October, all seventeen
crew were lost; the day before, *UC 16* sailed for Boulogne and is presumed
lost on the Zeebrugge mines on 4 October after the body of its watch officer
was washed ashore in Holland.[71] Together, during their careers, these
three u-boats are credited with sinking 156 ships and damaging twelve
others. Whichever side one takes in the debate about *UC 44* off Waterford,
and whether Gerth's declared u-boat route from Zeebrugge would have
been mined sooner or later, and to greater or lesser intensity, the whole
suggests that the cost to the Germans of *UC 61*'s intelligence was beginning
to mount.

Before the end of World War I, 375 u-boats of thirty-three separate classes
belonging to seven general types had been commissioned. The Admiralty,
from spies, from captures, wreck inspections and interrogations of survivors,
had gathered a considerable amount of information. Manuals circulated
with details of each type and of its armament. The basic information was
all in place. However, this was a time of dramatic innovation. Each side
jostled for any advantage in offensive and in anti-submarine measures.
No less than winning the war was at stake. All of the sunken or captured
boats that could be reached carried potentially important information and
equipment and this importance increased with the arrival of any new class
of u-boat and with the passage of time. The need to review any u-boat
which became available was urgent.

Amidst all the classes and sub-classes of World War I u-boats, the important difference came down to three types: the u-boat, which became a long-range raider; the ub-boat, a coastal torpedo attack boat; and the uc-boat, a coastal mine-layer which, after dropping its mines, became a coastal raider. There were three series of uc-boat; fifteen boats in the early Series 1 (*UC 1 – UC 15*), all built by 1915; sixty-four boats in the mainstream Series II (*UC 16 – UC 79*); and sixteen boats in the more advanced Series III (*UC 90 – UC 105*), which only came into service from July 1918.[72] While Series II was a continuous series, the thirty-one boats after *UC 49* might be considered the more advanced. Their production was spread across five constructions yards and it was the day-to-day lack of cohesion between these yards that led the leader of *UC 61*'s fitting out party, Petty Officer Peter Kleinsorg, to complain about the many and confusing design differences.[73]

UC 61 was one of four boats built for a cost of around two million marks each at the Weser Yard in Bremen. For the Allies, the first capture of a Series II uc-boat would be a major coup; so much detail was unknown or guessed.

Three Series 1 uc-boats provided information before *UC 61*'s stranding. *UC 2*, off Yarmouth, and *UC 12*, off Taranto Harbour, Italy, were destroyed by their own mines with all hands lost in June 1915 and March 1916. *UC 2*, which was also later rammed, was examined by Royal Navy divers and parts of the boat were raised; *UC 12*, was raised, re-commissioned by the Italians and named *X-1*.[74] The third Series I boat, *UC 5*, was by far the most famous of its day. *UC 5* was the first u-boat to penetrate the English Channel, laying mines off Boulogne. After a twenty-nine-patrol career in which thirty ships were sunk and seven more damaged, *UC 5* grounded on the Shipwash Shoal, near Felixstowe, in April 1916; the boat was scuttled, but the explosive charges caused limited damage.[75] Little intelligence was discovered as much material had been destroyed by the crew.[76] After securing two mines which were bumping about inside in two-feet of water, the holed boat was patched up and towed to dock. *UC 5* was later taken to Temple Pier on Victoria Embankment in London and opened to the Press, including the naval correspondent of *The Times*.

Several requests for permission to photograph the UC 5 *having been received, the Admiralty announce that there is no objection to such photographs being taken, both while she is on her way up* [The Thames] *and while she is moored.*

Many postcards followed; *UC 5* was taken on a publicity tour ending in Central Park, New York, and the hull, later used to stimulate war-bond sales and recruiting, was sold for scrap in Montreal in 1923.

On 22 May, nearly a month after stranding, the Admiralty instructed that all books and papers recovered from *UC 5* should be send to NID.[77]

Unlike UC 2 *and* UC 12, *this small minelayer was virtually intact, and her construction could be studied intensively. Such study was important because some features of the smallest minelayers would be preserved in the designs of her newer and larger sisters* [the Series II uc-boats].

Grant listed five uc-boats from which during the war 'divers took special materials' that were therefore 'highly significant'; he added to the list *UC 12* in Italy and *UC 61*, which needed no divers.[78] There were four Series II boats from which information was gathered before *UC 61*'s stranding, all in 1917, and a brief examination of the circumstances of their demise allows the importance of *UC 61*'s inspection to be placed in context.

UC 39 was forced to the surface by depth charge and hit by gunfire by destroyer HMS *Thrasher* off Flamborough Head on 8 February with seven dead and seventeen survivors.[79] The first u-boat men on deck, including the commander Oberleutnant Otto Ehrentraut, were killed by a shell. HMS *Thrasher* kept firing because the u-boat kept her engines running even though the men on deck had their hands up in surrender. When the skipper of a Swedish steamer, held captive from that morning, waved a white flag and the engines were switched off by a petty officer, the firing stopped. *UC 39* didn't sink for a further two hours and thirty-five minutes after capture. The affair was a great embarrassment to the Royal Navy who had the boat in tow – and the event was kept secret. Following a court of enquiry on 13 February 1917 into the sinking of the interestingly named HMS *UC 39*, Lieutenant L. Ommanney, the commanding officer of the destroyer HMS *Itchen* which had the tow, was sent to court martial. Ommanney 'received distinct orders by signal to make sure that *UC 39* would float or to beach her'. He did neither. The boat was boarded and documents taken off including the engineering officer's notebook, but it was admitted that no effort was made to search for or to patch up the damage.[80] After over an hour of towing when shallow water could easily have been made, and during a towing manoeuvre, *UC 39* suddenly and quickly sank in deep water. The commanding officer got off on a legal technicality because of the framing of the charges; the Admiralty was not happy about the acquittal which the fourth sea lord saw as 'very fortunate' for the *Itchen*'s captain. 'This officer probably did his best, but his best was not good enough; and he didn't rise to the occasion.' This was the Admiralty's first chance to get hold of a complete Series II uc-boat and they lost it. A few days later, Hall received a letter with a crumpled piece of paper picked up in the street.[81] It was orders from the submarine school at Kiel from January, 'without doubt dropped by a *UC 39* crew member when they were being conveyed across London', thought Hall. Sixteen months later, a diver visited *UC 39*, but 'it was thought too old to be worth investigating'.

A few weeks later on 23 February 1917, *UC 32* blew up on its own mines near Roker Pier lighthouse off Sunderland; there were twenty-three dead and three survivors including her captain, Herbert Breyer. That month, the newly formed NID team, led by Trench, inspected their first uc-boat wreck, lying in thirteen metres of water in three broken sections.[82] 'Items' were recovered, including a torpedo.[83] The machinery history book was published in May.[84] The survivor's interrogations have not been found, but the interview with one of UC 32's crew, acting warrant officer Bernhard Haack, is on record.[85] On 25 January, Haack was in a boat travelling to a stopped British trawler, the *Mayfly*, with the intention of sinking her with bombs when UC 32 was attacked by *Speedwell II* and quickly submerged leaving Haack behind. Haack gave his interrogators reasonable detail concerning UC 32 and other u-boats that he knew.

On 8 May 1917, UC 26 was rammed and depth-charged by British destroyer HMS *Milne* while in the act of submerging.[86] The u-boat's commanding officer was 'dilatory' and could have got away, but was slow down the hatch and his boat was hit in the conning tower. UC 26 hit the bottom at forty-six metres with a 'considerable bump'. The second in command, sub-lieutenant Heinrich Petersen, and others managed an escape when compressed air allowed the hatches to be open; he rose slowly owing to his heavy clothing and suffered just a mild attack of the 'bends'.[87] The incident has relevance for two reasons: first, Petersen, one of the two survivors, kept a diary which survived with him, and he also gave on interrogation useful information regarding uc-boats; second, the Dutch press carried reports received from Germany that eight crewmen had reached the surface of whom the English deliberately only saved two.[88] A translation of Petersen's diary was distributed amongst the Dover Patrol on NID's suggestion 'as it is thought that this diary would make encouraging reading for our patrols'.[89] Hall of the NID instructed that all letters home from the two survivors were to receive 'special examination' and 'any doubtful letters' were to be forwarded to him personally.[90] Commander V. Campbell of HMS *Milne* received the DSO; Lieutenant L. Pearson, the DSC; and four crew, the DSM.[91]

The last opportunity was an encounter with UC 29 whose sinking was another exploit in one of the most lauded careers of the Allied naval war.[92] On 7 June, UC 29 attacked HMS *Pargust*, a Q-ship commanded by Commander Gordon Campbell, who had already been awarded the DSO for sinking U 68 and the Victoria Cross for sinking U 83.[93] *Pargust* was hit by a torpedo. Lured in close, UC 29 submerged when hit by *Pargust*'s suddenly disclosed deck guns, and then reappeared and was hit by some forty shells; Germans came to the deck and waved and Campbell ordered 'Cease Fire'. 'In a typically unsportsmanlike trick', UC 29 then made off 'at a fair speed' so Campbell reopened fire and sank the u-boat. *Pargust* did not sink due to her deliberate cargo of heavy timber. Campbell received a bar to his DSO; two other men received VCs by ballot.[94] Two men who came to the deck early on to man the u-boat's gun had been washed overboard in the heavy seas. They were the only survivors and gave limited information, but one, Leutnant Hans Bruhn, disclosed that Series II engine cylinders were being carefully checked since May because 'a submarine failed to return when all of her twelve cylinders had failed'.[95] UC 26 left Ostend at the end of April 1917 to lay mines and 'this boat suffered from continuous defects'.[96] UC 31 had also turned back in November with engine problems and again in December when two cylinders failed. Robert Grant noted that these engine problems, as well as the mining difficulties of five more minelayers, all occurred in submarines built by Vulcan at Hamburg, and all belonged to the First Flotilla, stationed at Heligoland. 'Could sabotage have played a part?' Admiral Reinhard Scheer admitted that, in any event, after each cruise every u-boat needed docking because of the large amount of technical apparatus which needed careful overhauling and the damage due to the voyage or to enemy attacks had to be repaired. 'Generally speaking, after four weeks at sea a boat would need to be in the dockyard for the same length of time for repairs'.[97] Constant breakdowns also caused a great diminution of the total efficiency.

By the time of UC 61's stranding in July 1917, a fully-equipped Series 1 boat had been captured, another dived, and a third raised by the Italians. Since then, the navy had 'lost' a captured Series II boat at sea, and interviewed twenty-four survivors from four other boats, a few of whom gave useful information. UC 61 was therefore the great coup, the first Series II uc-boat to be captured and to be inspected fully by NID teams.[98] Despite the damage to UC 61, and it may have been in everyone's interest to play it up, the boat was going to be inspected with a fine-tooth comb.

> The divers who visited the then recently sunken u-boats did so for the sole purpose of intelligence gathering. Intelligence came mainly in the form of charts, codebooks, call signs, technical and personnel data. The intelligence war against u-boats was secret. Little except hearsay emerged until 1969–70 with the release of much of what is now known as ADM 116 and ADM 137 to the National Archives [in the UK]; within which is a rich source of data. The information vacuum, which lasted for over half a century after WWI, was fertile ground for rumour and hearsay; some of the legacies of which have endured to the present.[99]

In his preliminary inspection of the wreck of UC 61 on 31 July, Commander Spencer felt that much of the information already held by the Admiralty on UC 61 was 'largely correct'.[100] He cited the boat's armaments (although quoting four torpedoes rather than the correct five). There existed good outline drawings, two pamphlets with the main details and two books of plans were issued, and a third book with detailed descriptions was 'in the press'. He also notes that UC 61 was built at the Weser Yard in Bremen, a different yard from the boats from which previous information was gleaned and there might be points of minor difference. In fact, the engineering officer, Johannes Giese, made a point of complaining during his interrogation that these uc-boats were built at several yards. As a part of his training for commissioning, he visited *UC 74* at Blohm & Voss's yard at Hamburg for a month from 26 November 1916 and then *UC 71* in the Vulcan Yard at Hamburg from Boxing Day for two weeks. Giese said that he had to make a fresh study of the details of the mechanism in each boat 'on account of the radical difference in their arrangement'. Spencer concluded his letter that accompanied his report to Bacon:

> *These mine-laying boats are of course greatly inferior to the regular ocean-going type in both offensive and defensive qualities, but details of their fittings, etc, may prove worthy of study, as they are of such recent construction and there is no doubt that in general the fittings adopted will closely resemble those in the larger boats.*

One wonders how Spencer's dismissive views on the uc-boat's offensive capabilities were received. The uc-boats were primarily coastal minelayers only supposed to engage with their five torpedoes after all mines were laid. However, apart from all the damage, disruption and chewed up resources in management time, money and constant use of resources by all these mines – and this was considerable, and the benefit of computer hindsight some one hundred years later, sixty-four uc-boats conservatively sank 1,867 vessels and damaged a further 218, putting out of action some 3.4 million tons of shipping.[101] Twenty-six vessels were taken as prizes. Series II boats made 559 patrols and in them 981 men lost their lives, an average of over fifteen men per boat.

As a result of, or perhaps despite of, Spencer's report, a more thorough inspection for the NID was made by three officers led by Commander A. Sommerville on 3 August.[102] By this time, the wreck had sunk bodily into the sand so that the lower portion was inaccessible 'even at dead low water'. The wreck listed heavily to starboard and the after end, mostly blown off in Gerth's explosion, was now severed by recent rough weather and was lying some distance from the main part and was almost full of water. All small fittings and electrical gear were burnt out. However, Sommerville noted the good standard of workmanship, the use of metal where steel could have been used, 'there appeared to be no effort to save metal', the number of safety appliances in the fittings, and the salvage equipment.

David Townsend, who examined the evidence of the shell hole in *UC 61*'s conning tower, was also asked in 2016 to assess the main findings made by Sommerville and his team.[103] Because of the difficulty in obtaining iron ore and the capacity of smelters during war time, steel would have been used for the pressure hulls. However, felt Townsend, savings could be made by using mild steel on unpressurised structures such as the casing.

Mild steel is not as strong or as hard as steel. He found the mention of safety appliances in the report interesting.

> *These could range from isolating valves, to lifejackets, or hatch securing latches. There may have been some type of escape breathing hoods, but this is unlikely as there were no escape hatches. The main safety appliance would have been a wired buoy that could be made to float by compressed air and released to indicate the submarine's position on the seabed. Later ones may have been fitted with a telephone so that surface ships could communicate with a stricken submarine.*

Bacon asked immediately for one of the boat's two periscopes for inspection and Ronarc'h, back in his office in Dunkirk after taking control of the beach at Wissant, replied immediately offering to 'lend' one 'as soon as they have been dismounted'. In fact, he sent the periscope on the day of stranding. Bacon also asked on 30 July for details of a mine, which was thought to be of a new type; for one of the torpedoes found floating in the sea; and for details of watertight ammunition holders.[104] In order to have ammunition readily available upon surfacing, a ready use locker of ammunition was fitted outside of the pressure hull, close to the 88mm cannon. 'It would be interesting to the Allies,' said Townsend, 'to know how many shells could be fired before more ammunition had to be brought up, or the boat had to dive out of a gun action.' If the ammunition holders were kept dry, literally by bungs, what effect would dived pressure have on those bungs? Would they be hard to remove if the submarine had been deep, thereby preventing immediate firing of the gun? De Bon, marine commander at Calais, needed first to check with Ronarc'h whether he approved sharing information with the British Admiralty about the munitions box. Ronarc'h replied to the effect that de Bon should get on with it.[105] The gun mountings were taken off and sent to Paris, while the gun and its ammunition were sent to the French national ammunition factory at Sevran-Livrey, for testing.[106]

On 15 August, the British commodore at Dunkirk reported to Bacon that Ronarc'h had sent him a bottle of engine oil taken from *UC 61* at the request of the Admiralty.[107] The French had been asked for five bottles, but 'only one could be obtained as the oil tanks were practically burnt out'. The bottle was despatched on that day's duty destroyer. Oil for analysis was important as by determining the type and level of impurities in fuel, assessments could be made of the origin and quality of available fuel. Also, the amount and size of tiny shards in the oil sump would indicate the quality of metal being used in engine production and might help in assessments of the effectiveness of the British blockade on iron ore, especially that imported from Sweden by the Germans. The intelligence describing engine failures on uc-boats added weight to this type of investigation.

It should be noted that Bacon, in Dover, through whom many of NID's requests in addition to Bacon's own were sent, and Ronarc'h were firm friends.

> *I look back on my cordial relations with Admiral Ronarc'h as one of*
> *the brightest spots in a somewhat uphill and arduous command. He*
> *possessed great experience and shrewdness, yet he was always ready to*
> *enter into the spirit of a new adventure ... He was ever ready to smooth*
> *a local irritation and help our vessels as fully as his own.*[108]

Altogether twenty-nine aspects of *UC 61*'s construction and operations were investigated. Of these, in an impressive report, Sommerville noted sixteen features that were different to the general practice in use by the British, or were completely new. These would be of interest to NID to improve Allied combat effectiveness or to help improve British designs. He also made a good number of measurements, discussed details of construction work and listed another twelve lesser, but useful, features.

Here, half of Sommerville's main observations are provided for interest and, in some cases, combined with information from Spencer's report, with Townsend offering his comments.

The jumping wires were primarily used to lift nets or booms out of the way as the submarine found a way through harbour defences and net barrages, although in this case they doubled up as a wireless aerial. *UC 61* had double jumping wires which 'may relate to parallel wires for additional backup or that they were rigged fore and aft. As submarines developed, became quieter, and sonar became more sensitive, jumping wires were found to vibrate giving out detectable noise.' The jumping wires worked in tandem with a wire net cutter (the 'scissors' of Chapter 8), shown in a pen picture, and taken off *UC 61* at Ronarc'h's orders, consisting of 'two flat bars about ten feet long and secured at an angle of thirty degrees to the superstructure with ten short knife edges clamped between them'.[109]

Gyro and magnetic compasses were fitted. The straightforward magnetic compass 'gives the last resort for navigation but needs variation, deviation and magnetic influences to be taken into account'. A gyrocompass involves spinning discs that use the gyroscopic effect to keep it balanced and level to point to true north as opposed to magnetic north. As it is electrically driven, it is possible to have gyro repeaters in different positions for steering, navigation and attack solutions, something that cannot be done with a magnetic compass binnacle.

UC 61 had twin propellers driven on the surface by twin diesel engines. The steerage way is caused by the propeller flow over the rudder so, 'by placing a rudder behind each propeller maximum steerage can be obtained, and with smaller blades'. It would have also been possible to steer the boat by adjusting the speed of each propeller and even turning the submarine around by going ahead on one and astern on the other.

The inspecting officers and the Press were much interested in *UC 61*'s two hydrophones which were housed in a small recess in the starboard side of a well in the superstructure between the conning tower and the mine shafts. This equipment enabled those in the boat to detect sounds from attacking surface and underwater craft. Spencer drew a pen sketch of the apparatus. The hydrophones were about twelve inches apart, one facing to starboard, one to port, and were mounted on rubber, which was an advance to stop internal machinery noise interfering with the hydrophone results. Wires from each led to a common junction box and thence in an iron tube through the hull. The much-copied journalist Marius Alix, who first told the story of the stranding of *UC 61*, was allowed an early tour of the u-boat:

> *And finally, in the forward part of the vessel and left untouched by the fire, a curious acoustic system was found that allows a crew, even during travelling underwater, to hear all outside noise in a given perimeter. This is an invention from which, hopefully, we can profit.*[110]

The inspectors also found another well with a lid near the bow and drew a pen picture of it. The well was home for a folding boat, useful as quickly ready for inter-ship transfers, taking moorings to buoys, getting ashore, or even a means of escape for some of the crew in an emergency. 'One of the top makers was the *Klepper* company that also produced canvas and wood kayaks that were still being used by the British Special Boat Service in the 1970s and 1980s.'[111] This boat was particularly important later when Gerth was in an officers' prisoner of war camp at Boyardville on the French Atlantic coast.[112]

The main ballast tanks were flooded by opening a vent at the top of the external tank, allowing seawater to flood in. When the boat needed to surface, the vents were closed and, in the case of *UC 61*, high pressure air at 2,350 pounds per square inch (psi) was passed through a reducer to a lower pressure air of 176 psi and then blown into the ballast tank, displacing the seawater.

When tied up alongside, a submarine needs mooring bollards (Samson posts) situated proud of the casing. But, when dived, 'these posts would make noise and disrupt the hydrodynamic efficiency'. By twisting the bollard, it can be dropped down into a housing so that it is flush with the casing deck.

When being towed, *UC 61* needed to be able to slip the tow quickly in an emergency. This would normally be done in other boats from the foredeck. However, 'small submarines have notoriously dangerous casings that are often awash when underway, and so being able to slip the tow rope from the safety of the fin is quite important'.

Word of the treasure trove available aboard *UC 61* spread slowly through the British Admiralty; u-boat historian Paul Kemp described the intelligence haul as 'immense', without offering more proof than the periscopes and the minefield charts.[113] Veteran u-boat archaeologist Innes McCartney claimed 'much of the wreck was undamaged in the scuttling and was taken away for examination', although no detail or evidence is given.[114] On 16 August, the Board of Invention and Research (BIR) said that 'it would be of material assistance in connexion with the work now in hand' if copies of both the crew interrogation and the report by 'English' officers could be made available.[115] The BIR committee was responsible from 1915 for soliciting expert scientific assistance to solve tactical and technical problems.[116] Chaired by Sir Jackie Fisher, former First Sea Lord, the BIR recruited scientists working in six science and technology divisions, which assessed and evaluated invention proposals from the public, with a view to applying them to naval technology and tactics.

Even after *UC 61* had been long filleted by the French Navy and by the British Intelligence service, there was still more information that the wreck could provide. A major problem had dogged the Allies since the beginning of the war: how to sink a u-boat; in particular, what weight of explosive was needed to penetrate a u-boat's skin and how close did it have to be when it exploded. The problem came to a head in January 1916 when the British began work on two new 'Type D' depth charges for use from fast and slow ships.[117] As well as being constrained by pre-set depth mechanisms, 'the effectiveness of these prototypes was also limited by the fact that they did very little material damage to submerged u-boats unless they exploded within a short distance of the target'. The depth charges were usually simply dropped from the stern of the attacking ship so the 'degree of accuracy needed was difficult to achieve'. After some successful work by June, the problem again became urgent when the weapon was extended to use by smaller craft. Perhaps, *UC-61*'s hull could provide additional answers?

During August and September, only a few weeks after the stranding, a series of firing tests was organised to establish how much explosive was needed to penetrate *UC 61* when it was submerged at high tide.[118] It was a meticulous operation with details recorded of the size of the boat, its position and the depth of the pit into which it had sunk in the sand. After some preliminary tests in late August and early September using 75 mm shells firing at steps from 1,000 to 4,000 metres, and then the firing of two stationary bombs close to the hull, a new Belgian 70mm mortar, the Van Deuren, designed by General Pierre van Deuren, was given a trial.[119] Photographs were taken after each firing and copies of these and of the tests have been found at the French naval archive at Chateau de Vincennes. Everyone was well aware that ten mines remained trapped on board in twisted shafts, but it was hoped that they were not 'ultra sensitive to shocks' as they were deep in the water. On 4 September, twenty mortar bombs were fired from 550 metres directly at the part of the submarine containing the mines. No explosion resulted. At low tide the next day, the hull was examined closely, but no damage could be found. At high water, nineteen bombs with seventeen kilos of high explosive were fired. The fifth bomb did not explode; the tenth bomb appeared to trigger another explosion which was possibly the fifth bomb. The fifteenth bomb produced a powerful explosion. Observers standing on the dunes thirty metres from sea level saw 'the line of the horizon cut the plume at least half of its height from its base'. Inspection next morning 6 September – showed a total destruction of all of the forward part of *UC 61* up to the conning tower; all of the mines had exploded.

A commission had observed the tests and wrote a report in Calais, signed by their President, Biseuil, on their findings. On the final explosion, they wrote:

> *The characteristics were these: a vast and compact plume of water and sand with a zone forty metres diameter at the base, fifty metres high, which was maintained for [ten or more seconds] as though by a constant pressure at the base. That a spectator had the time to take away his photographic equipment is a case in point and he took a photograph at the moment when the plume was still at its maximum height.*

The commission estimated that an exploding shell of 75mm could be used effectively against a submarine on the surface or semi-submerged. The fragility of the projectile had raised concerns that it would break in contact with the thick steel of the hull of the submarine. However, although several traces of incomplete explosion had been noted, [one] firing showed that shells pierced without fracturing the thin steel of the superstructure and its cement ballast and that ... it was susceptible to perforate either with a delayed explosion or with an explosion on contact. In either case, the 'damage produced was major' and would cause the loss of the vessel or put it out of action for some time and 'prevent it diving through ingress of water with or without internal disruption'.

The conclusion from the tests was that a charge of six kilograms exploding in contact with the hull in five metres of water 'damages the hull causing a tear which would cause the loss of the vessel'. The report was sent on 15 September to Ronarc'h who wrote tersely on the bottom: '*UC 61* can no longer serve as a useful experiment.'

ENDNOTES

1   Showell, 'Preface', p. x, in Doenitz, *Memoirs.*
2   Interview with Matrose Paul Schindler, Seamen's Hospital, Brest, 13/3/1918 (SHD, Cherbourg, SSTe35).
3   Original notes, *SHD*, Cherbourg, SSTe35; French 'interrogatoire', *National Archives*, Washington, 45/520/JU/Box 572; English translation, *TNA*, London, ADM 137/3818.
4   *ICRC*, P 24350, officers; P 24301-3, other ranks.
5   *TNA*, ADM 137/2096.
6   *ICRC*, P 24350 and P 24301-3. At Montoire-sur-le-Loir on 24/10/1940 the famous handshake between Adolf Hitler and Maréchal Pétain took place signifying the start of organised French collaboration with the Nazi regime. The meeting took place in a railway carriage (wikipedia).
7   *TNA*, ADM 137/3876.
8   Preface, 'Behind the mask'. Beesly, *Room 40*, pp. 32-33. Because of the war-time increase in Trench's work, Hall announced to everyone's consternation, that he would enrol women. 'Women in a department dealing with secret matters was something quite new.'
9   James, *Code Breakers of Room Forty*, p. 121. Ramsay, *Blinker Hall*, p. 232.
10 James, *Code Breakers*, pp. 8-10. Beesly, *Room 40*, p. 266.
11 Ramsay, *Blinker Hall*, p. 233.
12 'In practice [u-boats] sent very many more [messages]. It was often necessary to signal that they had laid a minefield, were short of fuel, had an engine breakdown or had run out of torpedoes or ammunition. Operational information which could be of value to other u-boats was also signalled ...' (Hezlet, *Electronics and Sea Power*), pp. 141-42.
13 *TNA*, ADM 137/3818, p. 99. The Nauen station in the Brandenburg region of Germany was opened in 1906 by Telefunken and was the oldest radio transmitting installation in the world, initially powered by a 35HP steam tractor. See also, *SHD*, Vincennes, Box MV SS Gr 43, for confirmation.
14 Hezlet, *Electronics and Sea Power*, pp. 83-84. Kennedy, 'Imperial Cable Communications', *War Plans of Great Powers*, pp. 75-98. Ramsay, *Blinker Hall*, pp. 27-28. Devlin, *Too Proud*, p. 183.
15 Boyle, *Before Enigma*, pp. 26-27.
16 Wegener, *Strategy*, p. 73, fn. 3. Boyle, *Before Enigma*, pp. 22-7. Beesly, *Room 40*, pp. 3-7. Ramsay, *Blinker Hall*, Ch. II, pp. 23-38. Koerver, *War of Numbers*, p. 42.
17 Ramsay, *Blinker Hall*, pp. 30-33.
18 *TNA*, ADM 116/3421, p. 298.
19 Ramsay, *Blinker Hall*, pp. 36-37.
20 Hezlet, *Electronics and Sea Power*, p. 143.
21 James, *Code Breakers*, p. 121. Beesly, *Room 40*, p. 266.
22 Fürbringer, *Legendary*, p. 127.
23 *TNA*, ADM 137/3818.
24 Appendix 4, 'Crew of *UC 61*'.
25 Thomas, *Raiders*, pp. 233-34.
26 *TNA*, ADM 137/1383, p. 114.
27 *TNA*, ADM 137/1383, p. 116.
28 Bacon's underlining.
29 'Decision of 11/2/1915 Protection of the Channel Communications', Churchill, *World Crisis*, pp. 285-86.
30 Churchill, *World Crisis*, pp. 724-25.
31 For example, in *TNA*, ADM 137/4154, see *UC 16, UC 18, UC 64, UC 65, UC 70*.
32 Koerver, *German Submarine Warfare*, p. xix.
33 *TNA*, ADM 223/637. For submarine numbers see, also, *TNA* CAB 24/8, pp. 328-29, 24/3/1917.
34 *TNA*, ADM 137/3898, p. 96.
35 Ramsay, *Blinker Hall*, p. 233.

36 *SHD*, Vincennes, MV SS GR 43.
37 *SHD*, Vincennes, MV SS GR 43, p. 6.
38 Gibson & Prendergast, *German Submarine War*, p. 180.
39 *TNA*, ADM 137/2096, Dover Patrol Operations Packs, Vol. III; ADM 137/3898.
40 Also quoted in Robert Grant, *U-Boat Hunters*, p. 53.
41 *TNA*, ADM 137/2096, 7/8/1917.
42 *TNA*, ADM 137/2096. Bacon's underlining.
43 *TNA*, ADM 137/645.
44 *TNA*, ADM 137/2096, 3898.
45 *TNA*, PG 62061.
46 *BA-MA*, MSG 2/18641.
47 Grant, *Intelligence*, p. 115.
48 Ramsay, *Blinker Hall*, p. 231. See also Beesly, *Room 40*, p. 265; Compton-Hall, *Submarines*,
    p. 305; Dorling, *Swept Channels*, p. 128; James, *Code Breakers*, p. 116; Kemp, *U-Boats
    Destroyed*, p. 31; Messimer, *Verschollen*, pp. 282–84.
49 Gibson & Prendergast, *German Submarine War*, p. 196.
50 Preface.
51 Grant, *U-Boat Hunters*, p. 55.
52 *TNA*, ADM 116/1632.
53 Grant, *U-Boat Hunters*, pp. 54–55.
54 Low, *Mine and Countermine*, pp. 149–51.
55 *TNA*, ADM 137/645.
56 McCartney, 'Tin Openers'.
57 *TNA*, ADM 137/3875.
58 *TNA*, ADM 137/3866.
59 Chapter 8, 'Final patrol'.
60 *TNA*, ADM 137/1382. Grant, *U-Boat Hunters*, pp. 63–64.
61 Grant, *U-Boat Hunters*, p. 64.
62 For more impartial and detailed views, see Marder, *Dreadnought to Scapa Flow*, Vol. IV,
    pp. 323–349; Patterson, *Jellicoe*, pp. 177–209.
63 Keyes, *Naval Memoirs*, Vol. 2, pp. 156–57.
64 Bacon, *Memoirs*, Jellicoe, 'Foreword', pp. 10–11. See also Chapter IX.
65 Jellicoe, *Submarine Peril*, p. 50.
66 Strachan, *First World War*, pp. 202–3.
67 Sims, *Victory at Sea*, pp. 7–8.
68 Bacon, *Memoirs*, p. 167.
69 Grant, *Intelligence*, p. 65.
70 *Royal Navy Library*, Portsmouth, Leith, *History of British Minefields*, appendix. Only three
    copies of this work of over 500 pages were produced.
71 *UC 21*: ninety-nine ships sunk and six damaged, the fourteenth most successful u-boat of
    World War I; *UC 14*: fourteen ships sunk including the Italian battleship *Regina Margherita*
    with 675 dead; *UC 16*: forty-three ships sunk and six damaged (uboat.net). *UC 16* and *UC
    21* were two of the four boats in Ostend with *UC 61* during the bombardment of 5/6/1917;
    UC 21 was the 'third' boat, delayed by repairs, which failed to travel down the Bruges
    canal on 25/7/1917 with *UC 61* on the latter's last voyage.
72 *UC 80* – *UC 89* played no part in the war. Only three were launched with the others were
    not completed and broken up on the slipways at war end. U-boats *UC 106–192* also played
    no part in the war being either commissioned in 1919 and surrendered without engines
    or torpedoes, uncompleted, broken up, or had their contracts cancelled (Gröner, *German
    Warships*), pp. 34–35.
73 Germaniawerft, Kiel; Kaiserliche Werft, Danzig; AG Weser, Bremen; Blohm & Voss,
    Hamburg; and Vulcan in Hamburg (Gröner).
74 uboat.net. *UC 12*: The Italians discovered that this u-boat had been constructed in sections
    at the Weser Yard in Bremen (*UC 61*'s yard) and then shipped by rail and assembled at
    Pola, and that her crew was German (Compton-Hall, *Submarines*), p. 219. 'The knowledge
    that Germany, technically their ally, was assiduously mining their naval bases was a

contributing factor in Italy's decision in August 1916 to declare war on Germany' (Kemp, *U-Boats Destroyed*), p. 17.

75 uboat.net. *West Sussex Record Office*, Druitt MSS/429. *The Times*, 22/7/1916, p. 3.
76 McCartney, *Tin Openers*, p. 21.
77 Grant, *U-Boat Hunters*, pp. 49–50.
78 Grant, *U-Boat Hunters*, p. 32.
79 uboat.net. *TNA*, ADM 156/28. *TNA*, ADM 137/3876.
80 *TNA*, ADM 137/3875.
81 Grant, *U-Boat Hunters*, pp. 51–52.
82 Grant, *U-Boat Hunters*, pp. 52–53.
83 McCartney, 'Tin Openers', p. 22.
84 *TNA*, ADM 137/3875.
85 *TNA*, ADM 137/3060.
86 *TNA*, ADM 137/1287.
87 Compare Kurt Tebbenjohanns' escape from *UC 44* at Waterford (Preface).
88 *TNA*, ADM 137/3897.
89 Letter NID, 14/5/1917 (*TNA*, ADM 137/3897).
90 Letter NID 15/5/1917 (*TNA*, ADM 137/3897).
91 *TNA*, ADM 137/1287.
92 ADM 137/3897.
93 Chatterton, *Q-ships*, pp. 21, 39–46, 109, 161, 192–208, 246.
94 Campbell received a second bar to his DSO for a famous later exploit in *HMS Dunraven*, yet another Q-ship, after an eight-hour duel against *UC 71*, which escaped undamaged. *Dunraven* was sunk (Gibson & Prendergast, *German Submarine War*), p. 197.
95 Grant, *U-Boat Hunters*, pp. 128–29. 'Believed to be *UC 30*' (ADM 137/3897), p. 60 (4).
96 Gibson & Prendergast, *German Submarine War*, p. 180.
97 Scheer, *High Sea Fleet*, pp. 316–17.
98 Ramsay, *Blinker Hall*, p. 233.
99 McCartney, 'Tin Openers', p. 19.
100 *TNA*, ADM 137/3898, pp. 128–37.
101 Figures derived from a spreadsheet constructed from information on uboat.net, accessed 8/1/2017.
102 *TNA*, ADM 137/3898, pp. 117–27.
103 Chapter 8.
104 Periscope reference: TNA, ADM 137/2096. Mine reference: *DRASSM* report, No 2014–105, relating to submarine archaeology operation OA2533, 24/7/2014, courtesy of Alain Richard.
105 *SHD*, Vincennes, Box MV SS Gr 43, p. 29.
106 *SHD*, Vincennes, Box MV SS Gr 43, p. 2.
107 *TNA*, ADM 137/2096, 16/8/1917.
108 Bacon, *Dover Patrol*, p. 233.
109 *TNA*, ADM 137/3898, p. 135.
110 See Chapter 1: *La Bibliothèque nationale de France, Le Petit Journal*, 28/7/1917, p. 3.
111 klepper.com/en/company.html, accessed 4/1/2017.
112 Chapter 12, 'Prisoners of war'.
113 Kemp, *U-Boats Destroyed*, p. 30.
114 McCartney, *Maritime Archaeology*, p. 322.
115 *TNA*, ADM 137/1383, p. 156a.
116 Schneider, *Operations Research Applications*, p. 13. During its operation from 1915 to 1918, the board evaluated over 41,000 submissions.
117 Tarrant, *U-boat Offensive*, p. 27.
118 *SHD*, Vincennes, Box MV SS Gr 43, pp. 1–37.
119 landships.activeboard.com/t38307173/the-van-deuren-mortar, accessed 4/1/2017.

CHAPTER 11

The 'Immense Cemetery' of the Hunger Blockade

[The enemy ship] *was certainly directly helping to destroy Germany, and to carry on a system of war that thrust into the hands of innocent German children a slice of raw onion for their supper. We could not spare that ship, however much we might regret it. When I travelled about on leave and so often saw children whose angel souls shone through their pale starved bodies, or soldiers, themselves but skin and bone, carrying home their last loaf to their wives whose hour was nearly come, I was seized with fury against this inhuman enemy who had cut off Germany's food imports. And what I felt all my comrades on the sea felt too. It was the enemy's crime that forced sailors like ourselves to sink floating palaces, masterpieces of human ingenuity and workmanship.*[1]

After the Great War, many u-boat commanders, national heroes, told and sold their stories. The books, good and poor, contained hubris and derring-do mixed with occasional professional modesty. Amidst the excitement and the technical detail, two themes regularly explode; the captains' collective anger continues to leap from the pages. The first, Allied propaganda, particularly the vilification of the u-boat crews and their tactics, was covered in Chapter 9, 'Your truth, our truth'. The second, the effects of the economic blockade on the people of Germany, and especially their own families and friends, is the subject of this chapter. Both subjects help to explain motivation of the sailors and their captains. These men stayed the course despite the horrendous casualty rate. As u-boat commander Werner Fürbringer explained in his memoir, no other submarine force in history has 'persevered with the 83 per cent loss rate found acceptable by the Flanders U-Flotilla'.[2]

The Allied economic blockade began during the first days of the war, but was in planning long before.[3] Through experiment and organic growth, its increasing control of finance, communications and raw materials gradually undermined Germany's ability to prolong an effective conflict. Immediate effects were limited and, for many, hardly noticed. However, little by little, the resilience of Germany's economy was ground down and the welfare of much of the civilian population, especially the poor and vulnerable, was brought to a sorry pass. In Germany, the British distant blockade was commonly referred to as the *Hungerblockade*.[4] The German Board of Public Health claimed it caused the death of 762,796 German civilians from starvation and disease to the end of December 1918.[5] This figure was disputed by a subsequent academic study that put the death toll at 424,000.[6] A study published in 2014 suggested about 300,000.[7] Overall, 600,000 civilians died in the United Kingdom in excess of the peacetime mortality rate, or about 1.3 per cent, a higher rate than Germany.[8] 'This is explained partly by the influenza epidemic, with 200,000 victims, and by respiratory diseases such as bronchitis and tuberculosis which were connected with the general wartime conditions, like excessive war work and poor housing, rather than nutrition.' It does question the accuracy and comparability of the German numbers.

The actual number of blockade deaths is out of reach, partly because of an intermittent break down in record keeping and collation especially at the end of the war, partly because of the impossibility of absolute attribution, but mostly because of the world-wide influenza epidemic of 1918 that took, perhaps, 200,000 people in Germany and up to 100 million people globally.[9] There is no number for the blighted lives nor for the demoralised population. Deaths in 1919 and later are elusive. Can the death of a baby with malnutrition that succumbed to tuberculosis be laid wholly at the feet of the blockade? Why, anyway, was tuberculosis present in the population far above peace-time rates?

> *To the layman, malnutrition usually means a condition of actual starvation. The picture that presents itself to him is usually one of the emaciated infants seen in the magazines from time to time showing the famine sufferers in India. Malnutrition rarely goes so far, the individual usually dying from an infectious disease before an extreme condition of emaciation is reached. Observation carefully made over a period cannot fail to show the energy changes mentioned; casual observation cannot be trusted to give the correct impression.*[10]

The precise number of 762,796 was arrived at by adding together the excess of deaths in the civil population during each of the four years 1915 to 1918 over the number of deaths for 1913. Displaying a steadily increasing line on the graph, in 1915, 88,235 people died over the total for 1913; in 1916, 121,174; 1917, 259,627; and 1918, 293,760.[11] Some of these deaths, however, were due to overwork, worry and other conditions caused by the war for which the blockade was not directly responsible.[12] Civilian death rates per thousand in Germany varied from city to town and country.[13] They increased throughout Germany by 65 per cent from 1913 to 1918, but only by 43 per cent in rural Bavaria. In the largest cities they rose by 71 per cent, for example in Berlin, and by 76 per cent in Hamburg; in smaller towns like Oldenburg by 81 per cent, and by 93 per cent in the Ruhr district of Lippe.

Another estimate noted the 1,486,952 deaths on the battlefield and later through wounds, and the 134,902 soldiers who died through sickness, gave a total of 1,621,034. A later calculation put the number of Germans who lost their lives in military service at about two million, nearly 3 per cent of the total population, or 15 per cent of those enrolled in the army.[14] The number of permanently disabled was just over one and a half million of whom 400,000 were 'heavily disabled'. The number of German war losses was compared to the excess of deaths in the civil population over the same period and indicated that the excess of deaths in the civil population was about half as great as the army losses that were due in the main to military operations. Put crudely, the average German was only twice as likely to die unexpectedly in the trenches than if they had stayed at home. German life insurance companies reported that the death rate of the civil population was beginning to compete with the death rate on the battlefields.[15]

Some other factor was clearly at work on the home front. The German National Board of Health tried to make a financial estimate of the loss to the national wealth of their country caused by death and illness among the civil population. The Board estimated the value of the deaths at 8.4 billion Reichsmarks; the prevention of one million births, 8.4 billion; the reduction of the working capacity of the civil population by one-third, 30.3 billion. The Board then compared their total of 471 billion Reichsmarks with that of reparations demanded by the Allies of 20 billion Reichsmarks. In addition, they noted the cost of feeding up the population after the war at 3.5 billion Reichsmarks and a somewhat exaggerated 4 billion for replenishing livestock.

If the numbers are far from conclusive, there is much factual and anecdotal information. Pronouncements from the German government agencies and the Press need careful reading. On the one hand, the authorities felt the need to be thoughtful with the truth for fear of unnecessarily exciting the population; on the other hand, the public experienced shortages directly and needed no tuition. They had to be told of the many and frequent arrangements that were made for rationing and distribution. Information passed to front line troops was usually constrained and, in any event, the military controlled vast stocks of food and fed their men with larger portions with higher levels of nutrient than was allowed the civilians. It was often a shock to the average soldier to find the conditions endured by his family when he went home on leave.[16]

There are many autobiographies of individuals who lived in Germany throughout the war, including women from Allied countries. There are numerous official reports in French and English of the dreadful conditions suffered by many Allied prisoners of war held in Germany. Several American journalists were allowed free rein across the German and Austro-Hungarian empires until 1917. At the end of the war, from mid-December through to March 1919, there were ten official visits by small teams of British Army officers sent to assess publicly the food situation in the German-ruled territories and covertly the state of morale among the German officials, military and public to determine what possibility there might be for renewed fighting if the peace talks went badly. The Americans also sent independent missions.[17] The British had direct access to senior officials dealing with food provision to the general population and to the German Army as it steadily demobilised. Their visits entailed lengthy journeys using crowded trains which gave many opportunities for conversation with individuals of every nationality and political hue. Generally, the trains were still running, although often late, which consistently irked the travellers. The officers, who might be away for a few days or several weeks, took their own rations with them in large packing cases into which they delved in the carriage or used to send down supplies for their meals to be cooked in hotel kitchens. Destinations varied, but often concentrated on single towns like Berlin, Cassel, Frankfurt, Hannover, Hamburg and Leipzig. The reports, frank and to the point, were leaked to the press by the British government and soon published in April 1919 in a single document as *The Economic Conditions Prevailing in Germany*, printed on ninety-two pages by His Majesty's Stationary Office in London.

Since that time, only a small number of specialist histories have been written. Within about ten years, there were several official or semi-official records from individuals either connected with blockade organisation or contracted by various governments to place what was known on the record.[18] A lengthy hiatus followed; it seems the subject was not for discussion and, in any event, academic work of this sort was interrupted by World War II.[19] From the 1960s, as much new archival material became available, the blockade became a more popular field of investigation and there were several serious attempts to provide context and understanding. Most recently, it has been the turn of the revisionists who sought to provide new interpretations, often travelling to the margins: to demonise the policy and all who were involved; to find within the blockade's effects the springboard for the rise of Nazi Germany; or to dampen its hurt and weakening of the resolve of the German people and thereby lessen its contribution to the German military collapse.

Implicit in these collected reminiscences, official returns and historical tracts are two arresting truths, that the British agreed a strategy from before the beginning of the war to starve the German civilian population, and that the Allies continued the blockade when at its most efficient after war end for national motives thereby adding considerable to the death toll.[20]

The first point was summed up in 1904 by Admiral of the Fleet Sir Jackie Fisher, who commanded the Royal Navy between 1904 and 1910, and was 'no respecter of the laws of war'.[21] Fisher repeatedly asserted that any talk of restraint in war was dangerous nonsense, 'All is fair in war!' he declared in one of his prints, 'hitting in the belly or anywhere else! ... Moderation in war is an imbecility!'[22] Four years later, the Committee of Imperial Defence required only a short discussion to endorse the strategy. 'We are of the opinion that a serious situation would be created in Germany owing to the blockade of her ports, and that the longer the duration of the war the more serious the situation would become.'[23] This view was endorsed by cabinet secretary Maurice Hankey who told his prime minister that the effects of blockade were cumulative 'and the process inevitably slow. It may be that years must elapse before its effect is decisive. But when the psychological moment arrives and the cumulative effects reach their maximum and are perhaps combined with crushing defeats of the enemy, the results may not be merely material, but decisive.'[24] The French were at first largely indifferent, being concentrated on the land battles.[25] Later French concurrence, and especially the enthusiastic support of the Americans from 1917, made the blockade a fully-Allied operation and a most efficient instrument.

The second point was that at the armistice in November 1918 the food blockade was continued and even extended to ban herring fishing in the Baltic which for the first time came under Allied control. There were many reasons for the continuation, including a fear of German resurgence. The French, in particular, by then converts to the use of food as a weapon for both punishment and coercion, refused any relaxation until the full signing of the final Peace Treaty in 1919. The French were prepared for the German nation to receive relief food supplies, essentially pork and grain from the United States, which the Americans were keen to offload to profit their own farmers. However, the French refused to allow the Germans to use their own gold to pay for it or to import the all-important fertilisers. The transactions had to be paid for elsewhere, preferably by American loans. The French insisted they had first rights on any liquid assets held by their recent adversary and that this money was to be used solely for reparations to cover the devastation suffered by their people and industry over four years in occupied northern France. This attitude was hardened because, in retreat, the Germans had stripped French factories under their control of their assets and blown up and flooded the French coalfields in the area east of Lens to Valenciennes so as to 'make the production of coal impossible for five to six years'.[26]

The occupation of northern France reached such a degree of completion in instrumentalising the civilian population, expropriating wealth, and destroying the infrastructure that it merits without hyperbole the work 'total' ... Because the French zone was [small] ... it was possible to impose a much more complete degree of control. There was a permanent curfew, doors and windows were forbidden to be locked during the day; correspondence was forbidden except to prisoners of war interned in Germany. No travel was permitted without a pass (for which one had to pay), and by 1917 there was virtually no movement, as the economy ceased to function and the land disintegrated into isolated units ... Requisitions from each household were heavy from the start down to lavatory buckets, forks, coffee mills and lamps ... a team of 200 economic experts visited over 4,000 firms compiling detailed reports that were the basis for outright expropriation ... army commander Crown Prince Rupprecht fined Lille half a million francs as 'atonement' for a patriotic demonstration ... Very large numbers of mostly women and children, old and sick people, were removed from the occupied zone by war's end, probably as many as a million, almost 25% ... [27]

Notwithstanding the evident anger and hatred felt by the French, freely supported in the immediate aftermath of the armistice by the Belgians and the British, the German people saw the extension of the blockade, and the emaciation and death it brought, as an unwarranted and inhumane war crime. However, it is evident from a wide international reading that money was at the root of the continuation. Money as recompense had a significant bedfellow in the callousness brought about by four years of unrelenting and unsought slaughter. There was a determination to make sure that in the foreseeable future the Germans would be incapable of attacking France. This fear was with good foundation. Before signatures were appended to the peace treaty, a core of the Prussian military and naval authorities had begun preparations for the next war expected to begin in about twenty years.[28]

On the first day of the war, Berliners bought up massive food supplies and prices temporarily doubled.[29] A few months later, George Schreiner, an American journalist, was sent to Berlin to get to the bottom of one of the most famous of the famine yarns.[30] Supplies had deteriorated so rapidly that elephants were slaughtered at the zoo for food. The story became an enduring myth and Schreiner enjoyed an excellent meal of conventional steaks at a top Berlin hotel. 'There seemed to be something wrong with starvation. It was not progressing rapidly enough.' *Kriegsbrot*, 'war bread', quickly appeared, a combination of about 55 per cent rye, 25 per cent wheat and 20 per cent potato meal with sugar and shortening.[31] The bread was very palatable and the potato elements in it prevented its getting stale rapidly. Schreiner thought that 'it was more of a staff of life than had been believed, despite its name. It tasted best on its third day and on trips to the front I kept the bread as long as a week without noticing deterioration.'

However, the 'first crevasse' in food management quickly appeared and, for Schreiner, undermined another myth, that of exceptional German organisational efficiency which he saw as more of a willingness in the population to accept and to follow rules.[32] By Christmas in the first year, village butchers had been called up and less expert men were left in charge of the conservation of pork products. 'The result could have been foreseen, but it was not.' Farmers were keen to sell their pigs at best condition when high on fat and did not want to waste their home-raised grain. This attitude was encouraged by the government determined to ensure the grain and potatoes used in pig food was kept for the humans instead.[33] In the spring of 1915, the government ordered a mass pig slaughter, *Schweinemord*, and the result was a temporary glut, thousands of tons of improperly cured sausages, pickled and smoked hams, shoulders and sides-of-bacon. 'Vast quantities of them began to spoil. It was a case of having no pigs and no pork.' Local municipalities were responsible for securing stocks of cured meat and rationing them and for a time this rapidly improved shortages.

A lack of coordination and incompetence worked its way into food and raw material administration.[34] The Siege Law of 1871 was invoked by the Kaiser which placed Germany under virtual martial law. The Law was administered by twenty-four army-corps districts, not including Bavaria, each commanded by a general usually called from retirement who 'wielded an almost unlimited power in the case of civil administration practically exempt from either ministerial or parliamentary control'.[35] Variations in ability and policy were quickly evident and the balkanised system prevented Germany from developing a uniform and effective food policy.[36]

On 1 February 1915, the Federal Council for Germany issued an edict effectively nationalising all stocks of flour, wheat and rye.[37] Traders were forbidden from operating on their own account. Such measures had already been put into effect in Hungary. That month, potatoes ran short and the first riots occurred, one of which was reported by Officer Paul Rhein of the Berlin political police:

> *Thousands of women and children had gathered at the municipal market hall in Andreas Street to get a few pounds of potatoes. As the sale commenced, everyone stormed the market stands. The police ... were powerless against the onslaught. A life-threatening press ensued.*[38]

Berliners suspected in mid-February that the remaining pigs, hidden away on farms, were being fed precious potatoes. The local authority raised the wholesale price ceiling on potatoes to encourage more to be brought to market, but little materialised. Farmers protested a depleted harvest. The military had commandeered rail equipment making it difficult to transporting potatoes to Berlin. The shortage of men on the farms limited the ability to harvest and 'through no fault of their own' much of the crop rotted in the ground at first frost. These potato shortages led to the first attacks on the state by street protestors.[39] Observing a butter riot in late 1915, Officer Rhein noted that the 'bad humour' among lower-class women 'grows from day to day'. A common view was that the 'war will not be decided on the front but, rather, through Germany's economic defeat'. Even before the mid-war crises, food ruled popular morale and 'played a significant role throughout the war in transforming relations between state and society'.[40] In October, there were more than fifty food riots over butter and concentrated primarily in a tiny segment of working-class Berlin.[41]

By the time of the growing season of 1915, a large part of German's population was mobilised and the country districts were short of labour. Reserve stores had been 'exhausted by improvidence'.[42] Schreiner travelled to Berlin to investigate and found that the area put under crops had been extended on Government advice that all fallow lands should be sown. The generalised instruction pamphlets from the authorities failed to recognise that every farm had its individual problems. Four million men in uniform were now consuming without producing a single thing. Their replacements on the farms, Russian prisoners of war, often shirked, and old people, many retired and lacking in stamina and experience, had to cope.[43] By the end of the war, one estimate placed 900,000 prisoners as land workers.[44] Additionally, their 'heart was often not in the work', taxes were higher and village elders had often suffered family losses at the front. Allied to the shortage of trained farmers and the lack of draught animals was a paucity of fertilisers caused by the blockade.[45] On the poor, sandy soil around Berlin, particularly, the harvest was not good; there was not enough reserve nutrient in the soil for even one season. Ingenious utilisation of farm waste helped, but the work was hard and time consuming. The year had been wet and much of the grain had been ruined even after it was ripe. Yields would have been higher from working half the ordered land. Returns were unsatisfactory and much of the wheat passed into the hands of speculators who held it until their profit was satisfactory or they deliberately let it spoil to drive up prices. Drastic regulation became necessary to relieve conditions and there were growing numbers of intrusive and unfriendly inspections seeking food hoards.

In April 1916, a German study of the blockade's impact on civilian nutrition affirmed that 'no woman or child in Germany need go hungry even if no food can be brought in'.[46] Caroline Cooper, aged forty-three, wrote a series of weekly seldom-posted letters from July 1914 to December 1918 to her home in South Australia.[47] Why she chose to stay in Leipzig is not made clear; there is speculation she was a spy or had a secret love affair. In any event, her pragmatic discussion of the problems of finding food is revealing. Here are some extracts from 1916:

9 April *There are great discussions about the increase in crime among children of late. Yesterday came this new order: under eighteen-year-olds, nobody is allowed to go alone to cafes, tea-rooms, automats, restaurants, or cinematographs – not allowed to smoke or to receive alcoholic drinks – not allowed to go out after ten in the evening without a good reason ... Frau Jaeger and her housekeeper at the farm have even concealed a pig from the inspectors! And you find great sides of bacon and smoked sausages in the most unexpected holes and corners.*

16 April *The living question gets more and more complicated every week. Yesterday a long article assured us that crows, ravens and [jack] daws were very good eating if they were first well soaked in a thin camomile tea to rid them of the fishy taste. Well, it may be, and Leipzig is some way off the nearest battlefield, but still it is too near for me to care risking a diet of crows.*

23 April *Soap is running short! We have soap-cards now and may not have more than two pounds a month, but as kitchen soap costs five shillings a pound you can imagine that one would not be wasteful anyway. I am very luxurious this week with half a pound of Danish margarine in the house. A shipment of it arrived and the orders were that it was to be sold in quantities of not more than one tenth of a pound to one person and only to people with an income of no more than £80 a year. You had to take your income tax receipt with you when you bought it!*

18 June *I paid four shillings and six pence this week for a pound of bacon! Still when one has the chance of getting it (it was smuggled in from Denmark) one takes it at any price, for there is no butter or fat of any sort, and practically no meat, and potatoes have quite given out. There are rows and fights and arrests at the market every day for the people are furious that potatoes were sent away to Switzerland last month.*

25 June *The luxuries of life are getting cheap, but the necessities are very difficult to obtain. Once or twice a week we take a tram as far as it goes and then walk out four or five miles. There in the villages you can often get a supper of eggs and cheese in a little inn and this week we found some sausage, the first I had seen for months. We take bread and a herring or a tin of sardines in case we have no luck.*

6 August *We have found an excellent new food – it is a tinned extract of soya beans and is as good as meat, very nice in taste and very filling. And I have just heard that a consignment of smoked walrus, or sea-calf, has arrived and that it is both nourishing and pleasant in flavour! We are going off to the market early tomorrow morning to try to get some. I must eat walrus!*

13 August *The walrus isn't bad! We bought a big piece, smoked and pickled, and one day it makes sandwiches and another day it is stewed with beans and so on. It tastes rather like pickled beef, only that it is almost black and has a gamey flavour.*

3 September *Nothing is coming in from Scandinavia or Holland and one gives up the daily hunt for milk with a good conscience! We have got an egg-card now which entitles one to one egg a week, but I have not been able to find my one egg yet.*

24 September *Today here was a huge duck. Even private poultry owners are obliged to deliver the eggs to the municipality and are only allowed one egg a week like the rest of us, so Frau Jaeger firmly made up her mind to eat her poultry before any law on the subject came into force!*

22 October *[They] each bought a large piece of smoked whale and they say it is just beastly, but nourishing and they feel bound to eat it. This week, I must certainly get some and see what it is like. But we hear that the days of cooking are numbered, that public kitchens are to be started and that everybody, rich and poor, is to get their food from them. It is an attempt to equalise things and to prevent the rich from buying up everything by fair means or foul (generally the latter).*

An Englishwoman married into German nobility, Evelyn, Countess Blücher, was another who wrote a diary of her experiences although the position and the estates of her husband shielded her from much of the deprivation. Nevertheless, she was perceptive. This from 14 March 1916:

One hears that so much is due to over-organisation. The Magistrat forbids the selling of butter, sugar, etc. until all has been bought up and distributed equally and justly, In the meantime, masses of butter and other stuffs get spoilt. So, they say, the dairy gave their butter to a big soap factory for the making of soap, as the butter had got bad through lying by so long, and in this way it was not entirely wasted.[48]

American peace activist Madelaine Doty, after making her first trip to Germany in 1914, returned two years later:

As for the people, there is a sombre greyness about them. They, too, are thin. I didn't see a big girth anywhere. Germany is stomachless. It isn't that people have nothing to eat, but they have too little. The food they have isn't of the right kind. During the summer, there seemed to be plenty of vegetables, fruit and a fair supply of black bread, but this without grease, sugar or meal does not satisfy digestion. It's like trying to run a wagon without oil. It begins to creak. The German race begins to creak. As a whole, it is pale, thin and sunken-eyed. Sooner or later a crisis is inevitable.[49]

In 1920, the eminent and largely-forgotten British physiologist Ernest Starling presented a paper to the Royal Statistical Society that gave a rigorous, authoritative analysis of food consumption during the blockade.

The paper had been compiled by the Royal Society (Food) Committee comprising scientific heavyweights who went to some lengths to find the correct situation.[50] The analysis is largely forgotten today.[51] Starling found that the Germans were well provided for in 1914, on average 3,215 kilocalories per head per day; by early 1916, 2,500; by late 2016, 1,700. The daily allowance in Germany was several hundred calories, 28 per cent less than in the United Kingdom. Starling levelled blame at German farmers for hoarding produce and creating a black market which particularly disadvantaged poorer citizens. One attendee at the talk suggested that the 'malnutrition of Germany resulted from a few German ration books being brought to England and several million forgeries of these printed before being returned to Germany'.[52] This, it was claimed, threw the whole system into chaos because it was impossible for all of the forged coupons to be redeemed for food.

In general, during the first two years of the war Germany compared well with France and Great Britain. Stores had been accumulated in case of need and food was taken from conquered territories. The Allied interpretation was that all these requisitions, especially around Lille in France's Nord Department, were proof of the shortages in Germany itself.[53] 'Food must be seriously lacking in Germany as the German soldiers were stealing food stocks to send to their parents.' Historian Kramer saw these conquered supplies as the German's 'strongest asset to challenge the Allies' with their command of the labour, industry, agriculture and finances of occupied Belgium, northern France, north-eastern Italy, Romania, Serbia, Poland, Lithuania and the Ukraine, but others disagree.[54] 'These resources, although smaller than Allied global resources, were of considerable value.'[55]

By May 1916, intelligence documents were flowing into London about the worsening situation in Germany. Sailors on Norwegian ships sailing from Sarpsborg to Cuxhaven were met on arrival by 'boats full of people clamouring for food, particularly bread'.[56] German officers were 'frequently jeered at and insulted in the streets by civilians'. Some soldiers were being fed on a 'sort of mixture of starch and water'. Visitors reported hotel food as 'execrable, bread was practically uneatable, coffee ditto, meat almost too bad to eat, no butter. In a court case in Leipzig, a butcher was given a short prison sentence, not for selling cat meat, but for wrongly describing it as hare. As the butcher was led away, the crowd called out, 'Only give us more cats' which, as with dogs, were no longer to be seen of the streets. Reports from Italian general headquarters reported numerous demonstrations in Berlin. 'The crowds including large numbers of women which assembled in the principal thoroughfares of the city were eventually dispersed with some casualties by the troops'. Much more seriously, similar riots took place in Dresden, Leipzig and Mannheim, where 'after material damage was done by the populace', 200 people were killed by machine gun. Another report from Rotterdam by a returning agent described machine guns used in Berlin and Hamburg with women's bodies lying where they fell.[57] If true, it is difficult to find any angry reaction to this mass execution of, principally, women in the public streets. Did they not matter?

From the summer of 1916 onwards the food situation in Germany became progressively less tolerable. Chickering noted that the most serious conflicts between the City Council and the state's District Office in Freiburg occurred in the autumn.[58] 'Frustrations over the shortages of food burst onto the streets, as angry crowds gathered in front of stores in the old city in a futile hunt for eggs, butter, cheese, and potatoes.' Food had become the irreducible minimum. The potato harvest was 'unfavourable' and causing widespread concern.[59] The quantity of bread was barely sufficient to feed the population. Its price could no longer be increased 'if the masses were not to starve for lack of money instead of lack of food'.[60] Daily bread was now a luxury. All effort and thought was directed toward the winning of the scantiest fare.' Men and women 'no longer strove for the pleasures of life', but had to rise early and work late if they wanted their families to eat. 'During the day, all laboured and scrambled for food, and at night men and women schemed and plotted how to make the fearful struggle easier. The voracity of the tax collector and the rapacity of the war profiteer came to know no bounds.'

> Civilians were forced to deal with rigid competition for goods and services and an increasing dehumanising struggle for survival – an especially hideous struggle because it took place among fellow countrymen.[61]

Falkenhayn was sacked in August 1916 after the failure at Verdun and fell into a pit of self-delusion. Far from acknowledging the defeat, he convinced himself that the 'ratio of French to German dead was far, far higher than it was – he estimated 9:1 and then trimmed it to 3:1 or 5:2 when it was in fact 1.1:1.'[62] Hindenburg and Ludendorff took over the military and, soon, almost complete power in the country. Their immediate tour of the western front, including a conference of senior officers in Cambrai in September, produced no good news. Over 120,000 casualties had occurred on the Somme from June to August. The war was being lost. One of Hindenburg and Ludendorff's immediate decisions, the introduction of the 'Hindenburg Programme' was a reprise of Falkenhayn's earlier idea of making all civilians of both sexes from their late teens liable to conscription for war work.[63] This forced labour of 300,000 German factory workers was supposed to double munitions and triple artillery and machine gun production by May 1917. Inessential factories were closed. Food would only be supplied to those who worked. Hindenburg told Bethmann that the 'whole German people must live only in service to the Fatherland. Achieving success makes action necessary. *Every day is of importance.* The necessary measures are to be taken *immediately.*'[64] Hindenburg brushed aside Bethmann's 'impressive list' of reasons why the programme was 'doomed'. Overall, the programme was a disaster. The workers were not to be found without damaging other parts of the economy and the military intrusion into civilian life fostered political discontent. The programme furthered the work of the Allied blockade. Men, horses and fuel were taken from agricultural production for the army and munitions causing food shortages and food price inflation. The programme made a bad situation much worse and, by the end of 1918, edged Germany even closer to famine.

In late 1916, the potato harvest failed and was replaced largely by unpalatable rutabaga, swede turnips.[65] 'As increasing proportion of milled grain was used for human consumption so that the bread became repulsive and there were fewer residues to pass on to farm animals. Almost 20 per cent of bread corn escaped the authorities.' Despite its nutritional value, the rutabaga, was a 'loathsome guest'. 'One day, potatoes and rutabaga, the next day rutabagas and potatoes.'[66] Dairy cows and other farm animals, which had been happy with vegetables that were objectionable to human tastes, were forced to forego a major part on their own diet.

> The turnip, which had figured prominently as a fodder crop, because a regular stand-in for cabbage and a range of other vegetables and fruits in short supply. The 'war puree' that disgusted consumers in 1917 had been concocted out of turnips. Salads of turnip greens, dandelions and young nettles became common fare. Coffee disappeared, thanks first to the blockade and then to the scarcity of chicory. The shortage of barley combined with the army's privileged claims on beer made this beverage scarce; private deliveries ceased in 1916.

The realm of Ersatz encompassed 'virtually everything that had once graced a table'. Staple foodstuffs such as grain, potatoes, meat and dairy products became so scarce by the winter of 1916 that many people subsisted on a diet of Ersatz products that ranged from the worsening *Kriegsbrot* to powdered milk.

> Butter was made from curdled milk, sugar and food colour. Coffee was invented from tree bark, acorns or chicory, tea from raspberry or catnip leaves, textiles from nettles. Cooking oil was concocted from carrots, red beet and turnip; cockchafers and lime wood replaced fats. By the end of the war, some 11,000 Ersatz products were on sale in Germany, including thirty-three egg substitutes and 837 different kinds of sausage.[67]

The result was the infamous 'turnip winter' which remains to this day embedded in the German collective memory. German women, wearied by dreadful queues, by rationing, demonstrated in Berlin and in the other big cities; riots for butter, then for potatoes, broke out. 'Women fighting against the cost of living in most of the warring nations used the language of social justice. The effects of the blockade meant that German women had been the earliest and the most virulent in demonstrating.[68] Starling estimated that from November 1916 to May 1917, the body weight of the underprivileged urban population fell by 15–20 per cent. The city of Freiburg was the subject of a detailed study by Roger Chickering:

In mid-August 1916, the rains began in earnest. They continued without significant pause for the next three months, as conditions in South Baden turned raw. By the end of the summer, hunters were reporting full white tails on local foxes, weasels and martens – portents, they said, of a hard winter. It snowed in the Black Forest in August and September. On 20 October, snow flurries fell in Freiburg itself; three weeks later the Rhine Valley was white. A blizzard, which brought down telephone lines around the city in early December, then announced the longest, most bitter winter in memory. Amid these conditions the shortages turned drastic. The principle casualty was the potato, which local farmers had refused to harvest in the fall of 1916, anticipating higher controlled prices the following spring. Left in the wet ground while consumers searched the market in vain for them, potatoes fell victim to the blight in south Baden. The effects of the disaster soon spread. The cold weather exhausted the fuel supply. It strangled the local production of vital goods and their transport by boat or train.[69]

In January and February 1917, strikers in the Ruhr and in Berlin, female metal-workers at their head, demanded food or more wages to buy food. 'Any other people on earth would rise against a Government that had reduced it to so much misery', Cooper wrote in February.[70] Two months later strikers in her home town of Leipzig called for political change, but the demands were for reform, not revolution: equal and universal suffrage, the removal of military controls on political discourse, and a peace without annexations.[71] Elsewhere in Germany, the strikes were not politicised, or at least not overtly so. In Berlin, 200,000 workers, half of them women, staged a one-day demonstration to demand food.

The winter of hunger, the 'turnip winter', was followed by shortages of foods and raw materials that enfeebled resistance in the last years of the war.[72] Civilian morale buckled under the strain, and the regime was thoroughly discredited by its failure to provide sufficient food. That winter, there was a nationwide coal shortage after contracted deliveries to the gasworks began to fall significantly short in the autumn.[73] In early March, they varied daily from nothing to barely enough to supply Freiburg for several additional days. 'We are living from hand to mouth,' reported the director of the gasworks, noting that his reserves of coal would be exhausted in three days.

Some 2,500 calories a day are needed to sustain working life. The German National Board of Health estimated that rations per head of population had fallen in the autumn of 1916 to 1,344 calories, and in the summer of 1917 to 1,100 calories, insufficient even for infants.[74] The low digestibility of some of this food, and waste in cooking, reduced its nutritive value to about 1,000 calories. The minimum deficiency from January to August 1919 was 1,456 calories. This was now the breeding time for the diseases of malnutrition – diphtheria, dysentery, rickets (known in war-time Germany as the 'English sickness'), scrofula, scurvy, small pox and tuberculosis – all became commonplace.[75] In Freiburg, Chickering found that these dreadful diseases that traditionally thrived in war time threatened repeatedly to settle in the town.[76] Several cases of small pox surfaced in the spring of 1917. In the summer, soldiers brought dysentery; over forty patients, both civilians and soldiers, were hospitalised.

> *Although the disease then receded, soldiers brought it back in the summer of 1918 – assisted, in the judgement of medical experts, by the burgeoning local population of flies. In any case, during the last two years of the war, it killed some fifty people in the city. Diphtheria, which had struck in isolated instances during the first half of the war, reached alarming levels in late 1917 and early 1918, when about eight people died. The increasing incidence of scrofula and pulmonary tuberculosis was a constant concern; the number of fatal cases of the latter disease was more than 50% higher in 1917 than on the eve of the war.*

Cooper in Leipzig continued her letters into 1917:

> **22 January** *On Sunday mornings the provision shops are open from eleven to one and I spent that time today hunting for my dinner, no cabbage, no potatoes, of course, not even turnips! I gave it up and ended in a restaurant where I got a plate of porridge and dish of stewed toadstools, you know these are bright yellow and look most poisonous, but they are excellent.*
>
> **4 February** *Coal has run out, the electric light is cut off in most houses, the trams are not running, or only in the very early morning. All theatres, schools, the opera, and concerts and cinematographs are closed. Neither potatoes nor turnips are to be had. They were our last resort. There is no fish and Germany has at last ceased to trumpet the fact that it can't be starved out. Add to that the thermometer outside my kitchen window says 24 degrees Fahrenheit below zero.*
>
> **12 August** *There is an outbreak of something here that they don't call cholera, but which is certainly an extremely infectious dysentery. The hospitals are crammed and people are dying of it by the hundreds.*
>
> **19 August** *It is no exaggeration to say that the whole day goes in the*

search for what is necessary to live on just for that day. You have literally to go three times for every article of food. On a certain day, for instance, your egg, or ounce of butter, of one third of a pound of meat for the week has to be ordered by taking your card and having it stamped. Then, on the next day, you have to go and get that egg or whatever it is, and then you are inevitably told that it has not been delivered and that you must come in again at six or whenever the time may be!

Ernst Glaeser's autobiography *Jahrgang 1902*, 'Class of 1902', remembered his time as a teenager.[77]

It was a hard winter right to the end. The war now got past the various fronts and pressed home upon our people. Hunger destroyed our solidarity; the very children stole each other's rations. August's mother went twice to church every day, she prayed and grew thinner and thinner: all the food she could get was divided down to the last crumb among August and his sisters. Soon the women who stood in pallid queues before the shops spoke more about their children's hunger than about the death of their husbands. The war had shifted emphasis. A new front was created. It was held by the women against an entente of field gendarmes and controllers. Every smuggled pound of butter, every sack of potatoes successfully spirited in by the night was celebrated in their homes with the same enthusiasm as the victories of the armies two years before ... Soon a looted ham thrilled us more than the fall of Bucharest. And a bushel of potatoes seemed much more important that the capture of a whole English army in Mesopotamia.

A municipal doctor in Chemnitz wrote that the early effects of the war were kept from most of the children, but that this was 'mainly due to the self-sacrifice of the parents, and especially of the mothers, in their anxiety for their children'.[78] The women were worn away to skin and bone and with 'seamed and careworn faces' and one knows where the 'portion of food assigned to them has really gone'.

Potato shortages were not limited to the German civilian population. In July 1917, the Dutch drafted 2,000 soldiers into Amsterdam to control riots.[79] Some of the soldiers sided with the strikers and were withdrawn. The vegetable market was wrecked, warehouses broken into, sabres drawn, and at least one man died and many were wounded. The workers declared themselves no longer capable of heavy work and demanded 'better feeding, not on paper, but on the table'. That same month, sailors in some of the larger German ships went on strike or mutinied. There were many reasons, but the open complaint concerned the poor food served in the idle fleet.[80] This issue was exacerbated was the 'increasingly unbearable harassment of the men by their officers'. 'The men slaved and engaged in perpetual drill, but the officers sat about idle, cleaning and polishing their fingernails and combing their hair'. Horn in his account of the naval mutinies gives example after example, taken from contemporary records. All was worsened because, with the ships packed together, the difference in living conditions between officers and men was emphasised, especially the food.

The turnip winter of 1916-1917 resulted in a drastic curtailment of navy rations. Early in 1917, Warrant Officer Bernhard Haack was left behind in a boat when *UC 32* had to crash dive. Haack told his British interrogators that rations were 'not more than half those supplied in peace time' even allowing for the extra that was served to u-boat crews.[81] In the big ships, sailors were most commonly served a concoction called *Drahtverhau*, literally chopped barbed wire, composed of 75 per cent water, 10 per cent sausage, 3 per cent potatoes, 1 per cent yellow turnips, 0.5 per cent each of beef and vinegar and 0.25 per cent fat. The stokers particularly suffered in the engine rooms where special rations were often not issued. In hot weather, they 'fell down like flies' from exhaustion and heat prostration.[82] Naval regulations stipulated that each enlisted man was entitled to 1.32 Reichsmarks worth of food per day; officers 3.65 Reichsmarks of which 2.15 marks was spent on food while the rest went for drink, reportedly eight bottles of wine each a week. Food was cooked in three separate kitchens, for the officers, deck officers and the men. The men's requests for food committees were refused and their frequent and documented examples of sailors' funds, donations and rations stolen by their own officers were refuted.

> *If the officers had shared this hunger and privation with the men, common suffering might have improved their relationship and ameliorated the class conflict. But the class-conscious and caste-ridden German naval corps refused to avail itself of this opportunity. Instead it aggravated the conflict. Insisting on their privileges and determined to maintain their superiority over the men, the officers allowed a revolutionary situation to arise in the fleet by their stubborn maintenance of unequal rations.*[83]

The battleships and cruisers involved at Kiel and Wilhelmshaven, including the *Friedrich der Große, Helgoland, Hindenburg, König Albert, Nürnberg, Pillau, Prinzregent Luitpold* and *Westfalen*, were not ships on which either Gerth brother had served, but they had been officers on sister ships in the same ports. They were complicit in the attitudes of their fellow officers.

The Gerth brothers swopped the socially intense world of the big ships for the claustrophobic environment of the u-boats. However, before they reached their commands in Bruges and Pola, they both underwent u-boat training in mutinous ports. In their chosen new environment, caste separation was nigh impossible and food was common and utilitarian. Admiral Adolf von Trotha, later chief of staff of the High Seas Fleet and twice Erich's commanding officer, was a staunch defender of the officer corps. He described in great detail an imagined issue of food rations to his men and conceded, somewhat desperately, that the 'high morale and lack of revolutionary activity among the men who served on torpedo boats and submarines might be attributed to the fact that in addition to being exposed to the same dangers as the officers, they shared a common kitchen and ate the same food'.[84] The navy eventually brought the mutinies and strikes under control with ten death sentences, two of which were carried out, and a series of lesser sentences that came to a total of 360 years of imprisonment.

Among the civilians, 'the era of greed was on and a high tide in hoarding set in.' Almost everyone had a relative, a friend or acquaintance in the country. Sunday excursions became popular and weekdays could not be put to much better use. The many holidays called for by religious observance and, now and then, a victory over the enemy came to be a severe strain upon the country's food reserve.[85] 'The trains coming into the city often carried more weight in food than its passengers.' Why go to the retailer when the farmers were willing to sell to the consumer direct? 'Everyone filled garret and cellar with the things that the farm produced. Existing regulations already permitted the searching of trains. When the inspectors descended on the hoarding holidayers there was 'much surprise, gnashing of teeth, and grumbling'. The food illicitly brought in was confiscated. Desperate people turned next to the parcel post, but it was over-used and the Post Office turned over all food found to the authorities. Then the farmer came to market in the towns. Illicit goods were quickly sold – 'a drop of ink with a blotter'. When carts were stopped and searched, food under regulation was smuggled into the towns inside unbanned articles; mattresses were filled with macaroni. Inexperience brought poor storage methods and much food was spoiled in cellars. There were weevils, sprouting potatoes, smells, explosions and noisome disposals. Servants and neighbours became informers and the authorities began to search houses. However, most of the commercial hoards were unfound as money changed hands. In the last year of the war, it was estimated that about half of the registered quantities of meat, eggs and fruit, one third of milk, butter and cheese were withdrawn from the legal food economy.'[86] As their routes to market dried up, the farmers changed to more profitable black market goods. Their energies went into high profit items like butter and other fats instead of grain and this transfer led to even greater shortages.

Schreiner was back in Berlin where the good-natured corner shop of long-relationship with the families in its vicinity, the *Kleinkrämer*, 'grew more autocratic every time he opened his store'. It was a case of 'buy from me now or never buy from me again'. People had to go to him or go hungry.

When America entered the war in April 1917, Herbert Hoover, a life-long Quaker, was appointed the first head of the newly-created US Food Administration and quickly showed he understood the power wielded by the blockade and by the American agricultural industry. 'Food has gradually, since the war began assumed a larger place in the economics, the statesmanship, and the strategy of the war until it is my belief that food will win this war – starvation or sufficiency will in the end determine the victor. The winning of the war is largely a problem of who can organise this weapon – food.'[87]

> *The British elevation of the Hunger Blockade into a central weapon of the war encapsulated the extreme militarisation of food; a transnational economy of food aid developed under the American leadership that relied on the distribution of food as a method of political control; and wartime food crises provided fertile ground for political radicalisation across Europe and especially in Germany spawning new organisations and party platforms that coalesced around the experience and anticipation of hunger.*[88]

At the same time, the Food War Committee of The Royal Society predicted that deficiencies of protein and fat in diets would fall below the level required for maintaining the health and efficiency of the German nation. What it did not foresee was that during the last two years of the war 'there was an absolute insufficiency in the caloric supply, and that the greater part of the civilian population during this time were in a state of chronic starvation.'[89] The review by Starling in 1920 found that all the available food might have been sufficient, but the German government failed to control German farmers.

> *Substantial quantities of produce were retained for the producer's own uses: the German farmer 'not only did his best to maintain his stock alive, if necessary using for the purpose food which ought by law to have been applied to man, but he also with great persistence and determination insisted on eating as much as he did before the war. Therefore, one does not find the same miserable starved aspect of the population as may be observed in the cities of Germany. The German government failed to enforce laws and even winked at violations. Anthony Fokker with his aircraft manufacturing plant, routinely bought large quantities of food from the farmers at prices about ten times that offered by the Government to supply workers and their families. By 1918, about 25-33% of the total food energy was diverted into illicit channels. The abject failure was a major factor in the breakdown of the government in 1918 as well as the class divisions that so bitterly divided post-war Germany and the difficulties they had in re-establishing effective civil authority.*[90]

This view of farmers seems an over-confident statement considering the reality in much of the countryside. Chickering thought the war 'strangled German agriculture'.[91] The blockade cut imports on which German food supply had to a great extent relied. The economist August Skalweit summarised the dilemmas that he faced in the central bureaucracy in Berlin. 'An increase in Germany's own agricultural production to compensate for these losses to even a small degree was impossible because the effort would have claimed too many human and material resources that the country's military power would have suffered.' The losses in fertilisers, animal feed, horses and rural manpower were particularly damaging, for they robbed German agriculture of basic sustaining resources. 'The cumulative effects of this disinvestment compounded one another, and by the last two years of the war they had produced the gravest food crisis that Germany had seen in almost a century.' The minor officials, small businessmen and craftsmen were the people hardest hit, their enterprises shut down to save coal, officials overworked, underpaid and underfed. Even so, farmers were not deemed 'hard-working' like the industrial workers, *Schwerarbeiter*, who were, therefore, given extra rations, and favoured a minority of well-unionised workers in heavy industries. These failures of the rationing system deepened social inequalities in Germany.[92] The gap was compounded by the *Schleichhandel*, black market, but the 'overall failure was the miscalculation by the authorities of the impact of the blockade'.

In the last year of the war, there were serious shortages of clothing and housing.[93] The clothing supply had deteriorated sharply because of the shortage of raw materials and the use of inadequate substitute products. Shoes were in such short supply that soldiers would hack off their jackboot heels and post them home to their families then draw new boots from the store. As usual the management of these problems was hindered either by an excess of organisation or by the absence of any organisation at all. Thus, factories requesting shoes for their workers had to apply to the local War Office bureau, the factory inspector, and the local clothing distribution agency. These agencies, in turn, had to apply to the central agencies in Berlin. Getting materials for the repair of shoes required an appeal to no fewer than ten different Berlin agencies. No less serious was the shortage of soap. Coal miners could not wash properly after work and housewives were unable to keep clothing clean. Many German workers were now being forced to contend with lice. Finally, the flood of workers into the industrial productions centres and away from food production created a housing shortage and a rapid rise in rents.

The rations allowed were not always obtainable.[94] Many thousands of individuals could only be sure each day of five slices of bread, half a small cutlet, half a tumbler of milk, two thimblefuls of fat, a few potatoes and an egg-cup of sugar. 'These supplies were, however, only obtainable by waiting for long hours in food queues, exposed to the rain, snow and slush of the bitter

German winter; after obtaining them, the women as often as not returned in their soaking clothes to houses that were not heated or even warmed.' Most of the urban population were either cold, or wet, or hungry for the greater part of the day.[95] Schreiner travelled to Berlin again and set out to find a face in these food-lines that did not show the 'ravages of hunger'.[96]

> *Four long lines were inspected with the closest scrutiny. But among the 300 applicants for food there was not one who had had enough to eat for weeks. In the case of the younger women and the children the skin was drawn hard to the bones and bloodless. Eyes had fallen deeper into the sockets. From the lips all colour was gone, and the tufts of hair which fell over parchmented foreheads seemed dull and famished – a sign that the nervous vigour of the body was departing with the physical strength.*

After three years on a diet insufficient as to quantity and quality, indigestible, tasteless and monotonous, there was a marked influence on the vitality and efficiency of the great bulk of the urban population. This finally resulted in a 'mentality which rendered impossible any further efforts of attack or even resistance'.[97] The war no longer seemed of importance. 'Food filled their thoughts by day and their dreams by night, and the only desire was to end the war by any possible means that might lead to a slackening of the blockade and the free entry of food into the country.' The more fortunate could add a precarious, irregular supply of jams, green vegetables and nuts. Professor Berghahn saw that the poor, the weak and the elderly were 'very badly hit, whereas the better-off who had savings were able to obtain supplies on the black market at exorbitant prices. Infant mortality rose dramatically.'[98]

In the second half of 1918, individual rations, when available, were down to 12 per cent of the peacetime diet of meat, 5 per cent of fish, 7 per cent of fats, 13 per cent of eggs, 28 per cent of butter, 15 per cent of cheese, 6 per cent of beans and pulses, 82 per cent of sugar, 94 per cent of potatoes, 16 per cent of margarine and 48 per cent of bread.[99] In Freiburg, local animals hardly registered half their pre-war weight: cows weighed on average 155 kilograms; pigs forty kilograms, and sheep twenty.[100] At this time, 'almost three-quarters of all officially available food' went to the Germany army.[101]

> *During the final months of the war, as riots, strikes and hunger protests spread through the country's cities, the German army consumed 30% of the country's total bread grains and 60% of the country's beef and pork, leaving little more than horsemeat for the hungry home front.*

Support for the war beginning draining away in the summer of 1918. In June, Countess Blücher diarised that the 'food question is always the most important topic of the day. The less there is of it, the more we talk about it. The Austrians have already eaten up their stores and are grumbling and turning to Germany for fresh supplies. It is rather like turning from a sandy desert to a rocky mountain for nourishment.'[102] News of the reverses suffered by the German army on the western front had a significant effect.[103] The 'tired consensus' could not survive the crushing of the expectations of land victory that had been extravagantly promised by Hindenburg and Ludendorff in the spring of 1918. The belief that had always sustained the home front, sacrifice in the name of *durchhalten*, 'sticking it out', collapsed. The Kaiser and the navy's confidence in the ability of the u-boats to starve England into defeat in 1917 had not happened. Ludendorff wrote in his memoirs:

> *The waning morale at home was intimately connected with the food situation. In wide quarters a certain decay of bodily and mental powers of resistance was noticeable, resulting in an unmanly and hysterical state of mind which under the spell of enemy propaganda encouraged the pacifist leanings of many Germans ... This state of mind was a tremendous element of weakness. It could be eliminated to some extent by strong patriotic feeling, but in the long run could only be overcome by better nourishment. Our enemies' starvation blockade triumphed and caused us both physical and spiritual distress.*[104]

By October 1918, the High Seas Fleet was in full rebellion.[105] The food situation was dire and evident to all. Life was miserable without a solution in sight. Sickness was rampant and reaching into every home. Children and old people were dying everywhere. The will to endure was lost. Then, the influenza pandemic came to Germany and to Freiburg with soldiers who returned from France.[106]

> *By September, a quarter of a local regiment's reserves were already hospitalised with the disease. From the barracks and the military hospitals, the epidemic spread through the city like a rumour. In October, a quarter of the children in the public schools was sick, as were more than a third of the teachers. A week later, when half of the children were out, the city closed all the schools. This measure failed to halt the spread of the flu, as the arrival of cold, wet weather in mid-October forced people inside. Paralysis descended on the city.*

Scout leader Robert Baden Powell noted on 8 September with some satisfaction that 'the German race is being ruined; though the birth rate, from the German point of view, may look satisfactory, the irreparable harm done is of a different kind and much more serious'.[107]

The German request for an armistice was made on 3 October. Clemenceau asked Foch and Petain, his commanders, to draw up quickly the armistice

terms and to present them to the other military leaders on 24-25 October.[108]
Surprisingly with hindsight, the armistice terms were left entirely to the
military leaders. No politicians were directly involved. In the first draft,
made without the Navy, naval matters and the blockade were omitted.[109]
The non-negotiable terms were given to the horrified Germans who had
completely underestimated the strength of Allied enmity, particularly from
France, and were given seventy-two hours to respond or the fighting would
restart.[110] The provisional end to the fighting was agreed for 11 November.
What happened next – the refusal by the Allies to lift the food blockade – is
one of the darker episodes of modern Western European history.

In Paris in October, Clemenceau, Foch and Pétain agreed that 'the
blockade was to be maintained and the duration of the armistice was to
be short'. Clemenceau thought initially that it would take Germany only
twenty-five days to comply with the terms of the armistice and that when
fulfilled 'the supply of the enemy can be authorised'. This wording was
agreed unanimously by the Allies and was intended to prevent Germany
from using the armistice to rearm and resupply, and allowed for more
definite relief.[111] Clause 26 of the armistice eventually specified that the
blockade was to remain unchanged and that all German merchant ships
found at sea were to remain liable to capture.[112] It stated that the Allies
'should give consideration to the provisioning of Germany during the
armistice to the extent recognized as necessary'. Objectives had shifted
and the promise of relief was less clear. There was now a 'desire to
use the blockade to break American food prices', to gain a competitive
trade advantage, including taking over the German merchant fleet, and
to win political concessions. The clause was vague enough to allow
for misunderstanding and dispute. It was assumed in Berlin that trade
restrictions would end with the signing of the armistice or a preliminary
peace. 'If the German government had shown more foresight, it could
probably have traded submarines for food supplies.'[113]

Under Clause 34, the armistice had to be renewed month by month.
The bankers began to take control and the supplementary armistice of
December 1918 was negotiated by Belgian and French financiers without the
knowledge of England or America.[114] The French argued that each monthly
renewal allowed a proper opportunity to add new or forgotten conditions
under threat of invasion. Thus, a fortnight after the revolution at the 'lowest
ebb of their fortunes and their vitality' the Germans were forced to a fatal
agreement. They were prohibited from 'disposing abroad of any of her gold,
foreign securities or other liquid assets, because they were a pledge over
which the Allies held lien for the purposes of reparation'. The blockade,
therefore, continued and the 'remnant of Germany's financial resources for
purchasing food from the neighbouring neutrals was immobilised'. Germany
could buy no food and the starvation was to continue.

It is worth reflecting on the French objectives from the peace negotiations for they stand in danger of being viewed as callously and solely prolonging the blockade. The peace objectives of the French were probably the most easily understandable of the Allies. 'Foch could conceive of only two words which would spell success – 'Rhineland' and 'Reparations' – and these two words dominated his thoughts and actions.'[115] The Rhineland was necessary to provide security either though annexation or by the creation of a buffer state against later German aggression. If Germany's border was moved to the Rhine, France could at last breathe more freely. Reparations were a clear necessity for the war had been largely fought on French, and Belgian, territory and the Germans had stripped France's industrial heartland in victory and in defeat and taken their booty back home. Germany, itself, in terms of industrial infrastructure, remained largely undamaged. A third objective, that of German disarmament, must be added although it would prove to be a temporary expedient. On 12 November, Clemenceau called his subordinates to the French War Office and spent the next two days planning the French strategy necessary to negotiate the desired peace. Marshal Foch was to formulate disarmament plans; Lucien Klotz was to prepare figures for reparation claims; and Paul Cambon was to decide how to remove the German state permanently from the left bank of the Rhine. On 4 February, Hoover wrote to Wilson, 'The French, by obstruction of every financial measure that we can propose to the feeding of Germany in the attempt to compel us to loan money to Germany for this purpose, have defeated every step so far for getting them the food which we have been promising for three months.'[116]

In February 1919, a fact-finding commission organised by Winston Churchill recommended that as 'Germany is still an enemy country, it would be inadvisable to remove the menace of starvation by a too sudden and abundant supply of foodstuffs. This menace is a powerful lever for negotiation at an important moment.'[117] This statement fits poorly with Churchill's apologists who later claimed that Churchill 'did not fully appreciate conditions in Germany until the last weeks of February 1919' when he was told of 'cruel privations', presumably in the reports by British officers.[118] 'The German people suffered severely [after the war] but they had an advocate in Winston Churchill.' From being a weapon of war, the blockade, at one bound, became a 'guarantor of peace'.[119]

John Maynard Keynes was the British financial representative on the Supreme Economic Council and was appointed to the team that tried to find some way of feeding the German people while the peace negotiations wound their probably lengthy way. Keynes and colleagues met German delegations twice in Trier on the German border. The French openly wanted German gold to rebuild their country at whatever cost to the German people. However, Keynes was unsure why the British supported the continuation of the blockade with all the death that it would entail. At first, he thought it came down to the irresolution of Lord Reading who led the British team whom he thought was in an 'agony of doubt' and 'terrified of identifying himself too decidedly with anything controversial'. Keynes final deduction was more inhumane:

> I attribute [the continuation of the blockade] more profoundly to a cause inherent in bureaucracy.[120] The blockade had become by that time a very perfect instrument. It had taken four years to create and was Whitehall's finest achievement; it had evoked the qualities of the English at their subtlest. Its authors had grown to love it for its own sake; it included some recent improvements, which would be wasted if it came to an end; it was very complicated, and a caste organisation had established a vested interest. The experts reported, therefore, that it was our one instrument for imposing our peace terms on Germany, and that once suspended it could hardly be reimposed.

There have been numbers of books and articles which provide blow by blow accounts of the machinations and incompetence, administrative niceties, and straightforward greed, which dogged the discussions on the lifting of the blockade. Much of these support Keynes' attribution although the topic remains subject to revisionist scrutiny.[121] In effect, Article 26 was a continuation of the war by the Allies and the United States after the armistice. It became clear the 'blockade was for sale' should American money be found to pay for American pork or surplus or rotting food stocks.[122]

> There is a great problem in the situation of the enemy people – about 90 million. This problem is not one of going to their relief. It is a problem of relaxing the watertight blockade, which continues through the armistice, sufficiently so that they may secure for themselves the bare necessities that will give them stable government. Unless anarchy can be put down and stability of government can be obtained in these enemy states, there will be nobody to make peace with and nobody to pay the bill to France and Belgium for the fearful destruction that has been done ... Justice requires that government be established to make amends for wrongs done, and it cannot be accomplished through spread of anarchy.[123]

The failure of the Allies to lift the blockade and to improve the food situation after stocks held by the German army and the great estates ran out led to increased conflict with the Soldiers' Councils.[124] Workers in the town began strikes for shorter hours because of their physical weakness. Food was increasingly adulterated to make it go further and to increase profits. The lack of food 'encouraged the Freikorps, the defeated Officer Corps, to use it as a tactic in waging civil war'. Food became an even more direct weapon of power when supplies were withheld from the workers in central Germany and Upper Silesia who supported the Ruhr general strike.

It is remarkable how many clauses that the Allies insisted on in the armistice agreements, deliberately or inadvertently, worsened the famine. Under Clause 7, 5,000 locomotives and 150,000 wagons in good working order, with all necessary spare parts and fittings, were to be handed over within thirty-one days all of which curtailed the ability of the Germans to move food around their country. Within a further five days, 5,000 working motor lorries were to be delivered. Clause 23 declared that all German merchant ships found at sea were liable to capture. Clause 25 called for freedom of access to and from the Baltic to be given to the Allied naval and mercantile marines and this resulted in the halting of the German Baltic and North Seas fishing fleets.[125] Among the things left out of the original armistice agreement was the permanent seizure of the entire German mercantile marine which by the time of the third armistice extension was being underhandedly linked to the supply of food.[126] The argument was that unless Germany put her ships at the Allies' disposal it would be difficult to find enough ships to furnish the much-needed food. 'Germany, by her u-boats, had reduced shipping to a level at which all Europe risked starvation. If Germany wanted to be fed, it was only reasonable that the ships laid up in harbour should be lent to carry that food. 'Ships against food was, therefore a reasonable bargain. The bluff was far less dangerous, because Germany probably needed the food more urgently than [the Allies] the ships.' The Allies decided to confiscate a substantial part of what was left of Germany's livestock.[127] The American representative at Versailles, Thomas Lamont, recorded the event with some indignation, 'The Germans were made to deliver cattle, horses, sheep, goats, etc ... A strong protest came from Germany when dairy cows were taken to France and Belgium, thus depriving German children of milk.'

The fifth clause of the Armistice agreement required the Germans to vacate the left bank of the Rhine within one month. The Allied commanders waited five days before moving their armies forward to occupy this space and, during this time, the German command structure collapsed. No-one controlled the large quantities of food stocks in the forward bases during the first phase of the withdrawal of Hindenburg's armies from Belgium and France to the east of the Rhine.[128] The gap in the command structure was filled perforce by more than 10,000 spontaneous soldiers' councils. 'Necessity forced them to play a leading part in resolving the food crisis during the withdrawal of the German armies. By demoting their officers and by rapidly demobilising themselves' the soldiers' councils 'saved hundreds of thousands of families from hunger while protecting themselves from recriminations as deserters'. This alleviation from the effects of the blockade was temporary, but vital.

In the East, the Army wanted to keep food stocks available to the military because, despite the western armistice, there was armed chaos. The undefeated German forces were initially in controlled retreat westwards, but by December 1918 there were mass desertions by officers and men. The spaces abandoned by the Germans were fought over by local impromptu armies. Lenin, while fighting the White Russians on one side, ordered the Bolshevik army to drive into central Europe and to set up Soviet governments throughout the area and to foment revolution in Germany and Austria-Hungary. Independent forces from, principally, Poland, but also Ukraine, Lithuania, Estonia, Latvia and Belarus fought to stop them, while seeking independence.

For the Germans, it became a fight to control the food stocks with the Government, the Army, the Soldiers' Councils, city authorities and the looters all in play. The Army warned that millions would starve if the conveyance of supplies from the east was made impossible. 'We are faced with an unutterable disaster as the problem of food supplies threatens the future of the people. It is vital to save for the people at home, the enormous quantities of army food stockpiled in the west. Only an orderly retreat could save the situation and only if the food supplies were successfully sent on ahead. We should not consider ourselves but rather our homeland and our comrades in the west'.[129] At 5 December 1918, the German High Command controlled 30 per cent of national grain stocks and 60 per cent of meat supplies. From October to February army grain stocks reduced by about 70 per cent. Over the three months at the end of 1918, five million troops dispersed under their own Councils and redistributed one million tones of army food and from hoards seized from the great estates, factories and farms. By late 1918, Germany was moving to a state of total famine. The unequal distribution of these reduced supplies placed numerous poorer sections of the community in considerable jeopardy.[130] The French secret service reported on 13 January 1919 that 'immense stocks have become the loot of soldiers who are to be seen in all the large towns of Germany as well as Berlin selling cocoa, tea, flour, potatoes which are being punctually delivered'.

Some 230 million people were facing the prospect of the 'worst famine since the Thirty Years War' in the seventeenth century, and Europe's economy was 'so paralysed that these people could not save themselves by their own exertions before the harvest of 1919'.[131] The ration of fats in 1918 was, according to German estimates, only 12 per cent of the pre-war consumption, that of meat 18 per cent, and that of cereals 64 per cent; the death rate from tuberculosis had doubled, and rickets was general amongst children. Deaths from tuberculosis during the war was estimated at 160,000.[132] Beatrice Webb wrote in her diary in November 1918, 'Every day one meets saddened women, with haggard faces and lethargic movements, and one dare not ask after husband or son.[133]

The Baltic States and Finland were found to be in desperate distress and conditions were much worse in Anatolia and Armenia. 'Hunger had long drawn the life out of Vienna.' *The Times* concluded in November

1918 that the shortage of food in the newly-occupied territories in recent months was 'even worse' than could have been imagined.[134] However, the propaganda that British prisoners had suffered more than the rest of the population was proved another invention. The success of the parcel system meant that most prisoners were adequately fed until the outbreak of the German revolution.[135]

After four years of blockade across the country, the stock of pigs was slashed 77 per cent, that of cattle 32 per cent.[136] The weekly per capita consumption of meat reduced from 1,050 grams to 135; the amount of available milk down by half. Women's mortality was up 51 per cent, that of children under five by 50 per cent. Tubercular-related deaths were up 72 per cent, the birth rate down by half. Rickets, influenza, dysentery, scurvy, ulceration of the eyes, and hunger oedema were a common occurrence. Malnutrition, smuggling, black marketeering, and hoarding were widespread.

> This country is not 'perfidious Albion', but rather imperial Germany. The suffering caused was not by unrestricted submarine warfare, but rather by a surface blockade that in the eyes of Jay Winter did not fall far short of being a war crime.

Historian Winter went further. 'The fact that war was waged on women and children, on the elderly, in my view – after the Armistice – is a war crime'.[137] As Paul Vincent researched the famine, he 'grew increasingly convinced of the irrational antipathy resulting from four years of brutal warfare underlying the mentality that rationalised the post-war blockade'.[138] Four years of the world's most intense and successful propaganda played its part in hardening attitudes.[139]

The Germans were quite clear and direct about the consequences of the Allied decision.[140] Majority Social Democrat Scheidemann announced, 'We have no longer any meat. We cannot deliver potatoes because we are short of 4,000 rail cars every day. We have absolutely no fats left'. Vice Chancellor Payer, leader of the Progressive Party protested angrily on 25 October 1918 against the High Command's change of heart and suggestion to continue the war for another winter. The generals, clinging to the old-world order, pleaded that demands by its 'enemies' to the left, centre, amid its own soldiers, and overseas to remove the Kaiser would cost Germany its national and military honour. Von Payer, as a 'burgher and a civilian pure and simple', could see nothing of honour, but 'only the starving people'.[141] Ludendorff replied that things were leading to Bolshevism in the army and at home 'within a few weeks'. If Ludendorff was correct, it pointed to a grievous fault within his own military structure. His prediction, despite a maximum effort by the communists, did not turn out to be true.

Germany kept the pressure up with a detailed note delivered to London via the Swiss at Berne on 14 January 1919.[142] The situation in Germany since the armistice had worsened because of 'unfair interpretation and execution' of the conditions and 'conflicting promises'. 'The severe stipulations regarding the surrender of railway material has greatly hindered the homeward movement of the troops and the distribution of food and coal inside Germany.' There was fear that the provisions stored inside the old boundaries of the empire for the feeding of the German people 'may be lost'. These reports and supporting telegrammes carried on through February where the 'economic situation was growing more gloomy'. 'It is not in the interest of the Allies that Germany should succumb under the strain of the present crisis.' The British Foreign Office set out on 21 January in a memorandum to the Treasury its view on the four reasons for continuing the blockade.[143] The Treasury, the Board of Trade, the War Trade Department and the Department for Overseas Trade were all for removing 'to a large extent' the restrictions. Against them were the Foreign Office, the War Office, the Admiralty, and the Restriction of Enemy Supplies Department. It was the military against the merchants. The blockade was the most effective weapon left to the Allies for 'speedily obtaining peace terms', said the Foreign Office. The continuance of the blockade was 'calculated to secure an early peace'. If the blockade was discontinued, even for a short period, it would be 'impossible again to bring its machinery into operation'. Finally, the blockade meant co-operation; its abolition would bring the 'most fierce trade competition' among the Allies.

The Allies were still not sure of the real situation in the unoccupied zone to the east of the Rhine. On 26 January 1919, the Americans sent the Gherhardi Mission to Germany for a two-month stay to report on political developments; on 30 January Doctors Taylor and Kellogg went to investigate food conditions.[144] The British despatched teams of officers, discussed briefly at the beginning of this chapter, to produce first-hand reports and collectively they provided a good insight into the position on the ground and away from Allied direct scrutiny.[145] The officers concurred that Germany 'appears to be completely beaten and disorganised; further hostilities on any appreciable scale are more improbable'. The nation was on the verge of starvation. The scarcity of food was much more pronounced in the large towns than in the country districts, but the reduction of the food ration has been carried out so gradually that the 'masses are hardly aware of the extent of the reduction'.

The officers' consolidated observations are instructive; their mix of militaristic terseness and real shock at the effects of the famine and shortages ring true. The officers found that, because of the lack of raw materials, industry was nearly at a standstill. The lack of locomotives and rolling stock caused by the fulfilment of the armistice demand was crippling Germany through a lack of coal. There was a great shortage of petrol and other spirits. The thousands of men now disbanded would not be

UB 10 and *UB 13*, sister boats of Georg Gerth's *UB 12*, lie side by side in the part shelter of Zeebrugge mole. They are painted in camouflage and have 'eyes', typical of the Flanders u-boats. *Tomas Termote.*

A hatch had to be totally opened to be able to lower a torpedo into a torpedo room. The crew of *UC 64*, sister ship to Erich and Georg's uc-boats, is busy at the task in Bruges docks. *Tomas Termote.*

A *UCII* boat in the Bruges Zeebrugge canal showing its forward wire cutters and the covers of three of its six mine shafts. *Tomas Termote.*

An aerial view of the mole and harbour of Zeebrugge, approached from land through a sea lock. *Tomas Termote.*

Ludwig von Schröder, left centre, and Karl Bartenbach, surrounded by their officers on the steps of the casino at Bruges, 1917. Perhaps Georg Gerth is pictured? *Tomas Termote.*

Gott strafe England, May God Punish England (for the hunger blockade), was a ubiquitous motto, daubed on buildings, on cufflinks, and imprinted on brown coal bricks. *Brockhaus family archive*.

Hungry Berliners carve up a horse cadaver, 1918.

Käthe Kollwitz's famous etching of 1924 shows German children with their food begging bowls as a result of the British hunger blockade. The Kaiser refused Kollwitz a gold medal because 'medals were for men'.

Salomon Marx and his children, Eduard (in his sailor suit) and Eva, before WWI. *Family archive.*

Erich Gerth and Eva, widowed Countess, von Ahlefeldt, on their wedding day, 27 June 1919. *Family archive.*

Was will Spartakus?

Neuer Militarismus

Junkertum   Kapitalismus

·K·P·D·
(Spartakusbund)

Arbeiter, Bürger!

Das Vaterland ist dem Untergang nahe.

Rettet es!

Es wird nicht bedroht von außen, sondern von innen:

Von der Spartakusgruppe.

Schlagt ihre Führer tot!
Tötet Liebknecht!

Dann werdet ihr Frieden, Arbeit und Brot haben!

Die Frontsoldaten

'What does Spartakus want?' The young Communist wields a sword against a six-headed establishment serpent. Two of the heads, Charles I of Austria and Wilhelm II of Germany, have fallen; four remain, capitalism, new militarism, the Catholic church and the Prussian aristocracy. *German Communist Party poster, 1919.*

The poster, believed directly funded by Salomon Marx and pasted around Berlin early in 1919, which called for the murder of communist Karl Liebknecht.

Erich Gerth in raincoat and felt hat about to board an early Lufthansa flight.
Family archive.

During the night of 16 March 1945, RAF Bomber Command dropped 256
heavy bombs and aerial mines on Würzburg and followed them with
300,000 incendiaries. The fire storm saw temperatures reach 2,000 degrees
Centigrade and produced a proportionately higher rate of death and
destruction than during the attack on Dresden the month before.

Adolf Hitler and Joseph Goebbels visit Ufa in 1935. Not long afterwards, the film studios became a part of Goebbels's propaganda empire.

Erich Gerth's gravestone in the private garden of the German cemetery inside the Vatican, Campo Santo Teutonico. *Emanuele Ojetti.*

Eva and her four children, probably in the United States in the 1950s.
Family archive.

Georg Gerth's wife Maria and her three
daughters; Christa-Maria is the youngest.
Family archive.

Georg Gerth in later years; he died in
1970. *Family archive.*

The gravestone of Georg Gerth and his wider family in Würzburg. Georg and his wife, Maria, are recorded bottom right.

The mysterious 'compressor head', thrown out of *UC 61* in an explosion, and presented to the 4th Belgian Lancers in 1958. *Jacqui Squire.*

The author waits for entry to the atmospheric 'UC-61' bar in Rue de l'Arc de Triomphe, Paris. *Jacqui Squire.*

able to find work. Many returning soldiers were in a state of considerable exhaustion and dirt. Clothes at the depots for returning troops had been sold. There was a shortage of leather goods and warm clothing which cost five or six times as much as before the war.

The Germans were 'hungry, very hungry,' except for the super-rich who could afford to spend 100 Reichsmarks or more a day on food through illicit traders who pervaded the town. Good food was still obtainable in big hotels at very high prices. A 'long purse' would be needed to fill the German larder. For every day life, the use of substitutes for necessary articles of food was at a high degree of perfection. The present scale of rationing could roughly be maintained from January without outside assistance to the end of March, possibly till the middle of April. Prospects for the next harvest were not encouraging due to the lack of manures and to the abnormal numbers of field mice which, because of the mild winter, had attacked the seeds sown in the autumn.

A specific study In Düsseldorf and Cologne noted that the middle class was confined to rationed foods; they could earn enough to save, but not to buy food.[146] Children from seven to fourteen years betrayed unmistakable signs of insufficient diet and were living in poverty. They were noticeably pale and thin and, especially when gathered together in numbers, demanded sympathy.

> You think this is a kindergarten for the little ones. No, these are children of seven and eight years. Tiny faces, with large dull eyes, overshadowed by huge puffed, rickety foreheads, their small arms just skin and bones, and above the crooked legs with their disabled joints the swollen, pointed stomachs of the hunger oedema ... 'You see this child here', the physician in charge explained, 'it consumed an incredible amount of bread, and yet it did not get any stronger. I found out that it hid all the bread it received underneath its straw mattress. The fear of hunger was so deeply rooted in the child that it collected the stores instead of eating the food: a misguided animal instinct made the dread of hunger worse than the actual pangs.'[147]

There were eighty-one *Kriegsküchen*, communal kitchens, for the poor who were largely clad and shod in paper. The kitchens provided a hot midday meal of a basin of soup containing potatoes and either mangold wurzels or cabbage and a so-called meat extract, *viandal*, produced from plants. The soup was thin and unappetising. Twice a week, either a couple of small spoonfuls of stewed meat were added or cold sausage was issued and the soup was strengthened by stock made from stewed horse bones. Both taste and smell were odious. Unsavoury though they were, the authorities regarded the maintenance of these kitchens as vital. They held that if in winter, the masses could not put hot food into their stomachs, there would be 'riotous assemblies and disorders'. The kitchens were a 'bulwark against bolshevism'.

Cassel, in February 1919, was really and truly in a desperate state.[148] Germany was laid low, was quite helpless. There was no longer any danger of it being a menace to anyone, but menace could easily develop. The poor were 'suffering horribly'. Some of the most unfortunate cases were the German officials whose incomes were always small, and who could now exist only by their rations. Everyone's constitution had suffered so much that there was no power of resistance and, when illness came, it was hard to shake off. The mortality amongst women, children and the aged had been 'awful for years past', and was at its worst. Unless help came soon, 'total calamity' stared Germany in the face. Robbery, bankruptcy and general Bolshevism were certain and would spread across the country. The best form of help would be a partial, if not total, lifting of the blockade, the 'sense of which even the most broadminded German could not see'.

George Gedye, after being wounded and before becoming an eminent foreign correspondent, worked for the Allied High Commissioner for the Rhineland. He accompanied the British officers on some of their investigations and his reports in February 1919, published as the *Revolver Republic*, are harrowing.[149] He described his journey to Frankfurt as a 'valuable opportunity of inspecting a starving nation through a microscope'. His small party took fifty days' supplies in 'two enormous packing cases and several sacks of bread'.

> *The rationing of the civilian population was such that we felt ashamed to send down our good meat and vegetables to the hotel kitchen for cooking.[150] Uneatable meat only once a week, artificial butter, pith bread, acorn coffee, aniline jam – we saw and tasted them all among the queues of starving people awaiting their rations. In the slaughterhouse were a few emaciated carcasses (three weeks' supply), including two skinny tubercular cows. The most diseased portions of the latter were cut out and burnt, the remainder boiled and issued for human consumption.*

> *Hospital conditions were appalling. A steady average of 10% of patients had died during the war years from lack of fats, milk and good flour. Camphor, glycerine and cod-liver oil were unprocurable. This resulted in high infant mortality, especially from tuberculosis, kidney and stomach disorders. Old people were simply admitted so that they could die between clean sheets – no effort could be made to save them … We saw some terrible sights in the children's hospital, such as the 'starvation babies' with ugly, swollen heads. For three years the hospital had had no fish, no rice since 1914, no eggs for five months, and for five weeks no butter or fats.*

Gedye's report urged the immediate opening of the frontiers for fats, milk and flour, and confidently asserted that there was not the slightest danger of a broken Germany using the supplies to re-form her shattered army. Gedye noted that the 'terrible blockade was maintained as a result of French insistence and British compliance, with hopelessly inadequate relaxations from time to time, from November 1918 until the Treaty of Versailles was signed in June 1919'. In the Occupied Territory to the west of the Rhine, 'no severity of punishment could restrain the Anglo-American divisions from sharing their rations with starving German fellow-creatures; sentences of imprisonment relentlessly imposed by the Summary Military Courts on civilians for being in possession of Allied property' were powerless to prevent the hungry Rhinelanders from buying or stealing bully beef and bread from the troops.'

While receiving these reports from his officers in Germany, Arthur Balfour, the British Foreign Secretary during the armistice period, summed up the value to British interests of the continuation of the blockade in a memorandum of 21 January 1919.[151] He argued that it would 'speed the signing of the peace treaty and unite the Allies. It would help control the prices of Germany's food imports and prevent them going mostly to the rich. Most importantly, but as yet not put into practice, it would provide a direct supply of food and raw materials to those provinces and proletariats resisting Bolshevism.' Ironically, the first state of Germany to benefit from lifting of the blockade was communist-controlled Bavaria.[152] Balfour saw that the blockade was a substitute for war that would facilitate the speed-up of the demobilisation of the British Army of occupation and at the same time enable the victorious powers 'to avoid the danger of complete Bolshevism in Germany' by ensuring that the distribution of food and other supplies would remain under their control.

In the councils of the victors there ensued a tug of war. 'Endless discussion on the Supreme Economic Council availed nothing, since under the construction of the body there was no way through French obstruction.'[153] Lord David Cecil, British Minister of the Blockade, and American Food Commissioner Herbert Hoover wanted to see food get in.[154] Historian MacMillan saw Hoover's food and relief agency as 'by far the most effective' among the many Allied agencies.[155]

With $100 million from the United States and about $62 million from Britain, [Hoover] established offices in thirty-two countries, opened soup kitchens that fed millions of children, and moved tons of food, clothes and medical supplies into the hardest-hit areas. By the spring of 1919, Hoover's organisation was running railways and supervising mines. It had its own telegraph network. It waged war on lice, with thousands of hair clippers, tons of soap, special baths, and stations manned by American soldiers.

While not doubting Hoover's sincerity to relieve the Germans, Keynes thought the 'underlying motive of the whole thing' was Hoover's 'abundant stocks of low-grade pig products at high prices which must at all costs be unloaded on someone, enemies failing Allies'.[156] The other side 'wanted to keep the Germans on short commons until they signed a peace treaty, and the French, horrified by the devastation of their lands and in the battle zone, did not want the German gold reserves spent for any purpose whatsoever until reparations were paid'. 'Everything turned on the gold.'[157]

Secretary of State for War Churchill showed his resolve in the House of Commons on 3 March.[158] His lengthy statement came at the end of a long discussion on the army estimates and was in stark contrast to his rhetoric of 1914. As was his style, he borrowed language and sentiment already used by others, in the case from Herbert Hoover.

> At the moment, we are bringing everything to a head with Germany. We are holding all our means of coercion in full operation, in an immediate readiness for use. We are enforcing the blockade with rigour. We have strong armies ready to advance at the shortest notice. Germany is very near starvation ... Now is, therefore the moment to settle. To delay indefinitely would be to run a grave risk of having nobody with whom to settle and of having another great area of the world sink into Bolshevik anarchy ... Once Germany has accepted the terms, revictualling can begin ... It is repugnant to the British nation to use this weapon of starvation which falls mainly on women and children, upon the old, the weak and the poor, after all the fighting has stopped, one moment longer than is necessary to secure the just terms for which we have fought.

The problem for those wanting to re-victual Germany was to get the attention of the 'Big Four' – Clemenceau, Lloyd George, Orlando and Wilson – who were 'wrapped up in rearranging much of the world'. Keynes reported that they ...

> ... spent three afternoons debating how many votes Brazil should have on a sub-commission on which questions were not decided by voting; and they had in front of them a long programme of interesting deputations: Copts, Armenians, Slovaks, Arabs and Zionists crowded the ante-rooms of the Quai d'Orsay, and each of them was permitted to make in the presence of the Great Ones a set oration in an unknown tongue.[159]

The story of the final overcoming of the French objection to Germany paying for food with gold was told by Keynes, who was present:

> Meantime, Lloyd George was rousing himself. He can be amazing when

one agrees with him. Never have I more admired his extraordinary powers than in the next half-hour of this conference.[160] *So far, he had said nothing, but I could see from behind that he was working himself up, shaking himself and frowning as he does on these occasions. Now he spoke; the creeping lethargy of the proceedings was thrown off, and he launched his words with rage. This is the sort of thing he said, in this commonplace diction but with an air which swept away the spiders and their cobwebs. He wished to urge with all his might that steps should at once be taken to revictual Germany. The honour of the Allies was involved. Under the terms of the Armistice the Allies did imply that they meant to let food into Germany. The Germans had accepted our armistice conditions, which were sufficiently severe, and they had complied with the majority of those conditions. By so far not a single ton of food had been sent to Germany. The fishing fleet had even been prevented from going out to catch a few herrings. The Allies were now on top, but the memories of starvation might one day turn against them. The Germans were being allowed to starve whilst at the same time hundreds of thousands of tons of food were lying at Rotterdam. These incidents constituted far more formidable weapons for use against the Allies than any of the armaments which it was sought to limit. The Allies were sowing hatred for the future: they were piling up agony, not for the Germans, but for themselves.*[161]

The scales were tipped unexpectedly by General Herbert Plumer, the Commander of the British Occupation Army in Germany.[162] On 7 March 1919, the anguished general told Lloyd George in an outspoken telegram dramatically introduced to the Supreme Council in Paris 'that the rank and file of the army was sick and discontent and wanted to go home because they just could not stand the sight of hordes of skinny and bloated children pawing over the offal from the British cantonments'. The event smacked of contrived theatre, confirmed by Keynes, but it achieved its objective. 'When the civilian politicians mercilessly went on starving German children after the armistice, the British soldier fed them out of his rations; and it was from the army that the first Allied protest came against the infernal cruelty of the continued blockade'.[163] The Big Four allowed the import of 270,000 tons of grain and 70,000 tons of fat monthly, increases of 40 and 180 per cent, to the starving Rhinelanders.[164] It took another fortnight for the first food to arrive. By the end of May, Germany had received less than a month's recommended supplies.

'The starvation of the Germans across the imaginary line of Occupied Territory went on with but little amelioration until the beleaguered and disarmed nation purchased relief from the pangs of hunger with the signature to the Treaty of Versailles.'[165] Under pressure from the British and the Americans to gain control of Germany's merchant fleet and from the French to 'sequester its reserves of gold and hard currencies', food was withheld with increased severity to force the Germans to sign the Brussels agreement of 15 March 1919. No food was delivered before this agreement. Germany surrendered the whole of her merchant fleet and still had to pay over £100 million in gold Reichsmarks and £11 million in neutral currencies to the bank of the British Council in Rotterdam. In return, Germany was permitted to buy with her own money 370,000 tons of food a month until September 1919. The French delegation continued to object to the diversion of German gold from the proposed reparations account to the food account for the payment of relief supplies.[166] On the same day as the Brussels Agreement, The International Red Cross added their voice to the cries for food supply with a detailed letter to the President of the Peace Commission 'impelled by the cause of humanity alone'.[167]

On 7 May, Count von Brockdorf-Rantzau, the German chief delegate, indignantly told the Versailles assembly that, 'The hundreds of thousands of non-combatants who have perished since 11 November 1918 as a result of the blockade were killed with cold deliberation after our enemies had been assured of their complete victory.'[168] Allied preparations to reimpose the full blockade were well underway in case the arrival of food supplies strengthened Germany's combative resolve and they refused to sign the peace treaty.[169] The Blockade Council was instructed in April and on 18 June to make 'every preparation', including the despatch of destroyers to the Baltic. Upon the receipt of a telegramme from the Foreign Office containing the words 'Take action', principally British units were to begin patrols. Planning to receive prize ships was under way at the same time if the Germans did sign.

The blockade ended on 12 July 1919 with the signing of the Treaty of Versailles, but food shortages continued for some months longer and many more died in the interim because the relief was too slow or too late. By the end of October 1918, the reduction in the consumption of protein foods amounted to over 80 per cent.[170] From the end of the shooting war, which had claimed three million military lives in Central Europe to the conclusion of the state of hostilities, the continued food blockade brought about a quarter of a million additional deaths among the civilian population in Germany.[171]

In December 1918, the United Medical Societies of Germany held an extraordinary meeting at the Berlin Medical Society, their papers published in 1919 in a thirty-page booklet, *The Starving of Germany*. It was a cry from the heart of eight senior doctors and administrators, backed with copious research, who had lived through and dealt with the consequences of the food blockade and had great fear if it was not immediately lifted. Their papers were translated into English in an attempt to drive a change of political will. Much of its content duplicates examples already given. One paper with particular knowledge of conditions in Berlin is repeated as

Appendix 8. From the rest, here are a few quotes which deal with the general condition:

From year to year, there has been an increasing change in the mental attitude of the nation ... All enterprise, all initiative, all loftiness of thoughts, are reduced to unproductive depression. Even the child has forgotten how to laugh, play and romp about ... We lack trucks, and accordingly coals. Stagnation in the production of coal is not alone responsible for this distress. For example, the sugar industry is at a standstill, while the nitrogen industry cannot operate properly and threshing machines, not getting their fair share of coal cannot work fully. The lack of trucks prevents us from recovering in time perishable goods such as potatoes, beetroots, etc ... How much anxiety is there for the future when one thinks of the hundreds of thousands of orphans, doomed to find their way through life without any assistance, when further one thinks of the innumerable men and women irreparably injured by poor food, of consumptives who, for years to come – another class of war invalids – will require endless nursing and care ... One day reason will again be knocking at the peoples' doors, asking what is the good of supplying the immense cemetery of the Hunger Blockade with an unending succession of further tens of thousands of victims.

The long-term physiological and psychological impact of the hunger blockade upon Germany's children has received limited examination. As far back as 1916, there were intelligence reports of school attendance in Germany down by 50 per cent 'owing to a lack of sufficient food'.[172] A traveller in the same month said that it was a 'sad sight to see the children; hardly a single child did not bear obvious signs of being underfed'. A medical examination suggested 90 per cent were insufficiently nourished. After the war, when British doctors found that thousands of children were suffering from rickets, it was realised that the Germans thought it an infectious disease.[173] The importance of 'accessory food factors', shortly to be called 'vitamins', had already been clearly demonstrated in Great Britain and these findings had influenced the conclusions of the Royal Society committee on food. For instance, Vitamin B_1, Thiamine, found in rice bran, was discovered in 1910; Vitamin A, Retinol, found in cod liver oil, in 1913. 'This does not seem to have been accepted or acknowledged in Germany. This sad story signalled a fall from grace for German medical science which twenty years before had led the world.'

Tentative conclusions, based on medical research of the last three decades, more than suggests that prolonged malnutrition in infancy and childhood would have considerable and irreversible effect on brain development in the young.[174] The basis for this dreadful hypothesis is back in Trier in 1919 at the same time and place as Keynes' negotiations with his German counterparts over relaxing the blockade and providing food to German civilians. Smiley Blanton was a medical officer with the American Army of Occupation's Department of Sanitation and Public Health. By the time of the war, which he began by directing the psychiatric ward in the hospital at Fort Slocum, New York, Blanton was already a distinguished academic and medic with specialisation in child mental health and speech pathology. The American medical team at Trier began studying physical changes occurring in the local school children due to malnutrition, but encountered so many complaints from teachers and school officials concerning the mental deterioration of the children as shown by their poor school work, and the number of nervous disorders occurring, that it was decided to supplement the physical examination by a psychiatric study. It was a 'unique opportunity' for a high-volume investigation. Blanton explained that the study was restricted to the 6,500 children of the Volksschulen aged between five and a half and fourteen years because it was there that the changes caused by three years on a 'rigid and inadequate diet' were found to be greatest. 'From 40–50 per cent of the children suffered from a noticeable degree of malnutrition.' This contrasted with some 2,000 children seen in Bonn, Coblenz and Cologne. In these cities, Blanton found two reasons. First, the workmen in the large munitions factories received 'very high wages and could buy extra food which was often unlawfully obtained by the factory owners and sold at cost to the workers' and, second, that these city governments took 'excellent measures to prevent malnutrition amongst school children, including free breakfast or dinner for those unable to procure these meals at home'. Blanton felt able to say that conditions in Trier were not typical and were worse than those in general throughout the Rhine Province.

Blanton published his findings within weeks in an article, *Mental and Nervous Changes in the Children of Volksschulen of Trier, Germany, Caused by Malnutrition* (the period of compulsory school attendance), in the publication *Mental Hygiene* and this was reprinted quickly in New York as a pamphlet.[175]

In Trier, a city of about 55,000 people, the poor found during the winter of 1915 that the price of bread was too high. Later bread based on raw grain rye contained a 'great amount of waste material'. After the failure of the potato crop in the summer of 1916, there were 'weeks, even months, when the people had to substitute for potatoes the indigestible turnip, *Steckrüben*'. Milk supply in 1917 was down to 3,300 litres a day from a peace-time level of 18,000 litres. 'The success of people in obtaining extra food depended on their economic status. Those with extra money could always obtain food, such as butter, eggs and meat, even at the worst period of food shortage.' Trier was one of the German cities nearest the front; thousands of troops were stationed in the town and constantly passing through, taking over one-third of the schools; the city was often flooded with wounded after the great offensives; 'all of this created an atmosphere of unrest'. The town was bombed twenty-two times and the air alarm sounded ninety-seven times, mostly during 1918. The siren had a greater claim than the teachers on the attention of the children who were always waiting to rush to the cellars.

Blanton found that with almost every child the quality of school work had declined due to 'malnutrition but partly by war conditions'. The specific changes were a lack of nervous and physical energy, inattention during school hours, poor and slow comprehension for school tasks, poor memory for school work and a general nervous restlessness while in school. The number of children failing to pass their grades doubled to 15 per cent. However, children with 'superior or good average intelligence' could better withstand prolonged malnutrition. Between one-third and one-half of the children were so undernourished that they were unable to walk a few steps without considerable fatigue. So great were the energy changes that the play time had to be reduced and the 'violent running games had to be discontinued'. In the summer of 1918, 'most of the children were not taken for a swim in the Moselle because many were so weak it was feared they might drown'. Where the integrity of the nervous system had been affected by extreme malnutrition in infancy over a period, Blanton saw that normal intelligence had been compromised and that 'feeblemindedness may result'. He concluded that those from poorer stock suffered a 'general and sometimes permanent lowering of the whole intelligence level from even a moderate degree of malnutrition and that the change would be permanent'.

Blanton's findings were supported by other studies by English doctors and by the municipal doctor in Chemnitz in collaboration with the Berlin Teachers' Union in a pamphlet called *Hunger*.[176] 'The lack of mineral salts through the almost complete lack of meat ... produced an increase of irritability, which was noticed by nearly all teachers in their scholars ... stands in the closest relation to the nourishment of the brain ... Scholars who used to be quite clever showed themselves uninterested and absent-minded ... also the moods of depression which overcame the children when they thought about the misery and hunger in their homes ... the education authorities have lowered the standard of work ... Not only has the whole mental development of the school children been hampered in many directions by hunger, but the emotional life and the will power of the growing girls and boys have been menaced.'

Vincent in his authoritative study of the blockade, and particularly its casual extension, was horrified by these implications.[177] Blanton's study and its findings broke new ground. Vincent investigated subsequent work after World War Two, based on Blanton, and subsequently. In 1955, Stoch and Smythe launched a long-term study upon the hypothesis that 'under-nutrition during infancy may result in a failure of the brain to achieve its full potential size and it is not unreasonable to suppose that this may also predispose to inhibition of optimum intellectual and personality development.[178] In the late 1950s, Cravioto became the first researcher to demonstrate that 'malnourished pre-school-age children exhibited decreased mental age' and that as the children got older there was an increasing gap between their mental and actual ages.[179] 'Nutritional rehabilitation is less effective in producing mental recovery in younger individuals.' Studies with rats showed that a restriction of food intake from birth to twenty-one days resulted in a decrease number of brain cells.[180] These results were validated in a study of human children in 1966: 'When near starvation occurs during a significant part of the first year, failure to grow in length and head size is so striking that even under the best of circumstances significant permanent deficits occur.'[181] Lastly, in a list of many more, Margaret Mead concluded in 1970:

> It is true that the starving adult, his efficiency enormously impaired by lack of food, may usually be brought back again to his previous state of efficiency. But this is not true of children. What they lose is lost for good ... [since] deprivation during pre-natal and post-natal growth can never be made up.[182]

Vincent was not shy of confronting the elephant in the room. Assertions that prolonged and extreme hunger and privation had a deleterious psychological impact in the German children of World War I was, for him, amply supported by the evidence.[183]

> Whether one espouses the psychological argument that childhood deprivation fostered irrational behaviours in adulthood or the physiological assertion that widespread malnutrition in childhood led to an impaired ability to think rationally in adulthood, the conclusion remains the same: the victimised youth of 1915-1920 were to become the most radical adherents of National Socialism ... Historians have been struck by the Weimar era's generalised loss of confidence in omnipotent justice serving to regulate the course of human life ... The roots of National Socialism are significantly deeper than the World War I blockade ... However, one cannot intellectually dismiss the important possibility that blockade-induced starvation was a significant factor in the formation of the Nazi character. The defeat of Germany, the failure of the kaiser's military machine, the disillusionment and misery evoked by the war – these factors combined to undermine the naive faith which the greater part of the German people had traditionally placed in their autocratic militaristic social structure. During the chaos of November 1918, the Germans overthrew their rulers and began a process of self-scrutiny. But the process was thwarted. At the same time that the Germans expected a harsh peace, they also anticipated just treatment ... Retention of

the hunger-blockade symbolises the great lost opportunity of post-war Europe.[184]

From the end of the war, doubts began to appear publicly, especially in the United States, and mostly based on anecdotes. Questions were asked about the food supply position in Germany, about exaggerations of the famine, and its relative severity compared, say to Russia, Poland, the Balkans and the Austro-Hungarian empire; and about the use of 'famine' by the Germans to gain sympathy during and therefore to influence the peace talks.[185] In November 1918, a *Washington Post* editorial, 'Let Germany Starve First', said, 'Germans are drawing a little too heavily upon American incredulity and her magnanimity when they ask Americans to regard them as genuine converts to democracy, victims of their late rulers, and deserving of the fatted calf and forgiveness. The German conversion is too sudden and too voluble. Four years of atrocious crimes cannot be wiped out in a week or two of internal disorders and declamations on the beauties of democracy.'[186] Historian Weinreb reported debates in Congress in early 1919 over the distribution of food aid to Europe when 'many senators and congressmen expressed doubts about the level of hunger in Germany' and reported Wilson emphasising to Congress that 'money will not be sent for food for Germany itself, because Germany can buy its own food, but it will be spent for financing the movement of food to your real friends'. In July, *The Sunday Times* in London issued a warning lest 'the sentimental folk who cry out for pity for the German children forget that Germany used most of her milk for munitions purposes'.[187] These harsh, even crass, words contrast with the consensus historical view, 'Despondency and fatigue overwhelmed [Germany]. If the lack of food contributed to the German defeat it was not because the Germans were dying in vast numbers, but because the grinding misery of never having quite enough to eat wore down the morale of the people'.[188]

> *In spite of the delays, Hoover knew that sooner or later there would have to come a break in the blockade. Starvation was the wedge and fear of Bolshevism the hammer that would crack it open. With every passing day, the choice of the Allied government was being narrowed down by the consequences of their own policies. Millions of people, ragged, war weakened, and unemployed, were eating less than enough to sustain human life. In Germany, by no means the worst famine area on the map, the toll of the dead was officially 800 a day, and city after city fell into the hands of the revolutionists. Knowing a break in the blockade was inevitable, Hoover prepared for the moment by piling up 1,200 million pounds of fats and 100 million bushels of wheat in Copenhagen, Amsterdam, Rotterdam and Antwerp. But in Paris, the Big Four were talking about democracy and justice, and haggling over*

*the spoils of war. Yet there was no time when the Allies would not
have opened up the blockade if the United States had agreed to pay
Germany's food bill. To make matters even less logical, the Allies were
spending huge sums, far in excess of the total German gold reserves, in
helping the White Russians fight the Red Russians. Allied policies were
obviously contradictory and self-defeating.*[189]

In London, the cry against the continuation of the famine was led by Bernard
Shaw and members of the Labour Party. In July 1919, they rushed to print a
compilation of *Family Life in Germany under the Blockade*, gathered by Lina
Richter from reports by doctors, school nurses, judges and teachers. Shaw,
in his preface, said that it was 'easy to forget about the German children,
and work yourself up into a frenzy of determination that the Kaiser shall
be hanged to avenge the victims of the submarine campaign. In Cologne,
with famine-wasted children begging for the refuse of your meals, or
mutely watching every morsel you eat with a hungry eye, it is impossible'.
Richter was a Berliner, the daughter of one of the banking Oppenheims,
who became a teacher of philosophy at Leipzig University. During the
war, she supported a hospital donated by her family. She believed that,
even during the war, that if the people had known the full facts about the
Allied blockade it would have been banned, 'condemned by the loathing
of the whole world as the most horrible of all methods of war'.[190] Richter's
book is full of difficult observation. She notes that children born later in
the blockade averaged between four and five pounds in weight. 'Only in
rare cases could there be a joyful preparation for the expected child.' It was
almost possible to procure the necessary bed linen.

The German government signed the Treaty of Versailles partly because
it knew that refusal would mean a worsening of the famine. On 12 July
1919, eight months and a day after the armistice had been signed, the
blockade ended.

*In retrospect, the project of economic pressure as a divisive weapon
gives rise to unease.*[191] *No doubt Hankey would have answered, and
rightly, that it was merely a contingency plan, and that it was left to
Germany to start the war. This act placed a large credit in the moral
balance of the Allies, and, despite the early violation of maritime law,
they remained in moral credit at the end of the war. Their economic
blockade against the German home economy made no distinction
between combatants and non-combatants. Germany became a moral
void that the Allies, with their rhetoric of virtue and their large reserves
of food, were well placed to fill ... Those who invoke the law of nations
must be ready to live by its precepts. Clause XXVI of the Armistice
said that the existing blockade would remain in force, but the Allies
would 'contemplate the provisioning of Germany as shall be found*

necessary'. As A J Balfour said a few months later, 'Almost a promise has been made'. The Allies could only impose final justice on Germany by resorting to measures that they themselves had proscribed before the war. In doing so, they could no longer plead necessity. That is the key point. The legal position is debateable (legal positions always are), but the moral aspect was clear. As the blockade continued to inflict starvation on Germany into the winter of 1918-19, the Allies rapidly exhausted their moral credit. In depriving the Germans of food, the Allies applied military power for political and economic ends, in a way that increasingly sapped the determination of their officials and officers in Germany and at Versailles. Moreover, the Allies brandished the threat of renewed blockade to impose the peace treaty on the Germans. This weighed heavily with the Social Democrats in Germany when they decided to sign the treaty. In his reply to the Allied terms, which was addressed to his compatriots as much as to the Allies, the German delegate Brockdorff-Rantzau made a bid for moral equality:

Crimes in war may not be excusable, but they are committed in the struggle for victory, when we think only of maintaining our national existence, and are in such passion as makes the consciences of peoples blunt. The hundreds of thousands of non-combatants who have perished since 11 November, because of the blockade, were destroyed coolly and deliberately after our opponents had won a certain and assured victory. Remember that when you speak of guilt and atonement.

Six days' later on 18 July 1919, General Jan Smuts sent his highly-regarded farewell message to the English people:

A new life, a new spirit, is imperatively necessary ... The continent which is the mother-land of our civilisation lies in ruins ... with its peoples broken. Starving, despairing ... seeing only red through the blinding mists of tears and fears. It is the most awful spectacle in history, and no man with any heart or regard for human destiny can contemplate it without the deepest emotion ... No, it is not a case for hatred or bitterness, but for all-embracing pity, for extending the helping hand to late friend and foe alike, and for a mission of rescue work such as the world has never seen ... You cannot have a stable Europe without a stable, settled Germany, and you cannot have a stable, settled prosperous Great Britain while Europe is weltering in confusion and unsettlement next door ... In our policy of European settlement the appeasement of Germany, therefore, becomes of cardinal importance.[192]

In 1920, German agricultural output stood at only half its pre-war capacity and domestic food production did not reach its 1913 level until 1928.[193]

Several historians offered their summaries: 'The guilt of the world press in covering up the atrocity is compounded by the fact that the American and British public were told of the starvation itself, but were kept ignorant of the criminal policies of the Allies which produced it.'[194] 'The armistice had ended the fighting on land, but the naval blockade continued even tighter and compelled the German government to accept a deeply demoralising peace.'[195] 'The prolongation of the blockade was the victors' greatest mistake, leaving a residue of burning hate for future politicians to fan.'[196] 'Owing to the effectiveness of the blockade, privation wore down the military efficiency as well as the health and morale of the people of the Central Powers. These facts indicate that blockade, while it is less bloody than fighting on the battlefield, may in the long run do more injury to the physical welfare of the blockaded nation. Looked at from this point of view, blockade is more barbarous than fighting on the battlefield. There can be little question that the physique of the blockaded nations for several generations will suffer from ill nutrition of parents and children. Blockade thus extends the effects of war to a much larger number of human beings, and thus increases greatly the scope of war. For these reasons blockade should be condemned because it has been the constant effort of the humanitarian forces in modern civilisation to limit as narrowly as possible the scope of war.'[197] 'The long-term shortages, partly caused by the blockade, partly by the Central Powers' declining ability to pay for imports, but mostly by the enemies' ownership of the resources, were more decisive in shifting the military balance than shortages of food.'[198]

In 1924, Germany's international food relief stopped as the economy stabilised and hyperinflation ended. Hoover's programmes provided much food to the German nation, but used propaganda to institutionalise an image of the United States as the main provider of food relief, not for the undoubted debt and profits which accrued, but as an 'effective, even necessary, weapon in the fight against Bolshevism'.[199] Hoover famously dismissed the Bolshevik Revolution as a 'food riot'.

Three years later, the prominent agronomist Friedrich Aereboe published a study of the influence of World War I on agricultural production and 'concluded that Germany would have been better off if it had followed the liberal course of integrating into the world economy in the nineteenth century. Agriculture should have been scaled down, freeing up workers for industry to produce manufactured goods for export which would then, in turn, have paid for increasing imports of food and consumer goods.'[200]

In April 2007, the International Association for the Study of Obesity released the results of a recent study of European overweight.[201] It unexpectedly revealed that Germany had become the 'fattest country in Europe'. The country was embarrassed to find itself second only to the United States in its percentage of overweight population. ... Especially upsetting was the fact that the Germans had surpassed the English, who had long held the dubious title of 'fattest Europeans' in comparative weight tables.

ENDNOTES

1   Chief Petty-Officer Roman Bader, 'Bavarians in the Irish Sea', Neureuther, *U-Boat Stories*, p. 90.
2   Fürbringer, *Legendary*, p. ix.
3   Chapter 3, 'Planning a famine'.
4   Wegener, *Strategy*, p. 76, fn. 7.
5   Gesundheits-Amt Schaedigung der deutschen Volkskraft durch die feindliche Blockade (Denkschrift des Reichsgesundheitsamtes, 12/1918). Vincent, *Politics of Hunger*, p. 141.
6   Grebler, *Cost of the War*, p. 78.
7   Hull, *Scrap of Paper*, p. 168. Winter and Robert, *Capital Cities at War*, Vol. 1, p. 517. Roerkohl, *Hungerblockade*, pp. 309–13. Vincent, *Politics of Hunger*, throughout.
8   Kramer, 'Blockade' in Winter, *First World War*, Vol. II, p. 486.
9   Weinreb, *Modern Hungers*, p. 29. Strachan, *First World War*, pp. 328–29. Chapter 12, 'Prisoners of war'.
10 Blanton, *Mental and Nervous Changes, Trier*, pp. 30–31.
11 Rubner, 'Von der Blockade und Aehnlichem', *Deutsche Medizinische Wochenschridt*, Berlin, Vol. 45, No. 15, 10/4/1919.
12 Parmelee, *Blockade*, pp. 221–25.
13 Howard, 'Social and Political Consequences', pp. 167–68.
14 Grebler, *Cost of the War*, pp. 77–78.
15 *TNA*, FO 382/1836, f. 11663, 'Germany / Blockade', 9/1/1918. Howard, 'Social and Political Consequences', p. 165.
16 Remarque, *Im Westen nichts Neues*, the renowned semi-autobiographical novel, is studded with references to battlefield food and has a shocking home-coming scene. Remarque, incidentally, was wounded at Passchendaele in the battle to defend the Flanders u-boat canals. He later escaped the Nazis with an American visa facilitated by Marlene Dietrich who also appears in Chapter 15, 'Salomon Marx and the film business'. Remarque's second wife was another film actress Paulette Goddard; he was her third husband following Charlie Chaplin and Burgess Meredith.
17 Mayer, *Politics and Diplomacy*, p. 282.
18 Of particular use are the selected documents of the Supreme Economic Council, and other organisations, prepared and edited by Bane and Lutz, *The Blockade of Germany After the Armistice 1918-1919*; and the translation, also by Lutz, of parts of the officially authorised inquiry of the German parliament into the reasons for Germany's failure at the end of World War I, *The Causes of the German Collapse in 1918*.
19 Raico, review of Vincent, *Politics of Hunger*, partly citing Peterson, *Propaganda*, p. 83.
20 Chapter 3.
21 Offer, *Morality*, p. 100.
22 Fisher, '*Submarines*', 20/4/1904. *TNA*, ADM 116/942.
23 *TNA*, CAB 16/5.
24 Hankey, *Supreme Command*, Vol 2, p. 858. Strachan, *First World War*, p. 208.
25 Porch, *French Army*, p. 205.
26 Kramer, 'Blockade' in Winter, *First World War*, Vol. II, p. 484.
27 Hull, *Absolute Destruction*, pp. 248–57.
28 Chapter 14, 'Welcome home, Erich'.
29 Davis, *Everyday Life*, p. 24.

30   Schreiner, *Iron Ration*, pp. 4–5.
31   Schreiner, *Iron Ration*, p. 8.
32   Schreiner, *Iron Ration*, p. 14.
33   Weinreb, *Modern Hungers*, p. 23.
34   Vincent, *Politics of Hunger*, pp. 17–20. Berghahn, Imperial Germany, pp. 241–42. Herwig, First World War, p. 88.
35   Asprey, *German High Command*, p. 49. Hull, *Entourage*, p. 268.
36   Hull, *Absolute Destruction*, p. 204.
37   Dunn, *Blockade*, p. 128.
38   Davis, *Everyday Life*, p. 1.
39   Davis, *Everyday Life*, p. 65.
40   Davis, *Everyday Life*, p. 20.
41   Davis, *Home Fires*, pp. 80–84.
42   Schreiner, *Iron Ration*, pp. 55–57.
43   *TNA*, FO 371/2679, support from a report by a traveller from Cologne to Darmstadt and Mayence, received in London 20/5/1916, p. 42.
44   Teuteberg, 'Food Provisioning', Zweiniger-Bargielowska, *Food and War*, p. 61.
45   Blum, 'Living standards', p. 557.
46   *New York Times*, 'How Germany's Food Problem Was Met', 16/4/1916, quoted in Weinreb, Modern Hungers, p. 23.
47   Cooper, *Behind the Lines*, Letters 1914–1918.
48   Blücher, *English Wife*, p. 122.
49   Doty, *Short Rations*, p. 122.
50   Starling, 'Food Supply', pp. 225–54.
51   Kloot, 'Analysis of Energy Balance', pp. 186–89.
52   Henderson, *Ernest Starling*, pp. 117–19.
53   Becker, *Oubliés de la Grande Guerre*, p.46.
54   Chapter 4, 'Erich's war'.
55   Kramer, 'Blockade' in Winter, *First World War*, Vol. II, p. 488.
56   *TNA*, FO 371/2679,18/5/1916, pp. 17, 25, 41, 93, 116.
57   *TNA*, FO 371/2679, 1/5/1916, pp. 26, 99.
58   Chickering, *Urban Life*, p. 217.
59   *TNA*, ADM 137/3876, 'Extracts from Daily War Orders, German High Seas Forces', 'Potato Harvest', Berlin, 9/12/1916, pp. 119–22.
60   Schreiner, *Iron Ration*, pp. xii, 160.
61   Vincent, *Politics of Hunger*, pp. 8–9, 21–22.
62   Afflerbach, *Falkenhayn*, pp. 371, 506, quoted in Hull, *Absolute Destruction*, pp. 220–21.
63   Hull, *Absolute Destruction*, pp. 294–95.
64   Ludendorff, *Urkunden*, p. 67. Original emphasis.
65   A rutabaga is today called a swede, a cross between a turnip and a cabbage.
66   Chickering, *Urban Life*, pp. 270–71.
67   Dunn, *Blockade*, p. 129. A cockchafer is the May bug.
68   Becker, *Oubliés de la Grande Guerre*, pp. 73–74.
69   Chickering, *Urban Life*, pp. 209–10.
70   Cooper, *Behind the Lines*, p. 182.
71   Strachan, *First World War*, pp. 263–64.
72   Lutz, *Causes of German Collapse*, pp. 180–87.
73   Chickering, *Urban Life*, p. 225.
74   Dunn, *Blockade*, p. 133.
75   Parmelee, *Blockade*, p. 219. Blücher, *English Wife*, p. 169.
76   Chickering, *Urban Life*, pp. 346–47.
77   Glaeser, *Class 1902*, pp. 270–71.
78   Richter, *Family Life*, p. 15.
79   *The Daily Telegraph*, 5/7/1917, p. 1.
80   The following events are taken freely from Horn, *Mutiny on the High Seas*, principally pp. 32–137.

81   *TNA*, ADM 137/3060, p. 10.
82   Horn, *Mutiny*, pp. 41–42. Chapter 2, 'Kaisertreu'.
83   Horn, *Mutiny*, pp. 39–40.
84   Horn, *Mutiny*, p. 43.
85   Schreiner, *Iron Ration*, pp. 92–103.
86   Teuteberg, 'Food Provisioning', Zweiniger-Bargielowska, *Food and War*, p. 68.
87   Hoover, *Weapon of Food*, p. 197.
88   Weinreb, *Modern Hungers*, pp. 13–14.
89   Kloot, 'Analysis of Energy Balance', pp. 186–89.
90   Grebler, *Cost of the War*, pp. 79–83.
91   Chickering, *Urban Life*, p. 217.
92   Howard, 'Social and Political Consequences', pp. 163–64.
93   Teuteberg, 'Food Provisioning', Zweiniger-Bargielowska, *Food and War*, p. 68.
94   Tarrant, *U-Boat Offensive*, p. 45.
95   Bell, *Blockade*, p. 601.
96   Schreiner, *Iron Ration*, p. 76. Parmelee, *Blockade*, p. 227.
97   Kloot, 'Analysis of Energy Balance, pp. 190–91.
98   Berghahn, Imperial Germany, pp. 241–42.
99   Flemming, *Landwirtschaftliche Interessen*, p. 87.
100 Chickering, *Urban Life*, p. 219.
101 Lummel, 'Food Provisioning', p. 20, quoted in Weinreb, *Modern Hungers*, p. 22.
102 Blücher, *English Wife*, p. 231.
103 Chickering, *Urban Life*, pp. 553–54.
104 Ludendorff, *War Memoires*, Vol. 1, p. 349.
105 Chapter 13, 'Guilt and blame'.
106 Chickering, *Urban Life*, pp. 564–65.
107 Raico, *Great Wars and Great Leaders*, p. 202. Berlin Medical Society, *Starving of Germany*, Appendix 8, p. 6.
108 Vincent, *Politics of Hunger*, pp. 63–64.
109 Willis, 'Hoover and the Blockade', in Cox, *Modern European History*, p. 265.
110 A fuller account is given in Chapter 13.
111 Willis, 'Hoover and the Blockade', pp. 265–68.
112 Bouton, *Abdicates*, p. 251. Appendix 6.
113 Compare the American office of mediation of 1915 which did just this and which the Germans accepted and the British declined.
114 Keynes, 'Dr Melchior', *Two Memoirs*, pp. 22–23.
115 Cox, 'French Peace Terms', pp. 82–85.
116 Willis, 'Hoover and the Blockade', p. 286.
117 Howard, 'Social and Political Consequences', p. 183.
118 Manning, Scott, History Detectives – Churchill's Efforts to Feed Germany after the Great War, Finest Hour, p. 24 (winstonchurchull.org, accessed 25/5/2017).
119 Weinreb, *Modern Hungers*, p. 27.
120 Keynes, 'Dr Melchior', *Two Memoirs*, p. 24.
121 Willis, 'Hoover and the Blockade'. Davis, *Home Fires Burning*. Lutz, *Causes of the German Collapse*. Lutz & Bane, *Blockade After the Armistice*. Vincent, *Politics of Hunger*. There is a voluminous literature on the Treaty of Versailles and its consequences.
122 Willis, 'Hoover and the Blockade', pp. 277–78.
123 Herbert Hoover in Willis, 'Hoover and the Blockade', p. 282.
124 Howard, 'Social and Political Consequences', pp. 181–82.
125 Kloot, 'Analysis of Energy Balance', p. 191.
126 Keynes, 'Dr Melchior', *Two Memoirs*, pp. 27–28.
127 Blahut, 'Allied Attempt to Starve Germany', pp. 11–14.
128 Howard, 'Social and Political Consequences', pp. 171–78.
129 *TNA*, FO 371/3451, p. 152, 16/11/1918.
130 Howard, 'Social and Political Consequences', pp. 170–71.
131 Arnold-Forster, *Blockade*, p. 29.

132 Roerkohl, *Hungerblockade und Heimatfront*, p. 309, quoted in Weinreb, *Modern Hungers*, p. 29.
133 Cole, *Beatrice Webb's Diaries*, 17/11/1918, p. 137. Strachan, *First World War*, pp. 328–29.
134 *The Times*, 16/11/1918, p. 6.
135 Jones, *Violence*, pp. 262–63.
136 Herwig, 'Total Rhetoric', p. 1.
137 Winter, 'Versailles Treaty – Grand Bazaar', p. 2.
138 Vincent, *Politics of Hunger*, p. vi.
139 Chapter 9, 'Your truth, our truth'.
140 Howard, 'Social and Political Consequences', p. 169.
141 Kitchen, *Silent Dictatorship*, pp. 263–64.
142 *TNA*, FO 608/221, pp. 461–63.
143 *TNA*, T 1/12275.
144 Bane and Lutz, *Blockade*, pp. 35–41.
145 *Reports by British Officers on the Economic Conditions Prevailing in Germany*, 12/1918 to 3/1919.
146 *Reports by British Officers*, pp. 34–43.
147 Friedrich, *Before the Deluge*, cited by Keynes in Blahut, 'Allied Attempt to Starve Germany', pp. 11–14.
148 *Reports by British Officers*, p. 86.
149 Gedye, *Revolver Republic*, pp. 26–27.
150 Gedye, *Revolver Republic*, pp. 30–31.
151 Howard, 'Social and Political Consequences', pp. 185–86.
152 Blahut, 'Allied Attempt to Starve Germany', pp. 11–14.
153 Keynes, 'Dr Melchior', *Two Memoirs*, p. 41.
154 Kloot, 'Analysis of Energy Balance', p. 191.
155 MacMillan, *Paris 1919*, pp. 41–42.
156 Keynes, 'Dr Melchior', *Two Memoirs*, p. 26.
157 Keynes, 'Dr Melchior', *Two Memoirs*, p. 55.
158 *Hansard*, House of Commons Debates, 3/3/1919, Vol. 113, cc69–183.
159 Keynes, 'Dr Melchior', *Two Memoirs*, p. 41.
160 Supreme War Council, 8/3/1919, at the Quai d'Orsay in Paris.
161 Keynes, 'Dr Melchior', *Two Memoirs*, pp. 56–59.
162 Willis, 'Hoover and the Blockade', pp. 297–301.
163 Richter, *Family Life*, pp. 5–6.
164 Bane and Lutz, *Blockade*, pp. 35–41.
165 Gedye, *Revolver Republic*, pp. 32–33.
166 Howard, 'Social and Political Consequences', p. 184.
167 *TNA*, FO 608/72.
168 Blahut, 'Allied Attempt to Starve Germany', pp. 11–14. Howard, 'Social and Political Consequences', p. 161.
169 *TNA*, Cust 49/480; FO 608/72.
170 Flemming, *Landwirtschaftliche Interessen*, p. 87.
171 Howard, 'Social and Political Consequences', p. 162.
172 *TNA*, FO 371/2679, 18/5/1916, pp. 25, 49.
173 Henderson, *Life of Starling*, p. 119.
174 Vincent, *Politics of Hunger*, p. vii.
175 Blanton, *Mental and Nervous Changes*.
176 Richter, *Family Life*, pp. 24–27. Lorentz, Berlin, *Hunger*.
177 Vincent, *Politics of Hunger*, pp. 160–65.
178 Stock and Smythe, 'Nutrition during Infancy', pp. 546 onwards.
179 Cravioto, 'Application of New Knowledge', pp. 1803–9.
180 Winick and Noble, 'Cellular Response in Rats', pp. 300–6.
181 Graham, 'Growth during Recovery', pp. 740 onwards.
182 Mead, 'Changing Significance of Food', pp. 176 onwards.
183 The first links between food deprivation with National Socialism were made by historian

Loewenberg, 'Psychological Origins of the Nazi Youth Cohort', pp. 1457–1502.

184 Vincent, Politics of Hunger, pp. 162–64. Vincent cites Childers, Nazi Voter; Hamilton, Who Voted for Hitler?; Kater, Nazi Party; Kohn, Mind of Germany; Mosse, Crisis of German Ideology; and Viereck, Roots of the Nazi Mind.

185 Weinreb, Modern Hungers, pp. 34–48.

186 Bane & Lutz, Blockade of Germany, pp. 638–39.

187 Bane & Lutz, Blockade of Germany, p. 798.

188 Collingham, Taste of War, p. 25.

189 Willis, 'Hoover and the Blockade', p. 296.

190 Richter, Family Life, pp. 13, 17.

191 Offer, Morality, pp. 113–14.

192 Quoted in Richter, Family Life, p. 57.

193 Teuteberg, 'Food Provisioning', Zweiniger-Bargielowska, Food and War, p. 70.

194 Blahut, 'Allied Attempt to Starve Germany', pp. 11–14.

195 Offer, Working Classes, pp. 217–18.

196 Kloot, 'Analysis of Energy Balance', p. 191.

197 Parmelee, Blockade and Sea Power, pp. 254–55.

198 Kramer, 'Blockade', in Winter, First World War, Vol. II, p. 489.

199 Weinreb, Modern Hungers, p. 37.

200 Kutz, 'Kriegserfahrung und Kriegsvorbereitung', pp. 73–74. Cited in Collingham, Taste of War, pp. 26–27.

201 Berliner Zeitung, 'Deutsche führen Liga der Dicke an', 20/4/2007, quoted in Weinreb, Modern Hungers, p. 1.

CHAPTER 12

Prisoners of War

France's actions were completely contrary to those of the other Allied countries. Their evil intentions became clear – they wanted to exploit the prisoners as long as possible. No single measure of the French government would create more hatred than the cruel treatment of German POWs in the reconstruction zones from December 1918 ... As a consequence, a new protest movement arose in Germany accusing France of the 'murder of the souls of our prisoners'.[1]

The immediate interrogators at Wissant thought that the crew of *UC 61* was relieved to have finished with the discomfort, stress and every day danger of life in a u-boat. There was almost none of the 'East Prussian' arrogance that was shown the previous year by the crew of *UB 26* captured at Le Havre.[2] 'No side or bravado was shown.' Only one junior member of *UC 61* was defiant and refused to answer questions. On the contrary, Georg Gerth, the commander, was talkative, helpful and apologetic for his lack of military knowledge. In truth, the French interrogators found the crew a little disappointing.

Since the declaration of unrestricted submarine warfare in January, the rate of loss among the coastal submarines of the Flanders Flotilla had begun to rise. The simpler and safer days of 1916 were unlikely to return and crews knew that their chances of survival were decreasing. With hindsight, these u-boat personnel now had less than a 50 per cent chance of staying alive until the end of hostilities. 'The men of the fleet reckoned that a submarine rarely survived its tenth trip.'[3] Another piece of hindsight would have given the crew further pause. Three of their number would be dead before release and the remainder would all be incarcerated for almost a thousand days, half of which time would be after the ceasefire.

As the twenty-six men waded ashore, there was no evident animosity. Curiosity, certainly, as the village population moved to the beach. Perhaps even respect, tinged with a little fear. None of the guards, when they were eventually found, had to hold back an angry crowd of local people. The crew stood idly outside the town hall while they waited for the first decisions as to their future. The slight illegality of losing personal papers perhaps still rankled, but the crew were allowed to keep their tobacco and pieces of bread and sausage. After the early morning excitement, *UC 61* was no longer their responsibility.

The announcement that they were to walk more than twenty kilometres to Calais in a rising summer sun may have caused surprise as they watched French military vehicles stream into Wissant. The cars, though, held senior French officers and the lorries contained men and equipment concerned only with making safe the still burning u-boat and the dozens of munitions lying inside and outside the craft. The crew with an average age of twenty-three were all fit submariners less than a day into a patrol. Their Belgian mounted cavalry escort arrived importantly and prepared to herd the captives to their destination. One can imagine some choice exchange of words with the lancers. Many of these men were survivors from the retreat from Belgium into France of 1914 and had seen no action since then.[4] Some carried thoughts of families left behind in their occupied homeland and of friends dead in scattered horseback skirmishes; all these memories would have been leavened with a strong resentment based on the numerous horrific tales of German atrocities against supposed Belgian franc tireurs. However, pictures of the country walk to Calais through the villages of Hervelinghen and Saint-Inglevert suggest more of a stroll than of a tense affair with bayonets at the ready.[5]

The crew reached Calais in good order with some evidence of haughtiness, enjoyment even, as they marched along busy boulevards. Gerth's monocle caused comment. The lunchtime crowds, brought quickly by the news of the capture, were interspersed by a large number of gawping young female lacemakers.[6] This spectacle was in sharp contrast to Germany where from 1914 the streets would be cleared before the transport of military prisoners and, later, laws were passed to prevent any fraternisation.[7]

Whether in Germany or in France, the passage of prisoners in a town raised curiosity, and often hatred amongst the population, particularly if it was a question of a town near to the front.[8]

Perhaps the first sight of the impressive walls of the Calais Citadel gave the crew some concern. This was unmistakably a medieval prison fortress: a cobbled entry through tower and portcullis, arrow slots in thick stone double walls, windows with iron grilles, and a teeming interior full of motor transports, weaponry and many hundreds of potentially hostile enemy soldiers. However, imprisonment and twenty-four hours of close examination may not have been so immediately distressing for a group of men used to the conditions inside a cramped submarine.[9]

But what next? How long before they were moved? Where to? Would they go as a group? When would they be separated from their officers? Would they be punished for their avowed wartime trade of starvation? Some foodstuffs were already difficult to find locally. Prices were rising. Everybody seemed to know someone who knew someone who had been killed by a u-boat. Would treatment of imprisoned submariners be different from that meted out to soldiers captured in land battles?

> *Why didn't you stay at home? Why did you go to sea when you know what threatens? Why do you or your governments force us to destroy your ships wherever we can find them? Do you think we are going to wait until our own women and children starve and let you keep your bread baskets full before we defend ourselves? You have started it. You are responsible for the consequences. If you would discontinue your inhuman way of carrying on the war then we would let your sailing ships and steamers pass unmolested, when they do not carry contraband. You have wanted war to the knife. Good, we have accepted your challenge.*[10]

Direct expectations of the sailors came from news of their comrades who had already been captured. Prisoners of war were generally encouraged to send postcards and a fixed number of letters a month. Prisoners were allowed to write to whomever they pleased and that often included letters directly to friends and officers in their home units and also, in the case of commanders, to the families of dead crew. These letters were scrutinised and censored for militarily valuable information about tactics, units, equipment, commanders and morale as well as for news about broader concerns, particularly the three-year Allied blockade and its effects on industry and civilian life. Captured u-boat men reported prison conditions in England that were more boring than bad. Food was said to be better and more plentiful than at home. However, the unknown for the crew of *UC 61* was the condition of prison camps in France for most u-boat men who survived the loss of their vessel were taken to Britain. This was because much of the responsibility for patrolling the merchant shipping lanes, certainly those leading to the English coasts, and also for dealing with German maritime sorties into the North Sea and the English Channel, was the province of the Royal Navy. When the Royal Navy fished enemy sailors out of the water, they took them home with them.

Many u-boat officers were placed at Donington Hall in Leicestershire, which Kapitänleutnant Freiherr Edgar von Spiegel von und zu Peckelsheim, commander of *U 93*, found was the 'best prison camp in England, and if there were any better they must have been de luxe places indeed. It was one of the most beautiful country seats in England, a great grey castle in a perfect setting on green lawns and oak trees. Sheep were grazing on the meadows and birds singing in the trees.'[11] Peckelsheim was left in the water when his boat went down on being hit by a Q-ship. He was greatly surprised when he heard later that the boat had survived and been brought over 2,000 miles back to Wilhelmshaven by Leutnant Wilhelm Ziegner, 'scarcely more than a boy', on his first cruise. Engine-room Petty Office Walter Gach of *U 48* wrote home in December 1917:

> *You notice nothing of the war here. We were sent by rail to London and we shall shortly be leaving here for the camp. I have been here for eight days already, and we are very well off and could not wish for anything better. I am in a large room with five of my comrades and we do nothing else but eat and smoke and look out of the window. You see plenty of life here; there are no wooden soles or bicycles with wooden tyres here yet, and the butchers' shops have rows and rows of pigs hanging up. There is no prospect of starving England. I am glad the war is over for me.*[12]

Indirect expectation was a more concerning matter. Prisoners of war were used in various ways from early in the war as retaliatory bargaining chips: withholding access to food parcels or exercise, forcing punitive and dangerous labour or placing prisoners in the front line as human shields. Both sides publicised their retaliations widely in order to shame the enemy or to force a change in policy or behaviour by exciting public opinion.[13] This publicity would certainly have reached u-boat crews as newspapers from both sides were generally available to them.

For example, on 15 March 1915, Winston Churchill when First Lord of the Admiralty, described as 'pirates' thirty-nine men captured that month from two scuttled u-boats. *U 8* was trapped in nets, forced to surface and fired on by HMS *Gurkha* and HMS *Maori*; *U 12* was rammed and shelled by a British destroyer off Fife Ness leaving twenty dead.[14] While the men awaited a threatened trial at the end of the war for their alleged piracy, Churchill had them segregated in isolation in naval detention barracks at Chatham rather than placed in prisoner-of-war camps.[15] The conditions at Chatham were later acknowledged by the u-boat men as far from Spartan. However, compare Werner Fürbringer's view after being depth charged in *UB 110* in 1918 and before being sent north to a camp at Colsterdale near Manchester:

> *I was held for four weeks in the Detention Barracks, four gruelling weeks in solitary confinement, beset by agonising worries and a sense of grinding outrage.*[16]

Churchill's emotional and badly thought through response to unrestricted submarine warfare sought a quick and dramatic headline. The Germans responded in kind with the same number of carefully chosen upper-class British officers, some wounded, placed in much tougher conditions in

German camps. They endured weeks of solitary confinement, primitive sanitation, restricted exercise and semi-starvation. The outcry in the British Parliament was quick and intense.[17] Churchill's decision, with which he was not immediately identified by the Government, was called a 'great mistake' and a 'piece of absolute folly'. While serious charges of 'special treatment', apart from segregation of u-boat men at Chatham, were denied, the British parliamentarians were appalled, indignant and powerless at what they 'knew' as retaliations ordered personally by the Kaiser, 'the ever-present nightmare of the Slavonic force which besets the heart of the average German [and accounts] for the present frenzied lunacy of the German people. In these bestialities, they are playing the game of angry children; we will not follow them in that.'

Charges of piracy could not be sustained. 'On a purely practical point, a u-boat with a small crew crowded into a cramped space, could not possibly commit the essence of piracy, which surely was to board a prey, carry off its cargo and capture the vessel. U-boats had no hands to spare for prize crews and not much space for extra cargo or prisoners on board.'[18] Churchill was forced into a humiliating climb down which gave his many domestic enemies further and sufficient ammunition to remove him from office soon afterwards.[19]

From then on, Britain largely avoided carrying out any reprisal against prisoners of war. The Director of the Department of Prisoners of War at the War Office even viewed reprisals as un-British: 'Our national characteristics are opposed to the ill-treatment of a man who has no power to resist and this especially in the case of one who is not personally responsible for the acts complained of.'[20] U-boat personnel were still given 'differential treatment' in prisoner-of-war camps although nobody quite specified what this meant. King George made his own protest to the Prime Minister about Churchill's instruction. The king favoured 'generous and magnanimous consideration to our prisoners-of-war'.

Most captives had been taken on fluid battlefields which, on the western front, meant during the German advance and the French response of 1914. Trench warfare provided fewer and fewer opportunities for surrender. To obtain intelligence, patrols were despatched to drag individuals by force through the Allied lines.[21] From the beginning of 1915, French prison camps were, therefore, relatively stable in numbers except during the big offensives. By chance, official figures for the number of German non-officer naval and military prisoners held in France were released the day before UC 61's crew was captured: there were 44,016 of which 876 were in hospital, almost parity with those held in the United Kingdom.[22] It was not until the German Spring attack and subsequent collapse of 1918 that numbers rose dramatically. 'The British Army made more captures in 1918 than it did in the previous three years of the war combined.'[23]

However, taken over all fronts, 'the scale of captivity was staggering' and was almost the same as the 'risk of death'. In this, the Great War was different from previous conflicts. The huge number of eventual prisoners was a phenomenon without precedent in history involving between six and a half and eight million men, about one in every ten soldiers of all the nations involved. Eventually, there were 530,000 German prisoners held on French soil.[24] The sheer numbers forced the introduction of mass, industrialised, militarised captivity. Defensive battlefield technological advances were adapted in the construction of prisoner-of-war camps to ensure prisoners could not escape – barbed or electrified wire, sentry towers with machine guns, floodlights and guard dogs. Sophisticated railways ensured that food supplies regularly reached camps.

'The way prisoners are treated is also a way of waging war.'[25] French and German experience of managing prisoners came from the Franco-Prussian war of 1870 and initially they used the same camps, but these were soon found to be insufficient. There were too many prisoners to hold without causing epidemics and protests. In the first period of World War I, there was much improvisation. The French constructed pre-fabricated 'Adrian' barracks from light wood panels with tar paper roofs which were difficult to heat in winter. There were nearly 500 detention sites, either in mainland France or in its colonies. The main urban centres and their suburbs or the ports united several detachments under the one authority. The communes of less importance, or those in rural areas, grouped together prisoners who were then taken daily to factories, work sites or agricultural work. Each work company was to contain 425 prisoners 'not to be employed within range of enemy activity'.[26] The number of Germans employed in labour companies rapidly increased. By 26 January 1917, 22,915 German prisoners were working directly for the French war effort.[27] Combatants were required to operate their prison camps according to common law and military codes enhanced by external rules such as international conventions or rules adopted by the warring parties after agreements between them. Visitors to the camps, sent by neutral powers and humanitarian or charitable organisations, found that the methods employed did not always meet legislated standards.

The prisoner had become useful as a currency of exchange, as a hostage, and as an object of retaliation. Above all, the prisoner became a worker in the service of the economy of the country where he was held prisoner.[28] The requirement for manpower everywhere was too great to let this pool of prisoner labour remain unused. Prisoners could no longer be fed for doing nothing so, as a minimum, they could 'replace farm workers and other workers gone to the front, the wounded, the dead or those themselves prisoner of the adversary'. This supply became indispensable.

In rural areas, German prisoners were a blessing for the farmers.
Amongst them there were many who had worked the land in their own

country and it was with a real sense of pleasure that in captivity they took up their former occupations with agricultural machinery under the watchful eyes of the territorial guards. Throughout the war this foreign work force which carried out agricultural work benefited from excellent living conditions. [29]

The Red Cross calculated that at least two thirds of prisoners in France and Germany were sent to work detachments, sometimes far from the camp at which they were registered and to where their parcels were sent.[30] Conditions for prisoner-of-war labour companies attached to the French army were frequently poor often due to supply problems which dogged, particularly, the newly established camps.

However, cultural attitudes also played an important role; the indifference to these captives' welfare indicates a certain attitude that prisoners were expendable – revealing an ongoing process of brutalisation. Although never justified as an official reprisal, the treatment was also certainly perceived in terms of retaliation by the French personnel involved. [31]

While conceding this criticism, many French historians insist that the situation of German prisoners could never be compared to that of the French in the German zone.[32] From the end of 1916, the treatment meted out to prisoners in Germany became 'more and more rigorous'. French and English doctors not only accused their German colleagues of not being on top of things, but also to have provoked epidemics by willingly mixing Russian prisoners carrying typhus with other soldiers. 'One sees here how war is carried out by all means. Each one being persuaded by the determination of the other to beat them. The *war of the lice* counts as much as that of the cannons.'[33] Quickly, prisoners became dependent on the laws of the state which captured them. 'All appeal by prisoners for the regulations and laws of their own country would be useless; the prisoners being currently under just the laws of the captive government.'[34]

The Geneva Convention of 1906 allowed prisoners to be put to work, but excluded officers, civilians, churchmen, health workers, invalids, wounded and the incapable. Camp commanders spontaneously gave the prisoners tasks concerned with hygiene, cooking, laundry for the common good and to guard against idleness. Day-to-day life could change at any moment if the men were caught in a tornado of maltreatment inflicted upon them as retaliation. 'To the end of the war this menace hung over all camps and detachments.' 'The life of a prisoner went very slowly, sadly and exhaustingly.' Sexual frustration also afflicted prisoners 'although this was largely a taboo subject'.[35] There were also cultural fears that prisoners would lose their virility or return after the war with homosexual tendencies. Efforts were made in many camps to provide courses in reading, gardening, letter writing, sport, camp newspapers, theatre, music, choirs, hobby workshops, and learning a foreign language.

Minimum rules of laws of war agreed in various pre-war conventions, ratified by the British, French and German governments, had to be respected. There were regular bilateral agreements as the opposing governments struggled to find formulas to deal with the numbers. One of the new arrangements between the French and German governments, negotiated at Bern, Switzerland, came into force on the day of the capture of the crew of *UC 61*. The main points of The Hague Convention on Land Warfare of 1899, modified in 1907, quickly became outdated.[36]

Prisoners were not to be seen as captives of individuals, but of the captor state; they were not to be treated as individuals, but as legal, disarmed enemies. Prisoners 'must be humanely treated' and allowed to keep all their private property with the exception of arms. They could be employed in work, so long as it was not related to war operations, nor should it be exhausting or humiliating. The captor nation was responsible for feeding and clothing the prisoners, on the same peace footing as that of its own soldiers. Prisoners were not to be compelled by force to impart information about the military situation or their nation ... prisoners should be removed immediately after capture to camps at least thirty kilometres from the firing line.

Some of these agreements were quickly put aside, for instance on the level of feeding. By 1915, the Allied blockade was beginning take insidious effect. To emphasise the immorality of depriving civilians of food, the Germans decided to feed prisoners of war at the same level as German civilians.[37] Generally, German troops almost throughout the war received better rations that the civilian population. In response, the Allies fully utilised the right of prisoners to receive food parcels to ensure their men held prisoner by Germany were protected in some degree from their blockade's impact. Across western Europe, a complex and effective food parcel scheme developed. German prisoners held in France and Britain also received parcels sent from home. 'However, as the war progressed and the blockade's impact tightened, it became more difficult for families to send individual parcels; increasingly they received care packages bought directly from the International Red Cross.' Many prisoners, especially officers, could also receive money sent by bank mandate to purchase food locally. 'Overall, prisoners of war were the subject of a mammoth charitable aid effort during the war which encompassed both domestic and international organisations such as the International Committee of the Red Cross at Geneva, the Vatican and the Young Men's Christian Association.' This process drove a 'rapid modernisation of wartime humanitarian aid delivery and charity lobbying techniques'. With feeding of prisoners no longer solely the responsibility of the captor state, prisoners' access to food became a 'lottery, based on how well served their location was by rail and

444 SOUND OF HUNGER

by how much food either charities or their home state could provide'.

The Church of Rome's efforts in Germany to ameliorate the conditions of prisoners was led by the papal nuncio in Munich, Monsignor Eugenio Pacelli who became Pope Pius XII in 1939. Pacelli was to be a referee in 1922 for Georg Gerth's brother Erich's application to the German Foreign Office.[38] In 1915, Pacelli 'focussed on the plight of the vast populations of prisoners-of-war on both sides ... a whirlwind of administrative activity ... in every diocese where there were prisoner-of-war camps, bishops were required to enlist priests with appropriate language skills to set up links between prisoners and families'.[39] Working with the International Red Cross and the Swiss Government, Pacelli negotiated exchanges of wounded prisoners and, reportedly, as a result of his efforts, an estimated 65,000 prisoners were sent home. Pacelli's department also busied itself with searching for news of the missing and the dead, and managed funds supplied by the Holy See for the purchase of medicine and food.

Throughout the war there few naval men amongst prisoners taken by the French: while men from the Kaiserliche Marine could be counted in tens, and fliers by the handful, it was the German army that was counted in hundreds of thousands. This may have been a saving grace for the crew of *UC 61* because initial conditions for soldiers taken at the front by the French were usually not good. The rarity of u-boat men and the importance of their equipment and practices meant in-depth interrogations were far more likely than if they were foot soldiers. It also meant that there was no discernible special treatment or navy camps for sailors. Because their capture happened away from the trenches they were often taken to prisons either in metropolitan France or behind the front in the military zone. Newly-taken prisoners in the military zone were 'kept in large collection centres where conditions were generally overcrowded with very rudimentary sanitation' before being sorted into different categories for divergent treatment – Alsace-Lorrainers, Poles, officers, and skilled and unskilled workers.[40] There were regular claims of random beatings by guards. Prisoners were quarantined for fifteen days in these holding camps before moving to permanent wooden barracks with bunks or beds with sacks filled with straw and a blanket and no heating. Daily rations were meagre: ¼-¾ litres of coffee; up to two litres of noodles, rice or soup; 400-500 grams of white bread; sometimes with added beans, potatoes or lentils. This food had to suffice for a ten-hour day spent on heavy manual tasks such as forestry, road or railway building, quarrying or loading stores.

Even though many aspects of French prisoner of war labour companies are well documented, there is no complete cohesive plan of the entire French camp system or of their inhabitants. Broadly, camps fell into two categories, those run by the Army behind the front line and known to the Germans as *Gefangenen-Kompagnie* (G-K) companies and those in regions in metropolitan France run by the formal prisoner-of-war system. Some sources suggest that all the G-K companies were in the military zone and used for military labour. The Germans compiled and published an atlas in May 1918 of the eighteen metropolitan French regions and their many constituent camps.[41] For instance, in Region XVIII there were seven depots. Georg Gerth was imprisoned in one of these, the Île d'Oléron which was centred on Fort La Galissonnière. The depot was responsible for three camps at Jotonnière, Saint-Pierre-d'Oléron and Saint-Georges Chéray, together containing 192 prisoners. Other regions had dozens of depots, and some depots had dozens of camps. The atlas included the numbers of prisoners in each region and each camp was mapped. In the French military archives at the Chateau de Vincennes east of Paris, there are boxes of haphazard records. Many days can be spent on off-chance searches. By 1 June 1918, France had captured 243,590 German prisoners.[42] Of these, 46,664 were working in prisoner of war labour camps for the French army.[43] The remainder had been assigned to work in the French interior or consisted of prisoners who were exempt from working because they were officers or wounded.[44]

Today, there is a burgeoning record of millions of individual prisoners being developed by the International Committee of the Red Cross (ICRC) in Geneva.[45] All of the crew of *UC 61* were entered quickly into the system after capture showing a necessarily efficient process.[46] *UC 61*'s officers were quickly separated from the men.[47] The two sea officers, Gerth and Karl Dancker, the second-in-command, and Johannes Giese, the engineering officer, were received at Montoire-sur-le-Loir by 5 August. The twenty-three crewmen were taken to G-K 84 holding company, probably in the Oise, this move being recorded on an ICRC fiche on 27 August. These fiches identify individual *UC 61* crew members so that there is no doubt about provenance. They also give full name, rank, date and place of birth, and name and address of next of kin which has proved useful in discovering more information about individuals and their families. Individual fiches in the ICRC files, when found, often contain 'P' numbers, which provide online links to further documents, which mostly concern camp transfers and details of illnesses.

For German naval personnel, there is a short cut. Each combatant country was required to report to their adversary the whereabouts of captives held and also to report any movements between camps. German naval archives with limited numbers to track still hold some of the alerts received from the French.

The first German prisoner-of-war record found that includes the crew of *UC 61* is dated 15 May 1918 and lists u-boat crews held in France.[48] There is a second list, dated 10 July 1918, which shows that nine crew members had been moved, including Gerth to a more secure officer's camp following an escape attempt, while Max Eggers and Andreas Nagel joined Max Pucknus at port locations, and Paul Schindler was in hospital in Brest. These stories are covered later. The remaining five men, Otto Bock, Georg Gerigk, Adalbert Neumann, Willi Sänger and Michael Weidner, changed their work camps.

By far the most complete list is dated 31 March 1919, over four months after the end of the war.[49] It is typewritten and compiled by German naval staff from information sent to them by the French, and includes the date of entry of each man into the French prison system. This date is the same as the date of capture for those taken on the mainland or near the French coast; for men captured overseas the date indicates the time of landing in mainland France. Handwritten annotations have been made in pencil and pen as new information on individuals was received. The first date of registration on the list is 17 December 1914, the latest date is 27 May 1918. There are 471 captives named, officers and men, who are held in seventy-five named camps and eight separate numbered G-K companies with a small number of men whose work camp location was not known. This level of dispersal, especially for officers, suggests a policy of deliberate separation rather than chance allocation. The list may well be as far as possible complete because every expected vessel that provided prisoners can be found. The great puzzle of the lists is to find the location of the G-K companies. A G-K company, each with an alphanumeric identifier, is almost always a collection of small camps in a locality. Even if the general location of a G-K company is known, placing an individual prisoner in one of its constituent camps is all but impossible.

Many of the prisoners in the German list dated 31 March 1919 were from marine infantry and artillery regiments and were captured in the fluid fighting near the coast in December 1914 after the Battle of the Marne.[50] The three principal ships' contingents were from the armed cruiser SMS *Kaiser Wilhelm der Grosse*, a converted passenger liner; the light cruiser SMS *Königsberg* on which Erich Gerth served before the war; and SMS *Möwe*, a survey ship. *Kaiser Wilhelm der Grosse* eluded the British blockade and, for a few weeks in August 1914, operated as a commerce raider. On the 26th, just three weeks after breaking out into the Atlantic, she was surprised by the British light cruiser HMS *Highflyer* while lying in Spanish Saharan waters off the Rio de Oro. *Kaiser Wilhelm der Grosse* sank from gunfire in shallow water with the surviving crew putting ashore in the boats. The *Möwe* was scuttled at Dar-Es-Salaam, the administrative and commercial centre of German East Africa, later British Tanganyika and then independent Tanzania, under threat from British cruisers. The *Möwe* was intended to supply *Königsberg*, which met her fate from British monitors after hiding deep in the Rijufi River, about 200 miles south of Dar-Es-Salaam. What is remarkable is that the crews of these three ships who were able to reach land were only and gradually captured over the next two years. The crews of the *Möwe* and the *Königsberg*, in particular, took their ships' guns and joined with the *Schutztruppe*, the colonial troops in the African territories of the German colonial empire in east Africa.

They fought the Belgians and the British on Lake Tanganyika and also with Lieutenant Colonel Paul Emil von Lettow-Vorbeck, known to the Germans as the 'Lion of Africa', who commanded the one German force to invade British imperial territory.[51] Lettow-Vorbeck was a veteran of the Battle of Waterberg that forced the Herero into the Kalahari Desert to die of thirst in 1904, witnessed the declaration of von Trotha's Extermination Order, and the following year was sent to fight the Nama.[52] Lettow-Vorbeck surrendered his much reduced and emaciated East African force only at the end of the war. One of *Königsberg*'s officers, Oberleutnant Walter Rosenthal, held in the camp at Cholet on the River Moine with Oberleutnant Wilhelm Smiths, commander of *UB 26*, was an undoubted hero of the East African force.[53] He was captured by Belgian native Askaris after repeatedly swimming into an armed camp on Lake Tanganyika to discover information about warship building which would be damaging to the Germans. Rosenthal and a fellow officer, Odebrecht, took the 'most outrageous chances with their lives, disguising themselves with cork and blankets as natives and stealing ashore night after night'.

The three u-boats represented were crews from *UB 26*, entangled in nets and scuttled off Le Havre in the March of the previous year, twenty men; *UC 38*, depth charged by French destroyers in December 1917 in the Ionian Sea, eleven men; and *UC 61*, twenty-six men. Six naval flying officers from the seaplane station at Zeebrugge were held at different camps including Friedrich von Arnauld de la Perière, captured in 1916, the brother of Lothar, the Mediterranean u-boat ace, and the year class mate of cadet Erich Gerth.

One of the fliers, Joseph Kaspar, was held at the Montoire camp on the Loir River near Orléans with three other officers, Karl Dancker, *UC 61*'s second-in-command, Johannes Goldermann from the Flanders Flotilla torpedo boat *A 19*, and Hans Gayer of the Zeppelin *L 49*.[54]

Torpedo boat *A 19* was rammed and cut in two by the British destroyer HMS *Botha* on 21 March 1918.[55] It was part of a German force intercepted while bombarding Dunkerque as part of an investigation of defensive artillery to see whether the port could be captured.[56] Admiral Ludwig von Schröder, commander of the MarineKorps Flandern, and Georg Gerth's superior officer, thought a capture would aid both Hindenburg and Ludendorff's Spring offensive of 1918 and also protect and facilitate the Flanders Flotilla's u-boat campaign. Goldermann was one of a few lucky survivors picked up by a French destroyer; another, Köller, was in PoW company *Gefangenen-Kompagnie 84* at an unknown location alongside seven members of the *UC 61* crew, stokers Friedrich Becker, Christian Carstensen and Wilhelm Starke; radio operator Otto Bock; machinist Fritz Bödrich; seamen Willi Sänger and Johannes Giese, the naval engineer.

The presence of Giese, who gave evidence at the court of enquiry in 1920 into the loss of *UC 61*, suggests that there was, at least, an engineering officers' section at this camp. In the German navy at this time there was a 'decided effort to suppress and thwart the drive toward advancement of inferior social groups such as engineering officers and warrant officers'.[57] Naval engineers were looked down upon as technical personnel. In 1911, the inspector of the navy's education department suggested that engineers should be drawn from families of 'lower than middle-class background in the future' so that they would 'give up their social pretensions' and content themselves with the position 'they deserve'. Whether this subjugation by his own people extended to officer Giese's standing in his French prisoner-of-war camp is unclear.

The final large contingent of prisoners on this 1918 list of German marine prisoners in France was the crew of two Zeppelins, seen as naval craft, eleven men from *L 49* and fifteen from *L 50*. *L 49* provided one of the iconic pictures of World War I when it crashed nose down into woods at Bourbonne-les-Bains and became the first German airship to be captured intact. It was photographed the next day surrounded by French peasants by Albert Moreau.[58] Moreau was one of the French army photographers who attended the stranded *UC 61* on the beach at Wissant.[59] *L 49* and *L 50* were part of a group of eleven Zeppelins that bombed England on the night of 19 October 1917. On their return, they ran into headwinds and fog and eight accidentally crossed into central France. Four were lost, two destroyed by Allied gunfire, and two, *L 49* and *L 50*, were forced down by the French *Crocodile* squadron. 'Engineers took the *L 49* apart and developed a series of blueprints and reports to evaluate design improvements since 1914 ... The plans served as the basis for the development of airships after the war.'[60]

Eight of *UC 61*'s crew of twenty-six are accounted for at Montoire and G-K 84. Georg Gerth, the commander, was at Boyardville officers' camp on the French Atlantic Coast; Max Pucknus, the petty officer on loan for a single patrol from the battleship SMS *Schleswig Holstein*, was at Rouen-Croisset, possibly after early internment at Dieppe; reserve navigator Hubert Lengs was at the hamlet of Serres-Carpentras near to Avignon in the far south; machinist Paul Barthold at G-K 13, a community of camps including Bellinglise, Coup-Gueule, St Leger-aux-Bois and Choisy Aux Bac in the Oise region; stoker Paul Schindler at G-K 25; and the remainder, bar two, at G-K 90: seamen Max Eggers, Paul Ihn, Kurt Koch and Adalbert Neumann; machinist mates Georg Gerigk, Peter Kleinsorg and Alfred Naumann; stokers Franz Goosman, Karl Raabe and Michael Weidner; and b'swain's mate Andreas Nagel.

The second b'swain's mate, Franz Zäbische, was at G-K SA5 in 1918 which was at Pont-Sainte-Maxence and, again, in the Oise region, seventy kilometres from the front. In 1919, Zäbische was in Paris at the 'Bureau de renseingnements', literally an information office, or more probably the intelligence section of the French Deuxième Bureau counter-espionage section, which makes for an unsolved puzzle. What could a twenty-two-year-old junior petty officer have known that was of particular interest and required special attention in the French capital in 1919? There is just one oddity in Zäbische's war-time career offered up to his interrogators, his service on SMS *Vineta*. This posting may have confused or interested the French. In an effort to maintain security, a second SMS *Möwe*, a commerce raider that was causing great concern in the Atlantic, was temporarily renamed *Vineta*, after another auxiliary cruiser which had been withdrawn from front-line service. In this guise, *Möwe* set out on a series of short cruises during the summer of 1916 to attack Allied shipping off the coast of Norway. But then, this posting was equally claimed by one other *UC 61* seaman, Paul Ihn, who had no recorded special attention.

The final crew member was the one man not on the German prisoner list of 1919, seaman Willy Neumann. Neumann was twenty-three-years-old and had been with Gerth on *UB 12*, the only witness to all of Gerth's operational patrols. Neumann died less than three months into captivity on 17 October 1917.[61] The rapidity of the death of a supposedly fit young man so soon after capture offers just a hint of accident or brutality.

The two other crew members to die before release were Karl Raabe on 23 January 1920, of whom nothing further is known except that by the time of his death he had been moved to G-K 80B, and Paul Schindler on 26 July 1918 who has a most interesting story. The imprisonment of Max Pucknus and, later, Andreas Nagel at Rouen is part of an important wider tale of retaliation. Finally, the attempted escape by Georg Gerth by u-boat from his island prison needs detailed investigation.

Most prisoners survived captivity in western Europe.[62] About 25,000 German prisoners died in France. Death rates for British and French prisoners in Germany were around 7 per cent, Germans held in France had a death rate of 6.4 per cent and Germans held in Britain had a death rate of 3 per cent. 'Most significantly, too, these death rates were almost entirely other rank prisoner deaths.' In general, the main home front camps saw little disease except for the major typhus epidemic of 1915, which killed millions in Russia and Easter Europe particularly, and the 1918 influenza epidemic which was even-handed.[63] The death rate for the crew of *UC 61* was 11.5 per cent, but this is too small a sample from which to draw any conclusions.

Paul Schindler was born in 1895 in Kleinzschocher near Leipzig in Saxony, an unmarried son of Gustav and Mary.[64] He joined the 1st Werf Division at Freiwilly in October 1915 for ten months' training and then attended the School for Stokers in Kiel. After a spell at the u-boat base in Zeebrugge, he was ordered to Bremen to join his first u-boat, *UB 29*, and from there in December 1916 to *UC 61* for her commissioning. Schindler's timing was exemplary as on *UB 29*'s next patrol after he left, it was sunk by two depth charges from the destroyer HMS *Landrail*, south of Goodwin Sands, with all twenty-two hands lost.

Schindler died in Davos-Wiesen, Switzerland, a year to the day from his capture at Wissant. He was first taken on his own from Calais to G-K 25 which was headquartered at Roye, thirty-seven kilometres from the front line. Roye provided workers for two sugar beet refineries at Baurin and Wawignies, close to the Belgian border, at a claimed sixty and seventy kilometres from the front. Under the auspices of the agricultural authorities of the Somme, the company also provided workers for Tilloloy and Crépy-en-Valois where the furnaces were heavily bombed by the Germans early in 1918.[65] Schindler was moved by 13 March 1918 to the Seamen's Hospital at Brest.[66] He had bronchitis, but there is good reason to suspect that it developed into tuberculosis.

While in Brest, Schindler underwent a searching interview which was a little unusual, first because he was in hospital presumably because of the condition that was to kill him within four months and, second, because this was a long time after his initial interview with the rest of the crew at Calais.[67] The interview was conducted by Lieutenant de Vaisseau Cariou, commander of the French submarine Sirène, who used Engineer First Class Tasizza as his interpreter. Their handwritten report was discovered by chance in archives in Cherbourg. Cariou's command of the Sirène suggests this was an opportunistic encounter, more to do with his wish for personal knowledge rather than any official French naval request. Sirène was the first of four submersibles in its class, laid down in 1900 in Cherbourg and launched the following year. By 1918, these craft were antediluvian, indeed all were scrapped the following year. They were torpedo boats with four tubes which could go under water to just thirty metres. However, diving took six to nine minutes and was achieved by flooding the space between the inner and outer hull. One imagines that any commander of one of these vessels would have been keen to learn what a modern u-boat could achieve. It is interesting, though, that Cariou spent little time discussing UC 61 with Schindler and moved quickly on to a detailed and lengthy investigation of the capabilities of UB 29, Schindler's first posting. 'Given that the prisoner had been on board the grounded submarine at Wissant and thinking that all possible information had thus been gathered on this vessel, we decided to concentrate this interrogation on UB 29.'

Schindler's condition worsened quickly. As a result, he was accepted for participation in a great humanitarian experiment which was universally described as 'one of the few good things to have come out of the war'.[68] Article 2 of the Geneva Convention allowed the warring sides to send home prisoners incapable of taking up arms again because of their wounds. Repatriations could only happen through a neutral territory and needed the involvement of the president of the Swiss Confederation, Giuseppe Motta, and the papal nuncio, Eugenio Pacelli.[69]

Only the idea of humanity has given to the vigilant neutrality the character of compassion and human tenderness and without these general human qualities neutrality would have remained unsubstantial and lifeless.[70]

The French-German exchanges, the first to be organized, began through Switzerland in March 1915 and those between Germany and Britain followed in December through the Netherlands. Under the auspices of the Swiss Red Cross, very sick soldiers, amputees, the blind, the deaf, those paralysed or gassed, and those wounded about the face, and with advanced syphilis, were considered as non-combatants and transferred to their home country. As the war continued, the grounds for repatriation were gradually widened from purely physical to recognising the 'good of families' and also that, after eighteen months, 'captivity seemed to become almost impossible to put up with', which produced a category which became known as 'barbed wire psychosis'.

In the main camps, the prisoners suffered from a feeling of being crushed, overwhelmed, and at the same time they did not want to make a new life because of the monotony of their life with its limited horizons. Real life was elsewhere. Torn between a refusal to accept the camp, which was their personal defeat, their capture and the desire to live in the best possible way under their unfortunate circumstances, they often fell into what was called depression, which developed in some of them, certainly as the years passed, into a 'barbed wire psychosis', which transformed itself into a nervous illness.[71]

Negotiations concerning men with tuberculosis and other long-term diseases began in February 1915. These were men who could not be healed in less than a year. 'The authorities were under no illusion as to the possible duration of the war and needed to be assured that a tubercular patient, once cured, would not return to arms. 'Thus was born the original idea of internment in a neutral country like Switzerland, for those prisoners not sick enough to be repatriated, but too sick to be left in POW camps.' Men were chosen from the POW camps by joint nationality medical commissions for internment in the Swiss mountain resorts of Leysin, Montana, and Davos and also in Denmark, Netherlands, Sweden and Norway.[72] From 1916, Switzerland received the greatest number of French and German soldiers, about 30,000 a year. Prisoners were interned for the duration of the war, their own countries agreeing to return any who escaped.[73] In parallel, doctors and priests inspected the sanitary and spiritual requirements of the prisoners and sought ways of fighting epidemics, particularly typhus and tuberculosis.[74] In all, 219,000 prisoners were exchanged or interned in a neutral country during the course of the war.

More than 1,200 volunteer workers with the International Committee of the Red Cross dealt with all the requests for information on prisoners of war.[75] Each day the agency received 8–10,000 letters which they acknowledged and forwarded as quickly as possible. The archive of information grew to 400 metres long. Today, six million files have been restored and computerised.

Schindler followed a well-worn and successful path.[76] Initial tests were carried out at his prison camp where he put himself up for internment. All those selected were brought to Lyons where they were examined by a Commission of Control. Schindler passed and, together with other successful internees, went at 1525 by daily train from Lyons-Bretteaux under the guard of an officer, an NCO and seven soldiers to arrive at Geneva at 1930. Here, carriages were separated and sent to allotted destinations. For Schindler and other Germans this was Davos-Wiesen. The French were taken to Leysin-Montana. The first group of one hundred German internees taken from French camps, all suffering from tuberculosis, arrived in Davos on 26 January 1916.[77] There was a temporary reduction of internees in April 1917 due to a new agreement that soldiers cured of tuberculosis could go home on condition that they should not be ordered to fight again. By July 1919, 2,500 German prisoners had been interned which translated to a German colony of about 1,400 at any one time.

The men were quartered in hotels, boarding houses and sanatoriums.[78] Special consideration was given to 'hotels in distress because of the war' and it was necessary to choose those that were little frequented by foreigners to avoid 'promiscuous association'. 'These establishments in no way resemble hospitals; sleeping accommodation for large numbers are rare; the rooms are bright and attractive and can, as a rule, receive two, three or at the most four occupants.' Proprietors were paid six francs for the officers and four francs for the soldiers with an increase for tuberculosis patients for whom extra food on a planned menu was necessary.

The Swiss arranged an impressive array of educational courses for the German prisoners. Those who were students before the war or for whom a change of career would be necessary because of disability were encouraged to travel to the university towns and were enrolled for free.[79] It is unlikely that Schindler was well enough for this option, but around 400 men enrolled for a vocational college, the *Deutsche Internierten-Fachschule*, which was managed by the local German-language school in their own building or in the Davos Dorf Casino or the community centre.[80] There were seven classes, including general education and foreign languages, commercial studies, craftsman apprenticeships, examination studies, academic subjects at higher levels, practical hand skills, and a library with drawing facilities.

Internees like Schindler who died at Davos were initially buried at the Waldfriedhof Davos Platz.[81] Early in 1917, plans were made to establish a separate cemetery near the Wolfgang pass. The German Sanatorium, *Deutsche Heilstätte*, made available a plot of woodland which was inaugurated on 27 October 1918. The remains of forty-six internees, including Paul Schindler, were transferred to the new *Soldatenfriedhof*. Initially the graves had wooden crosses which were later replaced by granite stone with individual names carved. There is a small hall of honour where a commemorative plaque reads, 'Here rest in peace German warriors. In hospitable foreign parts far from home they also died for their fatherland.'[82]

The likely experiences of the three crewmen of *UC 61* who found themselves based at French port cities was decidedly tougher, especially at Rouen and Le Havre. Their captivity smacked much more of the German retaliation applied to Churchill's thirty-nine 'pirates' held at Chatham. Luckily for the *UC 61* crewmen Eggers, Nagel and Pucknus, their involvement came towards the end of the episode. Again, it was actions by the French and the British which sparked the crisis.

> *It seems only right that if the utilisation of prisoners can be made to prove beneficial, it should be the whole body of the people, ie, the state alone which should benefit by it. German labour belongs to the whole country; the whole country alone has the right to profit by it. Therefore, when prisoners are placed in ports where the dockers are paid six, eight or ten francs a day, the contractors should not be permitted to benefit by prison labour at one franc fifty a day.*[83]

In 1915 and 1916, the French decided, first, to put German officers on hospital ships as human shields as a response to u-boat attacks and, second, to send German prisoners-of-war to less sanitary camps in North Africa to ease overcrowding in France. Then, the French and the British began extensive long-term employment of German prison labour near the front, including the French use of German prison labour to work under shell-fire on the Verdun battlefield. The British changed their practice of always carrying their battlefield prisoners across the channel. They diverted some 1,500 carefully-monitored German prisoners of war from the UK to work in Rouen and Le Havre from April 1916.[84] These German prisoners formed the first permanent British prisoner work units in France and were intended to load and unload French ships and to ease congestion in French ports. In exchange, the French gave the British army direct access to forests and quarries, to be worked with prisoner labour. This helped overcome a tonnage crisis in spring 1916 caused by German submarine warfare and the difficulties of bringing wood and stone from the UK to the British army in France.[85]

There are copious reports of the Rouen work parties in the British Foreign Office files.[86] The prisoners' principal complaints concern being forced to work, day after day, in all weathers. 'Ceaseless rain was falling. We were given no choice, but to work. We were told that if we did not obey the signal within ten minutes and go to work, every tenth man would be court-martialled and shot ... Here you must either work or die.' The order applied equally to men with no experience of manual labour during which they were expected, for example, to carry sacks of flour weighing 200 pounds. Camps were rudimentary. Men lived in sheds without floors, the ground consisting of loose cinders. The roofs were not watertight. The walls had no lining and were 'very draughty'. There were no tables or seats.

'What began in 1916 as a limited German reprisal clearly deteriorated in the winter of 1916-17 into something much more ruthless.' German reactions may have been measured, but they always raised the stakes.[87]

> *Germany employed French prisoners from middle-class intellectual professions in marshland drainage work in a reprisal action in 1915. Yet it was the German army which carried out the most extreme reprisals of the Western Front belligerents. In 1916, it sent thousands of French and British prisoners to work on the eastern front, near the front line, in sub-zero temperatures in reprisal for the British decision to use German prison labourers [at French ports]. This 1916 action was followed by an additional German reprisal in 1917 when the German High Command ordered that all newly captured British and French other ranks, taken prisoner unwounded, were to be held near the front line and between 10,000 and 20,000 French prisoners from camps in Germany were to be sent to join them. They were to have 'no provision of protection from the weather; no hygienic care; only meagre food; long and exhausting work without any restrictions, including transport of munitions and fortification work under enemy fire'.[88]*

Allied soldiers were used as human shields in the front line. The French, particularly, could see their comrades labouring in front of them in the direct line of fire and, after some military indecision, this caused the deliberate loss of their own men. There was a great deal of resentment. As with the 'pirates', the Germans carefully publicised their retaliatory actions. This punishment was to be highly visible, carried out symbolically upon French prisoners whose real suffering would 'chastise the metaphorical body of the French nation for its misdeeds'. Outgoing post from French prisoners was forwarded with speed. 'In a very real way, therefore, the German spring reprisals of 1917 used violence as a spectacle and theatre.'[89] The French received a German ultimatum that, if France did not withdraw all German prisoner of war labourers to at least a distance of thirty kilometres behind the front, Germany would increase its retaliation.[90] The withdrawal of German prison labourers was to be carried out as swiftly as possible and completed by 5 May 1917.

> *The prisoner reprisals came at a very tense phase of the war for both Germany and France. Following the massive losses in the Somme and*

Verdun battles of 1916, the German military leadership decided to retreat to a stronger defensive position on the western front and to focus upon the outcome of the unrestricted submarine warfare campaign.

The French Commander-in-Chief, George Robert Nivelle, was adamant that the French should establish their own reprisal camps for German prisoners in retaliation. Nivelle also publicised the reprisals to his troops to deter French surrenders. 'The irony was that although ordinary soldiers endured hard labour under shellfire, this was seen as culturally acceptable. When demanded of prisoners, on poor rations, by the enemy, however, it was perceived as violently abhorrent.'

Even without a perceived need for retaliation, all sides introduced prisoner-of-war labour close to and at the front and it 'marked a deterioration in prisoner-of-war treatment'. Prisoners suffered 'physically and psychologically; they were often hit by shells from their own side and forced to work directly on their captor's war effort in breach of international law'. The International Red Cross at Geneva arranged prisoner exchanges, inspected camps and monitored prisoner treatment. However, such inspections were restricted to the home front: no neutral power or humanitarian agency was allowed access to prisoners of war working directly for armies at or near the front line. Eventually, the agreement that prisoners should be held at least thirty kilometres from the front was reinstated. From then, the French carefully recorded the distance of their camps from the trenches in their official documents. However, an order from the French 2nd Army command on disciplining prisoners stated:

Treatment ... must be conceived of in reprisal for the sufferings which our own have experienced in camps ... Any act of indulgence, any regard whatsoever for a Boche prisoner is a punishable act of weakness and will be the object of severe sanctions by the higher command. Any misdemeanour by a prisoner must be punished with the greatest severity and the punishment must be immediate and without mercy.[91]

It is impossible to say how closely the crew of *UC 61* were caught up in the dockyard work. Max Pucknus, the supernumerary, was initially at Dieppe, but was later moved to Rouen-Croisset. Andreas Nagel was from Krautsand, near the entrance of the Kiel Canal onto the River Elbe. His first postings were on the sister pre-dreadnought battleships ships *Kaiser Wilhelm II* and *Kaiser Friedrich III* before he volunteered for the u-boat service. Nagel served in both *U 11* and *UC 17* before *UC 61*. Nagel was originally in camp G-K 90, transferred to G-K 80B and, finally, to Rouen-Lev. Some prisoners were highly critical of conditions in Rouen including being spat on by French civilians in the street.[92] Seaman Max Eggers from Grömitz, near the city of Lübeck on the Baltic coast, went from G-K 90 to

Le Havre Abattoirs. His patrol aboard *UC 61* was his first and last voyage.

It was only in the autumn 1917 that those British reprisal prisoners working on the Russian front were finally sent back to camps in Germany when Britain ceased using German prisoner labour units in French ports. However, the British continued to expand its use of German prisoner labour companies across France.[93] This latter was likely the fate of most of the crew of *UC 61*. Twenty of them at some time lived in a numbered, unplaced work company, whose actual location possibly languishes in some administrative record in the Chateau de Vincennes.

This threat to life, whether through retaliation, brutish behaviour or hunger, was a long way from the world of the captured officer that Georg Gerth lived through. Central to how captivity was structured in 1914 to 1918 was the dominant belief that captured officers should receive a better standard of treatment than other-rank prisoners. This overwhelmingly led to captured officers being held in separate officers' prisoner-of-war camps, where they were allocated other-rank prisoners from their own country as orderlies and where conditions were generally far better than in the men's camps. Officer prisoners were also paid a salary and were exempt from working.[94] 'In those days of rigid class hierarchies, enemy officers were generally, if not always, treated with dignity and given pay according to their rank, provided with comfortable, heated lodgings inside separate areas of camps, sometimes even in hotels, and provided with a manservant.'[95] Officer prisoners suffered particularly from apathy, depression and a sense of shame at spending the war in captivity.[96]

The island of Oléron owed its initial importance to its position relative to the island of Aix which guarded the approach to the great port and arsenal of Rochefort. Cannon on Oléron could reach only half way to Aix. Engineers handed Napoleon a report advocating the construction of a 'stone ship' built on a sand and rock reef and capable of mounting guns able to bridge the gap. Construction work began in 1804 and used the small village of Boyardville for storage of men and material and port access to the site. The project was dogged by heavy storms, poorly-positioned rocks and British attacks. A second attempt in 1809 failed and it took another thirty years, after repeated tensions between the French and British, for work to restart. Fort Boyard finally appeared in the late 1850s by which time artillery range had increased and the fort's forty-seven cannon were redundant. Fort Boyard eventually became a prison and by the turn-of-the-twentieth century fell into disrepair. The French Navy chose the small, but bustling, Boyardville for underwater defence and, later, a torpedo training school, and built a naval academy there in 1876.[97] It is interesting that Gerth should be imprisoned next to a functioning torpedo school, his military speciality. The various Napoleonic buildings, barracks for the hundreds of Napoleonic construction labourers, large fortifications and Fort Saumonard (formerly Fort Galissonnière and Fort Napoleon), provided ideal prison camps. At the time of Gerth's arrival at Boyardville, Oléron had a small importance for its tourism, fishing, salt extracted from the marshes, good brandy, and for pine resin taken in the Saumonard Forrest and distilled on the mainland to provide turpentine and rosin.[98] In the way of rubber farmers, the *resiniers* placed a terracotta pot under cuts in pine trees. In 1990, Fort Boyard became famous as the site of an eponymous and popular French TV game show.[99]

The 'other ranks' were held in the old barracks at Boyardville alongside the torpedo school. Sixty-one officers were settled in a 'very good' prison camp on a 'charming and healthy site', either in town or in bungalows on the sea front near the port, and were served by thirteen batmen.[100] Small gardens for flowers and vegetables were maintained 'with care' by the orderlies and by the officers. Boyardville was inspected during a Red Cross tour in 1915. Lieutenant-Colonel Dr C Marvel noted that relations between the French guards and the interned were 'particularly good on the Isle of Aix and at Boyardville'.[101] The two daily meals were taken in two restaurants; the pension was sixty to seventy-five francs per month. A typical menu included coffee and bread for breakfast, a salad of haricot beans and potatoes at lunch and macaroni for supper. 'Several of them buy what they need and make meals themselves.' Recreational activities included reading, walks where the officers wanted within a limit of four square kilometres, music (pianos, violins and guitars) and chess. The lodgings were not far from a sandy beach where 'these *Messieurs* install themselves for games, taking in an ideal view and sunbathing whilst studying or reading books which are sent to them from Germany'.

After Georg Gerth's capture at Wissant, interrogation at Calais and move to Montoire, he was sent ten days later, 15 August 1917, to Boyardville.[102] For Gerth, this meant a move well away from the trenches, but ironically one which took him much closer to his own front line, the shipping lanes off Rochefort which he had patrolled in *UC 61* a few weeks before.

We in the officers' mess raised our glasses and drank toasts to one another and to the beautiful u-boat: 'Rich spoils! A happy journey home! Long live the u-boat!' That is the u-boat toast.[103]

In 1949, Albert Chatelle, interrupted by the second world war, continued his lucrative employment of writing war histories of the French coastal towns. It was the turn of Le Havre and Chatelle remembered his books on Calais and Boulogne of twenty years before when he wrote of the wreck of *UC 61* at Wissant.[104] He turned the last patrol of Gerth's u-boat into a Le Havre story, 'Un mouillage de mines et une évasion manquée'.[105] The city was a main port of entry for British soldiers into France; an estimated 1.9 million Tommies passed through. The port was heavily protected with warships, but the u-boats waited outside and several ships were torpedoed in the roadstead. The suburb of Sainte-Adresse on the cliffs with fine views overlooking the port and the Seine estuary was the seat of the Belgian government-in-exile from October 1914 until the end of the war.[106]

> *In the second fortnight of July 1917, Le Havre harbour narrowly escaped a major mine laying. UC 61 sailed from Zeebrugge on 25 July about 1300 in the afternoon, for her fifth cruise. Her orders were to lay mines in front of Boulogne and Le Havre and then to cruise along the Atlantic coast. UC 61 never arrived at Le Havre. In the night following her departure, she ran aground at low tide on the beach of Wissant, not far from Cap Griz Nez.*

Chatelle was mostly right, except that the *UC 61*'s mines on this patrol were destined for near the *Royal Sovereign* lightship off Eastbourne, and at Newhaven and Brighton on the English south coast.[107] There was no 'Le Havre' story. Chatelle was also still trying to turn *UC 61*'s stranding into spy speculation:

> *We don't really know whether the grounding was purely accidental or if the submarine had to come dangerously close to shore to land an officer who was in excess of the normal complement and on whom was found currency notes issued during the war by the Chambers of Commerce of Boulogne and Calais.*

This was even less right as the supernumerary was Max Pucknus and the one-franc banknotes were found on Hubert Lengs, the navigator / steersman, hardly someone to be put ashore as a spy. However, Chatelle's story then changed into a discussion of an escape attempt by Gerth from Boyardville. This story appears nowhere else and it was only after much searching that records of the extraordinary event were found in French naval archives on long-term loan from the Chateau de Vincennes to the depository at Cherbourg.[108] The following chronicle is constructed from the Cherbourg documents, which were written by French intelligence officers, and using background material as appropriate.

The French claimed that Gerth's camp at Boyardville contained many u-boat officers although that seems more than doubtful as they held very few throughout the war; the French captures involved *UB 26*, *UC 38* and *UC 61* and, of the latter, only Gerth was held there. Almost immediately, Gerth 'hatched a plot' to escape from Boyardville by u-boat. From 1917, following agreement between the French and German governments, a postal service using special postcards was organised with deliveries once every two months.[109] Officer prisoners were allowed to send two letters and four official postcards each month. Gerth wrote on 1 September to Leutnant Suadicani at Flanders Flotilla headquarters at Bruges and included a message written in secret ink. This request was made within two weeks of arrival so one can assume Gerth and other u-boat officers had received escape training.

> In the [French] postal report for July 1918, the censor noted that a proportion of prisoners expressed their dissatisfaction with captivity and their despair at being out of the German offensive. Yet, prisoners, the censor noted, were not depressed. Many were still 'filled with an unquenchable faith in the right arm of Hindenburg (Ludendorff) and are still religiously respectful of the Kaiser', awaiting some action by them which would bring about the final victory.[110]

The recipient of the secret message was Leutnant Günther Suadicani, commander of *UB 17* for just nine days in 1916. As this was Suadicani's only command and he sank no ships, one can assume that for some reason his suitability to command was questioned. Clearly not disgraced, Suadicani joined Korvettenkapitän Karl Bartenbach as his senior staff officer.[111] In this position, he was the appropriate man for Gerth to write to and to take the escape plan to Bartenbach for a decision. Also within the two weeks since his arrival, Gerth had signed up a co-plotter, described by the French as German officer, 'le Ct. Schwerdteger'. The surname is probably a misspelling of 'Schwerdtfeger', of which the Red Cross archives have more than one hundred. As all the ranks given in the French documents were French, the 'Ct.' could stand for a capitaine in the French Navy (German, kapitän) or a commandant (German, major) in the French army. None of the three Schwerdtfegers in the German naval officer list was taken prisoner.[112] In any event, no more is heard of Schwerdtfeger.

Gerth's letter was read by French intelligence as were all messages from prisoners. The secret ink was discovered, the letter let go, and the following exchange of letters monitored. Gerth said that he would be able to escape on a u-boat if he stood within several hundred metres of the Chassiron lighthouse. He asked for the u-boat to be there for five consecutive nights as 'only one night seemed to him to be very risky'. If the weather prevented boarding, he would signal by long flashes of a lamp. Gerth had a weak pocket torch. Gerth also asked Suadicani to indicate any better alternative pick-up point precisely.

One Suadicani response was dated 5 January 1918, intercepted by the French on the 10th and delivered to Gerth about the 14th. Time was already slipping away because of the delay caused by the French.

> Dear Gerth
> During the nights of 12–18 January, a submarine will cruise abeam of the Chassiron lighthouse and will wait for you to come out about 100 metres south of the lighthouse at low tide. You will have to climb as high as you can on the rocks and signal with your pocket torch. Possibly

you will give your surname as a sign of recognition. The berthon will be launched and come and fetch you. On 13 January, low tide is around midnight. The mission will only be possible if there is very calm weather; for a rescue to be made it would be at around five miles from the coast. In bad weather, this plan could not be attempted.

In case the plan cannot be executed during this fixed period, a new attempt will take place during the period of the following new moon. A better place for an escape then could perhaps be the west buoy situated to the west of Fort Boyard near the Saumonards Point? But for that it would need you to indicate to us as to whether we should count on this place, if it's surveyed and whether, to the right of this place, there are surveillance ships and warships moored. In addition, Rudi is currently on his way to this location to get information for a repeat trip in February. Further news follows.

A Berthon was a small collapsible boat carried on u-boats, designed and built from 1877 by the Reverend Edward Lyon Berthon of Romsey in southern England as collapsible lifeboats. Berthon was prompted in his work by a fellow cleric who survived the sinking of the passenger ship SS *Orion* in 1850. One assumes that the Germans had developed their own version. The boats had double linings of canvas, sectioned in two watertight envelopes; the deck could also double as a life raft.[113]

The plan was for Captain Prulières of the French Army secret police to carry out 'special surveillance' and either take the place of the escapees or let the men make their signals and seize them and the crew of the Berthon at the last moment. Gerth was apprehended by Prulières after he signalled with a torch from the rocks. The exact night is not given, but it would have been the 14th or one of the following four days. No Berthon or u-boat was seen. Within the month, Gerth was moved from Boyardville to the inland fortress prison at Carcassonne.[114]

The French list in detail their 'reception committee' which included a submarine and numbers of torpedo boats and patrol boats. 'Through the good offices of the Gascony Patrol division, I would kindly ask you to take every measure to watch these places with discretion during the period indicated with the view of surprising if possible the submarine which is going to attempt this operation.' The sea patrols were to be fitted with Walser apparatus, a type of hydrophone for picking up underwater noises.

Did any u-boats attempt to rescue Gerth and, if so, were they sunk on the way there or did they make it to Boyardville, reject the mission, and were they sunk on the way home? No mention has been found of a rescue operation in the Kriegstagebuch of possible u-boats, but this is not unusual. Special operations were often not mentioned or mentioned only cryptically. The coded note from Suadicani suggests two visits, one to attempt the pick-up and a second, which is 'in addition', to scout information for a repeat trip the next month if this should be necessary. 'Rudi' was currently on his way for this back-up mission. For Rudi to be identified with his short-form first name suggests he was known to Gerth. The only possible 'Rudi' was Rudolph Seuffer, commander of *UC 50*, which sailed from Zeebrugge on 7 January 1918 and was ordered to lay mines near the Loire and the Gironde and was in the Bay of Biscay at the right time conducting trade warfare. Seuffer would have met Gerth as they both received command of their uc-boats in the Flanders Flotilla in December 1916. Also, Seuffer was in the same sea cadet year, Crew 1905, as Georg Gerth's elder brother Erich and the two were the best of friends as evidence of a photograph and its caption shows.[115] However, Seuffer's *UC 50* was 'originally assigned to the High Sea Fleet's I Flotilla and wasn't reassigned to Flanders until July 1917, just a couple of weeks before Gerth took *UC 61* out on her final patrol'.[116]

UC 50 did not return to Zeebrugge. U-boat historian Robert Grant declared that it was 'highly probable' that *UC 50* blew up the day after sailing when the drifter *Brothers Jem* on watch in the Straights of Dover felt a heavy explosion and 'soon found a large quantity of oil and dead fish'.[117] The drifter was unable to investigate further because of bad weather. Messimer's *Verschollen* says that *UC 50* was rammed and depth charged off Dungeness on 4 February 1918 by HMS *Zubian* while homeward bound on the surface with the loss of all twenty-nine hands, but this is successfully refuted by u-boat experts.[118] Michael Lowrey of uboat.net explains:

> *What actually happened to* UC 50 *is very unclear. It is one of the two most missing of the Flanders-based submarines that did not return from patrol. By most missing, I mean that at this point, all we can say is that it sailed and did not return. In most other cases of missing Flanders-based U-boats we at least have some contact after they sailed (typically a ship sinking). Unfortunately, we aren't going to be able to use ship sinkings to determine whether* UC 50 *got to her assigned patrol area in the Bay of Biscay.* UC 50's *patrol area overlapped with that of the larger* U 84 *and* U 93, *neither of which returned from patrol. While some attacks on shipping were clearly conducted by* U 84 *or* U 93 *(and in one case clearly by* U 93*), there aren't any cases that are clearly attributable to* UC 50 *as there are no survivor statements describing a UCII. However, that may not mean much as several ships were torpedoed without the u-boat being observed.*

The likelihood is that Rudi never made it to check out potential pick up points around Boyardville. The loss of *UC 50* cannot be attributed to Gerth's escape attempt as the u-boat would have been sailing anyway, but it was the fifth u-boat to have an association with the demise of *UC 61*, alongside *UC 44* off Waterford and the three uc-boats sunk when new mines were laid on the u-boat route south of Zeebrugge the previous year.

Was there a second u-boat intended to collect Gerth and Schwerdtfeger from Boyardville? Or was *UC 50* attempting both missions? If there was a second u-boat, it was not from Flanders Flotilla as they are all accounted for, either in port or not in the Bay of Biscay. The previous boat in the area was *UC 17*, which arrived back in Flanders on 15 January. The next boat operating in the Bay of Biscay is probably *UB 59*, which only sailed on 20 January. There are only two candidates, already mentioned as in the vicinity, *U 84* and *U 93*, both of which were lost at around the right time to unknown causes.[119]

The problem with the involvement of either of these is that they were High Seas Fleet boats. Suadicani would have to arrange any escape attempt from Bruges with officers based in Germany. Lowrey feels that 'this seems a bit unlikely'. The fractured nature of the various u-boat commands and the difficulty of co-ordinating missions are accepted. However, Suadicani would not be operating without direction and, presumably, Karl Bartenbach would have the rank and reach to contact another command. There was an overall national imperative to get experienced u-boat commanders back to sea as quickly as possible to meet the monthly sinking targets; and there was the attraction of further rescues, if this first was successful. A larger u-class boat that was going to the area anyway would be convenient and be better provisioned to keep station for five consecutive nights while active during the day. A u-boat would have more room for two extra men and, also, might carry a larger collapsible Berthon to handle the five miles from boat to shore estimated by Suadicani.

U 84, commander Kapitänleutnant Walter Roehr, was lost around 15 January and was found near Penmarch, Finistère, in 2014. *U 84* was assigned to operate between Penmarch and Île de Ré. What is probably *U 93*, commander Kapitänleutnant Helmut Gerlach, is in the eastern English Channel which fits its ordered patrol area from the Channel Islands to Penmarch.[120] One other page in the French escape reports may shed light as it contains submarine contact reports thought relevant by them for, probably, 5 January 1918 (so not *UC 50*). Ten miles from the Chassiron lighthouse, on the northern point of the island of Oléron, a French aircraft, one of a pair, threw a bomb by hand at a submarine (no bomb launcher); the submarine replied by firing a machine gun which hit the wing of one of the planes, and then 'dived quickly and disappeared'. The same afternoon, about 1500, three French aircraft found 'the same' u-boat engaged in a fight with a British steamship. One plane attacked and 'fired a bomb straight on the bow of the submarine at ten metres'; the submarine dived and disappeared.

The reason for Gerth's move to Carcassonne was clearly well known among his fellow officers. On the same day, 16 February, that he arrived at his new prison, another coded letter was sent from Boyardville to Suadicani in Bruges and intercepted. It purported to come from a 'Capitaine' von Niessen. There was later correspondence:

The escape attempt by Lt Gerth has failed as the escape was discovered. The French know nothing about the way in which the escape should have been carried out. Gerth has been taken to the mainland and asks you to be kind enough to now place on me all the goodwill that you had shown to him up to now as several officers here would like to once again have the chance to fight on the front and in particular Cap. von Dewall, former commander of the fighting squadron (Army High Command). The possibility of an escape is guaranteed.

If you agree with us as we hope we would ask you to take into consideration the following: Fixed term for the new undertaking the nights of the new moon 10–15 May, the nights of 14–15 being included. The place for the escape remains that for the January escape. Delay for letters is fixed at five weeks. If the sending of the reply is no longer possible before the 5 April please put back the operation to the nights of the new moon in June, that is to say the nights of 7–12 of June, those of the 7–12 being included.

The reply will take place solely by the same method as the current letter if possible simply encoded according to the key: Üb immer Treu und Redlichkeit.

In haste

The prophetic code key *Üb' immer Treu' und Redlichkeit*, 'Always practise loyalty and honesty', deserves more than a footnote. It is the first line of the poem *Der alte Landmann an seinen Sohn*, 'The old countryman to his son', by Ludwig Hölty.[121] The lines became popular as the words to the tune sung by Papageno, *Ein Männchen oder Weibchen*, 'A little man or little woman', in Mozart's opera *Die Zauberflöte*, 'The Magic Flute'. When Friedrich Wilhelm III became king of Prussia in 1797, his wife Queen Luise ordered that the carillon of the Potsdam Garrison Church should play every hour her two favourite tunes, that played on the half hour was *Üb' immer Treu' und Redlichkeit* as an emblem of Prussian soldiers' virtues. The song became the unofficial Prussian national hymn. On 21 March 1933, the ceremony for the opening of the new Reichstag after the German federal election was called the *Day of Potsdam*. Adolf Hitler took his oath of office in the presence of President Hindenburg in the garrison church. Twelve years later during the *Night of Potsdam*, a British bomb attack caused the church bell tower to collapse and the carillon with its forty bells fell to the ground while constantly playing the tune *Üb' immer Treu' und Redlichkeit*.

Hauptmann Job-Heinrich von Dewall, von Niessen's accomplice, was a pilot and the commanding officer of KagOHL 2 who did not return from a bombing mission over Châlons in Champagne on 23 March 1918.[122]

This second attempt at escape from Boyardville by u-boat in May 1918 also failed and Dewall was quickly moved from the sea coast to Montoire.[123] ICRC records indicate that Dewall was moved from a camp at Auch, the historical capital of Gascony, back to Boyardville on 27 October 1918.[124] Dewall was finally released in March 1920. He went on to work in several senior positions in the German aircraft industry and in the Luftwaffe.[125] In 1942, he was appointed Generalleutnant, air marshal, when he became a freelance member of the war science department in Berlin. Ironically, Dewall died in September 1945 after going missing near Karlsbad, a presumed Czech prisoner of war.

Captain Prulières of the French Army secret police returned to carry out his 'special surveillance' and was landed covertly because it was 'important not to raise awareness in the camp at Boyardville which remains ignorant of this operation'. The French reception committee was even more involved and explicit than for Gerth's attempt. The French Minister of the Navy and his chief of staff, Vice Admiral Ferdinand-Jean-Jacques le Bon, intervened to organise the surveillance. The submarine *Brumaire* with its eight torpedoes left its base at La Pallice each day of the escape period to be in position for the evening and returning the next morning at 0200. Would this 1906 boat, finally launched in 1911, have been a match for a modern u-boat in an open fight? Torpedo boats followed *Brumaire* an hour-and-a-half later each day. Two patrol boats, 'if possible armed with Walsar apparatus', to the west of Pertuis Strait, between the island and Rochefort, moved at slow speed in order to use their hydrophones.

> *If the weather allows,* [Brumaire] *to moor as close as possible to the land in the south west of the lighthouse [Chassiron]. It will be ready to cast off immediately and hold itself only on a kedge anchor and a cable, ready to go, with a buoy. The ship must offer the smallest silhouette possible and ... to be ready for every eventuality it will be semi-submerged. If the* Brumaire *needs help it will launch rockets of whatever colour.*

This time, the u-boat was seen, not during the failed May operation, but in the June repeat, word of the failed endeavour and capture in May of Niessen and Dewall not having reached Suadicani. This latter operation has the hallmarks of a French trap. Semaphorists at Chassiron lighthouse first saw a fixed white light on 9 June, thirty miles west of the La Coubre lighthouse on the mainland, and then a u-boat was seen keeping watch, but not approaching Boyardville immediately. The white light was seen twice more from Chassiron that night at 2300 and 2345.

There is an another recorded escape attempt by u-boat, not off France, but off north Wales. In 1915, Korvettenkapitän Max Valentiner, commander of *U 38*, from Heligoland, was ordered to pick up three German officers who had broken out of their prison camp. Valentiner waited three days for the signal from shore and at dawn on 16 August he 'abandoned the mission, not knowing that the officers were hidden by a projecting rock on a beach five hundred yards away'.[126]

Gerth arrived at the barracks in Carcassonne Castle to join 200 other officers on 16 February 1918 where the incomplete local files have no record of his stay.[127] The previous year the imposing prison was occupied by internees, but in November 1917, the castle was handed over to the French General Directorate of POWs and the internees left for new accommodation. This was a matter of 'extreme urgency' for lodging officer prisoners.[128] Gerth might have reflected on similarities with his short stay at Calais the previous year where high towers and medieval walls with arrow-slits guard passageways to the barbican and the river. Much time seems to have been taken up, according to prison records, with complaints about the sugar ration from 1917 to 1921. Fifty-two German officers signed an urgent request for sugar ration cards shortly after Gerth's arrival.[129]

Georg Gerth's family have recently recovered a picture sent home to Germany from Carcassonne where Gerth is seated at a table with wine and reading by a petroleum lamp.[130] Gerth was able to indulge his life-long interest in philosophy, particularly at that time works by Hermann Hesse, Immanuel Kant, Friedrich Nietzsche and Rainer Rilke. Kant, thought to be Gerth's preferred philosopher, particularly condemned British imperialism and methods of trade.[131] During his solitary readings, so typical of his later reclusive character, Gerth may have expanded this condemnation to imperialism in general, and therefore, a gradual longer-term disassociation with the trappings of his own imperial ruler.

> *Enlightenment is man's release from his self-incurred tutelage. Tutelage is a man's ability to make use of his understanding without direction from another. Self-incurred is this tutelage when its cause lies not in lack of reason, but in lack of resolution and courage to use it without direction from another. Sapere aude!*[132] *'Have courage to use your own reason!'. That is the motto of enlightenment.*[133]

The family believed from what Gerth told them that he was well treated in his French prison. But then, they did not know that he had tried to escape and was sent quickly to a more secure site. Gerth briefly described this time in his curriculum vitae attached to a dissertation he wrote in May 1923 while studying at the University of Würzburg.[134] Note, particularly, his claims to 'two' escape attempts, which is not disputed, but not proven by research, and to 'severe special treatment' that did not happen at Boyardville before the escape attempt, but may have happened later.

> *After the destruction of my boat in late July 1917, I became a French prisoner of war. Two attempts to escape which I undertook to return to the service of the fatherland failed and this, in addition to my previous occupation as a submarine commander, resulted in severe special treatment. However, during my two-and-a-half years of captivity, I*

had the opportunity to study philosophy in which I have always had a
special interest.

Gerth's escape attempt may have solicited some unpleasant repercussions. The most serious crimes for a prisoner were trying to escape and refusing to work.

> [Escape] *rarely succeeded; most of the fugitives were re-captured. Throughout 1918, French headquarters produced instructions for stopping escapes, many of which could be explained by the relaxing of surveillance, an 'excessive familiarity with prisoners ... and serious breaches of camp rules.*[135]

> *Prisoners were unable to refuse work allocated to them and, although they were theoretically entitled to a subsistence wage, in accordance with international law, due to be paid to them at the end of the conflict, most never received it because of chaotic conditions at war's end.*[136]

Perhaps there was a greater expectation that officers, as a matter of honour, should try to regain their countries. This was certainly more likely since the abandonment of the parole system soon after the start of the war. Lower level escapees were often placed in special camps known as 'security measures'. At the end of a 'terrible year' in November 1917, French premier Clemenceau was alarmed 'about the growing, unstoppable and truly abnormal number of escapes by German POWs'. He was worried that the 'enemy can obtain precious and true information on our projects and at least on our troop movements; it makes a laughing stock of our surveillance, and such frequent escapes could lead us to believe whether they are led by criminals around the camps'. Clemenceau was told that successful escapes were much less than he believed, thirty escapees out of 19,000 prisoners in the military zone in December 1917, for example. 'But this idea of a prisoner/spy was widespread at a moment when both at the front and behind the lines morale had dropped.'

> *In December 1917, the Northern Army produced a resumé of all the escapes from 6 October to 6 December comprising three columns, 'Circumstances of escape', 'Responsibilities and sanctions', and 'Measures taken to ensure more efficient surveillance'. Sixty-nine prisoners escaped alone, in twos or threes and up to six at a time for twenty-four escape attempts. Fifty-one were retaken and were interrogated for the reasons and the circumstances of their attempt. In fourteen cases, the motive for escape was given as 'nostalgia', to which was twice added insufficient food. All these prisoners worked on detachments in the department of Oise and the Somme, in quarries, saw mills, sugar beet processing plants.*

They were not complaining of the hours they worked, nor of having been located so close to the front line. Their placements were quite reasonable at forty to fifty kilometres from the front. But this distance was not so great as to not be able to cross [the front line], with luck in one or two nights, which explains the number who definitely escaped.[137]

The French became preoccupied by a 'sort of general relaxation' in 1918 in the management of the camps and the work regime, attributing it to a growing tendency amongst the military that guarded the camps as 'not seeing in the prisoners but a loyal and upright soldier to whom the fortune of war was against'.[138] The *Deuxième Bureau* called on everyone connected with the camp system to understand the atrocities committed by the Germans to French prisoners to 'dissuade them from excessive compassion'. 'It is necessary to show them the truth about our adversaries of whom nobody in France, after three years of war, could be ignorant of their treacheries, savageries and crimes.' Perhaps, towards war end, the 'spontaneous practice towards German PoWs was developing in a humanitarian way' and chimed with the new approaches of the charitable, religious and humanitarian organisations, particularly the International Committee of the Red Cross.

There was one known interruption to Gerth's stay at Carcassonne.[139] Gerth was a victim of a 'phenomenon which touched every region of the world in a brief and concentrated period ... an explosive pandemic which swept through the final months of 1918'.[140] In September of his first year, he was transferred over 400 kilometres to the Military Hospital at Grenoble suffering from Spanish flu. Why did he travel so far? The influenza pandemic travelled to Europe with American troops early in 1918.[141] It acquired its signature as the 'Spanish flu' during an early excursion in the Iberian Peninsula in May. Two further waves affected most of the areas concerned for a period of a few weeks in the autumn and winter of 1918, the latter reaching into 1919. It was the second phase, when Gerth was infected, that was the 'most virulent and most deadly'. About 90 per cent of all flu deaths occurred between August and November 1918. It was the 'emotional and judgemental juxtaposition of the epidemic with the ending of the war' which excited major immediate comment.[142] The disease struck most and in the millions in Asia, with China and India to the forefront, but the 'historians were westerners and the awfulness of the flu was partly hidden as an addendum of the war'. It is also contrasted awkwardly with the proven leaps in medical practice brought about through dealing with war wounded. The allies frequently claimed that the epidemic's source was among the Germans, perhaps as the latest version of poisoned wells, corrupted milk and air deliberately contaminated with microbes. 'A new sickness is raging among the Germans: it is the oedema of the war. It begins with a general weakening ... caused by a lack of dietary fats.'[143]

'The dreadful hygiene conditions in prison camps supposedly added to this, allowing the flu into prisoners' home countries when they were repatriated.'[144] The effect of the blockade on weakening German civilians and soldiers alike was little discussed by the Allies. It is likely that Gerth was not long at Grenoble, incubation was brief and 'people fell seriously ill in a few hours'. Victims experienced a variety of symptoms: high fever, headaches, intense pain in the muscles and bones, inflammation of the pharynx and throat, a state of prostration, and perhaps coughs, intestinal pain, nausea, rash nerve pains and depressive states.[145] Approximations of deaths varied widely, but grew through various studies over the years. Jordan in 1927 suggested 21.6 million, about 1.2 per cent of the world's population.[146] In 1991, Patterson and Pyle estimated 30-40 million deaths, around 2 per cent.[147] By 2002, Johnson and Müller proposed between 50-100 million deaths, between one in twenty and one in forty of everyone across the world who survived the war.[148]

Prisoners' rations in France deteriorated in 1918, not due to shortages 'but rather to the impact of Franco-German negotiations'.[149] In April 1918, two extraordinary international conferences took place in Berne which brought together all agencies for humanitarian aid for prisoners.[150] These conferences resulted in two accords, signed between France and Germany in March and April, that recognised agreed standards for prisoner rations, punishments, working hours and working conditions.[151] Ironically, this actually meant a cut in bread rations for the average German prisoner in France. The April accord covered forty pages and was printed in two columns, German and French. Article 26 of the April Accord set rations of 2,000 calories for non-working prisoners, 2,500 for ordinary workers and 2,850 for workers engaged on heavy manual labour. Article 30 precluded bread from being sent to individual prisons, only cake and gateaux. Article 36 specified that no punishment should last longer than thirty days unless there was a break of a week between punishments. Additionally, it was 'formally forbidden to confiscate personal papers from POWs, but the State had the right to take copies'. A general had the right to his own batman, high ranking officers had to share one between four. Generals and high-ranking officers also had the right to two pillows. Officers were limited to five candles each.

Under Clause 10 of the Armistice Treaty, Germany was obliged to release all Allied prisoners immediately whereas the release date of German prisoners in Allied hands remained indefinite. The clause called for the ...

   ... *immediate repatriation without reciprocity, according to detailed conditions which shall be fixed, of all allied and United States prisoners of war, including persons under trial or convicted. The allied powers and the United States shall be able to dispose of them as they wish ... However, the repatriation of German prisoners of war interned in*

> Holland and in Switzerland shall continue as before. The repatriation
> of German prisoners of war shall be regulated at the conclusion of the
> preliminaries of peace. In addition, Clause 18 called for Repatriation,
> without reciprocity, within a maximum period of one month … of all
> interned civilians, including hostages under trial or convicted, belonging
> to the Allied or associated powers.

Of particular interest to Georg Gerth, perhaps, Clause 21 stated that 'all naval and mercantile marine prisoners of the allied and associated powers in German hands to be returned without reciprocity'.

The end of the war did not mean the end of captivity. An enormous gap, a further war crime to many minds, developed between French and German views of prisoner repatriation. The end of the war offered immediate liberty to the prisoners of the conquerors, 'those of the conquered found themselves hostages, unregulated by the suspended Berne Accords'. The optimism of Berne conferences quickly deteriorated following the end of the fighting.[152] The Armistice agreement did not authorize the return of German POWs before a definitive peace agreement. The fifteen months' maximum foreseen in April 1918 for the repatriation of the last prisoners became the minimum for the German prisoners. 'If during the war the prisoners had had a terrible outcome on both sides of the front line, for the German prisoners the defeat was going to be paid for twice.'

> While Allied prisoners returned from Germany rapidly in late 1918,
> released under the terms of the Armistice, German prisoners remained
> in British and American captivity until mid 1919 and in French
> captivity until 1920, retained by France as human reparations.'[153]

Marshal Ferdinand Foch proposed retaining German prisoners to compensate losses, to put the country back together again and reconstruct those regions which had been devastated and occupied. When it was pointed out to him that this measure would be contrary to the engagements undertaken by France, he replied that the situation did not allow such 'elegances'. The Allies agreed that German prisoners would not be repatriated until after the ratification of the Treaty of Versailles by Germany and by three of the other powers involved.[154] About 100,000 POWs were transferred into the French 'liberated zones' and formed working parties for departments like Nord-Pas-de-Calais, Champagne-Ardennes and Lorraine which had been at the front line.[155] Under the authority of General Antoine de Mitry, 700 camps, each averaging 400 men, took part in the reclamation of the region in the North and North East.[156] Men were sent from camps all across the country to reconstruct the war-ravaged regions. From January 1919 to January 1920, between 270,000 and 310,000 German prisoners worked under French command, and some 200,000 under the British, in atrocious conditions, clearing ordnance and debris from fields, trenches and canals.[157] 'This had the added advantage of removing prisoners from jobs to which demobilised French soldiers were returning.' Forced and dangerous labour became a lengthy and deliberate policy of the French Government. Captain T Hage, a Danish visitor, noted that if this work was extremely dangerous it was equally so for the French military and for the recently liberated prisoners from German camps.[158]

Britain and France regarded German prisoners as a 'bargaining tool and saw their labour as a form of living war reparation'.[159] The great disparity fuelled resentment in the camps and in Germany. In the tense atmosphere awaiting liberation, which was always being delayed, on 1 May 1919 there were 'seditious' demonstrations with red flags and posters hostile to France' at the camp at Île Longue.[160] Captain Hage conducted a study in the liberated regions of northern France, from Calais to Switzerland in 1918 and 1919. He made a connection between the number of escapes, punishments and 'serious incidents' in the camps between Armistice and the final application on 15 January 1920 of the clause of the Treat of Versailles which allowed the freeing of all prisoners.[161]

Initially, the German negotiators viewed the delay as a temporary stay on German prisoner repatriation which would be remedied as soon as all Allied prisoners reached home. The French viewed the situation rather differently. 'Thus, even after the fighting, the need for forced labour drove an escalatory dynamic leading to deterioration in prisoner welfare.' 'For France, in the immediate post-war period, German prisoners were dangerous perpetrators to be punished, not victims; they derived no compassion.'[162]

> German prisoners represented security, ensuring German compliance with French demands. They also represented a sizable army of military men to whom Germany had no access. As early as April 1918, the French believed that Germany wanted its prisoners back 'because she wishes to get back the military instructors of which she had need'. This mentality continued to govern French perceptions after the Armistice; an emasculated France, which had lost so many men in the war, would be more vulnerable once German prisoners returned home.[163]

The French decision to continue to use German prison labour caused immense and mounting anger in Germany and was seen in Germany as an irrational and cruel act 'motivated purely by a vindictive victor's desire for revenge'. A massive public relations campaign was launched to bring the prisoners home including a People's Union for the Protection of German War and Civil Prisoners and the German Women's League for the Repatriation of Prisoners of War. The latter sent a petition to Mary, wife of King George, Queen of the United Kingdom (and also Princess of Teck in the Kingdom of Württemberg) in 1919.[164]

Your Majesty

The blood-stained weapons have been laid down. A merciless death has laid one and a half millions of our children in foreign soil. An ocean of tears has flown on their account, and thousands of German hearts have been broken and died. The misery is not yet over. By the Armistice, Germany handed back all her millions of prisoners, but 800,000 German prisoners have been left in the hands of the conquerors to an uncertain fate, our poor sons, husbands, brothers. Now these prisoners, some of whom have been separated for four years from the bosoms of their families, find themselves condemned to hard perilous labour in restoring the ruins of France. The hearts of millions of German women are again torn. We know the great physical and spiritual longings of our dear ones. We know how in utter despair they stretch out their hands to us, their mothers and their children. Their cry for help rings hourly in our ears. Their tear-stained eyes follow us day and night, but we can do nothing to help them.

Author Gerhard Rose was commissioned by the *People's Union for the Protection of the German War and Civilian Prisoners* to write a book detailing the efforts made to seek repatriation. It was published in Berlin in 1920 during the first French repatriations and makes detailed and harrowing reading.[165] The book explained that in the fourteen months until the end of the war was legally validated by the Peace Treaty, German citizens who were in the hands of the Allies as war or civilian prisoners suffered under the same, or even worse, conditions than during the previous fifty-one months of war. The situation was 'adverse to all human feeling and sensible consideration; the desperation, disappointment and bitterness about the delay of the POWs' return caused the families to doubt the government and their own elected leaders and accuse them of being partly to blame for the lack of success'. The prisoners were under the impression that 'incompetence and lack of determination of their own people and its leaders had a share in their hard fate'. This opinion was strengthened by enemy propaganda.[166]

Some brief excerpts from the book demonstrate the strength of feeling in Germany:

'During these despotic times, each nation would show their true character in the way they treated foreign prisoners of war' – French *'sadism'* *became apparent ... The expectations raised by the negotiations at Berne and in The Hague regarding prisoner exchange were completely disappointing.* *'Mainly the French government was to blame for this as they had only reluctantly agreed to ratification of the treaty having been pressurised by the influential French* Association des familles des prisonniers de guerre.' *According to the treaty regulations, in the*

first five months, 60,000, or in the worst case at least 50,000 prisoners should have been released on each side but the actual figure was only 4,000 ... The actions after the Armistice showed that the 'principle of brutal exploitation of power over the prisoners was the key to their treatment'. German's enemies use POWs as 'human bargaining chips'. 'Hard and firm was the will of the enemy to commit the rape [of the German prisoners] and the German government and people were powerless to affect that will' ... The enemy wanted to 'satisfy their hate by retaining the prisoners'.[167]

Protestors in Holland on 25 May 1919 demanded the immediate return of German POWs and the suspension of the hunger blockade, a demonstration which had a particular impact on public opinion in England. On 24 July, the liberal press in Britain began to call for the repatriation of German prisoners. At the end of July 1919, Churchill explained in the House of Commons that 20,000 German POWs were needed for England's agriculture, the rest in France for reconstruction work. Rear Admiral von Reuter, late of Scapa Flow and now interned at Donington Hall, the most senior representative of the German forces in England, passed a petition to Prime Minister Lloyd George through the Swiss Legation in London in August.[168] 'The uncompromising attitude of the British Government shows that it is not fully informed about the psychology of prisoners or war ... Unjust and inhuman ... Every day longer in captivity lowers their vitality and lessens their opportunity in life.' The International Red Cross issued a formal protest letter, but Clemenceau refused to compromise, asking Britain and America to give France their German prisoners instead of repatriating them to Germany.

The Swiss failed to get permission to return the German prisoners interned in their country. 'Indignation, shock and despair turned into a storm first aimed against the behaviour of the enemy, the broken promises of the Entente, but was then directed against the German government.'[169] Politicians were called traitors. At a protest meeting at the *Berlin Philharmonie*, 10,000 women demanded the resignation of the government. By August, the public mood started to worsen, even in France.

Once the Versailles treaty was signed, British and American attitudes changed. They were now keen to return their German charges. Despite French reluctance, the British and Americans went ahead. The British began repatriation with one thousand healthy prisoners on 1 September 1919 and completed on 1 November 1919. Not least of the British concerns was that 5,000 British troops were employed on guard duty at a cost of £30,000 a day.[170] The trains that brought British prisoners home were no longer returned empty to Germany. Switzerland quickly released its interned German prisoners. In August, 150,000 prisoners returned from the western front, the largest part from English hands. Hearing the news,

Clemenceau again demanded the transfer of British-held German POWs to France for reconstruction purposes.

In November, General Neill Malcolm, chief of the British Military Mission to Berlin, telegrammed London asking whether it was possible to do anything to get prisoners returned from France. 'Their retention is causing very bitter feeling and is weakening the position of the Government which is accused of criminal indifference by all parties'. Across Germany, there was the 'deepest indignation and bitterness about the French barbarism'.

> *Despite the public opinion of the neutral world, France condemned German prisoners to captivity, indeed slavery, blackmail and exploitation ... It was an outrage against all principles of international law; a stigma France will never be able to wash off.*[171]

Clemenceau remained obstinate into 1920, even in the face of a majority of the French army and of the chairman of the Peace Commission. The Germans called him 'brutal'.[172]

> *If the repatriation of prisoners by our Allies began in September it is because the French government was unable to oppose it. None of our Allies was as badly injured in its emotions and its interests as the population of the north of France was. How can this population wandering in the ruins of their homes ... accept to see the German prisoners, employed upon work of the utmost urgency ... leave France before the time appointed by the Treaty of Versailles, which fixed the end of their captivity on the definitive ratification – the entry into force of the treaty.*[173]

The denigration of the French was endorsed by leading German politicians.[174] Walther Rathenau, shortly to become foreign minister in the Weimar Republic and, in 1922, assassinated in Berlin by the right-wing terrorist group *Organisation Consul*, wrote, 'It is outrageous ... that our prisoner fellow citizens do not return home'. He described the situation as 'slavery'. Philipp Scheidemann, who proclaimed Germany a republic during the revolution and, later, became the second head of government of the Republic, stated, 'I believe the whole world must join with us in crying out against this last insult to humanity'.

It was not until 21 January 1920 that France finally began to repatriate her German prisoners of war. Karl Raabe died two days later. Georg Gerth arrived home on 1 March.

ENDNOTES

1 Rose, *Krieg nach dem Kriege*, pp. 170–184.
2 *TNA*, ADM 137/3898.
3 Bouton, *Abdicates*, pp. 89–90.
4 *Royal Museum of the Armed Forces and of Military History*, Brussels, AU 9089/2, p. 108. Chapter 2, 'Kaisertreu'.
5 *Royal Museum of the Armed Forces and of Military History*, Brussels, Est I/2322, p. 5. *SHD*, Cherbourg, Box MV SS Gr 43, picture caption, p. 1.
6 *Le Petit Journal*, 29/7/1917.
7 Becker, *Oubliés de la Grande Guerre*, p. 41.
8 Dufour, 'Prisonniers du guerre', p. 11.
9 Interview, Schindler, Seamen's Hospital, Brest, 13/3/1918 (*SHD*, Cherbourg, SSTe35).
10 Spiegel, *202*, p. 64.
11 Peckelsheim, '*U 93*' in Thomas, *Raiders*, pp. 189–92.
12 *TNA*, ADM 186/38, p. 19, Gach to Fräulein Walpurin, Breslau, 2/12/1917.
13 Jones, 'Prisoners of War', in Winter, *First World War*, Vol. II, pp. 274–76.
14 uboat.net.
15 Jones, *Violence*, pp. 83–86.
16 Fürbringer, *Legendary*, p. 129.
17 *Hansard*, House of Commons debates 1915: 27/4, Vol. 71, c544 cc572–5, cc623–92; 5/5, Vol. 71, c1087, cc1201–30.
18 Winton, *Convoy*, pp. 8–9.
19 Willis, *Prologue to Nuremberg*, pp. 17–22. Hull, *Scrap of Paper*, pp. 297–98.
20 *TNA*, FO 369/1450, Major General Sir Herbert Belfield, 'Report on Directorate of Prisoners of War', 9/1920, pp. 57–58.
21 Dufour, 'Prisonniers du guerre', pp. 9–10.
22 *TNA*, FO 383/261, 25/7/1917.
23 Jones, 'Prisoners of War', pp. 267–79.
24 Dufour, 'Prisonniers du guerre', pp. 8–9. Kramer, 'Prisoners', pp. 76–77.
25 Delpal, 'Prisonniers de guerre', pp. 144–46.
26 Jones, *Violence*, p. 139.
27 SHD, Vincennes, 16 N 525, 'État des Prisonniers se trouvant dans la Zone des Armées le 26 Janvier 1917'.
28 Becker, *Oubliés de la Grande Guerre*, p. 111.
29 Dufour, 'Prisonniers du guerre', p. 17.
30 Canini, 'L'utilisation des prisonniers de guerre comme main-d'oeuvre'.
31 Jones, *Violence*, p. 148.
32 Becker, *Oubliés de la Grande Guerre*, pp. 116–122.
33 Becker, *Oubliés de la Grande Guerre*, pp. 105–22.
34 Becker, *Oubliés de la Grande Guerre*, p. 91.
35 Jones, 'Prisoners of War', p. 286.
36 Kramer, *Prisoners*, pp. 76–77.
37 Jones, 'Prisoners of War', pp. 273–74.
38 Chapter 16, 'Erich's Jewish problem'.
39 Cornwell, *Hitler's Pope*, p. 60.
40 Jones, *Violence*, pp. 241–43.
41 Bern, Deutsche Kriegsgefangenen-Fürsorge, *Atlas der Gefangenenlager in Frankreich in neun Karten*, 15/5/1918.
42 *SHD*, Vincennes, 16 N 525, 'État des Prisonniers se trouvant dans la Zone des Armées', 1/6/1918.
43 Jones, *Violence*, pp. 238–39.
44 *SHD*, Vincennes, 7 N 1993, '*Ministère de la Guerre, Sous-Secrétaire d'état la Justice Militaire, Note pour les Directions et Services*', 29/5/1918.
45 grandeguerre.icrc.org.
46 *ICRC*, P 24350, officers; P 24301–3, men.

47   Delpal, 'Prisonniers de guerre', pp. 148-152.

48   *BA-MA*, Freiburg, RM 86/18: RMA 10139, p. 128.

49   *BA-MA*, Freiburg, RM 20/504, pp. 73–88.

50   Chapter 2, 'Kaisertreu'.

51   Hoyt: *Germans who never lost, Möwe*, p. 52, *Königsberg*, pp. 145–9; and *Guerrilla: Colonel von Lettow-Vorbeck*. Zimmer, 'Crew of the *Möwe*'.

52   Olusoga & Erichsen, *Kaiser's Holocaust*, p. 254. Chapter 2.

53   Hoyt, *Germans who never lost*, pp. 179–83. Cholet is the source for the name of Madame Cholet of the BBC children's television programme, the *Wombles*, who as a cook affects a French accent, though she is actually no more French than any other Wimbledon Womble. After the war, Smiths became the German Consul in Messina, Sicily, and managed a company which produced citrus fruit essences (uboat.net).

54   The Loir River is a tributary of the River Sarthe.

55   Newbolt, *Naval Operations*, Vol. V, pp. 224–227.

56   Karau, *Naval Flank*, pp. 180–83.

57   Horn, *Mutiny*, pp. 7–8.

58   Keyzer, *Unseen Glass Plate Photographs*, pp. 176–77. Moreau joined the conflict at the Marne where he recorded the second Battle of Champagne in September 1915. He was noted for photographs of prisoners of war, trenches and corpses after which 'confusion' became his art-historical theme. Keyzer's book of first world War photographs contains a section on Moreau, pp. 171–192, which begins with a picture of *UC 61* 'washed up' on the beach at Wissant.

59   *ECPAD*, SPA 230M4573.

60   Syon, *Zeppelin!*, p. 85. *Illustrated London News*, 17/11/1917, Issue 4100, Vol. CLI, pp. 5–10.

61   Spindler, *Der Krieg zur See*, Band 4, p. 547.

62   Jones, 'Prisoners of War', pp. 283–86.

63   Arnold-Forster, *Blockade*, p. 29.

64   Davos Archives, Death Register, 9/232/176.

65   *SHD*, Vincennes, 'Emplacements des Camps de Prisonniers de Guerre', 16N2466, 16/11/1917.

66   *ICRC*, P 34594.

67   Interview with Schindler, written by mistake as 'Schurdler' (*SHD*, Cherbourg, SSTe35).

68   Kramer, *Prisoners*, p. 86.

69   Becker, *Oubliés de la Grande Guerre*, pp. 201–8.

70   Motta, 13/9/1915, quoted in Kühnis, 'Deutsche Kriegsinternierte in Davos', p. 3.

71   Becker, *Oubliés de la Grande Guerre*, p. 97.

72   Dufour, 'Prisonniers du guerre', p. 21.

73   Lindsay, edited, '*Swiss Internment of Prisoners of War, Experiment in International Humane Legislation*', p. viii.

74   Delpal, 'Prisonniers de guerre', p. 154.

75   Dufour, 'Prisonniers du guerre', p. 20.

76   Lindsay, '*Humane Legislation*', pp. 15–19. Yarnall, *Barbed Wire Disease*, Chapter 11, 'Exchanges, Internment and Agreements'.

77   Kühnis, 'Deutsche Kriegsinternierte in Davos', pp. 6–13.

78   Lindsay, '*Humane Legislation*', pp. 20–24.

79   Lindsay, '*Humane Legislation*', pp. 25–28.

80   Kühnis, 'Deutsche Kriegsinternierte in Davos', pp. 15–19.

81   Kühnis, 'Deutsche Kriegsinternierte', p. 22.

82   The cemetery is open to the public and is located behind the *Hochgebirgsklinik Wolfgang*, the former German Sanatorium.

83   *TNA*, MUN 5/139, 'Memorandum on the Employment of German Prisoners in France', 26/9/1916.

84   Jones, *Violence*, pp. 137–38, 140.

85   Ferguson, *Pity of War*, p. 371.

86   *TNA*, FO 383/185, 'Prisoners, Germany Files', 1916.

87   For a review of the legality of reprisals on prisoners of war, see Hull, *Scrap of Paper*, pp. 276–310.

88   Jones, 'Prisoners of War', pp. 274–76. Jones, *Violence*, pp. 151–59.

89   Jones, *Violence*, pp. 151–59.

90   *The Times*, 22/1/1917, p. 9.

91   *SHD*, Vincennes, 16 N 2468, D. 4, f. 140, Copie de la Note 2515, SP46, 15/9/1916, 'Ordre donné par Groupement ABC de la IIe Armée à titre de compte-rendu, aux armées le 22/10/1916'. Jones, *Violence*, p. 149.

92   Jones, *Violence*, p. 138.

93   Jones, *Violence*, p. 143.

94   Jones, 'Prisoners of War', pp. 283–86.

95   Kramer, *Prisoners*, pp. 77–78.

96   Jones, 'Prisoners of War', p. 286.

97   Admiral Amédée Courbet commanded the *École des Défenses Sous-Marines* (School of Underwater Defences) at Boyardville from 1874 to 1877. Ledieu, *L'Amiral Courbet, 1889*; Michon, *Guide Répertoire des Écoles de France*, 1896; Trève, *Quelques Pages de le Vie d'un Marin*, 1887, pp. 42, 59, 71.

98   Berbudeau, *L'Espion de Boyardville, Une Plage Inconnue*, 1893.

99   *Crystal Maze* was created as an alternative format for the UK market by the Fort Boyard team.

100 Dufour, 'Prisonniers du guerre', p. 15.

101 *Comité International de la Croix-Rouge*, Marval and Eugster, 'Rapports sur leurs visites aux camps de prisonniers en France et en Allemagne', 5/1915, p. 19, grandguerre.icrc/fr/Camps/Quiberon/304/fr, accessed 1/2017.

102 *ICRC*, P 27882.

103 Spiegel, *202*, p. 34.

104 Chatelle, *Base Navale du Havre*, pp. 235–36.

105 Mine laying and a lucky escape.

106 Sainte-Adresse is a sought-after location today, especially as a grateful Belgian king granted a large sum to defray the local taxes of residents.

107 *BA-MA*, RM 120–95, Flotilla Order No. 264, 24/7/1917.

108 *SHD*, Cherbourg, SSTe35, pp. 79–100.

109 Becker, *Oubliés de la Grande Guerre*, p. 37.

110 Jones, *Violence*, p. 245.

111 Suadicani stayed in the German Navy: Kapitänleutnant 28/4/1918, Korvettenkapitän 1/4/1927. He died 11/6/1953 (uboat.net).

112 Ehrenrangliste, 1914–1918, lists three German naval officers with a last name of Schwertfeger. They are Hans Schwertfeger, born 1880, Crew 1898, Korvettenkapitän 1915; Paul Schwertfeger, born 1892, Crew 1900, Kapitänleutnant 1910; and a possible twin, Hermann Schwertfeger, born 1892, Crew 1901, Kapitänleutnant 1912. None was a prisoner of war. Paul Schwertfeger underwent u-boat training in 1918, including time as the commander of the training boats *U 21* and *U 22*.

113 wikipedia. The Berthon Boat Company still operates in 2017 on the same site in Lymington, where the business moved in 1918, with a skilled workforce of one hundred specialising in the refit and repair of small yachts.

114 *ICRC*, P 33851, 16/2/1918.

115 Photograph of Erich Gerth and his 'best friend' Rudi Seuffer, both in uniform in a 'relaxed' pose with alcoholic drink in, possibly, an officers' mess in 1917. Photograph captioned later by Eva, Erich's wife (Family collection, shared 2018).

116 Lowrey, correspondence 11/8/2016 and following (uboat.net, WW1 forum).

117 Grant, *U-Boat Intelligence*, p. 79.

118 HMS *Zubian* was a composite destroyer made of the front end of HMS *Zulu* and the rear and mid sections of HMS *Nubian*. 'For now, the HMS *Zubian* sinking claim for *UC 50* is the standard, post-war British claim. The maximum patrol length for a Flanders UCII patrol through Dover however was only twenty days, which is a major red flag. Luckily, we don't need to rely upon that to reject the *Zubian* sinking claim, as *Zubian*'s attack was clearly against the homebound *UC 79* there is a clear match in *UC 79*'s *KTB*' (Lowrey, uboat.net). Also, Grant, *U-Boat Intelligence*, p. 81.

119   *BA-MA*, Freiburg, KTBs: *U 84*, RM 90/v/96; *U 93*, RM/97/1021; *UC 50*, RM 97/1034.
120   Michael Lowrey, WWI forum, uboat.net, 2/1/2017: *U 84*, *U 93*, and *U 95* all sailed within a few days of each other — 1/1/1918, 29/12/1917, 27/12/1917 respectively — from Germany. We also know that all three of these boats successfully got through the Straits of Dover outbound. First of all, *U 95* is not an option for a Bay of Biscay POW rescue mission. U 95's patrol area was the western English Channel (Spindler, *Krieg zur See*, Vol. V, p. 45). In recent years, the wrecks of three large u-boats have been found. The first located is off Hardelot. I was among the people involved in trying to identify this wreck. The submarine in question is of the *U 93* type. (By design, this could be *U 93*, *U 95*, or *U 109*). It was clearly lost while homebound and has massive damage to the stern (internal torpedo explosion?). The propellers were scrubbed and clearly exclude *U 109*. Based upon dates on the propellers, Axel Niestle concluded that the wreck was most likely that of *U 95* (propeller dates after *U 93* was launched, but before *U 95* was launched). The 16/1/1918 date was the apparent last contact date from Royal Nay files (but further west). This is what uboat.net's listing reflects. Then, a few years later, Innes McCartney dived a U 93 class wreck near the Lizard. Innes was under the opinion that the wreck off the Lizard is likely *U 95* and sunk on 7/1/1918 by ramming. (This was the attribution for *U 95* before the Hardelot wreck was found.) The Hardelot wreck, despite the propeller markings must thus be *U 93*. The Royal Navy 16/1 mention could easily be a misattribution or otherwise made in error. Also, from an operational prospective, the odds are higher that *U 93*, with its patrol area along the French coast, would return via Dover as compared to *U 95*, which was assigned to operate in the western English Channel. Innes' hypothesis is pretty strong. However, the alternative theory would be that the Lizard wreck is that of *U 109*. (It is hard to get *U 93* to off the Lizard.) The wreck Innes found is within a mile of a British minefield. The sinking claim for *U 109* is via mine off Gris Nez while sailing outbound through Dover on 26/1/1918. Upon closer examination, there really isn't all that strong a sinking claim there. U 109's patrol area was the St George Channel, and the Lizard would be along the way for her. Finally, the wreck of *U 84* was found off Penmarch about three years ago. I was involved in identifying that wreck. One area of particular concern was making sure the wreck was not *U 93* — and based upon certain design characteristics, we ultimately determined the wreck had to be *U 84*, not *U 93*.
121   wikipedia.
122   *ICRC*, P 18454. theaerodrome.com/forum.
123   *ICRC*, P 36281, 15/5/1918.
124   *ICRC*, P 30318.
125   Hildebrand, *Die Generale der deutschen Luftwaffe 1935–1945*, pp. 190–91.
126   Coles, *Slaughter at Sea*, p. 53. Valentiner was later branded a war criminal while operating in the Mediterranean. Wilhelm Canaris took over *U 38* at Pola.
127   *ICRC*, P 33851. Email, M Claude-Marie Robion, Archives d'Aude, 1/3/2107, 25/4–1/8/1918.
128   Ministry of War, telegram, 66693–3/11 of 29/10/17 (SHD, Vincennes, GR 16N 2472).
129   Archives d'Aude, 9R/1, 10R/17 &20, 'Prisonniers de Guerre Enemis', Ref. 354a/AD–2017.
130   Interviews with Georg Gerth's daughter, Christa-Maria Gerth, 15–16/11/2016.
131   Koebner, *Imperialism*, p. 276.
132   'Dare to know!' (Horace, *Ars poetica*). This was the motto adopted in 1736 by the Society of the Friends of Truth, an important circle in the German Enlightenment.
133   Kant, *Foundations of the Metaphysics*, p. 85.
134   'The brandy industry of the Saar territory since application of the Versailles Peace Treaty', Inaugural Dissertation written and submitted to the Faculty of Law and Political Science of the Bavarian Julius-Maximilian-University Würzburg in order to attain the degree of Doctor of Political Science by Georg Gerth, retired Lieutenant Captain, from Berlin, Würzburg 1923.
135   Delpal, 'Prisonniers de guerre', pp. 152–53.
136   Jones, 'Prisoners of War', p. 282.

137   Becker, *Oubliés de la Grande Guerre*, pp. 127–30. SHD, Vincennes, 16 N 2477, Arcis-sur-Aube, 12/12/1917.
138   Delpal, 'Prisonniers de guerre', p. 153.
139   *ICRC*, P 44693, 9/9/1918.
140   Rasmussen, 'Spanish Flu', in Winter, *First World War*, Vol. III, pp. 334–57. See, also, Hartesveldt, *1918–1919 Pandemic of Influenza*, 1992; Mickels, *Die spanische Grippe 1918/19*, 2010, pp. 1–33.
141   Chickering, *Urban Life*, pp. 564–65.
142   Vaughan, *Doctor's Memories*, pp. 428–29.
143   Lucien-Graux, *Les fausses nouvelles de la Grand Guerre*, Vol. V, p. 265.
144   Rasmussen, 'Spanish Flu', p. 339.
145   Rasmussen, 'Spanish Flu', p. 345.
146   Jordan, *Epidemic Influenza*.
147   Patterson & Pyle, 'Geography and Mortality'.
148   Johnson and Müller, 'Updating the Accounts'.
149   Jones, *Violence*, p. 239.
150   Becker, *Oubliés de la Grande Guerre*, pp. 255–66.
151   *BA-MA*, Freiburg, RM 20/505, 'Berner Bereinbarungen', 26/4/1918.
152   Becker, *Oubliés de la Grande Guerre*, pp. 255–66.
153   Dufour, 'Prisonniers du guerre', p. 23. Jones, 'Prisoners of War', p. 289.
154   Willis, 'Hoover and the Blockade', p. 291. Jones, *Violence*, pp. 300–2.
155   Dufour, 'Prisonniers du guerre', p. 9.
156   Delpal, 'Prisonniers de guerre', p. 155.
157   Kramer, *Prisoners*, p. 86.
158   Delpal, 'Prisonniers de guerre', p. 153.
159   Jones, *Violence*, pp. 260, 296.
160   Dufour, 'Prisonniers du guerre', p. 15.
161   Delpal, 'Prisonniers de guerre', p. 153.
162   Jones, *Violence*, p. 258–59.
163   Rose, *Krieg nach dem Kriege*, pp. 170–184.
164   *TNA*, FO 608/136, pp. 6–8, 22/2/1919.
165   Rose, *Krieg nach dem Kriege. Der Kampf des deutschen Volkes um die Heimkehr seiner Kriegsgefangenen.*
166   Rose, *Krieg nach dem Kriege*, pp. 9–13.
167   Rose, *Krieg nach dem Kriege*, pp. 14–21, pp. 56–57.
168   *TNA*, FO 608/136, pp. 68–71, 18/8/1919.
169   Rose, *Krieg nach dem Kriege*, pp. 129, 152–53, 164–67.
170   *TNA*, FO 608/136, pp. 26, 36.
171   Plassmann, *German prisoners of war in France*, wintersonnenwende.com, accessed 1/5/2017.
172   Rose, *Krieg nach dem Kriege*, p. 120.
173   Becker, *Le retour des prisonniers*, p. 73. *NA*, FO 608/136, von Lersner to Clemenceau, pp. 113–15, 7/11/1919.
174   Jones, PhD dissertation, "The Enemy Disarmed', p. 366.

CHAPTER 13

Guilt and Blame

[One] *function of international law is that it helps to reconcile the loser to his defeat, to accept its legitimacy and to acquiesce in his own punishment. That was clearly shown in the aftermath of the Second World War. The blockade policy after the Armistice deprived the Allies of such legitimacy. In retrospect, it converted a just war against the Kaiser into an unjust war on civilian populations, a war in which the means no longer justified the ends ... It planted the seeds of a new casus belli.*[1]

In the few months Erich Gerth was away, the Reich had shifted on its political and military axis. He left the Baltic for the Adriatic in May 1918, travelling through Berlin, just as Ludendorff's final great offensive began. When Erich returned four months later, his u-boat sunk and his flotilla disbanded, the German armies of the west were in retreat. The naval officer corps faced a battleship mutiny after they were stopped by their crews from taking their capital ships on a 'secret' suicide mission in the North Sea. Home front support for the war had all but collapsed as many ordinary people realised that victory was never going to come. Combined with increasing shortages of food and other life essentials, and mixed with debilitating propaganda, the atmosphere vacillated from toxic to plain bewilderment. Hindenburg fell into depression and Ludendorff's health broke as he called panic-stricken for an armistice at any price.[2]

The Kaiser realised that a return to Berlin to lead the fight back was fanciful. Like so much excess baggage, he was largely deserted by the military leadership, looking to secure their own future. Even his abdication was decided for him. The imperial train was redirected to the neutral Netherlands. Hearing that the Dutch border was under the control of 'revolutionaries', Wilhelm's party transferred to a small convoy of automobiles and did not arrive safely until the small hours of 10 November.[3] After some confusion, the Kaiser was welcomed for there was a centuries-old relationship, through the military and by marriage, between the Dutch and Prussian royal families. Thereafter, Queen Wilhelmina 'steadfastly refused to give way to Allied demands that the Kaiser be expedited for trial as a war criminal', an event which might have ended in a hanging. The formal instrument of abdication for both the German and Prussian thrones was not signed until 28 November.

The armistice was signed on 11 November, the day after the Kaiser's departure. Ludendorff had informed a startled Kaiser and government on 14 August that the war was lost. 'A mere two weeks later [Ludendorff] whose fateful influence and power had driven Germany to the brink of the abyss took an even more humiliating step, in an attempt to avert total military collapse, by demanding an immediate armistice and complete democratisation of the country's political life.'[4]

> *Continuation would involve undue sacrifice of life, so now we must make up our minds to abandon the further prosecution of the war as hopeless. There is still time for this. The German Army has yet the strength to keep the enemy at bay for months, to achieve local successes, and to cause further losses to the Entente. But each new day brings the enemy nearer to his goal, and makes him the less ready to conclude a reasonable peace with us. We must accordingly lose no time. Every twenty-four hours that pass may make our position worse, and give the enemy a clearer view of our present weakness. That might have the most disastrous consequences both for the prospects of peace and for the military position.*[5]

The High Command while 'unable to fight on was also unwilling to surrender'.[6] Hindenburg's great anxiety was that Matthias Erzberger, who headed the three-man armistice team appointed by the government, might demand that the General Staff join in signing the armistice. Asked by Erzberger for advice as was leaving for his meeting with Marshal Foch in the Forest of Compiègne, Hindenburg dodged the question. 'With tears in his eyes, Hindenburg clutched Erzberger's hand and urged him to do his patriotic duty.' Many of Erzberger's countrymen never forgave him for acquiescing to the 'shameful terms'. On 26 August 1921 in the Black Forest he was assassinated by two fanatics for the 'crime of 11 November'.[7]

The allies were not expecting victory when it came. They were planning for at least another year of war despite the expected collapse of Austria-Hungary and so were unprepared with their terms for armistice. Had the call for a ceasefire come during 1916 and 1917 there might have been a more sympathetic hearing as the dominant sentiment was to stop the bloodshed. However, the last months the war had been 'pursued with formerly unimaginable ferocity and sacrifice'.[8] Mistrust had grown among the Allies and this was coupled with a belief that German behaviour had been criminal and so the German nation should be forced to pay a high price for its crimes. The belief, while firm among the Allies, was enthusiastically endorsed by angry publics at large. 'Wrath gradually warped the reason of the victors and threw obstacles in the way of their governments in the matter of bringing the defeated power back into the society of nations.'

The French had most cause to be bitter and took the lead. Prime Minister Clemenceau asked the country's military heroes, Foch and Pétain, to quickly draw up the armistice terms and to present them to Allied commanders in chief on 24-25 October. Naturally, these terms were military in nature and designed to neuter the German's capability to wage war.[9] The terms were taken to Paris on 26 October where President Raymond Poincaré was so startled by their severity that he feared German rejection. Foch replied, 'Then we will continue the war'. Keynes thought little of Foch's capacity for this job:

> *I am certain that Foch's mind and character are an extreme simplicity – of an almost medieval simplicity. He is honest, fearless and tenacious. But nine-tenths of the affairs of mankind are blotted out from his vision, and his mind is not susceptible to attention to them. He is capable therefore in the appropriate circumstances of being as dangerous to the welfare of mankind as others have been who have added a narrow and impervious intellect to a strong and simple character.*[10]

Admiral Rosslyn Wemyss, Jellicoe's replacement as British first sea lord, constructed the naval terms, left out by Foch and Pétain. The whole 'agreement' of thirty-five clauses was presented in Paris on 27 October.[11]

The armistice was read aloud to the Germans representatives on 8 November; the content was far from what was hoped. There was to be no debate and if the terms were not accepted an invasion would begin. The military terms were severe enough: evacuation of all occupied land, including Alsace Lorraine, within fourteen days; evacuation of the left bank of the Rhine; three thirty-kilometres bridgeheads on the right bank at Mayence, Coblenz and Cologne; 5,000 guns, 25,000 machine guns, 3,000 *minenwerfer* (short-range mortars), 1,700 airplanes; 5,000 locomotives, 150,000 railway wagons and 5,000 lorries. In addition, there was to be immediate prisoner of war and civilian repatriation without reciprocity, repayment of stolen gold and an undefined requirement for reparation for damage done. Along with six battle cruisers, ten battleships, eight light cruisers, and fifty modern destroyers, Germany had to hand over all submarines, the latter within fourteen days. There was to be freedom of access to the Baltic and an evacuation of the Belgian ports with all equipment left behind. The issue of the German merchant marine was mislaid for the time being. The Allies' plan was simply to denude the Germans of their fighting capacity. The French also wished to reduce the area and the population of Germany as much as possible, preferably by treaty. The minimum objective was to make the Rhine the western frontier of Germany, cutting off the whole of the Left Bank. 'There was a real possibility that [this area] might have been cut off from Germany and subject to France.' It was known by the Germans as the 'Revolver Republic'.[12]

What particularly jolted the delegates was Article 26 which declared that the blockade was to remain unchanged and, vaguely, consideration would be given to provisioning Germany during the armistice 'to the extent recognised as necessary'. The German delegates were stupefied. In large measure, their country had been defeated by a blockade. They were not prepared to sign a document that sentenced their people to 'prolonged hunger and continuing starvation'.[13] Ludendorff stiffened and now demanded the continuation of the war, but his pervious armistice request had 'broken the back of whatever power of resistance remained to the German people'.[14] Walther Rathenau, the industrialist who had organised Germany's raw materials for the war effort and, incidentally in the process, supported the deportation of 700,000 Belgians to German factories, published an impassioned appeal for a *levée en masse*.[15] 'The people must be ready to rise in defence of their nation ... There is not a day to lose ... There will be enough men to be found who are yet sound, full of patriotic fervour ... All men capable of bearing arms must be combed out of the offices, the guard-rooms and depots ... Our front is worn out; restore it, and we shall be offered better terms.'

> *Everything seems upside down with Rathenau's appeal for an 'insurrection of the people'. The high priest of corporate management calling for an insurrectionary people's war? A German-Jewish civilian firing up a furor teutonicus? ... All this sounds surreal.*[16]

Hindenburg and the Kaiser at Spa telegraphed a horrified acceptance to Erzberger in Paris an hour and a half before the invasion was due to start. They included the largest of caveats.

> *The German government will obviously take care to complete its assumed obligations with all strength. But in the interests of candidness the relationship between Germany and her opponents, the undersigned are forced to indicate by the dictates of conscience that the completion of these conditions must plunge the German people into anarchy and famine and that, by no fault of the German government and people, a situation can arise whereby the further observance of all obligations will be made unlikely.*

All the ingredients for the tortured peace treaty negotiations, and the cause of so much anger and disavowal, were immediately in place. The blockade would continue at the whim of the Allies and it would be made worse by the Allies' unfettered access to the Baltic where the German fishing fleet was to be sequestered. 'The winter of 1918-19, even more than the war years, determined the Germans' and Austrians' folk memories of hunger as an instrument of war.'[17] The blockade and German prisoners of war were available as bargaining counters. The fight began between the Allies over whether Germany's gold should pay for food or French reparations and what the amount the reparations should be. However, should supplies became available, the lack of a merchant fleet, when remembered, and the trucks and wagons to move the food would certainly hinder relief. 'The tragedy of the armistice and later of the treaty is that the blood, destruction, propaganda and suspicion of four years prevented the most logical of men from viewing the issue objectively.'[18]

It is worth reflecting on what the German hierarchy might have expected. For many individuals separated directly from the fighting, Germany was not a beaten nation. There was no conflict on her soil; her armies were 'far into enemy territory'. The army was believed to be largely intact. At the start of the war, the Germany army had only one objective – a crushing military victory over France and Russia. 'Having grown up and been educated in a tradition of almost blind trust in the power, superiority, and intelligence of the German military, people tended to close their eyes and flee from the harsh reality into wishful thinking and imagine that the war had somehow ended differently than it had.'[19]

The end was meant to be very different. Bethmann's war aims in September 1914 when he still expected to beat both France and Russia were 'security for the German Reich in west and east for all imaginable time'. France was to be 'so weakened as to make her revival as a great power impossible for all time'.[20]

In the west, this meant the Briey ore fields in French Lorraine, war indemnity so high and continuous that the French would be unable to spend any serious sums on armaments for up to twenty years. A commercial treaty making France economically dependent on Germany, reliant on German exports and excluding British goods from France. Belgium split between Luxembourg and Germany with a rump vassal state including Flemish France, with the ports and military completely controlled by Germany. A Central European economic association through common customs treaties to include France, Belgium, Holland (with a German garrison at Antwerp and the mouth of the Scheldt), Denmark, Austria-Hungary, Poland and perhaps Italy, Sweden and Norway under German leadership and economic dominance. The creation of a continuous Central African colonial empire from west to east coast. In the east, Lithuania and Courland under German

dominion, large sections of central Poland annexed and the remainder
of Poland with Austrian Galicia to form a Polish state completely under
German control.

Such an extensive power grab could only have been introduced to a willing Reich. The big interest groups, led by the iron and coal industrialists, became the most active and rabid proponents of annexations'. Theirs had been a 'good war' as between 1912 and 1918, net earnings in the metal manufacturing industries rose from 34 million to 111 million Reichsmarks.[21] The industrialists were joined by many the politicians, especially those who were to lead the Weimar Republic.[22] Among these leaders was the industrialist and financier Walther Rathenau, the head of the great electricity combine, AEG. Bethmann's 'September War Aims Programme' had strong similarities with a document sent to the chancellor a few days earlier. Bethmann and Rathenau were neighbours in the country and dined together from time to time. What did they talk about on these evenings?[23] Were German gains in a possible war already being 'discussed before August 1914 round the table of Rathenau's exquisite dining room in Schloss Freienwalde?' Hindenburg incorporated the list into his own war aims programme, endorsed by the Kaiser, and Trotha recommended it to Ludendorff.[24]

The issue of war aims underwent a number of political mood swings with fundamental disagreements between the Reichstag and the military as various peace moves were mooted.[25] In September 1916, the Chief of the Admiralty Staff, Admiral Henning von Holtzendorff, listed the Belgian Congo; the Courland coast with Libau and Windau, and the islands of Moon and Oesel; the Danish Faroe Islands, 160 nautical miles west of the Shetland Isles, as necessary acquisitions in order to outflank Great Britain; and also the Cape Verde Islands, Tahiti and Madagascar.[26] In September 1917, Holtzendorff demanded German control of the Zeebrugge-Bruges-Ostend triangle as the navy's minimum war aim. After his dismissal shortly afterwards Tirpitz agreed and campaigned against the papal initiative of Benedict XV because it entailed German 'surrender' of the Belgian coast. The Kaiser admitted that this strip of coast should not be an obstacle to peace, but he feared the reaction of his naval executive officer corps. 'Renunciation of the Flanders coast,' the Kaiser pleaded, 'will rob my navy of its battle aim; it will gain nothing.' William demanded compensation for the navy if it should be forced to give up Flanders in the form of a 'strong, energetic expansion of our fleet' after the present war in order to prepare for the 'next Anglo-German war'.[27] Hindenburg informed the chancellor that he now backed this demand.

With Germany's aims now pipe dreams, the German people were in a 'dreamland' 'where everyone, without grasping the conditions and real consequences, could portray the future in fantastic, pessimistic or heroic terms'.[28] This is an incessant theme in contemporary and historical writing:

'political and social illusions, fear, anger, and desperation sprang up, all of which were so far from reality that it seemed as though the terrible sacrifices and efforts of the war had destroyed people's ability to judge their place in history realistically'.[29]

Friedrich paraphrases Kessler, whose diaries from 1918, especially in Berlin, give pertinent and sardonic eyewitness accounts.[30]

> *The people starved and dying by the hundred thousand, were reeling deliriously between blank despair, frenzied revelry and revolution. Berlin had become a nightmare, a carnival of jazz bands and rattling machine guns ... On the very day of [one battle in the centre of the city] the streets were placarded with a poster, 'Who has the prettiest legs in Berlin?' Profiteers and their girls, the scum and riffraff of half of Europe could be seen growing fat and sleek and flaunting their new cars and ostentatious jewellery in the faces of the pale children and starving women shivering in their rags before the empty bakers' and butchers' shops ... 'The really important thing during any crisis,' said one Berliner who remembers the days of the Revolution, 'is whether the street cars are running. If the streetcars keep running, then life is bearable. And so it should be recorded that on 9 November, the day the German Empire fell, the streetcars of Berlin* [Ernst Gerth's legacy[31]] *continued running. The phone functioned, too, and so do the systems that provided gas, water and electricity.*

The Germany that signed the western armistice on 11 November was a republic. The naval revolution spread to the city streets, gathered in the war weary, and was abducted by socialists and Bolsheviks. In quick order, the once-proud u-boats were declared failures and every serviceable craft ordered to Harwich to surrender. Most of Tirpitz's capital ships were escorted to Scapa Flow and the German merchant marine was eventually handed over to the Allies. French, British and American military were camped on the Rhine. Germany's colonies across the world were snatched by the victors. Fighting continued in the east to hold back the re-invented Polish and Russian armies from East Prussia where they sought to gain ground before extant borders were set by treaty. Two million soldiers marched home from France by December in reasonable order.[32] No sooner had the army returned than it 'disintegrated, drifting onto the streets or packing up and going home'. Yet it was quickly clear that the thousands of returning veterans 'represented an unanticipated political force'.[33] Within days, it was a peculiar civil war with control of food stocks, government offices and communications as the prizes. In many cities, like Berlin where Erich reported for work, street fighting was normal while, around the corner, theatres and nightclubs remained open. For a naval officer like Erich, still in uniform, there was no room to hide as epaulets were torn from shoulders in the street by revolutionaries with an insolent contempt that would have meant the death penalty a few months previously.

Most people were in shock. After so many promises of impending success, of personal sacrifices made in the name of victory, the loss of almost two million men, how could the impossible have happened?

One week after taking over the Supreme Command in 1917, Ludendorff and Hindenburg inspected the western front. They quickly deduced that Germany had to fortify its reserve lines and to go on the defensive to save manpower. A controlled retreat in France early in the year was minutely planned based on the Siegfried Line, fifteen to forty-five kilometres behind the front trenches. 'The enemy must find a countryside completely sucked dry in which his own mobility is made as difficult as possible. Nothing was spared, not the wells, which were made unusable, not even the orchards, which were felled to prevent soldiers from taking shelter under them.'[34] When the Allied troops went forward 'into the moonscape they were deeply shocked'.

His deep reserve positions secured, Ludendorff launched a series of offensives designed to break through the western front. In the three months from March 1918, all Germany waited impatiently for a victory that never came. For the last time, the German people 'were permitted to enjoy illusory military successes'; their only compensation for the 'economic deprivation, the social and moral disruption, and the political indecisiveness that plagued German society'.[35]

The March offensive, code-named Michael, and the three mini-offensives that followed it in April, May-June, and July 1918, 'repeated the old pattern: a rush to embrace an unrealistic risk, the attempt to master the risk by technical virtuosity or by contradictory measures or by sheer denial; the trust in a wonder weapon, and the omission of preparations for failure'.[36] Substantial quantities of ammunition had been stockpiled for fifty-two attack divisions; eleven *Stellungsdivisionen*, 'holding divisions' to deal with counter-attacks; and 6,263 guns with 2,400 ammunition trains. The enormous build-up was kept secret despite well-founded rumours that the 'final' German offensive would be against the British line, which had been extended and weakened to relieve the French.[37] 'Matters would have been much better if the 300,000 troops held in reserve in Britain against an invasion had been sent earlier, but they were eventually all transferred in a single fortnight.' Because of bad planning, poor reconnaissance and the lack of co-ordination with the u-boats, the Allied emergency troop transfer was almost unhindered in a strange parallel with the BEF's arrival in France in 1914. The German navy remained idle in port.[38] As at the beginning of the war, the Allies command problems continued. It was 'incomprehensible' that it took the strong possibility of a German victory in 1918 before they were forced to establish a central reserve and a supreme Allied commander.[39] 'A long history of Anglo-French rivalry stimulated suspicion.' There was a reluctance by British politicians to have their troops commanded by generals of other nations, but if 'there was to be a supreme commander it could only be provided by France'. Co-operation by the British and French navies especially in the Dover approaches continued successful.

> When the attack came on 21 March it was wildly successful in the first few days ... By 1918, Germany lacked every objective measure for such an operation: it had numerical parity but not superiority; it lacked adequate reserves (one million men remained in the east); it had fewer heavy artillery and airplanes than the Allies; and, above all, it lacked trucks, horses and horse fodder for the transportation needed to pour troops and supplies through the hole ... Ludendorff blurted out to Rupprecht, 'I forbid the word 'operation'. We are simply going to punch a hole and everything will happen from there. That is how we did it in Russia.' ... Ludendorff failed to prepare strong defences to shield retreating troops and check Allied counterattacks ... In the five months after the March offensive began, Germany suffered one million casualties either dead, wounded, missing or captured. From mid-July to the armistice, another 420,000 were killed or wounded and 340,000 were missing or captured.[40]

The Michael offensives of 1918 were undertaken 'in defiance of the opposition of some of the army's leading strategists and in complete disregard of the War Office's warning that Germany's supply of reserves would be exhausted'.[41] Germany lacked both the manpower and mobility to convert a breakthrough into strategic victory. Ludendorff's claims that the offensives were wearing the enemy down were 'ridiculous' as he gravely underestimated enemy strength. German lines were extended by ninety to one hundred and fifty kilometres and the number of men available to hold them were reduced by one million as reserves were 'squandered'. The Allied forces were supplemented by over two million fresh troops, mostly American. Ludendorff probed repeatedly for signs of weakness, wearing down his attack divisions and their supply systems. On 29 March, he switched the main attack from the British to the French in an opportunistic decision which reminded one senior officer of the debacle of the Marne in 1914. Every mobilised German division was involved before the assaults ground to a halt.[42]

Numerous units temporarily abandoned their attacks to raid plentiful Allied food and wine depots. In the last days, the daily energy figure for the 4.2 million men in the German army was below 2,900 kilocalories a day; there were also 2.5 million prisoners of war to feed.[43] There is much anecdotal evidence that the German Army was hungry: the American handbills 'scattered over the German trenches to encourage enemy desertion listed the rations they would be given as prisoners of war'. Even Ludendorff admitted the attraction of the Allied food to his hungry men. 'The enemy's machine guns continued to give our infantry much trouble; it should have grappled with them more vigorously, but often it wasted time looking for food.'[44]

> *The way in which the troops stopped around captured food supplies, while individuals stayed behind to search houses and farms for food, was a serious matter. This impaired our chances of success and showed poor discipline. But it was equally serious that both our young company commanders and our senior officers did not feel strong enough to take disciplinary action, and exercise enough authority to enable them to lead their men forward without delay ... It should always have been remembered that there were many men in the army who deserved no mercy whatsoever; of this the numerous deserters and skrim-shankers are melancholy proof. Others mutinied and greeted reserves coming up to the front with cries of 'strike beakers'. Still others deserted either en route from the east, at home, or at the front.*

Desertions presaged the end. One regiment in the east destined in July for rest was diverted to the western front. When these troops realised, they threw their rifles and packs out of the windows, stopped the train and fled across the fields.[45] Ludendorff's view after the war was that amid 'deeds of glorious valour' there was also behaviour which he confessed he would 'not have thought possible in the German Army; whole bodies of our men had surrendered to single troopers, or isolated squadrons'.[46] Retiring troops, meeting a fresh division 'going bravely into action', shouted out things like 'Blackleg' and 'You're prolonging the war'. The officers in many places 'lost their influence and allowed themselves to be swept along with the rest'.

The extent of the damage was demonstrated by Ludendorff's threats to try to stem desertions by a general order on 23 June 1918:[47]

1. *Every man going to the enemy will be punished with death on return to Germany.*
2. *All his property within the country will be seized.*
3. *He will lose his citizenship; his next of kin will have no right to receive an allowance.*
4. *If a man is suspected of having betrayed his country ... action will be taken against him for treason to his country.*
5. *It is useless to reckon on escaping the penalty by remission or by lapse of time.*

The Allies staged massive counter-attacks on 18 July at Villers-Coterêts, spearheaded by the new light Renault, Berliet, and Schnieder tanks which lost almost half their number, but turned the tide in the land war.

> In the summer, of 1918, as fresh troops and equipment poured in from
> the United States, the Allies attacked. On 8 August, the 'Black Day' to
> the German army, they smashed through the German lines. For four
> years, shifts in the lines on the Western Front had been measured in
> metres; now the Germans went back kilometre by kilometre, leaving
> behind guns, tanks and soldiers. Sixteen German divisions were wiped
> out in the first days of the Allied attack ... The Allies were moving
> slowly but inexorably toward Germany's borders and there was little the
> German High Command could do to stop them ... Germany was near
> the end of its appetite and supplies. In Berlin, housewives marched
> with their empty pots and pans ... Workers put down their tools ...
> the Reichstag demanded peace ... Bulgaria dropped away at the end of
> September ... Ottoman Turkey a month later ... then Austria-Hungary
> ... the loss of Romanian oil.[48]

The iron wall in the West that had for 'more than four years withstood
the shocks of the armies of the greater part of the civilised world was
disintegrating or bending back'.[49] With the breakthrough in the German
lines on the Somme on the 'Black Day', the German army 'lost its nerve
and fled in panic'.[50] The second setback just a few days after Villers-
Coterêts proved to be too much for Ludendorff. His severe depression over
several days meant that he was no longer able to give decisive commands.
He continued to block his government's efforts to make a clear statement
of its intention to restore Belgium's independence to pave the way for
peace negotiations. The unwillingness to face reality was most evident
in Ludendorff's conduct of military operations. He constantly refused to
retreat to strong defensive positions yet, immediately after the 'Black Day',
he announced that Germany 'cannot win the war any more, but we must
not lose it either'.[51]

None of the normal attributes of failure was present.[52] Most of Belgium
and the industrial heartlands of north-eastern France were in German
hands. By holding so much French territory, the army 'retained the
advantages of an offensive strategy' forcing the Allies to attack across 'fire-
swept battlefields'. The German army was undefeated and 'still stood deep
in enemy territory on all fronts when it laid down its arms, its front had
neither been broken through nor enveloped'. But, after the failure of the
spring offensives, the army was without reserves and sufficient armaments
to stop the impetus of the fast-arriving Americans. The German troops
were hungry and demoralised. Stout rear guard actions were practicable,
but the fight would inevitably have inched back to the Rhine and from
there into the heart of Germany. Losses would have considerable and the
morale tide had turned.

New recruits and soldiers returning from leave brought news of the misery to the front line were the troops themselves were hungry and ill. They stole the barley feed meant for the horses and ground it in their coffee mills to make flour pancakes.[53] The horses died; the soldiers' will to fight dissipated ... To many who witnessed these events, it appeared as though hunger was the victor, and that it was starvation among the army and civilians which had brought about a humiliating defeat.[54]

Propaganda supported by the news from the home front played a decisive part and is well-documented by historian George Bruntz.[55]

The army was weary and embittered. Great injustices and unfulfilled promises demoralised the troops. The absolute separation of the officers' corps, the scandalous stories of provision stores, opened the eyes of the men ... Hindenburg's Vaterlandische Unterricht, 'Fatherland Teaching', propaganda using film and talks and given by young officers, was laughed at. Hate was in the troops. Hate, not for the enemy who were suffering the same, but hate for those who prolonged the war.[56] None of which was helped by hearing of 'unspeakable conditions' at home.

The German soldier or sailor was worked upon from the air, through secret channels, through traitors at home. He was told 'truths' about the forces against him that had been suppressed by the German censors. It was foolish to try to oppose the whole world. Every possible weakness in the German character was cunningly exploited. When, early in July 1918, some of the German papers began to publish stories which gave indications of war-weariness, this material was immediately put into leaflets and distributed among the German troops.[57] One senior officer on the western front analysing the military reverses wrote, 'What caused the most damage was the paper war waged by our enemies who daily flooded us with hundreds of thousands of leaflets, extraordinarily well arranged and edited.'[58] The military collapse of Germany was due to a 'disintegration of morale both on the firing line and among the civilian population.'[59] It was the telling of the truth to the Germans by their enemies that finally caused the debacle at a time when the German Army 'was well equipped with supplies and ammunitions, and behind it still stretched line after line almost impregnable because of natural strength and military science'.

Propaganda activities on the front line were powerfully if inadvertently supported by news from home and by revolutionary claims.[60] Some twenty-nine billion pieces of mail were sent backwards and forwards from home and front during the war. Every day some ten million letters, postcards, telegrams and packages reached the front with many loved ones writing daily. 'Military censorship was bitterly resented.'[61] The radical socialists within Germany sent out leaflets blaming the capitalists and the government for the plight of the people. One stated:

> *What was bound to come has come! Hunger! In Leipzig, in Berlin, in Essen, and many other places there are riots started by hungry masses of people. Herr Bethmann-Hollweg says England is the cause of the hunger in Germany, and the other officials repeat this. The German government should have known it would come to this. War against Russia, France and England had to lead to the blockade ... Why has the government done nothing? Because the government, the capitalists, the Junkers, do not feel the pangs of hunger of the masses ... The workers can either continue in silent obedience and go to a sorrowful end or they can rise up, do away with the government and the ruling classes and force peace ... Arise, you men and women! Down with the War! Hail to the International Solidarity of the Proletariat![62]*

Hindenburg publicly joined the propaganda battle, but his target was the home front.[63] On 2 September, he appealed to the German people by poster to remain loyal and to pay no attention to the propaganda of the enemy and the revolutionists within Germany. The gradual disappearance of the morale of the German troops after the Spring offensives resulted in a 'concealed soldiers' strike' of perhaps one million shirkers and deserters.[64] This state was described by historian Knesebeck,

> *In the first year of the war the soldiers spoke of 'death in the field of honour'; in the second year, they spoke of 'giving our lives for the Fatherland', in the third year they spoke of 'falling in a foreign field in the fulfilment of our duty'; and in the fourth year they spoke of 'dying as a further offering to this terrible war'.[65]*

The Supreme Command, 'unable to learn from defeat or to relinquish the chimera of military victory, repeated the tactic over and over until Germany was so weakened that the Allies could begin the final attacks of the war'. On the Western front through October, fighting continued without let up. It was a more fluid battle so civilians and their property were more at risk.[66] In steady retreat, the Germans looted and pillaged. The 'virtual collapse' of civilian government gave Ludendorff and Hindenburg unprecedented power and allowed 'limitless violence'.[67] The Belgian deportations, the Hindenburg programme, the destruction of northern France, the all-or-nothing slaughter of the Michael offensives were mirrored at sea where the u-boats still torpedoed neutral shipping.

In an ultimate display of self-indulgent violence, the military leaders, denying defeat, called for Germany to risk destroying itself in a hopeless final battle, an *Endkampf*, inside Germany. On 31 October, Ludendorff wrote that he was prepared in the *Endkampf* 'to risk actual defeat', an annihilation of the German army on national soil. 'Cabinet members thought this was no empty threat and it seems likely that many high-ranking officers preferred actual defeat to capitulation'. Equating the army with the nation suggested the next step, national suicide. In this extraordinary Wagnerian scenario, the Kaiser, riding a white horse, would lead his army, senior officers at his side and hundred of thousands of willing foot soldiers behind, into a modern battlefield filled with tanks and blasted by artillery and raked by machineguns.[68] Presumably, as the smoke thickened, the throng would slowly disappear, their bodies never to be found. In this commitment to protecting the honour of the officer corps, the whole sorry morality and misguided logic of the Prussian military nation was on display. The Kaiser, apparently, thought about the idea for a while, a last chance to play glorious soldier, and preferred abdication.

Endkampf was not just a fevered part of Ludendorff's mental collapse. A month earlier, the Kaiser's navy caught the executive hysteria and planned its own, private nihilistic extinction. This time, for the navy and for the nation, the consequences were far more severe. These Armageddons were not directly unconnected, but 'both services clung to the old logic of ultimate risk, ultimate force'.[69] The navy was as reluctant to admit the failure of unrestricted submarine warfare as the army was to admit its own defeat on land, and both sought a 'honourable' solution which protected their officer corps from the humiliation of public failure. In July 1918, the admiralty had twice proposed extending the u-boat blockade to the coast of the United States. The navy was 'prepared to risk a cascade of war declarations by the neutral states that mostly steamed these waters, even though only three u-boats were available to enforce the blockade'. As late as a cabinet meeting on 17 October, Admiral Reinhard Scheer repeated the claim that sooner or later the u-boat campaign would be 'politically effective'. The truth was that u-boat successes were rapidly diminishing: 187 vessels sunk or damaged, totalling 372,457 tons, in August; 123 vessels, 276,942 tons, in September; and ninety-four vessels, 176,333 tons in October.[70]

The story of the 1918 mutiny by the Imperial fleet is still, today, covered in lies and obfuscation; many myths have been strewn in the path of research. As with the 1917 food-based mutiny, the best explanation of what occurred is found in Horn's meticulously-researched book on the subject.[71] The navy by its handling of the 1917 mutiny and its 'unregenerate conduct since that time' had made itself so detested by its enlisted personnel that a real mutiny was in the offing. The first recognition of the possibility of revolution was made in the Reichstag by a socialist on 5 July 1917. 'There is always talk of whether the revolution will come or not; we can only say that the German people are already in the midst of the revolution ... The feeling in Germany is such that things cannot go on as they are at present, for otherwise it will come to conflicts of the worst kind. The

Government ought to take to heart Goethe's words, "The revolution from below is always due to the sins of omission of those above".[72]

After four years of war and constant exposure to mistreatment by their officers, the best of whom had gone to the u-boats, the sailors and stokers of the German navy were ready to resort to any means to remedy their plight.[73] 'No socialist, no communist propaganda or subversion was required to bring them to that conclusion.' Their life in the navy had taught them better than any socialist pamphlet that their superiors were nothing more than 'better paid and better fed masters whose absolute power they could no longer stomach'. That is not to say that there was no attempt by the communists to rabble-rouse.[74] A good example is this wireless message addressed to the German sailors on 15 February 1918:

> *To the Sailors of the Baltic Fleet and all Oppressed Peoples*[75]
> *Do you hear our voice, and do you hear the cries and groans of your brothers, the soldiers who are drowning in their own blood, and the sailors who are meeting their death day by day in the misty sea and the cold depths of the seas and oceans? Do you hear the heart-breaking lamentations and the despairing sobs of mothers, brothers and children throughout Europe which is drenched in blood? Do you not see the approaching shadow of the black spectre of famine and his bony hand? If you hear and see all this, who do you keep silent? Give answer to our cry and to the appeals of your brothers. Follow the example of the Russian people ... Rise up like a hurricane, tear off the fetters of bondage, overthrow the thrones of tyrants, and free yourselves from the god you have created with your own hands – Capitalism ... Therefore, raise boldly the standard of revolt. Leave the sepulchre of the trenches; make an end to the despots.*

Admiral Scheer bears a large measure of responsibility for the collapse of the navy after August 1918. On 11 August, he was appointed chief of the admiralty staff. His officers 'hoped that he would pursue an aggressive form of warfare that would permit it to gain some fame and glory before the fighting ended'. Scheer quickly insisted that he be given the right to co-ordinate and plan all future naval policy following the advice of his close friend and Chief of Staff, Captain Magnus von Levetzow. Almost from the day he assumed office, Scheer played the role of a 'passive Hindenburg to Levetzow's dynamic and domineering Ludendorff'. The navy soon 'fell prey to the most narrow-minded, reactionary, and irresponsible policies of Levetzow' and of his close ally Admiral von Trotha who had recently assumed the job of Chief of Staff to the new Commander of the High Seas Fleet, Admiral Franz Hipper. Both Levetzow and Trotha were noted for their 'marked antipathy toward democracy, parliamentary government, and the idea of a negotiated peace' and had an 'absolute abhorrence for all those who stood opposed to militarism'. Levetzow thought Prince Max, the newly-appointed Chancellor charged with democratisation and bringing a fair peace, was a 'donkey' and a 'traitor'; socialists generally were a horde of 'red rascals'.

Almost a month before Ludendorff's proposed *Endkampf*, Captain Michaelis, Director of the German Navy Department, proposed to Levetzow that the High Seas Fleet be 'thrown into battle against the English' in order to preserve its future in the post-war world.[76] Michaelis wanted to revive the sagging morale of the German people by means of a 'visible military success'. Michaelis wrote, 'I know it is pure risk, but if there is no alternative, then a risk is justified. If it succeeds, then I am convinced everything has been won; it if fails, nothing more is lost than is the case anyway without it.' Quite quickly, Trotha gave his strong support, animated by his desire to preserve the honour of the officer corps. He wrote to Levetzow, 'It goes without saying that we live in dread fear of the thought that our fleet could shamefully allow itself to be destroyed from inside without having engaged in battle. An engagement, even if it means dying in honour, is still worthwhile because it would inflict a severe wound on England ... You must feel this as much as we do. Nevertheless, I implore you, do not permit the power of our fleet to be bargained away or allow it to die in disgrace.' Several years after the war, Trotha was unrepentant, 'Even if the fleet had been destroyed, our proud, old Imperial fleet with its officers and men would now be lying in immortal fame at the bottom of the sea instead of having been preserved in order to cover itself in cowardly fashion with disgrace, the humiliation of revolution and delivery for internment.'

> On 15–16 October, Levetzow drafted a memorandum advocating a Flottenvorstoß, 'final fleet thrust', that received Scheer's immediate approval. By 26 October, the German Empire was transferred into a democratic, parliamentary monarchy. The officer corps of the navy and the army were convulsed with shock and grief. Under the impact of these precipitous changes, the self-confidence and arrogance of these officers turned into fear, despair and humiliation. Bitter anger and resentment at their military and political defeat alternated with a mood of total despondency and near paralysis. But, among the lower classes, the workers, sailors and soldiers – the end of the war and the onset of popular government was met with an overwhelming feeling of relief. During the last tragic weeks of the war as an agonised Germany sought an armistice, these diametrically opposite responses were to precipitate a mutiny that caused the final collapse of the Imperial Navy.[77]

Horn provides strong archival evidence that it was an admirals' rebellion that was responsible for the navy's collapse. 'The German navy died when the upper echelons of the caste-ridden, irresponsible officer corps was unable to reconcile themselves to military defeat, the advent of parliamentary government and the end of their power and prestige and they rebelled against the government of Prince Max von Baden. This rebellion took the form of an attempt to order the High Seas Fleet out on a desperate and heroic but completely hopeless and illegal suicide mission against the British. Justifiably outraged by the admirals' rebellion, the enlisted men sabotaged the suicide mission by their refusal to sail. When the naval authorities then branded them traitors and threatened harsh reprisals, the enlisted men rose in a full-fledged military rebellion that swept away the power of a moribund and half-paralysed officer corps.'

Twenty-four battleships and cruisers waited in the harbours of Kiel, Wilhelmshaven and Hamburg. The Kaiser, the Army, except for Ludendorff, and the government were deliberately kept ignorant of the suicide plan despite formal and strict instruction that the military was from 26 October under civilian control.[78] In an ironic tug-of-war with Ludendorff's Endkampf, the Kaiser's Imperial presence and death was required first by his love-child. He was nominated to stand proudly on the bridge of one of his battleships as he led 60,000 sailors to sacrificial oblivion. Rumour and fact spread quickly, often fuelled by the boasting of arrogant officers. On 28 October, Hipper received an order from Scheer, delivered verbally by Levetzow, to steam out for one last grand battle. The crews refused to obey. The battleships *Thüringen* and *Helgoland* quenched their fires. 'In ordinary times, the mutiny would not have lasted much more than a day, but these were times of disintegration, when a revolt succeeds not because of its own strength but because of the weakness, loss of nerve, of the ruling authorities.'[79]

Despite much readily available evidence, the German fleet command grossly miscalculated the fighting effectiveness of the fleet and the depressed morale of the sailors.[80] Officers called on the men to 'keep a stiff upper lip', blinded to the 'dreadful misery prevailing in Germany's cities, where the populace, living without coal for fuel, without adequate clothing, and with empty stomachs, fell an easy prey to the dreadful flu epidemic that raged throughout Europe'. Insensitivity made it impossible for the officers to 'fathom the war-weariness and defeatism that spread with speed through the enlisted ranks as sailors and shipyard workers returned from the evacuated ports in Flanders [and the Adriatic] to Germany filled with rumours of military collapse, chaos, and treason'. Numerous acts of sabotage were committed on board torpedo boats and submarines. Martin Niemöller, *U 67*, wrote later,

> *In mid-October, the Western Front was pulled back and the coast of Flanders evacuated. We understood that this was a major strategic measure to fight for peace on a shortened front, possibly peace for Germany, cost what it might! We no longer had confidence in our Allies,*

> *but that the suicidal discord was nourished at this moment amongst the*
> *German people – that was the crime of 1918.*[81]

A revolt broke out at the submarine base in Emden. On 12 August 1918, some mutineers, whilst refusing to serve in the submarines, took a torpedo boat and fled to Norway; chased by cruisers, this torpedo boat was hit and sunk and, several days afterwards, 130 bodies of German sailors were washed up on the Jutland coast.[82] In September, there were revolts in almost all the submarine centres where some crews refused to embark. On 29 October, men failed to return from shore leave in Kiel and Wilhelmshaven. Insubordination on an unprecedented scale soon spread through the large ships. There was broad anti-war sentiment and hopes for Wilson's idea of an armistice. Rebellious sailors found support in the civilian population. By 30 October, even Hipper conceded that the suicide operation was off.[83]

Two of Georg Gerth's former commanders played minor roles in the ensuing panic. The Kaiser's brother, Prince Heinrich of Prussia, fled his home and headquarters at the Kiel Schloss, upset by the invasion of his residence when a band of mutineers openly insulted him.[84] Early in November, the prince decided to remove himself and his family from the centre of the revolt. His car was stopped by sailors, two jumping on the running-boards, and Heinrich allegedly shot one as he sped off.

On 4 November, Levetzow raised the idea of restoring 'order and strict shore discipline' by placing the entire German coast under one command as in Flanders. The next day, Scheer went directly to the Kaiser and persuaded him to order Admiral Ludwig von Schröder, the commander of the Naval Infantry Brigade in Flanders, to assume control over Kiel and to restore 'peace and order with an iron hand'. Schröder was well known in England as the 'murderer' of Captain Charles Fryatt after trial as a *franc tireur*.[85] Among Schröder's staff was Karl Bartenbach, head of Georg Gerth's Flanders u-boat flotilla. Schröder received his orders on 6 November and began at once to prepare a special train to leave for Kiel with a thousand-strong 'battle-hardened naval shock battalion with artillery and a good machine gun company'. Thirteen hours later, as he was about to depart for the 'merciless suppression of the Kiel uprising', he received orders rescinding his appointment. Prince Max got wind of the plan and persuaded the Kaiser that it would be suicidal to send an 'aggressive type' like Schröder to Kiel. If pitched battles had ensued in Kiel between the Flanders' hard men and 40,000 mutinous sailors and their civilian supporters, the history of the armistice and the fledgling German republic might have been very different.

Everywhere naval officers were in full retreat, without firm leadership, panic-stricken, discredited, fearful of exposure and incapable of coherent action. On 3 November, Levetzow, Hipper and Trotha met in Wilhelmshaven and began the myth-making. They claimed they had acted to meet an imaginary British naval attack. Their officers then raised the spectre of a Bolshevik revolution and were initially successful in concealing the real causes of the mutiny. Scheer and his staff recognised the value of this deception and put forth the 'massive smokescreen that [the navy] had been betrayed and destroyed by a Bolshevik conspiracy and the fearful, cowardly and un-German conduct of its enlisted men, who lacked the courage to face the enemy'. After the war, the navy 'invented all sorts of excuses for Sheer's underhanded and unethical behaviour'. Scheer later claimed that the revolt was a long and carefully-prepared and executed plan of the leaders of the revolutionary wing of the Social Democrats and for years spent much time in questionable acts searching for non-existent evidence that ended in a farcical parliamentary enquiry.

As early as 4 November, individual sailors and groups began streaming out of Kiel by truck, train and ship. On 5 November, 500 men of the Third Squadron of the High Seas Fleet, which was at the centre of the mutiny, landed near Lübeck. The entire town with its garrison surrendered to the revolt without a shot fired. The same day, Hamburg joined, then Wilhelmshaven. In four years of war, the Kaiser's Reich had 'rotted so badly that the sailors' ill-organised uprising spread without resistance to the rest of the northern ports and within a week to Berlin'. The 'Red Count', Harry Kessler, avowed republican and pacifist, wrote in his diary on 7 November,

> Events at Kiel, Lübeck, Altona, Hamburg and Hanover have as yet passed off fairly bloodlessly. That is the way all revolutions start. The thirst for blood grows gradually with the strains involved in setting up the new order ... The shape of the revolution is becoming clear: progressive encroachment, as by a patch of oil, by the mutinous sailors from the coast to the interior. Berlin is being isolated and will soon only be an island.[86]

Within a few days, an uprising in Munich deposed the Bavarian monarchy; insurgents calling themselves the Workers' and Soldiers' Councils seized control of Frankfurt, Leipzig, Stuttgart, and Düsseldorf, and trainloads of mutinous sailors from Kiel and the North Sea ports began streaming into Berlin.[87]

The Bolsheviks quickly entered the wider fray, but they had almost no influence in the initial naval rebellion. One piece of evidence is enough to complete the rebuttal. Two days after taking Lübeck, delegates of the Baltic fleet's Third Squadron presented a list of primary demands, all demonstrably unpolitical:

1. Reduction of the punitive powers of the First Officer.
2. Since the trust of the crews in their officers has vanished completely,

for the immediate future a representative of the crews shall be attached to the Admiral so that the crews can feel that things are being handled correctly.

3. The men must be granted the right of assembly to speak their minds.
4. All newspapers are to be made available.
5. Equal rations for enlisted men and officers.
6. Freedom not to salute officers when off duty.
7. For infractions not concerning matters of honour, no imprisonment but money fines.

Horn's conclusion is most serious. Apart from consistently and dishonourably lying about their intentions, and spreading blame in all directions, Scheer and his officers cared little about their actions undermining the armistice negotiations. 'By keeping his plans secret, Scheer defied the Kaiser, by-passed the responsible chancellor, violated the constitution, and thus committed an act that can only be described as mutiny or rebellion.'

General Wilhelm Groener took over as Deputy Chief of the General Staff when the Kaiser fired Ludendorff on 26 October in a short-lived attempt to stop Prince Max from resigning.[88] The tussle between a military reluctant to cede control of the armistice to the civilian government had become damaging. Groener busied himself with the successful return from France of the German armies and felt that the Kaiser should remain. By 8 November, Groener changed his mind about the reliability of the army which could now not feed itself. Fifty German officers from the front were shipped in to give their opinions to Hindenburg. It was felt that the army could not be risked against revolutionaries because it would likely not fire on fellow Germans. The same day, Bavaria and Braunschweig were declared socialist republics and across western Germany, city halls were seized by local councils of revolutionary workers and socialists.

During the last weeks of the war, the question of whether Wilhelm could remain as Kaiser was 'increasingly widely discussed'. This immediacy was heightened in a speech turned into a note from President Wilson on 14 October which called for the 'destruction of every arbitrary power anywhere that can ... disturb the peace of the world', particular like the one that which had controlled the German nation.[89] The decision was made in the inner circle that Wilhelm should abdicate as Kaiser, but not as King of Prussia.

The plan was overtaken by events when it was learned that Prince Max had been 'forced to announce Wilhelm's complete abdication two hours before'.[90] Word reached the prince that thousands of workers were marching towards the Reichstag.[91] The socialists had never demonstrated in the government quarter before. The police and army had always kept them at bay whether for the hunger demonstrations of 1890, the suffrage protest of

1910, or the war protests of 1914. This time the military 'melted away'.

> *On 9 November, Germany, lacking any firm guidance, bereft of all will, robbed of her princes, collapsed like a house of card. All that we had lived for, all that we had bled four long years to maintain, had gone. We no longer had a native land of which we might be proud. Order in state and society vanished. All authority disappeared. Chaos, Bolshevism, terror, un-German in name and nature, made their entry into the German fatherland.* [92]

Schicksalstag, the Day of Fate, the ninth of November, is much discussed in German history.[93] In 1918, it was the day when the monarchy of the Kaiser ended. In order to avoid bloodshed, Prince Max gave up trying to secure the abdication and, to ensure an orderly transfer of power to Friedrich Ebert and the Social Democrats, informed the Wolff News Agency of the intended abdication and thus forced a *fait accompli*. Social Democrat Philipp Scheidemann was pulled out of the Reichstag cafeteria to make the announcement from the second-storey balcony. Two hours later, Karl Liebknecht made his own announcement from the north balcony of the Stadtschloss, the imperial palace in the centre of Berlin, and declared Germany a 'Free Socialist Republic'.

At the announcement in Berlin, shouting people poured into the streets. 'The papers are torn from the sellers' hands. While one and all are wild with joy at the prospect of the war's end, they nevertheless feel shocked at *this* end'.[94] The manner in which the war ended – with an 'armistice', an abdication and no fighting on German soil – played a significant role in subsequent events. 'Things might have been different,' MacMillan writes, 'if Germany had been more thoroughly defeated'.[95] Kessler was in the city: 'In the Leipzigerstraße I encountered a fleeing crowd. Various people shouted that loyalist troops had arrived from Potsdam and shooting would start at any moment. I turned away into Wilhelmstraße but heard nothing ... So closes this first day of revolution which has witnessed in a few hours the downfall of the Hohenzollerns, the dissolution of the German Army, and the end of the old order of society in Germany. One of the most memorable and dreadful days in German history'.[96]

By the armistice, the total German army strength had fallen by over two million to 5.64 million.[97] Of this fall about one and a half million were killed, injured, missing or captured in the Spring offensive and following retreats. That meant there were three-quarters of a million deserters before the armistice. This was confirmed by the need from conscription for 637,000 to 950,000 above the casualty requirements to make good the army's losses.[98] This shortage of recruits plus the effects of influenza and the potato famine led to Ludendorff's panic demand. After the call for an armistice on 3 October, the rate of desertion and plundering accelerated.

'Those missing from home leave rose to hundreds of thousands in a general strike of a hopelessly defeated army.'[99] The generals impotently tried to ban soldiers' councils. Chancellor Scheidemann met these orders with hilarity, it was as 'effective as forbidding that it rain tomorrow'. Troops in the east were deserting at 10,000 a day and by the end of January the army of the west had 'vanished'.

Both Ludendorff and his armies had reached the end of their physical and psychological capacities although Ludendorff refused to admit either and instead 'retreated into his world of petty staff work, mentally broken'. The most important result was that Germany was now incapable of sustaining the longer, grudging defence that might have frustrated the Allies into a more equitable negotiation. Hindenburg's command never seriously considered this alternative even though an increasing number of senior officers were convinced that the war had been lost. Ludendorff refused to 'accept this bitter truth'. His position, which 'depended so much on military success, was steadily eroded, not only by the politicians who were anxious to seize the opportunity to assert the primacy of the political over the military, but also from within the ranks of the demigods of the supreme command'. If it was a case of defeat rather than stalemate then armistice talks should begin at once to avoid the collapse of the army and the real danger of collapse at home.

Kessler visited the Palace in Berlin and noticed that structural damage was 'surprisingly small'.[100] The private apartments of the Emperor and Empress, especially the dressing rooms were 'pretty badly looted'.

The Emperor's trinket stands, their glass shattered, have been cleaned out. It seems difficult to say how far the sailors have been responsible for the pillage. But these private apartments, the furniture, the articles of everyday use, and what remains of [their] mementoes and objets d'art are so insipid and tasteless, so philistine, that it is difficult to feel much indignation against the pilferers. Only astonishment that the wretched, timid, unimaginative creatures who liked this trash, and frittered away their life in this precious palatial haven, amidst lackeys and sycophants, could ever make any impact on history.

Most Germans outside of the military high command did not realise that Germany was finished militarily and therefore did not regard 11 November 1918 as a day of surrender. Hitler would capitalise on this; his promise to undo the 'unfair' Treaty of Versailles was a potent and popular theme during his rise to power. Despite failures in political direction and field leadership, both the army's and navy's officer corps remained strong and intact at a time when their continued existence should have been in doubt. The upheaval at the time of the Kaiser's departure and the lack of later Allied scrutiny east of the Rhine may well have saved them and provided time for planning and reconsolidation. By riding the political storm rather than making futile if heroic last stands, the unity of the officer corps was preserved to a remarkable degree and with it the initial discipline of the returning army.[101] Thus, the office corps was able to withstand all attempts at democratisation and was to become an anti-republican and reactionary force. 'The influence of the army was not broken even in defeat and political upheaval and by severing its traditional links with the monarchy at that critical juncture the army did not go the same way as the Hohenzollern dynasty, but remained a powerful and profoundly harmful force in German society.'

> *The military did not cut loose from the Kaiser institutionally, but also ideologically, and this turned out to be the most dangerous trend of all for the monarchy ... The Kaiser was replaced by something more abstract, flexible and useful: the future Germany, its security, its greatness. In short, nationalism finally triumphed over monarchism ... As the war dragged on, the officer corps joined other leading segments of pre-war Wilhelmine society in embracing the radical nationalism that had previously been the joint preserve of heavy industry and the national, anti-establishment opposition. The radical nationalists, such as the Pan-Germans, sections of the Navy League, came mostly from the bourgeois strata ... The new converts, Tirpitz, Ludendorff and Bauer among the most notorious, brought with them three idées fixes from the old officer corps: technical military considerations far outweighed mere politics in decisions affecting the nation, compromise with enemies (domestic or foreign) was unthinkable, and preparations must begin now (even in the midst of World War I) for the next inevitable war. The goal these gentlemen pursued was to establish a German-ruled autarkic fortress on the continent. No sacrifice was too great to achieve this end. Not even the Kaiser.[102]*

The suicidal aspect of one of the sacrificial plans, however, was carried out in spite of everything. Skeleton crews sank the German fleet after it had surrendered and been ushered to Scapa Flow.[103] The British harbour patrol panicked and crews in lifeboats, flying the white flag, were indiscriminately machine-gunned; nine were killed and twenty-one wounded.

> *The harsh British reaction can be seen as a result of the Grand Fleet's failure ... and its subsequent inability to seek further naval encounters, of the tensions and hatreds engendered by four years of warfare, and the realisation that they had been cheated at the last moment of the spoils of war. In moral terms, their actions constituted atrocities, but no British officer or sailor was ever brought to trial.[104]*

When the Scapa Flow crews finally returned home in January 1920, they were accorded a triumphant reception. Von Trotha greeted them with a triumphant gala reception. Masses thronged the shores, flags and banners were unfurled, and an army guard of honour greeted them as returning heroes. 'The occasion provided war-weary Germany with its first opportunity to celebrate.'

On 19 January 1919, a new national assembly was elected and Germany's first president, Freidrich Ebert, proclaimed a return to general peace and order and to efficient nutrition. It was an impractical, if courageous call. The food situation did not really improve until 1923 as hyper-inflation which reduced wages and a large wave of unemployment reduced customer demand. 'Only with the introduction of the new currency at the end of 1923 and the subsequent return to the free market system was it possible for Germany to gradually restore normal feeding.'[105]

The German government was incapable of fulfilling the terms of the armistice in its original fifteen days.[106] The deadline was extended three times, the last time on 16 February 1919 indefinitely. Europe in 1919 struck many observers as being closer to another war than to a prolonged peace. 'The peace treaty with Germany had to solve the most pressing material questions arising out of the war and simultaneously had to lay the groundwork for a stable international system. Far from aiming at a punitive settlement, the United States and the Allies, with the exception of France, sought to preserve Germany, but they all wished to contain its power to fight future wars.'[107]

Since the governments fostered much of this propaganda, the statesmen at Paris in 1919 were largely the prisoners of their own machinations. The press had co-operated willingly as atrocities make good copy. Propaganda of atrocities might be said to have contributed more than any other single factor to the making of a severe peace. Stories of atrocity aroused two of the strongest human emotions: hate and fear. Through them the public was convinced of the utter monstrosity of the enemy.[108]

From mid-December through to March 1919, there were ten official visits by small teams of British army officers to major German cities, including Berlin.[109] Their combined observations, albeit seen through a British prism, give a most useful assessment of the conditions facing the returning troops who had served away from the German heartland.

The Workers' and Soldier's Councils carried very little weight and were feared by the average citizen as likely to introduce Bolshevism owing to their incapacity as rulers ... Many in Berlin would be glad to see the capital occupied by Allied troops ... No mention was made of a possible restoration of the monarchy; all had lost all respect for the Kaiser ...

Over the course of four war-time winters, Germans would mobilise their energies, vitalise public life, and rearrange their political conceptions around the nation rather than the state or monarchy ... [the war] transformed German nationalism by giving it emotional depth and tying it to social reform and political entitlement ... traditional allegiances to the monarchy withered while new conceptions of the national community ranging from utopian socialism to crude Aryan racism proliferated.[110]

... Officers were turned away from their commands on arrival at their barracks where command was taken over by Council delegates ... There were not many officers in uniform in the streets ... There were 30,000 applicants for a position at the Deutsche Bank at 130 marks a month ... The Kaiser's palaces in Berlin and Potsdam had been looted and the Kaiser's suits sold to the mob at 30 marks each.

Germany, it is felt, has lost the war although her defeat has been due to economic pressure and internal disruption rather than to military inferiority. Germany must pay but only as any other loser pays. Her offence lies not in her conduct of the war, but in her losing it. Possibly the violation of Belgium neutrality should be considered in a particular light. The u-boat war was a gross political mistake, but ethically justified by the British blockade. Germany's conduct of the war has been magnificent.

The establishment of a stable government, the repression of Spartakists [communists] and the cutting of all unavoidable losses are most immediately desirable. The indiscretion of the late Kaiser and the behaviour of his late advisers may have justified the suspicion of Germany's aims. The removal of the late governing class strips harsh treatment of the new democracy of any excuse and will justify the belief that the Allies embarked on a war of conquest which they strove to deck with humanitarian aims ... The restoration of the colonies is essential to Germany; their retention would be a gross disregard of justice and incidentally inexpedient for them since the colonies are the natural and only peaceful outlet for the energies of a nation whose expansion cannot be checked ... Russia is the plague spot of Europe. Russian agents are corrupting German workmen and seeking to prevent the restoration of ordered government. Germany in combating Bolshevism in her midst and the Slavs and the Poles on her Eastern border are fighting the battle of all Western civilisation ... Germany is entitled to a peace of reconciliation (Versöhnung) since the conclusion of such was a term implicit in the acceptance of the armistice ... The origin of the war and the apportionment of guilt therefore are, and are likely to remain, obscure. Discussion therefore is unprofitable. It is absurd, however, to suppose that the Entente and Germany represent the forces of good and evil respectively.

The tone of the local press in any discussion of foreign politics is becoming increasingly confident, if not insolent. The return of the German colonies is peremptorily demanded; the already de facto loss of Alsace-Loraine is condemned as premature and oppressive. No opportunity is lost of impressing upon the public how rigorous and exacting are the Armistice conditions which the Allies, like a usurer, will only renew upon more and more onerous terms, the prolongation of the blockade is inhuman and the British are thereby daily murdering German women and children. A speedy peace is not in Germany's best interests since every day that the [Peace] Conference sits diminishes the Allies power through demobilisation and loss of will.

The flood of workers into the productions centres and away from food production created a housing shortage and a rapid rise in rents. The exaggerated importance of the industrial workers during the war created a new type of social injustice. The plight of the farmers was truly miserable. Their best horses had been requisitioned by the army. They did not have sufficient labour, and the peace with Russia now threatened their most important source of prisoners of war. They had been forced to engage in massive pig slaughters and they did not have enough fodder for the livestock that remained. They were encumbered by hundreds of regulations and victimised by periodic searches for hidden food stores (which certainly existed). Their land was ruined by over cultivation and the shortage of artificial fertiliser. In some cases, even the food producers did not have enough to stay alive. They were not deemed 'hard-working' like the industrial workers who had food premiums. The minor officials, small businessmen and craftsmen were the people hardest hit by the war, their enterprises shut down to save coal, officials overworked, underpaid and underfed. As usual the management of these problems was hindered either by an excess of organisation or by the absence of any organisation at all.

The Versailles peace treaty, fifteen parts and 440 articles, was signed finally on 28 June 1919 to take force on 10 January 1920. The blockade did not end until the treaty was ratified by the Reichstag on 9 July 1919 by 209 votes to 116 after vitriolic debate. Food entered at a quickening pace, but it was many months before basic supplies were readily available and even longer before they became affordable for the unemployed poor. The large shipments of food to Germany, announced by a formal treaty on 15 March were an expression of the almost panic-stricken reaction to reports from Berlin and other industrial centres painting a picture of near civil war.[111] Wilson pronounced, 'The real thing to stop Bolshevism is food'. Hoover 'clearly bore much of the responsibility for the delay in establishing an efficient Allied economic establishment', eventually establishing in February one similar to what had been in existence the October before.[112]

President Wilson's 'Fourteen Points' were fundamental background to all debate at the Peace Conference.[113] All countries had to pay lip service to the overall concept which, in large part, had brought them together as it formed the basis for the German's request to the United Sates for armistice. It was to be a 'peace without victory'.[114] The points seemed initially straightforward, many would argue simplistic, an honest but impractical attempt to force through a new world order. It turned out that almost everything was ambiguous and negotiable.[115] Each point attracted fervent antagonists. Here are views from opposite ends of the political spectrum, each a pariah in his own way. Léon Degrelle was a Belgian politician who joined the Waffen SS, reaching the rank of lieutenant colonel in Worrld War II, and became a revisionist historian in exile in Spain where he fulminated against Allied policy in World War I. Arno Mayer was a self-proclaimed dissident Marxist. In Mayer's view, the greatest failure of the peace treaty was that it was a triumph for the power of the old landed aristocracy that owned most of Europe, but this success was covered with the veneer of Wilson's new politics.

> The naïve may have believed that Wilson's Fourteen Points, which the Germans and the Allies had agreed on as the basis for the peace treaty, would serve as the basis for a new age, one without annexations or exactions. That was an illusion. The Allies' agreement was worth nothing. It was merely a subterfuge to disarm Germany in order to pursue a policy of gain, greed and vengeance.[116]

> The peacemakers ... of 1918–19 convened to settle the accounts of a multilateral, unlimited, and ideological conflict; to legalise a new territorial status quo; to agree on safeguards and sanctions against future transgressions by the major defeated enemy; and to explore ways of putting the peace and concert of Europe on more enduring foundations ... Each statesman pursued these overarching foundations while simultaneously striving to maximise the national interest of his own country ... These two sets of objectives were pursued within a framework of power politics. Conflicting national interests were accommodated through mutual compensations and concessions ... the major powers assumed responsibility for bringing and maintaining in balance the international system of sovereign states. They abrogated to themselves the right to settle all basic territorial, military, economic, and political issues before securing approval for their decisions from the

plenary congress or conference. The secondary and minor powers were
cast in the role of suitors, supplicants, or satellites.[117]

Wilson was an idealist who was sure that a new world order would stop
future wars. That meant, in Clause 1 of the 'Fourteen Points', ending the
traditional European national blocs formed and re-formed to achieve a
continental balance of power. 'Private international understandings of any
kind' were to be banned and diplomacy was no longer to be private, but
to be open and in the public view. Enforcement came in Clause 14 from
a 'general association of nations' – the League of Nations – which would
guarantee 'political independence and territorial integrity' for all states.
States were to de-militarise, Clause 4, to the 'lowest point consistent with
domestic safety' and trade was to enabled by, Clause 2, 'absolute freedom
of navigation upon the seas' and, Clause 3, the removal of 'all economic
barriers' through equal trading conditions. All of these, of course, failed
in the short to middle term when national might and necessity became
national right in future adversity. Clause 5 called for the settling of all
colonial claims where the interests of a colonial population was to receive
equal weight with that of the coloniser. In as much as this was a thinly-
veiled and altruistic attack on all the European colonial powers, it might
be said to have succeeded over time, but colonialism, even American
colonialism, came in many forms. Clauses 6 to 13 each dealt with particular
national issues, from the Ottoman Empire to an independent Polish state,
and attracted covies of interested parties with widely differing views.

Allied leaders ... suspected [Wilson] really believed his own rhetoric
about 'permanent peace' and 'the world must be made safe for
democracy'. They suspected as well that Wilson viewed himself as
the Angel of the Lord, coming to deliver Europe from decadence and
corruption, and they worried that the Fourteen Points, which no Allied
leader had endorsed, might have become Holy Writ in Wilson's eyes.[118]

The United States had joined the war in April 1917 and most historians
agree with Chancellor Bethmann that the war was definitely lost at that
point.[119] By the end, America had over one million troops in Europe
alone, and a navy that rivalled Britain's. Indeed, the Americans 'tended to
assume that they had won the war for the European allies' and that this
gave them moral power. Europe was so deep in debt that a US withdrawal
'would lead to the collapse of European countries'. The extraordinary and
unprecedented borrowing by France (two billion gold francs) and Britain
(£1,365 million) resulted in 'acute national impoverishment' in both
countries. Most European belligerents had large domestic war debts; the
victors had vast foreign ones as well but Germany did not. In addition,
the continental Allies had immense reconstruction costs.[120] 'Somebody

would have to pay to clear the fields and provide new ploughs, rebuild factories, purchase new equipment and tools, reconstruct bridges and railroads, drain and restore coal mines flooded during the armistice negotiations, and revive the economies of thoroughly devastated and denuded territories.' If the Allies, and especially France, had to assume reconstruction costs on top of domestic and foreign war debts, whereas Germany was left with only domestic debts, they would be the losers, and German economic dominance would be tantamount to victory. 'Germany's economic potential was regarded increasingly as the vehicle by which the Allies would carry their almost limitless monetary burden.'[121] America's new-found financial power gave particular weight to Wilson's morality, but no-one had really envisioned the closeness of American involvement, their personal fratricidal war within living memory, and to the forefront from 1914 an understandable desire to distance themselves from incessant European squabbling.

> *The United States had few claims which lessened the importance of reparations in its domestic politics. But the United States pursued its own interests as determinedly as other powers. Since it wished to sell food to Germany and agricultural surpluses would soon again be a political issue to America, the United States ensured that purchase of food was among the permitted uses of the first German payments under the treaty. Equally, it resisted Allied efforts to impose the burden of their war costs upon it. America's own war costs were modest and easily paid. Those of European belligerents were neither. None was eager to pay its own bills or anyone else's.*[122]

There were many impassioned debates amongst the Allies. France was 'particularly eager to end the war without the exorbitant sacrifices deemed necessary in any march on Berlin'.[123] However, their programme challenged Wilson's declarations at every point; 'an imposed peace on the basis of agreed terms, a permanent Grand-Alliance of military domination as against the voluntary co-operation of all Powers, victors and vanquished alike, in a League of Nations; dismemberment of Germany as against 'self-determination'; crippling indemnities as against 'just reparation'; disarmament of Germany as against 'general disarmament'.[124]

For the English, the 'stumbling block' was the call for absolute freedom of navigation. Lloyd George pointed out that Great Britain, which depended on the unrestricted utilisation of her fleet, could under no circumstance accept freedom of the sea as this would serve to neutralise England's power to blockade and he demanded that the Allies acknowledge the extent to which they had all benefitted from the blockade's ability to prevent 'steel, copper, rubber, and many other classes of goods from entering Germany'. 'No, I cannot accept the principles of freedom of the seas. It has got association in the public mind with blockade. It is no good saying I accept the principle. It would only mean that in a week's time a new Prime Minister would be here who would say that he could not accept the principle. The English people will not look at it.'

> *No two specialists have been more at variance than the partners in the late Entente Cordials – Great Britain and France. The difference has been fundamental. For France, the armistice meant for the people, the politicians, the diplomats and the soldiers but one thing – the extinction as far as was humanely – or inhumanely possible of Germany as a Great Power. Great Britain presented no such united front. Certainly, the masses of the civilian population, suffering from a bad rush of propaganda to the head, had ideas not dissimilar from those of the French. Perhaps in no belligerent country was the conception of the original, ineradicable sin of the enemy peoples more honestly, more thoroughly accepted by the masses. So effective had the 'barbarous Hun' legend already become. But, however genuinely such things were believed in 1917, it would be 1922 before it was almost gone. Behind the desire of the French masses to see Germany utterly destroyed as a power in Europe and her population diminished by every possible means was much natural fear, much of it purely human desire to 'hit back' for ruined towns and ravaged countryside, but most of all a deadly personal enmity.*[125]

Despite military defeat, Germany emerged from World War I less damaged in terms of economic resources than the other major European combatants, particularly France and Belgium.[126] Like Britain, Germany was one of the 'luckier' ones in that it emerged with its economy intact, if battered, and was spared invasion, denudation, and devastation.[127] However, the devastation in France's ten richest departments was so severe that German delegates on their way to Versailles by train 'could barely endure to look at it'. At the Verdun battlefield, 'not a living thing grew, not a bird sang'.[128]

> *The coal mines on which the French economy depended for its power were flooded; the factories they would have supplied had been razed or carted away into Germany. Six thousand square miles of France which before the war had produced 20% of its crops, 90% of its iron ore and 65% of its steel, were utterly ruined. Perhaps Wilson might have understood Clemenceau's demands better if he had gone early on to see the damage for himself.*

The German view was, naturally, at odds with that of the Allies. The new Foreign Minister, Count Ulrich von Brockdorff-Rantzau, felt the victory of morality and the final worldwide vindication of democratic principles was at stake. Germany had transformed itself in to a democracy as a 'concession in advance' to its adversaries. Proposals should maintain the status and dignity as one of the world's leading powers regardless of its military defeat which would be co-operative in its foreign policy and thus acceptable to the rest of Europe. As he admitted, Germany had no more military trump cards left.[129] Brockdorff-Rantzau was confident that economic reason would prevail at least among the Anglo-Saxon powers. The German government 'continuously pleaded for a loosening of the blockade'. Food imports for the starving masses, the German government argued, would keep Germany's 'general economy running and thereby prevent further dislocations and it would prevent social unrest and hence deflate communist influence.'

Whatever hopes there were among the German delegation were dashed on 7 May when they were handed the draft of the peace treaty with the provision that no negotiations, only written observations, were permitted. On studying the terms, the German delegation realised that even its worst fears had been exceeded.

Conspiracy historians Docherty & Macgregor declared that a 'starving, desperate nation had been confronted with the choice of admitting her 'guilt' at once or suffering an Allied occupation with every likelihood that an admission of guilt would ultimately be extorted in any case'.[130]

Germany occupied the situation of a prisoner at the bar, where the prosecuting attorney was given full leeway as to time and presentation of evidence, while the defendant was denied counsel or the opportunity to produce either evidence or witnesses.[131]

The rights to reparations in the treaty were 'drafted to justify massive and indeterminate reparations, did more than any other factor to poison international relations between the wars'.[132] The 'war guilt' clause in Article 232, *Die Kriegsschuldfrage*, emphasised damages caused by Germany and her allies on civilian victims by acts of cruelty, violence or mistreatment (including attempts to kill or attacks on health following imprisonment, deportation, internment, or evacuation, abandonment at sea or forced labour) in whatever place and to the survivors who were in charge of these victims.' Wilson also demanded that the invasion of neutral Belgium be put 'right'.[133] As a result, Germany admitted violating Belgian neutrality and to entering Northern France; it 'directly admitted waging aggressive war'.

'It was for this reason,' Brockdorff-Rantzau wrote, 'that the German government admitted Germany to be responsible: it did not admit Germany's alleged responsibility for the origin of the war or for the merely

incidental fact that the formal declaration of war had emanated from Germany.' If the Allies wanted to saddle Germany with reparations for the entire war, then Germany must respond by demanding reparations for the 'immeasurable injury' that German civilians suffered 'owing to the blockade, a measure opposed to the Law of Nations'.

Marks argues that Article 231 of the Versailles Treaty was designed to lay a legal basis for reparations and points out that it made no mention of 'war guilt' and the same clause caused no 'war guilt' interpretation when included in the treaties with Austria and Hungary.[134] In later years, German politicians and propagandists fulminated endlessly about 'unilateral war guilt'. Marks also points out that the next article, 232, narrowed German responsibility to civilian damages.

Much ink has been wasted on the fact that civilian damages were stretched to cover war widows' pensions and allowances for military dependents. In reality, since the German reparations bill was established in 1921 on the basis of an Allied assessment of the German capacity to pay, not on the basis of Allied claims, these items did not affect German liability but merely altered distribution of the receipts. The inclusion of pensions and allowances increased the British share of the pie but did not enlarge the pie.

Brockdorff-Rantzau was further shocked when the Allied commission would not specify the amount that Germany would have to pay in reparations. 'The Allies had a blank cheque, and even a German offer to double what Keynes had proposed was received negatively.' This represented 100 billion gold Reichsmarks which was twenty-five times more than the Germans had imposed on France after the 1870-71 Franco-Prussian War.[135] Germany saw no reason to pay and from start to finish deemed reparation a 'gratuitous insult'.[136] The actual amount of war reparation proved irrelevant; Germany ended up paying less than France had paid after 1871. 'What mattered was the rhetoric.'[137]

By the spring of 1919, Allied commanders were increasingly doubtful about the ability to successfully wage war on Germany. The German army had been defeated on the battlefield, but its command structure, along with hundreds of thousands of trained men, had survived. 'There were 75 million Germans and only 40 million French, as Foch kept repeating or as Clemenceau put it, 'There are 20 million Germans too many.' Who knew what resistance there would be as Allied armies moved further and further into the country? It was unlikely that the Allied would get as far as Berlin.'[138] American General Pershing was the only senior general to recommend a push beyond the Rhine, if necessary.

For much of the following short discussion on reparations, a debt is owed to the excellent texts of American historian Sally Marks, already much quoted, although it should be noted that her works have not received universal approval.[139] What Marks shows is that Germany by constant prevarication played for time, over many years wore down the intransigent French, always underpaid on agreements and even these payments were never on time, called bluffs wherever possible, and deliberately ruined the Reichsmark so that, far from being beggared by payments, Germany became the economic victor. Germany's financial strength was such that less than twenty years later, she was able to fund the continuation of the war.

The reparations total discussed at the peace conference was 'astronomic', ranging to sixteen times the amount actually set. The treaty specified that Germany make an interim payment of twenty million gold marks before 1 May 1921, by which time the Reparations Commission had to set the total liability. In fact twenty billion marks is approximately what Germany paid during the entire history of reparation. During the interim period, she paid less than eight billion marks, mostly as credit for transferred state properties. Technically none of this was considered reparation as it was fully consumed by prior charges, notably occupation costs and the expenses of provisioning Germany. In time, however, there developed a certain tacit recognition of the eight billion as reparations. There were periodic cash payments and deliveries in kind. Kind meant coal, timber, chemical dyes and pharmaceutical drugs. Reparations included certain one-time payments. Return of art treasures did not received reparations credit, but materials to replace the destroyed library of Louvain did. Similarly, supplies of livestock, agricultural implements, factory machinery, and construction materials in compensation for wholesale removals during the German retreat were credited to the reparations account.[140]

A 'substantial degree of realism' set in in 1921 when the committee announced a total German liability of 132 billion gold marks. It represented an 'assessment of the lowest amount that public opinion in receiving states would tolerate'. It had nothing to do with any ability to pay.

Reparations in money or in kind were almost never paid on time or to the full amount. By January 1923, the Germans had failed to meet thirty-fourth coal targets in thirty-six months even though there were large loans to facilitate coal shipments. Premiums were paid by the Allies for goods ostensibly to provide better food for miners. The Germans were also in default on timber. The French and Belgians insisted on the 'ultimate sanction' of the occupation of the Ruhr. 'Britain stood aloof, but rendered the occupation feasible by permitting France to mount it on British-controlled railways in the Rhineland.' Passive resistance from the Germans led to a full-scale military operation.

> *France had played her last trump card and must win this card or go down to permanent defeat. She was inherently weaker than Germany and had already failed to enforce delivery of alleged war criminals, to obtain German compliance with the military clauses of the treaty, or to gain any effective German participation in costly French reconstruction ... French premier Raymond Poincaré was above all making a final effort to force Germany to acknowledge her defeat and to accept the treaty. He well knew that the fundamental issues were not timber and coal but rather the survival of the Treaty and of France's victory in the war.*

Depreciation of the Reichsmark, begun during the war, continued at an 'erratic pace' and, by 1922, was 'acute'. The destruction of the German currency enabled German heavy industry to 'wipe out its indebtedness by refunding its obligations in worthless marks'.[141]

Between 1923 and 1924, US President Calvin Coolidge allowed American private citizens to draw up a new reparation plan. He was 'essentially handing over the business to US bankers led by JP Morgan'. The ultimate effect of German failure to pay reparations in substantial quantity was the 'transfer of the burden to the victors'.[142] Reconstruction still had to be paid for. Pensions for disabled veterans and war widows still remained. So did the Allied war debts. In the end, the victors paid the bills. The eventual German payment equivalent to twenty billion gold marks, five billion US dollars, was 'predominantly financed by foreign loans', many of which were eventually repudiated by Hitler. Germany had her way in the end at great cost to herself and to others. 'Since Germany would not pay, and the other Central Powers could not, reparations dwindled and died.'

Was Germany to blame for a 'defensive' war in which they had invaded Belgium and Northern France? To what degree had Germany acted in an uncivilised and illegal way in continuing the fight through its conduct in invaded countries and in introducing unrestricted submarine warfare? Was there any truth in Ludendorff's claim that the army was undefeated, and that he and Hindenburg were therefore blameless? Had the military been stabbed in the back by an unholy combination of subversion, propaganda, communist revolutionaries and by a lack of moral fibre amongst the men and women (and their children) who held the home front?

The lies and blame began well before the war ended and continued thereafter in a Government-sponsored conspiracy. On the cause of the Kiel revolt, Lieutenant Captain Erich Galster von Seydlitz said, 'The mutiny was not the result of discontent despite the fact that there were sufficient causes for it ... It would be too unjust to our men to say that this discontent led them to turn against their flag at such an inopportune moment. The mutiny was rather the result of the systematic efforts of the betrayers among our own people and the systematic work of the enemy propaganda.'[143] Tirpitz wanted to defend his reputation from the waves of recrimination that were likely to come from enemies of all sorts.[144] His Fatherland Party 'limped along on sheer momentum for a few more months'. Its propaganda, along with that of the army, concealed from the population how truly desperate the German military situation had become. As the military situation grew steadily worse there was little that they could do except make wild demands and look around for scapegoats for the failure of the system which they had done so much to create.[145] Ludendorff in October 1918 and his successor General Groener in June 1919 both 'tried to cover their tracks'.[146] The fact that it was the high command, led by Hindenburg and Ludendorff, whose panic-stricken insistence persuaded the government to ask for ceasefire negotiations has been driven out of the memory of most Germans by the dishonest propaganda of the *Dolchstoß*, the stab-in-the-back myth, which claimed that an undefeated army had been betrayed by revolution and by its country.[147] It was simply unthinkable that Germany's premier institution should fail. 'The most astonishing sign of the ubiquity of this conviction is the ease with which right-wing officers convinced most Germans, in the face of every physical and political indication to the contrary, that Germany had not in fact lost Word War 1.' The country manufactured its 'own feeling of victory out of the war'. It had instead been 'stabbed in the back' at home.'[148] Groener recommended to the Reichstag on 23 June 1919 that, because of the hopeless military situation, that the peace treaty be accepted and that revenge be taken at some future time:

> *The near future lies dim before us. It is still unclear when the German people will rise from their shameful national degradation, will stand together as one man, and take up the battle once more against external forces for the honour and dignity of generations to come.*

In an article in *The Star* in 1918, entitled 'The Watch on the Rhine', the British General Sir Frederick Maurice was asked how it was possible that an enemy which was so united, so determined to win, should collapse.[149] He said that it could all be attributed to the moral collapse of Germany – a stab in the back. Historians Martel and Joll, suggest that it was British Major-General Sir Neill Malcolm who, while in Berlin, provided the origin of the stab-in-the-back myth, a 'legend which has never entirely perished'.[150] In the autumn of 1919, while Malcolm was dining with Ludendorff, Malcolm asked why Ludendorff thought Germany lost the war. Ludendorff replied with a list of excuses, including that the home front failed the army. Malcolm asked him: 'Do you mean, General, that you were stabbed in the back?' Ludendorff's eyes lit up and he leapt upon the phrase like a dog on a bone. 'Stabbed in the back?' he repeated. 'Yes, that's it, exactly, we were stabbed in the back.' By the time Hindenburg came to give a farcical soliloquy to a parliamentary enquiry on 18

November, the legend was officially born. 'The good core of the army, that is its officer corps, could not be blamed for the defeat; rather, it had been stabbed-in-the-back, *von hinten erdolcht*, by certain pacifist elements at the home front.'[151]

The tactics of *Dolchstoß* were threefold. The German front was 'intellectual revolutionised' through the spread of leaflets, pamphlets and manifestos. There was a 'physical or spiritual revolution of the front' through the organisation of deserters. Then there was an organised revolutionisation of the home front 'through the centralisation of all the forces of Bolshevism'.[152] In fact, it was the other way around. Examination of letters by German officers, the mood of dissatisfaction was carried into the homeland by the troops on leave at a time when the homeland did not think of opposing the war and its leaders.[153] Historian Vincent suggested there was a small truth to *Dolchstoß*.

> *Only two groups may be said to have derived any benefits from the war: the industrialists and the workers employed in the war industries.*[154] *Their common support of black marketeers was symptomatic of the special position they had assumed in the economy, but it was also symptomatic of the special position they had assumed in the economy. Such benefits were derived at the expense of fellow Germans. In this respect, at least, there was some truth in General Erich Ludendorff's assertion that the army had been stabbed in the back. But the general overlooked the fact that the army had fashioned the knife.*[155]

Groener nailed the *Dolchstoß* lie in a statement, left in his personal papers:

> *It would be the greatest injustice to defame the German people for their collapse at the end of the last word war. They had sacrificed their youth on the battlefields. They had proven themselves by magnificent feats of arms in the field, in unrelenting work, in privations and sufferings in the homeland. They had been led to the mountain peaks of an illusionary world in which they were held by hope after hope of certain victory ... Who can be astonished at their disenchantment, as if they had fallen into a deep abyss upon learning that victory was not to be won ... In the end, the blame for the continued self-deception and the mistaken employment of defensive tactics rests on the military. The victories proclaimed to the people had been those of magnificent deeds by heroes, but they were not victories in the strategic and political sense which had been won by the talents of generals and statesmen.*[156]

The German government developed the denial of war guilt from the time of their invasion of Belgium and Northern France in 1914, enshrined it with large resources in the immediate aftermath of the war, developed it into an art-form through Hitler's rise to power, and even continued its promotion after the second world war. It is an extraordinary story of vilified scholars, with their travel and awards restricted; state-sponsored lying and disinformation; and corrupted school and university textbooks in Germany and throughout the western world, particularly, in the United States. Those who survived the war and sought meaning and direction from it, like the Gerth brothers, and several generations of German youth were taught the opposite of the truth. The myth of the blameless German nation surrounded by predatory and powerful enemies planning and acting in concert has passed into the national consciousness. In 1996, British historian Keith Wilson edited a volume, *Forging the Collective Memory*, which should be required reading. While all the articles have great value, the offering by Holger Herwig, 'Clio Deceived: Patriotic Self-Censorship After the Great War', has especial value and is used extensively in the following section.[157] Wilson's argument is that:

> Governments have never taken the view that they, and what they regard as their property, the official records of the governance of the state, exist for the sake of historians. If anything, and especially so far as recent international history is concerned, the collective view of governments has been that the situation has been, and must remain, the other way round.[158]

Herwig accepts the basic tenets of Fritz Fischer's *Griff nach der Weltmacht*, which appeared in 1961, and which 'convincingly documented that Vienna and Berlin opted for war in July 1914 in the belief that time was running out for both of them ... In both capitals [statesmen and soldiers] accepted the calculated risk of a general European war in order to shore up, and if at all possible to expand, Bismarck's position of semi-hegemony in Europe.'[159] Herwig declares that the efforts of the *German* 'guilt office' 'polluted historical understanding', both at home and abroad, well into the post-1945 period. He asserts that 'it serves no purpose to continue to believe that Europe 'slid' into war unknowingly in 1914, that no nation harboured aggressive tendencies during the July crisis, and that fate or providence alone designed this cruel course of events'.[160]

From the signing of the treaty in June 1919 through to the Third Reich, 'key elements' of the German bureaucracy mounted a 'massive and successful campaign. It included the *Kriegsschuldreferat*, War Guilt Section, of the Foreign Ministry, which used notably two recruited agencies, the Arbeitsausschuss Deutscher *Veranda* (ADV), 'Working Committee of German Associations', and the *Zentralstelle für die Erforschung der Kriegsursachen*, 'Centre for the Study of the Causes of the War', and *Untersuchungsausschuss*, a parliamentary enquiry. The *Schuldreferat* became institutionalised as the 'Guilt Office', directed by Bernhard Wilhelm von Bülow, a future state secretary, who was charged with 'containing the damage from the Allied contention that Germany had started the war'. The decision was made to work through adulterated scholarship.[161] Bülow's first task was to show that the Allies had 'for a long time systematically and jointly prepared for a war against Germany', that they, rather than Germany were to be accorded 'immediate guilt for provoking war' in 1914. This work included France's armaments outlays, Britain's intensive training of a continental army, Italy's provocations, and, most of all, Russia's stockpiling of financial means with which to conduct war. All these views were adopted by the German peace negotiation team in February 1919.[162]

The German cabinet approved the first phase of the revisionist campaign: the publication of Germany's pre-war diplomatic documents from 1871 to 1914.[163] 'The *Schuldreferat* controlled access to the documents and exercised veto power over publication.' The forty volumes appeared from 1922 to 1927, the first of any nation's records to be open to historians. *Die Grosse Politik* was tendentious and based in part on the 'suppression and destruction of records'.[164] The *Schuldreferat* also 'fed documents and legal briefs to the Reichstag committee investigating the war; orchestrated the suppression, delay, or timely publication and distribution of its lengthy, detail-ridden reports, created front organisations to combat the 'war-guilt lie' in Germany and abroad and secretly funnelled government money to these organisations; arranged countless conferences and public lectures; published and translated books and pamphlets, falsified memoires; and altogether dominated the public relations and historical scholarship on the origins of the war during the entire interwar period.'

> [The Schuldreferat] *did these things clandestinely and, because it was active in many countries, produced an international synergy of revisionist works in which the various recipients of its largesse reinforced one another and seemed part of an inexorable groundswell of enlightened opinion ... The enormous activity directed at American historians is well documented. It was remarkably successful. In the words of one scholar the 'Germans had won the battle of history'. Historian Herwig notes that the success of revisionism 'retarded critical appraisal of the origins of the war until the 1960s'. In fact, revisionism still dominates US high school history textbooks and reappears in recent works.*

The *Die Grosse Politik* initiative meant that other countries felt obliged to follow suit and to 'show that they too had nothing to hide'.[165] *British Documents on the Origins of the War*, eleven volumes between 1926 and 1938, and the French *Documents Diplomatiques Français, 1930–1953* followed. Eight volumes of Austro-Hungarian documents were published in 1930, and Italians documents after World War II.

Initially, the Germans believed that to achieve moderate peace terms on the basis of Woodrow Wilson's 'Fourteen Points', they must disprove the Allies' accusation of German guilt. The 'entire question of reparations seemed to be legally based upon the German acceptance of moral responsibility for the start of the war'.[166] In addition, the Allies might go ahead, if unchallenged, with demands that German war criminals be handed over for trial with required German records surrendered to support proceedings.

> It simply cannot be stressed enough that by linking the war guilt issue very early on in the campaign to revise the Versailles treaty, the 'patriotic censors' virtually precluded sober and rational investigation into the matter ... Only by rejecting Article 231 outright could German leaders hope to convince the Allies that the harsh terms ... were based on a misconception. If they could undermine the charge of war guilt, they felt they could press on with treaty revisions such as evacuation of occupied territories, redress of borders, above all in the East, and lowering of reparation payments.[167]

Work continued apace into the 1920s as the German government sought the arguments to ameliorate the reparations bill. There is not the space in this book to detail the variety of approaches used for the grand deceit, but the scale of the work of, for instance, the ADV after its founding without public knowledge in 1921 is demonstrative. The ADV claimed ties to up to 600 organisations, reaching, perhaps, 2,000 by 1931, mostly patriotic clubs, but including Caritas-Verband, the welfare organisation of the Catholic church; the World Council of Churches; and the German City League. Private contributions came from large industrial concerns such as IG-Farben and from commercial groups like the Hamburg Board of Trade. With this money ADV organised speakers, seminars, conventions, exhibitions, rallies and special information works, estimated in 1925 alone to be 1,456 undertakings. Articles were fed to 1,500 newspapers through the thirty-five major news agencies in Berlin. A random sample suggested that some 300 German newspapers published up to 1,700 articles disseminated by the ADV in one week. Millions of copies of sponsored and favoured books were placed freely in schools, hospitals, libraries, reception rooms of doctors and lawyers and workers' rest areas in industrial plants.[168]

Memoirs of important eye-witness were consistently obstructed or altered: pressure was brought upon the widow of Moltke the Younger, the general of the Marne, because 'Berlin' thought publishing undesirable; the same is rumoured about Hindenburg's papers.[169] Four other collections of papers from Tirpitz; Admiral George von Müller, chief of the Navy cabinet until 1918; Kurt Riezler, Chancellor Bethmann's *intimus*; and Prince Philipp zu Eulenburg-Hartefeld, trusted and maligned adviser to the last kaiser, were all obstructed, neutered or attacked in some way. Meanwhile, historians who toed the official line, like Gerhard Ritter, Bernhard Schwertfeger and Alfred von Wegerer, had their works lauded, funded and distributed. Further, Herwig points out, omitted from the debate are the cases where editors were engaged to ghost-write memoirs, for instance those of Admirals Karl Donitz and Erich Raeder, 'in order to preclude public debate on vital issues of national interest'.

Herwig identifies the non-German scholars, particularly American, who received lavish care from the Foreign Ministry and its agents, like Wegerer. He lists eminent historians who were contacted, including Sidney B Fay and Bernadotte E Schmitt. For some, like Schmitt, this resulted later in fierce political opposition by Wegerer to their future tours to Germany as an 'incorrigible' historian. Others, like Fay, had their books purchased for distribution, and were provided with free translations into French and German. 'The greatest attention and support was showered upon Harry E Barnes of Smith College who, in articles, depicted France and Russia as the villains.[170] Barnes was provided with research materials and his writings were propagated, his visits to Berlin, Munich and Vienna in 1926 funded.[171] At least one generation of university students in the United States was 'raised on the apologias' presented them by historians such as Fay and Barnes, and elsewhere by writers such a Edmund Morel in England and Victor Margueritte and Alfred Fabre-Luce in France, and their work found its way into 'countless general histories' (which were still in use in 1996). Morel wrote congratulating the American Senator Robert Owen, who read the praise into the congressional record, and questioned the German responsibility for the outbreak of war.[172] 'For the first time since that war ended a member of one of the world's legislatures has broken through this conspiracy of silence ... German militarism was a bogey of the heated fantasy. French militarism is a reality and set its iron heel on Europe at this hour.' Herwig thought that, as a result, 'British and French historical understanding of the origins of the Great War must have helped to undermine faith in the need to maintain irenic clauses of the 1919 treaty.'

After ten years, the 'cumulative effect of continuous activity' took its toll as several German states, such as Baden, Bavaria, Sachsen-Anhalt, Württemberg and Waldeck openly adopted ADV material for classroom instruction. The ADV routinely organised talks at high schools and seminars in universities on the issue of the 'war guilt lie'. 'By delaying an open and honest discussion on the origins of the First World War for four decades, the self-censors did their part to bring about a political climate', especially among the youth, that 'could only have paved the way for their favourable reception of Hitler's revisionist ideas.'[173] Historian Erich Hahn suggests that the traditional elite of the Wilhelmstraße was driven in part by personal interest and 'fought for its political survival by defending its credibility both at home and abroad. The war guilt issue thus served its purpose much in the same way as the stab-in-the-back legend served the army: as an escape from the political consequences of defeat. 'It was to be part of the genius of the patriotic self-censors that they managed through their collective efforts at pre-emptive historiography to escape the 'death sentence' of responsibility.'[174]

By 1930, the 'Germans had largely won the battle of history and they were ready to pass from the 'injured innocent' role of the twenties back to the 'fire-eating' stage.'[175] Hermann Hesse said that 'ninety or one hundred prominent men' conspired in the supposed interest of the state 'to deceive the people on this vital question of national interest. Hesse told Thomas Mann in 1931 that, in his opinion, 'of 1,000 Germans, even today, 999 still know nothing of [our] war guilt'.[176] On the fourth anniversary of his appointment as chancellor, Hitler told the Reichstag that he was officially revoking the German signature on the document wherein a weak government had been pressed to accept Germany's guilt for the First World War.[177]

> It may be a mistake to refer to Versailles and the other treaties made in Paris as a 'peace settlement'. The real legacy of Versailles was neither peace nor settlement, but rather a 'seventy-year crisis' marked by a continuing European civil war, the rise of communism and fascism as international movements, inflation, depression, the breakdown of the world economy, and a second world war yielding a divided Germany, and an occupied Eastern Europe.[178]

ENDNOTES

1   Offer, *Morality*, pp. 114–15.
2   Martel and Joll, *Origins*, p. 4. Strachan, *First World War*, pp. 59, 323–34. Klein, 'Misunderstood Defeat', in Boemeke, *Versailles*, p. 213.
3   Clark, *Iron Kingdom*, pp. 613–14. Clark, *Kaiser Wilhelm*, p. 343.
4   Horn, *Mutiny*, p. 198. MacMillan, *Paris 1919*, pp. 157–58.
5   Presentation by Major Freiherr von dem Busche, emissary of Ludendorff and the third OHL to parliamentary leaders in the Reichstag, 2/10/1918 (Ludendorff, *War Memories*, Vol. 2), p. 725.
6   Friedrich, *Deluge*, p. 29.
7   Vincent, *Politics of Hunger*, p. 70.
8   Vincent, *Politics of Hunger*, pp. 60–64.
9   Strachan, *First World War*, p. 322.
10 Keynes, *Dr Melchior: Defeated Enemy*, pp. 15–16.
11 Appendix 6, 'Armistice agreement'.
12 Gedye, *Revolver Republic*, pp. 39, 46.
13 Vincent, *Politics of Hunger*, p. 67.
14 Feldman, *Army, Industry and Labour*, pp. 459–63.
15 Friedrich, *Deluge*, pp. 28–29, 102.
16 Geyer, 'Insurrectionary Warfare', p. 460. This articles provides an excellent dissection of the German psyche over the two months that Ludendorff's panic call for armistice descended in to the 'stab in the back' theory.
17 Strachan, *First World War*, p. 319.
18 Vincent, *Politics of Hunger*, p. 73.
19 Klein, 'Misunderstood Defeat', in Boemeke, *Versailles*, p. 219.
20 Fischer, *War Aims*, pp. 103–106.
21 Feldman, *Army, Industry and Labour*, p. 469.
22 Holborn, 'Introduction', Fischer, *War Aims*, pp. xi–xii.
23 Joll, *Unspoken Assumptions*, pp. 7–8.
24 Herwig, *Admirals*, pp. 216–19.
25 Birnbaum, *Peace Moves*, p. 248.
26 Herwig, *Admirals*, pp. 214–20, 224.
27 Fischer, *War Aims*, p. 416. Herwig, *Admirals*, p. 220.
28 Troeltsch, *Spektator-Briefe*, p. 69.
29 Klein, 'Misunderstood Defeat', in Boemeke, *Versailles*, p. 205.
30 Friedrich, *Deluge*, pp. 27–28. Kessler, *Diaries*, pp. 11, 81.
31 Chapter 1, 'Brave new world'.
32 Friedrich, *Deluge*, pp. 29–30. Howard, 'Social and Political Consequences', pp. 172–78.
33 Fritzsche, *Germans into Nazis*, pp. 102–103.
34 Hull, *Absolute Destruction*, pp. 258–60.
35 Feldman, *Army, Industry and Labour*, pp. 459–63.
36 Hull, *Absolute Destruction*, pp. 299–309.
37 Newbolt, *Naval History*, p. 125.
38 Herwig, 'Dynamics', p. 98.
39 Porch, *French Army*, p. 209.
40 Hull, *Absolute Destruction*, pp. 299–309. The war memorials in German churches reflect the carnage. After the relative emptiness of 1917, the glut of names on the plaques from March 1918 is sobering.
41 Feldman, *Army, Industry and Labour*, pp. 493–94.
42 Herwig, 'Dynamics', p. 102.
43 Kloot, 'Analysis of Energy Balance', p. 190.
44 Ludendorff, *War Memories*, Vol. 2, pp. 608, 611–12.
45 *Tribune de Genève*, 24/7/1918. Bruntz, *Allied Propaganda*, p. 193.
46 Ludendorff, *War Memories*, Vol. 2, p. 683.
47 Bruntz, *Allied Propaganda*, p. 206.

48 MacMillan, *Paris 1919*, pp. 157–58. Feldman, *Army, Industry and Labour*, pp. 513–14.
49 Bouton, *Abdicates*, p. 114.
50 Kitchen, *Silent Dictatorship*, pp. 247–53.
51 Feldman, *Army, Industry and Labour*, p. 511.
52 Martel and Joll, *Origins*, p. 4.
53 Vincent, *Politics of Hunger*, p. 131.
54 Collingham, *Taste of War*, p. 25. Vincent, *Politics of Hunger*, p. 50. Howard, 'Social and Political Consequences', *German History*, pp. 163, 166, 172.
55 Bruntz, *Allied Propaganda*, p. 159.
56 Lewinsohn, *Die Revolution an der Westfront*.
57 Bruntz, *Allied Propaganda*, pp. 34, 193.
58 *Kölnische Zeitung*, 31/10/1918.
59 Creel, chairman of the American Committee on Public Information, *Everybody's Magazine*, 2/1919.
60 Bouton, *Abdicates*, pp. 100–101.
61 Ulrich, 'Feldpostbriefe im Ersten Weltkrieg – Bedeutung und Zensur' in Knoch, *Kriegsalltag*, p. 43. Cited in Fritzsche, *Germans into Nazis*, p. 38.
62 Read in the Reichstag, 6/4/1916. Cited in Lutz, *Birth of the German Republic*, p. 91. Bruntz, *Allied Propaganda*, p. 166.
63 Bruntz, *Allied Propaganda*, pp. 214–20.
64 Deist, 'Verdeckter Militärstreik im Kriegsjahr 1918', in Wette, *Der Krieg des Kleinen Mannes*, cited in Fritzsche, *Germans into Nazis*, p. 34.
65 Knesebeck, *Die Wahrheit über den Propaganda Feldzugund Deutschlands Zusammenbruch*, p. 117.
66 Strachan, *First World War*, p. 319.
67 Hull, *Absolute Destruction*, pp. 198, 318.
68 Clark, *Kaiser Wilhelm*, p. 341.
69 Hull, *Absolute Destruction*, p. 319.
70 uboat.net.
71 Horn, *Mutiny*, Chapters VI–VII. What follows is largely based on this work. Page citations are given, as appropriate, from other sources.
72 Bruntz, *Allied Propaganda*, p. 160.
73 Also, Padfield, *Dönitz*, p. 90.
74 Bruntz, *Allied Propaganda*, p. 146.
75 *British Daily Review of the Foreign Press*, VI, p. 904. *Fliegerabwurf-Schriften*, No. 36.
76 5/10/1918.
77 Horn, *Mutiny*, p. 206.
78 Asprey, *German High Command*, p. 483.
79 Friedrich, *Kaiser Has Abdicated*, pp. 19–21.
80 Padfield, *Dönitz*, p. 90.
81 Niemöller, Vom U-Boot zur Kanzel, p. 133, cited in Mueller, *Canaris*, p. 30.
82 Laurens, *Blockade and Submarine War*, pp. 194–95. Herwig, *Luxury Fleet*, p. 225.
83 Kelly, *Tirpitz*, pp. 424–25.
84 Chapter 6, 'War of the raven'.
85 Chapter 6.
86 Kessler, *Diaries*, pp. 4–5.
87 Friedrich, *Deluge*, pp. 19–21. Strachan, *First World War*, p. 319. Koerver, *German Submarine Warfare*, p. 211.
88 Clark, *Kaiser Wilhelm*, pp. 340–41.
89 Asprey, *German High Command*, p. 472.
90 Hull, *Entourage*, p. 291.
91 Fritzsche, *Germans into Nazis*, pp. 86–89.
92 Ludendorff, *War Memories*, Vol. 2, p. 766.
93 Bernhard Kellermann, *Der 9. November*, deals with the subject in novel form. 1848: Left liberal leader Robert Blum was arrested during the Vienna riots and executed in what was seen as a symbolic event in the crushing of the German revolution of the next year.

1923: The failed Beer Hall Putsch in Munich marked an early emergence and temporary downfall of the Nazi Party. 1938: *Kristallnacht*, 'The Night of Broken Glass', saw synagogues and Jewish property burned and destroyed on a large scale. More than 400 Jews were killed or committed suicide. 1989: The fall of the Berlin Wall ended German separation and ultimately led to German reunification and the fall of Communism in eastern Europe (wikipedia).

94   Friedrich, *Deluge*, p. 15.
95   Holbrooke, 'Foreword', in MacMillan, *Paris 1919*, p. vii.
96   Kessler, *Diaries*, pp. 8–9.
97   Tardieu, *Truth about the Treaty*, p. 142.
98   Howard, 'Social and Political Consequences', pp. 172–78.
99   Wheeler-Bennett, *Nemesis of Power*, p. 15.
100 28/12/1918, Kessler, *Diaries*, pp. 44–45.
101 Kitchen, *Silent Dictatorship*, p. 267.
102 Hull, *Entourage*, pp. 268–69.
103 Hull, *Absolute Destruction*, p. 319.
104 Herwig, *Naval Officer Corps*, pp. 269–70.
105 Teuteberg, 'Food Provisioning', Zweiniger-Bargielowska, *Food and War*, p. 70.
106 Vincent, *Politics of Hunger*, p. 71.
107 Boemeke, *Versailles*, 'Introduction', p. 2.
108 Read, *Atrocity Propaganda*, pp, vii–viii.
109 Chapter 11, 'Immense cemetery'.
110 Fritzsche, *Germans in to Nazis*, p. 28.
111 Schwabe, *Wilson*, p. 192. Klein, 'Misunderstood Defeat', in Boemeke, *Versailles*, p. 211.
112 Vincent, *Politics of Hunger*, p. 67.
113 Appendix 5, 'Wilson's fourteen points'.
114 Birnbaum, *Peace Moves*, pp. 251–52.
115 Strachan, *First World War*, p. 295.
116 Degrelle, *Born at Versailles*, p. 519.
117 Mayer, *Politics and Diplomacy*, p. 3.
118 Marks, *Illusion of Peace*, p.3.
119 MacMillan, *Paris 1919*, pp. 10–13.
120 Boemeke, *Versailles*, Marks, 'Smoke and Mirrors', pp. 337–38.
121 Vincent, *Politics of Hunger*, p. 15.
122 Marks, 'Smoke and Mirrors', pp. 339–40.
123 Vincent, *Politics of Hunger*, pp. 61–63.
124 Cox, 'French Peace Terms', *Modern European History*, pp. 82–85. Tardieu, *Truth about the Treaty*.
125 Gedye, *Revolver Republic*, pp. 12–14.
126 Schuker, *End of the French Predominance in Europe*, pp. 3–4.
127 Boemeke, *Versailles*, Marks, 'Smoke and Mirrors', p. 359.
128 MacMillan, *Paris 1919*, p. 28.
129 Boemeke, *Versailles*, Schwabe, 'Germany's Peace Aims', pp. 42–52.
130 Docherty & Macgregor, *Hidden History*, p. 351.
131 Barnes, *Genesis of the World War*, p. 35.
132 Offer, *Agrarian Interpretation*, p. 374. Becker, *Oubliés de la Grande Guerre*, p. 370. Jones, *Violence*, pp. 262–63.
133 Hull, *Scrap of Paper*, p. 9.
134 Marks, *Myths*, pp. 231–32.
135 Degrelle, *Born at Versailles*, p. 516.
136 Marks, *Myths*, pp. 254–55.
137 Strachan, *First World War*, p. 325.
138 MacMillan, *Paris 1919*, pp. 158–59.
139 Marks: *The Illusion of Peace*; 'The Myths of Reparations', and 'Mistakes and Myths'. For contrast see Eichengreen, *Golden Fetters*; Ferguson, *Pity of War*, p. 414; Feldman, *Die deutsche Inflation*, and *Great Disorder*; Kent, *Spoils of War*; Schuker, *American 'Reparations'*

to Germany; Steiner, *Lights That Failed*, pp. 198–200.

140 Marks, *Myths*, pp. 235–46.

141 Friedrich, *Deluge*, pp. 36–37, 121, 134.

142 Marks, *Myths*, pp. 254–55.

143 *Deutsche Zeitung*, 28/12/1918.

144 Kelly, *Tirpitz*, p. 422.

145 Kitchen, *Silent Dictatorship*, p. 249.

146 Boemeke, *Versailles*, Klein, 'Misunderstood Defeat', p. 213.

147 Strachan, *First World War*, p. 59.

148 Hull, *Absolute Destruction*, p. 109. Strachan, *First World War*, pp. 323–34.

149 30/11/1918.

150 *Virginia Quarterly Review*, Wheeler-Bennett, 'Ludendorff: The Soldier and the Politician',
     Vol. 14, No. 2, pp. 187–202. Martel and Joll, *Origins*, p. 4.

151 Herwig, 'Clio', p. 109.

152 Bruntz, *Allied Propaganda*, pp. 156–57.

153 Feldman, *Army, Industry and Labour*, p. 507.

154 Feldman, *Army, Industry, and Labour*, p. 469.

155 Vincent, *Politics of Hunger*, pp. 22–23.

156 Asprey, *German High Command*, 17/5/1922, pp. 491–92.

157 Herwig, 'Clio Deceived', Wilson, *Collective Memory*, pp. 87–127.

158 Wilson, *Collective Memory*, Wilson, 'Introduction', p. 1.

159 Herwig, 'Clio', pp. 87–90.

160 Lloyd George: 'Europe slid into war with roughly equal amounts of ignorance and
     naiveté' (Herwig, *Clio*, p. 119). Compare, Clark, *Sleepwalkers, How Europe went to War in
     1914*, written in 2013.

161 Hull, *Scrap of Paper*, pp. 7–11. Wilson, *Collective Memory*, Wittgens, 'Senator Owen', p. 128.

162 Herwig, 'Clio', pp. 92–93.

163 Germany and Auswärtiges Amt, *Die Grosse Politik der Europäischen Kabinette, 1871–1914*.

164 See Rosenburg, *Imperial Germany*.

165 Martel and Joll, *Origins*, p. 4.

166 Herwig, 'Clio', p. 94.

167 Herwig, 'Clio', p. 119.

168 Herwig, 'Clio', pp. 103–104.

169 Herwig, 'Clio', pp. 115–17.

170 Adler, 'War-Guilt Question', pp. 15–24. See this article also for attacks on Fay by Barnes.

171 Herwig, 'Clio', pp. 105–106.

172 Wilson, *Collective Memory*, Wittgens, 'Senator Owen', pp. 132–33, citing Congressional
     Record, 1st Session, 68th Congress, Vol. 65, 18/12/1923, pp. 355–99.

173 Herwig, 'Clio', pp. 106, 120.

174 Herwig, 'Clio', pp. 118–19, citing Hahn, 'German Foreign Ministry', pp. 56, 69; and
     Kautsky, *Wie der Weltkrieg entstand*, p. 13.

175 Adler, 'War-Guilt Question', p. 21. Wilson, *Collective Memory*, Evans, 'History as
     Propaganda', p. 170.

176 Herwig, *Clio*, p. 120, citing Klessmann, 'Als politischer Zeitkritiker net indict: Hermann
     Hesse', in *Die Zeit Metabasin*, Vol. 15, 14/4/1972, p. 10, Hesse to Wilhelm Schäfer, 1930.

177 Herwig, 'Clio', p. 107, citing Jäger, *Historiche Forschung*, p. 65.

178 Boemeke, *Versailles*, Jacobson, 'Soviet Union', p. 451.

CHAPTER 14

Welcome Home, Erich

'To go to Berlin was the aspiration of the composer, the journalist, the actor; with its superb orchestras, its hundred and twenty newspapers, its forty theatres, Berlin was the place for the ambitious, the energetic, the talented. Wherever they started, it was in Berlin that they became, and Berlin made them, famous.' And yet there was something ungainly and sprawling and fermenting about it. It was a capital city that, like some horrible adolescent, had yet to grow into its role. In some ways it was even worse – a sort of golem – something that had been created for the purpose of existing, like Weimar, a bubble, and a hyperventilating bubble at that.[1]

Erich Gerth left Pola in the Adriatic by train on 28 October 1918. With over a thousand kilometres to travel to Berlin, there were many reasons for possible delay. The Austrian fronts were collapsing to right and left. Vienna, particularly its railway system, was in the grip of the influenza epidemic making 8,000 wagons and passenger cars idle.[2] Erich was part of a large party, the Adriatic naval staff of Kapitän zur See Theodor Püllen, perhaps 300 men and officers from ten scuttled u-boats and two torpedo boats, and about 1,500 maintenance workers who would return to Kiel. Logistics were complicated. One train would be insufficient and the fragmented regional nature of the Austrian and German railway systems might suggest changes at least at Vienna, Dresden and Prague. Officers might wish to move ahead of the main party in travel accommodation suitable to their status. All were anxious to return home at speed so as to support the Fatherland's last stand. The German call to President Wilson for an armistice was made at the beginning of October. Although nothing had yet been agreed, the war was likely to end soon, but not before, it was assumed, the army and navy had placed Germany in the best negotiating position either by a daring, aggressive stroke or by strengthening their defensive lines on foreign soil. It would be another month before any of

Erich's comrade u-boat commanders reached the Baltic. However, their heroic and marathon race home to bolster the fleet would be in vain as they would sail into a humiliating and dangerous rebellion. While Erich was on the train, the crews of the High Seas Fleet battleships refused to put to sea for Admiral Scheer's 'honour by suicide' naval battle and were in revolt, especially at Kiel. Ludendorff, self-proclaimed saviour of the nation, had just been dismissed by a frustrated Kaiser.

Erich bought, probably, an edition of *Berliner Tageblatt* and read the major stories which emphasised the worsening situation: official negotiations underway between Turkey and the Allies, separating its fate from Germany; reactions to Ludendorff's 'resignation' from The Hague, Geneva and London; a written constitution after the collapse of the military bureaucracy to transfer power to the people; declaration of the Czechoslovakian state; notes to and from President Wilson; u-boat successes; attacks by the English at Famars, south of the River Schelde, and by the French at the Rivers Aisne and Oise, all reportedly failing.[3]

> *Berliners read newspapers. They read them so voraciously that the German capital emerged as the newspaper city par excellence with more papers than London. The media culture ... helped change the look and the feel of the city as newspaper kiosks sprang up at every major intersection and newspaper vendors prowled the streets shouting the day's headlines.*[4]

Tired from the journey, only a few weeks away from sinking a clutch of Italian fishing vessels and dragging his ailing u-boat back to port, Erich had a personal choice. He could either travel to barracks with his fellow captains or bid them farewell and make his way onto the street to find a tram or taxi. As Erich was one of the few officers in his flotilla whose home was in Berlin, perhaps he received an overnight dispensation from Kapitän Püllen. His mother lived alone in a rented apartment in Keithstraße 22, a few minutes from Berlin Zoological Gardens, her home since 1908.[5] Erich's short trip would have been a shock. Berlin had a 'bedraggled appearance'; once the cleanest city in the world, it was now filthy and so were many of its people.[6] The shortage of soap spread disease and the poor lacked boots and warm clothing. Poverty was on the streets, with long queues for food, haggard faces, the disfigured and the maimed. A large number of the men wore a motley array of untidy uniforms and semi-military attire. There were no cats or dogs, all eaten and their skins used for leather.

> *The great cities remained, the railway lines were more or less intact, ports still functioned. It was not like the Second World War, when the very bricks and mortar were pulverised. The loss was human. Millions of combatants – for the time of the mass killing of civilians had not*

yet come – died in those four years: 1.8 million Germans, 1.7 million Russians, 1.4 million French (a quarter of French men between eighteen and thirty – twice as many again of its soldiers wounded), 1.3 Austro-Hungarians, 743,000 British and another 192,000 from the Empire. Children lost fathers, wives, husbands, young women the chance of marriage ... but the tally of deaths does not include those who were left with one leg, one arm or eye, or whose lungs had been scarred by poison gas or whose nerves never recovered.[7]

When Erich found Hedwig, his mother, his surprise presence should have done much to raise her depression; she was prone to 'melancholia'.[8] With her husband dead for twenty-five years, her life was wrapped in her two surviving sons, both serving in the most dangerous profession of all. Georg sent regular news from his prisoner-of-war camp in France. And, now, here was Erich, her eldest, home unexpectedly and, if the news was to be believed, increasingly likely to survive the war. She scrambled to make a meal. Had she sufficient money to escape the worst of the famine? Or was it a diet of half-rotten potatoes, adulterated flour and a few carefully guarded scraps? During these last weeks of the war, Germany suffered from almost as many civilian deaths as from military ones, but the famine did not affect the population equally. Urban citizens, like those in Berlin, Catholics, low social classes and the highly-integrated regions along the Rhine river and the North and Baltic seas were hit the hardest.[9] The famine 'exacerbated deep inequalities and a new food hierarchy emerged in Germany'.[10] The lowest groups were families of soldiers living without a male bread-winner, single older people, and inmates of institutions.

The poor, the weak and the elderly were very badly hit,' wrote Professor Bergahn, an historian of German and modern European history, 'whereas the better-off who had savings were able to obtain supplies on the black market at exorbitant prices.'[11]

Among the cheerfulness and thanksgiving, Hedwig found a son whose military world had collapsed. Erich reported to naval headquarters and was given work which eventually lasted until the end of November 1921, over three years of unexpected employment. When the armistice was signed on 11 November, two weeks after Erich's return, the imperial navy was ordered to be reduced and was later limited by the peace treaty to a force of 15,000 officers and men.[12] Nothing definite is known of Erich's work at the Admiralty except that he claimed to have spent some time on official duty in Spain and in Italy. His story here is built on scraps of concrete information and conjectural straws.

Admiral Adolf von Trotha was appointed head of the newly-created Admiralty in Berlin on 26 March 1919. He was a Tirpitz disciple and had under his command following the peace treaty six old battleships, six cruisers, twelve destroyers and twelve torpedo boats. There was an absolute ban on naval aircraft and, particularly, on u-boats to put a block on any future submarine arm. Trotha began planning secretly and immediately for a fleet for when Germany regained her temporarily lost status as a great power. He told a staff member, 'I want to preserve the smallest seed so that when the time comes a useful tree will grow from it.'[13] 'Consequently [Trotha's] immediate aim was in the personnel field; discipline and pride had to be restored, a nucleus of dedicated officers formed who would be able to guide the later expansion.'[14] Trotha was allowed only 1,500 officers so 'only the best and most loyal need be selected'. Erich was one of the 'seeds', a small, tight group chosen from among the available submarine commanders.

Trotha has been met before within this story, at the mutiny of the battleships, when he was noted for his 'marked antipathy toward democracy, parliamentary government, and the idea of a negotiated peace'. He had an 'absolute abhorrence for all those who stood opposed to militarism'. His disdain had flowered to include those he saw as chiefly responsible for the navy's present humiliation, the Allies in general, but specifically the Republican politicians 'who, by signing the armistice, had robbed the armed forces of victory'. Trotha had a fruitful seam to mine as the naval officer corps was 'imbued from top to bottom with a thoroughly vengeful spirit against the Versailles treaty and the Allies, particularly against Britain, with a 'poisonous hatred' for their 'inconsiderate inhumanity, incitement to revolution and the hunger blockade'. Trotha had also been Erich Gerth's commanding officer for about a year in 1910 aboard the light cruiser *Königsberg*, which had a small complement of fourteen officers, and therefore knew him well enough to write his annual review.

A service analysis of the 498 German and Austrian u-boat commanders who served during World War 1 produces almost-accurate numbers and they tell an interesting story.[15] The top figure can be quickly reduced by the 159 captains who died in the war and by sixty or so more: Austrians who were not a part of the imperial navy and were not available to Trotha, and others in exceptional circumstances like long-term illness, detainment in Allied prisoner of war camps and early death, and some for whom today insufficient information is available to make an assessment of their service period. From the end of the war to the great cull demanded by the peace treaty, forty-one u-boat officers dribbled from the ranks at the rate of a few a month probably led by normal attrition, by firm suggestions that they leave, or they were men who had better places to go and therefore made individual decisions to resign. This still left Trotha with about 230 officers, all of whom he kept on strength as he selected his cream. At the peace treaty signing in November 1919, ninety-one of the remaining u-boat captains immediately left naval service. They were followed over the next four months by fifty-five more and, principally in August and September

1920, by a final, smaller cull of twenty-seven. Those remaining were the sixty chosen men. One of these was Erich Gerth who stayed with the service until the end of 1921 when he left to prepare his application for the Foreign Office. One can deduce that Erich as a 'chosen man' was strongly aligned to Trotha's views, got to know him well and left with his blessing. Trotha, many levels of rank Erich's senior, agreed to act as one of Erich's referees for his Foreign Office application the following year.

Generally, Trotha chose his sixty men well. Of the forty-six u-boat officers identified who stayed long-term in naval service after 1922, one half made admiral: eight konteradmirals; eight vizeadmirals, including Wilhelm Canaris; four admirals (Hermann von Fischel, Wilhelm Marschall, and Otto von Schrader, who was to be Georg Gerth's commanding officer in Norway in World War II); and four grossadmirals (Rolf Carls, Karl Dönitz, Alfred Saalwächter and Otto Schultze).[16] Most u-boat commanders assumed power with relish and through right from their fathers' powerful business institutions or landed estates. As with their British and French counterparts, their prejudices and confidence was reinforced by their training at the better schools and in the naval officer corps. These young men were far from natural democrats. It is also clear that they loved their country, believed in a future as a maritime merchant power and had relished the chance to fight, to destroy and, when appropriate, to kill to make it happen. That did not end because of the Versailles Treaty. Memoirs and reminiscences confirm that the men, as personal servants of the Kaiser, were decisively loyal to the monarchy, despite abdication, and were reluctant republicans. The Imperial German Navy had been 'in peace and remained in war a federal German institution directly under the emperor'.[17] A love of risk and danger surges through the pages of their many published reminiscences. Yet, for most of them, there was also a clear sense of day-to-day chivalry. The majority were committed, as far as possible, to a civilised war and believed they fought by its rules. In most of this, they were little different from their Allied counterparts.

Preoccupations at the Admiralty in this immediate post-war period can be reasonably deduced. There was the much reduced fleet to manage and new rules and regulations suitable to a republican navy to develop, but for the immediate future the remaining older capital ships were used principally for training. They were not about to go to sea to fight. There were detailed arrangements for the humiliating transfer of the modern fighting ships demanded by the terms of the armistice and peace treaty, but this was quickly concluded. For instance, on 20 November 1918, twenty u-boats were shepherded by Royal Navy destroyers into Harwich, the last twenty miles with British crews and with the White Ensign hoisted above the German flag.[18] Over the next eleven days, this main transfer took the total to 114 vessels; those boats under construction were broken up on the shipyard slipways in Germany.

In addition, the Admiralty had to play its part in developing both the obfuscation needed to protect the office corps from criticism for its role and decisions made during the war and the arguments to undermine the Allies' peace assumptions so that better terms dealing with reparations and rearmament could be demanded.[19] This political manoeuvring included defeating social democrat parliamentary investigations into the responsibility of the naval command in the mutiny of 1918, for which much blame lay at the door of Scheer and Trotha, and supporting the spurious claim that the revolt was a carefully planned Communist conspiracy. More immediately, covert assistance was given to the three naval paramilitary *Freikorps* formed to fight the revolutionaries. Specific arguments were needed to show that the Allies had started the war and that Germany was an innocent party forced onto the attack to defend herself against determined aggressors. Claims that unrestricted submarine warfare as a whole, and the conduct of individual u-boat captains in particular, were criminal actions which warranted trial, needed continual rebuttal.[20] In the case of the latter, captains that might be found guilty were spirited away to safety both before and after their trials. Finally, continuous support was needed for Ludendorff's and Hindenburg's insistence that the military, and by inference the navy, and this meant the whole meritorious officer corps, had been stabbed in the back by a consortium of communists, lying Allied propaganda and weak and unpatriotic elements in the home front.[21]

> *After the war was lost the German public opinion of its navy was at an all-time low; the navy had caused the war with England in 1914; further, it had caused the war with America in 1917 leading to the revolution in Germany in 1918. The assorted failures led to the ignominious scuttling of the Imperial High Seas fleet at Scapa Flow in June, 1919.*[22]

Despite outward resignation, the leaders of the new Republican navy remained determinedly against the social democratic constitution. Individual officers had to wrestle with their monarchist, anti-democratic consciences to decide whether they wished to take the new oath of allegiance. For most that did take the oath, like Erich in 1920, it was no more than a fig leaf.[23] In 1922, he still declared himself as 'Prussian' rather than 'German'. Another prominent sailor who chose to remain on active duty, Vice Admiral Wolfgang Wegener, did so despite the fact that he viewed the Weimar Republic as an 'unloved façade', but primarily so that he could have a chance to lay the intellectual groundwork for the future 'unavoidable struggle against the sea power of England'.[24]

Article 191 of the Versailles Treaty banned Germany from building, acquiring or operating submarines of any description. One further secret and most important task of the 'new' officer corps of the republican navy was to prepare for the next world war. That part of this work which is of interest here concerns rebuilding Germany's u-boat capability.

> *Whether one looks back on the Weimar years from the perspective of the late 1930s or forward from the 1920s toward the Nazi era, the idea that the Second World War had been 'implicit since the moment the first war ended' is simplistic.*[25]

A team of knowledgeable u-boat managers and commanders had to be assembled. The latest plans and components for the next series of u-boats had to disappear from dockyards and admiralty offices before Allied inspectors from the Inter-Allied Control Commission called. Overseas facilities were needed to evade the complete ban on any work by Germany on submarines. Naval strategists were immediately put to work. Among them was Kapitänleutnant Erwin Wassner of the naval high command in Berlin who in July 1922 published a paper suggesting that, in his war experience commanding five u-boats, surface attacks had been the most successful and that since lone u-boat operations were uneconomic against convoys 'in future it will be essential for convoys to be hunted by sizeable numbers of u-boats acting together'.[26] Future admirals Wilhelm Marschall and Karl Dönitz, the Führer of the Nazi u-boats and the final Führer of the Third Reich, agreed. 'The coming war may or may not involve war against merchant shipping', but u-boat officers must be trained to attack convoys. This strategy was propounded by many of the u-boat and command memoirs which were sucked up by an eager public looking for heroes and hope among the ruins of the Kaiser's reign.

Much of the clandestine operations formally came into operation after a few years, but the groundwork was laid while Erich was at the admiralty. When Dönitz arrived back in Kiel in July 1918 after his spell in a British prisoner-of-war camp, he was met by the adjutant of the navy station, Otto Schultze, his u-boat flotilla chief from Pola. Dönitz asked whether they would ever see u-boats again and Schultze said he thought it would take two years.[27] Leading the work was the chief of the submarine department, Karl Bartenbach. Bartenbach, it will be remembered, was the long-serving Flanders u-boat chief, responsible for the establishment of the Bruges u-boat base, and was then Georg Gerth's senior officer.[28] By the end of the war, Bartenbach was 'without doubt the leading German submarine expert'. Before Flanders, he commanded the Germany Navy's first submarine, *U 1*; was the first chief of the new German *U-Boots-Abnahmekommission*, co-ordinating submarine construction; and then head of the submarine school. Importantly, a strong *Kameradenschaft* was formed aboard *U 1*, between Bartenbach, his second officer Ulrich Blum and his chief engineer Heinrich Papenberg.[29]

The German Navy 'began cheating on the Treaty of Versailles in June

1919', one month after its ratification, when Blum, still a serving naval officer, proposed by letter to Krupp's managers the founding of a submarine construction office at the Krupp Germaniawerft shipyard in Kiel.[30] The object was to use former u-boat officers to market German submarine plans and knowledge to other nations and thereby keep the German u-boat flame alive. Krupp agreed and Blum along with Bartenbach and a number of other former German naval officers, began trying to interest other nations in their wares.

Bartenbach began his overseas post-war career in Costa Rica in 1920, 'probably conducting negotiations with Japan from there', or with Argentina, where he moved in 1921.[31] Canaris did similar work in Italy and in his old stamping ground in Spain and it was to these two countries that Erich claimed he travelled on undisclosed 'missions' while working for Trotha, probably under Canaris's direction. Canaris re-established the *Etappendienst* in Spain, work that he and Erich had also undertaken in South America.[32] Canaris found his old colleagues and friends from the war and he also 'recruited some new agents all around the world'.[33] Here also, there is the answer to a small puzzle. In his foreign office application of 1922, Erich did not mention his time as commander of the Kiel training u-boat, *UB 76*, nor his operational u-boat experience in the Adriatic, nor what his most recent function had been in the *Marineleitung*, the naval high command in Berlin. Erich was no shrinking violet when it came to demonstrating his achievements. The likely reason was that Erich's most recent work was highly sensitive and this need for continued secrecy extended well into the 1930s, at least until the bombshell of the Lohmann Affair, described later.

Under the auspices of the newly-formed Reichsmarine, Bartenbach was closely involved in the German Navy's negotiations with Krupp and two other German firms to set up a covert Dutch puppet company, *Ingenieurskantoor voor Scheepsbouw* (or Scheepsvaart), known as IvS.[34] Blum became the commercial director. This drawing office in a shipyard in The Hague was ordered to stay on the cutting edge by offering comprehensive expertise in submarine development and construction to aspirant naval powers. The principal clients consulting IvS were Argentina, Finland, Italy, Japan, Russia (at various times), Spain, Sweden and Turkey. IvS's technical director was the former chief constructor at the Germaniawerft at Kiel, Hans Techel, who shipped a large amount of submarine plans and components over the Dutch border to begin operations. Germaniawerft also controlled the Ing Fijenoord shipbuilding yard in Rotterdam. The link between IvS and the German Admiralty was provided by *Mentor Bilanz*, a dummy Berlin company, directed by former *U 64* commander Robert Moraht, who officially left the navy service in July 1920 and was one of Trotha's chosen men.[35]

The *Marineleitung* became a 'powerhouse of rearmament'. Among its senior members dealing with u-boats were Arno Spindler, naval chief of staff and future u-boat official historian, Canaris, Dönitz, Wilhelm von Löwenfeld, who had been commander of the Kurland naval installations on the Baltic while Erich was there for his secret mission in 1917 and who had led one of the most infamous *Freikorps*, Kapitän zur See Werth, and their leader, Rear Admiral Adolph Pfeiffer.[36] The German Navy backed IvS with one million Reichsmarks and promised an additional 120,000 per year, if needed. The money came from a secret slush fund, the *Sonderfond*, that the navy created at the end of the war. Initial funds, amounting to at least twenty-five million dollars, came from the sale of warships and u-boats scrapped in 1919 and 1920 under the Allies' direction. Unfinished u-boats must have been a large contributor to the fund; at the end of the war, 226 boats were being built with a further 212 projected.[37] Additional support for navy 'black projects' came from 'Weimar officials, who colluded to vastly overcharge for navy equipment and then diverted the profits to what they considered more worthy causes'. Funding was managed from perhaps as early as 1920 by Kapitän Walter Lohmann of the Naval Transportation Division who was given full charge by early 1923 of the disbursement of the navy's 'black' funds for clandestine purposes with the 'complete trust' of the navy's commander-in-chief, Admiral Paul Behncke.[38]

Most of this money was transmitted to recipients, including IvS, through a middleman, a Lohmann-supported bank, the Berliner Bankverein. In 1927, this illicit operation was exposed in the 'Lohmann Affair' and crashed with disastrous and humiliating results for the Navy and the Weimar Republic, discussed in the next chapter when a few more important characters have been introduced, and latterly came under review by the American Central Intelligence Agency from whose report details are taken.[39]

The best documented examples of the reach of IvS concerns their contracts with Finland and Turkey. Bartenbach moved in May 1924 to become naval advisor to the Finnish government on the recommendation of retired Admiral Tirpitz. He worked 'unostentatiously behind the scenes', principally on submarine projects, and was generally referred to by the Finns as 'our expert'. Dealing easily with competition from French and British firms, Bartenbach ensured that Finnish u-boat contracts went to IvS or to an associated Finnish business, Crichton-Vulcan of Åbo (a part-British company before the war). Crichton-Vulcan was roundly criticised in the Estonian press as being covertly German-owned at the time which was true, but denied by the Finns. The company was taken up by Krupp to build torpedo boats for the Russian Navy. Later ownership had been transferred to Dutch and Swedish hands to camouflage the firm's German control. Contracts awarded to Crichton-Vulcan were secretly re-signed with IvS. In March 1927, following complaints from the British and the French, the Conference of Ambassadors ruled that it was not possible to invoke Article 191 of the Treaty of Versailles to prevent the Dutch firm from constructing components for the Finnish submarines. The conference stated that Article 191 was only applicable to Germany itself and could not be invoked against a foreign German-controlled firm.[40]

Two u-boats, one of 250-tons at Åbo for the Finnish Navy and the other of 500-tons at Cadiz for the Turks, were built for the private account of IvS. At one stage the Russians, alarmed at developments in Finland 'instigated and financed a metalworkers strike at Crichton-Vulcan' through the Red International of Labour Unions, *Profintern*, which lasted for nine months. In 1927, an agreement was concluded with the King of Spain, with the assistance of Canaris, for the technical section of *Mentor Bilanz* to build a 750-ton u-boat in Cadiz. That same year, the British identified twenty Germans working in the Finnish Navy alongside Bartenbach who were actually in the employ of the German military. One of these men was multiple u-boat commander Werner Fürbringer, who worked with IvS, and was to write Erich's obituary. Fürbringer also acted in an advisory capacity when in 1926 Turkey placed a large order for submarines to be built at Rotterdam. Before delivery in 1928, German crews gained useful experience by putting the boats through extensive trials. The boats created the need for a training school in Turkey and in due course German crews, including Fürbringer, were shipped out to provide and attend clandestine courses. In 1930, the first practical u-boat training on active service, as distinct from retired officers like Fürbringer, took place. The Germans were disguised at civilian tourists and carried out trials on a 500-ton Finnish submarine from July to September.

> The very re-birth of the German u-boat service owed its greatest debt to such First World War veterans as Hans Schottky, watch officer on UB 19 and UB 117, Kurt Slevogt, U 71, and Werner Fürbringer, commander of six u-boats. These men laid the foundations for the future campaign of 1939-1945 from the selection and development of basic submarine designs to the earliest tactical training in fleet and commerce operations.[41]

In 1932, the Germans made a political decision to rebuild their submarine arm. Still bound by the restriction of the Versailles Treaty, the German navy decided in 1933 and 1934 to collect all of the components for sixteen u-boats, ordered initially through IvS, in guarded sheds in German shipyards. Fürbringer re-entered the German Navy in 1933 and was appointed senior instructor at the Kiel-Wik 'Anti-Submarine School' 'which was of course exactly the reverse of what its title stated'.[42] Designs for large 550-ton u-boats were drawn up in 1934, managed by an IvS subsidiary, *Schiffbaukontor*, in Bremen, and this vessel became Germany's most-produced submarine of the Second World War. Hitler announced on 16 March 1935 that 'after the final collapse of our former enemy's disarmament charade we have taken our military sovereignty in our own hands'.[43] An Anglo-German naval treaty allowing submarines construction was signed in June 1935. The first Nazi u-boat slid into the water eleven days later. That year, submarines *U 33* and *U 34* undertook illegal covert operations in Spanish waters, committing what many years later was deemed an act of piracy, by sinking Spanish submarine *C-3* on 12 December 1935. As Admiral Wilhelm Marschall, who worked with Erich in the Adriatic, said in his book *Torpedo Achtung! Los!* in 1938, 'The seed is sown! We, the war-generation, see it rise with our own eyes; it's a magnificent feeling to be here and to be able to help it happen. Heil to our Fuhrer!' On 17 November 1939, Kapitänleutnant Otto Schuhart, *U 29*, sank the British aircraft carrier *HMS Courageous* in the Western Approaches with the loss of 518 British lives.

> *Britain's sleepy complacency in allowing Germany to re-acquire u-boats (which must also be set against the backdrop of political appeasement of the era) was a direct result of the Admiralty's belief, persisting since 1918, that the u-boat danger had been mastered, and that u-boats would never again be able to present Britain with the problem she had faced in 1917 ... a case, to paraphrase AJP Taylor, of men seeing the past when they peer into the future ... This confidence was reinforced when Germany denounced unrestricted u-boat warfare in 1936 [for which] Churchill accused the Admiralty of the 'acme of gullibility'.*[44]

While still in the navy, Erich registered at the Friedrich-Wilhelms University in Berlin on 29 November 1918 as a student of law.[45] He was a youthful-looking thirty-two-year-old, sociable with an attractive personality, and a lover of parties. He attended an eclectic series of lectures in his first semester over the winter of 1918/19: Mathematical Foundations of Natural Sciences, Contemporary Economics, Theory of Law and State in Modern Times, Origins of Man, World Harmony, History of Architecture and German and a further two dealing with Prostitution and Venereal Diseases. In the Spring seminars of 1919, his lectures seemed more germane: National Economy, 'Proseminar', Philosophy, Foundations of Logic, Modern Psychology and Modern History. Were these subjects just a series of haphazard evening classes? Would this wide-spread selection have been made by a committed law student? How much time in any event would Erich have been allowed away from the Admiralty for study?

At the same time as he entered university, Erich met and fell in love with a wealthy, petite, vivacious, young widow, a countess, Gräfin Eva von Ahlefeldt, who was to provide the centre and the inadvertent ruination of his career.[46] The introduction was made by Wilhelm Canaris who had figured in so much of Erich's naval life since their years together as naval cadets. Canaris was a frequent visitor to the home of Eva's father, Honorary Consul Salomon Marx, a banker and entrepreneur of considerable wealth who wielded much influence in Jewish, financial and political circles.

Canaris, who came from Dortmund-Aplerbeck, less than thirty kilometres from Salomon Marx's birthplace of Schwerte, was 'an intimate family friend'.[47] Marriage for a naval officer before and during the war had been a 'complicated business'.[48] From 1899, the groom needed Imperial marriage consent, *Allerhöchsten Konsens*, for reasons both financial and social. Officers needed enough money to support a family, lest they be overwhelmed with debt. Brides, too, had to have financial means, and a wife with low social status was considered unsuitable.

> *Young officers searched for wealthy, socially acceptable young women so actively that, in 1894, the Marine Kabinett censured officers for advertising in the newspapers for a suitable match. Although there were no written rules, young officers were discouraged from seeking Jewish wives, even if the latter were financially and socially suitable. Marie Lipke* [Tirpitz's wife] *was wealthy and prominent enough to clear these hurdles. She was a baptised Protestant, born in West Prussia in 1860.* [Her father,] *Gustav Lipke was born in 1820 in Berlin to a wealthy assimilated Jewish banking and business family.*

There were evident similarities between Eva Marx and Marie Lipke, but, by the time of Eva's marriage to Erich Gerth, there was no Kaiser and the military world was upside down. With his marriage, Erich now had three male mentors, Trotha, Canaris and Marx. All sought the replacement of the socialist-led Weimar Republic and were vehemently anti-communist, particularly in combatting the Spartakist League, formed by communists Karl Liebknecht and Rosa Luxembourg. This shared fanaticism led them into manipulations, plots, the *Freikorps* paramilitary groups and direct involvement in the murders of the two communist leaders. It is easy to see how Erich was seduced into their schemes.

Eva Marx was born on 29 August 1895 in Cologne, the third child of Salomon and Helene Clara Schirmacher.[49] With the birth of his children, Salomon joined his wife as a Lutheran Protestant.[50] Erich, a Protestant, married Eva in Berlin on 27 June 1919; she was nine years his junior. The year before her second marriage, Eva converted to Catholicism and took two additional suitable Christian names, Marie and Ignatia.[51] Eva's conversion was followed by Erich, her new husband, shortly afterwards and their subsequent enthusiastic support to the Catholic cause, discussed later, was a central and important part of their future private and working lives.[52] There were two witnesses at the wedding, both from Berlin. The first was Eva's father, Salomon, aged fifty-three, of Brückenallee 29, Berlin, a fourteen-room villa with domestic staff in the up-market quarter of Tiergarten. The second was coroner and doctor of medicine Hugo Marx, forty-four years, of Alt Moabit 12A. Hugo was no doubt close family having travelled to New York from Hamburg with Salomon and his wife Helene aboard the *Kaiserin Augusta Victoria* in 1911.[53] There is no question that the marriage had Salomon's blessing. The records show that he fought hard over many years to secure his son-in-law's future career.

Eva's first marriage was to Leutnant der Reserve Graf Karl-Christian von Ahlefeldt-Eschelsmark, he was twenty-three, she nineteen, and took place in the Garrison Church at Stettin on the Baltic coast on 3 August 1914.[54] It seems to have been a rushed affair, the certificate carries no ages, places of birth or parents' names. No family was present. This may easily be explained as a love match brought forward by the call for mobilisation the day before. There was a pressing need for Ahlefeldt to get from Stettin to Flensburg in Schleswig-Holstein on the Danish border where his regiment, Füsilier Regiment 'Queen' 86, was based.

> *Officers and men were quietly recalled from furlough, mobilisation rosters appeared overnight in every newspaper and were posted on public buildings in every hamlet, village and city of the German empire, while heralds went round the towns blowing trumpets to summon reservists to the colours.*[55]

Ahlefeldt's regiment was appropriately connected as its commander-in-chief was Augusta Victoria of Schleswig-Holstein, the Kaiser's wife and second cousin. The Danish and Mecklenburg royal connections of the noble family of Ahlefeldt-Eschelsmark extended to the eleventh century.[56] On 8 August, Ahlefeldt left for the invasion of Belgium.[57]

> *Crimes of excess began almost immediately: human shields, punitive destruction of buildings, mass execution of non-combatants began on 5 August 1914, the first day of the real shooting war. They were widespread. Half of all German regiments in the western theatre of operations committed such acts. In the first two months of the war there were 129 major incidents of execution involving ten or more civilians. The acts were committed by common soldiers or low-ranking officers.*[58]

The regiment suffered heavy casualties while fighting at Liege and the Marne, before falling back and settling into trenches in 1915 at Moulin, Quennevières Farm, Dreslincourt and Pimprez. 'Fear of the franc-tireur was ubiquitous.'[59] Every one of the thirteen regiments taking part in the initial *Handstreich*, 'surprise attack', against Liège was 'involved in action against alleged *francs-tireurs*'. At this time, because of heavy losses, a demand for junior officers as air crew existed which was directly comparable to the call by the navy for u-boat commanders. Ahlefeldt volunteered and served as an observer in Kagohl 2, a unit of the *Luftstreitkräfte*, renowned for its 'aces', including the contemporary 'ace of aces' Freiherr Manfred von Richtofen, the 'Red Baron' with over eighty combat victories. Ahlefeldt was shot down and killed while flying in an 'LGV C' on a photo reconnaissance mission over Douaumont Fort on 1 April 1916 during the Battle of Verdun.[60] His victor was Sergeant Lucien Jailler of Escadrille N 15 who was flying, probably, a Nieuport 11. Ahlefeldt's body was recovered and a picture of his battlefield grave exists. The Kagohl's Staffelführer Hauptmann Claes reported in his letter to Ahlefeldt's mother that Karl-Chistian died in air combat with three French biplanes by a shot to the head. However, this was a common report to cover a more likely and more terrifying death. Karl-Christian von Ahlefeldt's line is extinct in Europe since 1964; Graf Friedrich Karl of the only surviving branch emigrated in 1890 from Denmark to the Argentine, married Maria Ramona Mendez and their descendants live in Buenos Aires.

At first view, Erich's initial meeting with Eva might be thought to have been made by Erich's class mate of '05, Kapitänleutnant Wilhelm von Ahlefeld, later of the Flanders torpedo boat service. However, the current family chronicler Heiko von Ahlefeld is confident that the two branches of the Ahlefeldt/Ahlefeld family were distant with no opportunity for an introduction. Similarly, he feels that there is no evidence that the noble Ahlefeldts discouraged Eva Marx's first marriage because she was a half-Jewish commoner, but who counted herself a Protestant. Heiko von Ahlefeld also suggests that, at the re-marriage, Eva should have relinquished her use of her noble title.

The Ahlefeldts made considerable sacrifice for the fatherland. One branch stemmed from Vizeadmiral Hunold von Ahlefeld, who died in 1919, and who was one of the first of the 'modern' sailors, joining the Prussian Navy in 1867. Three of his sons were killed and one, Oberleutnant zur See Paul-Friedrich, a crew member of *U 27*, was shot, most would say murdered, by British sailors in the infamous *Baralong* affair in August 1915 – 'a British disgrace'.[61] His eldest son, Wilhelm was the fellow cadet of Erich in the Class '05. He served on torpedo boats in the Flanders Flotilla, re-joined the navy in World War II, fell out with the Nazis, was dismissed, and shot himself in 1941 at the family seat at Gut Ludwigsburg near Eckernförde. Another von Ahlefeld, distantly-related to the above, Karl Gustav, was an officer on board the SMS *Prinz Adalbert* when its ammunition store was hit by a British torpedo in 1915 leaving just three survivors from a crew of 675, the worst German naval loss in the Baltic in World War I.[62]

There is an interesting u-boat connection: Karl-Christian von Ahlefeldt's mother was Franziska Eugenie Elisabeth Katharina Adelaide Carola von Dresky, a member of another long-lived noble family which contained at least one admiral and four Prussian generals.[63] Franziska's nephew (or second cousin) was Hans-Wilhelm von Dresky, commander of *U 33* from Wilhelmshaven, who was drowned in the Clyde off the Isle of Arran in 1940 while on a daring mine-laying mission. The intention was to place mines far inside the extended Clyde naval base and cause havoc in what

the Allies considered 'safe' waters. The voyage was thought so dangerous
that Hitler and Dönitz, now u-boat Führer, came in person to see the boat
away after the crew enjoyed a sex and drink party send off in a wooden
hut in the middle of a forest.[64] *U 33* was detected by the minesweeper HMS
Gleaner and was badly damaged in three separate depth charge attacks in
shallow water. Dresky brought his boat to the surface to allow his crew
to escape and then scuttled. Only seventeen men survived; twenty-five
including Dresky died from hypothermia in the freezing water. What makes
the tale from another war worth telling here is that the sinking brought the
first break-through in the attempt to read the Enigma code and happened
far away from the British cryptographers at their secret intelligence base at
Bletchley Park.[65] Dresky gave orders for the *U 33*'s Enigma machine's code
wheels to be distributed among some of the men and to be dropped into
the water once clear of the u-boat. One set of three wheels was collected by
the British and taken to Alan Turing and his code-breaking team.

Perhaps it is not surprising that Erich's interest in his university course
quickly dwindled. Within six months, Erich was married to a most eligible
and wealthy widow, a countess, who was able quickly to raise him above
the fray and to introduce him to a very different sort of world. He attended
just one course on the Philosophy of Art in the Winter Semester of 1920/21.
Erich then took complete leave of every other semester until, in July 1923,
the University cancelled his registration because of his non-attendance. His
final report of August 1925 noted that, 'Nothing negative has been reported
about his behaviour.' Something or someone persuaded Erich on a career in
the Foreign Office. Optimistically, in his formal application in December
1922, Erich explained that he had 'not yet' received his doctorate, but that he
had attended eight semesters between 1919 and 1922 studying Law, Political
Sciences, Philosophy and History as well as one course at the High School
for Political Sciences in Berlin.[66] In the year, between first missing lectures
at the university and applying to the Foreign Office, Erich worked in Berlin
in Salomon Marx's Internationale Handelsbank, which concentrated on real
estate, 'participating in the management of the business and thereby gained
practical commercial knowledge', and in the telegraphy company Vox
Maschinen.[67] The Vox-Haus, near Potsdamer Platz in Berlin-Tiergarten, was
bought in 1920 by the Vox record company and, in 1921, a broadcasting studio
was installed in the attic. The new medium of radio became hugely popular.
One of the first transmissions was the Christmas speech by Chancellor
Wilhelm Marx in December 1923; a photograph, dated 1924, shows guests at
the Vox-Haus including the papal nuncio Eugenio Pacelli. Both these men
were to contribute significantly to Erich's career.

Perhaps the benefits and hard work of a doctorate were now not necessary
for Erich's future. One other speculative thought: Berlin's universities
at this time were a hotbed of student politics: republicanism, socialism,
communism, anarchism. Could it be that Erich attended partly to gather

information on dissidents for the Admiralty or directly for Canaris? The idea is not so far-fetched as later events show. The period around Erich and Eva's wedding was a time of revolution and there was death on the streets, particularly in Berlin where the Gerth and Marx families lived. Erich was taking tentative, and quickly unsuccessful, steps towards a legal doctorate. He was still in the employ of the Admiralty, most probably working with Canaris and others on some aspect of the early stages of rebuilding the u-boat fleet. He was already deeply involved with leading anti-Republican, anti-communist militarists like von Trotha, Canaris, and his other colleagues among the commanders of the u-boat flotillas. Salomon Marx, Erich's father-in-law, was cut from the same stamp and, as one of the richest men in Germany, had the money to encourage extreme action. Eva would also have enjoyed a private income and Erich entered into a whirl of new contacts: Catholic leaders delighted with Eva as a high profile and attractive 'catch'; far-right activists; and senior commercial, political and industrial giants of the time who formed Salomon Marx's daily contacts. One can assume that many of these introductions took place at Salomon's home, particularly over dinner with the young couple in attendance. Kessler noted in his diaries in December 1918, presumably during the courtship,

> The Christmas Fair carried on throughout the blood-letting. Hurdy-gurdies played in the Friedrichstraße while street vendors sold indoor fireworks, gingerbread, and silver tinsel. Jewellers' shops in Unter den Linden remained unconcernedly open, their windows brightly lit and glittering. In the Liepzigerstraße, the usual Christmas crowd thronged the big stores. In thousands of homes the Christmas tree was lit and the children played around it with their presents from Daddy, Mummy and Auntie dear. In the Imperial Stables lay the dead, and the wounds freshly inflicted on the Palace and on Germany gaped into the Christmas night.[68]

After Germany's defeat, Marx was instrumental in setting up a bourgeois citizens´ council for Berlin as a focus for opposition to revolutionary groups of soldiers, workers and the communist *Spartakusbund*. It was founded on 18 November 1918 as the *Bürgerrat von Gross-Berlin* with Marx as deputy chairman and chairman of the finance committee and one of the five members of the managing committee. Later, he became the Bürgerrat's leader and also of the *Landesbürgerrat* of the Province of Brandenburg. On 5 January 1919, the *Reichsbürgerrat*, the national umbrella organisation comprising 300 citizens' councils countrywide was founded. 'The clear-sighted and energetic chairman of the Berlin Bürgerrat, Consul Marx was credited with this achievement.' The *Bürgerrat of Gross Berlin* actively supported two causes at opposite ends of the spectrum – the fight against the peace conditions the Allies set out at Versailles and the provision of fuel and food to the city's population. Marx organised public protests against the demands of the Entente and against the lack of food, especially meat and fat and heating materials as a result of the continuing blockade. One of his initiatives, the *Holzhilfe GmbH*, provided the poorer population of Berlin with firewood.

There is one further strand, the development of the *Freikorps*, to follow before events and protagonists come together with the murder of the Communist leaders Karl Liebknecht and Rosa Luxemburg.

Liebknecht and Rosa Luxemburg have met with a dreadful and fantastic end.[69]

The murder date of 15 January had a particular significance for Erich Gerth, but it would be some days before he realised it. One of the mines he laid with *UC 53* in the Straits of Messina the previous October hit the French passenger and general cargo ship *Chaouia* on the same day.[70] She quickly sank and 476 men, mostly Greek troops, lost their lives. The *Chaouia* was the penultimate boat of the war to be lost to a u-boat. It accounted for the twenty-second largest loss of life.

As war ended and the men came home, many to desert, where was armed authority to be found? Kurt von Schleicher, protégé of General Wilhelm Gröner, one-time organiser of Germany's economic warfare and the last chancellor of the Weimar Republic before Hitler took over the government in 1932-33, had 'devised a secret plan to combat the disintegration of the old regiments'.[71] In mid-December 1918, the Army Supreme Command approved Schleicher's plan and assigned an infantry commander, General Ludwig von Maercker, to organise an entirely new kind of volunteer force known as the *Freikorps*. Schleicher wanted only the 'most loyal and disciplined veterans, who could be organised into highly mobile storm battalions, each with its own trucks and artillery, signed on month by month'. The generals 'circumvented the problem of unreliable reservists and with the support of the skittish Social Democratic government organised the first *Freikorps* or freelance units, ostensibly to protect the Fatherland from subversion and plunder, but, in fact, to crush the radical left'.[72] A dozen early corps were formed, each of several thousand men, including three corps from the navy: the Hermann Ehrhardt Brigade; Colonel von Roden's 'Iron Brigade', loyal to Gustav Noske, who represented the government in negotiations during the Kiel naval mutiny; and the Löwenfeld Corps, 'the largest group, organised in Kiel, which included many former u-boat captains and crewmen among its ranks'.[73]

In something of an irony, it was these three corps of angry naval officers and reactionary leaders who were to define the fight against socialism in the capital. It was ironic because it was the sailors from the Baltic who

precipitated the revolution in 1918 by standing up to their weak and
ill-led officers of the High Seas Fleet, perhaps stiffened by the u-boat
commanders, and it was these self-same officers who, over the next year,
broke the revolution's back and crushed its temporary successes.[74]

> *Within a rather short time,* [the Freikorps] *were to become a collection
> of some 200 piratical bands, merciless in their attacks on civilians and
> loyal only to their unit commanders and seen as the only force able to
> stand up to the Communists.*[75]

There is a Gerth family memory, a story told many years later by Erich to
his son Marco, in which Erich claimed to have played his part as a member
of one of the naval *Freikorps* and to have 'manned the barricades in Berlin
against the Bolsheviks'.[76] If true, and there is already a suspicion that Erich
inclined to slight embellishment, then it is likely that he followed the
lead of his Adriatic comrades, Arnauld de la Perière, Canaris, Kukat and
Niemoller, all known *Freikorps* members of the Löwenfeld Corps, formed
in December 1918.[77] The story also adds credence to a possibly subversive
role for Erich at his university which he joined the month before. The
Corps disbanded in June 1920 and this coincided with his loss of interest
in his studies. There is no record of Erich in the lists of naval *Freikorps*, but
these are far from complete. His absence does, at least, suggest that he was
not a prominent member.

Löwenfeld was one of those with Dönitz and others who were identified
as leading the covert u-boat programme. Löwenfeld's assault battalion was
commanded by the legendary u-boat ace, Lothar von Arnauld de la Perière,
who had rescued Canaris from Spain in 1916, and the corps contained
'probably every naval officer in the vicinity' of Kiel.[78] Canaris was one of
Löwenfeld's 'first and closest collaborators' and it was within this corps'
organisation that Canaris began the 'outstanding intelligence bureau' that
later led him to senior power in the Nazi government.[79] In December, Canaris
was sent from the Baltic to Berlin by Löwenfeld, to contact groups 'possibly
preparing a kind of counter-revolution'. The Admiralty was ostensibly not
interested, but one can imagine that Trotha, another eventual member
of the Ehrhardt Brigade, gave him close attention. However, Canaris was
successful with the Garde-Kavallerie Schützen Division (GKSD), a 'royal
elite troop'. In March 1918, on Ludendorff's order, Hauptmann Heinrich
Waldemar Pabst had joined GKSD as its chief of general staff to convert it
from a cavalry to a rifle division.

> *Under Pabst, GKSD became the strongest counter-revolutionary unit in
> Germany, the 'backbone of all troops deployed'* ... *Pabst's main aim was to
> overthrow the Republic and its socialist leaders. He gathered like-minded
> men around him and, amongst the GKSD staff, were Kapitänleutnant*

Horst von Pflugk-Hartungg and his younger brother, Heinz. All were
fanatical militarists, anti-communists and enemies of the Republic.

Horst von Pflugk was a cadet member of the Crew of '07, and therefore
a close contemporary of Georg Gerth, currently languishing in a French
prison hospital recovering from influenza.[80]

Several of the Gerths' fellow u-boat commanders were at the forefront
of the *Freikorps*. Personal comrades were killed in action. Communism left
the u-boat crews largely unaffected, and they were still prepared to fight
on 'beyond the end of the war'.[81] Wilhelm Werner, a classmate of Erich
Gerth, sank sixty-five ships with *U 7* in the Mediterranean and *U 55* around
Britain. He was an unconvicted war criminal and later joined the Freikorps
of Paul von Lettow-Vorbeck before fleeing to Brazil. Lettow-Vorbeck, who
commanded the German troops in East Africa, ended the Spartakist uprising
in Hamburg without the use of force.[82] Two men of the Adriatic flotilla,
Heinrich Kukat and Martin Niemöller, were involved in 'one of the most
bloody and savage episodes of the whole German revolution'.[83] Kukat was
killed fighting pro-communist forces in the Ruhr uprising in 1920; Niemöller
commanded his own Academic Defence Corps of the *Freikorps* in the same
action. Niemöller briefly became a farmer before studying Protestant
theology and became a pastor in 1924 in Dahlem, a suburb of Berlin. He was
an early supporter of Hitler until his seizure of power in 1933. Niemöller
claimed that Hitler's writings on Aryan supremacy contradicted 'Christian
charity values'. In 1936, Niemöller signed a petition along with a group of
Protestant churchmen, calling for opposition to the Nazis' state control of
the churches, an action that prompted the mass arrest of nearly 800 men.
After a trial for 'activities against the state' he was eventually imprisoned
in Sachsenhausen and Dachau concentration camps from 1938 to 1945,
narrowly escaping execution. He later became an ardent pacifist.[84]

> *The u-boat men who headed for Kiel Harbour* [on their way home
> from the Adriatic] *were neither potential pacifists nor future
> democrats. Neither Niemöller nor Canaris had the least desire to
> be welcomed home to red flags and solders' councils. The eleven
> commanders agreed to enter harbour flying the Imperial ensign and
> the home-coming pennant, and swore that the red flag would never be
> hoisted on their boats.*[85]

It was a further irony that the German general staff provided Lenin's
'sealed train' that took Lenin and his followers home after the Russian
Revolution in the hope that he would sow disaffection among the Russian
soldiery.[86] 'The seeds were scattered beyond Russian borders' and came
back to haunt Germany's rulers. Lenin was a long-term, personal mentor
of Rosa Luxemburg and a supporter of Karl Liebknecht.

Karl Liebknecht had always been a 'lonely, high-strung and essentially likeable man'. His father, William, was one of the founders of German Socialism, a friend of Karl Marx, who 'combined Marxist revolutionary theory with practical, legal, political activity'.[87] In 1904, Karl Liebknecht told the SPD party conference, 'Militarism is our most deadly enemy and the best way of waging the struggle against it is to increase the number of social democrats among the soldiers'. In 1907, he published a fierce attack on Germany's military and served an eighteen-month sentence for treason.[88] Liebknecht broke ranks from his party at the end of 1914 to vote against war credits, the socialists accepting that it was a defensive war.[89] It was only when the SPD became convinced that the German government was conducting a war of conquest that they declined to pass further credits. Despite Liebknecht's parliamentary immunity, the army retaliated by putting him in a punishment battalion on the eastern front where he refused to fight and served by burying the dead. Because of his deteriorating health, he returned to Germany in October 1915.

> As a Reichstag deputy, however, he had the right to attend each session and he repeatedly asked embarrassing questions about the shooting of Belgian hostages and about the specific causes of the war – greeted with cries from other deputies of 'Nonsense' and 'Madness'.[90]

Expelled by the SPD in 1916 for his previous lone stand against war credits, Liebknecht began publishing a radical newspaper under the name of Spartakus, a small affair with only about 500 copies printed.[91] Liebknecht and Luxemburg developed the USPD, the Independent Social Democratic Party of Germany which briefly shared power with the SPD late in 1918. The USPD led in turn to the founding of the communist party and its attendant Spartakus League. In May 1916, while Liebknecht was giving an anti-war speech, mounted police charged the crowd and Liebknecht received a four-year prison sentence for high treason and 'contumacy to the authority of the state'.[92] In October 1918, the Spartakus group was active with appeals and their first national conference for nearly two years. 'The spontaneous mutinies among the soldiers must be supported by all means and be led towards an armed uprising for the struggle to gain the entire power for the workers and soldiers.' In other words, the working class could only be relied on to invoke the weapon of the strike. The move to a revolution required the leadership of the intelligentsia.

> The whole process was intended as a continual raising of revolutionary sights so that the ponderous and reluctant dragon of the German working class could finally be induced to snort and move.[93]

As the old order crumbled, Liebknecht was one of the first to be released under a general amnesty. He returned to Berlin on 23 October as a 'prophet vindicated' and with Lenin's full support. He was 'welcomed by huge crowds and carried shoulder-high by soldiers decorated with the Iron Cross'.

Rosa Luxemburg's relations with Liebknecht were politically close, but they were 'never personal friends'. She 'admired his courage and despised his slapdash existence'.[94] Luxemburg was an educated Polish Jew who moved to Zurich in 1889 where she met the founders of the first Russian Marxist party and received a doctorate in law and political science. It was also where she began her unusual love affair with Leo Jogiches, who became a stalwart if flaky party member. Jogiches lived next door to Luxemburg because he wished to keep their relationship secret. Luxemburg moved to Berlin in 1898 and, though women were not allowed to join political parties, offered her services to the SPD as a writer and speaker. In Berlin, she was 'confronted by a double prejudice' among Prussians who saw both Poles and Jews as 'irredeemably inferior'. She thought 'Berlin the most repulsive place: cold, ugly, massive – a real barracks, and the charming Prussians with their arrogance as if each one of them had been made to swallow the very stick with which he got his daily beating.' On a holiday in Finland, she met again with Lenin whom she found a pleasure to talk to. 'He is sophisticated, knowledgeable, with the kind of ugly mug I like so much.' Quickly becoming an activist, she roused a pre-war crowd of 6,000 SPD members. 'We are the millions of those whose work makes society possible ... we can show our reactionary rulers once and for all that the world can go on without Junkers and Earls, without councillors, and at a pitch even without the police, but that it cannot exist for twenty-four hours if one day the workers withdraw their labour.' She joined Liebknecht in condemnation of war. 'Once the majority of working people come to the conclusion ... that wars are nothing but a barbaric, unsocial, reactionary phenomenon, entirely against the interests of the people, then war will have become impossible even if the soldiers obey their commanders. We think that wars can only come about so long as the working classes either supports them enthusiastically because it considers them justified and necessary, or a least accepts them passively.'

In July 1916, Luxemburg was suddenly arrested, a police decision unresolved as to whether to place her on trial or just to keep her in custody.[95] She remained incarcerated until November 1918, mostly in the city jail in Breslau. She missed the amnesty that freed Liebknecht because it was thought to apply only to those serving specific sentences. After addressing an expectant crowd in Breslau's central square, she hastened in the afternoon to Berlin here she was 'greeted with joy by her old friends, but also with concealed sadness, for they suddenly realised what the years in prison had done to her. She had aged terribly and her black hair was gone quite white. She was a sick woman.'[96]

Adolph von Trotha, Tirpitz disciple, Erich Gerth's mentor, co-leader in 1918 of covert plans for Germany's fleet for the 'next war'.

Reginald Bacon, the 'cleverest man' in the Royal Navy, charged with blocking the Dover Straits to u-boats; maximised the intelligence gain from Georg Gerth's *UC 61*.

Karl Bartenbach, founder of the Flanders u-boat bases with a 'fanatical following' from his captains, including Georg Gerth; by war end Germany's leading submarine expert.

Wilhelm Canaris, the man with a finger in every secret pie, pre-war spy, leader of the Abwehr, close friend of Erich Gerth, Spanish royalty, assassins, and plotters to kill Adolf Hitler.

Maximilian Harden, Jewish intellectual, publisher, journalist, actor and critic; friend and business supporter of Salomon Marx; eventual fierce critic of the Kaiser.

Heinrich Brüning, Christian Democrat Chancellor, devout Roman Catholic and co-organiser with Erich Gerth of masses for peace in the 1930s; fled Germany in 1934.

Alfred Hugenberg, leader of Krupp, the steel and armament firm; bought Ufa, Germany's largest film studio; failed to outwit Adolf Hitler and was humiliated.

Maria de la Paz de Bourbon, Spanish infanta, daughter of Queen Isabella II, who recommended Erich Gerth for a position at the German Foreign Ministry.

Karl Dönitz, fellow u-boat commander to Erich Gerth in the Mediterranean, future German Führer, whose Berlin background closely mirrored that of the Gerth brothers.

Karl Liebknecht, a 'lonely, essentially likeable man', anti-war campaigner, Reichstag member, political prisoner, Communist, murdered by the Freikorps in 1919.

Martin Niemöller, another
of the Mediterranean u-boat
commanders with Erich Gerth,
became a pacifist, a pastor, and
was sent to Sachsenhausen
concentration camp.

Konstantin von Neurath,
whose diplomatic
sensibilities were upset
by Erich and Eva Gerth
in Rome, later Protector
of Bohemia and, finally, a
convicted war criminal.

Rosa Luxemburg, an educated
Polish Jew, mentored by
Vladimir Lenin, murdered
minutes after Karl Liebknecht,
found in the Landwehr Canal
four months later.

Ludwig von Schröder, Georg
Gerth's commander as head
of the Flanders MarineKorps,
signed Charles Fryatt's death
warrant; 'iron man' told
to suppress the Kiel naval
rebellion.

Walther Rathenau, head of electrical giant AEG, advisor to the Kaiser, friend to Salomon Marx, raised five million Reichsmarks for the Freikorps, Foreign Minister, machine-gunned to death.

Wilhelm Marx, leader of the central catholic party, twice German Chancellor, covered up German naval rearmament; his father was cousin to Salomon Marx.

From 4 January 1918, more than 100,000 soldiers and civilians demonstrated against the government in what became known as the Spartakist uprising. The revolutionary committee of the Communist Party, the KPD, called for a general strike which led to street battles between its supporters and the moderate Social Democrats (SPD), whose government was led by Friedrich Ebert, Philipp Scheidemann and Gustav Bauer. Luxemburg considered any revolt at that time would be a catastrophe and spoke out against it. The SPD newspaper building and other publishing houses were occupied by the Spartakus League. Schreiner captured the mood of long-repressed discontent, 'The Peoples of Europe are at one another's throat today because one set of capitalists is afraid that it is to lose a part of its dividend to another. The only way we have of getting even with them is to turn socialist and put the curb on our masters. The men in the trenches knew very well what they were fighting for. They realised that, now the struggle was on, they had to continue with it, but they had also made up their mind to be heard from later on.'[97] Two of Erich Gerth's later referees, the Prince and Princess Ludwig of Bavaria, were warned to take care as 'Luxemburg and company were looking for new hostages, people with names, officers of the old army, princes ...'[98] These descendants of the Spanish royal family saw Rosa as 'drunk with blood lust and hideous', the ringleader whose 'ferocity gave her an uncanny power over the lowest elements of the mob'.

The Police Headquarters was in the hands of the Spartakists where ...

> *Liebknecht was addressing a large crowd. He speaks with unctuous solemnity, like a parson, intoning his words slowly and expressively ... Only a part of his words were intelligible, but his sing-song inflexion carried over the heads of the silent and attentive crowd. When he ended there was a roar of approval, red flags were flourished, and thousands of hands and hats rose in the air. He was like an invisible priest of the revolution, a mysterious and sonorous symbol to which the people raised their eyes.*[99]

At the Reich Chancellery, it was Defence Minister Noske who suggested using military force against the insurrectionists and he was given wide-ranging powers by Chancellor Ebert to restore order.[100] Noske immediately set up his headquarters at Berlin Dahlem. One of 'most active' officers was Pabst, whose adjutant was Canaris. Noske asked Kiel for help and within a few days a force of 1,200 men of the 'Iron Brigade' left for the capital. Canaris arranged for the distribution of weapons, uniforms, equipment and rations. After a bombardment of several hours, the Spartakists vacated the SPD Vorwärts newspaper building.[101] 'Five intermediaries, who had negotiated the surrender of the building, were summarily tried and executed; three couriers were murdered.' Over 150 insurgents and seventeen *Freikorps* soldiers died.

> *On 13 January, the* Freikorps *were now mopping up the final doomed resistance in bloody and pitiless street-fighting in which deaths rose to over 1,000. Luxemburg, her cheeks sunken, her eyes dark with tiredness, wrote her final article. 'The leadership failed. But the leadership can and must be created anew by the masses and out of the masses … 'Order reigns in Berlin!' You stupid Lackeys! Your 'order' is built on sand. The revolution will 'raise itself up again clashing', and to your horror it will proclaim to the sound of trumpets: I was, I am, I shall be.*[102]

Noske 'marched 3,000 men through the city and government district to demonstrate their military strength and the resolve of the government'. There was no resistance. Liebknecht and Luxemburg went into hiding. Luxemburg wrote on 25 December that she had 'received urgent warning from official sources' that the assassins were looking for them both and 'we shouldn't sleep at home'.[103]

On 9 January 1919, Salomon Marx, the most influential man of the *Bürgerrat Gross-Berlin*, called upon 'every man capable of bearing arms who had previously done military service to join the Republican civic militia at once'. Bands of citizens armed themselves to fight against the Spartakusbund with the rallying cry, 'Shoot down the red dogs!' Bourgeois businessmen like Marx initially financed the *Freikorps* troops under whose protection many armed vigilante groups consisting of bourgeois voluntary fighters were formed. Walther Rathenau reputedly personally raised five million Reichsmarks to support the *Freikorps*.[104] The same day, Eduard Stadtler gave a speech at Berlin University where Erich Gerth studied and called upon all students to take up arms.

On 10 January, Salomon Marx organised a meeting of fifty representatives of banks, industry and trade, including Ernst von Borsig, Friedrich von Siemens and Hugo Stinnes. Eduard Stadtler who had just returned from Russian captivity and had become one of the leading anti-communist agitators gave a talk entitled 'Bolshevism as a world danger'. Following this meeting, the attendees from industry and banks set up a fund worth 500 million Reichsmarks with the aim of putting down the revolution. Historian Hintz questions this sum, but suggests an amount of twenty million Reichsmarks. The next day an organisation of academics demanded that all men in professional occupations joined forces to fight against Bolshevism.

> *A strong anti-Bolshevist propaganda is being carried out by the Government and Berlin is placarded with a variety of posters on the subject. One of the commonest represents a huge skull holding a dripping dagger in its teeth, the poster being in lurid colours and headed 'Die Gefahr des Bolshevismus'. Berlin in itself is a fair representation of the people at the moment. Dirt, disorder, dancing and death. The traffic is chaotic. Every dancing hall is filled to overflowing and, almost within*

the sound of their orchestras, Spartacists and Government troops shoot each other dead every day.[105]

Marx chaired daily meetings in the back room of a 'well-known' inn in the Unter den Linden where the Bürgerrat and Freikorps leaders exchanged information and plotted the arrest of Karl Radek, an Austro-Hungarian Jew and prominent Bolshevik who travelled with Lenin in the sealed train the year before. Radek had recently crossed into Germany illegally, arriving in Berlin a few weeks earlier. Marx also called for the killing of Liebknecht and Luxemburg on whose heads a reward of 100,000 Reichsmarks, at least unofficially, had been placed by right-wing private enterprise, with the probable backing of Philipp Scheidemann at the top of government.[106]

A poster appeared across Berlin:

> *Workers, Citizens!*
> *The fatherland is close to its downfall.*
> *Save it!*
> *It is not threatened from outside, but from the inside:*
> *The Spartakus Group.*
> *Strike their leaders dead!*
> *Kill Liebknecht!*
> *Then you will have peace, work and bread!*
> *The Front-line Soldiers*[107]

Writer Engelmann credits the 'man behind the scenes', Salomon Marx, with the financing and authorship of this propaganda poster.[108] The German Historical Museum, *Deutsches Historisches Museum*, however, argues that the pamphlets in their data base which can be directly linked to the *Bürgerrat Gross-Berlin* and Salomon Marx show a different line of attack, for example, calls for the speedy foundation of a national assembly or to promote a future co-operation with Austria.[109]

> *The street fighting in Berlin between 10-15 January culminated in an attack on an ill-considered and chaotic demonstration of extreme left socialists and communists and the deaths of the Communist party leaders, Karl Liebknecht and Rosa Luxembourg, on 15 January. The crushing of the so-called 'Spartakus revolt', in no way deserving of the name, and the 'white terror' that followed was a shattering defeat for the left-wing radicals. Strikes and armed conflicts took place in February and March, and for a brief period, 4 April – 1 May, a Soviet republic was established in Bavaria. All were suppressed.*[110]

On 16 January 1919, a day after the murders of Liebknecht and Luxemburg, the Dresdner Bank, Deutsche Bank and Disconto-Gesellschaft each transferred donations of 50,000 Reichsmarks into the account of Salomon Marx at *Bürgerrat Gross-Berlin*.

The murders themselves are well covered in many publications although, as always, there are long-lasting queries as to the complete facts.[111] 'From the early days of the revolution, shortly after they had both been released from the Kaiser's jails, Liebknecht and Luxemburg were targeted for destruction.' They were 'politically vital' as their deaths would remove the 'two most able and charismatic leaders of the German left'. They also exposed the 'guilt of the SPD' in agreeing to the elimination of their former party comrades and this left 'a legacy of bitterness that was to divide and fatally weaken the forces of German socialism for more than a generation'.

In brief, Pabst and the GKSD had their headquarters at the Hotel Eden in Berlin under the local command of Heinz von Pflugk-Harttung; his brother Horst, the cadet contemporary of Georg Gerth, was in the unit and present. Pabst had 'often met with Liebknecht and considered him a dangerous enemy'.[112] Civilian militia at Wilmersdorf arrested Liebknecht and Luxemburg at a safe house, possibly as a result of tip-off by a 'friend' and took them separately to the Eden where they were reportedly separately tortured. The government was informed of the arrests and private instructions were passed and understood. Late that evening, Liebknecht was taken to the rear of a waiting open car to a 'barrage of insults from soldiers and hotel guests'. Once seated, flanked by the Pflugk-Harttung brothers, Rifleman Otto Runge, on guard at the hotel revolving door, ran forward and hit Liebknecht with a 'savage blow' with the butt of his rifle. Faking a puncture near Berlin Zoo, Horst Pflugk-Harttung took Liebknecht by the arm, released him and then shot him several times from behind as if he was trying to escape. The 'unknown' body was later taken to the city morgue where it was identified. Luxemburg was interviewed by Pabst, who had also met her several times. She darned the hem of her coat and read *Faust* in the toilet. When word was received that Liebknecht was dead, Luxemburg was taken outside where Runge struck her twice on the head with his rifle and she was thrown into the waiting car. About forty metres from the hotel, Oberleutnant Kurt Vogel jumped onto the running board and shot her dead. The body was thrown into the Landwehr Canal where it was found by sluice gates four months later and identified only by clothing.

> In the early hours of 8 May 1919, the Landgericht courthouse at Berlin Moabit resembled an army depot. Units of GKSD was stationed at all entrances, on the streets patrols broke up large gatherings; the whole east wing of the courthouse swarmed with soldiers and visitors; reporters and witnesses were searched for weapons. Hundreds wanted to watch the trial ... British and American visitors were offering up to 5,000 Reichsmarks on the black market for a ticket.[113]

All of the men on trial had previously been released from custody. Only Vogel was charged with Luxemburg's murder. Liebknecht's accused were Otto Runge, Heinz and Horst Pflugk-Harttung and four others.[114] The chairman of the GKSD panel of military judges was Hermann Ehrhardt, the brigade commander of the men on trial. He was assisted by three lay judges, one of whom was Canaris who had role-played the evidence with the defendants, especially that of his two personal friends, the Pflugk-Harttungs. Unsurprisingly, there was 'ever-growing criticism' from Press, politicians and the workers' and soldiers' councils. All except two were acquitted: Vogel was cleared of murder, but found guilty of a number of minor disciplinary matters and sentenced to twenty-eight months' imprisonment; Runge, who was brought back for trial from the Danish border where he had been smuggled personally by Pabst, was sentenced to two years' imprisonment.

Three days after sentencing a 'Leutnant Lindemann' arrived at Moabit prison with authority to remove Vogel to Tegel penitentiary. 'Lindemann' and Vogel drove off and disappeared, Vogel to Holland. 'Lindemann' was Canaris. In a trial in 1933, Canaris's involvement was uncovered, including 30,000 Reichsmarks made available for the Pflugk-Harttung brothers to flee. Heinz was blown up in his car in Berlin in 1920 and died the same day of wounds.[115] It was a retribution bombing by Polish communists, Luxemburg's native comrades. In a later career that has all the hallmarks of Canaris's involvement, Horst co-ordinated the Fascist movement in Sweden. He became the leading German spy in Denmark where he set up a ring that operated secret broadcasting stations that dealt with nautical and hydrographical material.[116] At the same time, he worked for General Franco arranging the sinking of Spanish Republican fishing boats and was instrumental in the sinking of the Spanish Republican freighter *Cantabria* ten miles off Dover by the Spanish nationalist cruiser *Nadir* in 1938. In 1944, Horst commanded the Germany Navy docks in Bordeaux. He was arrested by the Americans and taken to Arizona for questionning, eventually released because he was not seen to be a Nazi, and returned to Germany in 1947.

Luxemburg's long-term lover, Jogiches, did not have long to live. On 10 March, he was arrested and identified at once. At police headquarters, one of the detectives in charge was an ex-Sergeant-Major Tamschick, a 'notorious bully'. He knew Jogiches as one of the leaders of Spartakus and shot him in cold blood at the first opportunity. No attempt to punish Tamschick was ever made.[117]

Demands from the military mounted on Noske to seize power and reject the peace treaty. Borsig-director Benningsen-Förde wrote on 12 February 1919 to Ernst Borsig that, 'The soul of the citizen councils is Consul Marx.' He has close links to the government. Marx's influence, and that of his family friend, Canaris, was ubiquitous. Marx belonged to the financial committee of the *Ausschuss Deutscher Verbände zur Schaffung einer Einheitsfront zur Bekämpfung der Schuldlüge*, 'Committee for the Creation of a United Front to Fight against the Guilt Lie'.[118] This committee became one of the biggest and most influential propaganda organisations of the Weimar Republic. Further, during the socialist March revolts, the Berlin Bürgerrat could be credited with setting up a regiment of 1,200 volunteers in Berlin at short notice, thus boosting the regular army troops.

It seems as if Salomon Marx's conscience was pricking him, particularly as a Jew, despite his conversion to Christianity. He asked the President of the Central Association of German Citizens of Jewish Faith, Dr Ludwig Holländer, for his views on Judaism and Revolution or Socialism. Holländer confirmed that Judaism 'strictly condemned subversive actions and that Jewish life was by its nature conservative'. Another prominent Jewish representative of the time, Dr Cäsar Hirsch, stated that 'revolutionary Jews were behaving contrary to the teachings of Judaism and had therefore stopped being Jewish'. Hintz believes that the motive for Salomon's role as a counter-revolutionary was the fact that he was deeply rooted in the traditionally conservative milieu of the educated and wealthy German-Jewish upper classes. Of course, there were Jewish protagonists on both sides of the political divide, revolutionaries and radical conservatives.

Under pressure to leave from the Swedish government and attracted by the rise of the *Freikorps*, Ludendorff returned to Germany in February 1919 to free rooms at the Adlon Hotel in Berlin.[119] He was given a private entrance to keep him away from the Allied Disarmament Commission, meeting in the same hotel, who wanted Ludendorff as a war criminal. Ludendorff plotted and met with, for instance, General Walther von Lüttwitz, commander of the troops in Berlin, including all of the *Freikorps* and who had helped suppress the Spartakists uprising; Pabst; and Wolfgang Kapp, the co-founder with Tirpitz of the short-lived Fatherland Party. In August 1919, Pabst founded the *Nationale Vereinigung*, an anti-republican organisation, in order to 'prepare the counter-revolution'.[120] Membership included von Lüttwitz, Ludendorff, Max Bauer, the former chief of staff, *Freikorps* leader Ehrhardt, Kapp, and, of course, Canaris.

In May 1919, leading figures involved in the eventual 'Kapp-Lüttwitz Putsch' to depose the government met at Marx's Brückenallee address to discuss plans. The *Reichsbürgerrat*, headed by Marx, published a pamphlet calling for the revision of the Versailles Treaty because its demands could not be met. Marx used a recent book by the British political economist John Maynard Keynes, *The Economic Consequences of the Peace*, to further his arguments. Marx gained widespread public attention by an event he organised in June on the day of the scuttling of the German fleet at Scapa Flow. The commander of the German fleet had been instructed to hoist the British flag above the German one during the transfer of the ships, a command that was seen as an humiliation by large parts of the German population. The German government had guaranteed that French flags seized during the war would be returned. In response, members of the *Freikorps* entered the Berlin arsenal and forced the guards to hand them over for burning at the memorial for Friedrich the Great. Many university students, perhaps including Erich Gerth six days before his wedding, were involved in the protest.

In the spring of 1919, the *Freikorps* were greeted as liberators by burghers in the cities where they smashed the general strikes of militant workers and the Spartakist uprising in Brunswick. They marched to Munich to lead the suppression of the Communist government in Bavaria, then moved to Silesia in search of Polish guerrillas. Once the *Freikorps* had 'murdered their way across Germany and finally disbanded', they left behind a loose confederacy of secret organisations, veterans' clubs, and rifle clubs which included Hitler's nascent *Sturmabteilung*.[121] At the same time, regional governments promoted the creation of local citizens' or home guards, *Einwohnerwehren*, to maintain law and order, so that more than one million men were enrolled in paramilitary activities in 1919 and 1920 with local armouries, veterans back in uniform, and rifles under the floorboards – all attesting to the deadly mobilisation that had taken place in hundreds of communities across the Reich.

On 29 February 1920, Defence Minister Noske ordered the disbandment of two of the most powerful *Freikorps*, the naval brigades of Löwenfeld and Ehrhardt. Ehrhardt refused to disband and staged a parade where Lüttwitz backed the unit. Noske then removed the brigade from Lüttwitz's command. Lüttwitz ignored the order, but agreed to a meeting with President Ebert. On 10 March, Lüttwitz, Ebert and Noske met. Lüttwitz reiterated that he would rather 'bring down the government' than disband.[122] He demanded the immediate dissolution of the National Assembly, new elections for the Reichstag, the appointment of technocrat *Fachminister* as Secretaries for Foreign Affairs, Economics and Finance, his own appointment as supreme commander of the regular military and the revocation of the orders of dissolution for the naval brigades.

One particular dispute where the public at large agreed with an infuriated Lüttwitz was the matter of war criminals. The Allies had just 'heightened the tension' by publishing a list of nearly 900 war criminals and demanded that they be surrendered to stand trial.[123] Civilian and military resistance to the charges were prominently made. Atrocities and war crimes included many types of incidents: behaviour to wounded soldiers and prisoners, the treatment of occupied or even home populations, aerial bombardment, economic blockade and unrestricted submarine warfare. 'These lay behind articles 227-230 of the Treaty of Versailles and the subsequent Allied attempts to bring German war criminals to trial in 1921.'[124] The list included the Kaiser and his entourage, Hindenburg, Ludendorff, Falkenhayn, Tirpitz, Scheer, von Trotha and

eighteen u-boat commanders.[125] After much negotiation, the Allies agreed
that the Germans could themselves conduct the trials of a much-reduced
list of forty-five persons, including Ludwig von Schröder for the murder
of Captain Fryatt.[126] In the end, only twelve people were tried in February
1921 in Leipzig and of these two were u-boat captains, Karl Neumann,
promoted Kapitänleutnant in 1918, who travelled home to Berlin from
Pola with Erich Gerth, and Helmut Patzig.[127] Most of the twelve were found
not guilty or given short prison sentences. Lowell, a u-boat historian, has
a particular view:

> But how about all of those atrocities which were so liberally attributed
> to the u-boats? Here, as with the subject of atrocities in general, it
> is difficult to find any sound evidence, anything more than rumour.
> The two particular crimes attributed to the u-boats were the sinking
> of hospital ships and the firing on lifeboats. In the first instance, the
> Germans cite the fact that ships often struck mines and were thought
> to be torpedoed. There are two authenticated instances where hospital
> ships appear to have been sunk deliberately. In the second instance,
> I ran across cases where lifeboats were said to have been fired upon.
> The Germans reply to this by pointing out at least one instance where
> a seemingly innocent lifeboat tried to sink a submarine with a sudden
> throwing of bombs, and it was scarcely more than human for the
> u-boat to open fire.[128]

U-boat commanders routinely asserted that the Allies deliberately used
hospital ships as troop carriers, abusing the Red Cross Convention. While
returning from a voyage in February 1915, *U 20* attempted unsuccessfully
to torpedo a hospital ship approaching Le Havre, her decks and rails
crowded with armed British troops bound for the front. Werner Fürbringer,
then one of commander Walther Schwieger's officers, said he could hardly
believe his eyes and 'confirmed Schwieger's own observation through the
periscope before the attack was made'.[129]

> The ship which was safe under the holy flag of humanity and mercy
> [the Red Cross] was loaded from bow to stern with artillery supplies
> and amongst the guns and ammunition there was crowded an army
> of soldiers and horses. Under the protection of the colours of the flags
> which they were so atrociously misusing they were proceeding in
> daylight on the way to the front.[130]

No Allied war criminals were tried which is, perhaps, the right of the
victor. The Germans certainly had a list of Allied war criminals with
Churchill and Haig right at the top. Allied hypocrisy and ruthlessness
was an ever-present in high strategy.[131] British Cabinet Secretary Maurice

Hankey was fond of quoting Machiavelli on the subject:

> When the entire safety of our country is at stake, no consideration of what is just or unjust, merciful or cruel, praiseworthy or shameful, must intervene. On the contrary, every other consideration being set aside, that course alone must be taken which reserves the existence of the country and maintains its liberty.[132]

As usual British admiral Jackie Fisher was more blunt. Hankey quotes him thus:

> As Fisher used to say, 'You can no more tame war than you can tame hell!' The only laws of war that are of any value are those which are mutually beneficial, such as arrangements for the Red Cross, flags of truce, and for the treatment of prisoners. Even these are apt to break down. To attempt more than this is certain to lead to mutual recrimination, where compromises fail and rules are broken, to prolong and embitter the war by exasperating public opinion on both sides, and to bring the whole fabric of international law into disrepute.[133]

Ebert and Noske rejected Lüttwitz's demands and told him that they expected his resignation the next day. Instead of resigning, Lüttwitz went to Ehrhardt and asked whether he would be able to occupy Berlin that evening. Ehrhardt said he needed another day, but in the morning of 13 March he could be in the centre of Berlin with his men.[134] Lüttwitz gave the order, and Ehrhardt began his preparations. At this point, Lüttwitz brought Pabst's *Nationale Vereinigung* into the plot, and included Kapp and Ludendorff.

> On the day of the Kapp Putsch, a new movie was playing at the Marmorhaus on the Kurfürstendamm. It was a story of murder and madness. And it was to become immensely popular. It was called 'The Cabinet of Dr Cagliari'. All through the war, there had been a growing interest in the new medium of moving pictures. The number of German theatres showing these novelties grew from 28 in 1913 to 245 in 1919 The German government saw political possibilities in the phenomenon ... and agreed to establish the powerful Universum Film A. G. (Ufa) for the creation of propaganda films.[135]

On the morning of 13 March, the Ehrhardt Brigade reached the Brandenburg Gate, where it was met by Lüttwitz, Ludendorff, Kapp and their followers.[136] Ludendorff claimed later that the meeting was accidental and that he was just out for a walk. The Reich Chancellery and the government quarter was occupied. Kapp declared himself Reichskanzler and formed a provisional government. Lüttwitz served as commander of the armed forces and Minister of Defence; von Trotha cabled naval stations to say that he had placed himself at Kapp's disposal and expected that the 'Navy will continue to obey my orders'.[137]

> *Kapp, founder of the Fatherland Party, an anonymous pamphleteer and unstable adventurer, has put himself at the head of* [the government] *as Chancellor. General Lüttwitz has treasonably gone over to him with the troops under his command and been rewarded with the appointment of Defence Minister ... It smacks more of farce than history. Berlin has evidently been taken over by the counter-revolutionary forces and the old Government has disappeared. Where to, nobody knows. The Social Democrats have proclaimed a general strike. That, it is to be hoped, will wring this gang's neck. Else the position would become extremely grave. If these people were to stay in the saddle, civil war, foreign intervention, and chaos would be almost inevitable.*[138]

The strike proclaimed by the fleeing government was 'more effective than anyone anticipated' and paralysed the country making it impossible for Kapp to govern. The Army refused to support the government, but all of the serving men, particularly in Kiel, were 'torn between their service duty and sympathy with family and friends supporting the strike'.[139] Kapp resigned on 17 March and fled to Sweden. He proved to be a 'leader of almost absurd incompetence, promulgating and rescinded instructions every day of this short five-day reign'.[140] In Kiel, communist groups stormed the naval arsenal, killing the commanding officer and fighting broke out between them and the men of the torpedo boats until von Löwenfeld's brigade went into action. Lüttwitz tried to hold on for another day as head of a military dictatorship, but then resigned. He was offered an amnesty, a false passport and money to leave the country. Ehrhard was allowed to march his brigade out of Berlin. A boy in the crowd laughed as they passed and was attacked with rifle buts. Several bursts of machine guns were fired into the crowd. At the same time, many *Freikorps* brigades marched to the Ruhr to put down a full-scale Communist revolution. The troops of the 'Red Ruhr' were well organised and, at first, beat back the *Freikorps* and took Duisburg, Düsseldorf, Hamborn and Mülheim. There were ferocious battles at Chemnitz, Dresden, Gera, Gotha, Jena, Leipzig and Weimar. The insurrection was seen by the Right as heralding union with Russia and providing a 'springboard for world revolution and world socialism'. Red Army recruitment offices were opened on the streets.

> *The atrocities accompanying and following the campaign ... matched previous patterns of behaviour that made the* Freikorps *so feared in Berlin, the Baltic and Bavaria the year before. Hundreds of Red Army*

> captives were 'shot while attempting to escape'. Scores of civilians who
> had played no part in the uprising, but were merely Trade Union
> officials or thought to have leftist affiliations were rounded up and
> shot after appearing before illegal Freikorps courts-martial ... The
> total casualties were never counted, but some indication of their scale
> can be estimated by the fact that Freikorps historian von Oertzen
> admitted that one thousand 'Reds' were shot in the first two days
> of the campaign. This, the last and most bloody full-scale military
> campaign waged by the Freikorps against fellow Germans, left an
> enduring legacy of hatred.[141]

A special committee of the Reichstag was set up to investigate the navy's
complicity in the Lüttwitz-Kapp putsch and 'some 172 officers, including
von Trotha, either retired or were discharged, but on 31 May those officers
deemed to have taken no part were reinstated'.[142] In 1922, 2,500 veterans of
the *Freikorps von Löwenfeld* were integrated into the grand total of 15,000
navy personnel allowed under the Treaty of Versailles, that is every sixth
man in the Reichsmarine which meant the 'incorporation of strongly
nationalistic and anti-republican attitudes in the inter-war navy'.[143] The
same legacy can be seen in the World War II appellation *Freikorps Dönitz*
for the entire submarine service of Nazi Germany.

Georg Gerth got off his train in Berlin in March 1920, returning from
almost three years in a French prison camp, the war now over, but perhaps
with the shame of his lost u-boat to return to haunt him. Apart from his
early escape attempt from Boyardville, Georg's active life had been dull
and repetitive. His head, however, was full of Hesse, Kant, Nietzsche and
Rilke, the philosophical studies of his internment. He had no immediate
future other than that which the Admiralty determined. The humiliating
Treaty of Versailles was signed leaving few fighting ships; every submarine
was gone. Georg left the railway station in the middle of the five-day Kapp-
Lüttwitz Putsch. He found the capital and his older brother Erich somewhat
changed. There was death and hunger in the streets; he needed to see if
his mother was safe and well. His sworn-leader, the Kaiser, was long gone
replaced by a shaky republican government run, hardly to be believed, by
socialists, most of whom were in hiding. Erich, the socialite and party-goer,
had married a rich ex-countess and was working covertly with Georg's old
boss from Flanders, Karl Bartenbach, and with Wilhelm Canaris, to provide
u-boats for the next war. For a lowly Kapitänleutnant, Erich had surprising
and powerful acquaintances: the head of the Admiralty, Adolf von Trotha;
ex-Minister of State Friedrich Wilhelm von Loebell; and Walther Rathenau,
head of the electrical giant AEG. Erich's father-in-law, Salomon Marx, was
of Jewish background, ran one of the country's most successful private
banks, and had fingers in many commercial pies. Marx was up to his neck
with right-wing extremists like Heinrich Pabst and Erich Ludendorff,

leader of the Imperial Army when Georg was last in Germany. With his widespread and determined network, Marx was trying to undermine the peace treaty, was complicit in the murder of communist leaders Karl Liebknecht and Rosa Luxemburg, and was integral to the current plot to overthrow the government. This would take some getting used to.

ENDNOTES

1   Historian Gay quoted by Hofmann, 'Translator's Introduction' in Roth, *What I Saw*, pp. 12–13.
2   Hollweg, *First World War*, p. 435.
3   *Berliner Tageblatt*, morning and evening editions, 553–558, 29–31/10/1918.
4   Large, *Berlin*, p. 88.
5   Berliner Adressbücher, 1799–1943, zlb.de/besondere-angebote/Berliner-adressbuecher (accessed 3/2017).
6   *Economic Conditions Prevailing in Germany*, Berlin, pp. 61, 67, 75.
7   MacMillan, *Paris 1919*, pp. xxv–xxvi.
8   Email, Christa-Maria Gerth, 18/3/2017.
9   Blum, 'Government decisions', pp. 565–66.
10 Teuteberg, 'Food Provisioning', Zweiniger-Bargielowska, *Food and War*, p. 68.
11 Tarrant, *U-Boat Offensive*, p. 45.
12 Wegener, *Naval Strategy*, p. xxxii, p. 207, fn. 4.
13 Herwig, *Naval Officer Corps*, p. 265.
14 Padfield, *Dönitz*, pp. 95–96.
15 These numbers vary understandably from source to source. Mulligan, *Sharks Not Wolves*, p. 40, cites 457 u-boat commanders in World War 1 of whom 152 were killed and thirty-three captured, for a total loss of over 40 per cent. Tennant, *U-Boat Offensive*, p. 77, records a loss of 178 u-boats, 511 officers and 4,576 men, 'an exchange rate of almost thirty ships of 69,000 tons per u-boat lost'. The most current and also the most respected listing is compiled by uboat.net and this is used as the principal source in these calculations.
16 Canaris, Dönitz, Erich Gerth, Marschall and Schultze served together in the Mediterranean (Chapter 4, 'Erich's war'.).
17 Herwig, *Dynamics*, p. 80.
18 Tarrant, *U-Boat Offensive*, p. 77.
19 Chapter 13, 'Guilt and blame'.
20 The first step in reassessment was to assemble the facts and this was undertaken by Konteradmiral Albert Gayer's four-volume series *Die deutschen U-Boote* (1920). His books became standard works which were republished in 1930. Korvettenkapitän Friedrich Lützow followed in 1921 with *Unterseebootskrieg und Hungerblockade*. Lützow concluded that Germany had strictly observed international accords whereas England's blockade was in contravention of all international and humane convention. In 1925, Vizeadmiral Andreas Michelsen wrote *Der U-Bootskrieg 1914–1918* '… not only to show the Volk just what the u-boat war meant in reality, but because I have a need to set the deeds of the u-boat crews in the proper light and to protect the u-boat arm against undeserved disparagement'. The Navy produced its multi-volumed *The War at Sea*, 1914–1918, edited by the Naval Archives which included contributions from Arno Spindler and Erich Raeder. Spindler later produced his monumental five-volume *Der Handelskrieg mit U-Booten*, discussed briefly in the 'Introduction' to this book, the fifth volume of which was suppressed by the Nazis as in it Spindler argued that the u-boats had been responsible for drawing the United States into the war (Hadley, *Count Not the Dead*), pp. 48–50.
21 Chapter 9, 'Your truth, our truth'.

22   Koerver, German Submarine Warfare, p. x.

23   Erich Gerth's application to the Foreign Office, 30/12/1922.

24   Wegener, Naval Strategy, p. xxxii.

25   Marks, '1918 and After', p. 40, commenting on Taylor, Origins of the Second World War, p. 267.

26   Padfield, Dönitz, pp. 101–103.

27   Padfield, Dönitz, p. 96.

28   Chapters 2, 'Kaisertreu' and 6, 'War of the raven'.

29   Forsén and Forsén, 'Secret Submarine Exports', Stoker, Girding for Battle, pp. 114–15.

30   The following section on the early u-boat rearmament is a composite account taken from a number of sources including Forsén and Forsén, 'Secret Submarine Exports', pp. 113–33; Mueller, Canaris, Chapter 9; Mulligan, Sharks Not Wolves, pp. 139–40; Padfield, Dönitz, p. 102; Saville, 'Development of German U-boat Arm'; Stoker, Naval Arms Trade, pp. 124, 145–49; Ten Cate, 'Das U-Boot als geistige Exportware'; Tennant, U-Boat Offensive, p. 77.

31   Details of Karl Bartenbach's post-war career were partly supplied by Gisella Bartenbach, his niece, in an interview with Forsén and Forsén in 1999.

32   Chapter 4.

33   Derencin, uboat.net.

34   Other German armaments firms that used Holland included the aircraft maker Fokker from 1919, Carl Zeiss Optical Works of Jena (Nederlandsche Instrumenten Compagnie NV) and Siemens, fire control equipment (F Hazemeyer's Fabriek von Electrische Signal-Apparaten NV) (Forsén and Forsén, 'Secret Submarine Exports'), p. 127, fn. 17.

35   Tarrant, U-boat Offensive, pp. 77–78.

36   Padfield, Dönitz, p. 111, 145. Padfield, Dönitz, p. 26. Löwenfeld had also been cadet Dönitz's navigating officer aboard the training ship, Hertha.

37   Compton-Hall, Submarines, p. 300.

38   Lohmann came to the fore through his work on negotiations concerning the Allies' appropriation of the German merchant fleet after the armistice and for his direction of emergency food supplies to Germany. Lohmann also managed the return from overseas of German war prisoners.

39   cia.gov/library/center-for-the-study-of-intelligence/kent-csi/vol4no2/htmlv04i2a08p_0001. htm, accessed 15/10/2017; copy at Appendix 10.

40   Stoker, Naval Arms Trade, p. 144.

41   Mulligan, Sharks Not Wolves, p. 25. Fürbringer, Legendary, p. ix.

42   Padfield, Dönitz, p. 119.

43   Hadley, Count Not the Dead, pp. 75–76, 80.

44   Tennant, U-boat Offensive, pp. 79–80. Germany and other powers signed the London Protocol to this effect in November 1936. Churchill, Second World War, Vol. 1, p. 126.

45   Humbold University, Berlin, archive, Erich Gerth, received 14/6/2017.

46   Interview, Christa Gerth, 15/11/2016.

47   Hintz, 'Salomon Marx', p. 103.

48   Kelly, Tirpitz, pp. 69–70.

49   Salomon and Helene married in the Free State of Danzig on 27/2/1892. Eva's two siblings were born in Danzig: Eduard, 23 November 1898, and Eleonore, 29/10/1903. Salomon was the son of businessman Eduard Marx and Bertha Hecht; Helene, was the daughter of businessman Richard Schirmacher and Clara Scharloch.

50   Interview, Christa-Maria Gerth, 15/11/2016.

51   Foreign Office file, Berlin. Eva's conversion to Catholicism confirmed in the records of the Campo Santo, Rome.

52   Erich Gerth converted to Catholicism after his marriage to Eva Marx, 6/1919, and before his application to the Foreign Office 12/1922.

53   The year before, 1910, Marx took his wife Helene, aged forty, and two children, Eduard and Eva, on a holiday to Tenerife aboard the Eleonore Woermann, sailing from Hamburg. Tourists began visiting Tenerife from Spain, the United Kingdom, and northern Europe in large numbers in the 1890s. They were attracted to the northern towns of Puerto de la Cruz and Santa Cruz de Tenerife.

54   The hyphen in Graf Karl-Christian was added eighteen years after his birth on the Kaiser's birthday in 1909, when the certificate was amended by court order.

55   Asprey, *German High Command*, p. 47.

56   Private letters and emails from Heiko von Ahlefeld, 9/2017. Also 'Ahlefeld', wikipedia, accessed 4/3/2017.

57   War Diaries of Dieter Finzen, www.war-diary.com/dieter_finzen.htm, accessed, 19/12/2016. 'Ahlefeld' is a simple, but close, variant of 'Ahlefeldt'.

58   Hull, *Absolute Destruction*, p. 209. Chapter 2.

59   Horne and Kramer, 'War between Soldiers', p. 187.

60   Forum correspondence: 1914–1918.invisionzone.com and www.theaerodrome.com, accessed 12/2016. Also, Franks, Bailey, Duiven, *Casualties of the German Air Service 1914–1920*.

61   Coles, *Slaughter at Sea, The Truth Behind a Naval War Crime*. Cole's book is a detailed indictment of British conduct by the Baralong's captain and crew. For original material, *HMSO*, London, 'Memorandum of the German Government in regard to Incidents Alleged to have Attended the Destruction of a German Submarine and its Crew ... and Reply of His Majesty's Government', Cd. 8144, 7/1916, 2½ pence. Also, for alterative views: Newbolt, *Naval History*, p. 94; and Chatterton, *Q-ships*, pp. 20–23. A third of Hunold von Ahlefeld's sons, Leutnant Heinrich, an observer in the German air force, was shot down over Italy on 12/2/1918 (Heiko von Ahlefeldt). Five other von Ahlefeldts died and their names are recorded on a family-held roll of honour. See also, Schoenermarck, 'The Eight Heroes of Ahlefeldt', *Helden-Gedenkmappe des deutschen Adels*.

62   Chapter 4.

63   Erich von Dresky, 1850–1918, Vizeadmiral; Eugen von Dresky, 1831–1892, Prussian Generalmajor; Gotthardt von Dresky, 1844–1912, Prussian Generalleutnant; Rudolf von Dresky, 1776–1852, Prussian Generalmajor; Justus von Dresky und Merzdorf, 1818–1899, Prussian General der Artillerie.

64   Hadley, *Count Not the Dead*, has a picture following p. 78 of Hitler and Dönitz wishing Dresky good luck.

65   Sebag-Montefiore, *Enigma*, pp. 67–77, has a blow-by-blow account of the mission, the on-board confusion, and the sinking.

66   Foreign Office application 30/12/1922.

67   Chapter 16, 'Erich's Jewish problem'.

68   Kessler, *Diaries*, 24/12/1918, pp. 41–42.

69   Kessler, *Diaries*, 16/1/1919, pp. 41–42.

70   Chapter 4.

71   Friedrich, *Before the Deluge*, pp. 38–39. Schleicher and his wife Elizabeth were murdered at their home on Hitler's orders on the 'Night of the Long Knives' in 1934.

72   Waite, *Vanguard of Nazism*, pp. 12–16, 35–37.

73   Mulligan, *Sharks Not Wolves*, p. 220. Jones, *Birth of the Nazis*, p. 64, Appendix A. Horn, *Mutiny*, p. 248.

74   Chapter 13, 'Guilt and blame'.

75   Friedrich, *Before the Deluge*, p. 39.

76   Telephone conversation with Marc Gerth, 14/1/2018.

77   Jones, *Birth of the Nazis*, p. 284.

78   Mulligan, *Sharks Not Wolves*, pp. 220–21. Mueller, *Canaris*, pp. 38–39.

79   Mueller, *Canaris*, p. 52.

80   Chapters 1, 'Brave new world', and 6.

81   Compton-Hall, *Submarines*, p. 300.

82   Chapter 11, 'Immense cemetery'. Jones, *Birth of the Nazis*, pp. 88–89, 173–74.

83   Jones, *Birth of the Nazis*, p. 192.

84   Niemöller, *From U-boat to Pulpit*.

85   Chapter 4. Mueller, *Canaris*, pp. 31–33.

86   Chapter 4. Compton-Hall, *Submarines*, p. 300.

87   Friedrich, *Before the Deluge*, pp. 18–19.

88   Liebknecht, *Militarismus und Anti-Militarismus*.

89   Rosenberg, *Imperial Germany*, p. 73.
90   Harmer, *Luxemburg*, p. 101.
91   Named after the Thracian gladiator Spartacus, the leader of the slave revolt against the Roman Empire in the Third Servile War in the last century before the birth of Christ.
92   Nettl, *Luxemburg*, pp. 388–89.
93   Nettl, *Luxemburg*, p. 439.
94   Harmer, *Luxemburg*, pp. 10, 22, 28, 79, 94.
95   Nettl, *Luxemburg*, p. 401.
96   Nettl, *Luxemburg*, p. 442.
97   Schreiner, *Iron Ration*, p. 66.
98   Princess Ludwig, *Through Four Revolutions*, p. 317.
99   Kessler, *Diaries*, 5/1/1919, p. 52.
100 Mueller, *Canaris*, pp. 41–42.
101 Nettl, *Luxemburg*, p. 483.
102 Harmer, *Luxemburg*, pp. 134–35, citing the *Die Rote Fahne*, the *Red Flag*, 14/1/1919. For other extracts, Nettl, *Luxemburg*, p. 485.
103 Nettl, *Luxemburg*, p. 473.
104 Friedrich, *Deluge*, pp. 28–29, 102.
105 *Economic Conditions Prevailing in Germany*, Berlin, pp. 61, 67, 75.
106 Nettl, *Luxemburg*, p. 485.
107 Stadtgeschichtliches Museum, Leipzig, PLA 487, GOS-Nr. p0006819.
108 Engelmann, *Germany Without Jews*, pp. 243–44.
109 Letter, German Historical Museum to Alfred Hintz, 17/5/2010.
110 Steiner, *Lights That Failed*, p. 10.
111 Mueller, *Canaris*, pp. 43–44. Jones, *Birth of the Nazis*, Chapter 6, 'The Twin Murders: Liebknecht and Luxemburg', pp. 70–83. Bouton, *Kaiser Abdicates*, pp. 225–36. Harmer, *Luxemburg*, pp. 135–37. Nettl, *Luxemburg*, pp. 486–94.
112 Mueller, *Canaris*, p. 40.
113 Mueller, *Canaris*, pp. 45–46.
114 Ulrich Ritgen, Heinrich Stiege, Bruno Schultze and Rudolf Liepmann.
115 Heinz had had an interesting war career in the Prussian infantry (severely wounded), joined the air force (the same path as Salomon Marx's daughter's first husband, Karl-Christian von Ahlefeldt), and flew over 300 bombing missions, including the first in 1915 on Paris (forum.axishistory.com, accessed 3/2017).
116 Gollomb, *Army of Spies*, pp. 88–89.
117 Nettle, *Luxemburg*, p. 493.
118 Chapter 9, 'Your truth, our truth'.
119 Friedrich, *Before the Deluge*, pp. 58–59.
120 Mueller, *Canaris*, pp. 51–52.
121 Fritzsche, *Germans into Nazis*, pp. 105, 122–24.
122 Mueller, *Canaris*, p. 52.
123 Yarnall, *Barbed Wire Disease*, Chapter 13, 'Leipzig: The Aftermath'.
124 Horne and Kramer, 'War Between Soldiers', p. 153.
125 Proposed list of those to be tried as war criminals (Bridgland, Outrage), pp. 193–94, corrected from uboat.net: **Hans Adam**, *U 82*, Galway Castle (actually sunk by **Heinrich Middendorff**, *U 82*); **Hubert Aust**, *UC 45*, *Golden Hope*; **Thorwald von Bothmer**, *U 66*, *Mariston* (actually sunk by **Erich Sittenfeld**, *U 45*); **Otto Dröscher**, *U 20*, *Ikaria*, *Tokomaru* (both actually sunk by **Walther Schwieger**, who also sank the *Lusitania*, which was not on the list); **Konrad Gansser**, *U 33*, *U 156*, *Clan Macleod*, *Belle of France* (actually sunk by **Otto Hersing**, *U 21*), *WC McKay*, *Artesia*; **Carl-Siegfried Ritter von Georg**, *U 57*, *U 101*, *Refugio*, *Jersey* City (actually sunk by **Leo Hillebrand**, *U 46*), *Teal*, *Richard de Larrinaga*, *Glenford*, *Trinidad*, *John G Walker*, *Lough Fisher*; **Alfred von Glassenapp**, *U 91*, *Haileybury*, *Birchleaf* (damaged), *Landonia*, *Baron Herries*, *Ethel*; **Heinrich Jess**, *U 96*, *U 90*, *Apapa*, *Destro*, *Inkosi*; **Wilhelm Kiesewetter**, *UC 56*, *Glenart Castle* (a hospital ship, his only sinking); **Constantin Kolbe**, *U 152*, *Clan Murray* (actually sunk by **Theodor Schultz**, *UC 55*), *Ellaston*, *Elsie Birdett*; **Heinrich**

von Nostitz und Jänkendorf, *U 152, Dwinsk*; **Karl Neumann**, *UC 67, Dover Castle* (a hospital ship); **Helmut Patzig**, *U 86, Llandovery Castle*; **Claus Rücker**, *U 103, Victoria*; (Rücker did sink a *Victoria* in 1915, two years earlier than claimed; there were four *Victorias* sunk in 1917 by other commanders); **Otto von Schrader**, *UB 64, Dartmoor* (actually sunk by **Rudolf Seuffer**, *UC 50*, who was the captain lost on his way to rescue Georg Gerth from Boyardville, Chapter 12, 'Prisoners of war'); **Max Valentiner**, *U 38, Glenby, Persia, Clan Macfarlane*; **Erwin Wassner**, *UC 69, Addah*; **Wilhelm Werner**, *U 55, Clearfield, Artist, Trevone, Toro, Torrington, Rewa, Guildford Castle* (the last two were hospital ships; his technique was to load survivors without lifebelts on his u-boat deck having wrecked their lifeboats, then submerge. Werner fled to Brazil, worked on a coffee plantation rather than stand trial, and returned in 1924 to join the NSDAP and later the staff of SS Reichsführer Heinrich Himmler. Werner was a classmate of Erich Gerth.).

126   Chapter 6.
127   Bridgland, *Outrage*, pp. 193–200. MacMillan, *Paris 1919*, pp. 164–65. Neumann sank the hospital ship *Dover Castle* off Algiers in 1917 (Bridgland, *Outrage*), pp. 151–56. *UC 67* was 'brought home' by Martin Niemöller when Pola was closed at war end. Neumann was found not guilty because he was 'following orders'. One of the worst atrocities of the naval war, which gathered the longest sentences, happened on 27 June 1918 when Oberleutnant Helmut Patzig, *U 86*, sank the Canadian hospital ship *Llandovery Castle* off Fastnet while travelling from Halifax in Canada to Liverpool (Bridgland, *Outrage*), pp. 176–92. Patzig ordered his u-boat to ram the life boats and shot at the survivors. Of a crew of 258, only twenty-four survived; another report in uboat.net claims 146 casualties. Patzig's senior officers, Ludwig Dithmar and John Boldt, were given four years' imprisonment. Patzig could not be found (he was in hiding in the Free City of Leipzig) and his officers 'escaped' on the way to their labour camp (Newbolt, *Submarine and Anti-submarine*), p. 125.
128   Lowell, *Raiders*, pp. 6–7.
129   Fürbringer, *Legendary*, p. 6.
130   Spiegel, *U-202*, p. 58.
131   Peterson, *Propaganda*, pp. 78–79.
132   Machiavelli, *Discorsi*, cited in Hankey, *Supreme Command*, I, p. 352 onwards, Chapter 'Belligerent Rights'.
133   Hankey, *Supreme Command*, I, p. 101. See, also Chapter 9 on propaganda. In 1911, a slightly penitent Fisher wrote, 'Perhaps I went a little too far when I said I would boil the prisoners in oil and murder the innocent in cold blood, etc, etc. But, it's quite silly not to make war damnable to the whole mass of your enemy's population, which of course is the secret of maintaining the right of capture of private property at sea ...'
134   Padfield, *Dönitz*, pp. 97–98. Friedrich, *Before the Deluge*, pp. 63–64.
135   Friedrich, *Before the Deluge*, pp. 64–65. Chapter 15, 'Salomon and the film business'.
136   Waite, *Vanguard of Nazism*, Chapter VI, 'In The Service of Reaction', pp. 140–167.
137   Mueller, *Canaris*, p. 54.
138   Kessler, *Diaries*, 13/3/1920, pp. 41–42.
139   Padfield, *Dönitz*, p. 98.
140   Friedrich, *Before the Deluge*, p. 72.
141   Jones, *Birth of the Nazis*, Chapter 14, 'The Red Army of the Ruhr', pp. 192–202. Friedrich Wilhelm von Oertzen, *Die Deutschen Freikorps, 1918-1928*.
142   Padfield, *Dönitz*, p. 99.
143   Mulligan, *Sharks not Wolves*, pp. 220–21.

CHAPTER 15

Salomon Marx and the Film Business

The forgotten, the unknown man, who was pulling the strings behind the scenes. A skilful diplomatic mediator with excellent links to the most influential men of his time in German business, politics, Jewry, and society. Marx was one of the best known and respected Berlin private bankers, with an active mind, full of vitality and energy, who enjoyed the highest esteem in the world of art and literature. Marx´s annual income from thirteen positions on the supervisory boards of different companies and his own private bank was more than 250,000 Reichsmarks.[1]

Salomon Marx, a 'small chubby man', played a large part in the story of Erich Gerth, his son-in-law from 1919.[2] Salomon came from a wide-spread and successful Jewish business family. He was born in Schwerte near Dortmund in 1866, attended grammar school in Höxter and Soest, and studied law at Freiburg, Berlin and Marburg universities. He worked for the Deutsche Bank, partly in London. There are two occupations for Salomon Marx in the Cologne address book at Ehrenfeld for 1896: one as a director of 'Ehrenfelder Terraingesellschaft', a real estate company; and another as an owner with Wilhelm Oldemeyer of 'Oldemeyer, Marx and Company', a factory which produced *papier maché* goods, folded boxes, packages for sugar cubes, and technical articles made from paper, cardboard and wrapping paper. Marx sought to deliver cardboard articles to the military and to try to begin an export business into Russia and to facilitate this he opened a branch of Oldemeyer in Danzig, current Gdansk, his wife's home town, where he had family ties to a timber company, Münsterberg. These plans failed through a lack of skilled manpower and slow orders.

One of the political aims of the German empire at that time was the industrialisation of West Prussia and of the cities Danzig and Posen, current Poznań. Despite Marx's struggles, one of the leading Prussian politicians

and civil servants, Gustav von Gossler, recognised a 'young, ideal candidate'
to further the state policy. Gossler approached other industrialists in the
Rhineland and, with an invested capital of 400,000 Reichsmarks, Marx
founded the company 'Ostdeutsche Industriewerke Marx & Co'. In April
1897, the 'Nordische Elektrizitäts-Aktiengesellschaft' was founded in
Gdansk with Marx as general director with a brief to build and operate
electrical light and power plants, steel and roller mills. The company was
successful, paying a 5 per cent dividend in 1897 and 8 per cent in 1898.
In the summer of 1897, the 'Norddeutsche Elektrizitäts-Aktiengesellschaft'
bought the 'Ostdeutsche Industriewerke' and, in 1898, the two companies
merged under Marx´s leadership to form the 'Nordische Elektrizitäts und
Stahlwerke AG'. After two successful years, one of its electricity subsidiaries
collapsed threatening bankruptcy. Because of the political importance of
Marx´s enterprises, Gossler and several Prussian politicians, including
the Lord Mayor of Danzig, Clemens von Delbrück, and the Prussian
Finance Minister, Count Georg von Rheinbaben, decided to support the
business by raising a further two and a half million Reichsmarks from the
Prussian State Bank. The Kaiser asked Fürst Henckel von Donnersmarck,
the magnate of the Upper Silesian heavy industry, for his views about
the Danzig recovery plan. Donnersmarck criticised Marx and the other
businessmen from the Rhineland involved in the project for their lack
of understanding of local conditions. However, others like Maximilian
Harden, the Jewish intellectual, publisher, journalist, actor and critic,
praised Marx's achievements. In correspondence between Harden and
Walther Rathenau, heir to AEG, the leading electrical company, and later
Foreign Minister, Marx was repeatedly mentioned positively. Harden said,
'the little Marx is *in summa* a jolly good fellow'; Marx is 'very good, tough
and calm'. Rathenau said he was 'full of personal respect' and was pleased
that 'the little one', 'the capital little fellow', had managed to secure the
deal with the government to save his company.

In 1906, Marx became a member of the industrial council of the
Darmstädter Bank in Berlin. He set up as an independent banker in
1912, founding 'Salomon Marx'. By 1910, Marx was travelling as 'Consul
Marx'. On 21 February 1913, he was appointed Honorary Consul to Berlin
representing the Grand Duchy of Oldenburg, a town in Lower Saxony in
North-West Germany near Bremen. He was also one of twelve recipients
of the Leopold Order of the Principality of Lippe which he received for
'special merits'.[3]

Marx changed the name and status of his bank in 1920 to 'S. Marx &
Co' and then in 1923 with a Jewish business partner, Alexander Elfer,
to the 'Internationale Handelsbank KGaA', situated at Jägerstraße 20 in
Berlin. The chairman of the supervisory board of the Handelsbank was
Minister of State Friedrich Wilhelm von Loebell who became a 'big-name'
referee for Erich Gerth's application to the Foreign Office.[4] 'Consul Marx'

belonged to numerous supervisory boards of German companies including Deutsche Bank, founded in 1870 as a specialist bank in foreign trade to combat British and French dominance in the world at large; the major Engelhardt Brewery, founded in Berlin in 1860; Groterjan & Co, banking and insurance; the Portland-Cement-Werke AG in Schwanebeck; and Carl Lindström, a Berlin-based record company, the forerunner of Parlophone, later recording label for *The Beatles*.

The firm of Lindström, together with Deutsche Bank which was always close to Marx's investments, three private banks, and the heavy industry concern of Fürst von Donnersmarck, and Robert Bosch, controlled the majority of shares of Ufa, Universum Film, headquartered in Babelsberg.[5] The board of directors also contained a 'respectable cross-section of the Wilhemite *haute bourgeoisie* with especially strong representation from Prusso-German financial and industrial capital'. Ufa was founded in 1917 with Ludendorff's direct involvement as a patriotic propaganda tool for the army command and the imperial government. Ludendorff's strategy was to establish German control over film supply in Central Europe, as well as in large parts of eastern and south-eastern Europe, and to influence the 'volatile mood of the people'. The directors of Ufa bought the 'Haus Vaterland' at the Potsdamer Platz in Berlin, a six-storey, pleasure dome with bars, restaurants and entertainment venue, 'a beacon of commercial kitsch'. Salomon Marx was seen as the 'founder' of the Haus Vaterland because of his considerable financial investment.

During the 1914 war, as a financial expert, Marx concerned himself with how the costs of war could be met and published his conclusions.[6] On 17 December 1917, he addressed a group of business leaders in Rhineland Westphalia and recommended that the repayment of war debts be postponed. On 30 October 1918, leading representatives of German finance capital, led by representatives of the Deutsche Bank, met at the Hotel Adlon in Berlin and issued a statement welcoming political reforms and calling for an immediate peace.[7] Can one doubt that Marx attended?

In his memoirs, Eduard Stadtler, founder of the Anti-Bolshevik party, described a dinner party on 24 October 1918 at the 'elegant upper middle class mansion of Consul Salomon Marx'. Stadtler had advocated that year the creation of a national socialist dictatorship; Anton Drexler, the founder of the Nazi Party, attended Stadtler's lectures in Berlin.[8] Among those attending was Kurt von Kleefeld, a baptised Jew like Salomon Marx, founder of the *Hansabund*, an economic organisation for German merchants and industrialists based in Berlin, and brother-in-law of Gustav Stresemann, briefly Weimar Chancellor in 1923, Foreign Minister for six years, and winner of the Nobel Peace Prize.[9] After dinner, the men withdrew for political talks to the gentlemen´s parlour where Marx explained how the progressive wing of the conservatives should merge with the progressive powers of the national liberals with the aim of forming a new political movement to carry out state reforms. Stadtler, however, pleaded to marry conservative Prussian militaristic ideals with the acceptable socialist content of the revolution. Marx was impressed with Stadtler´s views and asked him if he would write down his thoughts in a speech. Stadtler agreed, gave Marx the manuscript eight days later and received a fee of 200 Reichsmarks. At the beginning of November 1918, Marx gave the speech written by Stadtler at the packed Aeroclub and later printed the lecture as a brochure titled 'The organic principle of the state' under his own name.[10] 'The main task of the new party would be to help restore and strengthen German nationalism ... In the fight against Anglo-Saxon capitalism and imperialism and the Bolshevism of the East, Germany would emerge as the power of culture based on a true people's state ... Despite the defeat [in World War I], Germany would be politically ahead of its peers in the world.'

Salomon Marx was a member of the small initial founding group of the German National People's Party, the *Deutschnationale Volkspartei*, DNVP.[11] Before the rise of Hitler's National Socialist German Workers' Party (NSDAP), the DNVP was the major conservative and nationalist party in Weimar Germany, an alliance of nationalists, reactionary monarchists, anti-Semitic elements and the völkisch groups, and supported by the Pan-German League.[12] The party's right-wing diversity was both its strength and, eventually, as a disparate coalition, its weakness. Marx joined the executive committee of the party in December 1918, promising to finance the party with several hundred thousand Reichsmarks of his own money and was suggested as the party's treasurer. Marx decided to leave the DNVP in February 1919 because of the anti-Semitic propaganda supported by some members and also an insulting letter by party leader Oskar Hergt addressing 'the gentlemen of Jewish descent in the party'.

It is worth reflecting on the extent of Salomon Marx's known contacts in the 1920s. Salomon kept close contact with Wilhelm Marx, German lawyer, Catholic politician and a member of the Centre Party who was twice Chancellor from 1923 to 1925 and again from 1926 to 1928. Salomon Marx was cousin to Wilhelm Marx's father and this explains how Wilhelm came to be another referee later offered by Erich Gerth.[13] Marx was closely associated with the industrial and Jewish giants of the day: Fürst Henckel von Donnersmarck, Gustav von Gossler, Maximilian Harden, Friedrich Wilhelm von Loebell, Walther Rathenau of AEG, and the scions of the household-name-firms Bosch, Henckel, Krupp and Siemens; and the leading figures of heavy industry in Rhineland-Westphalia like Hugo Stinnes, owner of the Woermann and East German shipping lines, who organised the coal production in Belgium after the invasion at the request of Ludendorff; Emil Kirdorf, known as the 'Chimney Baron' for having Europe's largest coal mine enterprise; and Ernst and Conrad Borsig, railway and locomotive magnates.[14] Through long-term friendship Salomon was close to Wilhelm Canaris, also a friend of Erich Gerth, and established as a leading figure in the murky world of naval and national politics, and, through Erich, Admiral Adolf von Trotha, head of the post-war naval office in Berlin. These anti-republican, anti-socialist figures, introduced Salomon to Philipp Scheidemann of the SDP, to Prince Otto II of Salm-Horstmann, the anti-Semitic president of the Navy Association, the *Flottenverein*, and leading Pan-German, and to Kurt von Kleefeld, Gustav Stresemann, and the radical-conservative agitator Eduard Stadtler.

Marx's same-street neighbours at Brückenallee 29 in Berlin included Leo Arons, physicist and social democratic politician at number nine; Dietrich Bonhoeffer, the theologian later persecuted by the Nazis at number five; Botho zu Eulenberg, Prussian Minister President and Interior Minister, number two; Walter de Gruyter, publisher, number nine, Else Lasker-Schüler, writer and artist, at number sixteen with her studio at number twenty-two. The quarter was home to many other wealthy Jewish bankers and merchants, politicians and intellectuals.

In December 1921, Helene, Salomon Marx's wife and Eva Gerth's mother, died in Berlin.[15] No details are known, but just over a year later, Salomon must have caused a stir when he remarried to Charlotte Mayer-Schalburg, twenty years his junior, only three weeks after her divorce from her first husband became effective.[16] Charlotte, known as Lotte, was just ten years older than Salomon's own daughter, Eva. Lotte's husband had been Robert Mayer, a Royal Lieutenant, son of Royal General Lieutenant August Mayer. Robert and Charlotte married in 1906 and, in 1920, hyphenated their surname to include his mother's maiden name. In 1928, Salomon Marx took over the Nordische Bank in Berlin. In 1931, the Marxes moved home five miles in the south of Berlin from Brückenallee 29 to Lessingstraße 31, where they were joined by Eva's brother, Salomon's unmarried son, Dr Eduard Marx.

Meanwhile, Canaris, continuing his u-boat trade missions, in 1924 shipped aboard the steamer *Rhineland* for Japan. His instructions were to bring to fruition previous sales to the Japanese of sketches of u-cruisers and minelaying u-boats and to secure construction orders that would be supervised by German naval architects. The next year, and the following, Canaris was back in Spain on a similar task where he took time to meet Max Bauer, who fled there after the Kapp Putsch and was now military adviser to King Alfonso XIII.

> *The long-term value of Spanish-German co-operation cannot be underestimated. The Spanish Navy placed modern submarines at the disposal of the German naval forces for testing and manoeuvres. For the future German production of u-boats, these preliminary steps and the fact that Spain helped Germany keep up with new developments in submarine technology would prove of decisive importance.*[17]

On 8 and 9 August 1927, Kurt Wenkel, financial editor of *Berliner Tageblatt*, investigating the bankruptcy affairs of the film company Phoebus, stumbled on and published details of an extraordinary clandestine network of companies funded since 1923 through Kapitänleutnant Walter Lohmann's office at the Navy High Command.[18] Kreimeier, the biographer of Ufa, estimated that ten million Reichsmarks were transferred from Lohmann's secret fund to Phoebus to be used for rearmament.[19] 'The reach of these funds was considerable covering the naval intelligence service; submarine development with a bubble-free torpedo, aided by IvS and secret funds from Krupp in Kiel, Wesser in Bremen and the Vulcan Shipyard in Hamburg; aircraft and small boat production; and pilot and future officer training.[20] The background was straightforward. Lohmann was 'imbued with a mixture of too much zeal, arrogance and false patriotism and had become involved in a number of madcap schemes ... He continued to expand his armaments empire and had so lost sight of what he was doing that it finally collapsed'.[21]

Shortly before the Lohmann Affair broke, Canaris warned his superiors that matters were out of control. Undeterred, at the height of the ensuing uproar, Pfeiffer, Canaris and Spindler held a meeting on the funding necessary for Canaris' Spanish u-boat project and four million Reichsmarks were signed off from the Navy's own construction budget. The following spring, ex-u-boat commander Werner Fürbringer and his men, having carried out trials on a second German-designed submarine built for Turkey by Krupp's Rotterdam yard, delivered the boats to Constantinople, and both Fürbringer and his chief engineer stayed on to guide the Turkish u-boat school.

The cover-up mounted, first by the navy and then by the government, was extensive and to some degree successful in that the full extent and reach of the rearmament funding was not discovered. The government through Chancellor Wilhelm Marx tried to suppress knowledge of the government's involvement. Dönitz was involved in preparing the Navy's defence for the Reichstag. The German navy's dummy company, Mentor Bilanz, was liquidated in 1928 and a new covert operator 'Igewit', *Ingenieurbüro für Wirtschaft und Technik*, was formed as the Admiralty's u-boat technical section in such a way that the Navy and Government would not be compromised. Lohmann was sacrificed, as previously agreed with him, but was never prosecuted for fear the whole story would come out. He died, impoverished, shortly afterwards. Other famous heads to roll, most mentioned previously in this book, were Defence Minister Otto Gessler, Pfeiffer, Werth, von Löwenfeld and the navy chief, Admiral Hans Zenker. 'What is clear is that these were cosmetic changes.'

In 1927, as Phoebus suffered, Ufa also experienced financial difficulties and had to borrow money from the American film companies, Paramount and Metro-Goldwin-Meyer (MGM). It was Lohmann's concern about

America's 50 per cent ownership of Ufa that had led him to support Phoebus in order to maintain a major German-controlled presence in film production. Salomon Marx's pet project, Haus Vaterland, was used as a guarantee for a four million dollar loan. Marx was instrumental in negotiating the purchase of Ufa by Alfred Hugenberg, the mega industrialist from the steel and armament firm, Krupp, in Essen.[22] Only five of the original founders of Ufa continued as members of the supervisory board under Hugenberg´s chairmanship. Salomon Marx was one of them, taking responsibility for finance and for maintaining relations with the Americans.[23] In the early 1930s, Salomon and Lotte Marx, travelled several times to the United States on Ufa's business, and to holiday in Funchal, the latter also a holiday destination of Salomon and his first wife, Helene, and their two children in 1910 aboard the *Eleonore Woermann*. In 1928, Phoebus, its business mortally wounded, became dependent on United Artists (UA) and, as with Ufa, on MGM.[24] It was only a matter of time before the film industry would attract a German national front 'much given to chauvinist rhetoric to do battle against the omnipotence of the dollar'.

The overlap between Ufa and Phoebus, albeit fierce competitors at the production and distribution level, can now be seen with joint backing from senior industrialists, German banks and American film dollars. Hugenberg, together with Hugo Stinnes, Emil Kirdorf and, significantly, Wilhelm Beukenberg of Phoenix, formed the *Wirtschaftliche Gesellschaft*, 'The Economic Society', as a private association to administer a trust fund derived from the Ruhr industrialists' discretionary accounts to 'countermand threatening dangers in the economic and social fields'.[25] In January 1928, Ernst Hugo Correll, formerly sole executive of the politically and economically destroyed Phoebus, was appointed Ufa's production chief.[26] In 1930, Ufa, now the greatest German motion film company, produced one of Germany's greatest films, *The Blue Angel*, starring Marlene Dietrich. Correll identified totally with the nationalistic principles of Ufa's senior executives and co-operated with the National Socialists after 1933.

Alfred Hugenberg who became Ufa's master in March 1927 is integral to the wider story of Germany's political direction, as is Marx as his financial right arm.[27]

When still an unknown young attorney, Hugenberg founded the *Allgemeiner Deutscher Verbandd*, the 'Universal German Union', which in 1894 changed its name to the *Alldeutscher Verband*, the 'Pan-German League', the great protagonist for Tirpitz's navy and aggressive world economic expansion. In 1909, he made a big step up when he became chief executive of Krupp after its owner, Friedrich Krupp, committed suicide when his letters to his Italian lovers were published. Krupp left the company to his daughter, Bertha, but the Kaiser felt that Bertha, as a woman, could not be up to the job. Hugenberg had a long-term grudge against the communist Karl Liebknecht, the Social Democrat Reichstag member.[28] Liebknecht exposed industrial espionage by Hugenberg at Krupp in October 1912. A civil servant at the war ministry and four arsenal lieutenants supplied Krupp with extracts from contracts by competing firms. The firm's management did not 'even try to deny the allegations of bribery and industrial espionage with Krupp arguing in a press article that any attack on the firm of Krupp was an attack on the ability of the German state to wage war'. Several junior employees were convicted of corruption, but Hugenberg was never indicted. The sentences that were handed down were 'very lenient'.[29] Krupps were also charged at this time with orchestrating an international armaments ring from 1901, called the Harvey United Steel Company, which was designed to 'remove all excuse for competition between the major international armament firms in their united aim of encouraging the growth of jingoism, that the jingoism of one nation react on the jingoism of another to the profit of the armament manufacturer'.[30] Harvey's directors included representatives from Germany: Krupp, Dillingen; Britain: Vickers & Maxim, Beardmore, Coventry Ordnance, Armstrong Whitworth, Cammell Laird; France: St Chamond Steel, Chantillon-Commentry; Schneider, Cresuot; and Italy: Societa Degli Alti Forni Fondiere ed Acciaiene de Terni. As the industry's trade journal commented, 'It is the idlest of delusions to imagine that any nation is going to forego a quarter of a century of preparation and expenditure without trying whether it can recover in war something of what it has spent in peace.'[31]

In September 1914, Hugenberg dusted off the aims of the Pan-German League and, in collaboration with its then chairman Heinrich Class, prepared an extensive memorandum delivered to the Kaiser suggesting concrete war aims:

> *The ultimate goal was the security of the German people, security from future attacks and security for internal development. Germany needed a colonial empire to supply her with raw materials, a market for surplus products, and also a war indemnity to subsidise a system of rural colonisation and urban improvement. Belgium would have to remain under German control by right of conquest; France would have to cede valuable territory from the Swiss border to the channel coast; British sea power would have to be broken; and Russia would have to be confined to the boundaries existing at the time of Peter the Great. In addition to expanding its African colonies, Germany would have to unite central Europe (including Scandinavia, Finland, Rumania and Bulgaria) into a single economic unit.*[32]

Salomon Marx aided, one could say led, undoubtedly under Hugenberg's direct instruction, the taking of the German film industry into ultimately Nazi control. The 'Spiro Plan' of 1932, drafted primarily by Marx, cemented the centralisation of the film industry and 'asserted the priority of production over distribution, and argued for a state-controlled economy that would work against the forces of free competition'.[33] The plan favoured large premiere theatres owned by the big companies to the detriment of small theatres obliged to book films 'blind' for allocated times. It was a 'seamless transition from a media industry based on private capital to an essentially state-owned one that remained committed to the profit principle'.

The combination of Hugenberg's preference for, and trust in, Marx at Ufa, and Marx's delivery under direction of a 'Nazi-ready film industry', suggests that the two men's politics were similar. Hugenberg was notoriously intolerant of alternative views. There was a noticeable overlap between their business partners and dinner guests like Kirdorf, Stinnes, Albert Vögler and Freiherr Hans von und zu Löwenstein.[34] Hugenberg 'concentrated the financial resources of the Ruhr and made his office a central clearing house for the distribution of immense political funds'. Hugenberg, and by implication Marx, sought the total elimination of democracy and socialism.[35] 'Hugenberg had always been an outspoken nationalist and was resolutely opposed to any move that might be interpreted as a gesture of reconciliation to the hated Weimar Republic'.[36] He believed that only a patriarchal approach that 'viewed the corporation and the state as extended families could prosper the nation'. In industry, the entrepreneur as lord of his house had to have ultimate authority. In government, the Kaiser had to be a 'strong and determined leader who would decree the best for his subjects and rule with an iron hand'.

Hugenberg initially tried to work out of the limelight. During the inter-war period, he became the country's leading media proprietor. He patronised the radical masses who believed fervently in the nation state through his direction of regional newspapers, news agencies and film. He was a dominant figure in nationalist politics as leader of the National People's Party (DNVP) which, while never taking power in its own right, at least joined coalitions, briefly in 1925, but principally to join the cabinet in 1927 under Chancellor Wilhelm Marx.[37] The DNVP reached a peak of seats in 1924 with 103 places in the Reichstag, second only to the Social Democrats. The party's lists contained many famous names, including from among these pages, Karl Helfferich, Paul von Lettow-Vorbeck, Freiherr Hans von und zu Löwenstein, Eduard Stadler and Alfred von Tirpitz. Hugenberg pursued policies through his business and private life that considerably eased Adolf Hitler's rise to power and he served briefly in Hitler's first cabinet in 1933. 'The national opposition which ultimately triumphed was the tragic result of such tactics'.[38] The DNVP viewed the Versailles Treaty as a national disgrace, signed by traitors, which should be repealed; wished to restore the monarchy; and sought the reacquisition of all lost territories and colonies.

There was a wider background of murder and secret conspiracies to this period of which the killing of Liebknecht and Luxemburg was but a part. Many of these deaths had close links to Salomon Marx, and sometimes Erich and Eva Gerth, not as perpetrators, but in the loss of social, religious and business contacts. If the Weimar Republic failed through a lack of leadership, it was partly because the assassins 'cut down so many of the men who might have provided that leadership'.[39] A month after Liebknecht and Luxemburg's killing by the Freikorps, Kurt Eisner was shot in the back while on his way to the Bavarian parliament building in Munich to resign as prime minister.[40] Bavarian nationalist Anton Graf von Arco auf Valley drew the short straw in a lottery with colleagues for the honour of the task.[41] Valley 'was so covered in wounds inflicted by the infuriated mob and the red guards that he was left for dead', but recovered. Eisner was a journalist who organised the socialist revolution that overthrew the Wittelsbach monarchy in Bavaria, and declared a free state and a republic. He had spent spells in prison for criticising the Kaiser and for inciting strikes. He was also editor of *Vorwärts* after the death of Karl Liebknecht's father, Wilhelm.[42] After Eisner's death, a short-lived Bavarian Soviet Republic followed until ruthlessly suppressed by the Freikorps.

In the winter of the same year, Hugo Hasse was shot and severely injured on the steps of the Reichstag by Johann Voss, a deranged leather worker, and died a month later.[43] Hasse and Friedrich Ebert co-chaired the Council of the People's Deputies after the German revolution of 1918-1919; Hasse was later leader of the Independent Socialist Party. He defended social democrats in many legal cases including Karl Liebknecht after he published *Militarismus und Anti-Militarismus* in 1907. Hasse organised the anti-war rallies of the SPD in 1914, and with Liebknecht argued against war credits.

A year after the Freikorps-managed Kapp putsch misfired in March 1920, Matthias Erzberger, finance minister, was shot to death while walking in the Black Forest.[44] His greatest and most tragic legacy would always be his signature on the armistice for which he was never forgiven by the extreme right. The murder was master-minded by Manfred von Killinger who recruited two members of the ultra-nationalist death squad, 'Operation Consul', Heinrich Tillessen and Heinrich Schulz, former navy officers and members of the disbanded Ehrhardt Brigade. Erzberger had a varied career, leader of the Catholic Centrum Party, pre-dating future Chancellor Wilhelm Marx, and confidant of previous chancellor Bethmann.[45] It was always Erzberger's plan to use a German victory to gain control of the European continent 'for all time'. Tuchman called him a 'shrewd and able opportunist who represented whatever opinion was dominant ... a political flexibility unseen in Europe since Talleyrand'. He had 'no convictions, only appetites'. Erzberger served as chairman of the Armistice Commission and achieved other important legacies including new taxation measures heralding a redistribution of the tax burden in favour of the less-well-off. This particularly upset the political right-wing. Erzberger also stabilised the national finances and nationalised the railways which began as a result and for the first time to make a profit.

Within a few weeks in the summer of 1922, three close associates of Salomon Marx were attacked and one of them killed. The first was Philipp Scheidemann, joint chairman of the SDP parliamentary group with Hugo Hasse, who was killed the previous winter. It was Scheidemann who made the impromptu speech from a Reichstag balcony after the abdication of the Kaiser. 'The old and rotten, the monarchy has collapsed. The new may live. Long live the German Republic.' He formed the first democratically elected government, but resigned a few months later because of the harsh terms of the Versailles Treaty. He was the purported quiet support of Salomon Marx's poster calling for the murder of Liebknecht. Scheidemann was hated by the right who coined the term *Scheidemänner* as a derogatory terms for Weimar supporters. In June 1922, Scheidemann was attacked with prussic acid in a blinding attempt.[46] 'He survived, but lived with his scars.'[47] In 1926, Scheidemann exposed the clandestine co-operation between the *Reichswehr*, the post-Kaiser central military organisation in Germany until 1935, and the Red Army which was in violation of the Treaty of Versailles; this negotiation brought down the third cabinet of chancellor Wilhelm Marx.

Maximilian Harden, was initially the crusading editor of *Zukunft*, 'Future', and became an influential Jewish intellectual. He was godfather to Salomon Marx's daughter Eleonore and publicly praised Marx's business achievements. At first a monarchist, elitist, anti-democrat, anti-egalitarianist, Harden became a fierce critic of the Kaiser and his entourage and made open accusations of homosexual behaviour, then a criminal offence in Germany. These charges led to numerous trials and did 'sustained damage to the House of Hohenzollern'.[48] Harden supported the invasion of Belgium and demanded that Germany take over most of Europe after winning the war. 'Ibsen and Strindberg were his literary heroes; Nietzsche and the new prophets of Social Darwinism his philosophical guides.' After the war, Harden became a pacifist and supported the republic. In July 1922, Harden was beaten half to death with a heavy steel rod; he died five years later.[49] His assailants were Freikorps members Bert Weichardt and Albert Wilhelm Grenz who claimed that they had been incensed by Harden's writings. Grenz was imprisoned for four years, Weichardt less.

The third attack shocked the country. Foreign Minister Walther Rathenau was machine gunned as he was driven in his open-top car from his home to the Foreign Office in Wilhelmstraße.[50] His murderers then threw a hand grenade into the car for good measure. It was another murder by 'Operation Consul', led by Hermann Ehrhardt.[51] Rathenau had been warned many times about a pending attack, most significantly in May 1922 by Eugenio Pacelli, the papal nuncio, who had been tipped off by a priest.[52] Rathenau's friend and biographer, Count Kessler, felt that 'not since the assassination of Abraham Lincoln has the death of a statesman so shaken a whole nation'.[53] Over a million people marched in Berlin in homage, 150,000 in Munich and Chemnitz, 100,000 in Hamburg, Breslau, Elberfeld and Essen. As a regular dinner partner, one must assume that Rathenau also met Erich Gerth during his frequent visits to Brückenallee with Eva. Rathenau was killed in June 1922 and Gerth wrote his application to join the Foreign Office that December. Was Rathenau an inspiration for Gerth's choice of career, a mentor even? Foreign Office attachés, Gerth's designation next year, stood guard as Rathenau's coffin lay in state in the Reichstag.[54] There was a possible slight personal reason for a close private discussion between the two. Gerth's father, Ernst, was a founding manager of Berlin's first horse-drawn tram company. Rathenau, as a young man, superintended the introduction of electric trams in Genoa and his own conglomerate bought a streetcar firm in Madrid.[55]

Rathenau's father, Emil, bought the European rights to Edison's electric light patent in the first step to becoming one of Germany's most successful entrepreneurs, the renowned general manager of the *Allgemeine Elektrizitätsgesellschaft* (AEG), an innovator on a world scale, a system builder and an extremely rich and powerful man.[56] Maximilian Harden saw in him 'the Bismarck of Germany's industrial empire'. Walther Rathenau, the younger son and the least favoured by his father, was a student at the Wilhelm-Gymnasium in the wealthy Tiergarten district of Berlin, the classical sister of the Gerths' own school. After a shaky start in business, Walther came into his own. By 1904, he was officially involved on the boards of 107 companies, twenty-one of them foreign.

In 1907, Rathenau's growing commercial reputation saw him invited to join a team to visit Germany's African colonies.[57] His first report entitled 'The Development of the German East African Colony' was presented to the Kaiser in November and gave an overview of the chances for economic growth. It also discussed the failures and achievements of the German administration. His second report on South West Africa was much less well received and was banned from publication. Lieutenant-General Lothar von Trotha was sent to South West Africa with a military force to deal with the Herrero tribe who were protesting against the theft of cattle lands by German settlers. Trotha introduced a policy of not merely subjugating the Herreros, but of eliminating them.[58] 'The handling of the Herreros', wrote Rathenau, 'involved the greatest atrocity brought about by German military policy.' The Kaiser ennobled seven Jews during his reign, but never Rathenau. In addition to these seven, there were a number of converted Jews among these men of commerce and industry who accounted for a growing proportion of those given a 'von'.[59]

Rehabilitated by necessity by 1914 as an influential member of the international capitalist structure, Rathenau was a visiting friend of both the Kaiser and Chancellor Bethmann, who lived close by. Rathenau wrote,

'Three hundred men, all acquainted with each other, control the economic destiny of the Continent.'[60] He played a key role in convincing the War Ministry to set up the War Materials Department (KRA) of which he was put in charge in August 1914. KRA focussed on raw materials threatened by the British blockade as well as supplies from occupied Belgium and France. It set prices and regulated the distribution to vital war industries and this success of Rathenau's work went a long way to extending Germany's ability to stay in the war.

After the war, Rathenau's wife, Edith, entertained lavishly in their elegant villa, holding open house on Sunday afternoons, where the entire economic and cultural elite of the capital gathered for food, but more especially for lively and brilliant conversation.[61] It was here, in Königsallee, as well as at his own 'at-homes', that Salomon Marx mixed freely.

Rathenau continued to be affected by the insults 'hurled at him by the radical parliamentary right wing party, the *Deutschnationale*, led in the Reichstag by Rathenau's old war-time rival, Karl Helfferich'.[62] By the end of 1921, 'expressions of hostility became ever more threatening'.

> *Day by day speeches in the Reichstag and the various Diets [by the Nationalists led by the former Imperial Vice-Chancellor, Karl Helfferich], leading articles, vast popular meetings, pilloried him as the Jew responsible for the depths of shame to which Germany had been brought and for the ruin of the German middle classes. In the imagination of millions of impoverished and famished Germans, Rathenau became a sort of arch-traitor, in league with the Jews, the Bolsheviks, and the Entente to give the death-blow to Germany. An Upper Silesian semi-military organisation, Selbstschutz, used to tramp the roads singing, 'God damn Walther Rathenau. Shoot him down, the dirty Jew.'[63]*

Two months after signing the Treaty of Rapallo, which renounced German territorial claims against Russia from World War I, Rathenau was assassinated. During his last motor trip, he was passed by a Mercedes touring car with Ernst Werner Techow behind the wheel and Leutnant Erwin Kern and Hermann Fischer on the backseats. Kern opened fire with the sub-machinegun at close range, Fischer threw the hand grenade. Also in the plot were Techow's younger brother, Hans Gerd Techow, future writer Ernst von Salomon, and Willi Günther, aided and abetted by seven others, some of them schoolboys.[64] A memorial stone in the Königsallee in Grunewald marks the scene of the crime. The murder was soon cleared up. Günther bragged in public about his participation. After his arrest on 26 June, he confessed fully to the crime. Hans Gerd Techow was arrested the following day, Ernst Werner Techow, who was visiting his uncle, three days later. Fischer and Kern remained on the loose. After a daring flight, which kept Germany in suspense for more than two weeks, they were finally spotted at the castle of Saaleck in Thuringia, whose owner was a secret member of 'Operation Consul'. On 17 July, the pair was confronted by two police detectives. While waiting for reinforcements during the stand-off, one of the detectives fired at a window, unknowingly killing Kern by a bullet to the head. Fischer then took his own life. When they seized power in 1933, the Nazis wiped out public commemoration of Rathenau by destroying monuments to him, closing the Walther-Rathenau-Museum in his former mansion and renaming streets and schools dedicated to him. Instead, a memorial plaque to Kern and Fischer was solemnly unveiled at Saaleck Castle in July 1933 and in October 1933 a monument was erected on the assassins' grave.[65]

Once more, Canaris entered the scene because of suspected links to Rathenau's murder through his involvement with Ehrhardt and 'Operation Consul'. Canaris was identified as the chief activist at the Baltic Naval Station where he supported the radical right-wing putsch movement with financial and material help.[66] The money distributed by Canaris helped set up the Ehrhardt terror organisation to assist the rise of Hitler's SA and his putsch of November 1923. Canaris maintained secret hoards of weapons and misappropriated military equipment for 'Operation Consul' under the noses of the Allies, and the German Naval Command knew and tolerated it. The *Gauleiter* for 'Organisation Consul' in Holstein, Mecklenburg and Pomerania was Kapitänleutnant Kurt Wende whose adjutant, Erwin Kern, was later killed while on the run after the murder of Rathenau.

Canaris was now openly accused by the republicans in the Reichstag and in the Press as a supporter of terror. His past was put under the microscope, his contacts with 'Operation Consul', links to the Hitler Putsch, allegations about the Rathenau murder, his military links to Spain with secret funding, links to the Lohmann Affair, the escape of Otto Runge convicted in the murder of Liebknecht, and the funding of pro-Fatherland groups, including the *Wikingbund*, the renamed 'Operation Consul'. An investigation by members of the Reichstag into many of these matters refused to have Canaris as a witness because of his public taint.

Diarist Kessler claimed, and many thought it proven, that the death of Rathenau gave the French confidence to invade the Ruhr and to seek to set up the area as an independent state, the Rhenish Republic. Kessler had a lengthy argument by letter with French Prime Minister Raymond Poincaré.

At the very moment that Poincaré was prepared to strike a death-blow at German unity his more serious obstacle was suddenly removed; that is to say, the measure of confidence and trust which Rathenau as director of Germany's foreign policy had won for himself and his country. One blow cleared the way for a renewal of the prejudices which had made possible the Treaty of Versailles. Poincaré had to thank those responsible for the assassination of Rathenau when he found himself at liberty to occupy the Ruhr without encountering any serious opposition from French or British opinion.[67]

At the beginning of 1923, French and Belgian troops had marched in to the Ruhr to enforce payment of arrears of war reparations. About 130 German civilians died in a number of skirmishes. The government of Gustav Stresemann called a general strike throughout Germany.

Poincaré did not anticipate passive resistance. Though aware he was playing France's last trump in a decisive contest and critically short of troops and coal, he never considered barring food shipments to force the Ruhr miners back to work. Despite the recent precedent of Germany's refusal to feed civilians in territories it conquered in the war, he was neither so foolish or so brutal.[68]

Many among the Allies thought that to finance this resistance, the Germans printed money and 'there resulted the notorious period when the value of the Reichsmark fell by the day and by the hour until trunkfuls of paper were needed for the smallest purchase'. In another view, from historian Sally Marks, the French made a profit after costs of nearly 900 million gold Reichsmarks from their Rhineland adventure; German hyper-inflation was due to other causes.[69]

[Inflation] was a disastrous ploy, sweeping away the savings of the middle classes, bankrupting thousands, reintroducing hunger to the streets of the cities, further loosening the ties of society and unleashing a bitterness and restlessness that were harnessed by revolutionaries and nationalists for their own ends ... While the middle classes were ruined and workers thrown on the streets, the Army high command received one hundred million in gold at the height of the crisis for the purpose of rearmament outside Versailles limits; a portion of this was passed on to the Navy and incorporated in two secret rearmament funds.[70]

By the middle of 1923, the whole of Germany had become delirious. Whoever had a job got paid every day, usually at noon, and then ran to the nearest store, with a sack full of banknotes, to buy anything he could get, at any price. In their frenzy, people paid millions and even billions of marks for cuckoo clocks, shoes that didn't fit, anything that could be traded for something else.[71]

French occupation forces facilitated the minority Ruhr Separatists in many ways including providing considerable sums of money, permitted the carrying of arms and the carrying out of military manoeuvres 'both of which were, of course, forbidden to the loyal section of the population under threat of the severest penalties'.[72] In the chief towns of the Ruhr, from Düsseldorf to Trier, where Georg Gerth was still working, everything was done by the French civil and military occupation authorities to ensure the success of putsches designed to bring about the 'Rhenish Republic' including disarming the police before the main putsch took place and protecting the Separatists. The French withdrew in June 1930. They also abandoned 'one by one the cherished possessions of the Reparations Commission', the right of sanctions, economic occupation and military operations.[73]

Diarist Kessler in his biography of Rathenau said that, 'Political murder had at that time become one of the commonplaces of German public life to a degree hardly credible'.[74] Most of the victims were on the left wing of the political spectrum and 'only a few were prominent political figures'.[75] Kessler cites a pamphlet by Emil Gumbel, a statistical lecturer at the University of Heidelberg, 'Four Years of Political Murder, 1922, which names 354 assassinations by right-wing groups and twenty-two by left-wing groups during the four years after the war, all quite separate from those killed in civil war or street fighting.[76] Friedrich takes the analysis further.[77] For the twenty-two murders by the left, seventeen brought heavy sentences, including ten executions; for the right, 326 went unpunished. The average prison sentence for murder was fifteen years for left-wingers and four months for right-wingers. 'Organisation Consul' was making a 'concerted effort to undermine the republic by well-chosen political assassinations' and seemingly supported by the judiciary.[78]

The years 1922 and 1923 were also the time when Hitler and the Nationalsozialistische Deutsche Arbeiterpartei, the NSDAP, 'National Socialist German Workers' Party', formed the first incarnations of their two most influential party organisations, the *Jungsturm Adolf Hitler* and the *Jugendbund der NSDAP*, which would become the Hitler Youth, and the *Stabswache*, 'Staff Guard', quickly renamed the *Stoßtrupp-Hitler*, 'Shock Troop-Hitler', which became the infamous *Schutzstaffel*, the SS. The first coup in May took over a barracks and weapons, but 'the order to march never came'. In November, in the famous 'Beer Hall Putsch', sixteen NSDAP members and four police officers were killed in the attempted *coup d'état*. Hitler was arrested and put on trial for high treason in 1924.[79] Sentenced to five years' imprisonment at Landsberg, Hitler was pardoned by the Bavarian Supreme Court on Christmas Eve that year, but not before he had dictated the first volume of *Mein Kampf*, principally to his deputy Rudolf Hess.[80] The putsch attempt of the *Freikorps* in 1920 failed as did the two coup attempts by Hitler in 1923. By the end of 1924, there were signs that all of this activity was taking on a coherent political form. The most viable patriotic associations that emerged from among the scattered remnants of the *Freikorps* and Home Guards were the *Stahlhelm*, 'Steel Helmets', and the *Jungdeutscher Orden*, 'Young German Order', became 'major political forces'.[81] The *Freikorps* 'sank mostly into oblivion'.[82] It was only early in 1933 and Hitler's arrival in power that they were 'widely recognised as fascist *avant la lettre* and publicly commemorated as political heroes which is why most of the great histories of the *Freikorps* movement and memoirs of its veterans appeared after 1933. The *Freikorps* were in the vanguard of Nazism mainly because the Nazis declared them so.'

The first round of Germany's first-ever democratic presidential election in 1925 saw the stalking horse candidate of the German right, Karl Jarres, take almost 40 per cent of the vote, but still well short of the clear majority that was needed in this round. The SDP candidate, Otto Braun, and Wilhelm Marx of the Catholic Centre Party, were some distance off. Ludendorff with the fringe German Völkisch Freedom Party was in seventh place and this marked the demise of his last chance of becoming a serious politician. In the second round, Jarres withdrew in favour of a late entry, Paul von Hindenburg, who stood, supposedly reluctantly, as an independent. The democratic SDP and the Centre parties combined under Wilhelm Marx to ensure Hindenburg's defeat. Hindenburg won with 48 per cent of the vote, 900,000 more than Marx and took the presidency, which he held until his death in 1934. Hitler stood against Hindenburg for the Presidency in 1932 and lost, but gained 37 per cent of the popular vote.

No party obtained a Reichstag majority so Hindenburg ruled through presidential decree with an appointed chancellor, Franz von Papen. The Hitler and Nazi Party bandwagon steadily gained votes in several elections to 1932 through a mixture of Hitler's undoubted oratory as he criss-crossed the country by air, sweeping terror tactics and conventional campaigning. Papen left office and Hindenburg reluctantly appointed Hitler as chancellor, even though he was without an absolute Reichstag majority.

Marchers cutting their boots against asphalt streets, growing louder, cheers swallowing up the winter stillness, torchlights and searchlights advancing on the darkness ... the New York Times *later reported a 'gigantic demonstration that has not been witnessed' in Berlin, at least not since that November afternoon some fourteen years earlier, in 1918, when 'Fritz Ebert reviewed the masses'. The day was Monday 30 January 1933; Adolf Hitler had just been named Chancellor of Germany and stood overlooking Wilhelmstraße, reviewing a newer, larger, more threatening version of Germany's masses ... Newspaper trucks parked up and down the street, their cables and spotlights furbishing the big moment with electric excitement. By early evening, members of the SA, Sturmabteilung or stormtroops, and the SS Schutzstaffel, the party's smaller security guard, as well as the nationalist Stahlhelm, assembled in the Tiergarten for a full-dress parade through the Brandenburg*

Gate, down Wilhelmstraße, and into the old city of Berlin. What was not anticipated was the sheer number of civilian well-wishers who also gathered. In this ostensibly 'red' city, thousands of Berliners stood and cheered Hitler and Hindenburg, the President of the Republic. The old songs were dusted off including Deutschland über Alles, The Watch on the Rhine *and the Nazi anthem, the* Horst Wessel Song.[83]

Some argue that Hugenberg's major achievement by 1930 was to assist the growth of the Nazis to become the major political force on the right. 'The squat bespectacled Hugenberg did not have Hitler's personal magnetism and failed to exploit the economic and political crises which he had foretold'.[84] Hitler used his position to unleash a campaign of violence against all of the Nazi's left-wing parliamentary opposition during the 1933 election. Hitler took 44 per cent of the vote. On 7 March 1933, a supposedly communist-laid arson attack partially burned down the Reichstag. The Reichstag Fire Decree, signed the next day by Hindenburg, suspended most civil liberties in Germany, including habeas corpus, freedom of expression, freedom of the press, the right of free association and public assembly, the secrecy of the post and telephone and transferred state powers to the Reich government. The decree was quickly followed by the *Gesetz zur Behebung der Not von Volk und Reich,* an 'Enabling Act' to remedy the distress of the people. The amendment gave the German Cabinet, in effect Hitler as the new chancellor, plenary power to enact laws without the involvement of the Reichstag. It was approved by the Reichstag and Hindenburg on the same day, 24 March. With the support of all the non-socialist parties, Hitler assumed dictatorial power.

Hitler won such decisive elections in 1932 and 1933 because the Nazis departed from established political traditions in that they were identified at once with a distinctly popular form of ethnic nationalism and with the basic social reforms most Germans counted on to ensure national well-being.[85]

Hugenberg was a part of Hitler's first government which set up the Enabling Act. He held the posts of Reich and Prussian ministers of the economy and of food and agriculture in what the *Berliner Lokal-Anzeiger* claimed was the best position in the cabinet.[86] Hugenberg as an extreme nationalist was seen by Mussolini, and also by the French ambassador and the Polish government, as more dangerous and a greater threat to the *status quo* than even Hitler and the NSDAP. He immediately facilitated Ufa's use by Goebbels as a propaganda machine. On 29 March 1933, Ufa management fired several Jewish employees. In the summer, the Nazis created the Film Chamber of the Reich which excluded Jewish filmmakers from all German studios.

Hindenburg chose Hugenberg as a balance to the NSDAP members in the government. The plan was for Hugenberg to manipulate Hitler and 'restrain the radicalism of the Nazi movement'.[87]

> *Conservatives, convinced that society should be subject to the state and the regime could control the state, thought that they had outwitted the Nazis. In their hubris, Hugenberg and his associates could not imagine a revolution from below. Ensconced in his ministry, Hugenberg believed he could remodel Germany. Within five months, he was forced to admit that he had totally misjudged the political scene. The manipulators had become the manipulated. German nationalism and its leader were obsolete.*[88]

At Hitler's first cabinet, Hugenberg fought unsuccessfully to have the Communist party proscribed. Quickly, all of his other plans for power went astray. By June, Hugenberg admitted complete defeat and resigned. His life-long plans for the organisation of Germany were shattered.[89] Hugenberg was later reputed to have remarked, 'I've just committed the greatest stupidity of my life; I have allied myself with the greatest demagogue in world history.'[90] He made a despondent comment:

> *I am indeed of the opinion that we all have cause to go home and to crawl into our closets or go into the woods. In the last days and weeks it has been my chief goal to remain respectable in every way and not to allow my good name to be marred. I would hope that in a difficult situation I have succeeded in this and would find for that reason a great peace and relief. You don't know what you ought to say in days like these, but one thought has gone through my mind in these hours and I would still like to add it: if anyone should hear that I have committed suicide, do not believe it at all. I would not do it and I do not believe in suicide.*

Hitler's power became absolute when Hindenburg died next year and took with him the last hint of restraint. The Nazis did not persecute Hugenberg, but they 'circumcised his power'. 'Germany's new rulers treated him gently as a superfluous elder statesman.' Was this deduction by Hugenburg's biographer, Leopold, completely accurate? The Nazis may not have wished to publicly humiliate him and alienate his powerful industrial supporters or his ultra-right-wing political followers. Yet, they did need to neuter his power base and, therefore, his ability to cause further trouble. The Nazi state swallowed up Hugenberg's and Salomon Marx's Ufa as a coveted and persuasive tool and gave it to Joseph Goebbels, the Reich Minister of Propaganda. Hugenberg and his allies, including Salomon Marx, were forced to sell their shares. Marx was no longer needed and, perhaps, knew too much. Anyway, Marx was a born Jew and, therefore, now official prey.

ENDNOTES

1   Alfred Hintz, 'Salomon Marx (1866–1936) – Industrieller, Bankier und Politiker', *Berlin in Geschichte und Gegenwart, Jahrbuch des Landesarchivs Berlin*, 2011, pp. 101–130.

2   The following material comes from four principal sources: [1] Erich Gerth's personnel files at the Berlin Foreign Ministry and kindly retrieved by Martina Nibbeling-Wriessnig following the good offices of Emanuele Ojetti of Rome (Auswärtiges Amt, Politisches Archiv, Gz: 117–251.09: IH 004386–7, Personalia, Vols. 1–2; IB 004388, Personnel Finances 'Persönliche Geldangelegenheiten', Vol. 1; IBV 004389, Personalia, Vol. 2) with additional material from Matthias Löhr, also of the Foreign Office; [2] LABO Entschädigungsamt, Berlin, Restitution File, Salomon Marx, 1956, researched by Renate Rüb, archivservice-berlin; [3] Hintz, above; and [4] 'Salomon Marx', Deutsches Biographisches Archiv (Neue Folge), Microfiche NE 859, p. 207. Translations from the German are by Cathrin Brockhaus-Clark.

3   ordensmuseum.de/historische-oe/der-furstlich-lippischer-leopold-orden,   accessed 10/2017.

4   Loebell had one loose connection with Erich's past. Erich's father, Ernst, was a pioneer of Berlin's horse-drawn trams. Loebell was the driving force behind the construction of the Brandenburg urban railway with its five radial, networked routes into Berlin.Ihm zu Ehren erhielt auch eine Lokomotive den Namen „Landrat von Loebell", die am 25. März 1904 den Eröffnungszug der Strecke zog. In Loebell's honour, a locomotive was named 'District of Loebell', which in 1904 pulled the opening train. From 1901 to 1912, Loebell was chairman of the railway company (wikipedia).

5   Kreimeier, *UFA Story*, pp. 1, 30.

6   Marx, *Die Deckung unserer Kriegskosten*, 'The Coverage of our War Costs' (Berlin 1917), copy National Library.

7   Kitchen, *Silent Dictatorship*, p. 266.

8   Stadtler claimed to have encouraged Waldemar Pabst in the murder of Karl Liebknecht and Rosa Luxemburg (Stadtler, *Life Memories*, Vol. 3), pp. 46–49.

9   The Peace Prize of 1926 was received jointly with the French politician Aristide Briand for work on reconciliation between Germany and France which resulted in the Locarno agreements of October 1925.

10 Marx, *Das organische Staatsprinzip*, 1919, Deutsche National Bibliothek.

11 Hertzman, 'Founding of the DNVP', p. 26, fn. 9.

12 Walker, 'Nationalist People's Party', p. 627.

13 *LABO*, Berlin, file Salomon Marx/304.641, pp. C4–6, 'Duplicate of prosecution papers against Walter Firnhaber and Dr Eduard Marx, Berlin 28/7/1942.

14 In 1910, August Borsig, father of Ernst and Conrad, was one of the sixty richest men in Prussia. After the war, he financially supported the *Freikorps* Ehrhardt Brigade, helped found the Anti-Bolshevik League, and promoted Hitler and National Socialism. Stinnes was known as the *Inflationskönig*, 'Inflation King', for borrowing vast sums in Reichsmarks and repaying them when the currency collapsed. At the time of his early death in 1924, his empire held about 4,500 companies and 3,000 manufacturing plants. The company collapsed in 1930 and merged with AEG.

15 Helene Marx, née Schirmacher, born Danzig, 13/1/1869, died 5/12/1921, Berlin (Einwohnermeldekartei StA XIII a, Nr. 1977).

16 Charlotte Sommer, age twenty, married Robert Rolf Friedrich Ludwig Mayer, born 25/3/1883, died 1976, 15/10/1906, Berlin Charlottenburg. Surname change to Mayer-Schalburg 6/1920. Divorced 13/1/1923, registered 11/2/1923, five days after Charlotte's remarriage to Salomon Marx (Einwohnermeldekartei StA XIII a, Nr. 1977).

17 Mueller, *Canaris*, pp. 63–71.

18 Padfield, *Dönitz*, pp. 117–18.

19 Kreimeier, *UFA Story*, p. 166.

20 *CIA Report*: 'The Lohmann Affair', Studies in Intelligence 4, Heft 2, Spring 1960: A31–A38. RG059. Appendix 10.

21 Mueller, *Canaris*, pp. 73–74.

22 Hintz, 'Salomon Marx', pp. 111–13. Walker, 'Nationalist People's Party', p. 632.
23 Kreimeier, *UFA Story*, pp. 160–61.
24 Kreimeier, *UFA Story*, p. 129.
25 Leopold, *Hugenberg*, pp. 7–8.
26 Kreimeier, *UFA Story*, p. 129.
27 Kreimeier, *UFA Story*, p. 158.
28 Leopold, *Hugenberg*, p. 4.
29 Murray, *Krupp's International Armaments Ring*, p. 182.
30 Murray, *Krupp's International Armaments Ring*, Preface, pp. xiii, 174–75.
31 *Arms and Explosives*, 2/1894.
32 Leopold, *Hugenberg*, p. 6, citing extensive correspondence between Hugenberg and Class and, particularly, '*Denkschrift betreffend die nationalen und sozialpolitischen Ziele des deutschen Volkes im gegenwärtigen Kriege*', (Als Handschrift Gedruckt).
33 'Spiro', *Spitzenorganisation der Deutschen Filmwirtschaft*, the 'Council of the German Film Industry' (Kreimeier, *UFA Story*), pp. 184, 193–94.
34 Leopold, *Hugenberg*, pp. 4–5.
35 Leopold, *Hugenberg*, pp. xv–xvi.
36 Jones , 'Greatest Stupidity', p. 64.
37 Walker, 'Nationalist People's Party', p. 628.
38 Leopold, *Hugenberg*, p. xvi.
39 Friedrich, *Before the Deluge*, pp. 117–18.
40 Murdered 21/2/1919.
41 Princess Ferdinand, *Through Four Revolutions*, pp. 312–13.
42 Liebknecht's family descended from Martin Luther. While Wilhelm Liebknecht lived in exile in London through the 1850s, he joined the Communist League and became an intimate friend of the family of Karl Marx (Roth, Social Democrats), p. 49.
43 Shot 8/10/1919, died 7/11/1919.
44 Murdered 26/8/1921.
45 Tuchman, *August 1914*, pp. 360–61.
46 Attacked 4/6/1922; died 29/11/1939.
47 Friedrich, *Before the Deluge*, p. 118.
48 Volkov, *Rathenau*, p. 44.
49 Attacked 3/7/1922; died 30/10/1927.
50 Murdered 24/6/1922.
51 Martin Sabrow, 'Der Rathenaumord: Rekonstruktion einer Verschwörung gegen die Republik von Weimar', *Schriftenreihe der Vierteljahrshefte für Zeitgeschichte*, Issue 69, Munich, Oldenburg, 1994. Kessler, *Rathenau*, pp. 367–68.
52 Dalin, *Myth of Hitler's Pope*, p. 51.
53 Kessler, *Rathenau*, p. 380.
54 Kessler, *Rathenau*, p. 379.
55 Kessler, *Rathenau*, p. 360.
56 Volkov, *Rathenau*, p. 9.
57 Volkov, *Rathenau*, pp. 67–71.
58 Chapter 2, 'Kaisertreu'.
59 Clarke, *Kaiser Wilhelm*, pp. 351–2.
60 Rosenberg, *Imperial Germany*, p. 39. Friedrich, *Before the Deluge*, pp. 99–100.
61 Volkov, *Rathenau*, p. 57.
62 Volkov, *Rathenau*, pp. 197–98.
63 Kessler, *Rathenau*, p. 365. Volkov, *Rathenau*, p. 197, 'uniformed youth adorned with large swastikas'.
64 Friedrich, *Before the Deluge*, pp. 99, 106–7.
65 Rathenau is acknowledged to be, in part, the basis for the German nobleman and industrialist Paul Arnheim, a character in Robert Musil's novel, *The Man Without Qualities*.
66 Mueller, Canaris, pp. 57, 77, 79.
67 Kessler, *Rathenau*, pp. 380–81.
68 Marks, '1918 and After', p. 39.

69   Marks, '1918 and After', p. 30.

70   Padfield, *Dönitz*, p. 104.

71   Friedrich, *Before the Deluge*, p. 124.

72   Kessler, *Rathenau*, pp. 383–88.

73   Marks, 'Myths of Reparations', pp. 246–52.

74   Kessler, *Rathenau*, p. 362.

75   Volkov, *Rathenau*, pp. 196–97.

76   Gumbel, *Vier Jahre politischer Mord* (Verlag der Neuen Gesellschaft, Berlin-Fichtenau 1922).

77   Friedrich, *Before the Deluge*, pp. 117–18.

78   Volkov, *Rathenau*, p. 197.

79   Padfield, *Dönitz*, p. 107.

80   *Mein Kampf*, 'My Struggle', was originally entitled 'Four and a Half Years of Struggle against Lies, Stupidity, and Cowardice'.

81   Fritzsche, *Germans into Nazis*, p. 134.

82   Fritzsche, *Germans into Nazis*, pp. 122–24.

83   Fritzsche, *Germans into Nazis*, pp. 139–40.

84   Walker, 'Nationalist People's Party', p. 642.

85   Fritzsche, *Germans into Nazis*, pp. 8–9.

86   Leopold, *Hugenberg*, p. 137, citing *Berliner Lokal-Anzeiger*, 30/1/1933.

87   Jones, 'Greatest Stupidity', p. 76.

88   Leopold, *Hugenberg*, p. 139.

89   Leopold, *Hugenberg*, pp. 163–65.

90   Jones, 'Greatest Stupidity', p. 63.

CHAPTER 16

Erich and his Catholic and Jewish Problems

In Germany, they came first for the Communists,
And I didn't speak up because I wasn't a Communist;
And then they came for the trade unionists,
And I didn't speak up because I wasn't a trade unionist;
And then they came for the Jews,
And I didn't speak up because I wasn't a Jew;
And then . . . they came for me . . .
And by that time there was no one left to speak.[1]

Erich Gerth's application to the Foreign Office, much trailed in these pages, was made on 30 December 1922 after he had completed a year of developmental employment in two of Salomon Marx's companies. During this time, and at least until 1925, Erich and Eva lived in Berlin at Schwäbischestraße 8 in the south-west of the city near Barbarossaplatz.[2] After his acceptance on 1 March 1923, Gerth prepared for the examinations needed for diplomatic-consular duties. These he passed on 20 December 1924 with a Grade 2, 'good'. The exam consisted of three essays which received a mixed reception from the head of the examination committee, Gustav Stresemann. Stresemann, who had a distinguished Foreign Office career, was known to Salomon Marx as a brother-in-law of Kurt von Kleefeld, a frequent visitor to Marx's dinner parties.[3] Erich wrote his first paper of 108 pages on the 'German-English alliance negotiations between 1898 and 1901 against the background of the English imperial policy between 1895 and 1902 and the German naval policy since 1897/98', for which he received a Grade 2 as 'he worked more intelligently and independently than his colleagues'.[4] This essay might have come easily to Gerth as he could rely on his training and experience as a naval cadet and junior officer. However, his legal paper on the 'Jurisdiction of Foreign States' was considered only a Grade 4, 'Sufficient', as it 'did not refer to foreign law sources and lacked depth'. A third paper on the 'Dissolution of the Danube Monarchy', the Catholic Austro-Hungarian Empire, with ninety-two pages, was graded 1, 'Very good', perhaps benefitting from input from Eva's many contacts in the Bavarian Catholic community.

A much greater influence on his acceptance than these essay results came from the group of twelve stellar individuals who, as the application form requested, were 'able to give reference about you due to personal acquaintance'. For the first time, Canaris is not mentioned or needed, but one senses he is close at hand. Nor did the list include father-in-law Salomon Marx, but he was discreetly mentioned in answer to other questions. Nothing demonstrates better than these proffered referees Gerth's whirlwind rise into the world of prestige and influence following his marriage to Eva Marx.

The list had just one family member. Somewhat surprisingly, it was Frau Gräfin Franziska von Ahlefeldt-Eschelsmark in Silesia, Eva's ex-mother-in-law. Eva's first husband was killed in 1916.[5] Not only did Eva keep a close connection with her previous noble family, but was able to introduce her second husband amid sufficient good humour and respect for the Gräfin to provide a reference six years later.

Erich's previous boss, Admiral Adolf von Trotha, until 1920 chief of the *Oberste Marineleitung*, was an obvious, but serious, addition to the list for a lowly ex-u-boat commander.

Then came four of Salmon Marx's business and political contacts, all, presumably, meeting Gerth at social events at Brückenallee, and at which he evidently impressed: Minister of State Friedrich von Loebell, President of the *Reichsbürgerrat Berlin*, founded by Salomon Marx in January 1919. Leobell was also soon to become chairman of the supervisory board of Marx's Internationale Handelsbank, where Gerth spent part of his commercial training year before entry into the diplomatic corps; Foreign Minister Gottlieb von Jagow, who had retired in 1916, 'a quiet, unassuming and scholarly man, perhaps the worst speaker in the Reichstag'; Gustaf Schlieper, owner of the Berlin finance business, Diskonto-Gesellschaft, a leading German banking organisation and closely associated with Rothschild and Krupp until its 1929 merger into Deutsche Bank; and, finally, Ottmar Strauss, co-founder of the iron wholesaler Otto Wolff, one of the largest businesses in pre-war Germany. Strauss was a Jewish business contact of Salomon Marx from when they both lived and worked in Cologne.

The remaining six referees all came from the upper-reaches of the Catholic community in Germany. Salomon Marx would have introduced Erich to the son of his cousin, Senate President Wilhelm Marx, Chairman of the Catholic *Zentrum* Party of the Reichstag, already discussed in several places, and to become Chancellor for the first time next year. Erich's Foreign Office application was signed in Munich, suggesting he and Eva were living there in 1922 with ready social access to the remaining referees. Pre-eminent among Eva Gerth's contribution, acting as one referee, were their Royal Highnesses, Prince Ludwig Ferdinand von Bayern and his wife, his maternal first cousin, Princess Maria de la Paz de Bourbon, Infantin von Spanien whom he married in 1883. Maria de la Paz was the second-youngest daughter of King Francis and Queen Regnant Isabella II of Spain. Prince Ludwig, a Hapsburg, was a member of the Bavarian Royal House of Wittelsbach with royal links to Catholic Bavaria and Spain. As a gynaecologist, he was one of only a few European princes doing an ordinary job outside government or the military and, during World War I, worked as head of the surgery department of the Munich Military Hospital. The family were close to their distant relative, Kaiser Wilhelm, and frequently corresponded.[6] Princess Maria lived until the Bavarian Republic at Schloss Nymphenburg, near Munich. Next, Freiherr Karl von Papius was Legation Councillor of the Bavarian Embassy in Berlin and was Erich's godfather. He had strong links to Würzburg, the home town of the Leinecker family which married into the Gerth family.[7] Papius studied law at the universities of Munich and Heidelberg and passed the examination for public service in 1864 in Würzburg where he also received his doctorate two years later. Then came their Excellencies Pablo Soler and Diego von Bergen, ambassadors of His Majesty the King of Spain in Berlin. Finally, Monsignore Eugenio Pacelli, was the Vatican's papal envoy in Germany, based for much of his time in Munich, and who was to become Pope Pius XII in 1939.

It is possible that all these senior Catholics, joined by Eva and Erich, met at the Eucharist Congress in Rome in May in 1922 and which Princess Maria recorded as 'an important contribution to the cause of international goodwill'.[8] And, surely, Pacelli would have arranged, and been present at, a personal meeting between the Princess, his friend from Munich, and his pope. As she noted in her diary,

> *Pope Pius XI gave us a private audience. Again after many years I passed through those halls that I had crossed first as a child, and then as a young mother. Much has changed in the world, but the principles for which the Vatican stands remain eternal. In the same room where I had met Pius IX, I now met Pius XI ... For the first time in my life I spoke German to a pope. That gave me special pleasure.*

There is a note on Erich's Foreign Office file for April 1924 which suggests that Erich's new career in Berlin was not without question marks. 'It is advisable to transfer Gerth later as his first foreign post not to a diplomatic mission, but a busy general consulate, like St Petersburg or Poznań, and only to send him to an embassy after he has proven himself at a general consulate.'[9]

It is worth recalling that Erich was from a staunch Lutheran family and Eva's first marriage was as a Jew, the religion of her father. Eva converted to Catholicism in 1918 and Erich followed, possibly, in 1919, but certainly by 1922. Erich's early career in the Foreign Office, especially during holidays to Rome and his postings to Copenhagen and Paris, saw him identify with leading Catholics and the Catholic faith. Eva spent the winters in Rome if she could and Erich visited her there, at least in 1921 and again in 1924, when he needed to ask for leave to do so.

During this latter visit, Erich and Eva, seriously displeased the Ambassador, Konstantin Hermann Karl Freiherr von Neurath. Neurath took up his ambassadorship early in 1922 and found a 'totally disorganised embassy, a staff of well-paid but incompetent agents, and an Augean stable of legal cases concerning confiscated German property including even the old embassy building'.[10] In his personal relationships, Neurath adhered to a strict moral code, believing that decency and honesty were necessary forms for daily life. His favourite poem, which he often quoted and which was read at his funeral, 'caught this sense of a private man struggling to endure the stresses of a public world':

> *Think and be quiet*
> *Feel more than you show*
> *Bow down before God*
> *And you stay your own master.*

Neurath was a well trained diplomat with insights into world problems, formidable linguistic skills, and determined political and economic views. 'Above all, he mastered two difficult virtues: he could mask his feelings and private opinions from even the most astute observer, and he could remain calm in the most distressing circumstances.' He despised artificial solutions, which he claimed were concocted by intellectual scheming and marred by emotional involvement. Politicians and intellectuals, he implied, could enjoy such parties; a civil servant, especially in the foreign service, had to live by another code: recognition that personal desires and fantasies must be submerged in serving the nation's broader realities. Neurath 'did not like society and he despised politics'. On more than one occasion, he complained that the most difficult part of his life was the social whirl accompanying international diplomacy. All of these skills combined to help him develop a personal relationship with the preening Benito Mussolini which lasted for years and was of great benefit to Germany's foreign relations.

Neurath wrote in 1924 to the headquarters of the Foreign Office at Wilhelmstraße:[11]

For several months, a Herr Gerth, Attaché in the Foreign Office, has been staying here with his wife. The couple, the female part of which dresses and acts quite flamboyantly, almost exclusively keeps company with Vatican circles. It has been reported repeatedly to me by Germans that among themselves, even if they are together with Germans, they use the French language, although Herr Gerth as far as I know, was formerly a German naval officer and Frau Gerth is a daughter of the well-known Consul Marx in Berlin. The bad taste of this conduct, for which, by the way, the Romans have a very fine sense, seems to me topped by the fact that a few days ago Herr Gerth submitted the attached business card to me. I leave it to you to form your own opinion about this hopeful young colleague in the Foreign Service but considered it my duty to inform you about the Roman activities of the 'Attaché'. The card had the French text: 'E Gerth, Attaché au Ministère des Affaires Etrangères, Berlin'.

The French affectation, the access to money well above the salary of a junior diplomat, the winning ways within the Vatican, and the career precociousness did not sit well with the Neurath style. There is nothing in Neurath's character that suggests that he harboured long-term dislike, according to his biographer Heinemann, but Neurath thought Erich needed disciplining and to be taken down a peg. No 'Neurath effect' was immediately apparent, but his reappearance in Erich Gerth's story in 1933 did have serious impact.

Gerth was meant to report to the Embassy in Bucharest in March 1925 because of a 'terribly complicated personnel situation' and to prepare the Romanian White Book.[12] This, however, did not happen due to Gerth's ailing wife. Then, Erich went sick with a streptococcal infection and left with Eva for two weeks at the Pensione Lucchesi in Florence to recover. On 1 August 1925, Erich Gerth started his service at the embassy in Copenhagen and on 22 May 1926 was promoted to Legation Secretary. There is a testimonial of his work in Copenhagen.[13]

His personality is extraordinarily amiable and pleasing, demonstrating in his social interaction and in his relationships with the German colony as well as the local authorities, his gift to act as a balancing force and avoid conflict. He is also truly kind hearted. This is illustrated in particular in his relationship to the small Catholic-German community in Copenhagen. Before their departure the couple undertook with great skill and success to socially unite the younger members of the diplomatic corps at their house.

Erich held a minor position, dealing with consular matters, but it was noted that his potential was higher. His language skills in English and

French were described as just 'satisfactory'; he preferred Spanish. The testimonial continues: 'Once his wife's health has been restored, I would like to recommend for Gerth and his wife for reasons of the physical and moral climate, the Catholic South [of Europe] as employment area.' Somebody placed a question mark under the wording 'moral climate'. A Foreign Office source thought this last sentence 'very unusual'. While it is common to finish a performance testimonial with a recommendation for the next post, the 'repeated highlighting of the Catholic theme is a hidden comment that this young diplomat was one-sided and preferred to follow his specific personal interests'.

Eva's health did not improve and she stayed for long periods at the spa resort of Arosa, Switzerland. Erich tried to get a post in Geneva to be near her. At his urgent request, he was moved from 24 September 1926 to become Vice Consul in Genoa. On 3 July 1928, Gerth was transferred to the Paris Embassy. Erich Gerth's surviving personnel files in the Foreign Office concentrate on three topics: health issues, continuing contacts with the upper echelon of Catholic society, and promotion, or perhaps more accurately, the need for more income which is surprising given Eva's father's fortune which allowed her, for instance, to convalesce in Switzerland and Italy.

Gerth was proud of his health. He told the Foreign Office that he was 'completely healthy and fit to serve in the tropics. I have been examined several times for this and always found to be fit.'[14] This was called into question the following year when a doctor diagnosed a 'raised diaphragm and several nervous phenomena'. This caused the Foreign Office concern when seen together with his wife's frailty, and they insisted on medical confirmation, which was received, that he was ready for service. In September 1929, a doctor in Nassau in the Rhineland wrote that Gerth was suffering from a 'neurosis of the sympathetic nerve as a reaction to untreated inner secretoric [sic] exhaustion symptoms'. The heart had moved upwards, pushing the diaphragm, and 'leading to an unstable circulation and disturbances in the digestive organs'. The doctor felt that the condition was temporary, could be cured, and urged that treatment should not be interrupted. This last plea smacks a little of Erich fearing for his employment. He had an operation on his tonsils in Berlin and returned to his post in Paris in November 1929. When visiting Berlin, the couple always stayed with Salomon Marx at Brückenallee.

Erich was not lacking for 'career' friends in high places. Twice-chancellor Wilhelm Marx wrote from the Reichstag on 15 April 1930 to Foreign Minister Julius Curtius, saying that he had already spoken to State Secretary Baron Ago von Maltzan about Erich 'and found full comprehension' for the desire to either promote him or to adjust his service age to better recognise his military service. This was so that he would earn more. Curtius replied on 28 April 1930 regretting that all the posts in Paris that carried a promotion were taken, but that a recheck of Erich's service age level had been ordered. A further letter explained that Erich had already been treated in a privileged way and that no more could be done. Erich wrote asking 'not for a financial privilege *vis-à-vis* his fellows', but because at age 44, he would 'never be able to finance his family'. In August the following year, 1931, Salomon Marx, writing from his Handelsbank in Berlin, was on the financial case, this time emphasising to Dr Köpke at the ministry Erich's roles as u-boat officer and as a Catholic intermediary.[15] 'In the conversation which you kindly granted me yesterday, I also took the liberty to bring up the issue of my son-in-law's career. You kindly told me that the ambassador, Herr von Hoesch, would give him a good qualification and that my son-in-law was of great value in Paris, especially as a connection officer between the embassy and the high clergy and further Catholic-interest circles.' Marx asked that Erich be kept in Paris and promoted, citing Erich's 'long years in which he successfully served as a submarine commander'. As Köpke then left on holiday, his deputy, Ernest Freiherr von Grünau, Head of Personnel, dealt with the request, but turned it down initially with some sympathy. 'I am fully aware of the fact that the impossibility to grant you a financially better position by taking into account your many years of service as an officer comprises a certain severity.'

It may be that the determination of Erich and his father-in-law to increase Erich's earnings was because, unexpectedly, Eva was carrying a child. Son Marco was born on 10 January 1932 and, later that year, pressure told when Erich was promoted to First Secretary of the Paris legation.[16] Daughter Marie-Diana was born early next year. Eva went on to have four children while she was between thirty-seven and forty-two years, remarkable given that there were no children in the first thirteen years of marriage. Perhaps her earlier frailties, had been related to difficult pregnancies. Erich wrote to Grünau expressing his 'deep gratitude'.[17] Grünau, incidentally, an ex-member of the Kaiser's personal staff, had fought strongly against the introduction in 1917 of unrestricted submarine warfare.[18]

There is a confidential letter of 12 June 1931 with an obscured sender, possibly 'Brümmermann', from the address of the Foreign Office at Wilhelmstraße, and no addressee, except for the salutation *Lieber Freund, persönlich und vertraulich*, 'Dear friend, personal and confidential'. The letter says,

> *Frau Gräfin Dolly de Castellane, widowed Princess Fürstenberg, the wife of the current 'President' of the city of Paris, whose great social influence in Paris is known to you, gave me at my last journey through Paris the attached card and asked me to tell the German Chancellor, Dr Heinrich Brüning* [a devout Roman Catholic] *that Botschaftssekretär, 'Embassy Secretary', Gerth had undertaken to form close links with all organised Catholic powers in France. This relationship was in her*

opinion extraordinarily important not only for the work in Paris itself,
but also for the whole nature of German-French relations. De Castellane
therefore demands that Gerth should not be removed from Paris.[19]

Dorothée, 'Dolly', de Talleyrand-Périgord, daughter of Napoléon-Louis de
Talleyrand-Périgord, Duke of Talleyrand, Valençay and Sagan, and Pauline
de Castellane, was a great *salonière* and society lady. She married Jean
de Castellane after the death of her first husband, Prince Karl Egon IV of
Fürstenberg. At the beginning of the twentieth century, the Fürstenbergs,
were leaders and role models for the aristocratic *jeunesse d'orée*, 'gilded
youth', and presided over the group in a luxurious foreign lifestyle at their
Berlin mansion at Wilhelmstraße 23.[20] Kaiser Wilhelm I often dropped in
unexpectedly for tea. After her second marriage, Dolly was a rival in high
society circles in Paris to her cousin and aunt, Marie Radziwill: Radziwill
represented the *grandes dames* of the eighteenth and nineteenth centuries;
Dolly was the more Bohemian salon lady of the early twentieth century
as portrayed by Marcel Proust and fulfilling Balzac's ideal of the modern
elegant and correct woman, the *femme comme il faut*.[21] 'Their family went
to great lengths to avoid a meeting of these two powerful women at the
family's summer palace Rochecotte.'

Dolly was less exclusive in her choice of guests invited to her salon –
she embraced zeitgeist changes and received actresses and artists, and
by doing so established a link between the aristocracy and the demi-
monde.[22]

Dolly was described as a *valkyrie* with majestic beauty, looking as if she
had just returned from a visit at *Wotan*'s; other contemporaries saw her
as 'clever, a typical *grande dame*, but natural, free of any affectation.[23] Not
conventionally beautiful, her lively eyes and full red lips gave her an air
of joy of life.'[24] Her portrait was painted by Philip Alexius de László. Dolly
was fluent in German and French, the latter was spoken the world over in
'sophisticated circles' and this may have encouraged Erich and Eva Gerth's
performance in Rome that so upset Ambassador Neurath.

Dolly's proficiency in German meant that when she lived in France she
was able to act as an intermediary between both countries and cultures.
She became one of the most influential figures of her time: her city
palace was a meeting place for politicians, diplomats, scholars and artists
as well as high-ranking foreign visitors including good personal contacts
with Kaiser Wilhelm II whom, until the beginning of the war, she always
met during her annual visit to Berlin.[25] After the war, Dolly's 'overriding
political endeavour was to achieve a rapprochement between Germany
and France', which explains her determination to keep Erich and Eva
in Paris. Radziwill's biographer, Erbe, gives no information about Dolly's

Catholicism, but does describe Marie Radziwill's holy communions in 1851 and 1854 and a visit to Rome to attend the ceremonies, also in 1854, for the 'Proclamation of the Dogma of Mary's Immaculate Conception' by Pope Pius IX.[26] One can only assume the same level of devotion from her cousin. If so, Dolly de Castellane may well have joined Erich Gerth, Pacelli, Princess Maria and the rest at the Eucharist Congress in Rome in 1922.

Where in all this high society hobnobbing, with its swirl of parties and crystal glass chatter, is the thread? Were Erich and Eva just the consummate Catholic hosts and guests? Assessments of the Gerth brothers suggest this could be so. Georg, the serious ex-sailor and thinker, a preferred recluse, was chalk and cheese to Erich, the extrovert party goer.[27] And, yet, any consideration of Erich's career, withstanding the rigours of the naval cadet programme, the intricacies and danger of South American spying, the determination to see action in a u-boat, the selection by Trotha as one of his 'chosen men', the continued close association with Salomon Marx and Wilhelm Canaris, suggest another side to Erich comprising commitment and determination. Was there more behind Dolly de Castellane's sponsorship of a couple who she thought useful to her political purpose?

Family evidence comes down firmly on the side of Erich as a consummate peacemaker.[28] Erich came to the embassy in Paris in 1928 against the background of the 1925 Locarno Treaties of Reconciliation for which Aristide Briand and Gustav Stresemann, the respective Foreign Ministers of France and Germany, received the Nobel Peace Prize in 1926. This was the same Stresemann who made marked Erich's diplomatic essays in 1922.

> *Henceforth the spirit of Locarno would reign, substituting conciliation for enforcement as the basis for peace. Yet for some peace remained a desperate hope rather than an actuality. A few men knew that the spirit of Locarno was a fragile foundation on which to build a lasting peace.*[29]

Erich's son, Roger, explains that, against the background of Locarno, Erich 'viewed the mutual hostility and distrust between the two countries [as] the result of a rupture of Christian unity, fundamentally a spiritual problem requiring a spiritual approach to a solution'. After cultivating the key Catholic influencers in Paris and Germany, Erich organised a series of peace and reconciliation masses at Notre Dame des Victoires, the designated Catholic church for diplomats in Paris. At one of these masses in 1931, the German side was represented by Christian Democrat Chancellor Heinrich Brüning [mentioned by Dolly de Castellane] and on the French side by Auguste Champetier de Ribes, a jurist and junior minister in several governments, and later a French prosecutor at the Nuremberg Trials.

> *As a government delegate assisting Chancellor Brüning and convinced of the necessity for a Franco-German reconciliation, [Gerth] attended a*

mass for peace held on 19 July 1931 at Notre-Dame des Victoires church. Contacts were established between French and German democrats, but they were interrupted by the advent of Hitler [who] wrecked all hope of reconciliation. In the face of the insatiable demands of the new Chancellor of the Reich, Brüning advocated a policy of firmness, the only way, according to him, of safeguarding peace. He was appalled at the concessions granted to Germany at Munich which, six months later, resulted in the occupation of Czechoslovakia.[30]

This was the calibre of the people attracted to Erich's reconciliation work. Erich also used the figure of St Albert the Great, a leading philosopher and theologian of the thirteenth century, as a bridging figure between Germany and France.[31] *... It was at a great feast in 1933 for Albert the Great in a large public venue which Eva recalled often and described as looking like it had snowed because, in addition to many others, there was a large number of Dominican [nuns] attending in their white habits. It was celebrated as an important event of reconciliation.*[32]

Erich's very public espousal of the Catholic interest in the cause of reconciliation while in Copenhagen and Paris was a most risky undertaking for a young delegate in the foreign service of his country. The trail of distrust that clung to Catholic relations with the German and French states remained 'poisonous' well beyond Gerth's time as a junior diplomat.[33] Open embracing of the German Catholic community in Paris to aid post-war reconciliation was a dangerous strategy for Erich's political career. Support given to his initiatives by well-placed Catholic friends would be seen as a mixed blessing among his Prussian superiors at Wilhelmstraße.

There are some scattered places to look for further answers, in the turbulent recent history of the Vatican's relationships with France and Germany, and in the papers and biographies of Erich's referee, Eugenio Pacelli. Pacelli was not yet an anointed successor to Pope Pius XI, but he was recognised as a 'coming man' with his enormous self-confidence and evident intellect.[34]

The bitter struggle in the 1870s on the part of Bismarck to subject the Catholic church to state controls led to the term *Kulturkampf*, 'culture struggle'. Bismarck was looking for a common enemy to which he could divert dissatisfaction with the newly-created German reunification. He lighted on the concern that Catholics could not be fully loyal to Germany if their affairs were also ruled by the Vatican. Catholics could never be 'good' Germans. At the time of reunification the new German Empire included over twenty-five million Protestants, 62 per cent, and fifteen million Catholics, 36 per cent; these latter populations were geographically concentrated, particularly in the Polish east and in the Bavarian south. Education was separate, usually in the hands of the churches. There was little mutual tolerance or intermarriage. The ideological struggle was sparked by three promulgations from Rome: in 1854, the proclamation of Mary's immaculate conception; in 1864, an encyclical which condemned as false eighty philosophical and political statements, many of which countered the arguments for the foundation of the nation state, and forbade a large number of books; and, in 1870, the dogma of papal infallibility.[35] If the pope was always right, where did Germany stand? 'As far as the [German] liberal elites were concerned, Catholics were subjects of the Pope ... a foreign power within the state.'[36] Bismarck responded from 1871 with twenty-two laws, starting with threatening two years in prison for any clergyman who addressed political matters from the pulpit, the *Kanzelparagraf*. The next year, 'hated' Jesuits were expelled across the empire, not returning until 1917; all religious schools were to have government inspections; all religious teachers were moved from government schools; and, in December, diplomatic relations with the Vatican ended. In a move, which had repercussions for Erich Gerth, Catholics were banned from representing Germany abroad. 'Bismarck sought to lame Catholicism as a political force'.[37]

'The hatred of the Catholics can only be called fanatical', but the extent of the Catholic backlash took Bismarck by surprise.[38] Increasingly severe tit-for-tat measures followed between all parties including government attempts to control the appointment of bishops, marriage being deemed a civil ceremony, the banning of religious orders, confiscation of church property and the arrest of over 200 priests and 130 newspaper editors. 'With each new piece of legislation and every new outrage and arrest, the levels of Catholic anger grew, but Catholics did not riot in the streets or plot violent revolution.'[39] However, there was an assassination attempt on Bismarck in 1874. The year before, Pope Pius IX issued an encyclical,

No wonder, then, that the former religious tranquillity has been gravely disturbed in that Empire by this kind of law and other plans and actions of the Prussian government most hostile to the Church. But who would wish to falsely cast blame of the disturbance on the Catholics of the German Empire![40]

Over seven years, Bismarck's failing strategy brought considerable and lasting damage to relations between Rome and Berlin and within the German people. Bismarck capitulated to overtures from a new pope, Leo XIII, and most of the laws were rescinded by 1887, but the *Kanzelparagraf* lasted until 1953. In the elections on 1873, the Catholic Centre Party, founded to defend the position of the church in the new empire, doubled its membership in the Landtag and the next year secured ninety-one members in the Reichstag. Bismarck turned his attention to the socialists and this eventually brought his downfall.[41]

Similar determination for state control over church occurred in many European countries at this time, principally Italy, France and Spain. During Pacelli's career, Church-State affairs in France saw 'rampant anti-clericalism'.[42] The French government was antagonistic towards the Catholic hierarchy and clergy because of their perceived royalist tendencies. The government forbade religious orders from teaching and boasted that 13,904 Catholic schools had been closed. 'Elected at the height of the French anti-clerical persecution', Pius X had made it clear that he wanted no 'appeasement of the French republic' which responded by cutting off diplomatic relations with the Vatican, then passed an act separating Church and State in France.

Pacelli was despatched to Bavaria in 1917 as nuncio and appointed as a 'political' archbishop of Sardi, entrusted with the 'delicate and difficult task of gaining German support for the papal peace effort. The new pope, Benedict felt 'tormented by the spectacle of Christians waging war against Christians, Catholics against Catholics'. On election, Benedict published a protest to the world condemning the 'horrible butchery'.[43] Pacelli was upset by the ever-changing German attitude on peace, lamenting that 'when things went well militarily ... the Germans abandoned themselves to the most lunatic of illusions'.[44]

> *Pacelli set off in remarkable style from Rome for Munich. Not only had Pacelli commandeered his own private compartment, but an additional sealed carriage had been added to the train to transport sixty cases of groceries to ensure that his troublesome stomach would not be affected by the food of wartime Germany.*[45]

Pacelli was seen as a 'surprising, indeed extraordinary appointment'.[46] His previous international experience was limited and often unsuccessful: ceremonial rather than substantive visits to London in 1905, a criticised concordat with Serbia in 1914, and a brief visit to Vienna the following year. Yet, he was a renowned Germanophile, applauded for tireless work to ameliorate the condition of Allied and German prisoners-of-war, sympathetic to German interests and fitted easily as the epicentre of Bavarian Catholic society. In June 1920, Pacelli was accredited as apostolic nuncio to the Weimar Republic.

> *Soon after becoming Pope [in 1939], Pacelli told a group of pilgrims from Germany: 'We have always loved Germany where We were able to spend many years of Our life, and We love Germany even more today. We rejoice in Germany's greatness, rise, and well-being, and it would be false to assert that We do not desire a flourishing, great, and strong Germany.' German foreign minister von Ribbentrop, following a meeting, said: The Pope has always his heart in Germany and a*

great and lasting desire to reach a firm and lasting understanding with Hitler.'[47]

What were the public and private Catholic objectives of the time? Pacelli branded the Versailles Treaty an 'international absurdity', deplored the Spartakists, Liebknecht and Luxemburg, and was delighted with the fall of the 'Bolshevik' government in Bavaria with its Jewish leaders. He also declined to reprove the French for its invasion of the Ruhr on the grounds that it was not his place and, on the grounds of impartiality, the Vatican had not criticised the German invasion of Belgium.[48] Parallel with the schemes for the French takeover of the Ruhr Valley ran the French encouragement of Bavarian separatism, with the idea of forming a great German Catholic block against Prussia, to include perhaps Austria.[49] In pursuit of this aim, 'France was at one time even prepared to contemplate the Wittelsbach Monarchy being restored' of which Prince Ludwig Ferdinand von Bayern and Princess Maria de la Paz de Bourbon would have been close beneficiaries.

From the Vatican's point of view, the state of Bavaria with its large Catholic population and historic links with the Church of Rome, was an 'obvious starting point for the first state concordat'.[50] Between 1920 and March 1924, Pacelli concluded delicate negotiations with Bavaria which granted the Vatican broad power over the educational system and ensured the continuation of religious instruction in schools and universities.[51] It was passed by the Bavarian parliament by seventy-three votes to fifty-two.

With the move to Lutheran Berlin in 1925, Pacelli had a less favourable climate in which to negotiate. He was given three major papal tasks. Two were public: to negotiate concordats with Prussia and with the central German government seeking religious liberty, but also concessions on Catholic control on education. A third was secret: to resolve differences between the Soviet Union and the Vatican through the Soviet ambassador in Berlin. Pacelli found that the lay Catholic political leadership of Germany saw the nation's new situation as a striking opportunity. 'Having shown unquestioning loyalty through the war, German Catholics trusted that their days of inferiority, their days of having been regarded as Reichsfeinde, 'enemies of the Fatherland', had at last ended.'[52] Pacelli settled into a splendid residence in the Tiergarten quarter. 'Tall, elegant, in his purple silk cloak, he became a familiar figure in the capital, arriving in his limousine at the Reich and Prussian ministries, or sweeping into receptions at embassies.'[53] He threw parties for the diplomatic and official elite; Paul von Hindenburg, Foreign Minister Gustav Stresemann and other cabinet members were regulars. This is not where Erich Gerth made first acquaintance as Pacelli had already agreed three years before to become a referee. Canaris was, of course, never far away and knew Pacelli well when he was nuncio in Berlin.[54] In 1939, Joseph Muller, a Catholic lawyer, was sent after discussions with Canaris to the Vatican to re-establish connections with Pacelli, now Pope Pius XII. The object was to use the Vatican to make contact with the British Government to obtain their support for a coup attempt against Hitler and Himmler. On 12 January 1940, Pacelli spoke on the matter with the British Envoy Extraordinary and Minister Plenipotentiary to the Vatican, Sir Francis d'Arcy Godolphin Osborne, and again on 7 February, and received an assurance from the British Government transmitted by Pacelli to Berlin in which 'the will for a just peace' was guaranteed provided that Hitler was toppled.[55]

When word reached Berlin of the success, and the German embassy involvement through Erich Gerth, in the Mass of Reconciliation in Paris in 1933, Erich was recalled and 'told in no uncertain terms that reconciliation was considered defeatist thinking and, further, that henceforth the Bismarck attitude that no Catholic should ever represent Germany abroad was now re-instated'.[56] The final threat hurled at him was, 'By the time we get through with you, you will be lucky if you can sell newspapers on the corner.'

And then the wider world fell in – for Erich Gerth, for Salomon Marx and his family, for German Jews, and for the nation. Gerth was recalled from Paris to Berlin on 12 May 1933, but was briefly delayed because of work. On 30 September, he was placed in temporary retirement. 'For official reasons the dismissal of the legation secretary at the embassy in Paris, Erich Gerth, is urgently required. As there is currently no other position available his transfer into provisional retirement could not be avoided.' The certificate was prepared by Grünau, recent supporter from Personnel, signed personally by President Paul von Hindenburg and countersigned by the latest Foreign Minister, Konstantin von Neurath, who Gerth managed to upset nine years before in Rome. On 19 March 1934, Gerth was placed without review into final retirement. This was a bevy of powerful men to move one First Secretary. Overnight, Gerth's salary fell from a base of 6,000 Reichsmarks plus a further 7,000 as a Paris allowance to a pension of 420.50.[57]

After banning all other political parties on 7 April 1933, two months after coming to power, the Nazis introduced the 'Civil Service Restoration Act' which claimed to re-establish a 'national' and 'professional' civil service. Racially or politically unwanted civil servants were to be fired or forced into retirement, Clause 3(1).[58] In the first instance, the 'unwanted' were either members of the Communist party or were those who had just one Jewish grandparent, whatever their current religion. The stricture applied to anyone in government employ or needing a government licence to work: teachers, professors, judges, diplomats, lawyers, doctors, tax consultants, musicians and notaries. Hindenburg objected to the bill until three classes of civil servants were excluded: veterans who had served at the front, those who had been in the civil service since August 1914, and those who had lost a father or son in combat, Clause 3(2). Under Clause 6, civil servants could be forced into retirement without cause and this was Gerth's fate. When Hindenburg died in 1934, his exclusions were swept away. It was the first time since German Jews had been emancipated in 1871 that an anti-Semitic law had been passed in Germany. Albert Einstein resigned from the Prussian Academy of Sciences and emigrated to the United States before he could be expelled.[59] Erich's fellow u-boat commander from Pola, Martin Niemöller, now a pastor, spoke against Jews, but protected them in his church. In 1933, he co-founded the *Pfarrernotbund*, 'Emergency Covenant of Pastors', to combat the discrimination against Christians of Jewish background and particularly the discriminatory 'Aryan Paragraph' anchored in the 'Law for the Restoration of the Professional Civil Service'.[60]

Until the revelations about Erich Gerth's Catholic activities, disclosed in this book, the reason for the action against him was seemingly evident. Eva Gerth, though thoroughly Catholic, was half-Jewish by birth and her father, Salomon, was already under attack by the Nazis perhaps because he was Jewish, perhaps because he was cheek by jowl with Hugenberg, but also perhaps because the film company Ufa was coveted? No mention of any 'reason' was ever included in Gerth's file. Erich was to suffer by association. A simple route would be to use the Civil Service Act to force Erich and Eva back to Germany. The act's provisions were broad and could not be appealed. Gerth was not Jewish and had fought on the front line. A note in the files dated 8 September 1933 states that 'Gerth was a combatant according to the attached war service certificate by the Command of the Navy Station, Baltic Sea. He took part in the operations of the submarine flotilla in the Mediterranean, based in Pola and Cattaro'.[61] The certificate itself was returned to Gerth so that this defence was not available to those at the Foreign Office.

Was Neurath taking some sort of delayed retribution? It looks doubtful as a primary reason as he was as much caught up in events as Gerth. After his term at the Foreign Office, Neurath frustrated Hitler once too often and was sent away as Protector of Bohemia and Moravia when the area was taken over in 1939. Here, Neurath had, hopelessly, to deal with his deputy, Reinhard Heydrich, joint main architect of the holocaust and known as the 'Butcher of Prague'. Neurath ended his life as a 'war criminal', convicted after the second world war at Nuremberg as foreign minister of leading his country and his people into 'wars of aggression and crimes against humanity'. It was a prosecution, says his biographer, in which 'had he been given access to his documents, a defence lawyer who understood the court proceedings, and a court seeking historical truth rather than legal technicalities, he would have been acquitted'.[62]

Neurath, a virtuous and decent gentleman, had allowed his talents and capabilities to serve forces which he only imperfectly understood and frequently rejected personally. Perhaps in another time, good intentions

and private virtues would have sufficed. In Hitler's Germany they
proved disastrous to a baron born for another century. Neurath's story
is one of a man trying to tame a whirlwind. His fate reflects that of a
generation of well-meaning Germans and speaks to one of the great
questions of modern history: how could decent and honourable men
serve the evil that was National Socialism?[63]

Once you start these things, blind policies, there are often unintended consequences. Tirpitz's wife, Marie Lipke, was a baptised Protestant, born in West Prussia in 1860. Her father, Gustav Lipke, was born in 1820 in Berlin to a wealthy assimilated Jewish banking and business family and who, at eighteen, converted to Protestantism.[64] He was a lawyer who served in the Prussian Diet and in the Imperial Reichstag. Tirpitz, as with Erich Gerth, was married to a Jewess. Tirpitz's salary on retirement was 45,000 Reichsmarks, plus another 15,000 for office expenses. At his death in 1930, his pension was half his salary. Had Tirpitz lived until 1933 and the introduction of the Civil Service Restoration Act, he might have seen his pension cut to just 10 per cent, 4,500 Reichsmarks.[65]

There is now another, compelling, option for the termination of Erich Gerth's diplomatic career. His determined cultivation of the most senior Catholics in Paris and his attempts at Franco-German reconciliation was of serious concern to the Nazi direction of travel. The Catholic Centre Party was a prominent voice in the Weimar Republic, holding the chancellorship eight times, including under Wilhelm Marx, Eva Marx's relation. However, in the face of Nazi hostility, even this party dissolved itself in 1933 before Hitler could disband it. 'The clash of *Kulturkampf* in the German Empire laid the groundwork for the repression of Catholics in Germany and Europe under Adolf Hitler.'[66] It was the Nazi view, as with Bismarck, that to be a good German meant being a good Protestant. Protestant Christianity was positioned within the concept of Nazi anti-Semitism by removing the Old Testament and presenting Jesus as the original anti-Semite.

National Socialism was antithetical to Catholicism. Nazi leaders and
members who had come from a Catholic background were apostates
and often bitterly opposed to Catholicism. By the time that the Nazis
were in power, it was clear to them that institutional Catholicism was
opposed to National Socialism and that being a loyal Catholic meant
being loyal to a power that was not German.[67]

In power, the Nazis were intent on destroying Catholic influence in Germany. A rapprochement with the French was the opposite of official policy; the long-term plan was the continuation of the first world war. Erich Gerth in Paris could not be more out of step with his new masters if he had tried.

On 8 April 1934, Gerth wrote a painful letter from Villa Patroncinio, Malaga, in Spain, to Grünau. 'For health reasons I am unable to travel ... I can't believe otherwise than the approach of the Foreign Office against me is based on insufficient information and erroneous considerations. It only remains for me to hope that one day this will turn out right and that an opportunity will be found to make up for the injustice committed to me and my family.'

A stream of further pleadings flowed from Gerth. 'My financial situation has deteriorated significantly during the night' ... 'news of my transfer to permanent retirement throws me completely off track and brings my family into the trouble which hit me at Easter' ... 'Heaven knows how I will get my feet back on solid ground'.[68] 'Difficulties of looking for a new livelihood as my health is very shaken by recent events and I can do little for the time being'... 'Whether we will come back after my recovery to Paris or somewhere else to take our place of residence, I don't know today ... in particular, where may I manage to find a new livelihood ... will my foreign pension be paid in time ... I'm dependent entirely on my pension which is only 300 Reichsmarks per month'.

Erich did regain his health and strength brought about by Spanish sun and by Eva cooking a vegetarian diet with fresh vegetables and fruits. Local orange growers advised that the diet should include the white pulp from inside the orange peels which contained many valuable nutrients, usually overlooked. On the couple's return to Germany in 1935, people who knew Erich before and after Spain said that he looked ten years younger.

This was also the year when the Nazis moved to finish with Salomon Marx and others in his family.[69] Marx was classed a *Volljude*, a full blooded Jew, as both his parents were Jewish and, therefore, his private bank was classified as a Jewish business. His share in Haus Vaterland was lost during an aggressive takeover by a company called Kempinski. The Nazis made him sell his shares in Ufa after the downfall of Alfred Hugenberg. In 1935, Salomon Marx's last positions on supervisory boards, once forty, were reduced from thirteen to four, causing a considerable reduction in his income. Marx tried to keep ownership of his Internationale Handelsbank, but he was forced into liquidation with a loss of several hundred thousand Reichsmarks. Salomon then had to sell all his real estate.

After the decree of the Nuremberg Laws, Salomon lost his right of citizenship of the German Reich.[70] He suffered constant harassment of his business, the arrest and imprisonment of his banking partner Alexander Elfer [who later escaped to New York], *termination of credits and loss of his honorary and supervisory positions. His home was regarded as a Jewish home and this meant that no domestic servants were allowed to be kept. His estimated income fell steadily: 1930, 80,000 Reichsmarks; 1931: 50,000; 1932, 40,000.[71]*

George Martos confirmed that he knew Salomon Marx well, both socially and as his doctor from 1925 until his death in 1936. Marx underwent a 'psychological and physical change' as a consequence of his loss of professional and social status.[72] Martos said Marx had an active mind, was full of vitality and energy, and enjoyed the highest respect in industry, art and literature. In 1933, when he first lost his honorary positions and later had to surrender the management of the bank 'for reasons of political persecution', he completely changed and due to an increasing paranoia suffered from bouts of *angina pectoris* which became increasingly frequent and severe. 'It is unquestionable that the persecution caused his early demise.'

Marx's son, Eduard, who as a doctor treated his father for the last five years of his life, confirmed the diagnosis.[73] Eduard claimed that Marx's angina was cured completely in the spa resort of Bad Nassau and he was fully able to work until 1931. He undertook a 4,500 kilometre car journey throughout Western Europe without any problems or medical issues. The first severe relapses occurred at the beginning of 1933. 'My father was worried about the increasing strength of the national socialists. As a leading businessman, he was also aware of the consequences that a seizure of power by the Nazis would have for him. My father was deeply affected by the deprivation of rights as a result of the Nuremberg Laws which he saw as a terrible injustice.' From 1935, Salomon Marx's health deteriorated rapidly, each act of harassment by the Nazis triggered new attacks and bouts of depression.

> *The loss of his supervisory positions in leading companies such as Ufa, Lindström and Engelhardt not only damaged him economically, but had a detrimental effect on his existing angina pectoris which up to then had caused him little discomfort. The feeling of suddenly being dubbed an undesirable and inferior human being by a government that acted unlawfully, the prohibition to keep domestic servants, to work in an executive position and all further restrictions and humiliations accelerated the course of his existing illness.*

Salomon's wife, Charlotte, described how the loss of economic and social status, financial worries and growing isolation led to his heart attacks and depression. In his last days, Salomon rarely left his flat. He died on 24 October 1936 of heart failure.[74] Charlotte received one quarter of his much reduced inheritance and his two children from his first marriage, Eduard Marx and Eva Gerth, three-eights each.

Could there be another reason for this early attack by the Nazis on a prominent and wealthy businessman who happened to be a Jew? Was Marx to be impoverished because of his importance to Hugenberg who had dared to try to manipulate Hitler?[75] Hugenberg might be allowed the façade of freedom, but his ability to respond to Nazi aggression had to be eliminated and Marx was a part of his potential toolbox. Action against Hugenberg and Marx would also deliver the Ufa film studios, a most useful propaganda tool, into Goebbels's hands.

Nazi steps against Salomon Marx extended to his family. In 1933, his younger brother, Karl Marx, who fought in the trenches in the first world war, lost his positions as a government councillor and building officer in the construction industry because of his Jewish heritage. He 'fell in 1945 as a member of a Jewish labour squad defending the city of Breslau'. Salomon's oldest brother, Otto Marx of Una in Westphalia, died aged eighty-three in the Theresienstadt, now Terezín, walled ghetto, near Prague. The ghetto was used as a transit centre for western Jews on their way to Auschwitz and other extermination camps.[76] No date has been found for Otto's death, but it is probable that he died while Konstantin Neurath was Protector of Bohemia.

In May 1935, the Gerth family moved from Spain back to Germany, probably motivated by the approaching Spanish Civil War. They moved into Ahornallee 6 in Berlin; Eva gave birth to Isabella in August. Erich was hired on 15 June by Fritz Werner Maschinenfabrik in Marienfelde, a 3,000 employee engineering factory. Erich explained to the Foreign Office that he was a junior employee in the machinery section and earned a low salary of 400 Reichsmarks. Fritz Werner made machine tools, but in 1938 became a small armaments plant with a contract from the Portuguese government. With war the next year, Werner's produced arms for the German army using forced labour from a camp at the Daimler-Benz street corner in Berlin. The slaves were housed in underground cells under Daimler Street. Eva was, therefore, in Belin when her father died in October 1936.

At the same time as he took the position at the Werner company, Gerth applied for work to the Air District Command VI in Kiel. The Command asked for background to his forced retirement from the Foreign Office. The request and reply were classified secret. The Foreign Office said that Gerth had 'proven himself during his career in the foreign service as a diligent and reliable official', but nothing came of the opportunity in the air force. The real reason for his retirement was not mentioned. Three years later, the opportunity returned and, perhaps, Gerth reapplied. By this time, the Nazi party had the final say in matters to do with Gerth so the Foreign Ministry wrote to Rudolf Hess, Deputy Fuhrer to Hitler, on 23 June 1938. Hess's department simply confirmed that in 1935 a favourable assessment had been sent to the air district command.

In 1937, Eva was expecting a fourth child and, well aware of the actions against her family, used the excuse of attending the Paris Exposition so that the birth did not happen in Nazi Germany.[77] The couple stayed in a rented top floor corner apartment in the Eighth Arrondissement from which Eva could see the basilica of the Sacré-Coeur from one window and the Eiffel Tower from the other. Eva was visited by Gestapo attached to the embassy,

Erich's old place of work. Even though Erich was no longer employed, a watch was kept on those on the 'list'. At her bedside, Eva was asked why the wife of a former delegate had a Jewish doctor, Levi Solal, for the birth. Eva replied that Solal was the best obstetrician in Paris which the Gestapo duly noted and left. Roger, who was born prematurely, was baptized Roger Andre Marie Rüdiger, plus six other names as was the custom.

Gerth's health issues flared up again. That summer, doctors found far too late *ulcerous granuloma* at the roots of several teeth which were extracted three at a time. The last doctor's declaration of that year confirmed that Erich had *angina pectoris*, chronic gout and kidney disease. However, the Foreign Office official doctor turned down a recommendation to send their disgraced pensioner Gerth to a sanatorium in Switzerland. In January 1938, Erich wrote that he had suffered for 'quite some time' from angina, cramps of the coronary blood vessels, circulatory disturbance, gout and renal colic.

Both Salomon's sons, Eduard and Dr Eberhard Marx, who lived at Gritznerstrasse 45 in Steglitz in the south-west of Berlin, were considered a *Mischling*, a mongrel, with first-degree mixed-blood, having one Aryan parent.[78] Because of this, Eduard was unable to marry his chosen Ilse Geue, seven years his junior, also a *Mischling*. In 1937, they travelled quietly to Glasgow, in Scotland, to marry 'illegally', violating the Nuremberg laws.[79] An employee at the Glasgow registry office tipped off the London Press about this 'very unusual foreign marriage'.

> *Our names and photos were on the title page of the* Daily Express *with the comment that we had flouted Nazi laws by getting married. The mentioned newspaper was also sold in Berlin. Lack of money forced us to return to Berlin where we were in constant danger of being arrested. The Schwarze Corps, 'Black Corps', launched a spiteful personal attack against me.* Eduard stated that he never knew how he and Ilse managed to escape arrest.

In 1938, Erich Gerth received a message from his long-term friend, Canaris, that a so-called *Aktion M* was being prepared which aimed at the extermination of all mixed-race persons. The lives of Eduard Marx and his sister Eva Gerth and her four children were now in immediate danger. 'We were urgently advised by Canaris to obtain Aryan certificates in order to escape this action' and an introduction was made to a 'professional genealogist', previous-Kapitänleutnant Walter Firnhaber. While working for the Fritz Werner company, Erich Gerth met Firnhaber in the Gerths' flat in Berlin in the autumn to discuss research designed to establish the ancestry of the paternal family of Erich's wife.[80] At this stage, the provision of fake documents was not mentioned. About two weeks later, Firnhaber returned to the flat and confirmed that it would be difficult, unsurprisingly, to obtain suitable documents for the paternal line of Gerth's wife, Salomon

Marx's Jewish family. Matters turned illegal when Firnhaber explained that he would be able to provide a forged, faultless, pure Aryan ancestor pass for Gerth and his family. At the same time, Firnhaber explained that he would have to increase his fee from 300 to 3,000 Reichsmarks.

Firnhaber was no fly-by-night. Production of the officially certified *Ahnenpass*, the Nazi's genealogical passport, was a major business as people scrambled to secure protection from the extermination camps. 'The Ahnenpass spawned its own cottage industry', competing with the state-licensed kinship researcher, *Berufssippenforscher*.[81] There were many 'how-to' guides, smart, printed documents for personal completion with the 'proofs', research services and arranged official scrutiny and approvals. One company, RNK Papier- und Schreibwaren in Berlin produced a product called 'Firnhaber's Little Ahnenpass', named after its designer, Walter Firnhaber. This was a passport-sized document which unfolded into a full genealogical table that could be viewed all at once. RNK sent an example to Martin Bormann, convicted murderer and Hitler's private secretary, who sent back his personal approval. RNK used Bormann's endorsement in a four-page advertisement and, as a result, got into a serious spat with the civil registrars' publishing house who saw RNK as gaining unfair advantage over all competition. Eventually, Bormann ordered Firnhaber to 'stop the advertisement and to remove all such items from commerce'. 'The producers of these products designed to prove racial purity fought for market share' with steely determination. Firnhaber's business was much damaged and there was more than a hint that Canaris, now leader of the Abwehr, and Germany's pre-eminent spy service, saw a useful and discreet service provider for his operation and was happy to recommend Firnhaber to Gerth, an old friend in need.

The story is taken up in prosecution papers prepared for an eventual trial of Walter Firnhaber and Eduard Marx.[82] Erich Gerth considered 3,000 Reichsmarks too much and decided to talk to Marx. He asked Firnhaber to return in a few days. Eduard Marx agreed to buy an ancestor pass for himself and to contribute to the fee. In the next few days, Marx and Erich and Eva Gerth met Firnhaber at the Gerths' flat and he was asked for seven ancestor passports for the Gerths, their four children, and Marx, but, interestingly, not for his wife, Ilse. Firnhaber initially demanded a fee of 5,000 Reichsmarks which he dropped to 4,500 Reichsmarks after negotiation. Marx and his sister, Eva, went to the 79th Depositenkasse of the Dresdner Bank and withdrew their share of the money and gave it all to Firnhaber in the street without a receipt.

Firnhaber then set about forging baptism and marriage certificates for Eduard and Eva's grandparents, Eduard and Bertha, née Hecht, Marx, the parents of Salomon Marx. On 21 September 1938, Firnhaber went to the Catholic parish office in Schwerte, Salomon's birthplace, where he asked for the baptism and marriage documents of randomly selected persons in the church register. He had copies made of these entries, written out in ink, and signed and stamped by the local priest. The same day in his hotel room, he removed the personal details on the copies with 'ink killer' and replaced them later in Berlin with the names and dates of Eduard and Bertha Marx. Satisfied with these forgeries, Firnhaber destroyed them and returned to Schwerte, this time with his own blank copies of baptism and marriage forms. When the parish assistant left the room, Firnhaber stamped the blanks with the original church seal. He later entered all the personal details of Eduard and Bertha Marx and copied the signature of the priest, had the documents certified by a notary, and burned the background evidence. In December, Firnhaber met with Marx and the Gerths and handed over their seven ancestor passports with certified duplicate copies of six supporting documents.

Firnhaber advised that, if possible, it was better not to use the ancestor passports in Germany. Gerth did not use the passports, intending them for travel abroad or in case he or his family encountered difficulties in getting foreign visas or in securing education for his children, especially his son, Marco, in his planned career, surprisingly, as an officer. Eduard Marx, however, went to his medical association in Berlin, showed his documents, and declared that he could now prove he was of pure German blood and that all the previous statements that he was a first-degree *Mischling* were wrong. Only Aryan doctors were eligible to join the 'Union of German Doctors' and display their sign at the door of their surgery and this was Marx's goal.[83]

When Marx later registered his doctor's car, he submitted his forged documents again. During these repeated ancestry checks, some irregularity was spotted and the matter was referred to the *Rasse- und Siedlungshauptamt*, the SS office for Race and Settlement. Canaris intervened personally with the investigation, but advised Marx that matters could only be delayed until late 1943. However, Firnhaber was implicated. After long and persistent denial, Firnhaber made a comprehensive confession which led to legal charges in July 1942 at which he, Eduard Marx and Erich and Eva Gerth were all named and accused.

Fear of the German government had becomes serious by 1939 when Erich and Eva tried to flee Germany for South America. They travelled to Portugal to get a Clipper flight but, when they arrived, found that the last flying boat had left.[84] Imagine the desperation at the airport and the bitter sweet consequences. Erich and Eva returned to Berlin. At least, that is the story and it comes only from family memory.[85] The first question is why, flight missed, they did not stay in neutral Portugal? The answer, one expects, was a need to return to their children. Second, why during their trip to Portugal did Erich and Eva leave their four children in Berlin with Eduard Marx, Eva's brother, and two nannies?[86] This was surely not an abandonment of their loved children on the brink of war. From many perspectives, Eduard was in as much danger as Eva. The thought is that only one of them was travelling onwards. Erich or Eva always intended an immediate return to Germany to resume care of the children and to make plans to follow when the other was settled. The remaining question is, then, who would help with refuge and a new life in South America? The suggestion is that it was the von Ahlefeldts, the family of Eva's first husband, Graf Karl-Christian, who was killed in 1916. It may be remembered that Frau Gräfin Franziska von Ahlefeldt-Eschelsmark, Eva's ex-mother-in-law, was in 1922 prepared to support Erich's application to the Foreign Office showing that a close relationship continued. Also, Graf Friedrich Karl, leader of the only surviving branch of Karl-Christian's family, emigrated in 1890 from Denmark to the Argentine, and his descendants lived near Buenos Aires. There is one further hint. Just before Christmas, 1922, Eva 'von Mark', a photographer in her twenties, Catholic, left Hamburg in first class aboard the steamer *Carias* for Santos, the port for São Paulo.[87] Was this Eva Gerth visiting the relatives of her dead first husband and cementing a contact that would later become valuable?

Weeks afterwards, the Gerth family left Berlin for good. At the end of 1939, Erich, Eva and the children took a train from Berlin for Rome. They rented an apartment at Via Zara 13, which was owned by an Italian Senator. The building was near where Via Zara runs into Via Nomentana, across from Mussolini's Villa Torlonia residence. Mussolini's wife, Donna Rachele, the daughter of a peasant family, did her own shopping in a nearby open air market. 'The people seemed to really like her. It was said in the neighbourhood that she was doing her own shopping because she did not think that her husband's 'dictator thing' would last and she did not want to get out of practice.'[88] Georg Gerth's son, Ernst, visited at this time. When Mussolini was dismissed by King Victor Emmanuel III in 1943, the Germans occupied Rome and began rounding up Jews and others on their lists. The senator returned to re-occupy his apartment forcing the Gerth family to find another lodging, which they did adjacent to the nearby Parco Paganini. One early morning, German troops surrounded the building and an officer knocked on the door looking for the previous occupiers, a Communist underground newspaper. When Erich answered the door, they realized they were too late and departed without incident.

Court papers, even after his death, gave Erich's occupation in Rome as a representative of Fritz Werner, the Berlin firm he had joined in 1935. He now worked in security, screening visitors and protecting the firm's war secrets. He flew to Germany from Italy several times on business. Erich continued ill and took nitro-glycerine tablets for his angina.

Erich had every incentive to seek some small sanctuary, at the least some safer distance, among the powerful Catholic community in Rome. 'It was prudent to escape the attention of the German government'.[89] Erich was caught up in a formidable mixture of threats and, today, it is difficult to know which, or which combination, was the most dangerous. Most immediately, the investigation into Eduard Marx and the confession of Walter Firnhaber were available to the Nazis and Erich and Eva were to be charged with offences concerning their false passports. Their co-conspirator, Eduard, had travelled illegally to Glasgow to get married and had been lauded in British newspapers for breaking the Nuremburg laws. Erich and Eva had run away to Portugal in an attempt to get one of them to South America, and this may have been known to the German authorities; they certainly knew they were now in Rome. There was unfinished business from 1933: first, Eva was a *Mischling* and her freedom and, eventually, that of her quarter-blood children would come to an end; second, Erich and Eva's public work in Paris among the French and German Catholic communities calling for reconciliation, and which had attracted so much official attention, had angered the Nazis. Eva's father, Salomon Marx, had been the right-hand man of Alfred Hugenberg, whom the Nazis had 'circumcised' for daring to try to manipulate Hitler. The Nazis had stolen Salomon's property, reduced him to a mental wreck, and probably sent him to an early grave. Some combination of these 'threats' might explain why the highest Nazis, Hindenburg, Neurath and Hess, all signed parts of the papers forcing Erich from the Foreign Office and ignored his pleas for reinstatement. Perhaps Neurath also harboured some dark personal memory. Finally, there was the awkwardness of knowing Wilhelm Canaris, Erich's friend and protector, and who knows how far their links really went. Canaris's time was running out, even in 1939. Heinrich Himmler, Reichsführer of the SS and acquirer of Ufa, was working to bring him down. Sooner or later, someone in the Nazi hierarchy might place all this damning information about Erich together and decide to take executive action.

Erich Gerth did not survive the war. He died in Rome on 12 December 1943, age fifty-seven, of *Herzschwäche*, 'heart disease'.[90] He was travelling in a car to the train station at Settebagni on his way to Germany; his eleven-year-old son, Marco, with him to wave goodbye, was sitting in the front seat. On the way they passed the airport where there were many destroyed *Luftwaffe* planes. Erich was sitting in the back between two men whom Marco had never seen before and never saw again. Erich did not speak, went red in the face, and died quickly. Eva was always convinced, although Marco, late in life, was not, that Erich had been assassinated. There was no autopsy. Unusually, there is only one photograph of Erich in his personal file in the Berlin Foreign Office. It is stuck firmly onto the bottom of his application of 1922, except that the top half, the half showing his face, has been torn off in a manner that would be a most unlikely accident. Staff searching the archive as research for this book thought that the picture had been deliberately defaced. Perhaps it is wrong to read too much into these things?

Erich was buried in the private garden of the German cemetery inside the Vatican, *Campo Santo Teutonico*, today inaccessible behind high walls to the crowds of tourists. The Vatican secretariat confirms that burial here required previous strict attendance to religious rules of a Catholic confraternity. There were only three other German internments during the war years: Theobald Heintzel, born the same year as Erich, a Prussian who served in a Munich infantry regiment in World War I, and an elderly couple, the Gieffers, Wilhelm and Filippine, who both died in their eighties. Eva wrote in January 1944, care of the German Embassy at the Holy See, to the Foreign Office asking for 1,000 Reichsmarks quickly for the costs of Erich's doctor and the funeral. She was told she would receive 509 Reichsmarks and she asked for the money and her widow's income to be sent to Erich's brother, Georg, who was living in Würzburg.

When Erich died, murdered Eva believed, she decided it was time to go into hiding. Marco, who previous to the American bombing of Frascati in September 1943, had been at the Mondragone Jesuit boarding school, now went into hiding with the Jesuits in Rome. The two daughters, Diana and Isabella, were already safe at their French boarding school, the Sacré-Coeur, atop the Spanish Steps. Eva found a place for herself and Roger in a convent of French nuns near the Trevi Fountain. The nuns had responded to the urging of Pope Pius XII, who had signed Erich's job application over twenty-five years before, for the convents of Rome to open their doors and hide people who were at risk of persecution, Jews and Christians alike. While hiding in the convent, Roger fell ill and required medication. Eva went to a pharmacy near Via Rasella just as Italian partisans attacked a column of German SS Police. Eva heard the explosion and shots. She knew what would happen next: nearby streets would be blocked and everyone rounded up as retaliation. Eva took a long detour and returned safely to the convent.

It was from the convent windows on the evening of 4 June 1944, after waiting all day for it to happen, that Roger caught sight of the first Allied troops.

> They came sauntering across the Piazza della Pilotta. They looked so casual, compared to the spit-and-polish German soldiers who had just departed, that I wondered how they could be the ones winning the war. And yet it was such a joyous occasion. For all practical purposes, the war for the Gerth family was now over. We finally felt safe. None of us thought about what awaited us when we would return to a devastated Germany.[91]

When Eduard Marx received his bill of indictment for falsification of documents and submission of forged Aryan certificates in 1942, he suffered his first severe heart attack and was unable to work for a long period. Matters got steadily worse. His brother-in-law, Erich Gerth, died at the end of the next year. At the same time, Canaris had been defeated in his power battle against Himmler and was unable to help further. Canaris was executed in 1945 in Flossenbürg concentration camp for his part in an assassination attempt on Adolf Hitler. Eduard's home, his father's last house at Lessingstraße 31 in Berlin, was destroyed by bombing at the end of 1943. Marx tried to establish a doctor's practice in Moabit, however he was ordered by the Commissioner for Jews in the Berlin Medical Association, SS-doctor Arno Hermann, to a post outside of Berlin as a locum. Hermann also told Marx in a telephone conversation that criminal proceedings for fraud had been filed against him and that 'he would soon discover the consequences'. Marx worked in Eichwalde where a local doctor, Machowicz, a staunch Nazi and close friend of Hermann, filed charges against Eduard for sabotage for writing too many sick notes for women working in arms factories, for wasting petrol, and also for his connection with Canaris. It was alleged that Eduard had lists of partisans in Eichwalde which should have been destroyed in case the plot against Hitler of 20 July 1944 did not succeed. In the evening of 22 November 1944, Eduard suffered 'several severe heart attacks' and left Eichwalde to escape arrest and to join his family in the remote village of Klein-Köris. He lived illegally until the end of the war without food ration cards and relied for help on a local shop owner, a friend of his wife.

In February 1944, Eduard was sentenced to twelve months in prison for possession of false identification papers, but he appealed in November. There were no further proceedings before the end of the war. 'The ancestor passports were returned to me and are my property. I also have the grey ID card for the politically and racially persecuted.'[92] The criminal charges against Erich and Eva Gerth fell away. In 1945, Firnhaber was also given a jail sentence, but the case was deemed 'political' and the criminal proceedings were suspended at war end.

After the liberation of Rome, the Gerth family moved to the Pensione Villa Mater Dei on the Viale delle Mura Aurelie, overlooking St Peter's basilica. This time was 'mostly a very happy memory for the Gerth children as there were also other families with children'. The villa was managed by an order of German nuns from Mainz and is now a residence for German bishops visiting Rome. Eva received a long letter from Georg, her brother-in-law, inviting the family to his home in Würzburg.

A further question arises, that of money. With Salomon Marx's death after the loss of his fortune, followed closely by the serious drop in Erich's income from the Foreign Office, one might assume that the Gerths were in dire straits. This was not the case. They lived for many months up to 1937 at a villa in Malaga and then felt comfortable enough to move to Paris to have their fourth child where they occupied a prestige apartment and enjoyed the services of the 'best obstetrician'. Back in Berlin, 4,500

Reichsmarks were spent on forged passports and papers. Erich and Eva then dashed to Portugal intending, at least, for one of them to fly to South America. After a return to Berlin, they took the train to Italy where, until Erich was 'murdered' in 1943 and Eva and the children went into hiding, they lived in apartments in the city centre. Marco and his two sisters were at boarding schools. After the Americans arrived in 1944, the family stayed in Rome for more than two years. It would seem that savings, added to by inheritance and a continuing small income from Salomon's estate, and a limited salary from the firm of Fritz Werner, was more than enough to get by.

The widowed Eva Gerth with her four children left Rome by train at 2020 on 4 November 1946 for Germany where they moved to Würzburg, the home of Georg Gerth's family. A loan made pre-war by Erich to Georg's Leinecker coffee firm was repaid and used for immediate living expenses. Eva and the children then stayed for a short time in Baden Baden on the edge of the Black Forest near the border with France. Eva and her eldest daughter also returned briefly to Italy. The family was given the choice by the National Catholic Welfare Conference of a paid-for emigration to either France or the United States. Eva shared the decision with her children and they chose America. They left Bremerhaven in Germany for Boston, USA, in 1949 on an assisted passage aboard the *USAT General M L Hersey*, 12,420 tons, a passenger ship built during 1944 for use as an American Navy transport.[93] At the time of Eva's voyage, the ship was one of five which had been transferred to the US Army for the carriage of displaced persons and refugees from Europe to the USA and Australia in support of the International Refugee Organisation (IRO).[94] The IRO was an intergovernmental organisation founded on 20 April 1946 to deal with the massive refugee problem created by the war.[95] The *Hersey*'s manifest shows that the Gerth party had eight trunks and seven valises.[96] This was a sizable collection of luggage. They were not coming back. Roger Gerth explains:

> *Unfortunately, we could not bring any money with us. We were told that US government regulations prohibited immigrants from bringing any hard currency out of Europe. I think that the US was investing significant amounts of money in the reconstruction of Europe and did not want the large number of departing immigrants to take money out, since this would be counter-productive to the money being pumped in. Therefore, we had to spend all of the money we had in Germany and had no money when we arrived in the USA. But we did have tailor-made clothes and other items bought with the money we otherwise could have brought with us. As luck would have it, my new clothes included a suit that had short pants and another one was in the knickerbocker style, neither of which were in fashion for boys in America.[97]*

Eva was fifty-four-years-old, fifty-three by the manifest; Marco, seventeen; Maria (Marie-Diana), sixteen; another Marie (Isabella), thirteen; and Roger, eleven. The family's destination was 53e Edgemere Drive South East, Grand Rapids, Michigan. They did not have a dollar to their name. Only Eva spoke any English. Well-clothed, maybe, but it was going to be a tough welcome.

ENDNOTES

1   Martin Niemöller, who brought *UC 67* home to Kiel in the dash from Pola in 1918 (Chapter 4, 'Erich's war'), wrote this famous and widely quoted poem about the persecutions by the Nazis. The poem exists in many versions, often modified to reflect a specific persecuted group. In a 1971 interview, Niemöller said that this was his preferred version.
2   *Berlin Telephone Directory*, 1923 (ancestry.com). Erich's number was Lutzow 89 67.
3   Chapter 15, 'Salomon and the film business'.
4   *Auswärtiges Amt*, Politisches Archiv, Gz: 117–251.09.
5   Chapter 14, 'Welcome home, Erich'.
6   Princess Ludwig, *Through Four Revolutions*, p. xiii and following.
7   Chapter 17, 'Georg amid the ruins'.
8   Princess Ludwig, *Through Four Revolutions*, pp. 334–35.
9   File note, 27/4/1924, unsigned (Obituary, Matthias Lohr).
10 Heineman, *Neurath*, pp. 3–4, 24.
11 Letter, Neurath to von Kühlmann, 4/10/1924 (Berlin Foreign Office personnel file, with thanks to Matthias Löhr and Martina Nibbeling-Wriessnig).
12 Foreign Office cables Nos. 31,42 (IH 1098), 5,31/3/1925.
13 Report 22 IB, 20/4/1926, signed by 'Mutius'.
14 30/12/1922.
15 Letter, Salomon Marx to Dr Köpke, 'Min. Dir.', Berlin', 7/8/1931. Reply 19/8/1931. Further letters 1,12/9/1932.
16 Marco Gerth born 10/1/1932, Marie-Diane 19/2/1933, Isabella 7/8/1935 and Roger 30/11/1937.
17 Letter 9/8/1933.
18 Matthias Lohr email.
19 Comte Jean de Castellane was a French cavalry officer who left the army in 1902 to stand successfully in legislative elections. He was disqualified for bribery and beaten in the subsequent by-election. He became a municipal counsellor in Paris from 1919 to 1944 and was vice-president of the municipal council in 1928 and then from 1930 to 1931. Chancellor Brüning established presidential government in the final days of the Weimar Republic, but was forced out when President Paul von Hindenburg refused to sign further decrees. He was author of a plan to reinstate the Hohenzollern monarchy in a British-style constitution. Hindenburg refused his support unless the Kaiser was called back from the Netherlands. When Brüning explained this would not be possible, Hindenburg dismissed him. Fearing arrest by the Nazis, Brüning fled Germany in 1934, settling in Switzerland, then the United Kingdom and, finally, the United States. Brüning warned the American public about Hitler's plans for war and, later, about Soviet aggression and expansion (wikipedia).
20 Erbe, *Das vornehme Berlin*, p. 25.

21 Honoré de Balzac, *La Femme comme il faut*. Erbe, *Das vornehme Berlin*, p. 154.

22 *Demi-monde*, people on the edge of respectable society. *Zeitgeist*, the defining spirit or mood of a particular period of history as shown by the ideas and beliefs of the time.

23 Grenaud and Marcailhou, *Boni de Castellane*, Book 1, p. 207. Richard Wagner's opera cycle, *Der Ring des Nibelungen*. In Norse mythology, a *Valkyrie* is one of a host of females who choose those who will live and die in battle, bringing their chosen to the after-life hall of the slain, *Valhalla*, ruled over by the god *Odin*. *Wotan* is a character based on the god.

24 Erbe, *Das vornehme Berlin*, pp. 204–8.

25 There was some criticism of Dolly's lack of national [French] feeling during the war, but this turned into resentment when her cosmopolitanism was reflected in a questionable attitude towards the Third Reich (Erbe, *Das vornehme Berlin*), fn. 690. Price Jean-Louis Faucigny-Lucinge, *Un gentilhomme cosmopolite*, p. 64, fn. states that Jean and Dolly de Castellane were collaborating with the German occupying power.

26 Erbe, *Das vornehme Berlin*, p. 37, fn.

27 Interview with Christa-Maria Gerth, 15/11/2016.

28 Email, Roger Gerth, 22/1/2018.

29 Marks, *Illusion of Peace*, p. 89.

30 Extracted by Roger Gerth from a French National Assembly document about Auguste Champetier de Ribes. See also, Guieu, 'Le rapprochement franco-allemand', *Les Cahiers Sirice*, 2016/1 ; Delori, 'La genèse de la coopération franco-allemande', *Revue française de science politique*, 2006/3.

31 Albert was a German Dominican friar, and later bishop, who became a highly acclaimed and successful professor at the University of Paris. To this day, there is a Rue Maître Albert in Paris, not far from the University.

32 Email, Roger Gerth, 22/1/2018.

33 Ulrich, *Bismarck*, p. 91.

34 Pacelli's papers while nuncio in Munich and Berlin, and his correspondence with German bishops while he served as secretary of state at the Vatican, were among the 30,000 files of the pontificate of Pope Pius XI opened to researchers in 2006. These were followed in 2007 by Pacelli's war-time diaries (Coppa, *Pius XXI*), p. xxi.

35 In 1864, the *Quanta cura* and *Syllabus of Errors*. In 1870, the infallibility dogma was declared at the First Vatican Council. Gross, *War Against Catholicism*. Bunson, 'German Catholics under the Iron Fist'.

36 Gross, *War Against Catholicism*, p. 248.

37 Ulrich, *Bismarck*, p. 91.

38 Gross, *War Against Catholicism*, p. 90.

39 Bunson, 'German Catholics under the Iron Fist', p. 25.

40 Encyclical *Etsi Multa*, EM 15, 21/11/1873.

41 Chapter 1, 'Brave new world'.

42 Cornwell, *Hitler's Pope*, pp. 45–46.

43 Cornwell, *Hitler's Pope*, p. 60.

44 Herber, 'Pacelli's Mission', p. 48.

45 Cornwell, *Hitler's Pope*, p. 62.

46 Coppa, *Pius XII*, pp. 74–75. Pacelli was appointed archbishop of Sardi on 13 May 1917 on the sudden death of his predecessor. Sardi, or Sardes, was not an actual diocese with a cure of souls, but one of the seven hundred dioceses of Eastern Christendom destroyed by the Muslim invasion (Cornwell, *Hitler's Pope*), p. 61.

47 Coppa, *Pius XII*, p. 74.

48 Coppa, *Pius XII*, p. 87.

49 Gedye, *Revolver Republic*, p. 39.

50 Cornwell, *Hitler's Pope*, p. 87.

51 Coppa, *Pius XII*, pp. 91–100.

52 Cornwell, *Hitler's Pope*, p. 80.

53 Cornwell, *Hitler's Pope*, p. 101.

54 Mueller, *Canaris*, pp. 180–82.

55　Osborne played a key part, as did Pacelli, in the plot in 1940 to overthrow Hitler. Osborne ran with others an escape line for up to 4,000 Allied soldiers on the run in Italy, almost all of whom survived the war (Chadwick, *Britain and the Vatican During the Second World War*), p. 86 and following. See the 1983 film *The Scarlet and the Black*, starring Gregory Peck.

56　Email, Roger Gerth, 22/1/2018.

57　IG 336 5/10, 9/10/1933.

58　Appendix 9, 'Law for Professional Civil Service'.

59　wikipedia.

60　Niemöller, *From U-boat to Pulpit*.

61　Personnel file, Berlin, 120–29 B 4/8, Kiel, 4/7/1933.

62　Heineman, *Neurath*, pp. 2, 226.

63　Heineman, *Neurath*, p. 246.

64　Kelly, *Tirpitz and the Imperial German Navy*, pp. 69–70.

65　Kelly, *Tirpitz*, pp. 410, 443–45.

66　Bunson, 'German Catholics under the Iron Fist', p. 27.

67　Steigmann-Gall, *Holy Reich*. Hastings, *Catholicism and the Roots of Nazism*.

68　Letter from Erich Gerth to Herr Freudenberg, Personnel Department, Foreign Ministry, 9/4/1934.

69　Chapter 15.

70　wikipedia: The *Nürnberger Gesetze*, Nuremberg Laws, were introduced on 15/9/1935 at a special meeting convened at the Nazi Party's annual Nuremberg Rally. The two laws were for the 'Protection of German Blood and German Honour', which forbade marriages and extramarital intercourse between Jews and Germans and the employment of German females under forty-five in Jewish households; and the 'Reich Citizenship Law', which declared that only those of German or related blood were eligible to be Reich citizens; the remainder were classed as state subjects, without citizenship rights. A supplementary decree outlining the definition of who was Jewish was passed on 14/11/1935 when the 'Reich Citizenship Law' came into force. The laws were expanded on 26/11/1935 to include Romani and black people. This supplementary decree defined Gypsies as 'enemies of the race-based state', the same category as Jews. Because of concern for the Olympics to be held in 1936 in Berlin, prosecutions under the two laws did not start until after the games finished.

71　*LABO*, Documents Marx Family 1951–58, file Salomon Marx/304.641, 'Declaration for the Entschädigungsamt by Dr Eduard Marx, 29/5/1956, p. A5.

72　*LABO*, Documents Marx Family 1951–58, file Salomon Marx/304.641, 'Certificate of Dr George Martos', 23/5/1956, p. A3.

73　*LABO*, Documents Marx Family 1951–58, file Salomon Marx/304.641, 'Declaration for the Entschädigungsamt' Dr Eduard Marx, 29/5/1956, p. A5.

74　*LABO*, Documents Marx Family 1951–58, file Salomon Marx/304.641, 'Letter by solicitor Dr Georg Lancelle, Berlin 4/10/1957, pp. M19–20.

75　Chapter 15.

76　The 7,000 Czechs that lived in the town before the Nazis took over were expelled during June of 1942, making way for some 50,000 Jews. About 155,000 Jews were brought to Theresienstadt during the war. Approximately 87,000 were deported to concentration camps farther east, while about 34,000 died in the ghetto. Of the more than 10,500 children who lived in the ghetto before being deported east, only 245 survived the war.

77　The 1937 Exposition Internationale des Arts et Techniques dans la Vie Moderne, 'International Exposition of Art and Technology in Modern Life', in Paris was the city's sixth International Exposition after fairs held in 1855, 1867, 1878, 1889, and 1900. It took place between 25/5–25/11, centred upon the Trocadéro, just across the Seine from the Eiffel Tower.

78　*Mischling* was used before the Nazi era as describing mongrel dogs.

79　Married in Blythswood, Glasgow, 9 or 17/5/1937. Ilse's parents lived at Kirchstraße 13 in Berlin. Her father Paul Geue was a foreman in an optical company; her mother was Elise Schultz.

80 *LABO*, Documents Marx Family 1951–58, file Salomon Marx/304.641, 'Duplicate of prosecution papers against Walter Firnhaber and Dr Eduard Marx, Berlin 28/7/1942, pp. C4-6.

81 Ehrenreich, *Nazi Ancestral Proof*, pp. 69–75.

82 This information was confirmed by Walter Firnhaber, now a district counsellor, in Wiesbaden, 23/10/1952 (*LABO*, Documents Marx Family 1951–58, file Salomon Marx/304.641), p. E41.

83 There were covert identification marks in the official list for doctors: a comma for non-Aryans, a semicolon for Jews.

84 The Boeing 314 Clipper was a long-range flying boat produced between 1938 and 1941. One of the largest aircraft of the time, it had a massive wing to achieve the range necessary for flights across the Atlantic and Pacific Oceans (wikipedia).

85 Telephone conversation, Marco Gerth, 15/1/2018; email, Roger Gerth, 19/1/2018.

86 After the second world war, on one of his trips to Germany, Marco Gerth, met again with one of his nannies.

87 Hamburg passenger lists, 20/12/1922 (ancestry.com).

88 Email, Roger Gerth, 20/1/2018.

89 Telephone conversation, Marc Gerth, 15/1/2018.

90 Freiburg, MSG2/18635, p. xiii.

91 Email, Roger Gerth, 20/1/2018.

92 *LABO*, Documents Marx Family 1951–58, file Salomon Marx/304.641, 'Affidavit by Dr Eduard Marx', Berlin-Schöneberg, 6/11/1957, p. A12.

93 Shipindex.org, ID 6903228, accessed 2/2017.

94 *The New York Times*, 'Shipping News and Notes', 29/1/1950.

95 In 1952, the IRO was replaced by the Office of the United Nations High Commissioner for Refugees (UNHCR).

96 Passenger Lists of Vessels arriving at Boston, NAI No. 2668739 (Massachusetts Passenger and Crew Lists, ancestry.com).

97 Email, Roger Gerth, 21/1/2018.

CHAPTER 17

Georg Amid the Ruins

[RAF] *Bomber Command's offensive against Germany in the Second World War was one of the most remarkable passage of arms in history. It began when Winston Churchill could see no other road to victory, as England stood alone in 1940. It was undertaken with almost messianic fervour by a generation of senior airmen determined to prove that strategic air power could make a unique and decisive contribution to war. It ended in a controversy, moral and strategic, which has been raging ever since. The cost was very high, 55,573 aircrew, almost all officers and NCOs [Non-Commissioned Officers], among the finest and most highly trained material in the British Empire, were killed ... The sacrifice was greater than the British Army's total loss of officers in the First World War.*[1]

Georg Gerth arrived in Berlin from his French prison camp during the week of the Kapp Putsch in March 1920. He found that a court of enquiry, held the previous month in Bremen, had already interviewed his engineer Johannes Giese on the reasons for the stranding of *UC 61* at Wissant in 1917.[2] Giese had also just returned from captivity. His short verbal account was counter-signed by a Leutnant zur See Scharper, holding the lowest officer rank in the German Navy, so this was no high-powered tribunal. By chance, Giese and Gerth were both from Charlottenburg so one could imagine that the two men met in Berlin to discuss the circumstances and atmosphere at Giese's hearing. One might also expect that Erich Gerth, at work in the Admiralty in Berlin, might have checked the temperature to reassure his younger brother. In any event, Gerth, a Kapitänleutnant, was not asked to travel to Bremen and, instead, hand-wrote his version of events over four sheets of paper, leaving the left hand side free for official notations.[3] There were a lot of initialled signatures. That it seems was the end of the matter.

Georg Gerth said a few years later that he took a position in the

International Law Department on the admiralty staff for nine months until he resigned in December.[4] In fact, he joined the navy team contributing to the Peace Commission negotiations. Files for his period in office were not found at the naval archives in Freiburg, but enough general material exists to build a satisfactory picture.[5] There is an immediate surprise: the commissary to the four-man team of noble officer sailors who headed the delegation was Leutnant z.S. Sharper who interviewed Giese at Bremen. Apart from the necessary formality of interviewing the commander of a lost ship, perhaps that whole episode was mostly to see if Gerth was suitable for his role in the Commission? Admiral Adolf von Trotha, the Admiralty chief, specified the sort of men he wanted. 'Fluent in at least one of the main languages (English or French), eloquent, confident, experienced travellers with extensive knowledge of the organisation of the navy and skilled in radio telegraphy and coding messages, cool, professional and discrete behaviour, observing the correct formalities at all times.'[6] This was a precise description of 'Raven' Gerth's skills, given that 'correct formalities' was a euphemism for 'loyal to the officer corps'.[7]

The main issue for Trotha was 'unfair unilateral obligations for Germany as outlined in the peace treaty regarding disarmament, surrender and destruction of German naval vessels, reduction of naval staff, impossibly short time limits'. He felt that the peace conditions had 'no basis in international law, put an extraordinary economic strain on Germany [and were] unacceptable for economic and financial reasons'. There were six sub-sections of the naval peace delegation which mainly concentrated on the trade war, the naval air force, and mine field clearance and, of course, Gerth could have been employed in any of them. However, it seems likely that he was used in either of the units covering 'Transition to Peace Time', especially in its dealings with naval POWs, although this work was largely concluded, or in the section for 'Submarines and Submarine War' whose responsibilities, said Trotha, covered

> *German submarines delivered to the Allies and USA, memoranda on the justification of the submarine war (4/2/1915) as well as the unrestricted submarine war (31/1/1917), list of vessels sunk or damaged by German submarines/naval forces/fighter planes, collection of material dealing with the accusations made against our submarines regarding cruel treatment of crews of sunk ships, materials about the Baralong case and similar cases, collection of news about submarine traps, Q-boats etc. especially with regard to the cruelties committed by the enemies in their warfare against our submarines.*

Gerth's short stay at the Admiralty suggests his mind had already turned to other matters. There is another possibility that his work placed him in contact with the French border town of Saarbrücken almost 500 miles away from the bustle and intrigue of Berlin. In 1920, Saarbrücken became the capital of the Saar territory administered by the League of Nations. Under Articles 47 and 48 of the Treaty of Versailles, the Saar coal mines were made the exclusive property of France for fifteen years as compensation for the destruction of French mines during the war.[8] Gerth resigned from the Peace Commission and immediately at the start of 1921 took a post in the Transport and Customs Department of the Saarbrücken Chamber of Commerce where smuggling was a primary concern.[9] His command of French and English would have been of great use in what must have been a chaotic period. Gerth noted that 'in addition to my official job, I managed the Association of the Distilleries of the Saar Territory' with a great emphasis on brandy and gin production.[10] Within a few months, he began studies at the University of Würzburg and, from the spring, worked for the Employers' Association at Trier.

The city of Trier, another Saar region border town, this time with Luxembourg, was the birthplace of Karl Marx, the philosopher and revolutionary socialist. It is worth a small diversion for coincidence sake for Trier has appeared in these pages before. It was in Trier in 1919 that John Maynard Keynes, the British financial representative on the Supreme Economic Council, twice met German delegates to try to alleviate the famine in Germany.[11] It was also in Trier that Smiley Blanton, the medical officer with the American Army of Occupation's Department of Sanitation and Public Health, conducted his ground-breaking study into the damage caused to young German children by malnutrition.[12] Blanton wrote in his report, printed in 1919,

> The city of Trier is situated on the Moselle River and is the centre of the wine industry for the Moselle Valley. It has about 55,000 inhabitants, the majority of whom are small shopkeepers, artisans and officials. There are several thousand factory workers in about thirty factories which include leather and tobacco factories and iron foundries. The rich people are chiefly wine merchants, many of whom have grown quite rich during the war. Before the war, there was much wine drinking among the poorer classes and much hard liquor was consumed as well. The people have large families and among the poor people malnutrition was common before the war. On the whole, I believe that we are justified in saying that the people of Trier are not so well developed physically and not so well off economically as the people in the neighbouring cities of Cologne, Bonn and Coblenz.[13]

There is some determination and planning evident in the moves to Saarbrücken, Trier and Würzburg, all within a year of Gerth's return to Germany. The triangle formed by the three cities has a longest commuting distance of under 200 miles. Support for this conjecture comes from an unusual direction, a study of Gerth's signature which was conducted in London in 2017 without any knowledge of Gerth's history.[14] If this analysis meets with some surprise, it is not new investigative ground. James Joll of Oxford University and professor at the London School of Economics wrote that the 'historian must seek his explanations where he can find them, even in unorthodox or unprofessional places. After all, even [Sir Lewis Bernstein] Namier [an historian of the British parliament with a legendary hatred of Germany] was not ashamed to use the services of a graphologist in reconstructing the character of the writer of manuscript documents'.[15]

> *The writer* [Gerth] *had a strong personality having lasting emotional energy and staying power. A man with a strong sense of purpose and conscientious attitude to all his endeavours. Gerth had a good analytical intellect and would seek his own answers for any projects rather than just accepting any information. Fairly outgoing but quick to react and could be defensive, impatient and subject to mood swings. A man with good coordination and manual dexterity and confident in his ability to succeed. He was able to inspire others with his ideas and take control demonstrating strong leadership qualities. An assertive individual with a strong desire to acquire which could be glory as well as to obtain and possess material objects. Highly competitive, willing to carry the fight, somewhat ruthless, with the desire to push forward and challenge. A man with great initiative, high goals, ambition and enduring determination.*

The glue to all this commuting was surely Gerth's second cousin, Maria Leinecker, whom he was to marry on 8 September 1921 in her home town of Würzburg. It is likely, therefore, that the couple were romantically linked from Gerth's return to Berlin or even from before the war. Maria's mother, Anna Maria (her preferred Christian name) Helene, was also a Gerth, a convert to Catholicism on marriage; her father and Georg's father were brothers who lived in Berlin.[16] So, Georg Gerth's mother-in-law was also his first cousin. Maria was just a few days short of her twenty-first birthday at marriage; Gerth was twelve years her senior. Memories of lost family photographs describe her as 'very pretty'. Georg stood 1m 80, had blond hair, clear, blue eyes and bad hearing, a notorious affliction of early submariners. He spoke German like a Berliner, English with an Oxford accent, and had good French.[17] He was always a student of philosophy rather than either a military man that he had been and was to be again, or a businessman that he was to become in order to earn his living. He learned Sanskrit, the liturgical language of Hinduism, in order to trace the path of Buddhism across south east Asia and, particularly, its translation into Zen or Japanese Buddhism. His other love was landscape painting.

It was a life-lasting love match, but also a good match for Georg as the

Catholic Leinecker family were rich, their wealth founded on a coffee, sugar and wine wholesale business, well-known in Würzburg. The family coffee firm was founded by Joseph Leinicker (sic) in 1815.[18] The Leinecker family home in Würzburg for some generations was a substantial detached house at Sanderring 22, Riemenschneiderstraße 1, and this eventually passed to Georg and Maria Gerth.[19] A combination of income from Saarbrücken and Trier, a pension from the navy and, presumably, accommodation and some Leinecker funds, saw Gerth through his doctorate at the Faculty of Law and Political Science at the Bavarian Julius-Maximilian-University, Würzburg. In 1922, he studied National Economics, Economic Statistics and, in 1922/23, added the Versailles Treaty, Population Statistics, and a Comparison of National and State Law. His 142-page dissertation, successfully submitted in May 1923, was titled 'The Brandy Industry of the Saar Territory since Application of the Versailles Peace Treaty'. He became a Doctor of Political Science, 'Dr rer. pol'.

No doubt the degree was part-time and Gerth's attendance was balanced with his employments, particularly at Saarbrücken. The document itself is mostly typed, but the appendices, tables and many corrections are hand-written.[20] Georg used freely information, data, business contacts, legal knowledge and personal experience that he gained during his employment. This insider knowledge of the brandy and spirits industry, current legislation, customs duties, taxes, commodity prices, main competitors, would eventually come in useful for an anticipated position as a manager in the Leinecker family business. Georg's lack of academic credentials apart from his school matriculation would not normally allow him to undertake post-doctoral studies. The explanation is probably that, after World War I, universities made allowance for a generation of young men who had missed further education because they had fought in the war, and fast tracked their subsequent academic careers. The same leniency occurred in many countries after World War II. It is unusual, however, to have such a practical subject for PhD study with its links to most recent current affairs, including the politically sensitive German-French relations after the ratification of the Versailles Treaty. As such, the dissertation is more of an up-to-date report than an in-depth piece of analytical study based on academic research and reflection.

The brandy and coffee industries, particularly among the many food infrastructures all but destroyed during the war, were struggling to get back to some kind of normality. As an example, in 1916, the German government issued five decrees which affected seriously the rights of the merchants.[21] The first two laid down strictures about the importation of tea and coffee, the next two regulated the sale of these, and the last dealt with substitutes for coffee. In future, the importation of both tea and coffee lay in the hands of the 'War Committee for Tea, Coffee, and their substitutes'. Merchants with stocks of 10kg of raw coffee and 5kg of tea or more 'must report these to the committee and must deliver them immediately when ordered to do so'. The committee settled the price to be paid as compensation. Chicory roots were a preferred substitute and could not be used as animal fodder. Only 350,000 sacks of uncommandeered coffee remained in Germany, enough for six weeks' civilian consumption. However, the Army and Navy had sufficient supplies for six months. The scarcity of coffee led many dealers to refuse to sell either coffee or its substitutes to their customers. The authorities forbade this, but a customer could not get more than 1lb at a time. Some merchants were fined five marks and sentenced to one day's imprisonment for selling roasted barley prepared to resemble coffee. The Reichstag then ordered the creation of a Board to control the sale of strong brandy. Spirits could no longer be used for lighting or cooking.

Gerth concluded that after a pre-war busy exchange of goods with Germany and France, the Saar territory in 1920 hardly imported or exported any brandy.

> French imports which dominated the Saar territory have been increasingly reduced and German imports have ceased almost completely. The local industry now provides the Saar territory with spirits, liqueurs and, partly, distilled wines, but there is little demand ... At the end of 1922, the brandy industry of the Saar is a predominantly stand-alone, self-contained economic unit. Because of the political breakdown of the German empire after the armistice, Germany was unable to protect its borders in the West against foreign trade. As a result the occupied territories were flooded with banned foreign goods. The German economy was hugely damaged by the duty free import of luxury foods, drinks and tobacco, toiletries and perfumes and especially spirits, brandy and liqueurs of French origin. Because of its geographical location, Saarbrücken became the hub of unlicensed trade. As for all of the occupied territories this time of effortless profit came to an end after the coming into force of the Versailles Treaty when the Saar territory joined the French customs area and all exports of goods to Germany had to follow German customs regulations.[22]

After his doctorate, Gerth immediately found employment as head of finance for the Richard Kahn Group of mainly automotive companies, founded in 1921. This important first commercial job meant a move back to Berlin where he stayed until 1925. While in Berlin, Gerth enrolled for one semester during the winter of 1923 at the Philosophical Faculty of the Friedrich-Wilhelms-Universität where he studied psychology.[23] He moved with Maria into his mother's apartment at Keithstraße 22. Maria often 'spoke enthusiastically' to her children about this time in the capital as 'she enjoyed taking part in big city life'.[24]

It was also a period of great unhappiness through family death and the murder of the Marx families' friends and business associates.[25] In September 1923, just before Georg and Maria arrived in Berlin, Georg's mother, Hedwig, was found dead at the Keithstraße apartment.[26] She was sixty-one years old and died from gas poisoning, *Gasvergiftung*, presumably at the apartment because the time of her death was recorded as seven in the morning. There is no indication on the official forms or in the newspapers of whether it was an accident or suicide, a case of accidental overnight gas escape or a deliberate ending of a life. Perhaps of significance was that the record was signed by the *Oberstaatsanwalt*, the Senior Public Prosecutor, at the Landgericht II District Court. Eighteen printed words were firmly deleted from the death record. The funeral at the Protestant Kaiser-Wilhelm-Gedächtniskirche, the Kaiser Wilhelm Memorial Church, was conducted with the 'assistance' of a cleric with the initial 'G'.[27] A church service was not at all normal for a declared suicide. Perhaps her remembered depression, her 'melancholia', her twenty-five year widowhood, her loneliness during the war, some ailment, became too much. On the other side, Christa-Maria Gerth, who never met her grandmother, remembers particularly that her own father, Georg, was 'very fond of his mother, more than Erich', and shared with her a tendency to depression. This insight makes matters the more sad because Hedwig died knowing that Georg was coming to live in Berlin for at least a few years.[28]

This was the time when the Gerth brothers began to establish their post-war careers: Georg, practical experienced gained at Kahn's, returned in 1925 to Würzburg as a manager in the Leinecker family firm, his career for the rest of his business life; and Erich at the Foreign Office. Relations between the brothers remained close even with the physical differences that separated them. At one time, Erich made a loan to the Leinecker company and this was repaid at a crucial time after the second world war.

Georg Gerth's second war was a very different affair to that of his brother, Erich, who was seeking refuge with his family in Rome. However, during the early years of the war, they did manage to meet up at least twice. Georg and Maria had four children who, as with Erich Gerth's children, arrived later in life, the last, Christa-Maria in 1939.[29] Georg developed a love of landscape painting, but his first passion remained philosophy. Maria had her own coffee shop in Würzburg, was celebrated locally as a painter and an artist, and was wealthy. None of Maria's three brothers married and Georg was destined to assume control of the company as the founding family died out or lost interest. The Leinecker family home in Würzburg, Sanderring 22, became the Gerth family home and it was from here that Georg dealt with the news of his brother's humiliation at the hands of the civil service. Georg, in the naval reserve as war approached, was appointed to the senior rank of Korvettenkapitän.[30] Membership of the Nazi party was a requirement for all German officers and Gerth signed up. He was called into the navy on 1 January 1940, six weeks after Christa-Maria's birth. Records of his war service are sketchy and the following relies on personnel records and various war diaries.[31]

Gerth was sent first as a *Marine-Nachrichten-Offizier*, 'naval intelligence officer', for a few months to Memel, now Klaipeda in Lithuania, on the Baltic coast, reporting to Base Commander Captain von Bredow. He arrived on 1 April in freezing conditions, arriving ships needed the help of ice breakers.[32] Hundreds of recruits for various training courses in radio and gunnery poured in. On 11 May, the first units of the 1st and 2nd u-boat training flotilla were moved to Memel, sailing in around lunch time and taking their moorings in the southern part of the winter harbour. On 15 June, Memel's coastal monitoring station reported that the Russians were invading Lithuania. All leave was cancelled. Memel was ordered to repel any crossing of the borders between Germany and Lithuania.

Gerth was next sent to Sandnessjöen on the island of Alsta in occupied north Norway, a town with just a few thousand inhabitants. He arrived on 1 October 1940, where he continued as intelligence officer, second-in-command to Kapitän Johannes Bachmann.[33] Bachmann, who commanded the light cruiser *Emden* before the war, was killed fighting the Americans in Willebadessen in 1945. The invasion of Norway from April to June 1940 took sixty-two days, the longest any country apart from the Soviets held out against the Nazis. The records immediately before Gerth's arrival show that military consolidation was the main activity: the preparation of a naval radio station at Bodø, the sighting of a surfaced submarine near Trondheim, six English fighter planes dropping mines, and the escape and recapture of downed English fighter plane crews from the island of Leka. Reinforcements arrived regularly, including the 10th Company, Infantry Regiment 263, one officer and sixty-nine men, and the promise of a fourth trained battery crew.

One of Gerth's first tasks was to take over the writing of the daily war diary for his commanding officer, a most personal task during his u-boat commands twenty-five years before. However, this time, Gerth's entries were of a different nature. On 10-12 October, popular concerts and social events were recorded: the *Regimentsmusik*, the musical band of the Infantry Regiment, played for German soldiers and the Norwegian population at a teacher training college, at a hospital, at an officer's home with tea, string music and the mayor as special guest of honour. On 14 October, the Admiral of the Norwegian north coast, Captain August Thiele visited to inspect the naval constructions and emplacements. Thiele was a recent hero who received the Knight's Cross of the Iron Cross for his command of the pocket battleship *Lützow* and his leadership of *Kampfgruppe V*, '5th battle group', during the invasion of Oslo. Thiele took command of the battle group after the sinking of the heavy cruiser, SMS *Blücher*, Konteradmiral Oskar Kummetz's flagship, in Oslo Fjord, after close fire from shore batteries. From Trondheim on 26 October, Thiele criticised Bachmann and Gerth on three grounds. The war diary for 1 October, Gerth's first day, reported the emergency landing of a seaplane and stated that 'the commander did not initiate anything as a secret messaging connection did not exist with Brønnøysund so the harbour master could not be contacted'. Thiele explained that, for notification of sea emergencies, a secret messaging connection was not required. Thiele then moved onto 'reports about promenade concerts, social evenings and tea invitations' which did not belong in a war diary 'even if they serve to entertain the members of the armed forces and help contact with the Norwegian civilians'. Finally, Thiele insisted that the war diary was to be signed personally each day by the local commander. There were no more signatory duties for Gerth. On 23 October, Gerth reported a message in Morse from the harbour master at Bodø regarding the stranding of a German steamer which, it turned out was the Norwegian steamer *Princess Ragnhild*, hit and sunk by an English mine. Seventy-one German soldiers were rescued alive, fourteen dead. Thiele later criticised the Bodø harbour master for the delay in rescue.

After an eventful two months in Sandnessjöen, Gerth moved to Warnemünde, near the city of Rostock on the Baltic, to take up duties as intelligence officer on 1 January 1941.[34] Gerth's duties here are not described, but he moved yet again after another few months to join Coastal Command, Western Baltic, at Kiel, on 1 October 1941. 'Dr Gerth' was appointed first Adjutant, third in line after the commander, Vice Admiral Werner Grassmann, killed in Berlin in 1943, who was a fellow sea cadet in Gerth's Crew of '07, and the Chief of Staff Captain Grattenauer.[35] On 1 April 1942, Gerth took on additional responsibilities as *Personalreferent*, 'Personnel Officer' and on 1 July added *Offizierpersonalreferent*, Officer's Personnel Officer, but now number four in line after the Assistant to the Chief of Staff, Willy Quaatz. With all of these quite rapid changes in appointment, there is a suspicion that the local admiralty staff did not know quite what to do with their fifty-four-year-old ex-u-boat commander, a philosopher with a doctorate, who was used to running his own successful brand-name business in peacetime. Perhaps his demeanour was insufficiently war-like? Perhaps, also, while a stout defender of Germany, the fate of his brother gave him second thoughts about his commitment to the Third Reich? Perhaps, even, his old classmate Grassmann rescued him?

At least Kiel was an eighteen-month appointment. On 1 January 1943, Gerth moved finally to the Torpedoversuchsanstalt, 'Torpedo Research Centre', at Eckernförde, as 'Head of Division' and stayed for almost two years.[36] Here, Gerth was finally dealing with a subject of which he had hands-on experience. It was also while Gerth was serving in Eckernförde that his brother, Erich, died in Rome. Georg Gerth retired from the navy for a second time on 1 November 1944, aged fifty-seven, less than a year later. Could the reason for this departure have any connection with the manner of his brother's death and his wife Eva's strong suspicion that Erich was killed by the Nazis? Had the hounding of Eva into hiding broken Georg's loyalty? Georg returned to the coffee and wine business of Leinecker in Würzburg and to tragedy. He never saw combat and was seemingly of limited use to the Third Reich in its final months.

On the night of 16 March 1945, RAF High Command in High Wycombe, England, decided to firebomb Würzburg using the half-timbered and cramped buildings of the old city as a tinder box.

> *Cities like Würzburg were primarily selected because they were easy for the bombers to find and destroy. Because they had a medieval centre, they were expected to be particularly vulnerable to fire attack.*[37]

Leading the attack was the same air group, using eleven Mosquito twin-engine bombers and 225 Lancaster heavy bombers, which the month before had burned Dresden. Proportional to the size of Dresden, Würzburg experienced an even higher rate of death and destruction. The Mosquitoes first marked the target with green flares, called 'Christmas Trees' by the Germans, as a marker for the main bombers. As a result of meticulous planning, each bomber was over the target for less than one minute. Then, Würzburg's roofs and windows were destroyed with 256 heavy bombs and aerial mines and, finally, 300,000 incendiary bombs rained down. A single area-wide fire storm saw temperatures reaching 2,000 degrees Centigrade. Returning bombers could see the flames from 240 kilometres away. Just one bomber was shot down by a German night fighter; five others were lost during or after the attack. The population had minimum warning and little protection from the heat. Many tried to reach the banks of the Main river on the edge of the town. An estimated 5,000 people were killed, only 3,000 were identified, and almost 89 per cent of the buildings in the historic town, 68 per cent in the suburbs, were obliterated in a raid that lasted seventeen minutes. This was a war-time record on several counts.[38] Specifically, this meant 21,062 homes and thirty-five churches destroyed. From June 1944 to March 1945, Würzburg suffered ten other air attacks, together killing over 500 people. Hildesheim was half-destroyed six days after the main Würzburg raid, Paderborn in another five days, and half of Plauen on 10 April. 'The final catalogue of air attacks could not be restrained even by Churchill.' Seventy German cities were area bombed by the RAF alone between 1942 and 1945 in 365 raids.[39]

> *It is right to say that the shockwave triggered by Dresden swept away what was left of the will to resist, as the Germans now feared that such a catastrophe could be repeated daily. Awareness of the inevitable defeat increased and the belief in miracles disappeared but, above all, here was the growing realisation that it would be better if the end came soon … better to have a terrible end than endless terror.*[40]

Officially, Würzburg was targeted as a traffic hub, but every large town is a crossroads. It was known that Würzburg's main war duty was as a hospital town, there were over forty hospitals in the centre at the time of the attack. On 14 February 1942, the Area Bombing directive was issued to Bomber Command. Bombing was to be 'focussed on the morale of the enemy civilian population and, in particular, of the industrial workers'.[41] Although never officially admitted at the time, the British were to carry out 'unrestricted area bombing' on a scale which dwarfed the 'unrestricted submarine warfare' of the first war and over which the British had used such demonic language. The over-riding drive behind the RAF raid on Würzburg was the determination of Air Marshall Arthur 'Bomber' Harris, to break the will of the German people by hitting unprotected civilian populations. The policy was much debated internally with leaders like Churchill frequently vacillating because of the horror of success.[42] Would it not be preferably to attack strategic targets like steel production, rail networks and oil supply?

> The ultimate aim of an attack on a town area is to break the morale of the population which occupies it. To ensure this, we must achieve two things: first, we must make the town physically uninhabitable and secondly, we must make the people conscious of constant personal danger. The immediate aim is, therefore, twofold, namely to produce destruction and fear of death.[43]

Christa-Maria Gerth remembers that nobody expected an attack this late in the war, especially as Würzburg was a hospital city.[44] The three sisters had been sent to the countryside for safety several months previously, but on this night all were back home again. Her brother had been conscripted into the navy and was serving in Denmark. During previous alarms, the family went with local residents into the low basement, the vaulted wine cellar, of their house in Sanderring 21, which survived this attack although the house did not. The Gerths were not in the cellar that evening.

> I do remember that in the late afternoon we walked towards Altertheim, about twenty kilometres from Würzburg. My parents knew the forest ranger in Irrtenberg. When we arrived, many other people had already come to this place so that we couldn't find accommodation in the forester's house. We went to a barn which was laid out with layers of straw. In the distance we saw the red light of fire. Würzburg was ablaze, but nobody moaned. Everyone present had escaped the fire storm alive – the only important thing.
>
> Sanitary facilities were missing completely. A tree trunk was placed above a dug-out pit and you had to balance on it when going to the

toilet, the so-called 'thunder beam'. After a short while, we moved into the forester's house with many other people. The ranger housed as many people as he could. I can't remember his face, only that he and his wife were helpful and kind. Years later we would regularly go on a trip to Irrtenberg in the summer and visit them. We were not hungry. We were under strict orders to lie down flat on the ground as soon as we heard a low-flying plane approaching. We played outside on the meadow and nobody was hurt. Then the Americans came. A few 'clever' villagers placed some tree trunks on the roads as barriers – a ridiculous idea as they were no obstacle for the tanks! In addition, it was completely unnecessary. The Americans were friendly to us, especially the children. They gave us chocolate and chewing gum and the first oranges of our life. In the day time, my parents were, I assume, in Würzburg and we had every freedom until they returned in the evening. This included smoking cigarillos in the ditch by the road until we were feeling sick.

Back in Würzburg, the Gerths were allocated two rooms in an undamaged house. 'This was the end of our freedom. The owners behaved in a hideous way and we had to creep on tiptoes through the house'. Brother Ernst returned, 'fortunately uninjured'. Then aunt Eva with her four children came from Rome.[45]

We suffered great hardship which I as a five-year-old could not fully comprehend, but sensed nevertheless. Würzburg presented a ghostly vision. Streets lined with ruins, mountains of rubble wherever you looked. There was a lack of water due to damaged water pipes. Fetching water in buckets and canisters from a public water pipe at restricted times became part of a daily ritual. Whingeing was not allowed!

Ernst went to Nürnberg, the first intact university in Franconia/Bavaria having completed the so-called *Notabitur*, 'Emergency A-levels', during the war. Both Christa-Maria's sisters attended the boarding school of the 'Angelic Young Ladies' in Bad Kissingen.

Life went on somehow. Everything was 'passed on' – shoes, dresses, coats, all second-hand. Then food tokens were introduced. We were never starving, but a roll, warmed up in the oven for breakfast on a Sunday was a rare highlight. And black marketing was flourishing. Even I noticed that. Women of Würzburg were standing on mountains of rubble and chipping bricks for re-use. These were the legendary Trümmerfrauen, 'Rubble Women', wearing aprons and head scarves.

Much of the family conversation concerned regaining their wealth. Georg was not allowed to work initially because, as a naval officer, his membership of the Nazi Party had been required. He had to go through a process of de-Nazification would took several months.

> *Entnazifizierung*, *'De-Nazification'*, *was an Allied initiative to rid German and Austrian society, culture, press, economy, judiciary, and politics of any remnants of the National Socialist ideology. Nazi Party members were removed from positions of power and influence. The Allies and the United States in particular [which controlled Würzburg] began to lose interest in the programme, and it was carried out in an increasingly lenient and lukewarm way until being officially abolished in 1951. The American government soon came to view the program as ineffective and counterproductive. Additionally, the program was hugely unpopular in Germany and was opposed by the new West German government.*[46]

However, Maria could work and she restarted the wine wholesale business immediately in adverse circumstances on the plot of the Old University. Of course, Georg did work, quietly, for his wife. During this 'grey' period, Christa-Maria went everywhere with her almost-unknown father and, as a six-year-old, developed a close relationship with him. For three months they walked the woods, told stories, read books, which included a personal present of a poetry book into which favourite poems were copied. The Gerths were given the chance to extend a barn in the *Josefshof*, 'Joseph's Court', on the outskirts of Würzburg as their home. They were surrounded by fields, cattle, and many German refugees who had come from the east.

> *We all went to school, three quarters of an hour one way, past the American barracks. On Fridays, when they got alcohol, I was sometimes a bit afraid as I had to walk alone for the last bit of my school route. I often ran rather than walked. Because there were only a few intact schools, teaching was organised in shifts, sometimes in the morning, sometimes in the afternoon, and the teachers, who were mostly of the older generation, demanded strict discipline. By hitting my fingers with the ruler, they forced me who was originally left-handed to use my right hand for writing.*

Georg was eventually allowed to work again and managed the Leinecker wholesale business. Slowly things improved everywhere. Blocks of flats were built replacing the ruins. Social housing became the order of the day for many years.

> *I also remember the currency reform. The newly allocated money was spread out on the big dining table, the D-Mark. We could get cream and fruit and rolls! Pure paradise. Many things had also been lost*

irretrievably in the war, but my family was fortunate that no family member had been killed.

Georg and Maria steadily rebuilt their life and business. All Gerth's landscape paintings with almost all of the family belongings were lost in the bombing. Gerth rekindled his interest in philosophy and Zen Buddhism. He read extensively; many of his books are still on Christa-Maria's shelves. He enjoyed ice cream, loved a cigar, a glass of red wine, his Meerschaum pipe, and, perhaps harking back to the u-boat days, a caged canary. The Leinecker business prospered, eventually owning four wholesale premises, two in Würzburg, and one each in Dortmund and Hildesheim, one of them managed briefly by a swindler.

Georg gradually cut back on work in the 1950s; he had the first touches of cancer. He kept in touch with his shipmates, especially from Crew '07. Their old comrades association worked hard to organise annual meetings and to send out regular newsletters many of which survive in the admiralty records at Freiburg.[47] In 1953, Gerth wrote from Würzburg that his health was 'not quite up to scratch any more'. His wife worked from early to late in her own business. His son, Ernst supported Georg at Leinecker's. The three daughters all still attended school, the oldest about to do her *Abitur*. 'Georg is very happy about every visit he receives from ex-crew visitors. He will try to visit 'Braune' in late autumn in Flensburg, take part in a crew meeting in Hamburg and afterwards be taken to Lüneburg.'[48]

Next year, Gerth was critically ill with several operations and 'endless stays in hospital'.[49] Flensburg was 'off'. His 'enjoyment of life had been dampened for years by the illness within him, but after his convalescence he hoped to return stronger than before'. In 1957, he pulled out of the 50th Crewfest.[50] Two years later, Gerth wrote that he feeling better again, but that he wanted to finally retire.[51] In 1962, he announced the wedding of his son Ernst with Miss Winni Ritter on 28/4/62 in Braunschweig.[52] Messages through the 1960s spoke increasingly and briefly about the effects of illness.[53] He lived at home 'like a hermit'.[54]

Maria died three months before Georg, but he was not told. For the last three years, he did not speak and lived in total silence, slept on a mattress on the floor kept in by side supports; suffered from dementia, holding a newspaper upside down, he was helpless and needed intimate care.

Death has reaped a rich harvest among our crew: On 19 June 1970, our crew sister Frau Maria Gerth died in Würzburg, aged 70. For many years she had cared for her husband who soon after WW2 often suffered from bad health, especially in the last five years in which he was bound to his bed and arm chair.[55] Suffering become harder year to year for 'Raven Gerth' who died on 13 September, aged 82.

According to naval custom, the senior living member of each annual Crew wrote the obituary.[56] In Gerth's case, this was the legendary Werner 'Fips' Fürbringer, who died aged ninety-one in 1982 in Brunswick, one of the most successful World War I u-boat commanders, sinking 102 ships.[57] He was in command of *UB 110* in the Flanders Flotilla at the same time as Gerth's service. On 19 July 1918 off the coast of Scarborough *UB 110* was damaged by depth charges, forced to surface, and rammed by the destroyer HMS *Garry*. Fips was captured. Fürbringer alleged that, after the sinking, HMS *Garry* hove to and opened fire with revolvers and machine guns on the unarmed survivors. During the ensuing massacre, Fürbringer watched the skull of an 18-year old member of his crew being split open by a lump of coal hurled by a Royal Navy sailor. The shooting only ceased when the convoy the destroyer had been escorting and which contained many neutral-flagged ships, arrived on the scene. Fürbringer later recalled, 'As if by magic the British now let down some life boats into the water.'[58] Twenty-three members of the crew died during the sinking and the alleged ensuing massacre. Lieutenant Commander Charles Lightoller, who was the most senior officer to survive the sinking of the *Titanic*, was awarded a bar to his Distinguished Service Cross for the sinking of *UB 110*. During the next war, Lightoller took his 'little ship', a small motor yacht, to the Dunkirk evacuation and brought back over 120 British servicemen.

Fürbringer wrote of Gerth, 'always the burning cigar between his fingers and the red wine in the background ... he spread a special atmosphere of comfort and was always open for any humour ... Gerth was reliable with high intellectual abilities, unshakable calm, and his personal style nominated him as a high-quality person and an outstanding officer ... he was highly popular and commanded maximum respect among his companions ... Way too early, his heavy suffering captured him. Only rarely, when you visited him at the end, did the memories light up his eyes.'

ENDNOTES

1   Hastings, *Bomber Command*, p. xi. Bomber Command's aircrew losses in World War II were about ten times higher that the German u-boat crew losses in World War I.
2   9/2/1920 (KTB, *UC 61*, addendum, V4), pp. 35–39, Cuxhaven.
3   Chapter 8, 'Final patrol'.
4   Curriculum vitae, Würzburg University, 5/1923.
5   *Freiburg*, RM 20/525, Reichs-Marine-Amt 11/1918–3./1919, and RM 21/1–2, Archiv der Marine, Vols. 1–2, 11/1918–1/1920, 2/1920–3/1920.
6   Letter, Trotha, Berlin, 22/10/1919 (RM 21/1, Vol. 1, 11/1918–1/1920).
7   *Cuxhaven*, Obituary, biographical profile, Georg Gerth, *Marine Offizier Vereinigung*, 'Navy Officers' Association', 11/2016.
8   There is a useful view of the Saar Territory in Reichstag discussions reported in Kessler, *Rathenau*, pp. 372–74. The Versailles Treaty also provided for a plebiscite at the end of

the fifteen-year period to determine the territory's future status. In 1935, more than 90 per cent of the electorate voted for reunification with Germany, while only 0.8 per cent voted for unification with France. The remainder wanted to rejoin Germany, but not while the Nazis were in power (wikipedia).

9   Records of the Saarbrücken Chamber of Commerce before 1944 were destroyed by World War II bombing (private email, Oliver Groll, 4/4/2016).

10   Curriculum vitae, Würzburg University, 5/1923. Cuxhaven, biographical profile.

11   Chapter 11, 'Immense cemetery'.

12   Chapter 11.

13   Blanton, *Mental and Nervous Change*, p. 7.

14   Ruth Myers, handwriting consultant, London, 3/2017.

15   Joll, *Unspoken Assumptions*, p. 9.

16   Anna Maria's parents were Heinrich Carl Wilhelm Emil Georg Ernst Gerth, brother to Ernst, Georg's father, and Friederike Wilhelmine Emilie Leben, married 18/7/1861 in Brandenburg (ancestry.com).

17   Interview, Christa-Maria Gerth, 15/11/2106. Berliners are well known in Germany for their fast, quick-witted, loud-mouthed, slightly vulgar, over-confident bordering on arrogant, way of speaking. This is summed up in the term *Berliner Schnauze*, 'Berlin snout/ gob'. The most comparable British dialect would be the Cockney dialect of Londoners. The chatty cabbies of both cities are similar in this respect. The German stage version of the musical *My Fair Lady*, which celebrated London and Cockney speech, was set in Berlin and used Berlin dialect.

18   Joseph Nikolaus Leinicker (with a middle 'i'), born 8/10/1789, Würzburg, merchant, died 20/10/1843, Würzburg, Maria's great-grandfather. The foundation date of the firm is found on company promotional literature celebrating 150 years of business in 1965.

19   Maria Leinecker's father was Oberstleutnant z.D. Josef Richard (preferred Christian name) Leinecker, a career soldier, who on 4/8/1914 was *Kommandant der Ersatzabteilung*, commander of the reserve, 11 Field Artillery Regiment, Royal Bavarian Army.

20   University of Würzburg archive, 1923, 10582.

21   *TNA*, FO 371/2679, 16/5/1916, p. 49.

22   Dissertation, 5/1923, University of Würzburg.

23   Matriculation No. 1861/114R, 6/11/1923 to 24/1/1924 (University email, Auste Wolff, 29/5/2017).

24   Personal email, Christa-Maria Gerth, 18/3/2017.

25   Chapter 15, 'Salomon and the film business'.

26   Hedwig Gerth, née Boch, born Aken, district of Calbe on the River Saale, 19/5/1862, died 12/9/1923 (Civil Registry Office Berlin III, Berlin-Tiergarten, 1923: No. 775), buried 15/9/1923 (Parish of the Kaiser-Wilhelm-Gedächtniskirche, Berlin-Charlottenburg).

27   The church was built in the 1890s and was badly damaged in a bombing raid in 1943. The present building, which consists of a church with a foyer and a separate belfry with a chapel, was built between 1959 and 1963. The damaged spire of the old church has been retained and its ground floor has been made into a blue-glass-walled memorial hall. The Church today is a famous landmark of western Berlin, nicknamed *Der hohle Zahn*, 'the hollow tooth' (wikipedia).

28   Christa-Maria Gerth email 183/2017.

29   Ernst Richard, born 25/9/1926 (no children), died 8/6/1995; Ilse Marie (married Nikolaos Paparafiu, no children) 24/8/1934, died 2016; Hedwig-Therese (married Alfred Kremheller, no children) 24/7/1936, died 27/1/2016; Christa-Maria 14/11/1939 (two sons).

30   Equivalent to Lieutenant Commander in the Royal Navy, Major in the British Army.

31   Georg Gerth's service during World War II has been found in *Freiburg*, RM 17, Navy Personnel Office – officer staff records.

32   RM 17/65: Document by the Memel Base Commander, Captain von Bredow, dated 29/3/1940. RM 45 I/83, KTB of the Base Commander, 1–6/1940.

33   RM 17/75: Document by Commander Sea Defence Sandnessjöen, dated 27/9/1940. RM 45 III/190 KTB, of the Commander, Sea Defence, 17/7/1940–31/12/1941, extract 1/7–31/10/1940.

34 RM 17/54: Document, Warnemünde, 30/12/1940, repeated in documents 19/3, 1/4 and 20/6/1941.
35 RM 17/54–5: Document, Kiel 7/4/1942.
36 RM 17/45: Document, Eckernförde, 21/12/1942 listing officer staff at the *Torpedoversuchsanstalt*, 1/1/1943.
37 Siebert, 'British Bombing Strategy in World War Two' (bbc.co.uk/history/worldwars/wwtwo/area-bombing_04.shtml), p. 4, 1/8/2001.
38 Overy, *Bombing War*, p. 397.
39 Hastings, *Bomber Command*, Appendix E, pp. 482–87.
40 Bergander, *Dresden im Luftkrieg*, p. 349, cited in Probert, *Bomber Harris*, p. 321.
41 Probert, *Bomber Harris*, pp. 132–33.
42 Hastings, *Bomber Command*, Chapter 7, 'Protest and Policy'; Overy, *Bombing War*, pp. 410–12, Chapter 10, 'Balance Sheet of Bombing'; Probert, *Bomber Harris*, pp. 147, 316–22; and much else throughout these books and others.
43 British Air Staff paper, 23/9/1941 in Harris, *Despatches on War Operations*, p.7.
44 Christa-Maria Gerth was four-years-old at the time so any discrepancies in memory and chronology can be readily forgiven.
45 These are memories of a long time ago. It is possible that Eva Gerth's visit to Wurzburg was some time after the war ended.
46 wikipedia.
47 Freiburg, MSG 2/18640, Crew 1907, Notes (1909–1978).
48 Message sheet No. 10, p. 2, 8/8/1953.
49 Message sheet No. 12, p. 1, 24/6/1954.
50 Message sheet No. 19, p. 1, 15/4/1957.
51 Message sheet No. 25, p. 2, 6/10/1959.
52 Message sheet No. 31, p. 2, 14/5/1962.
53 Message sheets No. 34, p. 3, 25/8/1963; No. 38, p. 3, 2/9/1965; No. 40, p. 2, 8/11/1966; No. 44, p. 2, 20/4/1968.
54 Interview, Christa-Maria Gerth, 15/11/2106.
55 Message sheet No. 51, p. 1, 3/12/1970.
56 Wegener, *Naval Strategy*, p. li.
57 *Cuxhaven*, Obituary, 11/2016.
58 Fürbringer, *Legendary*, pp. 118–21.

CHAPTER 18

The Long Arm of the War

Laziness and cowardice are the reasons why so great a portion of mankind, after nature has long since discharged them from external direction, nevertheless remains under lifelong tutelage, and why it is so easy for others to set themselves up as their guardians. ... If I have a book which understands me, a pastor who has a conscience for me, a physician who decides my diet, and so forth, I need not trouble myself. I need not think, if I can only pay – others will readily undertake that irksome work for me.[1]

1917: Insulting the Cavalry

Cavalry officers can be sensitive. After the crew of *UC 61* were successfully escorted to the Calais Citadel on 26 July 1917 that might have been the end of the matter, another small job concluded in four years of war. However, imagination was fired; elements of the Belgian Press were anxious to gain renown for their fighting forces. What had been a simple support role rapidly turned into something much more significant. Within a few weeks, the 5th Regiment of Lancers had actually brought the crew ashore. From there it was only a small step to a story that spread around the world of how a u-boat had been captured by the Belgian cavalry: *'Quand la Cavalerie belge captura un sous-marin allemande'*.[2]

There was already considerable antipathy among infantry regiments to the cavalry of all of the Allies. Originally intended to wait behind the front lines until the infantry achieved a bloody breakthrough, the plan at the start of the war was for the fast-moving horsemen to pour through the gap, fight gloriously with sword and lance, and cause havoc in the enemy's rear. The trouble was that there were few gaps and, in any event, when there was one it could not be charged by horses because of the mud, shell holes, trenches and barbed wire. Ludendorff declared that by 1916 'trench warfare offered no scope for cavalry'.[4] The reputation of the cavalry was made worse in several ways. The cavalry, always the senior regiment and perhaps with a certain arrogance, rode everywhere. Their units demanded precedence on the road, often leaving badly-needed foot soldier reinforcements waiting their turn at crossroads. Forage was the largest item by weight shipped from England to France, exceeding 'even ammunition' and it probably took 'more shipping space than was lost to German submarines'.[3] During the war, channel transports carried 5,916,104 tons of oats and hay, cavalry fodder by no means accounting for the total, while the amount of ammunition was 5,296,302 tons. By 1917 and the stranding of *UC 61*, many cavalry regiments on both sides of the front line were reduced to providing mounted infantry to plug gaps that were desperate and dangerous rather than to charge through them. Cavalry regiments, like the Belgian lancers, invariably took their rest and recreation far away from the front at a safer and more relaxed seaside, especially where there were wide beaches to exercise the horses. So it was for the 5th Regiment at Wissant.

Quickly, all the lancer units of the Belgian cavalry were given the life-time soubriquet, 'Submarines'.[5] In October, infantrymen of a company of the 11th Regiment of the Line treated a squadron of the 3rd Lancers, innocent parties all, with ironic comments, perceived as insults, 'se plaignant des injures', as they paused on the road giving way to the cavalrymen. The commander of the lancers complained to his opposite number, General Jules Marie Alphonse Jacques, 1st Baron Jacques de Dixmuide.[6] General Jacques founded Albertville in the Congo in 1894 and was one of those whose colonial behaviour was questioned by the British.[7] From early in 1917, Jacques commanded the 3rd Belgian Army division and was credited by the Belgian government with preventing Dixmuide from falling to the Germans for which feat he was elevated to Baron.[8] On hearing of the 'insults' to the lancers, Jacques 'immediately ordered a strict investigation' to find the culprits. 'Express orders' were given to 'avoid the repeat of similar events which I myself, as much as yourself, regret and which can affect the good relations between brothers-in-arms'.

The investigation found that an infantry soldier had shouted 'Submarines' at the passing lancers. He claimed it was a 'simple joke' and was not meant to be 'offensive to the cavalry'. If the soldier had realised that he might be misunderstood he would have shouted, 'Here are the conquerors of submarines'. However, the lancers needed greater appeasement. The soldier was placed in solitary confinement for four days and deducted twelve days of war pay supplement. The lieutenant in command of the infantry company was given six days of simple arrest for 'not immediately suppressing the discourteous act and for not reporting it to his senior officers'. A punishment of eight days' confinement to the camp area was given to the adjutant 'as commander of a platoon exercising on a road, leaving his troops at rest while a squadron of cavalry passed, and when one of his men was discourteous to this detachment did not find out the name of the culprit so as to inform his company commander'.

1920: Salvaging the Scrap

War over, the pieces of *UC 61* settled slowly into the Wissant sand and became a minor tourist attraction. Children played on and around the wreck. The serious matter of responsibility for the scrap needed to be decided. In 1920, M. R Mazerat for the Navy Ministry wrote to the Vice Admiral, Commander in Chief of the Maritime Prefecture at Cherbourg, explaining the position:

> *Following the various notes you have sent concerning the German submarine* UC 61 *grounded at Wissant, I bring to your attention* [the fact that] *this vessel is strictly speaking neither a wreck nor the spoils of war; it is military equipment abandoned by the enemy. All the same, given the little value that remains in the hull of* UC 61 *as all the useful parts have already been taken off by the Navy, I consider that it is advisable to pass it to the Administrator of the Maritime Area in Calais who will take charge of it as a wreck and will dispose of it as necessary.*[9]

Disposal began in the form of M. Charlemagne Honvault, citizen of Wissant, who, it may be remembered, was on duty on the morning of July 1917 at the nearest semaphore and customs post to where *UC 61* stranded. It was Honvault, national hero Coastguard 2nd class Stanislas Pierre Louis Serin, and the unnamed shrimp girl who first spotted the submarine, who combined to alert the authorities. The wreck remained since stranding in the same place on the beach and was quickly auctioned off in 1920 under the auspices of the *Inscription Maritime*, the 'Naval Register'. It was bought for 1,500 francs by Honvault who accepted the task of removal.[10] In truth, Honvault's intent was not so much removal, but the collection of 'large quantities' of bronze and copper. He intended to use *Melinite* explosive to expose *UC 61*'s interior.[11] Honvault was an hotelier, restaurateur and seller of timber salvaged from wrecks. He died in 1920, the same year as his purchase of *UC 61*. Honvault's son, Maurice Charlemagne Honvault managed the demolition in 1928.[12] In 2006, local diver Alain Richard tracked down Charlemagne's grandson, Lucien, still living in Wissant, and confirmed details of the story with Lucien's wife, Léone.[13] Honvault apparently recovered a significant amount of worthwhile metal from the wreck although there do not seem to be any figures. The family still operates a restaurant in Rue Gambetta in Wissant in 2017. Perhaps, the establishment might be renamed, or a least sub-titled, *Restaurant UC 61* in recognition of the u-boat's possible contribution to its development.

There was a surprise in store for Maurice and his workforce when they began their investigation of the wreck. They found a bronze torpedo launcher containing a self propelled torpedo, four metres long and 'weighing around 500-600 kilos'. It was live.[14] *UC 61* carried eighteen mines and five self propelled torpedoes. Two of the torpedoes were fired by commander Georg Gerth in his attempt to lighten the submarine and were later collected from the sea. Two more were salvaged from the wreck by the French military. The last torpedo, together with ten of the mines in buckled shafts, was left on board because a two-day storm sank *UC 61* one and a half metres into the sand and made removal impossible. After an experimental Belgian mortar produced a 'huge explosion', the wreck was raised in the air and fell on its side.[15] Everyone present believed that the remaining munitions had been destroyed.

Another French hero entered centre stage to save the day. An 'honourable fellow citizen', M. Carton, a retired head Artificer, offered to defuse the torpedo 'on a voluntary basis'. During the war, Artificer Carton of Calais trained and educated military teams in the defusing of bombs, torpedoes, shells and mines. In 1928, he still travelled to areas outside Calais and Boulogne to carry out his 'painstaking and dangerous work for love of his trade'.

The newspaper, *Le Miroir*, continued the story,

> *The torpedo was removed from the tube and it was decided to destroy it. To carry out this dangerous operation, it was necessary to move the lethal bomb to the foot of the cliffs at Blanc Nez. However, this was a most difficult operation. In effect, nobody wanted to lend a hand. Only a sailor from Wissant, M. Pourre, known as Mont Blanc, was prepared to help. M. Cousin from Sangatte offered his wagon. But it still needed a driver. This was how M. Leon Fournier, a man of private means living at rue de l'Amiral-Courbet, Calais, agreed to stand-in. Accompanied by these two men, Carton took the torpedo to the foot of the cliff and proceeded to destroy it. Thanks to his technical knowledge and dexterity, this operation was carried out in an excellent manner.*

According to Carton, said the newspaper, there were still two unexploded torpedoes in the wreck of the submarine. Perhaps unaccounted for may be a better description. This theory was clearly laid to rest as Honvault continued to work with his *Melinite*.

> *This new exploit pays tribute to our courageous fellow citizen who, during the war, proceeded to defuse all the aerial bombs falling on the town and submarine mines gathered up off Calais. We heartily congratulate M. Carton for this new exploit, which adds to the already long and extensive list of similar exploits, in hoping that one day the Government will be able to reward as it suits them the selfless devotion of this brave servant of the pyrotechnic art.*

1920 Onwards: Tourist Attraction

In the following years, the u-boat appeared as the focus of souvenir items sold in Wissant's tourist shops.[16] It was mentioned in war books and articles and became popular on the internet because of its 'capture' by the Belgian cavalry. A wash painting of *UC 61* on the beach featured in a 1920 book, *La Guerre Navale Racontée par Nos Amiraux*. In 1996, Robert Chaussois, in an edition of the regional newspaper *La Voix du Nord*, summarised the history of the u-boat comparing it to a North Korean submarine stranded on a South Korean beach.[17] The end of *UC 61* is cited by Gallois (1984), Gonsseaume (1988) and Dufossé (2002, 2014).[18]

1927–1930: U-boat Memorial

The symbol of the German 'u-boat sacrifice' is the famous 'U-Boot Memorial' on the 5.7 hectare site at Möltenort at the outskirts of Kiel Harbour. On 8 August 1927, some 3,000 naval veterans and visitors witnessed the laying of its foundation stone.[19] It would be the only common memorial site for the fallen comrades of both world wars; in 1969 a concourse was added bearing bronze tablets containing the names of submariners lost to the enemy in World War II. When officially opened on 8 June 1930, the towering structure overlooked the harbour exit – a saluting base for passing ships, a mecca for veterans, a gathering place for the German people on national occasions. When laying the foundation stone in 1927, the former Commander-in-Chief, Submarines, Admiral Andreas Michelsen's words were widely reported in the German press:

> *This is the memorial of the u-boat fallen whose graves are graced by neither stone nor flower. From the Baltic to the Black Sea and the most northern Arctic, they rest in unknown places in their battle-tried boats at the bottom of the sea. In vain does the hand of those left behind seek on charts and in atlases the spot where the beloved one rests to awake no more. Surely that is the very thing that obliges us to erect on their home soil a monument to those fallen, that it might be to us comrades and to others left behind a symbol of their graves.*

1929: Failing Future Prisoners of War

While the Great War set key precedents on the treatment of prisoners, these had limited impact in 1914 to 1918. It was only with the later rise of totalitarian regimes that the true horrific potential of some of the Great War innovations in captivity would become clear.[20] On the positive side, the International Committee of the Red Cross had played a major role in the inspection of camps, the transmission of information about prisoners, and humanitarian relief. The question of prisoners-of-war became less pressing with 'other priorities taking over'.[21] In spite of French efforts, it was not till later that international agreements were put in place for the protection of civilians. The ICRC campaigned for a new code 'to alleviate the conditions of prisoners of war' and this came about with the Geneva Convention of 1929 when the Convention of 1906 was revised and updated. On the negative side, the 'mass incarceration of civilian and military prisoners and their often harsh treatment were signposts on the road to the concentration camps of the later Fascist and Communist regimes'.

The ICRC failed in two later attempts, Tokyo 1934, and London 1938, and the Second World War broke out without having any ground gained and with grave consequences after 1939.

1941: The King is Dead

Kaiser II Wilhelm died at his borrowed home at *Huis Doorn* in the Netherlands never having returned to Germany after his flight in 1917. His wife, Augusta Victoria of Schleswig-Holstein, also died there in 1921, aged sixty-two. The manor house is now a museum.

1947: Goodbye Prussia

> On 25 February 1947, representatives of the Allied occupation authorities in Berlin signed a law abolishing the state of Prussia. From this moment onward, Prussia belonged to history.[22]

1951: Appealing for Restitution

Dr Eduard Marx claimed assistance for financial reimbursement and a pension from the *Entschädigungsamt*, the Berlin Compensation Office, established in 1951, for damage done to the family during the Nazi era. He applied on his own behalf, that of his step mother, Charlotte Marx, and, in 1955, that of his sister, Eva Gerth, now living in Buffalo, New York.[23]

Eduard described his own physical damage caused by his persecution as a half-Jew as 'cardiac insufficiency' following a heart attack from 1941 brought about by 'permanent persecution by the Gestapo, permanent threat of arrest and imprisonment in a concentration camp, ordered and carried out by the Berlin Chamber of Doctors and the Racial Political Office of the SS through Dr Arno Hermann, dismissal from positions of trust, and living illegally in inhuman conditions similar to imprisonment in Klein-Köris'. Eduard attached medical attestations by doctors Biedermann and Rosenhagen and other evidence and claimed for capital compensation of 10,000 Deutschmarks.

From Salomon Marx's death, his wife Charlotte Marx lived in a flat at the house in Lessingstraße from which she also received a small rental income. When the house was bombed in 1943, she lost almost all of her possessions except for a few pieces of furniture that had been stored elsewhere. A few salvaged valuables were sold. Charlotte applied for emergency aid. As late as 1956, aged seventy, Charlotte was without a pension and had to rely on financial support from her step son, Eduard, and from a son from her first marriage named Gert Mayer-Schalburg, each giving her 150 Deutschmarks per month. By this time, Eduard Marx had married again. His new wife was Jutta Therese Marie Luise Mayer-Schalburg, the daughter of his step mother, now also his mother-in-law.

Charlotte's claim for compensation rested on 'damage to life', a pension or financial compensation as Salomon Marx was 'killed by the violent actions inflicted by the Nazis or as a result of such measures', severe damage to property and possessions, damage to career and economic progress by restricting self-employment and by her dismissal from private employment. Her lawyer asked for accelerated processing of the compensation case as a *Katastrophenfall*, a catastrophic emergency, arguing that Charlotte, who registered her claim years ago, had been ill advised. Charlotte would have received a 'regular and considerable income' from the bank owned by her husband if he had died normally. Due to the liquidation of the bank enforced by the Nazis, valuable assets were lost. Her claim for compensation was also 10,000 Deutschmarks covering both a pension and a lump sum.

There was much delay. In expert opinion in 1958, a Dr Kreis stated,

> It cannot be accepted as likely that the death of [Marx] at the age of seventy in 1936 in Berlin was the result of damages caused by persecution as the existing coronary sclerosis which finally led to his death had not been affected by the influences of the persecution between 1933 and 1935 to such an extent that we would be justified to assume that there had been a causal connection between these influences and [his] death at the age of seventy.

Today, the papers relating to the inheritance court proceedings are not included in the file and are seemingly lost. What sum was finally paid by the authorities is unknown although there is a blank form from April 1958 that suggests a payment was made to someone. Also, in 1959, the Berlin *Kammergericht*, 'Superior Court of Justice' suggested a settlement without the amount identified to the 'Marx petitioners' on the basis of their original inheritance. Widow Charlotte received a quarter and children Eduard Marx and Eva Gerth, three eighths each.

1952: Reinstating the Pension

Eva Marx wrote to an acquaintance, a German parliamentarian, about her financial position. After investigation, the German government reinstated Erich's career as if he had not been forcible retired by the Nazis, adding expected promotions until his death in 1943. Eva's pension was adjusted upwards to the 'should-have-been' salary and her immediate money problems were relieved.

1958: Exhibiting a Compressor Head

In 1958, there was another *UC 61* surprise, when a 'compressor head' from the submarine mounted on a wooden frame was presented by a M. Pierre de Hauteclocque to the 4th Lancers.[24] The presentation prompted some small mysteries.

Was the piece really a 'compressor head'? Its function remains uncertain. It stands about 350cm high and is heavy enough to need two hands to carry it. It is stamped to work with pressures between 160 and 225 atmospheres and therefore needed to be robust. It is seriously crumpled which was likely caused by an explosion and this makes its lettering difficult to read. There is a letter 'M' with a crown on top [Imperial navy = Marine?]; the part word 'SAUER' [probably *Sauerstoff*, oxygen]; and the maker's name, the Maschinenfabrik Ges. [*Gesellschaft*, Company) Gelsenkirchen. The Berlin Sauerstoff Company merged with Gelsenkirchener Maschinenfabrik in 1905 and became known as Westfalia Maschinenfabrik. Westfalia produced oxygen rescue apparatus and regenerators for submarines during World War I. David Townsend, the submarine technical export who contributed earlier to the review of *UC 61*'s stranding, commented, 'I have not been able to find an equivalent in allied boats other than the possibilities of a compressed air reservoir for a pressurised water system, an internal blowing tank to pressurise a compartment in event of flooding, or, if pure oxygen, a reserve breathing apparatus.' Commander Chris Phillips suspected that 'as it specifically mentions *Sauerstoff*, it could be for adding oxygen to the atmosphere in the boat to allow for longer periods dived'.

There is some confusion about the origin of the exhibit. One report says that it was recovered from the beach in 1917 on the day of stranding and was blown out when the Germans set off their bombs which ruptured and set fire to their craft. Another story suggests it was a remnant from the Belgian mortar experiments of a few months after stranding and which sent a cloud of material thirty metres into the air. Yet another thought is that is was found by Honvault during his salvage. One imagines, however, that if it was found by Honvault it would have been sold for scrap value. Another tale is that Hauteclocque, a Frenchman and 'owner' of the exhibit, was serving in Africa in the 1950s alongside a detachment of 4th Lancers when he found out the background to the lancers' 'Submarines' name, and decided to make a gift of the memento. A version of this latter explanation seems most likely. Pierre de Hauteclocque was a member of the French

Foreign Legion and a cousin of the celebrated World War II French military leader Maréchal Leclerc de Hauteclocque.[25] Pierre de Hauteclocque saw service in Norway, England with Charles de Gaulle, battles at Dakar, Koufra, El Alamein and in Syria. He also served in Madagascar, Morocco and Indo-China, ending his career in, again, Morocco. He left the army as a lieutenant-colonel in 1958, the year he donated the 'compressor' to the Belgian lancers.[26]

The 'compressor' is now on display at a small, but excellent, *Museum Cabour WOII & 2/4 Lansiers* in De Panne, Adinkirke, in Belgium where Guido Mathieu is a most helpful and knowledgeable custodian.[27] The museum is also home for the trophies of the now combined 2/4th Lancers.[28] As the *UC 61* crew was escorted by the 5th Lancers, the exhibit's plaque is wrongly attributed and is also wrong in its commemoration of a u-boat capture as, according to the French Naval Ministry, *UC 61* was not captured, but rather abandoned. The exhibit is a cuckoo in the museum's nest, although a most interesting one.

1962[29]

Erich Gerth was not able through his work in Paris in the 1930s to bring about a reconciliation that might have prevented World War II. In 1962, his Catholic masses at Notre Dame des Victoires were mirrored in a similar ceremony.[30] President Charles de Gaulle and Federal Chancellor Konrad Adenauer 'understood the spiritual dimension of reconciliation' when they attended a Mass of Reconciliation at Rheims Cathedral, celebrated by Monseigneur François Marty, the archbishop, later cardinal and Archbishop of Paris. They had previously watched a parade of French and German troops at Mourmelon military camp. An Élysée Palace political event was not sufficient for the occasion. The choice of Rheims was meaningful on a number of levels. The Merovingian King, Clovis I, was baptised and Ludwig 1, the son Charlemagne, were crowned there. For centuries, the coronation of every French king was held in the cathedral. The city was occupied during the Franco-Prussian war, became a 'martyred' city in the first world war, and was where the German army surrendered to the Allies on 7 May 1945.[31]

1991 and 2008: English Memorabilia

About 1991, Tomas Termote, the underwater archaeologist quoted throughout this book, was pursuing his hobby of metal detecting through the magazine *Treasure Hunting*. He read an article from a detectorist in Devon or Cornwall in England; 'I cannot exactly remember where'. The detectorist sought more information on a low-quality copper ring he had found in a field which carried the inscription 'U-61 Wissant August 1917'.[32]

The ring is now with Termote.[33] The u-boat number is wrong, but there can be no doubt it refers to *UC 61*. It seems likely that the ring was made from a piece of copper pipe taken from the wreck during an August visit. This rules out one of the crew as its maker because the month is later than the crew's capture, the identifier is wrong, and the crew left the site immediately in July. Most probably it was made by a British seaman who visited the wreckage on the beach and picked out a souvenir piece of piping, made the ring and it was subsequently lost it when taken to England.

The English West Country connection continues. In 2008, at a local flea market in Somerset, Geoff Pringle bought a carved wooden lifeboat plaque from the *SS Broomhill*.[34] The *Broomhill*, a 1,700-ton collier bound from Penarth to Sheerness, was sunk on 9 May 1917 by *UC 61*.[35] Two brothers from Caernarvonshire were killed. The eighteen surviving crew rowed to Weymouth in their single lifeboat. The nameplate was likely a memory piece for a safe return. Pringle's business, oldnautibits, sold the item quickly.[36]

> *Sadly, it came with no history so I really can't add anything to the research I did at the time. Looking at the paintwork and ageing to the varnish, etc, I am sure it is as we have described and a period item. Seeing the Broomhill was lost in Lyme Bay, it is reasonable to assume the rescued crew members were landed after their ordeal in the West Country. It looks as though it may have had a paper label on the back at some stage which might well have confirmed the provenance but sadly nothing to read when we bought it.*

1994: Eva in the United States[37]

Why did the widow, former diplomatic wife and short-term countess, Eva Gerth, and her four children emigrate to America? Sometime during World War II, Erich told Eva, 'After the war, take the first ship to America.' Both he and Eva's father had been to the USA several times and were enthusiastic about what they saw. So, she had this in mind. To that can be added the general destruction and confusion in Germany that they found after returning there from Rome. And there was also the educational and economic opportunities for her children.

After arrival in Boston Harbour, the family was met by their primary sponsor, a distant relative of a Redemptorist priest friend in Rome. The sponsoring couple then drove them to Grand Rapids, Michigan, where they were initially split up, the children all going to different farm families and Eva to a well-to-do dentist's family, where she was to help with the cooking. After a short time of seeing her limited cooking ability, she was let go with the observation, 'This is not a cook, this is a countess!'

Eva then found a place to stay and work as a kitchen assistant at a Catholic boarding school for girls in Grand Rapids. After a month or so, Marc, Diana and Roger left the farms for other homes. The family was able to hold a reunion at Eva's girls school at Christmas. It was at that reunion that they received a phone call from a Jesuit priest friend who the whole family knew from Marc's years at the Jesuit boarding school at Mondragone. He invited them to come to Buffalo, New York, where he was now serving in a parish. In 1950, Eva moved ahead of the children from Grand Rapids to Buffalo. There she worked as a translator for Remington Rand and later taught foreign languages at a girls school. The children gradually joined her. A little later in the year the whole family was able to establish themselves independently in an apartment. At that time Marc and Diana started working while Isabel and Roger were still in school. Eva moved to Florida in 1955 with Isabel. She bought a four-bedroom house in Fort Lauderdale, Florida, part of which, in her enterprising way, could be rented out to winter tourists or could be used to welcome visiting family members and friends.

Eva returned to Europe several times while she was living in the United States. Her niece, Christa-Maria Gerth, remembers meeting her once in Germany although the visit is not dated. Eva's long-time preference for the sun won through, leading her, finally, to California where she moved initially to perform grandmother baby-sitting duties for Marc's family. After that she lived in Ventura, California and several other cities in southern California. She was living in Orange County when she died on 23 July 1994, a month before her ninety-ninth birthday. Eva was buried at Pacific View Memorial Park in Corona del Mar, California, over 6,000 miles from her beloved Erich at the Vatican. She was survived by her four children and thirteen grandchildren.

After having made the big decision to come to the United States, the family at various reunions always agreed that it was the best decision of their lives.

2005: Deciding to Forget?

Past the shady, pleasant Forêt de Soignes in Tervuren on the outskirts of Brussels in an enormous Louis XV-style palace built by King Leopold II is the *Royal Museum for Central Africa* .., 'On a typical day it will be swarming with hundreds of visitors, from schoolchildren filling in blank spots in workbooks to elderly visitors arriving in air-conditioned buses. The museum houses one of the world's largest collections of Africana.[38]

> *In 1999, a museum official acknowledged that possible changes in its exhibits were under study … In 2005, with much fanfare, the museum mounted a large temporary exhibit, 'Memory of the Congo: the Colonial Era', simultaneously publishing a lavishly-illustrated book of the same name. Both exhibit and book were examples of how to pretend to*

acknowledge something without really doing so. Among the hundred of photos the museum displayed, for instance, were four of the famous atrocity pictures from Morel's slide show.[39] But these were shown small and more than a dozen other photos, almost all of innocuous subjects like Congolese musicians, were blown up to life size. Another picture showed a hearing by Leopold's 1904-05 Commission of Inquiry, which a caption praised as 'a pioneering initiative in the history of human rights in Central Africa' ... The museum's book had a half-page photo of Captain Léon Rom, but made no mention of his collection of severed African heads, the gallows he erected in his front yard, or his role as a possible model for Conrad's murderous Mr Kurtz ... The book contained more than three dozen scholarly articles about everything from the bus system of Leopoldville to Congo national parks, but not a single article, not a single display case in the museum, was devoted to the foundation of the territory's colonial economy, the forced labour system. Nowhere in either book or exhibit could you find the word 'hostage'. This does not leave me optimistic about seeing the Congo's history fully portrayed in the Royal Museum in the future.
Adam Hochschild

2014: Safeguarding Surfers

The wreck of *UC 61* disappeared as the Wissant sands were moved around by fast tides and channel storms. However, local diver Alain Richard knew there was always the likelihood that it would reappear some day. 'We have seen the remains of the English trawler *Lord Grey* which was wrecked the same year as *UC 61* and which are still visible at the bottom of the foreshore to the southwest of the beach of Wissant, at Châtelet.'[40]

A survey conducted by SHOM in 1977 found that the wreck of *UC 61* was buried under the sand northeast of Wissant beach, towards Strouanne, to the right of Herlen Creek. The wreck site was deleted in 1985 following a general revision of SHOM charts.[41] After storms at the beginning of 2014 and high tides that March, wrecks reappeared along this stretch of coast including *SS Socotra*, south of Le Touquet, and the remains of the *UC 61*.[42] Mme. Laurette Maquignon was alerted of the reappearance by beach walkers. She reported its rediscovery and notified DRASSM, the *Département des Recherches Archéologiques Subaquatiques et Sous-Marins*, and the GPD, a divers' clearance group. Maquignon also discovered on the beach some 'Rommel Piles' that presented explosion hazards.[43] Alain Richard was appointed by DRASSM to investigate the wreck as it was a possible danger to surfers who practised at Wissant. He was also to pinpoint and to measure the site and to make safety recommendations. He found *UC 61* in two parts within a few metres of each other at the limit of the supervised beach swimming areas.[44]

After the survey, four buoys were installed to warn the surfers. Then the wreck disappeared again. The author with researcher and interpreter Jacqui Squire visited the site under the direction of Richard at low water on an ice-cream and shorts evening in July 2016 to find, against predictions, that *UC 61* had resurfaced.[45] The visit therefore allowed assessments to be made of the u-boat's original position on wrecking using contemporary photographs and also assessed probable firing angles to the hole in *UC 61*'s conning tower. *UC 61* stranded parallel to the dunes and facing Cap Gris Nez. Site measurements showed that the cannon had been fired from the sea and while *UC 61* was at sea.[46]

2015: Germany Apologises for Herero Genocide

In 1985, the United Nations' Whitaker Report declared that the German actions in South West Africa against the Herero and Nama peoples were one of the earliest attempts at genocide in the twentieth century.[47] In 2004, the German government recognised this and apologised, but ruled out financial compensation for the victims' descendants. In 2015, the German government and the speaker of the Bundestag officially called the events 'genocide' and 'part of a race war'. Personal reparations were refused, although Germany pays Namibia the highest aid payments per head of population compared to any other country. In 2017, representatives of the Herero and Nama announced a class action in New York was being brought against the German government for reparations.[48] The bleached bones of the Herero and Nama dead lying openly in the desert were photographed in 2016.

2016: Parisien Watering Hole

In 2016 in Paris, a new cocktail bar opened in the Rue de l'Arc de Triomphe.[49] Its grey, always locked front door is in an uninspiring street setting. Access is easy, but requires a combination of inquisitiveness and determination. Inside is unobtrusive and welcoming. The bar is long and narrow, the rough size and shape of the interior of a World War I submarine. The cocktails are good.[50]

> *UC-61 is the new venue by the guys behind 'La Conserverie'.[51] This tiny bar boasts a slightly quirky German submarine theme with various nautical bits and pieces, even a 'captain's quarters.' It's an easy place to miss. Hidden away on a quiet street with virtually no external signage and a buzzer you'll need to ring to gain entry. You could walk right past it. But that would be a mistake. It's a hip yet relaxed place with some great cocktails. The prices are on the high side, but they are reflected in the quality and the bar attracts slightly more savvy and*

sophisticated people who know their cocktails and value good service.
The atmosphere reflects this, convivial yet elegant, the kind of place
you can have a conversation while savouring your drinks and these are
drinks to savour.[52]

But why chose the name *'UC-61'*? Here is the email response of the founder,
Eric Bulteau, who specialises in restaurant and cocktail bar start-ups:

Apart from memories of a small boy who played on the remains of UC
61, we have no direct links with this boat. Its unusual story inspired us
and the bar space has implicitly guided the choice of name. We have no
intent to develop a 'museum' effect. The illusion is sufficient. Customers
are ready to play the game and to try to find out what is hiding behind
this enigmatic symbol 'UC-61' on the outside door. So, it is possible to
combine 'history' and 'a good drink'. Who would have thought it![53]

2016: *Würzburger Torte*

Georg and Maria Gerth's son, Ernst, became a professor of economics,
published several books, and emigrated to California. His last address in
1995 was thirty minutes' drive from his aunt Eva Gerth last address in the
same county.[54] There were many contacts and get togethers between Ernst
and Eva, and also her four children. Georg and Maria's two eldest daughters,
Ilse and Hedwig, lived together in Kiel after widowhood and both died in
2016. Christa-Maria stayed with her family until the Leinecker wholesale
shops were sold. Later, it was her 'duty' to work in the family coffee shop.
After her parents died and she was freed from their care, Christa-Maria
made a remarkable life as a sculptress, potter, translator, historian, and
developed a renowned *Kaffee und Kuchen* shop, still running, where her
Würzburger Torte, is held in high regard. She has two sons who live nearby.
Her most treasured possession are the books on philosophy left by her
father; his most precious gift is her commitment to Buddhism.

2016: Annoying Young Mothers

Back on Wissant beach, two young mothers shepherd their children
away from the small pieces of wreck of *UC 61*. Their annoyance is briefly
overheard,

Whoever put that dangerous metal there on a beach for toddlers? Who
would have thought anyone could be so selfish? What on earth were
they thinking of?

2017: Une Lecture Erronée[55]

When we were on the beach on 26 July, I had noticed that the presumed location of the wreck seemed to me to be a lot further than previously!! In fact, my GPS was giving a faulty reading with an error of 200/1000 minutes on the latitudinal coordinates: it was this that led us about 300 metres beyond the estimated position of the wreck!

Since then I have done another re-positioning with a new GPS, which conforms closely to the previous data. The rear of the wreck (much less visible) towards Cap Blanc Nez is at 50° 53' 556N – 1° 39' 794E. The central point, corresponding to the starboard side of the submarine is at 50° 53' 551N 1° 39' 782E. The far ends towards Cap Blanc Nez are at 50° 53' 552N – 1° 39' 785E, the other end towards the south is at 50° 53' 550N – 1° 39' 778E.

Alain Richard

2017: Centenary Thank-you

On 26 July 2017, some twenty archivists, historians, translators, enthusiasts and family members who had helped piece together the Gerths' story were invited to attend a day-long centenary event at Wissant where Georg Gerth stranded *UC 61* one hundred years before. Attendees, vicarious u-boat travellers all, came from Belgium, France, Germany and the UK.

Pride of place went to Frau Christa-Maria Gerth, the last-surviving child of Georg Gerth, and her two sons, Franz and Frédéric who travelled from Bavaria for their first visit to the area. Other important guests were Alain Richard, diver and u-boat wreck historian and writer, who produced the 1977 wreck report on *UC 61* for the Service d'Hydrologie et d'Océanographie de la Marine, and his wife Ingrid, who was then curating the travelling exhibition 'La Grande Guerre sous La Mer', which dealt with wrecks of the first world war, many of them u-boats, on the Opal Coast.

The *UC 61* commemorative party met in the morning inside Wissant Town Hall where to the hour one hundred years before, the crew were stripped of the personal documents (but allowed to keep their bread and sausage) and received their first cursory interrogations. These documents were recently found in Paris and photographs of them were shared with the party. Everyone then walked along the beach to the wreck site which was found using GPS and a metal detector. The wreck rises and falls within its covering of tidal sand. It was visible last autumn, but on this anniversary visit was under 1.5 metres of sand. Here, on the exact spot, in the sunshine, the circumstances of the grounding were discussed. Two weeks later, like a good submarine, *UC 61* had risen again.

The group then had lunch in a nearby restaurant when they were joined by town dignitaries and historians. About 100 pictures associated with the crew and the stranding were played on a looped slide show as a wall background. Commemorative t-shirts were distributed. The party then drove the twenty kilometres from Wissant to Calais Citadel, mostly following the route walked by the crew under its guard of Belgian lancers. At the Citadel, the main interrogations and first imprisonment occurred. Details of the interrogations were shared from original documents found recently in Cherbourg.

That evening, the *Art and History Society of Wissant* managed a conference, 'La mission inachevée de l'UC-61', which was attended by almost 200 people.[56] Christa-Maria Gerth was introduced by the society's president, M. Jean-Marie Ball, to a round of applause. Lieutenant-Colonel Henri Lesoin outlined the course of the naval war in the North Sea and the Channel with emphasis on the submarine war. Dr Chris Heal was then invited to give a presentation, with live interpretation by Jacqui Squire, on four points: a description of the last voyage, theories on the reason for the stranding with emphasis on the cannon hole found in the conning tower; the secrets of the wreck; and the fate of the crew, three of whom died during imprisonment, while the rest were held until March 1920. At the end, local historian, M. Gallois, introduced some documents and photographs about the final life of the wreck which were discovered only the week before.

At the lunch, Christa-Maria Gerth, as a survivor with her father of the loss of their home to World War II carpet bombing, gave a short, poignant and impromptu speech, interpreted by her eldest son Franz:

Thank you for allowing me to say a few personal words. This hadn't been planned at all, but then I never thought that this event here would touch me so much!

My father – like most men – never talked about the war, neither the first nor the second. I was only affected by the aftermath of WW2 as a child and could talk about this experience. But now here, 100 years later – a lump of iron in the sand, I see a vision of my father in front of me thanks to the research of you all and the photos that have emerged.

A young man, just like his older brother Erich, two years his senior, who joined the Imperial Navy straight after leaving school and then did his service for Kaiser and fatherland. Nobody knows if this was his lifetime dream; personally, I suspect it wasn't for he was a thoroughly philosophical and religious man. He also used the time of his captivity to study the works of the German philosopher Immanuel Kant. He was thirty years old when he stranded here in his submarine and became a French prisoner of war. Thirty strikes me as incredibly young when

I look at my son Frédéric who is even six years older than that. My father was treated fairly during captivity – he told me so himself and you have found out that he was also fair in his dealings with his crew and his enemies. I'm very glad about this as this is how I knew him in his civil life.

By your work, I have got to know my 'unknown' father. I am grateful for this; unfortunately, so late in my life. My father has been dead for more than thirty years, but you can still have conversations with the dead, this I now know.

I could finish here. But time went on and soon after WW1 followed WW2 – as devastating and cruel as the first one. I remember many things: hastily getting up in the middle of the night and taking refuge in the air raid shelter. Later heaps of rubble, queuing at a public standpipe, housing shortages, playing in the ruins. My home town, Würzburg, one of the most beautiful German cities, was literally reduced to rubble by the English – I'm sorry to say. But there was one of them, an Englishman – I've forgotten his name – who said, 'Stop!' and prevented our Residenz [the Palace of the Prince Bishops] from being totally destroyed. It is now a world heritage site.[57] His courage and his appreciation of values is praised every year on the anniversary of the date of destruction, 16 March 1945.

I cannot comment on the question of guilt. But I know what it means that we have had peace for many years now and I also know how threatened this peace is in our time. I would like to end quoting the words of British Prime Minister Theresa May – 'Enough is enough' – even if she used them in a different context.

Yes, it has been enough, but the fact that we can sit together as friends and talk about the war is a reason to celebrate.

Thank you.

ENDNOTES

1 Kant, *Foundations of the Metaphysics,* p. 85.
2 1914-1918.be/insolite_sous_marin.php.
3 *Statistical Abstract of Information,* Imperial War Museum, 1919, quoted in Marquis of Anglesey, *History of the British Cavalry,* Vol. 8, pp. 286–87. See also Liddell Hart, *First World War,* pp. 61–62.
4 Ludendorff, *Own Story,* Vol. 1, p. 457.
5 *Royal Museum of the Armed Forces and of Military History,* Brussels, AU 9089/2, p. 108. See also 4th Regiment HQ correspondence (Box 308, 26/7/1917).
6 Letter 31/10/1917, Baecken, *Historique du 5° régiment,* p. 131.
7 Chapter 2, 'Kaisertreu'.
8 Compare the achievements of Frenchman Pierre Ronarc'h in the same battle, Chapter 2.
9 Letter 22/5/1920, Bundle 70–75 (*SHD,* Cherbourg, Box MV SS Gr 43), p. 70.
10 Chatelle, *Calais Pendant La Guerre,* pp. 163–65.
11 Picric acid was the first high explosive nitrated organic compound widely considered suitable to withstand the shock of firing in conventional artillery. In 1885, based on research by Hermann Sprengel, a French chemist, Eugène Turpin patented the use of pressed and cast picric acid in blasting charges and artillery shells. In 1887, the French government adopted a mixture of picric acid and guncotton under the name *Melinite.* In 1888, Britain started manufacturing a similar mixture in Lydd, Kent, under the name *Lyddite* (wikipedia).
12 Richard, Coulon and Lowrey, 'L'odyesée de 5 sous marins allemands', *Sucellus,* pp. 61–85.
13 Conversation with Alain Richard at Wissant, 18/7/2016.
14 *Le Miroir,* 'On découvre une torpille dans l'épave du sous-marin allemand échoué à Wissant', 'A torpedo discovered in the wreck of the German submarine beached at Wissant', 30/6/1928 (*SHD,* Cherbourg, Box MV SS Gr 43).
15 Chapter 10,' Intelligence gift'.
16 A souvenir low-value envelope knife was recently found at the home of the Honvault family. It carries the legend, 'Souvenir du sous-marin Allemande échoué à Wissant 26 juillet 1917'.
17 Chaussois, 'Le cigare naviguait trop près de la cote', *La Voix du Nord,* 6–7/10/1996.
18 Philippe Gallois, 'Le Wissant d'hier et ses environs', *SI de Wissant –site des 2 Caps* (Print Forum, Lille 1984), p. 153. Christian Gonsseaume, Naufrages et fortunes de mer, Book 2 (Amis du Musée de la Marine d'Étaples, 1988), p. 285. Franck Dufossé, *Wissant, des origines aux années 1930* (AMA, 2002), p. 203; *Wissant 1914–1918* (Art et Histoire de Wissant, Mairie de Wissant 2014).
19 Hadley, *Count Not the Dead,* p. 57.
20 Jones, 'Prisoners of War', in Winter, *First World War,* Vol. II, pp. 289–90.
21 Delpal, 'Prisonniers de guerre', p. 156.
22 Clark, *Iron Kingdom,* p. xix.
23 *LABO,* Documents Marx Family 1951–58, file Salomon Marx/304.641, 'Claim form for Class B 'Damage to body and health', p. B1, and 'Claim for Class C Damage to liberty', p. C1, Dr Eduard Marx, Berlin-Schöneberg, 25/4/1951, both submitted 10/7/1951: 'Affidavit', p. C2, Eduard Marx, Berlin-Wilmersdorf, 17/1/1952; 'Power of Attorney' drafted, Eva Gerth, Buffalo, USA, certified by the German consulate, New York, 27/09/1955, p. M30; 'Application', Charlotte Marx, Berlin-Schöneberg, 9/9/1956, p. M1; 'Form claiming damage to career progress', pp. E1–E2, Charlotte Marx, 2/12/1956; 'Letter by solicitor, Dr Georg Lancelle', Berlin, 12/3/1957, p. M13.
24 Guido Mathieu, custodian, Museum Cabour WOII & 2/4 Lansiers, Moeresteenweg 141, 8660 Adinkerke, Belgium.
25 wikipedia.
26 Pierre de Hauteclocque married Nicole de Saint-Denis, an important member of the French resistance in World War II, receiving the Croix de Guerre, and later a prominent politician in Paris.
27 www.depanne.be/product/1083/museum-cabour-wo-ii-en-24-lansiers.

28 Museum Cabour WOII & 2/4 Lansiers, Moeresteenweg 141, 8660 Adinkerke; +32 58 42 97 53.

29 Email, Roger Gerth, 22/1/2018.

30 8/7/1962. Chapter 16, 'Erich and his Catholic and Jewish problems'.

31 Chapter 2.

32 Email, Termote, 17/8/2016.

33 Termote, *Krieg Unter Wasser*, p. 318.

34 Emails, Pringle, 29/2/2016.

35 *TNA*: ADM 137/1296; ADM 137/2692; ADM 137/4114.

36 Item 4377, oldnautibits.com.

37 Emails Marc and Roger Gerth, 21/1/2018.

38 Hochschild, *King Leopold's Ghost*, pp. 292, 312–13.

39 Chapter 2.

40 *Lord Grey*, trawler, lost 2 December 1917 (www.naval-history.net/WW1LossesBrRNA-L. htm, accessed April 2016). SHOM reference 21601059.

41 SHOM is the *Service d'Hydrologie et d'Océanographie de la Marine* – the French Navy Hydrology and Oceanography Service which edits all French sea charts. It is also responsible for the management of wrecks. SHOM wreck record 21601056, coordinates 50° 53'614 N – 1° 39'865 E (Euro 50) was invalidated in 1985.

42 On 26 November 1915, the British steamer SS *Socotra* ran aground off Le Touquet, France, while en route from Brisbane to London with general cargo (wrecksite.eu/wreck. aspx?2911), accessed 8/4/2016.

43 Underwater constructions to prevent landing craft gaining a French beach during an invasion by the Allies in World War II.

44 One section measured 4.35m by 2.55m with a height of 0.70m, lying to the northeast in the direction of Blanc-Nez at a point 50° 53'557 N – 1° 39'793 E. It is not far from the wreck point cancelled by SHOM 21601056. The co-ordinates on a Euro 50 tracking device processed on WGS 84 gave 50° 53'564 N – 1° 39'785 E. The second section lies towards Wissant and extends for 11.60m; the largest width is at the centre, 3.60m, while at each end the width is no more than 2,70m. In WGS 84 points, the average position is 50° 53'551 N – 1° 39'780 E (DRASSM report OA 2533, No, 2014–105).

45 18/7/2016.

46 Chapter 8, 'Final patrol'.

47 wikipedia. *BBC News*, 'Germany admits Namibia genocide', 14/8/2004. *International Business Times*, 'German official says Namibia Herero killings were 'Genocide', 13/7/2015. Also, *Spiegel Online*, 13/7/2015; *The Economist*, 11/5/2017.

48 *BBC News*, 12/10/2017.

49 uc-61.com.

50 Visit 12/10/2016.

51 The bar '*La Conserverie*' has now been relaunched as '*Le Fou*'.

52 worldsbestbars.com/bar/paris/champs-elysees/uc-61.

53 Private email, Eric Bulteau, 17/8/2106.

54 US Social Security Applications and Claims Index (ancestry.com).

55 Private email, Alain Richard, 6/9/2017.

56 *Memoire d'Opale*, Richard, 'Quatre Épaves', No. 9, 2017, pp. 47–67.

57 Frau Gerth can be forgiven a small lapse in memory which confused the 'Englishman' with an American, part of the occupying forces in the area of Würzburg at the end of the war. This unnamed American recognised that while the roof of the *Residenz* was destroyed, the precious wall and ceiling works below were mostly undamaged. He arranged quickly for extensive tarpaulins to be used to act as a makeshift roof and thereby saved the internal structure and its paintings from further damage (Private conversation with Dr Jarl Kremeier, *Die Hofkirche der Würzburger Residenz*, 1999, 1/9/2107).

Appendices

Kriegstagebuch *UB 12*

Date: 22 June – 4 November 1916[1]

27 June 1916

Left Bruges for Zeebrugge and Zeebrugge for outpost at night.

28 June

0200: Passed gap in enemy's net barrier, navigate via Schouwen Bank light vessel.

29 June

Heading for Thornton Bank. 0520: Hazy dawn. Sighted nine enemy destroyers about 1,000 metres off. Dived. Boat is being shot at by several guns. Because of great proximity of destroyers and adverse position between Schaar and Rabe Bank, stopped evasion. Decided to lay boat on sea bed. During diving heard strong approaching propeller noises. At 20 m. depth, depth charge – water bomb – detonated close to the boat. Boat undamaged. Boat on sea bed at 34.5 m. Being searched with device by destroyer for about an hour. 0640: Propeller noises fade, go to 9 m, sighted several destroyers and two monitors on Thornton Bank. 1445: Nordhinder Light Vessel. Three steamers sighted (one American steamer – *Healdton*, New York; one unlit steamer of about 2,000 tons without flag, neutrality badge or name, on course for Maas light vessel; one unlit steamer of about 5,000 tons without flag, neutrality badge or name, on western course. 2100: Laid on sea bed because of bad weather.

30 June

0700: Because wind and sea have not calmed decided to sail back. 1230: Anchored at Zeebrugge mole. Reported return to u-boat-flotilla. Received order to go to Bruges. 1530: Anchored in Bruges.

1–3 July

Bruges. Boat in docks for repair of hydroplane. Only limited steering movement possible.

Top Secret Flotilla Order, Bruges, 3 July 1916, signed Bartenbach

News of the enemy: Between 4-8 July a bombardment on Zeebrugge is said to be planned by English naval forces. *UB 12* on outpost north and west of Thornton Bank, *UB 17* on outpost east of Thornton Bank. Be aware of sailings of our own ub- and uc-boats and torpedo boats. Sail on 3 July evening. Attack enemy forces. Take carrier pigeons. Report important messages immediately, otherwise send daily one carrier pigeon message about observations and events. Report enemy forces at night via radio, if necessary alarm coast. Establish position and dimensions of the new net which has apparently been put up north of the old barrier. Destroy buoyage. Return 6 July. [*The small ub-boats conducted a determined campaign against the enemy barriers. By the Flanders coast they destroyed the marking buoys which were continually replaced by the enemy, and assisted the [larger] ub- and uc-boats to enter the harbour under the increasingly difficult conditions of navigation as well as rendering aid to the destroyers of the II Flotilla which were sent to relieve the pressure.*[2]]

3 July
Bruges to Zeebrugge
4 July
Zeebrugge. 0245: Passed gap in enemy's net barrier. 0500–1400: North of Thornton Bank. Searching in vain on changing courses for the new enemy net barrier as reported by planes about five miles north of the old net barrier. 1610: Heard gun fire in direction of Knocke. As gun fire at Zeebrugge expected headed towards it. Nothing was to seen or heard. Returned to Schouwen Bank. Found out from *UB 17* that it was apparently Dutch target practice.
5 July
0330: Westwards via Thornton Bank until about five miles west of Bligh Bank. Searching on changing courses for the new enemy net barrier. 1025: Injection valve of engine broken. Electronically heading for Thornton Bank. 1035-1300: Laid boat on sea bed west of Bligh Bank because of dense fog. Provisional repair of injection valve. 1345: Dived and ran attack against u-boat heading for Schouwen Bank. When passing it at about 3,000 m recognised it as one of ours, possibly UC. [*This was the last sighting of* UC 7, *homebound west of the Bligh Bank.* UC 7 *never reached Zeebrugge: the bodies of two crew members washed up on the Flanders coast while the bodies of commander Oberleutnant Georg Haag and Oberleutnant Fischer were recovered by Dutch fishing boats near the Schouwen Bank.*[3]] Thornton Bank. Headed for Schouwen Bank light vessel to check ship's position.
6 July
Schaar Bank – Nordhinder light vessel places position. Diving and underwater voyage practice. 1305: Sighted several destroyers and identified them as boats of the I. Flotilla. 1450: Passed Schouwen Bank light vessel. 1800: Zeebrugge. 2030: Moored Bruges.

7–12 July

Bruges. Maintenance works. Loading equipment.

Top Secret Flotilla Order, Bruges, 13 July 1916, signed Bartenbach

Outpost service at the barrier. Sail on 13 July in the evening. Observe activity of enemy vessels by the barrier. The area south east of Thornton Bank, especially the gap in the net barrier, is likely to be mined. On 16-17 July, the return of the u-boats *UB 18* and *UB 39* is expected. Advise boats not to use the Thornton Bank barrier gap. Return 16 July.

13 July

Bruges. 1110: Sailed for outpost duty.

14 July

Zeebrugge via Buoy 14 towards Schouwen Bank. North of Thornton Bank. Buoy S B 1, diving practice. Towards Bligh Bank. Dived before planes.

15 July

Stopped north of the gap in the enemy net barrier. Charged batteries. Diving and underwater practice near Schouwen Bank.

16 July

Net barrier. Schouwen Bank. Bligh Bank. Dived before one monitor, six destroyers. Returned past Schouwen Bank light vessel via buoy 14. 2215: Zeebrugge.

17 July

0100: Moored Bruges.

17–20 July

Bruges. Installation of 'NQ' antenna, Repairs.

21 July

Repair of fuel pump.

Top Secret Flotilla Order, Bruges, 20 July 1916, signed Bartenbach

Cruise on the steamer routes between Holland and England at commander's discretion. Sail 21/7. Take carrier pigeons. Return at commander's discretion, 25/7/16 at the latest. Nordhinder light vessel is to be avoided by a radius of five miles due to mines.

22 July

1750: Left Bruges, via Zeebrugge and barrier gap at Buoy 13 to Schouwen Bank light vessel. Underwater navigation practice.

23 July

Maas light vessel. 0530: Sighted nine destroyers. Started attack, but could not get close enough to shoot. 1615: Sighted net buoyed with glass balls. Dimensions could not be identified.

24 July

0800: Nordhinder light vessel. Heading for Lowestoft. 1105: Sighted

German u-boat. Later found out it was *UC 6*. 1350: Crossed path again with previously sighted German u-boat. Sighted several patrol boats and one plane.

25 July

Early morning heading for coast again in order to attack patrol vessels above water. No patrol boats or steamers to be seen. Turned around towards Nordhinder and Maas light vessels. 1510: Going northwards in order to check dimensions of the net seen on 23/7 in the afternoon. Identified this as a drifting piece of net. 1930: Sighted two freighter convoys. Intend to stop them as soon as outside steamer traffic at Maas light vessel. 2025: Two planes coming towards us. Machine gun shot. No response. Dived. 2110: Surfaced. Convoys are now out of reach. Cruised on steamer route.

26 July

0545: Sighted five steamers and at great distance several destroyers. 0700: Five destroyers heading towards us at great speed. Middle one is identified as small cruiser which passes at about 50 m distance. Two destroyers sail at around 600 m on both sides of the cruiser with long zigzag courses. Periscope apparently not sighted. 0705: Surfaced. Started return journey. 0915: Passed buoy SB 1, Schouwen Bank light vessel, buoy 13. 1420: Zeebrugge. 1540: Moored Bruges.

27–29 July

Repair works

30 July

1811: Bruges. Sailed for outpost, via Zeebrugge, passing barrier gap at Buoy 13. Schouwen Bank light vessel. Passed I. Flotilla sailing out. Diving tests.

31 July

1225: Sighted two destroyers. Did not attack as suspected boats belonging to Z-Flotilla, later confirmed. Went under water to Steendoep. 0445: Both depth manometers in the central unit fail due to blockage. Laid boat on sea bed. Cleared manometer. 0545: Surfaced. Conning tower hatch cannot be opened. Hook for holding the hatch in opened position has fallen onto the closed hatch and has got jammed there. Torpedo hatch is being opened and the hook is removed from the tower hatch. While doing this a plane approaching at great height is sighted. Closed torpedo hatch as quickly as possible while steering course changes at full speed. Then fast running. 0800-1200: Cruising at Schouwen Bank on different courses. 1200: Sighted two apparently Dutch torpedo boats northwest of B12. 1215: Surfaced. Cruising at Schouwen Bank. 1400: Started return journey via Buoy 14. 1740: Zeebrugge. 2140: Moored Bruges.

1–2 August

Bruges. Repairs.

3–11 August
Bruges. Maintenance.

12 August
0900: Bruges. Sailed for outpost. 1110: Zeebrugge. Passed mole.

13 August
Via Buoy 14. Heading towards Schouwen Bank light vessel. Under water navigation practice. 1125-2000: Cruising between Nordhinder light vessel and Schouwen Bank.

14 August
0730–0630: Under water navigation practice. 0630-1825: Going up and down between Bligh Bank and Schouwen Bank. Buoy SB 1. 1825: Laid boat on sea bed at Buoy SB 1 in order to repair an engine injection valve.

15 August
0600-0630: Under water navigation practice. 0630: Returned via Schouwen Bank, Buoy 13. 1500: Moored Bruges.

16–17 August
Bruges. Maintenance.

Top Secret Flotilla Order, Bruges, 18 August 1916, signed Bartenbach
[*Ambush at Sunderland.*] Five u-boats to sail from Bruges at 1800 on 18 August. Take up waiting position five sea miles apart in U-line II from 53° 33'N. 4° 09'0. to 53° 18' N. 4° 30'0 in order *UB 37, UB 19, UB 16, UB 6, UB 12*. The U-line will be occupied by the big boats until dark on 24 August; by the small boats until dark on 22 August. Then sail back. Own and enemy naval forces are to be anticipated. Trade war permitted only on return journey. Radio only in urgent cases to Bruges.

18 August
1820: Bruges. Sailed via Zeebrugge, Buoy 13. 1140: Dived before two destroyers, probably own from Z-Flotilla. 1146: Surfaced. Engine had to be turned off again immediately because of heavy banging in the second cylinder and sparking of the safety valve. It turned out that the fuel needle of the cylinder had got stuck in open position and needle, diffuser nozzle and nozzle plate had been burnt. The valve was fitted with a reserve needle, diffuser nozzle and nozzle plate, newly ground in and reinserted. During the repair went by electric power.

19 August
1425: As the repair took longer than originally anticipated laid boat on sea bed in order not to overuse batteries. 1730: Finished repair. Surfaced. Headed for Maas light vessel. 1700: Heading towards land for periscope control.

20 August
0300: Arrived at ordered position. Evaded busy traffic: steamers, fish trawlers, sailing boats so that boat remains unseen. 0700-09330: Under

water navigation practice.

21 August

Cruising on position.

22 August

0830: Started return journey.

23 August

Continued return journey via Maas light vessel, Schouwen Bank light vessel, Zeebrugge. 1030: Arrived at Bruges

24–27 August

Bruges. Maintenance.

28 August

Bruges. 1010: Sailed for outpost.

29 August

Zeebrugge, Middelkerke, heading for Westhinder Buoy. 1025: Patrols on net barrier: two monitors, two torpedo flotillas, four trawlers, six u-boat search vessels, five u-boat hunters. Decided to postpone an attack against the monitors to the late afternoon in order to shorten the time between shooting the torpedoes and nightfall as thorough u-boat searches can be expected. 12.53-1500: Laid boat on sea bed. 1540: Barrier patrol vessels on their way home Tried at full speed to hunt down monitor, but was too fast so gave up on attack. Travelled north towards Nordhinder light vessel.

30 August

1910: Schouwen Bank light vessel. Started return journey because of bad weather.

31 August

0145: Moored. Bruges.

Top Secret Flotilla Order, Bruges, 31 August 1916, signed Bartenbach

Sail on 2 September in the evening. Cruise in the Hoofden. Assume waiting position at own discretion. Take carrier pigeons. Enemy submarine at Schouwen Bank. Only attack in completely perfect position as own outpost boat is there. Return journey at night according to capability at latest on 8 September.

1 September

1015: Bruges. Sailed.

2 September

Zeebrugge, Middelkerke, Westhinder Buoy, Nordhinder light vessel, towards Maas light vessel.

3 September

Sighting of four destroyers. Three steamers sailing out from Hook of Holland. 1000: Met *UB 10*. Boats stay together in order to conduct joint trade war.

4 September

0600: Heading towards Ijmuiden. 1300: Started return journey to Maas light vessel. 1930: Off Scheveningen. Laid boat on sea bed because of bad weather.

5 September

1030: Stopped between Maas light vessel and Hook of Holland. Charged batteries.

6 September

Heading towards Nordhinder light vessel. 0845: Stopped American steamer *Eurana* from Savannah on westerly course. Turned out to be Belgian Relief steamer. Released. 1115: Stopped and repaired injection valve of engine. 1250: Interference removed. Cruise continued. 1615: Sighted steamer on westerly course. Hunted it down at full speed on electric motors. 1730: At Nordhinder light vessel. Forced steamer with flag signal and machine gun to stop. Norwegian steamer *Rilda*, 313 tons, carrying food from Rotterdam to London.[4] Sank steamer with explosive cartridges. Crew handed over to Dutch steamer *Batavia III* on easterly course.

7 September

Heading towards Maas light vessel. 0640: Sighted one destroyer each side ahead at portside and starboard going in opposite course. Dived. Ran attack against the destroyer closest on portside at full speed. At around 500 m shooting distance, at angle 90°, gave release command. Due to operating error of torpedo sailor, shot is not fired. Trainee engineer on hearing release command dives as practised on his own initiative. Accelerates again and goes to 9 m. Shooting at the attacked destroyer is no longer possible. The other destroyer has however come close, intending to sail in the wake of the first destroyer or go to the other side of the first destroyer. Shooting at this destroyer is just possible. 0704: Fired torpedo at about 500 m while turning boat. Shot failed. Very soon afterwards while diving heard propeller sounds above and depth charge detonation. Because of the speed of this attack, assumed that the destroyer had already seen the torpedo bubbles and turned towards them. Laid boat at 43 m on sea bed. Turned off compass. After the destroyers had been searching for a while with wires, a second bomb detonation closer to the boat. A third water bomb did not detonate according to radio message of destroyer. 0810: Propeller sounds fade. 0820: Gone to 9 m. Destroyer far off visible, departing to the west. 0840: Surfaced. To the west only smoke clouds visible. 0940: To the north the tops of masts and funnels of a steamer on westerly course appear. Headed towards it. Speed of diesel is not sufficient. Go electric for full speed. 1200: Stopped steamer with flag signal and machine gun. It is the Dutch steamer *Niobe*, 654 tons, carrying food to Bordeaux. Steamer is taken as prize. Steamer captain taken as hostage on board *UB 12*. 1230: Started return journey with steamer via Schouwen Bank light vessel. 2330: Zeebrugge. Moored steamer in port.

8 September
0830: Zeebrugge. Handed over steamer to prize commissioner in lock.
1020: Moored. Bruges.
9–12 September
Bruges. Maintenance.

Top Secret Flotilla Order, Bruges, 15 September 1916, signed Bartenbach
UBs 12, 17 and *38* to patrol the Dutch coast. Sail on 15 September in the
evening. *UB 12* to take up waiting positions from Terschelling to Haaks
light vessel. Carry out acute observations especially at night. Conspicuous
traffic of any vessel is to be reported immediately via radio or carrier
pigeons. Trade war is permitted in the day time. Reconnaissance flights
of own aircraft are to be expected. Return after five days. Recall via radio
before this time is likely.

13 September
Bruges. 2300: Sailed for outpost.
14 September
Moored Zeebrugge because of bad weather and heavy sea.
15 September
Received order to return to Bruges. 2115: Sailed via Zeebrugge.
16 September
Via Schouwen Bank light vessel to Maas light vessel.
17 September
Cruising on steamer path Ijmuiden-Smiths Knoll-Scheveningen-Maas
light vessel.
18 September
Cruising between Ijmuiden and Maas light vessel.
19 September
Cruising between Ijmuiden and Scheveningen. 1045: Sighted steamer
on south west course. Headed for it. 1135: Stopped Norwegian steamer
Ceres. Released as destined for Rotterdam. 1420: Near Ijmuiden. Noticed
that a lubricating oil bunker has run completely empty due to leaking
oil level glass. Remaining oil reserve is just sufficient for return journey
to Zeebrugge. Started return journey.
20 September
0110: Schouwen Bank light vessel. 0415: Passed Zeebrugge mole. 0615:
Moored Bruges.
21–25 September
Bruges. Maintenance.

Top Secret Flotilla Order, Bruges, 25 September 1916, signed Bartenbach
Sail on 26 September in the evening. Cruise in the Hoofden. Then take
up outpost position at own discretion. Return 30 September. Own U- and

torpedo boats are to be anticipated. Pay close attention to radio Bruges Great Programme.

26 September
1907: Bruges. Sailed. 0920: Passed mole in Zeebrugge.

27 September
Via Schouwen Bank light vessel to Nordhinder light vessel. Cruising on steamer route between Nordhinder and Maas. 0930: Replaced damaged fuel valve.

28 September
0010: Heading for Smiths Knoll. 0722: Sighted English fishing smack. Ran it down. 0752: Stopped fishing cutter *Marjorie*, LT 999 from Lowestoft. Sank using explosive cartridges.

1022: Sighted buoy of Hearty Knoll. Close by buoy English fishing cutter *Ethel*, LT 569. Fired machine gun rounds at fishing boat. Almost simultaneously the crew that was standing in front of the rear mast jumped aside and an immediately firing gun becomes visible. Missile/projectile hits water close by *UB 12*. Water column sprays high above tower. Dived. Gone to 9 m. Cutter equipped with an auxiliary engine. Runs zig zag courses. Sets the English trade flag on the great topsail. Its gun is estimated to be 7.6 cm. Departed. 1050: Surfaced. 'NA' is penetrated. Five big holes in the top deck. Explosive fragments are not found. Cruised on steamer route Smiths Knoll-Skagen. 1600: Hearty Knoll buoy. Sighted two fishing cutters sailing in keel line. Run them down. Dived at around 900 m distance. Approached at 9m depth. While *UB 12* was diving one of the cutters casts out its boat, takes it in tow and veers off. The other one keeps heading closer to us. Both fishing cutters set the English trade flag on the great topsail The cutter, LT 7210, which is heading towards us has in front of its rear mast a tetragonal canvas cover that from afar looks like a cabin hatch. When our periscope becomes visible athwart the cutter, the canvas cover is removed and a forwards turned gun appears and is weighted outboard. Calibre is apparently 7.6 cm. Simultaneously the cutter keeps turning towards us. Departed from fishing cutters. 1700: Surfaced. Heading towards Smiths Knoll Buoy 18. 1825: On course towards Nordhinder light vessel. 1912: Right ahead at short distance a u-boat hunter sighted heading at high speed towards us. He must see UB 12 as well. Dived. U-boat hunter drives above us and continued journey at 40 m. Propeller sounds cannot be heard after a short while. 1920: Gone to 9 m. U-boat hunter is a little astern close to us. Lies on opposite course Running apparently at very slow speed. Apart from the currently inconvenient position, an attack against the u-boat hunter in a smooth sea seems futile as we have been seen before. Therefore gone to 40 m again and continued journey. Strong, humming, high-pitched sound can be heard, like that of a high frequency radio transformer. Sound increases. Then propeller sounds become audible near us. As the u-boat hunter can probably hear our propeller sounds, laid boat on sea bed at 47 m. The sound and propeller sounds continue several times increasing and decreasing above us. It is unclear what the sound that drowns out the propeller sounds is. 2045: Nothing can be heard anymore, but decide to wait on sea bed for complete darkness. 2130: Gone to 9 m. 2135: Surfaced. Continued journey to Nordhinder.

29 September

0140: Continued to Nordhinder light vessel. 0925: Cruised on steamer route Nordhinder-Maas. 2105: Laid boat on sea bed.

30 September

0720: Surfaced. 0800: Warship-like vessel is sighted very far off on course towards us. Dived. Ran towards it. Vessel is recognised as Dutch warship *Zeehond*. For practice, carried on running at 9 m. 0957: Surfaced. Cruising on steamer route. 1100-1227: Running down Dutch steamer on westerly course. On approaching steamer turns out to be empty. 1230-1530: Cruising on steamer route Nordhinder-Maas. 1530: Started return journey via Schouwen Bank light vessel.

1 October

Zeebrugge. Bruges. Moored.

2–5 October

Bruges. Maintenance.

6–16 October

Bruges. Not sailing due to bad weather.

Top Secret Flotilla Order, Bruges, 17 October 1916, signed Bartenbach
For *UBs 12, 16, 17*. Sail on 17 October [handwritten correction of typed date '9'] in the evening. Take up waiting position in u-line: the u-line runs from a point 20 sm NW of Terschelling Bank light vessel in north western direction. *UB 16* to mark the direction on this point: *UB16*. Order of boats in the U-line from SE to NW: *UB 16, UB 12, UB 17*. Distance between boats: five sea miles. The U-line has to be occupied at dawn on 11 October [sic – uncorrected date]. Start return on 12 October [sic] at dusk. Trade war is permitted on return journey. Return after five days at the latest. Own and enemy naval forces are to be anticipated. U-boat danger at Terschelling Bank and Schouwen Bank. Pay close attention to Bruges Great Programme. Possible recall signal may be given following Great Programme.

17 October

1935: Bruges. Sailed. 1045: Passed mole at Zeebrugge.

18 October

Via Schouwen Bank light vessel towards Maas light vessel. Cruising on steamer route Maas-Nordhinder. Sighting of Dutch steamer and destroyer.

19 October

0125: Terschelling light vessel – heading for position according to order. 0500: Arrived at position. Cruising on position. 10000-1630: Sightings of German airships.

20 October

Cruising on position. Heading towards Terschelling light vessel.

21 October

1210: Ijmuiden light vessel. Heading for Smiths Knoll. 1810–1840: Opened blocked engine injection valve. 1840: Continued journey to Smiths Knoll.

22 October

0630: Gone to 9 m. Eleven English fishing cutters and further away two armed trawlers in sight. Running down fishing cutters. It was intended to get so close under water to the fishing cutters, which were sailing together in groups of two to three, in order that any armament could be established. 0845: Smiths Knoll Buoy 18. Due to continuous course changes of the cutters, this was given up. Surfaced. Running down two fishing cutters sailing windward in keel line. 0900: Both armed steamers open fire on us from a hopeless distance. Running towards us. 0903: The cutter in front which I am running down also opens fire from a gun of small calibre located in front of the rear mast. Dived. Steering southerly course. 1005: The armed trawlers and cutters are about 4,000 m off. Surfaced. Continued southerly course unchallenged. 1203: Three fishing cutters in sight. Dived. Running down cutters. 1224: The fishing cutters turn out to be Dutch. Surfaced. Navigating southerly course. The engine is smoking so much that the whole boat is constantly covered by smoke. Tried in vain to eliminate this. 1803: Gone on aft course. Heading for Nordhinder light vessel. 2040: Nordhinder light vessel. Started return journey via Schouwen Bank.

23 October

1930: Passing Zeebrugge mole. 0920: Bruges. Moored.

24–28 October

Bruges. Maintenance.

[Bartenbach, handwritten: The smoking of the oil engine can be attributed to the deformation of a connecting rod caused by water in the cylinder.]

29 October

1420: Bruges. Sailed. 1745: Passed mole Zeebrugge. 1900: Received call to return to Zeebrugge. 2200: Received order to moor at mole.

30 October

1340: Received order to return to Bruges. 1610: Moored at Bruges.

31 October

Bruges. Repairs.

1 November
Bruges. 2100: Sailed. 2335: Passed mole Zeebrugge.

2 November
0110: Dived before five destroyers (probably own ones). 0745: Dived before patrol vessel. 0910: At Buoy 2501. Exchanged news with *UB 10*. 0930: Established radio message connection with *UB 16*. 1040: Dived before u-boat. Started running attack. 1130: Recognised u-boat as *UB 10*. Surfaced. On course towards Nordhinder light vessel.

3 November
0?27: Sighted two English destroyers. Dived. 0?30: Ran continuous attacks against four mostly separately navigating English destroyers. Boat under water just before a torpedo shot because of the heavy sea. Torpedo shots misfired because of the frequent course changes of the destroyers. 1000: Surfaced. 1100: Dived before English destroyers. Departed northwards as attack was hopeless because of the heavy sea and also low battery. 1205: Surfaced as due to heavy sea neither trade war nor under water attack possible. Started return journey. 1455: Dived before English destroyers. Continued journey at 20 m. 1420: Surfaced. Destroyer visible far off. 1740: At Nordhinder light vessel. Stopped and recharged almost empty battery. 1950: Dived before steamer heading straight for us. Laid boat on sea bed. 2030: Surfaced. Heading for Schouwen Bank light vessel.

[*A quick dive, and the sound of the [destroyer's] propellers rushed over us. We were deep enough for safety, but the suction as the speeding torpedo boat dashed along jerked our sewing machine almost to the surface. If another destroyer had been following we should surely have been rammed.*[5]]

4 November
0330: Schouwen Bank light vessel. 0655: Passed Zeebrugge mole. 0907: Moored in Bruges. Handed over command of UB 12 to Oberleutnant Hans Ewald Niemer [*who was in command of UB12 while at Bruges dockyard for her bow conversion*].[6]

ENDNOTES

1   *Cuxhaven, U-Boot Museum*, Kriegstagebuch, *UB 12*, 27/6-4/11/1916, translated Cathrin Brockhaus, stylised and abbreviated by the author.
2   Gayer, *Submarine Warfare*, p. 21.
3   A wreck believed to be that of *UC 7* has been located by divers in recent years (uboat. net). Termote, *Krieg unter Wasser*, pp. 230-231.
4   *Clearance Certificate* for merchant vessel *Rilda*, issued by the Downs Boarding Flotilla (Boarding Officer of *HMS Chester*) on 16/2/1916, typed form completed by hand, in English.
5   Lowell, *Raiders*, 'UB-15, von Heimburg', p. 135.
6   5/11/1916-19/1/1917 (uboat.net).

The Holtzendorff Memorandum

Date: 22 December 1916

From: The Chief of the Admiralty Staff of the Navy Berlin, Admiral Henning von Holtzendorff

To: The Royal Field-Marshal, Chief of the General Staff of the Army, His Excellency von Beneckendorff und von Hindenburg

Most Secret!

I have the honour to respectfully submit to your Excellency in the attachment a memorandum on the necessity for the commencement an unrestricted campaign of submarine warfare at the earliest opportunity. The memorandum is essentially a continuation of the memorandum Ref. No. 22 247 I of 27 August 1916: The Merchant Tonnage Issue and the Supply of England in 1916, which has previously been submitted to your Excellency. Based on the detailed information attached to this memorandum, I would like to ask your Excellency to kindly follow the line of argument laid out below, and I hope to achieve agreement that it is absolutely necessary to increase our measures against England as soon as possible to the very limit of our abilities in order to exploit the favourable situation and to obtain a swift victory.

1. The war requires a decision before autumn 1917, lest it should end in the mutual exhaustion of all parties and thus in a disaster for us. Of our enemies, Italy and France are already so severely weakened in their economic foundations that they are kept in the fight only through England's energy and resources. If we succeed to break England's backbone, the war will immediately be decided in our favour. England's backbone is the merchant tonnage, which delivers essential imports for their survival and for the military industry of the British islands and which ensures the [kingdom's] ability to pay for its imports from abroad.

2. The current situation in respect to the merchant tonnage has already been mentioned in the memorandum of 27 August and is laid out in further detail in the attachment. In all brevity the situation is as follows: The [shipping] rates have reached outrageous levels, often as much as ten times as much [as in peacetime] for many important goods. We know with certainty from a variety of sources that merchant tonnage is lacking everywhere.

The current English merchant tonnage can safely be assumed to be in the order of 20 million gross register tons. 8.6 million tons of these are requisitioned for military purposes, and 1/2 million is employed in coastal trade. Approximately 1 million [tons] are undergoing repairs or are otherwise temporarily unavailable. Approximately 2 million tons are sailing for other allies, which leaves about 8 million tons of English merchant tonnage to provide for the supply of England. An analysis of statistical figures of ship movements in British ports suggests an even lower figure. In the months of July – September 1916 only 6¾ million tons were employed in the trade with England. In addition to that, other tonnage sailing in the trade with England can be assumed to amount to around 900,000 tons of enemy – non-English – and approximately 3 million tons of neutral tonnage. Hence, no more than 10¾ million GRT are at the disposal for the supply of England.

3. If the achievements in our battle against merchant tonnage have been encouraging thus far, then the exceptionally poor world harvest of grain, including feed grain, this year provides us with a unique opportunity, which nobody could responsibly reject. Both North America and Canada will probably cease their grain exports to England in February. Then that country will have to draw its grain supplies from the more distant Argentina, but since Argentina will only be able to deliver very limited quantities, because of the poor harvest, England will have to turn to India and mostly Australia. In the attachment it is explained in detail how such an increase in the length of the grain routes will require an extra 720,000 tons of tonnage for the grain shipments alone. In practice, the implications will be that, until August 1917, 3/4 million tons of the available 10¾ million tons will have to be employed for a service, which had hitherto not been required.

4. Under such favourable circumstances an energetic blow conducted with all force against English merchant tonnage will promise a certain success in a way that I have to reiterate and emphasize my statements made on 27 August 1916 that "our clearly defined strategic objective is to force a decision in our favour through the destruction of [enemy] sea transport capacity" and also that "from a military point of view

it would be irresponsible not to make use of the submarine weapon now." As things stand at the moment, I cannot vouch that a campaign of unrestricted submarine warfare will force England to make peace within five months time. This reservation needs to be made in respect to the unrestricted submarine warfare only. Of the currently conducted submarine warfare under cruiser a decisive result cannot be expected, regardless of the circumstances, even if all armed merchantmen are designated as legitimate targets.

5. Based on a monthly rate of destruction of 600,000 tons of shipping through a campaign of unrestricted submarine warfare, as pointed out previously, and on the well grounded expectation, elaborated upon in the attachment, that at least two fifths of the neutral tonnage sailing in the trade with England will be deterred by such a campaign, it stands to reason that the current volume English sea borne trade will be reduced by 39 per cent within five months. This would not be bearable for England, neither in view of her future position after the war, nor in view of her ability to continue the war effort. Already, the country is at the verge of a food crisis, which will soon compel it to attempt to undertake the same food rationing measures, which we, as a blockaded country, have been forced to adopt since the outbreak of the war. The preconditions for implementing such measures are totally different and infinitely more unfavourable than in our case. They do not have the necessary administration and their population is unused to submitting to such privations. Then there is another reason why the uniform rationing of bread for the whole population will not be possible in England at this point. It was possible for Germany at a time in which bread could be substituted by other foodstuffs. That moment has been missed in England. But with only three fifths of the current sea borne trade, the continued supply with [alternative] foodstuffs cannot be maintained unless a severe rationing of grain is imposed—provided the war industry is to be maintained at its current output level. The objection that England could have sufficient domestic stockpiles of grain and raw materials has been disproved in detail in the attachment.

In addition to that, the unrestricted submarine campaign would cut off England from the trade with Denmark and the Netherlands, which would result in an immediate shortage of fats, since one third of all butter imports and the entire margarine imports to England originate in Denmark and the Netherlands respectively. Moreover, by threatening the sea routes to Scandinavia and intensifying activities against the Spanish iron-ore trade, it would result in a scarcity of iron-ore and wood. This will automatically reduce the coal production for lack of wood. In consequence it would also reduce the output of pig iron, steel, and subsequently the production of munitions, which depends on both. Finally, it gives us the long hoped for opportunity to strike at neutral munitions shipments, and thus it will also provide a relief for the army.

By contrast, a submarine campaign according to cruiser rules, even assuming the possibility of indiscriminate attacks on armed merchantmen, would only yield a reduction of the tonnage sailing for England by 5 × 400,000 tons—about 18 per cent—or less than half of what could be achieved by unrestricted submarine warfare. Experience so far does not suggest that the authorization to torpedo armed merchantmen would improve upon the result of 400,000 tons of destroyed merchant tonnage, which has been achieved over the past two months. In fact, it is likely to merely compensate for a decline, which has to be expected in the course of progressing arming [of merchantmen]. I am aware that even a reduction of one fifth of English sea borne trade will have a severe impact on the English supply situation. However, I consider it unthinkable that the current English leadership under Lloyd George, who is absolutely determined, could be forced to make peace on these grounds, particularly since the constraints of fat, iron-ore, and wood scarcity—and the latters' impact on the munitions production—would not come into effect. Furthermore, the psychological effects of panic and terror cannot be exploited. These effects, which can only be achieved by a campaign of unrestricted submarine warfare are, in my view, an indispensable prerequisite for success. Just how important they are can be judged by the experiences made when we initiated submarine warfare in early 1915, or even during the brief period of the submarine campaign in March and April 1916, when the British believed that we were serious about it.

A further precondition [for success] is that the beginning and the declaration of unrestricted submarine warfare should coincide in a manner that leaves no room for negotiations, particularly between England and the neutrals. Only then will the effect of shock have the most profound impact on the enemy and the neutrals.

6. Upon the declaration of unrestricted submarine warfare the United States government will once more be compelled to make a decision whether or not to take the consequences of its previous position vis-à-vis the unrestricted submarine warfare. I am absolutely of the opinion that war with the United States is such a serious matter that everything has to be undertaken to avoid it. Fear of a diplomatic rupture however, should not lead us to recoil from the use of a weapon that promises victory for us.

At any rate, it is realistic to assume the worst case as the most probable one and to consider which impact an American entry into the war on the side of our enemies would have on the course of the war. In respect to the merchant tonnage this impact is likely to be negligible. It cannot be expected that more than a fraction of the interned central power tonnage in American – and perhaps in other neutral ports – can be put into the trade with England at short notice. The overwhelming part of it can be rendered useless in a manner that it will be unable to sail during the first, critical months. All preparations in this respect have been made. Also, there would be no crews available in the initial stages. The American troops would be of equally little import, if only for the lack of bottoms to carry them over here in great numbers; the same applies to American money, which cannot compensate the lack of tonnage. The only question that remains would be how America would react to a peace, which Great Britain would be forced to accept. It is unlikely that it would decide to continue the war against us, since it has no means to strike at us decisively, whereas its sea borne commerce would suffer from our submarines. Indeed, it is to be expected that it will join England in making peace, in order to restore healthy economic conditions.

Therefore my conclusion is that a campaign of unrestricted submarine warfare, launched in time to produce a peace before the harvest of the summer 1917 – i.e. 1 August – has to accept the risk of American belligerence, because we have no other option. In spite of the diplomatic rupture with America, the unrestricted submarine warfare is nevertheless the right means to conclude this war victoriously. It is also the only means to this end.

7. Since I have declared the time come to strike against England in autumn 1916 the situation has even improved tremendously in our favour. The crop failure, in conjunction with the impact of the war on England up to now, gives us the opportunity to force a decision before the next harvest. If we do not make use of what seems to be the last chance, then I see no other option than that of mutual exhaustion, without our succeeding to bring the war to an end on terms that will guarantee our future as a world power.

In order to achieve the required results, the unrestricted submarine warfare has to commence no later than 1 February. I request from your Excellency an indication, whether the military situation on the continent, particularly in regard to the remaining neutrals, would allow this schedule. The necessary preparations can be completed within three weeks time.[1]

---

1   *Freiburg,* Kriegsarchiv der Admiralstät (KdA), UM 5/11. Translation, Dirk Steffen, 'Holtzendorff Memorandum', *Journal of Military History*, January 2004, Vol. 68, No. 1, pp. 219–224.

Kriegstagebuch *UC 61*

Date: 13 December 1916 – 8 July 1917[1]

13 December 1916
Bremen: *UC 61* on building dockyard AG Weser. Put into service.

14–20 December
Bremen: Works in building dockyard.

21 December
Voyage to Kiel.

22 December 1916–19 February 1917
Kiel: UAK works.

20 February
Travelled through Kaiser Wilhelm Kanal to Brunsbüttel.

22–24 February
Travelled to Helgoland.

25 February
Helgoland. Exercises at the I. U-Flotilla. 1100: Hazy, part fog. Departed Helgoland for passage to Flanders. The accompanying outpost boat is lost in fog immediately after departure.

26 February
1150: Maas light vessel. As Zeebrugge port is to be entered only at night, patrolled steamer route Maas-Nordhinder. Sighted nothing apart from *UB 10*.

27 February
0130: Nordhinder light vessel. To Zeebrugge via Schouwenbank. 0920: Zeebrugge. 1115: Bruges. Moored.

28 February
Repairs.

Top Secret Flotilla Order, Bruges, 1 March 1917, signed Bartenbach
Sail on 1/3 to Square 106 alpha additional number 6 for trade war against convoys. Return 0500 6/3. Anticipate own torpedo boats and U-boats. Pay close attention to Bruges Great Programme.

1 March 1917

  2200: Sailed.

2–4 March

  0715: Arrived at position. Cruised in quadrant. Sighted nothing. Practice
  runs under water.

5 March

  0730: Headed towards Nordhinder light vessel to fix position. 0938:
  Nordhinder light vessel in 234° 10 sm off. Wind 6, sea 6, hazy. Sighted
  steamer, accompanied by two destroyers, dived, ran attack, both engines
  full speed straight ahead. Realised afterwards it was the English steamer
  Copenhagen on route to Holland. 0945: Bow torpedo shot at steamer,
  distance ca. 1,500 m, steamer speed 16 knots. Hit in the engine room.
  Steamer stops. Lies abeam of the sea, both destroyers circle around
  it. Went to steamer. The crew leaves the steamer in the ship's boats.
  Destroyers cannot go alongside in the heavy sea. Steamer lies without
  list, astern significantly lower. 1010: At 400 m released second torpedo
  at stopped steamer. Failed shot can only be explained by faulty course
  of torpedo, probably as a result of the heavy sea. Although going almost
  constantly full speed, boat cannot be held at depth. Several times comes
  above water with whole conning tower and is apparently being seen.
  Destroyer approaches *UC 61* at great speed. Went to depth. Departed.
  Afterwards, headed again towards site of the attack. Sighted nothing
  else in the very limited field of vision due to high sea. 1345: Surfaced
  very nearby destroyer. Dived. 14:20: Foggy. Surfaced. Hatches and thick
  spars and booms are floating around. Sighted nothing of the steamer.
  Immediately afterwards sighted two destroyers quite close. Dived.
  1505: Surfaced. Steamer is briefly visible through the fog. Tried to reach
  it. However steamer is not sighted again. 1550: Laid boat on sea bed
  because of dense fog. 1712: Surfaced. Visibility is slightly better. Started
  return to Zeebrugge via Schouwen Bank. 2355: Zeebrugge.

6 March

  0230: Bruges. Moored.

7–9 March

  Maintenance.

10–14 March

  Ostend: Docked in dry dock for repair of oil bunker and dip tank IV.

15–16 March

  Equipped for operation.

Top Secret Flotilla Order, Bruges, 17 March 1917, signed Bartenbach
Sail 17/3. Lay mines at spacing and depth settings at own discretion if possible
at turn of tide/slack tide/still water: *UC 17*: Beachy Head, Newhaven and
Keb (?); *UC 61*: [Tree Stones-Oar], Navar Point and Trevose Head; *UC 65*: off
Liverpool. Then trade war according to special instructions: *UC 17*: English

Channel coast middle; *UC 61*: English Channel coast Scillies; *UC 65*: Irish Sea. Return depending on capability and ammunition consumption, at the latest after 10 days (*UC 65*: 14 days). Anticipate own torpedo boats and u-boats in the Channel. Pay close attention to Bruges Great Programme.

17 March
1430: Sailed. Headed for Channel close to French coast. 2340: Buoy 5. 1150: Strong explosions starboard athwart. Lively shooting of a destroyer. Shell hits near *UC 61*. Dived. Laid boat on sea bed, 26 m. Ascertained after return, it was a previously not known advance of our VI. Flotilla shooting at an English destroyer. 1208: Surfaced. Sighted nothing. Continued. 1215: Destroyer illuminates water with search light. Apparently notices *UC 61*. Shoots. Dived. Laid boat on sea bed, 27 m 1220: Surfaced. Sighted nothing. Continued. 1540: Dungeness athwart. Overcast.

18 March
0610: Dived before destroyers. 0650: Surfaced. 1107: Dived before destroyers. 1143: Surface. Charged portside engines. 1400: Sighted sailing ship ahead. Ran it down. Stopped charging. 1420: Opened fire at sailing ship. As a result of the firing five trawlers are approaching from starboard at high speed. Distance of *UC 61* from sailing ship decreases only very slowly. 1500: As sinking the sailing ship before arrival of the trawlers is impossible, ceased fire. Dived. Two trawlers stay with the sailing ship; three come to the dived u-boat. 1600: Trawlers are far off. Continued. 1640: Two patrol vessels pass starboard. 1750: Passed *UC 21*. 2200: Casquets light beacon 183° about 18 miles.

19 March
1145: Lizard at 301° about five miles off. Portside nearby a u-boat hunter. Starboard further off a steamer and several destroyers. Dived. Carried on westerly course. 1455: Surfaced. Portside engines charging. 1540: Dived before destroyers. 1640: Surfaced.

20 March
0430: Wind NW 6-7, Sea 6-7, gusty, overcast. Gyro compass fails due to the swell. Continued to steer according to magnetic/marine compass. Compared courses according to bearing of Wolf Rock and Longship. 0650: Starboard astern sighted large steamer heading for Lands End. Sought convenient position for underwater attack. Attack above water impossible because of swell. While doing this *UC 61* is apparently noticed by a steamer located starboard ahead, also heading for Lands End. Suddenly heads for the coast where there are some patrol vessels very far off. 0745: Dived. Ran attack against first steamer. This seems in the mean time to have noticed the manoeuvre of the other steamer for it also changes its course by several points closer towards land. Distance is too far for safe shot. Cancelled shot. Stayed under water as several

smoke clouds are still visible from Cape Lizard. 0815: Two trawlers approach the boat. The depth control is faulty due to the swell so that the periscope is being noticed. Go to 40 m. Depth charges quite far off. The gyro compass levels itself now that swell ceases. 1020: Go to 10 m. The sea has increased so much that an underwater attack is impossible. Both trawlers follow, one to starboard and one to port quite close to the boat. They probably keep in touch with short range underwater telephony. Go to 50 m. Changed course. Both engines malfunction. 1245: The torpedo and engine bilge pumps have run full of water through a leaky connector/ bush owing to the negligence of the sailor in charge of the engine, without this having been reported. At 10 m the boat becomes front-heavy. The water rushes to the front. The anchors of the electric engines come under water. Both electric engines fail. The boat sinks with about 25–30° incline to 40 m. Surfaced with compressed air. Very swelling sea, snow and hail gusts which allow only very limited visual range. Trawlers are nowhere to be seen. Switched on oil engines. Left coast. Gyro compass fails again. 1500: Chief engineer clears engines. Heading towards Lands End. 1700: Dived before destroyer. As no trade war possible in the bad weather, travelled at 40 m. 1900: Surfaced. Portside engines charging. Evaded some patrol vessels and destroyers above water between Scillies and Lands End. 2350: Dived before destroyers. Starboard engine malfunctions.

21 March
0005: Surfaced. Continued. 0300: Both electric engines unstable. No chance to get them clear again. Cancelled operation. Started return. Evaded above water some patrol vessels and destroyers which were sighted far off.

22 March
0705: In order to wait for evening to continue, laid on sea bed, 42 m, athwart Beachy Head. 0800: Boat lies very badly. Therefore surfaced and cruised at low speed in the middle between Beachy Head and Treport. Gyro compass levels itself again. 1800: Continued. Passed Channel close to French coast. Sighted nothing apart from some steamer lights close to land. Green buoy at Calais not lit, otherwise shore lights and buoys as usual.

23 March
1217: Bruges. Moored. Handed over torpedoes.

24 March–24 April
Ostend floating dock: electric and bunker repair [special report of the flotilla to U-Boot Headquarters].

25–27 April
Bruges: Completion of repairs and equipment.

Top Secret Flotilla Order, Bruges, 25 April 1917, signed Bartenbach
Sail 25/4. Lay mines if possible at turn of tide with depth setting and
spacing at own discretion: *UC 61*: Needles, St. Alban's Head and Portland;
UC 65: in the inner Firth of Clyde; *UC 69*: Steamer passage at Belle Isle
and off Quiberon Bay. Conduct trade war according to special instructions:
UC 61 at the western exit of the English Channel; *UC 65* in the Irish Sea;
UC 69 in the Bay of Biscay. Return depending on capability and ammunition
consumption, at the latest after eighteen days. Sail and enter port only at
darkness. Anticipate own torpedo and u-boats. Recently several enemy
vessels sighted at Thornton which have possibly laid nets and mines. Pay
close attention to radio tower at Bruges.

28 April
0130: Sailed. Heading for Buoy 2501. Entered prohibited area. 0850: Buoy
2501 2.5 miles. Dived before three enemy planes. Showered with four
bombs. Boat on sea bed, 31 m. 1020: Surfaced. Ventilated boat. Sea bed
again. 2117: Surfaced. 2010: Heading for Channel close to French coast.
2352: Passed net barrier. Evaded above water two destroyers operating
in tandem.

29 April
0235: Colbart lightship athwart. Evaded two destroyers operating in pair
above water. Starboard charging and air pumping. 1200: Sighted steamer.
Stopped charging. Ran towards it. Identified as trawler with radio station
aboard. Dived. 1330: Dived. 1615: Dived before destroyer and trawler.
1900: Evaded patrol vessel above water. 2000: St. Catherine's Point. Port
engines charging and air pumping. 2245: Evaded destroyer above water.
stopped charging.

30 April
0005: Needles at 61°, St Catherine's Point at 106°. Boat on sea bed, 25 m,
in order to wait for time to drop mines. 0035: Surfaced. Headed for light
buoy. 0102: Needles. Under water dropped Barrier I (2 mines). 0105:
Surfaced. 0115: Needles. Above water dropped Barrier II (mines). 0122:
Headed for Anvil Point to drop mines. 0325: St Alban's Head. Dropped
Barrier III above water (3 mines). 0425: Portland at 250°. Starboard
engine for charging. 0830: Sighted sailing ship. Headed for it. Stopped
charging. 0907: Approached sailing ship under water. 0916: Surfaced.
English sailing ship *Little Mystery* with coals from England to France.
Stopped with gun shots. Sank with explosive cartridge. 1044: Sighted
trawler which from a very far distance opens fire. Moved out of sight
above water. 1125: Charged starboard engine. 1600: Evaded destroyer
above water. 1702: Sighted steamer. Headed for it. 1737: Dived. Let
steamer pass. 1835: Surfaced. Fired at steamer. Left by crew after
being hit. 1850: Approached under water. 1902: Surfaced. Armed yacht
nearby comes very quickly towards *UC 61*. Went alongside Argentine

steamer *Gorizia* from Montevideo, c. 3,000 tons. Attached two explosive cartridges. Explosive cartridges detonate while yacht navigates around steamer. Yacht first takes crew on board. Then stays close to the steamer. 2006: Sank steamer. Departed under water. 2050: Armed yacht and one destroyer nearby. Carried on running under water. 2152: Surfaced. Starboard engines charging and air pumping. Headed to Portland to drop mines. 2310: Ran down a big steamer without lights. 2355: Steamer sees *UC 61* in the moonlight shortly before shot and turns. Sailing to Portland.

1 May

0020: Dived before destroyer. 0045: Dived as probability too great to be seen above water in the bright moonlight by Shambles light vessel]. Headed towards light vessel. 0120: 100 m from Shambles. Under water dropped Barrier V (6 mines). 0143: Surfaced. Moved away from coast. 0215: Charged starboard engines. 0255: Ran attack on steamer with dimmed lights. Stopped charging. Steamer sees *UC 61* in the moonlight. Turns. Sounds alarm with steam whistle as two patrol vessels pass close by. Dived. 0323: Surfaced. 0410: Ran attack on dimmed steamer. Failed torpedo shot front. Steamer sees the strongly curved torpedo path and turns. 0430: Charging starboard engines. 1210: Dived before destroyer. 1855: Dived before plane. 1935: Sighted airship to west. 2000: Two sailing ships sighted. Headed towards them. 2130: Destroyer moves towards sailing ships at high speed. Dived. Destroyer stays with the sailing ships, therefore departed. 2225: Surfaced. 2255: Moonlight. Sighted steamer convoy accompanied by several trawlers and destroyers. Above water. Assumed position in order to attack in moonlight under water. *UC 61* becomes visible. Already seen from a very great distance and fired at. Dived. 2259: Two trawlers and one destroyer leave convoy and head towards diving site. Departed. 2315: Moonlight. Surfaced.

2 May

0032: Charged starboard engines. 0830: Sighted sailing boat. Headed towards it. Destroyer runs at great speed towards *UC 61*. Dived. Destroyer stays close to the sailing ship. Departed. 1205: Dived before two patrol vessels. 1253: Port engines charging. Heading towards Ouessant.

3 May

0045: Stopped charging. 1050: Sank French fish trawler with gun. 1230: Ar Men lighthouse. Sank French fish trawler with gun. 1800: Passed torpedo boat on opposite course. 2120: Sighted steamer. Ran it down. Fired. Crew left after several hits. 2135: Dived. Closed with steamer. 2145: Surfaced. Italian armed steamer *Giovannina* carrying oranges from Catania to Liverpool. Attached two explosive cartridges. Steamer does not sink immediately. Boat already in darkness. Put *UC 61* alongside and attached another two explosive cartridges. Steamer sinks. While going alongside, *UC 61*'s stern came hard against the ship's side. As a result of that the spindle which moves the muzzle door has been buckled and the muzzle door has been slightly opened. Muzzle door can not be moved any more.

4 May

Cruised off Loire. Muzzle door of the stern tube is uncoupled from the linkage arm and as a result it shuts tight by water pressure when diving.

5 May

0030: Sighted steamer in the Loire estuary, chased with course 218°. Distance too great for gun attack. With highest revolutions with addition of electrical motors, distance can be maintained. 0600: At dawn at 35 km open fire which is immediately reciprocated. Second and third shots from *UC 61* are hits. Then the gun height adjuster fails and jams. Combat is continued rolling motion. The steamer fires during the course of the combat about twenty smoke bombs which enforce temporary pause in shooting. *UC 61* achieves no more hits in the slow rolling sea, whereas the steamer has become very good at shooting. Seaman No 1 is slightly wounded at the foot by shrapnel. Dived. 0640: The steamer uses the opportunity and throws athwart to its heading a line of numerous fog bombs which cover the horizon over about 180° with dense fog. 0649: Surfaced. Height adjusting engine is being examined. A pressure valve is burst. Some fragments have got jammed in the gear ring. After their removal the height adjuster is moveable again. In the mean time, the steamer has become visible in the fog and has been chased. It has changed its course towards the Gironde [River]. Shooting is started again, but shots at the greatest elevation still short whereas the shots of the steamer are close to the boat again. 0730: As a result combat is aborted and headed for Loire again. 1520: Belle Isle. Cruised off Loire.

6 May

0600: Sighted convoy. Dived. Ran attack. Because of too great distance not able to shoot. 0807: Surfaced. Headed towards Audierne Bay for repair of stern armament.

7–8 May

0400-0500: Audierne Bay. Under land shelter started repair of stern armament. In order to facilitate the work, flooded dive tank I and trim tank. The spindle which moves the muzzle door was taken out and adjusted. The muzzle door could after this be completely shut, but still not yet completely opened. Could not be achieved even despite readjusting. From now on the motion linkage was only used to shut the muzzle door tight. For opening it was taken off and the muzzle door was picked up with a tightly attached rim which after some practice took about twenty seconds. At the same time the mean effective pressure piston of the portside injection air pump which had previously run hot was overhauled. The pump was taken apart, piston and cylinder ground with stone, piston rings exchanged. Working day and night, the pumps were reassembled in one and a half days. During the test run, the piston ran hot again. As the smoothing could not be carried out properly with the available tools, the piston was sawn open and the starboard engine supplies air to the portside engine during the further work. By adding compressed air from the main generator and electrical pumps both engines could nevertheless run full revolutions. The repairs represent a good achievement by the engine staff. The works were several times briefly interrupted by diving before a French trawler and a French torpedo boat which patrol the coast on a set course. Conserved rear torpedo. 0605: Sighted steamer close by at dawn. Shot at. Fire is tenaciously reciprocated. Distance is increased. 0640: Through a lucky hit, ammunition at the rear of the steamer goes up in great flames and continuing detonations. Steamer raises white flag. Crew disembarks hastily. French steamer *Nelly* from Oran with wine cargo for Rouen sunk with blasting cartridges. 1600: Ouessant at 70°. 1845: Sighted two sailing ships. Headed towards them. 1913: Dived before destroyer. Destroyer stays with sailing ships. 2030: Surfaced. Charged with port engines. 2230: Sighted steamer accompanied by trawler. While approaching *UC 61* is seen and shot at. Dived. 2345: Surfaced.

9 May

0500: Ouessant at 203°. 2350: Start Point at 316°. Heading towards it.

10 May

0055: Ran down two dimmed off steamers. Only very slowly come closer. 0300: Boat is seen by the steamer so turned away. Pursued, but at the steamer's high speed an artillery night combat is futile. 0555: Sighted steamer. Dived. Shot a rear torpedo. Did not see path. Torpedo has apparently suffered despite previous conservation because of too long lying in armed condition. 0620: Surfaced. 0653: Dived. Let steamer pass. Then surfaced and attacked. 0707: After some hits, lifeboats are launched. During the shooting, another steamer shoots from a great distance without a chance at *UC 61*. 0715: Blasting cartridges attached to English steamer *Broomhill* with coal cargo. Dived before patrol vessel. 0740: Sank *Broomhill*. Departed. 0836: Destroyer nearby. 1045: Surfaced. Shot at steamer. Far off, *UC 17* also shoots at a steamer. 1100: After our hits, lifeboats are launched. Norwegian steamer *Minerva* from Haugesund in ballast sunk with blasting cartridges. 1440: Alongside *UC 17*, thirty grenades taken over. 1800: Evaded two patrol vessels above water.

11 May

0312: Shambles light. 0710: Foggy. Quick dive before destroyer depth charge. 0815: Surfaced. 1000: Dived before patrol vessel. 1500: Cruised off Lag de la Hague, then headed towards Cherbourg. Steamer seen.

12 May

0400: Headed towards St Catherine's Point. 0800: Charging starboard engines. 1438: Sighted several steamers. Dived. Ran attack against a black painted c 1,500 ton steamer with flag whose nationality could not be identified. Steamer carried at the bow in white letters the name *Mia*, on its black funnel with a ring of white indistinct letters h from afar looked like a white funnel ring. Radio masts. In other respects the appearance of a common freight steamer. Steamer turns towards periscope. Go to depth and at full speed turn away. Depth charge near the boat. 1452: Go to 11 m, very briefly and carefully extended periscope. The steamer lies around 1,000 m off. Stopped. Behind the funnel, a funnel coat-like cover has fallen. On a platform there are two guns. At the stern, a slip for depth charges. Periscope has been seen again. Steamer close towards it. Go to 30 m. 1503: Two depth charges near the boat, fuses blowing out partly, bilge pumps failing, boat sinks to sea bed, 35 m. Further depth charge close to boat. Fuses are inserted again and departed at 25 m. 1550: Surfaced. The ventilation valve for stern bunker has popped open despite existing lock. The oil gushes out. 1600: Extremely hazy. Dived before destroyers. Later cruised off Portland.

13 May

0215: Dense fog. Some vessels nearby. Dived. 0245: Surfaced. Dense fog. Dived. 0635: Surfaced. As I am in the meantime far away from the coast, despite the fog approached coast above water. Charging starboard engines. 1200: Stopped charging. 1600: A little clearer. 1828: Suddenly clear and very visible. Aborted return course in order to try in the now clear weather to get rid of the torpedoes. 2200: Dived before destroyer. 2300: Ran above water attack against very strongly protected convoy. Boat is seen. Destroyer turns almost towards *UC 61*. Dived. Depth charge. 2334: Surfaced. Many patrol boats and destroyers nearby.

14 May

0400: Beachy Head. Wind, rainy. Return course. Dived very frequently before planes and destroyers.

15 May

0010: Colbart light vessel 310°. Passed channel close to French coast. 0303: Passed net buoys. 0610: Dived before planes. Left prohibited area. 0847: Zeebrugge. Passed mole. 1200: Bruges. Moored.

16 May

Bruges. Repairs.

17 May–5 June

Ostend. Floating dock. Repair of the moving apparatus of the muzzle doors at the rear torpedo tube and the door itself. Start of repair of the water pump which had run hot at sea. It appeared that the cooling chambers had been half filled with fine sand. Examination of a piston of each engine for revision of the piston pin. It became apparent that the white metal shells had been broken. When, as a result, all mountings were checked all displayed the same condition. Furthermore, at the starboard engine three and at the portside engine four mounting shells broken. The renewal of these seven shells and equipping all shells with new white metal linings was started.

6–11 June
Continuation of repair works of the engine plant and equipment.

Experiences: Different hand, Reichs Marine Amt [Imperial Navy Office]
1. Artillery:
   • The breakage of the pressure of the height adjusting engine has its cause in a material fault. The many material faults, defects and failures of the Ehrhard Gun let its exchange/replacement by the Krupp Gun seem desirable.
   • The equipment with a sighting mechanism better suitable for night use seems desirable.
2. Periscope:
   • The equipment of u-boats with a periscope that has optics better suitable for the night seems desirable.
3. U-Boat traps:
   • The steamer with which *UC 61* had a combat on 5/5 in the Bay of Biscay gave a radio SOS although it was definitely no Q-ship.

Top Secret Flotilla Order, Bruges, 3 June 1917, signed Bartenbach
Sail 3/6. Lay mines if possible at turn of tide. Spacing and depth settings at own discretion. *UC 47*: Bristol Channel; *UC 48*: In front of and north of the [] Estuary; *UC 61*: off Brest. Then trade war according to the special regulations: *UC 47*: Bristol Channel and south of Ireland; *UC 48*: in the Bay of Biscay; *UC 61*: Western exit of the English Channel.

12 June
Bruges. 1615: Sailed. 2145: Attempt at trimming. Front hydroplane is jammed in hard steering position on top. Return journey.

13 June
0515: Bruges. Moored. 0645: Through the Ostend Channel to Ostend.

14–19 June
Ostend. Repair in the hoist. The gear mechanism had become deadlocked.

20 June
Undocked. To Bruges above water.

21 June
Equipped/armed.

22 June
The gauge-cock of the front starboard bunker has become detached due to poor fastening. Repair.

23 June

Sail. 1600: Entered exclusion area. 1910: Trimming attempt. 2100: Buoy 2501. Heading for Channel close to French coast.

24 June

0120: Passed net barrier. 1600: Colbart light vessel. Dived before destroyer. Continued under water. 1136: Surfaced. 1320: Dived before destroyer. 1950: Evaded destroyer and airship above water.

25 June

Overcast, intermittent rain.

26 June

0147: Chenal Le Four. Dropped barrier I above water (6 mines). 2035: Sighted airship.

27 June

0127: Pierres Noires. Dropped barrier II above water (6 mines). 0145: Dropped barrier III above water (6 mines). 0300: French armoured cruiser Kleber runs onto the just dropped mines (radio message in uncoded language). 0600: Sighted [] at meeting/target point Z. The barometer falls significantly. Wind and Sea increase. As a result left meeting point. Headed for French coast. 0940: Dived before destroyer. As barometer keeps on falling journey further south to Bay of Biscay abandoned. Headed for English Channel coast at Start Point. 2000: Wind, Sea 5, rain, no visibility.

28 June

0800: Lyme Bay. Wind 4, sea 3, hazy. 1055: Dived due to dense fog. 1140: Extremely hazy. Surfaced. 1250: Dived due to dense fog. 1342: Hazy. Surfaced. 1512: Hazy. Dived. Ran several attacks against steamer, torpedo shot, then cancelled because of too small size. 1700: Surfaced. Shot at steamer. Achieved hit. Am being fired at by three trawlers which I had not noticed under water because of the very misted over periscope. 1725: Forced by trawlers to dive. Two depth charges quite far off. 1915: Foggy. Weather too bad for underwater attacks. Surfaced. 2354: Laid boat on sea bed, 38 m, because of dense fog.

29 June

0100: Fog. Surfaced hourly for visibility control. 0450: Hazy. Surfaced. 0635: Sighted big empty tank steamer with some trawlers. Dived Ran attack. 0703: Failed shot at tanker from 300 m out of stern tube. Failed shot can only be explained by undershot or other non-functioning of the C/03 D.-Torpedo. Re-loaded stern tube. 0925: Surfaced. 0940: Dived before destroyer. 1115: Surface. 1600: Wind 6, sea 6, overcast, rain gusts. 2045: Dived before patrol vessels. Ran at depths due to motion of the sea swell no possibility to shoot.

30 June

0010: Start Point at 250°. Wind, sea 7. Surfaced. 0355: Beachy Head at 249°. Wind and sea unchanged. Boat on sea bed, 38 m. Surfaced every two hours to check weather conditions. 1000: Went to 10 m. 1406: Clear, very visible. Surfaced. Charged. In the course of the afternoon dived several times before destroyers and patrol vessels. 2030: Met *UB 40*.

1 July

0015: Dived before patrol. 0440: Portland at 59°, ten miles. Dived before destroyer. Stayed under water to wait close by Portland for steamers. Sighted large number of steamers. No opportunity to shoot at bigger steamers. 1250: Surfaced. Immediately dived again before patrol vessels which could not be seen through the constantly very misted over periscope. 1420: Surfaced. Charged. Dived several times before patrols or evaded above water.

2 July

0510: Dived before destroyer. Stayed under water to wait for steamers. Had to omit several shooting opportunities as steamers too small. 1140: Failed shot from c. 300-400 m at bigger steamer out of stern tube. Failed shot can only be explained by undershot or other non-functioning of the C/03 D.-Torpedo. 1145: Laid boat on sea bed. Re-loaded stern tube. 1435: Went to 10 m. 1625: Surfaced. Charged. Dived several times before patrols or evaded above water.

3 July

0500: Dived near the coast at Start Point before patrols. 0536: Surfaced. Immediately dived again before patrol (misted over periscope). 1000: Ran underwater attack against large Norwegian steamer. Steamer turns shortly before shot, apparently accidental change of course. Surfaced to take steamer by gun. Trawler nearby which had not been seen under water forces boat to dive. 1430: Surfaced. Charged. Dived several times before patrols or evaded above water.

4 July

0100: Portland starboard athwart. Foggy. 0400: Sighted steamer. Above water for torpedo shot. Steamer at close distance turns out to be too small for torpedo. Stopped by gun fire. 0450: Norwegian steamer *Ran* sunk by blasting cartridges. 0655: Dived before steamer to run attack. Weather is however too thick for my misted over periscope. Because of that surfaced again and followed steamer at some distance as initially a trawler situated nearby makes shelling futile. Opened fire on steamer. However, after a few shots it gets lost in the thickening fog. 0810: Fog. Laid boat on sea bed. Surfaced hourly to check visibility. 1110: Surfaced. 1130: Sighted steamer. Ran attack. Steamer too small. Omitted shot. Surfaced in order to take under gun fire. There are however too many patrols nearby which I hadn't seen through the misted over periscope. 1230: Dived. Ran attack against bigger steamer. 1317: ailed shot out of stern tube from 300-400 m. Failed shot can only be explained by undershot or other non-functioning of the C/03 D.-Torpedo. 1330: Beachy Head at 343°. 1604: Surfaced. Charged. 1800: Met *UB 32*. Dived several times before patrols or evaded above water.

5 July

0900: Waited at Anvil Point for steamers. No shooting opportunity. 1300: Went out to sea to charge batteries. Dived frequently before patrols or evaded above water.

6 July

0829: St Catherines Point at 315°. Waited at Catherine Point close to land for steamers from dawn onwards under water. Very frequent traffic. Shot out of II. tube at loaded French steamer of c. 3,000 tons. Hit. 0834: Steamer sunk. 1400: Surfaced. Charged. 1830: Dived before destroyer. 2000: Wind 5-6, sea 5, increasing.

7 July

0430: Beachy Head at 0°, four miles. Dived before destroyer. Stayed under water in order to wait for steamer. 0800: Sighted convoy, consisting of a middle-sized passenger steamer (possibly auxiliary warship) and a deeply loaded steamer with four masts, numerous cargo booms/derricks, engine astern, no flag type like the Swedish iron steamers, size at least 6,000 tons, shepherded by four destroyers, two u-boat hunters and some trawlers. 0848: Shot out of I. tube at steamer with engine astern. Hit. Boat is rammed by escort. 0903: Went to periscope depth. The attacked steamer has sunk. The passenger steamer keeps at very slow speed close by the boat. Slightly astern of here lies a destroyer bow heavy up to the front funnel under water. Mast and bridge are missing. The whole escort goes at high speed around the damaged destroyer. A hit against the destroyer instead of the attacked steamer is out of the question. It had probably been damaged by ramming. 1055: Surfaced. Started return. 1730: Dived before two patrols. Laid boat sea bed, 35 m. 1910: Surfaced.

8 July

0004: Colbart light vessel. Passed net area close to French coast. 0255: Passed net barrier. 0700: Left exclusion area. 1105: Bruges. Moored Bartenbach: The blocking of the front hydroplane is the result of a construction fault. The stroke limitation of the hydroplane is effected by pinch screwing the thread end on the revolving spindle against the nut supporting the mounting on the front trim tank. Because the hydroplane had apparently frequently been pushed very hard into the end position a thread pitch/turn on the spindle had got jammed. In this position the spindle was jammed so tightly that after its extraction the nut had to be cut open.

Added by another hand:

9–13 July

Bruges North Port. Ongoing repair works.

14 July

Bruges to Ostend.

15–22 July

In dock in Ostend. Ongoing repair works.

23 July

Ostend back to Bruges.

23–25 July

Bruges North Port. Equipment for long distance journey.

25 July

1525: Sailed from Zeebrugge to lay mines at Royal Sovereign, Newhaven and Brighton and for trade war in English Channel.

26 July

At Wissant (Calais) stranded, boat blown up by crew, crew taken into French captivity.

---

1   *Cuxhaven, U-Boot Museum*, Kriegstagebuch, translated Cathrin Brockhaus, stylised and abbreviated by the author.

APPENDIX IV

Crew of *UC 61* and POW Camps

Date: 26 July 1917[1]

OFFICERS

Gerth, Georg Carl, 29, Kapitänleutnant, Active, born 3/3/1888 Berlin
3/4/1907 cadet entry; 10/1915 u-boat school; Bremen 12/1916; Commander
UB 12, joined *UC 61* 12/1916; POW, released 3/1920. Court of enquiry
Bremen 9/2/1920. Left naval service 31/1/1921. Died 13/9/1970
POW camps: Montoire 5/5/1917, Boyardville, Carcassonne

Dancker, Karl Otto Hermann, 27, Leutnant, Reserve, born 2/9/1890
Wolfhagen
Officer Hamburg Amerika Linie; in New York, returned on Norwegian ship
1/1915; adjutant *Kaiser Freidrick*: Wetting; submarine school 2/1916; *UC 24*
two months. Joined *UC 61* 12/1916
POW camp: Montoire 5/5/1917

Giese, Johannes Waldemar, Ingenieur Leutnant, Active, born 8/3/1891
Berlin
UA 10/1915; Libau 1/1916; seven months on *UB 6*, Flanders Flotilla, left
before ran aground 12/3/1917 Maas River, crew interned; *UC 74*; joined *UC
61* at Kiel 11/1916. Gave evidence at court of enquiry 9/2/1920
POW camps: Montoire 5/5/1917, 84

DECK PERSONNEL

Eggers, Max, 21, Seaman, III Marineinfanterieregiment, Active, born
3/1/1896 Grömitz
Next of kin: Heinrich Eggers, Wicheldorfstraße Grömitz, Neustadt Holstein
Seebatallion, Wilhelmshaven 12/1915; Battalion in Bruges 6/1916-5/1917;
reserve one month. Joined *UC 61* 6/1917. First voyage
POW camps: 90, 80B

Ihn, Paul Otto Franz, 22, Seaman, Active, born 1/1/1896 Pyritz

Next of kin: Franz Ihn, Rohrsdorf bei Bahn, Pomeranie
Fisherman; Kiel Matrose Division 10/1915-4/1916; *Augusta* to 9/1916; ten weeks signal school, Kiel; ten weeks *Veneta*; *UB 24*; Flanders Flotilla 1/1917. Joined *UC 61* 28/3/1917; third class passage Hamburg to Winslow via New York, Hamburg-Amerika Line, on *Westphalia*, 6/12/1923
POW camps: 90, 80B.

Koch, Kurt Richard, 19, Seaman, Active, born 26/3/1898 Berlin
Next of kin: Lonia Koch, Kleiststraße, Glasow Kreis, Brandenburg; mother Emilie Alwine Koch
Landstrurm-Infanterie-Bataillone, Würzburg II/B/7, joined 6/1915; u-boat volunteer; nine months Lübeck; Freiwilly to 4/1916; Kiel 1st Matrose six months; Freiwilly; UA to 8/1916; Flanders Flotilla reserve. Joined *UC 61* 3/1917
POW camps: 90, 80B

Lengs, Hubert Gaspar, 30, Steuermann, Reserve, born 16/10/1896 Dortmund
Next of kin: Elisa Lengs, Stirperstraße, Lippstadt
UA 1/1915; Libau; returned winter 1915/16; 2/1916 to Flanders; Kiel training ship *Hertha*; training *Acheron* three months; Flanders Flotilla; ship to Bremen. Joined *UC 61* 7/1917; first voyage. On watch on stranding, sounding route. Suspected spy with Boulogne currency. Spoke French well
POW camps: Arrived 15/8/1917, 84, 90, Croisset to St Aubin-Epinay 3/9/1917, Serres-Carpentras 30/9/1917

Nagal, Andreas Peter Klaus, 29, Bootsmannsmaat, Active, born 3/2/1888, Krautsand S/Elbe
Next of kin: Wilhelm Nagel, Krautsand S/Elbe, Hanover
Libau 1915, *Kaiser Wilhelm II* to 3/1915, *Kaiser Friedrich III* to 7/1915; 9-12/1916 Wilhelmshaven; Kiel *U11*; *UC 17* to 4/1917, commander Ralph Wenniger sick; reserve personnel to 6/1917. Joined *UC 61* 6/1917
POW camps: 90, 80B, Rouen-Lev

Neumann, Adalbert (Albert), 23, Seaman, Cook, Active, born 22/8/1894 Tolkemit
Next of kin: Albert Neumann, Tolkemit, Prusse Occ
Matrose Division, Kiel, 12/1915-12/1916; *Fürst Bismarck* nineteen weeks, UA, *Veneta*, cooking seven weeks, Flanders Flotilla 10/1916; reserve; *UB 40*; UAK Bremen 23/12196-3/1917; three trips to Biscay. Joined *UC 61* 12/1916
POW camps: 90, 80B, 12 (Orval, Ribecourt, Equipes de battage (Oise))

Neumann, Willy, 23, Seaman, Active, born 18/8/94 Soltemin bei Vollin
Next of kin: Albert Neumann, Soltemin bei Vollin

Matrose Division, Wilhelmshaven 8/1915-1/1916; 4/1916 Flanders Flotilla reserve for *UB 12*; joined *UC 61* 12/1916. Died in French captivity 17/10/1917
POW camps: None found

Pucknus, Richars Max, Oberbootsmannsmaat, Loan, born 14/6/1889 Tilsit
Next of kin: Fritz Pucknus, Frischstraße 26, Brunsbüttel (Koog Schleswig Holstein)
Supplement to crew. Month loan from battleship *Schleswig Holstein*. Joined *UC 61* 7/1917
POW camps: 86 to 90 1/3/1917, 84 to 90 15/8/1917, 90 to 13 22/8/1917, Zône to Rouen-Croisset 8/10/1917, Croisset to Dieppe 17/11/1917

Sänger, Willy Hans, 22, Seaman, Active, born 23/4/1896, Graudenz
Next of kin: Frau Z Sänger, Speicherstaße 32, Graudenz
Matrose Division, Kiel, 7/1915, one year, infantry; *UC 11*, Kiel, training ship 7-12/1916; training ship *UB 25*; *U 1* training ship; *U 9*. Joined *UC 61* Bremen 12/16, two months; re-joined 2/1917; two voyages: Biscay, Spain, and 6/1917; two weeks' leave
POW camps: 84, 24

Zäbisch, Franz Karl, 22, Bootsmannsmaat, Active, born 1/11/1895, Gippe (Kisterberg)
Next of kin: Heinrich Zäbisch, Cippe near Kisterberg, Saxony
Joined 1911, Flensburg Training School; 4/1912 *Hertha*; 4/1913 Flensburg; 11/1913 Torpedo Division, Wilhelmshaven; 1/1916 *V106* training ship, Kiel; then *V105*, *V108* to 5/1916. Promoted from Boy. UA 3/1916; 5/1916 *Vineta*; three trips *UB 11*, *UC 11*; one trip *UB 10*; *U 38* to Hamburg. Joined *UC 61* at Bremen 11/1916
POW camps: 90, Bureau de renseingnements, Paris

ENGINE ROOM
Barthold, Paul, 29, PO Second Class, Machinist mate, Reserve, born 12/10/89 Berlin
Next of kin: Mle Inge Balzerson, Flensburg Teichstraße 5, Schleswig Holstein
Volunteer. Braunschweig, one year; Torpedo School, Flensburg, eighteen months; Flanders Flotilla reserve from Kiel 5/1916. In charge electrical apparatus and services engines. Fitting-out party *UC 61* 6/1917
POW camp: 13 (Bellinglise, Coupe-Gueule, St Leger-aux-Bois, Choisy Aux Bac)

Becker, Friedrich, 22, First stoker, Active, born 1/6/1895 Ludwigshafen

1st Werft Division, 1/10/1915, eight months; UA Kiel, three months; training *UB 11*, *UB 5*; *Acheron*; Ostend Flanders Flotilla reserve 10/1916. Joined *UC 61* Bremen, 12/916. *UC 61* in shelter during Ostend bombardment
POW camp: 84

Bock, Otto, 22, Telegrapher, Ob. Gst, Active, born 4/2/1895, Hoisbüttel
Next of kin: Augusta Bock, Schmalem-becker, Hamburg Staras 18
2nd Werft Division, 1/10/1915, Wilhelmshaven; FelsburgFunk (radio) training school 16/1/1916; UA, 3/8/1916; *UB 12* to 11/1916; reserve to end 2/1917; joined *UC 61* 3/1917
POW camps: Zône des armées 84, Mouy-Bury, SA2

Bodrich, Fritz, 24, PO Second Class, Machinist mate, Active, born 6/12/1892, Seepothen
Next of kin: Frau Rebut, Siegelscheinstaße 3, Elbing, Prusse Occ
1st Werft Division Hesse, 1912; 10/1913 divisional training school six months' theory; *Lotharingen*, four weeks, 10/1914; UA Bremen to 1/1915; *U 3*, three months to 4/1915; Hamburg *UC 7*, eight weeks; Kiel; 8/1915-2/1916 to Flanders Flotilla; B&V shipyard, Hamburg; *UB 39*. Last two u-boats sunk after leaving. Fitting-out party *UC 61*, 11/1916
POW camp: 84

Carstensen, Christian, 23, Stoker, Active, born 27/11/1894, Flensburg
Next of kin: Karl Bostorf, Schloßstraße 44, Flensburg, Schl. Hols.
Kiel, 12/1915; *Fürst Bismarck*, stokers' school, 10/1916; UA; Flanders Flotilla; training, *UC 26*, two voyages; Kiel, joined *UC 61* 12/1916. Three notes from Oran found in wallet
POW camp: 84

Gerigk, George, 24, PO Second Class, Machinist mate, Active, born 30/7/1893 Prohlow
Next of kin: Frau Gerigk, Mickelsdorf, Prusse Occ
Torpedo division 1/10/1913, six weeks; one year Werft Division, Kiel; under officer school for torpedoes 1/4-9/1915, Kiel, six weeks. On 'Y' 1915 to 9/1916. Training ships U1, U 2, UB 25, UB 28, reserve 10/1916-1/1917; four-five cruises. Fitting-out party, *UC 61*, Kiel 10/1916. No more voyages. Returned 8/7/1917. Gerth 'not best commander'. In charge mines & torpedoes
POW camps: 90, 80B, Pont-Sainte-Maxence, SE5

Goosmann, Franz, 19, Stoker, Machinist trainee, Active, born 3/6/1898 Düsseldorf
Next of kin: Hermann Goosmann, Behrenstraße, Düsseldorf
Freiwilly, volunteer, 3/4/1916; 2nd Werft Division, six months' exercises;

UA Kiel end 8/1916, *Acheron*; training school, Flanders Flotilla, 9/1916, *UB 38*; joined *UC 61* Bremen 12/1916. Refused questions
POW camps: 90, 80B

Kleinsorg, Peter, 24, PO I, First machinist mate, Active, born 8/2/1893 Frechen
Next of kin: Bertel Kleinsorg, Frechen
Kiel, 1911, first trip *Wettin*; UA three months training ship *UC 11*; training ship *UC 1*. Fitting-out party, Bremen, *UC 61*, 11/1916. First under officer, Obermaschinemat. Complained of different mechanisms to other UC boats
POW camps: 90, 80B

Naumann, Alfred Ernst Hermann, 23, PO 2, Machinist mate, Active, 15/11/1894 Alt-Neudöbern
Next of kin: Hermann Naumann, Neu Petersheim, Brandenburg
1st Werft Division, Freiwilly, Maschinenschlosser, 5/1914; 21 months' infantry; *SMS Hessen* 7/1914; Norway; *Großer Kurfürst*, one year; Mechanics School, Kiel, six months, 1915; 3/1916 UA; course on practical techniques; worked on u-boats at Vulcan yard. UAK, four weeks, *Acheron*; Flanders Flotilla reserve 3 weeks, 6/1916; *UC 6*; *UC 1*, six weeks; Bremen 9/1916. Fitting-out party *UC 61* 12/1916
POW camps: 90, 116 (Villeneuve-s-Fere, Roncheres, Fere-en-Tardenois)

Petersen: No details: Suspect, only found on initial crew interrogation

Raabe, Karl, 21, Stoker, Active, born 8/10/1896 Essen
Next of kin: Wittor Raabe, W Buttmanstraße 34, Essen
Born, 3/10/1896; 1st Werft Division, 1/10/1916-1/1917, eight weeks, infantry course; joined *UC 61*, Kiel, 1/1917. Died in French captivity 23/1/1920
POW camps: 90, 80B

Schindler, Paul Emil, 22 Stoker, Active, Grosse Schlocher, born 9/2/1896 Leipzig
Nest of kin: Gustav Schindler, Wiegandstraße 34, Leipzig
Born 9/2/1895; unmarried son of Gustav & Mary Schindler; 1st Werft Division, 1/10/1915-8/1916; reserve Flanders Flotilla; *UB 29*; Bremen; joined *UC 61* 11/96. Died in internment in Davos, 26/7/1918. POW camps: 90 to 25 (Roye Cote, Tilloloy, Rosieres, near to Crépy-en-Valois) 26/8/1917; Seaman's Hospital, Arsenal, Brest (bronchitis) 2/5/1918; Davos-Wiesen, Switzerland

Starke, Wilhelm, 24, Lead stoker, First stoker, Active, born 26/9/1893 Dortmund

Next of kin: Johann. Starke, Silbenstraße 9, Dortmund
2nd Werft Division, 1/10/1914, eight months; UA Kiel, training six weeks, 5-6/1915; *Acheron*; workshop to 12/1915; then Flanders Flotilla; training, *UB 19*, one trip; reserve to 11/1916. Joined *UC 61* 12/1916
POW camp: 84

Weidner, Michael, Stoker, born 3/8/1895 Neustadt
Next of kin: Johann Weidner, Gasfabrikstraße 50, Weiden, Bavaria
1/10/1916; UA 1916; *UB 25*; *UB 16*, Flanders Flotilla, 1916; joined *UC 61* 1/1917
POW camps: 90, 80B

---

1   Some of the writing and typing on these documents is very poor; best efforts have been made. *Freiburg, Gefangenenkompanie*, 'POW company'; Kp. 150518; RM 20/504 31/3/1919; RM 86/18: RMA 10139, 15.5/1918; Gef. Kp. 100718; ancesrry.com; grandeguerre.icrc.org/en/List/480150/897/24302.

President Wilson's Fourteen Points

Date: 8 January 1918

It will be our wish and purpose that the processes of peace, when they are begun, shall be absolutely open and that they shall involve and permit henceforth no secret understandings of any kind. The day of conquest and aggrandizement is gone by; so is also the day of secret covenants entered into in the interest of particular governments and likely at some unlooked-for moment to upset the peace of the world. It is this happy fact, now clear to the view of every public man whose thoughts do not still linger in an age that is dead and gone, which makes it possible for every nation whose purposes are consistent with justice and the peace of the world to avow now or at any other time the objects it has in view.

We entered this war because violations of right had occurred which touched us to the quick and made the life of our own people impossible unless they were corrected and the world secure once for all against their recurrence. What we demand in this war, therefore, is nothing peculiar to ourselves. It is that the world be made fit and safe to live in; and particularly that it be made safe for every peace-loving nation which, like our own, wishes to live its own life, determine its own institutions, be assured of justice and fair dealing by the other peoples of the world as against force and selfish aggression. All the peoples of the world are in effect partners in this interest, and for our own part we see very clearly that unless justice be done to others it will not be done to us. The programme of the world's peace, therefore, is our programme; and that programme, the only possible programme, as we see it, is this:

1. Open covenants of peace, openly arrived at, after which there shall be no private international understandings of any kind but diplomacy shall proceed always frankly and in the public view.
2. Absolute freedom of navigation upon the seas, outside territorial waters, alike in peace and in war, except as the seas may be closed

in whole or in part by international action for the enforcement of international covenants.

3. The removal, so far as possible, of all economic barriers and the establishment of an equality of trade conditions among all the nations consenting to the peace and associating themselves for its maintenance.

4. Adequate guarantees given and taken that national armaments will be reduced to the lowest point consistent with domestic safety.

5. A free, open-minded, and absolutely impartial adjustment of all colonial claims, based upon a strict observance of the principle that in determining all such questions of sovereignty the interests of the populations concerned must have equal weight with the equitable claims of the government whose title is to be determined.

6. The evacuation of all Russian territory and such a settlement of all questions affecting Russia as will secure the best and freest co-operation of the other nations of the world in obtaining for her an unhampered and unembarrassed opportunity for the independent determination of her own political development and national policy and assure her of a sincere welcome into the society of free nations under institutions of her own choosing; and, more than a welcome, assistance also of every kind that she may need and may herself desire. The treatment accorded Russia by her sister nations in the months to come will be the acid test of their good will, of their comprehension of her needs as distinguished from their own interests, and of their intelligent and unselfish sympathy.

7. Belgium, the whole world will agree, must be evacuated and restored, without any attempt to limit the sovereignty which she enjoys in common with all other free nations. No other single act will serve as this will serve to restore confidence among the nations in the laws which they have themselves set and determined for the government of their relations with one another. Without this healing act the whole structure and validity of international law is forever impaired.

8. All French territory should be freed and the invaded portions restored, and the wrong done to France by Prussia in 1871 in the matter of Alsace-Lorraine, which has unsettled the peace of the world for nearly fifty years, should be righted, in order that peace may once more be made secure in the interest of all.

9. A readjustment of the frontiers of Italy should be effected along clearly recognizable lines of nationality.

10. The peoples of Austria-Hungary, whose place among the nations we wish to see safeguarded and assured, should be accorded the freest opportunity to autonomous development.

11. Rumania, Serbia, and Montenegro should be evacuated; occupied territories restored; Serbia accorded free and secure access to the sea; and the relations of the several Balkan states to one another determined

by friendly counsel along historically established lines of allegiance and nationality; and international guarantees of the political and economic independence and territorial integrity of the several Balkan states should be entered into.

12. The Turkish portion of the present Ottoman Empire should be assured a secure sovereignty, but the other nationalities which are now under Turkish rule should be assured an undoubted security of life and an absolutely unmolested opportunity of autonomous development, and the Dardanelles should be permanently opened as a free passage to the ships and commerce of all nations under international guarantees.

13. An independent Polish state should be erected which should include the territories inhabited by indisputably Polish populations, which should be assured a free and secure access to the sea, and whose political and economic independence and territorial integrity should be guaranteed by international covenant.

14. A general association of nations must be formed under specific covenants for the purpose of affording mutual guarantees of political independence and territorial integrity to great and small states alike.

In regard to these essential rectifications of wrong and assertions of right we feel ourselves to be intimate partners of all the governments and peoples associated together against the Imperialists. We cannot be separated in interest or divided in purpose. We stand together until the end.

For such arrangements and covenants we are willing to fight and to continue to fight until they are achieved; but only because we wish right to prevail and desire a just and stable peace such as can be secured only by removing the chief provocations to war, which this programme does remove. We have no jealousy of German greatness, and there is nothing in this programme that impairs it. We grudge her no achievement or distinction of learning or of pacific enterprise such as have made her record very bright and very enviable. We do not wish to injure her or to block in any way her legitimate influence or power. We do not wish to fight her either with arms or with hostile arrangements of trade if she is willing to associate herself with us and the other peace- loving nations of the world in covenants of justice and law and fair dealing. We wish her only to accept a place of equality among the peoples of the world, the new world in which we now live, instead of a place of mastery.

Armistice Agreement

Date: 11 November 1918 at 5 o'clock French time

Armistice Agreement: Military Clauses on Western Front

1. Cessation of operations by land and in the air six hours after the signature of the armistice.

2. Immediate evacuation of invaded countries: Belgium, France, Alsace-Lorraine, Luxemburg, so ordered as to be completed within fourteen days from the signature of the armistice. German troops which have not left the above-mentioned territories within the period fixed will become prisoners of war. Occupation by the allied and United States forces jointly will keep pace with evacuation in these areas. All movements of evacuation and occupation will be regulated in accordance with a note annexed to the stated terms.

3. Repatriation beginning at once to be completed within fifteen days of all the inhabitants of the countries above enumerated (including hostages, persons under trial or convicted).

4. Surrender in good condition by the German armies of the following war material: Five thousand guns (2,500 heavy, and 2,500 field), 25,000 machine guns, 3,000 minenwerfer, 1,700 airplanes (fighters, bombers – firstly, all of the D7s and all the night bombing machines). The above to be delivered in situ to the allied and United States troops in accordance with the detailed conditions laid down in the note (annexure No. 1) drawn up at the moment of the signing of the armistice.

5. Evacuation by the German armies of the countries on the left bank of the Rhine. The countries on the left bank of the Rhine shall be administered by the local troops of occupation. The occupation of these territories will be carried out by allied and United States garrisons holding the principal crossings of the Rhine (Mayence, Coblenz, Cologne), together with the bridgeheads at these points of a thirty-kilometre radius on the right bank and by garrisons similarly holding the strategic points of the regions. A neutral zone shall be reserved on the right bank of the Rhine between the stream and a line drawn parallel to the bridgeheads and

to the stream and at a distance of ten kilometres, from the frontier of Holland up to the frontier of Switzerland. The evacuation by the enemy of the Rhine-lands (left and right bank) shall be so ordered as to be completed within a further period of sixteen days, in all, thirty-one days after the signing of the armistice. All the movements of evacuation or occupation are regulated by the note (annexure No. 1) drawn up at the moment of the signing of the armistice.

6. In all territories evacuated by the enemy there shall be no evacuation of inhabitants; no damage or harm shall be done to the persons or property of the inhabitants. No person shall be prosecuted for offences of participation in war measures prior to the signing of the armistice. No destruction of any kind shall be committed. Military establishments of all kinds shall be delivered intact, as well as military stores of food, munitions, and equipment, not removed during the time fixed for evacuation. Stores of food of all kinds for the civil population, cattle, etc., shall be left in situ. Industrial establishments shall not be impaired in any way and their personnel shall not be removed.

7. Roads and means of communication of every kind, railroads, waterways, main roads, bridges, telegraphs, telephones, shall be in no manner impaired. All civil and military personnel at present employed on them shall remain. Five thousand locomotives and 150,000 wagons in good working order, with all necessary spare parts and fittings, shall be delivered to the associated powers within the period fixed in annexure No. 2, and total of which shall not exceed thirty-one days. There shall likewise be delivered 5,000 motor lorries (camion automobiles) in good order, within the period of thirty-six days. The railways of Alsace-Lorraine shall be handed over within the period of thirty-one days, together with pre-war personnel and material. Further, the material necessary for the working of railways in the countries on the left bank of the Rhine shall be left in situ. All stores of coal and material for the upkeep of permanent ways, signals, and repair shops shall be left in situ. These stores shall be maintained by Germany in so far as concerns the working of the railroads in the countries on the left bank of the Rhine. All barges taken from the Allies shall be restored to them. The note, annexure No. 2, regulates the details of these measures.

8. The German command shall be responsible for revealing within the period of forty-eight hours after the signing of the armistice all mines or delayed action fuses on territory evacuated by the German troops and shall assist in their discovery and destruction. It also shall reveal all destructive measures that may have been taken (such as poisoning or polluting of springs and wells, etc.). All under penalty of reprisals.

9. The right of requisition shall be exercised by the allied and United States armies in all occupied territories, subject to regulation of accounts with those whom it may concern. The upkeep of the troops of occupation

in the Rhineland (excluding Alsace-Lorraine) shall be charged to the German Government.

10. The immediate repatriation without reciprocity, according to detailed conditions which shall be fixed, of all allied and United States prisoners of war, including persons under trial or convicted. The allied powers and the United States shall be able to dispose of them as they wish. This condition annuls the previous conventions on the subject of the exchange of prisoners of war, including the one of July 1918, in course of ratification. However, the repatriation of German prisoners of war interned in Holland and in Switzerland shall continue as before. The repatriation of German prisoners of war shall be regulated at the conclusion of the preliminaries of peace.

11. Sick and wounded who cannot be removed from evacuated territory will be cared for by German personnel, who will be left on the spot with the medical material required.

Disposition Relative to the Eastern Frontiers of Germany

12. All German troops at present in the territories which before belonged to Austria-Hungary, Rumania, Turkey, shall withdraw immediately within the frontiers of Germany as they existed on 1 August 1914. All German troops at present in the territories which before the war belonged to Russia shall likewise withdraw within the frontiers of Germany, defined as above, as soon as the Allies, taking into account the internal situation of these territories, shall decide that the time for this has come.

13. Evacuation by German troops to begin at once, and all German instructors, prisoners, and civilians as well as military agents now on the territory of Russia (as defined before 1914) to be recalled.

14. German troops to cease at once all requisitions and seizures and any other undertaking with a view to obtaining supplies intended for Germany in Rumania and Russia (as defined on 1 August 1914).

15. Renunciation of the treaties of Bucharest and Brest-Litovsk and of the supplementary treaties.

16. The Allies shall have free access to the territories evacuated by the Germans on their eastern frontier, either through Danzig, or by the Vistula, in order to convey supplies to the populations of those territories and for the purpose of maintaining order.

Clause Concerning East Africa

17. Evacuation by all German forces operating in East Africa within a period to be fixed by the Allies.

General Clauses

18. Repatriation, without reciprocity, within a maximum period of one month in accordance with detailed conditions hereafter to be fixed of all interned civilians, including hostages under trial or convicted, belonging to the Allied or associated powers other than those enumerated in Article Three.
19. The following financial conditions are required: Reparation for damage done. While such armistice lasts no public securities shall be removed by the enemy which can serve as a pledge to the Allies for the recovery or reparation for war losses. Immediate restitution of the cash deposit in the national bank of Belgium, and in general immediate return of all documents, specie, stocks, shares, paper money, together with plant for the issue thereof, touching public or private interests in the invaded countries. Restitution of the Russian and Rumanian gold yielded to Germany or taken by that power. This gold to be delivered in trust to the Allies until the signature of peace.

Naval Conditions

20. Immediate cessation of all hostilities at sea and definite information to be given as to the location and movements of all German ships. Notification to be given to neutrals that freedom of navigation in all territorial waters is given to the naval and mercantile marines of the allied and associated powers, all questions of neutrality being waived.
21. All naval and mercantile marine prisoners of the allied and associated powers in German hands to be returned without reciprocity.
22. Surrender to the Allies and United States of all submarines (including submarine cruisers and all mine-laying submarines) now existing, with their complete armament and equipment, in ports which shall be specified by the Allies and United States. Those which cannot take the sea shall be disarmed of personnel and material and shall remain under the supervision of the Allies and the United States. The submarines which are ready for the sea shall be prepared to leave the German ports as soon as orders shall be received by wireless for their voyage to the port designated for their delivery, and the remainder at the earliest possible moment. The conditions of this article shall be carried into effect within the period of fourteen days after the signing of the armistice.
23. German surface warships which shall be designated by the Allies and the United States shall be immediately disarmed and thereafter interned in neutral ports or in default of them in allied ports to be designated by the Allies and the United States. They will there remain under the supervision of the Allies and of the United States, only

caretakers being left on board. The following warships are designated by the Allies: Six battle cruisers, ten battleships, eight light cruisers (including two mine layers), fifty destroyers of the most modern types. All other surface warships (including river craft) are to be concentrated in German naval bases to be designated by the Allies and the United States and are to be completely disarmed and classed under the supervision of the Allies and the United States. The military armament of all ships of the auxiliary fleet shall be put on shore. All vessels designated to be interned shall be ready to leave the German ports seven days after the signing of the armistice. Directions for the voyage will be given by wireless.

24. The Allies and the United States of America shall have the right to sweep up all mine fields and obstructions laid by Germany outside German territorial waters, and the positions of these are to be indicated.

25. Freedom of access to and from the Baltic to be given to the naval and mercantile marines of the allied and associated powers. To secure this the Allies and the United States of America shall be empowered to occupy all German forts, fortifications, batteries, and defence works of all kinds in all the entrances from the Kattegat into the Baltic, and to sweep up all mines and obstructions within and without German territorial waters, without any question of neutrality being raised, and the positions of all such mines and obstructions are to be indicated.

26. The existing blockade conditions set up by the allied and associated powers are to remain unchanged, and all German merchant ships found at sea are to remain liable to capture. The Allies and the United States should give consideration to the provisioning of Germany during the armistice to the extent recognized as necessary.

27. All naval aircraft are to be concentrated and immobilized in German bases to be specified by the Allies and the United States of America.

28. In evacuating the Belgian coast and ports Germany shall abandon in situ and in fact all port and river navigation material, all merchant ships, tugs, lighters, all naval aeronautic apparatus, material and supplies, and all arms, apparatus, and supplies of every kind.

29. All Black Sea ports are to be evacuated by Germany; all Russian war vessels of all descriptions seized by Germany in the Black Sea are to be handed over to the Allies and the United States of America; all neutral merchant vessels seized are to be released; all warlike and other materials of all kinds seized in those ports are to be returned and German materials as specified in Clause Twenty-eight are to be abandoned.

30. All merchant vessels in German hands belonging to the allied and associated powers are to be restored in ports to be specified by the Allies and the United States of America without reciprocity.

31. No destruction of ships or of materials to be permitted before evacuation, surrender, or restoration.

32. The German Government will notify the neutral Governments of the world, and particularly the Governments of Norway, Sweden, Denmark, and Holland, that all restrictions placed on the trading of their vessels with the allied and associated countries, whether by the German Government or by private German interests, and whether in return for specific concessions, such as the export of shipbuilding materials, or not, are immediately cancelled.

33. No transfers of German merchant shipping of any description to any neutral flag are to take place after signature of the armistice.

Duration of Armistice

34. The duration of the armistice is to be thirty days, with option to extend. During this period if its clauses are not carried into execution the armistice may be denounced by one of the contracting parties, which must give warning forty-eight hours in advance. It is understood that the execution of Articles 3 and 18 shall not warrant the denunciation of the armistice on the ground of insufficient execution within a period fixed, except in the case of bad faith in carrying them into execution. In order to assure the execution of this convention under the best conditions, the principle of a permanent international armistice commission is admitted. This commission will act under the authority of the allied military and naval Commanders in Chief.

The Limit for Reply

35. This armistice to be accepted or refused by Germany within seventy-two hours of notification.

F FOCH
R E WEMYSS
ERZBERGER
OBERNDORFF
WINTERFELDT
VON SALOW

Kaiser Wilhelm's Abdication

Date: 28 November 1918

I herewith renounce for all time claims to the throne of Prussia and to the German Imperial throne connected therewith.

At the same time I release all officials of the German Empire and of Prussia, as well as all officers, non-commissioned officers and men of the navy and of the Prussian army, as well as the troops of the federated states of Germany, from the oath of fidelity which they tendered to me as their Emperor, King and Commander-in-Chief.

I expect of them that until the re-establishment of order in the German Empire they shall render assistance to those in actual power in Germany, in protecting the German people from the threatening dangers of anarchy, famine, and foreign rule.

Proclaimed under our own hand and with the imperial seal attached.

Amerongen

WILLIAM

Paper, Dr A. Weber, Municipal Officer of Health, Berlin, at Berlin Medical School

Date: 18 December 1918

If the City of Berlin in the present problem is allowed to have its say, this, apart from the local interest, is in the first place justified by the fact that Berlin, being the largest community of Germany, for evident reasons has to face an especially hard struggle with food difficulties, and that figures relating to Berlin express with special distinctness the unfavourable influence on the health condition of its inhabitants.

In Berlin also an increased mortality commenced at the beginning of December 1916, the aged being first overtaken. They would primarily succumb to diseases of the upper organs of respiration, especially inflammation of the lungs and tuberculosis.

The increase of tuberculosis commenced somewhat later in January 1916, when the increased mortality, which at the beginning had been limited to the age above fifty to sixty years, gradually commenced taking hold also of younger people, down to the age of about ten.

While old and sickly people or those debilitated by tuberculous or other chronic infection mainly fell victims to the above mentioned diseases behind the front as a consequence of war conditions, acute intestinal troubles, including dysentery, carried off in the months from June to September 1917 even strong persons, and influenza and inflammation of the lungs in July and October 1918, frequently took the healthiest and strongest.

There died, in fact, in October 1918, of influenza and inflammation of the lungs alone 2,770 persons, as compared with a total mortality of 2,360 in October 1917. The influenza epidemic drove the total mortality in October 1918 to the unheard of number of 5,385, in November 1918, to 3,478. Women suffered especially since 1,771 out of a total of 2,770 persons dying in October 1918 of influenza and inflammation of the lungs were of the female sex.

Though it is not admissible to bring the influenza epidemic into direct connection with war conditions – it would also have appeared if we had been in peace – there cannot be any doubt but that not a few of those carried away by secondary inflammation of the lungs and other complications have perished on account of the insufficient resistance they offered to infection because of poor alimentary conditions.

To this should be added another circumstance which would seem to justify our discussing the influenza epidemic which unfortunately still keeps us under its sway.

Very great indeed on account of the enormous spread of the disease is the number of those who after an attack of influenza suffer from consecutive phenomena, being unable to recover completely. Their convalescence is slow and difficult, such as is frequently observed also in the cases of other diseases during the present war. In order to improve the condition of such people, to make them efficient workers again, first-class and easily and digestible articles of food are necessary, milk and fat above all.

While the total of deaths for 1916 does not show any distinct increase, the year of 1917 shows a strong rise. The total mortality in 1917 was 34,122, as compared with the average for 1913/1916, amounting to 28,362. There thus died in the city of Berlin in 1917, 5,760 persons, viz. 23 per cent, in excess of the average for 1913/1916. Practically all ages are concerned in this surplus mortality, but particularly from the age of ten upwards.

If now, in order to get an idea of the year 1918 which has not yet come to an end, the total mortality of the first nine months of 1918 (viz, 23,437) be compared with the average of the first nine months 1913/1916 (viz. 21,190), it is seen that in the time from the first of January to 20 September 2,247 persons, viz. 10.6 per cent, more than the average of the first nine months of 1913/1916, have died. Adding the enormously high influenza mortality already mentioned for the months of October and November 1918, we may already affirm that the total mortality in 1918 will attain, nay, probably exceed somewhat that of 1917. This distinctly shows how much the state of health has been impaired in the course of the last two years of war. Under no circumstances can this state of affairs be allowed to continue.

Special attention should be paid to tuberculosis, a disease connected with the greatest dangers for the national heath.

Tuberculosis mortality – the following figures are relative only to tuberculosis of the lungs and throat, not to other forms of tuberculosis – in the city of Berlin in the years of 1913/1916 was, on an average, 3,375, in the year of 1917, 5,046. In 1917 there died in the city of Berlin 1,671 persons, that is, 49.5 per cent more than the average of the years 1913/1916, of tuberculosis of the throat and lungs.

Tuberculosis mortality during the war shows a greater rise than the total mortality.

If here also, in order to form an idea of the year 1918, the first nine months of 1918 be compared with the corresponding period of 1917 and with the average of the first nine months of 1913/1916, an increase of tuberculosis amounting to 54.58 per cent is obtained for 1917, and increase of 48.68 per cent for 1918. When separating the figures relative to males from those relative to females, males are found to show in 1917 an increase of 43.47 per cent, in 1918 an increase of 30.62 per cent, women on the other had – these figures on account of special war conditions are more convincing – in 1917 an increase of 68.72 per cent, in 1918 an increase of 71.67 per cent.

Women, especially those of the age of working efficiency, have suffered severely from tuberculosis. Even in 1918, the cases of tuberculosis with them show a further increase as compared with 1917.

In January last, I elsewhere stated the opinion that our population no longer having any reserve matter of its own body to draw upon, we should under no circumstances renew experiments such as those of the Swede-turnip period in 1917, that any further deterioration of our feeding standard was bound to lead to the most fatal consequences. Since then the populations has held out nearly another year. Thanks to regular potato supplies, somewhat more abundant than in 1917, the test has been stood somehow or other. At what sacrifice, however, especially among our women, this holding out has been bought, you have seen from the figures here communicated. For two years now with regards to our food standard we have been on the borders of the possible and bearable. According to what has been said today, we are on the edge of a precipice for there can be no doubt that any further deterioration of our food standard is bound to lead to the breakdown of the health of our population. Unless we soon get fats and cereals from abroad, we should unavoidably – at the very latest from February on – on account of the rapid decline of out potato and corn stocks, fall victims to a state of general underfeeding or even famine, which would cause the mortality, first of women and children, afterwards that of the remaining population, in spite of peace, to swell to such an extent that even on the basis of war conditions we cannot now form any idea of.

Law for the Restoration of the Professional Civil Service

Date: 7 April 1933

The Reich Government has enacted the following Law[1], promulgated herewith:[2]

Clause 1:

1. To restore a national professional civil service and to simplify administration, civil servants may be dismissed from office in accordance with the following regulations, even where there would be no grounds for such action under the prevailing Law.
2. For the purposes of this Law the following are to be considered civil servants: direct and indirect officials of the Reich, direct and indirect officials of the Laender,[3] officials of Local Councils, and of Federations of Local Councils, officials of Public Corporations as well as of Institutions and Enterprises of equivalent status ... The provisions will apply also to officials of Social Insurance organizations having the status of civil servants ....

Clause 2:

1. Civil servants who have entered the service since 9 November 1918, without possessing the required or customary educational background or other qualifications are to be dismissed from the service. Their previous salaries will continue to be paid for a period of three months following their dismissal.
2. They will have no claim to temporary pensions, full pensions or survivors' benefits, nor to retain designation of rank or titles, or to wear uniforms or emblems ....

Clause 3:

1. Civil servants who are not of Aryan descent are to be retired; if they are honorary officials, they are to be dismissed from their official status.
2. Section 1 does not apply to civil servants in office from 1 August 1914, who fought at the Front for the German Reich or its Allies in the World War, or whose fathers or sons fell in the World War. Other exceptions may be permitted by the Reich Minister of the Interior in coordination with the Minister concerned or with the highest authorities with respect to civil servants working abroad.

Clause 4:

1. Civil servants whose previous political activities afford no assurance that they will at all times give their fullest support to the national State, can be dismissed from the service ....

Reich Chancellor Adolf Hitler
Reich Minister of Interior Wilhelm Frick
Reich Minister of Finance Graf Schwerin von Krosigk

ENDNOTES

1 *Gesetz zur Wiederherstellung des Berufsbeamtentums.*
2 *Reichsgesetzblatt*, Vol. I, 1933, p. 175 (The Public Law Journal).
3 The name for federal states in German-speaking countries.

CIA Report: The Lohmann Affair

Date: 7 April 1933

APPROVED FOR RELEASE: CIA HISTORICAL REVIEW
PROGRAM: 22/9/1993
Historical Document: Posted: 8/5/2007; Last Updated: 1/7/2008[1]

Achievements, extravagances, and exposure of a clandestine German interbellum operation in military research and development.

THE LOHMANN AFFAIR

The Weimar Republic's attempts in the twenties to circumvent the Versailles restrictions on its armed forces produced clandestine operations which in their financing, cover devices, and hazards of exposure present a close parallel with intelligence operations. One such series of undercover research and development projects, carried out by a Captain Walther Lohmann of the German Naval Transportation Division, got out of hand and became a source of acute embarrassment to the Weimar Ministry of Defense. The affair was hushed up, and in more recent times has been virtually overlooked by historians. Sufficient material is now available, however, for a scrutiny of Lohmann's work, its oddities and blunders, and for an account of the way the German Cabinet successfully veiled its true nature after some of the clandestine activities had been exposed in the press.[2]

Walter Lohmann, the son of a one-time director of the *North German Lloyd* shipping line, served inconspicuously as a non-combat logistics specialist during the European war of 1914-1918. He won recognition in navy circles afterward, however, for his work on a sub-commission which negotiated the disposition of the German merchant fleet and for his direction of shipments of emergency food supplies to Germany. He also managed the return from overseas of German war prisoners. In 1920, while on the first of two trips to Leningrad to negotiate with the Russians regarding the release of captured German merchant ships, he met the comely German-born Frau Else Ektimov, destined later to play a role in his downfall. He subsequently arranged for the return of the lady to Germany and for her support.

In October 1920, he assumed command of the Naval Transport Division of Navy headquarters in Berlin, a post concerned primarily with logistical matters. For this reason, and also because he enjoyed the complete trust of Admiral Paul Behncke, then commander in chief of the Navy, he was given full charge in early 1923 of the disbursement of the Navy's 'black' funds reserved for clandestine purposes.

Achievements

Initially, these funds included large sums – amounting in dollars to at least twenty-five million – obtained from the sale of warships and submarines scrapped in 1919 and 1920 at the order of the Allied Powers. Later, some two and a half million were added as the Navy's share of the so-called 'Ruhr funds', monies voted by the Reichstag and used to strengthen the armed services above Treaty limit at the time of the French occupation of the Ruhr. Subsequently, smaller sums totalling about two and a quarter million were obtained or diverted from other sources. Most of this money was transmitted to recipients through a Lohmann-supported bank, the *Berliner Bankverein*, which acted as a middleman between the Naval Transport Division and the various projects funded.

Only one inspector, a man of Lohmann's own choice, was assigned to audit the funds, and he had no authority to question the wisdom or validity of the captain's disbursements. His presence afforded a partial check against improper book-keeping and ordinary waste, but none to hinder Lohmann from supporting whatever projects he chose. Admiral Behncke and Minister of Defense Otto Gessler, trusting Lohmann to use the money for worthwhile undertakings, seem to have given him carte blanche, an opportunity which appealed to his Hanseatic spirit.

Between 1923 and 1927, Lohmann financed nearly all of the clandestine and semi-clandestine projects of the Navy. Most of these were established with the initial concurrence of his superiors, and many required the closest cooperation with several divisions of the naval staff; but some were founded and supported solely on the captain's initiative without the knowledge of even the commander in chief of the Navy. This independent activity was protected by the necessity for strict secrecy in clandestine operations and by Lohmann's extremely broad powers.

The projects which dealt with aircraft and submarine design and development were for the most part soundly conceived, well executed, and extremely important for the future development of the Navy and the Luftwaffe. With subsidies from Lohmann, three German shipyards operated a highly successful submarine design bureau in The Netherlands which maintained contact with Navy headquarters through a dummy firm known as Mentor Bilanz. The 'Dutch' bureau, *Ingenieurskantoor voor Scheepsbouw* (IvS), designed a submarine which Lohmann and Captain Wilhelm Canaris (later to become the Abwehr chief of ambivalent loyalties) in 1926 arranged to have built at Cadiz in Spain. The purpose was to train German technicians and to develop a prototype medium-size submarine, which among other features had torpedo tubes designed to eliminate the large bubble of air that normally betrayed a submarine's position when a torpedo was fired.

Lohmann's work in aircraft development was equally significant. The firms of *Heinkel, Dornier,* and *Rohrbach* enjoyed his subsidies, and in 1926 he purchased outright the *Casper Aircraft Company* to obtain facilities for the type-testing of 'commercial' aircraft which closely resembled the fighter, bomber, and reconnaissance planes being built abroad by such firms as *Boeing, Vickers,* and *Douglass.* By 1927, Germany had several successful prototypes, and the Swiss subsidiary of *Dornier* was about to embark on the design and development of the 'DO X' flying boat, a twelve-engine giant larger even than the famous *Boeing Clippers* of Pan-American, to meet the requirement for a patrol seaplane capable of landing and refuelling at sea. Only an unacceptably low service ceiling made it necessary to abandon this design.

The training of airmen was at the same time not overlooked. Battle-experienced pilots of the Lohmann-financed *Severa* flying service based at Noordnay and Holtenau conducted tactical exercises with the fleet and trained a dozen young naval officers each year in the art of flying.

Extravagances

As Lohmann's list of projects grew – including also such things as the secret construction of motor torpedo boats and subsidies to various small-boat shipyards and yachtsmen's associations – his ambition increased proportionately. By about 1926, he seems to have become convinced that he could perfect a massive structure of clandestine projects financed by profitable commercial ventures bolstering the rapidly dwindling 'black' funds. He then stepped into another world, the world of commerce and business, where his successes were lamentably few. He had become the victim of *Maßlosigkeit, '* gross intemperance'.

Two projects which attempted to combine money-making with what might today be termed 'defence-related research' bordered on the fantastic. One company was founded to exploit an experimental method of raising sunken ships by surrounding them with ice, and another sought to extract motor fuel from potatoes. These accomplished nothing, and both aroused much public ridicule when they were later exposed. Another device, a coal-pulverizing machine, came to grief in the course of experiments and the Lohmann-financed company which sponsored it went bankrupt.

But it was the *Berliner Bacon Company* which came to be described by German Socialists as the most odiferous of Lohmann's schemes. This project was initiated primarily as a money-maker in the spring of 1926. Lohmann proposed to wrest from the Danes the lucrative British bacon market by offering a German product cured by a new process especially for the Englishman's palate. He had incidentally in mind that the fast refrigerator ships he hoped to acquire for the bacon trade would be useful in wartime as troop transports.

His ambitions, however, exceeded his ability to analyse the British market potential, and by mid-1927 his company was bankrupt.

Lohmann's downfall stemmed from his relations with the *Phoebus Film Company*, in 1927 the third largest producer of motion pictures in Germany. Beginning in 1924, Lohmann granted subsidies to this firm on condition that it produce films of a 'national' character designed to stimulate the 'fatherland consciousness' of the German people. He also hoped to use its overseas offices to establish an intelligence network in former enemy countries where Germany was not allowed a naval attaché.

The captain probably had personal reasons for supporting *Phoebus* as well. Prior to his association with the company, he had become a close personal friend of one of the directors, and afterward a member of a hunting club organized by him. Through this man Lohmann secured for his friend Frau Ektimov a position with Phoebus at a salary of 1,000 marks a month, enough to enable her to support her aged mother and young son in comfort. Frau Ektimov, employed for 'representation', did no work, and she had apartments in a house purchased by Lohmann. Lohmann's personal relations with her are nevertheless officially said to have been above reproach, motivated solely by a desire to help her; and *honi soit qui mal y pense*. He also seems not to have appropriated any of the 'black' funds for his own use.

Between 1924 and 1927, Lohmann provided *Phoebus*, a company capitalized at approximately $1,000,000, with a total of over $2,500,000. He informed his superiors of only one of five separate grants, a government-guaranteed loan from the *Girocentral Bank* in Berlin in March 1926. In order to obtain their signatures on this guarantee, Lohmann resorted to a stratagem, informing them that the *Lignose Company*, a producer of raw film, had also guaranteed the loan and that in the event of default it would stand the loss instead of the government. He neglected to add that he had in effect bribed one of Lignose's officials with a $2,500 'negotiating fee', and that he had given this man a written assurance that *Lignose* would not have to pay. In the early half of 1927, he arranged two more government-guaranteed loans which he kept secret from his superiors by affixing his own signature in the name of the Reich.

Despite this massive aid, *Phoebus* continued to lose money. In 1927, it was in such serious financial difficulties that it failed to convene its regular annual stockholders' meeting or issue a financial report. By August, disaster was impending for both Lohmann and *Phoebus*. The company was falling behind in payments on its loans, and penalties were mounting rapidly. None of Lohmann's various money-making projects had paid off, and the 'black' funds were near exhaustion.

Exposure

Kurt Wenkel, one of the financial writers of the *Berliner Tageblatt*, a liberal daily of high quality, had been following the declining fortunes of the German film industry with close attention. He was well aware of the financial condition of *Phoebus*, and by mid-July had begun to suspect that *Phoebus* enjoyed official support. At about this time, he became acquainted with a former director of the company, Isenburg, who had resigned in disgust in 1926 and knew of Lohmann's dealings with *Phoebus*, of the several government-guaranteed loans, and of Lohmann's relations with Frau Ektimov. Evidently, for reasons of spite, he told all this to Wenkel, who took care to check the story independently and then in articles on 8 and 9 August created a sensation by exposing the shameful scandal.

Wenkel, however, was apparently not aware of Lohmann's real clandestine mission. For him, the *Phoebus* relationship constituted an attempt by the Navy to strengthen right-wing elements in Germany. His articles briefly mentioned some of Lohmann's other activities, including subsidies to a boatbuilding yard, but only as attempts to help industries that had some war potential. One of his disclosures, however, had it been pursued, could have exposed most of Lohmann's work, his connections with the *Berliner Bankverein*.

Lohmann had bought a controlling interest in the *Bankverein* in March 1925 in order to use it as a covert financing agency for his projects. But the private bankers who remained shareholders were greatly displeased at the depreciation of its stock caused by failures such as that of the *Berliner Bacon Company*, and their discontent made them serious security risks. If any of them emulated the vindictive Isenburg and talked to the press, there was grave danger that the Lohmann affair might become not only a scandal but a revelation of serious German violations of the Versailles Treaty.

Antidotes

The German Cabinet and Chancellor Wilhelm Marx were therefore anxious to smooth the affair over as rapidly as possible. Lohmann was suspended from office, an official Cabinet inquiry was begun, and a retired official of the Prussian State judiciary, was placed in charge of Lohmann's office for the purposes of investigation and audit. Publicity was curtailed and Wenkel silenced by pressure on the *Berliner Tageblatt*. Two radical journals continued to carry articles through late August, September, and October, but neither had good enough contacts in navy or industrial circles to make further damaging disclosures. Chancellor Marx consulted directly with various important party leaders to insure silence in political quarters.

In November, the Cabinet began a series of meetings on the affair. As prophylactic action against future extravagant indiscretions by one individual or one component of the government, it decided to establish a 'Supervisory Commission for the Secret Tasks of the Armed Forces' composed of the heads of the Army and Navy, the Reich Finance Minister, and the President of the General Accounting Office, *Rechnungshof*, to supervise and approve all clandestine projects of the services. Within the Navy a special 'B' budget for funds diverted from publicly budgeted items was placed in the charge of a regular budget officer who had no authority to initiate or control projects. Although illegal operations were ultimately on a considerably larger scale than during the Lohmann era, rising from $1,700,000 in 1928 to $5,250,000 in 1933, there was no further abuse of the powers conferred by secrecy.

Lohmann, much in disfavour, was nevertheless punished only by forced retirement on a reduced pension. There seem to have been two reasons for this clemency: first, that extensive investigations showed he had not appropriated official funds for himself; and second, that an elaborate court-martial would have brought on the very thing the government wanted most to avoid, publicity which might disclose violations of the Versailles Treaty. Lohmann was a broken man, however, and he died only three years later of a heart attack. His widow had so little money that she was unable to pay the necessary inheritance taxes. Of Frau Ektimov's fate there is no word.

Before the Reichstag and the world public the Cabinet was able to obscure the fact that violations of the Versailles Treaty had occurred. The matter had to be brought to the Reichstag for approval of a special appropriation to pay off the government-guaranteed loans to *Phoebus*; but the Cabinet announced in advance the resignation of both Defence Minister Gessler and Navy commander Zenker, who, as Lohmann's superiors, had to accept responsibility for the scandal. In the Reichstag discussions, the question of why Lohmann had engaged in such unusual activities was never fairly asked. Violation of the Treaty was charged only once, by the young and fanatical Communist deputy Ernst Schneller, who declared correctly that Lohmann had been involved in submarine production in Spain. He ruined the effectiveness of an otherwise good case, however, by continuing with wild allegations that Germany's former enemies were assisting her in this work preparatory to a combined capitalist assault on that bastion of socialism, the USSR. This was such hackneyed tripe that the responsible German press did not bother to print his charges. The French news agency Havas carried them, but only in routine fashion and without comment.

Abroad, the fact that Lohmann's work violated the Versailles Treaty was completely missed by the press. Furthermore, the reports of the American

Embassy in Berlin were brief and incurious regarding Lohmann's motives. British and French diplomatic reporting is not available, but an examination of the German Foreign Office records fails to disclose even a memorandum of conversation on the subject between these embassies and the Wilhelmstrasse. The conclusion seems inescapable that either the vaunted British and French intelligence services were caught napping, or, as seems more likely, the policy-makers in Paris and London chose to ignore the affair. To them, the apparent collapse of the German Navy's efforts to circumvent the Treaty was perhaps a matter for quiet amusement rather than for alarm or indignation.

ENDNOTES

1   www.cia.gov/library/center-for-the-study-of-intelligence/kent-csi/vol4no2/html/ v04i2a08p_0001.htm.
2   The following materials were used in the preparation of this article: captured documents of the German naval staff, in custody of the Division of Naval History, US Navy; the record of proceedings of the German Cabinet and documents of the German Foreign Ministry, in custody of the US Department of State at the National Archives; records of the Berlin Embassy of the Department of State, now available to the public at the National Archives; documents of the German Reichstag and the files of several German newspapers, including *Berliner Tageblatt,* available at the Library of Congress. In addition, the writer has consulted the published memoirs of former German Defence Minister Otto Gessler, *Reichswehrpolitik in der Weimarer Zeit* (Stuttgart, 1958).

Bibliography

Abel, Theodore, *Why Hitler Came into Power* (1938, reprint Harvard University Press, 1966)

Adler, Selig, 'The War-Guilt Question and American Disillusionment, 1918–1928', *The Journal of Modern History*, Vol. 23, No. 1, 1951, pp. 1–28

Afflerbach, Holger, Falkenhayn: Politisches Denken Und Handeln Im Kaiserreich, Beitrage Zur Militargeschichte (Oldenbourg Wissensch, 1994)

Albertini, Luigi, trans. Masset, Isabella *The Origins of the War of 1914* (1952; Enigma Books, New York 2005), 3 Vols.

Anglesey, The Marquis of, *A History of the British Cavalry 1816–1919*: Vol. 8: *The Western Front, 1915–1918, Epilogue, 1919–1939* (Leo Cooper, London 1997)

Arnold-Forster, W, *The Blockade 1914–1919, Before the Armistice – and After* (Oxford Pamphlets on World Affairs, No 17, Clarendon Press 1939)

Ascherson, Neal, *The King Incorporated, Leopold II in the Age of Trusts* (Allen & Unwin, London 1963)

Aspinall-Oglander, Cecil, *Roger Keyes, Being the Biography of Admiral of the Fleet Lord Keyes of Zeebrugge and Dover* (Hogarth Press, London 1951)

Asprey, Robert B, *The German High Command at War, Hindenburg and Ludendorff and the First World War* (William Morrow, New York 1991)

Bacon, Admiral Sir Reginald H
   The Dover Patrol, 1915–1917, Vols. 1&2 (Hutchinson, London 1919)
   The Concise Story of the Dover Patrol (Hutchinson, London 1932)

Baecken, Charles, *L'Historique du 5th Régiment de Lanciers* (Maréchal de Logis)

Baker, Nicholson, *Human Smoke, The Beginnings of World War Two, The End of Civilisation* (Pocket Books, London 2009)

Bane, Suda Lorena, and Lutz, Ralph Haswell, *The Blockade of Germany After the Armistice, 1918–1919; Selected Documents of the Supreme Economic Council, Superior Blockade Council, American Relief Administration, and Other Wartime Organizations* (Stanford University Press, 1942; Howard Fertig, New York 1972)

Banks, Arthur, *A Military Atlas of the First World War* (Leo Cooper, Barnsley 1997)

Barnett, L Margaret, *British Food Policy During The First World War* (Allen & Unwin, Winchester, Mass., 1985)

Barrett, Michael B, *Operation Albion, The German Conquest of the Baltic Islands* (Indiana University Press, 2009)

Bauer, Hermann, *Als Führer der U-Boote im Weltkriege* (Koehler & Amelang, Leipzig 1941)

Beesley, Patrick, *Room 40: British Naval Intelligence 1914–1918* (Hamish Hamilton, London 1992)

Becker, Annette, *Oubliés de la Grande Guerre, Humanitaire et culture de guerre 1914–1918, Populations occupées, déportés civils, prisonniers de guerre* (Pluriel 2012)

Bell, A C, *A History of the Blockade of Germany and of the countries associated with her in the Great War: Austria-Hungary, Bulgaria, and Turkey 1914–1918* (HMSO, London 1937)

Bell, Christopher M
 'Sir John Fisher's Naval Revolution Reconsidered: Winston Churchill at the Admiralty, 1911–1914', *War in History*, 18(3), 2011, pp. 333–56
 'On Standards and Scholarship: A Response to Nicholas Lambert', *War in History*, 20(3), 2013, pp. 381–409
 Churchill and Sea Power (Oxford University Press, 2013)

Bendert, Harald
 Die UB-Boote der Kaiserlichen Marine 1914–1918. Einsätze, Erfolge, Schicksale (E S Mittler, Hamburg 2000)
 Die UC-Boote der Kaiserlichen Marine 1914–1918, Minenkreig mit U-Booten (E S Mittler, Hamburg 2001)

Birnbaum, Karl E, *Peace Moves and U-Boat Warfare: A Study of Imperial Germany's Policy towards the United States April 18, 1916 – January 9, 1917* (Almqvist & Wiksell, Stockholm 1958)

Bittner, Lieutenant Colonel D F, *Royal Marines Spies of World War One Era*, Part One, 'Captain B F Trench, RMLI' (Royal Marines Historical Society, No. 15, Portsmouth 1993)

Blahut, Fred, 'The Allied Attempt to Starve Germany in 1919', *The Barnes Review*, April 1996, pp. 11–14

Blanton, Smiley, *Mental and Nervous Changes in the Children of the Volksschulen of Trier, Germany, Caused by Malnutrition* (The National Committee for Mental Hygiene, New York 1919); reprint from *Mental Hygiene*, July 1919, No. 3, pp. 343–386

Blet, Pierre, trans. Johnson, Lawrence J, *Pius XII and the Second World War according to the Archives of the Vatican* (Gracewing, Herefordshire 1999)

Bloch, Ivan Stanislavovich, *Is War Now Impossible?: Being an Abridgment of 'The War of the Future in Its Technical, Economic & Political Relations'* (Grant Richards, London 1899; eprint War College Series 2017)

Blond, Georges, *The Marne, The Battle that Saved Paris and Changed the Course of the First World War* (Prion, London 2002)

Blücher, von Wahlstatt, Evelyn M, *An English Wife in Berlin: A Private Memoir of Events, Politics and Daily Life in Germany Throughout the War and the Social Revolution of 1918* (Constable, London 1920)

Blum, Matthias, 'Government Decisions Before and During the First World War and the Living Standards in Germany During a Drastic Natural Experiment', *Explorations in Economic History*, Vol. 48, Issue 4, Dec 2011

Boemeke, Manfred F; Feldman, Gerald D; and Glaser, Elisabeth, eds., *The Treaty of Versailles, A Reassessment after 75 Years* (The German Historical Institute, Washington, DC; Cambridge University Press 1998)

Bondevik, Lovholt, Harbitz, Stormo and Skerjal, 'The Storegga Slide Tsunami – Deposits, Run-up Heights and Radiocarbon Dating of the 8000-Year-Old Tsunami in the North Atlantic', *American Geophysical Union*, Fall Meeting 2006, No. OS34C-01

Bouton, S Miles, *And The Kaiser Abdicates, The German Revolution November 1918– August 1919* (Yale University Press 1920; reprint Wildside Press 2016)

Bowles, Thomas Gibson, *The Declaration of Paris of 1856: being an account of the maritime rights of Great Britain; a consideration of their importance; a history of their surrender by the signature of the Declaration of Paris; and an argument for their resumption by the denunciation and repudiation of that declaration* (Low, Marston, London 1900; Relnk Books, Delhi, India 2017)

Bown, Stephen R, *A Most Damnable Invention, Dynamite, Nitrates, and the Making of the Modern World* (Thomas Dunne, New York 2005)

Boyd, Julia, *Travellers in the Third Reich, The Rise of Fascism through the Eyes of Everyday People* (Elliott and Thompson, London 2017)

Boyle, David, *Before Enigma, The Room 40 codebreakers of the First World War* (Real Press, 2016)

Bradbury, Ray, *The Sound of Thunder & Other Stories* (1990; Harper Perennial, New York 2005)

Brandt, Karl, *Management of Agriculture and Food in the German-Occupied and Other Areas of Fortress Europe, A Study in Military Government*; Germany's Agricultural and Food Policies in World War II, Vol. 2 (Stanford University Press, Bridgland, Tony, *Outrage at Sea, Naval Atrocities in the First World War* (Leo Cooper, Barnsley 2002)

Bridgman, Jon M, *The Revolt of the Hereros, Perspectives on Southern Africa* (California University Press, 1992)

Bruntz, George G, *Allied Propaganda and the Collapse of the German Empire in 1918* (Stanford University Press 1938; SN Books reprint, India 2017)

Buchan, John, *The Complete Richard Hannay Stories* (Wordsworth Classics, Ware 2010)

Bunson, Matthew, 'German Catholics under the Iron Fist: Bismarck and the Kulturkampf', *This Rock*, December 2008, pp. 22–27

Canini, Gerard, 'L'utilisation des prisonniers de guerre comme main-d'oeuvre 1914–1916', Les Fronts invisible, nourrier, fournir, soigner (Pressue universitaire de Nancy, 1984), pp. 247–262

Carter, Geoffrey, *The Royal Navy at Portland Since 1845* (Maritime Books, Liskeard 1987)

Carpenter, Captain Alfred F B, *The Blocking of Zeebrugge* (Herbert Jenkins, London 1922)

Chambers, Frank P, *The War Behind The War 1914–1918, A History of the Political and Civilian Fronts* (Faber and Faber, London 1939)

Chatelle, A, and Le Bon, E, *Boulogne et sa marine pendant la guerre 1914–1918* (Imprimeries réunies, Boulogne-sur-Mer 1921)

Chatelle, Albert, and Tison, G, *Calais Pendant La Guerre 1914–1918* (Librairie Aristide Quillet, Paris 1927)

Chatelle, Albert, *La Base Navale du Havre et La Guerre Sous-Marine Secrète en Manche 1914–1918* (Les Éditions Médicis, Paris 1949)

Chatterton, E Keble
  Q-ships and their story (Sidgwick and Jackson, London 1922; facsimile reprint 2016)
  The Big Blockade (Hurst & Blackett, London 1932)

Chickering, Roger
  We Men Who Feel Most German, A Cultural Study of the Pan-German League, 1886–1914 (George Allen & Unwin, Boston, USA 1984)
  The Great War and Urban Life in Germany, Freiburg, 1914–1918 (Cambridge University Press, 2007)

Churchill, Winston S, *The World Crisis 1911–1918* (1930, reprint Four Square, London 1964); The World Crisis 1915 (Thornton Butterworth, London 1923)

Clark, Christopher
  Iron Kingdom (Penguin, London 2006)
  Kaiser Wilhelm II (Penguin, London 2009)
  The Sleepwalkers, How Europe went to War in 1914 (Penguin, London 2013)

Clausewitz, von Carl, trans. Graham, J J, *On War* (Wordsworth Classics, Ware 1997)

Cobb, Stephen, *Preparing for Blockade 1885–1914, Naval Contingency for Economic Warfare* (Ashgate, Farnham 2013)

Coles, Alan, *Slaughter at Sea, The Truth Behind a Naval War Crime* (Robert Hale, London 1986)

Collingham, Lizzie, *The Taste of War, World War Two and the Battle for Food* (Allen Lane, London 2011)

Compton-Hall, Richard, *Submarines at War 1914–1918* (1991, reprint Periscope Publishing, Penzance 2004)

Connolly, James B, & Schenk, Karl von, *U-Boat War 1914–1918: Two Contrasting Accounts from Both Sides of the Conflict at Sea During the Great War: The U-Boat Hunters; The Diary of a U-Boat Commander* (Leonaur, 2008)

Consett, Rear Admiral M W W P, *The Triumph of Unarmed Forces (1914–1918): An account of the transactions by which Germany during the Great War was able to obtain supplies prior to her collapse under the pressure of economic forces* (Williams and Norgate, London 1923; electronic reprint 2016)

Coogan, John W, *The End of Neutrality, The United States, Britain, and Maritime Rights 1899–1915* (Cornell University Press, 1981)

Cooper, Caroline Ethel (the Letters of), *Behind the Lines, One Woman's War 1914–18*, ed. Denholm, Decie (Norman & Hobhouse, London 1982)

Corbett, Sir Julian, *Some Principles of Maritime Strategy* (1911; Conway, London 1972)

Corbett, Sir Julian S, and Newbolt, Henry, *History of the Great War, Naval Operations*, (Longmans Green, London 1920–31), 5 Vols.

Cornwell, John, *Hitler's Pope, The Secret History of Pius XII* (Penguin, London 2000)

Coppa, Frank J, *The Life & Pontificate of Pope Pius XII, Between History and Controversy* (Catholic University of America, Washington DC 2013)

Cox, Frederick J, 'The French Peace Plans, 1918–1919: The Germ of the Conflict Between Ferdinand Foch and Georges Clemenceau' in Cox et al, eds., *Studies in Modern European History in Honor of Franklin Charles Palm* (Bookman, New York, USA, 1956), pp. 81–104

Cravioto, Joaquin, 'Application of New Knowledge of Nutrition on Physical and Mental Growth and Development', *American Journal of Public Health*, No. 53, 1963, pp. 1803–9

Cron, Hermann, trans. Colton, C F, *Imperial German Army 1914–18: Organisation, Structure, Orders of Battle* (*Geschichte des Deutschen Heeres im Weltkrieg 1914–1918*, Berlin 1937; reprint Helion, Solihull 2002)

Cruttwell, C R M F, *A History of the Great War 1914–1918* (Granada, St Albans 1936)

Dalin, David D, Rabbi, *The Myth of Hitler's Pope, How Pope Pius XII Rescued Jews from the Nazis* (Regnery Publishing, Washington DC 2005)

David, Patrick and Serge, *14–18 La Guerre Maritime en Manche et en mer du Nord* (Du Bout du Monde)

Davis, Belinda J, *Food Politics, and Everyday Life in World War I Berlin: Home Fires Burning* (University of North Carolina Press, 2000)

de Chair, Admiral Sir Dudley, *The Sea is Strong* (Harrap, London 1961)

Degrelle, Leon, *Hitler: Born at Versailles*, Vol. 1, *The Hitler Century* (Institute for Historical Review, Costa Mesa, California 1987)

Delanoy, Gilbert, *Guerre 1914–18, Citations à L'Ordre de L'Armée des Formations and des Bâtiments de la Marine Française*

Delpal, Bernard, 'Prisonniers de guerre en France, 1914–1920', pp. 145–159, in Gueslin, André; Kalifa, Dominique; *Les Exclus en Europe, 1830–1930* (Ouvrières, L'Atelier, Paris 1999)

Devlin, Patrick, *Too Proud to Fight, Woodrow Wilson's neutrality* (Oxford University Press, 1971)

Ditte, Général, *Calais (1914–1918)* (Militaire Universelle, Fournier, Paris)

Docherty, Gerry, and Macgregor, Jim, *Hidden History: The Secret Origins of the First World War* (Mainstream Publishing, Edinburgh 2013)

Doenitz, Grand Admiral Karl, *Memoirs: Ten Years and Twenty Days* (1958; Frontline Books, Barnsley 2015)

Dorling, Taprell (Taffrail), *Swept Channels being an Account of the Work of the Minesweepers in the Great War* (Hodder and Stoughton, London 1935)

Dorpalen, Andreas, *Heinrich von Treitschke* (Kennikat, New York 1973)

Doty, Madelaine Zabriskie, *Short Rations: An American Woman in Germany 1915–1916* (Century, New York 1917)

Doyle, Arthur Conan, 'Danger! Being the Log of Captain John Sirius', pp. 7–31, also 'Preface', pp. 5–6, in *Danger! and Other Stories* (1912; Serenity, Rockville, Maryland 2011)

Dufeil, Yves, *Kaiserliche Marine U-Boote 1914–1918, Dictionnaire Biographique des Commandants de la Marine Imperiale Allemande* (Histomar, 2016)

Dufossé, Franck

    Histoire de Wissant, des origines aux années 1930 (Éditions AMA, Paris 2002)

    Wissant 1914-1918 (Art et Histoire de Wissant, Mairie de Wissant 2014)

Dufour, Pierre, 'Les prisonniers du guerre allemands', *14-18: Le magazine de la Grande Guerre*, August/September/October 2016, pp. 8-23

Edmonds, James E, *Military operations: France and Belgium, 1914*, Vol. 1: 'Mons, the Retreat to the Seine, the Marne and the Aisne, August–October 1914' (Official History: Imperial War Museum, London 1992)

Eichengreen, Barry, *Golden Fetters: The Gold Standard and the Great Depression 1919-1939: Gold Standard and the Great Depression, 1919-39* (Oxford University Press, 1992)

Ehrenreich, Erich, *The Nazi Ancestral Proof, Genealogy, Racial Science and the Final Solution* (Indiana University Press 2007)

Ehrenrangliste Der Deutschen Marine 1914-1918, CD (Deutsches Wehrkundearchiv, Helion)

Eley, Geoff, 'Reshaping the Right: Radical Nationalism and the German Navy League, 1898-1908', *The Historical Journal*, Vol. 21, No. 2, June 1978, pp. 327-354

Emmerson, Charles, 1913, *The World Before the Great War* (Vintage, London 2013)

Engelmann, Bernt, *Germany Without Jews* (Bantam, New York 1984)

Erbe, Günter, Das Vornehme Berlin, Fürstin Marie Radziwill und die grossen Damen der Gesellschaft 1871-1918 (Böhlau Verlag, Köln 2015)

Essen, Léon van der, *The Invasion & The War in Belgium from Liège to the Yser with a Sketch of the Diplomatic Negotiations Preceding the Conflict* (Fisher Unwin, London 1917)

Ewart, John S, *The Roots and Causes of the Wars (1914-1918)*, Vols. 1&2 (George Doran, New York 1925)

Farago, Ladislas, *The Game of the Foxes, British and German Intelligence operations and personalities which changed the course of the Second World War* (Pan, London 1974)

Fayle, C Ernest, *Official History of the Great War: Seaborne Trade*, Vol. 2, 'Submarine Campaign', Vol. 3, 'The Period of Unrestricted Submarine Warfare' (1920-4; Imperial War Museum, London 1997)

Feldman, Gerald D

    Army, Industry and Labor in Germany 1914-1918 (Berg, Providence, Rhode Island 1966)

    The Great Disorder: Politics, Economics, and Society in the German Inflation, 1914-1924 (Oxford University Press, 1997)

    Die Deutsche Inflation / The German Inflation Reconsidered: Eine Zwischenbilanz / A Preliminary Balance (Gruyter online, 2011)

Ferdinand, HRH Princess Ludwig, of Bavaria, Infanta of Spain, *Through Four Revolutions 1862-1933 set forth from her diaries and correspondence by her son HRH Prince Adalbert of Bavaria* (John Murray, London 1933)

Ferguson, Niall

    The Pity of War (Penguin, London 1999)

The House of Rothschild, The World's Banker 1849–1999 (Penguin, New York 2000)

Fischer, Fritz, *Germany's Aims in the First World War* (Chatto & Windus, London 1977)

Flemming, Jens, *Landwirtschaftliche Interessen und Demokratie, Ländliche Gesellschaft, Agrarverbände und Staat 1890–1925* (Verlag Neue Gesellschaft, Bonn 1978)

Fletcher, R A, *In the Days of the Tall Ships* (Brentano's, London 1928)

Forstnerr, Georg-Gunther von, König, Paul, Peckelsheim, Baron Spiegel von Und Zu, *U-Boat War 1914–1918:* Vol. 2 – *Three accounts of German submarines during the Great War: The Journal of Submarine Commander von Forstnerr, The Voyage of the 'Deutschland' & The Adventures of the U-202* (Leonaur, 2010)

Forstner, Georg-Gunther von, *The Journal of Submarine Commander von Forstner (1916, abridged; USA 2016)*

Frey, Marc, 'Bullying the Neutrals, The case of the Netherlands', in Chickering, Roger, Förster, Stig, eds., *Great War, Total War: Combat and Mobilization of the Western Front, 1914–1918* (German Historical Institute and Cambridge University Press, 2000), pp. 227–244

Friedman, Norman, introduction, *German Warships of World War I: The Royal Navy's Official Guide to the Capital Ships, Cruisers, Destroyers, Submarines and Small Craft, 1914–1918* (1918, reprint Greenhill Books, London, 1992)

Friedrich, Otto

    Blood and Iron, From Bismarck to Hitler the von Moltke's Family's Impact on German History (Harper Collins, New York 1995)

    Before the Deluge: A Portrait of Berlin in the 1920s (Harper, New York 1996)

Fritzsche, Peter, *Germans into Nazis* (Harvard University Press, 1998)

Fuehr, Alexander, *The Neutrality of Belgium* (Funk and Wagnall, London 1915)

Fürbringer, Werner, *FIPS: Legendary U-boat Commander 1915–1918*, trans. & ed., Brooks, Geoffrey (1933; Leo Cooper, Barnsley 1999)

Gayer, Captain Albert, *General Survey of the History of the Submarine Warfare in all Theatres of War, 1914–18* (Stencilled and printed, Naval War College, Newport RI, 1930)

Gedye, George Eric Rowe

    The Revolver Republic: France's Bid for the Rhine (Arrowsmith, London 1930)

    Fallen Bastions, The Central European Tragedy (Gollancz, London 1939)

Gerwarth, Peter, *The Vanquished: Why the First World War Failed to End, 1917–1923 (Allen Lane, UK 2016)*

Geyer, Michael, 'Insurrectionary Warfare: The German Debate about Levée en Masse in October 1918', *Journal of Modern History*, Vol. 73, No. 3, 2001, pp. 459–527

Gibbons, Don C, 'Say, Whatever Became of Maurice Parmelee, Anyway?', *The Sociological Quarterly*, Vol. 15, No. 3 (Summer, 1974), pp. 405–416

Gibson, Hugh, *A Journal from Our Legation in Belgium* (Doubleday, Page, New York 1918)

Gibson, R H, and Prendergast, Maurice, *The German Submarine War 1914–1918* (John Constable, London 1931; reprint Periscope Publishing, Penzance 2002)

Glaeser, Ernst, *Class 1902* (1928; University of South Carolina, 2008)

Gleick, James, *Chaos, Making A New Science* (Vintage, London 1988)

Goffic, Charles le, trans. Simmonds, Florence, *Dixmude: The Epic of the French Marines (October 7–November 10 1914)* (1916; CreateSpace, USA 2014)

Gollomb, Joseph, *Army of Spies* (Macmillan, New York 1939)

Goss, Michael B, *The War Against Catholicism: Liberation and the Anti-Catholic Imagination in Nineteenth-Century Germany* (University of Michigan Press, 2004)

Grainger, John D, ed., *The Maritime Blockade of Germany in the Great War: The Northern Patrol, 1914–1918* (Ashgate, Navy Records Society 2003)

Graham, G G, 'Growth during Recovery from Infantile Malnutrition', *Journal of the American Medical Women's Association*, No. 21, 1966, pp. 740 onwards

Grahame, Kenneth, *The Golden Age* (1895; CreateSpace Independent Publishing Platform, (2017)

Grant, Robert M
   U-Boats Destroyed: The Effect of Anti-Submarine Warfare 1914–18 (1964, Periscope Publishing, Penzance 2002)
   U-Boat Intelligence, Admiralty Intelligence Division and the Defeat of the U-boats 1914–1918 (1969, Periscope Publishing, Penzance 2002)
   U-Boat Hunters: Code Breakers, Divers and the Defeat of the U-Boats, 1914–1918 (Written unpublished 1971; Periscope Publishing, Penzance 2003)

Gray, Edwyn A
   The Killing Time: The German U-boats 1914–18 (Seeley, Service 1972)
   British Submarines at War 1914–1918 (reprint Pen & Sword Maritime, Barnsley 2016), first published as *A Damned Un-English Weapon* (Charles Scribner's Sons, 1973)

Grebler, Leo, Winkler, Wilhelm, *The Cost of the World War to Germany and to Austria Hungary* (Yale University Press, New Haven 1940)

Grelling, Richard ('A German'), translated Gray, Alexander, *J'Accuse* (Hodder and Stoughton, London 1915)

Greenhill, Basil
   The Mariner's Mirror, 'The Rise and Fall of the British Coastal Steamer', Vol. 27, Issue 3, 1941, pp. 243–259
   The Merchant Schooners, Vol. II (David & Charles, Newton Abbot 1968)

Grimes, Shawn T, *Strategy and War Planning in the British Navy, 1887–1918* (Boydell Press, Woodbridge 2012)

Gröner, Erich, *German Warships 1815–1945*
   Vol. 1: Major Surface Vessels (1983; Conway, London 1990)
   Vol. 2: U-Boats and Mine Warfare Vessels (1968; revised and expanded by Jung, Dieter, and Maass, Martin, 1983; translated by Thomas, Keith, and Magowan, Rachel, Conway Maritime Press, London 1991)

Guichard, Louis
   Au Large (1914–1918) (La Renaissance du Livre, Paris 1919)
   Bleu Marine (Société d'éditions géographiques, maritimes et coloniales, 1927)
   Les Guerres des Enseignes (La Renaissance du Livre, Paris 1929)
   The Naval Blockade 1914–1918, trans. & ed. Turner, Christopher R, (Phillip Allen, London 1930)

Fouqueray, Charles, *La Guerre Navale Racontée par Nos Amiraux* (Librairie Schwarz, Paris 1920)

Hadley, Michael L, *Count Not the Dead, The Popular Image of the German Submarine* (Mc-Gill-Queen's University Press, Montreal 1995)

Hankey, Lord, *The Supreme Command 1914–1918*, Vols. 1&2 (George Allen & Unwin, London 1961)

Harmer, Harry, *Rosa Luxemburg* (Haus, London 2008)

Hashagen, Ernst, *The Log of a U-boat Commander or U-boats Westward – 1914–1918* (Unwin, London 1931)

Hampshire, A Cecil, *The Blockaders* (William Kimber, London 1980)

Hastings, Derek, *Catholicism and the Roots of Nazism: Religious Identity and National Socialism* (Oxford University Press, 2011)

Hastings, Max, *Bomber Command* (1979; Pan Books, London 2010)

Haws, Duncan, *Merchant Fleets – Britain's Railway Steamers – Eastern and North-Western Companies + Zeeland and Stena* (TCL Publications, Hereford 1993)

Heimburg, Heino von, *U-Boot gegen U-Boot* (Scherl, Berlin 1917)

Heineman, John L, *Hitler's First Foreign Minister, Constantin Freiherr von Neurath* (University of California Press, 1979)

Henderson, John, *A Life of Ernest Starling* (Oxford University Press, New York 2005)

Henig, Ruth, *Versailles and After 1919–1933* (Methuen, London 1984)

Herber, Charles J, 'Eugenio Pacelli's Mission to Germany and the Papal Peace Proposals of 1917', *The Catholic Historical Review*, Vol. 65, No. 1, January 1979, pp. 20–48

Herwig, Holger H

    'Admirals versus Generals: The War Aims of the Imperial German Navy, 1914–1918', *Central European History*, Vol. 5, No. 3 (September 1972), pp. 208–233

    The German Naval Officer Corps, A Social and Political History, 1890–1918 (Clarendon Press, Oxford 1973)

    The First World War: Germany and Austria-Hungary 1914–1918 (Arnold, London 1997)

    'The Dynamics of Uncertainty: German Military Policy during The First World War' in Millett, Allan R, and Murray, Williamson, eds., *Military Effectiveness*, Vol. 1, *The First World War* (Allen & Unwin, Winchester, Mass., USA 1988), pp. 80–115

    'Total Rhetoric, Limited War: Germany's U-Boat Campaign 1917–1918', *Journal of Military and Strategic Studies*, Vol. 1, issue 1, May 1998, and in Chickering, Roger, Förster, Stig, eds., *Great War, Total War: Combat and Mobilization of the Western Front, 1914–1918* (German Historical Institute and Cambridge University Press, 2000), pp. 169–188

    The Marne, 1914, The Opening of World War 1 and the Battle That Changed the World (Random House, New York, 2011)

    'Luxury' Fleet: The Imperial German Navy 1888–1918 (George Allen & Unwin, London 1980; reprint Routledge, Abingdon 2014)

Herzog, Bodo, *Deutsche U-Boote 1906–1966* (Pawlak, Koblenz 1990)

Herzman, Lewis, 'The Founding of the German National People's Party (DNVP),

November 1918–January 1919', *The Journal of Modern History*, Vol. 30, No. 1, March 1958, pp. 24–36

Hezlet, Vice Admiral Sir Arthur

The Submarine and Sea Power (Peter Davis, London 1967)

Electronics and Sea Power (Stein and Day, New York 1975)

Hinchcliffe, John & Vicki, *Dive Dorset: A Diver Guide* (Underwater World Publications, Teddington 1999)

Hintz, Alfred, 'Salomon Marx (1866–1936) – Industrieller, Bankier und Politiker', *Berlin in Geschichte und Gegenwart,* Jahrbuch des Landesarchivs Berlin, 2011, pp. 101–130

Hitler, Adolph, *Mein Kampf* (1924; Jaico, Mumbai 1988)

Hobhouse, Emily

'Report to the Committee of the Distress Fund for South African Women and Children of a Visit to the Camps of Women and Children in the Cape and Orange River Colonies' (Friars, London 1901)

The Brunt Of The War And Where It Fell (1902; reprint Read Books, 2013)

Hobson, John Atkinson

Capitalism and Imperialism in South Africa (Tucker, New York 1900)

The Psychology of Jingoism (Grant Richards, London 1901)

Hobson, Rolf, *Imperialism at Sea, Naval Strategic Thought, the Ideology of Sea Power and the Tirpitz Plan, 1875–1914* (Brill, Boston 2002)

Hochschild, Adam, *King Leopold's Ghost, A Story of Greed, Terror and Heroism in Colonial Africa* (Pan, London 2006)

Holloway, S M, *From Trench to Turret, Royal Marines Letters and Diaries 1914–1918* (Royal Marines Museum, Portsmouth, 1987)

Hollweg, Konteradmiral Karl, *Unser Recht Auf Den U-Bootskrieg* (1917; Nabu reprint, USA 2016)

Hollweg, Theobald von Bethmann, trans. Young, George, *Reflections on the World War,* Vol. 1 (Butterworth, London 1920; digital reprint Forgotten Books, 2015)

Horn, Daniel, *Mutiny on the High Seas, The Imperial German Naval Mutinies of World War One* (Leslie Freewin, London 1973)

Horne, John and Kramer, Alan, 'War Between Soldiers and Enemy Civilians, 1914–1915', in Chickering, Roger, Förster, Stig, eds., *Great War, Total War: Combat and Mobilization of the Western Front, 1914–1918* (German Historical Institute and Cambridge University Press, 2000), pp. 153–168

Howard, Keble (Bell, J Keble), *The Zeebrugge Affair* (George H Doran, New York, 1918)

Howard, N P

'Men against Fire: Expectations of War in 1914', *International Security*, Vol. 9, No. 1 (Summer, 1984), pp. 41–57

'The Social and Political Consequences of the Allied Food Blockade of Germany, 1918–19', *German History*, Vol. 11, No. 2 (June 1993), pp. 161–188

Hoyt, Edwin P

The Germans Who Never Lost (Sphere, London 1970)

Guerrilla, Colonel von Lettow-Vorbeck and Germany's East African Empire (Collier Macmillan, London 1981)

Hull, Isabel V

> *The Entourage of Kaiser Wilhelm II, 1988–1918* (Cambridge University Press 1982)
>
> *Absolute Destruction, Military Culture and the Practices of War in Imperial Germany* (Cornell University Press 2005)
>
> *A Scrap of Paper, Breaking and Making International Law during the Great War* (Cornell University Press 2014)

Humphreys, Roy, *The Dover Patrol 1914–18* (Sutton Publishing, Stroud 1988)

James, Admiral Sir William, *The Code Breakers of Room Forty* (St Martin's Press, New York 1956; reprint Literary Licensing, 2016)

Jamieson, Alan G, 'Martyr or Pirate? The Case of Captain Fryatt in the Great War', *The Mariner's Mirror,* Vol. 85, No. 2, 1999, pp. 196–202

Jane's Fighting Ships of World War I (1919; reprint Studio Editions, London 1990)

Janicki, D A, 'The British Blockade During World War 1: The Weapon of Deprivation', *Student Pulse,* 6(06), 2014

Jasper, Willi, trans. Spencer, Stewart, *Lusitania: The Cultural History of a Catastrophe* (Yale University Press 2016)

Jellicoe, Admiral of the Fleet, The Right Hon. The Earl, *The Submarine Peril: The Admiralty Policy in 1917* (Cassell, London 1934)

Johnson, Niall, and Müller, Jürgen, 'Updating the Accounts', *Bulletin of the History of Medicine,* 2002, pp. 105–15.

Joll, James, *1914: The Unspoken Assumptions* (Weidenfeld and Nicholson, London School of Economics and Political Science 1968)

Joll, James, and Martel, Gordon, *The Origins of the First World War* (Pearson, Harlow 2007)

Jones, Heather

> *Violence against Prisoners of War in the First World War: Britain, France and Germany, 1914–1920* (Cambridge University Press, 2011)
>
> 'The Enemy Disarmed: Prisoners of War and the Violence of Wartime: Britain, France and Germany 1914–1918', PhD dissertation (Trinity College, University of Dublin, December 2005)

Jones, Larry Eugene, 'The Greatest Stupidity of My Life: Alfred Hugenberg and the Formation of the Hitler Cabinet, January 1933', *Journal of Contemporary History,* Vol. 27, No. 1, January 1992, pp. 63–87

Jones, Nigel, *The Birth of the Nazis, How the Freikorps Blazed a Trail for Hitler* (Robinson, London 2004)

Jung, Hans, 'The New Berlin Horse Railway Company', *Traffic History Sheets,* Berlin, Issue 4, 1960, pp. 17–18

Kant, Immanuel

> *Foundations of the Metaphysics of Morals and What is Enlightenment?* (1785; Bobbs-Merrill, Indianapolis, USA 1959)
>
> *Kant's Critiques* (1787; Wilder, Radford, Va 2008)

Karau, Mark D, *The Naval Flank of the Western Front, The German MarineKorps*

Flandern 1914–1918 (Seaforth Publishing, Barnsley 2003)

Kessler, Count Harry

    Walther Rathenau, His Life and Work (Howe, London 1919)

    The Diaries of a Cosmopolitan 1918–1937 (Weidenfeld and Nicholson, London 1971)

Keyser, Carl de, and Reybrouck, David van, *The First World War, Unseen Glass Plate Photographs of the Western Front* (University of Chicago 2015)

Kelly, Patrick J, *Tirpitz and the Imperial German Navy* (Indiana University Press, 2011)

Kemp, Paul, *U-Boats Destroyed, German Submarine Losses in the World Wars* (Arms & Armour, London 1997)

Kennedy, Greg

    'Intelligence and the Blockade, 1914–1917: A Study in Administration, Friction and Command', *Intelligence and National Security*, No 5, October 2007

    'The North Atlantic Triangle and the blockade, 1914–1915', *Journal of Transatlantic Studies*, Vol. 6, No 1, 2008

Kennedy, Paul

    The War Plans of the Great Powers 1880–1914, edited (Allen &Unwin, London 1979)

    'Britain in the First World War', in Millett, Allan R, and Murray, Williamson, eds., *Military Effectiveness*, Vol. 1, *The First World War* (Allen & Unwin, Winchester, Mass., USA 1988), pp. 31–79

Kent, Bruce, *The Spoils of War: The Politics, Economics, and Diplomacy of Reparations 1918–1932* (Oxford University Press, 1992)

Keyes, Sir Roger, *The Naval Memoires of Admiral of the Fleet, Scapa Flow to the Dover Straits 1916–1918* (Thornton Butterworth, London 1935)

Keynes, J M, *Two Memoirs, Dr Melchior: A Defeated Enemy and My Early Beliefs* (Hart-Davis, London 1949)

King, M S, *Woodrow Wilson: Warmonger, A Brief Analysis of How America was Deceived Into World War I* (Author, USA 2016)

King-Hall, Sir William Stephen Richard, *The Diary of a U-boat Commander* (Amazon reprint)

Kitchen, Martin, *The Silent Dictatorship, The politics of the German High Command under Hindenburg and Ludendorff, 1916–1918* (Croom Helm, London 1976)

Kloot, William van der, 'Ernest Starling's Analysis of the Energy Balance of the German People During the Blockade 1914–1919', *Notes and Records of the Royal Society of London*, Vol 57, No 2, May 2003

Koebner, Richard, and Schmidt, Helmut Dan, *Imperialism, The Story and Significance of a Political World, 1840–1960* (Cambridge University Press, 1965)

Koerver, Hans Joachim

    German Submarine Warfare 1914–1918 in the Eyes of British Intelligence (LIS Reinisch, Steinbach 2012)

    War of Numbers 1914–1916, The Kaiser's Navy Gone Rogue (LIS Reinisch, Steinbach 2016)

Kramer, Alan R, 'Prisoners in the First World War', Chap. 4, in Scheipers, Sibylle, ed,

Prisoners in War (Oxford University Press, 2010)

Kreimeier, Klaus, *The UFA Story, A History of Germany's Greatest Film Company 1918–1915* (University of California Press 1999)

Kühnis, Beni, 'Deutsche Kriegsinternierte in Davos während des 1. Weltkrieges' (Extended A-level Project Essay, 2014)

Kutz, Martin, 'Kriegserfahrung und Kriegsvorbereitung. Die agrarwirtschaftliche Vorbereitung des Zweiten Weltkrieges in Deutscheland vor dem Hintergrund de Weltkrieg I – Erfahtung', *Zeitschrift für Agrargeschichte und Agrarsoziologie*, No. 32, 1984, pp. 59–82, 135–163

Ladd, Brian, *The Ghosts of Berlin* (University of Chicago Press, 1997)

Langmaid, Captain Kenneth, *The Approaches are Mined!* (Jarrolds, London 1965)

Lambert, Nicholas A

  Sir John Fisher's Naval Revolution (University of South Carolina Press 1999)

  'On Standards: A Reply to Christopher Bell', *War in History*, 2012, 19(2), pp. 217–240

  Planning Armageddon: British Economic Warfare and the First World War (Harvard University Press, London 2012)

Langsdorff, von Werner, *U-Boote am Feind, 45 deutsche U-Boot-Führer erzählen* (Bertelsmann, Gütersloh 1937)

Large, David Clay, *Berlin, A Modern History* (Allen Lane, London 2000)

Larn, Richard & Bridget, *Shipwreck Index of the British Isles: Isles of Scilly, Cornwall, Devon, Dorset* (Lloyd's Register of Shipping, London 1995)

Laurens, Alphonse

  Le Blocus et la Guerre sous-marine, 1914–1918 (Libraire Armand Colin, Paris 1924)

  Histoire de la Guerre Sous-Marine Allemande, 1914–1918 (Société d'Éditions, Paris 1930)

Leith, Captain Lockhart, *The History of British Minefields 1914–1918* (Admiralty private use, 1920, charts added 1932, Library of the Royal Naval Museums, Portsmouth)

Lentin, A, *The Versailles Peace Settlement: Peacemaking with Germany* (The Historical Association, London 1993)

Leopold, John A, *Alfred Hugenberg, The Radical Nationalist Campaign against the Weimar Republic* (Yale University Press 1977)

Liddell Hart, B H, *History of the First World War* (1930; Cassell, London 1973)

Lindsay, Samuel McCune, Swiss Commission in the United States, edited, *Bulletin of Social Legislation on the Henry Bergh Foundation for the Promotion of Humane Education, No. 5, Swiss Internment of Prisoners of War, An Experiment in International Humane Legislation and Administration* (Columbia University Press, New York 1917)

Lipkes, Jeff, *Rehearsals: The German Army in Belgium, August 1914* (Leuven University Press 2007)

Loewenberg, Peter, 'The Psychological Origins of the Nazi Youth Cohort', *American Historical Review*, No.76, 12/1971, pp. 1457–1502

Low, Professor A M, *Mine and Countermine* (Hutchinson, London 1940)

Lowenthal, David, *The Past is a Foreign Country* (Cambridge University Press, 1986)

Lubbock, Basil, *Last of the Windjammers*, Vol. 1 (Brown, Son & Ferguson, Glasgow 1927)

Ludendorff, Erich von

    Ludendorff's Own Story: August 1914–November 1918, Vol. I (1919, Harper; reprint Kessinger Legacy, USA 2016)

    My War Memories, 1914–1918, Vol. II (Hutchinson, London 1919)

Lutz, Ralph Haswell, *The Causes of the German Collapse in 1918: Sections of the officially authorized report of the Commission of the German Constituent Assembly and of the German Reichstag, 1919–1928, the selection and the translation officially approved by the commission* (1934; Archon, USA 1969)

McCartney, Innes

    Lost Patrols: Submarine Wrecks of the English Channel (Periscope Publishing, Penzance 2003)

    British Submarines of Word War I (Osprey, Oxford 2008)

    The Maritime Archaeology of a Modern Conflict: Comparing the Archaeology of German Submarine Wrecks to the Historical Text (Routledge, Abingdon 2015)

    'The *Tin Openers* Myth and Reality: Intelligence from U-boat Wrecks During WW1', *Proceedings of the Twenty-Fourth Annual Historical Diving Conference*, Poole, November 2014, www.researchgate.net/publication/275957885

    'The Historical Archaeology of World War I U-boats and the Compilation of Admiralty History: The Case of (UC79)', *UNESCO Conference, Bruges*, 26 June 2014, chapter July 2015, researchgate.net/publication/280925727

    'Paying the Prize for the German Submarine War: U-boats destroyed and the Admiralty Prize Fund, 1919–1932', *The Mariner's Mirror*, Vol. 104:1, February 2018, pp. 40–57

McDermott, John, 'Trading with the Enemy: British Business and the Law During the First World War', *Canadian Journal of History / Annales Canadiennes d'Histoire*, XXXII, No 2, Aug 1997

McDowell, Duncan, *Steel at the Sault* (University of Toronto Press, 1988)

Macintyre, Captain Donald, *Jutland* (Evans Brothers, London 1957)

MacMillan, Margaret

    Paris 1919, Six Months That Changed The World (Random House, London 2003)

    The War That Ended Peace (Profile, London 2014)

Mahan, Captain Alfred Thayer

    The Influence of Sea Power upon History 1660–1805 (1890, Bison, London 1980)

    The Influence of Sea Power upon the French Revolution and Empire 1793–1812, Vol. II (Sampson, Low, Marston, London 1896)

Manning, T D, *The British Destroyer* (Putnam, London 1961)

March, Edgar J, *British Destroyers, A History of Development 1892–1953* (Seeley Service, London 1966)

Marder, Arthur J

    Portrait of an Admiral; the life and papers of Sir Herbert Richmond (Harvard University Press, 1952)

From the Dreadnought to Scapa Flow, The Royal Navy in the Fisher Era 1904 – 1919

Vol. I: *The Road to War: 1904–1914* (Oxford University Press, London 1961)

Vol. II: *The War Years: To the Eve of Jutland 1914–1916* (1965; Seaforth Publishing, Barnsley 2013)

Vol. IV: *1917: Year of Crisis* (1969; Seaforth Publishing, Barnsley 2014)

Vol. V: *Victory and Aftermath January 1918–June 1919* (Oxford University Press 1970)

Marks, Sally

The Illusion of Peace, International Relations in Europe 1918–1933 (MacMillan, London 1976)

'The Myths of Reparations', *Central European History*, Sep. 1978, Vol. 11, Issue 3, pp. 231–255

'1918 and After. The Postwar Era', in Martel, Gordon, ed., *The Origins of the Second World War Reconsidered, The AJP Taylor Debate after twenty-five Years* (Routledge, London 1986)

'Mistakes and Myths: The Allies, Germany, and the Versailles Treaty, 1918–1921', *The Journal of Modern History*, Vol. 85, No. 3, Sep. 2013, pp. 632–659

Marreo, Javier Ponce, 'Logistics for Commerce War in the Atlantic during the First World War: The German *Etappe* System in Action', *The Mariner's Mirror*, Vol. 92, No. 4, November 2006, pp. 455–64

Martel, Gordon

ed., *The Origins of the Second World War Reconsidered, The AJP Taylor Debate after twenty-five Years* (Routledge, London 1986)

The Origins of the First World War (1987; Longman, London 1996)

Martin, Roy, & Craigie-Halkett, Lyle, *Risdon Beazley: Marine Salvor* (Authors, Southampton 2007)

Massie, Robert K

Dreadnought: Britain, Germany, and the Coming of the Great War (1991; Vintage, London 2007)

Castles of Steel: Britain, Germany and the Winning of the Great War at Sea (Vintage, London 2007)

Mayer, Arno J

Politics and Diplomacy of Peacemaking, Containment and Counter-Revolution at Versailles 1918–1919 (Weidenfeld and Nicolson, London 1968)

The Persistence of the Old Regime, Europe to the Great War (Croom Helm, London 1981)

Mead, Margaret, 'The Changing Significance of Food', *American Scientist*, No. 58, 1970, pp. 176 onwards

Messimer, Dwight R

The Merchant U-boat: Adventures of the 'Deutschland', 1916–18 (Naval Institute Press, Maryland, USA 1988)

Find and Destroy: Antisubmarine Warfare in World War I (Naval Institute Press, Maryland, USA 2001)

Verschollen: World War I U-Boat Losses (Naval Institute Press, Maryland, USA

2002)

Messinger, Gary S, *British Propaganda and the State in the First World War* (Manchester University Press 1992)

Molodowsky, N, 'German Foreign Trade in 1899–1913', *The Quarterly Journal of Economics*, Vol. 41, No 4, Aug 1927

Mommsen, Wolfgang J, 'The Debate of German War Aims', *Journal of Contemporary History*, Vol. 1, No. 3, July 1966, pp. 47–72

More, Sir Thomas, *Utopia* (Everyman, London 1928)

Morel, Edmund D

    The Congo Slave State, A Protest against the new African Slavery; and an Appeal to the Public of Great Britain, of the United States, and of the Continent of Europe (Richardson, Liverpool 1903)

    The Fruits of Victory. Have our Statesmen Won the Peace our Soldiers Fought For? (Union of Democratic Control, London 1919)

    Military Preparation for the Great War, Fact versus Fiction (Labour Publishing, London 1922)

    The Secret History of a Great Betrayal (Owen, Washington 1924)

Mueller, Michael, trans. Brooks, Geoffrey, *Canaris, The Life and Death of Hitler's Spymaster* (Greenhill, Barnsley 2017)

Munro, Dana C, Sellery, George C & Krey, August C, *German Treatment of Conquered Territory being Part II of 'German War Practices'* (The Committee of Public Information, Washington DC, USA, 1918; reprint Kessinger Publishing, 2016)

Mulligan, Timothy P, *Neither Sharks Nor Wolves* (Chatham, London 1999)

Murray, H Robertson, *Krupp's and the International Armaments Ring, The Scandal of Modern Civilisation* (Holden & Hardingham, London 1915)

Murray, Stewart Lygon, *The Reality of War, a Companion to 'Clausewitz'* (Hodder and Stoughton, London 1914)

Nettl, Peter, *Rosa Luxemburg* (Oxford University Press, London, abridged 1969)

Neureuther, Karl, and Bergen, Claus, eds., *U-Boat Stories. Narratives of German U-boat sailors* (*Wir leben noch!*, 1931; reprint The Naval & Military Press, Uckfield 2005)

Newbold, J T Walton

    The War Trust Exposed (National Labour Trust, Manchester 1913)

    How Asquith Helped the Armaments Ring (National Labour Trust, undated pamphlet)

    How Europe Armed for War 1871–1914 (1916; reprint Isha, New Delhi 2013)

Newbolt, Henry

    A Note of the History of the Submarine War (George Doran, New York 1917)

    Submarine and Anti-Submarine, The Allied Under-Sea Conflict During the First World War (Leonaur, 2013 reprint)

    A Naval History of the War, 1914–1918 (Hodder and Stoughton, London 1919–20)

Niemöller, Martin, *From U-boat to Concentration Camp: The Autobiography of Martin Niemöller* (William Hodge, London 1939)

O'Brien, Patrick, 'The Economic Effects of the Great War,' *History Today*, Vol. 44,

Issue 12, Dec 1994

Offer, Avner

'The Working Classes, British Naval Plans and the Coming of the Great War', *Past and Present*, no. 107 (May 1985), pp. 204–226

'Morality and Admiralty: 'Jacky Fisher', Economic Warfare and the Laws of War', *Journal of Contemporary History*, Vol. 23 (Jan 1988), pp. 99–118

The First World War: An Agrarian Interpretation (Clarendon Press, Oxford 1989)

'Bounded Rationality in Action: The German submarine campaign, 1915–18' in Gerrard, Bill, ed., *The Economics of Rationality* (Routledge, London 1993), pp. 179–202

'The Blockade of Germany and the Strategy of Starvation, 1914–1918', in Chickering, Roger, Förster, Stig, eds., *Great War, Total War: Combat and Mobilization of the Western Front, 1914–1918* (German Historical Institute and Cambridge University Press, 2000), pp. 169–188

Ogden, C K, *Sailing Directions of the North Coast of France*, Part 1 (Imray, Norie & Wilson, London 1908)

Olusoga, David, and Erichsen, Casper W, *The Kaiser's Holocaust, Germany's Forgotten Genocide and the Colonial Roots of Nazism* (Faber and Faber, London 2010)

Osborne, Eric W, *Britain's Economic Blockade of Germany 1914–1919* (Routledge, Abingdon 2013)

Osman, Lt.-Col. A H, *Pigeons in the Great War: A Complete History of the Carrier Pigeon Service during the Great War, 1914 to 1918* in *Pigeons in Two World Wars* (Racing Pigeon Publishing, London 1976)

Overy, Richard, *The Bombing War, Europe 1939–1945* (Penguin, London 2014)

Paddock, Troy R E, ed., *A Call to Arms: Propaganda, Public Opinion, and Newspapers in the Great War* (Praeger, Westport, CT, 2004)

Padfield, Peter, Dönitz, *The Last Führer, Portrait of a Nazi War Leader* (Victor Gollancz, London 1984)

Pakenham, Thomas

The Boer War (Abacus, London 1991)

The Scramble for Africa 1876–1912 (Weidenfeld and Nicolson, London 1997)

Parmelee, Maurice, *Blockade and Sea Power: The Blockade, 1914–1919, and its Significance for a World State* (Hutchinson, London 1924)

Paterson, Lawrence, *Black Flag, the Surrender of Germany's U-Boat Forces 1945* (Seaforth, Barnsley 2009)

Patterson, A Temple, *Jellicoe: A Biography* (Macmillan, London 1969)

Patterson, David, & Pyle, Gerald, 'Geography and Mortality', *Bulletin of the History of Medicine*, 1991, pp. 4–21.

Peterson, H C, *Propaganda for War: The Campaign Against American Neutrality, 1914–17* (University of Oklahoma Press, 1939)

Pitt, Barrie, *Zeebrugge* (Ballantine Books, New York 1959)

Phillips, Ethel, 'American Participation in Belligerent Commercial Controls 1914–1917', *The American Journal of International Law*, Vol. 27, No 4, Oct 1933

Pohl, Hans-Joachim

'The New Berlin Horse Railway Company. The Traffic Access White Lake, Lichtenburg', *Traffic History Sheets*, Berlin (Issue 1, 1986, pp. 2–11, Issue 2, 1986, pp. 32–38).

(with Bauer, Gerhard) 'Neue Berliner Pferdebahn-Gesellschaft (NBPf)' (Berlin: Transpress Verlag 1987), pp. 91–96

Poolman, Kenneth, *Armed Merchant Cruisers* (Leo Cooper, London 1985)

Polybius, *The Histories,* trans. Waterfield, Robin (Oxford World's Classics, Oxford University Press 2010)

Porch, Douglas, 'The French Army in the First World War' in Millett, Allan R, and Murray, Williamson, eds., *Military Effectiveness*, Vol. 1, *The First World War* (Allen & Unwin, Winchester, Mass., USA 1988), pp. 190–228

Probert, Henry, *Bomber Harris, His Life and Times* (Greenhill, London 2006)

Quigley, Carroll, *Tragedy and Hope, A History of the World in Our Time* (Macmillan, New York, 1966)

Raico, Ralph

    Review, Vincent, *Politics of Hunger, Review of Austrian Economics*, Vol. 3, No. 1, 12/1989

    Great Wars and Great Leaders, A libertarian Rebuttal (Ludwig von Mises Institute, Auburn, Alabama 2010)

Ramsay, David, *'Blinker' Hall: Spymaster, The Man who Brought America into World War 1* (Spellmount, Stroud 2009)

Ranft, Bryan McL, ed

    'The protection of British seaborne trade and the development of systematic planning for war, 1860–1906' in *Technical Change and British Naval Policy 1860–1939* (Hodder and Stoughton, Sevenoaks 1977)

    The Beatty Papers 1902–1918, Vol. 1 (Scholar Press, Navy Records Society, Aldershot 1989)

Read, James Morgan, *Atrocity Propaganda 1914–1919* (Yale University Press 1941)

Reader, W J, *'At Duty's Call', A Study in Obsolete Patriotism* (Manchester University Press 1988)

Reichs-Marine-Amt

    Vorschriften für die Ergänzung des Seeoffizierekorps nebst Ausführungsbestimmungen (Reichs-Marine-Amt, Berlin 1909)

    Vorschriften für die Ausbildung der Seekadetten auf den Schulschiffen (Reichs-Marine-Amt Berlin, 1910)

Remarque, Erich Maria, *All Quiet on the Western Front* (1929; Vintage, London 1996)

Reports of British Officers on the Economic Conditions Prevailing in German, December 1918 – March 1919; Cmd-52, Army (HMSO, London 1919)

Richard, Alain, and Coulon, Jef, 'La guerre sous-marin en 1914–1918 dans le Détroit du Pas-de-Calais: armes utilisées par les sous-marins allemands et lutte anti-sous-marins des alliés', *Sucellus: Dossiers archéologiques, historiques et cultural du NORD-PAS DE-CALAIS*, No. 56, 2005, pp. 41–58

Richard, Alain, Coulon, Jef, and Lowrey, Michael, 'L'odyssée de 5 sous marins allemands, mouilleurs de mines, coules en 1917–19 dans le Detroit du Pas-de-

Calais UC26 – UC46 – UC61 – UC64 – UC79', *Sucellus:* No. 57, 2006, pp. 61–85

Richardson, Matthew, *The Hunger War, Food, Rations and Rationing 1914–1918* (Pen & Sword, Barnsley 2015)

Richie, Alexandra, *Faust's Metropolis, A History of Berlin* (Harper Collins, London 1999)

Richter, Lina Speiss, *Family life in Germany under the blockade*, preface Shaw, Bernard (National Labour Press, London, 1919)

Ritter, Gerhard, *The Schlieffen Plan* (Oswald Wolff, London 1958)

Ronarc'h, Admiral Pierre-Alexis, *Souvenirs De La Guerre*, Vol. 1 (Payot, Paris 1921)

Rose, Gerhard, *Krieg nach dem Kriege. Der Kampf des deutschen Volkes um die Heimkehr seiner Kriegsgefangenen* (Dem Rockbound zum Schultze der deutschen Krieges- und Zivilgefangenen, Berlin 1920)

Rosenberg, Arthur, *Imperial Germany, The Birth of the German Republic 1971–1918* (1928; Oxford University Press, New York 1970)

Rössler, Eberhard, trans. Erenberg, Harold, *The U-boat, The evolution and technical history of German submarines* (Arms & Armour Press, London 1981)

Roth, Guenther, *The Social Democrats in Imperial Germany. A Study in Working-Class Isolation and National Integration* (Bedminster Press, Totowa, New Jersey, 1963

Roth, Joseph

    What I saw, Reports from Berlin 1920–33 (Granta, London 2013)

    Job, The Story of a Simple Man (1930; Granta, London 2013)

Ruge, Friedrich, *Scapa Flow 1919, The End of the German Fleet*, trans. Masters, Derek, ed. Watts, A J (Ian Allen, London 1973)

Rüger, Jan, *The Great Naval Game, Britain and Germany in the Age of Empire* (Cambridge University Press, New York 2007)

Russell, Bertrand, *Justice in War Time* (Spokesman, Nottingham 1917)

Ryheul, John, *Marinekorps Flandern 1914–1918* (E S Mittler, Hamburg 1997)

Sands, Philippe, *East West Street* (Weidenfeld & Nicolson, London 2016)

Saville, Allison Winthrop, 'The Development of the German U-boat Arm, 1919–1935' (PhD dissertation, University of Washington, USA, 1963)

Scheer, Reinhard, Admiral, *Germany's High Sea Fleet in the World War* (1919; Shilka Publishing, Truro 2013)

Schierbrand, Wolf von, *Kaiser's Speeches Forming A Character Portrait of Kaiser Wilhelm II* (Harper Brothers, New York 1903)

Schneider, William, *Operations Research Applications for Intelligence, Surveillance and Reconnaissance: Report of the Defense Science Board Advisory Group on Defense Intelligence (Diane Publishing, Darby, PA, 2009)*

Schoenermarck, A, ed., *Helden-Gedenkmappe des deutschen Adels* (Petri, Stuttgart 1921)

Schreiner, George Abel, *The Iron Ration: The Economic and Social Effects of the Allied Blockade on Germany and the German People* (John Murray, London 1918)

Schröder, Joachim, *Die U-Boote des Kaisers: Die Geschichte des deutschen U-Boot-Krieges Gegen Großbritannien im Ersten Weltkrieg* (Bernard & Graefe Verlag, Bonn 2003)

Schuker, Stephen A

The End of the French Predominance in Europe, The Financial Crisis of 1924 and the Adoption of the Dawes Plan (University of North Carolina Press, 1976)

American Reparations to Germany, 1919–33: Implications for the Third World Debt Crisis (Princetown University, USA, 1988)

Schwabe, Klaus, Woodrow Wilson, Revolutionary Germany, and Peacemaking, 1918–1919: Missionary Diplomacy and the Realities of Power, trans. Kimber, Rita and Robert (University of North Carolina Press, 1985)

Sebag-Montefiore, Hugh, Enigma, The Battle for the Code (Cassell, London 2000)

Sedrati, Mouncef, Anthony, Edward J, 'Confronting coastal morphodynamics with countererosion engineering: the emblematic case of Wissant Bay, Dover Strait', Journal of Coastal Conservation, Springer Verlag, 2014, 18 (5), pp. 483–494

Seligmann, Matthew, Spies in Uniform, British Military and Naval Intelligence on the Eve of the First World War (Oxford University Press 2006)

Seligmann, Matthew S, Nägler, Frank, and Epkenhans, Michael, eds., The Naval Route to the Abyss, The Anglo-German Naval Race 1895–1914 (Ashgate, Naval History Society, Farnham 2015)

Simonds, Frank H, How Europe Made Peace Without America (Heinemann, London 1927)

Simpson, Colin, Lusitania (Penguin, London 1983)

Sims, William Sowden, The Victory at Sea, The Allied Campaign Against U-Boats During the First World War 1917–18 (1920, reprint USA, 2016)

Siney, Marion C, The Allied Blockade of Germany 1914–1916 (University of Michigan Press 1957)

Spies, S B, Methods of Barbarism? Roberts and Kitchener and Civilians in the Boer Republics, January 1900–May 1902 (Human and Rousseau, Cape Town 1977)

Spiess, Johannes, Six Ans de Croisières en Sous-marin (Payot, Paris 1927)

Spiegel, Edgar, Baron von und zu Pecklesheim, The Adventures of the U-202, An Actual Narrative (1917; Project Guttenberg EBook 2010)

Spindler, Arno

Der Krieg zur See 1914–1918: Der Handelskrieg mit U-Booten, Band 3, Oktober 1915 bis Januar 1917 (E S Mittler, Berlin, 1934)

Der Krieg zur See 1914–1918: Der Handelskrieg mit U-Booten, Band 4, Februar bis Dezember 1917 (E S Mittler, Berlin 1941; reprint 1964)

Starling, E H, 'The food supply of Germany during the war', Journal of the Royal Statistical Society, No. 83, pp. 225–254, 1920

Strachan, Hew, The First World War (Pocket Books, London 2006)

Steigmann-Gall, Richard, The Holy Reich: Nazi Conceptions of Christianity, 1919–1945 (Cambridge University Press, 2009)

Sutherland, Jon, and Canwell, Diane, U-Boats at World Wars I and II: Rare Photographs from Wartime Archives (Images of War) (Pen & Sword Maritime, Barnsley 2009)

Steffen, Dirk, 'The Holtzendorff Memorandum of 22 December 1916 and Germany's Declaration of Unrestricted U-boat Warfare', The Journal of Military History, Vol. 68, No. 1, 1/2004, pp. 215–224

Steiner, Zara, *The Lights That Failed, European International History 1919–1933* (Oxford University Press, 2005)

Stock, M B, and Smythe, P M, 'Does Nutrition during Infancy Inhibit Brain Growth and Subsequent Intellectual Development?', *Archives of Disease in Childhood*, No. 38, 1964

Stoker, Donald J

    Girding for Battle, The Arms Trade in a Global Perspective, 1815–1940 (edited with Grant, Jonathan A, Praeger, Westport, Connecticut 2003), Chapter 6, Forsén, Björn, and Forsén, Annette, 'German Submarine Exports, 1919–35', pp. 113–33.

    Britain, France and the Naval Arms Trade in the Baltic 1919–1939, Grand Strategy and Failure (Routledge, Abingdon 2012)

Sun Tzu, *The Art of War* (500 BC; Hodder Mobius, London 1981)

Swayze, Alan, *The End of World War I: The Treaty of Versailles and Its Tragic Legacy* (Crabtree Publishing, Hove 2014)

Swetman, Deryck, 'The Flanders U-Boat Flotilla, A Nest of Vipers Spawned by Allied Intelligence?', MA Maritime Studies, *University of Portsmouth*, 2003/2004

Tardieu, André, *The Truth about the Treaty* (Bobbs-Merrill, Indianapolis 1921)

Tarrant, V E, *The U-boat Offensive 1914–1945* (Cassell, London 1989)

Ten Cate, J H, 'Das U-Boot als geistige Exportware: Das Ingeniuerskantoor voor Scheepvaart N.V., 1919–1957' in Melville R, et all, ed., *Deutschland und Europa in der Neuzeit, Festschrift für Karl Otmar, Freiherr von Aretin, zum 65* (Stuttgart, 1988)

Tennent, A J, *British Merchant Ships Sunk by U boats in World Wars I and II* (Pen & Sword Maritime, Barnsley 2009)

Termote, Tomas

    Krieg Unter Wasser: Unterseebootflottille Flandern 1915–1918 (E S Mittler, Hamburg 2015)

    War Beneath the Waves: U-boat Flotilla Flandern 1915–1918 (Uniform, London 2017)

Terraine, John

    Mons, The Retreat to Victory (Batsford, London 1960)

    Business in Great Waters, The U-Boat Wars, 1916–1945 (Leo Cooper, London 1989)

    The Smoke and the Fire (Leo Cooper, London 1992)

Terry, C Sanford, ed., *Ostend and Zeebrugge, April 23: May 10, 1918, The Dispatches of Vice-Admiral Sir Roger Keyes and other Narratives of the Operations* (Oxford University Press, 1919)

Thomas, Lowell, *Raiders of the Deep* (Garden City Publishing, New York 1932)

Thomazi, A, 'La Guerre Navale dans la Zone des Armées du Nord' (1924; Payot, Paris 1928)

Tooley, Hunt, *The Western Front, Battle Front and Home Front in the First World War* (Macmillan, Basingstoke 2003)

Trentmann, Frank, and Just, Flemming, editors, *Food and Conflict in Europe in the Age of the Two World Wars* (Macmillan, Basingstoke 2006)

Tuchman, Barbara W, *The Guns of August – August 1914* (Four Square, 1964)

Tucker, Spencer C, ed., *The European Powers in the First World War, An Encyclopedia* (Garland Publishing, New York 1999)

Turner, L C F, *Origins of the First World War* (Edward Arnold, London 1970)

Ullrich, Volker, trans. Beech, Timothy, *Bismarck* (1998; Haus Publishing, London 2015)

Vagts, Alfred, *A History of Militarism: Civilian and Military*(Revised edition; Free Press, New York 1967)

Vigness, Paul G, *The Neutrality of Norway in the World War* (Stanford University 1932; Kessinger Reprint, USA, 2016)

Vincent, C Paul, *Politics of Hunger: The Allied Blockade of Germany, 1915-19* (Ohio University Press, 1985)

Volkov, Shulamit, *Walther Rathenau, Weimar's Fallen Statesman* (Yale University Press 2012)

Waite, Robert G L, *Vanguard of Nazism, The Free Corps Movement in Postwar Germany 1918-1923* (1952; Norton, New York, 1969)

Walker, D P, 'The German Nationalist People's Party: The Conservative Dilemma in the Weimar Republic', *Journal of Contemporary History*, Vol. 14, 1979, pp. 627–647

Ward-Jackson, C H, *Stephens of Fowey, A Portrait of a Cornish Merchant Fleet 1867-1939* (National Maritime Museum, London, Maritime Monographs and Reports, No 43, 1980)

Warner, Philip, *The Zeebrugge Raid* (William Kimber, London 1978)

Webster, Sir Charles, and Frankland, Noble, *The Strategic Air Offensive Against Germany 1939-1945*, Vol. III, Victory, Part 5 (1961; Naval & Military Press, Uckfield 2006)

Wegener, Vice Admiral Wolfgang, trans. Herwig, Holger H, *The Naval Strategy of the World War* (1929; Naval Institute Press, Annapolis, Maryland 1989)

Weinreb, Alice, *Modern Hungers, Food and Power in Twentieth-Century Germany* (Oxford University Press 2017)

Weintraub, Stanley, *A Stillness Heard Around The World: The End of the Great War: November 1918* (Oxford University Press, 1985)

Weir, Gary E, *Building the Kaiser's Navy, The Imperial Naval Office and German Industry in the von Tirpitz Era, 1890-1919* (United States Naval Institute, Annapolis, Maryland 1992)

Westerman, Percy F, *The Thick of the Fray at Zeebrugge, April 1918* (Blackie and Son, London, 1919)

Williamson, Gordon, *U-boats of the Kaiser's Navy* (Osprey, Oxford 2002)

Willis, Edward F, 'Herbert Hoover and the Blockade of Germany, 1918-1919' in Cox et al, eds., *Studies in Modern European History in Honor of Franklin Charles Palm* (Bookman, New York, USA, 1956), pp. 81–104

Willmott, H P, *World War I* (Dorling Kindersley, London 2012)

Wilson, Keith, edited, *Forging the Collective Memory, Government and International Historians through Two World Wars* (Bergahn Books, Oxford 1996)

Wilson, Michael, & Kemp, Paul, *Mediterranean Submarines* (Crécy, Wilmslow 1997)

Wilson, Michael, *Baltic Assignment, British Submariners in Russia: 1914-1919* (Leo Cooper, London 1985)

Winick, Myron, and Noble, Adele, 'Cellular Response in Rats during Malnutrition at

Various Ages', *Journal of Nutrition*, No. 89, 1966, pp. 300–6

Winter, Jay, ed, *The Cambridge History of First World War*, Vols. I–III (Cambridge University Press, 2014)

Winter, Jay, and Prost, Antoine, *The Great War in History: Debates and Controversies, 1914 to the Present* (Cambridge University Press 2005)

Winton, John, *Convoy: The Defence of Sea Trade 1890–1990* (Michael Joseph, London 1983)

Wislicenus, Georg, *Deutschlands Seemacht, sonst und jetzt* (1895; Grunow, Leipzig 1901)

Woodward, E L, *Great Britain and the German Navy* (Clarendon Press, Oxford 1935)

Yarnall, John, *Barbed Wire Disease, British and German Prisoners of War, 1914–1919* (History Press, Stroud 2011)

Zimmer, Gustav, 'The Crew of the *Möwe* on Lake Tanganyika', *The Naval Review*, Vol. X, No. 4, November 1922, pp. 650–60

Zweig, Stefan, trans. Bell, Anthea, The *World of Yesterday* (1942; Pushkin, London 2009)

Zweiniger-Bargielowska, Ina, Duffett, Rachel, and Drouard, Alain, editors, *Food and War in Twentieth Century Europe* (Ashgate, Farnham 2011)

Anonymous, *La Guerre Navale Racontée Par Nos Amiraux* (Librairie Schwartz, Paris, undated)

Anonymous, *The Starving of Germany*, Papers read at Extraordinary Meeting of United Medial Societies held at Headquarters of Berlin Medical Society, Berlin, 18 December 1918 (Berlin, 1919)

Index

NOTE: Ranks and titles are generally the highest mentioned in the text.